D1187616

WITHDRAWN

THE RUSSIAN EMPIRE AND SOVIET UNION

A GUIDE TO

MANUSCRIPTS AND ARCHIVAL MATERIALS IN THE UNITED STATES

Steven A. Grant and John H. Brown

**KENNAN INSTITUTE
FOR
ADVANCED RUSSIAN STUDIES**

G. K. HALL & CO., 70 LINCOLN STREET, BOSTON, MASSACHUSETTS
1981

Library of Congress Cataloging in Publication Data

Grant, Steven A.
The Russian Empire and Soviet Union.

Includes index.
1. Soviet Union—Archival resources—United States.
I. Brown, John H. (John Halit) 1948- . II. Kennan
Institute for Advanced Russian Studies. III. Title.
Z2491.G66 [DK17] 016.947'0072073 81-6306
ISBN 0-8161-1300-9 AACR2

MANUFACTURED IN THE UNITED STATES OF AMERICA

PREFACE

This guide to manuscripts and archival material pertaining to Russia and the USSR is the fruit of four years of work by a team of Research Associates of the Kennan Institute for Advanced Russian Studies led by Dr. John H. Brown and Dr. Steven A. Grant. Their assignment was enormous in scope and they carried it out with distinction. In the course of their work, the editors and researchers contacted more than 7,500 institutions and individuals in the continental United States, Hawaii, and Alaska. Hundreds of collections that had heretofore escaped scholarly attention were brought to light, while dozens of other major collections were catalogued for the first time. Their contents might now become known in detail not only to scholars but, in some cases, to their owners, many of whom had earlier sought in vain for authoritative information on the materials they have inherited or otherwise acquired. All those interested in the history and culture of the peoples of the USSR will therefore be grateful to the editors for the thoroughness and persistence they have shown.

The project received support from the Research Division of the United States Office of Education and also from the National Endowment for the Humanities. Such support could be utilized more effectively because of the strong backing the project has received at every stage from the staff and Fellows of the Woodrow Wilson International Center for Scholars, of which the Kennan Institute is a part. Indeed, the very conception of this scholarly aid derives from The Wilson Center's commitment to serve the needs of those engaged in fundamental research in many fields of the humanities and social sciences.

S. Frederick Starr
Secretary, Kennan Institute for Advanced Russian Studies, The Wilson Center

INTRODUCTION

This guide lists materials in U.S. archives and manuscript repositories that relate to the Russian Empire, Soviet Union, and the many distinct nationalities therein. The materials described in the guide are extremely diverse in character. They cover the broadest possible range of subjects: political, historical, social, economic, diplomatic, artistic, literary, religious, military, musical, and other matters. The combined subject and name index at the end of the volume is the key to locating desired materials in the approximately 650 different entries.

Scope

The guide covers public and private institutions, including university libraries and archives, public libraries, museums, ethnic organizations, church and business archives, federal and state governmental archives, and both public and private historical societies. Some collections owned by private individuals are also noted.

All research for entries was completed by the spring of 1979.

Among the types of materials listed in the guide are the following: correspondence, reports, organizational records, account books, essays, literary manuscripts, diaries, journals, memoirs, autobiographies, photographs, films, tape recordings, and graphic material. With the exception of certain mimeographed materials and rare clippings, nearly all printed matter has been excluded. Those seeking published books, periodicals, theses, and the like should refer to appropriate catalogs of library collections. However, unpublished facsimiles, photo reproductions, and microfilms of originals (even of originals subsequently published) have been taken to be archival materials in this guide.

An attempt has been made to cover all nationalities and regions within the present territory of the Soviet Union. For the most part, the emphasis throughout has been on the homelands of these people, rather than on their emigration and life in the United States or elsewhere. However, some documents pertaining to émigré life have been included.

Method of Collecting Data

The careful user of this guide will doubtless turn up instances in which coverage of a given collection or repository is less than complete or in which items are imprecisely described. Given the large number of collections involved, this is inevitable, the more so since the authors and their assistants could actually visit only the most important collections and repositories in or near Boston, Chicago, New York, Philadelphia, San Francisco, and Washington, D.C. For the many collections not examined in person, the authors have relied upon published finding aids, descriptions supplied by curators and librarians in writing or by telephone, photoreproductions of card catalog entries, and the like. Many entries on collections or individual items are thus based closely on information published elsewhere or supplied by others. Wherever possible, the sources have been duly acknowledged in the text. If the authors have anywhere failed to provide such acknowledgments, they would like here to express their gratitude to their informants.

Form of Entries

Entries are in alphabetical order by state, by city, and thereunder by repository, institution, or individual. Within each entry collections are again in alphabetical order.

Every effort has been made to assure that each collection listing provides the following information: name of the person, organization, or subject involved; dates of birth and/or death of pertinent individuals; dates of existence or operation of institutions and organizations covered; the quantity of materials preserved in the collection; a general description of the collection as a whole, with a more detailed description of the Russian-related holdings; reference to pertinent citations in the National Union Catalog of Manuscript Collections and other finding aids; and special conditions affecting access to the collection. Some repositories also provided their own identification or location numbers for collections; these have been incorporated as well.

Due to the diversity of cataloging systems and to the fact that collections were in varying states of organization, it was not always possible to adhere to this ideal format. Even when it has been followed, the same term may have different meanings in the context of different collections. For example, a "box" in one collection may be substantially larger than the same unit of measure in another. For more information or for clarification, researchers should always directly contact the repository or individual concerned.

Restrictions on Access

The conditions of access to the various collections listed in this volume vary greatly, as do restrictions affecting the use of materials. The ultimate authority on such matters is the repository itself, and failure to observe any restrictions will only complicate access to the collection by other users. It is therefore strongly recommended that researchers ascertain beforehand not only the restrictions on access to collections, but also regulations affecting literary rights and the duplication of materials.

Transliteration

Most transliterations of names have been left in the form in which the different repositories reported them with the exception of more common names, such as Trotskii, Dostoevskii, Chaikovskii, etc., which have been standardized for ease of reference. When the spelling used by a repository differs from this, the standardized spelling used here has been indicated in square brackets following the particular entry. When the repository itself did not transliterate Russian names, the authors have made a transliteration based on the Library of Congress system. This procedure simplifies work in the separate repositories as researchers must locate materials by the repository's own listings. However, the lack of a standardized transliteration system throughout the U.S. means that the researcher sometimes has to use his or her imagination in identifying the Russian original. In order to reduce confusion on this point, the authors have frequently introduced Library of Congress transliterations in parentheses after the repository's version. Most importantly, alternative forms are cross-referenced in the index.

Toward Future Research

This guide does not pretend to be an exhaustive coverage of all Russian/Soviet-related materials in archives and manuscript repositories in the United States. For some entries in the volume, the collections listed may represent only highlights of relevant holdings. Much work remains to be done, particularly in church archives and private collections. Computerized data banks and machine-readable collections will also have to be culled at some future point. One should note as well that the microfilm revolution is proceeding at so rapid a pace that the accessibility and reproduction of many items and collections listed herein will soon be greatly broadened.

Steven A. Grant
John H. Brown
Washington, D.C. 1980

ACKNOWLEDGMENTS

This guide has benefited from the generous cooperation and assistance of numerous individuals who work in the archives and repositories listed. Without their help the project could not have been completed.

For funds to support the research and writing of the book, we are grateful to the International Education Division of the Office of Education (Department of Health, Education, and Welfare) and especially to the National Endowment for the Humanities, which supplemented its original major grant with additional funds.

For timely advice throughout the project we are deeply indebted to our consultants Dr. Patricia Kennedy Grimsted and the late Dr. Sergius Yakobson. In particular we must thank Dr. Grimsted for her help in preparing our data sheet and for her extremely helpful critical reading of portions of the manuscript.

In the early stages of the project, much research on the spot was performed by Dr. Gilbert S. Doctorow (in the areas of New England and New York City) and especially by Dr. Michael Shaw, on the West Coast.

Several people have assisted with various tasks at different times in the project: Mr. Christopher Crowner, Ms. Susan Eget, and Ms. Nina Beck.

Although it would be impossible to thank individually all those on whose help we relied, we owe special debts of gratitude to the following: Nancy Sahli, George Voght, and the staff of the National Historical Publications and Records Commission; Harriet Ostroff of the National Union Catalog of Manuscript Collections at the Library of Congress; Stephen Corrsin, Elizabeth Valkenier, and the staff of the Bakhmeteff Archive at Columbia University; Charles S. Palm and the staff of the Hoover Institution Archives; Ronald D. Landa, Charles S. Sampson, and others at the Historical Office of the Department of State; J. Dane Hartgrove and others at the National Archives; and, for information about various ethnic groups, Edward Kasinec, Lubomyr Wynar, Mrs. V. Valaitis, Endel Aruja, and Halyna Myroniuk.

Finally, our greatest debt is to Nancy Nawor Blanpied, who prepared the index, and to William Bruce Pitt, who edited her work. The Stakhanovite effort which Nancy gave to this laborious task deserves more thanks than these few words can convey. *Molodets!*

BIBLIOGRAPHICAL NOTE

The two main guides used for locating collections were the Library of Congress's The National Union Catalog of Manuscript Collections (1959-) and the National Historical Publications and Records Commission's Directory of Archives and Manuscript Repositories (1978). Also consulted were Philip M. Hamer, A Guide to Archives and Manuscripts in the United States (1961) and the various guides prepared in the 1930s and 1940s by the Historical Records Survey, a unit of the Works Projects Administration. Most information on Armenian manuscripts was taken directly from Avedis K. Sanjian, A Catalogue of Medieval Armenian Manuscripts in the United States (1976). Seymour de Ricci and William J. Wilson, Census of Medieval and Renaissance Manuscripts in the United States and Canada (1935, 1962) was also helpful in finding materials. Lubomyr Wynar and Lois Butler, Guide to Ethnic Museums, Libraries, and Archives in the United States (1978) and Philip P. Mason, Directory of Jewish Archival Institutions (1975) provided information on ethnic organization archives. For music manuscripts, the basic reference work was Otto E. Albrecht, A Census of Autograph Music Manuscripts of European Composers in American Libraries (1953)--revised edition in preparation. Steven A. Grant, Scholars' Guide to Washington D.C. for Russian/Soviet Studies (1977) was used for research in the Washington area and contains information not included in this book. Many of the other guides used in this book are cited in Frank B. Evans, Modern Archives and Manuscripts: A Select Bibliography (1975).

ABBREVIATIONS

ALS	. . . .	autograph letter signed
DS	. . . .	document signed
LS	. . . .	letter signed
TLS	. . . .	typed letter signed
NUCMC	. . . .	National Union Catalog of Manuscript Collections

ABBREVIATIONS OF STATES

Alabama	AL
Alaska	AK
Arizona	AZ
Arkansas	AR
California	CA
Colorado	CO
Connecticut	CT
Delaware	DE
D.C.	DC
Florida	FL
Georgia	GA
Hawaii	HI
Idaho	ID
Illinois	IL
Indiana	IN
Iowa	IA
Kansas	KS
Kentucky	KY
Louisiana	LA
Maine	ME
Maryland	MD
Massachusetts	MA
Michigan	MI
Minnesota	MN
Mississippi	MS
Missouri	MO
Montana	MT
Nebraska	NB
Nevada	NV
New Hampshire	NH
New Jersey	NJ
New Mexico	NM
New York	NY
North Carolina	NC
North Dakota	ND
Ohio	OH
Oklahoma	OK
Oregon	OR
Pennsylvania	PA
Puerto Rico	PR
Rhode Island	RI
South Carolina	SC
South Dakota	SD
Tennessee	TN
Texas	TX
Utah	UT
Vermont	VT
Virginia	VA
Washington	WA
West Virginia	WV
Wisconsin	WI
Wyoming	WY

GUIDE

ALABAMA

AL 1
ALBERT F. SIMPSON HISTORICAL RESEARCH CENTER
Maxwell Air Force Base, Alabama 36112
(205-293-5958, 5962)

1 Elmer E. Adler (1892-1970). On assignment in Moscow in 1942 and in command of the U.S. Army Middle East Air Force, Major General Adler played an important role in delivery of lend-lease aircraft to the USSR in late 1942 and early 1943. The delivery route was via the Persian Gulf. The papers include correspondence on lend-lease aircraft and data on the Moscow mission, October-December 1942, which concerned an Anglo-American offer to send an air contingent to the Caucasus, operate, and maintain it.

2 William H. Blanchard (1916-1966). Papers, ca. 3 in. The major general was, as deputy director of operations, SAC, a member of the U.S. Air Delegation to the USSR in 1956. Among his speeches, notes, talking papers, and photographs are materials on a Tushino Air Show, the Kubinka Airfield, Zhukovskii Air Engineer Academy, the aircraft designer A. N. Tupolev, and N. S. Khrushchev. The papers are restricted by a security classification in part.

3 John K. Cannon (1892-1955). On 2 August 1944, General Cannon met with Soviet Colonel General Nikitin to discuss the U.S. military mission in Moscow. Besides the U.S. mission, the papers, mostly copies, relate to the conduct of World War II and the Russian air force. They include his report and some illustrations, 2 folders, ca. 90 pp., and approximately 20 photographs. Materials are under a security classification restriction at present.

4 German Air Force Monographs (1953-1958). Ca. 3% of 84 ft. Comprised of voluntary contributions from former leading German military personnel and of captured German aircraft records, these materials contain references to doctrine, tactics, and military operations of the Soviet Air Force in World War II. Some items have been translated and edited for publication; others are available in translated, unedited form. Inquire at the repository. (NUCMC 68-1991)

5 Thomas Dresser White (1901-1965). Papers, 1901-64, ca. 5% of 2 ft. Air Force officer. As a first lieutenant, White (later Chief of Staff of the U.S.A.F.) was assistant air attaché to the U.S. Embassy in Moscow, February 1934 to early 1935. His diaries, 6 vols., cover his stay in the USSR in 1934. Among 16 folders of personal correspondence, arranged chronologically, are letters from 1934-35 containing much information on the Soviet Union. Some photographs are also on Russia. White's primary interest in this material was the state of Soviet aviation, though general information on the USSR in the 1930s appears as well. (NUCMC 77-830)

6 Note: According to Mr. James Eastman, Chief of the Research Branch, "Spread throughout our collection is material concerning the transfer, delivery, and supply of lend-lease aircraft to the Russians in World War II. Also data are included in HQ army air force and various bomb unit records and periodic histories on Operation Frantic--the use of Russian bases for shuttle-bombing Germany in 1944." For some possible further leads, the researcher might wish to consult the bibliography in Richard C. Lukas, Eagles East: The Army Air Forces and the Soviet Union, 1941-1945 (Tallahassee: Florida State University Press, 1970).

Finding Aids: For all of the papers listed above, two publications are useful. The first is United States Air Force History: A Guide to Documentary Sources (Washington, D.C., 1973), compiled by Lawrence J. Paszek; the other is Personal Files in the US Air Force Historical Collection (Albert F. Simpson Historical Research Center, 1975), pamphlet, 29 pp.

AL 2
ALABAMA DEPARTMENT OF ARCHIVES AND HISTORY
624 Washington Avenue
Montgomery, Alabama 36130
(205-832-6510)

Arthur Pendleton Bagby (1794-1858). Papers, 1848-49, 7 items. U.S. minister to Russia. Letters to his wife in the United States, 17 June 1848-14 May 1849. Beginning with his stopover in London on the way to Russia, the letters concern his diplomatic mission and various aspects of Russian life, including accommodations, the nobility and peasants, weather and snow removal, Count K. R. Nesselrode, architecture, Russian political and military aspirations, moral depravity and crime, religion, Moscow, and the underground telegraph "by which the Emperor communicates with his ministers."

AL 3
AMELIA GAYLE GORGAS LIBRARY
MANUSCRIPT SECTION
UNIVERSITY OF ALABAMA
Drawer 2
University, Alabama 35486
(205-348-5512)

William Charles Cravner (1883-1963). Family papers, 1803-1963, ca. 5,020 items. Methodist and Episcopal minister. Contains journals, scrapbooks, photograph album, and memorabilia, a small part of which relates to a trip W. C. Cravner took with his wife to Russia. Library restrictions. Unpublished finding aid (NUCMC 68-1450).

ALASKA

AK 1
ALASKA PACIFIC UNIVERSITY LIBRARY
Anchorage, Alaska 99502
(907-276-8181)

Melvin Ricks, translator. Collection of translations of 7 Russian journals of Alaskan and Siberian exploration. Also, his "Alaskan Bibliography 1924-1965."

AK 2
ARCHIVES OF THE CATHOLIC DIOCESE OF FAIRBANKS
1316 Peger Road
Fairbanks, Alaska 99701
(907-456-6753)

1 or 2 folders of materials pertaining to ecumenical relations between the Russian Orthodox Church and the Roman Catholic Church. The materials, which date back to the 1950s, include letters and reports that touch on the needs and status of the Eastern rite churches in the Southwest and South central part of the State of Alaska. Limited to specific requests.

AK 3
ALASKA NATIVE LANGUAGE CENTER
UNIVERSITY OF ALASKA
Fairbanks, Alaska 99701
(907-479-7874)

The Center's holdings include nearly everything the Russian Church or Russian scholars ever published in or on Alaskan Native languages plus a very small amount of unpublished material on the same subject. Also, all Soviet Eskimo language publications, ca. 75 titles since 1932, a very rare collection. The comprehensiveness and rarity of these holdings qualifies them as archival in nature.

AK 4
UNIVERSITY ARCHIVES AND MANUSCRIPT COLLECTION
UNIVERSITY OF ALASKA
Fairbanks, Alaska 99701
(907-479-7261)

1 Alaska Commercial Company (San Francisco). Records, 1868-1922, ca. 70 ft. Ledgers, log books, correspondence, copy books, loose papers, etc., ca. 95% handwritten; in English and Russian. Successor trading company to the Russian-American Company and Hutchinson, Kohl & Co.; succeeded in turn by the Northern Commercial Company. The company operated trading stations in 4 administrative districts: Kodiak, Unalaska, St. Michael, and the Pribilof Islands. This collection concerns chiefly the Kodiak District. The Company had no direct links to Russia after the U.S. purchase of Alaska in 1867 but there were contacts with Russians and their descendants in Alaska. Unpublished guide (NUCMC 73-1).

2 Alaska History Documents. Records, 18th-20th c., 15 bound vols. and 4 boxes. Includes abstracts of records in the Alaska Church Collection at the Library of Congress, the Yudin Collection, documents relating to the Bering Sea controversy, excerpts from the Russian Orthodox American Messenger, excerpts from Dr. V. V. Gsovski's "Memorandum on the Legal Status of Alaska Natives under the Russian Government," reports from the governors of the Russian American Company, confession of Ivan Petrov, the Brainerd Collection, Richard Olney Collection, material concerning the reorganization of the government of Alaska, reports of the Alaska Engineering Commission and the Alaska Railway Division of the Interior Department, and material pertaining to the reindeer industry in Alaska. (Vol. 13 of these documents has been microfilmed: M/F 30.) Also, 4 boxes of research notes relating to the Alaska History Documents Project, which produced the preceding 15 vols. of materials. Unpublished index.

3 Robert Campbell (1808-1851). Hudson's Bay Company clerk. Journal, 1 box, with references to Chief Shakes of Wrangell, who traded Russian goods in the interior of Alaska.

4 Richard Henry Geoghegan (d. 1944). Correspondence, 1938-44, 1,500-2,000 pp. Scholar and Sinologist. Letters to Jay Ellis Ransom pertain in part to Russian, Siberian, Aleutian, and Asiatic linguistics, and to Geoghegan's translations from Bishop Ivan Veniaminoff's Aleutian writings.

5 Historical Photographs Collection. Ca. 120 photos of Russian Orthodox churches, governmental buildings, Siberian Eskimos in Alaska, Siberia, and Kamchatka ca. 1897, etc. Index.

6 Russian American Company. Records, 1802-67, on microfilm. Correspondence of the company's governors general in Alaska with the board of

directors in Russia, 1802-66; copies of similar communications, 1818-67; ships' logs, 1851-67; and journals of exploring expeditions, 1842-64. All in Russian; some copies. Originals in the National Archives. (M/F 7)

7 Russian Orthodox Church. Records, 1825-1966, 11 reels of microfilm. Documents recovered from the basements and belfries of parish churches in Alaska. Consists of priests' journals, worship service journals, church registers, school journals, metrical records, confessional lists, marriage inquests, and financial accounts. Originals at St. Herman Pastoral School, Kodiak, Alaska. (M/F 59)

8 Siberian Military Documents. Collection, ca. 1744-85, ca. 100 items. Routine orders, reports, petitions, etc. of the Yakutsk Infantry Regiment. Primarily from 1744-49, during the reign of Elizabeth; one document from the reign of Peter III, and several from that of Catherine II. Also, 2 photos of the documents. Materials were found in a church loft at Kenai, Alaska. They are too fragile for handling.

9 Petr Aleksandrovich Tikhmenev (1725-1863). Historical review of the formation of the Russian-American Company and its activity. With translations by Dmitrii (Dimitri) Krenov. 1 microfilm reel. (M/F 11)

10 Ivan Veniaminov. Russian cleric in Alaska. Diary, 1821-37, 1 microfilm reel. (M/F 46)

Finding Aids: "Guide to Manuscript Holdings--Work File with M/F" (30 June 1978), a computer print-out used for the preceding descriptions. There are also unpublished finding aids for each of the collections cited.

AK 5
ALASKA STATE HISTORICAL LIBRARY
333 Willoughby Avenue (Mail: Pouch G)
Juneau, Alaska 99811
(907-465-2925)

1 Innokentii, Metropolitan of Moscow (1797-1879). Papers, 1821-40, 3 vols. Includes correspondence relating to the Russian Orthodox Church in Alaska, papers of the Irkutsk Consistory, and Veniaminov's account of his trip to California in 1836. Manuscript in Russian, laminated. Microfilm only. (NUCMC 65-1712)

2 George E. Pilz (b. 1845). Typewritten letter, 1922, 31 pp., to James Wickersham, with "Reminiscences of the Oldest Pioneer Miner in Alaska."

3 Vladimir Stafeieff. Agent of the Western Fur and Trading Company. Journal or diary, 1 vol., in Russian, reflecting activities and observations at Nuchok, Kodiak, Tyonok, and Douglas, 1880-92. (On loan)

4 U.S. Bureau of Customs. Alaska customs records, 1867-1914, 264 vols. Includes 1 vol., 74 pp., by customs agents William Sumner Dodge and Hiram Ketchum, Jr., a manuscript record of events preceding and following the transfer of Alaska from Russia to the United States. Remaining records, uncatalogued, contain correspondence to and from U.S. customs agents in Alaska (Sitka, Juneau, Skagway, etc.) concerning commerce, vessels, and other matters. (NUCMC 65-1715)

5 David B. Walker (b. 1841?). Papers, 1864-69, 8 items and 1 vol. Sailor. Includes letters, 1868, with instructions from the American Russian Commercial Company to him, and journal concerning voyages on the Russian vessel Olga and the American Russian Commercial Company vessel Cesarewitch, and Walker's commencing as superintendent of ice works on Wood Island, Kodiak, and Kenai, Alaska. (NUCMC 70-1437)

6 Note: The library holds a number of other manuscript items pertaining to the history of Alaska, some of which may contain information about Russians or Russian activity.

Finding Aid: Guide to the Russian Holdings (Juneau, 1971).

AK 6
KODIAK PUBLIC LIBRARY
319 Benson Avenue
Kodiak, Alaska 99615
(907-486-3312)

Gabriel Ivan Davidov, "Account of Two Voyages to America by the Naval Officers Khvostov and Davidov, with Extracts from Davidov's Diary, 1810-1812" and Ivan Veniaminov, "The Russian Orthodox Church in Russian America, 1793-1853," both in Russian America, a bound typescript compiled by N. Gray (1925). Published in a new translation by Richard A. Pierce.

AK 7
ST. HERMAN'S PASTORAL SCHOOL
Mission Road
Kodiak, Alaska 99615
(907-486-3524)

The Archive of the Russian Orthodox Church in Alaska, currently housed at St. Herman's, is a major collection on Russian Alaska. Recovered in recent years from parish churches, the several hundred documents, rare books, and periodicals in this archive represent a collection largely complementary to the massive records of the Orthodox Ecclesiastical Consistory deposited with the Library of Congress in 1928. Parish records form the core of the holdings. Almost all the documents concern the Kvikhpak (Yukon) River Mission, founded at Ikogmute in 1845. The records cover over 100 years of Alaskan history. Physically, most of the records are in the form of large (8x13 in.) ledger books or soft-bound documents, in some cases damaged by weather, fire, mold, or mice. A brief outline of the kinds of parish records in the archive (taken from the Smith Survey cited under Finding Aids):

Journal. Kept by the priest to keep his superiors informed of his activities, the journal might cover only mission headquarters duties or it might also extend to travel among the parishioners. Particularly important is the journal of Father Jacob Netsvetov, 1845-53.

Journal of Worship Services. A record of the priests' official work, by the late 19th c. this type of journal was predominant. One example of the genre is Igumen Amfilokhii's record of his missionary work in the Chukchi region of Siberia, 1909-10.

School Journals. In the 1880s (post-Russian times) the parish school was the only educational institution in many outlying areas. The school year ran from November to April or May; instruction was in church law, Russian, English, calligraphy, geography, and arithmetic.

Vedomost' (Church Register). Included a physical description and brief history of the parish, its churches and chapels, and a biography of all clerical staff members. Equally important were its list of mission villages and their religious and social composition as well as cartographic and travel information.

Metrical Records. Accounts (annual) of births, baptisms (including adults), marriages, and deaths in the mission's jurisdiction. The name, social status, tribe, residence, and age of the parties involved appear in these records. After 1867 this type of document generally disappeared, though one large ledger of marriage inquests from the American period provides valuable genealogical data.

Confessional Lists. These records listed all village inhabitants in the parish, indicated if they were Christian, and even detailed the number of those receiving communion. Appended was a list of new converts, by village. Note: Both the Confessional Record and the Metrical Records often contain the sort of personal commentary more frequent in a priest's Journal.

Financial Accounts. An inventory of church/chapel property or general capital, annual income from candle sales and purchase of supplies, general income and expenses (usually by the month), clerical salaries, and donations/contributions.

Correspondence. See further under Finding Aids.

Miscellaneous Records. These include fragments, undated items, recent (post-1935) documents, manuscript fragments in the Yupik language, some material relating to Siberia, and one piece predating the mission's founding--instructions on marriage by Bishop Innocent in 1841.

Note: Parish records in the archive are on 11 reels of microfilm, available for loan or purchase. Plans are to develop a complete microfilm set of the Russian Orthodox American Messenger from the Alaska Archive, the Library of Congress materials, and holdings at the University of California at Berkeley and elsewhere. A contemplated second edition of the Preliminary Survey would serve as a guide to all of this material also (including a list of Messenger articles on Alaska).

Restriction: All original materials are closed to researchers; microfilm available (see above).

Finding Aids: Most important is the currently out of print, 135 pp., paperbound Preliminary Survey of the Documents in the Archives of the Russian Orthodox Church in Alaska (Boulder, Colorado: Western Interstate Commission for Higher Education, 1974) by Barbara Sweetland Smith.

ARIZONA

AZ 1
ARIZONA COLLECTION
CHARLES TRUMBULL HAYDEN LIBRARY
ARIZONA STATE UNIVERSITY
Tempe, Arizona 85281
(602-965-3145)

1 Barry M. Goldwater (b. 1909). Papers, 1867-1971, 155 ft., additions expected. U.S. Senator and Republican canidate for President, 1964. Correspondence, voting and congressional records, speeches, writings, 172 scrapbooks, 1948-65, photos, clippings, 121 reels of tape recordings, and other material. Scattered throughout are items pertaining to communism and the USSR. Unpublished guide and subject/name card index (NUCMC 72-24).

2 Carl T. Hayden (1877-1972). Papers, 1877-1972, 1,500 ft. U.S. Senator from Arizona. Includes State Department files with correspondence and miscellaneous historical documents, 1948-68, about the Cold War, communism, Lend-lease,

Soviet consular treaties, and trade agreements between the USSR and U.S. Subject and title index.

ARKANSAS

AR 1
SPECIAL COLLECTIONS
UNIVERSITY OF ARKANSAS LIBRARY
Fayetteville, Arkansas 72701
(501-575-4101)

James William Fulbright (b. 1905). Papers, 1941-60, 470 ft. U.S. senator from Arkansas, 1945-75, and chairman of the Senate Foreign Relations Committee, 1959-75. Constituent, official, and personal correspondence, memoranda, legislative bills and other records pertaining primarily to his governmental, political, and diplomatic activities and interests. Materials on the 1946 Fulbright Act, which provided for scholarly exchanges between the U.S. and other countries, the Fulbright-Hays Act (Mutual Educational and Cultural Exchange Program) of the early 1960s, U.S. foreign relations and military affairs, Wisconsin Senator Joseph Raymond McCarthy, the U-2 Incident and Paris Summit collapse of 1960, the Voice of America, exchange programs with the Soviet bloc, U.S.-USSR relations, and diplomat Charles E. Bohlen. Unpublished finding aids include a "File Title Inventory," "Index to File Titles," "Index to Selected Correspondents," and a "Third-Party--Selected Subjects--Proper Noun--Key-Word Index."

An additional accession of records, 1961-75, 650 cu. ft. of Senatorial correspondence, files, and other documents, is inaccessible until preliminary processing can be completed.

CALIFORNIA

CA 1
XENIA JOUKOFF EUDIN--PRIVATE COLLECTION
538 Clubhouse Drive
Aptos, California 95003

Born in Poltava, emigrating to the U.S. in 1932, Xenia J. Eudin was a research associate of the Hoover Institution at Stanford University from 1932-68. During these years she edited and translated, in collaboration with others, 4 books of documents on the Russian revolution and civil war. Currently in her possession are 5 manuscript books of her own, all being prepared for publication. Her 5 typescripts, each approximately 500 pp. in length, cover the following subjects, in translated and annotated documents: (1) the White and the Volunteer Army, 1918-20; (2) the Bolshevik westward thrust toward defeated Germany and Austro-Hungary and the anti-Soviet Northwestern Army's attempts to block it, 1918-20; (3) domestic opposition and the Cheka, 1918-21; (4) peasant opposition, 1918-21, in European Russia and Siberia; and (5) front organizations and the Comintern, 1921-62: a. pre-World War II organizations, 1921-41, and b. Soviet communist peace and international youth and students, 1945-62. The last 2 are nearly in final form.

The preceding materials and additional documents in her possession discuss such people and topics as the generals Nikolai N. Iudenich and Anton I. Denikin, V. I. Lenin, Leon Trotskii, I. V. Stalin, V. Molotov, A. A. Zhdanov, the collapse of the Imperial Russian Army, the formation of the Red Army, the post-World War II communist peace movement, and Soviet youth and students. Access is by consent of X. J. Eudin only. Most of the manuscripts and documents are currently being prepared for publication; all rights reserved.

CA 2
HIGHGATE ROAD SOCIAL SCIENCE RESEARCH STATION, INC.
32 Highgate Road
Berkeley, California 94707
(415-525-3248)

Molokan Christian Church Collection. Materials, ca. 1909-present, gathered by Ethel and Stephen P. Dunn. Primarily printed matter and photo and microform copies, but also business correspondence, literary manuscripts, manuscript books, and diaries. Also, a tape-recorded description of a flight to freedom in the Near East and rare or unique émigré Molokan periodicals and monographs, plus some titles published in Tiflis in the 1920s. Materials concern Molokan communities in Russia, particularly the Caucasus; Harbin, Manchuria; the United States; and Canada. Besides information on Molokan customs, history, practice, and theology, there are also data on the Dukhobors and Slavic Evangelical Christians. Information about these holdings may be obtained by writing Mrs. E. Dunn, Secretary, at the above address. Access is restricted to qualified scholars; literary rights are subject to permission of the Molokan church bodies involved.

CA 3
MORRIS GOLDSTEIN LIBRARY/WESTERN JEWISH HISTORY CENTER
JUDAH L. MAGNES MEMORIAL MUSEUM
2911 Russell Street
Berkeley, California 94705
(415-849-2710)

Morris Goldstein Library

1 Simon Belkin (b. 1889). Papers, 1919-29, ca. 500 items. Representative of the Jewish World Relief Organization. First American Jewish relief worker to arrive in the Ukraine during the civil war years of 1918 and after. He remained seven months, gathering information about pogroms (e.g., in Kiev), political activities of Russian Jews, and Jewish agricultural settlements. Materials in Yiddish and in Russian (the latter mostly unidentified) include protocols from his discussions with Soviet relief authorities and data from the All-Russian Union of the Jewish Working Masses. Among the organizations with which Belkin dealt and had information about were the Federation of Ukrainian Jews, the Kievan city committee of the Jewish Communist Party, the Jewish Section of the Bolshevik Central Committee (central bureau), Ukrainian United Jewish Socialist Labor Party, and the Jewish/Social Committee in Moscow. Also, material on the question of Soviet Jewish emigration and ca. 100 photographs of Ukrainian Jewish pogrom victims and of relief efforts. Unpublished partial list of items.

2 Max Lilienthal (1815-1852). Correspondence, 1839-45, 38 letters. Principal of a newly opened Jewish school in Riga, 1840-45. He took the post at the request of Nicholas I. Minister of Education S. S. Uvarov solicited his aid as an intermediary between the regime and Jews in reforming education and establishing Jewish schools. Lilienthal traveled in the Pale of Settlement in 1842, took part in the work of a commission on Jewish reform, May-August 1843, and left Russia in 1845. The letters, mostly in German and French, concern educational reform and Russian Jews. They mention Uvarov, the Chevalier Dukstaduchinskii, de Vrochenko, Vorontsov, and educational ukazy of 22 June 1842 and 3 November 1844. Unpublished list of letters with dates, places of origin, and addresses.

Western Jewish History Center

3 Michael Caminetsky (1850-1932). Family papers, 1869-1881, 17 items. Author. Includes materials from Russia and a family tree. Michael and Rivka Caminetsky came to Winnipeg, Manitoba, Canada, in 1882.

4 Leopold Lerner (1897-1971). Papers, 1940s-1971, 9 scrapbooks. Businessman. Material relating to San Francisco, Israel, Russian and national Jewish life. Includes an interview and biographical data.

Finding Aid: Suzanne Nemiroff, Catalog of Manuscripts Collections (1977), for the WJHC only.

CA 4
PROFESSOR GLEB STRUVE--PRIVATE COLLECTION
1154 Spruce Street
Berkeley, California 94707
(415-525-4638)

Prof. Struve holds the papers of his father, Peter B. Struve (1870-1944)--political leader, economist, and historian--and his own scholarly papers and literary correspondence. Details of the two collections are not available at this time and both are currently closed to outside researchers. Ultimate disposition of the papers is undetermined. Prof. Struve will attempt to respond to scholarly inquiries.

CA 5
MANUSCRIPTS DIVISION, BANCROFT LIBRARY
UNIVERSITY OF CALIFORNIA
Berkeley, California 94720
(415-642-3781)

1 George Russell Adams (b. 1845?). "A Story of the First American Exploring Expedition to Russian America . . . 1865-1867," microfilm. Experiences as a member of the Western Union Telegraph Company's expedition for the Russian Extension, under Colonel Charles S. Bulkley and Major Robert Kennicott. Includes a separate account of his trading venture to Alaska, 1868.

2 Alaska Miscellany. 10 items, ca. 1878-1915. Translations from Russian articles by Alexander Petrovich Sokolov and Peter Simon Pallas; extracts taken from the transcribed journal of James Douglas; notes on Alaska trade digested, 1877, from commercial correspondence of Agapius Honcharenko in San Francisco with Oppenheim & Company of London, 1868-73; letter from George Washington McCrary, Secretary of War, to H. H. Bancroft (Washington, D.C., 3 December 1878), 1 p., signed, concerning papers formerly belonging to the Russian American Fur Company; LS from Richard Wigginton Thompson, Secretary of the Navy, to Bancroft (Washington, D.C., 13 February 1879) about a report on the Aleutian Islands by the U.S. North Pacific Surveying

Expedition; 1 p. report on the fishing grounds on the Alaska Coast (188-?) and the need of fisheries exploration by the U.S. government; list applying to Russian America: "Omissions in Ivan Petrov's Translation of Tikhmenev's 'Historical Review . . . of the Russian American Company', of "Materials for the History of Russian Possessions . . .', and of Veniaminov's 'Letters . . .'" (1915?) 6 ll.; and ALS from Paul Schumacher (Los Angeles, 2 July 1878) to [William Healey Dall], 2 pp., thanking him for publications about Alaska Indians and archaeology. In 3 separate collections.

3 Konstantin Sergeevich Alekseev (1863-1938). [Rabota aktera nad soboi. Ca. 1923], 220 ll., in Russian, holograph and typescript, with revisions: early draft of An actor prepares, an exposition of his techniques of creative acting; and copy of a letter by A. Koiransky (17 November 1960) concerning the manuscript. Also, a photocopy of the Alekseev manuscript.

4 José Joaquín de Arrillaga (1750-1814). Correspondence, 1794-1814, 1 portfolio. Governor of Upper California. Letters written by him to M. Castro and to him from F. M. Calleja, Viceroy of Mexico, concerning Russian deserters and illegal Russian trading in California. (Mainly from the T. W. Norris and Cowan collections)

5 David Prescott Barrows (1873-1954). Papers, 1892-1954, 33 cartons and 8 boxes. Professor of political science and president of the University of California, Berkeley, 1919-23. Diaries, notebooks, scrapbooks, clippings, and notes, including material on his service as lieutenant colonel and intelligence officer with the American Expeditionary Forces in Siberia, 1918-19. Also, miscellany about communism and the USSR and subject files on Russia.

6 Fedor Bashmakov. 6 documents, 1829-31. Papers relating to his trial for sorcery at Sitka in 1829, translated by Ivan Petrov in 1878 from originals held by Rev. A. Mitropolsky at Sitka.

7 M. P. Berry. "Developments in Alaska" [San Francisco, 1879], 22 ll., interview recorded at the Bancroft Library, with interjections by Ivan Petrov, on the British Columbia boundary, inadequacy of existing charts, gold discoveries and potentialities, white settlements, salmon fisheries, and resources of the country.

8 Bible. New Testament. Selections. Manuscript (n.d.), in Church Slavic.

9 E. Blashke. ". . . O baidarkakh i o Lis'evskikh Aleutakh . . . 1848," 50 pp., transcript of "A Few Observations on Handling the Kayak and on the Aleuts of Lis'ev Island" (Morskoi sbornik, vol. I, 1848).

10 Dmitrii Bragin. Report of a Four Years' Voyage to [the Aleutians, from Okhotsk, 1772-1777?], 7 ll., translation of a narrative published by Peter Simon Pallas in Neue nordische Beyträge, vol. II, pp. 308-24.

11 [Charles S. Bulkley]. Journal of the U.S. Russo-American Telegraph Expedition, 1865-67, microfilm copies of correspondence and reports while he commanded the Western Union Telegraph Company's expedition for the Russian Extension. Original held by the Library Association of Portland, Oregon.

12 Manuel de Jesús Castro (b. 1821). Collection, 1828-75, 2 boxes. Prefect at Monterey. Primarily official letters and documents sent to him concerning military affairs, mission matters, elections, land transactions, and Russians in California. Also microfilm copy. Permission required to use originals.

13 Catherine II (1729-1796). Russian empress. Document, 22 September 1784, presumedly signed by Catherine, conferring an honorary title on General Simon for his services to the state.

14 Zakhar Chichinov (b. 1802). "Adventures of Zakahar Tchitchinoff, an employee of the Russian American Fur Company, 1802-1878" [Kodiak, Alaska, 1878], 52 pp., dictation recorded by Ivan Petrov, with an explanatory note. Reminiscences about Alexander Baranov, in whose house Chichinov lived at Sitka before going to California in 1818; life at Fort Ross; sea lion and sea otter hunting along the Pacific Coast; relations with the Spaniards; Tarakanov's 1824 hunting party; later experiences at St. Paul's on Kodiak Island; smallpox epidemic of 1836; salvage operations at Kenai Bay; life at Sitka and on Kodiak.

15 George Chismore (1840-1906). Papers, 1866-81, 3 vols. Surgeon. Served on the Western Union Telegraph Company's expedition for the Russian Extension. Typed transcripts of logbook, 1866, and other papers.

16 Edward Conway. Correspondence and papers, 1861-76, microfilm. Letterbooks, diaries, and other material concerning his service as superintendent, Collins Overland Telegraph Company, and assistant engineer for the Western Union Telegraph Company's Russian Extension. Originals in the British Columbia Provincial Archives.

17 R. B. Crittenden. Forty-niner and California legislator, farmer at Fort Wrangel, Alaska, from 1878. "Agricultural Capabilities of Alaska" [ca. 1890], 6 pp.

18 Cutting Packing Company. San Francisco. "Alaska Fisheries" [ca. 1885], 5 ll.

19 Nannielou Hepburn (Reier) Dieter (b. 1926). Correspondence and papers, ca. 1947-74, 1 box. Radio astronomer. Letters from her colleagues, Bart J. Bok, Cecilia H. Payne-Goposchkin, and Soviet astronomer Solomon P. Pickelner;

photographs; and her notebook from a 1947 astronomy course. (History of Science Collection)

20 James Douglas (1803-1877). Journals, 1840-1843, microfilm. Extracts made in 1878 of 5 journals kept in the service of the Hudson's Bay Company, 22 April 1840-25 September 1843, describing travels in Oregon, Washington, British Columbia, Alaska, and California, by land and sea. Originals in the British Columbia Provincial Archives.

21 Clarence John Du Four (b. 1879). Papers, 2 cartons. Mainly notes and transcriptions relating to his thesis on John A. Sutter and his life in California. Includes notes and draft of an article on the "Abandonment of the Russians in California."

22 Early Commerce in the North Pacific. Lists of vessels and masters, mostly from New England ports, 1787-1807, 3 ll.

23 George Foster Emmons (1811-84). Naval officer. Typed excerpts from his journal (19 August-2 November 1867), 21 ll., relating to his command of the U.S.S. Ossipee, conveying the U.S. and Russian commissioners to Sitka for the Alaska transfer ceremonies.

24 José Fernández (1799-ca. 1875). Signed manuscript: Cosas de California (Santa Clara, California), 19 August 1874, dictation recorded by Henry Cerruti for H. H. Bancroft. Reminiscences about early California, including Russians at Bodega and Ross, 193 pp., with clippings pasted in. Also on microfilm.

25 Charles R. Flint (1850-1934). 9 letters, 1917-18. Correspondence relates primarily to Russia, written when he was chairman of the American Committee for the Encouragement of Democratic Government in Russia. (In Chester H. Rowell Papers)

26 J. C. Glidden. 1 item, 1883. Seaman. Signed holograph (?), 15 ll., reminiscences of 2 voyages to Alaska in command of a sailing vessel, 1870-71, the first to the Gulf of Nushahak, the other to Kodiak and Afognak islands and Cochokmac Gulf. Describes construction of a bidarka, the Aleuts, church building, and services at St. Paul's.

27 Eliab Grimes (1780-1848). 2 items, 1820-22. Sea captain. A journal for 23 May 1821-1 February 1822 was kept mainly aboard the schooner Eagle on a trading voyage to California and return to the Sandwich Islands. Describes visits to Fort Ross, San Francisco, and other Spanish cities.

28 De la Guerra Family. Papers, 1752-1955, 4,179 items. Spanish landowners in California. Correspondence and reports, handwritten in Spanish, from the period 1810-41, concern Russians in California, Fort Ross, Russo-Spanish relations in California, Russian shipping, and the fur trade. Microfilm copies of originals in the Santa Barbara Mission Archives in California. Unpublished calendar for the papers available at the Mission and at the Huntington Library in San Marino.

29 Gurdon Hall (b. 1812). 1 item, 1844-47. Seaman. Journal of a Whaling Voyage from Stonington [Connecticut] around the World by Way of the Cape of Good Hope on to the Northwest Coast of America . . . on Board the Ship, Charles Phelps, Gilbert Pendelton, Jr., Command[ing] . . . . [1844-1847], 230 pp., signed holograph. The Charles Phelps hunted whales off the coast of "Kamzcatka" (Kamchatka) in the fall of 1845.

30 Warren Heckrotte. "The Discovery of Humboldt Bay: A New Look at an Old Story," n.p., n.d., 32 ll., photocopy of a typescript. Concerns the role of the Russian-American Company in the discovery and development of the Bay, with comments on early Russian maps of the area and on the voyage of the O'Cain under Captain John Winslip in 1806. Notes at end of paper, pp. 23-32.

31 Agapius Honcharenko (1831-1916). 4 collections, 1850-73, 22 items and 10 vols. Editor of the journal Svoboda [Alaska Herald]. (a) "Address to the People of Alaska" (1868), 2 ll., translation of an address originally printed in Russian in the San Francisco Alaska Herald, concerning the position of Americans and Aleuts in view of the transfer of sovereignty from Russia to the U.S.; (b) Alaska Scrap Book, 1868-70, 2 vols., clippings mostly from San Francisco newspapers, some in Russian, and two letters from Honcharenko, 1877 and 1909, concerning material he supplied to the Bancroft Library; (c) correspondence between Prince Dmitrii Petrovich Maksutov, chief of the Russian colonies in America, and Sergei Stepanov, supervisor of St. Michael Redoubt, 10 letters, 1867-68, in Russian; list of credits of the employees and Aleuts by sections, to 1 July 1867, 2 pp., in Russian; copy of the form of contract, 1850, between the Russian-American Company in St. Petersburg and its employees, translated from the Russian into Swedish, then to English, 8 pp.; 7 letters and petitions of Russian and Aleut residents in the Aleutians, addressed to American and Russian officials, 1868-73, and an account of Russian missionary activities relating to schools on Sitka Island, in Russian; letter of protest, 1872, by Russian traders living at St. Michael Redoubt, addressed to Honcharenko in San Francisco, 2 pp., printed in English; facsimile of a seal belonging to Rev. Pëtr Salamatov, converted Aleutian tribal chief; and (d) "Marine and Shipping Intelligence from the Alaska Herald and other papers" [1867-73], 8 vols., with some newspaper clippings included, holograph.

32 Innokentii, Metropolitan of Moscow (1797-1879). The priest Ivan Evsieevich Popov-Veniaminov, later Metropolitan Innokentii, visited Fort Ross and several California missions in 1836. His "travel journal" from Sitka to California and return covers the period 1 July-13 October 1836. Copied from the original in the Alaska Archives at Juneau. Includes a 1951 translation by Richard A. Pierce. Each item 10 ll.

33 Charles James (1817-1901). Papers, 1863-72, 2 vols. Customs collector. Vol. 2 holds an invitation to a ball in San Francisco, 17 November 1863, honoring Admiral Popoff and the Russian squadron.

34 Hiram Warren Johnson (1866-1945). Papers, ca. 1895-1945, 145 boxes and 49 cartons. U.S. senator from California, 1917-45. Includes 1 carton of subject files relating to Russia, 2 letters from the Russian Consulate in San Francisco, 1913, and 1 letter from the Russian Consolidated Mutual Aid Society, 1931. Probably more Russian-related material in other subject files.

35 John Coffin Jones. U.S. consul in the Sandwich Islands. Letter to the secretary of state in Honolulu, 12 March 1837, 2 ll., concerning the Russian threat to California in light of the recent "revolution" there; with a letter of transmittal from Colonel Thomas M. Spaulding (1936). Typed transcript from the National Archives.

36 Iëromonakh Juvenal (d. 1796). 1 item, 1796. Priest. Journal of one of the earliest missionaries of Alaska, 74 pp. Experiences at Three Saints Harbor, Pavlovsk, Kenai River, and Ilyamna, 19 June-29 September 1796, when Father Juvenal was stabbed to death by the natives. Translation by Ivan Petrov, 1878. Original in possession (1878) of Rev. Innokentii Shashnikov at Unalaska.

37 John Henry Kinkead (1826-1905). 2 items, 1884-ca. 1886. First appointed governor of Alaska, 1884. Dictation ("In Nevada and Alaska. 1884") concerns his early life, business background, trip to Alaska with a U.S. expedition in 1867, stay at Sitka until 1871, military and U.S. commissioners, the transfer of sovereignty, social and economic conditions in Alaska, and return to Nevada in 1871. His biographical sketch (ca. 1886), 2 pp., touches only briefly on his appointment as Alaskan governor after definition of that territory as a civil and judicial district. 2 separate items.

38 Ivan Konny-gen (b. ca. 1833). "The Nulato Massacre" (San Quentin Prison, California, 1879), 6 pp. Statement recorded by Ivan Petrov concerning the killing of Lieutenant Barnard of the British navy and others in an attack on Fort Nulato in 1851, the principal instigator of which was Konny-gen's uncle, Larion.

39 Peter Kostromitin (b. 1798). 1 item, 1878. Russian-American Company official. "Early Times on the Aleutian Islands. Life of Peter Kostromitin, 1798-1878," 16 pp. Recorded, with explanatory note, by Ivan Petrov. Life in Unalaska, visit of Captain L. Hagemeister, ca. 1819-20, influence of Father Veniaminov in Christianizing the Aleuts, and the Russian-American Company.

40 G. Kromchenko. "Zhurnal plavania . . . 1822 g. . . . 1824," 174 pp., excerpts from the "Journal of the Voyage of Kormchenko in 1822" (Severnyi arkhiv, vols. X-XI, 1824).

41 Charles Krüger (b. 1828). 1 item, 1885. Russian-American Company worker. Born in Riga, joined the Russian-American Company in 1853. His statement, 12 pp., describes trip around the Horn to Sitka, work there until the Company ceased operations, Indian difficulty in 1854, and events surrounding the transfer of sovereignty to the U.S. in 1869.

42 Jerome Barker Landfield (1871-1954). Photocopy of typescript entitled "Operation Kaleidoscope, A Mélange of Personal Recollections," 219 pp., n.p., n.d. Education and career, travel in Russia, Siberian gold mines, marriage to Princess Louba Lobanov-Rostovsky, and teaching at the University of California.

43 Thomas O. Larkin (1802-1858). Papers, 1822-58, 20 boxes. Merchant, diplomatic agent, and U.S. consul at Monterey, California before U.S. acquisition. Personal, official, and business correspondence. Much information on the Russian-American Company, ca. 1840-51 (accounts with, evacuation of Bodega, supplies to Kamchatka, John Augustus Sutter's debts to, contracts with the Hudson's Bay Company and a man named Thompson, need for wheat, and ships in America). Correspondence of J. A. Sutter with M. Tebennof. References to the Crimean War (Allied Powers' attitude to Russia, Turkey's declaration of war, recruitment), and to vessels named Moscow (several, 1845-47), Petersburg, Bhering, Baltic, and Mazeppa. Correspondence with Pedro Kostromitinof (Petr Kostromitinov) of the Russian-American Company, 1845, and with A. Etholen, governor of the Russian-American Colony, 1844-45. Reference to Fort Ross, ca. 1843. The Larkin Papers have been published, 10 vols. (Berkeley, 1951-64), edited by George P. Hammond, and an Index for the publication appeared in 1968, edited by Anna Marie and Everett G. Hager.

44 List of Vessels of the Siberian Fleet, From 1714 to 1853. 8 ll. From the Okhotsk Archives, copied from Morskoi sbornik, 1855.

45 Alexander Petrovich Maksutov (b. 1832). Papers, 1854-1925, 1 microfilm reel. Russian prince, officer. Manuscripts, photos, maps, pamphlets, and service record relating to his military career, the Crimean War, Battle of Petropavlovsk (1854), etc.

46 Emma Jane McIntyre (b. 1846?). 1 item, 28 pp., 1874. "Observations of Life on the Pribilof Islands. St. Georges Island, Alaska," holograph, written for her mother while her husband, Captain William J. McIntyre, was resident agent on St. Georges Island for the Alaska Commercial Company. Notes on the geography, climate, flora, fauna, natives, daily life; plus an explanatory note by her daughter, Julia McIntyre Merriman, and tear sheets of two articles concerning the Pribilov Islands.

47 Mexico. Archivo General de la Nacíon. Provincias Internas, 1689-1830. Microfilm. Information on Russians in California. Also, record prints and transcripts of selected items. Unpublished finding aid.

48 John Franklin Miller (1831-1886). 1 item, 6 pp., ca. 1885. President of the Alaska Commercial Company. Statement concerning lease of Pribilov Islands by the U.S. Government. The Alaska Commercial Company leased the islands in 1870. Also, a biographical sketch of Miller.

49 Nicholas Tiho Mirov (b. 1893). Diary, 1917-64, 812 pp. in 2 vols. Plant physiologist and professor of Russian geography at Berkeley. Diary, partly in Russian, has photographs and clippings pasted in. Russian revolution, civil war, departure from Russia via Siberia and Manchuria, arrival in the U.S., 1923, career in industry, and teaching. Requires written permission of Professor Mirov. Also, 2 cartons of unprocessed papers.

50 Gustave Niebaum (b. 1842). 5 items, 1883-85. Finn employed by the Russian-American Company from 1858, captain of the steamboat Constantine. "Sealing in Alaska" (San Francisco, 1883), 70 ll., with commentary on Alaska's resources, potentialities, people, living conditions, and recent commercial development; biographical materials; statement on Alaska fur interests; and statement on the transfer of Alaska to the U.S. 2 separate holdings.

51 Joseph Rous Paget-Fredericks (1905-1963). Collection, ca. 1925-63, 9 boxes, 3 cartons, and 1 portfolio. Dance collection, with letters from Russians, primarily dancers, and about Russian dancers, especially A. Pavlova and V. Nijinsky; Paget-Fredericks's reminiscences and writings about his father, Vladimir Borisovitch Freedericksz, and about Pavlova, S. Diaghilev, L. Bakst, Nijinsky, and Olga Spessivtseva; and notes, memorabilia, etc. relating to Pavlova, T. Toumanova, and Isadora Duncan.

52 Ivan Petrov (1842-1896). 5 collections, ca. 1877-84. Associate of H. H. Bancroft. (a) Alaska Archives, from Oonalaska (i.e., Unalaska) and St. Paul's Island [1878?], 35 pp., census data for Unalaska, baptismal records at Sitka (1805-19); translation of a petition by inhabitants of Unalaska for the removal of Ivan Laduigin, an objectionable character, in 1878; translation and Russian text of a Chief's Address to Sea Otter Hunters, n.d.; (b) Dictation, ca. 1884, 5 ll. Information on hunting of sea lions and sea otters; the dome of the Greek church at Sitka; Russian motives for selling Alaska; establishment of the Greek Church there; attitude of the inhabitants toward the sale of Alaska and the American succession; and transfer of the property of the Russian-American Company; (c) signed holograph of Petroff (Petrov)--"Journal of Trip to Alaska in Search of Information for the Bancroft Library" (San Francisco, 1878), 76 pp. Aboard the U.S. Revenue Cutter Richard Rush (11 July-27 October 1878) he visited sites in Washington, British Columbia, Sitka, Kodiak, Delarof, Belkovsky, Ilinlink, Unalaska, Makushin, St. George, St. Paul, Tchitchtagov, and other Alaskan points; (d) "The Management and Personnel of the Russian-American Company from its Beginning to its Dissolution" [San Francisco, 1877], 21 ll., signed holograph, a brief history which Petrov entitled "The Russian Hunters and Trappers on the American Northwest Coast"; and (e) "Memorandum on . . . departure for Alaska. May 7, 1879," 3 ll., signed holograph concerning Bancroft's History of Alaska, outlining parts still to be written, with a letter to Petrov from John M. Morton, Washington, D.C. 4 February 1879.

53 Alphonse Louis Pinart (1852-1911). Collections (many), ca. 1871-1878, 2 boxes and 22 items. French linguist and scholar. (a) Alaska Papers [ca. 1871-77], 2 boxes, manuscripts in English, Russian, French, German, Latin, and Alaskan dialects; sketch maps and drawings of Alaskan terrain with legends in French, Russian, and English; ethnological notes on the Aleuts and others; miscellaneous reference notes, mostly bibliographical; linguistic notes relating to Russia and Siberia, Kamchatka, Sakhalin Island, the Kurile Islands, the Ainus, the Aleutian Islands, and Alaska, recorded in Russian, German, and native dialects; (b) 21 transcripts of articles from Russian publications, ca. 1875, about Alaska, the Aleutians, and Siberia from 1729 to ca. 1871, mostly in Pinart's hand. Includes early reports on Kamchatka and the Chukotsk Cape; voyages by Grigorii Shelekhov, Ivan Vasil'ev, Andrei Ustiugov, Lieutenant Voronovskii, and Alexander Kashevarov; dispatches by Kiril Timofeevich Khlebnikov, and Ferdinand Petrovich Wrangel; news notes; and ethnological observations, especially on the Eskimos and Chukchis. Most reflect activities of the Russian-American Company.

54 Rossiisko-Amerikanskaia Kompaniia. Several collections, 104 microfilm reels and 6 other items. (a) "Les Russes aux Iles Hawaii" [1809-22], 206 pp., transcripts in Russian, English, and French, mainly by Alphonse Pinart, of documents supposedly in Russian archives, titled by Pinart. Summaries of two letters by Leontii Hagemeister, 1809, describing the Hawaiian Islands and making recommendations as

to Russian occupation; fuller reports by Vasilii Berkh and Ivan Kuskov, 1817; instructions of Governor A. Baranov on sending Dr. Yegor Scheffer to the Islands, 1815; Scheffer's handling of Russian affairs there, 1816-19; his correspondence with the Company and with nationals of other countries; commercial negotiations with the natives; and related documents; plus English translation by George Vjacheslau Lantzeff (1949?) of the first 121 pp.; also in microfilm; (b) instructions to Baranov, governor in America, 18 April 1802, 11 ll., translated by Ivan Petrov, concerning the conduct of foreign relations and the company's affairs, directing Baranov to establish through settlement the Russian claim to America south of 55°; (c) correspondence, Sitka, Alaska, 1802-67, 85 vols. on 104 reels. Records of the Russian-American Company, created in 1799 by Paul I as a monopoly to carry on the Russian fur trade on the North American continent, with political and economic control of Alaska until its purchase by the U.S. in 1867. In Russian, longhand: 40 vols. of letters sent by the governors general, 1818-67; 25 vols. of letters received by the governors general, 1802, 1817-66; and 20 logs of vessels and journals of exploring expeditions, 1842-67. Consists of microfilm, record prints, and some Cyrillic transcripts made for Robert J. Kerner, a Berkeley professor, supplemented by film from the National Archives. Originals in the Records of the State Department at the National Archives; (d) "Kratkoe istoricheskoe obozrenie obrazovania i deistvii Rossiisko-Amerikanskoi Kompanii s samogo nachala uchrezhdenia onoi, i do nastoiashchago vremeni," 163 pp. (n.d.), a translation of which by Ivan Petrov is listed below under Russian America; (e) "Opis' delam Rossiisko-Amerikanskoi Kompanii s 1781 po 1825 god," 77 pp., inventory of documents and communications received, pertaining to the affairs of the Russian-American Company, 17 August 1781-27 August 1824, with a letter (1866) to P. V. Falk. See under Russian America for a translation of the same or a similar inventory; (f) "Otchet R. A. K. . . . 1846," 1 p., transcript by A. Pinart: "Report of the Russian-American Company," concerning two expeditions in search of a water route north of the Nikolaevsk and Konstantinovsk redoubts; and (g) 2 manuscripts in Russian, bound in 1 vol.: a diary of Vladimir Romanov, ca. 1831, 19 pp., and a statement of commercial conditions of the company in 1831, delivered to shareholders, 18 pp. The diary concerns Romanov's visit to Alaskan settlements and the condition of the company's offices in Novoarchangelsk, Sitka, Kodiak, and Unalaska.

55 Russia. Archives. Microfilm of records relating to Russians in Alaska, 1732-96. Journals, logbooks, and reports by Vitus J. Bering, A. I. Chirikov, Nikolai Golovnin, Sofron Khitrov, G. F. Müller, Grigorii Shelikov, Vice-Admiral Sanders, G. W. Steller, Sven Waxel, and Kharlam Yushin. From negative and positive photostats obtained in Leningrad for the University of Washington in Seattle.

56 Russia, Gosudarstvennyi Sovet. "Mnenie . . . 1865-66," viii + 3 pp., facsimile of a manuscript Opinion of the Council of the Empire, confirmed by His Majesty the Emperor, concerning the charter of the Russian-American Company and the regulations for the Russian-American colonies, 14 June 1865, with amendment, 2 April 1866.

57 Russian America. Collection of translations, ca. 1758-1866, 7 vols. All but one are from Russian publications, most done by Ivan Petrov, 1876-80. They concern the early history of Siberia, Alaska, and the Russian-American Company, the Fort Ross colony in California, and Russian voyages in the Pacific. Includes works by P. Tikhmenev (partial translation by Petrov; the library also has a manuscript translation of the complete work by Michael Dobrynin and Dimitri Krenov made in 1938-40), Vassili Petrovich Tarakanov, Metropolitan Innokentii of Moscow [i.e., Ivan Veniaminov], Kiryll Khlebnikov, Grigorii Shelekhov, Real State Councillor Kostlivtzov, Dmitry Zavalishin, A. Zagoskin, Ivan Ogorodnikov, Aleksiei Markov, Vassili Berg, and Gavrila I. Davidov. There is an unpublished list of transactions of the Russian-American Company from 1781-1825 compiled from documents preserved in its archives, 15 pp. Other references: A. Baranov, vessels sailing to and from the Russian American colonies in 1849-52 (a list), Cape Chukhotsk, the Aleutians, and the fur trade.

58 Russian Consulate (San Francisco, California). 3 letters, 1902, from Paul Kosakevitch of the Imperial consulate. (Frederick S. Stratton Collection)

59 Russian Émigré Collection. 1 box at present. Printed matter, clippings, and mimeographed typescripts. Concerns the Russian emigration in California, the Tubabao (Philippines) displaced persons camp, etc. Currently uncatalogued, the material includes issues of rare periodicals and an autobiography of A. Lenkov, 13 pp.

60 Russian Historical Society. 1 portfolio, 1937-38. Form letters, programs, printed album, and clippings, all relating to the Society's efforts to raise funds to maintain Fort Ross as an historic site.

61 Russian Missionary Activities in the Aleutian Islands. 5 items, ca. 1840-1904. Fragment in Russian and Aleut from the Book of Matthew, ca. 1840, 100 pp.; copies of 2 sermons in Aleut, 1842, by I. Veniaminov, later Innokentii, Metropolitan of Moscow, 23 pp.; journal of an unidentified priest, in Russian, 23 August 1847-6 March 1849, 24 pp.; diary in Russian, 1861-63, kept by I. Shaishnokov,

priest at Unalaska, 38 pp.; and copy of a mimeographed periodical, The Orthodox Alaska (Unalaska, January 1904) in Aleut, Russian, and English.

62 Russians in Alaska. Documents relative to the history of Alaska, 18th-20th c., 11 vols. on microfilm (positive). Made from copy in the Library of Congress. Typed transcripts of documents, or excerpts therefrom, made, 1936-38, from material in the U.S. Department of State Archives, Division of Manuscripts and Slavic Division of the Library of Congress, and the U.S. Department of the Interior. Russian documents translated by T. I. Lavrischeff. Contents: vols. 1-4 (reel 1), Alaska Church Collection, the Yudin Collection, and the Golder Collection from the Library of Congress; logbooks of ships of the Russian-American Company; reports of governors of the company and excerpts from company archives; vols. 5-7 (reel 2), excerpts from Russian Orthodox American Messenger, 1897-1901; miscellaneous documents from Alaska Territorial Library, Juneau; material from Library of Congress relating to Bering Sea controversy; excerpts from Erastus Brainerd Collection relating to activities of the Seattle Chamber of Commerce in connection with the Klondike gold rush; vols. 8-10 (reel 3), material relating to the problem of reorganizing the government of Alaska, 1914-31; material relating to Ballinger-Pinchot controversy; annual reports of the Alaska Engineering Commission, 1917-22; vol. 11 (reel 4), annual reports of the Alaska Engineering Commission and Alaska Railroad, 1922-26; and reports of the Manager of the Land and Industrial Department, 1916-17.

63 St. Petersburg Finnish Colony. Ornate document, November 1910, signed by members of the Finnish colony in St. Petersburg, 1 p., expressing gratitude to Paul Miliukov for his efforts on behalf of the Finnish nation.

64 Martin Sauer. Digest by Ivan Petrov of a part of Sauer's Account of a Geographical and Astronomical Expedition to the Northern Parts of Russia (London, 1802)--about Captain Joseph Billings' second voyage, 1791-92, from Kamchatka to the American coast, 5 ll.

65 Charles Melville Scammon (1825-1911). Papers, 1849-1911, 6 boxes, 2 portfolios, and 2 packages. Journal and letterbook concerning the Western Union Telegraph Company's expedition for the Russian Extension, 1865-67. Scrapbooks, maps, pictures, and papers.

66 Grigorii Ivanovich Shelekhov (1747-1795). 1 item, 122 pp. Russian fur merchant, founder of first permanent Alaskan settlement on Kodiak Island. Transcript of the German edition (St. Petersburg, 1793) of his Rossiiskago kuptsa Imenitago Ryl'skago grazhdanina . . . pervoe stranstvovanie s 1783 po 1787 god . . . (Grigori Schelechof Russischen Kaufmanns . . . Reise . . . in den Jahren 1783 bis 1787. . . .). For Ivan Petrov's translation of the 1812 edition, see under Russian America.

67 George V. Sheviakov (d. 1973). "My Life" (1970), photocopy of typescript, xii + 305 ll., with copies of photographs inserted. Childhood in Russia, experiences during the revolution, service in the White Army, escape to China and residence there, emigration to the U.S., work in fisheries in Alaska, Russian colony in San Francisco, career as psychologist and professor.

68 The Sitka Times. Sitka, Alaska. 1868. Handwritten weekly newspaper, edited by Barney O. Ragan, vol. I, nos. 1, 6-8 (19 September, 24 October-7 November 1868), 16 pp.

69 Alexander Petrovich Sokolov (1816-1858). 3 items, 1852. Transcripts by A. Pinart, in Russian, of articles published in Zapiski Gidrograficheskogo Departamenta. References to the River Mednaia, Serebrennikov, the Chukchi, Captains Shishmarev, Krenitsin, and Levashev, the Aleutian Islands, Kamchatka, Ushakov, Elistratov, Khvostov, and Davydov.

70 Vasilii Sokolov (b. 1820). Sitka parish clerk. "The Voyage of Alexander Markoff from Okhotsk to California and Mazatlan in 1835" (Sitka, 1878), 14 pp. Statement recorded by Ivan Petrov, plus explanatory note. Visit to San Francisco, Monterey, and Hawaii in 1835; ravages of smallpox in Alaska, 1836; influence of the Russian-American Company and the Church on Alaskan life; circumstances of his becoming parish clerk; and the effect of American acquisition of Alaska.

71 Ivan Soloviev. Extracts from the Journal of Soloviev during the years 1770-75, 9 ll., translation of an abstract by P. S. Pallas, published in Neue nordische Beyträge, 1781, vol. 2, pp. 325-41.

72 Spain. Archivo General de Indias, Seville. Papeles de Estado, 1773-1821 [Selected legajos]. Microfilm, and record prints and/or transcripts of selected items. Information on Russians in America. Unpublished guide.

73 Konstantin Stanislavskii. See under Konstantin Sergeevich Alekseev, the actor's real name.

74 Andrew Jackson Stone (1859-1918). Papers, 1896-1918, 1 carton. Traveler, naturalist, and businessman. Visited Fort Wrangel in 1896. Diaries and reports on his extensive travel in the Pacific northwest and Alaska, 1896-1903. (NUCMC 65-1819)

75 Heinrich Storch (1765-1835). 1 item. Historian. Extracts in German from his Russland unter Alexander dem Ersten. Eine historische Zeitschrift . . . (St. Petersburg, 1804), made for A. Pinart. Documents pertaining to the organization of the Russian-American Company, 1798-99, 34 pp.

76 William Sturgis (1782-1863). "Fur Traders in the North Pacific" (1799), 35 ll., extracts from his journal, 15 February-17 May 1799, on board the Eliza, Captain Rowan, while trading for sea otter on the Northwest Coast; also, his reminiscences of the Northwest Coast, 1799-ca. 1804. Microfilm copy of the first item listed under Voyages to the Alaska Coast.

77 John Augustus Sutter (1803-1880). Letters, 1840-46, 35 pp. German-born early California settler and entrepreneur. Extracts from his letters to Antonio Suñol, relating primarily to business matters, with some references to Russians in California. Also photocopy and transcripts of the letters.

78 Alexander Smith Taylor (1817-1876). "Notes on the Indianology of Alaska . . ." (Santa Barbara, California, 1867), 27 ll., signed holograph, addressed to J. Ross Browne. Ethnology, linguistics, and natural history of Alaska.

79 Thomas Taylor. Depositions by Peter Rupi and Michael Petetin, interpreted from the Russian by A. Honcharenko, in the case of Thomas Taylor vs. the Alaska Commercial Company (1871). Concerns the company's sealing and trading operations.

80 Petr Aleksandrovich Tikhmenev (d. 1888). Materialy dlia istorii russkikh zaselenii (St. Petersburg, 1861), 11 pp., translations of documents and reports of Captain N. Golovnin relating to the Russian-American Company, from Tikhmenev's book, vol. 1, pp. 2-123. More extended translation under Russian America. Also, "Historical Review of the Origin of the Russian-American Company and its activity up to the present time," 2 boxes, translated by Michael Dobrynin, 1940, as part of a WPA project.

81 Bernice (Jameson) Todd, comp. The Bear--The Mercy Ship: Excerpts from the letters of Lieutenant Commander Clement Joseph Todd's 3 trips to Alaska on the Coast Guard Cutter Bear (n.d.), iv + 52 ll., photocopy of the manuscript, photographs inserted. Excerpts from his diary letters, 1921-23, describe his experiences in Alaska and Siberia and mention encounters with Eskimos. Includes biographical information on Todd.

82 Manuel Torres. "Peripecias de la vida Californiana, 1843-1850," 120 ll., signed manuscript, dictation recorded by Henry Cerruti, San Francisco, 27 April 1876, concerning customs, manners, and people in early California, with observations on the Russians at Bodega and Fort Ross. Also on microfilm.

83 U.S. Coast Guard. Microfilm. Selected documents relating to the Western Union Telegraph Expedition, 1865-67. Mention of Captain Charles M. Scammon and Colonel Charles S. Bulkley. Originals in the National Archives.

84 Stephan M. Ushin (b. 1832). Diary and notes, 1874-95, 3 microfilm reels. Clerk in the Sitka post of the North Western Trading Company and a clerk under Prince D. Maksutov before 1867. Local affairs, especially church matters, and incoming news. Originals in the Library of Congress ("Alaska Historical Documents"). Also, excerpts from the diary translated in 1935-36 by Tikhon Lavrischeff, microfilm.

85 Mariano Guadalupe Vallejo (1807-1890). Collection, 1780-1875, 36 boxes. California military and political leader. Correspondence (business and personal), official documents, reports, and financial papers, most in Spanish but with English translations for some. Correspondence with officials of the Russian-American Company and other Russians at Fort Ross or other points: Kiril Timofeevich Khlebnikov, 3 letters, 1828-37, Petr Kostromitinov, 15 letters, 1834-41 and 1852, Ivan Kuprianov, 3 official letters, with translations and/or transcripts, 1840, Aleksandr Gavriilovich Rotchev (Rochev), 9 items, 1838-41, Iliashevich, 2 items, 1833-34, and Zajario Chichinov, 1 letter and transcript, 1834. There are also copies of articles of agreement between the Spanish and the Russian-American Company, 3 items, 1841; trade and shipping data for cargoes on such vessels as the Kiakhta (1825-28), Baikal (n.d.), the Young Tartar (1827), Okhotsk (1828), and Rurik (1824); business correspondence between the Russians named above and William Edward Petty Hartnell, 7 items, including drafts and copies, 1833 and 1840, Luis Antonio Argüello, 1828, Ignacio Martinez, and Juan Bautista Alvarado; letters written at the Russian River by Lindsey Carson, 1851, and Michel Laframboise, 1838; an unsigned official letter, n.d., concerning the governor of the Russian colonies in America, draft; a letter from John Bautista Rogers Cooper, Monterey 5 December 1840, to Kostromitinov, rough draft; an official letter from José Figueroa, Monterey 10 April 1833, to the governor of the Russian settlements on Sitka and at Fort Ross, fragment, copy; and a public notice of a decree issued by the Cortes of Spain, ca. 1813, concerning a treaty with Russia dated 20 July 1812, printed, signature partly destroyed. Vallejo wrote 8 letters to Russians in 1840-41, with transcripts, a letter draft in 1838 to Kostromitinov, and some documents relating to the establishment of Novoarkhangelsk (Nuevo Arcángel) in 1836-38 (copies). Also, 1 letter of Ferdinand Petrovich Vrangel, 1830, and a statement, 22 December 1831, by Dionision Zarembo, Khlebnikov, and Paul Shelekhov (copy). Materials are bound in 3 rough categories, each in approximate chronological order. Easier access might be through the published finding aid, arranged by author: Doris Marion Wright, A Guide to the Mariano Guadalupe Vallejo Documentos para la Historia de California 1780-1875 (Berkeley, 1953).

86 Platon M. G. Vallejo (1841-1925). Memoirs of the son of Mariano G. Vallejo (preceding collection), 52 ll. Mainly a biography of his father, with notes on California military affairs, the American conquest, and Russians in California. Arranged for publication by J. H. Wilkins.

87 Voyages to the Alaska Coast: Logbooks and Journals. Microfilm, 2 items, 1799-1816. (a) Journal of William Sturgis on board the Eliza, 13 February-17 May 1799, holograph, 59 pp.; trade for sea otter in Alaskan waters, Indian trading, and 2 brief vocabularies. See also under William Sturgis; and (b) journal kept by an unidentified passenger or supercargo, mainly in logbook form, of voyages on the Atahualpa, Behring, Albatross, Isabella, and Pedlar, 1811-16, 330 pp., voyages to the Sandwich Islands and the Alaska coast; originals in the Massachusetts Historical Society.

88 James C. Ward. "Three Weeks in Sitka," 12 ll., extracts made by Ivan Petrov from a manuscript cited in Bancroft's History of Alaska. Ward describes Sitka in the summer of 1853.

89 Sven Larsson Waxell (1701-1762). 1 item, ca. 1750. Swedish seaman and explorer in Russian service. "Auszug so wohl aus meine, als aus andere officiers auf den Kamschatkischen Expedition . . . Journalen . . . ca. 1750," 211 pp., signed holograph (photocopy). Account of Vitus Bering's second expedition, 1733-41, with maps and illustrations. Original in Public Library in Leningrad. Note: M. A. Michael's published English translation is from a Danish translation, not the original German.

90 Ferdinand Westdahl. "Alaska. 1878," 19 ll., interview at Anderson Island, Puget Sound; experiences on the Pacific Coast since 1865, especially with the Western Union Telegraph Expedition; the Russian settlements in Alaska as they were in 1866-67.

91 J. W. White (b. 1829). 1 item, 1885. Commander of the Revenue Cutter Lincoln. "Statement on Alaska," 12 pp., concerns the captain's intervention (1867) in the slaughter of the fur seals on the Pribilov Islands.

92 William L. Wiggins (1817?-1880). 1 item, 1877. California pioneer. Reminiscences, 23 ll., recorded by Thomas Savage. Arrival at Bodega in July 1840; Mexican and Russian officials. Available on microfilm. (Bancroft Collection)

93 Lascente Alekseevich Zagoskin (1808-90). Transcript in Russian of an article on the Redoubt of St. Michael in the southern part of Norton Sound, 32 pp., from Zapiski Gidrograficheskogo Departamenta (1846, vol. 4, pp. 86-101). First 7 pp. translated by Ivan Petrov in the Russian America collection.

Finding Aid: A Guide to the Manuscript Collections of the Bancroft Library, edited by Dale L. Morgan and/or George P. Hammond, 2 vols. thus far (Berkeley, 1963-).

CA 6
MARK TWAIN PAPERS
BANCROFT LIBRARY
UNIVERSITY OF CALIFORNIA
Berkeley, California 94720
(415-642-6480)

21 letters and postcards by Ossip Gabrilowitsch to Mrs. William Churchill (Fanny) Hammond, of Holyoke, MA.; 2 undated and the rest written 1901-34. There is also one letter to Mrs. Edward Allen Reed (mother of Fanny Hammond), 15 March 1917. The letters are generally brief, accepting or declining invitations to visit or dine with the Hammonds, or letters of thanks after such visits have taken place. In a few, Gabrilowitsch gives details of his concert schedules and programs. Also included are 12 letters by Clara Clemens Gabrilowitsch to Mrs. Hammond, 1915-48, and 1 letter by Nina Gabrilowitsch to Mrs. Hammond, 1931.

CA 7
MEDIEVAL MANUSCRIPTS COLLECTION
BANCROFT LIBRARY
UNIVERSITY OF CALIFORNIA
Berkeley, California 94720
(415-642-6481)

Bible. Manuscript. New Testament. Gospels. Armenian. Four Gospels, on heavy waxed paper, illuminated, 409 pp., 16th c., bound in velvet and lined with leaves from an earlier Armenian manuscript. (MS UCB 113 and 2MS BS 2554 A7)

CA 8
ORAL HISTORY COLLECTION
BANCROFT LIBRARY
UNIVERSITY OF CALIFORNIA
Berkeley, California 94720
(415-642-3781)

1 California--Russian Émigré Series. Transcripts of tape-recorded interviews conducted by the staff and others. The typed transcripts are deposited in the Bancroft Library and the original tape recordings remain in the Regional Oral History Office. The ongoing Russian émigré series began in 1960. Among those interviewed thus far, in 3 separate series, by Richard A. Pierce, Alton C. Donnelly, and Boris Raymond (Romanoff):

2 Paul Dotsenko (b. 1894). "The Struggle for the Liberation of Siberia, 1918-1921," 144 pp., 1960 (Series I; Pierce). Photographs inserted.

Activities in Socialist Revolutionary Party in Russia, imprisonment and exile in Siberia, political activities after the Revolution, emigration to the U.S. in 1923. Also includes text of a speech delivered in June 1954: "Fight for Freedom in Siberia: Its Success and Failure."

3 Valentin Vassilievich Fedoulenko (1894-1974). Russian Émigré Life in Shanghai," 171 pp., 1967 (Series II; Raymond). Photographs inserted. Experiences during World War I and with the White Army; life as a refugee in Shanghai; Japanese occupation of Shanghai during World War II; removal to the Philippine Islands in 1949 and refugee camp at Tubabao; arrival in San Francisco, 1950; efforts to bring in other Russian refugees; Russian colony in the Bay Area. With this, as a second volume: his recollections of days in a Russian military academy, in Russian, and material relating to Russian refugees.

4 George Constantine Guins (1887-1971). Government official and professor. "Professor and Government Official: Russia, China, and California," 378 pp., 1966 (Series II; Raymond); and "Impressions of the Russian Imperial Government," 84 pp., 1971 (Series III; Pierce). Photographs inserted. First interview: life in pre-revolutionary Russia; experiences during Revolution and Civil War; life in Harbin, China, as professor and official of the Chinese Eastern Railway; emigration to the U.S., 1941. Also included, as vol. 2: photocopies of articles written by him, bibliography, curriculum vitae, etc. Second interview: comments on events in Russia between the revolutions of 1905 and 1917; career as official in the Ministry of Agriculture; discussion of Russian administrative system. Included also: copies of biographical sketch and obituary.

5 George Hoyningen-Huene (b. 1900). Photographer. "George Hoyningen-Huene, Photographer," 47 pp., Los Angeles, 1967 (interview conducted by Elizabeth I. Dixon for the UCLA Oral History Program). Life in pre-revolutionary St. Petersburg; emigration after the Revolution; teaching at Art Center School, Los Angeles; career as a fashion illustrator and as a motion picture photographer.

6 Aleksandr N. Lenkoff (Lenkov), (1896-1975). Soldier. "Life of a Russian Emigré Soldier," 64 pp., 1967 (Series II; Raymond), plus "Report to Subcommittee on Russian Émigré Project," 4 pp., and "Bibliography of Works on Far Eastern Emigration," 16 pp. Photographs inserted. Experiences during the Russian Revolution and with the White Army in Siberia; life in China, 1922-48; including service with a Russian detachment in the Chinese army; emigration to the U.S. The report and bibliography are Raymond's. A second volume contains a map drawn by Lenkoff to accompany the interview and an issue of a monarchist publication he edited.

7 Elizabeth Malozemoff (1881-1974). Teacher. "The Life of a Russian Teacher," 444 pp., 1961 (Series I; Donnelly). Photographs and maps inserted. Life as a teacher in pre-revolutionary Russia and Siberia; experiences during the Revolution; escape through China; residence in Oakland; Russian émigré societies; studies and teaching at UC Berkeley.

8 Jacob Marschak (1898-1977). Professor. "Recollections of Kiev and the Northern Caucasus, 1917-18," 78 pp., 1971 (Series III; Pierce). Photographs inserted. Recollections of early years in the Jewish community in Kiev; interest in Russian revolutionary movement; experiences as member of the Menshevik faction of the Social Democratic Party during the Revolution and Civil War. Included also: brief biographical sketch and list of selected publications of Marschak.

9 Victorin Mikhailovich Moltchanoff (1886-1975). "The Last White General," 134 pp., 1972 (Series III; Raymond). Photographs inserted. Military training in Russia; experiences during World War I and the Revolution; anti-Bolshevik movement; military events during the Civil War in Siberia; emigration to California in 1923; Russian émigré settlement in San Francisco.

10 Nicholas (Miklos) Nagy-Talavera (b. 1929). "Recollections of Soviet Labor Camps, 1949-1955," 100 pp., 1972 (Series III; Pierce). Photographs inserted. Reminiscences of a Hungarian émigré, covering his imprisonment during World War II in Auschwitz; his return to Hungary and work with anti-communist underground; imprisonment in Soviet labor camps in Siberia, outer Mongolia, the Arctic, and Central Asia.

11 Boris Shebeko (1900-75?). Engineer. "Russian Civil War, 1918-1922," 284 pp., 1961 (Series I; Pierce). Photographs and maps inserted. Experiences with the White Army on the southern and Siberian fronts; emigration to China, and to the U.S. in 1923.

12 Michael M. Shneyeroff (1880-1961). "Recollections of the Russian Revolution," 270 pp., 1960 (Series I; Pierce). Photographs inserted. Participation in the Russian revolutionary movement, 1900-17; experiences during the Revolution; emigration to the U.S. in 1921. Also includes 2 items donated by Shneyeroff to supplement his interview: "When I Was Young," 80 pp., Berkeley, CA., 1957--recollections of his participation in the revolutionary movement as a member of the Socialist Revolutionary Party; and "What I Remember" (1 microfilm reel, negative), Berkeley, 1952--typescript in Russian, memoirs as member of the SR Party, 1901-21.

Note: All interview transcripts are indexed and there is a master card index to persons and subjects in the Regional Oral History Office (Room 486, Bancroft Library). The transcripts are duplicated in photo-offset; copies are available at the Department of Special Collections at UCLA and other repositories (individual or series). The office at Berkeley will supply a list of these other locations on request. All transcripts are open but permission is required to quote. All transcripts available in microfiche from Microfilming Corporation of America (1620 Hawkins Avenue, P.O. Box 10, Sanford, North Carolina 27330).

Finding Aid: Catalog of Regional Oral History Office (Berkeley, December 1965).

CA 9
PICTORIAL COLLECTIONS
BANCROFT LIBRARY
UNIVERSITY OF CALIFORNIA
Berkeley, California 94720
(415-642-6481)

1 Robert B. Honeyman, Jr. Collection. 796 paintings, drawings, and watercolors, 18th-19th c. Western Americana. Includes:

Langsdorff Group. 36 items, ca. 1803-10. Depict the round-the-world journey of Nikolai Petrovich Rezanov, high chamberlain to Alexander I, 1803-1807, one of the first great Russian marine expeditions. The twofold purpose of the trip: to establish Russian trade with Japan (unsuccessful) and to investigate and develop the fur-trading colonies of the Russian-American Company. Rezanov found the settlements in poor shape, bought an American ship (the Juno) and its goods in New Archangel, and went to California to trade the cargo for food to bring back to the colonies. Georg Heinrich von Langsdorff (1774-1852) was physician and naturalist on the expedition. This German remained in Russian service for some years, attained the rank of councilor, eventually served as consul-general to the Brazils for Russia.

Some of the artists represented in this group include, besides Langsdorff, Ivan Petrovich Korukin (a shipbuilding expert who accompanied the expedition), Alexander Orloffsky, and Wilhelm Gottlieb Tilesius von Tilenau (a naturalist with the expedition).

Subjects of the art works: St. Peter and St. Paul in Kamchatka (design of Major Herrmann von Frederici); scenes of the island of Nukahiwa in the Marquesas, of the Sandwich Islands, Sakhalin, Kodiak, the Aleutian Islands, Kurile Islands, Japan, Sitka (dancers), Alaska, Oonalashka, California (San Jose and San Francisco), and Tenerife (Canary Islands). Langsdorff's "View of the Spanish Establishments of San Francisco in New California [as seen from the ship Juno]" is the first known view of that city.

There is important supplementary (background) material on the Langsdorff Group in the inventory prepared by Mr. Warren R. Howell.

Finding Aid: All of the above information is taken directly from the Catalogue of Original Paintings, Drawings and Watercolors in the Robert B. Honeyman, Jr., Collection, compiled by Joseph Armstrong Baird, Jr. (Berkeley, 1968).

2 Soviet Postcards and Posters. 4 separate collections. (1) 30 Soviet propaganda postcards, from the Tom Mooney Papers (1905.5284 [1-30] PIC); (2) Soviet propaganda posters, chiefly 1930s-1940s, 114 items. Inventory with TASS numbers, artists, dates, and descriptions (USSR: 1-1307, not continuous); (3) Soviet war posters, reproduced by Russian War Relief, Inc. (New York, 1945), 8 color plates (fD746.5 R8); and (4) "Torzhestvo leninskikh idei" (Moscow, 1977), 19 posters in 1 portfolio (pfs DK 254 L4 T6).

CA 10
MUSIC LIBRARY
UNIVERSITY OF CALIFORNIA
240 Morrison Music Building
Berkeley, California 94720
(415-642-2623)

Igor Stravinsky (1882-1971). Orpheus, complete score, 96 pp., holograph on transparent paper, Hollywood 23 September 1947, signed; and sketches illustrating the work (1 envelope).

Finding Aid: Published catalog for manuscript materials is in preparation.

CA 11
PACIFIC FILM ARCHIVE
UNIVERSITY ART MUSEUM
UNIVERSITY OF CALIFORNIA
2625 Durant Avenue
Berkeley, California 94720
(415-642-1437)

The Archive has about 50 silent Soviet films from the 1920s, most of which are on long-term loan from the Moscow Film Institute. Only a dozen titles, in 16 mm copies, are part of the Archive's permanent collection. Among the directors represented are D. Vertov, S. Eisenstein, F. Ermler, L. Kuleshov, Ya. Protazanov, and E. Shub. The Archive also has 30 Georgian films, features and shorts, covering the period from the 1920s to the present.

This collection is also on long-term deposit. Credits, synopses, and program notes are available for most films. Researchers must call or write in advance, presenting a valid research need. Appointments for screening must be made at least 3 weeks in advance. Films may be screened on a projector or flatbed viewer; a nominal screening fee is charged.

CA 12
WATER RESOURCES CENTER ARCHIVES
UNIVERSITY OF CALIFORNIA
Berkeley, California 94720
(415-642-2666)

B. A. Shumakov. "Quantities of water and time for irrigation of the principal irrigated crops on the North Caucasus," manuscript, 110 ll., translated by D. B. Krimgold from the original Russian report issued in 1929 by the People's Commissariat of Agriculture.

Finding Aid: Dictionary Catalog of the Water Resources Center Archives, 5 vols. (Boston: G. K. Hall, 1970).

CA 13
CHARLES K. FELDMAN LIBRARY
THE AMERICAN FILM INSTITUTE
CENTER FOR ADVANCED FILM STUDIES
501 Doheny Road
Beverly Hills, California 90210
(213-278-8777)

Sergei M. Eisenstein (1898-1948). Soviet film director. 3 portfolios of original drawings (reprints). These works include sketches he made for his proposed joint venture with Upton Sinclair, Que Viva Mexico!, theater drawings, and pieces relating to his film Ivan the Terrible.

Note: The library's published materials, with an emphasis on Russian film and filmmakers, is one of the best collections for Soviet area specialists in southern California. Books are at present uncataloged, shelved in random order in the Archives, ca. 15 ft.

CA 14
EDWARD LAURENCE DOHENY MEMORIAL LIBRARY
ST. JOHN'S SEMINARY
5012 East Seminary Road
Camarillo, California 93010
(805-482-4115)

1 Estelle Doheny Collection. Includes an Armenian manuscript, four Gospels, A.D. 1659 (MS. 367); and an ALS of Petr Ilich Chaikovskii [Peter I. Tschaikowsky], 22 January 1882, in French, introducing Mr. and Miss Burmeister to an unidentified recipient.

2 Henry L. Oak (1844-1905). Collection, 1769-1848, ca. 1,650 items. Autographs of California pioneers, i.e., persons who came to the area before 1849. Contained in 1 album, arranged under subjects, one of which is "Russians" (others are "merchants, missionaries, officials civil and military" and "traders and trappers"). Includes a brief printed biography of each signer, mostly clippings. Unpublished index (NUCMC 61-2735).

Restriction: Requires written permission of the curator/librarian of the Estelle Doheny Collection.

Finding Aid: Catalog of Books and Manuscripts in the Estelle Doheny Collection, 3 vols. (Los Angeles, 1940-55).

CA 15
SPECIAL COLLECTIONS DEPARTMENT
HONNOLD LIBRARY
CLAREMONT COLLEGES
Claremont, California 91711
(714-621-8000 x 3977)

1 James Mavor (1854-1925). Collection of Russian Economic History, 1875-1924, 33 ft. Economic historian. Contains journals, publications by the Russian government, statistical compilations, monographs, pamphlets, and articles pertaining to Russian economic development, and economic and political thought, and to such figures as S. Witte, the Socialist Revolutionaries, V. I. Lenin, and the Bolshevik Party. Manuscript materials include several early 20th c. peasant rent books; 7 scrapbooks with manuscript translations, mostly of selections from Archives of the Russian Revolution, manifestos, decrees, correspondence, and reports; 2 document cases of Mavor's translations of Russian publications; and annotated and corrected proof of the 1914 edition of his Economic History of Russia, 2 vols., with comments by J. Brime. In addition, the collection contains published works of literature by 19th c. Russian authors and others in Russian translation. Unpublished finding aid.

2 Gregory P. Tschebotarioff (b. 1899). Collection, ca. 1907-73 (excluding published material), ca. 15 ft. Author, retired consulting engineer. Books, pamphlets, photos, correspondence, typescripts, and clippings. Unpublished materials include:

A large manila envelope with an original photograph of Tschebotarioff's childhood friend, Mitya Heering, taken at a play put on by children at the Pavlovsk palace of the

Grand Duke Constantine Constantinovich, ca. 1907.

Correspondence with the State Museum of Revolution (Moscow), 1967-68.

Correspondence and newspaper clippings on the Rodion Berezov deportation case, 1950-57. Included are letters to Senator H. Alexander Smith and Berezov himself.

Several cardboard file boxes with correspondence pertaining to the first official U.S.A.-USSR soil engineering exchange, 1959.

Cardboard file box with reviews and letters on Tschebotarioff's book, Russia, My Native Land. A U.S. Engineer Reminisces and Looks at the Present (New York: McGraw-Hill, 1964).

2 binders with typewritten texts left out of Russia, My Native Land. These include "Cossackia and Other Fantasia in Washington"; "Past History and Present East-West Tensions"; and "Are Both Sides Captives of Their Own Propaganda?"

A cardboard file box with correspondence pertaining to Tschebotarioff's trips to the Soviet Union as a tourist (1968) and as a member of the Eighth International Conference on Soil Mechanics, 1973.

Data related to the background of Colonel Oleg Golenewsky and his role as a pretender to the Russian throne.

Cardboard file box of correspondence with Tschebotarioff's old Russian army friends and other related data.

Cardboard file box of correspondence with Soviet engineering friends.

Bound typescript, 215 pp., "Zapiski inzhenera," by V. E. Sproge (Zurich, 1963). The main interest of these notes are Sproge's impressions on large construction projects in the Soviet Union between 1920 and 1940, including a detailed description, pp. 103-40, of the 1926 "Dnieprostroy" negotiation with the American Colonel Hugh L. Cooper. Unpublished finding aid.

CA 16
DEPARTMENT OF SPECIAL COLLECTIONS
UNIVERSITY LIBRARY
UNIVERSITY OF CALIFORNIA
Davis, California 95616
(916-752-1621)

1 Higgins Library of Agricultural Technology. Ca. 350,000 items, 1860-present. Photographs, correspondence, pictures, advertising literature, etc., ca. 1,200 items, pertain to Russian agricultural equipment, practices, and history, 1930-present. Materials filed by subject and manufacturer. Described in Don Kunitz, "The Higgins Library: A Source for the Study of Agricultural History," Agricultural History 49 (1975).

2 Iazykov Collection. 273 items, 1613-1936. Photographs, pictures, oil paintings, and engravings of members of the Romanov dynasty, Russian architecture, and military uniforms during the reign of Paul I. Also printed documents (including religious tracts and political pamphlets); manuscript materials, including orders of the Empress Elizabeth; and miscellaneous memorabilia. Items in both Russian and English. Register.

3 Radical Pamphlet Collection. 7,000 pamphlets, 1917-47. Ca. 350 items concern Russian political movements and programs, the Revolution, communism, and other political aspects of Russian history. Includes works of V. I. Lenin, J. Stalin, K. Marx, and L. Trotskii.

CA 17
BARBARA DYE CALLARMAN (MRS. DON)--
PRIVATE COLLECTION
7413 Via Amorita
Downey, California 90241
(213-927-5255)

Mrs. Callarman is in possession of 2 items pertaining to the life of her great-grandfather, Joseph Kirk (1818-89), an American civil engineer who went to Russia ca. 1843 to set up machinery for spinning hemp and who helped construct the St. Petersburg-Moscow railroad with George Washington Whistler. The items are a Russian passport to Kirk and his family, dated 1849, and the wedding certificate of Kirk and Charlotte Elizabeth Meyer, 1844, signed by the German Lutheran minister in St. Petersburg. Mrs. Callarman also has some genealogical data on the Kirk and related families in the U.S. An advance telephone call or letter is requested.

CA 18
ORAL HISTORY PROGRAM
HISTORY DEPARTMENT
CALIFORNIA STATE UNIVERSITY
Fullerton, California 92634
(714-773-3580)

1 Leon Banen (O. H. 1432). Russian-Jewish immigrant. Interview with his daughter, Leah Gilbert, at age 82, 10 hrs.; life in tsarist Russia, service in the Jewish Legion during World War I. Transcript with index and pictures.

2 Andrew Erdeley (O. H. 1498). Hungarian emigrant. 17 hrs., discussion concerning Eastern Europe in World War II, Siberian prisoner of war camps, the Russian secret police, and the Hungarian revolt of 1956. This series of interviews has been edited and published under the title Struggle for Human Rights. Indexed, with pictures.

3 Al Lyon. Complete life history, ca. 100 hrs. taped, when 80 years old. Lyon left Russia at age 16. These memoirs, bound, 3 vols. entitled Popoo: An Autobiography of Al Lyon, were a legacy for his grandchildren.

4 Edmund Mueller (O. H. 1410). Interview at age 78 with his son Albert, 3.5 hrs.; service in the White Russian Army during the Revolution and Civil War years, and life in Siberian prison camps. Typed transcript in English, 34 pp., single-spaced, translated from Polish tape, with index and pictures.

5 Nelson Rupp (O. H. 1268). American soldier and male nurse in a World War I hospital. Reminiscences on tape, 2 hrs., of the Allied intervention in Archangel, 1917-18.

Note: All interviews except Lyon's will be available in the future from the Microfilming Corporation of America.

CA 19
YURY M. GURVICH--PRIVATE COLLECTION
3441 Maryann Street
La Crescenta, California 91214
(213-249-5169)

Mr. Gurvich, a recent émigré from the Soviet Union, has a number of items relating to science and technology in the USSR. The series "Apparatus and Methods of X-Ray Analysis" (numbers 7-10, 13-16) for 1970-75 was published by the Special Design Office of X-Ray Equipment (SKB RA, Leningrad) in a limited edition of 1,500 copies. The same office issued Briefs of Reports of the Ninth, Tenth, and Eleventh All-Union X-Ray Conferences with a circulation of only 300-500 copies. In Gurvich's possession also is a copy of his own thesis--"X-Ray Spectral Slurry Analysis of Polymetal Ore Concentration Products"--prepared for defense and publication but never printed because of his emigration. All materials are in Russian. Inquire concerning access.

CA 20
ARCHIVES BRANCH
FEDERAL ARCHIVES & RECORDS SERVICE, GSA
24000 Avila Road
Laguna Niguel, California 92677
(714-831-4220)

This repository has some of the microfilms of materials in the National Archives (Washington, D.C.) that pertain to Russia/USSR. For more details, see Charles South, List of National Archives Microfilm Publications in the Regional Archives Branches (Washington: National Archives and Records Service, 1975). Original Russian-related materials not found in the National Archives in Washington are located in RG 36, Records of the United States Customs Service, which contains a series, Records of the San Pedro Office, with records of goods requisitioned by the USSR from the U.S. in 1943-45 under the terms of the Lend-Lease Act. The material is arranged by ships within separate envelopes and includes crew lists and ships' provisions. Finding aid.

CA 21
DEPARTMENT OF SPECIAL COLLECTIONS/ARCHIVES
UNIVERSITY LIBRARY
CALIFORNIA STATE UNIVERSITY
Long Beach, California 90840
(213-498-4087)

Dorothy Healey (b. 1914). Collection, 1928-present, 160 ft. Chairman of the southern California division of the Communist Party of the United States of America. Primarily published materials and internal Party documents. Includes 27 letters, postcards, and manuscript notes from an invited trip to the Soviet Union, April-June 1961. Unpublished index of names and subjects. Additions expected.

CA 22
NICHOLAS I. ROKITIANSKY--PRIVATE COLLECTION
24910 La Loma Court
Los Altos Hills, California 94022
(415-941-6765)

Collection on Russians in California, primarily 19th c., ca. 20 items. Includes 1817 map of California, maps pertaining to the Russians in northern California, portraits, photos, illustrations of Fort Ross, and translations of Spanish documents. Inquire concerning access.

CA 23
ASTA ARISTOV--PRIVATE COLLECTION
106 N. Serrano
Los Angeles, California 90004

Asta Aristov (nee Tersky), born in Estonia, 26 September 1936, holds a collection, 2 boxes, of largely family papers. From the family of her husband Oleg come documents dating from 1725 (proof of nobility, records of Aristov family holdings in Kiev, and other rodoslovnye or kupchie items), plus diplomas and documents from the 1890s and early 1900s. From her father, Alexander Tersky, she has memoirs of the Russian Civil War (excerpts appeared in the Los Angeles émigré publication Pervopokhodnik). Some papers concern the arrest of her mother, Elsa Piass, in 1937. Other materials include printed matter, personal and business correspondence, diaries, and manuscripts, which cover life in tsarist Russia and the USSR, especially in the 1930s. Also, letters from Russian friends since the late 1960s depict émigré and Soviet life, 1950s-1970s. Among literary manuscripts in the collection are an unpublished translation of M. Rozanov's novel Prisoner Rozanov, about Soviet concentration camps, and a rough translation of the children's classic by P. Ershov, The Little Humpbacked Horse. Numerous article drafts describe various aspects of life in the USSR and the U.S. References to the Black Hussar Regiments of Kiev, the Russian-American Cultural Society (established in 1975 in Los Angeles, with E. Tersky [nee Piass] as secretary), and the émigré publications Novoye Russkoye Slovo and Rodnye Dali. There are, in addition, ca. 1,500 photographs and slides of pre-revolutionary Russia and the Soviet Union. Permission from A. Aristov required.

CA 24
JEWISH INSTITUTE OF RELIGION
HEBREW UNION COLLEGE
3077 University Avenue
Los Angeles, California 90007
(213-749-3424)

5 posters, 1917-30, depicting the anti-religious policies of the Soviet government. 1 poster, ca. 1917, presents the theme of anti-Semitism as counterrevolutionary.

CA 25
HOLY VIRGIN MARY RUSSIAN ORTHODOX CATHEDRAL
650 Micheltorena Street
Los Angeles, California 90026
(213-666-4977)

In 1970 the Russian Orthodox Church in North America officially became an autocephalous church, independent of the Moscow patriarchate. Its name is now the Orthodox Church in America. The history of the Church and its activities provides substantial insights into the history of the Russian émigré community in this country. 8 file drawers, ca. 20 ft., of the Holy Virgin Mary Cathedral, a part of the Orthodox Church in America: parish records, accounts, correspondence, reports, office files, and other materials (printed and unprinted) from its founding in 1923 to the present. These sources concern the Cathedral and its parish as well as the general Orthodox community. The materials cover the Cathedral's relations with other Russian Orthodox Church authorities in the United States, Europe, and Japan, primarily since 1957; negotiations with the Orthodox Church in the USSR for autocephaly, 1969-70; and records of the annual meetings of the All-American Sobor, 1970-. Concerning the operations and scope of the parish there are birth, marriage, and death records from 1923. Among Church officials named in the correspondence are the Archbishop Ioann Shakhovskoi and Metropolitan Leonty. Researchers must obtain permission from parish authorities to utilize the holdings; at present they should contact the archpriest Dimitri Gisetti for more information. Other records of the Holy Virgin Mary Russian Orthodox Cathedral are held by the chancery of the Orthodox Church in America, Box 675, Syosset, New York 11791.

CA 26
A. N. KOSCHIN--PRIVATE COLLECTION
4150 Holly Knoll Drive
Los Angeles, California 90027

Mrs. A. N. Koschin (Kozhina), widow of the prominent Soviet architect Sergei Nikolaevich Kozhin, has prepared the memoirs (zapiski) of her husband for publication. The manuscript of the book is in her possession. Contents cover the art and architecture worlds of the Soviet Union in the 1920s and early 1930s. Among the persons Kozhin knew and wrote about were Academician I. V. Zholtovskii; the architects (brothers) A. A., L. A., and V. A. Vesnin, founders of constructivism in the USSR; Le Corbusier, on a visit to Moscow; Fedor Shaliapin, the singer; Galina Ulanova, the ballerina; the writer Mikhail Bulgakov; the artist and stage designer Mstislav Dobuzhinskii; Evgenii Vakhtangov, theatrical director; and the Bauhaus group in Germany. The memoirs concern only his years in the USSR, although Kozhin, in Europe during World War II, emigrated to America and worked 16 years with a leading American architect, Richard Noitra. There are also several photographs of Kozhin, Le Corbusier, and Soviet architects; three are of Le Corbusier in a Russian village, with a peasant woman, in front of an old peasant izba. Write concerning access.

CA 27
ANDREW LOSSKY--PRIVATE COLLECTION
DEPARTMENT OF HISTORY
UNIVERSITY OF CALIFORNIA
Los Angeles, California 90024
(213-825-4368/4601)

Professor Lossky, son of the philosopher Nicholas O. Lossky, has transferred the bulk of his father's and grandmother's (Marie Stoyunine) papers to Paris. He retains at his home in this country some carbon copies of some of his father's works (nearly all published), photographs of the Lossky and Stoyunine families, from the 1880s onward, photographs of his father's friends (mainly Russian philosophers), and personal letters to him from his father and other family members and friends, 1935-present.

Ultimate disposition of the papers is uncertain at this time. Access to most of the materials is limited to scholars known to Professor Lossky or recommended by someone known to him, and possible only during the academic year (he is away in the summer).

CA 28
THE PHILOSOPHICAL RESEARCH SOCIETY
3910 Los Feliz Boulevard
Los Angeles, California 90027
(213-663-2167)

Armenian Manuscripts. Four Gospels, fully illuminated, on vellum, A.D. 1684 (Armenian era 1133), in Bolorgir, text copied at Zeithoun in Cilicia (Monastery of the Holy Mother of God) by the scribe Khatchatour; 2 leaves from a lectionary, A.D. 1671; and 1 leaf from the Acts of the Apostles, 15th-16th c.

CA 29
BIOMEDICAL LIBRARY
CENTER FOR THE HEALTH SCIENCES
UNIVERSITY OF CALIFORNIA
Los Angeles, California 90024
(213-825-6940)

1 Haymaker Archive. 14.5 ft., 18th-20th c. Includes some correspondence, documents, and photographs--used in the preparation of the book The Founders of Neurology by W. Haymaker and F. Schiller (2nd ed., 1970)--that pertain to Russian science. Uncataloged.

2 Miscellaneous Typescripts. Materials for the 19th-20th c., some relating to the Russian Empire or Soviet Union, chiefly in the fields of neurology, psychology, neurophysiology, and the history of these subjects. Cataloged.

CA 30
MUSIC LIBRARY, MUSIC HALL
UNIVERSITY OF CALIFORNIA
1102 Schoenberg Hall
Los Angeles, California 90024
(213-825-4881)

1 Joseph M. Rumshinsky (1881-1956). Papers, ca. 1910-56, 115 items. Composer. Born in Vilna, he studied music in Russian conservatories. Emigrated to the U.S. in 1924. Stage shows, songs, dance music, 8 scripts, his biblical opera Ruth, notes for productions of his works, clippings, and obituaries. Unpublished inventory.

2 Ernest Toch (1887-1964). Archive, 1906-present, ca. 20,000 items (additions expected). Includes his manuscripts, holographs, recordings, and oral history reminiscences of him. 1 oral history was done by Nikolai Lopatnikoff.

CA 31
SPECIAL COLLECTIONS DEPARTMENT
UNIVERSITY RESEARCH LIBRARY
UNIVERSITY OF CALIFORNIA
Los Angeles, California 90024
(213-825-4879)

1 Armenian Manuscripts. Minasian, Heghen, and Khantamour Collections, 14th-20th c., ca. 7 ft., 80 vols., 100 items, and 11 albums. Includes Bibles, commentaries on Biblical texts, ritualistic texts (ritual books, menologies, lectionaries, sermons, psalters, calendars of feasts, books of hours), poetry texts (e.g., canticles), medical and pharmacological books, works on logic and rhetoric, a dream book, works on astronomy, and miscellanies, 14th-18th c.; business and personal correspondence, account books, local histories, historical and semi-autobiographical novels, music, folklore, dictionaries, plant lore, medical works, commentaries on Biblical texts, and statistical information (particularly on Armenian communities in India), 19th-20th c., ca. 100 manuscripts and typescripts, partly in English; personal journals, short stories, scholarly works, correspondence, business papers, government edicts, and encyclicals, in Armenian and English, relating to the life of Armenian communities in Iran, India, and California, ca. 7 ft.; and 11 albums of photographs plus 80 loose photos of individuals and families, groups, historical monuments, etc., mostly 20th c., taken in Iran, California, Turkey, Greece, and other locations. A published guide to the early manuscripts is in preparation by Professor A. K. Sanjian.

2 Richard Cobden (1804-1865). Papers, ca. 1833-65, 225 items. British political economist, statesman, and reformer. While traveling in the Russian Empire in 1847, Cobden wrote letters home to his family (brothers, sisters, and wife). The letters, August-September 1847, came from St. Petersburg, Moscow, and Königsberg (present Kaliningrad). Unpublished register.

3 Cornelius Cole and the Cole Family. Papers, 1833-1943, 57 boxes. 2 folders in separate

boxes contain personal correspondence regarding the Russian-American Fur Company and Russia's ambassador to the U.S., Baron Edouard de Stoeckel, in 1855-66. References are in Elmo R. Richardson's The Papers of Cornelius Cole and the Cole Family, 1833-1943. A Guide to Collection 217 (UCLA Library Occasional Papers, no. 4, 1956).

4 Edward Gordon Craig (1872-1966). Papers, ca. 1883-1966, 25 boxes and 20 oversize packages. English stage designer and producer, son of Ellen Terry. Manuscripts, correspondence, ephemera, photographs, original drawings, and prints. In 1908 and succeeding years Craig was involved in designing the production of Hamlet presented at the Moscow Art Theatre, December 1911-January 1912. Among 32 letters from Craig to Ellen Terry in 1908-11, some concern the production of the Moscow Hamlet (box 8, folders 10-12). Box 11, folder 4 contains photographs of model stages and figures for Hamlet, ca. 1909 and 1913, 1 with holograph notes; and folder 13 (same box) holds 5 photos of production designs for Hamlet, 1908-11. There are 23 cut-out, one-dimensional cardboard figures of varying size for the model stage used in the Moscow Art Theatre production of Hamlet, 1909-11, colored with charcoal, crayon, and watercolor (box 13, folders 1-22, and oversize item "K"); and 5 more similar figures of wood, colored with paint and charcoal, variants of the cardboard figures, used for mock-up of the MAT production (box 13, folders 23-27). In box 14 are original prints (inked) of black figures Craig developed from the wood and cardboard silhouettes used in his model stage to illustrate scenes he envisioned for the MAT production of Hamlet; the one-dimensional figures were inked in black and pressed on thin paper or cloth, 12 items, 1907-1908. Box 10 (folder 6) has press clippings and advertising material relating to Craig's earlier work and current designs for the Hamlet production of December 1911-January 1912, 10 clippings, in Russian, 1911-12, and 20 postcards with photographs of the actors in the Moscow production, taken by K. A. Fetser, Moscow, 1912. Finally, there are 3 catalogs of exhibitions of drawings and models for Hamlet and other plays by Craig, 1912-13, in London, Manchester, and Leeds. Unpublished register.

5 George Hoyningen-Huene (b. 1900). Russian-born American photographer. Transcript of an interview completed under the auspices of the UCLA Oral History Program. Recollections of the Russian Revolution, 1917-21, his career as a fashion and motion picture photographer, and his photographic studies of various countries.

6 Roger Mennevee (b. 1885). Collection, ca. 1910-65, ca. 1,200 ft. French editor, publisher, and owner-manager of the monthly review Les Documents politiques, diplomatiques et financiers. Clippings, publications, and notes. These materials provided information for Mennevee's research and writing. They cover such subjects as the tsarist Okhrana from 1881 to the 1917 Revolution; the Cheka and other secret services plus Soviet espionage, particularly in the U.S., from 1917 to the Khrushchev years; pre-1914 Russian funds invested in the French press; emigration and émigré organizations, 1914-23; Russian debts; Bolshevik propaganda and activity between the wars; and anti-Bolshevism. Among people involved and noted in specific items are generals A. P. Koutiepoff, 1930, and E. K. Miller, 1937, Aleksandr Kerensky, V. M. Zenzinov, and the defector Viktor Kravchenko. Unpublished register, ca. 100 pp. (NUCMC 70-86)

7 [Olga Konstantinovna]. A calendar of selections from the works of Mikhail Lermontov used as a memory book, with manuscript inscriptions throughout, compiled by Olga Konstantinovna, granddaughter of Paul I. The book, Izo dnia v den', izvlecheniia iz sochinenii Lermontova na kazhdyi den' goda ([n.p.], 1886), is bound in black morocco with a heavy silver crown and the initials OK affixed to the cover. (Under Lermontov in the catalog)

8 Maria Ouspenskaya (1876-1949). Papers, ca. 1922-42, 4 boxes and 1 package. Russian-American actress. Materials for publicity, motion picture scripts, notices, photographs, and reviews. Unpublished register.

9 Eva Robin. Papers, ca. 1887-1959, 6 boxes. Activist. Correspondence, diaries, speeches, essays, photographs, and miscellaneous manuscripts concerning women's rights, prison reform, her visits to the Soviet Union, and other matters. Unpublished register.

10 St. Petersbourg (St. Petersburg, Russia). Album of photographs, 12 images, ca. 10 x 15.5 cm, identified in manuscript.

11 Edgar Evertson Saltus (1855-1921). Holograph manuscript entitled "The imperial orgy; an account of the tsars from the first to the last," n.p., n.d., ii + 208 ll. First published by Boni & Liveright, New York, 1920.

12 Alberto Muller Schaertlin. "The yellow count, with the Japanese check of 138 million yen . . . [New York, 1935]." Typescript with some holograph corrections, unpublished; an account of a swindle based on fraudulent papers from the Russo-Japanese War.

13 Waldemar Westergaard (1882-1963). Collection of typescripts, photocopies, microfilms, manuscripts, and personal correspondence; 217 boxes. UCLA professor of history. Materials concern Russo-Danish relations, 1513-1726; Sweden and Russia in the sixteenth century; Livonian affairs, 1523-57; and the Triple Alliance of 1668-72. Much of the material consists of copies of documents in various repositories in the Baltic states and in western Europe. Unpublished register. (NUCMC 61-1060)

Note: In addition, the Special Collections Department has copies of the University of California, Berkeley, Oral History Project manuscripts that relate to Russia. For information on this extensive series, see the entry for Bancroft Library, UC Berkeley.

CA 32
SPECIAL COLLECTIONS
EDWARD L. DOHENY, JR. MEMORIAL LIBRARY
UNIVERSITY OF SOUTHERN CALIFORNIA
University Park
Los Angeles, California 90007
(213-741-6058)

1 Mischa Bakaleinikoff (1890-1960). Papers, ca. 1945-60, 11 ft. Russian-born composer for motion pictures. Manuscripts of his motion picture scores. (NUCMC 70-1265)

2 Original Leaves from Famous Bibles, 1121-1935, 60 ll. Includes 1 leaf from an Armenian lectionary, A.D. 1671 (fR090 B582o).

3 William H. Standley (1872-1963). Papers, 1892-1958, 25 ft. U.S. navy admiral and ambassador to the USSR, 1943-43. Personal and official correspondence, reports, memoranda, and printed materials. In 1941 the admiral was a member of the (W. Averell) Harriman-Beaverbrook Commission concerned with Lend-lease. Other subjects covered: the Frankel Ruble Affair; Soviet-Finnish and Soviet-Polish relations; the second front in World War II; Soviet air forces, agriculture, railroads, and iron and steel industries; and Soviet recognition of the Free French (Committee on National Liberation) in North Africa. Among the figures mentioned in the papers are J. Stalin, V. Molotov, I. Maisky, M. Litvinov, and A. Vyshinsky. Includes background information reports, 19 pp., on cities and oblasts of the Urals region prepared for Standley before his trip there in August 1943 (includes a map and concerns such cities as Ufa, Magnitogorsk, Sverdlovsk, and Cheliabinsk), and Stanley's log, 13 September-18 October 1941, of the Harriman-Beaverbrook mission, 50 pp. Unpublished guide (NUCMC 64-964).

CA 33
NIKOLAI N. MORSHEN (MARCHENKO)--PRIVATE COLLECTION
1072 Hellam Street
Monterey, California 93940

N. N. Morshen holds the papers of his father, the novelist Nikolai Vladimirovich Narokov. These consist of manuscript drafts of published and unpublished writings, mostly from the 1950s-1960s, in Russian. Among the items is the Russian draft of the published novel Mnimye velichinye (Imaginary Numbers), translated into English and published as Chains of Fear (1958), a portrayal of the purge and terror years of the 1930s. There are also notes and other papers, typed and handwritten, in 3 manuscript boxes. Note: N. N. Morshen (Marchenko) is also an author and poet. Permission of N. N. Morshen (Marchenko) required; qualified scholars only.

CA 34
HELEN PASHIN--PRIVATE COLLECTION
2761 Kipling Street
Palo Alto, California 94306

The papers of Nicholas Pashin (d. 1976), journalist and Russian literature and language lecturer at Stanford University, and of his brother, the novelist Sergei Maximov, are now in the hands of Pashin's widow. The materials, ca. 1946-1976, are in 2 file cabinets, ca. 18 ft., and include personal and business correspondence, literary manuscripts, and printed matter. Some Maximov manuscripts deal with life in Soviet concentration camps, e.g., those for the novels Denis Bushuev and Bunt Denisa Bushueva (published in 1950). N. Pashin has translated George Orwell's 1984, the only Russian translation of this work so far made. Permission of Mrs. Helen Pashin required; serious scholars only.

CA 35
ELIZABETH STENBOCK-FERMOR--PRIVATE COLLECTION
2315 Columbia Street
Palo Alto, California 94306

Family archive of Vladimir Timofeevich Sheviakov (ca. 1859-1930), former assistant minister of education in Imperial Russia and professor of biology at Irkutsk University. Ca. 500 holograph letters in Russian, and some photographs. Most of the letters are from Sheviakov to his children, especially George Sheviakov, former professor of psychology at San Francisco State University. The correspondence, largely written from Irkutsk but also from Prague and Italy, details living conditions, the economic situation, the first Five-Year Plan, and the food supply in that Siberian city in the 1920s and 1930s. Some letters from a son, Boris, arrested in 1936, describe daily life in a Soviet concentration camp, where he died; and letters from Mrs. Kovalevskii, Boris Sheviakov's daughter and a Soviet archaeologist (Academy of Sciences of the USSR). Other items are by Mrs. Sheviakov and by an American Red Cross nurse, Charlotte Ketty, telling about the Sheviakov family in 1930, in English. A portion of the letters was written in Western Europe in the late 1920s, when V. T. Sheviakov was sent abroad on a scientific mission. Dated envelopes accompanying the letters contain Imperial Russian stamps used in the late 1920s.

Mrs. Stenbock-Fermor can provide some biographical data on the family and information about events noted. Permission of Mrs. Stenbock-Fermor and of Mrs. T. Miloslavsky required. Mrs. Miloslavsky, daughter of V. T. Sheviakov, reserves all rights to the material.

CA 36
INSTITUTE ARCHIVES, I-32
CALIFORNIA INSTITUTE OF TECHNOLOGY
Pasadena, California 91125
(213-795-6811 x 2433)

Paul S. Epstein (1883-1966). Papers, 1880s-1966, 1 ft. Émigré professor of theoretical physics at Caltech, 1921-53. Born in Warsaw of well-to-do Jewish parents, he was raised mostly in Minsk. He spent his student days in Moscow, ca. 1901-1905, where he received his master's degree in 1909. He became assistant professor of physics at Moscow University that same year. From 1910 Epstein studied and taught abroad (Munich, Zurich, and Leyden) until emigrating to the U.S. in 1921. Personal correspondence, photographs, 11 tape recordings (untranscribed), and holograph reminiscences. In the recollections he talks about his mother, Sara Lurie Epstein, an intellectual who knew Fedor Dostoevskii in St. Petersburg (Dostoevskii mentions her in his Diary of a Writer for March 1877). She had correspondence with the novelist that was apparently destroyed after her death in 1897. Other family members noted in Epstein's correspondence include his sister, Hedwig Lurie Epstein, and three cousins (Sadi and Vera Lurie Mase, and Rashel Lurie). Because his major work was done in Germany and America, Epstein's papers are not primarily concerned with Russia, especially after 1910. For the 1930s, however, there is some information about the plight of European (and Soviet?) Jews. Qualified scholars only. Unpublished guide.

CA 37
NORTON SIMON MUSEUM OF ART AT PASADENA LIBRARY
Colorado and Orange Grove Boulevard
Pasadena, California 91105
(213-449-6840)

Blue Four Galka Scheyer Collection. Ca. 800 letters, mostly 1924-45. Correspondence of the artists Wassily Kandinsky, Paul Klee, Lyonel Feininger, and Alexei Jawlensky with Galka Scheyer. Jawlensky was born near Torzhok in 1864, traveled frequently to Western Europe, and emigrated in 1914. Kandinsky, born in Moscow (1866), was also in the West often, finally leaving the Soviet Union in 1921. Letters not in English have all been translated. Due to their fragile condition, the originals are kept in a vault; only photocopies are available for researchers. Open to scholars by appointment only. There is a list of the Jawlensky letters, arranged by date of composition. (NUCMC 65-2000) All of the letters will eventually be available on microfilm at the Archives of American Art.

CA 38
ARCHIVES BRANCH
FEDERAL ARCHIVES & RECORDS SERVICE, GSA
1000 Commodore Drive
San Bruno, California 94066
(415-876-9009)

This repository has some of the microfilms of materials in the National Archives (Washington, D.C.) that pertain to Russia/USSR. For more details, see Charles South, List of National Archives Microfilm Publications in the Regional Archives Branches (Washington: National Archives and Records Service, 1975).

CA 39
THE THOMAS WHALEY HOUSE
2482 San Diego Avenue
San Diego, California 92110
(714-298-2482)

Thomas Whaley (1823-1890). Papers, 1799-1953. 25,070 items. Merchant, San Diego city official, and councilman at Sitka, Alaska. Includes Whaley's Russian passport, probably obtained during a European tour 1844-46, and documentation on his contacts with Russian officials in Alaska 1867-68. There are also newspaper clippings on Seward's purchase of Alaska. (NUCMC 62-2092) Available only to qualified scholars and researchers.

CA 40
AMERICAN RUSSIAN INSTITUTE
90 McAllister Street
San Francisco, California 94102
(415-861-3813)

This institute was established in 1932 by Dr. Holland C. Roberts to promote cultural exchange and to improve relations between the United States and the Soviet Union. Some 500,000 letters, 20-30 ft. of personal and business correspondence, reflect the Institute's interest in the preceding subjects as well as its work with international peace movements. Its contacts in the USSR include the Soviet Peace Committee in Moscow, other committees in the 15 republics, the Novosti press agency, Pioneer, and the Helsinki World Peace

Council. Cultural exchange materials cover tours and tour arrangements for Soviet delegations, both of organizations and of individual citizens. The Institute also screens classical and modern full-length feature films on Soviet life. Permission of the Executive President (currently Sonia B. Kaross) required.

CA 41
BANK OF AMERICA ARCHIVES, #3218
P.O. Box 37000
San Francisco, California 94137
(415-622-4997)

The firm's archives hold materials (correspondence and reports) on loan negotiations and extension of credit to the USSR, 1928 and 1942, visits of senior bank officers to the Soviet Union, 1961 and 1964, the Marshall Plan, and foreign branch banking. They make reference to the Amtorg Trading Corporation. Access is limited to employees. There are unpublished inventories for most of these items.

CA 42
BAY AREA COUNCIL ON SOVIET JEWRY
106 Baden Street
San Francisco, California 94131
(415-585-1400)

This organization, which assists Jews who seek to emigrate from the USSR, has records and documentation on ca. 1,500 refuseniks, Soviet Jews who have not obtained permission to emigrate. The material, from the late 1960s to the present, includes personal correspondence, reports, films, photographs, and a card file of all refuseniks known to the organization. The Bay Area Council is a member of the Union of Councils for Soviet Jews, a national organization composed of 24 groups throughout the United States.

CA 43
CALIFORNIA HISTORICAL SOCIETY LIBRARY
2099 Pacific Avenue
San Francisco, California 94109
(415-567-1848 x 391)

1 Alaska Commercial Company. Records, 1868-1918, 2 vols. Shortly after the U.S. purchase of Alaska from Russia, Hutchinson [Hayward M.], Kohl [William], & Co., shipping merchants and wholesale fur dealers, was established to facilitate the transfer of equipment and holdings from the Russians to the Americans. This company negotiated with the Imperial Russian government concerning, most importantly, the fur and seal trade but also about the leasing of certain islands, the purchase of stock, boats, buildings, and even furs. Hutchinson, Kohl, & Co. soon became known as the Alaska Commercial Company. The two volumes contain minutes of the company's board of trustees meetings, beginning on 19 October 1868. Vol. 1, handwritten, 260+ pp., to 6 January 1904; vol. 2, mostly typed, ca. 140 pp., to 1918. They also include copies of the company's articles and bylaws. Other members of the company were August Wasserman, Louis Sloss, Louis Gerstle, and Leopold Boscowitch. The materials are also available on microfilm, 1 reel. (Ms 28)

2 William Burling. Business receipts, 1866-68, 1 folder. Includes material pertaining to Russians on the west coast of America. (Ms 261)

3 Joseph L. Folsom (1817-1855). Business papers, 1834-70, ca. 2.5 in. Army officer. Contains some material relating to Russians in the Pacific Northwest in the late 1860s. (Ms 758)

4 William McKendree Gwin (1805-1885). Papers, 1841-85, 1 folder. Senator, 1851-55. Includes material pertaining to Russians in the Pacific Northwest. (Ms 897)

5 Edward Huff. Correspondence, 1880-1908, 2 vols., ca. 400 letters. American businessman. Huff worked in Nicolaefsk on the Amoor River in Siberia, managing a hardware store and perhaps engaging in export/import trade. The letters, to his wife in San Francisco, describe the countryside, the winters, his social life or lack thereof, and his business. He also attempts to placate his wife for his absence. He earned ca. $2,500 per year but his wife complained about their separation. Also included: a list of vodka prices, and ca. 25 letters in Russian to various business people from Huff's company with his signature. Many of the letters are extremely faded. (Ms 3090)

6 Joseph Mora Moss (1809-1880). President of the American-Russian Commercial Company. 2 letters to him, 31 December 1849 and 30 April 1864. 1, from the governor of the Russian colony in New Archangel, Sitka, notes the mild winter and lack of ice. (Ms 1520)

7 Eugene Sullivan. Papers, 1852-98, 1 folder. San Francisco businessman. Includes a bill of sale, 31 March 1866, involving the American-Russian Commercial Company. (Ms 2100)

8 Mariano Guadalupe Vallejo (1808-1890). Commandante of San Francisco. Passport issued to an unidentified American for a visit to the Russian settlement of Fort Ross, 29 August 1838, in Spanish. (In the Faxon Dean Atherton Papers) (Vault Ms 5)

CA 44
SUTRO LIBRARY
CALIFORNIA STATE LIBRARY
2495 Golden Gate Avenue
San Francisco, California 94118
(415-557-0374)

1 Italian Renaissance Mss. Ms. 166, dated Venice 13 January 1426, in Latin, is a sale of a Russian slave named Maria by Ser Luigi Loredan, son of the late Giovanni, to Ser Gabriele Barbarigo, son of the late Antonio. There is also a reference to "a slave named Maria" in Ms. 124.

2 Sutro Library Hebraica. Ca. 167 items. Medieval religious works, mostly of Yemenite provenance. Ms. 163, Matityahu ben Samuel Kohen Mizrahi, "Kol mevaser," ca. 1830, 120 ll., contains some incidental information on the Jewish communities of Azerbaijan, Kurdistan, and Persia which the author visited on his way to Palestine.

Finding Aids: William M. Brinner, Sutro Library Hebraica: A Handlist (1966); George T. Dennis, "An Inventory of Italian Notarial Documents in the Sutro Library, San Francisco," Manuscripta, Vol. IX (1965).

CA 45
CONSTANTINE V. GALSKOY--PRIVATE COLLECTION
3100 Vicente Street
San Francisco, California 94116
(415-564-7764)

Mr. Galskoy is in possession of a collection of ca. 100 unpublished manuscript poems of his father, Vladimir Galskoy (1908-1961). His father was born in Orël. The poems, written in emigration 1920-61, are all in Russian. Various West European émigré publications have printed numerous poems by Vladimir Galskoy. Constantine Galskoy is currently preparing transcripts (typed) of the poetry. Requires written permission of C. Galskoy, who retains the literary rights.

CA 46
MUSEUM OF RUSSIAN CULTURE
2450 Sutter Street
San Francisco, California 94115

Founded in 1948, this museum of ethnic history holds, besides a 6,000-volume library, substantial archival materials on Russian history and emigration. At present it publishes an occasional Sbornik Muzeia Russkoi Kul'tury and a bulletin. The museum and archives are open, without charge, on Wednesday and Saturday afternoons only (except holidays).

1 Anonymous Manuscript Collection. Ca. 50 handwritten pp., 1877-ca. 1905. Several items on the Russo-Turkish War of 1877-78 and on the Russo-Japanese War; and some pornographic poetry, unpublished but circulated in Russia at the turn of the century. The items are believed to have been collected in France.

2 Archives of the Russian Orthodox Mission to Peking, China. Records, including correspondence, 1925-45, ca. 350 items.

3 Arkhiv Russkogo Sel'sko-Khoziaistvennogo Obshchestva. Printed matter, 1940s-1950s. Concerns soil research, chemicals, fertilizers, and agriculture (including farming in Siberia).

4 Arkhiv russkogo studentskogo obshchestva pri kaliforniiskem universitete v Berkele. Records, 1920-40, ca. 6 boxes. Includes materials on the Chinese Eastern Railway, the Amur Cossack brigade, the Russian Revolution, and the Siberian Civil War, 1919-21.

5 Arkhiv russkogo muzeia. Records, 1945-present. Correspondence, publications, etc. concerning the activities of the MRC, excluding current business.

6 Arkhiv Vitiazei. Mostly printed matter, 1949-62. From and about boy scout organizations in Europe, the U.S., and the Philippines (Tubabao IRO camp).

7 Antonina R. von Arnold-Cherbakoff. Material on the San Francisco and Bay Area émigré communities (several folders).

8 Roman Appolonovich von Arnold. Imperial Army officer, police chief and civic leader in Harbin, China. Autobiography, 1880-1917, 400 pp.

9 Konstantin P. Barskii. Member of San Francisco Russian Center, secretary of the organization Representatives of the Russian Emigration in America, active in anti-Soviet political movements. Minutes of meetings, and lists of Russian groups.

10 A. T. Bel'chinko (d. 1953). Collection, ca. 1890s-1940s, 6 ft. Diplomat. Bel'chinko was Russian consul-general in Hankow, China, until 1917, then honorary Portuguese consul (ca. 1918-43). He emigrated to the U.S. ca. 1944. Business and personal correspondence and reports pertain largely to his consular activities; also, diary and memoir material on life in St. Petersburg at the turn of this century. Some reports, in English and French, detail local conditions and the Japanese military occupation of Hankow in the late 1930s. As leader of Russian Emigrants Association, Bel'chinko collected biographical information (ca. 1,000 registration sheets plus photographs) for Russian émigré citizens of Hankow.

11 Valentina Ia. Belskaia (fl. 1930s-1940s). Active in the Russian Orthodox Church in America. Many photos, some from 1890 in Russia.

12 Polina Vassilievna Swatikova-Bereznaia. Manuscript of a Russian grammar.

13 Timothy A. Berezney. Editor of the émigré newspapers Nash put' and Russkoe obozrenie in the 1950s. Short memoir; Russian grammars; materials in English on the Sixth Congress of the Communist Party of the USSR; and a manuscript by his wife entitled "Joseph de Maistre et la Russie" (1961), 162 pp.

14 A. Bilimovich. Professor of economics. Manuscript analysis of Marxism, 200 pp.

15 Nadezhda A. Birskaia-Okuntsova. Memoirs, 269 pp., 1890-1970; and materials on the Russian Orthodox Church (in the USSR and abroad) and on anti-Semitism.

16 Vasilii Vladimirovich Bolgarskii. Physicist and chemist, teacher (pre-1919) at the universities of Perm and Kazan. Correspondence and personal documents. He also taught at the Polytechnical Institute in Harbin, 1920-52.

17 Elmira Adolphovna Baibakova von Brandt. Typescript, 68 pp., reminiscences of her brother-in-law M. M. Nenadich, secretary of the Serbian Legation to St. Petersburg in 1914, later minister of court to Yugoslavia under Alexander I (1914-41).

18 A. Budberg. Dnevnik barona A. Budberga, 1919.

19 Sergei Chasov. Editor of San Francisco newspaper Russkaia zhizn'. Typescripts of plays and screenplays, most in Russian, written between 1944 and 1950.

20 Pavel Chelishchev (Tchelitcheff or Tchelitchew) (1898-1957). Collection, ca. 1900-64, ca. 6 boxes. Russian-French painter. Materials relating to his career and to the Chelishchev family, gathered by his sister, Alexandra (Choura) Tchelitcheff-Zaoussailoff. Includes 200 pp. typed biography of Chelishchev and his family, in Russian, English summary, 5 pp.; the document inscribing Chelishchev in books of the Russian nobility; correspondence; 3 photograph albums from the 1930s; a roll of drawings; some personal effects (paints and palettes); and printed matter. Materials are in Russian, French, and English.

21 David Chubov. Russian Orthodox priest in Switzerland. Autobiographical essay; correspondence about Western refugees, prisoners of war, and émigrés in Western Europe and Argentina; and letters from the Empress Maria Feodorovna, Grand Duke Nikolai Nikolaevich, Prince N. L. Obolenskii, Metropolitan Antonii, and generals A. P. Kuteopov and P. N. Krasnov.

22 Collection of Far Eastern Russian Newspapers and Magazines. 1920s-1945. Includes partial runs of Vestnik Manchurii, Zaria, Novosti zhizny, Russkii golos, Shanghaiskaia zaria, Russkoe slovo, Novaia zhizn', Aziia, Tientsenskaia zaria, Vozrozhdenie azii, and Rozhdestvenskii rubezh.

23 Jacob Lvovich Deich (b. 1896). Journalist. Papers of an émigré in Harbin, Shanghai, and the U.S.

24 Document Collection. Ca. 900 items, ca. 1800-ca. 1917. Letters, diaries, autographs, diplomas, copies of imperial prikazy, and historical documents. A substantial part of the collection consists of individual service records, ca. 100 ll. There is also a handwritten daily log (Dnevnik) of a Cossack troop elder who accompanied an Imperial Russian mission to Peking in 1831, ca. 100 pp.

25 Vladimir A. Dordopolo. Journalist and poet. Issues of Rossiia, 1949-59, containing his articles.

26 A. Efimov. Ca. 1,000 items. Materials on the Civil War years (1919-22) in Siberia and the Priamurskoe pravitel'stvo. Arranged in 4 folders, they comprise: (a) mimeographed copies of prikazy and ukazy of the Priamurskoe pravitel'stvo, September 1921-August 1922; (b) copies of telegrams, documents, prikazy, and service record lists of various military units; (c) biographic sheets and service records for soldiers of the Ussuriiskoe kazach'e voisko; and (d) a handwritten draft of Efimov's book Izhevtsy i votkintsy (Concord, California, 1975), which describes a 1918 revolt in Siberia against the Soviet regime.

27 Ivan V. Emil'ianov. Economist, political leader, and professor. Born in Tobolsk, Siberia, he became chief economist for and later president of the Provisional Government bank in Kharkov, then head of the city's government in 1919. On emigrating he became director of Selskosoiuz in London, 1920-21, the purchasing arm for some 20,000 Russian cooperative associations. Emil'ianov was an economics professor at Prague University before coming to the U.S. in 1927. He taught economics at Rutgers University. Author of 42 monographs and ca. 1,000 articles on cooperatives, agriculture, and industry. His papers cover most aspects of his career in Russia and abroad. Personal and professional correspondence, photographs, typed and handwritten manuscripts of his works, documents, and printed matter. Includes bulletins of Selskosoiuz and his correspondence for 1920-21; reports from 2 agencies he was apparently connected with in the 1920s-1930s--the All-Russian Red Cross based in Paris, and the Commission pour la Reconstitution de l'Industrie Minière et Metallurgique de la Russie Meridionelle.

CALIFORNIA - MUSEUM OF RUSSIAN CULTURE CA 46

28 Evgenii Aleksandrovich Federov. Army officer, served under Baron R. F. Ungern-Sternberg in the Civil War. Diary, 1919-21.

29 A. V. Fedin. 3 versions of his unpublished work "Upadok gosudarstvennosti. Sushchestvuiushchogo v mire napriazhennogo polozheniia," in Russian and English, 109 pp.

30 Valentin Vassilievich Fedulenko (b. 1894). Rol' byvshikh soiuznikov Rossii po otnosheniiu k belomu dvizheniiu v Sibiri (1961).

31 Aleksandr A. Gefter (1918-1957). Author and painter, émigré in Paris. Literary manuscripts and photographs. Note: The museum holds a large number of his paintings.

32 Pavel Genzel' (Paul Haentsel) (d. 1949). Papers, ca. 1929-1948, ca. 1,000 items. Economics professor. Born in Moscow in the late 19th c., he taught economics at Moscow University 1908-28. Emigrating to the U.S. in 1929, Haentsel taught at the University of Chicago and then, from 1930, at Northwestern University. Letters, lecture notes, and printed matter. His assessment of conditions in the Soviet Union, especially economic plans and reality, 1929-48. Unpublished finding aid.

33 E. Glink. Typescript account of life in a Soviet concentration camp, 1934-42, 50 pp.

34 A. S. Golovkin. Letters, photos, and printed matter concerning the Russian Popular Monarchist Movement, 1950s.

35 George Grebenschikoff. Émigré writer. Letters, literary manuscripts, photographs, and personal documents.

36 Alexander Tikhonovich Grechaninov (1864-1956). Composer. Settled in the U.S. in 1939. Holograph of his autobiography entitled "My Life," ca. 150 pp.

37 M. P. Gromov. Pharmacologist. Lecturer in Harbin, compiler of unpublished Russo-Japanese medical dictionary and Russo-Japanese-English military dictionary.

38 George C. Guins (1881-1971). Collection, ca. 1917-1971, ca. 8 ft. Government official and professor. Guins was a minister in the Kolchak government (Siberia), later a resident of Harbin, and emigrated to the U.S. in 1941. He lectured at Berkeley, 1948-52. Primarily his lectures (most in English) at the University of California and typed manuscripts; also, personal memorabilia, documents from the Ministry of Supply, 1917-18, letters and documents from Harbin, 1931-41, and other papers. Unpublished finding aid.

39 Oleg Ivanovich (1902-1957). Émigré physicist, engineer, and mathematician. In France to 1940, then in U.S. Materials on career and a Russian engineers' group in France.

40 Vasily S. Iljin (b. 1888). Plant physiologist in Venezuela, 1940-1950s. Letters and photos about Russian colonies in Venezuela and Argentina; also drafts of scientific works.

41 Evgeniia Sergeevna Isaenko. Papers, 8 ft., ca. 5,000 pp. Writer (pseudonym: Pechatkina), singer, and actress in San Francisco. Correspondence, drafts of novels, photos, and printed matter. Many letters concern émigrés, 1930s-1960s.

42 Paul Ivanukov. Writer. 3 manuscripts of his novels written in 1923. "Life's Whirlpool" is typed and in both Russian and English versions; "The Swamp" and "Two Loves" are in Russian only. Each manuscript is ca. 200 pp.

43 A. Izenbek. Archaeologist and military historian. Emigrated to Western Europe in 1926. Research materials on Genghis Khan and Tamerlane in India, 13th-15th c.

44 Vasilii Osipovich Kappel'. General in the Imperial and White Russian armies. Articles about him from Russkaia zhizn' (San Francisco), 1947-52.

45 Nicholas S. Karinsky. "A History of Aviation in Russia (from its beginnings to 1918)," typescript, 150 pp.

46 H. Kas'ianov. "Temnye dela pochtennykh sfer," 189 pp. in 2 vols. (1947).

47 Estafy Kerner. A travel account entitled "The Voyage from Vladivostok to Japan, Australia, and New Zealand," in 1914, 170 pp.

48 Dmitrii L. Khorvat. Collection, 1899-1921, ca. 2,000 items, ca. 8,000 pp. Army officer (lieutenant-general), director of the Chinese Eastern Railway, ca. 1917, and a "supreme plenipotentiary" of the Omsk Provisional Government for the Far East in the Civil War. He was also a member of the Allied Control Commission, which dealt with the Chinese Eastern Railway in the Civil War. Business and personal correspondence, reports, office files, diaries, intelligence reports, and bulletins of the American Expeditionary Forces on Siberia and European Russia, telegrams, and diplomatic reports, mostly in Russian (many English and/or French translations). Covers the Siberian Civil War and Allied intervention there, the Chinese Eastern Railway, and major events in the Far East. Correspondents include Derber, prime minister in the Siberian government; Cossack Ataman G. M. Semenov; the Harbin consul-general M. K. Popov; and the ambassadors Boris Bakhmet'ev (Washington), V. Nabokov (London), V. A. Maklakov (Paris), V. N. Krupenskii (Tokyo), and Prince Nikolai Aleksandrovich Kudashev (Peking). Unpublished finding aid.

49 Vasilii F. Kibal'chich (Basile Kibaltchitch). Director of Russian Symphonic Choir (le Choeur

Russe), 1908-40. Correspondence, including some with A. Arkhangel'skii, 1908-24; photographs; account books; music scores; and printed matter.

50 Georgii Titovich Kiaschenko (Kiiashchenko). Imperial Army general. Correspondence, photos, documents, and printed matter concerning émigré benevolent, political, and military groups; also, notes and a sketch of General Lavr Kornilov's "rebellion," 1917-18, handwritten, 50 pp.

51 I. A. Kolchin. Choirmaster. Clippings, many of them reviews, about performances of Russian choirs led by Kolchin, from Zaria (Shanghai), Russkaia zhizn' (San Francisco), and Novaia zaria, 1937-54.

52 B. N. Kompaneiskii (1885-1965). Papers, 1 box, ca. 1,000 pp. Professor and author. Born in St. Petersburg, he went to Berlin in 1942, to Argentina in 1948, where he died. Taught psycho-physiological sciences at the Universidad Nacional de la Plata in Argentina, wrote works on the physiology of color and also plays, stories, novels, and fairy tales under the pseudonym N. Kovaleriskii. Unpublished typescripts (carbon copies), in Russian, of many of his writings. Unpublished finding aid.

53 T. K. Korotun (b. 1887). Chairman of the Stuttgart YMCA, 1940s. Material on the San Francisco émigré community and church.

54 Vladimir Petrovich Kulaeff. Far East civic leader. Documents from the Imperial Ministry of Communications, ca. 1915-1918, plus several rare books and grammars.

55 Aleksandr A. Kurenkov (Koor) (b. 1891). Imperial Army captain. Came to the U.S. in 1923. Materials on the monarchist movement in the emigration (ca. 1950).

56 Letter Collection of Prominent Russian Writers and Personalities. Ca. 100 items, 1860-1900. Letters from A. Amfiteatrov, Leonid Andreev, Konstantin Bal'mont, A. Chirikov, Aleksandr T. Grechaninov, Y. Grot, S. Kalivanis, Aleksandr Ivanovich Kuprin, A. M. Remizov, Ilia Repin, Nicholas Roerich, Grand Duke Konstantin, I. Sevrin, Fedor Shaliapin, Igor Sikorskii, Fedor Sologub, I. Sviatogor, N. A. Teffi, Count Aleksei Tolstoi, L. Tzvetaeff (Tsvetaev), and others. Unpublished list of letters.

57 Letters of Famous Russians Collection. Ca. 400 items, 1930s-1971. Written to Olga A. Morozova in answer to her request for biographical information to be used in her (still unpublished) "Biography of Famous Russians." Most date from the 1930s. Letters are in manila folders in alphabetical order by name of respondent: Professor A. F. von Ahnert (P. A. Ark), with an autobiographical sketch; I. V. Baikov (7 letters); General E. P. Beliaeff; Volikovskii (3 letters); Valentin Bulgakov; G. Grebenshikov (Grebenshchikov); Xenia Jukova-Yudina (Joukoff-Eudin); Lydia Krestovskaia; L. D. Liubimov; P. A. Martynov, with autobiographical details and samples of his poetry; Archbishop Ioann Shakhovskoi; and K. Zworykin, among others.

58 Iu. I. Lodyzhinskii (1888-1950). Active in the Russian Red Cross and in anti-communist groups. Materials on the White Armies, the Russian army of Yugoslavia (both early 1920s), the Lausanne trial of Maurice Conradi for assassinating Soviet Ambassador V. V. Vorovskii, Lt. General Kusonskii, Count P. D. Dolgorukov, S. N. Il'in, and Artsibashov.

59 Anatoly Stepanovich Loukashkin. Material on White Russian colonies in Manchuria and Shanghai and on espionage activities in these places, on the Civil War, and on Russia in 1905; and biographies of V. P. Vologodsky, colonels V. V. Vrashtel and S. S. Tolstoff, generals M. K. Dicterichs, V. O. Kappel, and D. L. Khorvat, Admiral A. V. Kolchak, and U.S. Vice-Admiral J. K. Stark.

60 Elizaveta Andreevna Malozemov (b. 1881). Papers, 1930-65, ca. 5 boxes. Lecturer in Slavic languages at UC-Berkeley. Includes papers of her husband A. P. Malozemov and their son Andrei. She emigrated from the USSR in 1920. Personal correspondence, photos, maps, notes, and printed matter. Correspondents include friends in the Soviet Union in the 1930s, the author N. V. Narokov, and the writer S. Gornii. Covers conditions in the USSR in the 1930s and 1940s, the Soviet army in the 1940s, and life in emigration in the U.S.

61 Grand Duchess Maria Aleksandrovna. 520 letters, 1870-88. Daughter of Alexander II and wife of the duke of Edinburgh. Correspondence mostly with her father and mother, particularly the latter, mainly on family matters. Includes some letters of her parents to her. Letters are legible and in fair condition but unsorted. Permission required from the museum president and curator. The letters are stored in a bank vault.

62 M. Marsova Autograph Collection. 20 letters, 1860s-1890s. Assembled by a Russian émigré in Tokyo. Letters from Russian bellelettrists of the last century, including Ivan Aksakov, Bertenson, Ivan Goncharov, Aleksei Maikov, L. Maikov, Matveev, Nazhivin, Nikolai Nekrasov, S. G. Petrov (Skitalets), A. A. Shenshin (Fet), Count M. Sologub, and Fedor I. Tiutchev. Letters are stored in a bank vault. Unpublished list of letters.

63 Materialy ob ob"edinenii soiuz russkikh shoferov v Parizhe. Ca. 100 items, 1926-43. Records of the group, including appeals for support.

64 Iu. P. Miroliubov (d. 1968). Papers, 4 boxes. Author, inventor, and editor of the periodical

Zhar-ptitsa (1948-57). Correspondence (personal and "to-the-editor"), typescript novels (e.g., "Beregites'," ca. 250 pp., written 1944-46), essays, other writings, (e.g., "Skitaniia po Evrope," 326 pp., handwritten), blueprints, and other materials for his inventions, principally electrical conductors. Also, his personal library.

65 Viktor Monkovich (Vile). "Twenty days on board the transport ship 'General Sturgis,' 1949," ca. 200 pp., handwritten.

66 Olga Alexandrovna Morozova. Collection of biographies of prominent émigrés that she prepared in the 1930s-1940s, handwritten, 400 pp.; and a typescript, 284 pp., entitled "Tubabao, The Camp of IRO for Russian White Emigrants from China" (IRO = International Relief Organization), written 1949-51. The primary focus in the biographies is the life of emigrants in the Far East, where Morozova herself was a civic leader, writer, and amateur historian.

67 V. Mort. Correspondence, diaries, notes, and manuscripts concerning Russians interned at Lake Lipari in Italy, 1949, Soviet Russia and Vladivostok, 1918-22, and the California emigration in the 1920s; also, poetry and letters to Aleksandr Leonidovich and Evgeniia S. Isaenko (some of the poetry signed by M. Nadezhdin).

68 Arthur C. Murray. Canadian captain, senior officer of the Inter-Allied Board to Supreme Dictator of Siberia, Admiral Kolchak. 1 notebook, handwritten, 100 pp., on Siberia in the 19th-20th c.; "The Siberian Icy March of the White Russian Army in 1919-1920," typescript, 126 pp.; and 5 pp., typed, of data on this march.

69 Andrei Mikhailovich Naidenov. 6 manuscripts (1 typed) about the threat of communism and the struggle against it, 1917-1960s, including a "Letter to Svetlana Alliluieva."

70 Boris Nedzvetskii. Correspondence, reports, and printed matter concerning Russian scouts/explorers (razvedchiki) in Shanghai, China, and the Tubabao (Philippines) refugee camp, 1937-50; also, notes on Russian history (Catherine II and G. Potemkin) and maps of Russia.

71 Abram Moisseevich Netupsky. Autobiography: "From Sakhalin Island to San Francisco, 1875-1945," typescript, 139 pp.

72 Obshchestvo iuristov vo Frantsii. Records, 1941-49, 7 folders, ca. 1,200 pp. Materials relating to the Society of Russian Lawyers in Emigration, the Union of Russian Jurists, the Association of Russian Lawyers in New York, and the Committee on Displaced Persons, all of which worked with the French group on behalf of Russian DPs after World War II, particularly those in Germany. References to K. Nikolaev, A. A. Gol'denveizer, P. A. Sokolov, and Vladimir Melnikov.

73 Iosif Konstantinovich Okulich (1871-1948). Papers, 1917-?, ca. 6 ft. Member of the Soviet of Trade and Industry, July 1917, participant in the Union of Siberian Creamery Associations, 1918, and representative plenipotentiary in the U.S. for the Priamurskoe pravitel'stvo of Siberia, 1921-22. Most of the material concerns his activity on behalf of anti-Bolshevik groups, including his efforts in 1918 to enlist British support for Admiral A. V. Kolchak and the Priamur government. Many letters between Okulich and the British Foreign Office deal with the Allied intervention in Siberia and at Murmansk and the need of icebreakers for Vladivostok. Personalities mentioned include U.S. Secretary of State Charles Evans Hughes (letter to him about Japan's seizure of former Russian territory in 1921); Maurice Paleologue, last French ambassador to Imperial Russia; Eduard Benes, an autograph; and the émigrés Pavel Genzel' (Haentsel) and I. P. Tolmachoff.

74 Aleksandr S. Orlov (b. ca. 1888). Lawyer and actor. Graduated Moscow University in 1913; emigrated to Harbin in 1931; actor in Shanghai, 1941-49; lecturer in China and the U.S. Many photos and some letters about his career, 1913-1960s. His book The Dust of Backstage appeared in 1934.

75 Dmitrii Petrovich Panteleev. Secretary for the Russian Orthodox Mission in Peking, ca. 1918-1942. Correspondence, reports, and printed matter.

76 M. P. Panteleev (1887-1953). Opera singer. Performance reviews and clippings.

77 A. Paveninskii. 3 notebooks, 2 April-2 December 1946, 3 ft., holograph, part diary and part historical essay, the whole entitled "Bor'ba za Rossii i ee svetloe budushchee; lichnye vzgliady," 280 pp.; and 18 large folders of newspaper clippings about life in the USSR, 1930s-1940s, from Russkaia zhizn' and other Russian and English sources.

78 Peter Vasil'evich Pavlo. Correspondence, reports, and printed matter concerning the Russian Orthodox Church in Exile (San Francisco), church affairs, and the construction of the Holy Virgin Mary of Kazan Cathedral. Many prelates are mentioned. Unpublished finding aid.

79 Vitali Ivanovich Petrapavlovskii. Papers, ca. 1917-1920s, ca. 1,000 pp. Government official and anti-communist. Served the Provisional Government and then various anti-Bolshevik governments, including Kolchak's in Siberia; chief representative of the Russian Government Control Commission in the U.S.A. from May 1917

to 1924. Materials, arranged in 5 folders in rough chronological order, include personal and business letters, reports, telegrams, and documents. His work involved quality control of supplies purchased. Includes his correspondence with U.S. Secretary of State Robert Lansing, and subpoenas from the U.S. Senate to testify about U.S. intervention in the Civil War.

80 Sergei Ivanovich Polikarpoff. Russian vice-consul in Manchuria, 1912-16. Materials from Imperial Ministry of Foreign Affairs, rare photos, and reports on early history of Russian aviation.

81 V. Ponomarenko. Collection, 16th c.-1960s, ca. 3 ft. Ataman (hetman) of the Zabaikal Cossack Stanitsa in San Francisco. Unpublished manuscripts, ca. 3,000-4,000 pp., literary and historical, diaries, memoirs, biographical sketches of individual Cossacks, maps, and documents, collected for an unfinished history of the Transbaikal Cossacks. Concerns the history of the Cossack settlement in Siberia since the 16th c. and, mostly, their history since 1900, especially the period of World War I and after. Some items also on the San Francisco settlement (stanitsa) from the 1940s to the 1960s, the Civil War in Siberia, and the Allied intervention and anti-Bolshevik organizations in Manchuria or elsewhere, ca. 1921. Includes a holograph memoir by Ataman G. M. Semenov, "About Myself," with a supplement entitled "The World-Wide Struggle Against the Bolsheviks" (1921); and a manuscript by I. I. Serebrennikov, F. K. Myl'nikov, and I. Razmakhnin about the Caucasus front, 1915-17, typed and handwritten, 511 pp.

82 Vladimir A. von Reimers. Teacher of civil engineering in Imperial military academies. Materials on Russians in Paraguay, 1930s-1940s.

83 Alexander Nikolaevich Rojdestvensky (Rozhdestvenskii) (b. ca. 1882). Assistant procurator in the Tiflis Superior Court, 1908-18. Personal documents, typed manuscripts, and printed matter. Three typescripts relate to the Rojdestvensky family and to Alexander Nikolaevich's career: "Memoirs of an Assistant District Attorney of the Tiflis Superior Court, 1908-1918," 200 pp.; "Family Chronicle, 1882-1918," 200 pp.; and "Abroad: France (Toulouse, Algiers, and Paris), 1920-1940," 200 pp. A typescript, 50 pp., concerns the conquest and colonization of the Caucasus. Includes a rare publication, the Voyage du Chevalier Jean Charden en Perse par la Colchide, 1672-1673 (Paris, 1821).

84 Vladimir Mikhailovich Rudnev. District attorney of Ekaterinoslav district court; appointed by the Kerensky government to a commission investigating wrongdoing of the tsarist regime. Handwritten memoir, 19 pp., about Nicholas II, the Romanov family, Rasputin, etc.

85 Russian-American Historical Society. Records, 1937-48. Precursor of the MRC. Includes material on the Russian Museum in Prague and the Russian Orthodox Church in Alaska.

86 Russian Center in San Francisco, California. Records, ca. 1940-64, 2 notebooks.

87 Russian Child's Welfare Society, Inc. (Outside Russia). Records, 1926-69. Organization headquartered in New York City with branches in Seattle, Hollywood, and St. Louis.

88 Russian Workers' Association--ARTEL (San Francisco). Records, 1952-57. Nikolai Skore, president.

89 Aleksandr Vladimirovich Samoilovich. Archpriest of the Russian Orthodox Church in Emigration/Abroad. Materials on church hierarchs and communities in Berlin, Brazil, and the U.S., 1941-68.

90 Reverend Father Innokenty Seryshev. Orthodox priest in Tomsk, Manchuria, Japan, and Brisbane, Australia. Personal correspondence, ca. 1,000 pp., extensive photograph collection (negatives), and an historical essay. Many autograph letters to Seryshev in Japan from Russian émigré writers describing life and conditions in the emigration. Photos of famous emigrants from the USSR. Handwritten essay entitled "The Essence of the Great People's Rebellion in Siberia, 1919," 150 pp., which deals with the collapse of the Kolchak government.

91 A. Severianin. "Memoirs about the lost native land," handwritten, ca. 100 pp., concern life in pre-1917 Russia.

92 Aleksandr Iakovlevich Slobodchikov (1875-1946). Lawyer and teacher. Correspondence and papers relating to his career in Manchuria, Harbin, and Shanghai; items on Soviet-Chinese diplomacy, liquidation of the Russo-Asiatic Bank in Harbin, 1926, banking, and trade.

93 Society for the Protection of Russian Children in San Francisco and Other Cities (U.S.). Records, 1926-40, 1 folder, ca. 200 pp.

94 Vasilii K. Sokovnin. Ukrainian, emigrated in 1946 to Austria and then to Western Europe. Memoir material, extensive personal correspondence, historical manuscripts, and printed matter. Ca. 1,350 letters exchanged between Sokovnin and individuals in the USSR, 1946-55. Copy of his 24 goda pod igom bol'shevikov, 1917-41 gg. Otryvki vospominanii (Kiev, 1943), published under German rule, with his handwritten revisions and foreword for a second edition, 244 pp. "Chto proshlo--togo ne budet--kartinki minuvshego. 1878-1917 gg.," handwritten, 100 pp., describes his early years. Typescript written in Austria entitled "Pod chuzhoi vlast'iu (Ruminy v Odesse, Okt.

1941-Apr. 1, 1944)," 65 pp., plus handwritten version of the same, 68 pp., with supplement and clippings, 12 pp.

95 Maria Sozonovichova (Sozonovitch-Kozhin) (b. 1896). Opera singer and journalist in Belgian Congo. Born in Warsaw. Printed matter.

96 A. N. Speranskii. Imperial army officer. Diary/notebook, battle orders, plans, maps, and information on Russian troops in France, all during World War I.

97 Natalia P. Sukhareva-Trubova (b. 1905). Born in Samara, emigrated to the U.S. 11 composition books, holograph, 1,100 pp., describing her life from 1905-43, largely in the U.S., mostly in Russian.

98 P. V. Swatikova. See under P. V. Swatikova-Bereznaia.

99 Nikolai Nikolaevich Tagantsev. Imperial senator. Memoirs in 3 manuscripts: "N. S. Tagantsev, zapisok ego syna N. N. T.," handwritten plus several pages of typed excerpt, 18 pp. "Iz moikh vospominanii, 1918-1919 (Ot"ezd iz Petrograda)," handwritten, 42 pp.; and "Delo general Sukhomlinova," handwritten, 65 pp., typed, 36 pp.

100 Vladimir Yakovlevich Tolmacheff. Papers, ca. 3 ft. Émigré scholar. Correspondence, diaries, and drafts of studies on the archaeology, geology, and fauna of Manchuria.

101 Sergei S. Tol'stov. Imperial army officer. Correspondence, reports, and personal documents. The captain commanded the armies and naval forces of the Primoria region in 1917-19. Material on his service near Lodz in World War I, and on the Siberian Civil War and its aftermath (especially in Vladivostok).

102 Vakhan Totomiiants. Russian émigré scholar. Typed drafts and printed matter concerning economic history.

103 Alexander Nikolaevich Vagin (Varguin) (1884-1953). Imperial army general, chief of staff of the Irkutsk military region in 1919, and journalist. Emigrated to Harbin in 1920. Papers on his career as a journalist and the emigration, 1937-55.

104 Pavel Georgievich Vaskevich. Imperial consul in Dairen, Japan. Memoirs and clippings, 1930-53.

105 Vladivostok-Genzan Collection. Ca. 100 items, 1922-24. Documents and letters concerning the White Russian and American Expeditionary forces in the 2 areas. Many are signed by General Dmitrii Antonovich Lebedev, army chief of staff under Admiral A. V. Kolchak, and are addressed to Vice-Admiral J. K. Stark of the U.S. Navy.

106 Boris Nikolaevich Volkov (b. 1894). Official, author, and poet. Literary manuscripts, voluminous correspondence, and some poetry. Born in Ekaterinoslav, Volkov was a student on the jurisprudence faculty of Moscow University 1912-15. He was in the stretcher-bearer corps during World War I. Sympathetic to the Provisional Government, he fled Irkutsk in 1917 through Mongolia to China, 1921. ("Ripley's Believe It or Not" reports that he covered 1,200 miles on foot in just 5 days and 10 hours.) Volkov emigrated to the U.S. in 1923. An unpublished autobiographical novel, "Conscript to Paradise," written in the 1930s, records his experiences in 1914-23: participation in the Siberian Civil War, investigation of the Pan-Mongolian movement for anti-Bolshevik forces, employment in Mongolia by the ministries of finance and interior of Baron R. F. Ungern-Sternberg's government, and work for the import-export firm the Gilchrist Company in Kalgan and Ulan Bator (Urga). There are English and Russian versions of this novel. Also, his unpublished work "Na chuzhaia berega" and some poetry from 1913. Much of the correspondence is with his publishers and translator. Other correspondents include General Dmitrii L. Khorvat and A. Serebrennikov.

107 A. P. Vorobchuk-Zagorskii. Maps, photos, and essays concerning émigrés in the Far East, 1930-42, including generals Grigorii Afanas'evich Verzhbitskii and D. L. Khorvat.

108 Vysshii monarkhicheskii sovet. The first 143 issues of this weekly serial published in Berlin, 14 August 1921-7 February 1926.

109 L. Zauer. "Questions of Life and Death," handwritten, 360 pp.

110 Sergei Vasil'evich Zozulin. Member of the Yugoslav Russian Pedagogical Society. Emigrated ca. 1919. Personal documents (1912-1940s).

111 Note: The Museum has an extensive clippings collection on a variety of subjects; photograph albums; and much additional manuscript material, particularly pertaining to the Civil War and the emigration in Siberia and the Far East.

CA 47
NATIONAL MARITIME MUSEUM
Foot of Polk Street
San Francisco, California 94109
(415-556-8177)

Russian-related materials include 25 photos of American soldiers taken at Vladivostok, ca. 1920, and photocopy documents, under 1 ft., pertaining to Russian activities at Fort Ross, California.

CA 48
ORTHODOX CHURCH IN AMERICA
DIOCESE OF SAN FRANCISCO AND WESTERN AMERICA
2040 Anza Street
San Francisco, California 94118
(415-752-4126)

The Russian Orthodox Church has been in America since the eighteenth century, but it has been autocephalous only since 1970. An integral part of the Russian community in this country, the Church with its records provides invaluable information concerning pre- and post-1917 émigrés of the Orthodox faith. The records of this diocese, extending from 1947 to the present, include materials on the diocese administration and all its affairs, relations with higher (Chancery) and lower (parish) authorities, émigré organizations, church-affiliated groups, and the Council of Bishops. The Orthodox Church and its missions in Japan, Australia, South America, and elsewhere are subjects touched upon in this collection of correspondence, reports, files, account books, photographs, and printed material. There are also literary manuscripts. Among the more interesting topics covered in the papers are the Church's efforts to acquire the icon of Our Lady of Kazan in 1963 and its negotiations with the Moscow Patriarchate for autocephaly in 1969-70. The names of the metropolitans Ireney and Leonty and the Archbishop Ioann Skakhovskoi are mentioned in connection with various matters noted above. Permission from diocese authorities is necessary to use the collection, ca. 20 ft.

CA 49
RUSSART CORPORATION
3402 Geary Boulevard
San Francisco, California 94118
(415-668-4080)

This travel bureau _cum_ art and culture society promotes cultural contacts between the United States and the Soviet Union. One important part of its program is the weekly showing of new and recent Soviet films in San Francisco. Russart purchases and retains copies of most of these films, though some are borrowed or rented. Films are both 35 mm and 16 mm. Interested scholars may want to contact Russart's president, Dmitry P. Gribanowski, about the possibility of using this film collection for individual research projects. A partial listing of Russart film holdings follows.

1 _Armed and Very Dangerous_ (Vooruzhёn ochen' opasen), 90 min. (1977), dir. Vladimir Vainshtok. Based on the California stories of Bret Harte. In Russian.

2 _Ballad of a Hussar_ (Gusarskaia ballada), 95 min., dir. Tikhon Khrennikov. Musical set in period of the Napoleonic Wars of 1812, with colorful costumes and beautiful scenery. In Russian.

3 _Blockade_ (Blokada), 165 min., dir. Mikhail Ershov. Four-part tale of the siege of Leningrad during World War II. With Iu. Solomin, E. Lebedev, I. Akulova. In Russian.

4 _Buying a Daddy/Dimka_ (Ya kopiel papo), 80 min. (1965), dir. Ilya Frez. Dubbed in English.

5 _Chekhov's Love-Likka_ (Syuzhet dlya nebolshogo rasskaza), 86 min. (1972), dir. Sergei Yutkevich. A co-production of Mosfilm Studio and Teleia-Film (France). In Russian.

6 _Daughter-in-law_, 82 min. (1974), dir. Khojakuli Narliev. A Turkmen film. Subtitled in English.

7 _Duel_ (Duel'), 98 min. (1974), dir. Iosif Heifitz. Based on a Chekhov short story set in a town in the Caucasus. Subtitled "A Bad Good Man"; English subtitles.

8 _Empty Trip_ (Porozhnii reis), 98 min. A rural romance.

9 _Gentlemen of Luck_, 92 min. (1973), dir. Alexander Sery. Comedy about thieves, mistaken identity, and impersonation. Dubbed.

10 _Grown-up Kids_ (Vzroslye deti), 80 min. Comedy.

11 _Hot Snow_, 90 min., dir. Gavriil Yegiazarov. Based on the novel by Yuri Bondarev, about fighting near Stalingrad in December 1942 and the Nazi effort to reach the entrapped Field Marshal Paulus. With Georgi Zhenov, Anatoli Kuznetsov, Boris Tokarev, and Tamara Sidelnikova. Dubbed.

12 _In Love_ (Vliublennye), 85 min. About the post-war generation of Russian young people. With Anastasiya Vertinskaya. In Russian.

13 _Jacob_ (Yakov Bogomolov), 97 min., dir. Abram Room. Based on Maksim Gorkii's play about the infatuation of a wealthy Russian tycoon for the wife of an engineer. With Anastasiya Vertinskaya, Nina Shatskaya, Igor Kvasha, and Alexander Kalyagin. English subtitles.

14 _The Living Corpse_ (Zhivoi trup), 145 min., dir. Vladimir Vengerov. Screen version of Leo Tolstoi's play, in 2 parts. In Russian.

15 _Lovers' Romance_ (Romans o vliublennykh), 140 min. (1975), dir. Andrei Mikhalkov-Konchalovskii. 2 parts. English subtitles.

16 _Office Story_ (Sluzhebnyi roman), 145 min. (1977), dir. El'dar Riazanov. Romantic comedy set in a statistical bureau. English subtitles.

17 Oh, That Nastya! (Okh, uzh eta Nastia!), 84 min. (1975), dir. Iurii Pobedonostsev. Story of a mischievous, day-dreaming little girl. English subtitles.

18 Olessia (Olesia), 95 min. Based on A. Kuprin's story of a sorceress's beautiful daughter. With Lyudmila Chursina. In Russian.

19 Only "Veterans" Engage in Combat (V boi idut odni "stariki"), 92 min. (1976), dir. and starring Leonid Bykov. A comedy. English subtitles.

20 Ordinary Fascism, 128 min., dir. Mikhail Romm. A look at mankind's fate and the birth and collapse of fascism. Award winner at Leipzig film festival. English narration.

21 Pirosmani, 85 min. (1973), dir. Georgy Shengelaya. Georgian film about the Georgian primitive artist Niko Pirosmanishvili, early 20th c. English subtitles.

22 Privalov's Millions (Privalovskie milliony), 170 min., dir. Yaropolk Lapshin. Based on the novel by D. Mamin-Sibiryak. A young Siberian steel mill owner tries to improve the lot of his employees. 2 parts. English subtitles.

23 The Red Snowball Tree (Kalina krasnaia), 100 min. (1974), dir. and starring Vasilii Shuksin. Humorous but biting tale of a recidivist. English subtitles.

24 The Slowest Train (Samyi medlennyi poezd), 96 min. About friendship and solidarity among ordinary Russian people. In Russian.

25 The Song Teacher (Uchitel' peniia), 88 min. (1974), dir. Naum Birman. A musical comedy. English subtitles.

26 Spartacus (Spartak), 90 min. (1977), dir. and written by Vadim Derbenev and Iurii Grigorovich. Film version of Aram Khachaturian's ballet. English subtitles.

27 The Steppe (Step' razdol'naia), 160 min. (1978), dir. and adapted by Sergei Bondarchuk. Based on a Chekhov story. In Russian.

28 A Strange Woman (Strannaia zhenshchina), 150 min., dir. Iu. Raizman. A woman bored with her husband falls in love with a seemingly more free-spirited man. In Russian.

29 Striped Voyagers (Polosatyi reis), 84 min. Comedy about a ship transporting tigers for a circus. With Yevgeny Leonov and Margarita Nazarova, a lion tamer.

30 The Talents and Their Admirers (Talanty i poklonniki) (1974), dir. Isidor Annensky. Based on a play by A. N. Ostrovskii. English subtitles.

31 The Village Detective (Derevenskii detektiv), 90 min., dir. Vladimir Lukinsky. Comedy poking fun at a rural district militiaman. With Mikhail Zharov, Lidia Smirnova. In Russian.

32 With You and Without You (S toboi i bez tebia), 86 min. (1974), dir. Rodion Nakhapetov. A rural love triangle set in the early 1920s. English subtitles.

33 Yegor Bulytchev and Others (Egor Bulychev i drugie), 130 min. Based on the play by Maksim Gorkii. 2 parts. In Russian.

34 Note: These films come from such film studios as Mosfilm, Lenfilm, Gorkii, and Sverdlovsk.

CA 50
RUSSIAN LIFE (RUSSKAYA ZHIZN')
2460 Sutter Street
San Francisco, California 94115
(415-921-5380)

Inquiries concerning the contents and possible use of the archives of this newspaper should be directed to the editor.

CA 51
NICHOLAS A. SLOBODCHIKOFF--PRIVATE COLLECTION
448 43rd Avenue
San Francisco, California 94121
(415-751-1572)

Mr. Slobodchikoff possesses 6 manuscripts, essentially memoir material, of his father and of another Russian. Alexander Y. Slobodchikoff (1875-1946) was a lawyer in tsarist Russia and in Harbin, Manchuria. 5 typescripts concern his career and experiences: "Several Reasons for the Failure of the White Movement under Admiral Kolchak and the Committee of the Constituent Assembly (Komuch)," a "diary" about the Siberian Civil War, 1917-20, 93 pp., and the Komitet uchreditel'nogo sobraniia (Komuch), formed in Samara (now Kuibyshev) by members of the Socialist Revolutionary and Constitutional Democrat parties; "Memoirs about St. Petersburg University, 1893-1898," 2 pp., where he studied under the law faculty; "The Rebellions of the Natives of Turkestan during the German War, 1914-1916," 19 pp.; "Memoirs of a Russian Lawyer at the Chinese Court" in 1920-43, 14 pp.; and "What my children and grandchildren should know (family chronicles)" for the years 1869-1918, 10 pp. All are in Russian. Related items on deposit with the Museum of Russian Culture, Inc. in San Francisco (q.v.), which Mr. Slobodchikoff currently heads.

The sixth item is the text of a lecture delivered by Second Lieutenant Kwitkin, an Imperial army officer, at the Officers' Club of the 142nd Zvenigorod Infantry Regiment on 29 January 1897 ("Eastern War of 1877-1878--Sketches and Notes.--Beginning of the campaign and first attack on Plevna"). 154 pp., in Russian.

Access to all of these items is through the Museum of Russian Culture, 2450 Sutter Street, San Francisco, California 94115.

CA 52
ARCHIVES OF AMERICAN ART
M. H. DE YOUNG MEMORIAL MUSEUM
SMITHSONIAN INSTITUTION
Golden Gate Park
San Francisco, California 94118
(415-556-2530)

This repository, like each of the regional centers of the Archives of American Art, has microfilms of much of the original materials kept at the Archives' Washington Center. It also holds items on microfilm from originals in other hands. Some of these materials pertain to the Russian Empire/Soviet Union. For details, see the entry under the District of Columbia.

CA 53
SPECIAL COLLECTIONS
RICHARD A. GLEESON LIBRARY
UNIVERSITY OF SAN FRANCISCO
San Francisco, California 94117
(415-666-6718)

1 Suffrage Movement. Marie MacNaughton. Papers, ca. 1890s-1940s, ca. 200 items. 1 folder holds "Materials concerning her husband Arthur Powell Davis, pt. II." Davis (1861-1933) was a hydraulic engineer who studied irrigation problems in Turkestan. 1 letter to him from a Russian translator (J. S. Grin-?), in Moscow, 12 July 1931, informs him that his (Davis's) report has been translated and taken to the Narkomzem office. It also mentions a Mr. Reingold, who was off to Transcaucasia for 2 weeks, and a Mr. Wilbur. A letter from A. Kainarsky in Moscow to Mrs. Arthur P. Davis in Berlin speaks of the weather and of Mr. Kainarsky working very hard. The contents of an envelope postmarked Tashkent, 27 February 1931, addressed to Mrs. C. W. MacNaughton, may not be the original enclosure (and are ungermane). There is also a blank novelty postcard made in the USSR (picture of a bee stinging a dog, with a noisemaker device implanted in the card).

2 Note: The library's special collections also have a fairly extensive pamphlet collection (R. T. Clark Pamphlet Collection relating to World War I; ca. 1,000 items) with many items about the Soviet Union and the nationalities, mostly from 1915-28. It includes works on the Ukraine, Baltic countries, and the Caucasus. Many titles checked were not at the Library of Congress.

CA 54
HISTORY DEPARTMENT #921
WELLS FARGO BANK
475 Sansome Street
San Francisco, California 94111
(415-396-3209)

The Corporate Archives of Wells Fargo and Company contain records for 1911-27 concerning accounts with and funds remitted to Russian banks. For example, there are references to the St. Petersburg (Petrograd) International Commercial Bank in the company's "Subsidiary Journal" (Foreign Bank Account Transaction Record; 4 vols., 1911-17), in the Wells Fargo and Co. Express "Bank Ledger" for 1916-27, and in 3 different parts of the records of the Treasurer's Office: "Summary of Foreign Postal Remittances," September 1912-May 1915, "Bank Balances" for September 1911-October 1916, and the "Foreign and Investment Bank Account," 1916-18. Records of the Wells Fargo Nevada National Bank contain a report of 5 June 1915 with an appended Schedule A which notes an account with the Commercial Bank of Siberia and a Schedule B noting funds remitted to the Russo-Asiatic Bank. Examination of materials requires prior permission from the archivist.

CA 55
B. J. SCOTT NORWOOD--PRIVATE COLLECTION
SCHOOL OF BUSINESS
SAN JOSE STATE UNIVERISTY
San Jose, California 95192
(408-277-2290)

Professor Norwood, a specialist on Soviet industry and trade, has a collection of more than 10,000 individual slides, 1968-present, covering Soviet geography (cities, towns, villages, countryside) and economy (factories, plants, mines, power stations). Arranged by topics. Permission in advance required.

CA 56
THE HUNTINGTON LIBRARY
1151 Oxford Road
San Marino, California 91108
(213-792-6141)

The Huntington Library specializes in four general areas of interest: British History, Literature (post-1600), American History, and Medieval and Renaissance manuscripts. Materials pertaining to Russia enter only peripherally in a few collections; therefore, the listings exclude data on total size and inclusive dates of holdings.

1 Armenian Manuscript. Four Gospels dated 1724.

2 Beaufort Collection. Report, by Alexander Dalrymple, first hydrographer of the British Admiralty, on the Russian Empire, 1779-1808, 12 pp. The report, dated 3 March 1808, shows the empire's vulnerability in Siberia and the Far East; comments on the possible seizure of Kamchatka, Russian fur trade, and the possibilities of a British assault on Russian Pacific and North American possessions; and estimates Russia's military and population strength in Siberia. (In part, NUCMC 71-1045)

3 Thomas Hastie Bell (1867?-1942). Author. Correspondence with and about Catherine Breshkovsky (Ekaterina Breshko-Breshkovskaia), his biographical essay on Breshkovsky in 1934, 11 pp., photocopy, and information on post-1917 Russian relief work and Soviet Russia. References to Alexander Kerensky and to the anarchists Peter Kropotkin and Alexander Berkman. About half the materials are photoreproductions.

4 Robert Alonzo Brock (1839-1914). Historian and collector. Transcript of a toast "made by American Minister to Russia Colonel Charles Steward Todd in response to a toast in Amity with Russia" (1843), the latter apparently made by a Count Worozow Daschkoff (Vorontsov-Dashkov).

5 Henry Clay (1777-1852). Statesman, senator, Secretary of State (1825-29). Correspondence with and reports from Russian envoys to the United States regarding Russian-American relations and trade, damage claims of American merchants and ship owners against the tsarist government, and Russian Pacific Coast settlements (Treaty of 1824). There are references to Baron de Tuyll, Russian Envoy Extraordinaire and Minister Plenipotentiary to the U.S.; Count Khristofor Andreevich Lieven, Russian ambassador to London, 1812-34; Baron Pavel Alekseevich de Krudener, also Envoy Extraordinaire and Minister Plentipotentiary to the U.S.; Count Karl Robert Nesselrode, foreign minister of Alexander I and Nicholas I; Baron de Mallitz, Russian chargé d'affaires; Madame Daschkoff (Dashkova); and the 1826 Convention of St. Petersburg.

6 Samuel Cooper (1725-1783). Scholar and Congregational minister. Letter (1 February 1781) from James Lovell discusses Russian and Danish neutrality in the American Revolutionary War.

7 Ellesmere Collection. Papers of the Egerton family, Earls of Ellesmere, 1150-1800. Thomas Egerton, 1st Viscount Brackley, was lord keeper of the great seal under Elizabeth I and lord chancellor of England under James I for almost 20 years. He was thus intimately concerned with diplomatic affairs. His great-grandson, John Egerton, 3rd Earl of Bridgewater, was first lord of trade and also a member of the Privy Council of William III. Among the papers are: copy of a letter from Tsar Boris Godunov to Queen Elizabeth I dated December 1598; "A Declaracion of the proceedinge of mr. Fraunces [Francis] Cherry sente as a messenger by her Majestie Elizabeth I, Queen of England, to the Emperor of Muskovia," 24 March 1598/99; "Reasons to induce his Majestie [James I] to the loane of monie unto the greate Emperor of Russia, now required by his Ambassador Alexsey Evanour," 5 May 1614; "An Information to the Right Hon. Lords of the High Court of Parliament concerning the state of the Russia trade" [reign of James I]; and notes by John Egerton concerning trade with Russia in William III's reign.

8 Galvez Collection. 4 letters and reports discussing Russian interest in settlements in California during the 1760s, sent by Carlos F. de Croix to José de Galvez, Marques de la Sonora (in Spanish).

9 Guerra Family. Correspondence, 1810-41. Photocopies of letters written in Spanish. About 35 of them mention Russians in California, Russian ships and shipping, and a Russian expedition to San Francisco. (Originals of the letters are in the Santa Barbara Mission Archive and Library, Santa Barbara, California [q.v.])

10 Charles Henry Janin (1873-1937). American mining engineer. Personal and business letters, reports, photographs, and account books, 1915-36. Most relate to mining operations (gold and platinum) in Siberia; some letters, articles, and notes concern Russian politics and domestic affairs.

11 Andrew Johnson (1808-1875). U.S. president. Letter of 20 June 1867 authorizes his Secretary of State W. H. Seward to seal the proclamation of the treaty ceding Russian possessions in North America to the U.S.

12 William Alexander Leidesdorff (1810-1848). Ca. 5 letters concern John A. Sutter (of gold rush fame), his property dealings with the Russian-American Company and its representatives, and his debts to the company (1840s). Some letters are to Tobenhoff.

13 Jack London (1876-1916). American writer. Correspondence. About 14 items concern the Russo-Japanese War in 1904; letters from

1913-15 refer to Russian socialism.

14 Charles Ross Parke (1823-?). Doctor. Parke served Nicholas I as a surgeon in the Crimean War. His diary for 1855-56, ca. 150 pp., describes his experiences in the Russian army. A 1905 letter from Count Sergei Witte thanks Parke for his service to Russia; a newspaper clipping recounts his career.

15 Raphael Pumpelly (1837-1923). Papers, 1839-1916, ca. 3,500 items. American mining engineer. He worked in Russia, Japan, and China. 1 volume contains notes on his trip from St. Petersburg to Peking via Siberia and Mongolia in 1864. More of his notebooks and some diaries of his wife, Eliza S. Pumpelly, describe a Trans-Caspian expedition in 1901-02. (NUCMC 71-1083)

16 Walter Scribner Schuyler (1850-1935). Papers, 1817-1932). Brigadier general. Served with the Russian army in Manchuria in 1904. Detailed report by him on the Russian army in Manchuria, an order from General Alexei Nikolaievich Kuropatkin to Manchurian forces, 19 September 1904, and descriptions of the Battle of Mukden. Many years earlier, as president and general manager of the Sierra-Alaska Mining Company, Schuyler traveled in Russia. Letters to his family, 1875, describe Russian society and manners.

17 Stowe Collection. Includes "A Short Account of the Revenues of the [Russian] Empire," ca. 1763, handwritten 4 fols.; a "Declaration on the use of the Sib[erian] Corps of 45,000 men," dated 29 June 1799, a copy; and the "Account of his mission to the Southern parts of Russia," August 1806, by the British envoy William Eton. Eton's mission was to purchase naval stores for Malta and to obtain information on commerce in southern Russia. The Stowe collection also contains papers of George Grenville (1712-70), British prime minister in 1763-65: 8 vols. (secret and confidential letterbooks) of diplomatic correspondence and dispatches, 1761-62. Each book is approximately 250 pp. Some letters, in French and English, speak of Peter III, the Seven Years' War, and Russo-British relations.

18 Frederick Jackson Turner (1861-1932). American historian. Letter from Thomas Powderly Martin, a YMCA worker in Vladivostok, 9 September 1918, describes events in Russia (Vladivostok) during the Revolution and Civil War.

19 Mariano Guadalupe Vallejo (1808-1890). Spanish official and soldier. Includes his correspondence and reports relating to an investigation of Russian activities in and around Fort Ross, California, 1830s.

Finding Aids: There are unpublished reports, calendars, or inventories for almost all of these holdings. In addition, various issues of the Huntington Library Bulletin, Norma Cuthbert's Huntington Library Lists (1951), and Herbert C. Schulz's Ten Centuries of Manuscripts in the Huntington Library (1968), all published by the library, contain references to some of the collections listed above. A series of 4 volumes is now in progress: Guide to American Historical Manuscripts in the Huntington Library appeared in 1979. The Guide to British Historical Manuscripts in the Huntington Library should be published by 1982, as should the other two volumes in the series.

CA 57
SANTA BARBARA MISSION ARCHIVE AND LIBRARY
Old Mission Santa Barbara
Santa Barbara, California 93105
(805-682-4713 x 24)

1 California Mission Documents. Records, 1521-1938, ca. 4,800 items. Some materials relate to Russo-Spanish relations and to the peace of 1803, the Russian settlement at Fort Ross, and Russian barter trade with the Spanish in San Francisco (correspondence, diaries, and reports, 1803-33). Also, information about the conversion (to Catholicism), baptism, and marriage of various Russians. (NUCMC 75-782)

2 De la Guerra Family. Papers, 1780-1885, ca. 2,000 items. Spanish landowners in California. Personal and business letters and reports, all handwritten in Spanish, contain references to Russians and Russian settlements in California, Russian ships, and Russians sent to Mexico. Copies of these original documents are in the Bancroft Library (Berkeley, California) and the Huntington Library (San Marino, California). (NUCMC 75-784).

Restriction: The Mission Archive is open only to qualified scholars.

Finding Aid: Father Maynard J. Geiger, Calendar of Documents in the Santa Barbara Mission Archives (Washington, D.C., 1947), an unpublished loose-leaf binder, describes these and all the Mission's collections.

CA 58
THE MOST REVEREND JOHN SHAKHOVSKOY--PRIVATE COLLECTION
27 East Arrellaga Street
Santa Barbara, California 93101

Arkhiepiskop Ioann Shakhovskoi (b. 1902). Papers, 1924-present, over 7,000 items. The archbishop's papers contain a variety of manuscripts, photos, diaries, correspondence, printed matter, and published works. Over 4,000 letters, 1924-present, to and from writers and poets in and outside of Russia, personal and theological-clerical, on philosophical, spiritual, and literary matters; 72

scripts of lectures in Europe, 1931-45; over 1,400 scripts of broadcasts for the Voice of America radio program; books in prose, 18, and poetry, 11; 82 brochures; over 700 articles, some translated into English, German, Japanese, Spanish, Yugoslavian, and Finnish; hundreds of press comments and reviews of his publications and lectures; books and journals edited by him, 1925-78; and photographs and other material for his autobiography. Born in Moscow; educated at the St. Petersburg Imperial Lyceum and in Paris and Louvain, Belgium; briefly at Mt. Athos, 1926; a priest in Yugoslavia, 1927-31, and Berlin, 1932-45; emigrated to the U.S. in 1946; dean of St. Vladimir Seminary, New York City, and bishop of Brooklyn, 1947-50; bishop, 1950-61, and archbishop of San Francisco and Western U.S., 1961-present. Pseudonym as poet: Strannik (Pilgrim). Inquire concerning access.

CA 59
JACKSON LIBRARY ARCHIVES
GRADUATE SCHOOL OF BUSINESS
STANFORD UNIVERSITY
Stanford, California 94305
(415-497-2163)

Alaska Commercial Company. Records, 1868-1942, 18 ft., ca. 20% directly relevant. Correspondence, reports, office files, minutes, charters, stock journals, ledgers, contracts, bills of sale, and maps. This company succeeded the Russian-American Company, formed in 1776, as the firm most directly involved in business development in Alaska. Well documented are company activities in the St. Michael's administrative unit (1 of several, including also Unalaska, Kodiak, and the Pribilov Islands). Minutes for meetings of the board of directors of the 2 companies which came out of this firm after 1901 are also included. The company dealt with Russian agents, purchased Russian properties, and had relations with both the Russian government and the Russian Orthodox Church. Finding aid (unpublished).

CA 60
MANUSCRIPTS DIVISION
DEPARTMENT OF SPECIAL COLLECTIONS
C. H. GREEN LIBRARY
STANFORD UNIVERSITY
Stanford, California 94305
(415-497-4054)

1 Ames Family. Papers, 1782-1927, ca. 102 items. 1 ALS of Timothy Pickering (1745-1829) to Fisher Ames (1758-1808), congressman and statesman. Pickering, a Revolutionary War general, secretary of state, and U.S. senator, writes from Washington, D.C. on 9 April 1806 concerning a report of A. Gallatin and a rumor that a minister will be sent to St. Petersburg and Constantinople, whose "real" purpose will be to promote trade in the Black Sea region, 2 pp. (M 3)

2 Albert M. Bender (1866-1941). Papers, 1871 and 1915-48, ca. 165 items. Book and art collector/patron. Correspondence of Clara Clemens Gabrilowitsch, the daughter of Mark Twain and wife of Ossip Gabrilowitsch, Russian pianist and conductor. (NUCMC 67-2061) (M 25)

3 George A. Clark Fur Seal Controversy Papers, 1890-1918, 1.5 ft., ca. 600 items. Clark (1864-1918) was secretary of the Bering Fur Sea Commission of 1896-98 and of a special investigation of seal herds for the Bureau of Fisheries in 1909 and 1912. Most of these items, 1890-1918, are letters to and from Clark and David Starr Jordan. There are also printed and manuscript articles by Clark about the fur seal controversy, a volume of photos of seals and seal islands, and typescripts about the Bering Sea controversy, Russian sealing, the Fur Seal Conference of 1897, and the Pribilov Islands. In addition, the collection has some remarks on fur seals by a Russian named Veniaminov. (NUCMC 67-2066) (M 118)

4 James Deitrick (b. 1864). Papers, 1900-18, ca. 475 items. Businessman and engineer involved in railroad construction in America, China, and Siberia. Relevant holdings, ca. 80 items, include personal and business correspondence, office files, diaries, memoranda, and printed matter, 1912-17, as well as 6 maps of Russia, 1910-15. The collection has copies of agreements between Deitrick and the Russian Land Reclamation Company, Ltd.; his plans for land reclamation and agricultural development in Russia, for the establishment of a bank, for mining ventures, and for railroad construction (e.g., a letter to Nicholas II about extending the Trans-Siberian line); and materials on the sale of ships, gasoline, and submarines to the ministries of war and of the navy in 1915. Among the people mentioned in the papers are Grand Duke Alexander, Count Musin-Pushkin (assistant secretary of agriculture in 1915), Alexei S. Ermoloff, G. Kozakow, Sergei D. Sazonov, Alexander Krivocheine (Krivoshein), E. E. Skorniakov, J. Polkhovskii, Baron E. Ropp, and Generals Aleksei Andreevich Polivanoff (Polivanov) and Mikhail Alekseevich Beliaev. The Russian Volunteer Fleet is also noted. Unpublished finding aid. (NUCMC 67-2067) (M 140)

5 Sergei Gorny (1882-1949). Papers, ca. 1933-49, ca. 30 items. Pseudonym of the literary critic and writer Aleksandr Avdeevich Otsup. Most of the items are handwritten correspondence between Gorny (in Berlin) and the fiction writer Vladimir Pimenovich Krymov (1887-1968) in Paris. Before emigrating, Krymov had edited the periodical Stolitsa i usad'ba in Petrograd, 1913-17. Besides the letters, from 1933-49, there are also some printed materials. There

are references to Vera Kovarsky, A. Iaromolinsky, Madame Bakhmeteff, and Macedonian refugees.

6 Harwood Family. Papers, 1770-1959, ca. 555 items. A clipping from a French newspaper has a copy of an undated letter from K. R. Nesselrode to Reshid Pasha, foreign minister of the Porte (container 1, item 67); and there is a signed letter of Anna Pavlova, the ballerina, to George P. McNear, 6 March 1922, seeking support for her Home for Russian Children in Paris (container 2, folder 25, item 224). (M 206)

7 John Paul Jones (1747-1792). Papers, 1785-88, 1 vol. Naval hero. Copies of items held in Soviet repositories (photostats, typed, and handwritten) made by Frank Golder. There are letters, reports, diaries (excerpts), and notes about his career as an admiral in the Russian Black Sea Fleet to 1794; and data on naval battles (including Ochakov) during the Russo-Turkish War of 1787-91. Correspondence between Catherine II and Grigorii A. Potemkin and between Jones and Potemkin, in French, document Jones's quarrels with Prince Charles Henry Nicholas Otto von Nassau-Siegen (a Dutch adventurer and Russian admiral) and with Potemkin. S. R. Vorontsov, A. V. Suvorov, and V. Dolgorukii are others mentioned in the papers. Jones was at first well received, but he was later accused of violating a young girl (the charges were subsequently dropped, as these materials relate). Note: This collection appeared in NUCMC 67-2059, which listing no longer applies. Unpublished finding aid. (M 62)

8 V. P. Krymov. See under Sergei Gorny.

9 John Franklin Miller (1831-1886). Papers, 1848-86, 2 ft., ca. 3,750 items. Lawyer Civil War general, and U.S. senator from California. Correspondence, financial-business-legal papers, documents, photos, clippings, and printed matter, some of which concerns the Alaska Commercial Company and his work as chairman of the Senate Foreign Relations Committee. Unpublished guide. (M 59)

10 Miscellaneous Small Collections. Contains 2 items of Ivy Litvinoff, the British wife of the diplomat Maxim Litvinoff: TLS to Jeanette (?) Hitchcock, 9 December 1943, with cover; and undated manuscript notes on a book by D. H. Lawrence with a bibliography of Litvinoff's publications.

11 Elmer E. Robinson. Collection, 1779-1944, ca. 67 items. Signed letter from A. Troyanovsky of the USSR embassy in Washington, D.C. to Dr. Ray Lyman Wilbur, president of Stanford, thanking him for his cordial reception at Stanford, 1 February 1935; and an autograph of the dancer Anna Pavlova, n.d. Unpublished finding aid. (M 145)

12 Russian Manuscripts. Collection, 1765-1919, 35 items. Printed, handwritten, and typed documents in Russian and English found in the effects of Dr. Frank A. Golder: folder 1, Golder correspondence from 1919, including a list of transcripts from Russian archives that he obtained for the Library of Congress; folder 2, school certificate in Russian and Chinese from the American Methodist Gimnasium in Harbin; folder 3, printed pamphlets on commercial navigation, 1903-1904; folder 4, extract of an Act of Administration of British Columbia, in Russian, 2 August 1858; folder 5, notes on a company of adventurers trading in Hudson's Bay, in Russian; folder 6, notes in Russian about the Russian-American Company plus letters from the Ministry of Finance's department of trade and manufacturing to the administration of the Russian-American Company, 19 June 1865 letter has the company's by-laws; 8 June 1861 letter extends company's existence; folder 7, typed bibliography, in Russian, 2 copies, relating to the Russian-American Company and to exploration of the Russian Far East; folder 8, unidentified document, handwritten copies of letters from the archive of the Naval Ministry to a Prince Mikhail Volodimirovich, and to others, about V. Bering's expedition and exploration of Siberia, 1724-25; G. Vernadskii's handwritten review of Golder's Russian Expansion on the Pacific 1614-1850 (Cleveland, 1914) and Vernadskii's letter to Golder from Moscow, 26 May 1915; folder 9, apparent minutes of a discussion at the Academy of Sciences, 18 January 1861, concerning D. Butkov's work on Peter the Great's expedition to the Caucasus and Caspian Sea (signed by Kunik, Zernov, and Brosset, the secretary), in French, and notes retyped from the Gazette de France regarding the exploration of Kamchatka and St. Petersburg in 1764-65, also in French; folder 10, 2 photographs, 1 of a document on Bering's first expedition and the other of a map of the route from Judowa Cross to Okhotsk; folder 11, typed introduction to the second edition of Iu. Smel'niktskii's "On the Volga." Unpublished finding aid. (M 199)

13 William Milligan Sloane. In Sloane's published Life of Napoleon Bonaparte (New York, 1896) there are affixed many original sources. Volume 4 has an ALS, 1 p., of Napoleon's General Jean Victor Marie to Count Daschkoff (New York, 18 June 1812) sending regards to the count and Madam Daschkoff and mentioning Kurakin and Rumiantsev. In Volume 7 is a letter of J. Poniatowski to the Interior Minister Luszczewski about Galicia, 9 January 1810.

14 Sloss Collection. Ca. 30 items, 1821-1947. Collection of musicians' autographs and songbooks includes an autograph, photo, and ALS of Mischa Elman (b. 1891) from 1913-14; and a songbook in Aleut. (M 126)

15 Joseph Strauss (1870-1936). Papers, n.d., 93 items. File 365, bundle C, contains 74 plans or sketches for the Palace Bridge in St. Petersburg, 1911-12, a Strauss Trunnion Bascule Bridge. (M 163)

In addition, the Department of Special Collections holds the collections of the Memorial Library of Music, which contain:

16 Mily Alexeivich Balakireff (1837-1910). "Reverie pour le piano par Mili Balakirew," signed manuscript, 10 April 1903, with emendations, title page holograph, dedication to Monsieur Serge Trailine; and "Russia. Poëme symphonique pour orchestre par M. Balakirew" (St. Petersburg, [1893]), inscribed to Louis Albert Bourgault-Ducoudray by the composer.

17 Alexander Porphyrievitch Borodin (1833-1887). "The Bogatyrs," fragment, signed, 9 September 1867, 1 leaf, 1 p., with a sketch for the tavern scene from his unpublished opera.

18 Cesar Antonovich Cui (1835-1918). "Le flibustier," a lyric comedy in 3 acts, poem by Jean Richepin (Paris, ca. 1893), first edition inscribed to M. Thierry by the composer and the author; and "Vingt poèmes de Jean Richepin" set to music by Cui (opus 44), piano and vocal score (Paris, [1892], inscribed to Madame Mathilde Colonne by the composer.

19 Camille Erlanger (1863-1919). "Poëmes russes," set to verse by Catulle Mendes and music by Erlanger, first edition (Paris, ca. 1915), inscribed by Erlanger, comprising "Aubade" by A. A. Fet, F. Tiutchev's "Les larmes humaine" and "Printemps," "Les seuls pleurs" by N. A. Nekrasov, "L'ange et l'âme" of M. Lermontov, and Turgenev's "Fédia."

20 John Field (1782-1837). Irish pianist, a pupil of Clementi, spent most of his life in Russia (his nickname was "Russian" Field). His nocturnes set the form and style for these pieces and were models for Chopin. He was pianist to the tsar. The library has the original manuscript of Nocturne no. 5 (L'incendie par l'orage), 2 ll., 3 pp.--his best known nocturne--from the collection of a Prince Dolgorouki with his stamp; a first edition of A new fantasia for the piano forte . . . dedicated to His Imperial Majesty, the Emperor of Russia by John Field of Petersburgh (London, [1835], inscribed by Field; a first edition of an introduction and rondo for piano (London, [1834]), also inscribed by the composer; and an untitled composition for piano, a fragment of the original manuscript from ca. 1794, when Field was only 12 and in England.

21 Alexander Konstantinovich Glazunoff (1865-1936). "Huitième symphonie, op. 83" (Paris, 1907), proofsheets signed by Glazunov with his corrections throughout, inscribed to Leonid Davidovich Kreutzer in Russian, 13/26 July 1907; "Preludio e fuga," arranged for organ, a signed fragment, 1 l., 2 pp.; "Stenka Razine," a symphonic poem for orchestra (op. 13), Leipzig, [1888], first edition, with Glazunov's signature on the title page; and the "2me symphonie en fa # mineur," op. 16 (Leipzig, [1889], first edition inscribed to L. A. Bourgault-Ducoudray by the composer--with an ALS to Alexander Petrovich, Berlin-Wilmersdorff, 23 January 1931, inserted. The letter concerns Glazunov's move to Berlin and publication of his works.

22 Michael Ivanovitch Glinka (1804-1857). "[Chao-Kang. Ballet]," 2 variations (Allegro and Brilliante), original manuscript, signed (ca. 1830), 4 ll., 7 pp., composed in Milan, Italy.

23 Alexander Gretchaninoff (1864-1956). "[Sur les champs jaunes]," original signed manuscript, ca. 1900, 3 ll. (title-page + 4 pp.), piano and vocal score, Russian text.

24 Alexis Feodorovich Lvoff (1799-1870). "Les adius," hymn composed on the occasion of a student graduation from "l'institut patriotique" in St. Petersburg, signed original manuscript, 6 ll., 11 pp., complete score; and an original manuscript of the Russian national anthem (his arrangement of Felice de Giardini's "God Save the Czar"), 7 ll., 12 pp., signed by Lvov, 1833, and inscribed to C. Pipinski, 2 March 1834.

25 Francesco Morlacchi (1784-1841). "Kaiser Nicolaus," an original, signed manuscript, 1833, cantata for solo voice and male chorus and piano--a hymn to glorify the Russian tsar for the king of Saxony (Morlacchi was director of the Dresden opera, 1810-41), 4 ll., 6 pp.

26 Nikolai Andreevitch Rimskii-Korsakov (1844-1908). "Antar," symphony for orchestra, taken from an Arab tale of Sennkowsky, arranged for piano and 4 hands by Nadejda Pourgold (St. Petersburg, [1878]), first edition, inscribed by the composer, with explanations, additions, and corrections in his hand on 56 of 170 pp.; and "Mlada," an opera-ballet in 4 acts, words after Guédénoff (Leipzig, 1891), first edition, inscribed to Michael Delines by Rimskii.

27 Anton Gregoryevich Rubinstein (1829-1894). First edition of "Allegro appassionato for piano," op. 30, no. 2 (Leipzig, ca. 1859), inscribed to Mme. Charles Poisson by Rubinstein; first edition of "Balletmusik" for orchestra from the opera Der Dämon (Leipzig, ca. 1875) with inserted manuscript fragments signed, Paris 6 March 1884, 1 l. (1 p.) and an ALS to an unidentified publisher in London, 6 July 1859, referring to a fugue and a violin concerto; "Fantaisie pour le pianoforte," op. 77, original signed manuscript, 15 ll. (title-page + 27 pp.); and "Zwölf Leider des Mirza-Schaffy aus dem Persischen," op. 34, signed original manuscript, ca. 1860-64, 16 ll. (title-page + 30 pp.), 12 poems by Friedrich Martin von

Bodenstedt, whose pseudonym was Mirza-Schaffy, with a portrait of Rubenstein inserted.

28 Igor Stravinsky (1882-1971). "Danses concertantes. Concerto for small orchestra," in 5 movements, composed in 1941-42, 76 ll. (147 pp.), original manuscript, with title-page in Stravinsky's hand, inscribed "I give this manuscript to Stanford University, Igor Stravinsky. Hollywood, January 9th, 1948"; and first editions of 16 published works (music or other writings), all signed or inscribed by Stravinsky (e.g., Circus polka composed for a young elephant, New York, ca. 1944; Les noces in French translation, London, [ca. 1922]; Le sacré du printemps, Moscow, ca. 1913; Petrouchka, Berlin, [ca. 1910]; L'oiseau de feu, Moscow, [1910]; and Scherzo à la Russe, New York, [ca. 1945]).

29 Sergius Ivanovich Taneieff (1856-1915). First edition of "Dix mélodies," op. 17 (Leipzig, 1905), piano and vocal score, title-page in Russian, inscribed by Taneev.

30 Peter Ilich Tchaikovsky [Chaikovskii] (1840-1893). ALS to Count Moisevitch, Tiflis, 22 October 1890, inserted in a first edition of Eugene Oniegin (Moscow, 1878); signed manuscript fragment, 14 March 1889, 4 bars of music to accompany the words "Die deutsche Sprache ist schön! . . . aber furchterlich schwer!!" inserted in a first edition of Pique-Dame (Moscow, 1890); and "Suite no. 3 for orchestra," op. 55 (Moscow, [ca. 1886], first edition, inscribed to Charles Lefebvre by the composer.

Finding Aid: For the musical holdings there is Nathan van Patten's Catalogue of the Memorial Library of Music, Stanford University (Stanford, California, 1950), from which all of the preceding information was taken.

CA 61
ARCHIVES, HOOVER INSTITUTION ON WAR, REVOLUTION AND PEACE
STANFORD UNIVERSITY
Stanford, California 94305
(415-497-3563)

This repository has grown, by donations and purchases from private individuals and organizations, into one of the most significant archives in the U.S. for the study of Russian/Soviet affairs and matters relating to all of the nationalities of the USSR. The description that follows omits the Hoover Institution's library holdings, namely printed matter such as books, serials, government publications, and published ephemera. Moreover, many collections that could reasonably be expected to contain Russian/Soviet-related material--such as those pertaining to the world wars, international organizations like the United Nations, and individuals involved with international relations in general--have been excluded from this description as well.

The authors are pleased to acknowledge the generous assistance and cooperation offered this project by the staff of the Hoover Institution Archives. They have permitted us to quote verbatim from their recently published Guide to the Hoover Institution Archives (Hoover Institution Press, Stanford, Calif., 1979) by Charles G. Palm and Dale Reed, which was supported by a grant from the National Endowment for the Humanities. We have made some annotations on their card catalog entries, based in part on NUCMC entries and in part on de visu examination of materials.

1 "Accessories to the Crime." Memorandum, n.d., typescript, mimeographed. 1 folder. Relates to the territorial dispute between Germany and Lithuania regarding Memel.

2 Arthur E. Adams. History, 1960. "Bolsheviks in the Ukraine: The Second Campaign, 1918-1919," typescript, 2 vols. Includes bibliography.

3 Aehrenthal, Aloys Leopold Baptist Lexa von Graf (1854-1912). Memoirs (in German), 1895. "Memorie [sic] des Freiherrn von Aehrenthal über die Beziehungen zwischen Österreich-Ungarn und Russland, 1872-1894" (Memoirs of Baron von Aehrenthal on Relations between Austria-Hungary and Russia, 1872-1894). Typescript, 1 vol.

4 Agence Télégraphique de Petrograd. Daily news bulletins (in French), 1915-16. Typescript, 5 vols. Press service. Relates to world military and political events.

5 Nikolai Akaemov. History (in Russian), 1930. "Kaledinskie Miatezhi" (The Kaledin Rebellion). Holograph, 1 folder. Relates to the White Russian movement led by Aleksei Maksimovich Kaledin during the Russian Civil War. Kaledin (1861-1918) was chosen head of the Don Cossacks in 1917; when the revolt failed, he committed suicide.

6 Konstantin Konstantinovich Akintievskii (1884-1962). Memoirs (in Russian), n.d. Typescript, 1/2 ms. box. General, Imperial Russian Army. Relates to activities of the Imperial Russian Army during World War I and to the White Russian forces during the Russian Revolution and Civil War, 1914-21. Includes an English translation.

7 Ralph G. Albrecht (b. 1896). Papers, 1926-61. 2 ms. boxes, 1 album. American lawyer; associate trial counsel, Nuremberg War Trials, 1945-46; counsel to German corporations, 1950-53. Correspondence, memoranda, writings, notes, leaflets, clippings, and photographs relating to the Nuremberg war crime trials, the Schuman Plan, European Coal and Steel Community, the

dismantling of German steel plants, the settlement of German external debts, and the National Government of Georgia (Transcaucasia) in 1926. Preliminary inventory. (NUCMC 75-610)

8 F. Alekseev. Painting (photograph), n.d., 1 envelope. Russian artist. Depicts the Winter Palace and Peter and Paul Fortress in St. Petersburg.

9 Mikhail Vasil'evich Alekseev (1857-1918). Miscellaneous papers, in Russian, 1905-18. Photocopy, 1/2 ms. box. General, Russian Imperial Army; commander-in-chief, Russian Imperial Armies on the southwestern front, during World War I; chief of staff to Tsar Nicholas II, 1915-17; and organizer of the anti-Soviet Volunteer Army in south Russia, 1918. Correspondence, notes, diaries, and military orders relating to Russian military activities during World War I, and to the Russian Revolution and Civil War. Preliminary inventory.

10 Alexander II, Emperor of Russia (1818-1881). Decree, in Russian, 1859. Printed, 1 folder. Emperor of Russia. Relates to the status of Russian 5% bank notes and of investments in Russian banks.

11 Alexandra (Empress Consort of Nicholas II, Emperor of Russia). Photographs, n.d., 1 envelope. Depicts Empress Alexandra of Russia.

12 Ronald Allen (1891-1949). Letter, 1944, to his mother. Holograph, 1 folder. Military attaché in Russia. Relates to a discussion between R. Allen and Herbert Hoover in the Waldorf Towers on current world affairs.

13 America First Committee, 1940-42. Records, 1940-42. 338 ms. boxes, 20 photographs, 50 posters, 3 motion pictures. Private organization to promote U.S. nonintervention in World War II. Correspondence, minutes of meetings, reports, research studies, financial records, press releases, speeches, newsletters, campaign literature, form letters, clippings, mailing lists, films, photographs and posters. The group opposed Lend-lease. Register (NUCMC 68-411).

14 American Committee for the Encouragement of Democratic Government in Russia. Records, 1917, 1 folder. Organization of American civic leaders sympathizing with the Russian Revolution of February 1917. Correspondence and printed matter relating to American public opinion regarding the February Revolution.

15 American Engineers in Russia Collection, 1927-33, 4 ms. boxes. Correspondence, writings, articles, and answers to questionnaires relating to economic conditions, wages, housing, living costs, and relations with Russian administrative personnel, of American engineers in Russia. Contains lists of: persons familiar with conditions in the USSR, technical assistance contracts, and firms having contacts with the Soviet Union. References: Amtorg Trading Corporation, the First Five-Year Plan, industrial management, mining, and railroads. Register (NUCMC 68-412).

16 American Russian Institute, San Francisco, Collector. Photographs, 1950-56. 3 envelopes. Depicts scenes in Latvia; Latvian and Russian authors, artists, and scientists; and a conference in the Soviet Union commemorating the 13th anniversary of the death of the American botanist Luther Burbank, 1956. Includes photographs of the Soviet geneticist Trofim D. Lysenko.

17 Amerikas Latweetis. Translations of articles, 1939-41. 1/2 ms. box. Organ of the American Latvian Workers Union (previous title, Strahneeku Zihna). Relates to the Soviet occupation of Latvia, 1940-41, Latvian foreign relations, the Latvian Communist Party, and the Latvian press in the U.S.

18 Wladyslaw Anders (1892-1970). Papers, in Polish, 1939-46. 34 ft. Polish military officer, commander-in-chief of the Polish Armed Forces in the USSR, commander-in chief of the 2d Polish Corps in Italy. Orders, reports, card files, questionnaires, accounts, Soviet government documents and publications, photographs, microfiche and printed matter relating to World War II, the Polish armed forces in Russia, the Polish 2d Corps in Italy, Polish citizens arrested and deported under German and Soviet occupations, Polish foreign relations, the Polish government in exile in London, and Polish Jews. Preliminary inventory.

19 Edgar Anderson (b. 1920). Study, n.d. "The Baltic Area in World Affairs, 1914-1920." Typescript, 1 ms. box. American historian. Relates to military and political aspects of Baltic affairs.

20 Roy Scott Anderson (d. 1925). Papers, 1920-22. 1/2 ms. box. American advisor to various officials of the Chinese government, 1903-25. Letters and reports relating to the Chinese economy, Chinese foreign relations with Japan, Russia, and the U.S., and historical and political events in China.

21 N. N. Andreev. Letters received, in Russian, 1921-23, from his son. Photocopy, 1 folder. Relates to impressions of the Civil War in Russia formed during a trip from the Crimea to Vladivostok.

22 Nikolai Aleksandrovich Andrushkevich. Writings, in Russian, 1931-36. Holograph, 1/2 ms. box. Histories entitled "Posledniaia Rossiia" (The Last Russia), 1931, and "Prokliatyi korabl" (The Damned Ship), 1936, relating to the Russian Civil Was in Vladivostok and the Far East, 1919-22, and to travels in Eastern Europe, the Near East and Asia.

23 Vladimir Petrovich Anichkov. Memoirs, in Russian, n.d. "Vospominaniia" (Reminiscences). Typescript, 1.5 ms. boxes. Manager of the Volga Kama Bank and head of the Alapaevsk District. Relates to the Russian Revolution and Civil War in Siberia, 1917-22. Includes a typescript translation (photocopy) by his daughter, Nathalie Nicolai. References: economic conditions, the Czech legion, the murder of the Romanov family, Grand Duke Sergei Mikhailovich, and N. I. Sokolov (chief investigator of the Imperial family's deaths).

24 Boris Vladimirovich Annenkov (1890-1927). Orders, in Russian, 1920. Handwritten, 1 folder. Cossack Ataman and White Russian military leader. Orders, in Russian, of the 1st Assault Mounted Battery of the partisan detachment of B. Annenkov relating to the Russian Civil War and Ataman Grigorii Mikhailovich Semenov.

25 V. P. Antonenko. History, in Russian, ca. 1922. Typescript, carbon copy, 1 vol. Kratkaia istoriia smieny pravitel'stv vo Vladivostokie s 31 ianvaria 1920 g. do evakuatsii oktiabria 1922 g. (Brief History of the Changeover of Government in Vladivostok from 31 January 1920 until the Evacuation of October 1922).

26 Gvido Augusts, Collector. Miscellany, 1940-66, 1 folder. Passbooks, permits, orders, certificates, deeds, and inventories relating to daily life in Latvia under Nazi occupation, to the status under the Nazis of property previously seized in Latvia by the Soviet government, and to post-war Soviet rule.

27 N. Axentieff. Memorandum, n.d. Typescript, 1 folder. Relates to relief needs of Russian refugees living in exile. Sent to Herbert Hoover during or immediately after the Russian Civil War.

28 Nancy Babb (d. 1948). Papers, 1917-25. 1 ms. box. American Relief Administration and American Friends Service Committee relief worker in Russia, 1917-25. Correspondence, reports and memoranda relating to American Relief Administration and American Friends Service Committee work in Russia. (NUCMC 71-1090)

29 A. Balk. Memoirs, in Russian, 1929. Typescript, carbon copy, 1 vol. "Posliednie piat' dnei tsarskago Petrograda, 23-28 febralia 1917 g.; dnevnik posliedniago Petrogradskago gradonachal'nika" (The Last Five Days of Tsarist Petrograd. 23-28 February 1917: The Diary of the Petrograd Mayor).

30 V. P. Balykov. Speech, in Russian, 1935. Typescript, 1 folder. Representative of the Russkoi Fashistskoi Partii (Russian Fascist Party) in Japan. Calls for patriotic unity among Russians in the struggle against bolshevism in Russia.

31 Suda Lorena Bane (1886-1952). Documentary history, 1943. Galley proofs, annotated, of Organization of American Relief in Europe, 1918-1919. Relates to World War I relief activities of the American Relief Administration and U.S. Food Administration. Edited by S. L. Bane and Ralph Haswell Lutz. Published in Stanford by the Stanford University Press, 1943.

32 Henri Barbé (b. 1902). Memoirs, in French, n.d. "Souvenirs de militant et de dirigeant communiste" (Reminiscences of a Militant and Leading Communist). Typescript, part carbon copy, 1 vol. Member and leading official in the French Communist Party, 1920-34, and in the Executive Committee of the Communist International, 1927-31.

33 Alvin B. Barber (b. 1883). Papers, 1919-22. 5 ms. boxes. American Relief Administration worker; European Technical Adviser for Poland, 1919-22. Correspondence, reports, and memoranda relating to Polish railways, coal, oil, and timber resources, Danzig, Upper Silesia, and the Ukraine. (NUCMC 68-415)

34 William S. Barrett. Diary, 1918-20. "America in Russia, or the Diary of a Russian Wolfhound." Typescript, 1 folder. Captain, U.S. Army. Relates to the U.S. intervention in Siberia during the Russian Revolution.

35 Thomas C. Barringer. Papers, 1922-25. 2 ms. boxes. District Supervisor, American Relief Administration in Russia, 1921-23. Correspondence, reports, memoranda, photographs, and clippings relating to relief operations of the American Relief Administration in 2 famine areas in Russia.

36 Nicolas Alexandrovich de Basily (1883-1963). Papers, in Russian and French, 1881-1957. 25 ms. boxes, 4 envelopes. Imperial Russian diplomat; deputy director, Chancellery of Foreign Affairs, 1911-14; member, Council of Ministry of Foreign Affairs, 1917. Correspondence, memoranda, reports, notes, and photographs, relating to Russian political and foreign affairs, 1900-17, Russian involvement in World War I, the abdication of Tsar Nicholas II, and the Russian Revolution and Civil War. Includes drafts of N. A. de Basily's book Russia Under Soviet Rule. Register (NUCMC 75-615).

37 Eva de Basily-Callimaki (1855-1913). Papers, in French, 1867-1913. 2.5 ms. boxes. Russian art critic and author. Correspondence, writings, notes, clippings, printed matter, photographs, and memorabilia relating to French and Western European art history, and to Jean Baptiste Isabey, the French miniaturist. Includes a draft of the biography Isabey by E. de Basily-Callimaki.

38 Vladimir J. Bastunov, Collector. V. J. Bastunov collection on the Russian Imperial

Army, in Russian, 1897-1917. 4 ms. boxes. Imperial orders, military orders, personnel rosters, and casualty reports relating to the operations of the Russian Imperial Army and its personnel.

39 N. S. Batiushin. History, in Russian, n.d. "V chem byla sila Rasputina" (What Comprised the Strength of Rasputin). Typescript, carbon copy, 1 vol. Relates to Grigorii Rasputin, 1871-1916.

40 Walter Russell Batsell. Memorandum, 1925. "Memorandum on the Union of Soviet Socialist Republics." Typescript, 1 folder. American visitor to European Russia, 1925. Relates to political conditions in the Soviet Union, and to Soviet foreign policy.

41 Robert I. Baxter, Collector. Map, n.d. Hand drawn, 1 folder. Represents the region around Archangel, Russia, indicating the route followed by a military expedition from Tiagra to Archangel, August-September 1918.

42 General Bazarevich. Papers, in Russian, 1919-24. 5 ms. boxes. Russian military attaché in Belgrade, Yugoslavia. Correspondence and orders relating to White Russian military activities in Gallipoli, Bulgaria, and Yugoslavia, and to the Civil War, Volunteer Army, Kuban Cossack Army Corps, P. N. Vrangel, A. I. Denikin, and N. Iudenich. Preliminary inventory (NUCMC 71-1091).

43 Major General Bazarov. Papers, in Russian, 1904-06. 1 ms. box. Major general, Imperial Russian Army. Reports, orders, field maps, correspondence and clippings, relating to the Russo-Japanese War and General A. N. Kuropatkin. Preliminary inventory (NUCMC 71-1092).

44 Laura Helene Bekeart. Study, n.d. "The A.R.A.: Herbert Hoover and Russian Relief." Typescript, 1 folder.

45 Eduard Benes (1884-1948). Speech, in Russian, 1921. Typescript, 1 folder. Foreign minister of Czechoslovakia, 1918-35, president of Czechoslovakia, 1935-38 and 1939-48. Relates to Soviet-Czechoslovakian foreign relations.

46 Emmanuil Pavlovich, Bennigsen (b. 1875). Translations of papers, 1914-19. Typescript, .5 ms. box. Colonel, Imperial Russian Army. Diary extracts, letters and poems, relating to Russian military activities during World War I, and to activities of the White Army of General Denikin during the Russian Civil War. Includes an account of the February 1917 Revolution by Grafinia Bennigsen.

47 Reinhard Berbig. Memoirs, in German, n.d. Typescript, 1 folder. Soldier, German army. Relates to the eastern front during World War II, 1941, and to Russian prisoner of war camps, 1945-53.

48 Dr. Bereczky. Radio address, in Hungarian, n.d. 1 phonorecord. "Ungarischer Aufruf" (Hungarian Summons). Denounces Soviet communism.

49 Gaston Bergery (1892-1974). Papers, mainly in French, 1924-73. 38 ms. boxes. French attorney, diplomat, author, journalist, and politician; secretary-general, Inter-Allied Commission for Reparations, 1918-24; director of the cabinet, Ministry of Foreign Affairs, 1924-25; ambassador to the Soviet Union, 1941. Correspondence, telegrams, reports, memoranda, lists, speeches and writings, posters, and leaflets relating to French political events and foreign relations, France during World War II, and the Front Populaire.

50 Abram Bergson (b. 1914). Report, 1950. "Disposition of the Gross National Product of the USSR in 1937, 1940 and 1948." Typescript, mimeographed, 1 folder. Relates to the allocation of Soviet economic resources. Written by A. Bergson and Hans Heymann, Jr., under the auspices of the Rand Corporation.

51 Stephen M. Berk History, n.d. "The Coup D'État of Admiral Kolchak: The Counterrevolution in Siberia and East Russia, 1917-1918." Typescript, .5 ms. box. American historian. Relates to activities of anti-Bolshevik forces in Siberia during the period October 1917 to November 1918. Discusses Bolshevik administration, the Czech legion, Siberian Duma, Izhevsk revolt, cooperatives, Kadet Party, and Admiral A. V. Kolchak.

52 Berlin-blockade (1948-49). Photographs, 12 envelopes. Depicts scenes in Berlin during the blockade and airlift of 1948-49. Preliminary inventory.

53 Mikhail Vladimirovich Bernatskii (b. 1876). Collector. Miscellany (in Russian, French, and English), 1916-18. 1 folder. Reports, correspondence, and statistics relating to the financing of the Russian war effort during World War I (credit, loans, banks, and foreign trade). Includes records of state revenues and expenditures to July 1917. Preliminary inventory (NUCMC 71-118).

54 Alfreds Berzins (1899-1977). Memoirs, in Latvian, n.d. Typescript, photocopy, 1 folder. Latvian politician; deputy minister of the interior, 1934-37; minister of public affairs, 1937-40. Relates to Latvian politics, 1934-40.

55 Lieutenant Bielevskii. Collector. Miscellany, in Russian, 1917. 1 folder. Military reports and memoranda relating to the abdication of Tsar Nicholas II, and to disintegration of discipline in the Russian army during the Russian Revolution. Preliminary inventory.

56 Alfred Bilmanis (1887-1948). Collector. A. Bilmanis collection on Latvia, mostly in Latvian, 1944-48. 1 ms. box. Serial issues,

mimeographed bulletins and manuscripts of writings relating to Latvia during World War II and to postwar Latvian refugees in Sweden, West Germany, Argentina, and the U.S. (NUCMC 71-119)

57 (Henri Jean) Bint (b. 1851). Dossier, in French and German, 1903-1917. Handwritten and typescript, photocopy, 1 folder. Dossier of the Swiss police relating to Bint, an agent of the Russian secret police (Okhrana). Originals in the Swiss federal archives.

58 K. Bizauskas. Memorandum, 1924. Typescript, 1 folder. Lithuanian minister to the U.S. Relates to the political composition of the Lithuanian government.

59 Dimitur Blagoev (1856-1924). Translations of writings, n.d. Typescript, .5 ms. box. Bulgarian communist leader. Unpublished translations by Olga Hess Gankin of two published books by D. Blagoev: Prinos kum istoriiata na sotsializma v Bulgariia (Contributions to the History of Socialism in Bulgaria), 1906, and Moi vospominaniia (Memoirs), 1928. Blagoev was a student in Russia and Social Democratic leader, 1883-86.

60 Raymond L. Bland. Papers, 1919-41. 3 ms. boxes, 3 envelopes, 3 medals. Statistician, American Relief Administration, 1919-24; member, President's Committee on War Relief Agencies, 1941. Correspondence, reports, memoranda, financial records, and printed matter relating to the work of the American Relief Administration in Europe and Russia, 1919-24, and the President's Committee on War Relief Agencies, 1941. Register.

61 Adolfs Blodnieks (1889-1962). Memoirs, in Latvian, n.d. "Ministrn Presidenta Amata" (In the Office of Prime Minister). Holograph, 1 folder. Prime minister of Latvia, 1933-34. Relates to Latvian politics and to the Karlis Ulmanis coup d'état in 1934.

62 A. Bogdanov (b. 1872). Writings, in Russian, 1923-30. Holograph, .5 ms. box. Relates to travels in Russia, Siberia, and Manchuria, gold-diggers in the Amur Republic of Zheltuga, and the Russian Revolution and Civil War in Siberia.

63 Nikolai Vasil'evich Bogoiavlensky. Correspondence, in Russian, 1928-37. 1 folder. Russian émigré in the U.S. Relates to foreign relations between the United States and Russia, and to political activities of Russian immigrants in the United States.

64 Vasilii Georgievich Boldyrev (b. 1875). Translation of excerpts from memoirs, n.d. Direktoriia, Kolchak, Interventy: Vospominaniia (Directory, Kolchak, Intervention: Recollections). Typescript, .5 ms. box. General, Imperial Russian Army; White Russian military leader. Relates to the Russian Civil War in the Siberian Far East, activities of anti-Bolshevik forces, and Allied intervention in Siberia.

65 Burnett Bolloten (b. 1909). Papers, in Spanish, Catalan, French, English, and Italian, 1936-78. 55.5 ms. boxes, 10 scrapbooks (cited in B. Bolloten's The Grand Camouflage), 7,264 items on over 60,000 frames of microfilm, 2 crates, 4 ft., and 1 portfolio. American author; newspaper correspondent in Spain for United Press of America, London Bureau, 1936-38. Manuscripts of writings by participants in the Spanish Civil War; extensive series of day-by-day clippings from the Spanish, French, Italian, and English press on the Spanish Civil War for the period 1936-46; reports; periodicals; newspapers; and other printed matter relating to the political, military, and international aspects of the Spanish Civil War (including Soviet involvement) and used as research materials for a book, entitled The Grand Camouflage (1961), by B. Bolloten. Includes an original manuscript of a published book, entitled The Spanish Revolution, the Left and the Struggle for Power during the Civil War, by B. Bolloten, 1978. Collection also includes over 12,000 bound newspapers and 900 books and pamphlets that have been integrated into the general library holdings. Register. Crates and portfolio closed during the lifetime of B. Bolloten.

66 Bolshevik Leninist Party of India. Bulletin, 1947. Typescript, 1 vol. Includes draft resolution by the Central Committee of the Bolshevik Leninist Party of India relating to the political situation in India.

67 Bolshevik posters, in Russian, 1917-18. 25 posters and proclamations relating to the Russian Revolution. Preliminary inventory.

68 Lieutenant Colonel Borkowski. Collector. Borkowski collection on Poland, mainly in Polish, 1939-44. 1.5 ms. boxes. Correspondence, reports, memoranda, government documents, bulletins, speeches, writings, and maps relating to Polish-Soviet relations, Polish military operations under French and British command. Preliminary inventory.

69 Serge Botkine. Papers, in Russian, German, French, and English, 1918-30. 8 ms. boxes. Russian refugee in Germany. Memoirs, correspondence, reports, memoranda, and printed matter relating primarily to Russian émigrés in Berlin, elsewhere in Germany, and in other European countries after the Russian Revolution. Preliminary inventory (NUCMC 68-417, in part).

70 Anna Bourguina. Study, in Russian, 1938. "Rabochii Vopros pri Arkhangel'skom Pravitel'stve" (The Labor Question in the Archangel Government). Typescript, 1 vol. Relates to the period of the Civil War in Russia, 1918-20.

71 Burle Bramhall. Collector. B. Bramhall collection on the Petrograd Children's Colony (in Russian), 1973-76. .5 ms. box. American Red Cross business manager in Siberia, 1919-20. Reminiscences of several of the 781 Russian children known as the "Petrograd Children's Colony," who were sent by their parents from Moscow and Petrograd in 1918 because of wartime shortages, were stranded in the Ural Mountains, evacuated from the war zones via Vladivostok by the American Red Cross, and restored to their families in 1920 following a global ocean voyage. Includes a description of the reunion of American Red Cross staff members and members of the Petrograd Children's Colony in Leningrad, 1973.

72 Albrecht Paul Maerker Branden (b. 1888). History, n.d. "Submarines in World War I." Typescript, carbon copy, 7 vols. Relates to British, German, Austrian, French, Italian, and Russian submarines.

73 Alexander Breese (1889-1976). Papers, 1915-44. .5 ms. box. Russian-American meteorologist; Meteorological Physics Section, U.S. Weather Bureau, 1942-44. Correspondence, passports, certificates, letters of recommendation, and printed matter relating to meteorology.

74 Marie Annenkov Breese. Memoirs, n.d. "Another Look at Russia." Typescript, 2 folders. Member of the Russian nobility; émigré to the U.S. after the Russian Revolution. Relates to the history of the Annenkov family, the Russian Revolution and Civil War, and émigré life in the U.S., 1922-43.

75 Gerald B. Breitigam. History, 1923. "The Retreat of the Hundred Thousand." Typescript, 1 folder. American journalist. Relates to the Russian Revolution and Civil War.

76 Ekaterina Breshko-Breshkovskaia (1844-1934). Miscellaneous papers, in Russian and English, 1919-31. 2 ms. boxes, 5 envelopes. Russian Socialist Revolutionary Party leader. Writings, correspondence, biographical data and photographs relating to the life of E. Breshko-Breshkovskaia. Includes drafts of the book by E. Breshko-Breshkovskaia, The Hidden Springs of the Russian Revolution (Stanford University Press, 1931); a biographical sketch of E. Breshko-Breshkovskaia. Preliminary inventory (NUCMC 71-121).

77 Brookings Institution Seminar on Problems of U.S. Foreign Policy, Stanford, 1948. Records, 1948. 2 ms. boxes. Mimeographed working memoranda prepared for the seminar relating to diverse aspects of current U.S. foreign policy throughout the world. Includes a mimeographed report from the Russian Research Center, Harvard University, and a State Department pamphlet.

78 Louis Edgar Browne (1891-1951). Papers, 1917-56. 2 ms. boxes. Correspondent of the Chicago Daily News in Russia and Turkey, 1917-19. Dispatches, correspondence, printed matter and photographs relating to political conditions in Russia during the Russian Revolution, Allied intervention in Russia, and political conditions in Turkey at the end of World War I. Covers French intervention at Odessa, Czech troops, Russian-Ukrainian conflicts, Japanese intervention in Siberia, Germans in the Ukraine, and Soviet foreign relations, particularly with the United States. Preliminary inventory (NUCMC 71-122).

79 Paul Brunelli. Memoirs, in Russian, n.d. "Moia Letopis' - Leib Gvardii v Ismailovskom Polku" (My Chronicle - Izmailovsky Guards Regiments). Typescript, photocopy, 1 folder. Colonel, Imperial Russian Army. Relates to activities of the regiment during the year 1897.

80 Court Councillor de Brunet. Papers, in French, Russian, Swedish, and German, 1809-14. 1 ms. box. Russian consul general in Norway. Correspondence, proclamations and reports relating to Russian foreign policy and commerce in the Baltic.

81 Aleksandr Aleksandrovich Bublikov. Essay, in Russian, 1923. "Likvidatsiia Likholiet'ia" (Liquidation of Troubled Times). Typescript, 1 vol. Relates to Russian reconstruction and public finance after the Russian Civil War.

82 Baron Aleksei Pavlovich Budberg (1869-1945). Papers, in Russian, 1919-20. 1 ms. box. Lieutenant general, Russian Imperial Army. Memoirs and diaries relating to Russian military activities during World War I, and to White Russian military activities in Siberia during the Russian Civil War.

83 Jan Bulhak. Photographs, 1925. 1 envelope. Depicts various locations in Poland, primarily Warsaw, Vilna, Lwow, and Krakow.

84 Evgenii Grigor'evich Buliubash. Papers, in Russian, 1954-64. 1 ms. box. General, Russian Imperial Army. Correspondence, clippings, printed matter, and photographs relating to Russian Imperial military forces before, during, and after the Russian Revolution and Civil War, and to activities of the Russian émigré community in the U.S.

85 Viktor M. Bunin (b. 1896). Memoirs, in Russian, n.d. Typescript, carbon copy. "Deviatyi val; vospominaniia uchastnika russkoi grazhdanskoi voiny 1918-1920 g.g." (The Highest Wave: Reminiscences of a Participant in the Russian Civil War, 1918-20). 1 vol.

86 James Bunyan (1898-1977). Papers, in Russian and English, 1917-63. 2.5 ms. boxes. Russian-American historian. Excerpts from published sources, documents, and notes (primarily in Russian) relating to the Ukrainian government, Russia, Siberia, and the Far Eastern Republic during the Russian Civil War in 1919, used by

J. Bunyan as research material for his book, The Bolshevik Revolution, 1917-18 (1934); drafts, notes, charts, and printed matter (primarily in English) relating to Soviet economic, administrative, agricultural, and industrial organization and planning, 1917-63, used by J. Bunyan as research material for his book, The Origin of Forced Labor in the Soviet State, 1917-1921 (1967); and drafts of the latter book.

87 Elmer Granville Burland. Report, 1925. "If the United States Should Negotiate a Commercial Treaty with Soviet Russia." Typescript, 1 folder. Relates to the prospects for a U.S.-Soviet trade agreement.

88 P. G. Burlin. Writings, in Russian, 1941. Typescript, 1 folder. Imperial Russian Army officer. Study entitled "Kratkaia Spravka o Russkom Kazachestve" (Brief Note on the Russian Kossacks), and a report entitled "Proiskhozhdenie Kazakov - Doklad" (Cossack Parentage - A Report), relating to Russian Cossack daily life, and class and military structure. Also, correspondence with General P. P. Stavitskii concerning the Japanese-Chinese War of 1938.

89 Vladimir L'vovich Burtsev (1862-1942). Papers, in Russian, 1906-35. 1 ms. box. Russian revolutionary; later anti-Bolshevik. Memoirs, essays, correspondence, and printed matter relating to the Menshevik and Social Revolutionary movements before 1917, Evno Azef and other Okhrana agents, and counter-revolutionary movements during the Russian Revolution. Includes communications between Burtsev and Admiral A. V. Kolchak, L. Bernstein, and General P. N. Wrangel in Istanbul, 1921. (NUCMC 71-123)

90 Byelorussian Central Council, New York. Memorandum, 1954. Typescript, mimeographed, 1 folder. Relates to forced labor and national policy of the Soviet Union towards Byelorussia. Addressed to the United Nations.

91 I. Bykadorov. Papers, in Russian, 1919-20. .5 ms. box. General, Imperial Russian Army. Mandates, orders, and circulars relating to the Civil War in the south of Russia. Includes a list of the main events in the history of the Don Army prepared by I. Bykadorov.

92 Alonzo Bland Calder (b. 1892). Papers, 1911-56. 45 ms. boxes. American consular official; stationed in China, 1920-41 and 1945-48. Memoranda, reports, correspondence, clippings, photographs, and pamphlets relating to U.S. foreign and economic relations with China in the interwar period and immediately after World War II, and to U.S. foreign and trade relations with Russia, Egypt, and Malaya.

93 John Kenneth Caldwell (b. 1881). Memoirs, n.d. Typescript, 1 folder. American diplomat; consul at Vladivostok, 1914-20; consul general at Tientsin, China, 1935-42; ambassador to Ethiopia, 1943-45. Relates to U.S. foreign relations and commerce with Japan, Russia, Australia, China, and Ethiopia, 1906-45, and to U.S. participation in international narcotics control agencies. Reference to the Russian Railway Service Corps.

94 Hannah Brain Campbell (b. 1880). Memoirs, 1945. Typescript, 1 folder. American Red Cross worker in Siberia, 1917-20. Memoir entitled "Adventure in Siberia," as told to Sarah E. Mathews, relating to activities of the American Red Cross in the eastern part of Russia, 1917-20; and memoir entitled "Children's Ark," relating to the return of Russian children by the American Red Cross to their parents in Russia in 1920.

95 Bob Carleton. Song, ca. 1939-40. Let's Send a Buck to Finland. 1 phonorecord. Appeals for American aid to Finland during the Russo-Finnish War. Words by Cliff Dixon and music by B. Carleton.

96 Philip H. Carroll (1885-1941). Papers, 1917-39. 1 ms. box. Captain, U.S. Army, 1917-20; American Relief Administration (ARA) worker in Germany and Russia, 1920-22. Memoranda, outlines of procedures, organization and personnel charts, preliminary programs, routine charts, and specimen forms relating to activities of the U.S. 348th Field Artillery in France and Germany, 1917-20, of the ARA in Hamburg, Germany, 1920-21, and of the ARA Russian Unit Supply Division in Moscow, 1921-22. Includes correspondence with Herbert Hoover, 1934-39, relating to U.S. politics. (NUCMC 75-618)

97 Lieutenant Carter. Letter, 1919. Holograph, 1 vol. British army officer. Relates to British military intervention against the Bolsheviks in northern Russia. Includes typewritten copy of original.

98 (Georges) Catroux. Photograph, n.d. 1 envelope. Depicts General Catroux, French ambassador to the Soviet Union, 1945-48.

99 Druzina Ceská. Records, in English, Czech, and Russian, 1918-20. Typescript, 1 folder, 21 pp. Czechoslovak Legion in Russia. Orders, leaflets, and writings relating to the activities of the Legion during the Russian Civil War. Includes a history of the Legion, entitled "The Operations of the Czechoslovak Army in Russia in the Years 1917-1920."

100 (Anastasia Nikolaevna) Chaikovskii. Collection, in Russian and German, 1920-32. 3 ms. boxes. Interviews, correspondence, notes, newspaper clippings, and other printed matter relating to the case of A. N. Chaikovskii, a woman claiming to be Grand Duchess Anastasia, daughter of Tsar Nicholas II of Russian. Alias, Anna Anderson. Preliminary inventory (NUCMC 71-1089).

101 Kia-Ngau (Chia-ao) Chang (b. 1889). Papers, in Chinese, 1945-57. 12.5 ms. boxes, 2 oversize boxes, 4 panels of calligraphy. Chinese

banker; governor of Central Bank of China; president of Bank of China; minister of Railways and Communications, 1935-42; chairman, Northeast (Manchuria) Economic Commission, 1945-47. Diaries, reports, instructions, statistics, and printed matter relating to economic conditions in Manchuria at the end of World War II, Chinese-Soviet negotiations for the return of Manchuria to Chinese control, and daily commodity prices of Chinese products, 1950-57. Includes some materials collected from Japanese organizations and calligraphy by Liang Ch'i-ch 'ao (1873-1929). Preliminary inventory. May not be used before 1 August 1984 without written permission of Kia-Ngau Chang.

102 David Chavchavadze. History, 1950. "The Vlassov Movement: Soviet Citizens Who Served on the German Side, 1941-45." Typescript, mimeographed, .5 ms. box.

103 A. V. Cheriachoukin. Papers, in Russian, 1918-19. 1 folder. Ambassador of the Don Cossack Republic to the Ukraine during the Russian Civil War. Correspondence, reports, and dispatches relating to the activities of the anti-Bolshevik movements during the Russian Civil War, and relations of the Don Cossack Republic with the Germans and with Allied representatives in Odessa. Preliminary inventory.

104 Cherkasskii Family. Papers, in Russian, 1837-1974. 1.5 ms. boxes, 1 oversize roll. Russian Imperial noble family. Diaries, correspondence, books, memorabilia, writings, genealogy, clippings, printed matter, and photographs relating to the careers, experiences, and genealogy of the Cherkasskii family, the Russian Revolution and Civil War, the Russian Orthodox Church abroad, and the Russian Imperial Army.

105 Viktor Mikhailovich Chernov (1873-1952). Writings, in Russian, n.d. Typescript, .5 ms. box. Leader of the Russian Partiia Sotsialistov-Revoliutsionerov. Relates to activities of the Partiia Sotsialistov-Revoliutsionerov (Socialist Revolutionary Party) during the Russian Revolution.

106 (Lieutenant General) Chichagov. Photographs, 1903. 1 envelope. Depicts Lieutenant General Chichagov with a group of Russian military officers.

107 Georgii Vasil'evich Chicherin (1872-1936). Letter, 1918, to Allen Wardwell. Typescript, photocopy, 1 folder. Soviet commissar of foreign affairs, 1918-30. Calls for the condemnation of atrocities by anti-Bolshevik forces in Russia.

108 James Rives Childs (b. 1893). Memoirs, n.d. Typescript, .5 ms. box. American diplomat; American Relief Administration worker in Russia, 1921-23; chargé d'affaires in Morocco, 1941-45; ambassador to Saudi Arabia, 1946-50; ambassador to Ethiopia, 1951-53. Relates to relief work and social conditions in Russia, U.S. foreign relations with Balkan and Near Eastern countries, diplomacy regarding Morocco in World War II, and the role of Iran in world politics, especially in relation to Russia.

109 China - communist posters and records, in Chinese, ca. 1949-53. 63 posters, 19 phonorecords. Propaganda relating to Chinese revolutionary history, mutual aid teams, policy towards minorities and marriage reforms, Sino-Soviet friendship, Mao Tse-tung, and Lu Hsun. Preliminary inventory.

110 Nicholas Chuhnov. Open letter, in Russian, 1951, to Harry S. Truman, president of the U.S. Typescript, mimeographed, 1 folder. Editor of The Banner of Russia (New York). Objects to a comparison of Iosif Stalin to Emperor Alexander I made by President Truman. Includes a translation of the letter (printed).

111 Felix Cielens (1888-1964). Papers, in Latvian and English, 1913-45. 2.5 ms. boxes. Minister of Foreign Affairs of Latvia, 1926-28; Latvian minister to France, 1933-40. Memoirs, writings, correspondence, memoranda, and printed matter relating to Latvian foreign relations and political conditions. (NUCMC 71-127).

112 Marmaduke R. Clark (d. 1964). Papers, 1918-20. 1 ms. box, 9 envelopes. Senior secretary, Young Men's Christian Association; with the American Expeditionary Forces in Siberia. Correspondence, memoranda, writings, newspaper clippings, memorabilia, and photographs relating to Y.M.C.A. activities in Siberia, political developments during the last stages of the Russian Civil War, and the Allied intervention.

113 Frederick W. B. Coleman (b. 1874). Diaries, 1909-38. Holograph, .5 ms. box. American diplomat; minister to Estonia, Latvia, and Lithuania, 1922-31; minister to Denmark, 1931-33. Relates to U.S. military activities during World War I, and to U.S. foreign relations with the Baltic states and Denmark.

114 Ethan Theodore Colton (b. 1872). Papers, 1918-52. 7 ms. boxes. American relief worker with the European Student Relief and the Young Men's Christian Association in Russia. Correspondence, reports, manuscripts of writings, and clippings relating to European Student Relief activities in Russia and other European countries, 1920-25; and to social conditions, the educational system, and the status of religion in Russia in the 1920s and 1930s. Includes the memoirs of E. T. Colton and 13 anti-religious Soviet posters.

115 Commission of Inquiry into Forced Labor. Report, 1950. Typescript, mimeographed, 1 folder. Relates to forced labor in the Soviet Union and Eastern Europe. Report made to the United Nations Economic and Social Council.

116 Communist International. Executive Committee. Instructions, 1922. "Concerning the Next

Tasks of the CP of A." Typescript, photocopy, 1 vol. Relates to the Communist Party, U.S.A. Seized by the U.S. Department of Justice during a raid on a secret convention of the Communist Party, U.S.A. at Bridgman, Michigan, 1922. Includes a cover letter signed by Nikolai Bukharin, Karl Radek, and Otto Kuusinen.

117 Conference on the Discontinuance of Nuclear Weapon Tests, Geneva, 1958-. Proceedings, 1961. Typescript, mimeographed, 1 folder. Proceedings of the 274th-276th and 278th-279th sessions, 21-23 and 27-28 March 1961, relating to proposals for a nuclear test ban treaty.

118 Merian C. Cooper (1894-1973). Papers, 1917-58. 1 ms. box. Brigadier general, U.S. Air Force; pilot with the Kosciuszko Squadron in Poland, 1919-21; chief of staff, China Air Task Force, 1942. Correspondence, memoranda, and memorabilia relating to the American Relief Administration and the U.S. Food Administration in Poland, the Kosciuszko Squadron during the Polish-Russian wars, 1919-21, General Douglas MacArthur, Lieutenant General Claire Chennault, U.S. defense policy, air power, and communist strategy.

119 Robert A. Cotner. Writings, 1959. Holograph, 1 folder. American Relief Administration worker. 2 essays, entitled "The Nature of Marxian Communism" and "Some Thoughts Regarding Communism and the World Situation."

120 George N. Crocker. Papers, 1950-73. 7 ft. American journalist and author. Writings, reports, and printed matter relating to political issues in the United States and international affairs. One of his books was Roosevelt's Road to Russia.

121 Czechoslovakia. Armada. 1. Ceskoslovensky Armadni Sbov v SSSR. Miscellaneous records, in Czech, 1941-45. 3 ms. boxes, 1 envelope. First Czechoslovakian Army, an Allied military unit on the eastern front in World War II. Correspondence, telegrams, orders, diaries, proclamations, newspapers, periodicals, clippings, and photographs relating to the organization, training, and activities of the First Czechoslovakian Army under General Ludvik Svoboda on the eastern front, 1941-45. References to the battles of Kiev, Sokolov, Bila Cerkev, and Kharkov, and to N. S. Khrushchev, I. V. Stalin, General K. K. Kokossovskii, and the 373rd Soviet Artillery Regiment. Preliminary inventory (NUCMC 75-624).

122 Czechoslovakia - invasion, August 1968. Collection, in Czech and French, 1968. 1 ms. box, 1 microfilm reel, 1 motion picture reel. Reports, leaflets, newspapers, cartoons, and photographs relating to the Russian invasion of Czechoslovakia, August 1968.

123 Roberts Dambitis. Memorandum, in Russian, 1940. Typescript, carbon copy, 1 vol. Minister of War in Latvia. Request addressed to Andrei Ia. Vyshinskii, deputy chairman of the Council of People's Commissars of the Soviet Union, that Latvian military units be allowed to remain in Latvia.

124 William Lafayette Darling (1856-1938). Diary, 1917. Typescript, 1 vol. American civil engineer; member, U.S. Advisory Commission of Railway Experts to Russia, 1917. Relates to the Russian railway system, May-December 1917.

125 E. Alfred Davies. Diary, 1919. 1 folder. U.S. army officer. Relates to the evacuation of the American Expeditionary Forces in Siberia from Omsk to Irkutsk, 4 September-4 October 1919.

126 Benjamin B. Davis. Papers, 1919-20. .5 ms. box, 2 envelopes. American Red Cross worker in Siberia, 1919-20. Correspondence, writings, diary, reports, pamphlets, postcards, and photographs relating to American Red Cross activities in Siberia, primarily in Vladivostok.

127 Loda Mae Davis. Papers, 1943-47. 1 ms. box. United Nations Relief and Rehabilitation Administration official. Writings, reports, correspondence, and memoranda relating to U.N.R.R.A. relief in Europe at the end of World War II, particularly to food procurement in the U.S. and distribution in Italy, Greece, Yugoslavia, and the Soviet Union.

128 Richard Hallock Davis (1913-1972). Miscellaneous papers, 1949-50. 1 folder, 1 envelope. American diplomat; student, Russian Institute, Columbia University, 1949-50; U.S. deputy assistant secretary of state, 1960-72. Lecture notes relating to Russian history, government, economics, and literature taken at the Russian Institute at Columbia University, course syllabi, and 3 unidentified photographs.

129 Robert E. Davis. Reports, 1917-19. Typescript, 1 folder. Major, U.S. Army; American Red Cross worker in Kuban area, Russia. Relates to the work of the American Red Cross, and the political and military situation in south Russia, 1917-19. Addressed to Colonel Robert E. Olds, American Red Cross commissioner to Europe. Refers to the Volunteer Army, General A. I. Denikin, A. Kerensky, and the Cheka.

130 George Martin Day. Papers, 1922-37. .5 ms. box. Professor of Sociology, Occidental College, Los Angeles. Writings, correspondence, and questionnaires relating to social conditions, education, and religion in the Soviet Union, and to the adjustment to American society of Russians living in the Los Angeles area in 1930.

131 Jane Degras. Study, n.d. "Revisiting the Comintern." Typescript, photocopy, 1 folder.

Relates to the history and organization of the Communist International.

132 Kseniia Denikina. Chronology, in Russian, n.d. Typescript. "Khronologiia Sobytii vo Vremia Grazhdanskoi Voiny v Rossii" (Chronology of Events during the Civil War in Russia). Relates to the southern and western fronts during the Russian Civil War.

133 Jonė Deveikė (1907-1965). Papers, in Lithuanian, 1930-63. 1.5 ms. boxes, 1 package. Lithuanian attorney, historian, and journalist. Correspondence, notes, reports, and memorabilia relating to social and political conditions of Lithuanians in France and Germany. Register. Correspondence between Jonas Dainauskas and J. Deveikė, 1 package, is restricted until 15 September 1999.

134 Georgi M. Dimitrov (1903-1972). Writings, in Bulgarian, n.d. Typescript, photocopy, 1 ms. box. Bulgarian émigré politician; secretary-general, International Peasant Union; president, Bulgarian National Committee. Includes memoirs relating to Bulgaria and Bulgarian émigré politics, and unpublished articles relating to the Bulgarian Agrarian Union between World Wars I and II, world agriculture, and agriculture in the Soviet Union. Register. May not be quoted without written permission of Charles A. Moser.

135 Sergei Vasil'evich Dmitrievskii. Translation of biographical sketch, ca. 1932. "V. M. Molotov." Typescript, carbon copy, 1 vol. Translation by D. M. Krassovsky of an excerpt from Sovetskie Portrety (Soviet Portraits) by S. V. Dmitrievskii.

136 Dnieprostroi. Photographs, 1931-32. 1 envelope. Depicts the construction of Dnieprostroi waterpower electric plant and its opening on 10 October 1932.

137 Lev Eugene Dobriansky (b. 1918). Papers, 1959-77. 2 ms. boxes. Ukrainian-American economist and author; chairman, National Captive Nations Committee. Correspondence, messages, pamphlets, programs, proclamations, reports, resolutions, and clippings relating to U.S. foreign policy, the National Captive Nations Committee, the Ukrainian Catholic Church, China, and Mao Tse-tung.

138 Princess Barbara Dolgorouky (b. 1885). Memoirs, in Russian, n.d. Typescript, photocopy, .5 ms. box. Russian aristocrat. Relates to the Romanov family, the Russian Imperial Court, and the Russian Revolution and Civil War, 1885-1919.

139 Dom Polskich Dzieci. Oudtshoorn, South Africa. Records, in Polish, 1942-47. 3 ms. boxes. Polish Children's Home, founded in 1943 for the care of Polish war orphans from Russia. Correspondence, telegrams, notes, memoranda, clippings, accounts, lists, protocols, reports, inventories, and published materials relating to the evacuation of the war orphans from Russia to Oudtshoorn, the establishment and operation of the Home, and the care and education of the orphans. Register.

140 General Domanenko. Study, in Russian, n.d. Holograph, 1 vol. "Sluzhba General'nago Shtaba v Divizii i Korpusie" (General Staff Service in the Division and Corps). Relates to organization of the Imperial Russian Army.

141 James Britt Donovan (1916-1970). Papers, 1940-70. 106 ms. boxes. American lawyer and educator; associate general counsel, Office of Scientific Research and Development, 1942-43; general counsel, Office of Strategic Services, 1943-45; assistant to U.S. chief prosecutor, trial of major German war criminals, Nuremberg, 1945; negotiator of Abel-Powers spy exchange with USSR and of the Cuban prisoners exchange following the Bay of Pigs; president of the New York City Board of Education, 1963-65. Correspondence, reports, memoranda, studies, drafts of book manuscripts, scrapbooks, notes, photographs, and printed matter relating to the U.S. Office of Scientific Research and Development and the Office of Strategic Services during World War II, the Nuremberg war crime trials, the Rudolph Abel-Gary Powers spy exchange, the Cuban prisoner exchange following the Bay of Pigs landing, and the New York City Board of Education. Restricted in part. Preliminary inventory.

142 Cecil Dorrian. Papers, 1912-26. 1 ms. box, 6 envelopes. American journalist; war correspondent, Newark Evening News, 1914-26. Clippings, writings, postcards, and photographs relating to World War I, postwar reconstruction in Western Europe, the Balkans, the Near East, and the Russian Revolution and Civil War.

143 Paul Dotsenko. Speech transcript, 1954. "The Fight for Freedom in Siberia: Its Successes and Failures." Typescript, photocopy, 1 folder. Relates to Siberia during the Russian Revolution, delivered in New York City, June 1954.

144 D. P. Dratsenko. Miscellaneous papers, in Russian, 1919-20. 1 folder. General, White Russian Army. Military reports, orders, and correspondence relating to the Russian Civil War in the Caucasus, political and military conditions in Georgia, and British foreign policy in Transcaucasia. Preliminary inventory.

145 Aleksandr Aleksandrovich Drenteln (1868-1925). Memorandum, in Russian, n.d. Typescript, photocopy, 1 folder. Relates to the life of A. A. Drenteln, major general, Imperial Russian Army, and adjutant to Tsar Nicholas II.

146 William Young Duncan. Papers, 1918-20. Photocopy, .5 ms. box. American clergyman; Young Men's Christian Association chaplain with the Czechoslovakian Legion in Siberia, 1917-20. Diary and letters relating to the Russian Revolution and Civil War and the Allied intervention in Siberia, 1918-20. Quotations may not be published without permission of Donald G. Duncan, during his lifetime. Any publication using the collection as a source must carry acknowledgment. A copy of any such publication must be provided to D. G. Duncan free of charge.

147 Joseph H. Dunner (b. 1908). Study, n.d. Typescript, .5 ms. box. "Germans Under the Hammer and Sickle: The Administration of the Soviet Zone of Germany from 1945 to 1953." American political scientist.

148 East German economic policy. Memorandum, in German, 1949. Typescript, 1 folder. Relates to the bases of economic reorganization in the Soviet Zone of Germany.

149 "Economic Conditions of Kuban Black Sea Region." Translation of study, n.d. Typescript, 1 folder. Relates to the topography and economic conditions of the Kuban District, Russia, during the Russian Civil War.

150 J. Edison. Photographs, 1918-21. 5 envelopes. Depicts demonstrations, military personnel, railways, and scenery in northern China and southeastern Siberia.

151 Donald Drew Egbert (1902-1973). Study, n.d. Typescript, photocopy, 2 ms. boxes. "Communism, Radicalism and the Arts: American Developments in Relation to the Background in Western Europe and in Russia from the Seventeenth Century to 1959." American historian. Relates to the effects of Marxism and Communism on American art, and the relationships between works of art and the social, economic, and political beliefs of the artists who produced them, 1680-1959. A revised version of this study was published under the title Socialism and American Art in the Light of European Utopianism, Marxism and Anarchism (Princeton, 1967).

152 Edward H. Egbert (d. 1939). Papers, 1914-21. 1 ms. box. Chief surgeon, American Red Cross detachment in Russia, during World War I; executive secretary, Catherine Breshkovsky Russian Relief Fund. Correspondence, notes, clippings, printed matter, and photographs relating to the Russian Revolution, relief work in Russia, and Ekaterina Breshko-Breshkovskaia. Includes correspondence with E. Breshko-Breshkovskaia and Herbert Hoover. Preliminary inventory (NUCMC 68-420).

153 "Egerskii Vestnik" (Eger Herald). Bulletins, in Russian, 1925-32. Typescript, mimeographed, 1 folder. Relates to the history of the Russian Imperial Army regiment, Leib-Gvardii Egerskii Polk, especially during the Russian Civil War, and to activities of veterans of the regiment. Issued by a regimental veterans association.

154 "Ekonomicheskoe Polizhenie Sov. Rossii" (The Economic Situation of Soviet Russia). Memorandum, in Russian, ca. 1923. Typescript, 1 folder.

155 S. A. Elachich. Memoirs, in Russian, 1934. "Obryvki Vospominanii" (Scraps of Reminiscences). Typescript, carbon copy, 1 vol. White Russian leader. Relates to the Russian Revolution, the Omsk Government of Admiral Aleksandr Kolchak, and the Czechoslovakian Legion in Siberia.

156 Eliashev. Study, in Russian, 1923. "Dva Puti Sovetskago Zakonodatel'stva" (Two Methods of Soviet Legislation). Typescript, 1 folder.

157 Colonel Theodore Elyseev. Memoirs, 9 vols., 5 bks., 4,670 pp. The colonel's memoirs, entitled "Ispoved' odnogo stroevogo ofitsera," concern mainly the years 1910-20 and cover his family, service in a Cossack cavalry regiment, military training, World War I on the Turkish front, the Russian Revolution and Civil War in the South, capitulation to the Red Army of ca. 40,000 Cossack troops and officers and their internment in a concentration camp. There are many pictures and maps, and much detail about the Cossacks. Includes references to the Kuban Cossacks, Baron (General) P. N. Wrangel, Colonels (later Generals) V. Naumenko, S. Toporkov, and N. Babiev, and the Kornilov cavalry regiment of Cossacks.

158 George H. Emerson. Papers, 1918-19. .5 ms. box, 1 envelope. Colonel, U.S. Army; commanding officer, Russian Railway Service Corps; and chief inspector of the Interallied Technical Board. Correspondence, reports, maps, photographs, and clippings relating to the activities of the Russian Railway Service Corps, the political situation in Russia during the Russian Civil War, and the Czechoslovakian Legion in Siberia. References: General D. L. Khorvat, Admiral A. V. Kolchak, Ataman G. M. Semenov, the evacuation of Omsk, and the death of the Romanovs. (NUCMC 71-135)

159 Fritz Theodor Epstein (b. 1898). Papers, in German, 1914-48. .5 ms. boxes. German-American historian. Writings, clippings, correspondence, and orders relating to Allied intervention in Russia during the Russian Revolution, German military government of Strasbourg during World War I, the trial of Menshevik leaders in Russia in 1931, and the authenticity of the diaries of Joseph Goebbels. Includes an unpublished history, entitled "Russland und die Weltpolitik, 1917-1920: Studien zur Geschichte der Interventionen in Russland" (Russia and World Politics,

1917-1920: Studies on the History of the Interventions in Russia).

160 Julius Epstein (1901-1975). Papers, 1939-72. 180 ms. boxes. American journalist and author. Correspondence, speeches, and writings, clippings, photographs, and printed matter relating to World War II, communism, forced repatriation of Russian prisoners to the Soviet Union following World War II, the Katyn Forest massacre, unreported deaths of Soviet cosmonauts, and the efforts of J. Epstein to obtain restricted government documents on these subjects.

161 Erasmus-Feit family. Papers, in Russian, 1895-1956. 3 ms. boxes. Family of Baron Erasmus-Feit, Russian Imperial Army officer. Correspondence, scrapbooks, memorabilia, printed matter, and photographs relating to the daily lives of Russian émigrés in China and the U.S., and family matters.

162 P. Ergushov. History, in Russian, 1938. "Kasaki i Gortsy na Sunzhenskoi Linii v 1917" (Cossacks and Mountaineers on the Sunzhenskii Line in 1917). Typescript, 1 folder. Colonel, Imperial Russian Army. Relates to White Russian military activities during the Russian Revolution.

163 Petr Zacharovich Ermakov. Memoirs, n.d. "The Massacre of the Romanoffs." Typescript, photocopy, 1 folder. Participant in the execution of the Russian royal family, 1918. Written by Richard Haliburton, as told by P. Z. Ermakov.

164 Estonia. Riigi Kohus. Records, in Estonian, 1936. Photocopy, 1 folder. Estonian State Court. Indictment and summary of police interrogation of witnesses, relating to charges made against Andres Larka, Johannes Holland, and others accused of involvement in the 1935 attempted coup against the Estonian government by the organization Eesti Vabadussojalaste Liit (the League of Veterans of the War of Independence).

165 "Estoniia i Pomoshch Golodaiushchim" (Estonia and Aid to the Starving). Essay, in Russian, 1921. Typescript, 1 folder. Relates to civilian relief in Estonia at the end of World War I.

166 Maria von Etter. Papers, in Russian, 1895-1916. 1 folder, 1 album. Russian aristocrat. Letters of appointment, commendation, and appreciation, certificates, and awards relating to the charitable volunteer work of M. von Etter. Includes a record book of patients at the Russian Red Cross von Etter Infirmary, 1915-16, and a memorial album with an engraved sterling silver plaque dedicated to Ivan Sevastianovich von Etter from the Russian Imperial Kiev officers under his command, containing photographs and autographs of the officers.

167 (General) Etterg. Photograph, ca. 1877-78. 1 envelope. Depicts the Russian General Etterg, commandant of Adrianopol' during the Russo-Turkish war.

168 European War, 1914-18, Russia. Collection, n.d. Typescript, 1 folder. Translations of editorials from Russian newspapers, July-August 1914, relating to the outbreak of World War I, and to the entry of Russia into the war.

169 Evengelische Kirchen in Deutschland. Hilfswerk. Letters, in German, 1949. Typescript, 1 folder. Relates to food relief received from the Church World Service in Soviet-occupied Germany.

170 Far Eastern Republic Collection (1917-21). 1 ms. box. Memoranda and copies of proclamations and correspondence relating to the creation of the Far Eastern Republic and to Japanese intervention in Siberia. Includes a mimeographed copy of the constitution of the republic and a memorandum from the Far Eastern Republic Special Trade Delegation to the U.S. government.

171 Far Western Slavic Conference, Stanford University, 1959. Proceedings, 1959. 7 phonotapes. Conference of Slavic studies scholars in the Western U.S. Relates to the history, politics, foreign relations, economy, society, and literature of the Soviet Union and Eastern Europe.

172 Linn M. Farish. Circular, 1940. Typescript, mimeographed, 1 folder. Reprints extracts from an article by L. M. Farish, entitled "Huge Reserves, Poor Technique Characterize Soviet Oil Industry," published in Mining and Metallurgy in June 1940, and letters to the editor prompted by this article, published in Mining and Metallurgy in July 1940, relating to a comparison of economic conditions in the U.S. and the Soviet Union.

173 Percival Farquhar (1864-1953). Papers, 1922-28. 4 ms. boxes. American engineer. Correspondence, memoranda, and reports relating to negotiations between P. Farquhar and associates and the Soviet government concerning the development of Russia's iron ore and steel resources, and to the work of American engineers in the Soviet Union. Includes reports on the Makeeva Steel Works, the Krivoi Rog Iron Ore District and Ekatrina and Donets Basin railway developments. (NUCMC 68-423)

174 Dmitri I. Fedichkin. Papers, in Russian, 1918-19. .5 ms. box. Colonel, Imperial Russian Army; commander-in-chief, Izhevsk People's Army, 1918. Writings, correspondence, and handbills relating to the Russian Civil War, and the rebellion of workers and peasants in Izhevsk against the Bolsheviks, 1918. Includes an English translation of "The Izhevsk Rebellion."

175 Georgii Fedorov. Memoirs, in Russian, n.d. Typescript, carbon copy, 1 vol. "Iz Vospominanii Zalozhnika v Piatigorskom Kontsentratsionnom Lagere" (From the Recollections of a Prisoner in the Piatigorsk Concentration Camp). Relates to the Russian Civil War in the Kuban region.

176 (Grigorii Fedorovich) Fedorov. Collection, in Russian, 1967-73. 1 folder. Brochures, pamphlets, newspaper articles, and photographs relating to the public life of G. F. Fedorov (b. 1891), Soviet government official.

177 Ladislav K. Feierabend (1891-1969). Papers, in Czech, Slovak, and English, 1922-75. 20 ms. boxes. Czechoslovak agricultural economist; minister of agriculture, 1938-40; minister of finance, Czechoslovak government in exile (London), 1941-45. Correspondence, speeches, writings, memoirs, photographs, and printed matter relating to agricultural administration, Czechoslovakia in World War II, and Czechoslovak foreign relations with Germany and the Soviet Union. Preliminary inventory. Personal papers closed until 1998.

178 Jules Feldmans (1889-1953). Papers, 1919-55. 18 ms. boxes, 1 envelope. Latvian diplomat. Correspondence, memoranda, and reports relating to the Russian occupation of the Baltic states in 1940, displaced persons in Germany, immigration, and Latvian émigré organizations after World War II. Register (NUCMC 75-622).

179 Alan Ferguson. Correspondence, 1938-39, with William Sidney Graves. Holographs, photocopy, 1 folder. American soldier; member, 31st Infantry Regiment, in Siberia, 1918-19. Relates to the history of the American Expeditionary Forces in Siberia.

180 Willem Karel Hendrik Feuilletau de Bruyn (b. 1886). Study, 1946. "The Aims, Methods, and Means of Soviet Russia in Asia and the Middle East." Typescript, carbon copy, 1 vol.

181 N. H. Field. Memorandum, 1946. Typescript, 1 folder. Unitarian Service Committee relief worker in Germany. Relates to relief work in the Soviet Zone of Germany.

182 Finland in the Russian Revolution. Reports, 1919-20. Typescript, 1 folder. Relates to political conditions in Finland during the Russian Civil War, Finnish independence, Karelian nationalism, and German intervention in Finland and the Baltic states.

183 "Finliandets" (Finnish). Bulletins, in Russian, 1963-72. Typescript, mimeographed, .5 ms. box. Organ of the Society of the Household Troops of the Finland Regiment, an organization of veterans of this regiment of the Imperial Russian Army. Relates to activities of members.

184 Finnish independence movement collection. In Finnish and Swedish, 1900-1903. .5 ms. box. Pamphlets, bulletins, and maps relating to the Russification program in Finland and to the Finnish independence movement.

185 George Fischer (b. 1923). Study, 1950. "Soviet Defection in World War II." Typescript, mimeographed, .5 ms. box. American author and historian. Relates to Russian collaborators with Germany during World War II and especially to the Russian Army of Liberation under General Andrei Andreevich Vlasov. May not be quoted or reproduced without permission of G. Fischer.

186 Harold Henry Fisher (1890-1975). Papers, 1917-74. 32 ms. boxes, 4 card file boxes, .66 ft., 5 envelopes, 1 album. American historian; director, Hoover Institution on War, Revolution and Peace, 1943-52. Clippings, printed matter, notes, correspondence, pamphlets, articles, microfilm, and photographs relating to the Soviet Union, the San Francisco Conference organizing the United Nations, the Civil War in Spain, Herbert Hoover and the American Relief Administration, and the history of Finland. Register.

187 Harold M. Fleming (b. 1900). Papers, 1922-23. 1 ms. box. American Relief Administration worker in Russia. Correspondence, writings, maps, and clippings relating to the American Relief Administration in Russia, economic conditions, and political and social developments in Russia after the Revolution.

188 V. E. Flug. Writings, in Russian, 1926-33. Holograph, 2 ms. boxes. General, Imperial Russian Army. Includes a study entitled "Pekhota" (Infantry), 1926, relating to infantry organization and tactics, and a memorandum, 1933, relating to activities of the Russian 10th Army in September 1914. Register.

189 F. F. Foss. Papers, 1890-1917. 20 envelopes, 4 albums, 38 oversize prints, 1 oversize package, .5 ft. Engineer in Russia. Photographs and memorabilia relating to the development of industry in prerevolutionary Russia.

190 General Frederichs. Papers, in Russian and French, 1835-76. 5 ms. boxes. Imperial Russian military attaché in France. Correspondence, memoranda, notes, and printed matter relating to Franco-Russian relations and Russian military policy. Preliminary inventory (NUCMC 71-1096).

191 O. J. Frederiksen. Letters, 1924. Typewritten transcripts, 1 folder. Relief worker in Leningrad, 1924. Relates to the flood in Leningrad and to the dismissal of students from Russian universities.

192 Arthur M. Free. Collector. Photographs, 1914-18. 8 envelopes. Depicts German troops and war scenes on the eastern and western fronts during World War I, and scenes of the negotiation of the Treaty of Brest-Litovsk, 1918. Captions in German.

193 Roger Adolf Freeman (b. 1904). Papers, 1950-74, ca. 195 ft. American economist; senior fellow, Hoover Institution on War, Revolution and Peace, 1962-75; special assistant to the president of the U.S., 1969-70, and other government positions. Correspondence, memoranda, reports, studies, speeches, writings, and printed matter relating to governmental problems in the state of Washington, 1950-55, fiscal problems of Bolivia, 1957, international economic development, taxation (federal, state, and local), intergovernmental relations in the U.S., public and private education from lower schools to university in the U.S. and the Soviet Union, public welfare in the U.S., and the growth of American government. May not be used without permission of R. A. Freeman, the director of the Hoover Institution, or the director of the Domestic Studies Program of the Hoover Institution.

194 Joseph Frejlich. Collection on Poland and world affairs, 1894-1968. 54 ms. boxes. Clippings, correspondence, and writings relating to Polish socialism, World War II, the Yalta conference, Poles in the United States and Canada, and the Russian Orthodox Church.

195 French Communism. Translations of newspaper articles, 1919-20. Typescript, 1 folder. Relates to the development of a French Communist party and to its adherence to the Third International. Translations of articles from French and Russian newspapers.

196 French leftist press. Newspaper articles, in French, 1917-19. Transcripts, typewritten, 1 folder. Relates to the movement for a Third International and to the mutiny of French sailors in the Black Sea. Articles from leftist French newspapers.

197 Alfred Hermann Fried (1864-1921). Papers, in German, 1914-19. 5 ms. boxes. Austrian pacifist. Diaries, correspondence, clippings, and notes relating to the international peace movement, particularly during World War I, pacifism, international cooperation, and the World War I guilt question (including Russian culpability).

198 Ernst Friedlander. Memoir, in German, ca. 1920. "Imprisonment in Siberia." Typescript, 1 vol. Austrian soldier taken prisoner during World War I. Includes incomplete translation.

199 Jacob G. Frumkin. Statement, 1957. Typescript, 1 folder. Notarized statement relating to a German offer to negotiate a separate peace with Russia in 1917. Includes second statement on same subject by Ilja Trotzky.

200 Adaline W. Fuller (b. 1888). Papers, 1919-20. 1 folder. American Relief Administration worker in Poland, 1919-20. Correspondence and memoranda relating to the work of the American Relief Administration in France, Belgium, Poland, and Russia. Includes letters from Clemens Pirquet and George B. Baker.

201 Benjamin Apthorp Gould Fuller (b. 1879). Papers, 1918-19. 4 ms. boxes, 2 envelopes. Captain, U.S. army; member, American Section, Supreme War Council of the Allied and Associated Powers, during World War I. Memoranda, daily bulletins, and photographs relating to military developments, especially on the Italian front, and to political conditions in Europe and Russia. Preliminary inventory.

202 Margarete Gaertner. Writings, n.d. Typescript, 1 folder. Relates to the interwar dispute between Germany and Lithuania over Memel, East Germany under Soviet occupation after World War II, and the Berlin blockade of 1948-49. Preliminary inventory.

203 Adam J. Galinski (1894-1973). Papers, in English and Polish, 1945-71. 4 ms. boxes. Polish resistance leader during World War II; German prisoner, 1944; Soviet forced labor camp prisoner, 1956. Correspondence, reports, personal documents, writings, photographs, and printed matter relating to conditions in Soviet forced labor camps, and to twentieth century Polish history and culture.

204 John A. T. Galvin. Collector. Reproductions of paintings, n.d. 1 envelope. Depicts scenes from the Franco-Prussian War, the Boxer Rebellion, and the Russo-Japanese War, including the battle of Tsushima Straits. Also includes miscellaneous scenes, mainly of Japan.

205 Peter A. Garvi (1881-1944). Writings, in Russian, n.d. Typescript, .5 ms. box. Russian socialist. "Vospominaniia Sotsialdemokrata" (Memoirs of a Social-Democrat), relating to the Russian Social-Democratic Workers Party, 1906-17; "Professional'nye Soiuzy Rossii v Pervye Gody Revoliutsii" (Trade Unions of Russia in the First Years of the Revolution); and "Rabochaia Kooperatsiia v Pervye Gody Russkoi Revoliutsii, 1917-1921" (Workers Cooperatives in the First Years of the Russian Revolution, 1917-1921). The memoirs have been published.

206 Olga Hess Gankin. History, 1940. Typescript and holograph, 2 ms. boxes. Research associate, Hoover Institution on War, Revolution and Peace. Drafts and notes for her book, The Bolsheviks and the World Wars: The Origin of the Third International. Relates to Russian political events and the Russian Army during World War I, Bulgarian political events during World War I, and the Communist International.

207 C.A. Gaskill. Diary, 1920. Typescript, 1 folder. Colonel, U.S. Army; American Relief Administration worker and technical adviser to Poland, 1919-21. Relates to conditions in the Ukraine during the Russian Civil War, 1-16 June 1920.

208 Milan Gavrilović (1882-1976). Papers, in Serbo-Croatian and English, 1939-76. 55 ms. boxes. Yugoslav journalist, politician and diplomat; ambassador to the Soviet Union, 1940-41; member, Yugoslav government in exile, London, 1941-43. Correspondence, speeches, and writings, office files, and printed matter relating to Yugoslavian politics and government, Yugoslavia during World War II, the Yugoslav government in exile, Draza Mihailović and the Chetnik resistance movement in occupied Yugoslavia, relations between the Kingdom of Yugoslavia and the Soviet Union, and the activities of Serbian émigré groups following World War II. Preliminary inventory. Closed until 21 August 1995.

209 E. Genkin. Translation of report, 1924. "A Few Words about Mongolia." Typescript, 1 folder. Relates to the development of the communist movement in Mongolia. Original report published in Tretii S'ezd Mongolskoi Narodnoi Partii (Third Congress of the Mongolian People's Party), 1924.

210 Genoa. Economic and Financial Conference, 1922. Records, in English, French, and Italian, 1922. 2 ms. boxes. Minutes of meetings, agenda, committee reports, draft proposals, a roster of delegates, and telegrams sent and received by the Italian delegation relating to European economic reconstruction and to European economic relations with Russia.

211 M. Georgievich. Study, in Russian, n.d. "Vstriechnyi Boi Divizii i Korpusa" (Encounters of Battle Divisions and Corps). Typescript, 1 folder. Relates to Russian military organization during World War I.

212 Georgii Mikhailovich, Grand Duke of Russia (d. 1919). Letters, in Russian, 1914-18, to his daughter, Princess Kseniia. Holograph, 2 ms. boxes. Russian aristocrat; special military representative of Tsar Nicholas II during World War I. Relates to political and military conditions in Russia during World War I, the Russian Revolution, and family affairs. Register.

213 German Army, World War I. Photographs, ca. 1914-18. 3 envelopes. Depicts German troops, battlefields, and war equipment, in France, Belgium, and Russia during World War I.

214 [German Prisoners of War in Russia]. Memoir, 1946. Typescript, photocopy, 1 vol. Authored by an unidentified German prisoner of war. Relates to conditions of imprisonment of German prisoners of war in Russia during World War II.

215 German refugee reports, 1948. Typescript, 1 folder. In German. Relates to social and economic conditions in Silesia and East Prussia under Polish and Soviet rule. Written by refugees from Silesia and East Prussia.

216 Germany. Oberste Heeresleitung. Records, in German, 1914-18. 2 ms. boxes. Intelligence and other reports, leaflets, radio news scripts, clippings, and press releases relating to political conditions in Russia and the Netherlands, Allied and Bolshevik propaganda, German propaganda, and military positions at the front during World War I.

217 Germany. Reichsfuehrer SS, und Chef der Deutschen Polizei. SS, und Polizeifuehrer im Distrikt Galizien. Report, in German, 1943. Typescript, photocopy, 1 vol. "Loesung der Judenfrage in Galizien" (Solution of the Jewish Question in Galicia).

218 Germany. Reichskommissar beim Prisenhof Hamburg. Extracts from records, in German and Latvian, 1939-44. Transcripts, typewritten, 1 folder. Prepared by Heinz von Bassi from originals at the German Military Archives, Freiburg/Br. Prize Court of the German Admiralty. Relates to the seizure of Baltic ships on high seas during World War II, and to indemnification questions.

219 (Aleksandr Alekseevich von) Gerngros. Photograph, 1901. 1 envelope. Depicts General A. A. von Gerngros, chief of Russian Railway Guards, Chinese Eastern Railway.

220 Gesamtverband Deutscher Antikommunistischer Vereinigungen. Records, in German, 1935-44. 172 ms. boxes, 3 pamphlet boxes, 1 ft. Anticommunist propaganda agency of the German government. Writings, reports, and clippings relating to the international communist movement and to the Jewish question. Covers the Comintern, Soviet domestic affairs and foreign relations, the Red Army, the Soviet secret police, show trials, espionage and sabotage, and the Baltic nations. Preliminary inventory.

221 B. Gessen. Memorandum, in Russian, n.d. Typescript, 1 folder. "Transportnyia Sredstva i Transportirovanie" (Means of Transport and Transportation). Relates to transportation systems in Russia during the Russian Civil War.

222 Iosif Vladimirovich Gessen (1866-1943). Papers, in Russian and English, 1919-20. 4 ms. boxes. Russian journalist and Constitutional Democratic Party leader. Reports, letters, and leaflets relating to the White Army in the Russian Civil War. Includes 2 translations of I. V. Gessen's memoirs, V Dvukh Vekakh (In Two Centuries), one entitled "Reminiscences," translated from the Russian by E. Varneck, and a second entitled "Legality versus Autocracy," edited and annotated by Ladis K. D. Kristof. Preliminary inventory.

223 Hugh Simons Gibson (1883-1954). Papers, 1903-54. 81 ms. boxes, 11 cu. ft. boxes, 12 ft. American diplomat; ambassador to Poland, 1919-24; ambassador to Switzerland, 1924-27; ambassador to Belgium, 1927-33 and 1937-38; ambassador to Brazil, 1933-37. Diaries, writings, correspondence, reports, minutes of meetings, and printed matter relating to U.S. foreign relations, international disarmament negotiations, the League of Nations, and relief work in Europe during World Wars I and II. Preliminary inventory.

224 Mikhail Nikolaevich de Giers (1856-1924). Papers, in Russian, 1917-26. 53 ms. boxes. White Russian diplomat; chief diplomatic representative of Baron Vrangel' to the Allied Powers, 1920. Correspondence, reports, telegrams, and memoranda relating to the Russian Civil War, the Paris Peace Conference, and White Russian diplomatic relations. Includes dispatches from White Russian diplomats in various countries. References: Generals N. Iudenich, A. I. Denikin, and P. N. Vrangel', Zemgor (Union of Russian Zemstva and Towns), Russian Red Cross, Omsk government, and various White Army units. (NUCMC 68-426)

225 Horace N. Gilbert. Report, 1931. "The Russian Industrialization Program." Typescript, 1 folder. American visitor to Russia.

226 Benjamin Gitlow (1891-1965). Papers, 1918-60. 17 ms. boxes. American Communist leader; later anti-Communist writer. Writings, correspondence, minutes of meetings, clippings, and printed matter relating to communism and socialism in the U.S. and Europe. Preliminary inventory.

227 Vladimir F. Gniessen. Memoirs, n.d. "Through War and Revolution: Memoirs of a Russian Engineer." Typescript, 1 ms. box. Engineer and colonel, Russian Imperial Army. Relates to Russian military activities during World War I, and White Russian military activities, especially in Turkestan, during the Russian Civil War.

228 Gold mines and mining - Russia. Collection, in English and Russian, n.d. 1 folder. Studies, maps, and mine records relating to the gold mining industry in the Russian Far East, Transbaikalia, and Outer Mongolia.

229 Frank Alfred Golder (1877-1929). Papers, in English and Russian, 1812-1930. 40 ms. boxes, 1 envelope. American historian; American Relief Administration worker in Russia. Correspondence, diaries, memoranda, articles, pamphlets, and photographs relating to Russian history in the late nineteenth and early twentieth centuries, the Russian American Company in Alaska, the Russian Revolution, and American Relief Administration work in Russia. Preliminary inventory (NUCMC 68-660).

230 Sergei Alexandrovich Golovan. Papers, in Russian, 1918-21. 6 ms. boxes. White Russian military attaché to Switzerland. Correspondence, military orders, communiqués, and clippings relating to the Russian Civil War, and White Russian military relations with Switzerland. Preliminary inventory (NUCMC 71-1099).

231 Nikolai N. Golovin (1875-1935). Papers, in Russian, 1912-43. 16 ms. boxes. General, Imperial Russian Army. Correspondence, speeches, writings, and printed matter relating to Russian military activities during World War I, and to the Russian Civil War. Register (NUCMC 68-662).

232 Golubev. History, in Russian, 1926. Typescript, 1 vol. Relates to White Russian military activities in Mongolia during the Russian Civil War, and particularly to Baron Roman Ungern-Shternberg.

233 Julián Gómez Gorkin (b. 1901). Translation of play, in French, n.d. Typescript, 1 folder. "Douze Fantômes Revivent leur Histoire" (Twelve Phantoms Relive Their History). Relates to conditions in tsarist Russia during the early twentieth century.

234 Millard Preston Goodfellow (1892-1973). Papers, 1942-67. 5 ms. boxes, 2 envelopes. Colonel, U.S. army; deputy director, Office of Strategic Services, 1942-46; political adviser to the U.S. commanding general in Korea, 1946. Correspondence, reports, printed matter, and phonotapes relating to Office of Strategic Services operations in North Africa and the Far East during World War II, and to postwar reconstruction in Korea. Includes correspondence of Ilia and Beatrice Tolstoy, 1942-43. Register.

235 Allan Erwin Goodman (b. 1944). Papers, 1947-75. 126 ms. boxes, 2 card file boxes, 3 binders, 16 notebooks, and 7 envelopes. Consultant on Vietnamese affairs, U.S. Department of State and Rand Corporation, 1967-71. Writings, reports, correspondence, clippings, notes, interviews, and printed matter relating to the Vietnamese war, the Paris peace talks of 1968-73, elections in South Vietnam from 1967-71, the South Vietnamese legislature, migration to Saigon, urbanization and political and demographic change in Southeast Asia, counterinsurgency, and Soviet-U.S. detente. Register. Users must sign a statement agreeing not to identify any persons mentioned in unpublished material in the collection (deceased U.S. citizens may be identified after 2 January 1980). Also 2.5 ms. boxes and 12 notebooks are closed until 2005.

236 (Ivan Logginovich) Goremykin. Photograph, n.d. 1 envelope. Depicts I. L. Goremykin, prime minister of Russia, 1914-16.

237 (Maksim) Gorkii (1868-1936). Collection, in Russian and English, 1921. 1 folder. Russian novelist. Appeal, handwritten in Russian, by M. Gorkii, 1921, relating to the need for foreign relief to aid Russian intellectuals; and 4 essays (typewritten) by Soviet scholars relating to the literary, political, and humanitarian ideas of M. Gorkii.

238 Willard L. Gorton (b. 1881). Papers, 1927-32. 2 ms. boxes. American civil engineer; consultant to the Soviet government in Turkestan, 1930-32. Correspondence, reports, clippings, and photographs relating to reclamation and irrigation projects in Turkestan. Preliminary inventory (NUCMC 68-663).

239 Malbone Watson Graham (1898-1965). Papers, 1914-56. 15.5 ms. boxes. American political scientist. Pamphlets, bulletins, writings, memoranda, and clippings relating to the League of Nations, and to political conditions and diplomatic relations in Finland, the Baltic States, the USSR, and Eastern Europe from the Russian Revolution to World War II. Preliminary inventory (NUCMC 71-138).

240 Aleksandr Aleksandrovich Gramotin. Report, in Russian, 1919. Holograph, photocopy, 1 folder. Captain, Imperial Russian Army. Relates to activities of the Russian Imperial family during the Russian Revolution.

241 Donald Grant (b. 1889). Writings, 1920-35. 1 folder. British author and lecturer; director, European Student Relief, 1920-25. Notes, diary entries, letter extracts, and a pamphlet relating to social conditions and relief work in Russia and Eastern and Central Europe, 1920-22, and to the economic and social policy of the socialist municipal government in Vienna, 1919-34.

242 William Sidney Graves (1865-1940). Papers, 1914-32. 3 ms. boxes. Major general, U.S. Army; commanding general, American Expeditionary Force in Siberia, 1918-20. Correspondence, reports, monographs, and photographs relating to the Allied intervention in Siberia, 1918-19. Preliminary inventory (NUCMC 71-139).

243 Walter A. Grayson. Papers, 1918-20. .5 ms. box, 3 envelopes. First lieutenant, U.S. Army; served with American Expeditionary Force in Siberia, 1918-20. Military intelligence studies, photographs, clippings, and memorabilia relating to activities of the U.S. 27th Infantry Division in Siberia, 1918-20.

244 Thomas T. C. Gregory (1878-1933). Papers, 1918-32. 3 ms. boxes, 1 album, 2 envelopes. American lawyer; American Relief Administration director for Central Europe, 1919. Correspondence, reports, memoranda, and printed matter relating to the work of the American Relief Administration in Central Europe and Russia, the fall of the 1919 Bela Kun Communist regime in Hungary, and the 1928 presidential campaign of Herbert Hoover. Register (NUCMC 75-633).

245 Joseph Coy Green (b. 1887). Papers, 1914-57. 21 ms. boxes, 2 envelopes. American diplomat; chief of inspection, Commission for Relief in Belgium, 1915-1917, director for Romania and the Near East, American Relief Administration, 1918-19. Diary, correspondence, writings, reports, pamphlets, clippings, maps, and printed matter relating to the Commission for Relief in Belgium, American Relief Administration activities in Romania and Transcaucasia, and the Herbert Hoover presidential campaign in 1920. Register (NUCMC 68-664)

246 (N. I.) Grigorovich. Photograph, n.d. 1 envelope. Depicts N. I. Grigorovich.

247 David Davidovich Grimm (b. 1864). Papers, in Russian, 1919-34. 4 ms. boxes. Russian educator; rector, Petersburg University, 1899-1910; assistant minister of education, Russian Provisional Government, 1917. Correspondence, memoranda, press reports, printed and other material relating to the Russian émigré community in Finland and other parts of Europe, and to the Russian Civil War. Register.

248 Pavel Pavlovich Gronskii (1883-1937). Study, n.d. "The Effects of the War upon the Central Government Institutions of Russia." Typescript, carbon copy, 1 vol. Relates to the political structure of Russia during World War I and the period of the 1917 Provisional Government.

249 Kazimierz Grzybowski. Study, n.d. "Soviet Public International Law Doctrines and Diplomatic Practice." Typescript, mimeographed, 2 ms. boxes.

250 P. D. Gubarev. Report, in Russian, 1919. Typescript, 1 folder. "Vremennoe Polozhenie ob Upravlenii Terskim Voiskom" (Temporary Situation of the Command of the Tersk Forces). Chairman, Main Circle, Tersk Forces. Relates to the Russian Civil War in the Tersk area.

251 (Aleksandr Ivanovich) Guchkov. Photographs, n.d. 1 envelope. Depicts the Russian politician A. I. Guchkov.

252 George C. Guins (b. 1887). Papers, in Russian, 1918-21. 1 ms. box, 1 envelope. Russian educator; White Russian political leader during the Russian Civil War. Correspondence, writings, reports, and declarations relating to the Russian Revolution and Civil War in the Siberian Far East, the activities of the anti-Bolshevik forces in Siberia, and the Japanese intervention.

253 Ivan Emel'ianovich Gulyga (b. 1857). Memoirs, in Russian, 1923. Holograph, 1 vol. "Vospominaniia Starago Plastuna o Velikoi Voinie, 1914-1917" (Reminiscences of an Old Scout

about the Great War, 1914-1917). Imperial Russian Army officer; commanding officer, Kubansko-Terskii Plastanskii Korpus, during World War I. Includes a biography, typewritten in Russian, of I. E. Gulyga by Karaushin.

254 Vladimir Iosifovich Gurko (1862-1927). History, in Russian, n.d. Typescript, 1 ms. box. Cherty i Siluety proshlago: Pravitel'stvo i Obshchestvennost' v Tsarstvovanie Nikolaia II (Features and Figures of the Past: Government and Opinion in the Reign of Nicholas II). Imperial Russian government official. Translation published (Stanford, 1939). Russian manuscript includes 2 chapters omitted from published translation.

255 Ketty Guttmann. Memorandum, in German, n.d. Typescript, 1 folder. "Los von Moskau! Erlebnisse einer Kommunistin" (Free of Moscow! Experiences of a Communist). German communist. Relates to the disillusionment of K. Guttmann with Soviet rule in Russia.

256 Hague International Peace Conference. Photographs, 1899-1907. 2 framed photographs. Depicts delegates to the first and second Hague Peace Conferences, 1899 and 1907. Includes an identification chart for the second photograph.

257 Andrew A. Halacsy. Memoirs, n.d. Typescript, photocopy, 1 vol. Hungarian prisoner in Russia during World War II. Relates to conditions in Soviet forced labor camps.

258 Stephen P. Halbrook. Study, 1973. Typescript, .5 ms. box. "Anarchism and Marxism in the Twentieth Century Revolution." Relates to the influence of anarchist and Marxist theories on the Russian and Chinese revolutions, and on revolutionary movements throughout the world.

259 Charles L. Hall. Papers, 1922-23. 1 folder, 1 envelope. Major, U.S. Army; American Relief Administration worker in Russia. Photographs and memorabilia relating to famine conditions and American Relief Administration work in Orenburg and Samara, Russia.

260 Maxwell McGaughey Hamilton (1896-1957). Papers, 1916-57. 4 ms. boxes. American diplomat; chief, Division of Far Eastern Affairs, U.S. Department of State, 1937-43; ambassador to Finland, 1945-47. Reports, memoranda, correspondence, lectures, press releases, and printed matter relating to U.S. foreign policy toward China, Japan, the Soviet Union, and Finland. Includes a report and series of interviews with Japanese, Chinese, and other government officials concerning economic and political conditions in Japan and Manchuria, 1933-34. Register (NUCMC 71-140).

261 Minard Hamilton (1891-1976). Papers, 1913-30. 1 ms. box. Captain, U.S. Army; executive officer, American Relief Administration operations in the Baltic States, 1919. Diary and correspondence relating to activities of the 313th Machine Gun Battalion in France during World War I, food distribution by the American Relief Administration in the Baltic States, and civil aviation in China, 1929-30.

262 W. P. Hammon (1854-1938). Papers, 1915-30. 3 ms. boxes. American businessman; associated with Yuba Manufacturing Company, San Francisco. Correspondence, reports, contracts, shipping lists, specifications for dredging equipment, annotated maps, and photographs relating to mining operations in China, Siberia, Korea, Malaya, and Poland. Preliminary inventory (NUCMC 75-635).

263 Lansing V. Hammond. Collector. World War II, 1900-45. 2 file boxes, 1 ft. Photographs and drawings depicting British, Russian, Japanese, German, American, and other ships and airplanes from World War II. Includes a section of photographs illustrating the history of aviation.

264 Ernest Lloyd Harris (1870-1946). Papers, 1918-21. 6 ms. boxes. American consular official; consul general, Irkutsk, Siberia, 1918-21. Reports, memoranda, and correspondence relating to the Russian Civil War in Siberia, the Czechoslovakian Legion, political and economic conditions in Siberia, and U.S. policy in Siberia. Register.

265 Gladys Harris. Collector. Photographs, 1919. 1 envelope. Depicts the headquarters of the American Expeditionary Forces in Siberia, and officers of the Japanese and Czechoslovak forces in Vladivostok.

266 Graf Dimitri F. Heiden. Memoirs, in Russian, n.d. Typescript and holograph, .5 ms. box. Russian aristocrat. Relates to the involvement of Russia in World War I and the Russian Revolution and Civil War; also reminiscences about Dostoevskii, Solov'ev, and Tolstoi. Register.

267 Alexander Helphand (1867-1924). Receipt, in German, 1915. Holograph, photocopy, 1 folder. Russian-German Socialist. Receipt for funds from the German government for furtherance of revolutionary activities in Russia.

268 Loy Wesley Henderson (b. 1892). Memoirs, n.d. Typescript, photocopy, 3 ms. boxes. American diplomat; secretary of embassy to the Soviet Union, 1934-38; assistant chief, Division of European Affairs, U.S. Department of State, 1938-42; director, Near Eastern and African Affairs, U.S. Department of State, 1945-48; and ambassador to India, 1948-51. Relates to American Red Cross Relief work in Russia and the Baltic States, 1919-20, and in Germany, 1920-21, and to U.S. foreign policy and U.S. relations with Ireland and the Soviet Union between the two world wars. Closed during the lifetime of L. W. Henderson.

269 Alexandre Heroys. Memorandum, in French, 1918. Typescript, 1 folder. "Situation Politique et Stratégique sur le Front Roumain et en Russie en 1917 et 1918" (Political and Strategic Situation on the Romanian Front and in Russia in 1917 and 1918). Relates to Russo-Romanian military activities during World War I and to the Russian Revolution.

270 Boris Vladimirovich Heroys. Papers, in Russian, 1917-20. 8 ms. boxes. General, Imperial Russian Army; chief, Special Military Mission to London sent by General Nikolai Iudenich, White Russian military commander, during the Russian Civil War. Correspondence, reports, communiqués, and printed matter relating to the Russian Revolution, anti-Bolshevik activities in Northwest Russia, 1919-20, and liaison between the White Russian forces and the British War Office. Preliminary inventory (NUCMC 68-658).

271 Noe Herrera. Collector. Miscellany, n.d. 2 albums. Photographs and magazine illustrations depicting V. I. Lenin and Iosif Stalin.

272 George Davis Herron (1862-1925). Papers, 1916-27. 26.5 ms. boxes, 16 vols., 4 scrapbooks. American clergyman and lecturer; unofficial adviser to Woodrow Wilson, president of the U.S. Correspondence, interviews, lectures, essays, notes, and clippings relating to the League of Nations, territorial questions, prisoners of war, and other political and economic issues at the Paris Peace Conference. 1 vol., bound, concerns the Russian Revolution and Civil War, aid to Russian POWs in Switzerland, and U.S. support for anti-Bolshevik forces. Also, correspondence, 12 letters, February-September 1919, between Herron and General P. N. Wrangel. Preliminary inventory (NUCMC 68-667).

273 Joseph John Hertmanowicz. Papers, 1916-41. .5 ms. box. Official, Lithuanian Council of Chicago. Writings and speeches, memoranda, and resolutions relating to the history, economy, and foreign policy of Lithuania and to the movement for Lithuanian independence. Includes appeals from Lithuanian-American organizations to the U.S. government urging recognition of the independence of Lithuania. Preliminary inventory.

274 George Alexander Hill (b. 1892). Papers, n.d. 1 folder. British Secret Service agent. Memoirs, typewritten, entitled "Reminiscences of Four Years with N. K. V. D.," relating to Anglo-Soviet secret service relations during World War II; and radio broadcast transcripts, entitled "Go Spy the Land," relating to British intelligence activities in Russia, Turkey, and the Balkans, 1917-18. May not be quoted without permission of G. A. Hill.

275 Sidney Hillman (1887-1946). Letter, 1923, to Mrs. M. S. Alderton. Typescript, 1 folder. American labor leader; president, Russian-American Industrial Corporation. Solicits stock purchases in the Russian-American Industrial Corporation, a company investing in Soviet industrialization.

276 Serge E. Hitoon. Memoir, 1936. Typescript, 1 vol. "From Aral Sea to the Western Turkestan." White Russian Army officer. Relates to the Russian Civil War in Mongolia.

277 Frank Harvey Holden. Miscellaneous papers, 1916-23. 1 folder, 1 envelope. American Relief Administration worker in France and Russia, 1919-23. Letter written by F. H. Holden in Moscow in 1923, relating to Russian operations of the American Relief Administration; and photographs of the German cruiser Wolf, its crew, and ships encountered and sunk by it during its raiding cruise in World War I, 1916-17.

278 Victor Chi-tsai Hoo (1894-1972). Papers, in English and French, 1930-72. 7.5 ms. boxes. Chinese diplomat, minister to Switzerland, 1932-42; vice minister of Foreign Affairs, 1942-45; United Nations assistant secretary-general, 1946-72. Diaries, correspondence, clippings, reports, memoranda, and photographs relating to Chinese political events and foreign relations, international diplomatic conferences, Sino-Soviet relations, and the United Nations.

279 Herbert Clark Hoover (1874-1964). Papers, 1897-1969. 306 ms. boxes, 90 envelopes, 1 album, 1 microfilm reel, 18 motion pictures, 31 phonotapes, 10 phonorecords. President of the U.S., 1929-33. Appointment calendars, correspondence, office files, speeches and writings, analyses of newspaper editorials, printed matter, photographs, motion pictures, sound recordings, and other material relating to the administration of relief during and after the two world wars, Hoover's relationship with Woodrow Wilson, U.S. politics and government, and the philosophy and public service contributions of Herbert Hoover. Includes photocopies of selected files from his presidential and Commerce Department papers that are located at the Herbert Hoover Presidential Library, West Branch, Iowa. Register.

280 Hoover Institution on War, Revolution and Peace. Russian Provisional Government Project. Translations of documents, 1955-60. 10 ms. boxes. Project for publication of a documentary history of the Russian Provisional Government of 1917. Results published as Robert Browder and Alexander Kerensky, eds., The Russian Provisional Government, 1917 (Stanford: Stanford University Press, 1961).

281 Hoover Institution on War, Revolution and Peace. Soviet Treaty Series Project. Records, 1957-59. 12 cu. ft. boxes, 2 file drawers, 1 ft. Correspondence, memoranda, notes, bibliographies, and translations of published

material used in the preparation of A Calendar of Soviet Treaties, 1917-1957, by Robert M. Slusser and Jan F. Triska (Stanford University Press, 1959; Hoover Institution Document Series #4).

282 Hoover Institution on War, Revolution and Peace. Supreme Economic Council and American Relief Administration Documents Project. Records, 1930-37. 21 ms. boxes, 45 vols. Project for compilation of selected Supreme Economic Council and American Relief Administration documents. Typed copies of minutes of meetings, reports, correspondence, press releases, and clippings relating to economic policies of the Supreme Economic Council and its predecessor, the Supreme Council of Supply and Relief, and to relief activities of the American Relief Administration in Europe and Russia. Preliminary inventory.

283 Harry L. Hoskin (b. 1887). Papers, 1917-73. .5 ms. box, 7 envelopes. American officer, Russian Railway Service Corps, 1917-20. Correspondence, clippings, reports, affidavits, court proceedings, and photographs relating to activities of the Russian Railway Service Corps in Siberia, and to subsequent legal disputes regarding the military or civilian status of members of the corps.

284 Emmett A. Hoskins. Memoirs, 1970. Typescript, 1 folder. "In the Service of the United States Navy, May 26, 1917-August 6, 1919." Sailor, U.S. navy. Relates to American naval operations in the Far East and Siberia.

285 Hungary, history, 1918-45. Photographs, 1942. 1 folder. Depicts Hungarian troops on the Russian front during World War II.

286 Hungary. Kueluegyminisztērium. Miscellaneous records, in Hungarian, 1915-22. .5 ms. box. Hungarian Foreign Ministry. Reports, memoranda, and orders relating to Austro-Hungarian military activities during World War I, domestic opposition to the war, socialist activities, Bolshevik propaganda, problems of minority nationalities during and after the war, postwar land reform, and the formation of soviets in Hungary. Preliminary inventory.

287 Hungary under Soviet rule. Studies, in Hungarian and English, 1958. Typescript, mimeographed, 1 folder. Relates to Soviet influence in Hungary, forced labor camps in Hungary, and Hungarian minorities in other Communist countries. Written by various Hungarian anticommunist ēmigrē organizations in the U.S.

288 Jay Calvin Huston. Papers, in English and Russian, 1917-31. 14 ms. boxes, 2 envelopes. American consular official in China, 1917-32. Writings, pamphlets, leaflets, and clippings relating to cultural, political, and economic conditions in China, and to communism and Soviet influence in China. Includes documents seized from the Soviet consulate in Canton, December 1927, and the diary and papers of the vice-consul M. Hassis. Preliminary inventory (NUCMC 71-146).

289 Lincoln Hutchinson. Papers, 1923-35. 2 ms. boxes. American Relief Administration worker. Correspondence, writings, and reports relating to American Relief Administration activities, food conditions in Germany following World War I, and technical assistance provided by American engineers in the Soviet Union.

290 Iakov Arkad'evich Iakovlev (b. 1896). Translation of a pamphlet, 1923. Typescript, mimeograph, 1 vol. Derevnia Kak Ona Est' (The Village as It Is). Relates to social, economic, political, and cultural conditions in Russian villages in 1923. Also includes an article by P. Aksenov, entitled "How the Village Lives" (published in Pravda, 1923).

291 A. Iaremenko. Translation of extracts from a memoir, n.d. Typescript, 1 vol. "Diary of a Communist." Russian communist. Relates to the Russian Civil War in Siberia, 1918-20. Translation of "Dnievnik Kommunista," published in Revoliutsiia na Dalnem Vostoke (Revolution in the Far East) (Moscow, 1923).

292 Izvestiia Revoliutsionnoi Nedeli (News of the Revolutionary Week). Extracts from newspaper articles, in Russian, 1917. Typescript, 1 folder. Petrograd newspaper. Relates to the February 1917 Revolution in Petrograd. Includes texts of Russian government decrees, and appeals and resolutions of Russian political groups.

293 John L. Iliff. Collector. Slides, 1936. 1 ms. box. Depicts the Caucasus region and the reconstruction of Moscow. Used in a Russian 7th grade class.

294 I. S. Ilin. Collector. Newspaper clippings, in Russian, 1931-32. 1 oversize package, .5 ft. Relates to Japanese military activity in Manchuria. From Russian-language newspapers in China.

295 "Importance de la Georgie en tant que Voie de Transit" (The Importance of Georgia as a Route). Study, in French, n.d. Typescript, mimeographed, 1 folder. Relates to the commercial geography of Georgia.

296 Harold Adams Innis (b. 1894). Memoir, 1946. Typescript, 1 vol. "Ottawa to Moscow." Canadian delegate to the 220th anniversary celebration of the founding of the Akademiia Nauk SSSR, Moscow, 1946. Relates to the visit of Western scholars to the celebration.

297 Institute of Pacific Relations. American Council. Records, 1925-60. 21 ms. boxes, 1 album, 1 envelope. Correspondence, reports, memoranda, study papers, press releases, printed

matter, and photographs relating to the study of political, social, and economic conditions in the Far East, and of U.S. foreign policy in the Far East by the American Council of the Institute of Pacific Relations. From the papers of Ray Lyman Wilbur, president of the American Council of the Institute of Pacific Relations. Register (NUCMC 75-637).

298 Institute of Pacific Relations. San Francisco Bay Region Division. Records, 1944-47. 26 ms. boxes, 1 card file, .16 ft. Private organization for the study of the Far East and of U.S. foreign policy in the Far East. Correspondence, reports, memoranda, studies, and printed matter relating to the study of political, social, and economic conditions in the Far East and of U.S. foreign policy in the Far East. Register (NUCMC 72-1467).

299 Vladimir Nikolaevich Ipatieff (1867-1952). Photographs, 1870-1939. 1 envelope. Depicts the site of the execution of the Imperial Russian family in 1918; and V. N. Ipatieff, relatives and friends.

300 Radu Irimescu. Papers, in Romanian, 1918-40. 5 ms. boxes, 5 albums, 11 envelopes. Romanian diplomat and politician; minister of air and navy, 1932-38; ambassador to the U.S., 1938-40. Correspondence, reports, dispatches, memoranda, clippings, and photographs relating to Romanian politics and foreign policy, and to the development of aviation in Romania. Includes correspondence with the Russian legation in Bucharest, 1935-36. Register.

301 Istoricheskaia Komissiia Markovskogo Artilleriiskogo Diviziona. History, in Russian, 1931. Typescript, mimeographed, 1 vol. "Istoriia Markovskoi Artilleriiskoi Brigady" (History of the Markovskii Artillery Brigade). White Russian military unit. Relates to activities of the Markovskii Artillery Brigade during the Russian Civil War. Edited by Colonel Zholondkovskii, Lieutenant Colonel Shcharinskii, and Captain Vinogradov.

302 Nikolai Nikolaevich Iudenich (1862-1933). Papers, in Russian, 1918-20. 21 ms. boxes. General, Russian Imperial Army; commander, Northwestern White Russian armed forces, 1918-20. Correspondence, memoranda, telegrams, reports, military documents, proclamations, maps, and printed matter relating to the campaigns of the Northwestern White Russian armed forces, communism in Russia, relations with the Allied Powers, and activities of White Russian representatives in Europe. Preliminary inventory (NUCMC 68-671).

303 N. L. Iunakov. Memoir, in Russian, 1927. Holograph, 1 vol. "Moi Posliednie Miesiatsy v Dieistvuiushchei Armii: Vospominaniia Byvshago Komanduiushchego Armiei, Oktiabr'-Dekabr' 1917 goda" (My Last Months in the Active Army: Reminiscences of a Former Army Commander, October-December 1917).

304 (Kniaz', Feliks Feliksovich) Iusupov. Photograph, n.d. 1 envelope. Depicts Prince F. F. Iusupov of Russia and his wife.

305 Vsevolod Nikanorovich Ivanov. Translation of extracts from study, n.d. Typescript, 1 folder. "Manchuria and Manchukuo, 1932: Observations and Prognoses." Relates to the Chinese Eastern Railway, 1898-1930. Translation by Elena Varneck, of excerpts from "Manchuria i Manchugo, 1932: Nabliudeniia i Prognozy."

306 "Iz Vozzvaniia k Karel'skomu Naseleniiu Kemskogo Uezda" (From the Appeal to the Karelian Populace of Kemsk Region). Appeal, in Russian, 1919. Typescript, 1 folder. Relates to the Russian Civil War. Written by a group of White Russian leaders.

307 John F. de Jacobs. Memoir, 1925. Typescript, 1 vol. "The American Relief Administration and My Crime." Interpreter for the American Relief Administration in Russia. Relates to the arrest of J. F. de Jacobs by Soviet authorities.

308 Konrad Jacun. Study, in Polish, n.d. Typescript and printed, 1 folder. "Antagonizm Azyi i Europy" (Antagonism between Asia and Europe). Relates to the Eurasian nature of Russian civilization.

309 Mieczyslaw Jalowiecki (b. 1886). Memoirs, in Polish, 1964. Typescript, 7.5 ms. boxes, 8 oversize boxes. Polish-Lithuanian agricultural expert, architect and engineer; chairman, Vilnius Agrarian Association. Relates to historical events in Russia and Lithuania before, during, and after the Russian Revolution and Civil War; Poles in Lithuania; and agricultural developments in Lithuania, 1881-1939. Includes watercolor drawings and sketches of scenes and manor houses in Lithuania and Poland.

310 Pierre Thiébaut Charles Maurice Janin (b. 1862). Extracts from a diary, in French, 1918-20. Typewritten transcript, 1 folder. General, French army; commander of Czechoslovak and other Allied forces in Siberia, 1918-20. Relates to Allied intervention in the Russian Civil War. Extracts published in Le Monde Slave, 1924-25.

311 Harry A. Jennison. Letter received, 1920. 1 folder. YMCA worker in Russia. Relates to conditions in Russia during the Russian Civil War. Written by a White Russian Army colonel.

312 Arnold E. Jenny (1895-1978). Papers, 1917-69. 4.5 ms. boxes, 2 envelopes. Young Men's Christian Association worker in Siberia, 1919-20, and in Germany, 1945-46. Correspondence, diary, reports, memoranda, and printed matter relating to relief work in Siberia during the Russian Revolution, and among displaced

persons in Germany at the end of World War II. Register (NUCMC 75-640).

313 Benjamin O. Johnson (b. 1878). Papers, 1917-23. Photocopy, 1 ms. box. American engineer; colonel, Russian Railway Service Corps, 1917-23; president pro tempore, Inter-Allied Technical Board, 1920-21. Correspondence, reports, memoranda, diplomatic dispatches, instructions, and printed matter relating to the Russian Railway Service Corps in Siberia, the Inter-Allied Technical Board, and the Trans-Siberian Railroad during World War I and the Russian Civil War. Preliminary inventory (NUCMC 75-641).

314 Lester J. Johnson. Collector. Miscellany, in Norwegian and German, 1940-47. 1 folder. Circulars, memoranda, proclamations, clippings, and miscellanea relating to regulation of the civilian population in German-occupied Norway during World War II, war damage insurance in Norway during World War II, and the postwar Soviet-Norwegian dispute over the establishment of military bases on Spitsbergen.

315 William H. Johnson. Papers, 1917-19. 1 folder, 2 envelopes. American soldier, assigned to 31st Infantry Regiment during World War I. Diary, correspondence, and photographs relating to activities of the 31st Infantry Regiment in Siberia.

316 Evelyn Trent Jones (1892-1970). Papers, 1925-69. 1 ms. box, 1 envelope. American journalist; wife of Manabendra Nath Roy, Indian communist leader. Correspondence, notes, pamphlets, clippings, and photographs relating to M. N. Roy and the communist movement in India.

317 Jefferson Jones. Collector. Miscellany, 1914-18. .5 ms. box, 4 envelopes. Photographs, drawings, posters, printed matter, and miscellanea relating to activities of the Japanese Army in China during World War I, especially to the siege of Tsingtao, 1914; to the Russo-Japanese War of 1904-1905; and to the palace of Kaiser Wilhelm II on the island of Corfu.

318 Francis Michael Juras (b. 1891). Papers, mainly in Lithuanian, 1912-77. Photocopy, .5 ms. box. Lithuanian-American Roman Catholic priest and author. Newspaper and magazine clippings, printed matter, writings, photographs, and memorabilia relating to the career of F. M. Juras and to cultural activities of Lithuanians in the United States.

319 Boris M. Kader. Collector. B. M. Kader collection on Peresylnaia Tiurma, in Russian, 1906. 1 folder. Articles, notes, and poems, written by the prisoners of Peresylnaia Tiurma in Petrograd for their secret magazine "Tiurma" (Prison). Includes description of the material by B. M. Kader, editor of "Tiurma." Preliminary inventory.

320 Jakob Kaiser. Speech transcript, in German, 1947. Typescript, mimeographed, 1 folder. Relates to cooperation between the occupation authorities in Berlin and in the Soviet zone of Germany. Delivered at a meeting of the Union der Ostzone und Berlin in Berlin, 12 July 1947.

321 Lieutenant Kapnist. Papers, in Russian, French, and Czech, 1919-20. 1 folder. White Russian Army officer. Orders, telegrams, and correspondence relating to the liaison work of Lieutenant Kapnist with General Pierre Janin, French army officer and commander of Czechoslovak and other Allied troops in Siberia during the Russian Civil War.

322 Vladimir Oskarovich Kappel'. Collection, in Russian, 1920. 1 folder. Orders, memoranda, and correspondence relating to the "Icy March" campaign of V. Kappel' (1881-1920), White Russian Army general, in Siberia during the Russian Civil War.

323 George F. Karcz (1917-1970). Papers, 1917-70. 37 ms. boxes, 4 card file boxes, .66 ft., 1 phonotape. American agricultural economist; professor, University of California, Santa Barbara. Correspondence, writings, research notes, statistical surveys and reports, and miscellanea relating to Soviet and East European agriculture and economics. Register (NUCMC 75-642).

324 Jan Karski (b. 1914). Papers, in Polish, 1939-44. 7 ms. boxes, 24 envelopes, 27 microfilm reels. Liaison officer and courier of the Polish government in exile (London) to the Polish underground, 1939-43; author, Story of a Secret State (1944). Correspondence, memoranda, government and military documents, bulletins, reports, studies, speeches and writings, printed matter, photographs, clippings, newspapers, periodicals, and microfilms relating to events and conditions in Poland during World War II, the German and Soviet occupations of Poland, treatment of the Jews in Poland during the German occupation, and operations of the Polish underground movement during World War II. Preliminary inventory.

325 Bronis J. Kaslas (b. 1910). Papers, 1918-74. 4 ms. boxes. Lithuanian historian. Writings and rare printed matter relating to Eastern European politics, the Russian occupation of Lithuania, Lithuanians in foreign countries, the Baltic States, Poland, and the Paris Peace Conference of 1946. Preliminary inventory.

326 George Katkov (b. 1903). Study, ca. 1968. "Soviet Historical Sources in the Post Stalin Era." Typescript, photocopy, 1 folder. Relates to the history, organization, and operations of Soviet archival administration and publication policy since 1954.

327 Aleksandr Vasil'evich Kaul'bars (b. 1884). Study, in Russian, n.d. Typescript, 1 folder. "Vozdushnyia Voiska" (The Air Forces). Relates to Russian aerial operations during World War I.

328 Karl Johann Kautsky (1854-1938). Essay, in German, 1938. Typescript, photocopy, 1 folder. "Der Demokratische Marxismum: Zum Vierzigsten Geburtstag der Russischen Sozialdemokratie" (Democratic Marxism: On the Fortieth Anniversary of Russian Social Democracy). German socialist leader. Relates to the history and future prospects of socialism in Russia. Includes postcard photograph of K. J. Kautsky.

329 Eugene M. Kayden. Memorandum, 1918. Typescript, 1 folder. "A Memorandum on the Political Changes in Russia since the Revolution." Staff member, Bureau of Research, U.S. War Trade Board.

330 Josef Kayser. Papers, in German, 1943-45. 1 ms. box. German army chaplain; Russian prisoner of war during World War II. Reports, correspondence, a diary, and sermons relating to German prisoners of war in Russia and to the Working Council on Religious Questions of the National Committee for a Free Germany, an organization of anti-Nazi German Christians concerned with the reconstruction of Germany after World War II.

331 Harold Kellock (b. 1879). Letter, 1918, to Lincoln Steffens. Holograph, 1 vol. Publicity secretary, Finnish Information Bureau in the U.S. Relates to American relations with the revolutionary governments of Finland and Russia.

332 Aleksandr Fedorovich Kerenskii (1881-1970). Miscellaneous papers, in Russian and English, 1945-65. 1 ms. box. Premier, Russian Provisional Government, 1917. Correspondence and writings relating to the Russian Revolution and personal matters. Includes a history by Kerenskii, entitled "The Genesis of the 'October Revolution' of 1917," and correspondence with Vasilii Maklakov, Michael Karpovich, and Anatole G. Mazour. Preliminary inventory (NUCMC 72-1471).

333 Aleksandr Keskuela (1882-1963). Papers, in German, 1915-63. 2 ms. boxes. Estonian socialist; reputed intermediary between V. I. Lenin and the German government during World War I. Correspondence, writings, and memoranda relating to personal experiences and to international Socialist and Communist movements. Preliminary inventory (NUCMC 71-149).

334 Dmitrii Leonidovich Khorvat (b. 1858). Memoirs, n.d. Typescript, carbon copy, 1 vol. Lieutenant general, Imperial Russian Army. Relates to Imperial Russian administration of the Chinese Eastern Railway, and to White Russian military activities in the Far East during the Russian Civil War.

335 (Alan Goodrich) Kirk. Photograph, n.d. 1 envelope. Depicts Admiral A. G. Kirk, U.S. Navy.

336 George Kitchin (1892-1935). Memoirs, in Russian, n.d. Typescript, carbon copy, .5 ms. box. "Zakliuchennyi OGPU" (Prisoner of the OGPU). Russian concentration camp prisoner. Relates to conditions in Soviet concentration camps, 1928-32. Translation published as Prisoner of the OGPU (New York: Longmans, Green, 1935).

337 Kititsyn. Order, in Russian, 1920. Typescript, mimeographed, 1 folder. White Russian naval officer. Relates to White Russian naval activities at Vladivostok.

338 V. Klemm (b. 1861). Writings, in Russian and English, 1922-26. Holograph and typescript, 1 folder. White Russian political leader during the Russian Civil War. Autobiographical sketch, typewritten, 1926; a history, handwritten in Russian, entitled "Ocherk Revoliutsionnykh Sobytii v Russkoi Srednei Azii" (Sketch of the Revolution in Russian Central Asia), 1922; and a translation, typewritten, of the above.

339 N. N. Kniazev. Translation, n.d. Typescript, 1 vol. "The Legendary Baron (From Reminiscences about Lieutenant-General Baron Ungern)." Relates to Baron Roman Ungern-Shternberg, White Russian military leader in Mongolia during the Russian Revolution. Translation of "Legendarnyi Baron," published in Luch Azii, 1937.

340 Nicolai Koestner. Miscellaneous papers, in English and French, 1920-21. 1 folder. Estonian consul in New York City. Writings, press summaries, and memoranda relating to diplomatic recognition of Estonia by the U.S. and other countries, and to the admission of Estonia to the League of Nations.

341 Vladimir Nikolaevich Kokovtsov (1853-1942). Translation of memoirs, 1935. Typescript, 1 ms. box, 1 envelope. Out of My Past: The Memoirs of Count Kokovtsov. Russian statesman; minister of Finance, 1904-14; chairman of the Council of Ministers, 1911-14. Relates to Russian political conditions, 1904-17, and to the Russian Revolution. Translation published (Stanford: Stanford University Press, 1935). Edited by H. H. Fisher and translated by Laura Matveev. Includes photographs used to illustrate the book.

342 Aleksandr Vasil'evich Kolchak (1873-1920). Correspondence, 26 May-4 June 1919, with heads of government of the Allied and Associated Powers. Typescript, mimeographed, 1 vol. White Russian leader during the Russian Civil War. Relates to conditions for Allied support of the forces of Admiral Kolchak.

343 Mikhail Viktorovich Kolobov. Memoirs, in Russian, n.d. Typescript, carbon copy, 1 vol.

"Bor'ba s Bol'shevikami na Dal'nem Vostokie (Khorvat, Kolchak, Semenov, Merkulovy, Diterikhs): Vospominaniia Uchastnika" (Struggle with the Bolsheviks in the Far East: Reminiscences of a Participant). Relates to White Russian military activities in Siberia during the Russian Civil War.

344 Constantine Nikolaevich Kologrivov. Memorandum, 1917. Typescript, photocopy, 1 folder. Captain, Imperial Russian Army. Relates to Tsar Nicholas II's Personal Combined Infantry Regiment and 4th Imperial Family Rifle Guards Regiment. Memorandum addressed to Cornet Sergei Vladimirovich Markov of the Crimean Horse Regiment.

345 Paul Komor. Extracts from a letter received, 1951, from an unidentified White Russian émigré in Shanghai. Typescript, 1 folder. Relates to political and economic conditions in China.

346 Kommunisticheskaia Partiia Sovetskogo Soiuza Tsentral'nyi Komitet. Politicheskoe Biuro. Photograph, n.d. 1 envelope. Depicts members of the Political Bureau of the Central Committee of the Communist Party of the Soviet Union, including Andrei A. Andreev, Lavrentii P. Beriia, Lazar M. Kaganovich, Mikhail I. Kalinin, Nikita S. Khrushchev, Anastas I. Mikoian, Viacheslav M. Molotov, Nikolai M. Shvernik, Iosif Stalin, Kliment E. Voroshilov, and Andrei A. Zhdanov.

347 Kommunisticheskaia Partiia Sovetskogo Soiuza. Tsentral'nyi Komitet. Politicheskoe Biuro. Resolutions, in Russian and German, 27 January 1934-14 March 1936. Handwritten and typewritten transcripts, 1.5 ms. boxes. Politburo of the Communist Party of the Soviet Union. Includes some photocopies.

348 General Konokovich. Report, in Russian, n.d. Typescript, 1 folder. "Opisanie Boia 15 Iulia 1916 Goda pri Der. Trysten, Kol. Kurgan i Der. Voronchin" (An Account of the Battle of 15 July 1916, near Trysten Village, Kurgan Settlement and Voronchin Village). Major general, Imperial Russian Army.

349 "Konspiracja w Kraju pod Okupacja Sowiecka" (Conspiracy in the Country under Soviet Occupation). Report, in Polish, n.d. Typescript, 1 folder. Relates to resistance to Soviet occupation forces in Poland at the end of World War II.

350 Konstantin Nikolaevich, Grand Duke of Russia (1827-1892). Extracts from letters, in Russian, 1881-82, to State Secretary Aleksandr Golovnin. Typescript, 1 folder. Relates to his travels in Western Europe, and the political situation in Russia.

351 Konstitutsionno-Demokraticheskaia Partiia. Miscellaneous records, in Russian and French, 1920-24. 2 ms. boxes. Constitutional Democratic Party of Russia. Minutes of meetings, resolutions, reports, and correspondence relating to the Russian Revolution and to activities of the Konstitutsionno-Demokraticheskaia Partiia in exile. Preliminary inventory.

352 Lavr Georgivich Kornilov (1870-1918). Writings, in Russian and English, 1917. 1 folder. General and commander-in-chief, Russian army, 1917. Translation, typewritten, of a speech, and copy, typewritten in Russian, of an order, both relating to conditions of morale and discipline in the Russian army in 1917.

353 M. Korol'kov. Memoir, in Russian, 1928. Typescript, 1 vol. "Iz Vospominanii Voennago Iurista" (From the Reminiscences of a Military Lawyer). Relates to administration of military justice in the Imperial Russian Army, and to military discipline at the time of the Russo-Japanese War. Published in 1929 as Grimasy zhizny.

354 Eugénie A. Korvin-Kroukovsky. Diary, in Russian, 1917-18. Typescript, 1 folder. Relates to events in Petrograd during the Revolution of 1917, and to the escape of E. A. Korvin-Kroukovsky to the United States via the Far East, 1918.

355 Vladimir Andreevich Kosinskii (1866-1938). Study, in Russian, n.d. Typescript, 2 ms. boxes, 1 envelope. "Russkaia Agrarnaia Revoliutsiia" (Russian Agrarian Revolution). Professor of Political Science and Economics, Moscow University. Relates to agrarian reforms in Russia, 1905-17.

356 Ferenc Koszorus (1899-1974). Writings, mainly in Hungarian, 1954-70. Typescript, .5 ms. box. Colonel, Hungarian army. Relates to Hungarian, German, Soviet, and international military strategy during World Wars I and II. Includes a letter and notes from F. Koszorus to General Omar Bradley, 1953. Register.

357 Pavel Alekseevich Koussonskii. Papers, in Russian, 1918-26. 12 ms. boxes. Lieutenant general, White Russian Army; staff officer under Generals Denikin, Wrangel, and Miller, 1918-25. Correspondence, reports, telegrams, orders, circulars, proclamations, lists, maps, and charts relating to the general headquarters of the Volunteer Army of the Armed Forces in South Russia; to the Caucasian, Crimean, and other campaigns of the Civil War; to the evacuation and resettlement of General Wrangel's army; and to Russian émigré military and political life in Europe. Register (NUCMC 68-707).

358 Rose Kraft. Collector. Miscellany, ca. 1941-65. 3 envelopes, 1 box of slides. Photographs depicting military campaigns in the Pacific during World War II; color slides depicting scenic views in mainly European

countries; and programs of Russian theater and ballet performances. Preliminary inventory.

359 Kramatorsk Machine Tool Factory. Kramatorsk, Russia. Photographs, n.d., 1 envelope. Depicts the Kramatorsk Machine Tool Factory.

360 Petr Nikolaevich Krasnov (1869-1947). Letter, in Russian, 1937. Holograph, 1 folder. General, Imperial Russian Army; and White Russian leader in the Russian Civil War. Relates to personal matters.

361 Vitol'd Krassovskii. Memoirs, in Russian, 1927. Typescript, 1 folder. Imperial Russian Army officer. Relates to Russian military activities during World War I, and to White Russian military activities in southwestern Russia during the Russian Civil War.

362 Eduards Kraucs (b. 1898). Papers, in Latvian, 1945-77. .5 ms. box, 1 envelope, 474 filmstrips, 3 motion picture reels, 1 album. Latvian-American photographer and television cameraman. Autobiographical sketch, scrapbook, films, and photographs relating primarily to Latvian refugees in Germany and the U.S. Includes translations. Preliminary inventory.

363 Sergei Mikhailovich Kravchinskii (1852-1895). Papers, in Russian, 1892-1908. 1 ms. box. Russian socialist and novelist. Correspondence, writings, and extracts from printed matter relating to nineteenth century Russian revolutionary movements. Includes material relating to S. M. Kravchinskii and to the 1905 Revolution. 1 letter is in English. (NUCMC 71-150)

364 Boris Aleksandrovich Kriukov (b. 1898). Papers, in Russian, 1917-23. 4 ms. boxes, 9 envelopes. White Russian Army and marine corps officer. Memoranda, military, and naval intelligence reports, civil, naval, and military orders, correspondence, and photographs relating to the Russian Revolution and Civil War in the Siberian Far East, especially operations of the Amur Flotilla (Red) and the Siberian Flotilla (White). Includes protocols of the Vladivostok Zemsky Sobor, 1922. Register (NUCMC 75-646).

365 (Aleksandr Vasil'evich) Krivoshein. Photograph, n.d. 1 envelope. Depicts the White Russian political leader A. V. Krivoshein.

366 "Krizis Partii" (Party Crisis). History (in Russian), n.d. Typescript, 1 folder. Relates to the history and structure of the Communist Party of the Soviet Union, 1905-23.

367 Aleksandr Nikolaevich Krupenskii. Papers, in Russian, French, and Romanian, 1918-35. 9 ms. boxes. Marshal of Bessarabian nobility; president, Bessarabian provincial zemstvo; Bessarabian delegate to the Paris Peace Conference, 1919-20. Correspondence, memoranda, lists, extracts, summaries, reports, appeals, protests, protocols, press analyses, maps, forms, notes, drafts, clippings, newspaper issues, journals, bulletins, and pamphlets relating to the Bessarabian question, to relations between Russia, Romania, and Bessarabia, to the occupation and annexation of Bessarabia by Romania, 1918, and to the Paris Peace Conference. Register (NUCMC 72-1473). Consult Archivist for restrictions.

368 Krymskoe Kraevoe Pravitel'stvo. Miscellaneous records, in Russian, 1918-19. 2 ms. boxes. Crimean regional government. Files of the president of the Council of Ministers, minister of foreign affairs, minister of justice, and minister of internal affairs, relating to the relations of the Crimean regional government and the Constitutional Democratic Party with the Russian Volunteer Army and with the Allies. Persons involved: M. M. Vinaver, S. S. Krym, V. D. Nabokoff, N. N. Bogdanoff, General A. I. Denikin, and Admiral A. V. Kolchak.

369 Zdenek Krystufek. Study, in Czech, 1972. Typescript, .5 ms. box. "Sovetský Vzor Vlády V Ceskoslovensku" (Soviet Model of Rule in Czechoslovakia). Professor of Political Science, University of Colorado. Relates to Soviet rule in Czechoslovakia, 1946-1968.

370 Kornel Krzeczunowicz. Study, in Polish, n.d. Typescript, .5 ms. box. "Ostatnia Kampania Konna" (The Last Cavalry Campaign). Relates to Polish cavalry operations in the war against Russia, 1920.

371 Sylvester E. Kuhn. Papers, 1920-76. 1 folder. Private, U.S. Army; soldier in the 31st Infantry Regiment in Siberia, 1918-20. Correspondence, reminiscences, and photocopies of documents relating to the American Expeditionary Forces in Siberia during the Russian Revolution, and especially to the Posolskaia incident.

372 Boniface Semenovich Kutzevalov. Study, in Russian, n.d. Holograph, 1 folder. "Ubiistvo Generala Romanovskago" (The Assassination of General Romanovskii). Captain, Imperial Russian Army. Relates to the assassination of the White Russian military leader Ivan Pavlovich Romanovskii in the Russian Embassy in Istanbul, 1920.

373 Antoni Wincenty Kwiatkowski (1890-1970). Papers, mainly in Polish and Russian, 1917-69. 45 ms. boxes, 1 album, 4 envelopes. Polish scholar. Writings, correspondence, reports, memoranda, research and reference notes, clippings, and photographs relating to Marxism-Leninism, dialectical and historical materialism, communism and religion, and the Communist International. Includes an autobiography and biography. Register (NUCMC 72-1474).

374 Lager Altengrabow, Germany. Prison camp newspaper issues, in Russian and German, 1920. Typescript, mimeographed, 1 folder. Relates to conditions at Lager Altengrabow, Germany, and to political events in Russia and Germany. Issued by Russian prisoners of war in the camp. Preliminary inventory.

375 Aleksei Aleksandrovich von Lampe (1885-1960). Papers, mainly in Russian, 1917-26. 10 ms. boxes. General, Russian Imperial Army; Russian military agent in Germany, 1922-26; Russian military representative to Hungary, 1921-26. Correspondence, reports, memoranda, orders, newsletters, clippings, leaflets, maps, pamphlets, and printed matter relating to operations of the offices of the Russian military agent in Germany and the Russian military representative to Hungary, Russian counter-revolutionary activities, political events in Russia, and activities of Russian civilians and military personnel in Europe. Includes the office files of the delegation of the Russian Society of the Red Cross for Relief to Prisoners of War, 1919-22. Register (NUCMC 71-151).

376 Arthur C. Landesen. Papers, in Russian, 1926-33. 3 ms. boxes. White Russian consular agent in San Francisco, 1926-33. Correspondence, memoranda, and miscellanea relating to White Russian consular activities in San Francisco. Preliminary inventory (NUCMC 72-1475).

377 Robert Lansing (1864-1928). Miscellaneous papers, 1916-27. 1 folder. Photocopy of originals at the Library of Congress. Secretary of State of the U.S., 1915-20. Diaries, correspondence, and memoranda relating to U.S. foreign policy during World War I and to the Paris Peace Conference in 1919.

378 Alexis V. Lapteff. Papers, 1921-71. 1 folder, 1 envelope. American Relief Administration worker in the Ufa-Urals district of Russia, 1921-23. Memoirs, reports, and photographs relating to relief work in the Ufa-Urals district. Preliminary inventory.

379 Maurice Laserson (b. 1880). Papers, in English, French, German, and Russian, 1920-49. 1.5 ms. boxes, 1 envelope. Russian finance, commerce, and law expert. Correspondence, writings, reports, government documents, printed matter, and photographs relating to life in Russia prior to the 1917 Revolution, the persecution of Jews in Russia and their emigration to Germany, 1904-1906, Soviet financial and commercial policy, 1918-25, the purchase of 600 locomotives by the Soviet government from Sweden, 1920, and the German Socialist Karl Liebknecht. (NUCMC 72-1476)

380 "Latvia Before and After the Establishment of an Authoritative Regime." Memorandum, 1935. Typescript, mimeographed, 1 folder. Relates to the abolition of parliamentary democracy in Latvia in 1934.

381 Latvia. Sūtniecība (Sweden). Records, mostly in Latvian, 1917-39. 14 ms. boxes. Correspondence, memoranda, and reports relating to Latvian foreign relations and to Latvian-Swedish relations. Register.

382 Latvian refugee school certificates. In Latvian and English, 1945-47. Printed and handwritten, 1 folder. Certificates of completion of elementary school by students in Latvian refugee schools in Germany.

383 Latvian social customs. Memorandum, n.d. Typescript, mimeographed, 1 folder. Relates to baptismal, wedding, and burial customs in Latvia.

384 Latviesu Centrālā Komiteja. Records, in Latvian, 1918-48. 122 ms. boxes, 2 motion picture reels. Latvian émigré organization. Memoranda, reports, correspondence, registration forms, printed matter, and motion pictures relating to conditions in Latvia under Soviet and German occupation, and to Latvian displaced persons during and after World War II. Preliminary inventory.

385 K. I. Lavrent'ev. Memoir, in Russian, 1925. Typescript, 1 folder. "Urginskiia Sobytiia 1921 Goda" (Events in Urga in 1921). White Russian. Relates to White Russian activities in Mongolia during the Russian Revolution.

386 Sergei Lavrov. Memoir, in Russian, 1942. Holograph, 1 folder. "Sobytiia v Mongolii-Khalkhie, 1920-1921 godakh - Voenno-Istoricheskii Ocherk - Vospominaniia" (Events in Mongolia-Khalkha, 1920-1921 - A Military-Historical Essay - Reminiscences). Major, Russian Imperial Army. Relates to Baron Roman Ungern-Shternberg and White Russian military activities in Mongolia, 1920-21.

387 William C. LeGendre. Letter, 1925. Holograph, 1 folder. American businessman. Relates to proposals in the U.S. for a negotiated end to World War I and Polish independence, 1916-17. Also includes translations (typewritten) of excerpts from Prawda Dziejowa, 1914-1917 (The Truth of History, 1914-1917), by Jerzy Jan Sosnowski, Russian diplomatic representative in the U.S. during World War I.

388 Jānis Lejins (b. 1897). Papers, in Latvian and English, 1940-78. 2 ms. boxes, 1 envelope. Member of the Latvian parliament, 1931-40; subsequently an émigré in Canada. Correspondence, writings, clippings, other printed matter, and photographs relating to the annexation of Latvia to the Soviet Union, conditions in Latvia under communism, Latvian émigrés in Canada and the U.S., and anti-communist Latvian émigré movements.

389 Rudolf Leman (b. 1897). Memoirs, in German, n.d. Typescript, .5 ms. box. "Geschichte der Goldenen Zwanziger Jahre in Russland" (History

of Twenty Golden Years in Russia). German chemist in Russia, 1920-30. Relates to economic conditions in Russia, especially Siberia, in the interwar period, and to Economic policy of the Vysshii Sovet Narodnogo Khoziaistva.

390 Vladimir Il'ich Lenin (1870-1924). Miscellaneous speeches and writings, in Russian, 1903-40. 1 folder, 1 phonotape. Russian revolutionary leader; premier of Russia, 1917-24. Pamphlet (mimeographed), by V. I. Lenin, entitled "K Studenchestvu: Zacachi Revoliutsionnoi Molodezhi" (To the Students: The Tasks of Revolutionary Youth), 1903; leaflet (printed), by V. I. Lenin and V. Bonch-Bruevich, entitled "Usluzhlivyi Liberal" (The Obliging Liberal); photocopy of the table of contents (printed) of Stat'i i Rechi o Srednei Azii i Uzbekistane (Articles and Speeches about Central Asia and Uzbekistan), by V. I. Lenin and Iosif Stalin, 1940; and recordings of speeches by V. I. Lenin, 1919-20.

391 Mademoiselle de L'Escaille. Letters, in French, 1863-1921. Holograph, 1 folder. French governess. Letters from individuals connected closely with the Russian Imperial family, relating to personal matters in the lives of the Russian Imperial family. Includes translations of some letters.

392 Nikolai Nikolaevich, Herzog von Leuchtenberg. Diary, in Russian, 1918. Holograph, photocopy, 1 folder, 1 envelope. Relates to activities of White Russian forces under General Krasnov in southern Russia during the Russian Civil War.

393 Isaac Don Levine (b. 1892). Miscellaneous papers, 1957-58. 1 folder. American journalist and author. Memorandum (mimeographed), 1958, and transcripts of hearings (printed) of the U.S. Senate Internal Security Subcommittee, 1957, both relating to the dispute between I. D. Levine and Martin K. Tytell regarding the authenticity of documents used by I. D. Levine in his book, Stalin's Great Secret (New York, 1956), as proof that Iosif Stalin had been a tsarist spy.

394 Eugene L. Levitsky. Writings, in Russian, n.d. Typescript, photocopy, 1 folder. Imperial Russian Army officer. History, entitled "Ataka" (Attack), relating to the operations of the 2nd Ufim Cavalry Division during the Russian Civil War in May 1919; and memoirs, entitled "Fevral'skie Dni" (February Days), relating to Russian military operations, 1916-17, and to the Russian Revolution.

395 Roger L. Lewis (d. 1936). Papers, 1917-19. .5 ms. box, 1 envelope. American journalist and Red Cross worker in Russia. Reports, notes, correspondence, printed matter, clippings, photographs, and memorabilia relating to operations of the American Red Cross in Archangel, Russia. Preliminary inventory.

396 Olberts Liepins (b. 1906). Papers, mainly in Latvian, 1948-72. 1 ms. box. Latvian journalist. Correspondence, clippings, writings, and reports relating to Latvian domestic and foreign affairs, and Latvians in the United States.

397 Lietuvia Salpos Draugija Prancūzije. Correspondence, in Lithuanian, 1947-50. .5 ms. box. Lithuanian Relief Association, France. Relates to Lithuanians serving in the French Foreign Legion. Closed until 14 December 2004.

398 Teresa Lipkowska. Letter, in Polish, 1941, to Stanislaw Mackiewicz. Typescript, mimeographed, 1 folder. Polish journalist and author. Relates to conditions in Soviet concentration camps and the success of the Polish government in securing the release of its citizens from them.

399 Lithuania. Photographs, ca. 1920-29. 1 envelope. Depicts various sites in Wilno, Lithuania.

400 Lithuanian National Council in America. Miscellaneous records, 1918-25. Typewritten transcripts, .5 ms. box. Organization of Lithuanian-Americans. Correspondence, resolutions, and reports relating to the movements to secure Lithuanian independence and U.S. recognition of Lithuania.

401 Lev Nikolaevich Litoshenko (b. 1886). Study, in Russian, 1927. Typescript and holograph, 5 ms. boxes. Study by L. N. Litoshenko and Lincoln Hutchinson, sponsored by the Committee on Russian Research, Hoover War Library, Stanford University, relating to agricultural policy in the Soviet Union. Includes a translation (typewritten) entitled "Agrarian Policy in Soviet Russia." Register.

402 Dmitrii Nikolaevich Liubimov (b. 1864). Memoirs, in Russian, n.d. Holograph, .5 ms. box. Chief of staff, Imperial Russian Ministry of the Interior. Relates to political conditions in Russia, 1902-1906.

403 Edith Livermore. Photographs, 1913-20. 1 envelope. Depicts activities of the German army during World War I, military parades and training exercises in Berlin, war damage in France, a 1913 parade in honor of Tsar Nicholas II at Potsdam, and British troops on parade in London.

404 Ivor M. V. Z. Livingstead. History, n.d. Typescript, carbon copy, 1 vol. "The Downfall of a Dynasty." Relates to the fall of the House of Romanov in Russia.

405 Georges Lodygensky. Writings, in French, n.d. .5 ms. box. Russian physician. Memoirs, entitled "Une Carrière médicale mouvementée" (A Turbulent Medical Career), relating to medical practice in Russia during World War I, the

Russian Revolution, and Civil War, 1908-23; and history, entitled "Face au communisme-Le-Mouvement anticommuniste internationale de 1923-1950" (In the Face of Communism - The Anti-communist International 1923-1950), relating to the operations of the International Anti-communist Entente.

406 Joseph B. Longuevan. Collector. J. B. Longuevan collection on Siberia, 1918-20. 1 folder. Reminiscences, letters, and printed matter relating to activities of the U.S. 31st Infantry in Siberia, and to the Russian Revolution in Siberia.

407 V. Lonzinov. Memorandum, ca. 1930. Typescript, mimeographed, 1 folder, 1 envelope. Relates to the emigration of German Russians from Russia to Germany, and to conditions in Russia causing the emigration. Includes a photograph of German Russian children in Kiel, en route to Canada.

408 Zekeriia Lordkipanidze. Indictment, in Russian, 1937. Typescript, carbon copy, 1 vol. Relates to the indictment of Zekeriia Lordkipanidze and others in Georgia on charges of treason, counter-revolutionary activity, sabotage, and subversion.

409 Louis Loucheur (1872-1931). Papers, in French, 1916-31. 12 ms. boxes, 1 envelope. French industrialist, statesman, and diplomat. Correspondence, speeches, notes, reports, and photographs relating to industry in Russia during World War I, inter-Allied diplomacy during World War I, war reparations, and post-war French and international politics. Preliminary inventory (NUCMC 68-676).

410 Jay Lovestone (b. 1899). Papers, 1906-76. 634 ms. boxes. General secretary, Communist Party, U.S.A., 1927-29, and Communist Party (Opposition), 1929-40; executive secretary, Free Trade Union Committee, American Federation of Labor, 1944-55; assistant director and director, International Affairs, American Federation of Labor-Congress of Industrial Organizations, 1955-74. Correspondence, reports, memoranda, bulletins, clippings, serial issues, pamphlets, other printed matter, and photographs relating to the Communist International, the Communist movement in the U.S. and elsewhere, Communist influence in U.S. and foreign trade unions, and organized labor movements in the U.S. and abroad. Published materials are opened. All other materials are closed until 5 years after the death of J. Lovestone.

411 Aleksandr Sergeevich Lukomskii (d. 1939). Papers, in Russian, 1914-39. 4 ms. boxes, 1 envelope. General, Russian Imperial Army; White Russian military leader under Generals Kornilov and Denikin, 1917-19. Correspondence, memoranda, reports, writings, notes, and printed matter relating to Russian military operations during World War I, and to the Russian Civil War. Register.

412 Arthur B. Lule. Memorandum, 1924. Typescript, 1 folder. Latvian consul, New York City. Relates to the political composition and policies of the government of Latvia.

413 Gibbes Lykes. Papers, 1919-23. 2 ms. boxes. Captain, U.S. Army; supervisor, Ukrainian district, Russian Unit, American Relief Administration. Reports, dispatches, correspondence, and photographs relating to relief work in the Ukraine and to political conditions in Hungary during the Hungarian Revolution.

414 Bessie Eddy Lyon. Papers, 1918-20. 1 folder. Stenographer, American Red Cross Commission in Siberia, 1918-20. Letters and reports relating to activities of the American Red Cross Commission in Siberia and the political and military conditions in Siberia during the Russian Civil War.

415 Marvin Lyons. Interviewer. Interview summary, 1965. "Conversation with a Chekist." Typescript, 1 folder. Relates to an interview of a former member of the Chrevychainaia Komissiia po Bor'be s Kontr-revoliutsiei i Sabotazhem (CHEKA), the Soviet secret police agency, who served as political commissar of the 29th CHEKA Brigade in 1919, regarding CHEKA activities, 1917-22. Includes a photograph.

416 Geoffrey McDonnell. Papers, 1918-19. 1 scrapbook. Lieutenant colonel, Canadian army. Photographs, correspondence, and memorabilia relating to the activities of the Canadian and other Allied expeditionary forces in Siberia.

417 Katherine S. McLean. Papers, 1918-20. 1 folder, 1 envelope. Young Women's Christian Association worker, Camp Fremont and Camp Kearny, California, 1918-19. Memoranda, clippings, photographs, and miscellanea relating to Y.W.C.A. work among American soldiers stationed at Camps Fremont and Kearny, and Czechoslovakian soldiers evacuated to these camps from Siberia.

418 N. Makarov. Study, in Russian, n.d. Holograph, 1 folder. "Na puti k Krisizmu Sotsial'nago Rationalizma: Sotsial'no-ekonomicheskie Ocherki o Rossii i eia Revoliutsii, 1917-1920" (On the Path to a Crisis of Social Rationalism: Social-economic Essays on Russia and its Revolution, 1917-1920).

419 Nestor Ivanovich Makhno (1889-1935). Memoirs, in Russian, 1932. Pechalnye Stranitsy Russkoi Revoliutsii (Sad Pages of the Russian Revolution). Printed, 1 folder. Russian anarchist leader. Relates to the role of the anarchists in the Russian Civil War. Published serially in the Chicago Rassvet.

420 Grigorii Grigor'evich Makhov (1886-1952). Study, in Russian, 1952. Typescript, carbon copy, 1 vol. "Sel'skoe Khoziaistvo Ukrainy" (Agriculture in the Ukraine).

421 Vasilii Alekseevich Maklakov (1870-1957). Papers, in Russian and French, 1917-56. 22 ms. boxes. Ambassador of the Provisional Government of Russia to France, 1917-24. Correspondence, reports, diaries, and clippings relating to Russian foreign relations with France, the Russian Revolution, and Russian émigrés in France after the revolution. Correspondents and references include: Boris A. Bakhmeteff, A. F. Kerensky, A. V. Tyrkova-Williams, N. V. Volsky (Valentinov), M. M. Karpovich, B. I. Nicolaevsky, P. B. Struve, S. P. Melgunov, Pavel N. Miliukov, F. Rodichev, E. D. Kuskova-Prokopovich, and M. M. Vinaver. Preliminary inventory (NUCMC 71-1108 and 68-678).

422 "Manchurian Manifesto." Press release, 1946. Typescript, mimeographed, 1 folder. Protests Soviet influence in Manchuria. Signed by a number of American anti-communists.

423 Friherre Carl Gustav Emil Mannerheim (1867-1951). Telegram, 1940, to Elsa Durkheimer. 1 folder. Field marshal and commander-in-chief, Finnish army, 1939-44. Relates to the Russo-Finnish War.

424 Mariia Feodorovna (1847-1928). Empress Consort of Alexander III, Emperor of Russia. Letters, in Danish, 1881-1925, to Alexandra, Queen Consort of Edward VII, King of Great Britain. Holograph, 15 ms. boxes. Relates to matters of state and family. Preliminary inventory. Closed until 2 January 2001 or until publication of the letters by Princess Eugenie of Greece. Thereafter, may be used with written permission of Princess Eugenie, or, after her death, of Prince Vasili Romanov or the director of the Hoover Institution.

425 Maritime Province, Siberia. Komissiia po Obsledovaniiu Obstoiatel'stv Sobytii 4-6 Aprelia vo Vladivostoke. Report, in Russian, ca. 1920. Typescript, carbon copy, 1 vol. Commission for Investigation of Circumstance of the Events of 4-6 April in Vladivostok. Relates to activities of Japanese troops in the Maritime Province of Siberia during the Russian Civil War.

426 Anatolii Markov. Study, in Russian, n.d. Typescript, 4 vols. "Entsiklopediia Belago Dvizheniia: Vozhdi, Partizany, Fronty, Pokhody i Narodnyia Vozstaniia Protiv Sovetov v Rossii" (Encyclopedia of the White Movement: Leaders, Partisans, Fronts, Marches and Popular Uprisings against the Soviets in Russia). Relates to White Russian activities during the Russian Civil War and after, 1917-58. Includes biographical sketches.

427 Herbert Marshall. Study, 1975. Typescript, photocopy, 1 folder. "The Fate of the Great Soviet Film Artist, Sergo Paradjanov." Professor, Center for Soviet and East European Studies in the Performing Arts, at Southern Illinois University. Relates to the arrest and imprisonment in the Soviet Union of Sergei Iosipovich Paradianov, Soviet film director. Includes a petition for the release of S. I. Paradianov.

428 Ludwig Christian Alexander Karl Martens (1874-1948). Letter, 1919, to Boris Bakhmetev. Typescript, photocopy, 1 folder. Demands that B. Bakhmetev, ambassador of the Russian Provisional Government to the U.S., hand over all property of the Russian government in the U.S. Written by L. C. A. K. Martens and Santeri Nuorteva, Soviet diplomatic representatives in the U.S.

429 R. C. Martens. Letters, 1942-46. Typescript, 1 ms. box. Lithuanian émigré in the U.S. Relates to diplomatic, economic, and political events during World War II.

430 Iulii Osipovich Martov (1873-1923). Writings, in Russian, 1920. Typescript, 1 vol. "Oborona Revoliutsii i Sotsial-Demokratiia: Sbornik Statei" (Defense of the Revolution and Social-Democracy: Collected Articles). Russian Menshevik leader. Relates to the Russian Revolution and Civil War.

431 A. P. Martynov (d. 1951). Memoir, in Russian, n.d. Holograph, 1 ms. box. Director, Moscow Office, Okhrana (Russian Imperial police), 1912-17. Relates to activities of the Okhrana, 1906-17. Published (Richard Wraga, ed.) in 1972. (NUCMC 75-655)

432 General Martynov. Study, in Russian, 1925. Typescript, mimeographed, 1 folder. "Soobrazheniia ob Ustroistvie, Obuchenii i Upotreblenii Budushchei Russkoi Kavalerii" (Considerations on the Organization, Training and Utilization of the Future Russian Cavalry). Lieutenant general, Russian Imperial Army.

433 Zakhar Nikiforovich Martynov. Papers, in Russian, 1914-77. 1 ms. box. Imperial Russian soldier in the convoy of His Imperial Majesty Emperor Nicholas II. Correspondence, writings, reminiscences, printed matter, clippings, and photographs relating to the Russian Imperial Army, Russia's role in World War I, the Russian Revolution and Civil War, and anti-communist movements in the U.S. Includes a cigarette case from the desk of Tsar Alexander III, a dagger presented to Tsarevich Aleksei Nikolaevich when he was made ataman of the Cossacks, and the St. George's Cross awarded to Z. N. Martynov for his military service.

434 Tomás Garrique Masaryk (1850-1937). Proclamation, in Czech, 1919. Typescript, photocopy, 1 folder. President of Czechoslovakia. Issued to the Czechoslovak army in Siberia.

435 John Wesley Masland, Jr. (1912-1968). Papers, 1945. 21 ms. boxes, 1 envelope. Staff member, International Secretariat, United Nations Conference on International Organization, San

Francisco, 1945. Reports, minutes of meetings, directories, notes, and printed matter relating to the UN Conference on International Organization at San Francisco and the founding of the United Nations. Preliminary inventory.

436 Sergei Semenovich Maslov. Study, in Russian, n.d. Typescript, mimeographed, 1 vol. "Kolkhoznaia Rossiia: Istoki, Nasazhdenie i Zhizn' Kolkhozov, ikh Priroda, Evoliutsiia i Budushchee Znachenie dlia s. Khoziaistva, Krest'ianstva, Gosudarstva" (Collective Farm Russia: Sources, Propagation and Life of Collective Farms, their Nature, Evolution and Future Meaning for Agriculture, Peasantry, Government).

437 Evgenii Vasil'evich Maslovskii. Letters, in Russian, 1945, to Baron Sergei Evgen'evich Ludinkhausen-Wolff. Holograph, 1 folder. Russian Imperial Army officer. Relates to Russian military activities in northern Persia before World War I, and in the Turkish campaigns of General Iudenich during World War I.

438 Frank Earl Mason (b. 1893). Papers, in English and German, 1915-75. 4 ms. boxes, 7 envelopes. American journalist; Berlin correspondent and president, International News Service. Correspondence, reports, journalistic dispatches, and other material relating to German and Soviet politics and diplomacy in the interwar period, and to Allied military administration of Germany at the end of World War II. Includes a copy of the logbook of the submarine that sank the Lusitania, 1915, and correspondence with Georgii Chicherin and Karl von Wiegand. Preliminary inventory.

439 Sarah E. Mathews (b. 1880). Papers, 1918-20. 1 folder, 1 album, 1 envelope. American Red Cross worker in Siberia, 1918-20. Memoirs, diary, reports, clippings, and photographs relating to the disposition of the remains of Tsar Nicholas II and his family, social and political conditions in Siberia, and relief work of the American Red Cross in Siberia during the Russian Civil War.

440 Matveev. Study, in Russian, 1939. Holograph, 1 vol. "Gibel Rigo-Shavel'skago Otriada" (Downfall of the Rigo-Shavel'skii Detachment). General, Imperial Russian Army. Relates to Russian military operations during World War I.

441 Antonina Alexandrovna Maximova-Kulaev. Memoir, 1932. Typescript, 1 folder. Russian physician. Relates to her service as a surgeon in a Red Army hospital in Koslov, Russia, and to the occupation of Koslov by White Russian forces in 1919.

442 Henry Mayers (b. 1894). Papers, 1930-66. 7 ms. boxes, 1 scrapbook. American advertising executive; member, Committee for Freedom for All Peoples; chairman, Cold War Council. Correspondence, speeches, writings, and printed matter relating primarily to the Cold War Council.

443 Baronessa Maria F. Meiendorf (1869-1962). Memoirs, in Russian, n.d. Typescript, .5 ms. box, 1 scrapbook. "Moi Vospominaniia" (My Reminiscences). Russian aristocrat. Relates to social conditions in tsarist Russia, the Russian Revolution and Civil War, and Russian émigré life afterwards. Includes a printed copy of the memoirs (clippings from Russkaia Zhizn' [San Francisco]).

444 Sergei Petrovich Mel'gunov (1879-1956). Papers, in Russian, 1918-33. 17 ms. boxes. Russian historian and editor; author of The Red Terror in Russia. Clippings, writings, correspondence, and reports relating to the Russian Revolution and Civil War, and the operations of the Soviet secret police. Correspondents include N. V. Chaikovsky and E. Breshko-Breshkovskaia. Preliminary inventory (NUCMC 68-680).

445 "Memorandum on the Present Condition of the Union of the Soviet Socialistic Republics and Its Population." Memorandum, 1931. Typescript, mimeographed, 1 folder. Relates to economic and social conditions in Russia.

446 Henry Cord Meyer (b. 1913). Miscellaneous papers, in German and English, 1916-50. Photocopy, .5 ms. box. American historian. Correspondence and printed matter relating to the ideas of Paul Rohrbach, German nationalist author, regarding pan-Germanism, German territorial expansion, and the German occupation of the Ukraine in 1918. Includes correspondence of P. Rohrbach. Preliminary inventory.

447 Johannes Mihkelson. Collector. Miscellany, 1949. 1 folder. Study, typewritten, and leaflet, printed, relating to the Communist system in Estonia, and to Estonian and Latvian émigré politics.

448 Stanislaw Mikolajczk (1901-1966). Papers, in Polish and English, 1938-66. 137 ms. boxes, 19 cu. ft. Polish politician; prime minister, government in exile (London), 1943-44; second vice premier and minister of agriculture, 1945-47; president, International Peasant Union, 1950-66. Correspondence, speeches and writings, reports, notes, newsletters, clippings, photographs, tape recordings, and printed matter relating to communism in Eastern Europe and Poland, agriculture in Poland, Polish politics, especially during World War II, Polish-Soviet relations, the International Peasant Union, the Polskie Stronnictwo Ludowe, and Polish émigré politics. Consult archivist for restriction.

449 Pavel Nikolaevich Miliukov (1859-1943). History, n.d. Typescript, carbon copy, 1 vol. "From Nicholas II to Stalin: Half a Century of Foreign Politics." Russian historian. Relates to Russian diplomatic history.

450 Evgenii Karlovich Miller (1867-1937). Papers, in Russian, 1917-24. 12 ms. boxes. General,

Russian Imperial Army; representative of General Wrangel in Paris during the Russian Civil War. Correspondence, reports, and military orders relating to White Russian military and diplomatic activities during the Russian Civil War. Preliminary inventory (NUCMC 68-682).

451 Nikander Ivanovich Miroliubov (1870-1927). Papers, in Russian, 1918-27. .5 ms. boxes, 1 envelope. White Russian political leader; chairman, Special Committee for the Investigation of the Murder of the Romanov Family. Correspondence, memoranda, reports, and clippings relating to the investigation of the deaths of the Romanovs, 1918-20, the creation of the first Far Eastern Republic, and Russian émigré organizations in the Far East, 1921-27. Register (NUCMC 72-1480).

452 General Mirovicz. Papers, in Russian, 1914-16. 1 folder, 1 envelope. General, Imperial Russian Army. Reports, orders, maps, and photographs relating to military operations of the Second and Third Finland Rifle Brigades in 4 battles on the Riga Front and in the Carpathian Mountains. Preliminary inventory.

453 Anna V. S. Mitchell. Papers, 1920-44. 6 ms. boxes, 9 envleopes, 4 medals. American relief worker. Correspondence, memoranda, reports, clippings, memorabilia, and photographs relating to World War I relief work in France, 1915-20, and relief work with Russian refugees in Istanbul, 1921-36. Register (NUCMC 75-658).

454 Leon Mitkiewicz (1896-1972). Papers, in Polish, 1918-69. 8.5 ms. boxes. Colonel and chief of Intelligence, Polish army; military attaché to Lithuania; Polish representative, Allied Combined Chiefs of Staff, 1943-45. Diary, correspondence, writings, and printed matter relating to Polish foreign relations with Russia, Czechoslovakia, the Baltic States and other countries, 1914-44; the Warsaw uprising of August 1944; and World War II Allied diplomacy. Register (NUCMC 75-659).

455 (Viacheslav Mikhailovich) Molotov. Photographs, 1945. 1 envelope. Depicts the Soviet political leader V. M. Molotov at an American Russian Institute reception in San Francisco.

456 Mongolia (Mongolian People's Republic). Velikii Khuraldan, 1st, Ulan-Bator-Khoto, 1924. Translation of protocols, 1933. Typescript, carbon copy, 1 vol. "New Mongolia, or, The Protocols of the First Great Assembly of the Mongolian People's Republic." Translation by J. Attree.

457 Mongol'skaia Narodno-Revoliutsionnaia Partiia. 3d Congress, Ulan-Bator-Khoto, 1924. Translation of report, 1933. Typescript, carbon copy, 1 vol. "The Third Assembly of the Mongolian People's Party, Urga, August 1924." Translation by J. Attree.

458 Hugh Anderson Moran (b. 1881). Papers, 1916-33. 2 ms. boxes. American clergyman; Young Men's Christian Association worker in Siberia and China, 1909-18. Correspondence, writings, clippings, maps, posters, and photographs relating to the Russian Civil War, political and economic conditions in Siberia and Manchuria, and relief work in Siberia and Manchuria, especially in the prisoner of war camps, during the Russian Civil War. David Francis was a correspondent. Preliminary inventory (NUCMC 68-683).

459 Valerian Ivanovich Moravskii (1884-1940). Papers, in Russian, 1917-34. 20 ms. boxes. White Russian political leader in Siberia during the Russian Civil War. Correspondence, reports, proclamations, and photographs relating to White Russian political activities in the Far East, the first and second anti-Bolshevik Siberian governments, 1918-22, and the Council of Plenipotentiary Representatives of Organizations of Autonomous Siberia. Preliminary inventory (NUCMC 72-1481).

460 Moscow. Conference, 1943. Photographs, 1 envelope. Depicts American, British, and Soviet delegates to the Tripartite Conference in Moscow in October 1943.

461 T. H. Vail Motter. Collector. Newsletter, 1941-42. Typescript, mimeographed, 1 ms. box. Newsletters issued aboard the U.S. Army transport ship Siboney, 29 December 1941 to 1 February 1942, relating to ship activities and war news. The ship transported the U.S. military North African mission, the U.S. military mission to Iran, and the U.S. military mission to the USSR from New York to Eritrea and Iraq.

462 Mueller and Graeff Photographic Poster Collection (ca. 1914-45). 4 ms. boxes. Photographs of posters relating primarily to Germany during World Wars I and II, German political events in the interwar period, and the Spanish Civil War. Includes posters from the Soviet Union, France, and a number of other countries. Preliminary inventory.

463 Malcolm Muir. Memorandum, 1957. Typescript, 1 vol. "Notes to the Staff on My Russian Trip, June, 1957." American journalist; Newsweek correspondent. Relates to social conditions in the Soviet Union.

464 Mikhail Georgievich Mukhanov. Papers, in Russian, 1862-1963. .5 ms. box. Russian aristocrat. Correspondence, printed matter, reports, and photographs relating to conditions in Russia before, during, and after the Revolution of 1917, and to experiences of various members of the Mukhanov family. Includes letters from the great-uncle of M. G. Mukhanov, Georgii Bakhmeteff, Russian Imperial diplomat; from the great-great-grandfather of M. G. Mukhanov, Marshal Mikhail Kutuzov, to his wife; and from

Grand Duke Nikolai Nikolaevich to the father of M. G. Mukhanov, 1924.

465 Janis Muncis (1886-1955). Miscellaneous papers, in Latvian, 1925-51. 1 ms. box. Latvian stage designer and producer. Photographs, certificates, diplomas, sketches, and memorabilia relating to mass propaganda open air theatrical productions during the Ulmanis regime in Latvia, 1934-39.

466 Vilhelms Munters (1898-1967). Miscellaneous papers, in Latvian and German, 1939-72. Photocopies, 1 folder. Minister of Foreign Affairs of Latvia, 1936-40. Correspondence, memoranda, and press releases relating to Latvian-Soviet relations and to the imprisonment of V. Munters in the Soviet Union, 1941-54.

467 S. Muraveiskii. Translation of pamphlet, n.d. Typescript, 1 folder. Data on the History of the Revolutionary Movement in Central Asia: Result of a Brief Study of the Soviet Party Schools and Political Primary Schools. Translation by Xenia J. Eudin of Ocherki po Istorii Revoliutsionnogo Dvizheniia v Srednei Azii: Opyt Kratkogo Posobiia dlia Sovpartshkol i Shkol Politgramoty, published in Tashkent in 1926.

468 Ekaterina Ivanova Murav'eva. Papers, in Russian, 1914-48. 6 ms. boxes. Russian refugee in France. Correspondence, memoirs, and notes relating to the Russian Revolution and political events in Russia and abroad. Correspondents include V. A. Maklakov, P. N. Miliukov, Vera Figner, and other leading Russian political figures. Preliminary inventory.

469 Merle Farmer Murphy. Memoir, n.d. Typescript, 1 folder. "Record of a Russian Year, 1921-1922: Daily Life in Soviet Russia." American Relief Administration worker in Russia, 1921-22. Relates to social and economic conditions in Russia.

470 Jamal Muzaffar. Writings, 1957. Typescript, .5 ms. box. Writings, including "American-Soviet Policy toward Egypt, 1953-1957"; "The Question of Fertile Crescent Unity," relating to pan-Arabism; and "Terror of the Red Fox and Reform of the Grey Wolf," relating to the Turkish revolution of 1918-23.

471 Karol Mysels. Translations of extracts from letters, 1945-46. Typescript, 1 folder. Letters written to K. Mysels by a relative living in a Polish refugee camp in New Zealand, relating to the experiences of Polish refugees in Russia and elsewhere during World War II.

472 K. Nagy. Collector. Collection on Hungary, in Hungarian and English, 1942-62. 2 ms. boxes. Interview, transcripts, reports, clippings, and printed matter relating to the Hungarian Revolution of 1956, political events in Hungary during World War II, the Sanders espionage trial, 1950-51, and the Wynne-Penkovskii espionage trial, 1962. Preliminary inventory.

473 "Nakaz Bol'shogo i Malago Voiskovogo Kruga Voiska Terskago" (Order of the Large and Small Military Union of the Tersk Unit). Memorandum, in Russian, 1919. Typescript, 1 folder. Relates to the bylaws of a White Russian officers' association.

474 National Polish Committee of America. Postcards, ca. 1914-18. 1 envelope. Depicts scenes of destruction in Poland during World War I, coins of Lithuania and Poland, and Polish-American soldiers in France during World War I.

475 National Republic, 1905-60. Records, 1920-60. 826 ms. boxes. Anti-communist American magazine. Clippings, printed matter, pamphlets, reports, indices, notes, bulletins, lettergrams, weekly letters, and photographs relating to pacifist, communist, fascist, and other radical movements, and to political developments in the United States and the Soviet Union. Register.

476 Nationalsozialistische Deutsche Arbeiter-Partei. Waffenschutzstaffel. 15. Grenadier-Division. Records, in Latvian and German, 1941-45. 4 ms. boxes, 86 maps. Volunteer Latvian Legion in Waffen-SS during World War II. Correspondence, memoranda, military orders, and printed matter relating to activities of the Latvian Legion Police Battalions and Regiments. Preliminary inventory. Access requires the written permission of the Latvian Welfare Association, Inc.

477 Aleksandr Nikolaevich Naumov (1868-1950). Memoirs, in Russian, 1929-37. Typescript, 12 vols. "Iz Utsielievshikh Vospominanii" (From Surviving Memories). Russian Imperial minister of Agriculture, 1915-16. Relates to political conditions in Russia during the reign of Tsar Nicholas II and during the Russian Revolution and Civil War.

478 Nicolai Vissarionovich Nekrasov. Translation of speech, 1917. Typescript, 1 folder. Minister of Finance, Russian Provisional Government. Relates to the financial situation of the Provisional Government. Speech delivered in Moscow, August 1917.

479 Nicholas I, Emperor of Russia (1796-1855). Order, in Russian, 1828. Printed, 1 folder. Illustrates and describes various medals and awards.

480 Nicholas II, Emperor of Russia (1868-1918). Miscellaneous papers, in Russian, 1890-1917. 1.5 ms. boxes, 1 oversize roll. Imperial orders, printed, signed by Tsar Nicholas II, 1905 and 1908; letters, handwritten and typewritten copies, from Nicholas II to prime minister P. A. Stolypin, 1906-11; facsimile of

the abdications of Nicholas II and Grand Duke Michael, 1917; Nicholas II's diary, handwritten copy; 2 religious books belonging to the Romanov family that were found in Ekaterinburg after their murder; and other materials relating to the reign of Nicholas II. Includes a colored reproduction of a painting of Nicholas II.

481 Boris Ivanovich Nicolaevsky (1887-1966). Collection, 1827-1966, ca. 250 ms. boxes plus unprocessed material. Member of the Social Democratic Party since his youth, a Menshevik, director of the Marx-Engels Institute in Moscow ca. 1918-21, director of the International Institute of Social History of Amsterdam, émigré scholar in the United States after 1942, and authority on Soviet Russia. Correspondence, reports, diaries, literary and other manuscripts, photographs, party records, account books, maps, charts, and miscellaneous historical documents. Concerns the Russian revolutionary movement, particularly the Mensheviks, the Socialist Revolutionary Party, the Russian Social Democratic Labor Party, the Russian Revolution and Civil War, the Second and Third Internationals, Iu. O. Martov, P. B. Aksel'rod, Viktor M. Chernov, Fedor (Theodor) Dan, Angelica Balabanova, and much else pertaining to Soviet Russia. Transcriptions of many of the handwritten letters are available. Includes papers of Gregor Aronson: typescript essays on the Russian labor movement and trade unions and on Minsk under German occupation, ca. 1917-20; 4 typed essays by Solomon Schwartz, a former Menshevik, on factory committees, trade unions, wages, and social insurance in the period 1917-21, all in Russian, dated 1935; manuscript by V. Chernavin on the Civil War in the South; and Iu. F. Semenov's papers concerning the Kadet Party and the National Center in southern Russia, 1918-19. The Nicolaevsky Archive has its own curator, currently A. M. Bourgina. Register for parts of the collection in progress.

482 Gerhart Niemeyer (b. 1907). Papers, in English and German, 1935-67. 2 ms. boxes. German-American political scientist. Correspondence, speeches and writings, clippings, conference procedures, and printed matter relating to communism, international organization and world security, and the foreign policy of the U.S. and the USSR.

483 Evgenii Aleksandrovich Nikol'skii. Memoirs, in Russian, 1934. Typescript, 1 folder. Russian Imperial Army officer. Memoirs entitled "Sluzhba v Glavnom Shtabie i Glavnom Upravlenii General'nago Shtaba" (Service in the Main Headquarters and Main Directorate of the General Staff) and "Biezhentsy v Velikuiu Voinu" (Refugees in the Great War), relating to the Russian General Staff, 1903-1908, and Russian refugees during World War I.

484 E. Kh. Nilus. Editor. History, in Russian, 1923. Printed and typescript, with map and diagrams, 4 vols. "Istoricheskii Obzor Kitaiskoi Vostochnoi Zhelieznoi Dorogi, 1896-1923 g.g." (Historical Survey of the Chinese Eastern Railway, 1896-1923). Commissioned by the Board of Directors of the Chinese Eastern Railway, Harbin.

485 Graf Feodor Maksimilianovich Nirod (b. 1871). Memoirs, in Russian, n.d. Typescript and holograph, 1 ms. box. "Prozhitoe" (What I Have Lived Through). Russian Imperial Army officer. Relates to Russian military life, 1892-1917, including the Russo-Japanese War, Russian participation in World War I, and the Russian Revolution.

486 Anatolii Nosovich. Writings, in Russian, n.d. Typescript, photocopy, 1 folder. General, Russian Imperial Army. Histories entitled "Ulany Ego Velichestva, 1876-1926: Imperator Aleksandr II; Imperator Nikolai II" (Uhlans of His Majesty, 1876-1926: Emperor Alexander II and Emperor Nicholas II), and "Leib Gvardii Ulanskii Ego Velichestva Polk v Velikuiu i Grazhdanskuiu Voinu: Kratkow Proshloe Polka v Emigratsii" (Uhlan Household Troops of His Majesty's Regiment in the European and Civil Wars: A Brief History of the Regiment in Emigration).

487 "Note on the Indebtedness and Credit of the Soviet Government." Memorandum, 1931. Typescript, mimeographed, 1 folder. Relates to the financial situation of the Soviet Union.

488 Friedrich Wilhelm von Notz. Letter, in German, 1975, to John C. Buchanan. Typescript, 1 folder. Colonel, German army. Relates to the unsuccessful attack of the 1st Vlasov Division against the Soviet bridgehead at Erlenhof, Germany, south of Frankfurt a. Oder, 13 April 1945. Includes a translation of the letter.

489 Novaia Zhizn' (New Life) (1917-18) Leningrad. Newspaper articles, in Russian, 1917-18. Typewritten transcripts, 1 vol. Relates to the role of the railroad workers' union, Vserossiiskii Ispolnitel'nyi Komitet Zheleznodorozhnogo Soiuza (Vikzhel'), in the Russian Revolution.

490 Nyman. Memorandum, ca. 1949. Typescript, 1 folder. "On Nature of War Against the Soviet Union." Anti-communist Russian émigré living in the United States. Relates to the prospects for war between the U.S. and the USSR.

491 Theodor Oberlaender. Memoranda, in German, 1943. Typescript, mimeograph, 1 folder. First lieutenant, German army. 2 memoranda, entitled "Buendnis oder Ausbeutung?" (Alliance or Exploitation?) and "Deutschland und der Kaukasus" (Germany and the Caucasus), relating to Germany's relations with the occupied territories in Eastern Europe, especially the Caucasus Region.

492 Charles A. O'Brien. Papers, 1918-23. .5 ms. box, 1 scrapbook. American Red Cross worker in Siberia, 1919-20. Diary, notes, photographs, postcards, clippings, and memorabilia relating to American Red Cross activities in Siberia, and the Russian Civil War and Allied intervention in Siberia.

493 Gleb Nikolaevich Odintsov. Papers, in Russian, 1928-73. 3 ms. boxes, 1 oversize framed photograph. Colonel, Russian Imperial Army. Correspondence, writings, clippings, printed matter, documents, and photographs relating to the Russian Imperial Army, events in Russia before, during, and after the Russian Revolution and Civil War, the Romanov family, and other Russian dignitaries and nobility.

494 M. Oiderman. History, n.d. Typescript, .5 ms. box. "Estonian Independence." Relates to the history of Estonia during the Russian Revolution and to the establishment of an independent Estonian state. Prepared under the auspices of the Estonian Foreign Office.

495 Theo Olferieff. Study, 1932. Typescript, 1 vol. "Soviet Russia in the Orient." Relates to military defenses in the Soviet Far East.

496 "Olonetskaia Kareliia." Memorandum, in Russian, 1919. Typescript, 1 folder. Relates to Russian influence in Karelia during the Russian Civil War.

497 One Hundred Years of Revolutionary Internationals. Conference, Hoover Institution on War, Revolution and Peace, Stanford University, 1964. Proceedings, 1964. 1 ms. box, 10 phonotapes. Sound recordings and conference papers relating to the history of Marxist doctrine and of the communist movement.

498 Fritz E. Oppenheimer (1898-1968). Papers, 1945-67. 2 ms. boxes. Legal adviser to the U.S. secretary of state, 1947-48. Minutes of meetings, reports, speech, and printed matter relating primarily to the meetings of the Council of Foreign Ministers at Moscow, London, and Washington, D.C., 1947. Includes an eye-witness account by F. E. Oppenheimer of the signing of the German surrender to the Allies in Berlin, 8 May 1945.

499 Thomas James Orbison (1866-1938). Papers, 1919-22. 2 ms. boxes. Chief, Latvian Mission, American Relief Administration European Children's Fund, 1919-20. Diaries, writings, photographs, and memorabilia relating to relief work in Latvia at the end of World War I. Preliminary inventory (NUCMC 72-1485).

500 P. Ostroukhov. Collector. Newspaper articles, in Russian, 1918-20. Typewritten transcripts, 1 folder. Relates to the Russian Civil War in Siberia. Articles published in Siberian newspapers.

501 "Oto Zdrada Narodu Radzieckiego" (This Is a Betrayal of the Soviet People). Translation of newspaper editorial, in Polish, 1963. Typescript, mimeographed, 1 folder. Relates to the policies of the Soviet government under Nikita Khrushchev. Editorial published in the Chinese newspaper Zenminzipao.

502 Ulan Otorchi. Memoir, in Russian, 1928. Typescript, 1 folder. "Ozero Tolbo: Vospominaniia o Nachalnom Periode Mongol'skoi Revoliutsii" (Recollections from the Initial Period of the Mongolian Revolution). Mongolian Communist. Relates to the Communist movement in Mongolia during the Russian Revolution.

503 Anton Zakharovich Ovchinnikov. Memoirs, in Russian, 1932. Holograph, 1 vol. Russian Red Army soldier. Relates to guerrilla warfare in the Russian Far East, 1918-20.

504 Oskars Ozels (1889-1975). Memoirs, in Latvian, n.d. Typescript, photocopy, 1 folder. "Pieredzejumi Riga Bermonta Dienas" (Experiences in Riga During Bermondts' Campaign). Latvian engineer and educator. Relates to the Bermondt-Avalov campaign in Riga, October-November 1919, during the Russian Civil War.

505 Ignacy Jan Paderewski (1860-1941). Papers, in Polish, English, and French, 1894-1941. 6.5 ms. boxes, 1 envelope, 1 album. Polish statesman and musician; premier, 1919. Correspondence, speeches, writings, clippings, printed matter, and photographs relating primarily to the establishment of an independent Polish State, the Paris Peace Conference, Polish politics in the interwar period, the occupation of Poland during World War II, and the musical career of I. J. Paderewski. Includes some correspondence with his sister Maria Paderewski in the USSR. Preliminary inventory. Personal financial materials in 4 folders closed until 1 January 1992. No handwritten material may be reproduced.

506 Konstantin Paets (1874-1956). Letters, in Estonian, ca. 1954. Holograph, photocopy, 1 folder. President of Estonia, 1921-24 and 1931-40. Relates to the imprisonment of K. Paets in the Soviet Union, and appeals to the United Nations to bring about civil rights and independence in the Baltic states. Includes a translation and a press release from the consulate general of Estonia, New York, 1977, explaining the acquisition and content of the letters.

507 Sergei Nikolaevich Paleologue (b. 1887). Papers, in Russian, 1920-33. 34 ms. boxes. Chairman, Board of the Government Plenipotentiary for the Settlement of Russian Refugees in Yugoslavia. Correspondence, reports, and memoranda relating to the activities of the Board of the Government Plenipotentiary for the Settlement of Russian Refugees in Yugoslavia. Preliminary inventory (NUCMC 68-685).

508 Olga Valerianovna Paley (b. 1865). Memoirs, n.d. Holograph and typescript, .5 ms. box. Memories of Russia, 1916-1919. Morganatic wife of Grand Duke Pavel Aleksandrovich of Russia. Relates to the Russian Revolution and Civil War. Memoirs published.

509 Fedor Fedorovich Palitsyn (1851-1923). Memoirs, in Russian, 1918-21. Typescript, 1 ms. box. General, Russian Imperial Army; chief of staff, 1905-1908. Memoirs, entitled "Perezhitoe, 1916-1918" (My Experience, 1916-1918), 1918, and "Zapiski Generala F. Palitsyna" (Notes of General F. Palitsyn), 1921, relating to Russian military activities during World War I, and to White Russian military activities during the Russian Civil War.

510 Sir Bernard Pares (1867-1949). Miscellaneous papers, 1919. .5 ms. box. British historian. Correspondence, notes, memoranda, and diary relating to political conditions in Western Siberia during the Russian Civil War.

511 Paris. Congress, 1856. Miscellaneous records, in French, 1857-58. Holograph, .5 ms. box. Commission established by the Congress of Paris of 1856. Protocols of meetings and report relating to the reorganization of the Romanian principalities of Wallachia and Moldavia. (NUCMC 75-663).

512 Paris. Peace Conference, 1919. U.S. Division of Territorial, Economic and Political Intelligence. Miscellaneous records, 1917-18. 7 ms. boxes, 3 card file boxes, .5 ft. Organization created to prepare background information for the U.S. delegation to the Paris Peace Conference; known as the Inquiry. Memoranda, notes, and reports relating to political and economic conditions in the Ottoman Empire and Latin America, proposals for new boundaries in Asia Minor, creation of an independent Armenia, and boundary disputes in South America.

513 Tõnu Parming. Study, 1977. 1 folder. "From the Republic of Estonia to the Estonian Soviet Socialist Republic: The Transfer of Rule and Sovereignty, 1939-1940." Estonian-American historian. Published as Chapter 1 of The Estonian S.S.R.: A Case Study of a Soviet Republic (Boulder: Westview Press, 1977), edited by Parming and Elmar Järvesoo.

514 Partiia Narodnoi Voli. Collection, n.d. Typescript, 1 folder. Translations of articles and declarations relating to the Narodnaia Volia and other nineteenth century Russian revolutionary parties, including the Partiia Sotsialistov-Revoliutsionerov.

515 Partiia Sotsialistov-Revoliutsionerov. Miscellaneous records, in Russian, 1914-23. Russian Socialist Revolutionary Party. Reports and minutes relating to the activities and views of the party, and to the Russian Revolution.

516 Stanley N. Partridge. Papers, 1918-45. 1 ms. box. Colonel, U.S. Army; served with American Expeditionary Force in Siberia. Photographs, postcards, and letters relating to conditions in Siberia, China, and Japan, 1918-20; and U.S. military facilities in New Guinea and the Philippines, 1943-45.

517 Boris T. Pash. Papers, 1918-76. 1 ms. box, 4 envelopes, 3 albums, 62 reels of film. Colonel, U.S. army; military intelligence officer. Correspondence, memoranda, reports, orders, writings, photographs, films, and printed matter relating to the naval forces of General Nikolai Iudenich during the Russian Civil War; the Russian refugee camp in Wuensdorf, Germany, in 1922; U.S. military intelligence service activities, including the Baja Peninsula mission to investigate the possible establishment of a Japanese base in Mexico in 1942, and the Alsos mission to determine the status of German nuclear development in 1944-45; and to allegations made in 1975 of the involvement of B. T. Pash with Central Intelligence Agency assassination plots.

518 Vladimir D. Pastuhov (1898-1967). Papers, in English, French, Russian, and Chinese, 1927-38. 58 ms. boxes, 13 albums, 1 envelope, 3 oversize packages, 2 ft. Secretary, League of Nations Commission of Enquiry in Manchuria, 1931-34. Correspondence, memoranda, reports, interviews, maps, photographs, and printed matter relating to the investigation of the Manchurian incident of 1931.

519 Patouillet. Diary, in French, 1916-18. Typescript, carbon copy, 1 vol. Frenchwoman in Russia. Relates to conditions in Petrograd and Moscow during World War I and the Russian Revolution, October 1916-August 1918.

520 Iv. Pavlov (pseud.). Memoir, in Russian, n.d. Typescript, 1 vol. "Notes of an Oppositionist: Reminiscences, Impressions, and Encounters." Russian member of Trotskiist opposition group, 1924-28. Relates to the Trotskiist opposition in Russia.

521 Dimitrii Petrovich Pershin. Papers, in Russian, 1916-36. 2.5 ms. boxes. White Russian diplomat. Correspondence, diaries, writings, notes, and clippings relating to White Russian and Soviet activities in Mongolia during the Russian Revolution, and the Russian émigré population during the Russian Civil War and subsequent years. Includes a memoir, handwritten, entitled "Baron Ungern, Urga i Altan-Bulak: Zapiski Ochevidtsa o Smutnom Vremeni vo Vneshnei (Khakhaskoi) Mongolii v Pervoi Treti XX-go Veka" (Baron Ungern, Urga and Altan-Bulak: An Eyewitness Account of the Troubled Times in Outer (Khalkha) Mongolia during the First Third of the XXth Century), relating to counter-revolutionary events in Mongolia

during the Russian Revolution, and a translation, typewritten, by Elena Varneck of the memoir.

522 V. A. Pertsov. Translation of diary extracts, 1919. Typescript, carbon copy, 1 vol. White Russian military aviation cadet, 1919. Relates to the evacuation of White Russian military personnel from Kurgan in Western Siberia to Spassk, near Vladivostok, July-August 1919.

523 Constantin A. Pertzoff (b. 1899). Letter, 1932, to Harold H. Fisher. Typescript, photocopy, 1 vol. White Russian soldier in the Russian Civil War. Relates to the question of Allied responsibility for the downfall of Admiral Aleksandr Kolchak during the Russian Civil War.

524 (Arkadii Nikolaevich) Petrov. Certificates, in Russian, 1918. Typescript, 1 folder. Relates to the appointment of A. Petrov to official positions under the White Russian Omsk government in Siberia.

525 Ivan Petrushevich (1875-1950). Papers, 1910-41. 6 ms. boxes, 5 microfilm reels. Ukrainian journalist. Diaries, correspondence, speeches and writings, memoranda, and clippings relating to the Ukraine during the Russian Revolution, Ukrainian territorial questions, the cooperative movement in the Ukraine, and Ukrainians in Canada and the U.S.

526 Werner Philipp. Translation of a study, n.d. Typescript, mimeographed, 1 folder. "The Historical Conditioning of Political Thought in Russia." Relates to the Russian tradition of political theory. Original study, entitled "Historische Voraussetzungen des politischen Denkens in Russland," published in Forschungen zur osteuropaeischen Geschichte (Bd. 1, 1954).

527 Carrie Pickett. Papers, 1919-21. .5 ms. box, 1 envelope. American Red Cross nurse in Siberia and Poland, 1919-21. Letters, reports, citations, photographs, and memorabilia relating to the activities of the American Red Cross in Siberia and Poland. Includes an account of various operations of the Czechoslovak Legion in Siberia. (NUCMC 75-665)

528 Richard A. Pierce. Study, 1957. Typescript, carbon copy, 1 vol. "The Origins of Bolshevism in Russian Central Asia." Prepared for the Columbia University Research Program on the History of the Communist Party of the Soviet Union.

529 Antonius Piip. Writings, in English and French, 1920-32. Typescript, mimeographed, 1 folder. Prime minister of Estonia, 1920-21. Relates to the independence of Latvia, diplomatic recognition of Estonia, Estonian membership in the League of Nations, and relations between Estonia and the Soviet Union.

530 Malcolm Pirnie. Papers, 1917-18. .5 ms box, 1 envelope, 1 album. American Red Cross worker in Russia, 1917. Diary transcripts, correspondence, photographs, clippings, and miscellanea relating to Red Cross relief work in Russia and to conditions in Russia during the Russian Revolution.

531 Valerian Platonovich Platonov (b. 1809?). Papers, in Russian, French, and Polish, 1815-84. 3 ms. boxes. Russian state secretary for Polish affairs, 1864-66. Correspondence, reports, and printed matter relating to Russian governmental administration in Poland, political, economic, and religious conditions in Poland, and the Polish revolution of 1863-64.

532 (Viacheslav Konstantinovich) Pleve. Photograph, n.d. 1 envelope. Depicts the tsarist Russian government official V. K. Pleve.

533 Aleksandr I. Pogrebetskii. Translation of excerpts from a study, n.d. Typescript, 1 folder. "Monetary Circulation and Currencies of the Russian Far East during the Revolution and Civil War." Original study, entitled Denezhnoe Obrashchenie i Denezhnye Znaki Dalnego Vostoka za Period Voiny i Revoliutsii, published in Harbin, 1924. Translation by Elena Varneck.

534 Pokrovsk, Russia. Kantonnyi Ispolnitel'nyi Komitet. Reports, in Russian, 1926-27. 1 ms. box. Cantonal Executive Committee in Pokrovsk, capital of the Volga Germans. Relates to the activities of the local soviets, local administration, and economic questions.

535 Poland. Records, in Polish, 1918-45. 976 ms. boxes. Records of the Polish government in exile in London, 1939-45. Correspondence, memoranda, and reports relating primarily to foreign relations and other governmental functions of the Polish government in exile during World War II. Includes some records of the Polish Republic relating to political conditions in Poland and to Polish foreign relations between the 2 world wars. Preliminary inventory.

536 Poland. Ambasada, Russia. Records, in Polish, 1941-44. 54 ms. boxes. Polish embassy in the Soviet Union. Reports, correspondence, accounts, lists, testimonies, questionnaires, certificates, petitions, card files, maps, circulars, graphs, protocols, and clippings relating to World War II, the Soviet occupation of Poland, the Polish-Soviet military and diplomatic agreements of 1941, the re-establishment of the Polish embassy in Moscow, Polish prisoners-of-war in the Soviet Union, deportations of Polish citizens to the Soviet Union, labor camps and settlements, relief work by the Polish Social Welfare Department delegations among the deportees, the Polish Armed Forces formed in the Soviet Union, evacuation of the Polish embassy to Kuibyshev,

evacuation of Polish citizens to the Middle East, the Katyn massacre of Polish officers, and the break-down of Polish-Soviet relations in April 1943. Includes material on the Communist Party of the Soviet Union and the Soviet government, 1928-29. Register.

537 Poland, Ambasada, U.S. Records, in Polish, 1918-56. 118 ms. boxes. Polish embassy in the U.S. Reports, correspondence, bulletins, communiqués, memoranda, dispatches, instructions, speeches, writings, and printed matter relating to the establishment of the Republic of Poland, the Polish-Soviet War of 1920, Polish politics and foreign relations, national minorities in Poland, the territorial questions of Danzig, Memel, the Polish Corridor, and Galicia, the Polish emigration abroad, Poland during World War II, and the Polish government in exile in London. Register.

538 Poland. Konsulat Generalny, New York. Records, in Polish, 1940-48. 7 ms. boxes. Polish consulate general in New York City. Correspondence, telegrams, memoranda, reports, agreements, minutes, histories, financial records, lists, press summaries, photographs, and printed matter relating to the German and Soviet occupation of Poland during World War II, activities of the Polish government in exile (London), and displaced Polish citizens after World War II.

539 Poland. Ministerstwo Prac Kongresowych. Miscellaneous records, mainly in Polish, 1940-44. 11.5 ms. boxes. Ministry of Preparatory Work Concerning the Peace Conference, Polish government in exile (London). Essays, bulletins, reports and studies relating to Poland's boundary disputes following World Wars I and II, events and conditions in Poland under German and Soviet occupation during World War II, Polish-Soviet relations, communism in Poland, and twentieth-century Polish agriculture, economy, foreign relations, history, politics, and government. Preliminary inventory.

540 Poland. Ministerstwo Spraw Wewnetrznych. Issuances, in Polish, 1942-44. Typescript, mimeographed, 16 ms. boxes. Ministry of the Interior of the Polish government in exile (London). Reports and bulletins relating to Polish politics and government, social conditions in Poland, the German and Soviet occupations of Poland, and the Polish underground movement during World War II. Includes reports and studies prepared by the Ministries of National Defense and Military Affairs. Preliminary inventory.

541 Poland. Polskie Rzadowe Centrum Informacyjne, New York. Records, in Polish and English, 1940-45. Ca. 70 ms. boxes. Polish Information Center, New York. Clippings, primarily from U.S. sources, correspondence, administrative files, press reviews and summaries, bulletins and printed matter relating to World War II, the German and Soviet occupations of Poland, the persecution of Jews in Poland, and the spread of communism in Eastern Europe.

542 Poland, Polskie Sily Zbronjne. Miscellaneous records, in Polish, 1940-45. 10 ms. boxes. Armed forces of the Polish government in exile (London). Correspondence, telegrams, memoranda, bulletins, reports, military orders and instructions, personnel rosters, lists, charts and maps relating to the Polish army in the East and in the USSR, conditions and events in the Soviet Union, Polish civil and military personnel in the Soviet Union, relations of the Polish army in the USSR with the Soviet military command, and operations of various branches of the Polish armed forces in Eastern Europe and the Middle East. Preliminary inventory.

543 Poland. Rada Ministrow. Reports, 1946. Typescript, mimeographed, .5 ms. box. Council of Ministers of the Polish government in exile in London. Reports, entitled "Facts and Documents Concerning Polish Prisoners of War Captured by the U.S.S.R. during the 1939 Campaign" and "The Mass Murder of Polish Prisoners of War in Katyn," relating to the Katyn Forest massacre.

544 W. P. von Poletika. Miscellaneous papers, in German, 1941-47. 1 folder. German economist. Reports, studies, bibliographies, and proclamations relating to Soviet agricultural policy, and to German agricultural policy in occupied parts of Russia during the two world wars.

545 Politicheskyi Obedinennyi Komitet. Miscellany, in Russian, 1921. 1 folder. Russian émigré organization. Memorandum (mimeographed) relating to the program of the Politicheskyi Obedinennyi Komitet, and bulletins (typewritten) relating to the Politicheskyi Obedinennyi Komitet and to political developments in Russia.

546 Polpress. Press releases, 1945-46. Typescript, 1 folder. The Polish news agency in Moscow. Relates to Polish political and diplomatic events.

547 "Poltavskiia Eparkhial'nyia Diela" (Poltava Diocese Affairs). Broadside, printed in Russian, 1917. 1 folder. Relates to the situation of religion in Poltava, Ukraine, during the Russian Revolution.

548 Ellen Graefin Poninski. Memoir, in German, n.d. Typescript, carbon copy, 1 vol. "Aufzeichnungen nach Täglichen Notizen über die Jahre in Potsdam, 1945-1949" (Notes from Daily Notations on the Years in Potsdam, 1945-1949). German aristocrat. Relates to conditions in Potsdam under Soviet occupation after World War II.

549 Ithiel de Sola Pool (b. 1917). Collector. I. S. Pool collection on American Trotskiism,

1905-48. .5 ms. box. Mimeographed letters and circulars, pamphlets and leaflets relating to American Trotskiism, especially to factional disputes within the U.S. Socialist Workers Party, 1938-40, and to Trotskiist activities in the anti-fascist, antiwar labor movements. Includes some radical non-Trotskiist material.

550 Zarko Popović (b. 1896). Papers, in Serbo-Croation, 1940-74. 2 ms. boxes. Colonel, Yugoslav army. Military attaché to the Soviet Union, 1939-41. Correspondence, reports, memoranda, and clippings relating to Yugoslav-Soviet relations, the Yugoslav coup d'état of 27 March 1941, relations of the Yugoslav government in exile with the U.S. and Great Britain, the "Scandal of Cairo," and Draza Mihailović and the Yugoslav resistance movement during World War II. Register. Closed until November 1984.

551 Nikolai Nikolaievich Poppe (b. 1897). Interview, in Russian, n.d. 17 phonorecords. Specialist in Mongolian culture. Relates to the Akademiia Nauk SSSR (Soviet Academy of Sciences) and government-scholar relations in the 1920s-early 1930s. Poppe was one of the first academy members to defect from the Soviet Union. Interview conducted by Sergei Yakobson ca. 1950.

552 "The Port Arthur Diary." Translation of table of contents, n.d. Typescript, 1 folder. Diary of an unknown Russian relating to the siege of Port Arthur during the Russo-Japanese War, January 1904-April 1905. Translation by Elena Varneck.

553 Posolskaia Incident collection, 1920. 1 vol. Transcripts of testimony, summaries of conferences, declarations, and notes relating to the capture of the armored train of Ataman Grigorii Semenov, White Russian military leader, by the U.S. 27th Infantry Regiment at Posolskaia, Siberia, and to alleged atrocities committed by the troops of Ataman Semenov.

554 Stefan Thomas Possony (b. 1913). Papers, in English and French, 1940-77. 27 ms. boxes. American political scientist; senior fellow, Hoover Institution on War, Revolution and Peace. Correspondence, writings, reports, research notes, bibliographic card files, term papers, examination papers, periodical articles, and newspaper clippings relating to military science, technology, national defense, international relations, Soviet foreign policy, revolution in the 20th c. and communism.

555 Wilber E. Post. History, 1918-19. Typescript, carbon copy, 1 vol. Relates to the Russian Revolution and Civil War in the Caucasus region, Allied intervention in the area, and economic conditions in the Caucasus. Written by W. E. Post and Maurice Wertheim.

556 Poster collection. Ca. 40,000 posters. Posters from many countries relating to the two world wars, political conditions in the twentieth century, and various other subjects. Collection includes primarily propaganda posters issued by the French, German, United States, and British governments during World War I and II and by the Russian Bolshevik and German Nazi parties. Some Soviet posters are also present.

557 E. Postnikova. History, in Russian, 1924. Typescript, 1 vol. "R.S.F.S.R." Relates to the Russian Socialist Federated Soviet Republic during the Russian Civil War, 1919-21.

558 Sergei Nikolaievich Pototskii (b. 1877). Papers, mainly in Russian, 1903-46. 40 ms. boxes, 2 card file boxes, .33 ft., 1 envelope. Major general, Russian Imperial Army, military attaché to Denmark, 1915. Correspondence, telegrams, reports, protocols, lists, orders, circulars, accounts and receipts, card file, and photographs relating to Russian Imperial military agencies in Copenhagen and Berlin, the Russian Imperial Passport Control Office in Copenhagen, the Russian prisoner-of-war and refugee camp at Horserød, the Russian Red Cross, military benevolent émigré organizations and activities, and Russian participation in World War I and the Russian Civil War. Register (NUCMC 71-1114). Consult archivist for restriction.

559 Michal Potulicki (b. 1897). Papers, in Polish, 1933-45. 2.5 ms. boxes. Polish law professor, principal legal adviser, Foreign Ministry, Polish government in exile (London), 1941-45; secretary general, Inter-Allied Research Committee (London). Bulletins, reports, studies, correspondence, notes, and clippings relating to Polish politics and government, German war crimes, Germany during World War II, prisoners of war in Germany, the German invasion of Poland, and Polish relations with Britain, France, and the Soviet Union. Includes bulletins, reports, and studies of the Inter-Allied Research Committee (London) relating to German propaganda during World War II, the German mentality, and nazism. Preliminary inventory.

560 Pravda (Truth). Translation of newspaper article excerpts, in German, 1917. Typescript, 1 folder. Bolshevik newspaper. Relates to the social democratic peace conference in Stockholm, and to the suppression of the Bolsheviks in Russia during the "July Days." Excerpts are dated July-August 1917.

561 Preparatory Commission of the United Nations. Records, 1945. Microfilm, 1 reel. Commission for work preparatory to the founding of the United Nations.

562 "The Present State of Latvia's Railways and the Views for the Future." Report, n.d. Typescript, mimeographed, 1 folder.

563 Press: Archangel, Russia. Translations of newspaper article extracts, 1918-19.

Typescript, 1 folder. Relates to the Russian Civil War, November 1918-July 1919. Translated from Archangel newspapers.

564 Princeton Listening Post. Transcripts of radio broadcasts, 1939-41. Typescript, 12 ms. boxes. Monitoring station for European radio broadcasts during World War II. Transcripts of news broadcasts from London, Paris, Rome, Berlin, and Moscow relating to war news, December 1939-May 1941.

565 Hjalmar Johan Fredrik Procopé (1889-1954). Papers, in Finnish, 1939-45. 8 microfilm reels. Finnish diplomat and politician; minister of Foreign Affairs, 1924-25 and 1927-31; minister to the U.S., 1939-44. Correspondence, diplomatic dispatches, memoranda, and reports relating to Finnish foreign relations during the Russo-Finnish War and World War II. Consult archivist for restriction.

566 Dimitri Pronin (b. 1900). History, n.d. Typescript, photocopy, .5 ms. box. "Europe in Flames." Relates to the Soviet and German occupation of Poland, 1939-45.

567 Propaganda, Communist, Russia. Collection, in Russian, 1929-31. Printed, 1 folder. Leaflets and posters propagating atheism and communism. Issued in the Soviet Union.

568 Protocols of the Wise Men of Zion. Writing, in Russian, n.d. Handwritten, 1 folder. "Sionskie Protokoly" (Protocols of Zion). Anti-Semitic propaganda tract.

569 F.A. Puchkov. Translation of history, n.d. Typescript, 1 vol. "The Icy March." Relates to White Russian military activities in Siberia during the Russian Civil War. Original published under the title "Vos'maia Kamskaia Strelkovaia Diviziia v Sibirskom Ledianom Pokhode" in Vestnik Obshchestva Russkikh Veteranov Velikoi Voiny. Translated, with commentary, by Elena Varneck.

570 Chester Wells Purington. Report, 1921. Typewritten transcript, 1 folder. American mining engineer. Relates to political and economic conditions in eastern Siberia, and to Japanese intervention in that area, during the period 1918-21. Report submitted to the U.S. State Department and U.S. Army Military Intelligence Division.

571 Kaarel Robert Pusta (1883-1964). Papers, in Estonian, French, and English, 1918-64. 20 ms. boxes. Estonian diplomat; foreign minister of Estonia, 1924-25. Correspondence, speeches, writings, memoranda, reports, printed matter, and photographs relating to Estonian politics and diplomacy, Soviet-Baltic State relations, the League of Nations, international law, and Estonian émigré politics. Preliminary inventory.

572 Gavriel Ra'anan. Study, 1977. Typescript, photocopy, 1 folder. "The Zhdanovshchina, Soviet Factional 'Debates' over International Policies and the Tito 'Affair.'" Relates to Soviet foreign policy decision-making in the early post-World War II period, the Stalin-Tito break, the political struggle between A. A. Zhdanov and G. M. Malenkov, and other Soviet internal controversies and debates. May not be used without written permission of G. Ra'anan.

573 Max Rabinoff (b. 1877). Autobiography, n.d. Typescript, .5 ms. box. "Web of My Life." Russian-American impresario. Relates to unofficial diplomatic and commercial relations between the United States and the Soviet Union during the 1920s.

574 Karl Radek (1885-1939). Letter, in German, 1919, to Paul Levi. Holograph, photocopy, 1 folder. Russian communist leader; relates to the communist movement in Germany.

575 Winifred V. Ramplee-Smith. Collector. W. V. Ramplee-Smith collection on the Russian revolution, in Russian and English, 1915-17. 1 ms. box, 1 folder, 1 envelope. Pamphlets, leaflets, clippings, and postcards relating to the February 1917 Revolution in Russia. Includes fragments of burned records of the tsarist secret police (Okhrana), which Ramplee-Smith surreptitiously removed from the Okhrana's St. Petersburg office files, then being burned by Bolshevik soldiers. Preliminary inventory.

576 Poul Ranzow Engelhardt (b. 1898). Memoir, 1961. Typescript, carbon copy, 1 vol. Major, Danish army; colonel, Viking Division, Waffen-SS. Relates to the German occupation of Denmark during World War II and to the formation of the Viking Division of Scandinavian and Dutch volunteers within the Waffen-SS to fight against the Soviet army.

577 Grigorii Efimovich Rasputin (1871-1916). Note, in Russian, 1916. Holograph, photocopy, 1 folder. Adviser to Tsar Nicholas II and Tsarina Alexandra of Russia. Includes explanatory letter by Peter S. Soudakoff, 4 March 1966, and an affidavit copy certifying the authenticity of Rasputin's handwriting.

578 Red Cross. U.S. American National Red Cross. Records, 1917-21. 217 ms. boxes, 38 vols., 2 scrapbooks. American charitable organization. Correspondence, memoranda, reports, financial records, and photographs relating to relief work in Europe, the Middle East, China, and Siberia during and immediately after World War I. Preliminary inventory.

579 Red Myth. Motion picture, 1961. 13 reels. Relates to the history of communism. Produced for television by KQED-TV, San Francisco, in cooperation with the Hoover Institution on War, Revolution and Peace.

580 Fedor Petrovich Rerberg (b. 1868). Memoirs, in Russian and French, 1922-25. Holograph and typescript, 1 ms. box. Russian Imperial Army officer; chief of staff, X Corps, and chief of staff, Sevastopol' Fortress, during World War I. Relates to the X Corps, the Sevastopol' Fortress during World War I and the Russian Civil War, and White Russian and Allied military activities in the Crimea during the Russian Civil War.

581 "Revel'skaia Gavan' i Bol'sheviki" (Revel Harbor and the Bolsheviks). Report, in Russian, 1921. Typescript, carbon copy, 1 vol. Relates to commerce conducted through the port of Tallinn, Estonia, during the Russian Civil War.

582 Elliott H. Reynolds. Letters to Helen B. Sutleff, 1918-19. Holograph, 1 folder. Private, U.S. army. Relating to activities of the American Expeditionary Force in Siberia.

583 N. M. Riabukhin. Translation of memoir, n.d. 1 vol. "The Story of Baron Ungern-Sternberg." Russian staff physician to Baron Roman Ungern-Shternberg. Relates to activities of White Russian military forces under Baron Ungern-Shternberg in Mongolia during the Russian Civil War.

584 Gardner Richardson. Papers, 1911-24. .5 ms. box, 2 albums, 2 envelopes, 1 portfolio. Official of the Commission for Relief in Belgium and of the American Relief Administration in Austria. Photographs, resolutions, and letters of gratitude relating to relief work in Styria, Austria, and in Odessa, Russia, and to the University of Vienna Children's Clinic.

585 Treaty of Riga, 1920. Translation of preliminary peace treaty and armistice, 1920. Typescript, 1 folder. Treaty between Poland and Russia, signed at Riga, 11 October 1920, halting the Russo-Polish War.

586 Arthur C. Ringland. Papers, 1921-60. 1 folder. American Relief Administration worker in Czechoslovakia, 1921-22. Memoranda and printed matter relating to League of Nations cooperation with American Relief Administration activities in Russia, the attitude of Aleksandr Kerensky in 1921 toward American Relief Administration activities in Russia, and subsequent Soviet attitudes toward American Relief Administration activities in Russia.

587 Fedor Izmailovich Rodichev (1854-1933). Memoirs, in Russian, 1924. Typescript, 1 folder. "Vospominaniia F. I. Rodicheva o 1917 godu" (Reminiscences of F. I. Rodichev about 1917). Leader of Russian Konstitutsionno-Demokraticheskaia Partiia; member of all Gosudarstvennaia Dumas; minister for Finnish affairs in the Provisional Government, 1917. Relates to events in Russia during the 1917 Revolution. Includes a biographical sketch of F. I. Rodichev by his daughter, Alexandrine Rodichev, 1933.

588 Mikhail Vladimirovich Rodzianko (1859-1924). Papers, in Russian, 1914-21. .5 ms. box. President, Gosudarstvennaia Duma of Russia. Correspondence, writings, and reports relating to Russian efforts in World War I, the Russian Revolution and Civil War, and the anti-Bolshevik movements. Includes letters and reports to Generals Wrangel and Denikin. Preliminary inventory.

589 Leighton W. Rogers. Memoir, n.d. Typescript, 1 folder. "An Account of the March Revolution, 1917." American official, Petrograd branch, National City Bank, 1917. Relates to the Russian Revolution of February 1917.

590 Tadeusz Romer (b. 1894). Papers, in Polish, 1913-75. 9 reels. Microfilm of originals at the Public Archives of Canada. Polish statesman, diplomat, and professor; ambassador to the Soviet Union, 1942-43; minister of foreign affairs, Polish government in exile (London), 1943-44. Correspondence, memoranda, speeches, writings, reports, telegrams, minutes of meetings, clippings, and printed matter relating to political events in Poland, Polish foreign relations, and Polish émigré politics. Many references to the USSR. Preliminary inventory. May not be used without the permission of T. Romer or his representative until 10 years after the death of T. Romer.

591 Sergei Aleksandrovich Ronzhin. Study, in Russian, 1925. Typescript, 1 folder. "Zhelieszn'yia Dorogi v Voennoe Vremia" (Railroads in Wartime). General, Russian Imperial Army. Relates to the use of railroads in Russia during World War I.

592 Robert Rosenbluth. Reports, 1919. Typescript, 1 folder. American Relief Administration worker in Russia, 1919. Reports, entitled "General Résumé, Russian Situation" and "Memorandum on Russian Affairs," relating to political and economic conditions and relief needs in Russia.

593 Rossiisko-Amerikanskaia Kompaniia. Summaries of laws, in Russian, ca. 1700-1860. Typescript and printed, 1 folder. Laws made by the Russian government to regulate settlements established by the Russian-American Company on the Pacific coast of North America.

594 Fedor Rostovtseff. Papers, in Russian, n.d. 2 ms. boxes. Russian émigré teacher in France. Writings, reports, notes and outlines for lectures, clippings, memorabilia, and syllabi for courses in Russian high schools in Paris, relating to Russian history from 1850 to 1940, French history, and logic. (NUCMC 71-1118)

595 Joseph Slabey Roucek (b. 1902). Papers, 1920-49. 38 ms. boxes, 2 envelopes. American sociologist and political scientist. Correspondence, writings, clippings, photographs, slides, and miscellanea relating to Slavs in the U.S., and politics, social conditions, and

education in Eastern Europe, especially the Balkan countries. Also, information on the educational system and political development of the Baltic states in the 1930s-1940s. Register (NUCMC 75-669).

596 Anatolii Nikolaevich Rozenshil'd-Paulin. Diary extracts, in Russian, 1915-16. Typescript, carbon copy, with 5 maps. 1 vol. General, Russian Imperial Army, commanding general, 29th Infantry Division. Relates to operations of the 29th Division during World War I and to the imprisonment of A. N. Rozenshil'd-Paulin in a German prison camp.

597 Ilya Alexeevich Rudneff (1892-1969). Papers, in Russian, 1913-23. 1 ms. box, 3 envelopes. Colonel, Russian Imperial Air Forces. Correspondence, photographs, and miscellany relating to Russian aviation in World War I, and White Russian military activities during the Russian Civil War (NUCMC 71-1119).

598 Arthur Ruhl. Series of articles, 1925. Typescript, 1 folder. "Russia Revisited." American visitor to Russia. Relates to social conditions and the situation of industry, education, and religion in Russia.

599 (Sergei Vasil'evich) Rukhlov. Photograph, n.d. 1 envelope. Depicts the tsarist Russian government official S. V. Rukhlov.

600 Russia. Armiia. Kavkazskaia Armiia. Miscellaneous records, in Russian, 1915-16. 1 folder. Russian Imperial Caucasian Army. Orders, reports, and a map relating to Russian military operations in Transcaucasia during World War I.

601 Russia. Armiia. 10. Korpus. War journal, in Russian, 1914. Typescript, 1 vol. Russian Imperial 10th Army Corps. Relates to activities of the 10th Corps at the outbreak of World War I, 10-31 August 1914.

602 Russia. Armiia. Leib-Gvardii Kirasirskii Ego Velichestva Polk. Collection, in Russian, 1916-74. 7 ms. boxes, 1 album. Correspondence, diaries, reports, memoranda, newsletters, books, photographs, and printed matter relating to the activities of the Imperial Russian Kirasir Household Troops Regiment of His Majesty before and during the Russian Revolution and Civil War and to the activities of surviving members in foreign countries after their emigration from Russia. Preliminary inventory.

603 Russia. Departament Politsii. Zagranichnaia Agentura, Paris. Records, mainly in Russian, 1883-1917. 203 ms. boxes, 10 vols. of clippings, 163,802 biographical and reference cards, 8 ft. of photographs. Russian Imperial Secret Police (Okhrana), Paris office. Intelligence reports from agents in the field and the Paris office, dispatches, circulars, headquarters studies, correspondence of revolutionaries, and photographs relating to activities of Russian revolutionists abroad. Preliminary inventory (NUCMC 71-1120).

604 Russia, famines. Photographs, 1922-23. 1 envelope. Depicts Russian famine scenes.

605 Russia. Gosudarstvennaia Duma. Collection, in Russian and English, 1906-16. 1 ms. box, 1 envelope. Proclamations, speeches, photograph, and translation of proceedings of the Russian Duma, relating to activities of the Duma and to political conditions in Russia.

606 Russia, history, Revolution of 1905. Photograph, n.d. 1 envelope. Depicts a poster commemorating the Russian Revolution of 1905.

607 Russia, history, Revolution, 1917-21. Collection, in Russian, ca. 1917-21. 1 ms. box. Miscellaneous posters and broadsides, and photocopies of newspaper and periodical articles, relating to the Russian Civil War.

608 Russia. Kabinet Ego Imperatorskago Velichestva. Ispolnitel'naia Kommissiia po Ustroistvu zemel' Glukhoozerskoi Fermy. Account book, in Russian, 1900. Holograph, 1 vol. Russian Imperial Cabinet Executive Commission for the Organization of Lands of the Glukhoozerskaia Farm. Relates to expenses of digging canals on the Glukhoozerskaia Farm, an estate of Nicholas II, Tsar of Russia.

609 Russia. Konsul'stvo, Breslau. Records, in Russian and German, 1860-1914. 10 ms. boxes. Russian consulate in Breslau. Correspondence, intelligence reports, orders, and printed matter relating to Russian-German relations, especially commercial relations. Preliminary inventory.

610 Russia. Konsul'stvo, Leipzig. Records, in Russian and German, 1830-1914. 7 ms. boxes. Russian consulate in Leipzig. Correspondence, reports, and printed matter relating to Russian-German relations, especially commercial relations. Preliminary inventory (NUCMC 68-417).

611 Russia. Legatsiia (Hesse). Records, in Russian and German, 1857-1913. 17 ms. boxes. Russian legation in Hesse (Hesse-Darmstadt until 1866). Correspondence, reports, circulars, instructions, telegrams, and printed matter relating to Russian-German relations. Preliminary inventory.

612 Russia. Legatsiia (Saxe-Weimar-Eisenach). Records, in Russian, French, and German, 1902-1908. 2 ms. boxes. Russian legation in Saxe-Weimar-Eisenach. Correspondence, orders, reports, and printed matter relating to Russian-German relations. Preliminary inventory.

613 Russia. Legatsiia (Wuerttemberg). Records, in French, Russian, and German, 1828-1904. 16

ms. boxes. Russian legation in Wuerttemberg. Correspondence, reports, orders, memoranda, and notes relating to Russian-Wuerttemberg relations. Preliminary inventory.

614 Russia, photographs, 1887-1977. 6 envelopes, 1 album, 20 glass slides. Photographs and postcards depicting members of the Romanov family and Imperial Russian nobility, military officers, statesmen, Russian churches, icons, art objects, cities, buildings, and scenes of daily life before 1917. Includes some post-1917 émigré subjects. Various sources, various dates.

615 Russia. Posol'stvo (France). Records, in Russian and French, 1917-24. 36.5 ms. boxes. Russian embassy in France. Correspondence, reports, memoranda, and notes relating to relations between France and the Russian Provisional Government, the Russian Revolution, counter-revolutionary movements, the Paris Peace Conference, and Russian émigrés after the revolution. Register (NUCMC 71-1121).

616 Russia. Posol'stvo (U.S.). Records, mainly in Russian, ca. 1914-33. 260 ft. Russian Imperial and Provisional Government embassies in the U.S. Correspondence, telegrams, memoranda, reports, agreements, minutes, histories, financial records, lists, and printed matter relating to Russia's role in World War I, the Russian Revolution and Civil War, activities of the Russian Red Cross, Russian émigrés in foreign countries, and operations of the embassy office. Includes files of the Russian military attaché in the U.S., the Russian financial agent in the U.S., and numerous Imperial Russian and Provisional Government embassies and legations that closed after the Russian Revolution and Civil War.

617 Russia. Shtab Verkhovnogo Glavnokomanduiushchego. Miscellaneous records, in Russian, 1914-17. 1 ms. box. Supreme Command, Russian Imperial Army. Military orders and directives issued by the Supreme Command, 1914-15, and clippings collected by the Supreme Command, 1914-17, relating to World War I military campaigns, principally on the eastern front.

618 Russia. Sovet Ministrov. Miscellany, 1914. 1 folder. Translation, typewritten, of a summary report on the meeting of the Council of Ministers of Russia, 11 July 1914, relating to the reaction of the Russian government to Austro-Hungarian demands made against Serbia; and a memorandum, typewritten, by Robert C. Binkley, relating to the significance of this document in assessing war guilt for the outbreak of World War I.

619 Russia. Voenno-Morskoi Agent (Germany). Records, in Russian and German, 1873-1912. 3 ms. boxes. Russian naval agent in Germany. Correspondence, reports, orders, and printed matter relating to Russian-German naval relations, and to Russian purchases of ships, ordnance and naval equipment from German firms. Preliminary inventory.

620 Russia. Voennoe Ministerstvo. Report, in Russian, ca. 1916. Typescript, carbon copy, 1 vol. "Kratkii Otchet o Dieiatel'nosti Voennago Ministerstva za 1916 god." (Brief Report on the Activities of the War Ministry for the Year 1916). Russian Imperial War Ministry. Relates to Russian military activities in World War I.

621 Russia. Voennyi Agent (Japan). Records, in Russian, 1906-21. 16 ms. boxes. General M. P. Podtiagin, Russian military attaché in Japan. Letters, telegrams, contracts, minutes, receipts, memoranda, reports, accounts, declarations, requests, orders, instructions, packing and shipping specifications, invoices, insurance policies, bills of lading, blueprints, tables, diagrams, certificates, and lists relating to the Japanese army, political movements in Japan, and the purchase by the Russian army of military supplies from Japanese firms. Register (NUCMC 72-1487).

622 Russia (1918-20) Vooruzhennye Sily Iuga Rossii. Nachal'nik Snabzheniia. Records, in Russian, 1916-26. 6 ms. boxes. Chief of Supply, White Russian Army. Correspondence, reports, receipts, and accounts relating to the payment of Russian soldiers in Bulgaria and Yugoslavia, financial subsidies to refugees, administration of refugee camp facilities, and the composition and distribution of units of the First Army Corps and the Don Corps. Register (NUCMC 68-653, in part).

623 Russia (1918-20) Vooruzhennye Sily Iuga Rossii. Sudnoe Otdielenie. Records, in Russian and Bulgarian, 1918-27. 9 ms. boxes. Justice Department, White Russian Army. Correspondence, reports, memoranda, orders, and affidavits relating to administration of military justice in the White Russian Army, Russian émigrés in Bulgaria, the political situation in Bulgaria, and the composition and distribution of the First Army Corps and the Don Corps. Register (NUCMC 68-653, in part).

624 Russia - World War I. Collection, in Russian, 1916-22. .5 ms. box. Photographs, calendars, and paper cut-out caricatures relating to Russia during World War I. Includes lithographs of Russian troops, a pictorial booklet on Russian wounded, photographs of an unidentified Russian officer and his family, caricatures of the belligerent powers, and Bolshevik calendars.

625 Russia (1917 Provisional Government). Photographs, 1917. 1 envelope. Photographs issued by the Russian Provisional Government, depicting scenes of the Russian Revolution.

626 Russia (1917 Provisional Government) Vserossiiskoe Uchreditel'noe Sobranie. Translation of proceedings, 1918. Typescript, 1 vol. All-Russian Constituent Assembly. Relates to the opening session of the assembly, 5 January 1918.

627 Russia (1917-R.S.F.S.R.) Chrezvychainaia Komissia po Bor'be s Kontr-Revoliutsiei i Sabotazhem. Photographs, ca. 1920. 1 envelope. Depicts atrocities committed by the Soviet secret police against White Russian forces in Kiev.

628 Russia (1917-R.S.F.S.R.) Tsentral'naia Komissiia Pomoshchi Golodaiushchim. Translation of report, 1922. Typescript, 1 ms. box. "Totals of the Struggle against Famine in 1921-22: Collection of Articles and Reports." Central Famine Relief Committee of the Soviet government. Translated by the Russian Unit Historical Division of the American Relief Administration.

629 Russia (1918-20) Dobrovol'cheskaia Armiia. Glavnyi Kaznachei. Account books, in Russian, n.d. 1 folder. Treasury of the White Russian Volunteer Army. Relates to the financial operations for the Russian Volunteer Army.

630 Russia (1918-20) Donskaia Armiia. Orders, in Russian, 1918-20. 1 ms. box. White Russian Don army. Relates to the Russian Civil War in the south of Russia.

631 Russia (1918-20) Vremennoe Sibirskoe Pravitel'stvo. Miscellaneous records, in English and Russian, 1918-19. 1 folder. Proclamations, memoranda, and reports issued by the Vremennoe Sibirskoe Pravitel'stvo (Provisional Government of Autonomous Siberia). Also includes some issuances of the U.S. Army forces in Siberia relating to the Provisional Government, and to the Civil War in Siberia.

632 Russia (1923-27, USSR) Narodnyi Komissariat po Inostrannym Delam. Diagrams, in Russian, 1927. Handwritten, 1 vol. Soviet Commissariat for Foreign Affairs. Illustrates the organization of the commissariat.

633 Russian Civil War in Georgia. Newspaper clippings, in Russian, 1920. 1 folder. Relates to the Russian Civil War in Georgia and elsewhere in Transcaucasia. Printed in Georgian newspaper.

634 Russian Commercial, Industrial and Financial Union. Committee for Study of Economic Conditions. Translation of study, 1931. Typescript, mimeographed, 1 folder. "Farm 'Collectivization' in Soviet Russia." Relates to agricultural policy in the Soviet Union.

635 Russian Imperial military documents. World War I, in Russian, 1915-17. 1 folder. Reports, orders, and maps relating to Russian Imperial military operations during World War I, the 7th Army Corps, and 13th Infantry Division. Preliminary inventory.

636 "Russian Public Debt: The Problem of the Distribution." Translation of study, 1923. Typescript, mimeographed, 1 folder. Relates to the financial situation of the Russian government. Study published in Agence Économique et Financière, 2 August 1923. Translated by S. Ughet.

637 Russian Review. Records, 1941-73. 10 ms. boxes. 3 cu. ft. boxes. Monthly periodical published at the Hoover Institution on War, Revolution and Peace. Correspondence, subscription files, unpublished articles submitted for publication, clippings, and printed matter relating to Russian and Soviet literature, politics and government, history, and political and scoial movements, before and after the Russian Revolution of 1917.

638 Russia's Five-Year Plan. Motion picture, n.d. 2 reels. Relates to the first Five-Year Plan, 1928-32. Includes sound track.

639 "Russie: Bulletin des Années 1917-1922" (Russia: Report on the Years 1917-1922). Bibliographical essay, in French, ca. 1922. Typescript, 1 folder. Relates to publications during the period 1917-22 on the subject of Russian history.

640 Viktor Nikolaevich Russiian. Study, n.d. Typescript, 1 folder. "The Work of Okhrana Departments in Russia." Major general, Russian Imperial Army. Relates to the structure and operations of the Russian secret service in Russia before the Revolution of 1917. Includes a draft with corrections and annotations.

641 John Russing. History, n.d. Typescript, 1 folder. "Petrograd Lancers in Service to their Country." Relates to activities of a Russian army regiment during World War I.

642 Russkiia Vedomosti (Moscow). Translation of excerpts from articles, 1918. Typescript, 1 folder. Moscow newspaper. Relates to instances of religious persecution of the Russian Orthodox Church in the Soviet Union. Includes accounts of events at the Alexandro-Nevskaia Lavra and the All-Russian Church Congress in Moscow, January-February 1918.

643 Russkoe Aktsionernoe Obshchestvo dlia Primeneniia Ozona. Issuances, in Russian, 1911-12. 1 folder. Russian Joint Stock Company for the Adaptation of Ozone. Relates to the establishment of a filter-ozonizing station in St. Petersburg.

644 Russkoe Slovo. Translation of excerpts from articles, n.d. Typescript, 1 folder. Russian newspaper. Relates to the activities of

Roman Malinovskii, a tsarist agent who infiltrated the Bolshevik Party in Russia.

645 Russo-Japanese War. Newspaper clippings, 1904-1905. 5 ms. boxes. Clippings from the U.S. press, principally in San Francisco, relating to the Russo-Japanese War.

646 Russo-Romanian relations. Report, in French, 1912. Transcript, typewritten, 1 folder. Relates to conversations between an unnamed Russian grand duke and a number of Romanian political leaders regarding Romanian foreign policy and Russo-Romanian relations. Written by the grand duke and addressed to Tsar Nicholas II.

647 T. Ryskulov. Excerpts from a study, in Russian, 1925. Typescript, 1 folder. Revoliutsiia i Korennoe Naselenie Turkestana (Revolution and the Indigenous Population of Turkestan). Relates to the Russian Revolution in Turkestan, 1917-19. Study published in Tashkent in 1925.

648 Edward G. Sabine. Collector. Photographs, ca. 1921-23. .5 ms. box. Depicts famine victims and American Relief Administration relief activities in the Samara region of Russia.

649 Konstantin Viacheslavovich Sakharov (b. 1881). Letter, 1933, to William S. Graves. Typescript, carbon copy, 1 vol. Relates to the book by W. S. Graves, America's Siberian Adventure, 1918-1920.

650 Ludmila (Tschebotariov) Safonov (b. 1897). Memoirs, ca. 1974. Typescript, photocopy, .5 ms. box. "Only My Memories." Russian émigré in the U.S. Relates to life in Russia 1900-19, immigration through the Far East and arrival in the United States, and work with displaced persons in Europe during World War II.

651 Voldermars Salnais (1886-1948). Papers, mainly in Latvian, 1918-45. 1.5 ms. boxes. 2 envelopes. Latvian diplomat; delegate to the League of Nations, 1921-34; minister to Sweden, Norway, and Denmark, 1937-40. Correspondence, reports, clippings, printed matter, and photographs relating to Latvian independence movements, foreign relations, and women's organizations, Latvians in Siberia, the Latvian National Council in Siberia (Vladivostok), and the Office of the Latvian representative in the Far East and Siberia. Includes some materials collected by Milda Salnais. Register.

652 Samizdat. Collection, in Russian, 1961-71. Photocopy, 1 folder. Underground Samizdat writings relating to political conditions, civil liberties, and non-Russian nationalism in the Soviet Union. Includes a protest of Latvian communists against Russian national domination.

653 Michael S. Samsonow (1900-1973). Papers, in English and French, 1919-67. .5 ms. box, 1 envelope. Hungarian-American historian. Memoirs, writings, and a photograph relating to Tsar Alexander III of Russia, Russian émigrés in Hungary after the Russian Revolution, and the provisions for a veto in the United Nations Charter.

654 William Sander. Collector. On occupied Germany, in German, 1945-49. 2 ms. boxes. Writings, correspondence, reports, and photographs relating to political, social, and economic conditions and to repression of civil liberties in the zone of Germany under Soviet occupation. Some items relate to the western zones of occupation and to the condition of German refugees from the area east of the Oder-Neisse line.

655 Clyde Sargent. Extracts from letters, 1941-47. Typescript, 1 folder. Professor, Cheeloo University, Chengtu, China, 1941; member, U.S.-USSR Joint Commission in Korea, 1947. Relates to the Sino-Japanese War, social conditions in China in 1941, and conditions in North Korea in 1947.

656 N. V. Savich. Memoir, in Russian, n.d. Typescript, 1 folder. Member of the Russian Duma. Relates to the Russian war program for 1917.

657 Petr Panteleimonovich Savin. Papers, in Russian, n.d. .5 ms. box. Captain, Russian Imperial Army. Photocopy of writing, entitled "Gibel' Generala Millera" (The Demise of General Miller), relating to the death of the White Russian military leader, E. K. Miller; and correspondence and printed matter relating to the writing and to Russian émigré anti-communist activities, 1917-68.

658 Boris Viktorovich Savinkov (1879-1925). Writings, in Russian and English, 1920-24. 1 folder. Russian Socialist Revolutionary Party leader. Letter, typewritten in Russian, to Baron Petr Wrangel, White Russian military commander, 1920, relating to White Russian military activities; and translation, typewritten, of the testimony of B. Savinkov at his trial for counter-revolutionary activities, 1924.

659 Lieutenant Savintsev. Diary, in Russian, 1920-21. Typescript, 1 folder. White Russian Army officer. Relates to the Russian Civil War in Siberia, August 1920-January 1921.

660 Sergei Dmitrievich Sazonov (1861-1927). Papers, in English, French, German, and Russian, 1915-27. 4 ms. boxes, 1 envelope. Russian diplomat; minister of foreign affairs, 1910-16. Memoirs, clippings, photograph, and correspondence relating to Imperial Russian foreign policy, and the Russian Revolution and Civil War.

661 Max Schnetzer. Report, in German, 1945. Typescript, 1 vol. "Tagebuch der Abenteuer:

Endkampf um Berlin, Reise durch Russland." (Diary of an Adventure: Final Struggle in Berlin, Journey through Russia). Swiss journalist. Relates to conditions in Berlin and in Russia in the spring of 1945, immediately before the German surrender.

662 Miroslav G. Schubert (b. 1895). Papers, in Czech and English, 1936-77. 2 ms. boxes. Czechoslovak diplomat; chargé d'affaires in Brazil, 1921-25; chargé d'affaires in Iran, 1927-32; counsellor and deputy envoy to Germany, 1934-38; consul general in Munich, 1945-48. Correspondence, speeches, writings, memoranda, reports, clippings, and other printed matter relating to World War II, the Soviet occupation of Czechoslovakia in 1945, international affairs in Europe during the interwar period, the Communist movement in Czechoslovakia, and the coup d'état of 1948.

663 Gero von Schulze-Gaevernitz (1901-1970). Papers, 1945. Photocopy, 2 folders. Special assistant to Allen W. Dulles, chief, Office of Strategic Services Mission in Europe during World War II. Letters relating to liaison between Allied forces and anti-Nazi groups, and the capitulation of German troops in Italy and southern Austria, and a report relating to a journey to Russia in 1923.

664 Hans Georg Schulze (d. 1941). Diary, in German, 1941. Holograph, 1 vol. Soldier, German army. Relates to campaigns on the Eastern front during World War II.

665 Eugene Schuyler. Biography, 1883. "Peter the Great, Emperor of Russia: A Study of Historical Biography." Holograph, 1 ms. box.

666 Alexis von Schwarz (b. 1874). History, in Russian, n.d. Typescript, carbon copy, 1 vol. "Opisanie Boevykh Dieistvii pod Ivangorodom s 8-go po 22-e Iiulia 1915 goda" (An Account of Combat Operations around Ivangorod from 8 to 22 July 1915).

667 Seine (Dept.) Préfecture de Police. Memoranda, in French, 1933-36. Typescript, 1 folder. Prefecture of Police in Paris. Relates to the presence of members of the family of Leon Trotskii, Russian revolutionary, in France, 1933, and to the theft of papers of Leon Trotskii from the International Institute for Social History in Paris, 1936.

668 Kārlis-Ludvigs Sēja (1885-1962). Papers, in Latvian, German, and English, 1934-71. 1 folder, 1 envelope. Latvian diplomat to the U.S., Great Britain, and Lithuania. Correspondence, photographs, and memorabilia relating to the displacement of the Sēja family during World War II, and to the arrest of L. Sēja by Soviet authorities at the end of the war. Preliminary inventory.

669 Evgenii Petrovich Semenov (b. 1861). Translation of articles, 1921. Typescript, 1 folder. "German Money to Lenin." Relates to allegations of German government subsidies to the Bolsheviks. Written by E. P. Semenov and Pavel Miliukov. Published in Poslednie Novosti, April 1921.

670 Grigorii Mikhailovich Semenov (1890-1945). Memoirs, in Russian, ca. 1937. Typescript, photocopy, 1 folder. "Istoriia Moei Bor'by s Bol'shevikami" (History of My Struggle with the Bolsheviks). Cossack ataman; White Russian military leader in Siberia during the Russian Civil War. Includes photocopy of a biographical sketch, typewritten in Russian, of G. Semenov, ca. 1937.

671 Ivan Innokentievich Serebrennikov (b. 1882). Papers, in Russian, 1906-48. 25 ms. boxes, 29 albums, 11 envelopes. Russian journalist; official, Siberian government, Omsk, 1917-18. Diaries, correspondence, writings, photographs, clippings, and notebooks relating to A. V. Kolchak, the Russian Civil War in Siberia, Russian émigrés in the Far East, and Chinese history and culture. Register. Consult archivist for access.

672 Marc Sevastopoulo. Letters received, in French, 1957-59, from Nicholas A. de Basily. Holograph, 1 folder. Relates to the Sevastopoulo family genealogy.

673 Nadezhda L. Shapiro-Lavrova. Memoir, in Russian, n.d. Typescript, 1 folder. Resident of Blagoveshchensk, Siberia. Relates to the Russian Civil War in the Blagoveshchensk area, and to the trial of A. N. Alekseevskii, a Socialist revolutionary, by the Bolsheviks in Blagoveshchensk in 1918. Includes a translation, typewritten, of the memoir by Elena Varneck.

674 Sergei Afanasevich Shchepikhin. Papers, in Russian, 1919-20. 1 ms. box. General and chief of staff, White Russian Army, 1919-20. Diaries and writings relating to the retreat of the Russian Volunteer armies toward Siberia, the government of Grigorii Semenov, Japanese intervention in the Siberian Far East, and the military activities of the Ural Cossacks against the Bolsheviks.

675 Dmitrii Grigorevich Shcherbachev (1855-1932). Papers, in Russian and French, 1914-20. 8 ms. boxes. General, Russian Imperial Army. Correspondence, orders, reports, and printed matter relating to Russian prisoners of war in Germany during World War I, counter-revolutionary movements during the Russian Revolution and Civil War, General A. I. Denikin and the Volunteer Army, Admiral A. V. Kolchak and the Siberian Army, and Bolshevik relations with Western European countries and the U.S. Preliminary inventory (NUCMC 71-1123).

676 Boris Sheiman. Translations, 1936-39. Typescript, .5 ms. box. Soviet statutes and articles published in Soviet journals, 1932-

38, relating to the Soviet judicial and penal systems, labor, social, and welfare legislation, and the legal position of the family in Soviet society. Preliminary inventory.

677 Klavdii Valentinovich Shevelev (b. 1881). Papers, in Russian, 1919-48. Photocopy, 1 folder, 1 envelope. Rear admiral, Russian Imperial Navy. Birth certificate, White Russian Naval Ministry identification document, International Refugee Organization documents, and photographs relating to the naval career and émigré life of K. V. Shevelev.

678 Ivan Fedorovich Shil'nikov. History, in Russian, 1933. Typescript, 1 folder. "Voevyia Dieistviia i Zabaikal'skogoi Kazach'ei Divizii v Velikoi Voine 1914-1918 Goda" (Military Operations of the Zabaikal Cossack Division in the Great War of 1914-1918). Published as 1-aia Zabaikal'skaia Kazach'ia Diviziia v Velikoi Evropeiskoi Voine 1914-1918g (1st Zabaikal Cossack Division in the Great European War, 1914-1918) (Harbin, 1933).

679 Demitri B. Shimkin. Study, 1949. Typescript, mimeographed, 1 folder. "The Mineral Self-Sufficiency of the Soviet Union." Relates to the extent and distribution of Soviet mineral resources and production.

680 (Andrei Ivanovich) Shingarev. Photograph, n.d. 1 envelope. Depicts A. I. Shingarev, minister of finance in the Russian Provisional Government, 1917.

681 Nikolai Vsevolodovich Shinkarenko (1890-1968). Memoirs, in Russian, n.d. Typescript, 7 pamphlet boxes, 2 ft. Russian Imperial Army officer; brigadier general of the Cavalry of the White Russian Army; Spanish Foreign Legion officer. Relates to Russian cavalry operations in World War I, White Russian military operations in the Russian Civil War, Spanish military operations in Africa, and Francoist military operations in the Spanish Civil War. Includes copies of letters and photographs. Pseudonym: N. Belogorskii. 1 sealed folder closed until 1 January 1985. (NUCMC 71-116)

682 John Amar Shishmanian (1882-1945). Papers, in English, French, and Armenian, 1903-45. 1 ms. box. Captain, French Foreign Legion, during World War I. Correspondence, printed matter, photographs, and memorabilia relating to the Armenian-Turkish conflict at the end of World War I, and to the Armenian question at the Paris Peace Conference. Preliminary inventory.

683 P. V. Shkurkin. Study, in Russian, n.d. Typescript, mimeographed, 1 folder. "Mozhet-li v Kitae Privit'sia Kommunizm?" (Can Communism Become Acclimated in China?). Includes translation, typewritten.

684 Andrei Grigor'evich Shkuro (1887-1947). Letter, in Russian, to Grand Duke Andrei Vladimirovich, 1932. Typescript, mimeographed, 1 folder. General, White Russian Army. Relates to Russian émigré politics.

685 M. M. Shneyeroff (b. 1880). Papers, in Russian and English, 1918-57. 1 ms. box. Member of the Russian Socialist Revolutionary Party. Memoirs, writings, and photographs relating to the Russian revolutionary movement in the early twentieth century, E. Breshko-Breshkovskaia, and V. Chernov. Preliminary inventory. Quotations limited to 500 words consecutively, and to 5000 words from any manuscript.

686 "Short Review of the Development of Latvian Literature." Memorandum, n.d. Typescript, mimeographed, 1 folder.

687 Kenneth O. Shrewsbury. Papers, 1919-22. 1 ms. box. American volunteer in the Kosciuszko Squadron. Photographs, clippings, and miscellanea relating to the activities of volunteer American aviators who formed the Kosciuszko Squadron of the Polish Army during the Polish-Russian War, 1919-21.

688 Iakov Shutko. Collector. Miscellany, in Russian, 1916-17. 1 folder. Reports, orders, and correspondence relating to Russian troops stationed at La Courtine, France, during World War I, and to revolutionary movements among the troops.

689 Dimitrii Andreevich Shvetzoff (b. 1902). Memoir, n.d. "Captivity and Escape of Horse-guardsman Dimitrii A. Shvetzoff in 1919-1921." Typescript, photocopy, 1 folder. Soldier, Russian Imperial Horse Guards. Relates to the activities of the Russian Imperial Horse Guard Regiment during the Russian Revolution and Civil War.

690 Ona Simaite (1894-1970). Papers, in Lithuanian, 1941-70. 2 ms. boxes, 1 envelope. Lithuanian librarian and literary critic. Correspondence, notes, memorabilia, and photographs relating to underground aid to the Jewish ghetto inhabitants of Vilnius, Lithuania, during the German occupation, 1941-44. Register.

691 Vladimir Evgenievich Skalskii. Memoir, n.d. Typescript, photocopy, 1 folder. Russian Imperial Army officer. Relates to the escape of V. E. Skalskii from Bolshevik captivity, 1918.

692 "Slaviane v Amerikie" (Slavs in America). Report, in Russian, 1917. Typescript, 1 folder. Relates to Czechs, Slovaks, Russians, Ukrainians, Yugoslavs, and Poles in North and South America, their national organizations, and political activities during World War I. Written by a Russian diplomatic agent in the U.S.

693 Edward Ellis Smith. History, 1962. Typescript, carbon copy, 1 vol. "The Department

of Police, 1911-1913; From the Recollections of Nikolai Vladimirovich Veselago." Relates to the Russian Imperial secret police.

694 Henry Bancroft Smith (b. 1884). Papers, 1919-28. 28 ms. boxes, 1 cu. ft. box. U.S. Grain Corporation agent, technical adviser to Poland, and commercial attaché in Poland, 1919-23; special representative, U.S. Department of Commerce, 1923-28. Diaries, correspondence, reports, memoranda, financial records, printed matter, and photographs relating to American food relief in Europe, economic reconstruction in Poland, agricultural market conditions in Europe and Russia, the Russian famine of 1921-22, and Anglo-Soviet treaties. (NUCMC 68-693)

695 Jack A. Smith. Study, 1950. Typescript, 1 folder. "White Russian Emigrants and the Japanese Army in the Far East." Relates to White Russian military activities and Japanese intervention in Siberia during the Russian Civil War.

696 Robert Smith. Reports, 1932-34. Typescript, .5 ms. box. American visitor to Manchuria and Mongolia. Relates to political and economic conditions in Manchuria and Mongolia, and to Soviet-Japanese relations.

697 (Walter Bedell) Smith. Photograph, n.d. 1 envelope. Depicts General W. B. Smith, U.S. Army.

698 I. S. Smolin. Translation of memoir, n.d. Typescript, 1 folder. "The Alapaevsk Tragedy: The Murder of the Russian Grand Dukes by the Bolsheviks." White Russian Army general. Relates to the discovery of the bodies of members of the Russian royal family at Alapaevsk, Russia, in 1918. Translated by W. Yourieff.

699 Konstantin Vasil'evich Snigirevskii (d. 1937). History, in Russian, 1937. Holograph, 1 folder. "Aleksandrovskii Komitet o Ranenykh" (Aleksandrovskii Committee for the Wounded). Major general, Russian Imperial Army. Relates to a Russian organization founded in the 19th c. for the care of wounded soldiers.

700 Société Agricole Arménienne. Report, in French, ca. 1919. Typescript, mimeographed, 1 vol. "La Situation Agricole en Arménie Occidentale, Années 1913 et 1917-1918: Rapport" (The Agricultural Situation in Western Armenia, for the Years 1913 and 1917-1918: Report).

701 Soiuz Voinstvuiushchikh Bezbozhnikov. Leningradskii Oblastnoi Sovet. Appeal, 1932. Typescript, 1 folder. "To Our Comrade Atheists in Capitalist Countries." Leningrad Regional Council of the Union of Militant Atheists. Calls for international struggle against religion.

702 Grigorii Iakovlevich Sokolnikov (1888-1939). Translation of study, 1931. Typescript, .5 ms. box. Soviet Policy in Public Finance, 1917-1928. Soviet commissar of finance, 1922-26; deputy commissar of foreign affairs and ambassador to Great Britain, 1929-34. Translation published (Stanford, 1931).

703 V. Sokolnitskii. Translation of memoir, n.d. Typescript, 1 folder. "Kaigorodovshchina" (Kaigorodoviana). Colonel, White Russian Army. Relates to the activities of Aleksandr Petrovich Kaigorodov, Cossack ataman and White Russian military leader in Mongolia during the Russian Civil War, 1919-21.

704 Boris N. Sokolov. Writings, 1931-32. Typescript, mimeographed, .5 ms. box. Writings, entitled "Soviet Dumping," 1931, and "Industry in the USSR in 1931," 1932, relating to Soviet commerce and industry.

705 Nicolai Alekseevich Sokolov (1882-1924). Report, in Russian, 1919. Holograph, 2 folders. White Russian official; Judicial Investigator for Especially Important Cases. Relates to the investigation of the murder of Tsar Nicholas II and his family. Intended as a supplement to the report by Lieutenant General M. K. Dieterichs. Includes translation (typewritten).

706 Dmytro Solovei. Memorandum, in Ukrainian, 1944. Typescript, 1 folder. "Istoriia Ukrains'koi Kooperatsii: Korotkyi Populiarnyi Vyklad" (History of Ukrainian Cooperation: Popular Short Version). Relates to the history of agrarian cooperatives in the Ukraine.

707 Emeliian I. Solov'ev (1898-1945). Memoirs, in Russian, n.d. Typescript, photocopy, 1 folder. Russian forced labor camp prisoner. Relates to conditions in the Solovetski Islands concentration camp in the Soviet Union, 1925-32.

708 Herbert Solow (1903-1964). Papers, 1924-76. 12 ms. boxes. American journalist; editor, Fortune Magazine, 1945-64. Correspondence, speeches, writings, memoranda, depositions, clippings, and other printed matter relating to the communist movement in the U.S., the Non-Partisan Defense League, the Commission of Inquiry into the Charges Made Against Leon Trotsky in the Moscow Trials, Soviet espionage in the U.S., Zionism, the Nuremberg trial of major German war criminals, 1945-46, and post-World War II international business enterprises. Includes some papers of Silvia Salmi Solow, 1964-76.

709 (Aleksandr Isaevich) Solzhenitsyn. Collection, 1975-78. 2 ms. boxes. Articles, publicity leaflet, photographs, and a sound recording relating to the visits of the Russian novelist A. I. Solzhenitsyn to the Hoover Institution on War, Revolution and Peace in June 1975 and May 1976; clippings relating to A. I. Solzhenitsyn's literary works; his public statements regarding civil rights in the USSR; and the text of his Harvard

University commencement address, 8 June 1978, with clippings reflecting U.S. public reaction to it.

710 "Some Books of Reference on Estonia." Bibliography, 1933. Typescript, 1 folder.

711 Peter Soudakoff. Writings, in Russian and English, n.d. Typescript, 1 vol. Relates to the Romanov dynasty, Leon Trotskii, and the Russo-Japanese War.

712 Boris Konstantinovich Souvarine (b. 1895). Papers, in French and Russian, 1925-71. 2 ms. boxes. Russian-born French journalist and author; French communist leader, 1919-24. Correspondence, writings, clippings, printed matter, and other material relating to the French Communist Party, the Communist International, Marxism, Soviet agricultural and economic policies, and political events in twentieth-century Russia. Includes correspondence with Ekaterina Kuskova, Sergei Prokopovich, Nikolai V. Volsky, D. Riazanov, and the Marx-Engels Institute (Moscow). Preliminary inventory.

713 "Soviet Ruble, Gold Ruble, Tchernovetz and Ruble-Merchandise." Translation of newspaper article, 1923. Typescript, mimeographed, 1 folder. Relates to the circulation of currency in the Soviet Union. Original article published in Agence Économique et Financière, 18 July 1923. Translated by S. Ughet.

714 Soviet Union, emigration list. In Russian, ca. 1975. Holograph, photocopy, 1 folder. Relates to the procedures required for a Jewish Soviet citizen in 1975 to procure a visa to emigrate from the Soviet Union to Israel. Includes a translation, and miscellaneous items pertaining to the problems of emigrating from the Soviet Union.

715 Sozialdemokratische Partei Deutschlands. Collection, in German, 1929-49. 1 ms. box. Reports, pamphlets, and leaflets relating to the 1929 election campaign of the Social Democratic Party of Germany; clandestine antifascist activities of the party, 1933-38; and social and economic conditions in Soviet-occupied East Germany in 1949. Includes a few communist pamphlets from the 1930s. Preliminary inventory.

716 Merrill Ten Broeck Spalding. Papers, in English, Russian, French, and Flemish, 1922-45. 1.5 ms. boxes, 1 card file box, 2 envelopes. American historian. Correspondence, notes, clippings, and other printed matter relating to economic conditions and labor in Russia from 1917 to World War II. Includes newspaper and periodical issues published in Belgium immediately after its liberation in 1945, and reproductions of paintings at the Tretyakov State Gallery, Moscow.

717 "Spravki o Glavnokomanduiushchikh Frontami, Komandirakh Armiiami, Komandirakh Korpusov i Proch" (List of Commanding Officers of the Russian Imperial Army, Arranged by Units, at the Time of World War I). List, in Russian, ca. 1916. Holograph, 1 vol.

718 Clayton I. Stafford. Memoir, n.d. Typescript, 1 folder. "Incident in the Crimea, 1920." Sailor, U.S. navy. Relates to a U.S. naval visit to the Crimea during the Russian Civil War, 1920.

719 (Iosif) Stalin. Photograph, n.d. 1 envelope. Depicts the Soviet political leader I. Stalin.

720 Boris Stanfield (b. 1888). Interview, 1976. 1 phonotape. Russian-American journalist; reporter for Izvestiia, 1917-20. Relates to the Revolution and Civil War in Russia. Interview conducted by Anatole Mazour at the Hoover Institution on War, Revolution and Peace, 15-16 November 1976.

721 Clarence T. Starr. Papers, 1923-41. 1 ms. box. American mining engineer in the Soviet Union, 1928-31. Correspondence, writings, notes, transcripts of testimony, and printed matter relating to the Soviet coal mining industry, forced labor in the Soviet Union, and efforts to secure an embargo on Soviet imports into the U.S.

722 "The State Bank of the Republic of Soviets." Translation of newspaper article, 1923. 1 folder. Relates to banking institutions in the Soviet Union. Original article published in Agence Économique et Financière, 25 April 1923. Translated by S. Ughet.

723 Isaac Nachman Steinberg (b. 1888). History, n.d. Typescript, 1 vol. "The Events of July 1918." Relates to the assassination of Graf Wilhelm von Mirbach-Harff, German ambassador to Russia, in 1918.

724 Eric Steinfeldt. Collector. Photographs, 1918. 1 envelope. Depicts scenes at Vladivostok, the Allied intervention, and the Czech Legion.

725 Ivan Stenbock-Fermor. Collector. Miscellany, ca. 1800-1913. 6 coins, 1 map. 6 Russian Imperial coins and 1 19th c. map of St. Petersburg.

726 Afanasii Ivanovich Stepanov. Papers, in Russian, 1956-61. 1.5 ms. boxes, 1 envelope. Soviet engineer. Correspondence, legal documents, memoranda, reports, engineering diagrams, and photographs relating to proposals for technological innovations in the Minsk Motorcycle Factory, the Soviet judicial system, administrative procedures and trade unions, Soviet factory management operations, daily life, and social conditions in the Soviet Union. Compiled by A. I. Stepanov for use in

a memoir to have been entitled "V Poiskakh Spravedlivosti" (In Search of Justice).

727 Aleksandr Stepanovich Stepanov. Outline of projected memoirs, in Russian, 1932. Typescript, 1 folder. White Russian Army officer. Relates to secret military organizations in Siberia, 1918-20.

728 Vanda Kazimirovna Stepanova. Memoirs, in Russian, ca. 1918. "Zapiski Velikoi Voiny 1914-1918 g." (Notes on the Great War, 1914-1918). Holograph, 1 vol. Nurse, Russian Imperial 12th Army. Relates to activities of the 12th Army during World War I.

729 Frederick Dorsey Stephens (b. 1891). Papers, 1909-45. 1 ms. box. American relief worker in World Wars I and II. Correspondence, photographs, printed matter, and miscellanea relating to relief activities of the Commission for Relief in Belgium, 1914-16, of the American Relief Administration in Russia, 1921-22, and of the Finnish Relief Fund, 1939-40.

730 Stepno-Badzheiskyi Volost (Russia) Collection. In Russian, 1919. 1 folder. Memoranda and reports relating to the gathering of the harvest that was abandoned by the inhabitants of the Stepno-Badzheiskyi District in Russia in 1919.

731 J. E. Wallace Sterling. Collector. J. E. W. Sterling collection on world affairs, 1937-51. 5 ms. boxes. Communiqués of the belligerent governments printed in the New York Times, 1942-45, relating to military operations during World War II; and reports from diverse sources relating to Japanese foreign policy, 1937-39, postwar Japanese educational reform, postwar Soviet foreign policy, and the Chinese Revolution of 1949.

732 John Frank Stevens (1853-1943). Papers, 1917-31. .5 ms. box. American civil engineer; chairman, U.S. Advisory Commission of Railway Experts to Russia, 1917; president, Technical Board, Inter-Allied Railway Commission for the Supervision of the Siberian and Chinese Eastern Railways, 1919-22. Memoirs and correspondence relating to railroads in Siberia and Manchuria during the Russian Revolution, and to Allied intervention in the Russian Revolution.

733 (Petr Arkad'evich) Stolypin. Photographs, n.d. 1 envelope. Depicts the tsarist Russian government official P. A. Stolypin.

734 Russell McCulloch Story (1883-1942). Papers, 1917-21. .5 ms. box, 1 envelope, 6 boxes of slides, 2 ft. War Work secretary, Young Men's Christian Association in Russia, 1917-18. Letters, photographs, and glass slides relating to relief work in Russia, conditions in Moscow and elsewhere in Russia during the Russian Revolution, and the Czech legion; and depicting scenes in Japan, Russia, and western Europe. Preliminary inventory.

735 Lev Pavlovich Sukacev (1895-1974). Translation of memoirs, n.d. "Soldier Under Three Flags: The Personal Memoirs of Lev Pavlovich Sukacev." Typescript, photocopy, .5 ms. box. Lieutenant, Russian Imperial Army; major, Albanian army; colonel, Italian army. Relates to Russian military activities during World War I and the Russian Civil War; Albanian military activities, 1924-39; and Italian military activities during World War II. Original memoirs published in Novoe Russkoe Slovo, 1972.

736 (Vladimir Aleksandrovich) Sukhomlinov. Photograph, n.d. 1 envelope. Depicts the tsarist Russian government official V. A. Sukhomlinov.

737 Vilis Sumans (1887-1948). Miscellaneous papers, in Latvian, French, and German, 1925-48. .5 ms. box, 1 envelope. Latvian diplomat and statesman; director of Administrative and Political Departments, Ministry of Foreign Affairs, 1919-24; delegate to the League of Nations Assemblies, 1922-30; minister to Italy, 1924-26, to France, 1926-34, and to Spain and Portugal, 1928-33. Correspondence, memoranda, bulletins, press excerpts, clippings, photographs, memorabilia, and other materials relating to Latvian foreign relations, 1925-48.

738 N. Sviatopolk-Mirsky. Collector. Postcards, n.d. 1 envelope. Patriotic Russian Imperial postcards, 3 from the collection of Tsarina Alexandra. Includes a photograph of Tsar Nicholas II and Tsarina Alexandra. Preliminary inventory.

739 "Svodki o Politicheskom i Ekonomicheskom Polozhenii v Sovetskoi Rossii za 1922 god" (Summaries of the Political and Economic Status of Soviet Russia for 1922). Reports, in Russian, 1922. Typescript, 1 folder.

740 Swiadkowie Historii (They Witnessed History). Compilation of sound recordings, in Polish, 1965. 4 phonorecords. Original speeches and radio addresses and later reminiscences of leading Polish statesmen, diplomats, and military officers relating to twentieth-century Polish history, especially the Polish-Soviet Wars of 1918-21 and the World War II period. Recorded by the Polish Broadcasting Department of Radio Free Europe.

741 C. T. Swinnerton. Letter, 1917. Typescript, 1 folder. American visitor to Russia. Relates to events in Petrograd during the Russian Revolution, 12-27 March 1917.

742 E. Sychev. Report, in Russian, n.d. Typescript, 1 folder. "Vozztanie v Irkutske" (Uprising in Irkutsk). General, White Russian Army. Relates to the uprising in Irkutsk, and

the liquidation of the rule of Admiral Aleksandr Kolchak in the region of Irkutsk in the period from 23 December 1919 to 5 January 1920.

743 (Tibor) Szamuely. Photograph, 1919. 1 envelope. Depicts the Hungarian communist leader T. Szamuely with the Russian communist Nikolai Podvoiskii.

744 Georgii Aleksandrovich von Tal'. Memoir, in Russian, n.d. Typescript, with 1 map, 1 folder. "Memuary ob Otrechenii ot Prestola Rossiiskago Gosudaria Imperatora Nikolaia II" (Memoirs on the Abdication of Emperor Nicholas II). Commandant, Imperial train of Nicholas II, Tsar of Russia, 1917.

745 Alexandre Georgievich Tarsaidze (1901-78). Papers, in English, Russian, French, German, and Georgian, 1648-1978. 33 ms. boxes, 9 oversize boxes, 16 reels of film, 1 box of film fragments. Georgian-American author and public relations executive. Correspondence, speeches, writings, research notes, printed matter, photographs, engravings, lithographs, and maps relating to the history of Georgia (Transcaucasia), the Romanov family, Russian-American relations, and the Association of Russian Imperial Naval Officers in America. Includes photocopies of Romanov family letters, photographs of Russia during World War I by Donald C. Thompson, and a documentary film of Nicholas II. Preliminary inventory.

746 Alexis B. Tatistcheff. History, 1971. "The Family of Princes Obolensky." Typescript, photocopy, 1 ms. box. Relates to the Obolensky family and its rise to prominence in Imperial Russia, 1862-1917.

747 Nikolai Tchernigovetz. Essay, in Russian, ca. 1976. Typescript, 1 folder. "Pisateliu Solzhenitsynu ot Immigranta Staroi Revoliutsii" (To Author Solzhenitsyn from an Immigrant of the Old Revolution). Russian émigré in the U.S. Criticizes Aleksandr Solzhenitsyn for anti-monarchist views and presents a personal evaluation of events in Russia 1917-76.

748 Tikhon, Patriarch of Moscow and All Russia (1865-1925). Letter, in Russian, 1918, to the Soviet Council of People's Commissars. Transcript, typewritten, 1 folder. Relates to the situation of religion in Russia. Includes a photocopy of a translation, typewritten, of the above by Peter Nicholas Kurguz, 1962.

749 Anatolii Pavlovich Timofievich (d. 1976). Papers, in Russian, 1890-1976. 2.5 ms. boxes, 1 memorabilia box, .5 ft. Russian physician. Correspondence, clippings, and printed matter relating to various members of the Romanov family and other Russian dignitaries and nobility, events in Russia before, during, and after the Russian Revolution, and the Russian emigration to foreign countries. Includes a towel and cloth napkin with the crest of Tsar Nicholas II from Ekaterinburg, and a handmade rug presented to the Dowager Empress Mariia Fedorovna by the students of the Kievo-Fundukleevskaia Zhenskaia Gimnaziia in Kiev, 1915.

750 Charles C. Tinkler. Papers, 1930. 1 folder. American engineer working in the Soviet Union in 1930. Correspondence and miscellanea relating to social conditions in the Soviet Union, anti-religious campaigns, and construction on the Golodnaia Steppe Irrigation Project.

751 Nicolas Titulescu (1883-1941). Papers, in French and Romanian, 1923-38. 15.5 ms. boxes. Romanian statesman and diplomat; minister of finance, 1920-22; ambassador to Great Britain and delegate to the League of Nations, 1922-27; minister of foreign affairs, 1927-28 and 1932-36. Diaries, correspondence, memoranda, reports, writings, clippings, and printed matter relating to Romanian politics and diplomacy, and to Romanian-Soviet negotiations, 1931-32. Register. May be used only if name of user and copy of any publication based on collection are made available to Mme M. Y. Antoniade.

752 Laurence Todd (b. 1882). Memoirs, 1954. Typescript, photocopy, 1 ms. box. "Correspondent on the Left." American journalist; Federated Press labor reporter, 1919-33; TASS correspondent, 1933-52. Relates to political, economic, and labor developments in the U.S. and Europe.

753 M. P. Tolstoi. Miscellaneous papers, in Russian, 1858-1903. .5 ms. box. Russian countess. Memorandum notebook listing major military and state officials, 1858; and photographs of the 1903 Russian Imperial costume ball in St. Petersburg.

754 Lev Nikolaevich Tolstoi (1828-1910). Miscellaneous papers, in Russian, 1853-1904. 3.5 ms. boxes. Handwritten and typewritten transcripts of originals located in the Biblioteka SSSR imeni V. I. Lenina, Moscow. Russian novelist. Diaries and writings relating to the life and works of L. N. Tolstoi. Includes drafts of the novels by L. N. Tolstoi, Anna Karenina and War and Peace. Preliminary inventory.

755 P. A. Tomilov. History, in Russian, n.d. Typescript, 1 ms. box. "Sievero-Zapadnyi Front Grazhdanskoi Voiny v Rossii 1919 Goda" (Northwestern Front of the Civil War in Russia, 1919).

756 "Trinadtsat' Let Oktiabria" (Thirteen Years of October). Study, in Russian, ca. 1930. Typescript, mimeographed, 1 folder. Relates to economic progress in the Soviet Union since the Russian Revolution.

757 (Lev) Trotskii collection, 1921-70. 1 folder, 1 envelope, 1 motion picture reel. Letter, typewritten photocopy, from L. Trotskii (1879-1940), Russian revolutionary leader, to Robert T. Lincoln concerning Soviet-American relations, 1921; excerpts, typewritten copy, from the English translation by Charles Malamuth of the book by L. Trotskii, Stalin: An Appraisal of the Man and His Influence; photographs and a motion picture film of L. Trotskii in Coyoacan, Mexico, 1938; and a newspaper article from La Vanguardia Espanola, 1970, by Maria Serrallach concerning the family of L. Trotskii in Barcelona before the Spanish Civil War.

758 Gregory Porphyriewitch Tschebotarioff (b. 1899). Correspondence, in Russian and English, 1941-75. Typescript and holograph, 1 folder. Lieutenant, Russian army, 1916-21, subsequently émigré in the U.S. Relates to the Don Cadet Corps during the Russian Revolution, and to relations between the U.S. and Russia in 1941.

759 Artem Dmitrievich Tsitlidze. Indictment, in Russian, 1937. Typescript, 1 vol. Charges A. D. Tsitlidze, Shalva Konstantinovich Alaverdashvili, and others with counter-revolutionary activities, including terrorism, subversion, and sabotage, in Georgia.

760 N. Tsurikov. Appeal, in Russian, n.d. Typescript, mimeographed, 1 folder. "Svoim i Chuzhym: O Tragedii 22 Sentiabria" (To Ours and Others: About the Tragedy of September 22). Member, Russkii Obshchevoinskii Soiuz, a Russian émigré association. Relates to the circumstances surrounding the disappearance of generals E. K. Miller and N. Skoblin, and calls for anti-bolshevik unity among Russian émigrés.

761 Eduardas Turauskas (1896-1966). Papers, mainly in Lithuanian, 1934-58. 9 ms. boxes, 1 envelope. Lithuanian diplomat and journalist; ambassador to Czechoslovakia, Yugoslavia, and Romania, 1934-39; political director, Ministry of Foreign Affairs, 1939-40. Correspondence, memoranda, reports, printed matter, clippings, and photographs relating to the Soviet occupation of Lithuania, 1940-41, and Lithuanian foreign relations in Europe, 1934-41. Register.

762 Leon G. Turrou. Memorandum, 1926. Typescript, 1 folder. "An Unwritten Chapter." American Relief Administration worker in Russia. Relates to a meeting between L. G. Turrou and Feliks Dzerzhinskii, Soviet Cheka director and commissar of transport, in 1922, regarding transport of American Relief Administration supplies.

763 "USSR Lend-Lease Program." History, 1945. Typescript, carbon copy, 1 vol. Relates to American military assistance to the Soviet Union during World War II.

764 USSR - photographs, 1950-64. 7 envelopes, ca. 230 items. Depicts cultural sites and events, industrial plants and workers, scenes from daily life, and government leaders in the USSR.

765 USSR propaganda, 1945-50. Photographs, 1 envelope, ca. 45 items. Depicts Soviet achievements in the fields of medicine, agriculture, and industry. Used in a Soviet exhibit. Includes printed slogans.

766 "Ulany Ego Velichestva, 1876-1926" (His Majesty's Lancers, 1876-1926). Commemorative history, in Russian, 1926. Typescript, mimeographed, 1 folder. Relates to the history of the Uhlan troops of the Russian Imperial Army.

767 Z. Unams. Memoirs, in Latvian, 1946. Typescript, .5 ms. box. "Latviesu Tautas Tragedija" (The Latvian National Tragedy). Latvian citizen. Relates to the Soviet and German occupations of Latvia, 1940-45.

768 (Baron Roman Fedorovich) Ungern-Shternberg. Collection, 1921. 1 folder. Copy, typewritten, of a pamphlet entitled "Letters Captured from Baron Ungern in Mongolia," reprinting correspondence of Baron Fedorovich Ungern-Shternberg (1887-1921), White Russian military leader; and translation, typewritten, by Elena Varneck, of a military order issued by Baron Ungern-Shternberg relating to White Russian activities in Mongolia during the Russian Revolution.

769 United Nations. Conference on International Organization, San Francisco, 1945. Sound recordings of proceedings, 1945. 146 phonorecords. Founding conference of the United Nations. Recorded by the National Broadcasting Company. Preliminary inventory.

770 United Nations. Conference on International Organization, San Francisco, 1945. Pictorial works, 1945. 5 envelopes. Depicts delegates to, and scenes at, the United Nations Conference on International Organization.

771 United Nations, pictorial works, 1945-53. 2 envelopes. Depicts United Nations activities, including founding ceremonies in San Francisco, and officials, including Eleanor Roosevelt, Dean Acheson, Henry Cabot Lodge, Jr., Sir Gladwyn Jess, Prince Faisal Al-Saud, Dr. Mohamed Fadil Al-Jamali, Sir Mohammad Zabrulla Khan, and Dr. J. M. A. H. Luns.

772 U.S. Advisory Commission of Railway Experts to Russia. Correspondence, 1931-36. .5 ms. box. Correspondence of former members of the U.S. Advisory Commission of Railway Experts to Russia, relating to the Russian Revolution and activities of the commission in Siberia, 1917-23. (NUCMC 71-175, in part)

773 U.S. American Relief Administration. Russian Operations, 1921-23. Records, 1919-25. 336 ms. boxes. U.S. government agency to provide relief after World War I (unofficial agency

after 28 June 1919, incorporated 27 May 1921). Correspondence, telegrams, memoranda, reports, agreements, minutes, histories, financial records, lists, press summaries, and photographs relating to relief operations, food and public health problems, agriculture, economic conditions, transportation and communications, and political and social developments in Soviet Russia. Register (NUCMC 68-413).

774 U.S. Army, American Expeditionary Force, Siberia. Collection, 1918-20. 2 ms. boxes. Press releases and a report relating to the Russian Civil War, and U.S. military activities in Siberia, 1919-20. Includes a report by Edwin Landon, colonel, U.S. Army, relating to conditions in Western Siberia and eastern Russia, 1918. Preliminary inventory (NUCMC 72-1495).

775 U.S. Army. European Command. Historical Division. Studies, in German and English, 1945-54. 101 pamphlet boxes, 25 ft. Typescript (carbon copies of original studies located at the U.S. National Archives and Records Service). Relates to German military operations in Europe, on the eastern front (including the Battle of Moscow, 1941-42) and in the Mediterranean Theater, during World War II. Studies prepared by former high-ranking German Army officers for the Foreign Military Studies Program of the Historical Division, U.S. Army, Europe. Contains evaluations of Russian armed forces and combat methods. Published guide, U.S. Army, European Command, Historical Division, Guide to Foreign Military Studies, 1945-54: Catalog and Index (1954), and Supplement (1959).

776 U.S. Committee upon the Arbitration of the Boundary between Turkey and Armenia. Report, ca. 1920. Typescript, carbon copy, 2 vols.

777 U.S. Consulate. Leningrad. Dispatches, 1917. Typescript, carbon copy, 1 vol. Relates to events in Petrograd during the Russian Revolution, 20 March-10 July 1917.

778 U.S. Department of State. International Information Administration. Translations of Soviet documents, 1937-42. Typescript, mimeographed, 1 folder. Relates to sentencing of individuals to forced labor, and to the administration of forced labor camps in the Soviet Union. Translated by the U.S. International Information Administration in 1953.

779 U.S. Department of State. Office of Foreign Liquidation. Report, 1945. Printed, 1 folder. Relates to U.S. lend-lease aid to the Soviet Union, 1941-45. Includes text of an agreement between the U.S. and Soviet governments on disposition of material in inventory or procurement in the U.S. at the end of World War II.

780 U.S. Federal Security Agency. Radio broadcast series, 1939. 24 phonorecords. "Americans All: Immigrants All." Relates to the immigration of various nationalities and ethnic groups to the U.S. (including Slavs). Preliminary inventory.

781 U.S. Information Agency. Radio broadcasts, in English and Chinese, 1961-65. 3 phonotapes. Sound recordings prepared for broadcast on Voice of America, including a program entitled "Have You Been Told?" 1961, relating to Soviet nuclear test resumption (transcript included); and interviews of W. Glenn Campbell, director of the Hoover Institution on War, Revolution and Peace, and of Dennis J. Doolin, Eugene Wu, and Yuan-li Wu, fellows of the Hoover Institution, 1965, relating to activities of the Hoover Institution in the area of Chinese studies.

782 U.S. Military Mission to Armenia. Photographs, 1919. 1 envelope. Depicts U.S. Army officers in Armenia, and conditions in Armenia at the end of World War I. Preliminary inventory.

783 U.S. Reparations Mission to Japan. Photographs, 1946. 1 album. Mission headed by Edwin W. Pauley, which investigated the condition of Japanese industries in Manchuria. Depicts Manchurian industrial plants, showing destruction or removal of equipment by Soviet occupation forces.

784 U.S. Subversive Activities Control Board. Records, 1950-72. 70 ms. boxes, 6 cu. ft. boxes. Quasi-judicial U.S. Government agency. Related to Communist and Communist-front activities in the U.S., and such groups as the Communist Party and National Council of American-Soviet Friendship. Preliminary inventory.

785 B. H. Unruh. Studies, in German, 1948. Typescript, 1.5 ms. boxes. German historian. Relates to the emigration of German Mennonites from the Soviet Union, 1921-33. Includes typewritten copies, in German, of documents relating to the Mennonites in Russia 1820-70.

786 Vasilii Vasil'evich Uperov (1877-1932). Papers, in Russian, 1916-17. 1 ms. box. Major, Russian Imperial Army; chief of staff, 5th Infantry Division, 1915-17. Reports, orders, maps, and diaries relating to activities of the 5th Infantry Division on the Western front during World War I. (NUCMC 71-1127)

787 Ivan Upovalov. Translation of memoirs, 1922-23. Typescript, 1 folder. "How We Lost Our Liberty." Russian Menshevik. Relates to the Russian Civil War in the areas of Votkinsk and Izhevsk, Russia, in 1918. Original memoirs, entitled "Kak My Poteriali Svobodu" and "Rabochee Vosstanie Protiv Sovetskoi Vlasti," published in Zaria (Berlin), 1922-23. Translated by Elena Varneck.

788 Leslie Urquhart. Letter, 1917. Typescript, 1 folder. American living in Petrograd. Relates to the Russian Revolution and its prospective outcome, as of May 1917.

789 Nikolai Vasil'evich Ustrialov (b. 1890). Papers, in Russian, 1920-34. 1 ms. box. Russian historian. Correspondence and writings relating to the Russian Revolution, the White governments in Omsk, 1918-19, Eurasianism, and the Smenovekhovstvo movement. Pseudonym: Skitalets. (NUCMC 72-1497)

790 Freda Utley (1898-1978). Papers, 1911-77. 92 ms. boxes. British-American author, lecturer, and journalist; director, American-China Policy Association. Correspondence, writings, and printed matter relating to social and political conditions in Russia, Japan, and China in the interwar period; the Sino-Japanese conflict; World War II; U.S. relations with China; Germany in the post-World War II reconstruction period; social and political developments in the Middle East; and anti-communism in the U.S. Preliminary inventory.

791 Utro Petrograda (Petrograd Morning). Newspaper issues, in Russian, 1918. 1 package, .5 ft. Newspaper of the Petrograd Printing Workers Union. Relates to the Russian Civil War, 1 April-29 July 1918. Annotated with identifications of pseudonyms used in the newspaper.

792 Ekaterina Nikolaevna Vagner. Papers, in Russian, 1876-1936. 2 ms. boxes. Russian Social Revolutionary. Correspondence, writings, diaries, and printed matter relating to revolutionary movements and events in Russia. Includes the "Reminiscences" of N. N. Dzvonkevich (father of E. N. Vagner), a study of the Strelnikovskii trial in Odessa, and letters from Ekaterina Breshko-Breshkovskaia. Preliminary inventory (NUCMC 68-422).

793 Edwin H. Vail. Letters, 1922-24. Typescript, 1 folder. Relief worker in Russia. Relates to social and economic conditions in Russia, and to Quaker relief work in Russia.

794 A. P. Vaksmut. Memoir, in Russian, n.d. Holograph, 1 folder. "Konets Kaspiiskoi Flotilii Vremeni Grazhdanskoi Voiny pod Komandoi Generala Denikina" (The End of the Caspian Flotilla during the Civil War under the Command of General Denikin).

795 Erika Valters. Letters, in Latvian, 1946-48, to Valia Turin. Typescript, 1 folder. Member of the Latvian Red Cross. Relates to Latvian Red Cross work in Belgium.

796 Mikelis Valters (b. 1874). Papers, in Latvian, 1923-40. Photocopy, .5 ms. box. Latvian diplomat and statesman; deputy premier; ambassador to Italy, Poland, and Belgium. Reports to Janis Balodis, Latvian deputy prime minister and minister of war, 1938-40, and minutes of the First and Second Conferences of Latvian Envoys Abroad, at Riga, 1923 and 1935, all relating to Latvian diplomacy.

797 Elena Varneck. Papers, n.d. 5 cu. ft. boxes. Russian-American historian. Research notes, drafts of writings, and translations relating to a proposed publication entitled "Revolution and Civil War in Siberia and the Far East," pertaining to events of the Russian Revolution and Civil War in Siberia.

798 Dimitrii Stepanovich Vasil'ev (d. 1915). Miscellanea, in Russian, 1907-75. 1 folder. Russian Imperial naval attaché in the U.S. Marriage and death certificates, 1907 and 1915. Includes Bulletins of the Russian Imperial Naval Academy, 1973-75, and a document concerning the Russian Military-Naval Agency in the United States, 1915-18.

799 E. Vasil'ev. Memoirs, in Russian, n.d. Holograph, .5 ms. box. "Zapiski o Plienie" (Notes on Prison). Russian soldier. Relates to the imprisonment of E. Vasil'ev in a German prison camp during World War I.

800 Mariia Petrovna Vatatsi (b. 1860). Papers, in Russian, 1917-34. 1.5 ms. boxes. Wife of a tsarist government official in the Caucasus. Memoirs and correspondence relating to family affairs, political conditions in Russia, 1904-17, White Russian activities during the Russian Civil War, and the Kuban Republic.

801 William Henry Vatcher, Jr. (b. 1920). Papers, 1939-65. 18 ms. boxes, 4 envelopes. American political scientist; member, United Nations Armistice Negotiations Team in Korea, 1951. Correspondence, writings, pamphlets, leaflets, slides, and photographs relating to South African political parties; Afrikaner and African nationalism; the Afrikaner Broederbond; U.S., Japanese, and North Korean propaganda and psychological warfare methods during World War II and the Korean War; and the Trans-Siberian Railroad. Register.

802 George Vernadsky (1887-1973). Miscellaneous papers, in English and Russian, 1935. .5 ms. box. Russian-American historian. Notes, handwritten and typewritten, for a projected social and economic history of Russia during the period 1917-21; and a copy, typewritten in Russian, with translation, of a letter to A. F. Iziumov, relating to the views of G. Vernadsky on serfdom in Russia.

803 Nina Vernadsky. Memoirs, in Russian, n.d. Typescript, .5 ms. box. Russian teacher. Relates to the Russian Revolution and Civil War. Includes an incomplete translation.

804 Maurice Verstraete (b. 1866). Memoirs, in French, 1949. Typescript, 1 ms. box. "Sur les Routes de mon Passé" (On the Paths of My Past). French diplomat; consul in Moscow, 1894-96; secretary of embassy to Russia, 1897-1900; consul general in St. Petersburg, 1901-

18. Relates to French relations with Russia, and historical and political events in Russia 1894-1918.

805 Major General Veselovzorov. Commentary, in Russian, n.d. Holograph, 1 folder. "Ustav Unutrennei Sluzhby" (Regulations of Routine Garrison Service). Russian Imperial Army officer. Relates to regulations of the Russian Imperial Army.

806 George M. Vesselago (b. 1892). Papers, in Russian, 1904-70. 8 ms. boxes, 1 envelope. Lieutenant commander, Russian Imperial Navy. Correspondence, writings, printed matter, clippings, and photographs relating to Russian naval operations during World War I and the Russian Revolution and Civil War. Register.

807 Sergei Sergeevich Viazemskii (d. 1915). Correspondence, in Russian, 1915. 1 folder. Captain, Russian Imperial Navy. Relates to Russian naval operations during World War I, especially the battles in Riga Bay in defense of the Irbenskii Strait.

808 George Victor. Memoirs, n.d. Typescript, mimeographed, 1 folder. "Odyssey from Russia." Relates to emigration of G. Victor from Russia via Turkey and western Europe to the U.S. around the time of the Russian Civil War.

809 Rose Georgievni Vinaver. Memoirs, in Russian, 1944. Typescript, 1 vol. Wife of Maxim Moiseevich Vinaver, a leader of the Russian Constitutional Democratic Party and foreign minister of the Crimean regional government, 1918-19. Relates to political conditions in Russia, the Russian Revolution, and the Crimean regional government.

810 A. K. Vinogradov. History, 1922. Typescript, 1 vol. "The Fortunes of the Roumiantzow Museum." Director, Rumiantsev Museum, Moscow. Relates to the museum, and especially to its library. Includes photographs.

811 IA. A. Violin. Study, in Russian, 1922. Typescript, carbon copy, 1 vol. Uzhasy Goloda i Liudoedstva v Rossii v 1921-22 g.g. (The Horrors of Famine and Cannibalism in Russia in 1921-22).

812 Mark Veniiaminovich Vishniak (1883-1976). Papers, in Russian and English, ca. 1910-68. 14 ms. boxes. Russian historian; Socialist Revolutionary Party leader. Correspondence, writings, and clippings relating to Russian and Soviet history, Russian revolutionists, Russian émigrés, and political conditions in the Soviet Union. Preliminary inventory (NUCMC 72-1498).

813 Vladimir K. Vitkovskii. Memoir, in Russian, 1933. Typescript, mimeographed, 1 folder. "Konstantinopol'skii Pokhod: Iz Vospominanii o Gallipoli" (The Constantinople March: From Reminiscences about Gallipoli). Lieutenant general, Russian Imperial Army. Relates to the evacuation of White Russian troops at the end of the Russian Civil War.

814 (Graf Sergei Iul'evich) Vitte. Photograph, n.d. 1 envelope. Depicts the tsarist Russian government official S. I. Vitte.

815 Ivan Alekseevich Vladimirov (1870-1947). Paintings, 1918-23. 40 paintings. Russian artist. Depicts scenes of privation and revolutionary justice in Petrograd and elsewhere in Russia during the Russian Revolution and Civil War. Register.

816 Algirdas Vokietaitis. Papers, in Lithuanian, English, and German, 1943-44. 1 folder. Lithuanian underground representative in Sweden during World War II. Photocopies of clandestine printed matter, and translations of declarations and clandestine radio broadcasts, of Lithuanian resistance groups during World War II, relating to their struggle against German and Soviet occupation.

817 Feliks Vadimovich Volkhovskii (1846-1914). Papers, in Russian, 1875-1914. 24 ms. boxes. Russian revolutionist and journalist; Socialist Revolutionary Party leader; editor, Free Russia (London). Correspondence, writings, photographs, periodicals, diary (1894-98, 5 vols.), and clippings relating to revolutionary movements in Imperial Russia. Volkhovskii was a member of the Ruble Society, head of the Odessa Chaikovtsy in the 1870s, banished to Siberia in 1890, and an exile in London thereafter. References to famines in the 1890s, the student movement, the Irkutsk massacre of 1899, the Potemkin revolt, Russian volunteers in the Balkan Wars of 1912-14, E. Breshkovskaia, P. Kropotkin, S. M. Kravchinskii (Stepniak), V. Zasulich, V. Figner, G. Plekhanov, and R. Luxemburg. Preliminary inventory (NUCMC 71-177).

818 Vladimir Mikhailovich Volkonskii (1868-1953). Memoir, n.d. Typescript, photocopy, 1 folder. Relates to the canonization of Saint Serafim of Sarov by the Russian Orthodox Church, 1903.

819 Boris Volkov. Writings, in Russian, 1921-31. Typescript, .5 ms. box. White Russian Army officer. Relates to the Russian Civil War in Siberia and Mongolia, the career of the White Russian commander, Baron Ungern-Shternberg, the capture of Troitskosavsk, and the massacre of officers on the Khor River. Includes a translation, typewritten, by Elena Varneck, of 1 manuscript.

820 Leon Volkov (1914-1974). Papers, 1948-74. 7 ms. boxes. Lieutenant colonel, Soviet air force, during World War II; editor and journalist for Newsweek magazine, 1953-74; consultant on Soviet affairs to the U.S. Departments of State and Defense. Diaries,

correspondence, speeches and writings, reports, clippings, press excerpts, and printed matter relating to social and political conditions in the Soviet Union, Soviet foreign policy, international politics, and Russian refugee life. Register.

821 Petr Vasil'evich Vologodskii. Papers, in Russian and English, 1918-25. .5 ms. box. Prime minister, White Russian Omsk government, 1918-19. Diaries, resolutions, reports, and translations of diary excerpts relating to the Omsk government, the Russian Civil War in Siberia, and economic conditions in Siberia. Also, material on the first Congress of Representatives of Trade, Industry, and Urban Homeowning of Siberia and the Urals, 1918.

822 Nikolai Vladislavovich Vol'skii (1879-1964). Papers, in Russian and English, 1908-64. 10 ms. boxes, 1 envelope. Russian revolutionary and author. Correspondence, writings, clippings, reports, and photographs relating to Russian revolutionary movements and émigré life, Imperial Russian and Soviet agricultural and economic policies, labor movements, Menshevism, and political events in Russia. Correspondents include Leon Trotskii, S. N. Prokopovich, G. Alexinsky, N. Andreev, G. Aronson, M. Aldanov, S. P. Melgunov, V. Maklakov, B. Nicolaevsky, M. M. Karpovich, Boris Sapir, M. Vishniak, R. Wraga, and B. Zaitsev. Vol'skii's pseudonyms: N. Valentinov and E. Yurevsky. Preliminary inventory (NUCMC 75-681).

823 Antonina R. Von Arnold. Study, 1937. Typescript, 1 folder. "A Brief Study of the Russian Students in the University of California." American social worker. Relates to the adjustment of Russian émigré students at the University of California, Berkeley, to American university life.

824 Dimitri Sergius Von Mohrenschildt (b. 1902). Papers, 1917-70. .5 ms. box, 1 envelope. American historian; editor, Russian Review. Correspondence, writings, printed matter, and photographs relating to acquisition of Russian historical materials, and the Russian Orthodox Church in the U.S. Includes letters from Sergei A. Von Mohrenschildt, Russian military historian and father of D. S. Von Mohrenschildt, describing political and economic conditions in Poland under Soviet and Lithuanian occupation, 1939-40. Register.

825 Karl Henry Von Wiegand (1874-1961). Papers, in English and German, 1911-61. 88 ms. boxes, 6 binders, 1 stack of oversize mounted clippings, 2 swords, 1 shield. American journalist; Hearst Newspaper foreign correspondent, 1917-61. Correspondence, dispatches, writings, photographs, clippings, and printed matter relating to European diplomacy and German politics between the world wars, the Sino-Japanese War, the European Theater in World War II, the Cold War, the postwar Middle Eastern situation, and U.S. foreign policy.

826 Colonel Vorotovov. Memoirs, in Russian, n.d. Holograph, 1 folder. White Russian Army officer. Memoirs, entitled "2-i Orenburgskii Kazachii Polk v 1918-1920 g.g." (The 2d Orenburg Cossack Regiment in 1918-1920) and "V Zabaikal'ie i na Primorskom Frontie v 1920-21 g.g." (In the Zabaikal and on the Maritime Front in 1920-21), relating to the Russian Civil War.

827 P. Voskevich. Collector. Photographs, ca. 1905. 1 envelope. Depicts Imperial Russian and Imperial Japanese officers during negotiations for settling new boundaries on Sakhalin Island, and the Russian embassy staff in Tokyo.

828 Arthur Voyce (d. 1977). Papers, ca. 1948-60. 27.5 ms. boxes, 2 card file boxes, .25 ft. American art historian. Correspondence, writings, notes, photographs, slides, clippings, and other printed matter relating to Russian art and architecture 15th-20th c.

829 Mariia D. Vrangel' [Wrangel]. Papers, in Russian, 1919-44, ca. 42 ft. Mother of General P. N. Wrangel, commander of the White Russian forces in southern Russia. Correspondence, writings, pamphlets, periodicals, newspapers, photographs, clippings, and printed matter relating to the life and military career of P. N. Wrangel, the anti-Bolshevik campaigns of the armed forces in Southern Russia, the Russian Revolution and Civil War, communism in Russia, and the activities of Russian refugees in foreign countries. Preliminary inventory.

830 Baron Petr Nikolaevich Vrangel' [Wrangel] (1878-1928). Papers, in Russian, 1916-23. 94.5 ms. boxes, 18.5 ft. Commander-in-chief, White Russian Volunteer Army, 1920. Correspondence, memoranda, reports, military orders, dispatches, printed matter, and photographs relating to the Russian Revolution and Civil War, the operations of the Volunteer Army and the Armed Forces of Southern Russia, evacuation of White Russian military personnel and civilians from the Crimea in 1920, and the resettlement of Russian refugees first in Istanbul and subsequently in various European countries. Preliminary inventory.

831 Vsesoiuznyi Mendeleevskii S'ezd po Teoreticheskoi i Prikladnoi Khimii, St. Petersburg, 1911. Photograph, 1911. 1 envelope. Depicts delegates to the All-Union Mendeleev Congress on Theoretical and Applied Chemistry.

832 V. I. Vyrypaev. Memoir, in Russian, n.d. Typescript, .5 ms. box. "Vladimir Oskarovich Kappel': Vospominaniia Uchastnika Beloi Bor'by" (Vladimir Oskarovich Kappel': Memoirs of a Participant in the White Struggle). Soldier, White Russian Army. Relates to the

Russian Civil War, and the activities of the Volunteer Army detachments under the command of V. O. Kappel'. Includes partial translation.

833 E. Carl Wallen (1889-1961). Papers, 1918-23. 1 ms. box. American photographer. Photographs depicting relief work in the Caucasus, Turkey, and other areas of the Near East at the end of World War I. Includes a few papers of Mary Jane Steel (Mrs. E. C. Wallen) relating to her service as a Red Cross nurse in the Near East at this time, and a photograph of President Warren G. Harding in 1923.

834 Warren B. Walsh. Translations, n.d. Transcript, photocopy, .5 ms. box. Diary of A. Balk, prefect of police of Petrograd, 1917, relating to the Russian Revolution of March 1917, and correspondence between Nicholas II, Tsar of Russia, and P. A. Stolypin, president of the Council of Ministers of Russia, 1906-11, relating to political conditions in Russia. Translated, with explanatory notes, by W. B. Walsh. May not be quoted without permission of W. B. Walsh.

835 Harold George Washington (1892-1961?). Collector. Miscellany, 1918-20. 1 ms. box. Depicts social conditions, railroads, and Allied troops in Siberia and Manchuria during the Russian Revolution. Includes some postcards of buildings and war damage in France.

836 Geoffrey White. Papers, 1939-68. 9.5 ms. boxes. American Trotskyist leader. Correspondence, writings, reports, resolutions, minutes, discussion bulletins, and printed matter relating to American Trotskyist politics, the Socialist Workers Party, and the formation of the Spartacist League. Includes a few items relating to the Communist Party of the U.S. and the Independent Socialist League.

837 James H. Whitehead. Collector. J. H. Whitehead collection on Siberia, 1918-20. 2 albums, 1 envelope, ca. 400 photographs and postcards. Depicts activities of members of the American Expeditionary Force in Siberia and the Russian Railway Service Corps, General William S. Graves, Czech and Russian military forces, and the living quarters of Tsar Nicholas II at Ekaterinburg.

838 Prince Serge Wiasemsky. Translations of miscellaneous papers, 1923-24. Typescript, 1 folder. Leader of the Russian National Progressive Party in England. Renunciation by S. Wiasemsky of landholdings in Russia, resolutions of the Russian National Progressive Party, and a memorandum on the dynasties of Russia.

839 Edward Frederick Willis (b. 1904). Writings, n.d. Typescript, 1 ms. box. American historian. Writings, entitled "Herbert Hoover and the Russian Prisoners of World War I"; "Herbert Hoover and the Blockade of Germany, 1918-1919"; and "The Genesis of the Bonus Army," relating to the Bonus Expeditionary Force march on Washington, 1932.

840 Samuel Graham Wilson. Letter to Ella W. Stewart, 1916. Holograph, 1 folder. Relief worker in Armenia. Relates to relief work in Armenia during World War I.

841 Nicholas Wiren. Sword, n.d. Belonged to N. Wiren, Russian émigré who was probably an Imperial Russian military officer.

842 "Die Wirtschaftliche und Soziale Entwicklung in der Sowjetischen Besatzungszone Deutschlands, 1945-1949" (Economic and Social Development in the Soviet Occupation Zone of Germany, 1945-1949). Study, in German, 1949. Typescript, mimeographed, 1 vol.

843 Wirtschaftspolitische Gesellschaft. Memorandum, 1935. Typescript, mimeographed, 1 folder. "Memellanders on Trial for Treason before the Military Court at Kovno." Political Economy Society, a German organization. Relates to the trial of German nationalists from Memel in Lithuania.

844 Wlodzimierz Wiskowski. Collector. W. Wiskowski collection on Poland, in Polish, 1914-19. 5 ms. boxes. Writings, reports, memoranda, booklets, leaflets, magazines, newspapers, memorials, and speeches relating to political conditions in Poland during World War I, and the development of Polish nationalism. Register.

845 (Zara) Witkin. Collection, 1933-37. .5 ms. box. Writings and correspondence relating to Z. Witkin, an American construction engineer in Russia, 1932-34. Includes a memoir by Z. Witkin, and a biographical sketch of him by Eugene Lyons.

846 Bertram David Wolfe (1896-1977). Papers, 1903-77. 150.5 ms. boxes, 2 card file boxes, 1 oversize box, 6 microfilm reels, 4 phonotapes, 19 envelopes. American historian; representative of the Communist Party, U.S.A., to the Communist International, 1928-39; author of Three Who Made a Revolution (1948) and other works on communism. Writings, correspondence, notes, memoranda, clippings, other printed matter, photographs, and drawings relating to Marxist doctrine, the international communist movement, communism in the Soviet Union and in the U.S., literature and art in the Soviet Union and in Mexico, and the Mexican artist Diego Rivera. Register.

847 Henry Cutler Wolfe (1898-1976). Papers, 1921-23. 1 folder, 1 envelope. American Relief Administration worker in Russia. Printed matter, identification card, medals, and photographs relating to conditions in the Samara Province of Russia and operations of the American Relief Administration.

848 George Wolfram (b. 1907). Papers, in Russian, German, and English, 1943-54. 1 folder. Russian member of Vlasov forces during World War II. Letters, clippings, photographs, and a diary relating to the Vlasov movement and to Russian refugee life after World War II.

849 Erich Julian Wollenberg (1892-1973). Memoirs, in German, n.d. Typescript, photocopy, 1 ms. box. German communist leader and journalist. Relates to the Bavarian Soviet Republic of 1919, the development of the German communist movement to 1933, activities of the Communist International, and the development of communism in the Soviet Union to 1933. No more than 500 words may be quoted.

850 Paul N. Woolf. Collector. Photographs, 1906. 1 envelope. Depicts people, scenic views, military parades, and captured weapons in Japan after the end of the Russo-Japanese War. Preliminary inventory.

851 Barry Lee Woolley (b. 1947). History, 1974. Typescript, photocopy, .5 ms. box. "Adherents of Permanent Revolution: A History of the Fourth (Trotskyist) International." Relates to the American and international Trotskyist movements. Closed until 1 January 1980. Thereafter and during his lifetime, access requires the written permission of B. L. Woolley.

852 Graf Hilarion Woronzow-Daschkow. Collector. Count H. Woronzow-Daschkow collection on Imperial Russia, in Russian, 1903-11. 3 oversize boxes, 2 ft. Printed photographs from the "Album of the Masquerade Ball at the Winter Palace in February 1903," depicting members of the Russian nobility; and a book, entitled Kazanskii Sobor, 1811-1911, v Sanktpeterburge (The Kazan Cathedral, 1811-1911, in St. Petersburg).

853 Richard Wraga. Study, 1959. Typescript, mimeographed, 1 folder. "Basic Problems of Soviet Foreign Policy: Methods and Means." Presented at the Eleventh Conference of the Institute for the Study of the USSR, held at Munich in 1959.

854 Ivan D. Yeaton (b. 1906). Papers, 1919-76. 1 ms. box, 7 envelopes. Colonel, U.S. army; military attaché in the Soviet Union, 1939-41; commanding officer, Yenan observer group in China, 1945-46. Memoirs, reports, memoranda, correspondence, orders, citations, charts, and photographs relating to his military career, Soviet military strength in 1941; U.S.-Soviet relations, 1941-49; organization of U.S. military intelligence during World War II; lend-lease operations; U.S. relations with the Chinese communists, 1944-46; and the inspection of U.S. army procurement contracts, 1952-53. Register. Philip Faymonville file closed until 1 January 1996.

855 Hui-Ch'ing Yen (1877-1950). Memoirs, 1946. Typescript, 1 ms. box. "An Autobiography." Chinese diplomat and statesman; minister of foreign affairs, 1920-22; premier, 1924 and 1926; ambassador the the Soviet Union, 1933-36. Relates to Chinese politics, diplomacy, finances, and famine relief.

856 Young Men's Christian Associations. Miscellaneous records, 1917-20. 68 ms. boxes, 5 folios, 79 envelopes, 40 albums. International social and charitable organization. Clippings, printed matter, posters, and photographs relating to activities of the Young Men's Christian Association in the United States and Europe during World War I. Includes material on Russia, Russian liaison, and Russian work, particularly in Siberia (box 57); Russian posters (box 67); and photographs/glass plates of Siberia, Russia, and Russian POWs in Austria (envelopes HHHHH-JJJJJ, PPPPP, and QQQQQ). Register.

857 Ivan Yurchenko. Writings, in Russian, n.d. Holograph, 25 ms. boxes. Russian émigré in the U.S. Relates to various aspects of philosophy, religion, and the sciences. Preliminary inventory.

858 Arsenii Zaitsov. Study, 1931. Typescript, mimeographed, 1 folder. "Military Aspect of the Five Year Plan of the U.S.S.R." Relates to Soviet economic and military policy.

859 Constantine L. Zakhartchenko (b. 1900). Papers, 1920-76. 1 ms. box. Russian émigré; aeronautical engineering designer; assistant chief engineer, Shiuchow Aircraft Works, Kwan-tung, China, 1934-43. Correspondence, certificates, airplane designs, blueprints, technical and financial reports, telegrams, contracts, and photographs relating to engineering and military aspects of Chinese aviation.

860 Sergei Vladislavovich Zavadskii. Biography, in Russian, 1933-35. Typescript, 6 vols. "Zhizn' V. R. Zavadskago, Razskazannaia Synom" (The Life of V. R. Zavadskii, as Told by His Son). Relates to Vladislav Romual'dovich Zavadskii, Russian Imperial courtier.

861 Konstantin Nikolaevich Zavarin. History, in Russian, n.d. Typescript, .5 ms. box. "Rechnaia Boevaia Flotiliia na reke Kame v 1919 godu" (The Fighting River Flotilla on the Kama in 1919). Relates to the river warfare campaigns and tactics of the White Russian forces on the Kama River in Siberia during the Russian Civil War, 1918-19. Written by K. N. Zavarin and Mikhail Smirnov.

862 Jay K. Zawodný. Interview transcripts, n.d. Typescript, 1 folder, 1 microfilm reel. Interviews, conducted by J. K. Zawodny, of former Soviet factory workers residing in the United States, relating to labor conditions in the Soviet Union, 1919-51.

863 Nicholas A. Zebrak. Papers, in Russian, 1920-31. 1 ms. box. Chief of police, Russian Concession, Tientsin; adviser to the local Chinese administration. Correspondence, clippings, and pamphlets relating to Russian émigrés, police administration, and welfare and veterans organizations in China.

864 K. Zershchikov. Memoir, in Russian, n.d. Typescript, photocopy, 1 folder. "Sobstvennyi Ego Velichestva Konvoi v Dni Revoliutsii" (His Majesty's Personal Convoy in the Days of the Revolution). Colonel, Russian Imperial Army. Relates to the bodyguard of Tsar Nicholas II in 1917.

865 V. Zenzinov. Translations of excerpts from letters and diaries, 1939-40. Typescript, 1 folder. Letters and diaries of Soviet soldiers during the Russo-Finnish War, relating to conditions at the front, living conditions in the Soviet Union, and personal matters. Translated and compiled by V. Zenzinov. Includes photocopies of the original letters and diaries, in Russian. Published (?) as Vstrecha s Rossiei (1945).

866 Harold Zinkin. Collector. Tabernacle, ca. 1835-45. Russian tabernacle, inscribed "Ral'k, Supplier for the Imperial Court."

867 Vladimir Aleksandrovich Zubets. Memoir, in Russian, 1933. Typescript, 1 vol. "Na Sluzhbie v Kitaiskoi Armii" (Service in the Chinese Army). Russian émigré in the Chinese Army after the Russian Revolution. Translated by Elena Varneck. Includes photographs.

868 Nikolai Zvegintsov. Papers, in Russian, 1920-22. 1 ms. box. Russian Imperial naval officer. Correspondence, writings, and memoranda relating to activities of the White Russian military forces during the Russian Civil War. Register.

CA 62
LIBRARY, HOOVER INSTITUTION ON WAR, REVOLUTION AND PEACE
STANFORD UNIVERSITY
Stanford, California 94305
(415-497-2058)

1 David Hunter Miller (1875-1961). My Diary at the Conference of Paris, with documents, privately printed (New York, 1924); also, positive microfilm copy, 22 reels. The original consists of 21 vols. of documents, memoranda, his diary, minutes, annotations, bulletins, maps, diagrams, and a list of personnel. Among the questions discussed were those relating to post-war boundaries, new states and minorities, and the problem of Poland and the Ukraine. Materials cover 19 November 1918-29 May 1919. (Call nos. (V) D642 M647 and Microfilm D642 M647a) In addition, under the same title, the library holds a separate set of 29 vols. of the S-H Bulletin (Bulletin of the American Commission to Negotiate Peace), nos. 1-1428, 2 February-7 December 1919, only nos. 1-398 of which are reproduced in vols. 17-18 of the preceding work. These 29 vols. (Paris, 1919) are supplied with a typescript index, unpaged, n.p., n.d., 1 vol. The Bulletin covers the period of the Council of Ten, the Council of Five, Council of Four, early meetings of the Council of Heads of Delegations, and documents relating to all their activities. (Call no. (V) D642 P229 f)

2 Paris. Peace Conference, 1919. Notes of a meeting of the Heads of Delegations of the Five Great Powers; also known as Minutes, Heads of Delegations (Paris, 1919-20), 13 vols. Text is in French; the Five Great Powers were Britain, France, Italy, Japan, and the U.S. (Call no. (V) D642 P227)

3 Paris. Peace Conference, 1919. Recueil des actes de la Conférence (Paris, 1922-34), 8 vols. in 18. French. Includes material on the Baltic nations and other territorial questions, and on all the matters discussed at the Peace Conference. (Call no. (V) D642 P228)

4 Note: In addition to the items listed, the Hoover Institution Library holds microfilm copies of over 350 archival and manuscript collections held privately or at other repositories. A part of them pertains to such subjects as the Communist International and communist parties of Europe in the interwar period, the eastern front in World War II, the Russian Civil War, Russian German relations 1914-20, Central Asian history, Russian-Persian/Iranian relations, the Communist Party of the Soviet Union, the Menshevik movement, the occupation of Lithuania, foreign students in the USSR, the Romanov family, the Russian unit of the American Relief Administration, the Soviet economy, the Shakhta affair, 1928, prominent Germans in the USSR in 1944, and Soviet internal affairs in the 1930s. Some of these items are records from the National Archives and various U.S. governmental agencies. All of the microfilmed collections are listed in the Guide to the Hoover Institution Archives by Charles G. Palm and Dale Reed.

CA 63
ESTONIAN AVIATION ARCHIVE (EESTI LENNUALA ARKHIIV)
c/o Anatol Rebane
22523 Shadycroft Avenue
Torrance, California 90505
(213-540-0208)

The archive contains about 2,000 photographs (ca. one-quarter originals) pertaining to Estonian military and civil aviation.

Includes photos of Estonian air clubs and the first Estonian commercial airline, 1923-26. The archive also has about 100 oral history interviews of Estonians involved in their country's aviation history. Materials in the collection have been gathered by Mr. Rebane during trips abroad. Much of the material has yet to be processed and catalogued, and additional items are coming in continuously. At present, holdings cover the period 1918-42. Researchers must write to Mr. Rebane well in advance, identifying themselves satisfactorily and indicating the purpose of the research.

COLORADO

CO 1
WESTERN HISTORICAL COLLECTIONS
UNIVERSITY OF COLORADO LIBRARIES
Boulder, Colorado 80309
(303-492-7242)

1 Robert Campbell (1808-1851). Fur trader for the Hudson's Bay Co. and explorer in western Canada. Memoirs, typed copy, 89 pp., contain references to Russians.

2 Women's International League for Peace and Freedom. Records, 1915-65, ca. 4 of 87 ft. Reports, correspondence, and miscellaneous historical documents on the Russian situation in 1915, Russian famine relief, 1921, the Cold War, 1946, the Hungarian uprising of 1956, the first conference of American and Soviet women held in the U.S., Bryn Mawr College, 1961, and a 1964 meeting between U.S. and Soviet women in Moscow. Some of the original material pertaining to the WILPF is located within member countries and their national sections and also at the International Headquarters in Geneva. Unpublished guide with subject listings by storage box.

CO 2
ARCHIVES BRANCH
FEDERAL ARCHIVES & RECORDS CENTER, GSA
Building 48, Denver Federal Center
Denver, Colorado 80225
(303-234-5271)

This repository has some of the microfilms of materials in the National Archives (Washington, D.C.) that pertain to Russia/USSR. For more details, see Charles South, List of National Archives Microfilm Publications in the Regional Archives Branches (Washington: National Archives and Records Service, 1975).

CO 3
GERMANS FROM RUSSIA IN COLORADO STUDY PROJECT
COLORADO STATE UNIVERSITY
Fort Collins, Colorado 80523
(303-491-5911/6854)

This research center has a collection of materials, both published and unpublished, pertaining to the Germans from Russia (sometimes erroneously called the "Volga Germans"). Unpublished materials include statistical data; a small amount of correspondence; and taped and transcribed oral interviews of Germans who emigrated from Russia. These interviews relate in part to conditions in Russia and to reasons for emigrating to the United States. A new and growing component of the collection consists of statistical and documentary material pertaining to the history of the German Russians under Soviet rule.

Note: These materials complement the collection assembled by the American Historical Society of Germans from Russia in the Greeley (Colo.) Public Library.

Finding Aid: Sidney Heitman, ed., German-Russians in Colorado (Ann Arbor: University Microfilms International, 1978).

CO 4
FORT COLLINS PUBLIC LIBRARY
201 Peterson Street
Fort Collins, Colorado 80524
(303-493-4422)

Oral History Interview Project. Includes several interviews with or about Russian-Germans who immigrated to the Fort Collins area. Some are duplications of holdings at Colorado State University and are not listed in the catalogue. Pertinent interviews which have been catalogued include those with Heinrich Glantz (who came to the U.S. with his parents in 1907), Bruce Patterson, Mrs. Revilo Reid, and Mrs. W. E. Scriven (née Ellda Schmidt).

CO 5
ARCHIVES AND HISTORICAL LIBRARY
AMERICAN HISTORICAL SOCIETY OF GERMANS FROM RUSSIA
PUBLIC LIBRARY
919 Seventh Street
Greeley, Colorado 80631

COLORADO - AHSGR ARCHIVES AND LIBRARY CO 5

The Society's archives are housed at the Greeley Public Library; its international office is located at 631 D Street, Lincoln, Nebraska 68502. The archives contain a substantial number of autobiographies, memoirs, and biographies of individuals or families, all unpublished, many in typescript and/or photocopy. Some are rather lengthy (up to 200 pp.); others are just a few pages long.

Another large number of manuscripts concern the history of German colonists in Russia/USSR (in the Ukraine, along the Volga, and in Siberia), their emigration, and their new life in the U.S. (Many have been "published" by the authors themselves in very limited editions.)

Some holdings are unpublished M.A. theses and doctoral dissertations. Many are photocopies of documents or publications (often excerpts) held elsewhere. These items include a marriage register from the New Saratovka Church Book, 1765-1804, photocopy, lists of colonies in Russia (with their locations, founding dates, and population statistics), and some privately-recorded phonograph records of Russian-German songs.

The archives also include more than 30 maps of interest. 4 show places of origin of Black Sea Germans in Germany (genealogical maps); 3, migration routes; 14, the original mother colonies of the Russian-Germans; and 6, the areas of the world where Russian-Germans currently live. There are also 3 charts on Russian-German history and a map of Russian-German settlements in the U.S. and Mexico. Most of the historical maps cover both the 18th and 19th c.

Note: Except for very rare items, all materials are available through interlibrary loan.

Finding Aid: The indispensable publication is the Bibliography of the AHSGR Archives and Historical Library, Greeley, Colorado 1976 (Lincoln, Nebraska: AHSGR, June 1976), compiled by A. Giesinger, E. S. Haynes, and M. M. Olson with E. Fromm--an annotated listing of the more than 550 books, articles, and manuscripts in the library.

CO 6
SPECIAL COLLECTIONS BRANCH
DFSLB/SC
THE ACADEMY LIBRARY
USAF Academy, Colorado 80840
(303-472-4674)

1 George de Bothezat (1882-1940). Papers, 1911-73, 2 boxes. Aircraft designer. Born in St. Petersburg, de Bothezat attended the Technological Institute of Kharkov, 1902-1905, did graduate work in Kharkov, and came to the United States in May 1918 as a lecturer and scientist. Under contract to the United States government, he built the "De Bothezat Helicopter," one of the first helicopters to carry out passenger flights. Captain Boris Sergievsky and Baron Vladimir Kuhn von Poushental assisted de Bothezat in the development of the rotary-wing aircraft. Series 7 of the de Bothezat collection consists of technical data written in Russian and of copies of 2 patents issued to Bothezat for his ideas regarding the first helicopter. Series 8 contains news clippings and correspondence to and from Poushental pertaining to his assignment as de Bothezat's special assistant. It also has materials on the Russian colony Poushental founded to preserve the customs of Russian emigrants. Unpublished finding aid.

2 Follett Bradley (1890-1952). Papers, 1905-67, 1.2 ft., 3,000 pp. Air force officer. In August 1942, General Bradley went to Russia with the rank of minister to open an airway for lend-lease aircraft to Russia from the United States through Great Falls, Alaska, and Siberia. By December 1942, when Bradley returned to the U.S., 8,000 airplanes had been delivered to the Soviets. The most significant part of the collection deals with this "Bradley mission." Series 2 consists of reports, 1942, 1947, documenting the plans (and confusion) of the Russians and Americans involved in the airplane delivery. Series 3 has 1 folder of messages Bradley received and sent on his mission. Series 8 contains news clippings relating to Bradley's work in Russia, and Series 9 has photographs illustrating the mission. Unpublished finding aid.

3 Jarred V. Crabb (b. 1902). Papers, 1929-61, 1.6 ft., 4,000 pp. Air force officer and deputy chief of staff for Operations, Far East Air Forces, 1949-52. Includes a journal describing the first encounter of North American F-86 Sabres with Soviet-built MiG-15s during the Korean War on 17 December 1950. Unpublished finding aid.

4 Robert LeGrow Walsh (b. 1894). Papers, 1918-57, ca. .5 ft., 1,000 pp. Air force officer. In 1944, Major-General Walsh was a member of the United States Military Mission in Moscow. Series 3 of his papers is a detailed analysis of the Poltava mission, 1944, during which American aircraft used Soviet airfields for shuttle-bombing of enemy territory. Poltava, Mirgorod, and Piryatin (all near Kiev) were the airfields used by the Americans. The series, which contains graphs of manpower, equipment, planes, bombs, and fuel, is a partially bound typescript with a record of planes used and photographs of the Poltava area and of American and Russian military personnel. Series 4 is a copy of a speech given at a meeting of the Russian Relief Inc., New York Committee, 18 December 1945, at Madison Square Garden. For having participated in

this meeting, Walsh was later criticized by Walter Winchell on a radio program and accused of being a communist. Series 1, correspondence, 1928, 1942-57, includes letters to and from Generals William Mitchell, H. H. Arnold, Carl Spaatz, and Ira Eaker. Series 5, newsclippings, 1925-50, is a folder of photographs and comments relating in part to Walsh's work. Unpublished finding aid.

Restriction: Individuals desiring to use manuscript materials must apply in writing to the Directorate of the Libraries, DFSLB, USAF Academy Library, USAF Academy, CO 80840.

CONNECTICUT

CT 1
BRIDGEPORT PUBLIC LIBRARY
925 Broad Street
Bridgeport, Connecticut 06604
(203-576-7417)

Historical Collections. Includes the Russian Famine Relief Fund, Bridgeport, Connecticut. Records, 1892, 2 in. Correspondence, account book, receipts, bank book (Bridgeport National Bank), and pledge lists of locally-organized fund to aid starving Russian peasants. Activities were coordinated by Major William B. Hincks, treasurer. Bridgeport citizens raised $1,978.50, sent to Kidder, Peabody & Co., Boston, agents, to be forwarded to the U.S. minister in St. Petersburg.

CT 2
R. GORDON WASSON--PRIVATE COLLECTION
42 Long Ridge Road
Danbury, Connecticut 06810
(203-748-0123)

Collection of manuscript and unique printed documents pertaining to mushrooms in Eastern Europe (Latvia, Lithuania, Poland, and other countries). Includes folk names and folklore of mushrooms in these lands. Inquire concerning access.

CT 3
MANAGER OF LEGAL RESOURCES
OFFICE OF GENERAL COUNSEL
GENERAL ELECTRIC COMPANY
Fairfield, Connecticut 06431
(203-373-2485)

Correspondence on and contracts and terminations thereof between International General Electric and Soviet organizations pertaining to purchase and/or patent licensing of electrical apparatus and machines. Also, an agreement between Radio Corporation of America and the State Electro-Technical Trust of Weak-Current Factories pertaining to exclusive licensing of "radio fields of use." By prior appointment only. Contact Ms. Mary Fisher.

CT 4
MRS. C. B. FALLS--PRIVATE COLLECTION
Sugar Hill
Falls Village, Connecticut 06031

Mrs. Falls is in possession of photograph prints, in brown, of some pictures used in James H. Hare's A Photographic Record of the Russo-Japanese War (1905). Mrs. Falls also has a copy of Hare's book inscribed to her husband.

CT 5
CONNECTICUT HISTORICAL SOCIETY
1 Elizabeth Street
Hartford, Connecticut 06105
(203-236-5621)

1 Samuel Colt (1814-1862). Papers, 1808-69, ca. 8 boxes. Firearm inventor. Includes 6 (10?) letters written from Russia in the 1850s.

2 Daniel Coit Gilman (1831-1908). Attaché of the American legation at St. Petersburg. 9 letters, typewritten copies, from Gilman when he was in Russia, 4 April-19 June 1854.

3 Thomas Hart Seymour (1807-1868). Papers, 1781-1868, 4 ft., ca. 3,500 items. Lawyer, editor, congressman, governor, and U.S. minister to Russia, 1853-58. Correspondence, papers, and memorabilia concern all phases of his career; ca. 5% relate to Russia. A travel diary from 1858 includes a description of his journey through Russia. Brief list of contents (unpublished). (NUCMC 66-411)

4 C. Wendel and H. J. Sanford (Ms. 68954). Correspondence, May-July 1854, manuscript, 2 ff. Concerns cholera in Russia, October, no year given, at Moscow, Kiev, Kharkov, Orël, Simferopol, and the Berdiansk district; and Russian colonies in America.

5 Note: The Society also has a collection of Russian medals given to it by Thomas Hart Seymour. The medals date from before Peter I to the reign of Alexander II.

CT 6
ARCHIVES UNIT
CONNECTICUT STATE LIBRARY
231 Capitol Avenue
Hartford, Connecticut 06115
(203-566-3690)

1 Colt Patent Firearms Manufacturing Company. Records, 1847-1919, 30 ft. Includes letters of Company agents in Russia in the 1870s and 1880s. (RG 103) Unpublished guide (NUCMC 60-827 and 71-1612).

2 Fisher. His report upon the trade of St. Petersburg; list of American vessels arrived at and departed from Cronstadt in 1820; list of American ships passed the sound in 1820; list of goods exported from St. Petersburg, 1819, 28 pp. Made for Bach, Bayley & Co., and sent to James Luke & Bros., Philadelphia, Kept in main vault (947.F2). (Probably Miers Fisher, Jr.)

3 Jonathan Trumbull (1710-1785). Papers, 1631-1784, 29 vols. Colonial governor of Connecticut, 1769-84. Report that the empress [i.e., Catherine II] exacted a contribution from the clergy (August 1773); comment on the friendly attitude of the empress [toward?], September 1780; declaration to support rights of neutrality mentioned, September 1780; and report of Empress of Russia favoring the Jesuits, March 1783. Unpublished subject index. (M.H.S. Connecticut Colonial Official Papers)

Finding Aid: Guide to Archives in the Connecticut State Library by Robert Claus, 2nd ed. (1978).

CT 7
CASE MEMORIAL LIBRARY
HARTFORD SEMINARY FOUNDATION
111 Sherman Street
Hartford, Connecticut 06105
(203-232-4451)

1 Armenian Manuscripts. The library holds the following 21 items (or groups of items): Four Gospels, A.D. 1222; four Gospels, A.D. 1299 and later; four Gospels, A.D. 1307-31; four Gospels, A.D. 1656; menologium, A.D. 1659; calendar of feasts, A.D. 1658; perpetual calendar, A.D. 1664; calendar, composed by the Vardapet Anton of Constantinople, A.D. 1732; hymnal, 17th c.; collection of canticles, 16th-17th c.; hymnal, 17th c.; prayer book, hymnal, and calendar, 17th c.; sermons and other texts, 16th c.; miscellaneous texts, 17th c.; Story of the Seven Wise Men and the King's Son (Sindbad), 17th-18th c.; commentaries on the divine liturgy, and the Catechism of Cyril of Jerusalem, A.D. 1706; historical and other works, A.D. 1590s; miscellaneous texts, 16th c.; phylactery, A.D. 1749; and phylactery, A.D. 1796.

2 James Young Simpson (1873-1934). Papers, ca. 1923-28, 50 letters plus miscellaneous papers. Science professor in Great Britain and the U.S. Simpson wrote about Russian political affairs. Unpublished finding aid.

3 Matthew Spinka (1890-1972). Ca. 300 letters, 1941-50, plus articles and clippings. American historian of the Russian and other East European churches. Unpublished index.

4 Alexander A. Stacey (1878-1949). Papers, ca. 300 items. Lawyer, journalist, publisher, and clergyman. Stacey, ne Alexander Alexandrovich Tarbeyeff, was born in Moscow and graduated from Moscow University. Before 1917 he practiced law, wrote for newspapers, and was a publisher. He also wrote some books that appeared in print. He emigrated to the U.S. after the revolution, arriving in 1923. Papers include 70 letters, an autobiographical essay, typescript, 17 pp., 160 sermons from 1930-46, some addresses, and a few articles. Also, his unpublished M.A. thesis and Ph.D. dissertation (1939 and 1941), both on the Patriarch Nikon.

Finding Aids: Nafi Donat has prepared 2 unpublished guides: Archival Material in the Case Memorial Library (Hartford, June 1976) and The Archives of the Case Memorial Library (Hartford, 1972 [1975]).

CT 8
THE WATKINSON LIBRARY
TRINITY COLLEGE
Hartford, Connecticut 06106
(203-527-3151)

Edward V. Wratislaw (1820-1888?). Papers, 1836-81, 1 ft., ca. 200 items. Hungarian-born Civil War officer. Letters, broadsides, and other papers concerning the Hungarian Revolution of 1848-49. Other materials relate to his service in the U.S. Civil War and to his life before and after emigration to the U.S. Some of the material is in Hungarian. As the collection is uncatalogued, relevant items could not be ascertained. But there might be possible references to Russia in the early material of the collection. (NUCMC 71-508)

CT 9
WADSWORTH ATHENEUM
600 Main Street
Hartford, Connecticut 06103
(203-278-2670)

The Serge Lifar Collection of Ballet Set and Costume Designs contains 182 oils, watercolors, and drawings--works of avant-garde artists in pre-revolutionary Russia and of Paris émigrés after the First World War. These are designs executed for Diaghilev ballets and peformers, acquired by Sergei Diaghilev and Lifar, and, after 1933, by the Atheneum.

Among the holdings are:

Leon Bakst (1866-1924). 11 items: Costume designs for La Fee des Poupees (ca. 1909), Scheherazade (1910-18), Daphnis et Chloë, Les Femmes de Bonne Humeur (1917), Le Spectre de la Rose (1911), and The Sleeping Princess (1921); a portrait of V. Nijinsky as the faun in L'Après-Midi d'un Faune (1912); and a portrait of Nijinsky as the rose (in Le Spectre de la Rose, 1911).

Andre Bauchant (1873-1958). 3 items: Backdrop of Perseus and Andromeda (1926; never produced) and backdrops for Apollon Musagete (1927-28).

Alexander Benois (1870-1960). 29 items: Costume designs and/or backdrops for Le Rossignol (ca. 1914?), Le Pavillon d'Armide (1909-11), Petrouchka (1911-25), and Giselle (1924).

Christian Berard (1902-49). 5 items: Setting, costume designs, and sketch for La Nuit (1930?).

Georges Braque (1882-1963). 4 items: Act curtain design for Les Facheux (1924), costume designs for Zephire et Flore (1925?), and curtain design for Les Sylphides (1926?).

Giorgio de Chirico (b. 1888). 24 items: Composition ca. 1929; backdrops, costume designs, program cover, setting designs, and/or curtain designs for Le Bal (ca. 1929?) and for Bacchus et Ariane (ca. 1931?).

Paul Colin (b. 1892). 2 items: Costume designs for L'Orchestre en Liberté (1931?).

Jean Cocteau (1891-1963). 1 item: Portrait of Serge Lifar (1931), with unfinished pencil sketches of Lifar's head on the reverse.

Andre Derain (1880-1954). 10 items: Detail for backdrop for La Boutique Fantasque: and setting and costume designs for Jack in the Box.

Mstislav Doboujinsky (1875-1957). 1 item: Setting for Les Papillons (1914).

Max Ernst (b. 1891). 5 items: "Still Death" (1925), oil on canvas; and curtain designs for Romeo and Juliet (1926-27).

Naum Gabo (b. 1890). 2 items: Costume designs for La Chatte (1927).

Nathalie Gontcharova (1881-1962). 4 items: Setting and costume designs for Les Noces (1923?) and costume designs for L'Oiseau de Feu.

Juan Gris (1887-1927). 4 items: Program cover (Pierrot), 1924; and costume, setting (?), and curtain (?) designs for Les Tentations de la Bergère (1924?).

Constantine Korovine (1861-1939). 6 items: Costume design for a Tartar bowman (ca. 1906) and costume designs for Polovtsians for Prince Igor (1908-1909).

Michael Larionov (1881-1964). 6 items: Costume designs for Soleil de Nuit (ca. 1918?); setting design for Le Renard (1929); design for make-up for Kikimora in Les Contes Russes (1916?); and curtain and setting designs for Sur Le Borysthene (ca. 1931).

Marie Laurencin (1885-1957). 3 items: Costume designs for Les Biches.

Fernand Leger (1881-1955). 4 items: Pen and ink drawings from ca. 1911-19; and backdrop for La Creation du Monde.

Louis Marcoussis (1883-1941). 1 item: Portrait of Serge Lifar (1933), pencil on paper.

Henri Matisse (1869-1954). 1 item: Sketch for the curtain for Le Chant du Rossignol.

Joan Miro (b. 1893). 2 items: Curtain design for Romeo and Juliet (1925) and project for a stage set, perhaps for Romeo and Juliet (1925).

Amedeo Modigliani (1884-1920). 1 item: Portrait of Leon Bakst, 1917, pencil on paper.

Eugene Mollo (b. 1904). 6 items: Grotesque figures in various media, 1928-30, not realized.

Pablo Picasso (1881-1973). 6 items: Self portrait with two female nudes (1903); woman's head (1906); sketches of dancers (1925-26); sketch of a seated saltimbanque (ca. 1923); and sketch for the setting for Le Tricorne.

Pedro Pruna (b. 1904). 10 items: Program cover (1925); backdrop, set, costume, and stage decoration designs for Les Matelots (1925); and curtain and backdrop designs for La Pastorale.

Isaac Rabinovitch (b. 1894). 1 item: Costume for a drunkard, design, 1927 (possibly for S. Prokofiev's Love for Three Oranges).

Sir Francis Rose (b. 1909). 5 items: Projects for settings (1932); portrait of Isadora Duncan (1926); and project for a ballet (1929).

George Rouault (1871-1958). 2 items: Scene designs for Le Fils Prodigue.

Prince Alexander Schervasnidze. 4 items: Backdrop and costume designs for Les Créatures de Prométhée (1931).

Jose-Maria Sert (1876-1947). 1 item: Costume designs for Le Astuzie Femminili (1920?).

Dimitri Steletsky. 3 items: Setting and costume designs for Czar Theodore (ca. 1915).

Leopold Survage (b. 1879). 6 items: Set and costume designs for Mavra (ca. 1922?).

Pavel Tchelitchew (1898-1957). 9 items: 2 portraits of Serge Lifar (both ca. 1928); drawing of Lifar in Giselle (ca. 1928); and projects for program covers, setting, and costume designs for Ode (ca. 1928).

Finding Aid: All of the preceding information was drawn from the published catalog The Serge Lifar Collection of Ballet Set and Costume Designs (Hartford, ca. 1965).

CT 10
MYSTIC SEAPORT, INC.
Mystic, Connecticut 06355
(203-536-2631 x 264)

1 Silas Enoch Burrows. Correspondence, 1818-48, typed copies, 78 pp. Substantial portion relates to his financing of repairs for the Russian corvette Kensington and his subsequent efforts to obtain reimbursement from the Russian government.

2 Miers Fisher, Jr. ALS, 12/24 July 1810, from Fisher in St. Petersburg to an unnamed correspondent (probably in the U.S.) summarizing trade possibilities in Russia, 6 pp.

3 Henry W. Hiller. Papers, ca. 1855-1935, 7 vols., 485 items, of Hiller and his wife, Liuboff Gouberoff Hiller. Correspondence, documents, diary, notes for speeches, photographs, and other materials dealing with his career as a whaler, an agent for William H. Boardman & Co., U.S. consul in Russia (Nicolaivsk, Siberia), and later as a buyer for Tiffany & Co., New York City. Also, typed copies of many of the items, arranged by subject in 5 vols. Reference to the Crimean War. (Collection 77)

4 Kermit Family. Papers, ca. 1790-1860, 5,500 items. New York shipping family. Documents and correspondence directed to and from family members, primarily Captain Henry Kermit (d. 1813), captain and entrepreneur, and his sons, Henry and Robert, merchants and shipowners. Letters written from all over Europe and the eastern U.S. Also, letters from ship's captains on their voyages, and from agents and commercial firms. Letters contain political and social news as well as business information. Some groups of papers relate to individual ships owned by the Kermits: purchase, outfitting, voyages, etc. Some references to Russia. Unpublished finding aid. (Collection 68)

5 [Logs]. Ships' logs are catalogued by their ports of call. There are entries for Russian ports.

6 George Warren (fl. 1830s). 1 vol. Shipping agent. His letter copybook for 1831-36. Warren was in Calcutta, India; Havana and Matanzas, Cuba; and St. Petersburg. He sent letters to many commercial firms, particularly in Great Britain. The amount of Russian-related material, if any, could not be determined. (NUCMC 68-951)

CT 11
NEW HAVEN COLONY HISTORICAL SOCIETY
114 Whitney Avenue
New Haven, Connecticut 06510
(203-562-4183)

1 Ingersoll Family. Papers, 1676-1874, ca. 3 ft., 2,050 items. Includes a diary of Ralph Isaacs Ingersoll (1789-1872), 16 November 1846-30 May 1848, written on his diplomatic mission to Russia. He was U.S. minister there in 1847-48. The diary recounts his stopover in Paris on the way to St. Petersburg and his reception by Nicholas I, and contains accounts of expenditures to be reimbursed by the U.S. government. Unpublished register. (MSS #58)

2 Women's Collection. 2 ft., 330 items, 1704-1930. Contains a Russian passport, issued in 1856 to Amelia Griebel (1839-1915), later Mrs. Peter Borgen. Unpublished register. (MSS #68)

CT 12
BEINECKE RARE BOOK AND MANUSCRIPT LIBRARY
YALE UNIVERSITY
1603A Yale Station
New Haven, Connecticut 06520
(Telephone numbers within body of entry.)

The Beinecke Library, devoted exclusively to rare books and manuscripts, now holds over

450,000 volumes and several million transcripts in 5 major collections: the General Collection of Rare Books and Manuscripts, the (Yale) Collection of American Literature, the Collection of Western Americana, the German Literature Collection, and the James Marshall and Marie-Louise Osborn Collection of English literary and historical manuscripts. Additional historical manuscripts are in the Manuscripts and Archives Department of the Sterling Memorial Library.

General Collection
(203-436-0628)

1 Armenian Manuscripts. The library has the following 6 items or sets: Brief exposition of the seven sacraments of the (Armenian) church, 17th-18th c.; miscellany, A.D. 1688; menologium, A.D. 1648; collection of canticles, A.D. 1415; four Gospels, A.D. 1594; and ritual book, A.D. 1694.

2 Russian Collection. This diverse holding includes materials by or about the following individuals, in their own or others' collections: Georgii Adamovich (1894-1971); Iurii Annenkov (1889-1975); Nina Berberova (b. 1901): over 1,000 letters from writers, scholars, and political figures; Robert D. Brewster: 6 albums containing 2,000-3,000 informal, unpublished photographs of the Russian Imperial family taken between ca. 1906 and 1914, plus about 35 letters to Anna Vyrubova from the family during their imprisonment by the Provisional Government and the Bolsheviks (1917-18); Ivan Bunin (1870-1954): several hundred of his letters; Boris Filipoff (b. 1905): 5,500 letters to him; Roman Goul (b. 1896); Zinaida Hippius (1869-1945); Georgii Ivanov (1894-1958); Iurii Ivask (b. 1907); Vladimir Korvin-Piotrovskii (1901-1967); V. I. Lenin (1870-1924): over 100 books and pamphlets by and about him, fragments of 2 autograph letters, a corrected typescript, and an unpublished manuscript of which some chapters were written by Lenin; Czeslaw Milosz (b. 1911); Irina Odoevtseva (b. 1901); Iurii Ofrosimov (b. 1895): 1,500 letters to him; Aleksei Remizov (1877-1957); Andrei Sedykh (b. 1902): ca. 400-500 items, including correspondence to him as editor of the émigré newspaper Novoye Russkoye Slovo and literary manuscripts; Fedor Stepun (1884-1970?): 10,000 letters to him; Iurii Terapiano (b. 1892); and Mark Weinbaum (1890-1973).

All of the collections in the Russian archives are restricted and require the permission of the Curator of the Slavic and East European Collections and/or the donors to see.

3 George Stewart. Typed translations of articles from Pravda, Izvestiia, and other Russian-language newspapers printed in the USSR and elsewhere, plus some miscellaneous papers. All items concern social and religious conditions in Russia, 1923-27.

4 Ezra Stiles (1727-1795). Papers and records, 22 microfilm reels. Minister, educator, and president of Yale. Include references to St. Petersburg, Cossacks, Siberia, commerce, the army, iron mines, the Volga River, and weather conditions. Published guide book for the microfilm edition.

American Literature
(203-436-0236)

5 Langston Hughes (1902-1967). The famous black poet and author visited the Soviet Union in 1932-33, with a group filming a movie about black American life. His autobiographical I Wonder as I Wander (New York, 1956) describes his experiences. The library has an extensive collection of his correspondence and manuscripts of his books, poems, and plays, among which are references to the USSR. (In the James Weldon Johnson Memorial Collection)

6 Note: The Joel Barlow papers in this division are also believed to contain Russian-related material. Barlow (1754-1812) was a diplomat, poet, and commercial agent.

Western Americana
(203-436-0235)

7 Alexander Andreevich Baranov (1746-1819). Dated 4/16 October 1816, New Archangel (Sitka), letter, 3 pp., to Mr. Abram Johns, in Boston, former tutor to Baranov's children. Baranov, head of the Russian-American Company in Alaska from 1790 to 1818, writes of his family, life in New Archangel, and of the settlement at Fort Ross, New Albion, California.

8 "Carta reducida de los payses del norte, en que se demuetra el verdadero Estrecho de Anian, o Paso del Norte, . . y las costas e islas del Mar del Sud, particularmente donde hacen el comercio los Rusos por el Kamschatka," 51 pp. (?). In ink and water color, the map shows English, Russian, and Spanish exploration.

9 Ludovik Choris (1795-1828). Paintings and sketches, 1815-18, 44 items. Artist, member of the Kotzebue Expedition. Water color paintings and sketches of the Aleutian Islands, Bering Sea, Alaska, and natives of those regions.

10 Descripcion geographico historica de la California y Tierras situadas al Nord-Ouest de la America hasta el Estrecho de Anian, segun las ultimas observaciones: y de las Islas de Anadir, Eleuteras, y de Bering. 241 pp., ca. 1790. This manuscript, in a very neat hand throughout, is in 15 chapters and 2 parts; the second part describes voyages and discoveries of the Russians. The anonymous author apparently had access to all published accounts of exploration of the 16th-18th c.

and to Spanish archival reports, the sources cited in the footnotes.

11 Documents on Russians in California. 4 items, ca. 1825. Drawn up in Mexico by the Junta de Fomento de Californias, signed or produced by Francisco de Paula Tamariz (and in one case, by Lucas Alamán). 1 describes plans for opening a road to New Mexico and a U.S. Congress pact with the Russians, 11 April 1825, 6 pp. A second, 1825-26, 24 pp., reports on Russians in California and details a political-military plan for their expulsion ("Exposicion . . . sobre la recuperacion del puerto de la Bodega ocupado Los Rusos. . . ."). 2 others describe Russian activity along the Pacific Coast, 9 pp. and 14 pp.

12 Ralph Haskins (1779-1852). Seaman. "Journal of a Voyage from Boston to the North West Coast of America, Thence to Canton, and Back to Boston--Kept on Board Ship Atahualpa by Ralph Haskins in the Years 1800, 1801, 1802 & 1803," 4 vols. Journal covers only the period 30 August 1800 to 25 June 1802, when the Atahualpa was still on the Northwest Coast. Contains references to the Russians there. Vol. 2 contains the "Blotter" and vol. 3 the "Ledger" of the Atahualpa.

13 Alexander, Freiherr von Humboldt (1769-1859). German explorer, scientist, and natural philosopher. 2 ALS/memoranda, 7 pp., in French but with translation and annotation, concerning international boundaries, the American Northwest Coast, California, and Russian activities on the Pacific Coast. Undated (but ca. 1829), one or both written in Bodega, California.

14 Fray Antonio de San Jose Muro. "Al Plan de Conquista, Poblacion de lo Reconocido en el Sur el ano de 1779 se anade algunas Reflexiones por la noticia cierta de los Establecimientos Rusos; y de haber subido. . . ." In this manuscript, 11 pp., Muro, a member of the Bethlehemite Community of Mexico, expresses fears of the Russian Pacific Coast settlements and reveals a plan for Spanish conquest and colonization of that coast north to the 68th parallel. He describes Russian attitudes toward the Catholic Church, the area's riches and natural resources, and reasons for the Spanish ministers to heed his plan. (MS 355)

15 Alexander Hunter Murray (1818-1874). Scot who joined the Hudson's Bay Co. in 1846. In his Yukon travels, he observed native customs and the ways of Russian fur traders in the area. Manuscript, 86 pp., entitled "Journal of an Expedition to build the Hudson's Bay Company post on the Yukon." Written in the form of a letter to Murdo McPherson, Esq., in May-June 1848, the piece appeared in print as Journal of the Yukon, 1847-48, edited by L. J. Burpee, in 1910.

Finding Aid: Volume 1 of A catalogue of the Frederick W. and Carrie S. Beinecke collection of Western Americana, compiled by Jeanne M. Goddard and Charles Kritzler (New Haven, 1965), is on manuscripts. In 1952 the library published A catalogue of manuscripts in the collection of western Americana founded by William Robertson Coe, Yale University Library (New Haven), compiled by Mary C. Withington.

Osborn Collection
(203-436-8535)

16 Lord Robert Grosvenor, 1st Baron Ebury (1801-1893). Statesman. His manuscript journal, 185 pp., autograph (?), for 3 May-26 September 1826 describes the duke of Devonshire's special mission to Russia on the occasion of Nicholas I's coronation. Lord Robert was a member of the delegation. He apparently wrote the journal later from a diary kept during the tour.

17 Thomas John Gisborne (fl. 1830s). Correspondence, 1832-33, 9 items. Representative of the Russia Company of London in St. Petersburg. His letters (to A. H. Thomson or Henry Bonar, Robert Cattley, a Mr. Birch, and Lord Sydenham) discuss the Russia Company, the British Factory in St. Petersburg, and Russian political and business matters. 34 pp., 2-5 pp. each, June 1832 to January 1833, 7 ALS, 2 copies.

18 Samuel Harrison (fl. 1850s). ALS, 12 pp., to a Major Brown, 17/29 September 1854 from Berlin, describes his journey from St. Petersburg to Berlin.

19 Charles William Stewart Vane, 3rd Marquis of Londonderry (1778-1854). Copy of a letter, 8 October 1836, Moscow, 7 pp., to Princess Daria Khristoforovna (Benckendorff) Lieven, containing his impressions and descriptions of Russia.

20 Frances Anne Emily (Vane-Tempest) Stewart, Marchioness of Londonderry (1800-1865). ALS, 18 August 1836, Hamburg, Germany, 3 pp., to Prince Khristofor Lieven, in French, discusses her trip to St. Petersburg.

21 George Macartney, 1st Earl Macartney (1737-1806). Papers, 1764-68, 2 boxes. Diplomat. Notes, memoranda, and drafts concerning his embassy to Russia in 1764-67, including a complete copy of the treaty he negotiated; accounts of travel in Russia and general descriptions of the country, including a treatise on Siberian natural history and fossils found there; a history of the Imperial Academy of Sciences at St. Petersburg; a description of major Russian court figures in 1767; documents on Polish affairs and Russian court protocol; and some papers from before and after his stay. Among the letters written

by Macartney are some to Sir John Goodricke, the duke of Grafton, M. de Panin, another duke, Russian officials, and Richard Stonhewer (all from St. Petersburg, all but one copy). There are also copies of a letter from Catherine II to George III, 10 April 1768, and from George III to Catherine II, 12 November 1767, concerning Macartney's mission. 2 of his correspondents who were also in St. Petersburg at this time were John Glen King, 14 ALS, 1769-71, and Robert Thorley. Among the other items in this collection are Macartney's "Answers to questions on Russian matters" (ca. 1765), his Livre de Visites (St. Petersburg, 1765), his "Instructions to Henry Shirley with a list of papers delivered to him" (St. Petersburg, 3/14 May 1767), and Samuel Swallow's "Address of thanks of the British merchants at St. Petersburg to Lord Macartney," copy, St. Petersburg, 1765. Available on microfilm. Unpublished finding aid.

22 Milutin Family. Papers, ca. 1860-75, 2 portfolios and 1 vol., bound. Correspondence of Nikolai Aleksandrovich Milutin (Miliutin) (1818-1872) and his wife. Chiefly pertaining to the couple's life and his career after his retirement from the post of assistant minister of the Interior in 1861. Important subjects covered include the emancipation of the serfs, student unrest in October-November 1861, and Milutin's role in the suppression of the Polish revolt of 1863. Correspondents include his brother General Dmitrii A. Miliutin, Prince Cherkassy, George Samarin, N. Kh. Bunge, Konstantin Kavelin, and I. S. Turgenev. Also, Madame Milutin's memoirs and an unfinished story entitled "Memoirs of a Governess," 37 pp. Material in Russian and French transcription. Unpublished finding aid.

23 [Joost Willemsz Nieuwkerck] (1587-1645). [Account of Russia, possibly prepared for the merchant family Marselis], autograph (?) manuscript, in Dutch, ca. 1632, 17 11.

24 The Present State of the Russian Empire. 12 11., January 1863. Anonymous manuscript in English.

25 Sergei Prokof'ev (1891-1953). Composer. TLS, 15 April 1925, Bellevue, to Schlomo B. Lewertoff, in French, saying he is too busy to go to Cologne, 1 p. (Else Thalheimer Lewertoff Papers)

26 Russia Company, London. "A list of the Court of Assistants of the Right Worshippfull the Muscovia Company for y[e] Year. 1723," 1 p.

27 [Travel diary]. An anonymous diary, 2 vols., of a tour through Holland, Hanover, Oldenberg, Holstein, Denmark, Sweden, Russia, Poland, and Prussia, June-September 1835. Volume 1 consists of "Rough Notes" made on the trip, Vol. 2 of a "Journal" compiled from the notes.

CT 13
BENJAMIN FRANKLIN PAPERS
YALE UNIVERSITY
1603A Yale Station
New Haven, Connecticut 06520
(203-436-8646)

Included are photostatic copies of documents relating to Franklin that pertain to Russia. Location of the original manuscripts can be provided. Use of the photocopies is in general restricted to the Franklin papers editorial staff.

CT 14
YALE COLLECTION OF FILMS
DEPARTMENT OF THE HISTORY OF ART
YALE UNIVERSITY
Box 2009, 56 High Street
New Haven, Connecticut 06520
(203-436-4958)

Russian/Soviet holdings, ca. 12 titles, 1912-29. These include Sergei Eisenstein's Strike, Battleship Potemkin, and October; Vsevolod Pudovkin's Mother, Storm Over Asia, and Chess Fever; Ladislas Starevich's Cameraman's Revenge (animation, 1912); Lev Kuleshov's By the Law; Abram Room's Bed and Sofa; Alexander Dovzhenko's Arsenal, and Dziga Vertov's Man With a Movie Camera. Scholars may view the films in New Haven at no charge; contact the curator in advance. Institutions, but not individuals, may borrow prints for exhibitions with a small charge.

CT 15
DIVINITY SCHOOL LIBRARY
YALE UNIVERSITY
409 Prospect Street
New Haven, Connecticut 06510
(203-436-8440)

1 Arthur Judson Brown (1856-1962). Papers, 1864-1967, ca. 8 ft. American Presbyterian clergyman, author, and leader of world ecumenical and missionary movements. The library holds his correspondence, diaries, writings, photographs, memorabilia, and printed matter. An important part of the 1909 diaries is his observations on the effects of the Russo-Japanese War on China and the Far East. As he was also active in World War I relief efforts, particularly in the Near East, it is possible that his papers contain other relevant items from that period. Unpublished register (NUCMC 76-1792). Note: These papers form part of the China Records Project.

2 John Raleigh Mott (1865-1955). Papers, 1862-1965, ca. 150 ft. American religious leader,

involved in the formation and/or direction of various organizations such as the World's Student Christian Federation (see below, separate entry), Student Volunteer Movement, YMCA, World Council of Churches, and International Missionary Council. Mott visited Russia in 1899 and 1909, and was part of a U.S. government commission to Russia (the Root Mission) in May-August 1917. There are letters, official reports, papers, recorded interviews, and diaries pertaining to these trips. The papers also include information about YMCA war work in Russia and Western Christianity's relations with the Russian Orthodox Church; copies of Mott's many speeches and addresses on Russia in 1917 and in the 1940s; and other source material. Finally, there are also biographical materials collected by Mott's biographer C. Howard Hopkins; these concern Mott's relations with E. T. Colton, Charles R. Crane, James Stokes, and Woodrow Wilson. (The Hopkins biography should appear in 1979.) A preliminary inventory of the papers is available but they are not yet in their final organized state.

3 World's Student Christian Federation. Official archives, ca. 1895-1920, plus other material to 1938, 225 ft. Contains correspondence between John R. Mott and Baron Paul Nicolay, 1899-1919, and between Mott and H. Witt, ca. 1899-1900; information on the work of James Stokes with young men in Russia; a "History of the school in Russia," New York, n.d., 36 pp., by Vladimir G. Simkhovitch; a typed report on conditions in Russia, n.d., 3 pp., by A. M. Reynolds; an interview with J. R. Reynolds, 1 February 1899, 1 p.; reports on European student relief work in Russia in 1924 compiled by O. J. Fredericksen (Moscow) and Frits Kuiper (Kazan); data on Russian universities ca. 1899-1924; the constitutions and regulations of various groups such as the Russian Student Christian Movement (Russian National Student Christian Union), the Students' Christian Association, ca. 1913 (?), and the Moscow university association; and correspondence with members of the Russian Student Christian Movement ca. 1907-20. Among the individual items noted are a report on the first general conference of the Russian Student Christian Movement outside Russia, held in Czechoslovakia 1-8 October 1923, typed, 3 pp.; information from Riga from the Russian student movement--strictly private and confidential (report sent by a Miss Bidgrain, n.d.), typed, 2 pp.; a 4 pp. pamphlet entitled "Why Save Russia?", London, 1922; and typed letters and reports of C. J. Hicks and a Prince Hilkoff concerning Russian railroads in the spring of 1899, 24 pp. In addition, the collection contains issues of rare periodicals: Duchovny mir studenchestva (Prague and Paris, 1923-25), nos. 1-3, and 5; The Russian student in the American college and university (published monthly by the Russian Student Fund, Inc., New York), vol. 1, nos. 1-5, 7-8; vol. 2, nos. 1-10; the Viestnik of the Russian Student Christian Movement in Paris, no. 10 (October 1926); and Russian Christian Thought, published by the National Russian Students' Christian Association in the U.S.A. (New York, Committee on friendly relations among foreign students), 1926; and the Institute of International Education's Guide Book for Russian Students in the United States, 4th series, bulletin no. 5 (New York 1923), 82 pp. An inventory of the collection is in progress.

CT 16
THE HISTORICAL LIBRARY
MEDICAL LIBRARY
YALE UNIVERSITY
333 Cedar Street
New Haven, Connecticut 06510
(203-436-2566)

Photographic File. Contains 2 photographs from 1929, one of Dr. Ivan Petrovich Pavlov alone and one of him with Dr. Harvey Cushing. There is also a postcard from Dr. Pavlov dated 1913.

CT 17
MUSIC LIBRARY
YALE UNIVERSITY
98 Wall Street
New Haven, Connecticut 06520
(203-436-8240)

1 Osip Solomonovich Gabrilovich (1878-1936). TLS, Detroit, Michigan 3 March 1919, to Horatio Parker, 1 p., with address, concerning performance of Parker's Northern ballad, typewritten copy laid in; telegram, Philadelphia, Pa. 24 February 1931, and 5 TLS, Detroit, Michigan 1926-31, to Max Smith (T. Max Smith Papers); and TLS to Gabrilovich (Gabrilowitsch) from Helen Love, New York 16 February 1917, plus ALS and 14 TLS to Helen Love, 1914-18, from Gabrilovich (Love Family Papers).

2 Leopold Godowsky (1870-1938). TLS to Helen Love, New York 3 January 1917, in the Love Family Papers.

3 Vladimir Horowitz (b. 1904). TLS from March 1954 in the Kirkpatrick Papers.

4 Nina Koshetz (1894-1965). ALS to Max Smith, New York City, n.d., in the T. Max Smith Papers.

5 Moritz Moszkowski (1854-1925). ALS to Horatio Parker, Paris (1912?), 2 pp., with envelope, in German, typed transcript laid in.

6 Leo Ornstein (b. 1895). Music manuscripts, 1913-present, 18 boxes (additions expected).

Composer. Comprises most of the existing holographs of Ornstein's works for voice, piano, chamber ensembles, and orchestra; photocopies of several manuscripts deposited at the Library of Congress; a photocopy of F. Martens' book on Ornstein; photographs of Ornstein at different ages; and a tape recording of "Tartar Dance" played by Andrew Imbrie. Also, correspondence to and from the Ornsteins, several programs of Ornstein's concert activity, biographical and critical essays written by Mrs. Ornstein, biographical clippings, and concert reviews. Register. (NUCMC 76-1795)

7 Vladimir de Pachmann (1848-1933). Autograph, 16 December 1891 (John Glenn Papers).

8 Quincy Porter (1897-1966). Papers, ca. 1921-66, 66 boxes. 6 TLS to him from the American-Soviet Music Society, 1946-47, TLS from him to the Society, 16 April 1947, minutes of a 1946 meeting of the Society, TLS of Serge Koussevitzky, 10 December 1942, plus correspondence listed under American-Soviet Music Society, TLS of Nicolas Slonimsky, 27 October 1961, and 2 ALS, 6 TLS, of Nicolai Lopatnikoff, 1965-66. Register (NUCMC 78-627).

9 Lazare Saminsky (1882-1959). ALS to Lucy Love, 2 October 1921, ALS to Helen Love, n.d., card to Helen Love, 9 October 1921, all in Love Family Papers; ALS to Max Smith, New York City, 7 April 1931, plus 2 ALS to Arthur Toscanini, n.p., 1931, in the T. Max Smith Papers; and 1 box of sheet music, 69 pieces, piano pieces for children published between 1936-41 by contemporary composers, for the Masters of Our Day educational series edited by Saminsky and Isadore Freed.

10 Igor Fedorovich Stravinskii (1882-1971). TLS to Richard Donovan, New York 2 February 1941, 1 p., with address; and 2 TLS to Bruce Simonds, Hollywood [Calif.], 29 November and 11 December 1943, in the YSM Papers.

11 Alexander Nikolayevitch Tcherepnin (1899-1977). Suite for harpsichord, op. 100, inscribed to Ralph Kirkpatrick (published, 1966), in the Kirkpatrick Papers.

12 Virgil Thomson (b. 1896). Papers, over 100 boxes. Composer and music critic. Correspondence and autographed manuscripts. Papers are in process. Among his correspondents were: Serge Koussevitzky, Nikolai Lopatnikoff, Nicolas Nabokov, Fabien Sevitsky, Nicolas Slonimsky, Leopold Stokowski, Igor Stravinskii, Pavlik Tchelitchoff, Alexander Tcherepnin, and Vladimir Ussachevsky. There is also a folder labeled "Soviet music controversy." Abbreviated register.

CT 18
HISTORICAL MANUSCRIPTS AND ARCHIVES DEPARTMENT
STERLING MEMORIAL LIBRARY
YALE UNIVERSITY
New Haven, Connecticut 06520
(203-436-4564)

1 Anonymous. Letter (found in A. Dumas's Vicomte de Bragelonne) in Russian from a member of the suite of the emperor or empress, 28 June, no year, signed "Vera" and addressed to "Dear Aunty." Duma's book was a copy from the Palace library at Tsarskoe Selo. (Miscellaneous Manuscripts Collection; herinafter, Misc. MSS.)

2 Gordon Auchincloss (1886-1943). Papers, 1917-34, 3.5 ft. Lawyer and diplomat. His diary for 1914-19 is particularly informative on the American intervention in the Civil War and for the attitudes of Colonel E. M. House and President Woodrow Wilson on this matter. Unpublished register (NUCMC 61-3683).

3 Hanson Baldwin (b. 1903). Papers, 1931-present, ca. 100 ft. Author and military editor of the New York Times. Includes extensive documentation relating to foreign affairs, papers of the Council on Foreign Relations, and subject files relating to the Soviet Union during World War II and the Cold War. Unpublished register (NUCMC 72-1873).

4 Belvedere Archives, 1918-22 (Archives of the Military Chancellery of the commander in chief of the Polish army). Microfilm, 31 reels. Documents of Jozef Pilsudski, chief of state and head of the Polish army, marked "T" to signify they are secret, are arranged imperfectly by subject and chronologically. Group II (files 27-45) concerns "Russia and all that developed out of it." Group IIB (files 15-26) is for "The Ukraine, Russia, Lithuania." File 21, for example, includes ca. 50 papers dealing with the Russian army of General von Bredov. The "Miscellaneous" file 84 contains documents concerning negotiations with the Soviet Red Cross in 1919; file 92 is a census of eastern territories, December 1919; file 95c has reports of the Intelligence Corps on the Baltic countries, 1920; and file 101 holds data on Polish-Soviet relations in 1919-20 (all in Group VII). The apparently separate documents of General T. Rozwadowski, chief of the Polish General Staff, for 1920, 3 files, also include materials on Latvia, Lithuania, and the Ukraine. (The originals of all the papers are in the Pilsudski Institute in New York.) Unpublished register.

5 Franz Borkenau. Writer. Undated memorandum sent to Henry M. Andrews concerning the Spanish Civil War and Russian foreign policy, typescript. (Misc. MSS)

6 Chester Bliss Bowles (b. 1901). Papers, 1924-73, 186 ft. Governor of Connecticut, 1949-51, a UN official in 1946-48, ambassador to India, 1951-53 and 1963-69, and U.S. representative, 1959-60. A specialist on foreign affairs and especially the USSR, Bowles served as under secretary for foreign affairs in 1961 and as President John F. Kennedy's special representative and advisor on Africa, Asia, and Latin American Affairs. Unpublished finding aid, 3 vols.; also, article in the American Archivist, 1975, no. 1. (NUCMC 77-2105)

7 Ekaterina Konstantinovna Breshko-Breshkovskaia (Catherine Breshkovsky) (1844-1934). Papers, ca. 1911-31, 1 box, 10 folders. First woman sent to the mines for a political offense, spent most of her life in prison or exile. Known as "The Little Grandmother of the Revolution." Papers include the typed manuscript of "How I Went Among the People, 476 pp.; handwritten manuscripts about herself and the people she met, 50 pp., some dated; "My Stay in Russia from 1896-1903," 10 pp.; extracts from her memoirs, Dni, Berlin, 20 January 1924, 5 pp., and her reminiscences of the revolution, 12 pp.; a manuscript she dictated to A. P. Toporkov in 1918, 58 pp.; articles about her by E. E. Lazarev, 1931, and M. M. Rosenbaum, 1917; and other magazine and newspaper articles about her, plus a pamphlet honoring her 80th birthday (Paris). Unpublished finding aid.

8 William Hepburn Buckler (1867-1952). Papers, 1907-37, 2.5 ft. Special agent for the U.S. State Department from 1914 to 1919, attended the Paris Peace Conference after World War I. He reported to Colonel E. House on European affairs. His notes include information on Russia and on his meeting with the Soviet diplomat Maxim Litvinov in Stockholm in 1919. Unpublished register (NUCMC 62-1109)

9 William C. Bullitt. Collection of materials from diverse sources, ca. 1917-10 primarily, on microfilm, 3 reels. Cf. NUCMC 61-3504 and 72-1881.

10 Georgii Vasil'evich Chicherin (1872-1936). Soviet foreign minister. 27 ALS to Louis Fischer. The correspondence, from various places, is dated 30 September-7 December 1929; February-September 1930; and 18 August 1932. The letters contain Chicherin's reflections and reminiscences on Russian history and foreign relations from tsarist times through the Pact of Locarno, 1925. (In Box 1 of the Louis Fischer papers, see below.) Unpublished register for the letters.

11 Edwin Rogers Embree (1883-1950). Papers, 1903-56, 9 boxes. Cultural anthropologist and official of the Rockefeller Foundation, 1917-27, and of the Rosenwald Fund, 1928-48. His journal for 1934 describes a trip to Russia. Unpublished register (NUCMC 68-1439).

12 Louis Fischer (b. 1896). Papers, 1929-62, ca. 40 items. Diplomatic historian. In addition to the Chicherin correspondence described above, the papers include letters of Boris Nicolaevsky, and typescripts with corrections of 4 of his books, including Russia, America and the World.

13 Langhorne Gibson (b. 1899). Papers, 1917-36, 3 ft. Author and curator of Naval History at Yale. The collection contains a notebook (ca. 1811) dealing with export trade to Russia.

14 Maksim Gorkii (1868-1936). Writer. ALS to Zinovie Issaevitch Grzhebin, 2 March 1925, concerning the arrest of A. N. Tikhonov and attempts to intervene on his behalf. The letter, 1 p., is signed with Gorkii's real name, A. Peshkov. A photocopy and French and English translations are included. (In the Clift Collection)

15 Howard Haag. Papers, 1921-61, 4 ft. YMCA worker and executive in the Far East. Much of the correspondence, notes, writings, and printed matter relates to Manchuria, Russia, China, and Japan, 1921-61. Unpublished register (NUCMC 72-1888).

16 Sophie Haberman (fl. 1900-11). 2 ALS. The letters, to her nephew and to a Mrs. Churgin, describe her experiences as a Russian immigrant in New York City (9 August 1900, 4 pp., and 20 March 1911, 10 pp.). (Misc. MSS)

17 Thomas Hazard (1758-1828). Letterbook, 1811-16, 1 vol. New Bedford, Conn., merchant. Contains copies of letters to various persons concerning business, trade, and shipping, in part involving Russia. (Misc. MSS)

18 Edward M. House (1858-1938). Papers, 1891-1938, 285 boxes. Statesman. In Colonel House's Subject File, boxes 182 and 207 contain letters, memos, and other papers on Russia. Most deal with post-1918 affairs but some are about 1917; Soviet-American relations is the major topic. Additional letters by government officials, observers, and others are in the general correspondence (alphabetically arranged). House's diary for 1912-26 is also a valuable source. One correspondent was William C. Bullitt. Unpublished register (NUCMC 61-3488).

19 Inquiry Papers, 1917-19. 29 boxes. Correspondence and reports relating to the settlement of World War I territorial problems in preparation for the Paris Peace Conference. Includes reports on Russian politics, education, commerce, and other subjects (boxes 20-21).

20 Victor Jeremy Jerome (1896-1965). Papers, 1923-67, 16 ft. Author and political activist. Correspondence, notes, writings. Polish-born Jerome's real name was Jerome Isaac Romain.

Coming to the U.S. as a boy, he became involved in political radicalism in the 1920s, joining the Communist Party in 1924. The bulk of the materials relates to his work in the Party, 1930-65, and Party organization and activities. He married Rose Pastor Stokes (see below). Jailed in the mid-1950s under the Smith Act, Jerome toured Eastern Europe after his release. In 1959-61 he edited V. Lenin's works in Moscow, returning to the U.S. in 1962. Among the papers are correspondence about his trial, manuscripts of 2 autobiographical novels, an incomplete draft of Rose Stokes' autobiography "I Belong to the Working Class," and a 1956 letter on Soviet persecution of Jews. Unpublished register (NUCMC 76-1434).

21 Alexander Keskula (1882-1964). Papers, in process, 400 items. Russian revolutionary, organizer of anti-tsarist underground movements. Memoirs (fragmentary); letters to him from Estonian and Russian socialists and revolutionaries, 1916-44; passports (under many false names); documents (e.g., receipt from a German consulate general showing Keskula had paid back all money he received as a German spy); his pro memorias to various governments, including the U.S.; 2 manuscript books (Die Natur- und weltgeschichtliche Funktion des Wahns and a study of Don Quixote); family papers, correspondence, photographs, printed matter, and books with his annotations. Permission of the curator of the Slavic and East European Collections required. Unpublished register.

22 Arthur Bliss Lane (1894-1956). Papers, 1904-57, 114 boxes. Ambassador to Poland from 1944-47. Lane often voiced his views on Polish affairs in questions of Soviet-American relations. Unpublished register. (NUCMC 61-3487)

23 Max Lerner (b. 1902). Papers, 1927-69, 42 ft. Political scientist. Correspondence, speeches, writings, notes, photos, clippings, and memorabilia in part concern his career and his activities during the Red scares of the 1950s. Unpublished register (NUCMC 76-1436).

24 Charles A. Lindbergh (1902-1974). Papers, ca. 1890-present, 650 boxes. Aviator. Includes some material relating to 3 flights to the USSR made by Charles and Anne Morrow Lindbergh in 1931, 1933, and 1938, with comments on Soviet airpower and society. Unpublished register.

25 Walter Lippmann (1889-1974). Papers, ca. 1906-74, 326 boxes, 115 ft. Journalist, author, and political commentator. Correspondence, writings, photographs, and printed matter document his personal and professional life. Includes material on foreign affairs and on Russia. Unpublished finding aid (NUCMC 62-71, in part).

26 John van Antwerp MacMurray (1881-1960). Papers, 1715-1960, on microfilm: 55,000 letters, 35 containers of writings, and 18 containers of printed matter and photos. Diplomat and specialist on Far Eastern affairs. In 1908-11 he was second secretary at the U.S. embassy in St. Petersburg. As chief of the Division of Near Eastern Affairs at the State Department, 1911-13, he was concerned with trying to remove tsarist restrictions on visits by Jewish-Americans to their Russian homeland. From 1933-38 he was minister to the Baltic countries. Most of the collection is correspondence and photos. Among his correspondents were V. N. Kokovtsov and George and Boris B. Bakhmetev. Includes papers of his father Junius. The originals of these papers are at Princeton University. Unpublished register (NUCMC 71-396, for Princeton). (Robert Anthony Collection)

27 William Cooper Moore (b. 1906). Yale College class of 1928. Typescript, 55 pp., entitled "Forty days and forty nights: A trip through Russia in 1931"; inscribed at the end: "Russia again, May 4, 1932--May 17, 1932 . . ."

28 Aleksandr Vasil'evich Osokin (d. 1974). Russian army officer. Memoirs, 133 pp., about the anti-Bolshevik forces in the Civil War (1917-22). In Russian, undated, the typed, signed manuscript apparently was produced in Paris. A newspaper clipping from La Pensée Russe, 4 October 1974, in Paris carries his obituary in Russian. (Misc. MSS)

29 Alexander I. Petrunkevich (1875-1964). Family papers, 1886-1932, 5 ft. Letters, 3 photo albums, other notebooks and albums. Ca. 250 letters of Alexander's father, Ivan Il'ich Petrunkevich, the famous zemstvo and liberal political leader. Many are from Nastia (Anastasia Sergeevna Petrunkevich), the elder Petrunkevich's second wife and widow of Count Vladimir Panin. Among the business correspondents were D. Lekhovich, Ksenia Denikina, and A. Tolstaia. The letters, arranged chronologically, date from 1886 on. Other materials include 2 albums of poetry, a notebook, and some slides. Charles E. Timberlake's "Source Materials on Russian and American History in the Alexander Petrunkevich Collection" appeared in the January 1967 Yale University Library Gazette; unpublished register.

30 Frank L. Polk (1871-1943). Papers, 1913-43, 28 ft. U.S. State Department official. His State Department files include correspondence with David R. Francis (ambassador in Petrograd in 1916); cables and correspondence with other embassy personnel to 1918; plus letters of John Reed, William C. Bullitt, and others. Some memos and reports concern Russian affairs, Russian-German relations, the railway situation, British diplomatic advances to Russia, the Allied intervention in Siberia, German influence in Siberia, the Red Cross, and Russian relief. His confidential diary reveals the changing views of U.S. State

Department officials and President Woodrow Wilson on Siberian policy and has information about the delegation of the high command in Siberia to Japan. Unpublished register (NUCMC 61-3497).

31 Alexander Polovtsoff (1857-1934). Papers, 1918-34, 6 boxes. Russian diplomat born in St. Petersburg. Polovtsoff served in the cavalry, 1888-92, and then entered the Ministry of the Interior. Later, in the foreign service, he served in Bombay, 1906-1909. In emigration after 1918, he translated literature and wrote historical essays. The papers include mostly notes, manuscripts, and typescripts of his writings (mainly historical studies of Peter I, other Russian monarchs, and noteworthy people). 1 typescript concerns protection of Imperial palaces after the 1917 Revolution. Only one of the historical works has been published: Les Favoris de Catherine la Grande (Paris, 1939). An autobiographical piece covers his youth and tsarist service. Unpublished register (NUCMC 68-1442).

32 Chester Wells Purington (b. 1871). Papers, 1917-25, 1 box. Mining engineer, traveled in Russia and Siberia ca. 1898-1900. Includes drafts of books and articles as well as correspondence relating to his travel in the Russian Empire, mines, and mineral resources.

33 Sergei G. Pushkarev (b. 1888). Papers, in process, ca. 20 ft. Russian historian. Correspondence, writings, reprints of articles, and related commentary. Some material concerns the personality and activities of Professor G. V. Vernadskii. Material by others relates to Professor Pushkarev's personality and activities. Also, clippings.

34 Russian Travel Questionnaires. 2 cartons, ca. 1960. Collection of questionnaires for travelers going to or returning from the USSR, apparently part of someone's Ph.D. research. They contain long, interesting comments on American impressions of Russia ca. 1960.

35 David Shub (b. 1887). Correspondence, 1912-63, 1 box. Revolutionary and author. Born and educated in Russia, he became a member of the Social Democratic Party in 1903. Shub lived in London, Paris, and Geneva, 1904-1905, mixing with Bolshevik and Menshevik leaders. Returning to Russia in September 1905, he took part in the Revolution, was arrested in late 1906, and exiled to Siberia. A year later he escaped and made his way to the U.S., 1908. For the next 50 years he remained in close contact with leaders of every faction of the Russian revolutionary movement. He wrote a standard biography of Lenin. Among Shub's correspondents, 1912-63, were A. R. Abramovich, M. A. Aldanov, Angelica Balabanoff, Vera Burtsev, Victor Chernov, Lydia Dan, Lev Deich, Vera Figner, M. Karpovich, B. D. Nikolaevsky, Catherine Prokopovich (Kuskova), and N. V. Vol'sky (Valentinov). Unpublished register (NUCMC 71-2040).

36 Walter Bedell Smith (1895-1961). Papers, 1949-50, 1 box. U.S. army officer, ambassador to the USSR, 1946-49. Draft copy, typed, signed, of the general's book My Three Years in Moscow (New York, 1950) with his own annotations and research notes. Also included is correspondence with U.S. agencies, 1949-50, mostly concerned with the process of getting security clearance for publication.

37 A. I. Spiridovitch (1873-1959). Papers, 1890-1950, 27 boxes. Chief of gendarmes and governor of Yalta. Manuscript books and documents on the following topics: the life of Nicholas II, his family, and Grigorii Rasputin; General Spiridovitch's memoirs; notes to a history of the Socialist Revolutionary Party and its forerunners; the governorship of Yalta; social movements in the late tsarist times; A. S. Pushkin and Russian literature; the Grand Duke Kiril Vladimirovich; the house of Romanov; the history of Bolshevism; the Jewish question; the reign of Nicholas II and the last years of the court at Tsarskoe Selo. Copies of some of the general's published works are also in the collection (e.g., The Revolutionary Movement in Russia, 2nd edition), often with his handwritten additions. There are items of P. Rachkovskii, 1890, and records (with a survey) of a department of police in the papers as well. In Russian. Permission of the Curator of Slavic and East European Collections required. Unpublished register.

38 Henry L. Stimson (1867-1950). Papers, 272 boxes. Secretary of war 1911-13 and again 1940-45, and secretary of state 1929-33. His papers and diaries, 1941-45 especially, shed much light on the origins of the Cold War and the work of his office in World War II. Both the papers and the diaries have been microfilmed (separately). The library produced a guide for each microfilm in 1973; the papers guide contains Russian references for several reels. Unpublished register (NUCMC 61-3472).

39 Anson Phelps Stokes (1874-1958). Papers, 1761-1960, 315 boxes. Author and canon of the National Cathedral. 1 box ("Portsmouth Treaty Papers, 1904-05") contains letters and documents, mostly unpublished, on the treaty ending the Russo-Japanese War, plus a copy of Harold Phelps Stokes's pamphlet Yale, the Portsmouth Treaty, and Japan. In a 1975 addition to the Stokes papers there is correspondence of Barnabas Sakai with important information on the signing of the Portsmouth Treaty in 1905 and material on Russian refugee relief in Istanbul. Unpublished register and correspondents list (NUCMC 74-1203 and 77-2112).

40 Rose Pastor Stokes (1879-1933). Papers, 1900-58, 13 boxes. Journalist and Communist Party member. She was born in Poland but emigrated

to the U.S. in 1890. After working in a Cleveland cigar factory for 12 years, she moved to New York City, 1903, and became a feature writer for the Jewish Daily News. In 1905 an interview led to marriage with a young millionaire socialist, James Graham Phelps Stokes. She then became radicalized, turning into a political activist and eventually joining the Communist Party. She divorced Stokes, 1925, and married Jerome Romain (see under Victor Jerome above). Stokes attended the fourth Comintern congress in the USSR in 1922. The papers include a photocopy of her unfinished autobiography (1879-1905); correspondence with Max Eastman, Eugene Debs, and Emma Goldman (1905-33); some drawings; and a copy of her report to the Comintern congress on the Negro question in America. Unpublished register (NUCMC 71-2041).

41 David Peck Todd (1855-1939). Papers, 1862-1939, 45 ft. Astronomer. Includes material on his trip to Russia to record the eclipse of 21 August 1914 (boxes 57-58). Unpublished register (NUCMC 77-2114).

42 Rosa Vinaver. Wife of M. M. Vinaver, Kadet Party leader and minister of justice in the Provisional Government. Typescript, carbon copy, memoirs covering the years 1905-21, 100 pp. They include valuable portraits of Kadet leaders. Location of the original is uncertain. (Misc. MSS)

43 Harry Weinberger (1886?-1944). Papers, 1915-42, 50 boxes. Lawyer and civil rights advocate. He defended many radicals, anarchists, aliens, and immigrants. Case files relating to Russian immigrants include those of Emma Goldman and Alexander Berkman; Jacob Abrams, Hyman Lachowsky, Samuel Lipman, and Mollie Steimer ("the Four Russians"); Wasily Andreyeff; Ethel Bernstein; and Bernard Sernacker. Unpublished register (NUCMC 74-1207).

44 William Williams Family. Papers, ca. 1750-1900, 2 boxes. Merchants. Includes a letterbook of Thomas Wheeler Williams (1789-1874) with copies of letters from various places, 1811-13; some relate to Russian commerce.

45 William George Eden Wiseman (1885-1962). Papers, 1916-19, 6 ft. British diplomat and banker. The major portion of the letters, cables, and other papers relates to Russian affairs from April 1917 to April 1919, particularly the Siberian intervention. Card index (NUCMC 61-3484).

CT 19
ALKA (ARCHIVES OF AMERICAN LITHUANIAN CULTURE)
P.O. Box 608
Putnam, Connecticut 06260
(203-928-7434)

The archives contain unpublished materials pertaining to Lithuanian writers, historians, and political figures. Among these are M. Krupuvicius, M. Vaitkus, and A. Giedrius. Also included are the archives of the Lithuanian consulate in New York (several big boxes) and of the Lithuanian Relief Fund of America. Finally, there are books, circulars, tickets, programs, and other items pertaining to Lithuania and its culture that were collected by Monsignor P. Juras. Some of the items in the archives were shown at the Lithuanian Pavilion in the 1939 World's Fair in New York.

CT 20
GENNADY PANIN--PRIVATE COLLECTION
209 Howe Avenue
Shelton, Connecticut 06484
(203-734-0096)

Born in Moscow in 1895, Panin spent his early years in St. Petersburg and Kazan. In the 1920s he moved in literary circles and was a writer of verses (including acrostics). Under Stalin he was imprisoned for 19 months. During World War II he worked for the Russian anti-communist newspaper (Golos Kryma) as a journalist and was evacuated with German troops to Austria and later to Germany, emigrating with his wife Frances (nee Shneider) to the U.S. in 1950. Collection includes diaries, memoirs of Petr Nikolaevich Shneider, and several hundred letters from notable people of the Russian emigration, often containing verses and information about their lives in Russia. Also, photographs and maps. Correspondents (and autographs) include O. Ia. Anop'ian, O. N. Anstej, G. Ia. Aronson, A. M. Arsharuni, Anna Akhmatova, Konstantin Bal'mont, Petr L. Bark, Vadim Bajan (pseudonym), Nina Berberova, Rodion M. Berëzov, Sarah Bernhardt, Vladimir F. Blagov, A. I. Buldeev, D. D. Burliuk, A. N. Vertinskii, Iurii N. Verkhovskii, M. A. Voloshin, Ia. Godin, Viktor Nikolaevich Denisov (pseudonym: Deni), I. V. Elagin, R. Ivnev, Nikolai Alekseevich Kliuev, A. P. Kraiskii, D. I. Krachkovskii (pseudonym: Klenovskii), Alla Ktorova, Prince Nikolai Kudashev, Ekaterina D. Kuskova-Prokopovich, Boris A. Lavrenëv, Fedor Markovich Levin, Lev A. Meij, Pavel I. Novitskii, Irina Odoevtsova, K. K. Fofanov (pseudonym: Olympov), V. Opalov, Valerii Pereleshin, K. P. Pobedonostsev, Iakov P. Polonskii, Vsevolod A. Rozhdestvenskii, Il'ya I. Sadof'ev, Lidia N. Seifullina, Sergei Nikolaevich Sergeev-Tsenskii, N. S. Tikhonov, Aleksei N. Tolstoy, K. A. Trenev, Afanasii A. Fet-Shenshin, Boris A. Filippov, M. N. Chudnov, Tikhon V. Churilin, Georgii A. Shengeli, and Pavel Iakovlev. Ultimate disposition of the collection is uncertain at this time. Inquire concerning access.

CT 21
COMBUSTION ENGINEERING, INC.
900 Long Ridge Road
Stamford, Connecticut 06902
(203-328-8771)

The company maintains records of sales and exports it has made to the USSR. Its activities date from the early 1940s. For information, the researcher should write directly to Combustion Engineering.

CT 22
UKRAINIAN MUSEUM AND LIBRARY
161 Glenbrook Road
Stamford, Connecticut 06902

The archives of the Museum and Library hold some materials of individuals and organizations. These include papers of Professor Mykola Chubaty (d. 1975), professor of church history (correspondence and other papers, ca. 1939-75, ca. 20 boxes); a few letters of Mykhaylo Hrushevsky (1866-1934), historian and first president of the Ukrainian Central Rada, from the early 1920s; literary manuscripts and correspondence of Bohdan Lepky; some papers of Professor Kyrylo Studynsky from the 1920s; material pertaining to the Shevchenko Scientific Society; correspondence of priests and other items relating to the church in the U.S. and in the Ukraine; and many periodicals and other printed matter. Access requires permission in advance; write and indicate specific research interests.

CT 23
WILLIAM S. LAUGHLIN--PRIVATE COLLECTION
DEPARTMENT OF BIOBEHAVIORAL SCIENCES
UNIVERSITY OF CONNECTICUT
Box U-154
Storrs, Connecticut 06268
(203-486-2556)

Collection of manuscripts, films, field notes, correspondence with Soviet scholars, records and specimens (ethnographic, archaeological, and anthropological), and books pertaining to research in the Aleutian Islands and Siberia (Commander Islands, Khabarovsk, Lake Baikal, and Novosibirsk), and to related field research in Alaska, Canada, and Greenland. Inquire concerning access.

CT 24
MR. THOMAS P. WHITNEY--PRIVATE COLLECTION
Roxbury Road
Washington, Connecticut 06793
(203-868-7353)

Mr. Thomas Whitney maintains a collection of published and unpublished materials and cultural objects and items pertaining largely to late 19th and 20th c. Russian art, literature, and culture. The total size of the collection is: several hundred works of art, ca. 10,000 published volumes including rare books and émigré publications; ca. 300 boxes of journals and newspapers, including émigré publications; ca. 100 boxes of monographs and archival materials including correspondence, manuscripts, etc., and in particular a large part of the archive of A. M. Remizov. The collection is closed to the public and facilities are not available to permit extended visits and study. Individual visitors or groups of scholars, students, and interested persons may be received to view the collection by advance appointment.

CT 25
JEWISH HISTORICAL SOCIETY OF GREATER HARTFORD
335 Bloomfield Avenue
West Hartford, Connecticut 06117
(203-236-4571 x 35)

This repository holds tape recordings, manuscripts, and newspaper/magazine clippings containing references to Hartford residents who emigrated from Russia in the late 19th and early 20th c. The archives are available to researchers only when the librarian is on duty.

DELAWARE

DE 1
ELEUTHERIAN MILLS HISTORICAL LIBRARY
Greenville, Delaware 19807
(302-658-2401 x 226)

1 Boeing-Vertol Division. Records, in process, 65 boxes and 14 vols. Contains the administrative papers of Harry S. Pack, director of customer relations. Some Executive Department correspondence from 1965 concerns the USSR. Restriction: All manuscript materials are covered by a time seal of 25 years; access by

application to the director of the library. (Accession 1375)

2 Edmund N. and Donald F. Carpenter. Collection, in process. Includes a letter of H. L. Scott, chief of staff, U.S. War Department, to the Russian army's chief of staff during World War I, 13 October 1915; and a letter of the first secretary of the Russian embassy to C. B. Landis, 11 October 1915. Both items are on microfilm, no. M66.15; neither may be reproduced. (Accession 889)

3 Jasper E. Crane (1881-1969). Papers, 1929-48, 26 boxes. Vice-president of E. I. du Pont de Nemours & Co., 1929-46. Includes materials on foreign relations (e.g., memoranda on Russia) and letters concerning war, munitions, neutrality, and contracts' terminations, 1939-44 (Series II, part 2, nos. 1039 and 1053). (Accession 1231)

4 E. I. du Pont de Nemours & Co. Miscellaneous records, Series II, 1902-52, ca. 2,600 items. Contains correspondence with foreign countries, including Russia, on patents, 1909-12 (Series II, part 3, no. 135); and materials on a process for manufacturing nitroglycerine, patented abroad (files for Russia, 1904-15)--Series II, part 2, no. 794. (Accessions 472 and 1305) (NUCMC 73-531)

5 Henry Francis du Pont. Collection of Winterthur Manuscripts, 1588-1926, 150,000 items. (NUCMC 60-1361). Family papers of the du Ponts, arranged in separate groups. Group 2: Papers of Pierre Samuel du Pont de Nemours (1739-1817) and his 2 wives. 480 items. Series B: Writings, memoirs, and political papers, 1763-1817. Some items from his service as inspecteur général du commerce of France, 1779-88, including material on commercial relations with Russia. Drafts of memoranda by du Pont de Nemours, a Monsieur le Gendre, and others, one of which is entitled "Mémoire sur le commerce de la France avec la Russie," ca. 1782-83?, 329 pp., with charts, tables, and an index, manuscript. Also, papers relating to the Gouvernement Provisoire of 1814, in which du Pont de Nemours was secretary general. 1 letter, 17 April 1814, from the keeper of the royal park at Mousseau to Baron de Jacken, gouverneur general de Paris, complains of the damage and destruction done to the park by the Russian Cossacks, 2 pp. (NUCMC 73-533). Group 9: Papers of Samuel Francis du Pont (1803-65) and his wife Sophie Madeleine du Pont (1810-88). 814 items. Series B: Letters to S. F. du Pont. Includes a letter from Captain Chikackoff (Chichagov?) of the Russian navy, 1858. Series E: Letters to Sophie Madeleine du Pont. Includes a news clipping entitled "A Daring Deed" which describes Lammot du Pont's part in delivering explosives to the Russians in the Crimean War (NUCMC 73-530). Group 10: Papers of Pierre Samuel du Pont (1870-1954), 1880-1954, ca. 1 million items. File 667, containing 18 items, concerns Imperial Russian government bonds, 1916-19.

6 Lammot du Pont (1880-1952). Papers, 1801-1954, 308 items. Transcripts in part. Includes correspondence of Thomas S. Grasselli and others pertaining to the role of Lammot du Pont (1831-84) in supplying gunpowder for the Crimean War. (NUCMC 73-529)

7 Haldeman Family. Papers, 1801-85, ca. 7,600 items. Correspondence, business, and personal papers, chiefly of Jacob M. Haldeman (1781-1857) and his son Richard Jacobs Haldeman (1831-1886), editor, congressman, and diplomat. Papers of Richard J. Haldeman include diaries of travel in Europe, 1852-55, when he was a student at Heidelberg and Berlin, and an attaché in the legations at Paris, Vienna, and St. Petersburg. (NUCMC 72-95)

8 François Damas Lainé. 2 diaries, 1814 and 1858. Includes a xerox copy of the diary of his father during his captivity in Russia in 1814. The copy cannot be reproduced. (Accession 1515)

9 Longwood Manuscripts. Collection, Group 7, 1778-1933, 550 items, including 199 vols. Notes and collections of Bessie Gardner du Pont, family historian and author, 1778-1933; Series A: Papers for the history of E. I. du Pont de Nemours & Co., 1804-1917. Records contain copies and extracts of business letters to and from the du Pont Co. regarding the sale of powder to the Russian fleet, 1863, and concerning cancelled contracts with the Russian government for pressed powder, n.d. (In part, NUCMC 60-1370)

10 Thomas Masters (d. 1844). Papers, ca. 1800-55, ca. 4,150 items. Merchant of Philadelphia and New York City. Business papers, mainly pre-1814, of Masters and his family and of the firms of Markoe & Masters, Masters & Markoe, and Masters, Markoe & Company. Series C, 1810-47, 215 items, includes a note on the state of commodities imported from America to Russia, indicating which were selling or in demand and which were not, St. Petersburg, 1809. This series is accession 189. (NUCMC 72-104)

11 New York Air Brake Company. Records, 1904-12, 12 items. 4 items concern a Russian patent on the company's invention of the J-valve (letters patent in Russian, 1910-12). (Accession 249)

12 Sun Oil Company. Houdry Process Corporation Records, in process. Contains administrative papers concerning legislation and Eugene Houdry's trip to Russia, 1938-47, 27 items; contracts and promotions concerning Russia, 1944-47, 40 items; lend-lease, 1939-43 and 1946, 100 items; and personnel training, 1942-45, 40 items. Restriction: access by application to the director of the library; the

company retains right of consent for reproduction or extensive quotation for publication. (Accession 1317)

13 Wood (Alan) Steel Company. Records, 1880, 34 items. Includes letters of Charles L. Gilpin from Russia which discuss Russian ironmaking, March-July 1880. All are on microfilm, no. M62.3. (Accession 340)

Finding Aid: A Guide to the Manuscripts in the Eleutherian Mills Historical Library. Accessions through the year 1965 by John Beverly Riggs (Greenville, 1970).

DE 2
SPECIAL COLLECTIONS
THE UNIVERSITY LIBRARY (MORRIS LIBRARY)
UNIVERSITY OF DELAWARE
Newark, Delaware 19711
(302-738-2229)

1 George S. Messersmith (1883-1960). Papers, 1907-55, 3.5 ft., 10 boxes. Diplomat and assistant secretary of state, 1937-40. 6 items relate to Russian diplomatic affairs. Subject index (NUCMC 62-1434).

2 Oral History Tapes Series. Includes interviews with, at present, 20 immigrants from Russia, the Ukraine, and Latvia; transcripts are available for those marked with an asterisk: Jacob and Florence Bronfin*, Robert Chaiken*, Max Chavin, Mrs. James N. Ginns (nee Sallie T. Topkis)*--2, Isidore Golden*, Louis Golin*, Uldis and Grieta Golts* (transcript only), Leon Hnida*, Goldie (Olga) Kagel*, Israel Plafker, Isadore Platt, Albert Raivy, Morris Salus, Abraham Seidel, Mrs. Leah Gold Seltzer, Isadore Silverman*, Phillip Simon, Mrs. Jacob Statnekoo, Morris Tomasis, Louis Weiner. Though available through Special Collections, the tape series is the project of the History Media Center. Permission to use the tapes must be obtained from the History Department of the University of Delaware (401 Kirkbride Hall; 302-738-2371).

DE 3
HISTORICAL SOCIETY OF DELAWARE LIBRARY
505 Market Street Mall
Wilmington, Delaware 19801
(302-655-7161)

1 James A. Bayard, the Elder (1767-1815). Lawyer, congressman, and diplomat. Includes letter declining ministry to Russia, offered by President Madison, in 1815.

2 James A. Bayard, the Younger (1797-1880). Lawyer, U.S. senator, and diplomatist. Papers, part of the Gallery Collection, 1750-1940, 300 items. Folder 14, box 60, contains 3 letters mentioning Russia; all are addressed to David Parish: (a) circular dispatch, 12 August 1812, from W. D. Lewis and Willing from St. Petersburg; (b) ALS, 26 March 1813, from Gouverneur Morris discusses the possibilities of President James Madison's accepting a Russian offer of mediation and perhaps a loan (in the War of 1812), 2 pp.; and (c) ALS, 28 June 1813, from Richard Forrest, 2 pp., reading in part: "God grant our envoy to Russia make a speedy and honorable peace."

3 Bird-Bancroft. Records, in process. Includes some correspondence between the Bancroft Company and the Mather firm from Imperial Russia, where they had a fabrics plant, 1870s-1880s. Letters pertain to dyes and machinery.

4 H. F. Brown (1867-1944). Collection, 1694-1898, ca. 1,380 items. Educator and collector. Folder 13, box 23, contains a letter from C. A. Rodney, 31 May 1817, to Count Peter von der Pahlen in Rio de Janeiro. This ALS discusses the War of 1812 and Russia's proffered intercession, 3 pp.

5 Allen McLane (1746-1829). Papers, 1777-1814, ca. 300 items (all photostats). Includes an ALS from William Duane, 7 February 1813, reporting no movement of the French in Russia and speaking of French activities at Vilna (folder 25, box 38). Originals in the New York Public Library.

6 Milligan-McLane. Collection, 1764-1843, ca. 114 items. Includes papers of George Baldwin Milligan (1791-1841). His letter of 29 August 1813 to his aunt describes his stay in St. Petersburg as companion of James A. Bayard.

7 Pierre Du Ponceau (1760-1844). Manuscript book, typescript, and his diary, 1777-78, with an account of his trip from Boston to Yorktown and to Washington's Valley Forge camp, written partly in Cyrillic and containing some Russian words. Because of its fragile state, researchers can use the diary only with permission of the executive director and under supervision.

DE 4
THE HENRY FRANCIS DU PONT WINTERTHUR MUSEUM
WINTERTHUR MUSEUM LIBRARY
Winterthur, Delaware 19735
(302-656-8591)

Joseph Downs Manuscript and Microfilm Collection. 1620-1914, 130,000 ms. items and 3,118 reels of microfilm. Includes 4 items pertaining to Russia: an insurance policy taken by Messrs. Wait & Pierce for the ship Friendship from Salem to Archangel, Salem, 1810; trade cards of foreign businesses at the Columbian Exposition, Chicago, 1893; a letter to Messrs. W. R. Rotch & Co. from J. D. Lewis, St.

Petersburg, Russia, 1828; and a letter to Messrs. Brown, Benson & Ives of Providence, Rhode Island, from Edward James Smith & Co., St. Petersburg, 1795, giving current prices. Register.

DISTRICT OF COLUMBIA

DC 1
OFFICE OF AIR FORCE HISTORY
HEADQUARTERS, UNITED STATES AIR FORCE
AIR FORCE DEPARTMENT
Forrestal Building, Room 8E082
1000 Independence Avenue SW
Washington, D.C. 20314
(202-693-7399)

This office maintains microfilms of the holdings of the Albert F. Simpson Historical Research Center in Maxwell Air Force Base, Alabama, which has a considerable amount of materials pertaining to Russia/USSR. A fuller description of some of these items can be found in the entry for the Simpson Center. Researchers may obtain a security clearance to examine pertinent classified documents up to secret by writing to AFSINC, Magazine and Book Division, Attn: Major Kahl, Kelly AFB, TX 78241.

DC 2
VOLTA BUREAU LIBRARY
ALEXANDER GRAHAM BELL ASSOCIATION FOR THE DEAF
1537 35th Street NW
Washington, D.C.
(202-337-5220)

1 box of pamphlets, correspondence, photos, and periodical clippings written and/or sent to the Bureau by N. and F. Rau, who were active in pre- and post-revolutionary Russian studies of deaf-and-mute problems. Most items date from the late 1920s or early 1930s and reflect the Raus's involvement in Russian medical problems.

DC 3
AMERICAN NATIONAL RED CROSS
17th and D Streets NW
Washington, D.C. 20006
(202-857-3712)

1 Record Group 4. 152 drawers, 1947-64. Contains correspondence with the Alliance of Red Cross and Red Crescent Societies of the USSR ("Russian Red Cross"). Materials on prisoners in the Soviet Union.

2 Record Group 5. 1965-present. Growing. Correspondence with "Russian Red Cross." Materials from current files are transferred to this record group after 3 years. The current files are kept in another part of the building and are restricted.

Note: Record Groups 1-3 have been transferred to Record Group 200 in the National Archives. Restricted to researchers with a valid reason for research.

DC 4
FILM LIBRARY
ARMY DEPARTMENT
The Pentagon, Room 5A1058
Washington, D.C. 20310
(202-695-5320)

5-10 motion pictures dealing with current Soviet armor and naval strength. Restricted. Inquire at the Film Library for details.

DC 5
REFERENCE LIBRARY
ARMY DEPARTMENT
The Pentagon, Room 5A486
Washington, D.C. 20310
(202-697-2806)

Still photographs of Soviet-related subjects. 300-500 items. Most of the photos are of captured World War II Soviet military equipment and of Soviet military operations in that war. A few photographs are of more recent equipment. Restricted. Inquire at the Reference Library for details.

DC 6
NATHALIE BABEL BROWN--PRIVATE COLLECTION
3016 Tilden Street NW
Washington, D.C. 20008

Nathalie Babel Brown holds materials of her father, the short-story writer Isaac Emmanuelovich Babel (1894-1941). These include his diary written while serving in S. Budyonny's cavalry during the Civil War, 1920, which formed the factual and imaginative basis for much of Red Cavalry; journalistic pieces, 1917-22, on the impact of the war and political upheavals on everyday; early stories, 1913-20; miscellaneous stories, 1920-39; film scenarios, 1926-39; and letters to his mother and sister, who had emigrated to Belgium, 1925-39.

Some of these materials have been published in Soviet and English-language editions of Babel's works. The Russian text of the correspondence has never been published, however, and only 1 film scenario is available in Russian (Wandering Stars, reprinted in 1972 by Ardis from a 1926 Moscow edition). Brief excerpts from the diary appeared in Literaturnoe nasledstvo, vol. 74. File materials at the moment are not available to readers. However, queries will be answered.

DC 7
INSTITUTE FOR CHRISTIAN ORIENTAL RESEARCH
THE CATHOLIC UNIVERSITY OF AMERICA
Washington, D.C. 20064
(202-635-5084)

Armenian Manuscripts. On the Heavenly Hierarchy by Dionysus the Areopagite, A.D. 1662; four Gospels, A.D. 1628; missal, A.D. 1648; Gospels, incomplete, 16th c.

DC 8
DEPARTMENT OF ARCHIVES AND MANUSCRIPTS
MULLEN LIBRARY
THE CATHOLIC UNIVERSITY OF AMERICA
4th Street and Michigan Avenue NE
Washington, D.C. 20064
(202-635-5065)

1 John Brophy (1883-1963). Papers, 1917-63, 25 ft. Labor leader and union organizer, involved in the AFL-CIO. 1 folder applies to his 1927 trip to the USSR as part of the Trade Union Delegation that observed labor conditions in the Soviet Union. There is correspondence about the trip and about discussions among the delegates, plus numerous postcards from Moscow, Kharkov, and the Ukraine, most addressed to his wife, Anita Brophy. He writes about the people, living standards, religion, the Communist Party, Petrograd (?), Leningrad, Moscow, the Peter and Paul Fortress, Red Square, the arts, ballet, social activities, festivals, industry, factories, working conditions, workers' attitudes, Workers' Conventions, the Donets coal basin, coal mines, salt mines, and agriculture in the Ukraine. (NUCMC 66-401)

2 Committee on Special War Activities of the National Catholic War Council. Part of the NCWC/USCC Records, 1917-present, ca. 900 ft. (additions expected). 1 folder contains correspondence regarding the Siberian War Prisoners Repatriation Fund, January 1920-July 1923. Unpublished finding aid.

3 Joseph Daniel Keenan (b. 1896). Papers, 1935-76, 8.5 ft. Labor leader. He was involved in the War Production Board and in labor unionization for post-World War II Germany. Includes correspondence for 1945-47 and an oral history account (prepared in recent years) concerning German labor issues then and Soviet attitudes toward them. Unpublished inventory.

4 Aloisius Cardinal Muench (1889-1962). Papers, 1906-63, 81 ft., 150,000 items. Papal nuncio to Germany after World War II, and official American representative to act as liaison officer between the church and the military occupation government in Germany. Cardinal Muench was in charge of Catholic relief work in post-war Germany, aiding religious and lay refugees, deportees, etc. Papers are divided into sections by specific agencies and years: (a) Vatican Mission Records and Correspondence, 1945-49. Includes letters from Father Octavian Barlea, of the Rumanian mission, who writes about Soviet persecution of the church in Rumania and other Rumanian matters. (b) Papal Relief Commission, 1946-59. Contains correspondence concerning financial assistance for priests, seminarians, and the laity in the Soviet Zone of Germany and the church in East Germany. A Memorandum to His Eminence Cardinal Stritch from Fr. William E. McManus of the National Catholic Welfare Conference, 23 October 1950, discusses, in part, Soviet plans for Western Germany. Also, correspondence detailing the work of the War Relief Services in Germany. (c) Refugee Priests, 1946-59. Includes documents relating to Latvian, Estonian, Lithuanian, Russian, and Ukrainian priests in Germany. (d) Liaison Consultant Omgus, 1945-59. Includes war crimes documents and reports; reports on the treatment of German POWs in the USSR, pamphlets on the Moscow trials, Malmedy, Landsberg Prison, and the Katyn Massacre; reports and correspondence on Soviet compulsory labor service, Miss Karin Vogt's life in a Russian forced-labor camp, a Russian officer's threat against the bishop of Berlin to force cooperation, and Alfred Lummer, a Russian POW returnee who saw 1,400 Vincentian sisters forced to become miners in the Soviet Union; surveys of the church in Germany and its negotiations for the emigration of German-Russian refugees; and correspondence between Muench and the vicar-general of the Ukrainian Catholic Church in Germany. (e) Prints and Photographs, 1947-59. Includes pictures of a priest released from a Russian prison camp, Muench speaking with prisoners from a Russian concentration camp, and Albertus Magnus College, Seminary for Refugees. Restriction: Call or write for details. Unpublished preliminary inventory.

5 Terence Vincent Powderly (1849-1924). Papers, 1871-1924, 90 ft. Labor leader and government official, U.S. commissioner-general of Immigration 1896-1912. Correspondence, reports, notes, writings, addresses, photos, and

clippings. Includes material on Jewish, Armenian, Slovak, etc. immigration to the U.S. in the late 19th c. Most, but not all, of the collection has been microfilmed by the Microfilm Corporation of America; for this part there is a published finding aid, edited by J. A. Turcheneske, Jr. (NUCMC 61-1317)

DC 9
MR. DAVID CHAVCHAVADZE--PRIVATE COLLECTION
3801 Windom Place NW
Washington, D.C. 20016
(202-363-7362)

Mr. Chavchavadze is related, on his mother's side, to the Romanovs. Materials in his possession include the memoirs of his mother and grandmother; letters of Grand Duke George Mikhailovich between ca. 1914 and 1918; and photoalbums of a personal nature. Individual researchers should contact Mr. Chavchavadze in advance regarding the use of his materials.

DC 10
NICHOLAS DANILOFF--PRIVATE COLLECTION
3713 Warren Street NW
Washington, D.C. 20016
(202-362-8281)

Papers of General Iurii N. Danilov (d. 1937), deputy chief of staff (quartermaster general) of the Russian army, 1909-15 (Nicholas Daniloff's grandfather). He was with Nicholas II at the latter's abdication, later supported General Lavr Kornilov, and even served reluctantly on the Soviet delegation to Brest-Litovsk, opposing a separate peace with Germany. After the peace treaty, he joined A. I. Denikin and General P. N. Wrangel in the Civil War. Emigrating in 1920, the general went to Paris, where he was associated with the Institut de France. Papers include his memoirs and writings (books and articles), notebooks in Russian relating to his exile in Paris, fragmentary correspondence from Baron Wrangel, typescripts on military developments in the Soviet Union, and other observations on developments in the USSR, 4 boxes. Among the manuscripts are: a book-length work entitled "On the Road to Collapse" (published in German); unpublished manuscript on military weaponry and strategy in the inter-war period; and an unfinished work, "On the Road to Bolshevism." Ultimate disposition of the papers will be to a university library. Telephone or write concerning access and for more information.

DC 11
DR. ROGER O. EGEBERG--PRIVATE COLLECTION
DIRECTOR, OFFICE OF PROFESSIONAL AND SCIENTIFIC AFFAIRS
HEALTH CARE FINANCING ADMINISTRATION
DEPARTMENT OF HEALTH, EDUCATION, AND WELFARE
330 C Street SW
Washington, D.C. 20201
(202-245-0348)

1 Dr. Egeberg was, for 4 years, the U.S. chairman of the U.S.-Soviet committee of scientists and administrators for cooperation and collaboration in the field of medicine. Since the program's inauguration in the early 1970s, the number of joint projects has grown to about 75, the large majority of which have been productive and successful.

Dr. Egeberg retains at present ca. 2 ft. of meeting agendas, discussion material, and official correspondence relating to the program. During his tenure (now ended), the Soviet co-chairman was Dr. Dmitri Venediktov, deputy minister of health of the USSR; Dr. Venediktov still has this position. Another Soviet figure who participated in the early discussions of the agreement was Dr. Boris Petrovsky, minister of health of the USSR. Dr. Paul Ehrlich, director of the Office of International Health, and his deputy Dr. Robert Fischer were also closely involved on the American side. At some time in the future, Dr. Egeberg's intention is to give these papers to Yale University. However, they must first be put into order, a process that may take some months.

2 In addition to these materials of an official nature, Dr. Egeberg and his wife have personal papers relating to an earlier trip to the Soviet Union in the early 1930s. A diary and perhaps a few photos survive from this early visit. Access to these papers is by written request only.

DC 12
PRINCE AND PRINCESS NICHOLAS GALITZINE--PRIVATE COLLECTION
4458 Greenwich Parkway NW
Washington, D.C.
(202-338-0806)

Prince Galitzine has in his possession an album of photographs of his family estate at Gremiach (near Chernigov), where he spent his childhood before the Revolution. (The estate was described in Stolitsa i Usad'ba, no. 50, 15 January 1916.) The Galitzines also have photos and portraits of relatives and a short unpublished biography by Prince Galitzine of his father, Basil Dimitrevich Golitsyn (1857-1928), curator of the Rumiantsev Museum in Moscow until 1917. The material is available for inspection only to qualified researchers.

DC 13
SPECIAL COLLECTIONS DIVISION
GEORGE WASHINGTON UNIVERSITY LIBRARY
22nd and H Streets NW
Washington, D.C. 20052
(202-676-7497)

Frederick R. Kuh (1895-1978). Papers, 1924-67, ca. 40 boxes. Journalist. Includes his diaries for 1938-44, personal correspondence, travel notes, clippings, scrapbooks, and other material. One of Kuh's news sources was Ivan Maiskii, Soviet ambassador to Great Britain in the 1940s. Some items pertain to Soviet foreign policy and to U.S.-Soviet relations. Kuh knew Secretary of State John Foster Dulles during the 1950s. Unpublished finding aid.

DC 14
DEPARTMENT OF SPECIAL COLLECTIONS
GEORGETOWN UNIVERSITY LIBRARY
GEORGETOWN UNIVERSITY
37th and O Streets NW
Washington, D.C. 20057
(202-625-3230/4160)

1 Victor M. Baydalakoff (1900-1965?), Papers, ca. 1932-65, 6.5 ft. Officer in the White Russian Army, 1918-22, founder and leader of the anti-Soviet National Workers Alliance (NTS), 1930-55. Materials primarily concern the founding and administration of the NTS in Germany, and the subsequent founding of the RNTS (Russian National Workers Alliance) in America, 1956. Also, extensive personal correspondence with other Russian émigrés, 1953-65. Restricted until 1 October 1982. Unpublished finding aid.

2 William R. Downs (1914-1978). Papers, 1929-77, 12 ft. Correspondent for United Press International and CBS and ABC networks. Includes manuscripts and correspondence. He reported the Battle of Stalingrad, Berlin airlift, and the Korean War, and covered the State Department and Department of Defense. Includes letters from Moscow, 1943-45 and 1950. Unpublished finding aid.

3 Robert F. Kelley (1894-1975). Papers, 1915-75, 7.5 ft. Diplomat and government official. U.S. and assistant military attaché to the Baltic provinces, 1920-22; foreign service officer, 1922-45; chief of the East European Affairs Division of the State Department, 1926-37; counselor of the American embassy in Ankara, Turkey, 1937-45; vice-president of the Radio Liberty Committee, 1945. Papers deal chiefly with Soviet domestic affairs, U.S.-USSR relations, and the founding of Radio Liberty. Finding aid.

4 Sophie A. Nordhoff-Jung (1867-1943). Papers, 1892-1939, .25 ft. Medical doctor on the staff of Georgetown University Hospital, cancer researcher. Includes 15 letters, 1901-1902, written to her from Moscow by the noted African explorer Paul Du Chaillu, who was traveling (cf. p. 124) in Russia at the time, plus a photograph of Du Chaillu taken in 1901.

5 Fulton Oursler Memorial Collection (1893-1952). Papers, 1886-1954, 33 ft. Journalist, editor, author. Includes correspondence with Upton Sinclair concerning the film (Que Viva Mexico!) Sinclair worked on with Sergei Eisenstein, 1930-31; correspondence between Sinclair and G. S. Viereck, in part about the first Five-Year Plan, 1930; and a copy of an Eisenstein letter. Unpublished partial finding aid.

6 Arthur Ransome (1884-1967). The Frank Kurt Cylke Collection, 1913-70, .25 ft. Book illustrator, journalist, and children's book writer. Manuscripts and ALS. He went to Russia in 1913, learning the language to study Russian folklore. He became war correspondent from the Russian front for the London Daily News during World War I and later special correspondent of the Manchester Guardian in Russia, China, and Egypt. Includes 2 ALS from St. Petersburg in 1914 and manuscript translations of Russian fairy tales. Unpublished finding aid.

7 Reverend Edmund A. Walsh (1885-1956). Papers, 1912-62, 21.5 ft. Jesuit priest, head of the Vatican Relief Mission to Russia in the early 1920s and of the American Relief Mission under Herbert Hoover. Ca. 3 boxes of material, 1922-33, deal with the famine relief mission, U.S. recognition of the USSR, Archbishop Jan Cieplak, and the persecution of Polish Catholic priests in the Soviet Union. Includes his correspondence with G. Chicherin and photographs of V. I. Lenin, the Imperial family, G. Zinoviev, L. Trotskii, and G. Plekhanov.

DC 15
HONORABLE W. AVERELL HARRIMAN--PRIVATE COLLECTION
3038 N Street NW
Washington, D.C. 20007

The Harriman papers will be made available to scholars at some future date, possibly through the Truman Library (Independence, Missouri). In the meantime, scholars are referred to materials from the papers that are included and drawn upon extensively in Ambassador Harriman's book, Special Envoy to Churchill and Stalin (1975).

DC 16
MANUSCRIPT DIVISION
MOORLAND-SPINGARN RESEARCH CENTER
HOWARD UNIVERSITY
Washington, D.C. 20059
(202-636-7480)

1 Paul Robeson (1898-1976). Papers. 120 ft. Singer, actor, political activist. About 75 letters from a Soviet delegation congratulating him on his birthday in 1973. There is also a large amount of unprocessed materials that has just been received. The newly-received, unprocessed material is restricted.

2 Aleksandr Pushkin. 80 color slides of the poet.

DC 17
SERGE KARPOVICH--PRIVATE COLLECTION
3546 T Street NW
Washington, D.C. 20007

Michael Karpovich Papers, ca. 15 ft. Michael Karpovich (1888-1959), Russian historian at Harvard University, came to the U.S. in 1917 with a diplomatic mission of the Provisional Government. He later became a professor of history and chairman of the Department of Slavic Languages and Literature at Harvard. He was also editor of Novyi Zhurnal in 1946-59.

Voluminous correspondence, especially with Russian authors and leading émigré figures, concerns literary, cultural, and historical matters. Papers also include his own lectures, speeches, manuscripts, bibliographical notes, and unfinished scholarly works. No catalogue exists at present but an inventory is in process. Access is closed pending completion of the inventory and permanent disposition of the papers. However, scholarly inquiries may be directed to Serge Karpovich at the above address.

DC 18
MRS. JEAN LEWTON--PRIVATE COLLECTION
404 10th Street SE
Washington, D.C. 20003
(202-544-0406)

Mrs. Lewton is in possession of ca. 70 letters, 1904-45, of her aunt, the Russian actress Alla Nazimova, who practiced the Stanislavskii method and first came to the United States in 1902 with the St. Petersburg players. The letters, in Russian and English, are addressed to Nazimova's sister, Nina Leventon, and deal with family matters, the theater, and other subjects. Also included in Mrs. Lewton's collection are family photographs and photographs of the Russian actor Paul Orlenev.

DC 19
NEAR EAST SECTION
AFRICAN AND MIDDLE EASTERN DIVISION
LIBRARY OF CONGRESS
Washington, D.C. 20540
(202-426-5421)

Armenian Manuscripts. Missal, A.D. 1722; Adam-Book and sermons, A.D. 1653; four Gospels, A.D. 1321; fragments from a lectionary, 17th c.; fragments from a Gospel, 17th c.; four Gospels, A.D. 1683-84.

DC 20
AMERICAN FOLKLIFE CENTER
LIBRARY OF CONGRESS
10 First Street SE
Washington, D.C. 20540
(202-426-6590)

Holdings concern primarily folklife and ethnic groups in the United States. Among its collections is the Chicago Ethnic Arts Project Collection of 335 sound recordings, ca. 3,700 color transparencies, black and white negatives representing ca. 300 rolls of film, field notes, and other written documentation, 1977. Information came from ethnic community leaders and artists. Among the ethnic groups whose music, dancing, and crafts were examined to note the impact of urban America were Lithuanians and Ukrainians. In general, these materials and other collections generated by the work of the Center will eventually go to the appropriate custodial branches of the Library of Congress.

DC 21
ARCHIVE OF FOLK SONG
LIBRARY OF CONGRESS
10 First Street SE
Washington, D.C. 20540
(202-287-5510)

Holdings include textual material, both printed and unpublished, and noncommercial recordings and tapes. There are materials pertaining to Russia, Russian-Americans, Armenians, Estonians, Lithuanians, Boshkirs (Bashkirs?), Russians in Alaska ca. 1808, Ukrainians, Laplanders, Mongolians, and Molokans.

DC 22
EUROPEAN LAW DIVISION
LIBRARY OF CONGRESS
10 First Street SE
Washington, D.C. 20540
(202-426-5088/5089)

Manuscript materials in the Division have not been thoroughly processed. A brief examination of holdings revealed: ca. 46 scrolls from the 17th and 18th c.; some original ukazy of Empress Anna Ivanovna, 1730s, a few with her autograph; draft of a law code prepared for Alexander I by the State Council, 1813-14; a number of photo albums with pictures of the Imperial family; reports and material relating to the White government at Omsk in the Civil War; material on the murder of the Imperial family at Ekaterinburg; Russian legal and political material, 39 files, pertaining to the legislative and other activities of the pre-Kolchak and Kolchak governments in 1918-19 and to Kolchak himself; and the Iakhontov papers. The latter include not only the final printed texts of minutes of the debates in the Council of Ministers in 1914 but also Iakhontov's pencil notes on the discussions. These papers shed much light on Russian politics, particularly the question of Polish autonomy.

DC 23
MANUSCRIPT DIVISION
LIBRARY OF CONGRESS
2nd Street and Independence Avenue SE
Washington, D.C. 20540
(202-426-5383)

The Manuscript Division of the Library of Congress, established in 1897, contains approximately 10,000 separate collections. Among these are the papers of roughly half of the persons who served as U.S. secretary of state and of 23 presidents from George Washington to Calvin Coolidge (other presidential papers, from Hoover to Johnson, are kept in presidential libraries). References to Russia undoubtedly abound in these papers, but no attempt has been made to describe all of these in detail (see note at the end of this entry). Russian-related materials in other groups of documents have been described as much as possible, mostly on the basis of available finding aids.

1 Cleveland Abbe (1838-1916). Papers, 1850-1916. 34 containers. Astronomer and meteorologist. Includes correspondence with Otto Struve, director of the Pulkovo Observatory, as well as Abbe's letters to his family when he was guest astronomer at the Pulkovo Observatory, 1865-66. The letters deal not only with scientific matters, but also with Russian social and cultural life, and include descriptions of St. Petersburg and its outskirts. There is ca. 1 ft. of Russian-related materials. Finding aid. (NUCMC 64-1556)

2 Academy of Natural Sciences of Philadelphia. Records, 1812-1925. 38 reels of microfilm contain references to several Russian organizations, including the Academy of Sciences (Leningrad), and the Légation impériale de Russie aux États-Unis. Finding aid.

3 Edward Goodrich Acheson (1856-1931). Papers, 1866-1936. 50 containers. Electrochemist, inventor, scientist, and businessman; travelled to Russia in 1913, when he discussed his company's product, Oildrag, with Russian government officials. 2 folders of correspondance, telegrams, calling cards, and other materials pertain to this visit. Included is an ALS from Count Witte, thanking Acheson for a photograph. Finding aid. (NUCMC 76-0140)

4 Carl William Ackerman (1890-1970). Papers, 1933-70. 228 containers. Journalist, educator, public relations consultant. 2 boxes of notes, memoranda, and telegrams on Ackerman's journey to Russia in 1918-19, when he traveled to Ekaterinburg and interviewed eyewitnesses to the execution of Nicholas II. There is also material on Ackerman's visit to Stalingrad, Moscow, and Baku in 1945. Finding aid. (NUCMC 72-1693)

5 Adams Family. Collection, 1776-1914. 2 containers, 225 items. Includes copies of letters of John Quincy Adams to A. H. Everett that touch on Adams's activities in Russia, where he was U.S. minister from 1809 to 1814. Also included are copies of some of Adams's dispatches to the secretary of State. Finding aid. (NUCMC 69-2025)

6 Adams Family. Papers, 1639-1889. 608 reels of microfilm (originals at the Massachusetts Historical Society). Contains numerous references to Russia. (NUCMC 62-1621)

7 Henry Justin Allen (1868-1950). Papers, 1896-1942. 214 containers. Governor of Kansas and U.S. senator; favored U.S. recognition of the Soviet Union. 2 folders of correspondence and printed materials dealing mostly with Allen's trip to the USSR and with the reactions of readers to his articles on Russia. Finding aid. (NUCMC 70-0936)

8 Henry Tureman Allen (1859-1930). Papers, 1806-1933. 78 containers. U.S. military attaché in St. Petersburg, 1890-95, and commander of the American forces of occupation on the Rhine until 1923. Correspondence, journals, military reports, Russian government decrees, and photographs (including of Russian army grand maneuvers, 1891), 1 ft. Subjects include U.S.-Russian relations, the Russo-Japanese War, and Soviet policy toward Rumania and Poland after World War I. There is also a letter from Theodore Roosevelt, 24 March 1894, asking Allen for an article on "your Russian hunting." Finding aid. (NUCMC 52-0260)

9 Joseph Wright Alsop. Papers, 1699-1970. 127 containers. Journalist. Some typescript articles pertaining to Russia. Finding aid. (NUCMC 71-1327)

10 Stewart Alsop. See Joseph Wright Alsop.

11 American Council of Learned Societies. Records, 1919-46. 548 containers. 15 boxes of correspondence, reports, office files, literary manuscripts, and financial reports pertaining to Russian studies in secondary schools; Slavic grants; U.S.-USSR exchanges of scholars in the humanities and social sciences; the Russian national character; Russian art, music, and painting; Soviet patriotism. Finding aid. (NUCMC 71-1329) Restricted.

12 American Institute of Aeronautics and Astronautics. Papers. 271 containers. 2 boxes of reports and (especially) printed materials and newspaper clippings pertaining to Russian engineers and aviators, including Alexander P. de Seversky, Igor Sikorsky, Stephen Timoshenko, and A. Toupeleff. The Sikorsky material includes photographs of the first helicopter he designed (1909) and of planes he built in Russia in the 1910s. Finding aid.

13 American Peace Commission to Versailles. Papers, 1917-19. 79 containers. Includes 10 reports on conditions in Russia in the 1910s. Finding aid. (NUCMC 59-0061)

14 American Psychological Association. Records, 1912-72. 262 boxes. 3 boxes of material reflect the Association's contacts with Russia and interest in Russian scientific developments. Included are reports by a group of U.S. psychologists who visited the Soviet Union in May-June 1960, as well as 4 folders of correspondence documenting the reactions to Senator Thomas J. Dodd's criticisms of a report by Ralph A. White on Soviet public opinion. Finding aid. (NUCMC 69-2027)

15 Chandler Parsons Anderson (1866-1936). Papers, 1894-1953. 65 containers. 1 box of correspondence, memoranda, telegrams, and contracts documenting Chandler's activities as legal adviser for the International Harvester Company claims against Russia, 1925-36. Includes correspondence between Anderson and Alexander Legge, Harvester president. Finding aid. (NUCMC 59-0243)

16 Hannah Arendt (1906-1975). Papers, 1935-75. 74 containers. Author, political scientist, educator. Correspondence pertaining to the Academic Committee on Soviet Jewry, to the conference on the Status of Soviet Jews, 1967-70, and to Hungarian refugee organizations, 1959-62. There are also notes on Bolshevism. Finding aid. (NUCMC 65-0891) Restricted.

17 Armenia-America Society. See Montgomery Family.

18 Henry Harley Arnold (1886-1950). Papers, 1907-50. 307 containers. U.S. general. Papers contain a considerable amount of material pertaining to Russian-American relations during World War II. Finding aid. (NUCMC 64-1557)

19 L. K. Artamonov. Papers, 1897-1929. 70 items. Russian army officer. Reports, photographs, memoirs, and other materials pertaining to the Special Russian Mission to Emperor Meneleke, Abyssinia, 1897-99, in which Colonel Artamonov took part. Finding aid.

20 Austria - Staatskanzlei. 40 containers. Contains copies of diplomatic materials pertaining to Russia, 1750-63. (NUCMC 67-0150)

21 Alexis Vasilevich Babine (1866-1930). Papers, 1901-30. 6 containers. Born in Russia and educated in the U.S., Babine was--after the Revolution--superintendent of schools in the Vologda area, instructor at the University of Saratov, and assistant to the American embassy in Moscow. He eventually emigrated to the U.S. 5 boxes and 1 large folder of materials (including correspondence, journals, lecture articles, notes, notebooks, diplomas, certificates, passports) pertain to Babine's life in post-revolutionary Russia, to the Bolsheviks, and to Russian universities. Also included is Babine's journal, typescript, in English, on day-to-day living in Saratov, 1917-20. (NUCMC 62-4591)

22 Newton Diehl Baker (1871-1937). Papers, 1898-1962. 276 containers. Secretary of War during the Wilson administration, 1916-21, and author of Bolshevism, Fascism, and Capitalism (1932). Among the Russian-related materials are memoranda on John Cadahy's book, Archangel: The American War with Russia, and on the North Russian and Siberian expeditions. Both memoranda are dated 1924. Finding aid. (NUCMC 66-1384)

23 Turpin C. Bannister. Collection. 1 container (5 items). Includes a letter, 1944, from Bannister to August Eccard, enclosing 4 photographs of St. Isaac's Cathedral in Leningrad.

24 Wharton Barker (1846-1921). Papers, 1870-1920. 29 containers. Philadelphia financier and publicist; participated in various business ventures in Russia in the late 19th c. Materials reflect Barker's interest in Russia trade, Russian railway concessions, the Russian navy, Ukrainian coal fields, and Russian-American relations. Among his principal correspondents were Captain L. P. Semetschkin and Constantine P. Pobedonostsev. Finding aid. (NUCMC 59-0148)

25 Clara Harlowe Barton (1821-1912). Papers, 1834-1918. 194 containers. Philanthropist and founder of the American Red Cross, Barton was concerned with the Russian famine of 1894 and participated in a Red Cross conference held in St. Petersburg in 1902. Several folders of correspondence, newspaper clippings, and other materials pertain to these contacts with Russia. Finding aid.

26 John Davis Batchelder. Autograph Collection, 1400-1960. 12 containers. Includes documents signed by Maksim Gorki, Peter I, A. S. Pushkin, G. A. Potemkin, Alexander I, Fedor

Rostopchin, Leo Tolstoi, Ivan Sergeevich Turgenev, and other prominent Russian-born personalities. Finding aid. (NUCMC 61-2074)

27 Bayard Family. Papers, 1797-1885. 7 containers. Lawyers and diplomats. Includes correspondence, diplomatic documents, and a diary of James A. Bayard (1767-1815) documenting his mission to St. Petersburg as a member of a U.S. delegation to end the War of 1812 under Russian mediation. Finding aid. (NUCMC 74-1065)

28 Becker Family. Collection, 1826-40. 1 container, 52 items. Some letters between members of the Becker family relating to business matters in Russia.

29 Edward L. Bernays (b. 1891). Papers, 1897-1965. 745 containers. Public relations counsel. Materials (including correspondence and 6 scrapbooks) dealing with Diaghilev's Ballet Russe and with the Russian exposition of 1929 in the U.S. Finding aid. (NUCMC 67-0588) Restricted.

30 Blackwell Family. Papers, 1830-1959. 96 containers. 3 boxes of materials (correspondence, photographs, postcards, printed matter) reflecting the interest of Alice Stone Blackwell (1857-1950), a reformer, author, and editor, in Russia and Russian poetry, which she translated. Included is Blackwell's correspondence with the "grandmother of the revolution," Catherine Breshkovskaia, which spans the years 1904-38. Finding aid. (NUCMC 69-2029)

31 Tasker Howard Bliss (1853-1930). Papers, 1870-1930. 496 containers. Army officer, scholar, diplomat; active in World War I. Several boxes of material, business correspondence, intelligence reports from the U.S. military attaché in Petrograd, maps, memoranda, pertaining to Russia, especially 1918-19. Subjects include the Allied intervention in Russia, the murder of Nicholas II and his family, Russian POWs in Germany, political conditions in Russia, anti-Bolshevik forces, and the situation in the Ukraine, Latvia, Lithuania, and Estonia around the time of the Revolution. Finding aid. (NUCMC 59-0259)

32 Charles Eustis Bohlen (1904-1974). Papers, 1940-70, 28 boxes. U.S. ambassador to the USSR, 1953-57. Research notes, drafts of Witness to History, and correspondence pertaining to the Soviet Union and to Bohlen's views on Soviet aims and intentions in the post-World War II era. Finding aid.

33 Bollingen Foundation. Records, 1939-73. 249 containers. 2 folders of correspondence relate to Vladimir Nabokov's translation of Eugene Onegin. There are also letters on the publication of scholarly monographs in Slavic studies between 1957 and 1962. Finding aid. (NUCMC 77-1494) Restricted.

34 William Edgar Borah. Papers, 1905-40. 881 containers. U.S. senator from Idaho, 1907-40; favored U.S. recognition of Soviet Russia. Included are letters between Borah and American business leaders on Russia, as well as correspondence with Raymond Robins. Finding aid.

35 Boris Leo Brasol. Papers, 1919-52. 64 containers. Prosecuting attorney under the Imperial Russian government, 1910-16, second lieutenant in the Imperial Russian guard, 1914-16, and lawyer in New York specializing in Russian law, 1918-53. Included are 6 boxes of "political correspondence," 1922-46; 4 boxes of "anti-Soviet correspondence," 1919-48; 6 boxes on the "Russian situation"; 3 boxes of correspondence and other papers concerning mainly the case of Herman Bernstein vs. Henry Ford, ca. 1925-27; and 10 boxes of Brasol's works on Russian literature and drama. Finding aid.

36 Mark Lambert Bristol (1868-1939). Papers, 1887-1939. 98 containers. Naval officer. 6 folders of materials pertaining to Russia, including dispatches sent by Newton Alexander McCully regarding the Denikin campaign, January-April 1920, and the Wrangel campaign, April-October 1920. Other subjects include Russian relief work, 2 folders, 1922-23, and Russian refugees, 1934-35. Finding aid.

37 Browning Family. Papers, 1824-1917. 3 containers, 900 items. Contains diagrams and studies of the bombardment of Odessa, 1854, evidently not by an eyewitness. Finding aid. (NUCMC 71-1341)

38 James Bryce. Papers, 1838-1922. Diplomat, historian, jurist. A newsletter, in French and English, regarding Russia.

39 Anson Burlingame (1820-1870) and Edward L. Burlingame (1848-1922). Papers, 1810-1937. 6 containers. Includes Anson Burlingame's correspondence with the empress of Russia. Finding aid. (NUCMC 59-0149)

40 S. E. Burrows. 1855-56. Collection, 8 items. Handwritten transcripts and facsimile letters, 15 March-14 November 1856, between Burrows and Count Nesselrode concerning the destruction of the Russian frigate Diana and the fate of its crew.

41 Harold Hitz Burton (1888-1964). Papers, 1918-63. 448 containers. U.S. senator and congressman. 1 folder of materials on Russia, including printed matter and a typescript of 1 of Burton's speeches on the Soviet Union. Finding aid.

42 Simon Cameron (1799-1889). Papers, 1824-92. 10 containers. U.S. minister to Russia, January-November 1862. The general correspondence covers the months Cameron was in

Russia. The papers also include 10 reels of microfilm reproducing the Cameron Papers in the Historical Society of Dauphin County, Harrisburg, Pennsylvania.

43 George Washington Campbell (1769-1848). Papers, 1793-1886. 6 containers. U.S. minister to Russia, 1819-20. A few items pertaining to Campbell's diplomatic service in St. Petersburg. (NUCMC 62-4616)

44 Thomas Capek (1861-1950). Collection. 19 containers. 1 folder of materials on a group of U.S. Czechs who set forth to establish a Utopian colony in Russia in the mid-nineteenth century. Finding Aid. (NUCMC 59-0044)

45 Truman Capote (b. 1924). Papers, 1947-59. 17 containers. Writer. Includes an unpublished, unfinished article entitled "Moscow." Restricted.

46 James McKeen Cattell (1860-1944). Papers, 1835-1948. 279 containers. Psychologist and publisher of scientific journals. 1 item: a typescript list of names of foreign psychologists, including several from Russia (1890-1917). Finding aid. (NUCMC 62-4684)

47 Philander Chase (1798-1824). Transcript of a journal (1818-19) with descriptions of St. Petersburg in the 1810s, when Chase served as U.S. navy chaplain on the U.S.S. Guerrière. The original of the journal is in the Kenyon College Library. (NUCMC 76-0148)

48 Raymond Clapper (1892-1944). Papers, 1913-44. 256 containers. Author, journalist, and radio commentator. Among the Russian-related materials are 2 boxes of newspaper clippings on Russia, 1930-40. Finding aid. (NUCMC 59-0052)

49 John Randolph Clay (1808-1885). Papers, 1 container (6 items). Contains the photostat negative of a draft of a report, 1824, by Clay, then secretary of U.S. Legation, Russia, to William Wilkins, U.S. minister at St. Petersburg.

50 Columbia University Oral History Collection. 16 containers, on microfilm. Microfilm of the oral history transcripts at Columbia University, many of which pertain to Russia.

51 Commerce (ship). Collection. 1 item: a French-language document, 21 pp., entitled "Lettre ecrite en forme de Memoire aux Interresses du Commerce de la Mer Baltique, envoyée à Londres et à Amsterdam au Mois de fevrier 1717."

52 Confederate States of America. Records, 1861-65. 125 containers, on microfilm. Materials on Lucius Q. C. Lamar's mission to Russia. Finding aid. (NUCMC 67-0593)

53 George Albert Converse (1844-1909). Papers, 1895-1908. 2 containers (250 items). U.S. naval officer. A few items pertaining to the Russo-Japanese War, including diagrams of Russian Imperial Navy ships. Finding aid. (NUCMC 71-1347)

54 Josephus Daniels (1862-1948). Papers, 1806-1948. 931 containers. Secretary of the Navy, 1912-21. 1 folder of materials (correspondence, reports, photographs, memoranda, and charts) pertaining to conditions in Russia, 1917-21, as seen by Americans both inside and outside the country. Finding aid.

55 Clarence Seward Darrow (1857-1938). Papers, 1894-1940. 36 containers. Lawyer, author, lecturer, and social reformer. 2 folders of printed materials on Leo Tolstoi. Finding aid. (NUCMC 71-1350)

56 Joseph Edward Davies (1876-1958). Papers, 1860-1957. 163 containers. U.S. ambassador to the Soviet Union, 1936-38, special envoy to confer with Stalin in May and June 1943, and special adviser to President Truman and Secretary of State James F. Byrnes at the Potsdam conference, July-August 1945. Over 10 boxes of material (including correspondence, diaries, and memoranda) contain references to Soviet personalities in the 1930s, lend-lease to Russia, and international conferences in the World War II era. Also included are materials used by Davies for his book, Mission to Moscow, and its sequel. Finding aid. (NUCMC 62-4609)

57 Elmer Holmes Davis (1890-1958). Papers, 1893-1957. 25 containers. News analyst of the Office of War Information, 1942-45. Russian-related materials include 1 folder of newspaper and magazine clippings on Russia, 1940-50. Finding aid. (NUCMC 64-1560)

58 Norman H. Davis (1878-1944). Papers, 1918-42. 93 containers. Economist and diplomat. 1 box of materials (primarily correspondence) pertaining to Davis's involvement in the Russian Student Fund, 1920-1930s. There are also progress reports on the work of Russian-born students in U.S. universities. Alexis von Viren is frequently mentioned in these papers. Finding aid. (NUCMC 59-0207)

59 Denmark. Danske Kaniellis Udenrigske Afdeling; Tygke Kancelliets Udenrigs Afdeling, 1558-1720. 16 reels of microfilm. Includes papers from the German desk, including selections from Russian dispatches. Finding aid. (NUCMC 67-161)

60 Peter A. Demens (P. A. Tverskoi) (1850-1919). Papers, 1893-1911. 42 items. Russian-born writer and entrepreneur; wrote about the U.S. for Russian publications. Newspaper clippings, drafts of articles and letters, and other materials illustrating Demens's interests and career. Mostly in Russian. The papers are not yet fully processed.

61 George Vernon Denny (1899-1959). Papers, 1934-60. 30 containers. Educator, radio personality, and executive. 1 folder of materials (mostly newspaper clippings) reflecting Denny's interest in Russia in 1959, when he was president, International Seminar and Town Meetings, Inc. Finding Aid. (NUCMC 68-2019)

62 Lavinia L. Dock. 1 container. 5 items pertaining to Dock's efforts to have Soviet nurses represented at international nurses' meetings. Finding aid.

63 Ira Clarence Eaker (b. 1896). Papers, 1918-60. 80 containers. U.S. general. Material on a U.S. military mission to Moscow on 5 May 1944, and on 20 March 1945. Finding aid. (NUCMC 66-1402) Restricted.

64 George Fielding Eliot (1894-1971). Papers, 1939-71. 23 containers. Author, journalist, and military analyst. 1 folder of newspaper clippings on the Soviet fleet in the Mediterranean, 1960-1970s. Finding aid. (NUCMC 76-0157)

65 Herbert Feis (1893-1972). 120 containers. Economist and historian. 5 boxes of materials used by Feis for his books on Russia. Finding aid.

66 Janet Flanner and Solita Solano (Flanner-Solano). Papers, 1925-67. 26 containers. Journalists and editors. Serveral items, including notes, typescript lectures, and photo negatives, pertain to George Ivanovich Gurdjieff. Finding aid. (NUCMC 70-0948)

67 Ford Peace Plan. Papers, 1915-18. 14 containers. The Ford Peace Plan was an expedition undertaken by Henry Ford and other Americans to bring peace to Europe during World War I. Its papers contain 4 folders of German translations of Russian press reports (1916). Finding aid. (NUCMC 60-0574)

68 John Watson Foster (1836-1917). Papers, 1872-1917. 1 container, 175 items. Includes 2 instructions from the U.S. Secretary of State William M. Evarts pertaining to Foster's service as U.S. minister to Russia, 1880-82. Finding aid. (NUCMC 68-2031)

69 France - Ministère des affaires étrangères. Records. 288 containers. Some materials on Russia. (NUCMC 67-964)

70 Frederick II of Prussia (1712-1786). 2 items. A facsimile letter, 1 February 1773, of Catherine II to Frederick II, in Russian. [In German Royalty and Nobility Collection]

71 John Philip Frey (1871-1957). Papers, 1891-1951. 35 containers. Labor leader and editor. 1 folder of correspondence reflects Frey's concern for the fate of American mechanics who left the U.S. to work in Russia in the 1930s. Finding aid.

72 George Gamow (1904-1968). Papers, 1915-75. 43 containers. Born in Odessa, Gamow was professor at the University of Leningrad, 1931-33, and, after his emigration to the U.S., professor at George Washington University. Included is an annotated typescript, "Getaway from Russia," and correspondence relating to Natasha Dobzhansky, Alexander Dorozynski, and T. Turkevich. Finding aid. (NUCMC 68-2034) 2034)

73 Harry Augustus Garfield (1863-1942). Papers, 1855-1961. 207 containers. Lawyer, educator, and college president. Materials on the activities of the Russian Famine Relief Committee in Cleveland, Ohio, during the 1890s. Also included is a confidential letter from J. M. Crawford, consul general of the U.S. in St. Petersburg, to James A. Garfield on the situation in Russia during the 1892 famine and on Russian reactions to famine relief, 26 March 1893, 4 pp., and an ALS from Leo Tolstoi, thanking the Cleveland Famine Committee for its help during the 1892 famine, 2/14 April 1892, 1 p. Finding aid.

74 Edmond Charles Genêt (1763-1834). Papers, 1756-1795. 53 containers. Includes materials pertaining to Genêt's diplomatic service in Russia (1787-89) as secretary to Comte de Ségur, French minister at the court of Catherine II. Finding aid. (NUCMC 59-0224) For a detailed description of the Russian-related materials in these papers, see Marc Bouloiseau, "Edmond C. Genêt à Saint-Pétersbourg," Bulletin d'histoire économique et sociale de la Révolution française (1968), pp. 15-51.

75 German Captured Materials. Records. 858 containers. Ca. 20 boxes of materials pertaining to Russia, 1938-44. Subjects covered include Germans in Russia, Russian literature in the libraries of Russian towns occupied by Germans, 1942, Soviet agriculture, religion in Russia, and other matters. See the Guide to Captured German Documents (1952) prepared by Gerhard L. Weinberg and the WDP staff under the direction of Fritz T. Epstein.

76 Arthur Huntington Gleason (1878-1923). Papers, 1863-1931. 13 containers. Editor, war correspondent, and socialist. Several folders of materials pertaining to Count Ilya Tolstoi. Finding aid.

77 Albert Gleaves (1858-1937). Papers, 1803-1946. 21 containers. Commander of the U.S. Asiatic fleet, 1919-21. References to the Japanese army in Russia after World War I, the evacuation of Czechoslovak troops from Russia, and conditions in Russia after the Revolution.

78 William Crawford Gorgas (1854-1920). Papers, 1857-1919. 39 containers. U.S. military officer and doctor. 1 folder of materials (correspondence, maps, photos) on the medical

and sanitary conditions of the U.S. Expeditionary Forces in Vladivostok. Finding aid. (NUCMC 62-4578)

79 Maksim Gorki (1868-1936). Papers, 1922-38. 1 container. Correspondence (original and copies) between Gorki, the Soviet author, and Khodasevich (1922-25); 5 letters from Gorki to Nina Berberova Khodasevich (1923-25); a lecture, in Russian, 33 pp., by Khodasevich, delivered in Paris in 1934. (NUCMC 62-4817)

80 Great Britain - Foreign Office. Records. 871 containers, partially on microfilm. Contains photostats of documents that pertain to Russia.

81 Frank Lester Greene (1870-1930). Papers, 1895-1930. 79 containers. U.S. congressman; involved in hearing, 1922, on providing an honorable discharge to members of the U.S. Railway Service Corps who were in Russia, 1917-18. 1 folder of materials (including correspondence, reports, and printed matter) document this hearing. Finding aid.

82 Adam Hrabia Gurowski (1805-1866). Papers, 1848-98. 4 containers. Author, panslavist, scholar; emigrated to U.S., where he wrote Russia as it is (1854). Contains a biography of Gurowski by Julius Bing, manuscript, ca. 200 pp.; notes taken by Gurowski, evidently for his book on Russia; and letters to Gurowski regarding his Russia as it is from American readers. Finding aid. (NUCMC 59-0141)

83 Green Haywood Hackworth (1883-1973). Papers, 1919-73. 19 containers. Judge, lawyer, public official. Accompanied Secretary of State Cordell Hull to the Moscow Conference, 1943. Materials on Soviet interests, 1944-45, United Nations Conference delegates in San Francisco from the USSR, April-May 1945, the Yalta Voting Formula, and the Teheran Conference. Finding aid.

84 Hale Family. Papers, 1698-1916. 34 containers. Includes comments by Alexander Hill Everett on Russia and an ALS, 2 pp., from James Ingerson, St. Petersburg, to James Savage, Boston, on the verdict on the Decembrists, 16 July O.S., 1826. Finding aid. (NUCMC 59-0139)

85 Elijah Walker Halford (1843-1938). Papers, 1867-1928. 2 containers. 400 items. Newspaper editor, soldier. Contains a letter from Emory Smith, U.S. minister to Russia, to Elijah Halford, 1892, with a description of famine relief.

86 Hamilton (ship). A clearance pass, 27 May 1801, signed by an unidentified Russian official at St. Petersburg for the ship Hamilton.

87 John Marshall Harlan (1833-1911). Family papers, 1810-1917. 53 containers. Lawyer and U.S. Supreme Court justice. Contains materials on Russia's role in the Bering Sea arbitration, 1892-93, in which Harlan took part as a U.S. representative. Finding aid. (NUCMC 76-0162)

88 Florence Jaffray Harriman (1870-1964). Papers, 1912-50. 30 containers. Author and diplomat. 1 folder of materials pertaining to the Russian Relief Fund, in which Harriman was involved in the 1940s. Finding aid. (NUCMC 61-1514)

89 Burton Harrison Family. Papers, 1812-1926. 62 containers. 6 folders of correspondence, notes, and literary manuscripts pertain to the visit to Russia of Mrs. Burton N. (Constance Gary) Harrison (1843-1920), a writer, in 1896. Articles on her Russian visit appeared in The Smart Set, March and April 1900. Finding aid. (NUCMC 70-0954)

90 Leland Harrison (1883-1951). Papers, 1915-47. 125 containers. Diplomatic secretary, American Commission to Negotiate Peace. 6 folders with correspondence and reports pertaining to Bolshevik Russia, to the activities of the Japanese and Germans in post-revolutionary Russia (1 thick folder, containing reports marked secret), and to a tentative plan for a Russian relief mission for the American Commission to Negotiate the Peace. Alexander Gumberg and Raymond Robins are mentioned pejoratively in the correspondence between Harrison and J. Butler. Finding aid. (NUCMC 59-0020)

91 John Haynes Holmes (1879-1964). Papers, 1906-67. 243 containers. Materials on communist organizations and Russia, as well as an autograph letter by Catherine Breshkovskaia. Finding aid. (NUCMC 71-1364) Restricted.

92 Harold L. Ickes (1874-1952). Papers, 1906-52. 466 containers. Secretary of the Interior, 1933-46. Includes Ickes' diary, which has references to Russia, 1933-51. There are also 2 folders of correspondence between Ickes and ordinary citizens regarding his views on U.S.-Soviet relations after World War II. Finding aid. (NUCMC 60-0145)

93 Philip Caryl Jessup (b. 1897). Papers, 1902-55. 277 containers. Jurist, biographer, educator. Russian-related materials include documentation on the Russian Institute, Columbia University, 1946-47, and Russian studies, 1943. Finding aid. (NUCMC 62-4576) Restricted.

94 John Paul Jones (1747-1792). Papers (part of the Force collection). U.S. naval officer. Materials pertaining to Jones's service in Russia in the 1780s. Finding aid.

95 George Kennan (1845-1924). Papers, 1840-1937. 136 containers. Siberian explorer, author, and journalist; cousin of George F. Kennan's grandfather. These papers can be divided into 3 parts:

DISTRICT OF COLUMBIA - LIBRARY OF CONGRESS DC 23

(a) 110 boxes of notes, published articles, lecture materials, newspaper clippings, and autobiographical materials, much of which pertains to Russia. Among the subjects dealt with are the Black Sea, bureaucracy, the Caucasus, Central Asia, Czargrad, Dukhobors, education, Finland, Friends of Russian Freedom, Georgia, civil service, Constitutional Democrats, courts, the Crimea, Irkutsk, Jews, Kalmucks, Kazan', labor unions, liberals, the Lena river strike, Moscow, nationalism, the nobility, nihilism, the Octobrists, Novgorod, Odessa, Petropavlosk fortress, prisons, religion, revolution, St. Petersburg, Siberia, the Social Democrats, socialism, terrorism, Tomsk, the Union of the Russian People, and the Y.M.C.A.

(b) 7 boxes of diaries, journals, and notebooks, 1865-1924.

(c) 18 boxes of correspondence, 1895-1937. Correspondents include Stepan Paderin (chief of Cossacks at Gizhiga), M. Vol'man (Wollman), Felix Vadimovich Volkhovsky, A. Bialoveskii, Vladimir Tchertkoff, Ivan Petrovich Beloveskii, T. Tsingovatov, Leo Pasvolsky, A. A. Bublikov, Serge Novosseloff, S. M. Oberoutcheff, S. A. Korf, Catherine Breshkovskaia, S. Kravchinskii-Stepniak, Robert Lansing, Alice Stone Blackwell, and numerous other government, cultural, and business figures from both Russia and the United States. Organizations from which Kennan received letters include the Iowa Russian Famine Relief Committee, the Russian Students' Society, the Friends of Russian Freedom, the Russkoye slovo, and the Fund for the Relief of Men of Letters and Scientists in Russia. Finding aid. (NUCMC 59-0212)

96 John Adams Kingsbury (1876-1956). Papers, 1840-1960. 117 containers. Medical doctor and social worker; visited Russia, took part in Russian-related organizations in the U.S., appeared before the Subversive Activities Control Board to explain the activities of the National Council of Soviet-American Friendship, and wrote about Soviet medicine. 4 boxes of materials, including correspondence, diaries, and literary manuscripts, reflect Kingsbury's interest in the Soviet Union and Soviet medicine. The American Russian Institute, 1933-34, and the American Council on Soviet Relations, 1938-39, are mentioned in these papers. Finding aid. (NUCMC 64-1572)

97 Alan Goodrich Kirk (1888-1963). Papers, 1919-61. 1 container, 125 items. U.S. ambassador to the USSR, 1949-52. A few items pertaining to Kirk's service in Moscow. Finding aid. (NUCMC 71-1369)

98 Ivan Alekseevich Korzhukhin (1871-1931). Papers, 1900-31. 2 boxes (1 item). A manuscipt book, "Materialy po istorii Chukhotskogo predpriatiia," which deals with the several unsuccessful efforts made by Korzhukhin, a geologist, and others to exploit mineral resources, particularly gold, in the Chukhotsk peninsula and surrounding area. The volume is illustrated with photos and a map.

99 George Frederick Kunz (1856-1932). Papers, 1783-1928. 4 containers. 2 boxes of materials, including correspondence, notes, typescript of articles, and printed matter, pertaining to Kunz's trip to Russia in 1892-93 to carry out mineralogical studies. Finding aid. (NUCMC 71-1373)

100 William Daniel Leahy (1875-1959). Papers, 1893-1959. 23 containers and 4 reels of microfilm. U.S. naval officer. Copies of letters written by Joseph Edward Davies in 1945 to F. D. Roosevelt that discuss in part Soviet aims and intentions. Finding aids. (NUCMC 60-1787)

101 Irvine Luther Lenroot (1869-1949) and Family. Papers, 1890-1964. 20 containers. U.S. senator from Wisconsin. Contains 1 folder of materials (mostly business correspondence) pertaining to the affairs of V. L. Bobroff, a consulting efficiency engineer from Milwaukee who was involved in an unsuccessful business deal, 1920, with the All-Russian Central Union of Consumers Society (Centrosoyus or Tsentrosoius). Finding aid. (NUCMC 65-0913)

102 Breckinridge Long (1881-1958). Papers, 1740-1948. 250 containers. Third assistant secretary of state under Woodrow Wilson, 1917-20. Includes correspondence, reports, newspaper clippings, and a diary, typewritten, 1918-21, pertaining to the Allied intervention in Siberia, the American Red Cross in Russia, and the Russian railway system. There is also a mimeographed account of a conference of the members of the Russian Constituent Assembly, 8-21 January 1921. Finding aid. (NUCMC 62-4958)

103 Nicholas Low (1739-1826). Papers, 1783-1865. 160 containers. Merchant. A few business letters from St. Petersburg, 1803-1807. Finding aid.

104 Alfred Thayer Mahan (1840-1914). Papers, 1824-1914. 23 containers. 1 folder of notes on the Russo-Japanese War by Mahan, the author of The Influence of Sea Power upon History, 1660-1783. Finding aid. (NUCMC 67-0618)

105 William Alexander Marshall (1849-1926). Papers, 1876-1906. 1 container, 100 items. U.S. naval officer. Material on the Russo-Japanese War, when Marshall was commander of the U.S.S. Vicksburg, then stationed in Korean waters. (NUCMC 72-1735)

106 James Murray Mason (1798-1871). Papers, 1798-1871. 9 containers. Diplomatic agent of the Confederacy in London. A small amount of correspondence between Mason and Lucius Q. C.

Lamar, appointed special commissioner of the Confederacy in Russia in 1862. (NUCMC 66-0234)

107 William Gibbs McAdoo (1863-1941). Papers, 1876-1941. 665 containers. Secretary of the treasury and U.S. senator from California, 1933-38. Finding aid. (NUCMC 59-0229)

108 McCook Family. Papers, 1827-1963. 28 containers. 1 folder of materials (mostly correspondence) on Alexander McCook's visit to Russia in 1896 as a U.S. representative to the coronation of the tsar. The letters describe official functions and a visit to Moscow. Finding aid. (NUCMC 59-0049)

109 Newton Alexander McCully (1867-1951). Papers, 1917-27. 1 container, 4 items. U.S. naval officer. Includes McCully's diaries in 1918, when he commanded U.S. naval forces in north Russia, and in 1920, when he was special agent of the State Department in south Russia. Finding aid. (NUCMC 76-0167)

110 James Patrick McGranery (1895-1963). Papers, 1938-72. 92.5 ft. Lawyer, attorney general. Office files on Russian property claims and on the Rosenberg case. Finding aid.

111 William F. Megee and Samuel Nightingale. Papers. 1 container, 47 items. Includes a letter, 9 September 1811, from the Brothers Cramer in St. Petersburg to John Rodgers, dealing with commercial matters.

112 George von Lengerke Meyer (1858-1918). Papers, 1901-17. 5 containers. U.S. ambassador to Russia, 1905-1907. Includes correspondence and a diary documenting Meyer's diplomatic service in Russia, Nicholas II, the Duma, social life in St. Petersburg, and the negotiations leading to the termination of the Russo-Japanese War. Finding aid. (NUCMC 65-0917)

113 Ogden Livingston Mills (1884-1937). Papers, 1920-39. 206 containers. U.S. congressman and secretary of the treasury. 1 folder of printed and/or mimeographed materials on Russia. Finding aid. (NUCMC 59-0035)

114 Elena and Leontovich Miranova. 1 playscript, "Dark Eyes," written by Elena Miranova in collaboration with Eugenie Leontovich that contains Russian themes and characters.

115 William Mitchell (1879-1936). Papers, 1907-46. 66 containers. Some items document General Mitchell's interest in Soviet aviation and Russia, which he visited in 1927. Finding aid. (NUCMC 59-0154)

116 Montgomery Family. Papers, 1771-1974. 33 containers. Boxes 21, 22, and 23 contain materials (primarily correspondence) pertaining to the activities of the Armenia-America Society, 1919-23, of which George Redington Montgomery (1870-1945) was director 1920-23. The Society aimed to bring peace in both Turkish and Russian Armenia and to assist Armenians in establishing a self-supporting nation. Finding aid.

117 John Bassett Moore (1860-1947). Papers, 1866-1949. 294 containers. International lawyer, diplomat. 1 scrapbook of newspaper clippings on Jewish emigration from Russia, 1811, and on other matters pertaining to Russian politics, trade, etc. in the 1910s. Finding aid. (NUCMC 61-328)

118 Maria Moransky. A typed letter signed 16 June 1937 to Miss Marie Trommer, editor, American Russian Review.

119 Alfred Mordecai (1804-1887). Papers, 1790-1946. 17 containers. Army officer and engineer; served on the U.S. military mission to the Crimea, 1855-57. Some of Mordecai's correspondence, ca. 1 letter album, addressed to his wife from St. Petersburg, Moscow, and Sevastopol, deals with the Crimean War and with his stay in Russia.

120 Roland Slettor Morris (1874-1945). Papers, 1910-43. 15 containers. U.S. ambassador to Japan, 1917-20; went on a special mission to Siberia, 1918. 3 boxes of correspondence, reports, memoranda, and maps pertaining to Russia and the Far East, conditions in Siberia during the Russian Civil War, the Japanese intervention in Siberia, and the Third Communist International. Finding aid. (NUCMC 60-0127)

121 Vladimir Vladimirovich Nabokov (1899-1977). Collection, 1923-58. 15 containers. Russian-born author. Manuscripts, typescripts, galley proofs, and corrected copies of Nabokov's novels, poems, articles, translations, book reviews, and other writings. Works in English include Pale Fire (on index cards), the screenplay of Lolita (on index cards), Invitation to a Beheading, The Real Life of Sebastian Knight, Conclusive Evidence, and other works. Works in Russian include Drygie berega, Dar, Tragediia Gospodina Morna, and Izobrazhenie Val'sa. There is alos a translation of Eugene Onegin and notes in regard to The Song of Igor's Campaign. Finally, there are several folders of general and special correspondence with Nabokov's agent, with Aldanov, Khodasevich, and Lukash, and with other writers and poets. Finding aid. (NUCMC 65-0921) Restricted.

122 National American Woman Suffrage Association. Records, 1850-1960. 98 containers. 5 items pertaining to Soviet bonds, the Russian famine, 1922, and Russian women. Finding aid. (NUCMC 71-1387)

123 Vladimir Ivanovich Nemirovich-Danchenko (1858-1943). Playwright, director, and writer.

Nemirovich-Danchenko's poem, in Russian, "Iorodiada" (Prague, undated).

124 Simon Newcomb (1835-1909). Papers, 1854-1936. 156 containers. Astronomer and mathematician. 2 folders of correspondence, in German and English, between Newcomb, astronomer and mathematician, and Otto and Herman Struve, Russian astronomers, ca. 1870-1900. Finding aid. (NUCMC 63-0384)

125 Reinhold Niebuhr (1892-1971). Papers, 1913-66. 33 containers. Theologian, philosopher, author. Included are articles on Khrushchev and the Cold War, Russia and America, and other Russian-related topics. Finding aid. (NUCMC 67-0622)

126 George William Norris (1861-1944). Papers, 1864-1944. 571 containers. U.S. senator from Nebraska; visited Russia in 1923, favored U.S. recognition of the Soviet Union. Among the Russian-related materials are several folders of documents on American prisoners in Russia, 1920, the Anna Lerner case, 1924, the Captain Paxton Hibben case, and American recognition of the Soviet regime. Finding aid. (NUCMC 62-2698)

127 John Callan O'Laughlin (1873-1949). Papers, 1895-1949. 109 boxes. Journalist, publisher, statesman; reported on the Russo-Japanese War from Moscow and St. Petersburg. 1 box of materials contains drafts of articles on Russia and Japan, 1904-1905, and typed extracts from Russian newspapers, 1904. Finding aid.

128 J. Robert Oppenheimer (1904-1967). Papers, 1927-67. 293 containers. Physicist. 3 folders of materials (including letters from George F. Kennan) pertaining to Russia. Finding aid. (NUCMC 71-1392)

129 William Orr (1860-1939). Papers, 1890-1939. 6 containers. Educator and author. 3 folders of draft articles on Latvia and Estonia. Finding aid. (NUCMC 65-0923)

130 Garfield Bromley Oxnam (1891-1963). Papers, 1823-1963. 137 containers. 2 folders of correspondence, pamphlets, and mimeographed materials documenting Bishop Oxnam's contacts with the Massachusetts Council of American-Soviet Friendship and the magazine Soviet Russia Today between 1942 and 1954. Finding aid. (NUCMC 64-0775)

131 Palmer-Loper Families. Papers, 1767-1900. 13 containers. Sea-captains and merchants. An ALS from Nathaniel Palmer to F. T. Bush, 13 March 1876, explaining how Krusenstern, the Russian sea-captain, named the Antarctic continent Palmer's Land in honor of the American discoverer of this continent. Finding aid. (NUCMC 64-1578)

132 Charles Ross Parke. A microfilm diary, 1855-56, of Dr. Parke, a U.S. medical doctor, who served the Russian government during the Crimean War.

133 Francis le Jau Parker (1873-1966). Papers, 1916-34. 11 containers. U.S. army officer; attaché in Petrograd, 1917, and observer with the Russian army. 5 folders of correspondence, reports, telegrams, newspaper clippings, and maps pertain to the Russian army in the 1910s, Parker's view on Russia's political future, and to other Russian-related subjects. Finding aid. (NUCMC 67-0625)

134 Leo Pasvolsky (1893-1953). Papers, 1937-53. 12 containers. Born in Pavlograd, Pasvolsky was the editor of the Russkoe slovo, 1917-20, and of the Amerikanskii ezhegodnik, 1917-18, and later a State Department official and economist. Included is some material pertaining to foreign policy and to conferences after and during World War II, including the Crimea Conference, 1945. Finding aid. (NUCMC 68-2062)

135 Robert Porter Patterson (1891-1952). Papers, 1940-51. 107 containers. Under secretary of war and secretary of war, 1940-47. Some materials pertaining to Russia, including a report by Averell Harriman on developments in the Soviet Union as reflected in the Soviet press. Finding aid. (NUCMC 62-4624)

136 Joseph (1857-1926) and Elizabeth (1855-1936) Pennell. Papers, 1835-1945. 377 containers. Materials on the stay in Russia of Anna Whistler and her son James McNeill Whistler; they were there with George Washington Whistler when he helped build the St. Petersburg-Moscow railroad. There is also correspondence between George Baker, U.S. minister to Russia, and Charles G. Leland. Finding aid. (NUCMC 66-1446)

137 John Joseph Pershing (1860-1948). Papers, 1882-1949. 417 containers. Albums containing a detailed survey of the equipment and operations of the Japanese army at the time of the Russo-Japanese War. Pershing was U.S. military attaché in Tokyo 1905-1906. Finding aid. (NUCMC 62-2729)

138 Amos Richard Eno Pinchot (1873-1944). Papers, 1863-1943. 273 containers. Lawyer and publicist. 1 folder of printed matter pertaining to Russia (1919). Finding aid. (NUCMC 59-0142)

139 Gifford Pinchot (1865-1946). Papers, 1830-1947. 3,235 containers. Agriculturalist, governor, and conservationist. Includes notes on a trip to Russia in 1902 and materials on Bolshevism, communism, foreign forests, and Russia. Finding aid. (NUCMC 59-0059)

140 Gregory Goodwin Pincus (1903-1967). Papers, 1920-67. 175 containers. Biologist and developer of the oral contraceptive. Includes

a translation of a Russian scientific work, 25 pp. Finding aid. (NUCMC 71-1398)

141 Viacheslav Konstantinovich Pleve (1846-1904). 18 items. Commander of the Petrograd military district for civil affairs. Thank-you notes, greetings, and a handwritten copy of "Gramota na prav, vol'nosti i preimushchestva blagorodnogo Rossiiskago dvorianstva" (1785).

142 Konstantin Petrovich Pobedonostsev (1827-1907). Papers. 6 rolls of microfilm. Correspondence of Pobedonostsev. The original material is located in the Lenin Library, Moscow. Finding aid.

143 Louis Freeland Post (1849-1928). Papers, 1864-1939. 7 containers. Lawyer and newspaperman. 1 folder of materials (probably research documentation) containing information on "Russian loan data," 1917-20. Finding aid. (NUCMC 71-1399)

144 Poushkin Society of America. Minutes, 1834-1955. 7 containers. Minutes, programs, correspondence, literary contest essays, postcards, newspaper clippings, and a card index to the words of Boris Godunov. Much of the material documents the activities of the Society and Russian émigré life and literatures. Among the individuals mentioned are Andrey Avinoff, Boris Brasol, Prince Serge Obolensky, Sergei Rachmaninoff, Michael Ivanovich Rostovstzeff, Igor Sikorsky, Pitirim Alexandrovich Sorokin, George Vernadsky, and other prominent Russians in emigration. Finding aid. (NUCMC 62-4882)

145 Mary Edith Powel (1846-1931). Papers, 1747-1922. 63 containers. Collector of materials pertaining to naval affairs. 3 folders of clippings (from newspapers, magazines, and other sources) pertaining to the Russian navy, primarily during the late 19th c. Finding aid. (NUCMC 69-2047)

146 Joseph Pulitzer (1885-1955). Papers, 1910-58. 193 containers. 4 folders of memoranda by Pulitzer, a journalist and editor, to his staff asking questions on Russia and speculating on what policies should be adopted toward it by the U.S. Trotskii is mentioned in these papers. Finding aid. (NUCMC 77-1566)

147 John Randolph of Roanoke (1773-1833). Papers, 1806-32. 5 containers. U.S. minister to Russia, 1830-31. Included are a diary and letterbook by John Randolph Clay, a nephew of Henry Clay who held diplomatic posts in Russia in the 1830s. Finding aid.

148 Grigorii Efimovich Rasputin (ca. 1871-1916). A negative photostat of a short note addressed to Chapin [?].

149 Kermit Roosevelt (1889-1943). Papers, 1885-1964. 174 containers. Explorer and businessman. Business correspondence dealing with the reentry of U.S. ships into Russian ports after the 1917 Revolution, as well as 1 folder of material relating to a trip taken by Roosevelt in the Soviet Union. Finding aid. (NUCMC 77-1569)

150 Jesse Robinson. A negative microfilm of 2 diaries, 1867, pertaining to Siberia. Robinson was a member of the Western Union Telegraph Expedition to Siberia in 1866-67.

151 Elihu Root (1845-1937). Papers, 1863-1937. 262 containers. U.S. secretary of state, 1905-1909; ambassador extraordinary at the head of the Special U.S. Diplomatic Mission to Russia, 1917. Several folders of materials pertain to Root's mission to Russia, including correspondence, maps, invitations, telegrams, calendars, and appointment books. There are also reports on Rear Admiral Glennon's movements in Russia, on the activities of John R. Mott with the Mission, and on the requirements of the Russian government in dollars according to the Russian minister of finance. Finding aid. (NUCMC 64-0778)

152 Dmitri Aleksandrovich Rovinsky. Undated ALS, in French, requesting catalogues of gravures.

153 Charles Edward Russell (1860-1941). Papers, 1914-18. 71 containers. Served on the Special Diplomatic Mission to Russia, 1917; wrote Unchained Russia (1918). Included are Russell's "Diaries of an Amateur Diplomat," which cover his Russian journey in 1917. There are also 10 folders of materials (including correspondence, reports, drafts of articles, notes, and postcards) dealing with Russia in the late 1910s. Finding aid.

154 Russia Miscellany. Ca. 1759-1917. 4 containers. Included are the following items: "Zapiska ob ustanovke Finbersbar i komnasov"; letters patent conferring the order of St. Alexander Nevsky on George Thomas Marye, U.S. ambassador to Russia, 24 February 1916, signed by Nicholas II; incomplete monthly lists of officers attending lectures at the Nicolaevsky Academy of the General Staff, St. Petersburg, 1881; a thanksgiving manuscript book for the victory of Russian troops over the King of Prussia at Frankfurt, 1 August 1759; a printed copy of the land decree of 26 October 1917; other materials.

155 Russia-Moscow. 3 containers. Includes copies of the following materials: Instructions to Count Pahlen from Alexander I, 1809; "Projet de depeche a M. de Stoeckl" (1854); Instructions to Baron Tuyll from Alexander I, 1817; papers of the Ruling Senate - Instructions to scientists of the Bering Expedition, 1732-33, 54 pp.; materials, 1868, from the archives of the Russian legation in Washington with translations by Hunter Miller; photostat negatives of ADS, 62 sheets, various sizes, pertaining to treaty negotiations leading up to the treaty of 1832 between the United States and

Russia, in French. See "Documents Relative to the History of Alaska," Volume III, pp. 322-39, available in the Manuscript Division.

156 Russia - Petrograd. 12 containers. Includes copies of materials made by Frank A. Golder in Petrograd archives in 1914. Most of the materials deals with Bering's Expeditions, the activities of the Russian-American Company and of Russians in Alaska, and with the sale of Alaska to the United States. Included are: report of the academician G. F. Muller on the discovery of new islands by Captain Shmalev, 1770, 4 pp.; a document on Francis Dana's mission to the court of Catherine II, ca. 1784, in French; documents containing data on Shelikhov, Baranov, and others; a refutation, in French, that American independence will be harmful to Russian trade, n.d., 6 pp.; documentation on the activities of Shelikhov, Golikov, and the first missionaries in Alaska, 1783-96, 44 pp.; report of the committee appointed to study interpretation of Article I of the Treaty of Ghent, 20 pp.; a life and scientific observations of Georg Wilhelm Steller; selections from a book of drawings of Alaskan scenes by Lieutenant M. Levashov; drawings of the port of Petropavlosk and other places by Ivan Elagin; historical calendar of the Russian-American Company for 1816; dispatches from Baron Stoeckl to State Chancellor Prince Gorchakov, 1860-64, ca. 2,000 pp. See U.S. Library of Congress, Manuscript Division, Handbook of Manuscripts in the Library of Congress (Washington: Government Printing Office, 1918), pp. 456-57. See also "Documents Relative to the History of Alaska," Volume III, pp. 322-39, available in the Manuscript Division.

157 Russia - Philanthropic Societies. Papers, 1865-76. 1 container. Reports, account books, and photographs relating to charitable and philanthropic organizations in Russia. The material, in Russian, German, and English, was collected in connection with the celebration of the 100th anniversary of American independence in Philadelphia. Organizations mentioned include the Bratoliubovnoe obshchestvo, the Benevolent Society for Governesses and French Teachers in Russia, and the Community for the Sisters of Charity at Pskov.

158 Russia - Valaam. 1 container, 4 items. Photographs of original drawings from Valaam monastery of the Elevoi, Kodiak, and Lesnoi Islands during 1819 made by the monk Kanowsky from memory in 1866. The materials were collected by Frank A. Golder.

159 Russian Orthodox Greek Catholic Church in Alaska. Records, 1772-1936. 1,015 containers. Donated to the Library of Congress by Russian Church officials in 1928 and 1964, these records consist primarily of ecclesiastical documents dealing with the administration of Alaskan parishes, including those in Atka, Belkovsky, Ikogmut, Juneau, Kenai, Kalesnoo, Kodiak, Kuskakwim, Nushagak, Nutchek, St. George Island, St. Michael Island, Sitka, Taitlek, Unalaska, and Unga. Documents include registers of births, marriages, and deaths; records of confession and communion; reports about churches and lists of clergy; records of divine services; records of income and expenditures of church funds; registers of converts to orthodoxy. There are also 23 diaries and travel journals spanning the years 1828-97; Imperial decrees beginning with Catherine the Great; letters, 1870, on the proposed union of the Russian Orthodox Church with the American Episcopal Church; private correspondence to clerics in Alaska from V. K. Sabler, Professor I. Glubokovskii (St. Petersburg Ecclesiastical Seminary), Professor N. Dobrov (Moscow Theological Seminary), and many others. Finally, there are documents pertaining to the Church and to the Russian-American Company before the purchase of Alaska. An unpublished register at the Library describes these records. The documents received in 1928 are described in the Alaska History Research Project, "Documents Relative to the History of Alaska" (1936-38). See also the article used extensively in writing this entry, John T. Dorosh, "The Alaskan Russian Church Archive," The Library of Congress Quarterly Journal of Current Acquisitions, Vol. 18, No. 4 (August 1961), pp. 192-203. Note: A detailed guide to the Records is being prepared; the Records will be microfilmed in the near future.

160 Russian Orthodox Church in Alaska. Typescript, 15 vols. "Documents Relative to the History of Alaska," made by the staff of the Alaska History Research Project at the University of Alaska, 1936-38. Included are calendars, indexes, transcripts of documents, and excerpts and translations of some of the records of the Russian-American Company (at the National Archives in Washington, D.C.) and of the following documents at the Manuscript Division: Russian Orthodox Greek Catholic Church records, the Yudin Collection, Russia-Petrograd, Russia-Moscow, Russia-Miscellany, and Russia-Valaam.

161 Eugene Schuyler (1840-1890). 1 letterbook, 300 items, 1873-78. Diplomat, author, and scholar. Letterpress copies of correspondence and writings pertaining to Schuyler's service as secretary of the American legation in St. Petersburg, 1873-76, and to his book, Turkistan: Notes of a Journey in Russian Turkistan, Khokand, Bukhara, and Kuldja (1876). There is also material relating to the advance of Russians into Central Asia, the Balkan question, and the Treaty of Berlin, 1878. On microfilm. (NUCMC 77-1570)

162 Hugh Lenox Scott (1853-1934). Papers, 1845-1934. 104 containers. Army officer and public official. Correspondence and reports by Scott during his membership, 1917-19, on the Root mission to Russia. Also, some

newspaper clippings on Russia. Finding aid. (NUCMC 62-4964)

163 Igor Ivanovich Sikorsky. 3 containers, 50 items. Russian-born aircraft designer. Printed matter (mostly), notes, photographs, correspondence, dating back to 1913, and the original manuscript (1936) of Sikorsky's "The Story of the Winged-S."

164 William Sowden Sims (1858-1936). Papers, 1856-1951. 149 containers. Some family letters pertaining to Sims's service in Russia, where he was U.S. naval attaché in the late 1890s. Finding aid. (NUCMC 77-1573)

165 Smirnov Archive. Collection. 1 container. Photostats of typewritten copies of P. Lavrov addressed to Rozalia Khristoforovna in the 1850s and 1880s. The originals are at the Internationaal Instituut voor Sociale Geschiedenis, Amsterdam.

166 Carl Andrew Spaatz (1891-1974). Papers, 1915-53. 352 containers. U.S. general. Some materials pertaining to Russia. Finding aid. (NUCMC 68-2075) Restricted.

167 Lawrence Edmund Spivak (b. 1900). Papers, 1927-73. 117 containers. Television commentator. 10 folders of correspondence from viewers of Spivak's T.V. show, "Meet the Press." Persons discussed in these letters include A. Mikoyan, Nikita S. Khrushchev, George K. Kennan, and Mikhail Menshikov (Soviet ambassador to the U.S.). Finding aid. (NUCMC 74-1074)

168 Joseph Stalin (1879-1953). A photograph of a published handwritten note praising Lenin, 1925, with a typewritten English translation. The note appeared in Rabochaia gazeta, January 1925, No. 17.

169 William Harrison Standley (1872-1963). Papers, 1895-1963. 14 containers. U.S. ambassador to the Soviet Union, 1942-43. Includes drafts of Standley's book, Admiral Ambassador to Russia. There is also correspondence pertaining to the anti-communist causes with which Standley was associated in the 1950s. Finding Aid. (NUCMC 71-1418)

170 Laurence Adolph Steinhardt (1892-1950). Papers, 1929-50. 89 containers. U.S. ambassador to Russia, 1931-41; handled the arrangements of the first lend-lease shipments to the Soviet Union. Some material on Russia and on Russian-Turkish relations. Finding aid. (NUCMC 65-0932)

171 John Frank Stevens (1853-1943). 1914-42. 1 container (80 items). Chairman of the American Railway Advisory Commission in Russia; president of the Inter-Allied Technical Board in charge of Russian railways. Included are correspondence, clippings, reprints, and biographical materials.

172 Stevenson Family. Papers, 1756-1882. 51 containers. Contains correspondence from the Russian minister in London to Andrew Stevenson (1785-1857) when he was U.S. minister to England, 1836-41. Finding aid. (NUCMC 76-0174)

173 Michael Wolf Straus (1897-1970). Papers, 1929-65. 22 containers. Consultant to the Senate Interior Committee, 1955-60. 1 folder of photographs, charts, drafts of articles, and notebooks pertaining to Soviet electricity and to Straus's trip to Russia in 1959.

174 Oscar Solomon Straus (1850-1926). Papers, 1856-1954. 53 containers. Businessman, diplomat, secretary of commerce. Some material reflects Straus's concern with the welfare and persecution of Jews in Russia. Finding aid. (NUCMC 60-0157)

175 Arthur Sweetser (1888-1968). Papers, 1913-63. 118 containers. Member of the Information Section, League of Nations Secretariat, 1919-42. 1 folder of correspondence, memoranda, and printed materials pertaining to the Russo-Finnish dispute, 1939. Finding aid. (NUCMC 69-2053)

176 Raymond Swing (1887-1968). Papers, 1935-63. 39 containers. Political commentator for the Voice of America, 1951-53, 1959-63. Some materials pertaining to Russia. Finding aid. (NUCMC 70-0977)

177 Thomas de Witt Talmage (1832-1902). Papers, 1843-1902. 33 containers. U.S. clergyman. Some materials (correspondence, scrapbook, notes) describing Talmage's visit to Russia in 1892, when he met Alexander III. Finding aid. (NUCMC 62-4819)

178 Georgii Gustavovich Telberg. Papers, 1915-40. 5 containers. Russian-born author, lecturer, and government official; participated in the Kerensky government. 2 ft. of materials (primarily Telberg's autobiography, and also newspaper clippings and lecture notes) relate to life in Russia, the Russian Revolution, and emigration. (NUCMC 61-1649)

179 Stephen Timoshenko (1878-1965). Papers, 1928-57. 4 containers. Educator and engineer. Lecture notes and other materials on Russian science. (NUCMC 64-1581)

180 John Willard Toland (b. 1912). Papers, 1941-66. 110 containers. Includes transcribed interviews with Russians involved in the destruction of Germany and the fall of Berlin. These interviews were used as source materials in Toland's The Last Hundred Days (New York, 1966). Finding aid. (NUCMC 68-2079)

181 Dimitry Tuneeff. Tuneeff's master's thesis, "Russian Libraries" (1932) and a biographical sketch, 1931, of G. V. Yudin.

DISTRICT OF COLUMBIA - LIBRARY OF CONGRESS DC 23

182 Ukrainian Congress Committee of America. A bound petition to President Gerald Ford on behalf of human rights in the Ukraine, 1976, 450 pp.

183 Hoyt Sanford Vandenberg (1899-1954). Papers, 1923-53. 97 containers. Chief of staff of the Air Force (1948-53). Materials on the USSR and on Soviet aircraft. Finding aid. (NUCMC 70-0984)

184 Volga Province - Russia. Records. 1 container (54 items). Spanning the late 18th and early 19th c., these 54 items, which include official documents and service records, pertain to the service and family history of the Ivanovs, a noble Russian family that lived in the Volga region.

185 Vozdushnye puti. Records, 1902-67. 6 containers. Contains 3 boxes of correspondence (1941-67) to R. N. Grynberg, the editor and publisher of Vozdushnye puti. Correspondents include Nina Berberova, Roman Goul, Vladimir Vladimirovich Nabokov, Vladimir Markov, Aleksandr Efimovich Parnis, Edmund Wilson, Joseph Brodsky, Max Hayward, Iurii Ivask, Michael Karpovich, Dmitri von Mohrenschildt, Temira Pachmuss, Aleksis Rannit, Gleb Petrovich Struve, Roman Jakobson, Vladimir Vasil'evich Weidle, Aleksei Mikhailovich Remizov, Natalie Baranoff, and others. In addition, there are 3 boxes of literary manuscripts, newspaper clippings, and photos (of Vladimir Nabokov, Khodasevich, Mayakovskii, and others).

186 Thomas James Walsh (1859-1933). Papers, 1910-34. 524 containers. U.S. senator from Montana. 1 folder of correspondence between Walsh and his constituents on Turkish atrocities in Armenia. Finding aid. (NUCMC 59-0261)

187 Stanley Washburn (1878-1950). Papers, 1912-45. 4 containers. Journalist and author; was in Russia with the John P. Stevens Railroad Commission to rehabilitate Russian railroads and participated in the Special Diplomatic Mission to Russia, 1917. Some materials pertaining to Russia. Finding aid. (NUCMC 60-0146)

188 Boris Weinberg. Educator. 1 item: "A Scheme of Itinerary of an Expedition for Studying the Aborigines of the North Siberia between Obi and Yenisei." Typed, 3 pp., in English, Tomsk, 17 June 1922.

189 William Allen White (1868-1944). Papers, 1859-1944. 452 containers. Author, editor, politician. Correspondents include Carl W. Ackerman, William E. Borah, and Raymond Robins. Finding aid. (NUCMC 59-0041)

190 Bertram David Wolfe. Papers, 2 containers. Author. Drafts of Wolfe's book, Three Who Made a Revolution. Finding aid.

191 Levi (1789-1851) and Charles Levi (1820-1898) Woodbury. Papers, 1638-1899. 105 containers. Contains the diary of Mrs. Gustavus Vasa Fox (Virginia Woodbury) when her husband was in Russia in 1866. Finding aid. (NUCMC 66-0235)

192 Wilbur (1867-1912) and Orville (1871-1948) Wright. Papers, 1881-1948. 120 containers. Some materials on the contacts of the Wright Brothers with the Russian government in the early 20th c. Finding aid. (NUCMC 60-0588)

193 Gennadii Vasil'ievitch Yudin - Russian-American Company. Records, 1876-1930. Correspondence, reports, tariffs, cargo registers, ships' logs, and other materials dealing with the exploration and colonization of Alaska by the Russian-American Company. Gregorii Ivanovich Shelikov, Fyodor Ivanov Shemelin, Lieutenant-General Ivan Pil', Matthew Lapatin N. P. Rezanov, Mikhailo Buldakov, and Alexander I are mentioned in these records. Finding aid. See "Documents Relative to the History of Alaska," Vol. 3, pp. 143-312, available at the Manuscript Division. (NUCMC 63-0410)

194 Gregory Ignatius Zatkovitch. Collection, 1918-ca. 1961. Lawyer, first governor of Carpathian Ruthenia, 1919-21. Includes a typescript of the Declaration of Common Aims of the Independent Mid-European Nations, 26 October 1918, adopted by their representatives, Independence Hall, Philadelphia, and signed by T. G. Masaryk, Zatkovitch, and others. There is also a document entitled "The Tragic Tale of Sub-Carpathian Ruthenia" and a picture postcard of the bust of Zatkovitch.

195 The following groups of documents have or may have materials pertaining to Russia or Russian-American relations:

(a) The papers of U.S. presidents, including Thomas Jefferson, Abraham Lincoln, James Madison, James Monroe, Theodore Roosevelt, and Woodrow Wilson. All these papers are on microfilm and have name indexes.

(b) The papers of U.S. secretaries of state, including Henry Clay, Bainbridge Colby, Charles Evans Hughes, Cordell Hull, Robert Lansing, and Henry Alfred Kissinger (restricted).

(c) The papers of Frederick Lewis Allen, Vannevar Bush, William E. Dodd, John William Draper, Tom Terry Connally, James John Davis, Henry P. Fletcher, Theodore Francis Green, Nelson Trusler Johnson, Jesse Holmes Jones, Peyton C. March, George Fort Milton, Charles Linza McNary, George Foster Peabody, Key Pittman, Donald Randall Richberg, Frances Bowes Sayre, Eric Arnold Sevareid, William Boyce Thompson, and Henry Agard Wallace.

Finding Aids: In addition to the finding aids mentioned above (most of which are unpublished draft "registers" that describe groups of documents in varying detail), there are also published descriptions of some holdings, including: Library of Congress, Annual Report for the fiscal years 1897 to date; Library of Congress, Handbook of Manuscripts (1918) and its supplements; Library of Congress, Quarterly Journal (until 1964 the Quarterly Journal of Current Acquisitions), 1943 to date; Library of Congress, Manuscript Sources on Manuscript: A Checklist (1975).

DC 24
MUSIC DIVISION
LIBRARY OF CONGRESS
10 First Street SE
Washington, D.C. 20540
(202-426-5507)

Original manuscripts

1 Leopold Auer (1845-1930). Aria Lenski, arrangement of score by Petr Il'ich Chaikovskii, 12 pp., for violin and piano, arranger's manuscript in ink [Eugene Onegin. How far ye seem behind me].

2 Aaron A. Avshalomoff (1894-1965). Symphony, no. 3 in B minor [1953], score, holograph in ink, on transparent paper, 169 ll. On titlepage? Dedicated to the memory of Serge and Natalie Kou-sevitzky. Plus a reproduction of the same (black-line print).

3 Victor Babin (1908-1972). Papers, 1935-73, of this Russian-born composer and pianist, ca. 174 items, include correspondence between him and his wife, letters from Vera Stravinsky, and the following musical items: Strains from far-off lands, three pieces for two pianos, four hands, based on folk melodies [Fantasies on old themes] (1943-45), score, holograph in ink, 31 ll., on transparent paper (published, 1948) [contains The piper of Polmood, Hebrew slumber song, and Russian village]; Twelve variations on a theme by Henry Purcell, for cello and piano (1945), score, 19 ll., and part, holograph in ink, on transparent paper (theme is a trumpet tune by J. Clarke, erroneously attributed to Purcell); Road to life, vocalise, holograph in pencil with additions in ink, for voice and piano, 4 pp.; Variations on a theme of Beethoven (Marcia alla turca, from Die Ruinen von Athen), piano [1957], holograph sketches in pencil, 11 pp. (published, [1960]); Etude 6, two pianos, score, holograph in pencil with emendations in ink, 14 pp.; Etude No. 5, two pianos, score (1937), holograph in pencil with emendations in ink, 6 pp.; Ballade heroique for cello and piano, score, holograph in pencil, 24 pp.; David and Goliath, score, holograph in pencil with emendations in ink, for piano, four hands, 24 pp. (published, 1954); Concerto no. 1 for two pianos and orchestra (1937), score, holograph in pencil and ink, 5 vols.; Three march rhythms for two pianos, four hands, score, holograph in ink, 26 pp., plus second holograph [194-?], 19 pp., in pencil (rough draft); Beloved stranger, eleven poems by Witter Bynner, for baritone or mezzo-soprano (1947), holograph in pencil, 24 pp., accompanied by sketches, 1 l., and with piano accompaniment; Drei Gedichte von Stefan Zweig, for voice and piano [1935], holograph in ink with pencil annotations, 11 pp.; Pour deux pianos (1934), score, holograph in ink with annotations in pencil, 14 pp.; Concerto no. 2, for two pianos and orchestra, score, publisher's first proof with composer's corrections in ink, 71 ll. (M. P. Belaïeff, 1961), accompanied by arrangement for third piano; and his arrangements of: Igor Federovich Stravinsky--Tango, arr. for two pianos [194-], score, 5 pp., arranger's ms. in ink with corrections in red pencil by the composer (published, 1962), two letters about the work from the composer to Babin in Russian (7 August and 5 September 1941) plus pencilled corrections for the music in Stravinsky's hand laid in, and another manuscript in ink [194-], 5 pp., with additions in pencil incorporating the composer's corrections; Petrouchka, ballet excerpts for two pianos [19--], score, 31 pp., Babin's holograph in pencil with emendations in ink (published, [1953]); Sergei Rachmaninoff--It's lovely here (Songs, op. 21, How fair this spot), arranged for two pianos (1939), score, arranger's holograph in pencil, 2 pp.; Floods of spring (Songs, op. 14, Spring waters), arr. for two pianos [195-?], score, 4 pp., Babin's ms. in pencil; Nikolai Andreevich Rimskii-Korsakov--Dance of the buffoons (from The snow maiden), complete sketch by V. Babin, arr. for two pianos [19--], score, arranger's holograph in pencil with emendations in ink, 14 pp.; Cradle song, arr. for two pianos [1937], score, Babin's holograph in ink, 3 pp.; Petr Il'ich Chaikovskii--Valse sentimentale ([Morceaux, piano, op. 51]), arr. for two pianos, score, arranger's holograph in pencil, 8 pp.; Johann Sebastian Bach--five organ sonatas arranged for two pianos: no. 1 in E♭ major, 13 pp., 1942; no. 2 in C minor, 18 pp., 1942; no. 3 in D minor, 18 pp. [19--]; the fifth, in C major, 23 pp. [19--]; and Sonata in G major, 18 pp. [19--]; Choral, Jesu, joy . . . (Herz und mund und Tat und Leben. Jesus bleibet meine Freude), arr. for two pianos, 4 pp. [1944]; and Recitativo and aria [Was mir behagt. Soll dann der Pales Opfer hier das letzte sein?], arr. for two pianos (1943), score, 4 pp.--all Bach items being the arranger's holograph in ink and/or pencil; Franz Peter Schubert--An die Musik, op. 88, no. 4, arr. for two pianos (1943), score, Babin's holograph in ink, 3 pp., plus unidentified sketch, holograph in pencil, 3 pp.; and Christoph Willibald Gluck--Melodie (no. 30) from the opera Orpheus and Eurydice, arr. for two pianos, four hands (1964), score,

Babin's holograph in ink on transparent paper, 4 ll. Contents lists available.

4 Nicolai Berezowski (1900-1953). Introduction and allegro, op. 8, composer's holograph, 45 pp., 1937, score for chamber orchestra--revision of his Poème of 1927 (in Elizabeth Sprague Coolidge Collection); and Poème, composer's holograph, score for chamber orchestra, 39 pp.

5 Aleksandr Porfir'evich Borodin (1834-1887). [Kniaz Igor: sketches], composer's holograph, 5 ll., mostly in pencil (n.d.), four orchestral sketches and one melodic phrase, score.

6 Petr Il'ich Chaikovskii (1840-1893). Aveux passionné [1892?], holograph in ink, for piano, 3 pp. See also under V. Babin.

7 Aleksandr Nikolaevich Cherepnin (1899-1977). Exploring the piano; twelve duets to explore the piano (1958), holograph in ink, 25 pp., with editor's blue and red pencilled corrections (published, ca. 1959), plus letters between the composer and the piano editor, Roberta Savler, and a copy of the published work laid in.

8 Muzio Clementi (1752-1832). Air Russe con basso di Clementi, autograph composition of 12 measures for piano (?) written on one side of one oblong leaf; on verso, unnamed autograph sketch.

9 Elizabeth Sprague Coolidge (1864-1953). Composer and patron of music. The Elizabeth Sprague Coolidge Collection contains manuscript pieces commissioned by and dedicated or presented to her, or commissioned by the Coolidge Foundation, including items by Russian-born composers. Some of these items appear individually in this entry (e.g., works of N. Berezowski, N. Lopatnikov, S. Prokofiev, and Igor Stravinsky). (NUCMC 67-642)

10 César Antonovich Cui (1835-1918). Kinzhal (from seven romances, op. 49, no. 7), song with pianoforte accompaniment (St. Petersburg, 1892), words of M. Lermontov, composer's holograph, 2 ll., dedicated to Aleksandr Andreevich Filonov; and [Three songs with pianoforte accompaniment], composer's holograph, n.d., 4 ll., published by V. Bessel in 1886 as op. 33, nos. 5, 1, and 7 (contains: Oni liubili drug druga--words of Lermontov, Solovei--A. S. Pushkin, and Metel'shumit--Pushkin). See also under Philip James.

11 John Field (1782-1837). Rondeau, for pianoforte, two violins, alto, and bass [Rondo, piano quintet in A♭ major] (St. Petersburg, ca. 1812), first edition of published score (incomplete, with string parts lacking), with additions, corrections, and fingerings in the composer's hand, written in ink and pencil on piano part and on slips pasted in for the purpose of performance as a piano solo; Andante, for two pianos, four hands, autograph, unpaged [3 pp.]; and Compositions for piano, holographs, seven numbers in one volume, for piano (n.d.), including: Preludio, 12 pp. [Composition without title], 5 pp., Concerto, 13 pp., Poco adagio, 3 pp., Rondo, 14 pp., Adagio, 11 pp., and Serenade, 3 pp.

12 Osip Solomonovich Gabrilowitsch (1878-1936). Collection, 1932-37, 80 items. Russian-born conductor and pianist; married Clara Clemens, daughter of Mark Twain, in 1909. (NUCMC 68-2091)

13 Alexandre Constantinovich Glazounov (Aleksandr Konstantinovich Glazunov) (1865-1936). Cortège triomphal, composer's holograph, n.d., 4 pp. score for orchestra (first 16 bars published as Cortège solonnel, op. 50); Preludio e fuga, 23 pp., for pianoforte, two hands, composer's holograph, signed and dated (at end): 31 iiulia 1926, Gatchina. Okonchatel'no pererabotano 17 avgusta 1929 g., Antib, A. Glazunov; Quartet, second sonata for piano [Quartet, strings, no. 7. Allegro giocoso] (1930), score, composer's apographs in ink, each signed at end, with an autographed portrait, 2 ll.; and [Musique pour le drame de C. R. Le Roi des Juifs], full score for chorus and orchestra, publisher's proof (M. P. Belaieff, Leipzig, 1915) with corrections and additions by the composer in red and black ink, signed and dated (St. Petersburg, 1913).

14 Leopold Godowsky (1870-1938). Papers, 1886-1938, ca. 12 ft. Pianist and composer. Business and financial papers, photographs, clippings, notes for a biography of Godowsky prepared by Leonard Saxe (his nephew and legal adviser), correspondence, much of it translated into English, and 52 music holographs, including his transcriptions of works by Bach, Schubert, Schumann, and Weber; ten pieces arranged for the left hand (inspired by Chopin's Études); Java, suite for piano, holograph in ink, 1924-25, 67 pp., with pencil emendations (published, 1925); Passacaglia, in B minor, for piano, holograph in ink, 27 pp., with emendations in blue pencil (1927); Yearning, poem no. 4, for piano, in ink (1931), 3 pp.; Alt Wien, for piano, in ink, 5 pp., 1919 (published, 1920); and Tyrolean (Schuhplatter), score, composer's manuscript arrangement, in ink, 4 pp., of the piano piece, 1915 (published, 1919).

15 Aleksandr Tikhonovich Grechaninov (1864-1956). The Lord's prayer (Otche nash, op. 107, no. 3), for soprano solo and mixed choir, composer's holograph, 2 ll., score (n.d.), title and text in English and Russian (published, English only, 1932); Missa oecumenica, for four solo voices, choir, orchestra, and organ, op. 142, partition (Paris, 1935), score, holograph in ink with additions and corrections in pencil, 148 pp.; and the same work, holograph in ink

with additions in pencil (Paris, 1935), 75 pp.; both the last two dedicated to the memory of Natalie Koussevitzky.

16 Alexei Haieff (b. 1914). Concerto for piano and orchestra (1949-50), score, holograph in pencil, 128 pp.; Eclogue [1945], score and part, holograph in ink (in memory of Natalie Konstantinovna Koussevitzky), 10 pp., plus two photocopies of this same work (negative and positive); and Eloge, for four flutes, bassoon, trombone, two pianos, and wood block (1967), 2 ll., score, holograph in ink on transparent paper (in memory of Serge and Natalie Koussevitzky), 62 ll.

17 Adolf von Henselt (1814-1889). Album leaf, composer's holograph, signed and dated: A. Henselt, Dresden, 16. sept. 1842 (three bars for pianoforte, two hands); and a second album leaf in the composer's holograph, signed and dated: A. Henselt, St. Petersburg, den 8ten marz, 1845 (pianoforte, two hands), with a portrait of the composer on the verso.

18 Boris Karlovich Ianovskii (1875-1933). Sulamit; muzykal'naia drama v 3-kh kartinakh [1916], holograph in ink, 170 pp., librettist unknown, but libretto based on A. I. Kuprin's Sulamif, piano-vocal score.

19 Tadeusz Iarecki (1888-1955). Quartet for two violins, alto, and violoncello, score and parts (1918), composer's holograph (Elizabeth Sprague Coolidge Collection).

20 Philip James (1890-1975). Partitur of arrangement for military band of Cesar Cui's Orientale (from Kaleidoscope), op. 50, no. 9, score, arranger's holograph in ink, 7 pp.

21 Dmitrii Borisovich Kabalevskii (b. 1904). Improvizatsiia, op. 23 (sic), no. 1, Improvisation, violin and piano, op. 21, no. 1, 1934, score, holograph in ink, 5 pp.; at end: D. Kabalevskii--9/iv. 1934 g. Moskva.

22 Anton de Kontski (1817-1899). Romance "Priez pour moi!!", words of Milleboye, music of Antonin de Kontski, unpaged autograph, piano accompaniment, French text.

23 Boris Koutzen (1901-1966). Second quartet for two violins, viola, and cello (1936), composer's holograph score, 1 l., 49 pp., dedicated to Mrs. Elizabeth Sprague Coolidge.

24 Jozef Kozlowski (1757-1831). Trois polonaises, executed on the occasion of the marriage of Nikolai Pavlovich and Alexandra Feodorovna, arranged for the pianoforte [1817?], holograph [?] in ink, 7 pp.; on title-page: Joseph Koslovsky, Amateur, à St. Petersbourg.

25 Fritz Kreisler (1875-1962). Papers, 1883-1945, 4 ft. Transcriptions for violin (S. Rachmaninoff's Prelude in G minor, 1945, 7 pp.) and for violin and piano (Rachmaninoff's Prayer--Preghiera--from the second movement of piano concerto no. 2, op. 18, in C minor [1940], score, 8 pp.; N. Rimskii-Korsakov's Fantaisie sur des thèmes russes, newly edited and freely arranged by Kreisler, 1928, score, 17 pp.; and P. Chaikovskii's Chant sans paroles, score, 3 pp.; and his reduction for violin and piano of Henri Wieniawski's Air russes, score, 7 pp. (published ca. 1929). Also, holograph works of A. Gretchaninoff and L. Godowsky.

26 Sergei Aleksandrovich Kusevitskii [Serge Koussevitzky] (1874-1951). Papers, ongoing, ca. 200 ft., of Serge and Olga Naoumoff Koussevitzky and of Natalie Ushkov Koussevitzky (1880-1942); and Archives of the Koussevitzky Foundation. Includes holograph scores owned by Koussevitzky, Russian-born composer and conductor of the Boston Symphony Orchestra (1924-49); holograph works commissioned by the Serge Koussevitzky Music Foundation since 1942, correspondence, financial and business records; concert programs, personal papers, correspondence with, inter alia, Vladimir Dukelsky, Nicolai Lopatnikoff, Nicolas Nabokov, Sergei Prokofiev, Igor Stravinsky, and Alexandre Tansman; and the holograph of at least one of his own compositions: Concerto for Double Bass and Orchestra, partitura, op. 3, in F sharp minor [1902], score, in ink with the composer's conducting marks in pencil, 100 pp., some pages being reproductions of a copyist's manuscript (published, [1907]). (NUCMC 67-650)

27 W. W. Kwiatkowski. Partitura from the opera Talisman in five acts, autograph full score, Polish text, signed by Kwiatkowski and dated: Pisal w Lublinie dnia 14 maja 1857.

28 Theodor Leschititzky (1830-1915). Die erste falte: un coup de hasard; frei nach dem Französischem von Mosenthal, opera in one act, partitur, one volume, autograph full score, vii + 208 pp., German text, first performed in Prague, 9 October 1867.

29 Anatol Constantinovich Liadov (1855-1914). Bagatelle, 1 l., composer's holograph in pencil, dated at end: An. Liadov, 18go oktiabria 89g. ("V al'bom Antonu Grigor'evichu Rubinshteinu"), for pianoforte, two hands.

30 Charles Martin Tornov Loeffler (1861-1935). Papers, 1882-1935, 6 ft., ca. 1,700 items. Composer and violinist. Correspondence, sketches, photos, literary works, programs, clippings, and musical holographs: Memories of childhood (Life in a Russian village), composer's holograph, n.d., 1 l., 49 pp., score for full orchestra (published, 1925), title in Russian (Skazochnyi mir o selie) and English; Une nuit de mai, rhapsody after Nicolai Gogol, for violin, orchestra, and harp [1891], score, holograph of earliest

version, in ink, 47 pp. (originally intended as the second movement for his suite Les veillées de l'Ukraine); the same work [189-?], score and part, holograph in ink, 42 pp., copyist's ms. of full score, in ink, with composer's additions and corrections in pencil and ink, 49 pp., laid in; the same work [189-?], score, holograph in ink, 16 pp., for violin and piano; Rhapsodie russe, for violin and orchestra, score, holograph in ink of the composer's reduction for violin and piano, 15 pp., with pencil sketches on p. 15, violin part extensively revised and incomplete, 3 pp., laid in: Les veillées de l'Ukraine after Nicolai Gogol [189-], score, holograph of suite for violin and orchestra, in ink, 116 pp. (omits second movement, Une nuit de mai, later reset as a separate work); same work, for violin and orchestra, violin principal [189-], holograph in ink, 25 pp.; same work, copyist's ms. in ink, parts, title-page wrapper in composer's hand (omits the third movement, Chansons russes); same work, suite for orchestra and harp [1891], score, holograph of early version in ink, 99 pp. (omits the second movement); and the same work, arranged for violin and piano [1891], score, holograph in ink (incomplete), 54 pp., with third movement missing. Music manuscripts reproduced on microfilm. (NUCMC 67-651)

31 Nikolai Lopatnikoff (1903-1976). Concerto for two pianos and orchestra, op. 33 [1949-50], orchestral score reduced for third piano by the composer, holograph in pencil, 18, 10, 17 pp. (published, 1953), L.C. copy imperfect (2 pp. of second movement wanting); Fantasia concertante, for violin and piano, op. 42 [ca. 1962], score, holograph in pencil, 18 pp. (published, 1967); Festival overture, for orchestra, op. 40 (1960), condensed score, holograph in pencil, 23 pp.; Music for orchestra, op. 39 (1958), condensed score, holograph in pencil, 17 pp.; Opus sinfonicum, for orchestra [1943], score, holograph in ink, 54 pp. (published, 1951); Quartet no. 2, for two violins, alto, and violoncello, op. 6 [1929], score and four parts, holograph in ink, 72 pp., dedicated to Elizabeth Sprague Coolidge (published by Belaieff, 1933), plus positive photocopy of this work; Quartet no. 2, for two violins, alto, and violoncello, op. 6a, arranged for piano, four hands, by the composer [193-?], holograph in ink, 88 pp.; Quartet no. 3, op. 36 [ca. 1956], score, holograph in pencil, 32 pp.; Piano sonata, op. 29 [1943], holograph in pencil, 22 pp. (published, 1946); Symphonie no. 2, in F minor, op. 24 [1939?], score, holograph in ink, 4 vols.; same work, Andante [194-?], condensed score, holograph sketches in pencil, 10 pp., of a new second movement to replace movements two and three of the original version (1939); Trio for piano, violin, and violoncello, op. 23 (193-], score, holograph in ink, 69 pp.; Variations and epilogue, for violoncello and piano, op. 31 [1946], score, holograph in pencil, 33 pp. (published, 1948); and Variazioni concertanti, op. 38 [1958], condensed score for orchestra, holograph in pencil, 34 pp.

32 Daniel Gregory Mason (1873-1953). Papers, 1902-35, 101 items. Includes correspondence between Mason and Osip Gabrilowitsch concerning Mason's music, mutual criticisms of compositions, and other matters. Among his holograph musical works in this collection are: Russians; songs for baritone and orchestra, op. 18 [1915-17], score, 1 vol., holograph in ink, with markings in red and blue pencil by Leopold Stokowski and Osip Gabrilowitsch, with historical notes in the composer's hand, words by Witter Bynner (published, 1920); scoring of the same work, Sketches of Negro quartet, for string quartet, score, 1 vol., holograph in pencil (published, 1930); and [Sketch book of Love songs, op. 15; an unidentified string quartet; Intermezzo for string quartet, op. 17; Russians, op. 18; Negro quartet, op. 19; and various piano pieces. 1915-16], 1 vol., holograph in pencil, with some sketches for Love-songs, op. 15 (orchestrated much later), a memo, September 1946, and lists of Mason's compositions (op. 1-23) and literary works on inside front and back covers in composer's hand.

33 Nikolai Karlovich Medtner (1880-1951). Papers, 1914-54, 4 ft., 1,912 items. Russian-born composer and pianist. Includes holograph sketches by Medtner in the margins of books of poems by Pushkin and Lermontov; a copy of his book Musa i Moda with his holograph corrections; correspondence with Sergei Rachmaninoff, 30 letters from Medtner, Aleksandr Fedorovich Goedicke (6 letters), Konstantin Klimov (74 letters), Leon and Olga Conus, and Mr. and Mrs. Serge Conus; and Khorovodnaia skazka [Russian round dance], from op. 58 [194-], score, holograph in ink, 27 pp., for two pianos (published, 1946). Restriction: A small group of letters is sealed until 1985. Unpublished guide (NUCMC 67-652).

34 Sophie Menter (1846-1918). Correspondence, 1865-1916, 102 items. Includes letters 1860s-1880s written by Mily Alexeyevich Balakirev. Other correspondents include Adolph von Henselt and Alexander Ilyich Siloti. (NUCMC 67-653)

35 Modern Music. Archives, 1924-46, 4 ft. Business papers of the periodical Modern Music, published quarterly by the League of Composers of New York City (earlier title: The League of Composers' Review). Includes typescripts of articles, photographs of contributors, some original drawings of composers, and a large number of letters, in part photocopies, by Lazare Saminsky and others. List of correspondents. (NUCMC 78-392)

36 Modeste Petrovich Moussorgskii (1839-1881). "Kinder-scherzo" dlia fortepiano, composer's holograph, 3 ll., dated at end: Fine. Selo Toshkovo, maia 28go, 1860?g.; dedicated to Nikolai Aleksandrovich Levashov.

37 Nicolas Nabokov (1903-1978). Serenata estiva (Summer serenade), for string quartet (1937), score, holograph in ink on transparent paper, 14 ll., dedicated to Mrs. Elizabeth Sprague Coolidge.

38 Nicolas Nicolaef (Nicolaev). Album leaf, for piano in F# major [1941?], holograph in ink, 4 pp. (published, ca. 1941); Concerto for piano in E minor [n.d.], score, 1 vol., holograph in ink; In modo russo [1942?], for piano, holograph in ink, 11 pp. (published, ca. 1942); La mouche, for piano, holograph in ink, 4 pp.; Ouverture [n.d.], score, holograph in ink, 84 pp., for orchestra; Poema-fantaziia [n.d.], score, for orchestra, holograph in ink, 96 pp.; Rêverie, for piano, holograph in ink, 2 pp.; Scherzo [1944?], for piano in G_b major, holograph in ink, 14 pp. (published, ca. 1944); and Song of the past, score and part, for violoncello and piano, holograph in ink, 4 pp.

39 A. A. Poluboiarinov. Kolybel'naia piesnia, composer's holograph (1896), 4 ll., dedicated to the Empress Aleksandra Feodorovna, with her portrait and that of the Grand Duchess Olga on the cover; song with pianoforte accompaniment.

40 Sergei Sergeevich Prokofiev (1891-1953). Quartet no. 1, op. 50, for strings (1930), score, holograph in ink, 33 pp., commissioned by the Elizabeth Sprague Coolidge Foundation (published, 1931), plus negative and positive photocopies of the same work; and Second concerto, op. 16, in G minor, for piano (1930), holograph, 1 l., two themes from the work, in ink.

41 Sergei Rachmaninoff (1873-1943). Papers, 1917-43, 24 ft. Composer and pianist. Includes financial papers, programs, books, articles, clippings by or about him, and correspondence with such figures as Mark A. Aldanov, Konstantin Balmont, Ivan A. Bunin, Mikhail M. Fedoroff, Mikhail M. Fokine, Alexander Glazounov, Boris D. Grigorieff, Ivan A. Ilyin, Nina Koshetz, Serge Koussevitzky, Emil Medtner, Nicolas Medtner, Nikita S. Morosov, Vladimir Nabokov, Gavriil Paitchadze, Anna Pavlova, Leonid Sabaneyev, Sophie Satin, Feodor Shaliapin, Eugene Somoff, Konstantin Stanislavsky, Leopold Stokowski, Alexandra Tolstoi, Ivan Wyshnegradsky, and Vladimir Wilshau, and with the American Relief Administration, the Committee for the Education of Russian Youths in Exile, the International Anticommunist League, Russian War Relief, Russian Students Fund Christian Association, and the Russian War Invalids Outside Russia. There is a card index for this collection, known as the Rachmaninoff Archives. In addition, the library holds the following manuscripts of his compositions: Oriental sketch [1917], 7 pp., holograph in ink, piano music, composer's copy of this work laid in (published, 1938), with his Andante semplice for piano, 2 pp. (published, 1919); Russian songs [Chansons russes], op. 41 [1926], holograph in pencil, 53 pp., for chorus (AAB) and orchestra, English words translated by Kurt Schindler (published, 1928); Concerto in G minor for the piano, no. 4, op. 40 [1927], score, holograph in ink, 171 + 4 pp., discarded sketches at end (published, 1928); Concerto no. 4 in G minor, for piano, op. 40, partition (Paris: Edition "TAIR," 1928), score, holograph revisions of composer in ink throughout, 144 pp. (published, 1944); Minuet (from L'Arlesienne Suite No. 1) by Georges Bizet, arranged for piano, holograph, 8 pp. (published, ca. 1923); Moment musical, op. 16 [Moments musicaux, No. 2], [1940], holograph in pencil, 11 pp., for piano (published, 1941); Mélodie, op. 3 [Morceaux de fantaisie, for piano], [1940], holograph in pencil, 11 pp. (published, 1941); Sérénade, op. 3, no. 5 [Morceaux de fantaisie], revised and as played by the composer [194-?], holograph in ink, 11 pp., piano music (published, 1941); Sérénade, op. 3, no. 5 (revised version) [194-?], holograph in ink, 9 pp., piano music (composer's incomplete copy published, 1941); Humoresque, op. 10 [Morceaux de salon], piano music [1940], holograph in pencil, 15 pp. (revised version published, 1941); Prelude in C-sharp Minor, op. 3, no. 2, 10 pp., n.d.--transcription for two pianos; Polka italienne, for piano, four hands, arrangement [193-?], score, holograph in ink, 5 pp.; [Rhapsodie sur un thème de Paganini, for piano and orchestra, op. 43 (1934)], score, holograph in ink, 176 pp., at end: 18e avgusta 1934. "Senar." Slava Bogu! (published, 1934), based on a theme from Paganini's Caprice, op. 1, no. 24; Symphonic dances, op. 45 [1940], score, holograph in ink, 196 pp., 2 pp. reversed in binding, pencil sketches on one page, at end: 29 oktiabria 1940, New York. Blagodariu Tebia, Gospodi! (published, [1941]); same work, arranged for two pianos [1940], score, holograph in pencil, 73 pp., sketches on one page, transcription by the composer (published, 1942); Symphony no. 3, op. 44 [1935-36], score, holograph in ink, 194 pp., at end: Koncheno. Blagodariu Boga! 6-30 iiulia 1936. Senar; and Variations sur un thème de Corelli, op. 42, for piano [1931], holograph in ink, 50 pp., based on Corelli's La folia (published, 1931). Published finding aid in Library of Congress Quarterly Journal (November 1951). See also under Victor Babin.

42 Rudolf and Richard Réti. Papers, ca. 12 ft. Papers of chess master Richard Reti (1889-1929) are in 5 boxes and comprise chiefly published works and printed matter. Also, correspondence, including 2 letters from the USSR:

ALS, n.d., in German, from A. Troitzky in Pensa, and ALS from the Moscow chess section secretary, 18 November 1926?, concerning business with Reti; photographs of such chess players as E. Bogoljubow and A. Nimzowitsch; signed; and Reti's own postcard from Moscow, 16 November 1925?.

43 Nikolai Andreevich Rimskii-Korsakov (1844-1908). Skazka o tsare Saltane; o syne ego slavnom i moguchem bogatyre kniaze Gvidone Saltanoviche i o prekrasnoi tsarevne Lebedi, opera in four acts with prologue (seven scenes), libretto of V. I. Bel'skii after Pushkin, St. Petersburg, 1900, 186 pp., for piano, on title-page, in ink, at end of five bars of holograph music: N. R-K. See also under Victor Babin.

44 Harry Rosenthal. Collection, on manuscripts and papers of Franz Liszt, 5 ft. Includes piano transcriptions of works by César Cui and other composers.

45 Anton Rubinstein (1830-1894). Ballade (Leonore de Bürger), for piano, two hands, op. 93, cah. 1, autograph, 7 pp., dedicated to a Monsieur Wenzel; Deux études, for the piano, two hands, op. 93, cah. 2, autograph, 7 + 1 pp., dedicated to Monsieur Kross; Deux sérénades, for piano, two hands, op. 93, cah. 6, autograph, 6 pp., dedicated to Sophie Smiriaguine; Doumka et Polonaise, for piano, two hands, op. 93, cah. 3, autograph, 4 pp., dedicated to Monica Terminsky; Scherzo for piano, two hands, op. 93, cah. 5, autograph, 4 pp., dedicated to Pierre de Tschsikofsky--all of the preceding bound within the same cover; and Deux marches funébres, no. 2, pour le convois d'un héros (n.d.), holograph, 1 + 4 pp., for piano, two hands (op. 29, no. 2).

46 Feodosii Antonovich Rubtsov (b. 1904). Compiler of a [Collection of White Russian folk songs. n.d.], in two portfolios, compiler's manuscript in ink, and some printed music sheets pasted on (unaccompanied melodies, White Russian words).

47 Lazare Saminsky (1882-1959). The daughter of Jephta; choreo-cantata, cantata-pantomime, op. 37 [1928], score, holograph in ink, 93 pp., for solo voices (STB), chorus (SATB), and orchestra, in English but with part of the text in transliterated Hebrew (published, ca. 1937); From east to west; a brotherhood of chants and dances, for violin and orchestra, op. 47 (1937), score, holograph in ink, 27 pp.; Hebrew rhapsody, op. 3, no. 2, holograph score for violin and orchestra (n.d.), 23 pp.; Julian, the Apostate Caesar, opera in three acts, op. 43 [193-?], book and music by Saminsky, score, holograph in ink, 233 pp.; Newfoundland air, a poem for chorus, op. 45, poem by Henry Thoreau (1935), score, holograph in ink, 6 pp. (published, ca. 1936); Le poème de la mer et du vent. Etude, op. 17, no. 3, holograph, 6 pp., footnote: Conceived in Paris 1919. Finished and finely (!) written New York 1921 (March); Pueblo, a moon epic, op. 45, orchestral score, holograph, 1 l. + 52 pp., dated "summer 1936, Rye N.Y.," plus a negative photostat of the same; Psalm 93: The Lord reigneth, op. 42, for chorus (SATB), organ, and piano (1931-33), score, holograph in ink, 8 pp.; Requiem, op. 54, for chorus, soli, and orchestra (1945), score, in Latin, holograph in ink, 20 pp. (fifth movement in English); Spring garden [Le jardin printanier], poem by Igor Sieverianin, op. 18, no. 1, En Georgie Caucasienne (au printemps, 1918), printer's first proof, 6 ll., with corrections, song with piano accompaniment, Russian, English transliteration, English, and French text, first line: Now is my garden full abloom with Spring, at head of title in composer's hand: To the Library of Congress, Washington, with deepest feelings of gratitude toward this noble country which sheltered my spirit and body. Lazare Saminsky 19/IV/23; Iière symphonie (Symphonie des grands fleures), op. 10 (1914), holograph, 2 ll. + 104 pp., orchestral score, title in French and Russian, plus a negative photostat of the same; Deuxième symphonie (Partition d'orchestre), autograph orchestral score, 1 l. + 73 pp., in caption-title: Op. 19. A Assoureti, Georgie, Juillet-Aout 1918 (with blue and red pencil markings of Mr. Mengelberg, who gave the first performance of the work); IV symphony, op. 33 (1927?), orchestral score, holograph, 93 pp.; and Three shadows, poems for orchestra, op. 41 (1935), holograph in ink, 5 pp., of piano sketches.

48 Albert Schatz (1839-1910). Collection of early opera libretti and research files, ca. 1541-1901, 30 ft. Primarily consists of over 12,000 printed libretti; also, "Operngeschichte Statistik"--60 card files of information about opera performances (title, composer, librettist, genre, number of acts, and date, city, and theater of premiere) plus shorter card catalogues of listings by title and librettist; notes; correspondence; manuscripts of articles; and clippings--all pertaining to the history of opera in Europe and the United States. Libretti and manuscripts have been microfilmed.

49 Kurt Schindler (1882-1935). Dunja, a Bessarabian song of the Danube, for mixed chorus and alto-solo, a cappella (ca. 1917), autograph, 5 ll., English version from the Little Russian by D. Taylor and Schindler; the dying harper (David of the White Rock [Dafydd y Gareg Wen]), English words by John Ozenford, Old Welsh folk melody, choral setting with harp accompaniment (ca. 1917), autograph, 4 pp., quartet for mixed voices; The goldfinch's wedding, humorous part-song of Little Russia after the setting by A. Koshitz, for mixed chorus a cappella, English version by Deems Taylor and Schindler [1917], holograph, 3 ll.,

written on one side; The home of liberty [Cariwyd y dydd], Old Welsh fighting song, English words by Walter Maynard, setting for mixed chorus by Schindler (1917), holograph, 4 pp., quartet for mixed chorus without accompaniment; El Paño, Spanish folksong from Andalusia, choral setting by Schindler (1917), holograph, 6 pp., sextet for mixed voices, unaccompanied; The prisoner in the Caucasus, Cossack lament for male chorus after a Little Russian folksong set by Kurt Schindler, English version by Deems Taylor and Schindler [1917], autograph part-song, a cappella, 6 ll.; Serenade de Murica, paraphrase for baritone solo and choral accompaniment (1917), autograph vocal score, unaccompanied, 7 pp.; The three cavaliers, humoresque, Russian folksong, choral setting and English version after a song by A. Dargomyshky, for mezzo soprano solo and mixed chorus, a cappella (1917), autograph, 5 ll.; and Alexander Tikhonovich Grechaninov's The hymn of Free Russia (March 1917) (Gimn svobodnoi Rossii), arranged and edited by Kurt Schindler (poem by Konstantin Balmont, music by Grechaninov), English translation by Vera and Kurt Schindler (1917), autograph song, piano accompaniment, 4 ll.

50 Arnold Schoenberg (1874-1951). Papers, ca. 1907-51, 4 ft. Includes a letter of Wassily Kandinsky concerning his esthetic philosophy (Schoenberg exhibited his paintings with the Blue Rider group in 1912). Also, the holograph musical work entitled A Survivor from Warsaw (1947), Schoenberg's personal and business correspondence, concert programs, and clippings. Requires permission of the Schoenberg estate to use; preliminary inquiries should be addressed to the Music Division.

51 Charles Louis Seeger (1886-1979). Collection, 1930s, 2 ft. (in process). Music and other materials relating to the Workers Music League (WML), an affiliate of the International Music Bureau, established in New York City in 1931. Includes WML songbooks, concert programs, news clippings, notes, and sheet music from the USSR, England, and the U.S.

52 Fabien Sevitzky (Koussevitzky) (1893-1967). Papers, 1933-52, 1 ft., 1,122 items. Russian-born conductor came to America in 1923. Papers include correspondence with Paul Kletzki and others attempting to find employment for Kletzki in the United States, and with Arcady Dubensky. (NUCMC 67-660)

53 Alexander Siloti (1863-1945). Papers, 1935, 11 items. Correspondence concerning his proposed emendations to the Scherzo of Beethoven's 9th Symphony. Correspondents include Sergei Rachmaninoff, Ernest Hutcheson, Pablo Casals, Walter Damrosch, and Joseph Achron. Also, listing of musical performances of works introduced into Russia by Siloti in the early part of this century.

54 Valentin Silvestrov (b. 1937). Eschatophony (1966), score for orchestra, holograph in ink, 101 pp., dedicated to the memory of Serge Koussevitzky; plus a photocopy of same.

55 Aleksandr Nikolaevich Skriabin (1872-1915). Cinquième sonate, for piano, op. 53, in F major [1911?], publisher's proof with the composer's corrections in red ink, 19 ll. (published, 1911).

56 Nicolas Slonimsky (b. 1894). Papers, 1895-1969, 24 ft. (additions expected). Russian-born conductor, composer, and musicologist who emigrated to the U.S. in 1923. Correspondents include Aaron Avshalomoff, Vladimir Dukelsky (Vernon Duke), Alexander Grechaninoff, Nicolas Nabokoff, and Serge Prokofiev. There are also drafts of his writings and over 20 holograph scores of Slonimsky, including Studies in Black and White. Partial contents list. (NUCMC 70-2026)

57 Patty Stair (1869-1926). Carpathian folk song, male voices with orchestra [1911], autograph full score, 16 pp., lent by the composer; and Refusal, words by A. Maykov, music by P. Stair (n.d.), autograph song, piano accompaniment, 4 pp., dedicated to Ernestine Schumann-Heink.

58 Leopold Stokowski (1882-1977). Symphonic transcription of Modeste Moussorgskii's Tableaux d'une exposition [194-?], score, arranger's manuscript in pencil of the suite originally for piano, 96 pp., program notes by the arranger, typescript, mounted on cover.

59 Igor Fedorovich Stravinsky (1882-1971). Agon, ballet for twelve dancers (1957), score, holograph in pencil, 88 pp., arranged for two pianos, accompaniment originally for orchestra (published, 1957); Apollon-Musagète, ballet in two scenes (1928), score for string orchestra, holograph in ink, 70 pp., with letter of authenticity from G. Paitchadze (22 October 1928) to Carl Engel laid in (commissioned by the Elizabeth Sprague Coolidge Foundation), plus negative and positive photocopies of the same; same work, photocopy (negative) of composer's reduction for piano, originally for string orchestra, 1927, 38 pp., plus a positive photocopy of the same; Babel, cantata for chorus, orchestra, and narrator, in English (1944), score, holograph in ink on transparent paper, 23 ll., chorus for men's voices, words from the Book of Genesis (published, 1952); the same work, condensed score, holograph in ink on transparent paper, 19 ll., plus a reproduction of the same (black-line print) (1944); Le baiser de la fée, ballet, score for orchestra, holograph in pencil with additions and corrections in red pencil at end: 30 oct. 1928 à minuit et à Nice, 167 pp.; Ballad for violin and piano from Le baiser de la fée, the violin part established in collaboration with Jeanne

Gautier [1951], score, holograph in ink on transparent paper, 17 ll., originally for orchestra (published, 1951); Cantata, for mezzo-soprano, tenor, female choir, and small instrumental ensemble, anonymous 15th-16th c. lyrics, in English, music by Stravinsky (1952), score, holograph in ink on transparent paper, 84 ll., accompaniment for two flutes, two oboes, English horn, and violoncello, holograph sketch in pencil, 4 ll., laid in (published, 1952); Canticum sacrem, as honorem Sancti Marci nominis (1955), piano-vocal score, in Latin, for solo voices (TB), chorus (SATB), and piano, accompaniment originally for orchestra, holograph in pencil on transparent paper, 56 ll. (published, 1956); Circus polka, for piano, composed for a young elephant [1942], holograph in ink, 14 pp. (published, 1942); Concerto in D for string orchestra (1946), score, holograph in ink, 57 ll. (published, 1947); Concerto pour piano et orchestre d'harmonie (1924), score, holograph in ink, 95 pp., with corrections in pencil and red ink, composer's addition of caption title with date, 1931, possibly refers to corrections, composer's notes on performance dates on inside back cover (published, 1936); Credo (orthodox), new 1964 version (1964), score, holograph in pencil on transparent paper, 6 ll., written in Church Slavonic language with phonetics in English letters (as the first one, 1932), for chorus (SATB) (published, 1966); Ebony concerto (1945), score for clarinet and jazz ensemble, holograph in ink on transparent paper, 45 ll., dedicated to Woody Herman and his orchestra (published, 1946), plus a photocopy of the same; Élégie (1944), for viola, holograph in ink on transparent paper, 3 ll. (published, 1945); same work, arranged for two violas [1944], score, holograph in ink on transparent paper, 3 ll.; same work, arranged for violin (1944), holograph in ink on transparent paper, 3 ll. (published, 1945); Elegy for J. F. K., by Wystan Auden and Igor Stravinsky (1964), score, for baritone and three clarinets, holograph in pencil, 5 ll.; 4 [i.e. Quatre] études pour orchestre (1928), score, holograph in pencil, 8, 10, 8, 21 pp.; The flood (1962), score, English, holograph of the musical play, in pencil, on transparent paper, 80 ll., text chosen and arranged by Robert Craft from the Book of Genesis and the York and Chester cycles of miracle plays (published, 1963); Eight instrumental miniatures (1962), score, 17 ll., for two flutes, two oboes, two clarinets, two bassoons, horn, two violins, two violas, and two violoncellos in varying combinations (published, 1963); Introitus, T. S. Eliot in memoriam (1965), score, for chorus (TB), harp, piano, four percussion players, viola, and double bass, Latin words, holograph in pencil on transparent paper, 10 ll. (published, 1965); Mass for a mixed chorus and a double wind quintet (1948), score, for solo voices (SATB), chorus (SSAATTBB), two oboes, English horn, two bassoons, two trumpets, and three trombones, holograph in ink on transparent paper, 15, 24, 28, 21, 10 ll. (published, 1948); Russian maiden's song (Devich'i pesni) [Mavra. Drug moi milyi], lyrics by B. Kochno after A. S. Pushkin, English translation by R. Burness, music by Stravinsky [1947], holograph in ink on transparent paper, 7 ll., accompaniment originally for orchestra (published, 1948); Monumentum pro Gesualdo di Venosa ad CD annum, 3 madrigals recomposed for instruments, 1960, score, holograph in pencil on transparent paper, 16 ll., based on madrigals from libro 5 and 6, by Gesualdo (published, 1960); Four Norwegian moods, for orchestra (1942), score, holograph in pencil, 47 pp. (published, 1944); Ode, in three parts, for orchestra [1943], orchestra score, holograph in pencil, 24 pp., in memory of Natalie C. Koussevitzky (published, 1947); Oedipus rex (1927), libretto by Jean Cocteau, based on Sohpocles' Oedipus tyrannus, holograph of the opera-oratorio in ink, 128 (i.e., 100) ll. (published, 1928); Petrouchka, holograph sketches in pencil of an arrangement for the Pleyela (player-piano), 4 pp., originally for orchestra; Three songs from William Shakespeare (1953), score, holograph in pencil on transparent paper, 8, 4, 5 ll., for mezzo-soprano, flute, clarinet, and viola (published, 1954); Suite pour violon et piano, after themes, fragments, and pieces of Giambatista Pergolesi (1925), score, holograph in ink with corrections in pencil, 21 pp. (published, 1926); Symphonie en ut, score, composer's holograph in pencil, 1 l. + 88 pp. + 1 l. + 89-209 pp., signed and dated in ink at end: Igor Strawinsky, Beverly Hills, August 19/1940, dedicated to the Chicago Symphony Orchestra on its 50th anniversary; Symphonies d'instruments à vent (1920-47), score, holograph in ink on transparent paper, 35 ll., to the memory of Claude Achille Debussy, revised version, for wind instruments (published, 1952); Tango, arranged for two pianos by Victor Babin [194-?], score, arranger's manuscript in ink, with corrections in red ink by the composer, 5 pp. (published, 1962), with two letters concerning the work from the composer in Russian, 7 August and 5 September 1941, and pencilled corrections for the music, in his hand, 1 l., laid in; another manuscript of the same work [194-], score, in ink, with additions in pencil, 5 pp., incorporating composer's corrections; Variations, Aldous Huxley in memoriam (1964), orchestral score, holograph in pencil on transparent paper, 13 ll. (published, 1965); facsimile of the preceding, with composer's extensive corrections and alterations in red and blue ink, plus another facsimile of the same, with composer's minor manuscript corrections, and publisher's first and second proofs, with composer's corrections, 25 ll. each, laid in; his arrangement of Petr I. Chaikovskii's Pas de deux (Bluebird) from the ballet The Sleeping Beauty, for small chamber orchestra (1941), score, arranger's manuscript in pencil, 26 pp. (published, 1953); and The Star-Spangled Banner, a standardized version of the melody (words by Francis Scott Key, music doubtfully ascribed to John Stafford Smith), harmonized by Walter Damrosch, published score (New York, [1937?]) with Stravinsky's red-pencil markings, apparently used as a source for his arrangements of the work: harmonization of the Star-Spangled Banner by Stravinsky (1941), score, arranger's ms. in ink, 3 pp., for chorus (SATB) and orchestra (published, 1941), with letters, photocopied sources, telegrams, and press notices laid in, plus a photocopy of this work without the laid-in material, and a second harmonization of the same work (1941), score, 3 pp., for chorus (SATB) and piano (published, 1941), plus negative and positive photocopies of this work.

60 Joseph Strimer (1881-1962). Horovod (Round dance with singing), for four-part mixed chorus, unaccompanied (ca. 1935), score, holograph, 1 l. + 5 pp., Russian text; his arrangement of a Gopak (after Moussorgskii and Ukrainian folk songs), for choir a cappella (four-part mixed chorus), Ukrainian text (ca. 1936), score, holograph, 2 ll.; arrangement of Chopin's Tristesse [op. 10, no. 3], for four-part mixed chorus and soprano solo, unaccompanied (ca. 1936), score, 2 ll., Russian text; and his arrangement of Yar-hmel (Spring-hops) from the opera La fiancée du Tsar by Nikolai Rimskii-Korsakov, for four-part mixed chorus a cappella (ca. 1936), score, 2 ll., Russian text.

61 Burnet Corwin Tuthill (b. 1888). His arrangement of Sergei Rachmaninoff's Serenade in B♭ minor [Morceaux de fantaisie] for piano, op. 3 1914, score, 7 pp., and part (published edition of A. Siloti [New York], with revisions in green pencil by the arranger, part in ink.

62 (Michelle) Pauline Viardot-Garcia (1821-1910). Etoile du soir, song with piano accompaniment, French text, holograph, 1 l., signed at the bottom: Pauline Garcia, and Francfort a 18 Aout 1838; [Vocal cadenza for an opera of Gluck], first line: Je vais braver le trépas, 1 l., holograph, signed and dated at end: Pauline Viardot, souvenir a monsieur [H. F.] Kufferath. Paris le 16 sebre. 1859; [Vocal cadenzas for various Italian operas] (1882?), holograph in pencil, 4 ll., written in an album, with the composer's visiting card bearing a holograph dedication to Antonia Kufferath for whom the cadenzas were written; and Vocalises and cadenzas for various opera arias (n.d.), pencil holograph, 23 ll., written for frau Gertrud Seeger-Engel.

63 Nicolai von Wilm (1834-1911). Humoreske, op. 47, no. 2, for piano, two hands (n.d.), autograph, 7 pp., with a note at the end: Dieses autograph schenkte mir der Autor beim abschied von Wiesbaden den 30. Nov. 1890 zugleich mit Op. 47. 1. Arthur Smolian; and Romance, op. 47, no. 1 (n.d.), for piano, two hands, 6 pp., with a similar note at the end.

Facsimile manuscripts (see also preceding section)

64 Johann Rudolph Zumsteeg (1760-1802). Das tartarische gesez, eine oper in zwey aufzugen, n.d., text by Friedrich Wilhelm Gotter, manuscript, perhaps autograph, 114 ll., full score, date of first performance, at Stuttgart, unknown.

65 Victor Babin (1908-1972). Etudes, two pianos (1936-38), score, positive photocopy of holograph, 25 pp.

66 Nikolai Lopatnikoff (1903-1976). Arabesque, for two pianos [194-], score, photoreproduction of holograph, 15 pp., with holograph corrections in pencil and a holograph, in ink, of five measures mounted (p. 14) to facilitate page turn, composer's arrangement from his unpublished orchestral work Russian nocturne no. 2 (published, 1948); Festival overture, op. 40 [1960], score, photoreproduction of holograph, 83 pp. (published, 1965); II [i.e., Seconde] symphonie, op. 24, in F minor [194-?], score, photoreproduction of holograph, 132 pp., Andante (second movement) replaces the second and third movements of the original version (1939); Symphony no. 3, op. 35 [195-?], score, photoreproduction of holograph, 153 pp. (published, 1956); and Variazioni concertanti, op. 38 [1958], score, photoreproduction of holograph, 112 pp. (published, 1968).

67 Aleksei Fedorovich L'vov (1798-1870). Piesn' russkikh [Bozhe, Tsaria khrani], arrangement for tenor and orchestra (1834), score, photocopy of holograph, 13 ll.

68 Nikolai Iakovlevich Miaskovskii (1881-1950). Symphonie no. 17, op. 41, in C# minor [1937], score, negative photocopy of holograph, 253 ll.

69 Sergei Rachmaninoff (1873-1943). Monna Vanna, piano-vocal score [1907], act one of an unfinished opera, positive microfilm copy of holograph in ink with pencil, 100 pp., sketches laid in, in slipcase with manuscript of the libretto by M. A. Slonov, plus negative microfilm of the same.

70 Lazare Saminsky (1882-1959). Eon hours, a concerto for vocal quartet, piano, viola, clarinet, and percussion, op. 44 (1935), piano-vocal score, positive photocopy of holograph, 27 pp.; From Psalm of the west, for chorus, organ, piano, and percussion, poem by Sidney Lanier [n.p.] (1947), score, reproduced from holograph, 4 pp.; and A sonnet of Petrarch (Gli angeli eletti), for flutes (or organ), violin, viola, piano, and three sopranos [1947], score, positive photocopy of holograph, 7 pp.

71 Igor' Fedorovich Stravinskii (1882-1971). Babel, cantata for chorus, orchestra, and narrator [n.p., 1945?], condensed score, blackline print from holograph, 19 ll.; Mass for a mixed chorus and a double wind-quintet [n.p., ca. 1946], score (1. vol.), reproduced from holograph; Petrouchka (ca. 1946), score, bal-

let, photocopy of holograph, 2 vols., 174 pp.; and Praeludium (ca. 1937), orchestral score, positive photostat of composer's holograph, 5 ll.

72 Note: In addition, the Music Division holds an album of autographs, mostly from Paris, 1834-53, 44 ll., compiled by Count Anatole Nicolaevich Demidoff (1812-1870), mainly pieces by prominent Western European composers (no Russians identified).

DC 25
RECORDED SOUND SECTION
MUSIC DIVISION
LIBRARY OF CONGRESS
10 First Street SE
Washington, D.C. 20540
(202-426-5508/5509)

Collections include the Office of War Information Collection, National Press Club Collection, United Nations Records Collection, 1946-63, and others with scattered Russian/Soviet-related material from the early 1940s to the present. Individual items include recordings of literary figures such as Andrei Voznesensky, Evgenii Evtushenko, M. Gorkii, Valentin Kataev, and A. Solzhenitsyn; of musical composers and musicians (e.g., Gregor Piatigorsky, Sergei Rachmaninoff, and Alexander Siloti); of singers like Feodor Shaliapin; and of political leaders such as Nikita Khrushchev and V. Molotov. Unpublished recordings are too vast to attempt a representative sampling, however. There are finding aids for some of the larger collections.

DC 26
PRINTS AND PHOTOGRAPHS DIVISION
LIBRARY OF CONGRESS
2nd Street and Independence Avenue SE
Washington, D.C. 20540
(202-287-6394)

1 Lot 159, on microfilm. Photos of Russian war anniversary, Washington, D.C., June 1942. Chorus and Paul Robeson on stage and backstage with autograph hunters; Mme Litvinoff, wife of Russian ambassador; Melvyn Douglas, conductor and soloist of Balalaika orchestra.

2 Lot 2444. 72 photographs, ca. 1918. Scenes of Vladivostok, Manchuria, and Siberian localities; military personnel, groups; Red Cross at work; headquarters building; officers of various nationalities; various official activities; close-up portraits of Russians and Americans; refugees. Photographs received through the Siberian commission of the American Red Cross.

3 Lots 2559, 2624 (Noble Collection). 29 postcard views of Portsmouth, New Hampshire, during the peace negotiations for the Russo-Japanese War, 1908, and 30 portraits and informal group photographs of Russian and Japanese peace envoys.

4 Lot 2691. Ca. 20 chromo-lithographic postcards, 1899. Scenes of Siberia: lakes, forests, snow; transportation by ox-cart, sled, and horse; pagodaed homes.

5 Lot 2692 (Tass Poster Collection). Ca. 115 colored posters, 1940-44 (?). The posters, issued by Tass during World War II, satirize the German war effort and call upon the Russian people to repel the invasion.

6 Lot 2746. 13 chromo-lithographs. Scenes from the history of Nizni-Novgorod from 1171-to 1612: election of princes; invasion by Tartar tribes; annexation in 1517 by the Russians; army saving Moscow from the Poles in 1612. Confiscated in Germany by U.S. military intelligence authorities.

7 Lots 2916-2919, 3027, 3029-30, 3052-53, 3147 (American National Red Cross Collection). Ca. 570 photographs, 1919-21. Life, war, and conflict in Siberia: U.S. troops and officials; Czechoslovak troops fighting Bolshevik forces; Cossack troops; General A. I. Denikin, General Skouro, P. N. Wrangel, Sultan Philimonoff, Countess Tolstoi, Mme Breshkovsky.

8 Lot 3098 (Pauley Mission Collection). 1 album of photographs from a Chinese source, showing Soviet troops moving equipment; a few photographs of Pauley during his mission to Manchuria, 1946.

9 Lot 3327 (Fugiwara Collection). 12 captioned photographs, 1897. Scenes of Eskimo life in Alaska and Siberia.

10 Lot 3372. 80 stereoscopic photographs, 1905. Scenes of the Russo-Japanese War: Russian soldiers in trenches, camps, barricades; guns and equipment; Russian priest praying over the dead; Red Cross activities; towns, destroyed buildings; waterfront, burning and sinking ships.

11 Lot 3635 (German Prisoner of War Camp Collection). 45 photographs, 1914-18. Photographs of Russian prisoners of war at German prison camps at Wunsdorf, near Berlin.

12 Lot 4027 (Spas-Nereditsy Collection). 164 mounted photoprints of the Byzantine 12th c. fresco paintings on the walls of the Church of the Savior at Nereditsa, made in 1903 by the Imperial Archeological Commission. From the library of the Russian Imperial family.

13 Lot 4487 (Taylor Collection). 75 photocopies of sketches by Bayard Taylor, American author, diplomat, and traveller, pertaining to salt

mines and prisoners being sent to Siberia, ca. 1860.

14 Lot 4708. Photocopies of original contemporary historical prints and reproductions of the Crimean War, 1853-56.

15 Lot 5090 (Yudin Collection of Siberian and Mongolian Sketches). Album of 333 original pencil and wash drawings, 1860-1910, of persons, landscapes, and buildings, probably made in Siberia and Mongolia.

16 Lot 5178 (Persian Gulf Command Collection). 14 photograph albums, 4,500 photographs. Official photographs of operations during World War II in Iran, concerning particularly the supply line for the shipment of war materiel to Russia.

17 Lots 5258-5270 (National Council of American-Soviet Friendship Collection). 404 photoprints concerning Russia in the late 1940s. Work and cultural activities; factories and schools; agriculture; Timiryazev Agricultural Academy activities; collection farms; life in the Buryat-Mongolian Autonomous Republic; elections; shrines associated with Pushkin; a congress of Soviet composers; other subjects.

18 Lot 5712 (Van Norman Collection). 75 captioned photographs, 1918-21. Included are pictures of Bolshevik prisoners in Poland.

19 Lots 5827-5839, 5842, 5849 (Diafoto Collection). Transparencies on the creation and development of the Bolshevik party in Russia; Novgorod; the works of I. V. Michurin and T. S. Lysenko; and the tundra zone.

20 Lot 6999 (Russian Gold Mining Collection). 9 photographs, ca. 1890, of Ariz, a village in South Central Asia, and of gold mining apparently in the vicinity.

21 Lot 7017 (Russian Toy Exhibit Collection). 12 photoprints, ca. 1900. Exhibits cases and general displays of toys and educational devices at an unidentified museum or exposition. Purchased as part of the library of G. V. Yudin in 1907.

22 Lot 7042 (Evreinova Collection). 15 photoprints, 1892. Russian churches and monasteries at Uglich. The portfolio containing the photoprints has the cover: Uglich i ego Dostoprimechatel'nosti. Fotograficheskii al'bom. Uglich, Izdanie K. Evreinova, 1892. Purchased as part of the library of G. V. Yudin in 1907.

23 Lot 7043 (Kuznetsov Collection). 43 photoprints, ca. 1885. Views in and near Nerchinsk in southeast Siberia, near the Mongolian-Manchurian border, showing gold mining buildings and operation. The materials relating to natives concerns mainly the Buryat tribes near Lake Baikal. The portfolio containing the photoprints has a title page: Al'bom 'vidov' Nerchinska Priislov i zavodov. Purchased as part of the library of G. V. Yudin, 1907.

24 Lot 7044 (Russian Southwest Railway Collection). 30 photoprints, 1890-94. Views of construction, stations, tunnels, locomotives, and groups of personnel along the line of the southwest railway along the Dniester River and in the Ukraine, 1890-94. The album containing the photoprints has a cover title: Obshchestvo Iugo-Zapadnye Zheleznye Dorogi, Postroika Nosvoselitskikh Vetvei. 1890-1894. Al'bom fotograficheskikh vidov.

25 Lot 7047 (Babine Collection). Ca. 150 items, 1883-1916. Includes postcards pertaining to the Russian revolution of 1905 and to the production of war materiel (116).

26 Lot 7048 (Russian Historical Portrait Collection). 1 album. Mostly clippings from published sources of Russian scientists, artists, and intellectuals, and of events connected with the revolutionary movement in Russia.

27 Lot 7198. 8 plates (14 reproductions of photographs), 1955. Scenes of collective farming in Siberia.

28 Lot 7213. 29 photographs, ca. 1917. U.S. troops in Khabarovsk and Valdivostok; views of Archangel; celebration of the Russian Revolution; a convict colony; the Peking-Paris auto race.

29 Lot 7354. 66 photographs and a pamphlet, 6 pp., 1954, pertaining to the celebration in the USSR of the tercentenary of the unification of the Ukraine and Russia.

30 Lot 7576 (Harbord Collection). 741 photoprints (in 10 portfolios), 1888-1900. Scenes of Georgia and other parts of Transcaucasia in the late 19th c. and perhaps early 20th c., from a Russian commercial house, assembled and presented by General James G. Harbord in 1923.

31 Lot 7702. 24 photographs, 1904-1905 [?]. Unidentified military personnel, mainly high-ranking officers, probably non-belligerent observers in the Russo-Japanese War.

32 Lot 7729 (Pershing Collection). 14 vols., 1902-21. Includes captioned photographs of the equipment and operations of the Japanese army at the time of the Russo-Japanese War.

33 Lot 7776. Photographs of the Peace Conference at Portsmouth, New Hampshire, after the Russo-Japanese War.

34 Lot 8823. 12 lithographs, ca. 1906. Scenes of the Russo-Japanese War: the landing of the Japanese army at Vladivostok, the battle of Ussuri, cavalry taking Khabarovsk.

35 Lot 8240. 57 wood engravings, 1879. Railroad-building and related activities in Rumania and Bulgaria during the Russo-Turkish War of 1877.

36 Lot 8488. 17 lithographs, 1878-79. Scenes of Bulgaria during the Russo-Turkish War, 1878-79.

37 Lot 8631. 27 photographs, 1904. Scenes of Jinsen, Korea, during the Russo-Japanese War.

38 Lots 8700-1, 8715. Ca. 65 photographs, 1959. Scenes of Siberia, Lake Baikal, Irkutsk, Ulan Ude.

39 Lot 9760 (Jackson Collection). 40 photographs, 1895. Scenes of Siberia and its people, including Vladivostok from the sea, churches and other buildings in Irkutsk, and Goldi tribesmen.

40 Lots 10332-10343 (S. M. Prokudin-Gorskii Collection). Ca. 2,700 photographs, 1909-12. The Marinska, a canal system joining the Neva to the headwaters of the Volga; Tolstoi in his study at Yasnaya Polyana; the area served by the rail line between the towns of Lodeinoye Pole and Kem; the Ural industrial area; the Caucasus; Russian areas involved in the Napoleonic campaign; Bukhara, Samarkand, and the Golodnaia steppe; the Volga River in various sections of Russia; engineering on the Oka.

41 Lot 10499. Ca. 10 photographs, 1961. President John F. Kennedy's meeting with Nikita Khrushchev in Vienna.

42 Lot 11119. 7 photographs. The Romanov family at Tsarskoe Selo during their internment in 1917.

43 Lot 11148. 550 photographs, 1904-25. Includes news photographs of members of the Russian Imperial family.

44 Lot 11116. Includes ca. 20 photographs, 1914-16, of Russian troops in France.

45 Lot 11170. 65 newsphotoprints, 1914-17. Includes items on the Russian army on the eastern front.

46 Lot 11457. 30 glass plate copy negatives, 1918-19. Allied military activities in Russia.

47 Carpenter Collection (Russia). Photographs, 1931, 2 ft. Russian émigrés and people and places in the Soviet Union.

48 Deck 1 (Chadbourne Collection). Includes original 19th c. Japanese woodcuts, printed in colors, on the visit of a Russian naval squadron in Nagasaki in 1804-1805.

49 Geographic File (Russia). Photographs, 2 ft. Buildings in Russia. Not cataloged.

50 Office of War Information Collection (Russia). Photographs, ca. 1941-45, 4 ft. Conditions in the Soviet Union; Nazi atrocities in Russia. Not fully cataloged.

51 Red Cross Collection (Russia). Photographs, 1910s, 4 ft., pertaining to conditions in Russia. Not cataloged.

52 Stereographic Collection (Russia). Ca. 650 stereographs pertaining to Russia. Included are scenes of the Russo-Japanese War, Kiev, Moscow, St. Petersburg, Cossacks, and of the tsar and royalty.

Note: The following collections, cited in Vanderbilt (see below), have been lost, dispersed, or become part of other collections: Alexander II Collection, Bristol Collection, William Eleroy Curtis Collection, Kun Collection, Kalugin Collection, Noyes Collection.

Finding Aids: In addition to the card catalogue, which describes collections in detail, see Paul Vanderbilt, Guide to the Special Collections of Prints and Photographs in the Library of Congress (Washington, 1955), used extensively in writing this entry.

DC 27
RARE BOOK AND SPECIAL COLLECTIONS DIVISION
LIBRARY OF CONGRESS
10 First Street SE
Washington, D.C. 20540
(202-426-5435)

1 Comte Nicolas de Romanzoff (Rumiantsov) (1750-1826). Russian minister of commerce and statesman. Presentation inscription, signed, in Gosudarstvennaia torgovlia 1802 goda v raznykh eia vidakh, 1 of 3 vols. for years 1802-1804 that contain detailed tables of Russian commerce. Inscription dated 6 July 1806. (Part of Thomas Jefferson Library, for which there is a multi-volume published guide.)

2 Lessing J. Rosenwald Collection. Includes ms. of part of chapter 3, part 2, of Nikolai Vasilevich Gogol's Mertvyia Dushi ([Moscow], 1855), 20 pp., with cover title and 13 original unpublished drawings of Pavel Petrovich Sokolov (1826-1905). A Catalog of the Gifts of Lessing J. Rosenwald to the Library of Congress, 1943 to 1975 (Washington, 1977).

3 Robert E. Sherwood (b. 1896). Playwright. Carbon typescript, 116 ll., of his drama "There shall be no night" (New York City, 1940) about the Russo-Finnish War.

4 John Boyd Thacher Autograph Collection. Section for European Notables includes: ALS, n.d., from the duke of Morny, 1811-1865, natural son of Hortense, queen of Holland, and married to Princess Sophie Troubetzkoi, to a friend, referring to his mother-in-law,

the Princess Troubetzkoi, and her husband, "les plus grands seigneurs de Russie, d'une fortune collossale, et aussi bonnes gens et simples que possibles" (item 1168); ALS, n.d., from Matilde Letitia Wilhelmine Bonaparte (1820-1904), daughter of King Jerome and married to Prince Anatole Demidov, letter of polite acknowledgment (item 1180); LS, Paris, 3 April 1839, from Prince Anatole Demidov (1813-1870) to Mr. Cherubini, requesting a loge at an approaching concert of the Conservatoire (item 1181); ALS, Breczin, 29 January 1813, from Romain Saltyk Gabriel Oginski to Baron Bignon, explaining that he had left Wilna 2 hours after the departure of Napoleon to avoid capture by the Russians and appealing for help, as he is without resources (item 1219); DS, Drysniaty 17 July 1812, of Charles Nicolas Oudinot (1767-1847), an order during the invasion of Russia, and an ALS, n.d., letter of thanks (item 1220); and DS, Walkowitz 16 October (1813?), of Joseph Anthony Poniatowski (1763-1814), an order to reconnoiter (item 1222). See The Collection of John Boyd Thacher in the Library of Congress, 3 vols. (Washington, 1931).

5 Triod Tsvietnaia. Liturgical manuscript, 16th-17th c., 1 vol. From a western Ukrainian monastery, possibly in the region of Zbarazh near Tarnopol; for the Ukrainian Catholic (Uniate) Church, with hymns and music, on paper; plus a detailed analysis in Russian of the manuscript by Dr. Panteleimon K. Kovaliv, a Ukrainian philologist and paleographer, 1959, 9 pp.

6 Note: There are additional Russian-related materials in such holdings as the Russian Imperial (Winter Palace) Collection, the personal library of the tsars (ca. 2,400 vols., some with presentation inscriptions written in English or Russian by members of the Imperial family) and the broadsides collection.

DC 28
CYRIL MUROMCEW--PRIVATE COLLECTION
3005 34th Street NW
Washington, D.C. 20008
(202-338-1429)

Collection pertaining to Sergei Alexandrovich Muromtsev (1850-1910), professor, jurist, a founder of the Kadet Party, and chairman of the first Duma--biographical data, photographs, and a collection of eulogies. Also, autobiography of Alexander Wolkoff-Mouromtsev, art critic, and some material relating to the Baku Oil Fields ca. 1912. Includes genealogical material concerning the family from the 14th c. to the present. Inquire concerning access.

DC 29
THE LIBRARY
NATIONAL ARBORETUM
24th and R Street NE
Washington, D.C. 20002
(202-472-9264)

The library has several thousand photographs of trees and plant specimens in Russia at the turn of the century up to the 1930s. The photos were taken by U.S. Department of Agriculture plant explorers, particularly Mr. Frank Meyer, 1906-17, and Messrs. Westover and Enlow, 1930s. Staff requests advance notice from those wishing to use the collection.

DC 30
NATIONAL ARCHIVES AND RECORDS SERVICE
8th Street and Pennsylvania Avenue NW
Washington, D.C. 20408
(202-523-3218)

The National Archives houses the records of the U.S. government and contains millions of paper documents, still pictures, maps, charts, and other materials. The great size of these holdings precludes a complete description of all their Russian-related materials.

All that has been done here, therefore, is to provide an overview of items pertaining to Russia/USSR among various National Archives record groups ("RG"). Some of these items may be widely scattered throughout a record group and may be difficult to locate. It is suggested, therefore, that researchers contact the National Archives operating unit in charge of specific record groups before attempting to examine the materials they contain. List of Record Groups of the National Archives and Records Service (October 1976, to be updated) lists which operating units (e.g., Diplomatic, Military) have responsibility for a given record group. Note: With a few exceptions, the total size and inclusive dates of record groups below are taken from the 1976 revised looseleaf edition of the Guide to the National Archives of the United States. These measurements and dates are, of course, subject to change and may be already outdated.

1 RG 1. Records of the War Labor Policies Board, 1918-19, 12 cu. ft. The War Labor Policies Board was created in 1918 to standardize labor policies of government agencies. Its records include a report by Herbert E. Cory, an assistant for the Board, on socialization in the Soviet Union.

2 RG 5. Records of the United States Grain Corporation, 1917-32, 198 cu. ft. Organized in 1919, the U.S. Grain Corporation was involved in Russian relief after World War I.

Its records include materials relating to the Baltic and Polish Missions of the American Relief Administration and to the interest of the Supreme Economic Council and the Inter-Allied Food Commission in the economic conditions of southern Russia.

3 RG 9. Records of the National Recovery Administration, 1927-37, 5,199 cu. ft. Formed in 1933, the National Recovery Administration (NRA) aimed to improve industry, trade, and employment during the Depression. Its records include letters and reports, 1933-34, that shed light on protests against Soviet exports of matches, horsehair, sunflower oil, manganese, and pearl essence.

4 RG 11. General Records of the United States Government, 1778-1974, 2,070 cu. ft. This record group contains international treaties and agreements signed by the United States. Among the Russian-related documents are the Convention as to the Pacific Ocean and the Northwest coast of America, 1824, the Treaty of Navigation and Commerce of 1832, the Convention Ceding Alaska, 1867, the Extradition Convention of 1887, and the North Pacific Sealing Convention of 1911. There are also small-scale maps of Russia in the 18th and 19th c. and a manuscript plan of Sitka, Alaska compiled in 1867 and later published in H. Ex. Doc. 125, 40th Congress, ed. session, Serial 1337.

5 RG 14. Records of the United States Railroad Administration, 1917-45, 1,353 cu. ft. The U.S. Railroad Administration (USRA) controlled railroads and other forms of transportation for the federal government. Its records include materials on the construction of 200 American locomotives for the Russian government and Soviet attempts to get this equipment. There are also records, 1919-22, pertaining to the seniority rights of former Russian Railway Service Corps employees who went back to work in the U.S. Finally, there are letters and memoranda on the unwillingness of Seattle longshoremen to ship arms and munitions to Siberia.

6 RG 18. Records of the Army Air Forces, 1914-52, 11,564 cu. ft. Originating in 1907, the Army Air Forces (AAF) was a predecessor of the U.S. Air Force. Its records contain materials on Soviet aviation, including a report by the Wright Aeronautical Corporation, 1932; letters on a flight from the USSR to the U.S. via the the North Pole; photographs of Kamchatka, and correspondence pertaining to Soviet aviation students in the U.S. and to Soviet requests, 1934-38, for Air Corps materiel.

7 RG 16. Records of the Office of the Secretary of Agriculture, 1839-1969, 7,949 cu. ft. The Department of Agriculture was created in 1862. Its records include correspondence on Bolshevism, 1919-20, 1922-23, 1926, 1930, communism, 1931-34, 1936-7, 1939, and the recognition of the Soviet Union, 1933-35. There are also materials relating to seed and plant distribution from foreign seed firms and consular officials.

8 RG 19. Records of the Bureau of Ships, 1775-1949, 17,194 cu. ft. The Bureau of Ships is the successor of several government agencies that handled ships and other craft. Its records include photos of Russian naval vessels, 1900 and 1915, correspondence on lend-lease naval equipment to the Soviet Union, 1941-45, and materials on tools and equipment bought by the Amtorg Corp., 1937-39.

9 RG 20. Records of the Office of the Special Adviser to the President on Foreign Trade, 1934-36, 57 cu. ft. The Office of the Special Adviser to the President on Foreign Trade was created in 1934. Its records include data on exports and imports between the U.S. and the USSR, 1922-34. There are also copies of commercial agreements, 1934-35, between the Soviet government and England, France, and Latvia.

10 RG 22. Records of the Fish and Wildlife Service, 1868-1961, 884 cu. ft. The Fish and Wildlife Service was created in 1940. Its records contain materials on the North Pacific Sealing Convention and considerable documentation on the Russian fur-seal industry in the Pribilof Islands during the early 19th c. There is also a report, dated 1917, on salmon fishing and canning operations in Siberia.

11 RG 24. Records of the Bureau of Naval Personnel, 1789-1956, 15,443 cu. ft. The Bureau of Naval Personnel handles the training of enlisted men. Its records include logs of vessels in Russian waters, ca. 1880-1945, and logs of ships assisting the Allied intervention in Russia. There are also various materials on the Second Leningrad (heavy) Artillery School, 1940; Soviet aviators in Alaska, 1941; Russian war relief; Soviet submarines; Soviet requests, 1941-45, for PT-boats, sub-chasers, and minesweepers; Soviet military personnel in the U.S. during World War II; and the operation of vessels provided to Russia under lend-lease. Finally, there are films of the role of the United Nations in Turkey to handle the Armenian problem.

12 RG 26. Records of the United States Coast Guard, 1789-1975, 10,760 cu. ft. Formed in 1915, the U.S. Coast Guard handles customs and navigation regulations. Its Alaska file includes correspondence from the secretary of State regarding illicit fur-sealing activities by American citizens who were seized by Russian authorities and sentenced to prison in Vladivostok (note: there is an Alaska file in RG 36). Also included are correspondence and communications of the Bering Sea Patrol (now the Alaska Patrol), 1926-40.

13 RG 27. Records of the Weather Bureau, 1819-1965, 2,833 cu. ft. The Weather Bureau was established in 1890. Its records include information on Siberian and Russian weather from 1829 on.

14 RG 28. Records of the Post Office Department, 1773-1971, 3,018 cu. ft. The Office of the Postmaster General was established in 1789. Included in the record group are materials relating to parcel-post rules, regulations, and rates in foreign countries, including Russia, 1911-12.

15 RG 29. Records of the Bureau of the Census, 1790-1970, 9,287 cu. ft. Formed in 1902, the Bureau of the Census gathers and makes available statistics for the use of the government and public. Data for Foreign Commerce and Navigation of the United States, a publication of the Bureau of Foreign and Domestic Commerce, are among its records. These machine and manual compilations, more detailed than the publication for which they are used, contain information on U.S. trade with the Soviet Union. RG 29 also has two series of monthly machine tabulations, 1934-38, on commerce by ships of various countries, including the USSR. There are also a few items pertaining to the Soviet census of 1958 and 1959.

16 RG 30. Records of the Bureau of Public Roads, 1892-1970, 2,480 cu. ft. The Bureau of Public Roads originated in 1893. Its records include photographs of prints of road construction in Russia.

17 RG 32. Records of the United States Shipping Board, 1914-38, 6,502 cu. ft. The U.S. Shipping Board, formed in 1916, regulated sea navigation and developed a merchant marine. Its records include memoranda and correspondence pertaining to coal, fuel, and other supplies for Russian relief, 1919-21, and to the regulation of passenger travel between the USSR and the U.S. by a commercial treaty, 1933-34.

18 RG 36. Records of the United States Customs Service, 1745-1965, 10,554 cu. ft. The Customs Service was established in 1789 and reached bureau status in 1927. Its Alaska File includes documents on how the treaty of 1867 influenced the Russian Church in Alaska. It also contains an 1867 report on the Aleutian Islands based on an article by Abraham Charitonoff and on inventories of public buildings by the governor of the Russian colonies in America.

19 RG 37. Records of the Hydrographic Office, 1837-1974, 2,051 cu. ft. The Hydrographic Office, which began in 1830, gathers and provides hydrographic and navigational information. Among its records are original charts from the North Pacific Surveying Expedition, 1854-55, relating to Bering Strait, St. Lawrence Bay, Seniavine Straits, Providence Bay, Nikolski Anchorage on Komandorski Island, eastern shore of Sea of Okhotsk, harbor of Ayan, Sakhalin Island, de Kastri Bay, northern Kurile Islands, Vladivostok harbor, and Wrangel Island. There are also annotated manuscripts and printed charts relating to routes of explorers in northern Siberia, Professor Nordenskiold's voyage along the north coast of Siberia, 1878, the loss of the U.S.S. Jeanette and landings at the mouth of the Lena River, 1881-82, and the location of Russian settlements in Alaska, ca. 1867.

20 RG 38. Records of the Office of the Chief of Naval Intelligence, 1882-1968, 3,720 cu. ft. Formed in 1915, the Office of Naval Operations is responsible for the coordination of operational activities by the Navy. Its records include naval attaché reports, 1892-1946, that deal with Russian military affairs and with political, economic, social, and diplomatic matters. Topics covered in detail include the Russo-Japanese War, the Russian Civil War, the Five-Year Plans, the Russo-Finnish War of 1939-40, World War II, communism, and ethnic and political minorities in the USSR. Other materials pertaining to Russia include the administrative files and general correspondence of the Office of Naval Intelligence, 1892-1944. These contain information on visits by Russian military personnel to the U.S., Soviet aviation, an hydrographic expedition to the Russian Arctic in 1924, and Russian economic and political affairs. Also included in these files are letters from Lieutenant N. A. McCully, 1904-1905, which pertain to the Russo-Japanese War and contain several hand-drawn maps. RG 38 also has McCully's diary, 15 August 1904-31 March 1908; it deals with operations by the Russians and Japanese in the Manchuria area and contains information on Manchurian coal deposits. Other Russian-related material include general correspondence, 1943-46, on lend-lease to the USSR, a flu epidemic in Moscow, Soviet decoration of U.S. naval personnel, ships built in the U.S. for the USSR, and a Soviet agreement with RCA. There are also Naval Armed Guard reports and logs on the operations and personnel of merchant ships that convoyed supplies to Russia after World War II. Finally, there are topographic and terrain maps of the USSR and 20 photographs of Soviet leaders who took part in the United Nations conference in San Francisco, 1945.

21 RG 39. Records of the Bureau of Accounts (Treasury), 1775-1948, 2,324 cu. ft. Established in 1940, the Bureau of Accounts coordinates accounting and financial transactions. Its records include 9 ft. (26 boxes) of materials pertaining to the fiscal relations between the U.S. and the USSR, 1917-41. These documents, originally part of the correspondence of the office of the secretary of the treasury, include correspondence, memoranda,

reports, claim files, newspaper clippings, and publications. They contain information on loans to Imperial Russia in World War I; Allied financial assistance to Russia; economic, financial, and political conditions in the USSR, 1917-20; decrees of 21 January 1918 on the repudiation of debts; U.S. claims against the USSR, Soviet claims against the U.S.; Japanese and English claims against the USSR; prohibition of trade with the USSR, 1918-20; Soviet gold, 1918-35; financing Allied armies in Siberia, 1918-20; recognition of the USSR, 1921-33; Soviet securities sold in the U.S.; and Soviet representatives in the U.S., 1918-40. Note: records relating to Estonia, Latvia, and Lithuania are filed separately from those of the USSR.

22 RG 40. General Records of the Department of Commerce, 1898-1954, 808 cu. ft. The Department of Commerce and Labor was formed in 1903. Included in the record group are correspondence, reports, and memoranda regarding commercial opportunities for American business in Russia, the purchase of Russian products, and statistics of Russian trade with the United States and other countries.

23 RG 41. Records of the Bureau of Marine Inspection and Navigation, 1774-1966, 11,858 cu. ft. Established in 1884, the Bureau of Navigation (renamed in 1936 the Bureau of Marine Inspection and Navigation) handled, among other matters, the administration of navigation laws. Its records contain data on Russian merchant and war ships in the early 1900s, as well as U.S. diplomatic documents from Riga on Soviet regulation of travel abroad by USSR citizens. There are also letters on the elimination of discrimination against Latvian vessels, 1923; lists of Latvian merchant ships, 1925-26; a 1926 agreement signed between Latvia and the U.S. for reciprocal recognition of ship-measurement certificates; and a report on Soviet views toward the First International Congress of Sailors and Port Workers, which took place at Altona, Germany, in May 1942.

24 RG 43. Records of International Conferences, Commissions, and Expositions, 1825-1968, 1,358 cu. ft. Included are materials on several conferences with references to the USSR: the Third World Power Conference, 1936, the International Conference on Electrical Communication, 1920, the Limitation of Armament Conference, 1921-22, the Moscow Conference of Foreign Ministers, 19-30 October 1943, the Tehran Conference, 1943, the Second Cairo Conference, 1943, the United National Monetary and Financial Conference, 1944. There are also Russian-related materials in records pertaining to the Advisory Commission of Railway Experts to Russia, the Russian Railway Service Corps, and the Interallied Railway Committee, 1917-22; the European Advisory Commission, 1943-46; the Council of Foreign Ministers, 1945-53; the Allied Control Council, Germany, 1945-50; the Far Eastern Commission, 1945-51; the Allied Council for Japan, 1946-52; and the U.S.-USSR Joint Commission on Korea, 1946-48.

25 RG 44. Records of the Office of Government Reports, 1933-47, 698 cu. ft. The Office of Government Reports, established in 1939, coordinated various federal programs that concerned relief and war efforts. Its records (and those of its successor agency, the Office of War Information, also included here) contain materials pertaining to the press clippings service organized by the agencies and public opinion surveys on American attitudes toward the war, the Allies, international organizations, and other matters. RG 44 also has various posters, in Russian and English, relating to weapon familiarization, anti-Nazi propaganda, and the Russian War Relief.

26 RG 45. Naval Records Collection of the Office of Naval Records and Library, 1648-1945, 2,966 cu. ft. The Office of Naval Records and Library, joined to the Office of Naval History in 1946, gathered and preserved records pertaining to naval affairs. Its subject file includes communications from Newton A. McCully when he was in the USSR; messages from the U.S.S. Olympia; and Office of Naval Intelligence records on the situation in northern Russia after World War I. Also included are the Asiatic Squadron Letters, 21 vols., 1865-85, which contain descriptions of Russian ports in the Pacific that were visited by ships attached to the Asiatic Squadron. In addition, the record group contains materials on U.S. submarine activities off the Russian Pacific coast; conditions and military forces in Vladivostok, 1919-20; the activities of the Russian Volunteer Fleet during the Russo-Japanese War; the Murmansk railroad after World War I; the activities in Russia of William H. Schuetze, who travelled from Moscow to Irkutsk in 1885; Russian economic and diplomatic affairs, 1890-1916; and on the activities of John Paul Jones, 1778-91. There are also various maps and charts, some of British origin, with information on the Baltic and Arctic territories of the USSR. Finally, there is a journal of Capt. James Biddle, 1817-19, which mentions the presence of the Russian vessel Kutusoff at Monterey, where her officers bought grain supplies for the Sitka colony.

27 RG 46. Records of the United States Senate, 1789-1974, 14,050 cu. ft. Included are the files of the Senate Committee on Foreign Relations, which contain hearings, committee papers, and petitions relating to U.S. concern for conditions in Russia during the Revolution and to American attitudes toward recognition of the Soviet Union. There are also the hearings of the Committee pertaining to the U-2 incident and to the summit conference in 1960; efforts to build a telegraph between the U.S.

and Europe; documents, filed under "Soviet tools," on equipment provided to Russia under lend-lease; records in the Truman Committee of the Senate on Soviet needs for rubber; and numerous resolutions and petitions pertaining to events and the treatment of Jews in Russia.

28 RG 51. Records of the Office of Management and Budget, 1905-71, 4,114 cu. ft. The Office of Management and Budget helps formulate federal fiscal programs. Files on specific legislation relating to Russia/USSR are interspersed in the general legislation files, 1921-38, general legislative history files, 1939-68, general subject files, 1921-38, and subject files of the director, 1939-68.

29 RG 52. Records of the Bureau of Medicine and Surgery, 1812-1951, 1,092 cu. ft. The Bureau of Medicine and Surgery, established in 1842, carries out various medical functions for the navy. Bureau correspondence for 1941-46 contains studies of war wounds and casualties in Russia, Mongolia, and Eastern Europe. Other materials forwarded by the naval attaché in Russia include bulletins on sanitary and health conditions, Soviet medical handbooks, and lists of courses given in the Russian Medical Academy. Finally, there are intelligence reports, 1922, on relief work in Russia and health conditions in the Ukraine.

30 RG 54. Records of the Bureau of Plant Industry, Soils, and Agricultural Engineering, 1879-1956, 2,916 cu. ft. The bureau, formed in 1943, carries out various functions pertaining to plants and seeds. Its records include materials on the exchange of agricultural data with the USSR, 1922-36.

31 RG 56. General Records of the Department of the Treasury, 1775-1974, 4,288 cu. ft. The records of the Department of the Treasury, which was established in 1789, contain 1 folder of correspondence pertaining to assistance to Russia during World War I, the purchase of Russian gold, and the deterioration of relations with Russia after 1946. This material is located in the correspondence of the office of the secretary of the treasury, 1917-33, 1933-56. There is also a volume, "Awards Granted Exhibitors from Russia at the World's Columbian Exposition, Chicago, 1893," which lists exhibits and awards in various areas, including agriculture, mining, and manufacture. Finally, there is correspondence on the dispatch of the boat Lincoln to inspect the Alaska territory in 1867.

32 RG 57. Records of the Geological Survey, 1853-1974, 2,334 cu. ft. Formed in 1879, the Geological Survey produces information on the country's geology and natural resources. Its records include materials on coal production in Russia, 1913-20; a notebook of S. F. Emmons, the geologist, on his field trip to Russia in 1897; and a report and correspondence, 1938-48, on Russian hydrological classification and terminology.

33 RG 59. General Records of the Department of State, 1764-1974, 23,206 cu. ft. This record group contains materials transferred from the State Department to the National Archives. Series within the record group that contain Russian-related materials include the following:

Instructions to diplomatic representatives, 1829-1906. Includes copies of instructions to U.S. diplomats in Russia.

Diplomatic dispatches, 1808-1906. Includes communications from U.S. ministers and ambassadors in Russia: John Quincy Adams, William Pinkney, George Washington Campbell, Henry Middleton, James Buchanan, William Wilkins, John Randolph Clay, George M. Dallas, Churchill C. Cambreleng, Charles S. Todd, Ralph I. Ingersoll, Arthur P. Bagby, Neill S. Brown, Thomas H. Seymour, Francis W. Pickens, John Appleton, Cassius M. Clay, Simon Cameron, Andrew G. Curtin, James L. Orr, Marshall Jewell, George H. Boker, Edwin W. Stoughton, John W. Foster, William H. Hunt, Alphonso Taft, George V. N. Lothrop, Lambert Tree, Charles Emory Smith, Andrew D. White, Clifton R. Breckrinridge, Ethan A. Hitchcock, Charlemagne Tower, Robert S. McCormick, and George von L. Meyer.

Notes to foreign missions in the United States, 1793-1906. Copies of the communications sent by the Department of State to foreign embassies and legations in the U.S., including those of Russia.

Notes from foreign missions in the United States, 1806-1906. Original communications and related enclosures received by the Department of State from foreign legations and embassies in the United States. Microfilmed.

Instructions to consular officers, 1800-1906. Includes copies of instructions sent by the Department of State to U.S. consular officers in Russia.

Dispatches from consular officers, 1789-1906. Dispatches and related enclosures received by the Department of State from its consular officers. Included are consular dispatches from the Amoor (Amur) river, Archangel, Batum, Moscow, Odessa, Petropavlovsk, Reval, Riga, St. Petersburg, and Vladivostok.

Numerical file, 1906-10. Includes instructions to diplomatic representatives, dispatches from diplomatic officers, notes to and from foreign missions in the United States, instructions to consular officers, and dispatches from consular officers. Included are communications from U.S. ambassadors to Russia in this period, John W. Riddle and William Woodville Rockhill.

Decimal file, 1910-49. Included are communications from U.S. ambassadors to Russia: Curtis Guild, George T. Marye, David R. Francis, William Christian Bullitt, Joseph E. Davies, Laurence A. Steinhardt, William H. Standley, and W. Averell Harriman.

Records of the International Commission on the North Sea Incident, 12-25 November 1905, 6 in. Includes materials on the investigation of the actions taken by the Russian fleet in the North Sea against British boats.

Miscellaneous petitions and memorials. Includes letters and a petition to the emperor of Russia relating to the massacre of Jews at Kischineff, Bessarabia, in 1903.

Analyses of reports on consular establishments of foreign powers, 1907-1908, 3 vols. Contains information on the consular establishments of Russia in various countries; for each post rank, salary, and staff is indicated.

Miscellaneous memoranda of conversations of the secretary of state, 1893-98, .5 in. Includes memoranda of interviews of the secretary of State with the Russian minister and other foreign diplomats regarding Korea and the U.S. annexation of Hawaii.

Records of the Kosloff Affair, 1815-16, 1 vol. Materials pertaining to the case of Russian Consul General Kosloff, accused of rape by the State of Pennsylvania.

Records of the Foreign Service Buildings Office. 1911-48. 15 ft. Included are 2 folders of correspondence and memoranda relating to the planning and building of the U.S. embassy in Moscow, 1931-34. The correspondence is with foreign service officers in Moscow, architects, contractors, and other officals. Some correspondence also relates to the negotiation of a lease with the Soviet Union.

Records of the Division of Current Information Includes reports, copies of translations, correspondence, and other materials pertaining to U.S.-Soviet relations and economic, political, and military matters relating to the USSR.

Records of the Office of the Counselor--general records. 1916-28. 104 ft. and 21 microfilm reels. Various materials pertaining to the "Sisson documents," communism, U.S.-Soviet trade, and other matters.

Miscellaneous manuscripts. Contain a receipt for transportation of the tsar's family to Ekaterinburg, 1918, and a Russian document pertaining to air navigation.

Records of the State Department Mission to South Russia, 1920, ca. 5 in. Includes messages to and from the secretary of State, letters, memoranda, notes, and reports pertaining to this mission. The purpose of the mission, in which Admiral N. A. McCully took part, was to observe local conditions and to contact General Anton I. Denikin.

Audiovisual records. Includes the plan and assembly room of the Hall of Nobility in Petrograd, 1915, and still pictures of the signing of the Russo-Japanese peace treaty, 1905.

Records of the Office of European Affairs (Matthews-Hickerson Files), 1935-47, 6 ft. The subject files of H. Freeman Matthews and John D. Hickerson, who both served as directors of this office, include some material relating to the Soviet Union, particularly concerning the second Moscow Conference in October 1944 and the Council of Foreign Ministers, 1945-47.

Records of the War History Branch, 1938-50, 29 ft. In December 1943 the State Department began work on a war history project, designed to document the role of the Department in World War II. Studies relating to the Soviet Union include those on the work of the geographical desks and on such topics as relations with Finland and the Lend-lease program. Index to titles and authors of studies.

Records of Harley A. Notter, 1939-50, 118 ft. Harley A. Notter held various posts in the Department of State 1937-50. The records of many World War II committees became part of the office files of Notter during his compilation of <u>Postwar Foreign Policy Preparation, 1939-45</u>, published by the Department in 1949. Various materials assembled by Notter during the preparation of his book were consolidated by the Department into a single collection. Records relating to the Soviet Union are scattered throughout.

Records compiled by the Official Views Section of the Division of International Organization Affairs and its predecessors, 1940-45, 45 ft. The Official Views Section and its predecessors kept a record of all official commitments or statements issued by Allied or neutral governments, whether publicly or confidentially, regarding the postwar settlements. Included are documents concerning the positions taken by the Soviet Union.

Acheson Files, 1941-47, 5 ft. Dean Acheson served as assistant secretary of state 1941-45 and under secretary of state 1945-47. His records include materials relating to lend-lease agreements with the Soviet Union.

Records of the Bureau of Intelligence and Research, 1941-61, 167 ft. The Research and Analysis Branch of the Office of Strategic Services prepared reports and studies on many subjects and countries during World War II.

There are over 8,000 reports in the numbered series and many of them relate directly to the Soviet Union or to subjects or areas of mutual interest to the United States and the Soviet Union.

Records Relating to the Tripartite Naval Commission and Tripartite Merchant Marine Commission, 1945, 6 in. These commissions, comprised of representatives of the United States, the United Kingdom, and the Soviet Union, met from August to December 1945 to develop recommendations for the allocation of captured German naval vessels and merchant marine ships. The records consist of correspondence and memorandums of the U.S. representatives, minutes of meetings, and the signed reports of the commissions.

Inspection reports on foreign service posts. 1906-39, 74 ft, The State Department began periodic inspections of U.S. consular posts in 1906 and U.S. diplomatic posts in 1925. The reports cover subjects such as personnel, quarters, office hours, U.S. government property, accounts and returns, summaries of business, estimates and allotments, trade and economic work, political reporting, visa and immigration work, citizenship and passport work, and other business. Included are reports on the U.S. embassy in Moscow, 1937, and U.S. consulates in Archangel, 1916, Batum, 1907, 1911, and 1913, Cronstadt, 1907, Moscow, 1907, 1911, 1913, and 1916, Odessa, 1907, 1911, 1914, and 1916, Omsk, 1911, Rostov-on-Don, 1911 and 1914, St. Petersburg, 1907, 1911, 1913, and 1916, Tiflis, 1916, and Vladivostok, 1907, 1909, 1911, 1913, 1916, and 1920.

Petitions on Behalf of Jan Pouren, ca. 1908, 3 ft. Petitions on behalf of Jan Janoff Pouren objecting to his extradition to Russia for alleged burglary, arson, and attempted murder. The petitions are arranged for the most part alphabetically by state of origin.

Records of the Office of News and its predecessors, 1909-63, 95 ft. Some of the series in these records are arranged by country or area and some relate to Russia. Included are State Department press releases, 1922-63, many of which pertain to relations with the Soviet Union. Also included are copies of George F. Kennan's lectures on the Soviet Union at Oxford University in 1957.

"Sisson Documents," 1917-21, 1 ft. Copies of a series of documents obtained in Russia in February and March 1918 by Edgar Sisson, a representative of the World War I Committee on Public Information, regarding direct cooperation between the Bolsheviks and Germany. With these documents are materials concerning the Department's investigation, 1919-21, of the documents' authenticity.

Records of the Division of Eastern European Affairs, 1917-41, 9 ft. Correspondence, reports, memoranda, studies, and published material maintained by this office. Virtually all these records relate to internal conditions in the Soviet Union or to relations between the Soviet Union and the United States. Included are 4 ft. of dispatches, chiefly from the U.S. legation at Riga, reporting on economic and political developments in the Soviet Union during the period 1913-26.

Records of the Office of the Counselor and Chief Special Agent, 1915-27, 103 ft. Includes material on Russian commercial and political activities in Latin America.

34 RG 60. General Records of the Department of Justice, 1790-1972, 18,264 cu. ft. The Department of Justice was created on 22 June 1870. Its records include documents, 1916, on claims that Russian nationals in the United States were using the Russian consulate in Chicago as a savings depository; some files on the handling of communist activities in the U.S. by the Department of Justice, 1919-39; and documents pertaining to the enactment of the North Pacific Sealing Convention.

35 RG 61. Records of the War Industries Board, 1916-33, 872 cu. ft. The War Industries Board was formed in 1917 to serve war industry requirements of the government. Its records include a general summary of contracts placed in the United States by the Supply Committee of the Russian government, January-November 1918; an estimate of the liquidated damages resulting from the cancellation of the entire Russian contract as of 15 December 1917; correspondence and list of materials relating to stored materiels belonging to the former Russian Imperial government and held for disposal by the Provisional Government, February-October 1918; and a purchase application of the Russian War Mission.

36 RG 63. Records of the Committee on Public Information, 1917-19, 85 cu. ft. Established in 1917, the Committee on Public Information handled government news during World War I and was assigned to keep up morale. The Russian Division of the Foreign Section of this committee (the Creel Committee) has records on American propaganda campaigns in the Soviet Union, 1918-19. These records include propaganda leaflets, bulletins, and news clippings from the Russian and Siberian press, and photostats on the "German-Bolshevik Conspiracy." RG 63 also has some documents on Soviet officials. For more documentation on the "German-Bolshevik Conspiracy," see RG 130.

37 RG 64. Records of the National Archives and Records Service, 1927-74, 646 cu. ft. Included are Soviet newsreels, training films, and a film, "June 13, 1942," on military activities in the USSR during the Nazi invasion.

38 RG 65. Records of the Federal Bureau of Investigation, 1897-1936, 29 cu. ft. The main function of the FBI is to investigate violations of federal law. Its records contain 2 microfilm series, Miscellaneous Files, 1908-21, 145 rolls, and Bureau Section Files, 1910-21, 81 rolls, that include investigative information on persons associated with communist organizations.

39 RG 69. Records of the Works Projects Administration, 1933-45, 4,647 cu. ft. The records of the Works Projects Administration, which handled federal work-relief programs, contain a bibliography of research on civilian defense and protection against air-raids in the Soviet Union.

40 RG 70. Records of the Bureau of Mines, 1895-1970, 3,231 cu. ft. The Bureau of Mines, formed in 1910, safeguards the lives of mineworkers and investigates ways to use mining resources more efficiently. Its records touch on several aspects of Russian mine and oil production, including U.S. use of Russian oil resources, 1917-21; the influence of the world oil situation on Russia and Sakhalin Island, 1917-22; petroleum resources of Baku and Azerbaijan, 1919-21; and the shipment of oil and coal from Russian ports on the Baltic, the Black Sea, and the Pacific Ocean, 1919.

41 RG 72. Records of the Bureau of Aeronautics, 1911-46, 4,065 cu. ft. Created in 1921, the Bureau of Aeronautics carried out various functions assigned to it by the secretary of the navy. Its records contain numerous Soviet information bulletins compiled by the Air Intelligence section during World War II. These bulletins deal with the allocation of raw and finished materials in the USSR, the Soviet Meteorology Mission in 1943, U.S.-USSR exchange of photographic equipment and prints, translation of Soviet technical data, and war relief efforts by Soviet civilians.

42 RG 74. Records of the Bureau of Ordnance, 1818-1946, 7,980 cu. ft. The Bureau of Ordnance and Hydrography, formed in 1842, was responsible for the production and distribution of armaments. Its records contain correspondence regarding the shipment of lend-lease materiel to the Soviet Union during World War II.

43 RG 75. Records of the Bureau of Indian Affairs, 1794-1967, 43,660 cu. ft. The Bureau of Indian Affairs was created in 1824. Included in the record group is documentation on an expedition to Siberia undertaken in 1891 by Sheldon Jackson to import Siberian reindeer and herders. There is also a motion picture, "A Trip to the Arctic with Uncle Sam," 1921, 1 reel, that documents a trip on the ship Bear from the Aleutian Islands to Plover Bay, Siberia, by way of Point Barrow, Alaska. It includes scenes of Eskimo life in the Arctic.

44 RG 76. Records of Boundary and Claims Commissions and Arbitrations, 1783-1952, 3,460 cu. ft. This record group includes documents relating to miscellaneous claims of United States citizens against Russia for the loss of vessels or cargoes seized, 1807-81, and records relating to the arbitration of claims of 4 United States vessels against Russia in accordance with a protocol of 26 August 1900. The Claims Against Buenos Aires (Argentina), Miscellaneous, 1816-43, has some materials on sealing operations by Russians off the Falkland Islands. There are also maps, used by the U.S. in the 1903 Convention regarding the U.S. Alaskan Boundary, that are of Russian origin.

45 RG 77. Records of the Office of the Chief of Engineers, 1776-1974, 12,308 cu. ft. The Corps of Engineers, U.S. army, was formed in 1802. Among its duties are the preparation of maps and the construction of various installations. Its records include 800 topographic maps of Russia at varying scales for use by the Defense Department, 1940-75; maps of "Bolshevist" disturbances in various nations, especially in Eastern Europe; maps on the Russo-Japanese War; manuscript maps of the Engineer Office of the American Expeditionary Forces, Siberia, 1918; maps of the Soviet Union, 1921-39, prepared by the Army Map Service and the Army Reproduction Plant; maps on Russian transportation networks in the 19th and 20th c.; and a map of Turkestan and the Russian dominions in Asia, 1885. Also included are a report on Russian iron production and its military use, 1870; materials on United States support of the Russian Railway Service Corps; 1 album of photographs on the Allied intervention in Siberia; and drawings and plans on the building of civil projects in Vladivostok and elsewhere in Russia. Finally, there is 1 reel of machine readable data, 1970, pertaining to Soviet trade with the U.S.

46 RG 80. General Records of the Department of the Navy, 1804-1965, 12,112 cu. ft. The James Forrestal papers, 1940-47, are among these records. They include speeches, letters, memos and articles on lend-lease supplies and the Russian political situation; comments on communist theory and practice, the Five-Year Plans and Soviet personalities; and minutes of the American Top Policy Group, 1944-47. RG 80 also contains the formerly classified correspondence of the secretary of the navy, which makes brief mention of radio stations in Russia and American designs for Soviet battleships and destroyers, 1927-39; correspondence pertaining to the Amtorg Trading Corp. and its commercial operations in the United States, 1939-42; and naval records, 1919-26, on Bolshevik activities in the Soviet Union.

47 RG 82. Records of the Federal Reserve System, 1936-69, 13 cu. ft. Formed in 1913, the

Federal Reserve System determines U.S. monetary policy. Its records include materials pertaining to the Eesti Bank, Estonia, 1924-54, the Latvijas Banka, Latvia, 1926-54, Lietuvos Bankas, Lithuania, 1931-54, the State Bank of the USSR, 1948, the Amtorg Trading Corp., 1924-30, and the Russian Embargo, 1918-43.

48 RG 83. Records of the Bureau of Agricultural Economics, 1840-1953, 2,978 cu. ft. Formed in 1922, the Bureau of Agricultural Economics carried out various research functions. Its records include materials on Russian crop area and production, 1864-1916, economic conditions, 1930-31, agricultural insurance, and rural credit. There are also materials on lend-lease to Russia and various studies pertaining to Russian agriculture.

49 RG 84. Records of the Foreign Service Posts of the Department of State, 1788-1957, 33,868 cu. ft. Many of the records in this record group are duplicated by documents in RG 59, but it does contain original materials, a large number of which pertain to trade and to consular activities. Included are dispatches sent to the Department of State, instructions from the Department, notes to and from the Russian government, consular letters sent and received, registers of correspondence, special consular reports, telegrams sent to the Department, passport applications, and letters to the Treasury Department. Cities from which communications were received include Riga, Warsaw, Reval, Odessa, Moscow, Vladivostok, Batum, Tiflis, St. Petersburg (Leningrad), Archangel, Chita, and Murmansk. Also included are personal correspondence, 1916-18, from Ambassador David R. Francis and the records of the United States Mission to the United Nations, 1945-49, 86 ft., which contain references to the Soviet Union and its foreign policy.

50 RG 85. Records of the Immigration and Naturalization Service, 1787-1954, 1,746 cu. ft. The passenger arrival records, 1883-1954, 11,476 rolls of microfilm, contain the names of Russian immigrants to the U.S. and of ship and airplane passenger and crew lists. There are also letters received, 1882-1906, and subject correspondence, 1906-32, that may include files relating to groups of Russian immigrants.

51 RG 88. Records of the Food and Drug Administration, 1877-1954, 979 cu. ft. Established in 1931, the Food and Drug Administration implements legislation designed to protect the health of American citizens. Its records include copies of Russian laws on the production and inspection of various foods and drugs, 1886-1913.

52 RG 90. Records of the Public Health Service. 1802-1974, 1,444 cu. ft. The Public Health Service, which originated in 1798, provides medical assistance and information. Its records contain the records of a United States Public Health Marine Hospital at Libau (Lepaya) in Western Latvia, 1909-13. These materials document epidemics, emigration, and health conditions in the Baltic area. There is also a translation of a report approved by the Imperial Plague Commission, 1912, entitled "Rules for the Prevention of an Outspread of Cholera or Plague on the Railways." Other pertinent materials include copies of U.S. consular reports on epidemics and other health matters in the Soviet Union, 1924-38; a copy of a report by Joseph E. Davies on Sochi, 1938; an account by Dr. O. H. Cox on Moscow hospitals and other medical establishments; and reports and correspondence pertaining to the Soviet Institute of Hematology and Blood Transfusion, 1940.

53 RG 92. Records of the Office of the Quartermaster General, 1792-1957, 23,198 cu. ft. The office of the quartermaster general handled supplies for the U.S. army. Its records include various materials on the equipment, supply, transportation, and organization of the Russian army between 1890 and 1914.

54 RG 94. Records of the Adjutant General's Office, ca. 1783-1925, 38,111 cu. ft. In operation since 1821, the adjutant general's office maintains the records of the U.S. army. Its records include reports and other materials by U.S. military observers during the Crimean War and the Russo-Japanese War. Among these observers were Capt. George B. McClellan and Capt. John J. Pershing.

55 RG 95. Records of the Forest Service, 1882-1973, 2,581 cu. ft. The Forest Service, a part of the Agriculture Department, first began its operations in 1881 under the name of Division of Forestry. Its records contain various materials on forestry in Russia, 1915-20.

56 RG 96. Records of the Farmers Home Administration, 1931-59, 2,481 cu. ft. The Farmers Home Administration, formed in 1946, provides assistance to small farmers. Among its records is a 1936 silent film, 16 mm, 18 minutes, on agricultural and industrial cooperatives in Russia and England.

57 RG 101. Records of the Office of the Comptroller of the Currency, 1863-1967, 12,178 cu. ft. The function of the Office of the Comptroller of the Currency, formed in 1863, is to manage the National Banking System. Among its records are reports, 1918, pertaining to the affairs of Russian branches (in Petrograd and elsewhere) of a New York City bank.

58 RG 102. Records of the Children's Bureau, 1912-49, 530 cu. ft. Among the functions of the Children's Bureau, created in 1912, is

to collect information pertaining to children. Its records include a League of Nations account on medical support for the USSR, 1921-22, and the names of people in the Soviet Union involved in childcare, July 1933.

59 RG 104. Records of the Bureau of the Mint, 1792-1960, 893 cu. ft. In the records of the Bureau of the Mint, which produces U.S. money, there are some reports by U.S. diplomats (some written directly to the Bureau) on Russian currency and on Russia's acquisition of gold and silver coins, ca. 1870-1915.

60 RG 107. Records of the Office of the Secretary of War, 1791-1948, 3,147 cu. ft. The records of the Office of the Secretary of War (now known as the secretary of the army) in clude documentation, 1940-47, concerning lend-lease operations to the Soviet Union, U.S. relations with the Soviet Union, and Soviet internal affairs. The record group also includes the records of assistant secretaries of War John J. McCloy and Howard Peterson, 1940-47, which contain correspondence, reports, and directives relating to communism in the United States, U.S.-Soviet foreign policy, lend-lease to the Soviet Union, and Soviet objectives in Finland, Rumania, Yugoslavia, and Hungary. There are also the records of the assistant secretary for air, which have cablegrams dated 1944-47 on internal Soviet affairs. Finally, there are materials concerning the U.S. Army's role in the transfer of Alaska from Russia to the U.S., and films on Soviet troops in Thuringia, on the Allied Council in Berlin, and on the Russian Commission in Korea.

61 RG 111. Records of the Office of the Chief Signal Officer, 1860-1954, 5,502 cu. ft. Formed in 1863, the Signal Corps handles signal duty equipment. Its records include newsreels and motion pictures pertaining to Soviet agriculture, the American Expeditionary Forces, the battle of Stalingrad, Vladivostok in World War II, Soviet mining operations in the 1940s, and the Yalta Conference. There are also still photographs of the American Expeditionary Forces in Siberia and the 339th Infantry in North Russia.

62 RG 112. Records of the Office of the Surgeon General, 1818-1949, 4,496 cu. ft. The International (Supply) Division files of this record group, 1942-47, contain documents relating to lend-lease and reciprocal-aid programs to Russia during World War II.

63 RG 113. Records of the Allied Purchasing Division, 1917-19, 14 cu. ft. In August 1917 the Allied Purchasing Commission was formed to buy material in the United States. Its records include material pertaining to Russian contracts and to the political situation in Russia 1917-18.

64 RG 115. Records of the Bureau of Reclamation, 1889-1963, 3,767 cu. ft. Material on irrigation in Turkestan, Siberia, and Russia, 1899-1903 and 1922-29.

65 RG 120. Records of the American Expeditionary Forces (World War I), 1917-23, 1912-29, 26,511 cu ft. Included in this record group are the records of the American Expeditionary Forces, North Russia, 14 ft., 1917-19. These documents throw light on the activities of the 3 American battalions sent by President Wilson in July 1918 to help Allied forces in Archangel. Among the materials are those of the chief of the American military mission to Russia, 1917-19, and of the inspector general, the judge advocate, and the chief surgeon who took part in the mission. AEF GHQ (Intelligence) has information on the military, political, and social conditions in Russia, both before and after the intervention. GHQ - Office of the Commander in Chief, 1917-20, contains correspondence and reports on the repatriation of Russian POWs in Germany after the 1918 armistice, the sending of American relief supplies to Russia, and conditions in Russia. GHQ - General Staff has material on the Kerensky government, the movement of Russian revolutionaries between Switzerland and Germany, March-April 1917, Finnish anti-Bolshevik forces and intentions, and other matters pertaining to Russia at the time of the Revolution. RG 120 also includes maps relating to operations in northern Russia (n.d., 14 items); maps accompanying reports from military missions, 1918-19, 29 items; enemy forces maps, eastern front, 1917-19, 26 items; maps of areas not on the western front, 1918-19, 86 items, showing fronts, situations, and orders of battle in Italy, the Balkans, Eastern Europe, the Near East, Rumania, Russia, and Portugal; a 1:500,000 topographic map of the Vladivostok area, 1909; 1:420,000 planimetric maps of Russia, 1918-19, 10 items; situation maps - Russia and Siberia, 1918-19, 35 items; and enemy order of battle maps - eastern front, 1917-19, 26 items.

66 RG 121. Records of the Public Buildings Service (GSA). 1801-1974, 8,654 cu. ft. The Public Buildings Service administers government buildings. Its records include photonegatives of posters drawn by American artists depicting life in Russia, 1939.

67 RG 123. Records of the United States Court of Claims, 1783-1952, 2,840 cu. ft. Formed in 1855, the U.S. Court of Claims is concerned with claims against the United States. Included in its records are documents, 1921-38, on Soviet efforts to be compensated for 2 ships being built for Russia that were requisitioned by the U.S. in 1917. Note: material on this topic can also be found in RG 205.

68 RG 125. Records of the Office of the Judge Advocate General (Navy), 1799-1943, 2,687 cu. ft. Established in 1880, the Office of the Judge Advocate handles legal matters for the navy. Its records may include materials on incidents involving U.S. naval personnel or U.S. naval vessels in Russian ports. There may also be records relating to investigations of Russian nationals working at U.S. naval installations and records of United States participation in international conferences dealing with laws of the sea.

69 RG 126. Records of the Office of Territories, 1878-1953, 753 cu. ft. The Office of Territories, formed in 1950, administers affairs pertaining to U.S. territories. Its records include letters on the hardship of carrying mail through Siberia; material on Soviet warships in the Philippines during World War II; and communist activities in the Philippines, 1917-36 (filed under "Bolsheviki").

70 RG 127. Records of the United States Marine Corps, 1798-1971, 2,269 cu. ft. The Public Information Division records include 30 ft. of material, 1941-45, consisting of story files, press releases, and marine corps publications that relate in part to the Soviet Union.

71 RG 130. Records of the White House Office, 1814-1971, 102 cu. ft. The White House Office, formed in 1939, is one of the 5 divisions of the executive office of the president. Its records include documents on the "German-Bolshevik conspiracy" (1918) obtained in Russia by Edgar Sisson, associate chairman of the Committee on Public Information, at the request of President Wilson.

72 RG 131. Records of the Office of Alien Property, 1878-1957, 1,545 cu. ft. The Office of Alien Property was responsible for dealing with property in the United States belonging to enemy powers and their citizens. Among its records are photos pertaining to the Soviet-German frontiers pact, 10 January 1941; reports, 1927-39, by agents of the Hamburg-American line with information on trade with Soviet ports; and 20 photographs of vacation spots in Russia, 1926.

73 RG 136. Records of the Agricultural Marketing Service, 1894-1968, 2,485 cu. ft. Formed in 1939, the Agricultural Marketing Service dealt with the marketing of agricultural products. Among its records are materials on the lend-lease of farm products.

74 RG 151. Records of the Bureau of Foreign and Domestic Commerce and Successor Agencies, 1899-1958, 1,419 cu. ft. Established in 1912, the Bureau of Foreign and Domestic Commerce compiled information on foreign commerce and markets. Its central file contains the following series pertaining to Russian trade: foreign service-executive Petrograd, 1916, with correspondence between the Bureau and commercial attachés in Russia; Russian trade with various countries, 1926-39, with material on Soviet trade agreements and trade-credit terms; Business conditions, with information on labor in the Soviet Union and on trade regulations in Russia and the Baltic states between 1921 and 1939; Trade with the United Kingdom, with data on Anglo-Russian trade, 1939-45; Trade with the United States, with correspondence between the Bureau and U.S. businessmen and exporting firms on Soviet credit reliability, Amtorg, and other matters; Foreign service-executive Petrograd, 1916, with currency; Business conditions, with information on exchange rates between the USSR and Latvia, Estonia, and Lithuania, 1921-39; Foreign credits and foreign loans, with data on loans to Russia and on late Imperial and Soviet bonds; American investment opportunities - Russia, with correspondence on the prospects of developing natural resources in Russia, 1915-17. RG 151 also has letters exchanged between the State and Commerce departments, 1921-22, on Japanese commerce in Siberia; correspondence, 1923-31, on car production in the Soviet Union; photos of Russian "new cities," 1930, of agricultural techniques, 1921-30, and of Soviet shipments of manganese, 1921-39; letters, 1922-35, on American famine relief in Russia; materials on a meeting of communist groups in Transcaucasia; and various documents, 1920-30, pertaining to the Soviet oil industry in Baku and elsewhere.

75 RG 153. Records of the Office of the Judge Advocate General (Army), 1800-1957, 6,316 cu. ft. The Office of the Judge Advocate General, Army, deals with army legal matters. Its records contain reports of investigations of criminal acts committed by Nazis (German and non-German) in the USSR, by Nazis against Soviet citizens in the Soviet Union, and by Soviet citizens against other Soviet citizens and persons of other nationalities. Also included are trial records of Nazis that shed light on the Katyn Forest massacre, the extermination of Soviet Jews, and the participation of Soviet judges in the International Military Tribunal, Far East.

76 RG 156. Records of the Office of the Chief of Ordnance, 1794-1969, 11,338 cu. ft. Founded in 1812, the Ordnance Department handled military supplies and equipment. Its records include correspondence, 1910-41, relating to Russian contracts with U.S. firms for rifles, spare parts, and other ordnance items.

77 RG 160. Records of Headquarters Army Service Forces, 1920-46, 2,021 cu. ft. The Services of Supply, renamed Army Service Forces in 1943, handled various service and supply duties. In the records of its International Division, 1940-47, the following series have Russian-related materials: Security-classified

correspondence, 1941-46; security-classified messages sent and received, 1941-46; security-classified historical file, 1940-46; security-classified correspondence, reports, and issuances relating to lend-lease aid and reciprocal aid policies and procedures, 1940-46; and correspondence of the Office of the Director of Defense Aid, War Department, and its successor, the Defense Aid Division, Services of Supply, 1941-42. The records of the Mission Branch contain information on military missions to the USSR, 1941-42. In the Civilian Supply Branch records there are reports, files, and correspondence relating to Russia/USSR. The Control Division records include a set of progress reports called "International Aid," 28 vols., 1943-45, information on items provided under lend-lease. In the records of the Strategic Logistics Branch there are studies relating to the USSR and to the possibility of developing supply routes through Siberia during World War II. Finally, there are 33 12" records used in Russian language training.

78 RG 165. Records of the War Department General and Special Staffs, 1870-1954, 11,003 cu. ft. This record group contains several series with information on the Soviet Union. The Military Intelligence Division Correspondence (M.I.D.) series, 1917-41, documents combat operations during the Civil War; the organization, strength, tactics, and equipment of the Soviet army; political, economic, and social conditions in the USSR; Soviet relations with other countries; and Soviet espionage activities. The War Plans Division Correspondence series, 1920-42, has information on lend-lease aid for the Soviet Union, air routes to Russia, negotiations over American use of Siberian air bases, and the Harriman Mission to Moscow. The English Translations of Foreign Intelligence Documents series, 1919-47, contains nearly 50 translations pertaining to Russia and the Soviet army. The German Military Records Relating to WWI series, 1917-19, copied from the original German documents by representatives of the U.S. Army War College at the Germany military archives at Potsdam, contains documentation on the mobilization plans and activities of the 8th German Army for the August-September 1914 campaign on the eastern front against the Russian army; on the 9th German Army campaign against the Rumanians and Russians, 1916-17; and on the operations of the 23rd German Reserve Corps and the 42nd German Infantry Division against the Russian army in September-October 1917. The Office of the Chief of Staff series, 1942-47, has information on the USSR in the central, secret, and top secret files. The Director of Intelligence series has data on the Soviet Union that is mentioned in the records of the interrogations of captured personnel. The Operations Division series, 1942-49, has various materials on the coordination of the Allied-USSR war effort, general war planning with the USSR, Soviet policies toward Japan, and U.S.-USSR post-war occupation. RG 165 also has maps of the Russo-Japanese War and photographs pertaining to Russian military matters.

79 RG 166. Records of the Foreign Agricultural Service, 1901-54, 961 cu. ft. The Foreign Agricultural Service is concerned with developing markets abroad for American agricultural goods. Its records include reports on various aspects of Russian agriculture by U.S. consuls, agricultural attachés, and special agents in Russia, 1903-45. The record group also has material on wood resources in the USSR, 1920-39, economic conditions in Russia, 1942-45, and Soviet foreign trade. Finally, there are machine readable files, dating from 1965 to the present, which contain detailed information by commodity of U.S. import and export trade with the rest of the world, including the Soviet Union.

80 RG 169. Records of the Foreign Economic Administration, 1939-47, 2,066 cu. ft. Formed in 1943, the Foreign Economic Administration handled various matters pertaining to foreign aid. Its records contain considerable materials on the Moscow mission, 1941-42, headed by W. Averell Harriman to negotiate lend-lease to the Soviet Union. Also included is a "History of Lend-Lease," completed by the Department of State, and supporting documents, 1939-47. In addition, the series Bureau of Areas, USSR Branch, 1944-45 has export licenses and other materials relating to the program of exports to the USSR during World War II.

81 RG 174. General Records of the Department of Labor, 1907-73, 1,548 cu. ft. This record group includes letters exchanged between Woodrow Wilson and the secretary of labor on selecting U.S. labor representatives to the American Special Mission (the Root Mission) to Russia; materials on the deportation of C. A. K. Martens, chosen by Chicherin in 1919 to establish trade relations with the U.S.; various pamphlets on the Russian army in World War I and on activities against the Bolsheviks; and materials pertaining to Soviet labor.

82 RG 178. Records of the U.S. Maritime Commission, 1917-50, 6,487 cu. ft. The U.S. Maritime Commission, established in 1936, was formed to promote the U.S. merchant marine. Its records include a series, Cargo, Mail, and Passenger Reports, 1918-46, which contains information on sailings of the U.S. merchant marine fleet from Soviet ports. These records are arranged chronologically by year and thereunder by name of ship.

83 RG 179. Records of the War Production Board, 1940-47, 2,123 cu. ft. Formed in 1942, the War Production Board (WPB) directed plans to produce and furnish war materiel. Its records contain materials documenting U.S. lend-lease to the Soviet Union. These materials include

correspondence with the Russian Purchasing Commission; the office file of Mose L. Harvey, assistant and deputy director of the Foreign Division of the WPB; and the correspondence file, 1942-45, and staff reports, 1942-45, of William L. Batt, U.S. member of the Combined Raw Materials Board and U.S. deputy member of the Combined Production and Resources Board; the reports and minutes, 1942-47, of the President's Soviet Protocol Committee; and the minutes of the Combined Aluminum and Magnesium Committee.

84 RG 180. Records of the Commodity Exchange Authority. 1921-52. 232 cu. ft. Formed in 1936, the Commodity Exchange Authority supervises trading behavior on commodity exchanges. Its records include an office file containing a Soviet government study of future markets, 1927-38.

85 RG 182. Records of the War Trade Board. 1917-35. 722 cu. ft. The War Trade Board, created in 1917, handled export and import licenses and other matters during World War I. Among its records are those of the Russian Bureau, Inc., 1918-20, which was established in November 1918. Materials in the record group document the Russian budget during World War I, trade between Russia and the U.S., Russian exports and imports, 1917-19, and the contacts of Russian companies with Germany in the 1910s.

86 RG 187. Records of the National Resources Planning Board, 1931-43, 1,400 cu. ft. Includes a speech by Dr. Karl Scholtz, February 1934, delivered to the Mississippi Valley Committee on Soviet agriculture, as well as a record of the ensuing discussion on the subject.

87 RG 197. Records of the Civil Aeronautics Board, 1934-77, 1,059 cu. ft. The Civil Aeronautics Board regulates and promotes international and domestic air travel. Its records include machine readable data, from 1968 to the present, pertaining to air traffic between the U.S. and the USSR by U.S. carriers.

88 RG 200. National Archives Gift Collection, 1783-1974, 7,294 cu. ft. The materials in this record group were donated to the National Archives by various groups and individuals. Included are the Charles Edward Rhetts Papers, which contain correspondence, memoranda, and reports pertaining to lend-lease supplies to the USSR and other countries, 1941-42. Recently received are the records of the American National Red Cross, 1881-1946, 33.31 cu. m., which include correspondence, reports, memoranda, and publications relating to Red Cross relief operations undertaken in Russia, Siberia, Armenia, Finland, Lithuania, Latvia, and Estonia as a result of floods, famines, droughts, epidemics, and wars. There are also films and/or newsreels on Soviet military equipment, on foreign dignitaries visiting the USSR, Soviet diplomats abroad (including the U.S. and the UN), Soviet troops in East Berlin, Vice President Nixon's trip to Eastern Europe and the USSR, and his tour of the American Trade Fair in Moscow with N. S. Khrushchev in 1959, the 1960 Paris Summit Conference, the meeting between President Kennedy and N. S. Khrushchev in Vienna in 1961, Khrushchev's visit to the U.S. in 1959 and to France in 1960, the signing of the Nuclear Test-Ban Treaty in 1963, the Russo-Finnish War, communism in Russia and Cuba, celebrations of the Bolshevik Revolution, the trans-Siberian railway, and other Russian-related subjects. There are taped speeches by Stalin, Trotskii, Molotov, and Khrushchev; a 1-hour tape, "Lenin and the People's Commissars"; photographs of German troops in Russia during World War II, and of the Soviet occupation of Vienna.

89 RG 205. Records of the Court of Claims Section (Justice), 1793-1947, 1,678 cu. ft. Includes records, 1921-38, of Soviet efforts to be compensated for 2 ships being built for Russia that were requisitioned by the U.S. government in 1917. There is also material on this matter in RG 123.

90 RG 208. Records of the Office of War Information, 1941-48, 4,630 cu. ft. Created in 1942, the Office of War Information handled information and propaganda efforts by the U.S. government during World War II. Its records include reports, photos, speech recordings, films (some of which were made in Russia) on the Soviet military, 1942-45, the USSR air command in Alaska during World War II, the Yalta Conference, Soviet delegates at the signing of the United Nations Charter, 1945, lend-lease to the Soviet Union, and the economy of the Ukraine, 1942-45.

91 RG 211. Records of the War Manpower Commission, 1936-47, 1,186 cu. ft. Formed in 1942, the War Manpower Commission (WMC) prepared the U.S. labor force for the war effort. Its records contain a considerable amount of documentation on Soviet labor from 1921 on, including data on trade unions, absenteeism, social insurance, and the migration of agricultural workers. There are also materials on Soviet industry, vocational training, welfare programs, veterans' pensions, and economic destruction during World War II. Finally, there is an index to publications pertaining to the USSR.

92 RG 217. Records of the United States General Accounting Office, 1776-1960, 36,987 cu. ft. Created in 1921, the General Accounting Office (GAO) audits the employment of public funds. Its records contain contracts used for the quartering of U.S. soldiers in Archangel, 1919.

93 RG 213. Records of the Foreign Claims Section (War), 1917-40, 40 cu. ft. The "General Correspondence of the Office of the

Special Representative of the Secretary of War, 1918-20" in this record group contains correspondence relating to a wartime contract for steel rails with the Russian government and to the ultimate disposition of the rails, which were stored in Japan.

94 RG 218. Records of the United States Joint Chief of Staff, 1942-56, 1,019 cu. ft. The Joint Chiefs of Staff are involved in strategic planning and make reviews of the major needs of the U.S. military. Included here are the records of the United Joint Chiefs of Staff (JCS) and of the Combined Chiefs of Staff (CCS) in the central decimal and geographic decimal files, 1942-56, which contain information on the armed forces of the Soviet Union during and after World War II, post-war occupation of Austria and Germany, Soviet domination of countries in Eastern Europe, Soviet influence in countries around the world, conditions in the Soviet Union, Soviet weapons, and U.S. plans for war in case of Soviet attack. Also included are the records of the Munitions Assignment Board, which helped to provide war equipment to countries in the United Nations, including the Soviet Union.

95 RG 219. Records of the Office of Defense Transportation, 1934-52, 1,095 cu. ft. Created in 1941, the Office of Defense Transportation served to make maximum use of the U.S. transportation network during World War II. Its records include reports, 1941-45, on the mail and communications system in the USSR; information on freight to be shipped from the U.S. to the Soviet Union, 1942-45; and a report by an American organization on how to improve Soviet railroads, 1930.

96 RG 220. Records of Temporary Committees, Commissions, and Boards, 1918-74, 2,158 cu. ft. Included are the records of the Subversive Activities Control Board, 1951-73, 161 ft., which contain materials on communist organizations, and records of the National Aeronautics and Space Council, 1958-73, 27 ft.

97 RG 226. Records of the Office of Strategic Services, 1919-46, 937 cu. ft. Formed in 1942, the Office of Strategic Services (OSS) gathered information for the Joint Chiefs of Staff. Its records include intelligence, naval, and military reports on Soviet natural resources, nationality problems in the USSR, and other social, political, military, and economic matters pertaining to Russia. There are also a considerable number of maps (mostly small-scale) of the USSR showing population distribution and density, administrative and political divisions, location of economic resources, transportation systems and routes, and routes of the trans-Siberian railroad.

98 RG 232. Records of the Petroleum Administrative Board, 1924-43, 405 cu. ft. Founded in 1933, the Petroleum Administrative Board regulated petroleum production according to the National Industrial Recovery Act and the petroleum code. Its records include materials on the oil resources of Estonia, Latvia, Lithuania, Asiatic Russia, and Sakhalin Island, 1925-29.

99 RG 227. Records of the Office of Scientific Research and Development, 1939-47, 3,004 cu. ft. The Office of Scientific Research and Development (OSRD) was established in 1941 to provide for scientific and medical research pertaining to national defense. Its records include materials on Soviet achievements in various fields of medicine; a report by the Special Aluminum Committee of the Combined Raw Materials Board describing Soviet bauxite resources, 1928-44; and a compilation of published Soviet materials on the control of rodents in agriculture.

100 RG 233. Records of the United States House of Representatives, 1789-1974, 17,201 cu. ft. The records of the House Committee on Foreign Affairs and of the House Committee on Un-American Activities are in this record group. These records contain materials on American attitudes to Russia, the Bolshevik Revolution, and the independence of Eastern European areas, including the Ukraine. There are also numerous bills, petitions, and resolutions pertaining to the abrogation of the U.S.-Russian commercial treaty of 1832, interest payments on Russian Imperial government bonds, U.S. mediation in the Russo-Japanese War, the extradition of Jan Pouren and Christian Rudowitz to Russia, the construction of telegraphic cables between the U.S. and Siberia, communist activities, and many other Russian-related subjects.

101 RG 238. National Archives Collection of World War II War Crimes Records, 1900-50, 1,620 cu. ft. Included is a copy of the Moscow Declaration, 1 November 1943, on how war criminals were to be treated by the Allied governments. There are also ca. 25 photographs of the Soviet legal and military personnel that collaborated with the United States counsel for the prosecution of Axis criminality; over 300 sound recordings from the courtroom at Nuremberg, 1945-46, with the voices and testimony of Russian witnesses and prosecutors; and films of concentration camps taken by Russian forces in 1945.

102 RG 242. National Archives Collection of Foreign Records Seized, 1941-, 1679-1954, 5,001 cu. ft. RG 242 contains microfilms of captured Nazi documents and other World War II materials pertaining to Russia. Records of the German Foreign Ministry and the Reich Chancellery, 1833-1945, 1 ft. and 6,005 rolls of microfilm, provide information on Nazi-Soviet relations. Records of the Reich Commissioner for the Strengthening of Germandom, 1939-45, 20 rolls of microfilm, have documentation on the resettlement of ethnic Germans

from the Soviet Union. Records of the Reich Ministry for the Occupied Eastern Territories, 1924-45, 152 rolls of microfilm, shed light on the Nazi administration of the Ostland (Estonia, Latvia, and Lithuania), the Ukraine, and White Ruthenia. Records of Other Reich Ministries and Offices, 1919-45, 1 ft., 23 rolls of microfilm, and 409 microfiche, have data relating to weather in the Soviet Union, 1941-42. Records of German Air Force Commands, 1932-45, 202 ft. and 197 rolls of microfilm, include records of German anti-aircraft units on shooting down Russian airplanes. Records from the Heere-archiv, 1679-1947, 169 rolls of microfilm, contain the papers of General Hans von Seeckt (1866-1936), which document Russian-German relations after World War I, and also the papers of General Wilhelm Groener (1867-1939), which have materials on the German occupation of the Ukraine and the Kiev Army Group of Field Marshal von Eichhorn, 1917-18. Records of the National Socialist German Workers' Party, 1915-42, 2,126 rolls of microfilm, contain information on the resettlement of ethnic Germans and foreign labor recruitment. Library of German microfilms, 1870-1945, 1,079 ft., has Russian propaganda leaflets and reports on the Russian army postal system, Soviet airborne troops, and industrial development in the USSR. Records of the All-Union Communist Party, Smolensk District, 1917-41, 28 ft., consist of materials, captured by German forces in 1941 and seized by U.S. forces in 1945, that document Communist Party activities in Smolensk. Records of the Soviet Purchasing Commission at Prague, 1936-41, 49 ft., provide information on business contacts between the Soviet Union and Czechoslovakia. Miscellaneous Russian Records, 1870-1947, 146 ft. and 6 rolls of microfilm, contain reports, publications, correspondence, and other materials on leading Soviet personalities and on economic, political, scientific, and military affairs in the Soviet Union. Miscellaneous Records, 1815-1945, 93 ft., contain military and civilian publications of Estonian and Lithuanian origin or language. Italian Records, 1922-43, 2 ft. and 825 rolls of microfilm, contain activity reports of the 8th Army (formerly the Italian Expeditionary Force in Russia) pertaining to operations on the Russian front. Japanese Records, 1928-47, 366 rolls of microfilm, include information on Japanese-Soviet negotiations and a report on the Soviet entry in World War II. Records Seized by U.S. Military Forces in Korea, 1921-52, 1,206 ft., contain publications and administrative and personnel files in Russian and other languages on Russian-Korean commerce, life in the USSR, and Eastern Europe. Cartographic Records, 1934-45, ca. 30,635 items, contain air reconnaissance maps of the eastern front, maps of the disposition of Red army units, situation maps prepared by the Soviets, Russian maps from captured German World War II records, and publications by the German navy high command on Siberian ice conditions. Audiovisual Records, 1913-54, 327,874 items, contain the Joachim von Ribbentrop collection, which includes ca. 250 photographs pertaining to the signing of the Nazi-Soviet Pact, Molotov's state visit to Berlin, November 1940, and other matters. Also included are several hundred Russian films, 1935-51, consisting of industrial, scientific, and travel documentaries on Soviet culture, music, and history, especially during World War II. There are also numerous photographs and slides pertaining to the Soviet Union and a Russian film on the death of Lenin, 1924.

103 RG 250. Records of the Office of War Mobilization and Reconversion, 1942-47, 189 cu. ft. The Office of War Mobilization and Reconversion (OWMR) was formed in 1944 to stimulate the production and efficient use of natural resources. Its records include materials on war relief in the USSR and on U.S. agricultural goods sent to the Soviet Union, 1941-45.

104 RG 253. Records of the Petroleum Administration for War, 1941-46, 2,192 cu. ft. The Petroleum Administration for War (PAW) was established in 1942. Its records contain much material on the lend-lease of oil goods to the USSR and on Soviet petroleum resources, needs, and production.

105 RG 255. Records of the National Aeronautics and Space Administration, 1914-69, 3,423 cu. ft. The National Aeronautics and Space Administration (NASA) was established in 1958 and preceded by the National Advisory Committee for Aeronautics, formed in 1915. Its records contain materials on Soviet aviation, 1915-63, including photographs, reports, and translations of Russian-language documents.

106 RG 256. Records of the American Commission to Negotiate Peace, 1914-31, 258 cu. ft. The American Commission to Negotiate Peace, established in 1918, prepared U.S. peace settlements after World War I. Its records include studies and other materials pertaining to Russian nationalities and the condition of the army in Russia at the time of the Revolution. Among its cartographic records is a "Russia and Poland Division," which contains 152 items illustrating the problems of establishing an independent Poland. There are also maps showing Eastern Europe, Armenia, and Russian settlements in Central Asia.

107 RG 260. Records of the United States Occupation Headquarters, World War II, 1942-71, 11,070 cu. ft. The records of the Office of Military Government for Germany, United States, and the records of the U.S. Element, Allied Commission Austria, both in this record group, contain references to Russia, the Berlin airlift, the industrial dismemberment of Germany, and German war reparations.

108 RG 261. Records of Former Russian Agencies, 1802-1922, 679 ft. Materials consist of records of Imperial Russian agencies that were obtained by the Department of State. Included are records of the Russian-American Company, 1802 and 1817-67, 23 ft., that contain (1) communications from the main office in St. Petersburg to governors general in America, 1817-66, 25 vols.; (2) outgoing communications of governors general at Novo-Arkhangel'sk, 1867, 49 vols.; (3) logs of company ships, 1850-67, 16 vols., on their journeys to Russia, the Hawaiian Islands, China, Siberia, and California; (4) journals of exploring expeditions, 1842-44, 1860-64, 2 vols., which contain the journals of Lavrentii A. Zagoskin and Capt. N. Arkhimandritov. Frequently mentioned in these records are the governors general of the company between 1799 and 1829: Aleksandr Andreevich Baranov, Leontii Andreianovich Hagemeister, Semen Ivanovich Ianovskii, Matvei Ivanovich Muraviev, and Petr Egorovich Chistiakov. Also included in RG 261 are records of Russian consulates, 1862-1922, 165 ft., which include the records of consulates at New York, Philadelphia, Chicago, San Francisco, Portland, Seattle, Honolulu, Montreal, and Vancouver. A final group of documents are records of the Russian Supply Committee, 1914-22, 603 ft., which consist of correspondence and other materials documenting dealings between the U.S. government and commercial firms for military supplies to Russia during World War I.

109 RG 248. Records of the War Shipping Administration, 1941-50, 280 cu. ft. Created in 1942, the War Shipping Administration (WSA) cooperated with other federal agencies to make maximum use of U.S. shipping. Its records include the records of the Office for the Russian Shipping Area, which pertain to the development of Soviet and East European shipping programs, 1941-46. There are also documents on U.S. lend-lease assistance to the USSR; reports by the Office of Strategic Services on Russian nationalities and political organization in northeastern Siberia; data on Soviet mineral and other exports to the United States; and reports on Soviet economic conditions and potentials.

110 RG 262. Records of the Foreign Broadcast Intelligence Service, 1940-47, 702 cu. ft. Created in 1941, the Foreign Broadcast Intelligence Service (FBIS) collected information on the broadcast programs of foreign countries. Its records include transcripts of broadcasts from the Soviet Union that touch on economic, military, and other matters. Also included is a recording of a talk by Stalin delivered in November 1942.

111 RG 263. Records of the Central Intelligence Agency, 1947-72, 135 cu. ft. The Central Intelligence Agency, formed in 1947, coordinates U.S. intelligence activities. Its records include transcripts of broadcasts from the Soviet Union and a speech given by N. S. Khrushchev in Kiev in October 1949.

112 RG 265. Records of the Office of Foreign Assets Control, 1943-45, 461 cu. ft. The Office of Foreign Assets Control, the successor of several agencies that regulated foreign assets in the U.S., was created in 1962. Its records contain reports on U.S.-owned property in the Soviet Union in 1943.

113 RG 272. Records of the President's Commission on the Assassination of President Kennedy, 1963-64, 363 cu. ft. Included are name files for Lee Oswald, accused of the assassination of President Kennedy, and his Russian-born wife, Marina. These files consist almost entirely of copies of documents in other series of the Commission's records, including investigative reports, correspondence, and internal memoranda. There are also name files for other persons that relate to Lee Oswald's residence in Russia, including 1 for the Russian defector Yuri Nosenko. There is also other material in the records relating to Russia that is not included in the Oswald name files, such as testimony by State Department and other government officials concerning Oswald's residence in the Soviet Union. The testimony has been published, as has much of the material in the Oswald name file, in the Report, 1 vol., and Hearings, 26 vols., including 11 exhibits of documents and photographs, of the Commission.

114 RG 304. Records of the Office of Civil and Defense Mobilization, 1939-61, 746 cu. ft. The Office of Civil and Defense Mobilization was created to assist the president in the mobilization of military, industrial, and civilian forces. Its records include correspondence pertaining to East-West trade in strategic commodities and raw materials.

115 RG 306. Records of the United States Information Agency, 1900-68, 1,326 cu. ft. Created in 1953, the United States Information Agency (USIA) collected and disseminated information on behalf of the U.S. government. Its records include ca. 2,000 photographs from the New York Times Paris office, 1920-40, 1945-50, of Russian/Soviet artists, writers (Ilia Ehrenburg, Maksim Gorkii), political figures (Stalin, Trotskii, Lenin, Kerensky, Dzerzhinskii, Tomskii, Zinoviev, Chicherin, Maevskii), and of events in the Soviet Union. There are also Russian-related materials in the records of the International Press Service of the Department of State, 1948-53, and in the Photographic Library of the USIA, 1953-65.

116 RG 307. Records of the National Science Foundation, 1956-73, 176 cu. ft. Created in 1950, the National Science Foundation is designed to promote research and education in the sciences. Its records include a U.S. flag

flown in 1967 at the Russian Antarctic station Molodezhnaya and English translations of Russian studies on the Antarctic.

117 RG 313. Records of the Naval Operating Forces, 1864-1974, 18,642 cu. ft. This record group, which contains materials on major operating force commands of the United States Navy, may have documents pertaining to visits by United States naval units to Soviet ports and to contacts between the Soviet and U.S. navies.

118 RG 319. Records of the Army Staff, 1940-69, 14,617 cu. ft. The Army Staff, formed in 1947, is the military staff of the secretary of the army. Its records include materials on U.S.-USSR policies in occupied countries after World War II (Japan, Germany, Austria), military contingency planning toward the USSR, and Soviet military potential and activities.

119 RG 326. Records of the Atomic Energy Commission, ca. 1964-71, 9 cu. ft. Created in 1946, the Atomic Energy Commission (AEC) controls the production and use of atomic energy. Its records include Russian educational documentaries, ca. 1964, on the peaceful uses of atomic energy.

120 RG 330. Records of the Office of the Secretary of Defense, 1940-65. The Office of the Secretary of Defense, formed in 1947, has responsibility for assuring the security of the U.S. Its records contain vast amounts of materials dealing with war planning directed toward the USSR. Much of this material is scattered throughout various general and special correspondence files and report files to the secretary, his principal assistants, and the heads of certain subordinate offices and divisions. Subjects discussed include the strategic and tactical use of nuclear weapons, European Defense Community agreements, the Mutual Defense Assistance Program, 1950-52, the Mutual Security Act, 1953, the Soviet role in the wartime and post-war period, and USSR-Iranian relations.

121 RG 331. Records of Allied Operational and Occupation Headquarters, World War II, 1938-54, 17,948 cu. ft. Inter-Allied operational headquarters carried out the plans of the Combined Chiefs of Staff (CCS), established in 1942. Its records contain materials on Russian-Allied military activities, missions of the Supreme Headquarters, Allied Expeditionary Force (SHAEF) to Russia, the handling of censorship by Soviet and American authorities, and the procurement of supplies for the USSR.

122 RG 333. Records of International Military Agencies, 1941-57, 150 cu. ft. International military agencies were formed by the United States and Allied nations to carry out mutual objectives during and after World War II. Records of the Tripartite Naval Commission, 1941-47, contain correspondence, messages, and memoranda among the members of the Commission representing the United States, Great Britain, and the USSR. The documents of the Korean Armistice include 2 original maps, 1 American and 1 Russian, denoting the agreed division of Korea by a joint U.S.-USSR survey at the 38th degree parallel in April 1947. Other references to the USSR can be found in the Records of the United Nations Command, 1950-57, 121 ft.

123 RG 334. Records of Interservice Agencies, 1916-58, 706 cu. ft. Interservice agencies were established during World War II to handle various matters connected with the war. The record group includes records of the United States Military Mission to Moscow, 1943-45, 23 ft., which includes reports, messages, correspondence and records pertaining to Operation Frantic, the shuttle-bombing of Axis-occupied Europe. Records of the National War College, 1943-54, 391 ft., contain library files on Soviet domestic affairs, military capability, and foreign relations.

124 RG 335. Records of the Office of the Secretary of the Army, 1926-70. The Office of the Secretary of the Army originated in 1947. Its records include documentation on the Soviet explosion of the atomic bomb, the U.S. airlift to Berlin, Soviet natural resources, and the military strength of the USSR.

125 RG 338. Records of the United States Army Commands, 1939-1960, 26,819 cu. ft. U.S. Army commands originated in World War II to carry out various functions. The record group includes records of other army field commands, 1940-53, 25,897 ft., which contain documentation on Soviet troop movements and American contacts with Soviet troops in Central Europe. Records of the U.S. Army Europe, 1939-60, 878 ft., include Intelligence Division interrogation reports on persons in the USSR or in Soviet-controlled nations, 1943-49, and Judge Advocate Division materials relating to criminal acts by Nazis inside the Soviet Union and against Soviet citizens outside the USSR. (Many copies of the Judge Advocate Division materials are in RG 153.)

126 RG 340. Records of the Office of the Secretary of the Air Force, 1942-56, 1,419 cu. ft. The Office of the Secretary of the Air Force, which originated in 1947, was responsible for war planning and for coordinating defense-related activities. Its Russian-related materials include documents on preparing for war against the Soviet Union, 1948-50.

127 RG 341. Records of Headquarters United States Air Force, 1935-63, 7,053 cu. ft. Headquarters U.S. Air Force, created in 1947, advises the president and the National Security Council on military affairs. Its records include correspondence, intelligence reports, aerial photos, radar reports, charts, and air attaché reports pertaining to the Soviet Union.

DISTRICT OF COLUMBIA - NATIONAL ARCHIVES DC 30

128 RG 342. Records of United States Air Force Commands, Activities, and Organizations, 1900-73, 1,465 cu. ft. Included is the General Goddard Collection, which contains photographs of the Soviet Zone in Berlin, 1945. There are also motion pictures with documentation on the 1949 May Day celebration, the defense of Moscow, Igor Sikorsky, Josef Stalin, and V. M. Molotov.

129 RG 345. Records of Joint Commands, 1942-56, 245 cu. ft. The system of joint commands, established in 1946, is designed to conduct military operations under a single commander when national security requires. Its records contain materials on military matters pertaining to the USSR.

130 RG 350. Records of the Bureau of Insular Affairs, 1868-1945, 1,645 cu. ft. The Bureau of Insular Affairs originated in 1898 to assist in the administration of Puerto Rico, Cuba, and the Philippine Islands. Included are records relating to the Philippine Islands, 1897-1938, 47 ft., that contain materials on Russian refugees in the Philippines, Russian consuls to and from Cuba, Bolsheviki, and Russian vessels served by the U.S.

131 RG 353. Records of Interdepartmental and Intradepartmental Committees (State Department). 1926-60. 164 cu. ft. Included in this record group are materials pertaining to U.S.-Soviet relations.

132 RG 354. Records of the Economic Research Service, 1934-71, 30 cu. ft. The Economic Research Service (ERS), created in 1961, provides information on various economic matters. Its records include machine readable data, 1961-71, on trade between the USSR and the Organization for Economic Cooperation and Development.

133 RG 360. Records of the Continental and Confederation Congresses and the Constitutional Convention, 1774-96, 312 cu. ft. Records of the Continental and Confederation Congresses, 1774-89, 415 ft., contain Item 86, Items from Ralph Izard and Others, 1777-84, which includes letters pertaining to Francis Dana's mission to St. Petersburg in the 1780s as envoy of the United States. The records also have materials relating to early Russian-American relations and to John Paul Jones's service in Russia.

134 RG 393. Records of the United States Army Continental Commands, 1821-1920, 10,401 cu. ft. Included are materials on the buildings and property that were part of the transfer of Alaska from Russia to the United States in 1867.

135 RG 395. Records of U.S. Army Overseas Operations and Commands, 1898-1942, 2,405 cu. ft. This record group includes the records of the American Expeditionary Forces in Siberia, 1918-20. Most of the material consists of war diaries written at American headquarters at Vladivostok; there are also diaries from local units at Shkotovo and the Suchan mines. Other materials include correspondence, cablegrams, telegrams, issuances, and photographs.

136 RG 407. Records of the Adjutant General's Office, 1917-, 1905-1958, 21,840 cu. ft. The adjutant general's office handles assignments, promotions, transfers, and other personnel matters for the army. Its records contain correspondence, reports, and other materials on lend-lease to the USSR, visits by Soviet officers to U.S. military installations during World War II, the award of Russian decorations to U.S. military personnel and vice versa, 1940-45, the Berlin blockade, 1948, Russian atomic bomb developments, 1949-54, U.S.-USSR joint occupation policies after World War II, and U.S. policies in regard to Soviet pressures in the eastern Mediterranean.

137 RG 457. Records of the National Security Agency/Central Security Office, 3 cu. ft. Included are comprehensive reports of political, military, economic, psychological, subversive, and other conditions in the Soviet Union.

138 The following record groups may contain materials pertaining to Russia/USSR:

RG 15. Records of the Veterans Administration, 1773-1969, 76,197 cu. ft.

RG 17. Records of the Bureau of Animal Industry, 1874-1953, 696 cu. ft.

RG 23. Records of the Coast and Geodetic Survey, 1806-1965, 3,238 cu. ft.

RG 81. Records of the United States International Trade Commission, 1909-68, 702 cu. ft.

RG 87. Records of the United States Secret Service, 1863-1971, 872 cu. ft.

RG 143. Records of the Bureau of Supplies and Accounts (Navy), 1885-1946, 3,906 cu. ft.

RG 189. Records of the National Academy of Sciences, 1900-64, 65 cu. ft.

RG 203. Records of the Office of the Chief of Finance (Army), 1792-1942, 480 cu. ft.

RG 389. Records of the Office of the Provost Marshall General, 1937-56, 684 cu. ft.

RG 401. National Archives Gift Collection of Materials Pertaining to Polar Regions, 1750-1974, 967 cu. ft.

Restrictions: There are various restrictions to some of the materials cited above, especially for more recent items. For details, contact the National Archives or see the National Archives Guide (1974) cited below.

Finding Aids: Guide to the National Archives of the United States (1974) is the most complete introduction to the materials in the National Archives. For Russian-related materials, see the guide on which much of this entry is based, Elizabeth Buck, comp., Materials in the National Archives Relating to the Russian Empire and the Soviet Union (1952) [National Archives Reference Information Paper no. 41]. This guide divides Russian-related materials by subject matter and historical periods (rather than by record groups) and could be of use to a researcher looking for information on a specific topic or event. The guide, however, is quite dated, especially on the post-World War II era. Inventories, preliminary inventories, and special lists to materials in individual record groups are mentioned in Select List of Publications of the National Archives and Records Service (revised, 1977). Microfilms of materials in the National Archives, and the publications that frequently accompany them, are listed in Catalog of National Archives Microfilm Publications (1974) and supplement (1979). Unpublished finding aids to various materials are frequently available at individual operating units of the National Archives.

DC 31
PHOTOGRAPHIC ARCHIVES
NATIONAL GALLERY OF ART
Constitution Avenue at 6th Street NW
Washington, D.C. 20565
(202-737-4215)

These archives contain ca. 1200 black and white photographs of Russian painting from the 15th to the 20th c. The Photographic Archives are a study collection of photographs of works of art. They may not be loaned or duplicated.

DC 32
NAVAL HISTORICAL CENTER
NAVY DEPARTMENT
Washington Navy Yard, Building 76
Washington, D.C. 20374
(202-433-2765)

500 photos relating to pre- and post-revolutionary Russia, overwhelmingly of ships. The greatest concentration of items dates from the 1950s. The staff requests advance notification from researchers who wish to use the collection.

DC 33
OPERATIONAL ARCHIVES
NAVAL HISTORY DIVISION
NAVY DEPARTMENT
Washington Navy Yard, Buidling 210
Washington, D.C. 20374
(202-433-3170)

At the start of World War II, the Office of Naval Records and Library (a predecessor of the present Naval History Division) began to collect the reports, plans, and diaries that flowed into Washington from combat naval commands. The collection formed during that war is the core of the holdings of the operational archives; its primary coverage is from 1939 to the present, although there are limited materials from earlier periods as well. Among the Russian-related sources in the archives are the following:

1 Early Records Collection. 1775-1975, 140 ft. Includes the original diary, 1904-1905, 2 vols., of Vice-Admiral Newton A. McCully. McCully was then a naval attaché in St. Petersburg and an observer with the Russian forces in the Russo-Japanese War. Aside from the diary, the collection holds a few additional Russian-related papers.

2 Immediate Office Files and Other Records of Individuals. Included here are materials by and on Secretary of the Navy James V. Forrestal, 1934-51, 2 ft.; Fleet Admiral Ernest J. King, 1941-46, 8 ft.; Fleet Admiral William D. Leahy, 1938-59, 9 ft.; and Vice Admiral Ralph A. Ofstie, 1942-55, 9 ft.

3 Records from Foreign Sources. 1914-45, 293 ft. Contains certain translated records of the German navy, essays by World War II German officers, and related studies, 1922-45, 98 ft. Russian-related materials include the war diary of the German naval command in the Black Sea, 1941-44; situation reports on the Mediterranean, Adriatic, and Black seas; and essays on German naval preparations for attacking the USSR and on Russian landings in the area of the Black Sea. The original German records used as a basis for these essays and translations were seized by the Allies at Tambach Castle in southern Germany late in World War II. Microfilms of these extensive archives have been transferred by the Navy to the Modern Military Branch of the National Archives.

4 Records Organized by the Operational Archives. Among these records the following contain materials on convoys to Russia in World War II: "Action and Operational Reports of Naval Commands," 1,200 ft.; "Records of the Tenth Fleet, Office of the Commander in Chief, U.S. Fleet," 349 ft.; and "War Diaries of Naval Commands," 833 ft. Some reports and other materials from U.S. naval attachés in Moscow in the 1940s are found in "Central Security - Classified Records of the Offices of the Secretary of the Navy/Chief of Naval Operations," 900 ft.; and "Records of the Top Secret Control Office, Office of the Chief of Naval Operations," 75 ft. There also is limited material on Russia in the "Records of the General Board of the Navy," 231 ft., and lend-lease and international conferences involving the Soviet Union are documented in "Records of the Immediate Offices of the Chief of Naval Operations/Commander in Chief, U.S. Navy," 25 ft.

Note: The Naval History Division also has copies, bound and indexed, of the Oral Histories in the collection of the U.S. Naval Institute in Annapolis, Maryland. Relevant holdings are described in the entry for the Naval Institute.

Finding Aids: The staff has prepared various card indexes and guides to the collections, including its "Information for Visitors to the Operational Archives" used in writing this entry.

DC 34
PHOTOGRAPHIC CENTER
NAVAL STATION
NAVY DEPARTMENT
Washington, D.C. 20374
(202-433-2168)

About 100 recent still photographs of Soviet ships, submarines, and aircraft.

DC 35
SCOTTISH RITE SUPREME COUNCIL ARCHIVES AND LIBRARY
1733 16th Street NW
Washington, D.C. 20009
(202-232-3579 x 32)

A letter from an organization of Russian Masons, dated 1817, asking for recognition from the Supreme Council. Published in the council's monthly The New Age (October 1973). There might be more Russian-related materials in the archives.

DC 36
S. M. SELCUK--PRIVATE COLLECTION
DIVISION OF INTERNATIONAL PROGRAMS (AFRICA AND ASIA)
NATIONAL SCIENCE FOUNDATION
Washington, D.C. 20550
(202-632-4342)

Mr. Selcuk has some materials, collected for a planned book, relating to his personal experiences in the USSR generally and in Azerbaijan in particular before emigrating. Some of his impressions are tape recorded. The holdings are at present closed to outside researchers, pending completion of the book.

DC 37
SHIPBUILDERS COUNCIL OF AMERICA
600 New Hampshire Avenue NW
Washington, D.C. 20037
(202-338-7722)

In division 16 of the Council's records, "Foreign Shipbuilding and Shipping," there are a number of items related to the Soviet Union. Among the holdings are materials on the following subjects: 16.002--Soviet maritime strategy, done by the Carrico-Center for Strategic Studies, 1967; 16.013--Soviet ships on order vs. U.S., 1962-72; 16.020--expansion of Soviet merchant marine into U.S. maritime trades, 1977; 16.021--Soviet oceans development, a Senate report, October 1976; 16.024--Soviet maritime activities in liner trades of the U.S., a staff report by the Federal Maritime Commission, October 1977; and 16.025--facts about the Soviet liner fleet and its effect on U.S. oceanborne trade, 1977. The Council maintains an unpublished list of these holdings.

DC 38
ARCHIVES
SMITHSONIAN INSTITUTION
900 Jefferson Drive
Washington, D.C. 20560
(202-381-4075)

Scattered throughout the administrative records and other materials held in this archive are undoubtedly additional items pertaining to the Russian Empire/Soviet Union. Time did not permit an examination of all collections, especially those concerned with international aspects of the Institution's work, which might hold material pertinent to this guide. The listing below represents only a sample of relevant holdings.

1 Assistant Secretary (Spencer F. Baird). Outgoing correspondence, 1850-77, 8 cu. ft. Arranged chronologically, these records include

correspondence with Russian/Soviet scientists. Indexes. (Record Unit 53; hereafter, RU)

2 Gustav Wilhelm Belfrage (1834-1882). Papers, 1866-82, .2 cu. ft., 80 items. Entomological collector and seller. Contains correspondence from entomologists in Russia. Unpublished description (NUCMC 74-968). (RU 7105)

3 Joseph Ashmead Clay (1806-1881) and John Randolph Clay (1808-1885). Papers, 1841 and 1859-66, .2 cu. ft., 100 items. John was a diplomat; Joseph, his older brother, managed his affairs. Both were amateur mineralogists. Includes material on mineralogical specimens obtained from Russia. Unpublished description (NUCMC 72-1232). (RU 7095)

4 William Healey Dall (1845-1927). Papers, ca. 1839-58 and 1865-1927, 22 cu. ft. Scientist, explorer, author, and government worker. Correspondence, notebooks, diaries, scrapbooks, financial accounts, field notes, maps, etc., relating to the Western Union Telegraph Expedition, and to Alaskan towns (such as Sitka), topography, mineral resources, flora and fauna, Alaskan Indians, Russian-Americans, and Alaskan politics, 1865-68. Also, notes, correspondence, and map of Robert Kennicott and information about Kennicott's death, plus additional material from Dall's later Alaskan explorations, 1871-76 and 1879-80. References to George Kennan, Cleveland Abbe, and Ivan Petroff. Unpublished description (NUCMC 71-1872). (RU 7073)

5 Robert Kennicott (1835-1866). Papers, 1863-65, 3 items, 22 pp. Alaskan explorer. 3 letters, 2 to Roderick MacFarlane of Winnipeg, Canada. (RU 7072)

6 National Institute. Records, 1839-63, 6.2 cu. ft. Contains some references to Russia. Unpublished description. (RU 7058)

7 National Zoological Park. Records, 1887-1965, 100 cu. ft. Includes some correspondence, 1938-39, on the exchange of animals between the U.S. and USSR. Unpublished description. (RU 74)

8 Registrar. Accession Records, 1834-1958, accretions to 1976, ca. 405 cu. ft. Includes some correspondence with Russian/Soviet scientists. Partially microfilmed. Unpublished finding aids. (RU 6999T)

9 Leonhard Stejneger (1851-1943). Papers, 1867-1943, 14.3 cu. ft. Scientist and museum curator. Served on the International Fur Seal Commission beginning in 1896. Manuscripts, notes, letters, reports, and photographs pertaining, in part, to his field trips in the North Pacific-Bering Sea area, 1882, 1895-97, 1922, and to fur seals and natives of that area. Also, manuscripts, notes, and correspondence concerning Georg Wilhelm Steller, a German naturalist on Vitus Bering's second expedition, a biography of whom Stejneger published in 1936. Unpublished description. (RU 7074)

10 United States National Museum. Permanent Administrative Files, 1877-1975, 224 cu. ft. Includes correspondence of Russian/Soviet scientists; also, records concerning the Smithsonian-Harvard expedition to the Altai Mountains in Siberia, 1912. Inquire concerning special conditions of access. Unpublished finding aids. (RU 192)

11 Western Union Telegraph Expedition. Collection, 1865-67, .3 cu. ft. Also known as the Russian-American Telegraph Expedition. Studied feasibility of establishing communications with Europe via Alaska, the Bering Straits, and Siberia. 3 divisions worked in Canada, Russian-America (Alaska), and Asia. Robert Kennicott headed the Russian-American division, which also made natural history collections. Members of the Scientific Corps which went to Alaska included William H. Dall, Henry M. Bannister, and Henry W. Elliott. Contains correspondence, mostly to Spencer F. Baird, copies of reports, copies of Kennicott's notes on natural history, and clippings. (RU 7213)

Finding Aid: Guide to the Smithsonian Archives (1978), from which the preceding information was quoted.

DC 39
ARCHIVES OF AMERICAN ART
SMITHSONIAN INSTITUTION
FINE ARTS AND PORTRAIT GALLERY BUILDING
8th and F Streets NW
Washington, D.C. 20560
(202-381-6174)

The Archives holds substantial materials concerning artists born in areas now comprising the Soviet Union. Items for any one artist may be scattered among several different collections. The following selective list includes figures for whom there are such materials as correspondence, photographs, oral history tape recordings, exhibition catalogues, clippings, notes, and other items. (Some of them left their homelands at an early age.) Boris Anisfeld, Alexander Archipenko, Saul Baizerman, Ilya Bolotowsky, David Burliuk, Marc Chagall, Serge Chermayeff, Nicolai Cikovsky, Gleb N. Derujinsky, Naum Gabo, John D. Graham (Debrovski), Morris Kantor, Jacques Lipchitz, Louis Lozowick, Louis Ribak, Joseph Schillinger, Ben Shahn, Moses and Raphael Soyer, Nahum Tschacbasov, Abraham Walkowitz, Max Weber, Adja Yunkers, and Feodor Zakharov.

In addition, these collections contain some material relating to the Russian Empire/Soviet

Union (amounts vary considerably; significance of references could not be checked): papers of Senator William Benton, William Merritt Berger, Maxim Karolik, Rockwell Kent, Hilla Rebay, Theodore Roszak, and William Reinhold Valentiner. Collections that also appear to have relevant holdings include: Alfred Hamilton Barr, Thomas Eakins, Albert Kahn, Elizabeth McCausland, J. B. Neumann, Hudson Walker, Robert Jay Wolff, and Sidney C. Woodward, and American Abstract Artists.

Much of the preceding material is on microfilm. A Checklist of the Collection, compiled by Arthur J. Breton, Nancy H. Zembala, and Anne P. Nicastro (Spring, 1975) will be revised periodically.

Note: Headquarters of the Archives of American Art is in New York City. Original research materials are in Washington. Researchers may use microfilm copies of the original material in Washington, New York, Boston, Detroit, and San Francisco, the 5 offices of the Archives. In cases when a branch does not have a copy of the desired material, an interlibrary loan system can generally provide the item(s).

DC 40
FREER GALLERY OF ART
SMITHSONIAN INSTITUTION
12th & Jefferson Drive
Washington, D.C. 20560
(202-381-5342)

Armenian Manuscripts. Four Gospels, 11th c.; four Gospels, 12th c.; four Gospels, A.D. 1253; four Gospels, 13th c.; four Gospels, A.D. 1263; psalter, 14th-15th c.; hymnal, A.D. 1651-52; four Gospels, A.D. 1668-73.

DC 41
NATIONAL MUSEUM OF HISTORY AND TECHNOLOGY
SMITHSONIAN INSTITUTION
Constitution Avenue between 13th and 14th Streets
Washington, D.C. 20560
(202-381-5017, information)

There is no central manuscript repository at the museum; instead, holdings are divided among various divisions according to subject. Along with textual matter, many of the divisions also have significant physical objects relating to the Russian Empire/Soviet Union. The listing below highlights only some of the manuscript and non-textual materials at a few of the divisions.

Department of History of Technology
Division of Mechanical and Civil Engineering

1 John A. Beemer (b. 1879). Papers, 1907-55, 1.2 cu. ft. Civil engineer. Correspondence, reports, maps, plans, drawings, etc., in part pertaining to his work as a consulting engineer for the Soviet government, 1929-31. He worked with the Trans-Caucasia Water Economy Service (Zakvodkhoz) in Georgia, particularly on the Samgory irrigation project, 1930. Reference(s) to V. V. Tchikoff, Giprovod, Amtorg, and the Magnitogorsk Dam. Unpublished folder list.

Department of National History
Division of Military History

2 Military and War Poster Collection. Ca. 1860s-1960s, 50 cu. ft. Contains military recruitment, bond and loan drive, labor and war production, and propaganda posters issued by various countries including Russia during World War I and the USSR in World War II. Unpublished finding aids.

Division of Naval History

3 Joseph Francis (1801-1893). Papers, 1842-87, .1 cu. ft. Inventor and manufacturer. Pioneered many developments in boat design and construction, including the use of corrugated iron and improvements in lifeboat design. While abroad in 1855-63, he contracted for a fleet of corrugated iron steamers for the Russian government. Papers concern primarily his work in Russia, 1858-62. Documents and letters concerning shipbuilding and testing in Russia, in Russian and English; Russian patents; emancipation proclamation of Russian serfs; and printed materials and resolutions addressed to Francis in 1885-87. Collection is unarranged.

Division of Numismatics

4 Willis H. Dupont Collection of Russian Coins and Medals (Prince Georgii Mikhailovich Collection). Ca. 1700-1900s, over 6,000 coins and ca. 4,000 medals. Some coins date from a much earlier period. Most of the medals are silver, some bronze.

5 Russian Paper Currencies Collection. Ca. 1800-1918. Number of items undetermined.

Division of Political History

6 Gustavus Vasa Fox (1821-1883). Papers, ca. 1866-72, 1 cu. ft. Assistant secretary of the navy, 1861-66. In 1866 he was chosen to lead an American delegation to Russia to congratulate Alexander II on escaping an assassination

attempt and, perhaps, to act as a secret negotiator for the purchase of Alaska. Papers documenting his trip to Russia include social correspondence, invitations, programs, and banquet menus, in French, Russian, and English. The Fox Collection also holds a snuff box presented to Fox by the tsar, some medals, a malachite box from the city of St. Petersburg, and some other objects. I. M. Casanowicz, "The Gustavus Vasa Fox Collection of Russian Souvenirs in the United States National Museum," Proceedings of the United States National Museum, vol. 38, no. 1725; and an unpublished description.

DC 42
TAMARA G. STRICKLAND--PRIVATE COLLECTION
3010 32nd Street NW
Washington, D.C. 20008

Papers of Lieutenant General David Constantine Gounsadze (1861-1924), commander of the Imperial Russian 12th Army, are in the possession of his granddaughter. These comprise 6 notebooks of memoirs written in longhand, his military service record, some reports, photographs, and maps, 1912-24. General Gounsadze details his personal military experiences and observations about operations of the 97th Lifland Regiment in July-August 1914, then under his command, on the East Prussian front. The Germans had to shift a quarter of a million troops from the western front to stem the Russian attack on the eastern front. The memoirs also cover the Warsaw front in 1915, the defense of Dvinsk, 1915, the Austrian front in 1916, and the Riga front in 1917. In 1918 the general joined the Volunteer Army fighting the Bolsheviks in the Caucasus; he discusses the White efforts against the Reds and the fall of the Crimea in 1920. General Gounsadze eventually made his way to Croatia, Yugoslavia, where he died. All material is in Russian.

DC 43
CURATOR'S OFFICE
U.S. SUPREME COURT
First Street NE
Washington, D.C. 20543
(202-252-3298)

Mrs. S. T. Konenkov. Typed copy of a letter (27 April 1939) from the wife of the sculptor to attorney F. Regis Noel in Washington, ca. 2 pp., unsigned. Concerns the marble bust of Justice Oliver Wendell Holmes executed by her husband, with amusing details about the length of Mr. Holmes' mustache. Accompanied by a letter, 28 April 1939, from Noel transmitting the Konenkov letter to the Supreme Court. Note: The bust itself stands in the Supreme Court Building.

FLORIDA

FL 1
HENRY SHELTON SANFORD MEMORIAL LIBRARY
520 East First Street
Sanford, Florida 32771
(305-321-0710)

Henry Shelton Sanford (1823-1891). Papers, 1769-1901, ca. 60 ft., 50,000 items. Lawyer, businessman, and diplomat. In 1847-48 he served as secretary of the American legation in St. Petersburg. Correspondence, diaries, biographical, and genealogical data, legal documents, speeches, accounts, and writings. Specific Russian-related items could not be ascertained. Researchers might examine his business correspondence for 1841-48 (box 13); general correspondence, 1847-49 (box 94), correspondence--letterbooks, 1845-48 (box 97), letters of introduction, 1844-47 (box 103); and correspondence with special persons (boxes 116, 122, and 133). Correspondents include Neil S. Brown, Cassius M. Clay, W. H. Hunt, and Ralph Isaacs Ingersoll, all ministers to Russia, and Colin M. Ingersoll and Edward H. Wright, both secretaries of the Russian legation. The Tennessee State Library and Archives in Nashville processed and microfilmed these papers, retaining a complete copy of the microfilm for its own collections. Published register (Nashville, 1960). (NUCMC 62-553)

GEORGIA

GA 1
RONALD R. RADER--PRIVATE COLLECTION
DEPARTMENT OF HISTORY
UNIVERSITY OF GEORGIA
Athens, Georgia 30602
(404-542-2053)

Professor Rader is in possession of a copy of the diary of Frederic C. Gill (1882-1956), a technical adviser in Russia in 1914-15 for the Russian Mining Corporation Ltd. (London). He was on assignment to that firm from the Sullivan Machinery Co. of the United States. He specialized in the operation of diamond-tipped drills. His work took him to Ust-Kamenogorsk and Zyryanovsk in the Zmeinogorsk region of East Kazakhstan.

The diary, handwritten, 190 pp., 6 x 10 in., contains comments on mining problems, the introduction of certain technology to the Russians, and the native peoples (and Russians) and their customs, way of life, etc. Gill also observes the impact of the First World War on this area, notes his own changing feelings (enthusiasm to frustration), and finally gives a detailed account of his trip up the Irtysh and westward on the trans-Siberian railroad as he returned home. There are also some picture postcards of the area in which he was stationed.

The material is open to scholars after 1 January 1981, subject to certain restrictions on its use.

GA 2
SPECIAL COLLECTIONS
MANUSCRIPT DEPARTMENT
UNIVERSITY OF GEORGIA LIBRARIES
Athens, Georgia 30602
(404-542-2972)

Olin Downes. Collection, 1920-40, 61 items. Contains 30 letters of Sergei Prokofiev to Gottlieb Ephraim, 20 postcards from Prokofiev, and 10 photos of his works, plus an article concerning the composer. Partial finding aid, unpublished. (Collection 233)

GA 3
RICHARD B. RUSSELL MEMORIAL LIBRARY
UNIVERSITY OF GEORGIA LIBRARIES
Athens, Georgia 30602
(404-542-5788)

Richard B. Russell (1897-1972). Papers, ca. 1933-71, 1,708 ft. U.S. senator from Georgia. Ca. 1 ft. of material (mostly constituent correspondence) in the International Series pertains to Russia. Additional Russian-related items are scattered throughout other series (e.g., Kennedy assassination, armed services, and especially speech/media) and in oral history transcripts. Unpublished guide. Access to the material is made by an application provided by the library. Note: The library also holds other collections of congressional papers which may contain materials relating to the USSR.

GA 4
ATLANTA HISTORICAL SOCIETY
3099 Andrews Drive NW
Atlanta, Georgia 30355
(404-261-1837)

1 Benjamin Mart Bailey (1880-1945). Papers, 1901-45, 4 ft. U.S. Army Officer (brigadier general). He served in the American Expeditionary Forces in Europe. There are 31 photographs (box 8, folder 1) of Company M, 31st Infantry of American Expeditionary Forces, in Suchan, Siberia, Vladivostok, and Khabarovsk, 1918-19. Included are photos of Russian officers in the Death's Head Battalion.

2 Mary V. (Mrs. E. L.) Connally (1850-1927). Papers, 1830-1930, 1.5 ft. Contains a scrapbook of European travels, 1894-1895, 95 pp., with photos, postcards, and souvenirs of travel to Moscow and St. Petersburg.

3 Pyatt Green ("Paul Grant"). Papers, ca. 1875-95, .5 ft. Box 1, folder 3, contains a typed manuscript by Green, 20 pp., "The Death of Russia's Day-Dream - a Story of the Romanoffs."

4 Antoinette Johnson Matthews (b. 1895). Papers, 1885-1974, 1.5 ft. In Box 3, there is a travel diary, summer 1961, describing a visit to Minsk, Leningrad, Moscow, Stalingrad, Sochi, and Yalta.

5 Clara Mildred Thompson. Papers, 1881-1975, 2.5 ft. Material pertaining to the Free Europe University in Exile, 1952, where Thompson was dean of women.

Finding Aids: Guide to the Manuscript Collection of the Atlanta Historical Society (1976) and unpublished finding aids for all the listed collections.

GA 5
ARCHIVES BRANCH
FEDERAL ARCHIVES & RECORDS CENTER, GSA
1559 St. Joseph Avenue
East Point, Georgia 30344
(404-763-7477)

This repository has some of the microfilms of materials in the National Archives (Washington, D.C.) that pertain to Russia/USSR. For more details, see Charles South, List of National Archives Microfilm Publications in the Regional Archives Branches (Washington: National Archives and Records Service, 1975). Original Russian-related materials not found in the National Archives in Washington include the files of the Office of Engineering Design and Construction in RG 142, Records of the Tennessee Valley Authority. These files, which contain reports, account books, blueprints, and correspondence, relate to the design, procurement, and shipment of hydroelectric power plant equipment to the Soviet Union by the T.V.A. under the lend-lease agreement (1942-45). Soviet engineers and electrical specialists mentioned include M. V. Maylshev, A. L. Artemov, N. M. Andrienko, V. N. Elfimov, A. G. Boiko, and N. P. Samsonov. Preliminary inventory.

HAWAII

HI 1
BERNICE P. BISHOP MUSEUM
1355 Kalihi Street (Mail: P.O. Box 6037)
Honolulu, Hawaii 96818
(808-847-3511)

1 Ray Jerome Baker. Includes a mimeographed "Brief report on a tour of Russia, July and August, 1958: visiting the cities of Leningrad, Kiev, Odessa, Yalta, Sochi, Kharkov, and Moscow," Honolulu, 1958, 20 pp. The photo collection has his "A tour of the Soviet Union and other European countries: lands of promise and progress" (1958), 3 vols. of photographs bound as books (negative nos. 50200-50857).

2 Martha W. Beckwith. Collection of clippings contains some items on Russians in Hawaii.

3 Louis Choris. Artist on board the *Riurik*, 1815-18, commanded by Captain Kotzebue. 46 original watercolor sketches, primarily of the Marshall Islands. Some of Kamchatka.

4 Peter the Great Museum of Anthropology and Ethnography (Leningrad). Contains a photographic reference file of Hawaiian ethnological objects in the collections.

5 Note: Additional Russian/Soviet-related materials (field notes, articles, clippings, a typed bibliography, etc.) appear in the Museum's published catalogue under the headings "Russians in Hawaii" and "Russians in the Pacific" as well as in the papers of Museum personnel who traveled abroad (e.g., M. Titcomb, P. Buck, and K. Embree).

Finding Aid: Dictionary Catalog of the Library of the Bernice P. Bishop Museum, 9 vols. (Boston: G. K. Hall, 1964), plus 2 supplements (1967 and 1969).

HI 2
HAWAII STATE ARCHIVES
Iolani Palace Grounds
Honolulu, Hawaii 96813
(808-548-2355)

1 Chamisso, Adelbert von. Typescript account of the voyage around the world on the *Riurik*, 1815-18. Translated from the German; Hawaiian section only.

2 Jackson, George E. G. Drawing of the Russian Fort Elizabeth at Waimea, Kauai, 1885. (Survey of ruins)

3 Russian Immigrants (Molokans). Documents concerning the Russian religious sect, 20 October 1905; letter, 7 April 1906, from Z. S. Spaulding to the governor on the worthlessness of the Molokans as laborers; letter, 27 July 1906, on use of Russians to colonize public lands at Kapaa, Kauai; registrar of conveyances to superintendent of public instruction pertaining to the leasing of lands in Kapaa, 27 January 1906.

4 Russia, Consul of. Letter, 24 January 1877, from the minister of the interior to Honolulu harbormaster.

5 Russia, Emperor of. Letter dated 17 September 1855, Alexander II to Kamehameha IV re death of Kamehameha III, read before Privy Council, 18 February 1856.

6 Russia, Proposed Treaty with. Letters, 17 and 20 July 1852, from R. C. Wyllie to the Danish minister of foreign affairs and to Captain Steen Andersen Bille, concerning the desire of Kamehameha III to sign a treaty with Russia; and letter, 20 April 1849, from the minister of foreign affairs to Captain Bille enclosing Wyllie's letter of 18 April 1849 to Captain Nevelskoi requesting him to use his influence for a treaty with Russia.

7 Russia, Treaty with. Signed in Paris, 19 June 1869, original, copy in Session Laws, 1870.

8 Russian-American Company. Letter, 28 December 1851, from the governor of the company in Sitka to the minsiter of foreign affairs introducing Lt. Turetyclm (?) of the Russian navy, visiting Honolulu on company business; and letter, 19 August 1851, introducing Mr. Pierre Kostromitinoff, San Francisco agent of the company.

9 Russian Settlements on the Amoor River. Broadside, 29 August 1860, notice of appointment of Henry H. Freeman as consul at these settlements.

10 Russians. Report sent to Privy Council, 7 August 1854, by R. C. Wyllie that he has heard reports of Russian designs against the Hawaiian Islands.

11 Russians in Honolulu. Letter, 9 April 1851, from the minister of foreign affairs to the lieutenant governor of Kamchatka informing him that the king will receive him, his lady, and other Russian gentlemen in Honolulu, Friday noon.

12 Note: Additional Russian-related materials can be found in the Reports of the Board of Immigration, Labor and Statistics (annual), which show steerage arrivals and departures for Honolulu, 1905-16, by ethnic groups; and in various ships' passenger manifests (e.g., the Glade, departing Bremen, Germany, and arriving Honolulu 27 July 1897, with many Slavic names of passengers aboard).

HI 3
HONOLULU ACADEMY OF ARTS
900 South Beretania Street
Honolulu, Hawaii 96814
(808-538-3693)

Louis Choris. 15 original watercolors and 12 lithographs of the Sandwich Islands. Choris was an artist aboard the Riurik, 1815-18, commanded by Captain Kotzebue.

HI 4
THOMAS HALE HAMILTON LIBRARY
UNIVERSITY OF HAWAII
2550 The Mall
Honolulu, Hawaii 96822
(808-948-8473)

1 Hawaiian and Pacific Collection. Diaries and logs relating to Hawaii, 1786-1883, 1 ft. In part transcripts, typed, and negative photocopies from the Bancroft Library, University of California, Berkeley, and the British Museum. Includes reports (1816-18) from Leontii Hagemeister, Yegor Scheffer, and Aleksandr Baranov of the Russian-American Company of Alaska, in translation. (NUCMC 62-1555)

2 Russian American Company. Records, 1802-67, 77 reels of microfilm. Correspondence and ships' logs. Originals in the National Archives.

3 Russian Consular Offices in Honolulu. Records, 1860-1907, in process. Being filmed by the National Archives for the Hamilton Library.

HI 5
KAUAI MUSEUM
4428 Rice Street (Mail: P.O. Box 248)
Lihue, Kauai 96766
(808-245-6931)

1 Alexander I. Medal given to Tomari, king of Kauai (1814).

2 Bering. Log, 1821. Several pages on microfilm and photocopy from Soviet archives of the Hawaiian portion of the log. Captain Bennett, commander.

IDAHO

ID 1
ARCHIVE OF PACIFIC NORTHWEST ARCHAEOLOGY
DEPARTMENT OF SOCIOLOGY/ANTHROPOLOGY
UNIVERSITY OF IDAHO
Moscow, Idaho 83843
(208-885-6751)

1 National Park Service. Manuscript report collection, 1969-77, ca. .5 ft. Materials on National Park Service excavations of Russian-American sites on federal land in Alaska. (Additions expected)

2 Sprague-Karklins. Trade bead literature collection, 1944-79, 3 ft. Includes many agency (federal and state) manuscript reports with data on "Russian" trade beads from the fur trade period found in sites in Alaska, British Columbia, Idaho, Oregon, and Washington. (Additions expected)

ILLINOIS

IL 1
HERBERT MARSHALL ARCHIVES
CENTER FOR SOVIET AND EAST EUROPEAN STUDIES
SOUTHERN ILLINOIS UNIVERSITY
Carbondale, Illinois 62901
(618-453-5174)

This archive, basically the personal acquisitions of Professor Herbert Marshall over more than 45 years in the Soviet Union and abroad, contains many rare and unique publications (especially periodicals) as well as manuscript holdings. It is particularly rich for the subjects of Russian and Soviet theater and film. For example, on the Soviet cinema, there are original manuscripts, stills, and photos of the famous directors Sergei Eisenstein and Dziga Vertov. Over 1,000 slides cover Russian and Soviet theater history; a collection of still photos, illustrations, slides, and filmstrips concerns Soviet cinema, Eisenstein, V. Pudovkin, A. Dovzhenko, and related topics. The Huntley Carter collection, named for a journalist and historian of avant-garde art in Russia and Germany in the 1920s, includes correspondence with Vsevolod Meyerhold, the Tairov Theater, Soviet institutions, and others, plus photographs and clippings, ca. 10 boxes. The Lionel Britton papers include shorthand verbatim transcription of a lecture delivered by Eisenstein in London in 1929. Other holdings include a large number of programs and brochures about theatrical productions of Meyerhold. Some material pertains to the Negro tragedian Ira Aldridge in Russia.

In the world of music, there are records of folk songs and more formal compositions, in Russian, Ukrainian, and other languages. Among the works for which Herbert Marshall has rendered English translations, and of which the archives holds usually the Russian (published or unpublished) and the English, are works by S. Prokofiev, D. Shostakovich, G. Sviridov, and N. Rimskii-Korsakov. Among the songs for which Marshall has provided English lyrics are the National Anthem of the Soviet Union (A. V. Alexandrov-S. Mikhailkov), Wait for Me (M. Blanter-C. Simonov), Times Are Not the Same (M. Koval-N. Aseyev), Happy Fellow Theme (Dunayevsky-Lebedyev-Kumach), Our Soviet Fatherland (Lebedyev-Kumach-Dunayevsky), and The Partisans Song (L. Knipper-V. Gusev).

Other materials in this repository are taped interviews with Soviet personalities and poets, Herbert Marshall's taped lectures on Soviet poetry, theater, cinema, and other topics, and a substantial number of translations of poetry and plays. Among the translated plays are Eugene Schwartz's The Shadow, A. Pushkin's Mozart and Salieri, and 3 works by Alexis Parnis: The Island of Aphrodite, The Wings of Icarus, and The Highway of Pasternak (on events of the Stalin era). Parnis was a Greek dramatist resident in the USSR. Poetry translations include Anna Akhmatova's Requiem, Joseph Utkin's The Story of Ginger Motele, Mr. Inspector, Rabbi Isaac and Commissar Bloch (about the 1917 Revolution and a Jewish settlement in Kishinev), Victor Bokov's Siberian Cycle (only part of this epic about life in a Siberian prison camp has been published; the English version is complete and unexpurgated), and Alexander Tvardovsky's Beyond the Beyond.

Other translations of plays: S. Aleshin, Once in Seville: Don Juan and Alone; Alexei Arbuzov, Years of Wandering; Maksim Gorkii, The Barbarians and Vassa Zheleznova; the Ukrainian playwright and Bolshevik leader Aleksandr Korneichuk, The Mission of Mr. Perkins in the Land of the Bolsheviks; L. Leonov, The Apple Orchard of Polovchansk; Tour and Sheynin, Face to Face and Smoke of the Fatherland; A. Grach, What Would Grandpa Have Said?; Yuri Germann, Bon Voyage; Igor Vsyevolozhsky, The Celebrated Wife; Valentin Zub, No Need to Get Upset; N. M. Karamzin, Sophia; M. Iu. Lermontov, Masquerade; Ivan S. Turgenev, Fathers and Sons (translated and adapted by Lionel Britton); and A. K. Tolstoi's historical trilogy, The Death of Ivan the Terrible, Tsar Fyodor, and Tsar Boris.

Another large part of the archives concerns the Yiddish theater in Eastern Europe. Some items of interest in this section are: correspondence of the Moskauer Judisches Theater (between Huntley Carter and Alexis Granowsky in the 1920s); bibliographies of over 450 works on the Yiddish theater in the USSR, in Yiddish, Russian, Ukrainian, German, etc., compiled by O. I. Lubomirsky, and of all works on the Yiddish and Byelorussian theater and culture housed in the library of the Jewish Academy in Cincinnati; and playbills, programs, and pamphlets on the Yiddish theater in Moscow, 1964, Vilna, 1966, and Petrograd, 1919.

A rough "Listing of materials in the Archives" (photocopy) is available.

IL 2
DEPARTMENT OF SPECIAL COLLECTIONS
DELYTE W. MORRIS LIBRARY
SOUTHERN ILLINOIS UNIVERSITY
Carbondale, Illinois 62901
(618-453-2516/2543)

1 Richard Aldington (1892-1962). Papers, 1910-62, ca. 8 cu. ft. Poet. Correspondence, literary manuscripts, and other papers. Traveled to the Soviet Union in 1962 where he was honored with a celebration for his 70th birthday. Unpublished finding aid.

2 George S. Counts (1889-1974). Papers, 1907-74, 3.25 cu. ft. Professor of education. Made 3 trips to the USSR, 1927, 1929, and 1936. Includes his diary for the 1929 auto trip through the Soviet Union. Also, correspondence and manuscript articles. He wrote extensively about Soviet education. Unpublished finding aid.

3 John Dewey (1859-1952). Papers, 1858-1970, 39 cu. ft. Educator and philosopher. Correspondence, diaries, and other matter. He traveled to the Soviet Union (Leningrad and Moscow) in 1928 with his daughter-in-law Elizabeth. Typescript copy of his diary, 19 May-4 August, contains comments on Russian educational practices, the Moscow Art Theatre, Russian Kunst Museum, and the Academy of Sciences. Also, materials relating to the

commission Dewey formed to inquire into the guilt of Leon Trotskii in the purge trials of the 1930s. Unpublished inventory.

4 Mordecai Gorelik (b. 1899). Author, playwright, and set designer. Papers unprocessed. Includes ca. 130 photographs of Soviet scene designs; probably other materials. Gorelik once visited the Soviet Union.

5 The Holy Door. Magazine records, 1964-66, 285 items. Includes 2 manuscripts, carbon and photocopies, of the Soviet poet Andrei Voznesensky, 1 being excerpts from "Oza," translated by "Bovar" (Patrick Shanley). Unpublished finding aid (NUCMC 69-1797).

6 John Howard Lawson (1894-1977). Papers, 1905-71, 50 cu. ft. Playwright and screenwriter, one of the so-called "Hollywood Ten." Papers include a photo album with pictures from his trip to Leningrad in 1961, and a copy of his play Parlor Magic, written in the USSR and produced there in December 1963. There is also material (e.g., phonograph records) on his testimony before the House Committee on Un-American Activities in 1947, which resulted in his blacklisting. Unpublished finding aid (NUCMC 71-1876).

7 Erwin Piscator (1893-1966). Papers, 1930-71, 57.6 cu. ft. Actor and director. He attempted to establish a German-speaking experimental theater in Engels, USSR, in 1936, with actors forced to leave Nazi Germany. A literary manuscript and correspondence deal with this effort. Unpublished inventory.

8 Unity Theatre in Great Britain. Records, 1936-70, 4.75 cu. ft. Essentially a part of the papers of Herbert Marshall (b. 1912). Relevant items include letters and translations of literary manuscripts. Marshall, the translator, was a film director who, in 1942-45, served as adviser to the Ministry of Information for films for Russia. As such he was in charge of production for Soviet, Czech, Polish, and Yugoslav films for Europe. Unpublished inventory.

IL 3
RYERSON AND BURNHAM LIBRARIES
THE ART INSTITUTE OF CHICAGO
Michigan Avenue at Adams Street
Chicago, Illinois 60603
(312-443-3666)

Louis H. Sullivan (1856-1924). Papers, 1903-24, ca. 60 items, 1 vol. Architect. Copybook of business letters, 1903-1905, contains several letters exchanged between Sullivan and Russian diplomats in the U.S. (Prince Nicholas W. Engalichoff, vice-consul in Chicago; Baron Schlippenbach, consul in Chicago) concerning the construction of St. Trinity Greek Orthodox Russian Church in Chicago. Also, microfilm copies. (NUCMC 66-762)

IL 4
BALZEKAS MUSEUM OF LITHUANIAN CULTURE
4012 Archer Avenue
Chicago, Illinois 60632
(312-847-2441)

Located next to Balzekas Chrysler-Plymouth, the Balzekas Museum of Lithuanian Culture is devoted to collecting and preserving Lithuanian cultural treasures. It opened on 22 June 1966, and consists of a library, archive, and art gallery. The archive of the museum contains valuable material, much of which is unpublished, including 25 file drawers on general subjects pertaining to Lithuania; ca. 5 file drawers on notable Lithuanians; 3 file drawers on Lithuanian clergymen and religious life; 8 file drawers, ca. 10,000 items, on Lithuanian artists and reproductions of their works; over 12,000 photos, presently being catalogued, relating to Lithuania; 50 manuscripts by Lithuanian playwrights; 3 file drawers on fighters for Lithuania's independence; 3 file drawers on Lithuanian doctors; a genealogy file containing 10,000 names; 4 ft. of bibliographical materials; and vast amounts of bibliographical materials on Lithuania.

On exhibit in glass cases on the first floor of the museum are letters from Dean Rusk and William Rogers to the chargé d'affaires of Lithuania commemorating anniversaries of Lithuania's independence, a photocopy of Lithuania's declaration of independence, 1918, and pictures (from published sources) of the signers of the declaration.

On the second floor of the museum, in the "Eminent Lithuanians Room," there are photos and/or drawings of Juozas Bachunas (1893-1969), Anthony O. Olis (1898-1958), Dr. A. M. Rackus (1893-1965), Juozas Zilevicius (b. 1891), Dr. Pijus Grigaitis (1883-1947), Dr. Petras P. Dauzvardis (1895-1971), consul general of Lithuania, Antanas Rukuiza (1887-1973), Leonardas Simutis (1892-1975), Right Rev. Msgr. F. M. Juras (b. 1891) (founder of the ALKA Museum in Putnam, Connecticut), Msgr. Dr. Joseph B. Koncius (1891-1975), Dr. Jonas Basanavicius (1851-1927), and Stanley P. Balzekas (b. 1893).

Also on the second floor on exhibit are photos of restaurant interiors in Lithuania; photos by Jonas Varnas of Vilnius metalwork; photos from published sources of outstanding Lithuanian women; and photos of prominent Lithuanian military leaders and Lithuanian troops.

IL 5
ARCHIVES DEPARTMENT
CENTER OF UKRAINIAN AND RELIGIOUS STUDIES
2247 West Chicago Avenue
Chicago, Illinois 60622
(312-489-1339)

The archives of the Center keep a sizeable amount of unpublished materials (including correspondence to the Holy See) on various Ukrainian-related topics, among them the organization of the Ukrainian patriarchal movement and the revival of religious spirit among Ukrainian Catholics in the U.S. Also, the Center is collecting some documentation on religion in the USSR. Materials are available to researchers on a restricted basis. For further information, contact Professor Vasyl Markus, director of the Center.

IL 6
CHICAGO HISTORICAL SOCIETY LIBRARY
Clark Street at North Avenue
Chicago, Illinois 60614
(312-642-4600)

1 John Armstrong (1758-1843). Papers, 1804-33, 5 items. Army officer, diplomat, and U.S. senator. Includes a letter to Lt. Col. Hamilton, 18 April 1815, discussing, among other matters, military opportunities for foreigners in Russia and military education abroad, particularly in France, 3 pp.

2 Philippe Buache. Papers, 1737-64, ca. 17 items. Includes an ALS to M. de Regemonte, 22 August 1747, requesting new maps of Russia belonging to a M. d'Argenson, 2 pp.

3 Cassius Marcellus Clay (1810-1893). Papers, 1844-89, 6 items. Statesman and diplomat. Includes a letter from St. Petersburg to Hubert P. Main concerning slavery, and other correspondence.

4 Charles Schuveldt Dewey (b. 1882). Papers, 1924-49, ca. 185 pp., 6 ft. Banker and U.S. congressman. He traveled often to the Soviet Union, 1928-29. He was interested in the country's economy, government, and people. Correspondence, speeches, reports, financial papers, and printed matter contain references to Polish-Russian trade, N. Bukharin, M. Kalinin, V. Molotov, and J. Stalin. In addition, Dewey was a financial adviser to the Polish government and director of the Bank of Poland in 1927-31. Some materials concern the Polish economic situation in the 1920s. Unpublished guide (NUCMC 66-1559).

5 Paul Howard Douglas (1892-1976). Papers, 1920s-1960s, ca. 700 ft. Economist and U.S. senator from Illinois, 1949-67. Senatorial papers, correspondence, scrapbooks, research files, phonograph recordings, audio and video tapes, films, and photographs. Includes material on foreign policy and the USSR.

6 John Fitzpatrick (1872-1946). Papers, 1890-1965, 11 ft. and 6 microfilm reels. President of the Chicago Federation of Labor and organizer for the American Federation of Labor. Primarily correspondence, 1913-30, including random letters, 1921-23, and other items from organizations and individuals interested in Russian relief. Other materials concern communism, socialism, and their pertinence to the labor movement. Unpublished inventory (NUCMC 69-102 and 71-897).

7 Sidney Lens (b. 1912). Papers, 1922-71, ca. 35 ft. Labor union official, editor, author, peace activist, and Marxist. Personal correspondence, manuscripts of and research files for many of his books and articles on American, labor, and radicalist history; Revolutionary Workers League papers and publications; and other union papers.

8 Edwin Lyman Lobdell (1857-1936). Papers, ca. 1908-40, 2 scrapbooks. Banker. 1 volume of the letters, writings, documents, and other papers of Lobdell and his family contains many items about his trip to Russia in 1908, especially his stay in Moscow. Also, letters to him from Nicholas A. Reitlinger, St. Petersburg, March 1909; Edward Osgood Brown, August 1917, about a Russian reception; and R. C. Martens, January 1920, about Lobdell's publication Russia and about the Russian peasant and Russian economy.

9 Clarence Manion (b. 1896). Papers, 1922-65, 13 ft. Lawyer, educator, lecturer, and broadcaster. A prominent conservative, he served on the American Bar Association's Committee for the Study of Communist Tactics, Strategy, and Objectives. Materials contain scattered references to Soviet-American relations. Additions to these papers are expected. Access to the papers requires Mr. Manion's written permission. Unpublished preliminary inventory (NUCMC 75-411).

10 Sterling Morton (1885-1961). Papers, 1891-1961, 22 ft. Businessman and philanthropist. Correspondence, speeches, articles, travel diaries, etc. pertaining to his conservative views on U.S. domestic and foreign policy. Reference(s) to USSR. Access restricted. Unpublished guide (NUCMC 75-415).

11 Lorado Taft (1860-1936). Papers, 1889-1938, ca. 200 items. Sculptor. Includes 2 letters to him from Nicholas Vachel Lindsay, 16 and 24 September 1921, asking him to aid Stephen Graham, an authority on Russia, during the latter's stay in Chicago. Enclosed is a printed list of Graham's travels and books.

12 United Charities of Chicago. Archives, 1867-1971, 30 ft. Includes correspondence of a

former staff member, Vincent Vokovich, ca. 12 items, 20 pp., 1920-27, which discusses Soviet economic conditions, the Russian scene, Siberian immigration, and commune life. (NUCMC 75-422)

IL 7
CHICAGO SYMPHONY ORCHESTRA LIBRARY
220 South Michigan Avenue
Chicago, Illinois 60604
(312-435-8133)

Nikolai Miaskowsky (1881-1950). Composer. Symphonie fantaisie no. 21, op. 51, composed for the 50th anniversary of the Chicago Symphony Orchestra, dedicated to Dr. Frederick Stock, July 1940. Requires advance written permission of the general manager of the Chicago Symphony Orchestra (at the above address).

IL 8
HAMMOND LIBRARY
THE CHICAGO THEOLOGICAL SEMINARY
5757 University Avenue
Chicago, Illinois 60637
(312-752-5757)

This repository, whose archives are in the process of being organized and catalogued, contains the papers of Albert Wentworth Palmer (1879-1954), a professor at and president of the Chicago Theological Seminary, who in 1919 was appointed special secretary of the YMCA to work with American troops in Siberia. 1 of his diaries, 1919, contains an account of his stay in Siberia and includes descriptions of Vladivostok, of American troops in Siberia, and of Russian life and mores. There is also a scrapbook, 1919, containing interesting photos of Vladivostok, of troops of various nationalities, and of a soldier standing in front of a Russian submarine. Part of the diary and some of the photos have been published in Alvin F. Brichtbill, Albert W. Palmer, A Life Extended, edited by Margaret Palmer Taylor (Athens, Ohio, 1968).

IL 9
ARCHIVES BRANCH
FEDERAL ARCHIVES & RECORDS CENTER, GSA
7358 South Pulaski Road
Chicago, Illinois 60629
(312-353-0161)

This repository has some of the microfilms of materials in the National Archives (Washington, D.C.) that pertain to Russia/USSR. For more details, see Charles South, List of National Archives Microfilm Publications in the Regional Archives Branches (Washington: National Archives and Records Service, 1975). Russian-related materials not found in the National Archives in Washington might be located in the records of the Circuit and District Court for Illinois, Indiana, Michigan, Ohio, and Wisconsin (1806-1946, 28,000 cu. ft. kept in this repository).

IL 10
CORPORATE ARCHIVES
INTERNATIONAL HARVESTER COMPANY
401 North Michigan Avenue
Chicago, Illinois 60611
(312-836-2149)

Corporate archives hold materials on the International Harvester Company in Russia. The firm's operations in Russia consisted of a manufacturing plant at Lubertzy (near Moscow), a general office in Moscow, and 11 branch houses, some with sub-branches, scattered throughout Russia and Siberia. The collection of Russian material, ca. 150 ft., consists of documents, records, correspondence, reports, and memoranda generated within the company's Russian sales and manufacturing organization, and between that organization and the corporate headquarters in Chicago. Material mainly 1909-25, with heavy concentration on the period ending in 1920. While not complete (it was not possible, for example, to save the records of the Lubertzy works or of the General Office in Moscow), the collection of material dealing with the operation of some of the branch houses, such as journals, ledgers, registers, inter-office memos, and general correspondence, is relatively intact and provides a view of how an American company conducted business in Russia prior to, during, and immediately following World War I.

In chronological order, some of the more important subjects on which the correspondence, reports, and memoranda focus may be listed as follows:

Pre-1914

Feasibility study of manufacture in Russia. Acquisition of Lubertzy Works. Start-up and organizational problems of Lubertzy Works. Tariff matters. Cost differential between Russian manufacture and Chicago manufacture.

1914-17

War-time financing of Russian business. Questions of exchange and the problem of credit. Shipment of goods to Russia--problems and risks involved. Depreciation of the rouble. Efforts to safeguard IH funds in Russia. The problem of getting funds out of Russia. Manufacturing difficulties caused by war-time shortages.

1917-20

Regulations imposed by Kerensky government and later by the Soviets on IH and other companies. Progressive deterioration of labor relations. Confiscation of some IH properties. Closing of all IHC branches and sub-branches.

1920-25

Closing of the General Office in Moscow. Seizure and nationalization of Lubertzy Works and subsequent denationalization.

1926-27

Re-nationalization of Lubertzy Works and final suspension of all IHC claims thereto.

Note: On exhibit in the archives is an unpublished blueprint of the layout of the Lubertzy plant.

Finding Aids: W. C. Caton's unpublished guide of 5 January 1976 has been quoted verbatim in the preceding description. See also the pamphlet International Harvester in Russia, 1850-1972. Both are available at the IH Archives.

IL 11
NATIONAL TRANSLATIONS CENTER
THE JOHN CRERAR LIBRARY
35 West 33rd Street
Chicago, Illinois 60616
(312-225-2526)

The National Translations Center has records of over 800,000 existing translations from some 40 languages, many of which are available directly from the Center's own collections. Translations of journal articles, conference papers, monographs, reports, and patents from all fields of theoretical and applied science, including medicine, are represented in the National Translations Center catalogue. Around 40% of these translations, many of which have not been published, are from Russian/Soviet sources. Translations Register-Index, published by the Center, serves as a finding aid to translations held in the Center's collection, as well as to those available from other sources.

IL 12
THE JUOZAS ZILEVICIUS LIBRARY OF LITHUANIAN MUSICOLOGY
2345 West 56th Street
Chicago, Illinois 60636
(312-737-8400)

This unique repository of Lithuanian musicology consists of over 400,000 published and unpublished items, most of which were donated by Professor Juozas Zilevicius, a scholar and composer who emigrated to the United States in 1929. Among the unpublished materials in the library are manuscripts of the operas "Dana" by Julius Gaidelis, "Du Kalavijai" and "Vaiva" by Vytautas Klova, "Dangute" by Zigmas Aleksandravicius, "Dalia" by Balys Dvarionas, "Gazina" by J. Karnavicius, and "Jurate ir Kastytis" by Kazys Viktoras Banaitis; and the cantata "Vilniaus Varpai" by Bruno Markaitis, S.J. One-act operas in the collection include "Juodasis Laivas" by Kacinskas, "Gintaro Krastas" by J. Gaidelis, and "Priesaika" by V. Marijosius. There are also manuscripts of Mikalojus Konstantinas Ciurlionis, including the symphonic poems "Miske" and "Jura" "Mes padainuosim"; the opera "Pagirenai" and the symphonic poem "Nemunas" by Stasys Simkus; manuscripts of Leonas Ereminas; the Albinas Strimaitis songs for chorus and the wedding dances as they were performed in the province of Suvalkija during the middle of the 19th c.; manuscripts of Juozas Jurcikonis, Vladas Jakubenas, Darius Lapinskas, Kazys Viktoras Banaitis, Vytautas Bacevicius, Juozas Groudis, Bruno Markaitis, S.J., Petras Sarpalius, Mikas Petrauskas, Julius Sinius, Antanas Pocius, Bronius Brudriunas, Vladas Adomavicius - Adonis, Domas Andrulis, Dr. Leonardas J. Simutis, Juozas Stankunas, Aleksandras Aleksis, Adomas Gediminas Grigaliunas - Glovarckis, Juozas Strolia, Jeronimas Kacinskas, Augustus Jankauskas, Rev. Juozas Zidanavicius (Seriju Juozas), Vladas Motekaitis, Aleksandras Mrozinskas, Antanas Vanagaitis, Povilas Ciurlionis, Rev. Vladas Budreckas, M.M., Sister M. Bernarda, M.M., Giedra Gudauskiene and many others. Also included are early compositional attempts of Lithuanian church organists in the United States, as well as numerous manuscripts written by Juozas Zilevicius himself.

Other unpublished materials include the Florijonas Valeika collection, ca. 100 manuscripts of waltzes, marches, etc. for military bands, and numerous volumes of manuscripts by Juozas Bertulis.

In addition to the materials mentioned above, the library maintains materials on American-Lithuanian musical activities; biographies of Lithuanian musicians; Lithuanian folk music and folklore; Lithuanian music after 1940; general items of musicological interest; auxiliary musicology; and phonograph records, magnetic recordings, microfilms, and piano rolls. Most of these materials are published.

This entry is based on the valuable finding aid by Professor Juozas Zilevicius (translated by Professor Leonardas J. Simutis), The Juozas Zilevicius Library of Lithuanian Musicology (Chicago, 1973).

IL 13
LITHUANIAN WORLD ARCHIVES
5620 South Claremont Avenue
Chicago, Illinois 60636
(312-778-2200)

This archive, one of the largest repositories of Lithuanian materials in the United States, maintains over 78 ft. of materials from after World War II to the present. Its holdings, which pertain to life both in and outside Lithuania, can be divided into 3 categories:

Records of Lithuanian organizations. Materials pertaining to Lithuanian organizations all over the world. These include the Lithuanian Community, the Lithuanian Catholic Youth Association, the Lithuanian scouts, and the Lithuanian charitable organization BALF.

Papers on and by prominent Lithuanians. Letters, memoirs, literary manuscripts, and other unpublished materials pertaining to Lithuanian writers, statesmen, artists. These include Vincas Kreve, Balys, Sruoza, Juozas Brazaitis, and many others.

Photographs. 8 file drawers of uncataloged photos on Lithuanian community activities throughout the world.

The World Archives also maintains 12,000 books pertaining to Lithuania, and large amounts of newspapers, magazines, and postcards. No restrictions, but it is advised that researchers make appointments with the director of the archive, Mr. Ceslovas Grincevicius. The archives are open to the public on Saturdays from 10 A.M. to 2 P.M.

IL 14
ARCHIVES OF THE LUTHERAN CHURCH IN AMERICA
LUTHERAN SCHOOL OF THEOLOGY
1100 East 55th Street
Chicago, Illinois 60615
(312-667-3500 x 230)

The Archives contain a small amount of materials pertaining to the immigration and settlement of Volga-Germans in the Great Plains area of the U.S. during the second half of the 19th c. There are also several letters written by the archbishop of Sweden, Nathan Soderblom, at the end of World War I, expressing concern for the fate of Lutherans in Russia. Access is at the discretion of the curator, but serious scholars are normally welcomed.

IL 15
DEPARTMENT OF SPECIAL COLLECTIONS
NEWBERRY LIBRARY
60 West Walton Street
Chicago, Illinois 60610
(312-943-9090)

1 Sherwood Anderson (1876-1941). Papers, 1904-41, 115 boxes. Author. Includes ca. 7 items (1 telegram) pertaining to his contacts with the USSR Society for Cultural Relations, 1932-37. References to I. Amdur, J. Robins, L. Cherniavsky, A. Aroseff, and Petrov. (NUCMC 59-199)

2 Yury Arbatsky (b. 1911). Collection on Balkan folk music, ca. 1934-55, size undetermined. Composer, musicologist, and authority on the music and customs of the Balkan rural population. Born in Moscow, where his father was a professor at the Imperial Polytechnic University, he fled the USSR with his family in 1924. Studied music in Prague, Dresden (with Sergei Rachmaninoff), and Leipzig. Fled from the Nazis to the Balkans, where he produced these manuscripts. "The Arbatsky Collection," Newberry Library Bulletin, 3 (1954), no. 6.

3 Edward Price Bell (1869-1943). Papers, 1889-1942, 53 boxes. Journalist. Includes 1 folder of correspondence between Mr. and Mrs. W. Tcherkesoff and Bell, 1904-30. 1 letter by Tcherkesoff, a Georgian nobleman, summarizes his life and career, 4 pp. (NUCMC 59-194)

4 Carte générale de la Sibérie et de la Grande Tartarie avec toutes les rivières, villes et ruisseaux, et les habitations des Tartares et Calmuques. Manuscript map, ca. 1670. Colored, scale: 1,000 Russian versts = 127 mm, drawn on a projection of straight parallels and converging meridians. 720 x 533 mm. (In Cartes marines, no. 115, Ayer Collection) Note: Some other maps of Europe and Asia, 15th c.-present, show parts of Russia.

5 Chicago Literary Club. Archives, 1874-present, 45 boxes (additions expected). Includes several articles by George Halperin on A. Chekhov, N. Gogol, and A. S. Pushkin, plus "A Doctor Looks at Communism. A Recent Trip to the USSR" (3 February 1936), also by Halperin.

6 Malcolm Cowley (b. 1898). Papers, in process, ca. 30 boxes (additions expected). Critic, poet, and author. Includes some correspondence with Soviet authors.

7 Floyd Dell (1887-1969). Papers, 1908-present, 3,520 items. Socialist in his youth, editor of the Masses, 1914-17, on staff of the Liberator, 1918-24, and later a novelist and playwright. A defendant in the Masses espionage trial. Correspondence, literary manuscripts, notebooks, photographs, etc. Includes an ALS, 19 May 1927, and a TLS, 1 October 1927, to him from Serge S. Dinamov in Moscow; ALS, 4 February 1930, from Mirra Komarovsky, 2 pp.; correspondence from Theodore Dreiser, 1911-28, 11 items; and Russian notebooks by an unidentified author, found in the collection, 2 items in 1 folder. (NUCMC 59-198)

8 William Vorhees Judson (1865-1923). Papers, 1896-1947, 790 items. Attaché with the Russian army in Manchuria during the Russo-Japanese War; U.S. military attaché in Russia, 1917-18. Contains maps, reports, correspondence, memoranda, and other materials pertaining to his activities in Russia, the Russo-Japanese War, and military affairs in Russia. (NUCMC 61-3088)

9 Daniel Nikitich Kashin (1773-1844). "Russkiia narodnyia pesni sobrannyia i izdannyia dlia peniia i fortepiano D. Kashinym i I. Prachem" [n.p., 1835], Ms., music interleaved with text of songs in Russian, in 2 parts, unpaged [294 pp.], 181 songs numbered continuously.

10 Obikhod (Orthodox Eastern Church. Liturgy and ritual). Nachalo vsenoshchnomu bdeniiu, Russian manuscript in Church Slavic, from the third quarter of the 17th c., on paper, rubricated, with musical notation ("kriuki"), 124 + 1 p., first leaf and some leaves at end wanting; with a prayer for the health of Tsar Aleksei Mikhailovich; plus a photostat (negative) of the same, 125 sheets. Alfred J. Swan, "The Newberry Obikhod," Newberry Library Bulletin, 4 (1956), no. 3.

11 Henry E. Phillips. "When the First Ship Landed in Alaska according to Thlinget tradition" (Sitka, 1922), with note by A. P. Kashevaroff, typescript, 6 pp. (Ayer Collection)

12 Russia. Sovereigns, 1613-43. Grant of land to Menshoi Ofanasievich Streshnev, Moscow, 1626, 1 sheet.

13 Russia. Sovereigns, 1682-89. Grant of land to Tikhon Nikitich Streshnev, Moscow, 1683, printed text with manuscript interpolation, within illuminated borders. Opening line is in viaz' (ligature), written in gold.

14 Frederick A. Stock (1872-1942). Correspondence, 1904-40, 60 items. Conductor of the Chicago Symphony Orchestra. Contains a letter, Moscow, 29 March 1935, from Nikolai Miaskovskii and another from Aleksandr Konstantinovich Glazunov, New York, 18 February 1930.

15 Alexander Tcherepnin (1899-1977). Composer. Musical scores, ca. 1935-55, 3 ft. Ca. 25 holograph scores.

16 Theodore Thomas (1835-1905). Papers, 185?-1926, 6 boxes. Conductor of the Chicago Symphony Orchestra. Includes an ALS, 31 July 1908, from W. Safonoff, from the Caucasus, 2 pp.; a postcard is enclosed. (NUCMC 60-1989)

17 Lambert Tree (1832-1910). Papers, 1821-1910, 12 boxes. U.S. minister to Russia, 1888-89. Ca. 20 items (mostly correspondence) pertain to his short service in Russia, including a draft statement, 6 pp., regarding diplomatic relations betweeen Russia and Mexico, 16 January 1889. George W. Wurtz, an American diplomat in Russia, is the most prominent correspondent. (NUCMC 60-988)

Finding Aids: Dictionary Catalogue of the History of Printing from the John M. Wing Foundation in The Newberry Library, 6 vols. (Boston: G. K. Hall, 1961), and supplement, 3 vols. (1970); Bibliographical Inventory to the Early Music in the Newberry Library, D. W. Krummel, ed. (Boston: G. K. Hall, 1977); List of Manuscript Maps in the Edward E. Ayer Collection, compiled by Clara A. Smith (Chicago, 1927); and A Checklist of Manuscripts in the Edward E. Ayer Collection, comp. Ruth Lapham Butler (Chicago, 1937).

IL 16
PHOTO LIBRARY
PLAYBOY ENTERPRISES
919 North Michigan Avenue
Chicago, Illinois 60611
(312-751-8000)

The Photo Library holds 1 folder containing the original color slides used for the March 1964 Playboy magazine feature on "Girls of Russia and the Iron Curtain Countries." Also included are 8 folders of photos of Russian and East European girls not published in the March 1964 issue. Use of the Photo Library is permitted only with special authorization from Playboy Enterprises.

IL 17
ARCHIVES
POLISH MUSEUM OF AMERICA
984 North Milwaukee Avenue
Chicago, Illinois 60622
(312-384-3352)

According to its curator, Father Donald Bilinski, the Museum archives may contain small amounts of unpublished materials (including oral history transcripts) pertaining to Polish-Russian relations. The archives may be used only by special written permission from the curator.

IL 18
ARCHIVES
MURRAY-GREEN LIBRARY
ROOSEVELT UNIVERSITY
430 South Michigan Avenue
Chicago, Illinois 60605
(312-341-3643)

1 Heisler Collection of Letters. Includes a holograph letter of the writer Ivan Sergeevich Turgenev (1818-1883), undated, addressed to a Mr. Pohl, probably an editor or journalist. Unpublished calendar. The letter is noted in a "Survey of Manuscripts and Local Historical Collections in Illinois," Illinois Libraries (April 1958).

2 Oral History Collection. 2 items. Interview with Irving Ross, 1.5 hrs., transcript, 26 pp. Garment worker. Born in Kovno, Lithuania, emigrated to the U.S. ca. 1905. 3 pp. of the interview touch on his father's life as a tailor in Lithuania, how the family was smuggled out of the country through Germany, and his education in Lithuania as compared to in America. Interview with Jacob Woolfe (b. 1888), 2 hrs., transcript, 31 pp. Laundry owner. Born in Russia, emigrated to the U.S. in 1905. References to the teaching of Yiddish and Hebrew in Russia and to the Red Scare of the 1920s.

IL 19
SISTERS OF SAINT CASIMIR
2601 West Marquette Street
Chicago, Illinois 60629

The convent's archives hold vertical files with official correspondence, clippings, 1907-present, pertaining to the congregation, photo albums, chronicles, diaries, and ephemera, in part pertaining to Lithuania. There is also a library and 3-room Lithuanian Museum, both of which are open to the public. Access to the archives is restricted. For more information, contact Sister M. Perpetua, Sisters of Saint Casimir.

IL 20
UKRAINIAN BIBLIOGRAPHICAL REFERENCE CENTER
2453 West Chicago Avenue
Chicago, Illinois 60622
(312-276-6565)

The center keeps bibliographical and reference materials, some of them unpublished, pertaining to the Ukraine. The library of the center is also a depository for the archives of the Ukrainian-American Library Association and of the Association for the Advancement of Ukrainian Studies.

IL 21
MEDICAL ARCHIVE AND LIBRARY
UKRAINIAN MEDICAL ASSOCIATION OF NORTH AMERICA
2453 West Chicago Avenue
Chicago, Illinois 60622
(312-276-6565, Museum)

The archive contains medical papers, clinical works, and historical studies by Ukrainian scholars of medicine, from the 19th and early 20th c. Holdings at present are primarily printed and published materials but some are manuscript. Access by appointment only.

IL 22
UKRAINIAN NATIONAL MUSEUM
2453 West Chicago Avenue
Chicago, Illinois 60622
(312-276-6565)

The museum holds a substantial amount of unpublished materials pertaining to the Ukraine. These include: 1 vertical file of letters and literary manuscripts of Father Stepan Musichuk (Musiychuk) (1894-1952), who wrote patriotic poems on the Ukraine; 2 vertical files of materials (including correspondence and a manuscript) by Stepan Ryndyk (1887-1972), a professor of mathematics who wrote satirical pieces; and the partial archives of the Ukrainian community in Chicago, primarily from 1932-33 or earlier (3 vertical files of newspaper clippings, protocols, correspondence, and other materials, some of which pertain to the Ukrainian pavillion at the Chicago World's Fair of 1932-33). The museum also has 5 vertical files of material on outstanding Ukrainian personalities, transcripts of Radio Liberty broadcasts from the 1950s to 1972, the archives of various Ukrainian organizations in Chicago, a large collection of photos concerning the Ukrainian community of Chicago (some on display, others stored), and framed photographs of churches in the Ukraine, on public display.

IL 23
DEPARTMENT OF SPECIAL COLLECTIONS
UNIVERSITY OF CHICAGO LIBRARY
1100 East 57th Street
Chicago, Illinois 60637
(312-753-4308)

1 Trevor Arnett (1870-1955). Papers, 1893-1955, 1,500 items. University and college administrator and trustee. Traveled to Russia in 1917. Unpublished guide (NUCMC 64-1324).

2 Saul Bellow (b. 1915). Papers, 1940-present, 27 ft. and still growing. American writer. Interest in Russia reflected in several items: 3 drafts of his preface to Dostoevsky's Winter Notes; draft of his article on Evgenii Evtushenko for The New York Review of Books (26 September 1963); and several drafts of an article on Nikita S. Khrushchev for Esquire (March 1961). Unpublished finding aid. (In part, NUCMC 69-1397)

3 William S. Benton (1900-1973). Papers, 1937-66, 22 ft. University of Chicago vice-president. Copy of a speech entitled "Soviet Education--Will America Meet the Challenge?" Unpublished finding aid.

4 Bulletin of the Atomic Scientists. Records, 1945-51, 13.5 ft. 6 folders of material (mostly newspaper clippings) on Russia and the atomic bomb, before and after 1949, and several folders on Russian-American relations. Unpublished finding aid (NUCMC 64-44).

5 Committee on Science and Freedom. Records, 1953-62, 13 ft. 1 folder of clippings on the Boris Pasternak affair; 1 folder of clippings on universities in communist countries; and several folders of material on the plight of Hungarian intellectuals in 1956. Unpublished finding aid.

6 Congress for Cultural Freedom. Papers in process and unavailable for some years.

7 William S. Culbertson (1884-1966). Papers, 1923, ca. 100 items. Notes and other materials connected with the 1923 round-table discussions of the Institute of Politics (Culbertson was a member). Documents include syllabi for a conference on "The international aspects of the Russian science. Unpublished finding aid (in part, NUCMC 64-86).

8 Federation of American Scientists. Records, 1946-70, 27.5 ft. Several folders of material, including newspaper clippings, on Russia and Russian science. Unpublished finding aid (in part, NUCMC 64-86).

9 Foreign Language Newspaper Files. 1876-1936, 21 ft. In autumn 1936 the Chicago Foreign Language Press Survey was organized under the Works Projects Administration of Illinois. Its purpose was to translate and classify news articles appearing in the foreign language press of Chicago in the 19th c. Files consist of 120,000 sheets of transcribed material from newspapers of 22 different foreign language communities of Chicago. 5,963 sheets are translated from Russian; 5,950 from Lithuanian; and 997 from Ukrainian. See The Chicago Foreign Language Press Survey: A General Description of its Contents (Chicago, 1946). Unpublished finding aid.

10 John Gunther (b. 1901). Papers, 1936-76, 136.5 ft. Journalist and author. Includes notes, drafts, interviews, correspondence, clippings, plus original and carbon copies, printer's proofs and galley proofs of his Inside Russia, Behind the Curtain, and other books. Unpublished finding aid (NUCMC 64-99).

11 Samuel N. Harper (1882-1943). Collection, 1905-36, 39.5 ft., ca. 40,000 items in 79 boxes. American scholar. The collection may be divided into 4 principal sections for purposes of description (though Harper himself organized it into 13 categories): (1) documents collected by Harper during his numerous visits to Russia, covering primarily the period 1905-17, largely records of meetings and other political activities of oppositional and unofficial groups, arranged in chronological order; (2) reports, diaries, unpublished notes and analyses of events, transcripts of interviews with Russian public figures in 1905-14; confidential reports to the U.S. State Department; accounts of his extended travels in the provinces of the Russian Empire and the Soviet Union; published and unpublished articles; detailed notes on regional conditions of land tenure on the eve of World War I, etc.; (3) correspondence reflecting Harper's concern with Russian affairs; among his correspondents: Boris A. Bakhmeteff, P. P. Batolin, Arkadi Borman, Alexander Braghin, Arthur Bullard, William C. Bullitt, William Henry Chamberlain, Count A. Cherep-Spiridovich, Charles R. Crane, Walter Duranty, David R. Francis, John Hazard, Loy W. Henderson, Maurice Hindus, J. Edgar Hoover, Colonel Edward M. House, Michael M. Karpovich, George Kennan, Robert J. Kerner, Maxim Litvinov, Prince G. Lvov, Paul Miliukov, John R. Mott, Vladimir Nabokov, Constantine Oumansky, Bernard Pares, Leo Pasvolsky, DeWitt C. Poole, Raymond Robins, John D. Rockefeller, Sergius I. Shidlovsky, Boris Skvirsky, Pitirim A. Sorokine, and Otto Struve; and (4) translations made by Harper for the State Department and for himself of Russian documents, articles and thousands of newspaper articles from the Russian press. Further details are in Paul A. Goble, "Samuel N. Harper and the Study of Russia: His Career and Collection," Cahiers du monde russe et soviétique, XIV (October-December 1973). Unpublished finding aid: "Samuel N. Harper Papers Guide" (1972), 107 pp. (Note: The Department of Special Collections also holds Harper's collection of pamphlets, some quite rare, from 1905-11 and 1917-29 primarily. There is an unpublished "Index to the Samuel Harper Collection of Russian Pamphlets" [1965], 130 pp.) (NUCMC 64-103)

12 Robert Maynard Hutchins (1899-1977). Papers, 1922-[51], 111 ft. and growing. Educator,

president of the University of Chicago. 2 folders of material on communism and Russia. Unpublished finding aid (In part, NUCMC 64-809).

13 Salmon Oliver Levinson (1865-1941). Papers, 1913-41, ca. 37 ft., ca. 50,000 items. Lawyer, internationalist, and philanthropist. Correspondence, diaries, documents, reports, memoranda, etc. Some material pertains to Russian war debts (World War I) and to his antiwar efforts. Unpublished finding aid (NUCMC 64-124).

14 Robert Morss Lovett (1870-1956). Papers, 1876-1950, ca. 1 ft. English professor and author. Correspondence, lectures, notes, clippings, and printed documents. Includes data on his interest in leftist causes and his involvement with the Dies Committee. Unpublished guide (NUCMC 64-127).

15 Charles Henry MacDowell (1867-1954). Papers, 1918-35, 2.5 ft. Technical adviser to the American Commission to Negotiate Peace, 1919. Consists primarily of the minutes of the Economic Commission, the Supreme Economic Council, the subcommittee on Germany, and other committees. Topics include Eastern Europe, relief for Odessa, reopening trade with Estonia, shipments through Bolshevik Russia, health conditions, trade restrictions, U.S. locomotives for Lithuania, Allied economic policy in Russia, and the situation in the Baltic states. Unpublished finding aid (NUCMC 64-129).

16 Charles J. P. Mahon (O'Gorman) (ca. 1800-1891). Papers, 1824-91, 5.5 ft. Irish politician and and adventurer. In the second half of the 19th c., he traveled to Russia, where he became a lieutenant in the tsar's army. Some of his papers document his journey to Russia. Unpublished finding aid (NUCMC 64-131).

17 Alexander A. Maximow (1874-1928). Papers, 1902-50, 23 vols. Professor of histology and embryology at St. Petersburg, 1903-22, and professor of anatomy at the University of Chicago from 1922. Among his papers is a manuscript Russian textbook on the principles of histology; other Russian-language materials also. Unpublished finding aid (NUCMC 64-134).

18 Minerva. Records, 1962-present, 16 ft. and growing. Scholarly journal edited by Edward Shils. Archive includes reports on scientific policy in the USSR by L. Lisichkin and V. Trapeznikov, and a folder on "Decision-making in Soviet Science Policy" by John Turkevich. Unpublished finding aid (NUCMC 69-1416, in part).

19 John Nuveen, Jr. (d. 1968). Papers, ca. 1922-66, 40 ft. Lawyer, politician, and University of Chicago trustee. 2 folders on Russia and communism, 1946-55. Unpublished finding aid.

20 Michael Polanyi (1891-1976). Papers, 1900-75, 23.5 ft., but some material remains uncatalogued. Scientist and philosopher. Polanyi wrote several books and articles about the Soviet Union; he visited the USSR in the early 1930s. His papers may contain materials relating to this visit. 2 of his correspondents were Soviet chemists, Alexander Frumkin and Nicolai Semenoff, who wrote asking him to stop attacking Soviet economic policies. There are manuscript articles on Soviet genetics, 1938, Russian science, 1943, politics in Russia and Germany, 1941, and planning and Soviet science, 1941. Unpublished finding aid.

21 Presidents' Papers. Ca. 1889-1965, 92 ft. and 14 cabinets. Papers of the presidents of the University of Chicago. Several folders of materials on scientific meetings held in the Soviet bloc, 1962, Slavic studies, 1942-47, The Journal of Slavonic Studies, and Russia in general. Unpublished finding aid.

22 Eugene I. Rabinowitch (1901-1973). Papers, 1954-71, 5 ft. Russian-born editor of the Bulletin of the Atomic Scientists and a leader of the Pugwash movement. The Pugwash conferences are meetings of international scientists to discuss the perils of the nuclear age. The papers reflect Rabinowitch's contacts with Soviet colleagues in the Pugwash Continuing Committee and details of the organization and planning of the conferences. Also, materials on science in the Soviet Union; mimeographed lists of Soviet research laboratories; mimeographed copies of Conditions of Research in Soviet Biology and of Human Science--Neither West nor East; a folder concerning the "Research Program on the USSR"; a folder of miscellaneous items (including clippings, speeches, and correspondence) about Soviet science and a trip to Russia by Katherine Lonsdale; and 3 folders with letters from Soviet academicians Topchiev and Skobeltzyn to Rabinowitch plus other materials. Unpublished finding aid (NUCMC 69-1418).

23 Julius Rosenwald (1862-1932). Papers, ca. 1862-1948, 33 ft. Chicago philanthropist. Includes 7 folders of material (mostly correspondence) on the settlement of Jews in southern Russia, 1920s; a folder about the Russian Information Bureau; 2 folders on Russian refugees in Istanbul and Germany; a folder on the abrogation of the Russian-American treaty of 1832; and 1 folder concerning the Zemstvos and Town Relief Commitee (1928-30). Unpublished finding aid (NUCMC 64-156).

24 Edward Shils (b. 1910). Papers are uncatalogued and unavailable at present. Some materials relate to a Rand study of the Soviet armed forces after World War II.

25 Emil Teichman (1845-1924). Papers, 1868-1925, 1 ft. British businessman of German descent.

In 1868 he joined the New York branch of Messrs. J. M. Oppenheim & Co., the leading fur merchants of London. As part of his work he dealt with the Russians regarding the Alaskan fur trade, traveling to Sitka for the purpose. He describes his travels in America and Alaska in his diary (handwritten copy in this collection). Also includes a typed version of diary made by his son, and a copy of the privately published edition (Cayne Press, 1925), plus correspondence, photographs, and memorabilia. Unpublished finding aid (NUCMC 64-172).

26 Leo Tolstoi (1828-1910). Russian author, moralist, and philosopher. Manuscript of his work "Story about Ivan the fool and his Two Brothers" (1886), 29 ll. (Codex MS 506) Unpublished description.

IL 24
MANUSCRIPT COLLECTION
UNIVERSITY OF ILLINOIS AT CHICAGO CIRCLE
P.O. Box 8198
Chicago, Illinois 60680
(312-996-2742)

1 Aldis Papers. 1872-1952. 6 ft. Materials pertaining to the relief of European refugees; correspondence and reports, 7 items, November 1916-January 1919, relating to the Russian Aid Committee. Unpublished finding aid.

2 A Century of Progress. Collection, 1928-44. 555 ft. Includes correspondence, press releases, schedules, etc., 1929-34, relating to the question of official Russian participation in the Fair (never realized), "Soviet Union Day," and the visit of Russian ambassador to the U.S. Alexander Troyanovsky to the exposition. Unpublished finding aid and card index.

3 Chicago Committee for a Sane Nuclear Policy. Records, 1955-66. 3 ft. Contains reports, newspaper clippings, and letters on U.S. and Russian attitudes toward disarmament proposals and nuclear testing, and congressional hearing report on the 1960 Moscow Workers' Parties Manifesto. Unpublished finding aid.

4 Chicago Council on Foreign Relations. Records, 1922-75. 36 ft. Includes speeches by primarily American journalists and public officials on foreign policy issues relating to American-Russian relations and Russia's world position. Unpublished finding aid.

5 Cook County Socialist Party. Papers, 1913-35. 200 items. Minutes containing scant references to Russia, including mention of Japanese-Russian disputes, political prisoners in Russia, and a resolution requesting the U.S. government to recognize the revolutionary Russian government.

6 Institute of Design. Collection, 1927-73. 5 ft. Formerly the New Bauhaus, the Institute of Design carried forward the concepts relating to art and technology begun by the German Bauhaus movement. Collection contains correspondence, exhibition announcements, and lectures of 2 Russian-born faculty, Serge Chermayeff and Alexander Archipenko. Unpublished finding aid available.

7 Frank McCallister (1908-1970). Papers, 1923-71. 23 ft. McCallister was an active member in SANE, World Federalists, and Turn Toward Peace; files on these organizations relate to U.S.-Russian relations, world peace, and disarmament. Unpublished finding aid.

8 Barratt O'Hara (1882-1969). Papers, 1948-68. 62 ft. U.S. representative from Illinois. Correspondence, reports, speeches, and office files relating to the USSR, its satellites, Soviet treatment of minorities, the Soviet military, and related subjects. Unpublished finding aid. (NUCMC 70-1551)

9 Victor A. Olander (1873-1949). Papers, 1884-1952. 21.5 ft. Trade-unionist. Extracts from correspondence and reports from Raymond Robins regarding the American Red Cross Commission to Russia in August-October 1917. Unpublished finding aid. (NUCMC 70-197)

10 Pamphlet Collection. 1850-1979. 15,250 items. Political pamphlets, including 1,450 dealing with Russia (1854-1979).

11 Women for Peace. Records, 1963-71. .5 ft. Contains numerous references to Russia in bulletins and letters on such topics as the Vietnam war, nuclear testing, and the arms race.

IL 25
RARE BOOKS ROOM
LOVEJOY LIBRARY
SOUTHERN ILLINOIS UNIVERSITY
Edwardsville, Illinois 62026
(618-692-2711)

Slavic Societies. Collection of materials relating to and issued by Slavic groups in North America, including Canada. Most are printed and date primarily from recent years. Stanley B. Kimball, ed., A Classified Catalog of the Slavic Imprint Collection at Lovejoy Library (1972).

IL 26
MUSIC LIBRARY
NORTHWESTERN UNIVERSITY
Evanston, Illinois 60201
(312-492-3434)

1 Anton Rubinstein. Piano sonata no. 4, op. 100, holograph, 15 pp.; 2 ALS, 23 June 1868 and 28 November 1871; and a musical incipit on a photo, dated 18 March 1883.

2 Sigismond Stojowski. Piano concerto, op. 3 (1890), holograph, 201 ll., bound.

3 Igor Stravinsky. "Fanfare" (1964), 2 pp. (John Cage Notations Collection)

Finding Aid: The first 2 listings above are in the portion of the Moldenhauer Archives, a very rich source for Russian/Soviet music, which has been transferred to Northwestern. The remainder of the archives is at present in Spokane, Washington. For most of the archives, the Music Library at Northwestern has a bound finding aid, unpublished, 3 vols., which does not distinguish between the part of the archives at Northwestern and that in Spokane.

IL 27
SPECIAL COLLECTIONS DEPARTMENT
LIBRARY
NORTHWESTERN UNIVERSITY
1935 Sheridan Road
Evanston, Illinois 60201
(312-492-3635)

Charles Gates Dawes (1865-1951). Collection, 1887-1951, ca. 200 ft. Military officer and U.S. vice-president, 1925-29. Diaries, correspondence, speeches, archival material, and clippings. Some material pertains to foreign policy questions involving the USSR. Unpublished finding aid (NUCMC 61-89).

IL 28
UNIVERSITY ARCHIVES
LIBRARY
NORTHWESTERN UNIVERSITY
1935 Sheridan Road
Evanston, Illinois 60201
(312-492-3354)

1 Kenneth Colegrove (1886-1975). Papers, ca. 1926-69, 84 boxes. Professor of political science. Includes 3 folders of correspondence, in French and Russian, relating to the Russian embassy and the Russian Institute of Columbia University, 1929-47. (Series 11/3/22/4)

2 Paul Haensel (Pavel Genzel') (1878-1949). Papers, ca. 1908-50, 1 folder. Economics professor, taught at Moscow University 1908-28. Contains a letter, biographical materials, and copies of his publications. (Biographical Files)

3 Vladimir N. Ipatieff (1867-1952). Papers, ca. 1867-1950, 10 boxes. Russian-born professor of chemistry. Taught in Russia and the Soviet Union, became an academician, but emigrated to the U.S. in the early 1930s. Correspondence, office files, diaries in English and Russian, writings, articles, memorabilia, and clippings. Biographical data and personal correspondence, much of it in Russian or French, from B. Babkin, N. T. Belgayev, B. Bogoyavlenski, G. Grebenstchikoff, his family (wife and son), P. F. Konstantinoff, M. Lisovsky, N. Longovoy, and others (box 1); letters of L. Markovitch, Mstislav A. Martynoff, his niece the Comtesse Kapnist, N. Pushin, A. Shubersky, A. Tchitchibabine, A. A. Titov, etc. (box 2); published memoirs (The Life of a Chemist: Memoires 1867-1930; 1945, in 3 parts) in boxes 3 and 4; diary ("Life in America") in English for 1932-42 (box 5); diary in Russian, writings, and memorabilia (box 6); and 4 other boxes of pertinent material. Note: A photograph file, which is separate, has related photos under Ipatieff's name. Mimeographed inventory of contents. (Series 11/3/8/2)

4 Kennicott-Bannister Collection. Papers, 1857-1905, 1 box. Papers of Robert Kennicott (1835-1865), naturalist, museum curator, and explorer, and of Henry Bannister (1844-1920), explorer and doctor. Members of the Western Union Telegraphic Expedition of 1865-66. Includes diaries, reports on Alaska sent back to William H. Seward, and 5 notebooks on the flora and fauna of Alaska. Also, some photos pertaining to the regions covered by the expedition. (Series 11/2/2)

IL 29
DR. GIVI C. GABLIANI--PRIVATE COLLECTION
2500 Payson Road
Quincy, Illinois 62301

Dr. G. C. Gabliani has in his possession some material relating to Georgia and the Caucasus covering the period just after World War I and during World War II. The collection is not open to the general public, but Dr. Gabliani may permit access to serious scholars on an individual basis.

IL 30
ILLINOIS STATE HISTORICAL LIBRARY
Old State Capitol Building
Springfield, Illinois 62706
(217-782-4836)

1 Norman Buel Judd (1815-1878). Papers, ca. 1860-65, ca. 11 items. Diplomat. Judd traveled to Russia while serving as minister plenipotentiary to Berlin, 1861-65. In 7 letters, September 1863, he describes the sites he visited (museums, palaces, "tourist attractions") and comments on the Russian peasantry and social class differences.

2 Scott W. Lucas (1892-1968). Papers, ca. 1918-68, 666 boxes and 7 microfilm reels. U.S. senator. State Department files include immigration and naturalization records (individual cases) covering many emigrants from Russia, 1939-40. Unpublished inventory.

3 Lawrence Y. Sherman (1858-1939). Papers, 1880-1936, 222 boxes. U.S. senator from Illinois, 1913-21. Personal correspondence and clippings concern Russia in 1918-20; other material is on the League of Nations. Unpublished inventory.

4 Nadezhda Lvovna Turchaninova (Nadine Turchin) (1826-1904). 1 item, 1863-64. Russian princess, wife of Brigadier General Ivan Vasilevich Turchaninov (John Basil Turchin; 1822-1901), a Russian noble who served in the U.S. Army during the American Civil War, 1861-64. Her diary, in French with English translation, for 26 May 1863-26 April 1864, contains her informed assessments of military affairs and other matters, 157 pp. The Journal of the Illinois State Historical Society published the diary, February 1977, after describing it in its February 1976 issue ("Manuscript Acquisitions"); also described in "New Notes" of The American Archivist (July 1976).

IL 31
RARE BOOK ROOM AND CLOSED STACK AREA
UNIVERSITY LIBRARY
UNIVERSITY OF ILLINOIS AT URBANA-CHAMPAIGN
Urbana, Illinois 61801
(217-333-3777)

1 Elias Czaykowsky (1909-1973). Papers, ca. 1946-70, 1 box and 4 bound vols. Public school teacher and writer in the Ukraine, electrical engineer in the U.S. Typescripts of 4 translations of Polish novels into Ukrainian (works from the 19th and early 20th c.); correspondence; 2 bibliographies of Ukrainian literature, over 200 pp. each; and 3 family histories/biographies of Ukrainian families in Czechoslovakia after 1918.

2 Vasyl' Grendzha-Dons'kyi (1897-1974). Papers, 1930s-1974, 2 boxes. Ukrainian writer and poet. Primarily photocopies of his literary manuscripts (novels and poems), correspondence, speeches, radio sketches, film scripts, articles, and other writings. Includes a bibliography of all his works, in Ukrainian, and a catalog of his works in 5 Western libraries, in English, both prepared by his daughter, Zerka Grendzha-Dons'ka Danyliuk. His memoirs, correspondence, and some documents are restricted.

3 Hugh Perkins (fl. 1830s). English traveler. Kept a manuscript diary during his stay in St. Petersburg, 1834-38, recording his impressions of Russian society and culture, 158 pp. (MS 914.745 P41j)

IL 32
UNIVERSITY ARCHIVES
UNIVERSITY LIBRARY, ROOM 19
UNIVERSITY OF ILLINOIS AT URBANA-CHAMPAIGN
Urbana, Illinois 61801
(217-333-0798)

1 American Library Association Archives. 1876-present, 735 cu. ft. and growing. Materials relating to the 50th anniversary conference of the ALA in 1926, including letters, photographs, and other documents concerning the visit of Mme. L. Haffkin Hamburger, a Leningrad librarian. The International Relations Office files for the World War II era contain several scattered folders pertaining to the Soviet Union. Some of these items are about the ALA Program Books for War Devastated Areas. A photograph file includes a few photos of Russian libraries. The archives of the Association of College and Research Libraries is thought to contain material relating to scholarly interest in the USSR. A series of hard-copy finding aids for this collection has been converted to an information retrieval system, which will be indexed for subjects and names.

2 William and Emmanuel H. Brandt. Collection, 1807-19, 8 cu. ft., 138,000 items. Business archives (records) of a London firm trading with Archangel, St. Petersburg, and the Hanse ports. Ca. 25% of the items (correspondence and reports) are in poor physical condition. Material on Jacob B. Rodde and Brandt, Rodde & Co., third largest trading house in Archangel. RS control card and supplementary finding aid. (RS 15/35/50)

3 Avery Brundage (1887-1975). Papers, 1908-75, 139 ft. President of the International Olympic Committee, 1952-72. Correspondence, office files, reports, and publications. Brundage, with the IOC from 1936, had frequent contact with Soviet athletes and officials. Perhaps 1% of the total collection holds information on Soviet sports, the influence of politics on athletics, Russian participation in international competition, and Moscow's attempts to become host for the Olympic Games. Brundage visited sports facilities in Russia and attended Olympic meetings there in 1954, 1962, 1967, and 1971. There is a finding aid: Avery

Brundage Collection, 1908-1975 (Köln, 1977), 275 pp. (NUCMC 77-1168) (RS 26/20/37)

4 Steven P. Hill (b. 1936). Papers, 1965-68, .1 cu. ft. Includes transcripts of tape-recorded interviews with Soviet filmmakers. (RS 15/20/20)

5 Samuel A. Kirk (b. 1904). Papers, 1933-67, ca. 7 ft. Professor of education and director of the Institute for Research on Exceptional Children. He visited the USSR in 1962 with a presidential mission studying Soviet treatment of mental retardation. In 1966 he traveled to the Soviet Union to attend the International Conference on Special Education sponsored by the International Congress of Psychology. Materials include letters, reports, speeches, and articles. RS control card. (NUCMC 69-258) (RS 10/14/20)

6 Simon Litman (1873-1973). Papers, 1865-1965, 5 cu. ft. Odessa-born professor of economics. Some information on life in Russia before 1905 and on Russian affairs until 1955. (NUCMC 77-1182) (RS 9/5/29)

7 Albert H. Lybyer (1876-1949). Papers, 1876-49, 19.3 cu. ft. History professor and statesman. He was on the American Commission to Negotiate Peace and on the King-Crane Commission after World War I. His academic specialty was the history of the Ottoman Empire and the Balkans. RS control card. (NUCMC 65-1925) (RS 15/13/22)

8 Philip E. Mosely (1905-1972). Papers, 1922-72, 40.6 cu. ft. Professor of international relations at Cornell, 1936-40, and Columbia, 1946-72, and president of the East European Fund, 1952-61. Correspondence, reports, manuscripts, articles, lectures, photographs, course materials, and clippings. Materials relate to Russian area studies, Russian travel, 1931-36 and 1956-61, State Department service, 1949-50 and 1959-71, security clearances, 1954-72, the East European Fund, 1951-64, Ford Foundation, 1952-68, Rockefeller Foundation, 1944-65, Council on Foreign Relations, 1952-62, Social Science Research Council, 1941-57, American Council of Learned Societies, 1948-49 and 1960-68, Columbia University's European Institute, 1950-71, and Russian Institute, 1963-70, Rand Corporation, 1950-70, War Documentation Project, 1951-55, Chekhov Publishing House, 1951-69, Bilderberg Group, 1957-68, Dartmouth Conferences, 1960-70, and his research on the Communist Party of the Soviet Union, 1955-65, zadrugas, 1937-41, and Transylvanian Saxons, 1934-36. Correspondents include John A. Armstrong, Cyril E. Black, Zbigniew K. Brzezinski, David J. Dallin, Michael Karpovich, Richard Pipes, Geroid T. Robinson, Leonard Schapiro, Timothy Sosnovy, and Sergė Zenkovsky. Inquire concerning possible restrictions. Unpublished finding aid. (RS 15/35/51)

9 Eugene I. Rabinowitch (1901-1973). Papers, 1930-68, 8.3 cu. ft. Russian-born scientist. Includes recollections of his emigration from Russia in 1918. RS control card. (NUCMC 69-271) (RS 15/4/23)

10 Slavic and East European Journal Editor's File. Records, 1970-76, 6 cu. ft. Correspondence, reviewers' evaluations, and similar material for manuscripts submitted for publication in the periodical. (RS 15/20/51)

11 Sound Recordings. 1936-present, over 3,600 hrs. Tape recordings of lectures given on campus. Includes talks by Manley O. Hudson, 1946, Alexander Kerensky, 1944, Foy D. Kohler, 1971, Countess A. Tolstoi, 1949, and others, plus speeches on Soviet-American relations. (RS 13/6/5)

12 George W. Swenson (b. 1922). Papers, 1957-77, ca. 1 cu. ft. Professor of electrical engineering and research professor of astronomy. He visited Russian radio astronomy installations in 1961. Correspondence, reports, and photos. RS control card. (NUCMC 67-478) (RS 11/6/21)

13 Joseph T. Tykociner (1877-1969). Papers, 1900-69, 23.4 cu. ft. Polish-born research professor of electrical engineering. Some items from the time he worked in Russia, 1900-18. (NUCMC 71-1171) (RS 11/6/20)

14 University High School Social Science Curriculum Study Center Materials. 1966-71, 2.3 cu. ft. Some manuals and teaching materials on Russia. (RS 10/12/8)

15 Note: In the future, either the university archives or the library's rare book room will receive physical custody of a significant collection of papers of Zinaida Hippius and Dmitrii Merezhkovskii (correspondence, diaries, writings), currently held by a university faculty member for research purposes.

Finding Aids: The library has published a Manuscript Guide to Collections at the University of Illinois at Urbana-Champaign (1976). The RS (Record Series) control cards noted serve as unpublished finding aids, and there is a duplicated "Description of Archival Resources for Research in Russian and East European History" dated 12 May 1977.

IL 33
INSTITUTE OF SLAVIC STUDIES
SLAVIC GOSPEL ASSOCIATION
139 North Washington Street
Wheaton, Illinois 60187
(312-690-8904)

The Institute, which trains missionaries for Slavic countries, has a library which includes both published works and also vertical files. Materials in the vertical file collection are, in part, documents from the Soviet Union in Russian and English; material from Russian research centers; and magazine or newspaper clippings, 1968-present, on nearly all aspects of Russian life and culture. (There are also reports from Slavic Gospel Association missionaries which are not open to the public.) The library hopes to expand its archives with documents on the early history of Evangelicals and Baptists in the Soviet Union. Restriction: Limited to those cleared by the director of the Institute or the head librarian of the Institute. The ISS Catalog briefly describes the library's holdings.

INDIANA

IN 1
PROFESSOR ROBERT F. BYRNES--PRIVATE COLLECTION
402 Reisner Drive
Bloomington, Indiana 47401
(812-336-5275, home)
(812-337-5484, work)

Professor Byrnes has, at his home, 3 valuable collections. The first is the correspondence between K. P. Pobedonostsev and Elizabeth Tiutcheva in the 1860s-1880s. Pobedonostsev (1827-1907) was the ober-procurator of the Most Holy Synod (1880-1905), a prominent conservative, and the close adviser of Tsars Alexander III and Nicholas II. The 5 reels of microfilm are from the Manuscript Division of the Lenin Library. Typed copies, in Cyrillic, are also available bound in notebooks.

Manuscript papers and letters (8 reels of microfilm) of the historian V. O. Kliuchevskii (1837-1911) are the second collection. The originals are in various Moscow libraries; Professor Byrnes's additional typed Cyrillic copies are also bound in notebooks. It should be noted that some of these items are not included in the published editions of Kliuchevskii's writings because they are drafts.

The final collection consists of files and personal papers from Professor Byrnes's work with the Interuniversity Committee on Travel Grants, which began sending American scholars to the Soviet Union to study 3 years before the first U.S.-USSR academic exchange agreement was signed. The International Research and Exchanges Board (IREX) adopted many of its principles and procedures, as have other organizations. Total amount of material is 4 filing cabinet drawers; these contain copies of some committee records from 1956-69 and copies of papers relating to Professor Byrnes's involvement.

Indiana University's Lilly Library has the originals of the Pobedonostsev letters, and the Library of Congress in Washington, D.C. has copies of them. IREX in New York has the full official files of the ICTG.

As published finding aids the researcher can consult Professor Byrnes's 2 books: Pobedonostsev (Indiana University Press, 1968), and Soviet-American Academic Exchanges, 1956-1975 (also IUP, 1976), for the first and third collections. His projected volume on Kliuchevskii will describe the second collection.

Researchers are requested to write in advance to arrange for access. The ultimate disposition of all these holdings will be Indiana's Lilly Library.

IN 2
BOOK DIVISION
LILLY LIBRARY
INDIANA UNIVERSITY
Bloomington, Indiana 47401
(812-337-2452)

Vidy sela Gruzina. Folio book, n.p., n.d., contains 7 plans and a colored map, all mounted: 2 house plans for the headquarters of his majesty's resident grenadiers, 1831; the same, n.d.; plan and facade of the house for the company school, consisting of 40 military men, 1829; plan for an officer's private quarters, n.d.; scene of an army moving from Zadniaia (?) to the village of Germianovo, 1826; view of the headquarters of his majesty's resident grenadiers as seen from the Volkhov River, n.d.; and a map of Novgorod province showing military installations, 1831.

IN 3
MANUSCRIPTS DIVISION
LILLY LIBRARY
INDIANA UNIVERSITY
Bloomington, Indiana 47405
(812-337-2452)

1 William Edward David Allen (1901-1973). Collection, 9th c.-1972, ca. 150 items. Historian. Contains medieval Russian charters; a 17th c. copy of a Sbornik, in manuscript, of 5 16th-17th c. Russian chronicles, 440 pp., in 3 different hands; 77 bawdy folk tales collected by A. Afanas'ev, bound, not all of which were published in his collections; ALS, 27 April 1879, from Ivan Turgenev to Charles

Tardieu, denying he is a French citizen; patent of hereditary nobility, 12 September 1720, of Catherine I; 17 gramoty (land grants), 1614-90; Georgian manuscript book of thanksgiving entitled Samadlobeli, 55 ll., dated 26 July 1746, with 4 large and 4 small illustrations; Ajmayil, an Armenian collection of prayers, invocations, and Bible passages, 3 sheets, illustrated, 21 February 1204 (i.e., 1755 A.D.); Prince Sulkhan Saba Orbeliani (1658-1725), first dictionary of the Georgian language, 323 ll. in 37 columns, an illustrated manuscript, 1724; handwritten and typed works on: the 4 rivers area in the Russian Civil War, 1918-19, Armenia and Georgia, and the Caucasus, in the years 1916-20, Kurds, Turkish Georgia, Anglo-Russian contacts, Ossetia (Osetiya) and the peoples of the northern Caucasus; correspondence and other material about the Ukraine, 1947-49, 1 box; 3 boxes of material on Turkestan; watercolors of military uniforms, 1788; and a carbon copy of Humphrey Higgins' translation of A. Tolstoi's Death of Ivan the Terrible.

2 Claude Gernade Bowers (1878-1958). Papers, 1868-1972, ca. 18,400 items. Journalist and diplomat. 8 letters, 14 October 1937-1 August 1938, Bowers received from Frank B. Hayne, who described his travel in the Soviet Union, some carbon copies. Unpublished finding aid.

3 Lewis Browne (1897-1949). Papers, 1878-1949, 4,786 items. Author. His diary for 1935 covers a trip to the USSR. Draft article, "A Jew goes to Russia. Prologue," is dated 9 September 1926; another article, "Experiences in Russia," is undated.

4 Robert Francis Byrnes (b. 1917). Collection, 1856-1904, 1,255 items. Historian. Materials gathered for his biography Pobedonostsev (Bloomington, 1968). Konstantin Petrovich Pobedonostsev (1827-1907) was a Russian university professor of law, tutor of Alexander III, senator, procurator of the Holy Synod, and the conservative eminence grise of the Russian court for many years. This collection contains photocopies, 8 vols., positive microfilm, and typescripts of letters in Russian and French to Pobedonostsev. Correspondents included Nikolai Barnov, Mrs. Anna Grigorevna (Snitkina) Dostoevskaia (Mrs. Fedor M. Dostoevskaia), Sergei Rachinskii, Sofia Rachinskii, Catherine Tiutchev, Mrs. Anna (Tiutchev) Aksakov, Mikhail Nikiforovich Katkov, Ol'ga Aleksieevna Novikova, and Sergiei Aleksandrovich Petrovskii. There are also 2 articles in English, 1 about Ol'ga Novikova ("Men and Women of the Day. 1900"), the other on Siberian gold fields ("I am once more on top") by Ernest Terah Hooley, a tsarist agent. Original manuscripts are in the Lenin Library in Moscow; microfilm negatives are in the Library of Congress.

5 Max Eastman (1883-1969). Papers, 1892-1968, 4,096 items. Author, editor of the Masses, 1913-17. Literary manuscripts, correspondence, writings. Among the manuscripts are: "The Anatomy of a Dictator," n.d., about V. I. Lenin; notes on Lenin's character; "Stalin's Purposes," in draft with collected materials, n.d.; "Stalin's Russia and the Crisis in Socialism," n.d.; "What the Russians learn about us," 1945, collected notes on Russian relations with the U.S.; and his notes on personnel in the Russian War Relief Society, 1940s. Manuscripts written by others and collected by Eastman include: Alexander Barmine, on Russian policy in Europe; an off-the-record address by Jan Ciechanowski, Polish ambassador to the U.S., at a meeting of the Cooperative Forum in Washington, D.C., 2 June 1943, copy enclosed in a letter to Eastman of 12 July; Vladimir N. Petrov on the "Soviet Gold Rush," n.d., English and Russian versions, and his outline of a piece entitled "War between U.S. and U.S.S.R. sooner or later is inevitable," n.d.; Robert Minor, "What happened in Russia"; and Paul Wohl, "A Cagliostro of the Underworld or The Real Story of Soviet Agent [W.] Krivitsky," n.d. The extensive correspondence includes letters to or from his wife, née Eliena Vassilyevna Krylenko, January 1924; Peter Berlinrut, August-October 1933; the author Julius Victor Stefan Epstein, October 1947; Charmion von Wiegand, a painter, December 1931 and February 1932; David Julievich Dallin, 8 and 23 November 1945; Eamon De Valera, August 1956; William Hazlett Upson, November 1941 and January 1942; Charles L. Tranter, December 1941; Robert Littell, December 1941; and Dmitri Fedotoff White, December 1941. Subjects discussed in these letters include Lenin, J. Stalin, the Soviet Union and its relations with the U.S., the Russian crown jewels, and the Russian War Relief Society. Other items: Eastman's incomplete translation of Lenin's "testament" and a supplement to it, 1922-23; a review of the International Publishers edition of Lenin's Collected Works, which Eastman called "Lenin Expurgated," n.d.; a report to Doubleday Doran publishers about Lenin's letters to his family, August 1936, a carbon copy; copy of concluding remarks on a sound track (Tzar to Lenin), omitted from a copy given to the Library of Congress; and a copy of a letter from Donald Ogden Stewart et al. to Mrs. Katherine Garrison (Chapin) Biddle discussing Soviet affairs (17 July 1939).

6 Montgomery Evans (1898-1954). Papers, 1918-52, 202 items. Book collector. Includes letter to him from the author Aleister Crowley, 28 November 1945, that discusses the Russians.

7 Francis Vinton Greene (1850-1921). Papers, 1876-1914, 12 items. General, historian, and engineer. Includes letter, 10 July 1883, to him from Thomas H. Anderson concerning the Russian army.

8 Powers Hapgood (1899-1949). Papers, 1915-51, 4,286 items. Union organizer. Includes a permit from the Permanent Commission of

Agricultural and Industrial Immigration for him to live in the autonomous industrial colony "Kuzbas" in Tomsk, Siberia, 24 July 1925; his work record from the People's Commissariat of Labor, July-November 1925; and a statement about Hapgood in the colony, 5 November 1925. All items in Russian.

9 Samuel Sidney McClure (1857-1949). Papers, 1865-1952, 24,244 items. Includes letter, 26 September 1911, from Henry Green to McClure that talks of Russian-American relations; and a typescript entitled "Russia's responsibilty," April 1916, by Albert Gróf Apponyi, a member of the Hungarian Parliament.

10 Paul Vories McNutt (1891-1955). Papers, 1899-1951, 31,922 items. Includes letter, 27 July 1938, to him from Harry Ervin Yarnell, a naval officer, mentioning current Soviet affairs.

11 Hermann Joseph Muller. Papers. Nobel Prize-winning physicist. Contains a considerable file of correspondence with many Soviet geneticists during the late 1920s, early 1930s, and later. There is much scientific and other material, including institute progress reports from the years Muller lived and worked in the Soviet Union. Also included is a fairly extensive file of both correspondence and printed articles relating to Lysenko and Lysenkoism in the Soviet Union in the late 1940s. The material is not yet fully cataloged.

12 Bonaro Wilkinson Overstreet (b. 1902). Papers, 1913-78, 63,004 items. Author, poet, and psychologist. Includes printer's copy of her 1960 book, The War Called Peace, which discusses Soviet foreign relations in the post-1945 era.

13 Upton Beall Sinclair (1878-1968). Collection, 1813-1967, 184 items. American author. Includes more than 50 letters, 1930-32, from Sergei Mikhailovich Eisenstein, plus other materials relating to the making of the film Thunder Over Mexico. There is also a telegram, 21 November 1931, to Sinclair from Iosif Stalin.

14 Slavic Manuscripts. Collection, 1817-1947, 34 items. Alexander I: certificate of promotion to major-general for Boris Poluektov, 1817; Nicholas I: promotion of Poluektov to lieutenant-general, 1826; Aleksandr Ivanovich Kuprin: "Pro drugoe," holograph, n.d., 4 pp., and "Lenin: opyt kharakteristiki," n.d.; Aleksei M. Remizov: "Iz knigi 'Zviezda nadzviezdnaia,'" n.d., holograph fragments; Ivan Bunin: "Neskol'ko slov angliiskomu pisateliu," n.d., holograph, 14 pp., and typed copy, and "O Gor'kom," n.d., holograph, 1 p.; and ALS, 26 December 1919, of Gennadii V. Yudin, the merchant and book collector, thanking a doctor for helping his son (written from Eastern Siberia). Other materials.

15 Frederick Tennyson (1807-1898). Papers, 1841-1922, 1,209 items. Poet. Letters discussing current Russian affairs: 3 from him to Mrs. Mary Isabella Irwin (Rees) Brotherton, 24 January 1872; 9 April 1878; and 16 December 1879, and 1 to him from Mrs. Brotherton, a novelist, 19 April 1881.

16 Richard Wigginton Thompson (1809-1900). Papers, 1837-99, 375 items. U.S. secretary of the navy. Volume 2 of his miscellaneous addresses contains a speech on Russian history delivered at the Eclectic Literary Society of the Indiana State Normal School in Terre Haute, 18 February 1882.

17 Lev Davidovich Trotskii (1879-1940). Papers, 1922-57, 201 items. Russian revolutionary and author. Primarily correspondence and materials exchanged between Trotskii and the writer Max Eastman. Among the correspondents: Eliena Vassilyevna Krylenko (who became Eastman's wife), Albert Boni, Nadezhda Konstantinovna Krupskaia (Lenin's wife), Maxim Lieber, Maurice Paz, Roger William Riis, Alfred Rosmer, Max Shachtman, Boris Souvarine, Joseph Usick Vanzler, Sara Weber, The Saturday Evening Post, and Harcourt, Brace, and Co., publishers. Other holdings: Eastman's notes from his first talks with Trotskii in 1922-23, when he was preparing a book about Trotskii; Eastman's impressions after living 3 days in Trotskii's home in 1932; notes of a conversation with Mrs. Natalie Ivanovna (Sedova) Trotskii after an attack on Trotskii in Moscow; an interview with Trotskii about Soviet economic difficulties in 1932; information on Eastman's efforts to obtain permission for Trotskii to visit the U.S. in 1933; and Eastman's translation of Trotskii's The Revolution Betrayed. A 1957 note from Eastman explains the loss and recovery of his translation of Trotskii's life of Lenin. There are also printed materials on Trotskii's wife, his death, his writings, and Eastman's translations of his works, plus Trotskii's works A Weakening of Stalin or a Weakening of the Soviet (n.d.) and New Moscow Amalgam: Three Trials (1937).

18 Aleksandr Romanovich Vorontsov (1741-1805). Correspondence, 1764-1814, 124 items. Imperial chancellor under Alexander I. Letters of Count Aleksandr Romanovich; Count Semen Romanovich Vorontsov (1744-1832), his brother and Russian ambassador to Vienna and London; and Ivan Larionovich Vorontsov-Dashkov, a relative of the Vorontsov brothers who inherited part of the estate of their sister, Princess Ekaterina Romanova (Vorontsova) Dashkova, when she died in 1810. The family, signing the name "Woronzow," writes to bankers in London and France primarily. The letters, mostly in French, concern financial accounts, the importing of wine, tobacco, and tea, a move from Pisa to London via Frankfurt, and the shipment of a set of armoires.

19 Jonathan Williams (1750-1815). Papers, 1738-1869, 7,197 items. Merchant, soldier, and

commandant of West Point. Includes letter from Princess E. R. Dashkova.

20 Wendell Wilkie (1892-1944). Papers, ca. 1938-45, ca. 200 of 500,000 items. American industrialist, anti-isolationist political leader, and Republican presidential candidate in 1940. Some items relate to his trip in 1941-42 when he visited the USSR and met with J. Stalin.

21 James Sprigg Wilson. Papers, 1918-19, 7 items. Chief surgeon of the American Expeditionary Force in Siberia, 1918-19. Scrapbook, letters, photos of Siberia, lists of American army personnel, and clippings, all relating to the colonel's experiences in the AEF. Among his correspondents were William Sidney Graves, major general commanding the AEF in Siberia; Fred P. Manget, acting commissioner of the American Red Cross in Siberia; and Kenneth Lewis Roberts, the author, who served as a captain in the Siberian AEF in 1918-19.

22 William Albert Wirt (1874-1938). Papers, 1899-1957, 22,232 items. Educator. Includes letter, 10 September 1919, from him to Arnold B. Keller, copy, and letter, 13 August 1919, from Keller to Henry G. Hay, Jr. discussing the Russian Educational Club of Gary, Indiana.

IN 4
MUSIC SCHOOL LIBRARY
SYCAMORE HALL
INDIANA UNIVERSITY
Bloomington, Indiana 47401
(812-337-8541)

1 Sergei Sergeevich Prokofiev (1891-1953). Concerto in G minor, no. 2, op. 63, for violin, negative film reproduction of the original in the Moscow State Library of the USSR, 1935, unpaged manuscript score; same, reproduced from composer's manuscript, 38 ll.; [The meeting of the Volga and the Don. Sketches], op. 130 [n.p., 1951], 1 vol. (various paging), photocopy of fond 1929, opis' 1, ed. khr. 128 of manuscripts in the Tsentral'nyi gosudarstvennyi arkhiv literatury i iskusstva; Symphony no. 3, op. 44, score, 196 ll., 1928, reproduced from composer's manuscript; Symphony no. 4, op. 47, in C major, 1929 (op. 112 in 1947), score, 171 pp. [n.p.], 1947, reproduction of holograph made by the Tsentral'nyi gosudarstvennyi arkhiv literatury i iskusstva; and Symphony no. 6, op. 111, Sketches [Moscow], TsGALI, 1 vol., various pagings, negative microfilm, reproductions of the composer's sketches ("inclusive dates: 1945-1947").

2 Igor' Fedorovich Stravinskii (1882-1971). [Histoire du soldat, Suite], ensemble parts for clarinet, bassoon, cornet, trombone, percussion, violin, and double bass, photocopy of manuscript; also, reproduction of same from manuscript [New York, E. F. Kalmus, 19--].

IN 5
ORAL HISTORY RESEARCH PROJECT
INDIANA UNIVERSITY
512 North Fess Avenue
Bloomington, Indiana 47405
(812-337-2856)

Waldemar John Gallman (b. 1899). Interview transcript, typed, 152 pp., plus introduction and index, 1975. Diplomat, ambassador to Poland. Conducted in 2 sessions by F. Gerald Handfield, Jr. Recording on 9 tape reels, ca. 8.5 hrs. Major emphasis on his 40-year career in the foreign service and on Great Britain. Numerous references to the Soviet Union, primarily U.S.-Soviet relations, ca. 1920-60. Mention of George F. Kennan and Fyodor Gusev. Duplicate copies of the transcript available.

Finding Aid: Guide to Indiana University Oral History Research Project and Related Studies (1977).

IN 6
UNIVERSITY ARCHIVES
INDIANA UNIVERSITY
Bryan Hall, Room 201
Bloomington, Indiana 47405
(812-337-1127)

Mark Veniaminovich Vishniak (1883-1976). Papers, ca. 1900-1920s, ca. 3 ft. Lawyer, professor, writer, and member of the Socialist Revolutionary Party in his youth. Includes correspondence relating to the Paris review Sovremenniia zapiski with M. Ossorgin, T. Stepun, and I. Fondaminskii-Bunakov. Also, correspondence with other important cultural figures of the Russian emigration. Access is restricted; inquire concerning conditions of access.

IN 7
PROFESSOR FELIX J. OINAS--PRIVATE COLLECTION
DEPARTMENT OF SLAVIC LANGUAGES AND LITERATURES
INDIANA UNIVERSITY
Ballantine Hall 502
Bloomington, Indiana 47401

Professor Oinas has ca. 5 notebooks containing his day-by-day remarks made in Russia (to the east of Lake Peipus) in 1942-43, when he worked as a member of the group sent there by Tartu University to investigate the situation of the Estonian minority. Professor Oinas's notes, written in Estonian, contain stories told by the Estonians about the history of their emigration to Russia and the conditions in Russia before and during World War II, list of place names, etc. This material has not been published, but was used in writing a detailed report (unpublished) about the

Estonians in the trans-Peipus region. Dr. Ilmar Arens, who resides in Sweden, has published studies based on this report. Scholars who would like to use this material should contact Professor Oinas at the given address.

IN 8
PROFESSOR ALEXANDER RABINOWITCH--PRIVATE COLLECTION
HISTORY DEPARTMENT
INDIANA UNIVERSITY
Bloomington, Indiana 47405
(812-337-7309)

Professor Rabinowitch is in possession of materials documenting the activities of his father, Eugene Rabinowitch, the founder of the Pugwash Conference. The materials include correspondence relating to personal, political, and scientific matters, some of which pertain to the Soviet Union. There are also manuscripts of some of Rabinowitch's works.

IN 9
ARCHIVES OF THE MENNONITE CHURCH
GOSHEN COLLEGE
1700 South Main Street
Goshen, Indiana 46526
(219-533-3161 x 327)

1 John Funk (1835-1930). Papers, 1852-1929, 35 ft. Mennonite bishop and publisher. Collection contains the following items: box 68, records of the Mennonite Board of Guardians, an agency set up to aid Russian Mennonite immigration; box 138, 1 notebook of the 1873 journey of 12 Russians to America in search of land; boxes 51-54, Funk's historical memorandum books with documents and clippings relating to Russian emigration. His correspondence also contains much data on Russian Mennonite immigrants in 1874. Unpublished inventory. (Hist. Mss. 1-1)

2 John Horsch Mennonite History Essay Contest. Collection, 1957-present, 5.75 ft. and growing. Collection of student writings, a few on Russian Mennonites. Among them are: Winston J. Martin, "Russian Mennonite Immigration to Manitoba with Special Reference to Aid Received from Ontario Mennonites, 1870-1880"; E. A. Isaac, "The Landless of the Molotschna [Molotschna being a Mennonite colony in Russia]"; B. Harry Dyck, "Johann Cornies [Russian Mennonite leader]"; Werner Funck, "The Cooperation of the Church Leaders with the Colony Government in Russia during the Years, 1859-1864"; John Kroeker, "Tensions between the Russländer and Kanadier in Canada"; Arlin Claassen, "Russian Mennonites in the Nineteenth Century, The Influence of Chiliasm on"; and Ruth Heinrichs, "A History of Susa Neustadter and Isaak Zacharias." (I-3-3)

3 Christian Emmanuel Krehbiel (1869-1948). Papers, 1893-1947, 1 microfilm reel. Mennonite pastor. A member of the Relief Commission to Russia in 1922-23. His diary describes his experiences, as do some letters. Originals are in the Mennonite Library and Archives in North Newton, Kansas.

4 Mennonite Central Committee. Records, 1920-present, 807 ft. and growing. Correspondence, reports, office files, and photographs. Over 36 ft. concern American Mennonite relief work in Russia during the post-World War I years and the resettlement of Russian Mennonites in Paraguay. These records are divided into 3 sections: Russian relief (IX-1); Maxwell H. Kratz, relief and immigration files, 1920-34 (IX-2); and Paraguayan immigration, 1920-33 (IX-3). The following MCC collections also include scattered references and documentation relating to Russian Mennonite refugees during World War II: general correspondence files (IX-6-1); data files (IX-12); Gronau files (IX-14); and European files (IX-19). Unpublished inventory.

5 Philip Wismer. Papers, 1874-80, 3 folders. Photocopies. Includes a memorandum book, records of the Ontario Mennonites, and a Russian Mennonite Aid Committee (Ontario) record book. All relate to Russian Mennonite immigration to Canada in 1874. Originals are in Ontario. (Hist. Mss. 1-180)

IN 10
INDIANA HISTORICAL SOCIETY LIBRARY
315 West Ohio Street
Indianapolis, Indiana 46202
(317-633-4976)

John Louis Hilton Fuller (b. 1894). Papers, 1917-18, 1 ft., 25 items. Banker. Correspondence, photographs, notes, and a diary, mostly typed, 144 pp. Materials pertain to his work as a trainee with the Petrograd branch of the National City Bank of New York, September 1917-August 1918. They touch on a variety of topics, including the Bolshevik Revolution and its aftermath, the takeover of foreign banks in December 1917, the moving of the foreign diplomatic and business community from Petrograd to Vologda in the spring of 1918, and the beginnings of foreign intervention in July-August 1918. Unpublished register.

IN 11
INDIANA DIVISION
INDIANA STATE LIBRARY
140 North Senate Avenue
Indianapolis, Indiana 46204
(317-232-3668)

1 William Dudley Foulke (1848-1935). Papers, 1849-1931, 622 items. Lawyer, author, and president of the American Woman's Suffrage Association. Includes ca. 6 letters and a newspaper article dealing with the political history of Russia and the status of Russian women in the years 1887-1904. 2 letters are copies of George Kennan letters in the Library of Congress. Collection is catalogued but not inventoried.

2 Pierce-Krull Family. Papers, 1834-1963, 8 boxes. Contains 2 letters from Henry D. Pierce, who traveled to Russia in 1890. Also, a piece entitled "Moscow, Holy Moscow" written in letter form (1894) by Theresa Pierce, who accompanied her father to Russia, which includes cultural, historical, and political information about pre-revolutionary Russia. Collection is inventoried and catalogued.

IN 12
DEPARTMENT OF RARE BOOKS AND SPECIAL COLLECTIONS
MEMORIAL LIBRARY
UNIVERSITY OF NOTRE DAME
Notre Dame, Indiana 46556

Elias V. Denissoff Slavonic Collection. The Right Reverend Denissoff (1893-1971) was born in St. Petersburg, the son of a political figure, and once served as secretary to the prime minister of Russia. He emigrated to the U.S. in 1948, holding positions as professor of philosophy at Illinois Benedictine College and the University of Notre Dame.

The collection consists primarily of books on Russian history, Russian church history of the 16th and 17th c., philosophy and theology of the Byzantine period, Russian philosophy, and geography of Russia.

There are also 700 microfilms on Muscovite church history drawn from holdings in the British Library (London); Vatican Library, and library of the Pontifical Oriental Institute (Rome); Bibliothèque Nationale, and Bibliothèque Slave (Paris); Staatsbibliothek, and library of the Orientale Institut (Berlin); and other libraries. (Denissoff's most famous work concerned the monk Maxim the Greek.)

Also in the collection is an 18th c. codex manuscript in several Old Russian hands that contains a chronicle of ecclesiastical history ("Letopis' keleinyi preosviashchennago Dimitriia mitropolita rostovskago i iaroslavskago ot nachala mirobytiia do rozhdestva Khristova") by St. Dimitrii Rostovski (1651-1709), a saint of the Russian Orthodox Church. The codex has a full-leaf illumination of St. Dimitrii writing the chronicle with a quill pen. Inquire about possible restrictions.

Note: The library also has a separate Elias V. Denissoff Collection on Descartes.

IN 13
ARCHIVES
LILLY LIBRARY
EARLHAM COLLEGE
Richmond, Indiana 47374
(317-962-6561)

Homer Lawrence Morris (1886-1951). Papers, 1908-51, 12 ft. Economist and educator. He was also an official of the American Friends Service Committee in 1905-51, serving as field director for famine relief for the AFS in Buzuluk, Russia, in 1919-22. Includes diaries, photographs, maps/charts, pamphlets, posters, and clippings, 1919-23, relating to his work in Russia. Unpublished finding aid (NUCMC 64-962, replacing 62-2167).

IN 14
DISCOVERY HALL MUSEUM
120 South Saint Joseph Street
South Bend, Indiana 46601
(219-284-9714)

Studebaker Company. Archives, 1852-1966, ca. 3,600 ft. There may be materials relating to foreign government contracts. Includes a presentation album given to Studebaker by the General Automotive Division of the Red Army in 1945. This album of photographs, 40 pp., captioned in Russian, shows Studebaker-made trucks in use by the Soviet army during World War II. Access currently restricted because the collection is still largely packed away and in process.

IN 15
DEPARTMENT OF RARE BOOKS AND SPECIAL COLLECTIONS
CUNNINGHAM MEMORIAL LIBRARY
INDIANA STATE UNIVERSITY
Terre Haute, Indiana 47809
(812-232-6311 x 2862/2863)

Eugene V. Debs (1855-1926). Papers, 1874-1945, ca. 7 ft. Labor leader and socialist. Contains several letters pertaining to Russia: from Charles F. Drake to Theodore Debs, 14 August 1943, regarding Drake's recent trip to Russia; from Joseph E. Cohen to Theodore Debs, 20 December 1930, in which Cohen discusses a trip to Russia by members of the Socialist Party; from Emma Goldman to Havelock Ellis, 8 November 1925, where she describes the failure of the Russian Revolution; from Emma Goldman to Eugene Debs, 18 March 1926, in which she portrays Soviet Russia as a crushing machine with a stranglehold on the masses. In addition to these letters, there is considerable correspondence in the collection with references to Russia, communism, and socialism. Annotated index cards.

IOWA

IA 1
DEPARTMENT OF SPECIAL COLLECTIONS
IOWA STATE UNIVERSITY LIBRARY
Ames, Iowa 50010
(515-294-6672)

1 Armenian Manuscripts. Leaf from Grigor Tat'ewac'i's Book of Questions, 16-17th c.; and leaf from a lectionary, A.D. 1671 (xf 220.8655/E290).

2 Ronald C. Bentley (b. 1899). Papers, 1926-63, ca. .1 of 2 ft. Radio broadcaster on farming for station WOI in Ames. He was a tour leader in 1958 for 29 Iowans who traveled to Western Europe and the Soviet Union. Includes some articles about the tour. Unpublished inventory.

3 Charles J. Hearst (b. 1904). Papers, 1935-68, ca. 1.6 of 5 ft. Farmer and livestock breeder. Diaries, speeches, and articles relating to his trip to the USSR in 1955 as part of a U.S. Farm Exchange delegation. Unpublished inventory.

4 George Heikens (1902-1976). Papers in process. Farmer. He worked as a swine expert in the Soviet Union in 1930-31.

5 Herbert Plambeck (b. 1908). Papers, 1936-70, ca. 2 of 14 ft. Farm broadcaster and public official. He accompanied the U.S. Farm Exchange delegation to the USSR in 1955. Some photographs and articles concern this trip. Unpublished calendar. (NUCMC 71-1779)

6 J. Stuart Russell (1892-1960). Papers, 1932-58, ca. 1 in. of 1.5 ft. Farm editor of the Des Moines Register and Tribune. In 1955 he covered the Russian agricultural visit to Iowa. Letters and articles concern the visit and the agricultural exchange. Unpublished inventory.

7 Lauren Soth (b. 1910). Papers, 1945-76, 19 ft. Economist, writer, and editor for the Des Moines Register and Tribune. Went to the USSR as part of the U.S. farm delegation. He received a Pulitzer Prize for his editorial suggesting the Soviet-American agricultural exchange in the first place. Unpublished inventory.

IA 2
PUTNAM MUSEUM (formerly, DAVENPORT MUSEUM)
1717 West 12th Street
Davenport, Iowa 52804
(319-324-1933)

1 James Buchanan (1791-1868). U.S. president, 1857-61. Letter, 19 January 1855, in which he briefly discusses the Crimean War, the peace conference at Vienna, and plans to seize Constantinople.

2 Propaganda Collection. Includes a poster, 21 x 15 in., printed and distributed by the Allen Bradley Co. of Milwaukee; and 3 handbills, 1 printed by the Student Peace Union of Chicago, the other 2 protesting Soviet activities in Lithuania. These materials were gathered as a result of N. Khrushchev's visit to Chicago in 1959.

3 Sonia Tolstoi (1844-1919). Wife of the novelist and philosopher Leo Tolstoi. Letter, 1892, from the countess thanking the recipient for American sympathy to Russians suffering from the famine.

Restriction: Access is restricted; inquire at the Museum.

IA 3
DIVISION OF HISTORICAL MUSEUM AND ARCHIVES
IOWA STATE HISTORICAL DEPARTMENT
East 12th Street and Grand Avenue
Des Moines, Iowa 50319
(515-281-5472)

1 Demetrius Gallitzin (1770-1840). Russian prince who became a priest, emigrated to the U.S. in 1792. Manuscripts of his sermons. (G 1354)

2 Iowa Commission for Russian Famine Relief (B. F. Tillinghast Papers). Records, 1892, ca. 500 letters. Correspondence relates to the commission and its work. The Iowa Historical Records Survey Project's Guide to Depositories of Manuscript Collections in the United States: Iowa (Des Moines, 1940) notes this collection. (NUCMC 62-651)

3 Iowa State Public Archives. Records, 1836-present, ongoing. Correspondence, reports,

and miscellaneous items relate to the Russian famine of 1891-92. Includes letters and reports on the famine, relief work, and a special commission established to render aid (GII, box 371); 47 letters appealing for aid, 1892, in GVIII, box 37; lists of contributors to the women's auxiliary, reports, and correspondence, ca. 50 pp., in GVIII; and ca. 100 more letters in TVI. There is a published guide book to the public archives.

IA 4
ARCHIVES
THE AMERICAN LUTHERAN CHURCH
333 Wartburg Place
Dubuque, Iowa 52001
(319-556-8151)

Iowa Synod Correspondence. File, 1850-1900. 10,000 items. Russian-related materials include ca. 200-300 letters, 1860-ca. 1900, written by members of a German Lutheran community in the St. Petersburg area. Mentioned is the leader of the community, the widow of the Russian army General von Helfreich; she helped to rouse support for the Wartburg Lutheran Seminary in Iowa. Also noted is Fraulein Augusta von Schwartz, an attendant in the home of the minister von Gamelaya, who at the age of 53 came to the United States to become housemother to the students at Wartburg Seminary. The letters are written in German script.

IA 5
THE HERBERT HOOVER LIBRARY
West Branch, Iowa 52358
(319-643-5301)

The Hoover Library was created to preserve materials pertaining to Herbert Hoover and his administration. Russian-related materials can be found in 5 of its holdings: the papers of Herbert Hoover; other manuscript collections; microfilms; oral history transcripts; and other materials.

The Papers of Herbert Hoover

1 Herbert Hoover (1874-1964). U.S. president, 1929-33, and secretary of commerce, 1921-29; visited Russia while employed as a mining engineer, 1909, 1911, 1913, and after World War I was active in relief aid to Russia and Armenia. His papers, which span his entire life, can be divided into several groups:

Pre-commerce period, 1895-1921, 75 ft. The general correspondence series, 1895-1921, 13 ft., includes correspondence with Woodrow Wilson, Edgar Rickard, Perrin C. Galpin, and Edward M. House. Some of these letters pertain to Russia and contain some of Hoover's observations on the Russian Revolution. The Subject File, 1913-21, 56 ft., includes materials on the American Relief Administration, 1 container, Russian relief, 1919-22, the Russian Mining Corporation, Ltd., 1914, and Russia, 1919-21. Also included in the Subject File is a "Mining" file that contains printed reports concerning the Atbasar Copper Fields, Ltd., 1911, the Irtysh Corporation, Ltd., 1916, the Kyshtim Corporation, Ltd., 1908-15, and the Russo-Asiatic Corporation, Ltd., 1914; maps of Russia and Siberia, 1888, 1889; and cables, reports, maps, and charts concerning the Antonoff Gold Mines, 1912. The pre-commerce period materials also include the American Relief Administration Documents, 26 vols., selected printed and typescript copies of documents concerning the European and Russian operations of the American Relief Administration. The original documents are in the Hoover Institution. 10 vols. devoted to Russian Operations.

Commerce period, 1921-28, 353 ft. Includes official and personal papers on: the American Relief Administration; the Bureau of Foreign and Domestic Commerce of the Commerce Department; Corn for Russia; the Foreign Policy Association; Germany and Russia; the National Information Bureau; the National Civic Federation; "Reds"; the State Department. There are also materials (under the heading "Russia") on Russia, general, 1921-28 and undated, approximately 1 container; the Far East Republic, 1921; Siberia, 1922-23; the Russian problem, 1921-28; Russian trade, 1921-28; Soviet propaganda in China; the Financial Attaché S. Ughet, 1922; the Ukraine, 1922; and on the book The Famine in Soviet Russia (extracts). Individuals mentioned in these papers include Allen W. Dulles, Mrs. Frank Fay, Harold Henry Fisher, James P. Goodrich, Paxton Hibben, Charles Evans Hughes, Lincoln Hutchinson, Litvinov, Edward Frank Wise, S. Slonim, and Leslie Urquhart.

Presidential period, 1929-33, 656 ft. The cabinet offices series, 30 ft., contains materials on the Eastern European Affairs Division of the State Department. The foreign affairs series, 22 ft., has materials on Russia, the Baltic States, and the Conference of Wheat Exporting Countries, 1931. The president's personal file series, 107 ft., includes documents on the Russia Student Fund, Inc.

Post-presidential period, 1933-64, 465 ft. The subject file series, 157 ft., includes correspondence and printed matter on Russia and materials on the Riga Agreement.

Special collections, 1853-1965, 625 ft. The "Articles, Addresses, and Public Statements" file, 1892-1964, 247 ft., includes some of Hoover's statements regarding Russia. The ,

"Clippings" file, 1920-64, 241 ft., chronologically arranged, has some materials on Russia/USSR.

Other Manuscript Collections

2 William Richards Castle, Jr. Papers, 1917-68, 12 ft. Chief, Division of Western European Affairs, Department of State, 1921-27; assistant secretary of state, 1927-30; ambassador to Japan, 1930; under secretary of state, 1931-33. Materials on Russia, 1931-33, and correspondence with Herbert Hoover and Charles Evans Hughes. Register. (NUCMC 72-1437)

3 James Westbrook Pegler (1894-1969). Papers, 1908-69, 80 ft. Columnist, Scripps-Howard Syndicate, 1933-34; columnist, King Features Syndicate, 1944-62; freelance writer and journalist, 1962-69. The heading "Russia" in the subject file series contains materials on Russia, 1941-64 and undated; the atomic bomb; 1949-50; the Constitution, 1936 and undated; investments in the U.S., 1956-57, 2 folders; the Katyn Massacre, 1953-54 and undated; recognition of the Soviet Union, 1939-41 and undated; Russian bonds, 1950. The subject file series also has materials on "Russian heirs," 1950-57, communism, and Philip R. Faymonville, 1942-54 and undated. The writings and speeches series has numerous references to Russia and Soviet-American relations. Register. 2 ft. restricted, but reviewed in 1980.

4 Hugh Robert Wilson (1885-1946). Papers, 1923-46, 2 ft. Chief, Division of Current Information, Department of State, 1924-47; chief, Executive Committee, Foreign Service Personnel Board, Department of State, 1924-27; assistant secretary of state, 1937; ambassador to Germany, 1938-39; member, Advisory Committee on Problems of Foreign Relations, Department of State, 1940. Correspondence with Joseph C. Green, John MacMurray, and Pierrepont Moffat is cross-referenced under "Russia." Register and index. (NUCMC 69-749)

5 There may be references to Russia/USSR in the following additional manuscript collections: Karl Baarslag, papers, 1927-65, 3 ft.; Edward Dana Durand (1871-1960), member, U.S. Food Administration, 1917-19, advisor to food minister of Poland, 1919-21, chief, Eastern European Division, Bureau of Foreign and Domestic Commerce, Department of Commerce, 1921, papers, 1906-59 (NUCMC 72-1438); Hugh Gibson (1883-1954), Department of State, February 1917, duty with Herbert Hoover, November 1918-April 1919, first Envoy Extraordinaire and Minister Plenipotentiary to Poland, April 1919, papers, 1910-30, 1946-47, 2 ft.

Microfilms

6 The following microfilms have references to Russia/USSR: American Commission to Negotiate Peace, general records, 1918-31, 563 reels, originals in record group 256, National Archives; Board of Trade (London), selected mining companies' materials, 1895-1921, 2 reels, originals at the Public Records Office in London; Calvin Coolidge, papers, selected portions, 1923-29, 160 reels, originals at the Library of Congress; Warren Gamaliel Harding, papers, selected portions, 1914-63, 202 reels, originals at the Ohio Historical Society; Herbert Hoover, selected documents from 11 collections, 1920-64, 1 reel, originals at the New York Public Library; Herbert Hoover, selected documents from 21 collections, 1914-64, 1 reel, originals at the State Historical Society of Wisconsin; Franklin D. Roosevelt - Winston Churchill, messages and related materials, 1939-41, 6 reels, originals at the Franklin D. Roosevelt Library; Henry L. Stimson, papers and diaries, selected reels, 1909-45, 135 reels, originals at Yale University Library; U.S. Department of State, records relating to the internal affairs of Russia, "Calamities and Disasters," 1910-29, 9 reels, originals in record group 59, National Archives; U.S. Department of State, records of the German Foreign Office received by the Department of State, "Captured German Documents on Microfilm," 1923-30, 4 reels, originals in record group 243, National Archives.

Oral History Transcripts

Note: The oral history transcripts cited below were made in 1966-71.

7 Horace M. Albright. 99 pp. Director, National Park Service, 1929-33. Mention of U.S. foreign policy regarding the USSR, 1933-45, pp. 95-96.

8 Samuel S. Arentz. 18 pp. Mining engineer who had mining contacts with Hoover. Mention of the USSR, pp. 11-12.

9 Martha Ellen Brumback. 38 pp. Research assistant to Herbert Hoover. Discussion of U.S. policy towards the USSR, 1919-67, pp. 17-19.

10 Elmer G. Burland. 36 pp. Deputy executive director, CARE, 1946. Mention of conditions in the USSR after World War II, p. 23.

11 Loren R. Chandler. 27 pp. Professor of surgery at Stanford, 1938-present. Discussion of the German invasion of the USSR, pp. 9-10.

12 Mark Wayne Clark. 27 pp. General, U.S. Army; chairman, Task Force on Intelligence Activities, Second Hoover Commission, 1954-55.

References to Soviet foreign policy in the post-World War II era, pp. 3-4, 6-13, 24-25; to Soviet military strategy in World War II, pp. 6, 10-11, 14-16; to Soviet economic policy, p. 30; and to Soviet intelligence and counter-intelligence, 1950s, pp. 24-26.

13 Arthur A. Curtice. 33 pp. Mining and petroleum engineer; business associate and friend of Herbert Hoover, Jr. Discussion of Soviet economic policy, p. 30.

14 Eleanor L. Dulles. 23 pp. Diplomat; served in the Office of German Affairs, Department of State. Discussion of Soviet foreign policy regarding Austria after World War II, pp. 2-7.

15 Dwight David Eisenhower. 36 pp. U.S. president, 1953-61. Discussion of Soviet propaganda, 1950s, p. 26. Portion closed until 2017.

16 Ralph Evans. 20 pp. Secretary to Secretary of the Interior Franklin K. Lane, 1919-20; secretary to U.S. Congressman Hull from Iowa, 1921-24. Discussion of U.S. foreign policy regarding the Soviet Union after World War I, pp. 5-6.

17 Harold M. Fleming. 21 pp. Member, American Relief Administration in Europe and Russia, 1922-23. Mention of conditions in the USSR in 1921-23, pp. 2-3, 5-12, 18-19.

18 George P. Harrington. 23 pp. Member, American Relief Administration (Poland and Latvia), 1919 and (Russia), 1922-23. Discussion of conditions in the USSR, 1921-23, pp. 9-17.

19 Olga von Nordenflycht Kaltenborn (Mrs. Hans). 27 pp. Husband was a news analyst. Discussion of Soviet military strategy after World War II, p. 14.

20 Edward A. Keller. 77 pp. Clergyman and economist; director, Bureau of Economic Research, 1935-52. Discussion of foreign policy regarding the USSR, pp. 51-52.

21 Irene Corgally Kuhn. 40 pp. Writer and commentator. Discussion of conditions in the USSR, 1920-21, p. 35.

22 Mr. and Mrs. David C. Lawrence. 73 pp. David Lawrence was president, U.S. News & World Report, 1948-73. Discussion of Soviet foreign policy in the 1960s and World War II, p. 16; mention of the treaty of recognition of Soviet Russia, 1933, pp. 45-46.

23 John J. McCloy. 12 pp. Assistant secretary of war, 1941-45. Discussion of Soviet military strategy during World War II, p. 3.

24 Neil MacNeil. 117 pp. Editor, author; worked for the New York Times. Discussion of the treaty of recognition of the USSR, 1933, pp. 45-46.

25 Raymond Moley. 43 pp. Assistant secretary of state, 1933; editor and author. Discussion of Soviet military strategy in World War II, pp. 37-39.

26 George G. Montgomery. 10 pp. Corporation executive. Mention of conditions in the USSR, 1960s, p. 4.

27 Felix M. Morley. 28 pp. Editorial writer, correspondent, college president. Discussion of Soviet foreign policy after World War II, pp. 6-8.

28 David Packard. 27 pp. President, board of trustees, Stanford University, 1958-60. Discussion of the Bolshevik Revolution, p. 11.

29 Byron Price. 29 pp. News editor. Discussion of foreign policy regarding the Soviet Union, 1932, p. 20.

30 Mr. and Mrs. Lawrence Kendall Requa. 38 pp. Requa and his father were mining associates and friends of the Hoover family. Discussion of the Bolshevik Revolution, p. 4.

31 Rudolph N. Schullinger. 19 pp. Physician to Herbert Hoover, 1958-63. Discussion of conditions in the USSR, 1921-23, p. 9, and Soviet foreign policy after World War II, p. 9.

32 Mrs. Helen d'Oyle Sioussat. 77 pp. Television commentator for Columbia Broadcasting System. Discussion of U.S. foreign policy regarding the Soviet Union after World War II, p. 9.

33 Robert G. Storey. 52 pp. Lawyer and college dean. Discussion of U.S. foreign policy toward the Soviet Union after World War II, pp. 34-36.

34 Cosmo Stravalli. 24 pp. Barber to Herbert Hoover. Discussion of Soviet foreign policy after World War II, p. 2.

35 H. Dudley Swim. 26 pp. Member, Northern Californians for the Hoover Report, 1949-58. Discussion of U.S. foreign policy regarding the Soviet Union, 1951, pp. 9-10.

36 Frederick E. Terman. 53 pp. Educator and electronics engineer. Discussion of the Bolshevik Revolution, pp. 27-29.

37 Payson Jackson Treat. 26 pp. Professor of history, Stanford University, 1909-45. Discussion of the military capacity of the Soviet Union, 1948, p. 24, and of the United Nations Relief and Rehabilitation Administration, 1940s, p. 25.

38 Walter Trohan. 48 pp. Newspaper correspondent; worked for the Chicago Tribune. Discussion of the Bolshevik Revolution, pp. 4-5.

39 Scott Turner. 82 pp. Mining engineer. Discussion of mining in the Soviet Union, pp. 9-11.

40 Henry C. Wolfe. 27 pp. Member, American Relief Administration, 1922. Discussion of conditions in the Soviet Union after World War I, pp. 1-10.

41 In addition, there may be references to Russia/USSR in the following oral history transcripts: Milton M. Brown, member, Finnish Relief Fund, 1939-43, 37 pp.; Robert B. Considine, newspaperman and author, 17 pp.; Charles S. Dewey, financial advisor, Republic of Poland, 1927-31; James H. Douglas, Jr., secretary of the air force, 1957-59, 35 pp.; Edward T. Folliard, reporter, 25 pp.; Adaline Fuller (Mrs. William Parmer, Jr.), member, American Relief Administration, European Children's Fund (Poland), 1919-20; Barry M. Goldwater, U.S. senator from Arizona, 1953-64, 1968-present, 11 pp.; Joseph C. Green, member, American Relief Administration (Rumania and Caucasus), 1918-19; career diplomat, Department of State, 1930-53, 49 pp.; Leslie R. Groves, chief of the Manhattan Development Project, 1942-47, 47 pp., restricted: portions closed until 1985; Henry Hazlitt, editor and author, 29 pp.; Marguerite Rickard Hoyt (Mrs. Graham), director, American Relief Administration, 1919-29, 45 pp.; Lyndon Baines Johnson, senator from Texas, 1949-61, U.S. vice-president, 1961-63, president, 1963-68, 22 pp.; George Killion, ambassador to the United Nations, 1966, 17 pp.; Arthur Krock, editor and correspondent, 22 pp.; Mary Pillsbury Lord (Mrs. Oswald), U.S. representative on Human Rights Commission, United Nations, 1953-61, 24 pp.; Eugene Lyons, United Press correspondent to Russia, 1928-34, 23 pp.; Mr. and Mrs. Frank Earl Mason, journalist, member, Hoover Economic Mission to Germany and Austria, 1947, 62 pp.; Thomas D. Morris, assistant secretary of defense, 1961-64, 14 pp.; William D. Pawley, special assistant to the secretary of state, 1948, 1951, special assistant to the secretary of defense, 1951-52; Thomas P. Pike, special assistant to the secretary of defense, 1957-58, 21 pp.; Gardner Richardson, chief, American Relief Administration, Hungary, 1919-20, Austria, 1920-23, 16 pp.; John L. Simpson, member, American Relief Administration, Central Europe and Yugoslavia, 51 pp.; Nadia de Kanel Slack, a Russian who worked with the American Relief Administration in Russia, 1922, 2 pp.; Truman Smith, military attaché and attaché for air in Germany, 1935-39, 17 pp.; Lewis L. Strauss, chairman, Atomic Energy Commission, 1953-58, 42 pp.; William Lindsay White, newspaperman and author, 50 pp., restricted: closed until 1985; Richard L. Wilson, newspaper editor, 13 pp.

Other Materials

42 The Library also has still photographs, motion pictures, and sound recordings pertaining to Hoover and his administration. There are photographs of mining operations throughout the world, Food Administration activities during World War I, and famine relief after World Wars I and II.

Finding Aids: In addition to the finding aids mentioned above, the Library has compiled an unpublished survey, 5 pp., "Resources for the Study of Russia and Soviet-American Relations - Herbert Hoover Library," which was used extensively in writing this entry. See also the Library's Historical Materials in the Herbert Hoover Presidential Library (September 1977).

KANSAS

KS 1
THE DWIGHT D. EISENHOWER LIBRARY
Abilene, Kansas 67410
(913-263-4751)

The Eisenhower Library was created to preserve materials pertaining to Dwight D. Eisenhower and his administration. Russian-related materials can be found in 3 of its holdings: manuscripts; microfilms; and oral history transcripts.

Manuscripts

3 estimates--"substantial," "moderate," and "a few scattered items"--are used to divide the manuscript collections described in this entry. These estimates are relative to the size of the collection; 200 pp. of materials, for example, would be considered "substantial" in a collection totalling 1 ft., while they might be considered "a few scattered items" in a collection totalling 1,000 ft.

1 The following manuscript collections contain a substantial number of materials pertaining to Russia/USSR: John Foster Dulles, secretary of state, 1953-59, papers, 1952-59, 29 ft., not processed; Dwight D. Eisenhower, papers as president of the United States, 1953-61, 122 ft., partly on microfilm; Dwight D. Eisenhower, records as president, White House Central Files, 1953-61, 3,241 ft. (NUCMC 71-1706), partly on microfilm; James C. Hagerty, press secretary to the president, 1953-61, papers, 1953-61, 47 ft. (NUCMC 76-1860); Christian A. Herter, under secretary, State Department,

1957-59, secretary of state, 1959-61, papers, 1957-61, 7 ft., not processed; C. D. Jackson, special assistant to the president for international affairs, 1953-54, papers, 1931-67, 36 ft., written permission required for examination (NUCMC 76-1863); C. D. Jackson, records, 1953-56, 4 ft., not processed; Emil F. Reinhardt, commanding general, 69th Infantry Division, 1943-45, papers, 1940-69, ca. 1 ft. (NUCMC 76-1875); Republican National Committee, news clippings and publications, 1932-65, 320 ft.; White House Office, office of the special assistant for national security affairs (Robert Cutler, Dillon Anderson, and Gordon Gray), records, 1952-61, 28 ft., partially processed; White House Office, office of the staff secretary, records of Paul T. Carroll, Andrew J. Goodpaster, L. Arthur Minnich, and Christopher H. Russell, 1952-61, 64 ft., partially processed; White House Office, Project "Clean Up," records of Gordon Gray, Robert Cutler, Henry R. McPhee, and Andrew J. Goodpaster, 1953-61, 27 ft., partially processed. There are finding aids to all these collections.

2 The following manuscript collections contain a moderate amount of materials pertaining to Russia/USSR: Stephen Benedict, assistant to Dr. Gabriel Hauge, research director of Citizens for Eisenhower, 1952-53, member, Eisenhower's personal campaign staff, September-November 1952, materials regarding General Eisenhower's 1952 campaign speeches, 1952, 2 ft.; Ezra Taft Benson, secretary of agriculture, 1953-61, papers, 1952-61, 2 ft., partly on microfilm; Combined Chiefs of Staff, conference proceedings, 1941-45, 1 ft.; Eleanor Lansing Dulles, Economic Office, State Department, 1942-45, U.S. representative, Bretton Woods Conference on International Monetary Fund, 1944, financial attaché, Vienna, 1945-49, Western European Division, State Department, 1949-51, special assistant, Office of German Affairs, State Department, 1952-62, professor, Georgetown University, 1963, papers, 1880-1971, 17 ft.; Dwight D. Eisenhower, papers, pre-presidential, 1916-52, 138 ft. (NUCMC 71-1682); Bryce N. Harlow, special assistant to the president, 1953, administrative assistant to the president, 1953-58, deputy assistant to the president for congressional affairs, 1958-61, records, 1953-61, 20 ft. (NUCMC 71-1687); Kevin McCann, member, staff of Dwight D. Eisenhower, 1946-51, special assistant and consultant to the president, 1953-57, president, Defiance College, 1951-present, material regarding writing of At Ease: Stories I Tell to Friends, and other publication projects of Dwight D. Eisenhower, 8 ft.; Carl W. McCardle, assistant secretary of state for public affairs, 1953-57, papers, 1953-57, 11 ft. (NUCMC 76-1867); Joseph Rand, secretary, Council on Foreign Economic Policy, 1954-61, records, 1954-61, 5 ft. (NUCMC 76-1874); Walter Bedell Smith, U.S. ambassador to the USSR, 1946-49, commanding general, 1st Army, 1949-50, director, CIA, 1950-53, under secretary of state, 1953-54, consultant, Special Projects Office (Disarmament), member, President's Committee on Disarmament, 1958, papers, 1942-61, 13 ft.; U.S. Council on Foreign Economic Policy, Office of the Chairman (Joseph M. Dodge and Clarence B. Randall), records, 1954-61, 37 ft., partially processed; U.S. President's Citizen Advisors on the Mutual Security Program (Fairless Committee), records, 1956-57, 7 ft. (NUCMC 76-1884); White House Office, office of the special assistant for science and technology (James R. Killian and George B. Kistiakowsky), records, 1957-61, 16 ft. (NUCMC 71-1705); White House Office, Staff Research Group (Albert P. Toner and Christopher H. Russell), records, 1956-61, 14 ft. (NUCMC 76-1882). There are finding aids to all these collections.

3 The following collections of manuscripts have only a few scattered items pertaining to Russia/USSR: Phillip E. Areeda, 1st lieutenant, USAF, Office of Air Force General Counsel, 1955-56, member, White House Staff for Economic Affairs and Higher Criticisms, 1956-58, assistant special counsel to the president, 1958-61, professor of law, Harvard Law School, 1963-present, papers, 1952-62, 9 ft. (NUCMC 73-479); Edward L. Beach and Evan P. Aurand, naval aides to the president, records, 1953-61, 13 ft., not processed; Joseph M. Dodge, chairman, Council on Foreign Economic Policy, 1954-56, member, President's Commission to Study the U.S. Military Assistance Program, 1958-64, consultant, National Security Council, 1959-64, papers, 1952-64, 5 ft. (NUCMC 76-1885); Milton S. Eisenhower, papers, 1940-present, 20 ft. (NUCMC 76-1855); Neil H. McElroy, secretary of defense, 1957-59, papers, 1948-62, 6 ft. (NUCMC 76-1868); Don Paarlberg, economic advisor to the secretary of agriculture, 1953-57, assistant secretary of agriculture, 1957-58, special assistant to the president and Food-for-Peace coordinator, 1958-61, records, 1954-61, 5 ft. (NUCMC 71-1698); Fred A. Seaton, U.S. senator, Nebraska, 1951, member, personal advisory staff to Dwight D. Eisenhower during 1952 campaign, assistant secretary of defense for legislative affairs, 1953-55, administrative assistant to the president, February 1955, deputy assistant to the president, June 1955, secretary of the interior, 1956-61, papers, 1946-72, 112 ft.; U.S. President's Committee to study the U.S. Military Assistance Program (Draper Committee), records--a component of Records of Presidential Committees, Commissions and Boards: Record Group 220--1958-59, 11 ft.; U.S. President's Science Advisory Committee, records--a component of Records of Presidential Committees, Commissions and Boards: Record Group 220--1957-60, 3 ft.; White House Office, cabinet secretariat records, 1953-60, 16 ft. (NUCMC 76-1879); White House Office, office of the press secretary to the president, press releases with

index, 1953-61, 10 ft., partly on microfilm. There are finding aids to all these collections.

Microfilms

4 The following microfilm collections may have Russian-related materials: Henry Cabot Lodge, U.S. representative to the United Nations and the U.N. Security Council, 1953-60, selected papers, 1942-52, 1 reel, location of originals --Henry Cabot Lodge; and microfilms of various records located in the Modern Military Records Division of the National Archives, Washington, D.C.

Oral History Transcripts

5 The Eisenhower Library has a number of oral history transcripts from the Columbia University Oral History Collection that have references to Russia/USSR. There are also transcripts of interviews with Dwight D. Eisenhower that are not located at Columbia.

Finding Aids: Aside from the finding aids mentioned above, see Historical Materials in the Dwight D. Eisenhower Library (May 1977).

KS 2
FORSYTH LIBRARY
FORT HAYS STATE UNIVERSITY
Hays, Kansas 67601
(913-628-4431)

Egla E. Steinle Olson. Interviews, 1958, 1 tape-recorded reel. In part, concerns Russian-Germans and Germans in Russia.

KS 3
MENNONITE BRETHREN HISTORICAL LIBRARY
TABOR COLLEGE
Hillsboro, Kansas 67063
(316-947-3121 x 254)

The library has a goal of acquiring materials (published and unpublished) that pertain to the history of the Mennonite Brethren Church. This branch of the Mennonites originated in the German colonies of southern Russia (Chortiza and Molotschna). A "Document of Secession," establishing the Mennonite Brethren, was written and signed in 1860 in the village of Elizabethtal.

The unpublished materials at the library are mainly records of the Mennonite Brethren Church in North America and the people from that church who came to North America in the first great wave of Mennonite emigration from Russia, 1874-75. Besides official church records, the library also has immigrants' diaries and correspondence, some of the latter to those who stayed in the Russian Empire.

KS 4
CLENDENNING HISTORY OF MEDICINE LIBRARY
UNIVERSITY OF KANSAS MEDICAL CENTER
Rainbow at 39th Street
Kansas City, Kansas 66103
(913-588-7040)

Crimean War. Collection, 1854-60, 1 box. These materials concern the Crimean War and include 32 letters, 3 pictures, clippings, and assorted other items. Correspondence originated in both the Crimea and London and correspondents included H. P. Wright, Lord Raglan, R. G. Gleig, C. H. Bracebridge, A. Tremayne, J. F. Burgoyne, W. E. Gladstone, and (holograph signed envelope) Florence Nightingale. The letters discuss the work of British army chaplains, field hospitals, the Light Brigade of Cavalry, the Battle of Tchernaya, and other subjects.

KS 5
PROFESSOR HERBERT GALTON--PRIVATE COLLECTION
SOVIET AND SLAVIC AREA STUDIES
UNIVERSITY OF KANSAS
Lawrence, Kansas 66045
(913-864-4236)

Noemi Solomonovna Galton (nee Merkin), the wife of Professor Galton and daughter of the noted historian of Jewish literature, Solomon Merkin (pseudonym Maks Erik), has in her possession copies of her father's letters written from prison in Kiev and from the Komi camp where he perished, 1936-37. By publication of this volume, the Galtons should also have the originals of these letters plus slides of Siberia, including scenes of the Lena and Amur rivers and Solovki. Written or telephone inquiries concerning these materials will be answered.

KS 6
DEPARTMENT OF SPECIAL COLLECTIONS
KENNETH SPENCER RESEARCH LIBRARY
UNIVERSITY OF KANSAS
Lawrence, Kansas 66045
(913-864-4334)

1 Anonymous. Travel-diary, 22 June-21 July 1828. Travel by an English lady through Warsaw, Smolensk, Moscow, Novgorod, and St. Petersburg.

KANSAS - UNIVERSITY OF KANSAS KS 6

Detailed account of the sights, costume, social services, village and town life, and travel mishaps. (MS B144)

2 Anonymous. Balance-books, 1810-18, 8 vols. Yearly summary accounts of an anonymous speculative trader in London. "Adventures" to Europe and the East and West Indies; cargoes mainly tropical produce. Some commerce with Russia. Gives ships' names. (MS E188)

3 [Catharine II] (1729-1796). [Manuscript collection of historical source material most likely copied for the Empress . . . c. 1770], text in Russian; contains "The manual of the Coronation of the Russian Grand Dukes . . ."; "A petition in connection with the Rebellion in May 1682"; and "Description of the new land of Siberia . . ." (MS E39)

4 Joannes Chrysostomus (d. 407). Saint, patriarch of Constantinople. Extracts from the works, in Russian, with some other works, Russia, 16th-17th c. (MS C38)

5 Graziani-Commendone Collection. Includes: (a) document in Lithuanian court Russian, issued by Zygmunt II Augustus (1565?); and (b) document in Lithuanian court Russian issued by Zygmunt II Augustus, 1569. (MS 62:V:1 and 62:V:2, respectively).

6 Nikolai Mikhailovitch Karamzin (1766-1826). Historian, writer, and political theorist. [Extracts from Karamzin's History of the Russian State and from other Russian historians, forming a short history of Russia, 862-1895. Russia?, 1895?], in Russian. (MS C156)

7 Korolevskaia kommissiia dlia razsliedovaniia voprosov kasaiushchikhsia sekty dukhobortsev v Britanskoi Kolumbii. Report, n.d., in Russian. (MS D44)

8 Frederick Lawless (b. 1847). [Album of travel photos and letters] from Ireland and abroad, including Russia, 1878-1920, ca. 53 photos and 9 letters mounted in album; also, clippings. (MS G20)

9 Memoire sur la cour de Russie et l'État russe. Moscow?, ca. 1746, 84 pp., paper. Report by an unidentified French diplomat on the persons at the Russian court and on conditions in Russia; probably unpublished. (MS C9)

10 Hugh O'Hagan (fl. 1840-1860). Correspondence, 1854-55, 33 items. Ship's surgeon. Letters written to his wife Nannie in Ireland, from the Crimean War, on board HMS Firebrand in the Black Sea and at Malta. Copies (by Nannie) in a scrapbook, which also contains maps, material relating to Captain Hyde Parker (1826-1854), and Crimean War clippings. (MS E118)

11 [Orthodox Eastern Church, Russian. Liturgy and ritual. Church Slavic.] Manuscript in Church Slavic, title page wanting, n.d. (MS A22)

12 Papers relating to the forces and intended operations in Russia, received from a Merchant connected with Riga. Riga, 17 September 1812, 7 pp. and docketing, 3 pieces. In English. Deployment of Napoleonic and Russian troops in the Baltic and Byelorussian areas in August and September. Probably a report by a secret agent for the British government. (MS P448)

13 Porter Family. Papers, 1794-1842, ca. 9 ft. English literary family. Includes correspondence of Sir Robert Ker Porter (1777-1842), who became historical painter to Alexander I in 1804 and married Princess Mary Scherbatoff in 1811. He was later British consul in Venezuela but returned to St. Petersburg, where he died. Among the papers: 65 ALS to his mother or sisters from England, Russia, Sweden, and Spain, 1794-1830; his letter book for 1824-29, containing copies of letters to and from Count K. R. Nesselrode, Alexander I, Nicholas I, etc.; letters from his daughter, Mary, in St. Petersburg, 1829-35, and from other Russian relations; a long series of ALS and unsigned, in French, 1805-26, to him from Princess Mary Scherbatoff--love letters, as well as some of his letters to her; his autograph journal, 1824-25, covering the end of his stay in Russia, sea-journey from Cronstadt, and time in England, ca. 75 pp.; correspondence of Prince Scherbatoff and Prince Alexander Galitzin; and many letters from his sister, Jane Porter (1776-1850), the historical novelist. Unpublished index of his letters, 1825-41. Also, Jane Porter's autograph journal in St. Petersburg, for a few days in March-April 1842, 11 pp. Collection is uncatalogued.

14 Poyer? Journal of travels on the Continent, including the Baltic coast (Rostock-Riga) in 1800-1801. Detailed descriptions of towns, social life, views, travel anecdotes; some interest in grain trade. (MS B126)

15 Russia Company. Collection, ca. 1696-98, 17 items. Petitions, etc., concerning the parliamentary actions against the company. From the North papers. (MS 104)

16 Solovetsky Monastery. Perepis'naia kniga (Solovki Island, Solovetsky monastery, after 1703, 180 folio pages), on paper. Cartulary of 38 documents. (MS C83)

17 George Strachey (1828-1912). Letter, 25 May 1855, concerning maps of Russia and the Aral Sea, and Mr. Arrowsmith. (Strachey at the Foreign Office?) (MS P302)

18 Sir Paul Vinogradoff (1854-1925). Russian-British historian. Istoriia srednikh viekov.

Lektsii prof. P. G. Vinogradova. Kurs 1901-1902 g.g. (Moscow, B. Rikhter, 1901); lithographed typescript of part of his lecture notes while at the University of Moscow, on the Middle Ages. First 56 pp. heavily corrected in pencil by Vinogradoff. (MS P418A:1)

19 Wasserbaue im Königreich Galizien. Ca. 1822, 147 items. Manuscript maps (colored) of planned improvements to the waterways of Galicia. Covers the drainage basin below the NE face of the Carpathians north as far as and including the Dnestr. With statistics and history of sites 1804-ca. 1823.

KS 7
UNIVERSITY ARCHIVES
UNIVERSITY OF KANSAS LIBRARY
Lawrence, Kansas 66045
(913-864-4188)

Oswald Prentiss Backus III (1921-1972). Papers, 1942-72, 52 cu. ft. University of Kansas professor of medieval Russian history and legal history. During the period 1957-66 he made several research, business, and pleasure trips to the Soviet Union. Ca. 13 cu. ft. of his papers contain the fruits of his contacts with the USSR. For example, there are copies of archival and library materials on medieval Russian history, particularly legal history. Some items concern the travels of Sigismund von Herberstein. Other items cover contemporary Soviet law and some unusual printed materials are on the Eurasian movement. Also, correspondence, office files, drafts of writings, literary manuscripts, etc. on book, serial, and faculty exchange programs that Professor Backus helped to establish and maintain. There is also a computer-based study of land grant provisions in Muscovite law. Unpublished accession record and box list of office records.

KS 8
MENNONITE LIBRARY AND ARCHIVES
(formerly, BETHEL COLLEGE HISTORICAL LIBRARY)
INFORMATION AND RESEARCH CENTER
North Newton, Kansas 67117
(316-283-2500 x 310)

1 Books and Documents Pertaining to Anabaptists-Mennonites the World Over, Including Russia. Ca. 750 books plus manuscripts. Documents on Russia concern famines and relief, 1920-24, and the second wave of Mennonite migration in 1924-30 (the first came in 1874-85). Also, letters, diaries, oral history interviews, photographs, and maps/charts about the Mennonites in Rusia, 1790 to the present. 1 M.A. thesis and some Ph.D. dissertations are on religious and church groups in Russia. Among the rare published materials are magazines published in Russia (e.g., Unser Blatt, 1925-28). Inquire about access restrictions. Unpublished register.

2 Peter Braun (1880-1933). Correspondence, 1922-33, ca. 80 items. Teacher. Material on the movement of Mennonites from Russia to Canada.

3 Dietrich Gaeddert (1837-1900). Papers, 1857-1903, 2.25 ft. Minister in the Alexanderwohl Mennonite Church in Russia, 1867-74. He led a group of Mennonite emigrants from Russia to near Inman, Kansas, in 1874, establishing the Hoffnungsau Mennonite Church at that time. Includes his diaries for 1857-65 and 1879-1900. (NUCMC 61-228)

4 A. A. Friesen (1885-1948). Papers, 1919-48, 9 boxes. Businessman. Includes information on Mennonites who left Russia for Canada.

5 Peter C. Hiebert (1878-1963). Papers, 1914-63, 52 boxes. Chairman of the Mennonite Central Committee. One of several Americans who went to Russia to administer relief in the years 1921-23. (NUCMC 74-456)

6 Cornelius Jansen (1822-1894). Papers, 1848-1918, 5 ft. Prussian consul and grain merchant in Berdyansk, Russia. Correspondence and diaries reflect his role in promoting Mennonite migration from Russia to America, for which activity he was expelled from the empire, 1873. Also, business records, pictures, a book manuscript, and clippings. (NUCMC 73-150)

7 Christian Emmanuel Krehbiel (1869-1948). Papers, 1893-1947, 7 ft. Mennonite pastor. He was engaged in relief work in Russia from March 1922 to March 1923. He kept a diary during this time and also wrote many letters to his wife and children. (NUCMC 61-199)

8 Mennonite Board of Guardians. Records, 1873-80, 1 box. Immigrant aid committee for Eastern European Mennonites, operating out of Summerfield, Illinois. Correspondence, contracts, and lists of immigrants. The group comprised Christian Krehbiel, David Goerz, John F. Funk, and Bernhard Warkentin. Many of the immigrants were from Russia. (NUCMC 62-4478)

9 Dietrich Neufeldt (1886-1958). Papers, 1912-57, 8 boxes. Writer and teacher. (Pseudonyms: D. Navall and Dirk Gora). Includes primarily writings about the Revolution and the activities of roving bandits such as N. Makhno. Also, information on the movement of Mennonites from Russia to Canada.

10 David Peters (1877-1956). Papers, 1949-56, 1 box. Mayor of a Russian village. Left

Russia toward the end of World War II, spent some years in Germany as a refugee, and came to America in 1949, settling in Kansas soon thereafter. Correspondence, memoirs, and an autobiography cover his life in Russia and experiences as a refugee. There are also maps of Russian Mennonite villages. (NUCMC 62-4476)

11 Peter Herman Unruh (1881-1943). Papers, 1906-22, 1 box. Pastor of the Alexanderwohl Mennonite Church. Relief worker in Russia, 1922. (NUCMC 61-313)

12 Abraham Warkentin (1885-1947). Papers, 1927-43, ca. 5 ft. Educator in Russia and minister in Germany and the U.S. He taught in the village of Alexanderwohl, Russia, 1904-12; left Russia in 1912 for Germany, where he was ordained a minister in 1920. Correspondence, a file on "Who's Who Among Mennonites," and other materials. (NUCMC 62-3609)

13 P. J. Wiens (1877-1945). Papers, 1904-43, 3.3 ft. Mennonite missionary. He traveled to Russia in 1906. (NUCMC 61-204)

14 Note: In addition to the preceding collections, there are many others which contain letters written from Russia to relatives in the U.S. after the migration of 1874, and correspondence from relatives dated in the 1930s.

Finding Aids: 2 published works would be useful for some of the collections described above: Peter C. Hiebert's Feeding the Hungry (1929) concerns American Mennonite Relief work in Russia in 1921-23; and Exiled by the Czar: Cornelius Jansen and the Great Mennonite Migration, 1874 by G. E. Reimer and G. R. Gaeddert (1956). In addition, there is an unpublished guide for each of these collections.

KS 9
SPECIAL COLLECTIONS
THE LIBRARY
PITTSBURG STATE UNIVERSITY
Pittsburg, Kansas 66762
(316-231-1589)

Haldeman-Julius Collection. Consists of 3,000 books, 8,000 Little Blue Books (published by E. Haldeman-Julius), 2,000 Big Blue Books, 20 ft. of correspondence, and 15 ft. of documents relating to the Haldeman-Julius publishing firm. Includes papers of Anna Marcet Haldeman-Julius (1887-1941), who, with her husband Emmanuel Haldeman-Julius (1889-1951), wrote 2 novels--Dust and Violence--that were translated into Russian by Peter Ochremenko. In late 1931 Mrs. Haldeman-Julius visited the Soviet Union to collect royalties for these 2 books. There are 17 letters dating from her visit and mentioning Anatolii Vasilevich Lunacharskii, Serge Brode, Anna Pavlova, Katia Yarros, Peter Ochremenko, and Anna Louise Strong. 2 letters, from Jane Addams and Elizabeth W. Clark, are copies; the originals remain in the possession of Mrs. Sue (Haney) Haldeman-Julius, the publisher's second wife and widow. Additional materials on the first Mrs. Haldeman-Julius' contacts with Russia have been published in the Haldeman-Julius Weekly.

KS 10
MANUSCRIPT DIVISION
KANSAS STATE HISTORICAL SOCIETY
10th and Jackson Streets
Topeka, Kansas 66612
(913-296-3251)

The Society holds several collections of U.S. congressmen and senators that each contain small amounts of material, generally legislative and constituent correspondence, pertaining to the Soviet Union, Cuba, the Korean War, Hungary, Vietnam, the United Nations, foreign affairs, communism, and disarmament:

Arthur Capper (1865-1951). Senator, 1919-49. 51 boxes.

Frank Carlson (b. 1893). Senator, 1950-69. 567 boxes.

Clifford Hope (1893-1970). Congressman, 1927-57. 263 boxes.

Chester Mize (b. 1917). Congressman, 1965-71. 96 boxes. Descriptive inventory.

KENTUCKY

KY 1
MANUSCRIPT DIVISION
KENTUCKY LIBRARY
WESTERN KENTUCKY UNIVERSITY
Bowling Green, Kentucky 42101
(502-745-4793)

1 American Association of University Women. Archive, 1949-76, 21 items. Comprises the papers of Aina Raits (b. 1913), a Latvian native. Following the Soviet occupation of her homeland and World War II, she became a displaced person. The Bowling Green branch of the AAUW adopted her and her family. In 1951

the family emigrated to Michigan. Includes 15 letters, 1949-52, 2 photographs, and an explanatory note, 1976, concerning these matters and mentioning the treatment the refugees received from the Russians in World War II.

2 Frank Leslie Chelf (b. 1907). Papers, 1897-1971, 8.3 ft. U.S. representative from Kentucky. He was a member of a congressional committee reviewing conditions in Europe and the USSR after World War II. Includes his diary in which he writes of his trip to Moscow, 15-18 August 1945, gives his impressions of Moscow, and notes relationships with the Russian people.

3 Clarence U. McElroy (1847-1928). Papers, ca. 1856-1928, 17 ft. Bowling Green lawyer. Includes 2 letters to him from Joseph W. Krueger, a member of the American Relief Administration, concerning a client of McElroy, Samuel Cristal (1861-1944). The letters, 8 and 25 May 1922, are in response to inquiries McElroy made on behalf of the Odessa-born Cristal, who was trying to help some of his family to emigrate to America.

KY 2
THOMAS MERTON STUDIES CENTER
BELLARMINE COLLEGE
2001 Newburg Road
Louisville, Kentucky 40205
(502-452-8187)

Thomas Merton (1915-1968). Collection, 1915-68, 30,000 items. Catholic religious thinker and writer. Ca. 40 Russian-related items, 1955-68 (with references to earlier periods in Russian history), include correspondence, tapes, typescript drafts for essays, and reading notes and commentaries pertaining to Boris Pasternak, Serge Bolshakoff, Igumen Chariton of Valamo, Nikita Sergeevich Khrushchev, Ivan Vasilevich Kireevsky, and Russian religious figures referred to as the "Russian mystics." Unpublished catalogues in the collection. Some restricted material; permission required prior to use.

KY 3
FILSON CLUB LIBRARY
118 West Breckinridge Street
Louisville, Kentucky 40203
(502-582-3727)

Cassius Marcellus Clay (1810-1903). Papers, 1844-1907, ca. 3 ft. Anti-slavery leader and U.S. minister to Russia, 1861-62 and 1863-69. Includes 21 letters he wrote from St. Petersburg in the course of his ministry there. They contain references to prominent Russian personalities and detail Clay's diplomatic work as well. (NUCMC 65-22)

KY 4
LAW LIBRARY, BRANDEIS ROOM
UNIVERSITY OF LOUISVILLE
BELKNAP CAMPUS
Louisville, Kentucky 40208
(502-588-6392)

Louis D. Brandeis (1856-1941). Papers, ca. 1870-1941, ca. 182 ft. Associate justice of the U.S. Supreme Court. Brandeis was interested in and received information about relief efforts for the Russian Jewish population during World War I. He was also concerned with the progress of military operations and the changes in Russian government at that time, receiving reports of observers and suggestions from others as to the solution of the Russian situation. Ca. 650 items, including incoming correspondence and reports, in section IV, World War (WW), 1917-20, of the collection are pertinent. Specific holdings noted: account of Lewis Straus, November 1917, of a discussion with Brandeis on the proper handling of the Russian question; and translations from *Pravda*, 28 April 1918, of 3 pieces by N. Lenin. Papers are in process of being microfilmed; a published guide to the microfilm edition should now be ready.

KY 5
PHOTOGRAPHIC ARCHIVES
UNIVERSITY OF LOUISVILLE
Louisville, Kentucky 40208
(502-588-6752)

The archives has 8 large albumin print photographs of Russian scenes (including of Moscow), 1860-70. There is also a small assortment of postcards with similar views.

KY 6
UNIVERSITY ARCHIVES AND RECORDS CENTER
UNIVERSITY OF LOUISVILLE
BELKNAP CAMPUS
Louisville, Kentucky 40208
(502-588-6674)

1 Ellis Freeman (b. 1896). Papers, 2 folders in the collection of presidents' papers. Professor. He owned Russian gold bonds. This and other activities embroiled Freeman in a legal dispute with the local American Legion during the mid-1930s. He left the University of Louisville in 1937.

2 Charles H. Parrish, Jr. (b. 1899). Papers, 1897-1969, 12.5 ft. Professor of sociology. His daughter, Ursula Parrish West, visited the Soviet Union in 1960. The collection includes material relating to that trip: 1 letter, an essay written on her return describing the experiences of a black teenager at a Komsomol youth camp, a small photo album, and some souvenirs. Also includes a 1953 tape recording of Dr. Rufus E. Clement, president of Atlanta University and candidate for the Atlanta school board, denying communist affiliation or sympathy.

LOUISIANA

LA 1
SPECIAL COLLECTIONS DIVISION
HOWARD-TILTON MEMORIAL LIBRARY
TULANE UNIVERSITY
Audubon Place at Freret Street
New Orleans, Louisiana 70118
(504-865-6695)

1 Hutson Family. Papers, 1807-1955, 12,488 items. Includes 8 letters from Albert Hutson to his family, written while he was with the U.S. Navy in Vladivostok, March-April 1919 and March-May 1921. He discusses the political situation, Cossack activities, the Bolsheviks, and U.S. and Japanese troops.

2 Donald Renshaw (d. 1961). Photographs of the USSR, 1921-23, 185 items. Member of the American Relief Mission in Moscow. Snapshots he took while in service show Moscow buildings, urban dwellers, country scenes, and peasants.

3 Daniel L. Winsor (fl. mid-19th c.). Correspondence, 1829-69, 129 items. Ship's captain and agent. Includes a letter, 6 June 1831, he received aboard the ship Coliseum in St. Petersburg from the ship's owner, John Brown of Boston, concerning his cargo. Partial inventory (NUCMC 64-1215).

MAINE

ME 1
MAINE STATE LIBRARY
Cultural Building
Augusta, Maine 04333
(207-289-3561)

Frederick C. Walcott. New York City businessman. Typescript of an address he delivered at the Maine War Conference, 8 May 1918, concerning war distress and relief in Europe, 11 ff. He speaks in passing of German-Russian fighting on the eastern front (in Poland particularly), the Russian Revolution, and problems of food supply.

Note: The Maine Vertical File holds a few clippings about Russians in Maine.

ME 2
SPECIAL COLLECTIONS DEPARTMENT
RAYMOND H. FOGLER LIBRARY
UNIVERSITY OF MAINE AT ORONO
Orono, Maine 04473
(207-581-7328)

Arnold Thomas Rubenstein (1888-1955). Collection, 1705-1950, ca. 5.5 of 9 ft. Historian. Collected official documents, clippings, and photographs for his unpublished book "1000 Years of Russian History," written under the pseudonym J. Thomas. Some of the materials are photocopies. Also, his notes for this work. Unpublished card index (NUCMC 74-432).

ME 3
MAINE HISTORICAL SOCIETY
485 Congress Street
Portland, Maine 04111
(207-774-9351)

George Tate (1746-1821). Correspondence, ca. 1780-1822, 17 items. English-born admiral in the Russian navy and Russian senator. 12 letters are to his youngest brother Robert Tate, 1780-1804, and 1 to his nephew George, son of Robert, 1805. These letters discuss family affairs, the admiral's trips to London and Maine, and naval engagements. Also, 2 letters from John Simpson: 14 May 1821, London, to George and Robert Tate about the admiral's death; and 3 August 1822, St. Petersburg, to George Tate. Finally, there are 2 pp. of Tate family records (births and baptisms) from a family Bible. Collection 198.

ME 4
THE TATE HOUSE
1270 Westbrook Street
Portland, Maine 04102

George Tate (1746-1821). Collection, 1780-1822, ca. 23 items. British-born American who became a Russian admiral. Typed and photocopies of 15 letters, 1780-1805, from Tate to his brothers and nephew, concerning his career, naval affairs, and his personal life; 2 letters, copies, from John Simpson to Tate's nephew, 1821-22, about the admiral's death and disposition of his estate; genealogical data from a family Bible and from a church register, British, photocopy; clippings; the admiral's will; and some of his personal effects. Most of the papers are duplicates of originals in the Maine Historical Society (Portland). In addition, Tate House often displays a miniature of the admiral from the collections of the Portland Museum of Art. An oil portrait of Tate is also extant and hangs at Tate House. Researchers seeking access to Tate House materials should contact Mrs. Frances Wilson Peabody, 4 Walker Street, Portland, Maine 04102 (the museum is not open year-round).

MARYLAND

MD 1
U.S. NAVAL ACADEMY MUSEUM
Annapolis, Maryland 21402
(301-267-2109)

1 John Paul Jones (1747-1792). Papers, 1762-92, ca. 35 items. American naval hero born in Scotland, served in the Russian navy. An ALS, 29 December 1789, Amsterdam, to the Hon. W. Short, Esq., chargé d'affaires of the U.S. embassy in Paris, includes references to Jones's service in Russia. (Miscellaneous Manuscripts Collection). Note: The museum also has photocopies of documents from Russian archives pertaining to Jones's stay in Russia in the Senior Collection.

2 Aleksandr Vasil'evich Kolchak (1874-1920). Russian admiral and counterrevolutionary leader. Holograph, signed document, 1918, from the admiral to the Russian ambassador in Washington concerning foreign intervention and aggression in Russia (rough draft). (Miscellaneous Manuscripts Collection)

3 William J. McCluney (fl. 1850s). U.S. naval officer. 1 letter of 9 is from Captain Joel Abbot, commanding officer of a U.S. squadron in the China Seas, to Captain McCluney, 29 October 1853, enclosing a copy of a letter from the secretary of the navy (not in this collection) commending McCluney for assisting shipwrecked Russians in Japan. (Christian A. Zabriskie Manuscript Collection)

4 James Monroe (1758-1831). U.S. president, 1817-25. 1 letter of 3, signed, 23 October 1816, sent by Monroe as secretary of state to the "prime minister" of Russia concerning the false arrest of the Russian Consul-General Kosloff (Kozlov). Included is a copy of a letter from Judge Joseph Hopkinson to His Excellency Andrew Daschkoff (Dashkov) of Russia giving details of Kosloff's arrest and imprisonment. (Miscellaneous Manuscripts Collection)

Finding Aids: Catalogue of Manuscripts (Annapolis, 1957) and Catalogue of the Christian A. Zabriskie Manuscript Collection (Annapolis, 1956); addenda have appeared.

MD 2
ORAL HISTORY COLLECTION
U.S. NAVAL INSTITUTE
Annapolis, Maryland 21402
(301-268-6110)

The following oral histories contain references to Russian-related activities (transcripts available for all):

1 Hanson W. Baldwin. 2 vols. Deals especially with the Middle East, Egypt, and Suez. Baldwin was with a British convoy from Cyprus to Suez at the time of the crisis, 1956.

2 Admiral Chester Bender. 1 vol. Former commandant of the U.S. Coast Guard. Mentions his meetings with the Russians (largely in London) at IMCO (International Maritime Consultation Organization).

3 Admiral Arleigh A. Burke. 1 vol. His discussion of the Soviets and seapower.

4 Vice Admiral John Chew. 1 vol. Head of U.S. Anti-Submarine Warfare, Pacific, 1960s. Russian references.

5 Rear Admiral Joshua W. Cooper. 1 vol. 1961-63 was head of U.S. Military Assistance Advisory Group in Norway. Many references to near neighbors of the Norwegians.

6 Admiral Robert Lee Dennison. 1 vol. He was in command of all U.S. forces in the Atlantic at the time of the Cuban Missile Crisis.

7 Admiral H. D. Felt. 2 vols. As a young officer he served in Russia in World War II. Later, 1960-64, he was commander in chief, Pacific, at the beginning of the Vietnam involvement.

8 Rear Admiral Samuel B. Frankel. 1 vol. Served at Murmansk and Archangel in World War II to handle lend-lease matters (1941-44). Earlier he was at Moscow and Kuybyshev when Moscow was under siege. He had post-World War II duties in the Far East--removing Allied POWs from Mukden, Manchuria; naval attaché to Nanking, China, 1948-50.

9 Admiral C. D. Griffin. 2 vols. Mentions his Far Eastern tours of duty, most particularly his final tour of duty as commander in chief, Allied Forces, Southern Europe, 1965-68.

10 Vice Admiral Andrew McB. Jackson. 1 vol. Served as U.S. representative, United Nations Military Staff Committee (1967). Other references include the Arab-Israel Six Day War.

11 Dr. Waldo K. Lyon. 1 vol. Navy scientist. Deals with his work in the Arctic Ocean areas.

12 Admiral David L. McDonald. 1 vol. Chief of naval operations, 1963-67.

13 Vice Admiral Kleber Masterson. 1 vol. Comments on Soviet trawlers and NATO exercises.

14 Rear Admiral George Miller. 1 vol. Contains his studies and extensive remarks about Soviet seapower, Soviet missiles, Soviet strategy, etc.

15 Rear Admiral Henry L. Miller. 2 vols. Refers to Russian spy ships, etc.

16 Rear Admiral Clarence E. Olsen. 1 vol. Interview dealing with his efforts and responsibilities to establish physical accommodations for U.S. delegation to the Yalta Conference. He was senior U.S. naval representative in Moscow at the time.

17 Rear Admiral Schuyler Pyne. 1 vol. Deals with wartime building of small ships in U.S. for Allies, etc. Later duty in rehabilitating Turkish navy.

18 Vice Admiral Lawson P. Ramage. 1 vol. References to submarines, modern developments, technology, etc.

19 Admiral Richmond (USCG). 1 vol. Mentions his many contacts with Russians while attending IMCO meetings (International Maritime Consultation Organization), mostly in London. He was former commandant, USCG.

20 Admiral Horacio Rivero. 1 vol. Pertains especially to his final tour of duty as a naval officer, commander in chief, NATO command in Mediterranean (CincSouth).

21 Admiral Edwin J. Roland. 2 vols. USCG. Refers to frequent meetings with Russians in connection with IMCO meetings. Roland was one-time commandant of U.S. coast guard.

22 Admiral James Russell. 1 vol. Deals especially with his contacts with Soviets in the Aleutians during World War II and when he had the NATO Command in the Mediterranean.

23 Admiral U. S. Grant Sharp. 2 vols. Served as commander in chief, Pacific, 1964-68 (Vietnam war).

24 Vice Admiral J. Victor Smith. 1 vol. Served as aide to Admiral Leahy at the Yalta Conference--vivid recollections. Later in his career he was senior United Nations officer at Panmunjam, Korea.

25 Admiral Willard Smith. 1 vol. Former commandant, U.S. coast guard. He had many contacts with Russians at IMCO meetings in London.

26 Admiral Alfred G. Ward. 1 vol. U.S. representative, NATO Military Committee, 1965-67; U.S representative to NATO Military Committee, Brussels, 1967-68; in command of U.S. Second Fleet at time of Cuban Missile Crisis.

27 Vice Admiral Chas. Wellborn, Jr. 1 vol. Mentions his tours as senior naval officer, U.S. European Command, and work as U.S. representative, United Nations Military Committee, New York.

Note: Several other histories are in process. Copies of all these volumes (bound and indexed) are at the Naval Historical Center in the Washington Navy Yard in Washington, D.C.

Restrictions: Most of these oral histories are available to accredited researchers. A few may require permission to cite or quote. Restrictions (if there are any) are noted in the Trustee Agreement in the forepart of the bound volume.

MD 3
THE FERDINAND HAMBURGER, JR. ARCHIVES
THE JOHNS HOPKINS UNIVERSITY
3400 N. Charles Street
Baltimore, Maryland 21218
(301-338-8323)

Office of the President. General correspondence, 1903-63, 113 ft. Ca. 4 folders contain correspondence, 1909-10, 1918-19, and 1921-24, concerning the American League to Aid and Cooperate with Russia, the teaching of Russian history at Johns Hopkins, and scholarships for Russian students at the university. A letter from the Seattle (Washington) Chamber of Commerce, 1918, contains data on Siberia. There is reference to Professor S. A. Korff's history lectures in 1909-10. Unpublished index.

MD 4
SPECIAL COLLECTIONS
THE MILTON S. EISENHOWER LIBRARY
THE JOHNS HOPKINS UNIVERSITY
Baltimore, Maryland 21218
(301-338-8348)

1 Isaiah Bowman (1878-1950). Papers, ca. 1918-47, ca. 4 filing cabinets. President of Johns Hopkins, 1935-48, and government official in both world wars. He kept a folder on Russia for the years 1943-45, when he was a special adviser to the secretary of state. Restriction: requires permission of the librarian to see. Subject headings list (NUCMC 63-217).

2 Daniel Coit Gilman (1831-1908). Papers, 1868-1907, 21,000 items. First president of Johns Hopkins, 1875-1901, and diplomat. He was attaché at the U.S. legation in Russia, late March-early July 1854. Ca. 24 letters to his family are from St. Petersburg; also, notes, some official documents, and passports relate to his Russian service, 3 folders. List of correspondents (NUCMC 60-2472).

MD 5
MARYLAND HISTORICAL SOCIETY
201 West Monument Street
Baltimore, Maryland 21201
(301-685-3750)

1 Bonaparte Family. Papers, 1785-1921, ca. 6 ft. Includes 1 letter, 2 October 1906, from Admiral George Dewey (1837-1917) to Charles J. Bonaparte (1851-1921), U.S. secretary of the navy, concerning naval matters in the Russo-Japanese War. Partial unpublished finding aid (NUCMC 67-1327). (MS 141)

2 William Carmichael (d. 1795). Papers, 1739 and 1779-91, 10 items. 1 letter, 8 February 1779, from Charles Carroll of Carrollton to him questions reports of Russia's plans to enter the American Revolutionary War. (NUCMC 67-1823) (MS 2143)

3 Anna Ella Carroll (1815-1894). Papers, 1854-90, ca. 550 items. Author and military strategist. Includes 1 letter, 24 January 1873, of Cassius M. Clay (1810-1903) discussing Russia and the American Civil War. Unpublished index (NUCMC 67-1361). (MS 1224)

4 Richard H. Douglass (1780-1829). Letterbook, 1816-18, 1 vol., ca. 1,600 items. Baltimore merchant. 1 letter, 4 October 1816, concerns trade in Russian goods. (NUCMC 67-1418) (MS 305)

5 Robert Gilmor (1774-1848). Papers, 1689-1848, 17 vols. and 1 folio. Baltimore art collector. Includes an album with data on Russian-American commerce in the second quarter of the 19th c. (NUCMC 67-1462) (MS 387.1)

6 Anna Melissa Graves (1889-1961). Papers, 1889-1961, 1 box, 38 items. World traveler, peace worker. Some correspondence concerns world peace, brotherhood, China, Korea, and Russia. (MS 2031)

7 Robert Goodloe Harper (1765-1825). Papers, 1701-1912, ca. 4 ft. Lawyer, U.S. representative from South Carolina, and U.S. senator from Maryland. Includes letter, 4 August 1808, from George Henry Rose which refers to the Russian navy; and a letter to Harper from Samuel Stanhope Smith, 9 January 1814, concerning Russia. Partial index (NUCMC 67-1490). (Harper-Pennington Papers, MS 431)

8 Hollyday Family. Papers, 1659-1934, 710 items, 7 vols., 1 box, and 1 file. Includes 1 letter, 8 August 1822, from Charles Ward to S. Carvill about Russia's peace with Turkey. (NUCMC 67-1511) (MS 453)

9 Alpheus Hyatt (1838-1902). Papers, 1859-1928, 30 items and 1 vol. Naturalist. The album contains a letter, 21 April 1865, of Cleveland Abbe (1838-1916) containing the metereologist's observations on Russia. (NUCMC 67-1523) (MS 1007)

10 Edna Claiborne Latrobe (d. 1949). Papers, 1926-27. 40 items. Relief worker. 1 manuscript, and a second excerpted from it, narrates her experiences and travels in the USSR, 1926-27. 27 photographs, with attached descriptions, are of Russia. Other items include circulars and letters of solicitation printed by the American Committee for the Relief of Russian Children at the time of Latrobe's service as a field inspector. (MS 2119)

11 Latrobe Family. Papers, 1796-1947, ca. 3 ft. and 31 vols. Includes diary of a European trip, 1847, and Russian correspondence, 1857-58, of John Hazlehurst Boneval Latrobe (1803-1891), artist, lawyer, inventor, and public official. On one trip to Russia, Latrobe secured from the tsar the sum of $60,000 as allowance for claims for a railroad from St. Petersburg to Moscow. There is a restriction on some of the material; inquire at the library. Calendar and partial index (NUCMC 67-1560). (MS 523)

12 Brantz Mayer (1809-1879). Papers, 1791-1934, 2 ft. and 2 vols. Lawyer, diplomat,

historian, and antiquarian. Includes 4 letters, 1844-49, to him from Charles Stewart Todd (1791-1871), an American diplomat in Russia. Partial index (NUCMC 67-1605). (Mayer and Roszel Papers, MS 581.3)

13 Claudia Old McKittrick (d. 1943). Diaries, 1923-37, 2 vols. Wife of a U.S. naval officer. Diaries of travel to the Far East, Near East, India, and Russia, the latter in the late 1920s. Written with "understanding and wit," according to the card catalog. (MS 2115)

14 Merchant's Exchange Reading Room. Record books, 1832-99, 72 vols. Records of arrivals and clearances in the port of Baltimore. Documents divided into: 32 vols. on arrivals; 9 vols. on foreign imports by port of origin; 21 vols. on vessels entering and clearing, and their cargo; 1 vol. on foreign exports; and miscellaneous other volumes. Includes data on commerce with Russia. (MS 610)

15 William Patterson (1752-1835). Papers, 1770s-1838, ca. 75 items, 4 vols., and 1 package. Baltimore merchant. Includes a letter, 5 June 1828, to him from Christopher Hughes (1786-1849) that discusses the Russo-Turkish War. (NUCMC 67-1630) (MS 1084)

16 William Pinkney (1764-1822). Papers, 1796-1926, 41 items and 2 vols. Lawyer, politician, and diplomat. U.S. minister to Russia, 1816-18. Includes a letter, 1823, of Charles Pinkney, his brother, about the Russian court. Partial index (NUCMC 67-1638). (MS 1388)

17 Redwood Collections. 1694-1940, 5 ft. Includes correspondence of John Greene Proud (1776-1865), a merchant, and other members of the Proud family. Proud's letterbooks, 14 March-17 July 1810 and 21 July 1810-19 July 1811, with copies of outgoing correspondence, contain many references to trade with Russia, difficulties getting cargoes to Russian ports during the English and French blockades, and politics obstructing trade. In 10 letters from Proud to Eliza Proud written in St. Petersburg, 1809-13, there are more references to trade with Russia, the French invasion of Russia, the fall of Moscow, and John Quincy Adams, plus descriptions of St. Petersburg, the Hermitage, churches, the harsh winter, outdoor sports, and social activities. A letter, 6 October 1809, of Proud and others, from Hamburg, to J. Q. Adams in St. Petersburg congratulates him on his mission and mentions American trade in Denmark. Another letter, 10 July 1813, of Proud to William T. Proud from London mentions the diplomatic mission of A. Gallatin and J. Bayard, which, with Alexander I in Silesia, cannot succeed. 2 letters, 2 January 1812 and 17 October 1813, from John Proud, Sr. to William T. Proud discuss the difficulties of doing business in St. Petersburg. There is also a letter, 16 November 1821, from Pierre de Poletica to Edward Johnson Coale, expressing, on behalf of Alexander I, the appreciation of the Russian government for Coale's services as vice-consul of Russia in the port of Baltimore and presenting him with a diamond ring. Finally, a letter, 2 October 1928, of G. D. Dorsey in Vichy, France, to Mrs. Francis T. Redwood mentions Pierre Botkine, a writer, of Montreux, Switzerland. Unpublished register and partial index (NUCMC 67-1658). (MS 1530)

18 White Family. Papers, 1764-1928, ca. 5,000 items and 30 vols. Includes account books for 1892 relating to the Russian Famine Relief Fund. Partial index (NUCMC 67-1755). (MS 1005.1)

19 Winans Family. Papers, 1838-1963, ca. 1,200 items and 81 vols. Contains papers of Ross Winans (1796-1877), a Baltimore engineer, inventor, and locomotive builder, and of his son Thomas (1820-1878). Family/company records and correspondence include a contract and accounts relating to the St. Petersburg & Moscow Railroad and its equipment. (NUCMC 67-1766) (MS 916)

Finding Aid: Manuscript Collections of the Maryland Historical Society by Avril J. M. Pedley (Baltimore, 1968).

MD 6
MARYLAND DIOCESAN ARCHIVES
MARYLAND HISTORICAL SOCIETY
201 West Monument Street
Baltimore, Maryland 21201
(301-685-3750)

The Maryland diocesan archives are on deposit in the Maryland Historical Society. They include papers on relations of the Episcopal Church with the Russian Orthodox Church in the 19th c., primarily between 1840 and 1878. Principal holdings concern the Russo-Greek Committee of the General Convention of the Episcopal Church, 1863-76, including correspondence of the Rev. Charles Reuben Hale (later bishop of Springfield) and the Rt. Rev. John Freeman Young (bishop of Florida) on efforts for cooperation or union between the churches and also their relations with the old Catholic churches of Europe. There are a few minor references to Russian activities in Turkey and elsewhere during the last century. Inquiries may be directed to Mr. F. Garner Ranney, historiographer of the diocese of Maryland, at the above address.

MD 7
THE WALTERS ART GALLERY
600 North Charles Street
Baltimore, Maryland 21201
(301-547-9000)

1 Armenian Manuscripts. 11 items: four Gospels, A.D. 966; four Gospels, A.D. 1193; four Gospels, A.D. 1262; four Gospels, A.D. 1455; four Gospels, A.D. 1475; four Gospels, A.D. 1488; four Gospels, early 17th c.; four Gospels, A.D. 1666; four Gospels, 17th c.; hymnal, A.D. 1678; and hymnal, late 17th c. Finding aid: Sirarpie Der Nersessian, Armenian Manuscripts in the Walters Art Gallery (Baltimore, 1973). Also cited in De Ricci and Sanjian, noted in the introduction of this book. (Walters nos. 10.537-10.547)

2 Catherine II (1729-1796). Papers, 1744-96 and undated, 56 items. Empress of Russia, 1762-96. Official letters and a few documents, all original, written by an amanuensis and signed by Catherine, some also signed by Peter III, and (primarily) brief informal notes in Catherine's own hand, generally comments or directions to her ambassadors or other staff. Some of the notes are in Russian, others in French, and 1 in German. Includes what curator Dorothy Miner thought to be the earliest known signature of Catherine, when she was 15 and the fiancée of the Archduke Peter. (NUCMC 65-2021)

3 Georgian Manuscripts. Four Gospels, A.D. 1687, written in ecclesiastical Georgian minuscules, on paper. Gold cover, decorated in cloisonné enamel, inscribed on the binding (in cursive warrior script) with the names of Lord Giorgi Kvinikhidze and Georgui XI, King of Karthli (Shah Nawas II), 1675-1709. Cited in De Ricci. (Walters no. 10.549)

4 Izbornik (Prayer Book). Dated 1079 A.D. but actually written by a 19th c. forger of medieval texts, Aleksandr Ivanovich Sulakasianis (1771-1828 or 1832). On vellum, in ustav script, with red velvet binding. It bears some indications of provenance. Cited in De Ricci. (Walters no. 10.548)

5 Paul I (1754-1801). Tsar. A land grant to Protosov, a member of the privy council, 9 February 1798, on vellum, bound in gold boards, with the imperial red wax seal attached. (Walters no. 10.515).

Restriction: All materials can be seen by appointment only.

MD 8
NATIONAL AGRICULTURAL LIBRARY
UNITED STATES DEPARTMENT OF AGRICULTURE
Beltsville, Maryland 20705
(301-344-3876)

1 Ralph Edward Hodgson (b. 1906). Papers, 3.5 ft. U.S. Department of Agriculture scientist. Includes manuscript, 130 pp., entitled "Notes on the Study of Animal Husbandry of the USSR (August 5, 1959-September 7, 1959)," a volume that describes Hodgson's visits to Soviet institutes, academies, and collective farms involved in animal husbandry.

2 Prince Family. Collection, ca. 1800-1860. 540 items. The Prince family operated Linnaean Gardens, where native European and Asian plants and trees were tested. There is a copy of a letter, 1847, from W. R. Prince to the Russian Imperial Gardens requesting that catalogues be sent to the Russian embassy in the United States. Published finding aid.

3 Lasar Volin (1896-1966). Russian-born economist. Original manuscript of A Century of Russian Agriculture, from Alexander II to Khrushchev (Cambridge, Mass., 1970).

MD 9
NATIONAL LIBRARY OF MEDICINE
HISTORY OF MEDICINE DIVISION
8600 Rockville Pike
Bethesda, Maryland 20014
(301-496-5405)

1 Albert Baird Hastings (b. 1895). Papers, 1915-76, 54 boxes and several vols. Biochemist and physician. During World War II he was in the Soviet Union on occasion. Includes correspondence, a diary, permits, etc., 1943-44, ca. 55 items in 6 folders that relate to Russia. There are restrictions on this collection.

2 James Sprigg Wilson. Papers, 1918-30, 13 items. U.S. army surgeon. Wilson was chief surgeon of the Medical Corps with the American Expeditionary Forces at Vladivostok in Siberia. Address, memorandum, letter, and photos pertain to the A.E.F.

3 Note: The History of Medicine Division also holds thousands of medical theses, mostly 19th-20th c., from Tartu University and other medical schools in the Russian Empire.

MD 10
ARCHIVES AND MANUSCRIPTS DEPARTMENT
McKELDIN LIBRARY
UNIVERSITY OF MARYLAND
College Park, Maryland 20742
(301-454-2318)

1 Baltimore and Ohio Railroad Collection. Includes the card catalogue of the B & O library, a useful bibliographic tool, which contains ca. 25 references to published materials, English language, on Russian railroads. An undetermined percentage of publications listed are available at McKeldin. (NUCMC 67-1290, 71-254, and 73-622)

MARYLAND - UNIVERSITY OF MARYLAND MD 10

2 Joseph Irwin France (1873-1939). Papers, 1884-1932, 10 cu. ft. Maryland and U.S. senator. Contains scrapbooks of newspaper clippings, many pertaining to Russia. Unpublished finding aid (NUCMC 75-772).

3 Romeo Mansueti (1923-1963). Papers, 1933-63, 10.5 cu. ft. Biologist, fish expert. Includes 1 box of clippings on Russian science. Unpublished finding aid (NUCMC 75-773).

4 Millard L. Tydings (1890-1961). Papers, 1918-50, 43 cu. ft. U.S. senator. Contains a few items on Finland, 1940, and Lithuania, 1945-49. Unpublished finding aid (NUCMC 73-655).

5 Note: The department is also in charge of a completely unarranged, uncatalogued, and stored collection of biographical data sheets for prominent Soviet citizens, gathered by the Munich Institute for the Study of the USSR (derived solely from published sources). Contains ca. 50 boxes (?), with information on perhaps 750,000 Soviet personalities (according to the Library of Congress). The material is currently unavailable to researchers and inquiries cannot be answered.

MD 11
OFFICE OF ARCHIVES
SISTERS OF MERCY OF THE UNION
10000 Kentsdale Drive
Potomac, Maryland 20854
(301-469-9221)

Crimea Materials. Includes photocopies of "Mission of the Sisters of Mercy in the Military Hospitals of the East 1854-1856," 2 vols., by Sr. M. Francis Bridgeman, and diaries of Sr. M. Joseph Croke and Mother M. Clare Moore who served in the Crimea. The originals of these materials are preserved in Kinsale, Ireland. Also included is the original copy of "Remembrances of Crimea" written by Sr. M. Joseph Lynch.

MD 12
AMERICAN LATVIAN ASSOCIATION
P.O. Box 432
Rockville, Maryland 20850
(301-340-1914)

25 file-drawer cabinets of annual reports, correspondence, organization records, photographs, and other materials pertaining to conditions in Latvia, Latvian organizations throughout the world, Soviet dissidents, and the Helsinki conference. Also included are the records of the Committee for a Free Latvia, 20 boxes. Much of the material is in the process of being catalogued and organized. Researchers should write or make appointments in advance.

MD 13
DR. JONAS BALYS --PRIVATE COLLECTION
1105 Chiswell Lane
Silver Spring, Maryland 20901

Lietuviu Tautosakos Lobynas (A Treasury of Lithuanian Folklore). Folklore manuscripts and tape recordings, 70 reels, 7 in. diameter. Materials concern Lithuanian calendar festivals; beliefs and customs related to childbirth, baptism, death, burial, and agriculture; and tales, superstitions, proverbs, and riddles (collected among Lithuanians in the U.S.). Some material was copied by hand in 1941-44 from the collections of the Lietuviu Tautosakos Archyvas (Lithuanian Folklore Archives) and Lietuviu Mokslo Draugija (Lithuanian Scientific Society) in Vilnius, Lithuania. At that time, Dr. Balys was director of the Lithuanian Folklore Archives.

Much of this material has appeared in the series Lietuviu Tautosakos Lobynas, edited by Dr. Balys, vols. I-VII, 1951-78, offset printed by Lithuanian Folklore Pub. of the Silver Spring address above. About 5 more vols. are planned, each ca. 300 pp. Serious scholars, by appointment only. (Note: The tape recordings are destined eventually for the Archives of Traditional Music at Indiana University, Bloomington, Indiana.)

MD 14
ROBERT J. MYERS--PRIVATE COLLECTION
9610 Wire Avenue
Silver Spring, Maryland 20901
(301-588-1335)

Mr. Myers has in his possession 2 boxes of material on Soviet social security, private insurance, and demography that he has acquired since 1958, plus a 250 ft., 8 mm movie film that he made in the USSR in 1958 when visiting there as a member of a U.S. group studying social security.

MASSACHUSETTS

MA 1
GEORGE IVASK--PRIVATE COLLECTION
263 Sunset Avenue
Amherst, Massachusetts 01002
(413-549-5342)

Professor Ivask is in possession of many unpublished materials of Russian writers. Among them: 3 books of memoirs of V. V. Rozanov (1856-1919), written by his daughters Tatyana, Vera, and Nadezhda, ca. 400 pp., only some chapters of which (Tatyana's) have been published; D. Darsky's 1952 book about Rozanov, 124 pp.; Rozanov's unprinted fragments and poems; a manuscript of K. Leont'ev's unpublished novel, ca. 100 pp., and his poems; memoirs of Rev. Sergius (Savel'ev), 1971, 469 pp.; and some Ivask family papers, including a private deluxe booklet on their genealogy (Moscow, 1910), only 15 copies printed. Also, ca. 6,000 letters of émigré writers, all concerning literary questions. Among these are 195 letters of the leading literary critic G. Adamovich (1894-1972), plus written or tape-recorded conversations with him; and correspondence with N. Andreyev, N. Arsen'ev, Sir Isaiah Berlin, J. Brodsky, I. Chinnov, Olga Chor (friend of V. Ivanov), V. Dukel'sky (Vernon Duke, the composer), Rev. G. Florovsky, G. Gazdanov, R. Goul', J. von Guenther, E. Izvol'sky, Archbishop John of San Francisco (Prince Shakhovskoy), J. Klenovsky, E. Mahler, V. Markov, N. Morshen (Marchenko), V. Pereleshin (Salatko-Petryshche), Anatol Renning, T. Rozanov, V. Terras, Rev. A. Schmemann, H. Stammler, Gleb Struve, Nikita Struve, V. Varshavsky, W. Weidlé, and others. The collection also includes ca. 30 hrs. of tape recordings. Note: Other parts of Professor Ivask's archives are at Yale University. Access is with the permission of Professor Ivask and the living authors.

MA 2
ARMENIAN LIBRARY & MUSEUM OF AMERICA
P.O. Box 147
Belmont, Massachusetts 02178

The Armenian Library & Museum of America has over 500 tape recordings of interviews with elderly Armenians in the United States, some of whom were born in Russia and fled through the Caucasus at the time of the Russian Revolution. The Library also has a number of diaries, photographs, memoirs, and unpublished archival materials, many of which deal with the plight of Armenians as a result of Turkish policies. Inquire concerning access.

MA 3
THE CONGREGATIONAL LIBRARY
AMERICAN CONGREGATIONAL ASSOCIATION
14 Beacon Street
Boston, Massachusetts 02108
(617-523-0470)

Fred Field Goodsell (1880-1976). Archives of the American Board of Commissioners for Foreign Missions, 1810-1975, 45 ft., 500 items. Goodsell was a secretary of the International Committee of the YMCA in Russia, Rumania, and Siberia (Vladivostok), 1916-19. Materials, in part typed transcripts, are correspondence from missionaries, manuscripts of religious writings, reports of missions' work, commonplace notebooks of Goodsell, ca. 450, 1913-1970s, and printed matter. Typewritten index of folders (NUCMC 76-880). Note: This collection represents Fred Goodsell's personal papers only; official archives of the American Board of Commissioners for Foreign Missions are in the Houghton Library at Harvard University.

MA 4
ARMENIAN REVOLUTIONARY FEDERATION (DASHNAKTSUTIUN)
HAIRENIK BUILDING
212 Stuart Street
Boston, Massachusetts 02116
(617-426-8479)

1 The Archives of the Armenian Revolutionary Federation contain several hundred folders of material dating from 1890 to the present. These materials concern the history and organization of the party, its activities in the Russian and Turkish empires, involvement in the Second Socialist International, and other subjects.

2 Archives of the Delegation of the Republic of Armenia to the Paris Peace Conference have also been integrated into the Federation's archives. Ca. 400 folders for the period 1915-22 deal with Transcaucasian governments, 1918-21, their foreign policies, interrelations, domestic affairs; relations with the Allied Powers, relations with Russian Whites, Soviet Russia, and other states in the region; and related topics.

The archives contain A.R.F. World Congress decisions, directives, and historical data, as well as the memoirs of prominent Armenian political and revolutionary figures.

Restriction: Access is to historians upon request. Contact must be established with the curator, currently Dr. K. Donabedian.

Finding Aids: Minutes of the first 3 A.R.F. World Congresses have been printed, as will others in the future. The archives are being microfilmed.

MA 5
DEPARTMENT OF RARE BOOKS AND MANUSCRIPTS
BOSTON PUBLIC LIBRARY
P.O. Box 286
Boston, Massachusetts 02117
(617-536-5400 x 318)

1 John Quincy Adams (1767-1848). U.S. president, minister to Russia, 1809-14. ALS, St. Petersburg, 6 October 1810, to William Plummer, president of the New Hampshire senate, discussing Russian policy toward Turkey, France, and Austria, 4 pp.; and ALS from Washington, 6 July 1818, to Plummer, then governor of New Hampshire, about the situation of U.S. diplomats in Russia and the return of William Pinkney to the U.S., 4 pp.

2 Samuel Adams (1722-1803). American Revolutionary War patriot. ALS, Baltimore, 25 December 1776, to John Warren, mentioning Russian troops in the British army, 4 pp.

3 A. H. Aiken. Autograph note from Archangel, November 1829, to a Mr. Storer.

4 Armenia. New Testament. Gospels. Illuminated manuscript, 311 ll., written by Gregory in the monastery of the son of Hussig, 1475.

5 Armenian Church. Liturgy and ritual. Services for the sacraments of baptism, etc.; written in Caesarea, 1798, 1 vol., 157 ll.

6 Vladimir Artsimovitz. ANS [191-?], from [Moscow?] to [Mary Boyle] O'Reilly, 3 pp.

7 Albert Bierstadt (1830-1902). American painter of Western scenes, born in Germany. ALS, New York, 19 October 1871, to William Alexander Smith, discussing Russian flags to be used in welcoming Alexis, grand duke of Russia.

8 Catherine II (1729-1796). Empress of Russia. Printed document, signed (1792), St. Petersburg, 2 pp.

9 Petr Il'ich Chaikovskii (1840-1893). Composer. ALS, Kiev, 3 November 1881, 3 pp., to unidentified recipient, explaining a delay in transmitting materials mistakenly sent to him instead of to the director of the Moscow Conservatory.

10 Maria Weston Chapman. AlS, Boston, 18 November [1852?] to C. Weston, commenting on N. I. Turgenev's Russia and the Russians.

11 Sir William John Codrington (1804-1884). British general. In the Crimean War he commanded a brigade at the battle of the Alma and a division at Inkerman, and succeeded Sir James Simpson as commander in chief in the Crimea, 11 November 1855. ALS [Sevastopol?], 13 June 1856, to [Sir George?] Grey, 1 p., about shipping 4 million cartridges to Nova Scotia.

12 George Mifflin Dallas (1792-1864). Vice president of the U.S., 1845-49. ALS, St. Petersburg, 8 July 1839, to Thomas Aspinwall, asking him to book passage on the steamer British Queen for New York, 3 pp.

13 Francis Dana (1743-1811). U.S. envoy to Russia, 1781-83. ALS, St. Petersburg, 14/25 October 1781, to the Honorable John Lowell, discussing his Russian mission, with which he is becoming impatient, and his desire to leave Russia, 2 pp.

14 Anna (Loring) Dresel. ALS, Riga (?), 21 July 1869, to John S. Dwight, with family news, 3 pp.

15 Frederick Temple Hamilton Blackwood, Marquis of Dufferin and Ava (1826-1902). British statesman and diplomat, ambassador to Russia, 1879-81. 2 ALS, St. Petersburg, 30 January and 28 March 1881, to Lady Walter Campbell, 20 pp.

16 Franz Fladermann (1799-1838). ALS, St. Petersburg, 10 October 1835, to Christoph Friedrich Otto, concerning back numbers of a botanical journal, 2 pp., in German.

17 Gotthelf Fischer. ALS, Moscow, 3 February 1810, to Benjamin Smith Barton, announcing Barton's selection as an honorary member of the Société Impériale des Naturalistes de Moscou and discussing other matters, 3 pp., in French.

18 J. L. Fruich. ALS, St. Petersburg, 26 February 1826, to an unidentified recipient, about travel plans, 2 pp., in German.

19 William Lloyd Garrison (1805-1879). American abolitionist. ALS, 7 June 1867, to H. E. Garrison, about meeting I. S. Turgenev and Professor E. de Laboulaye in Paris.

20 Fedor Gavrilovich Golovin (1766-1823). ALS, Stuttgart, 29 May 1814, to an unidentified recipient, 1 p., in French.

21 Maksim Gorkii (1868-1936). Russian writer. ANS, Boston 1906, to an unknown person, 1 p.

22 Curtis Guild (1860-1915). Ambassador to Russia, 1911-13. Papers, ca. 1873-1915, ca. 100 items. Correspondence, including ca. 35 letters from Russia. Papers are in process currently.

23 François Pierre Guillaume Guizot (1787-1874). Ca. 50 items. French statesman and historian. 2 ALS, Paris, 13 and 21 March 1855, to Mrs. and to Mr. Guglielmo Libri respectively, concerning Tsar Nicholas I.

24 Peter Kropotkin (1842-1921). Russian anarchist. 2 ALS, Cambridge, Mass. 1879, to Hugo Munsterberg; TLS, Berlin, 12 February 1919, to Munsterberg, 2 pp.; ALS, Harrow on the Hill,

England, 26 April 1890, to the editor of the Forum, L. S. Metcalf, regarding a promised article on intensive agriculture, 3 pp.; holograph list of books on Russian literature to be used in connection with his Lowell lectures in Boston, February/March 1901, 6 pp.; and a signed card, with a quotation, 29 July 1902, 1 p.

25 Karl Marx (1818-1883). Social philosopher and radical. Holograph notes from readings in Russo-Polish relations, 1763-67, taken in London, ca. 1850, 2 pp., in French.

26 Karl Anton Meyer (1795-1855). ALS, St. Petersburg, 8 November 1836, to Christoph Friedrich Otto, thanking him for some plants, 1 p., in German.

27 Mezhdunarodnyi konkurs pianistov, skripachei i violonchelistov imeni P. I. Chaikovskogo. Program for concert on 15 April 1958 in the First International Chaikovskii competition in Moscow, with autograph signatures of A. Khatchaturian, N. Khrushchev, N. Bulganin, D. Kabalevsky, Joyce Flissler, A. Mikoyan, Emil Gilels, Van Cliburn, etc.

28 Anastas Ivanovich Mikoyan (Mikoian) (1895-1978). Communist Party leader. Signature on part of a sheet of United Nations postage stamps.

29 Napoleon I (1769-1821). French emperor. Signed note, Moscow, 16 October 1812, to the Comtesse de Montesquieu, thanking her for a letter, 1 p.

30 Horatio Nelson (1758-1805). British naval hero. ALS, St. George Rostock, 26 May 1801, to Alleyne Fitzherbert, discussing negotiations with Russia and other matters, 2 pp.

31 Christoph Friedrich Otto (1783-1856). ALS, 28 February/12 March 1825, to him from an unidentified writer at the Jardin botanique impériale in St. Petersburg, 3 pp.

32 Boris Leonidovich Pasternak (1890-1960). ALS, Moscow, 19 September 1959, to Henri Mathot, thanking him for a pamphlet, 2 pp., in French.

33 William Pinkney (1764-1822). U.S. minister to Russia, 1816-18. ALS, [St. Petersburg], 6 July 1818, to Theophilus Parsons, noting the absence of the emperor and festivities in the capital, 3 pp.

34 M. Piolunkowski. Engineer. ALS, St. Petersburg, 12/25 January [ca. 1913], to Hugo Munsterberg, 2 pp.

35 Sergei Sergeevich Prokofiev (1891-1953). Composer. ANS, Moscow, 22 April 1934, to Mr. Zygman, about obtaining a score for him, 1 p.

36 Nikolai Andreevich Rimskii-Korsakov (1844-1908). Composer. 3 bars from Scheherazade, holograph, 1 p., 19 [December/] 1890.

37 William Ropes. Merchant. ALS, St. Petersburg, 15/27 August 1833, to the mathematician Nathaniel Bowditch, 1 p. Relates to the Russian Academy of Sciences.

38 Anton Rubinstein (1829-1894). Pianist and composer. ALS, Vienna, 5 June 1872, to a person identified only as the director of some body, concerning a trip to America and providing the score for "Die Kinder der Heide," 1 p.

39 Leopold Schefer (1784-1862). ANS, Moscow, 15 February 1825, to the "Calendar Deputation" [Ludwig Ideler?], 2 pp.

40 Friedrich Theodor von Schubert (b. 1758). ANS, St. Petersburg, 25 July 1819, to Nathaniel Bowditch, 1 p.

41 Eugene Schuyler (1840-1890). Secretary of legation at St. Petersburg, 1870-76. ALS, St. Petersburg, 4 August 1875, to Kate Field, concerning her requests in a letter to "our Representatives abroad," 3 pp.

42 Solovetsk. Canticle of a Russian religious sect, Fedoria, which did not recognize spirits; written in the convent of Solovetsk, n.d., 297 pp. Bought at Old Novgorod, January 1867, by Nathan Appleton.

43 James Thal. ALS, Moscow, 14/26 January, to Nathaniel Bowditch, 4 pp.

44 Leo N. Tolstoi (1828-1910). Philosopher and writer. ADS, 23 February 1875 [Paris?], to Mme. John Telfer, authorizing the translation of his writings, 1 p.; and ALS, 12 August 1900, to Morrison Davidson, 2 pp.

45 Leon Trotskii (1879-1940). Revolutionary leader and writer. Autograph postcard, signed, from Amherst, Nova Scotia, 17 April 1917, to M. Aronson, about a prisoner of war camp; plus 2 photographs, one of Trotskii and the other of his residence (?).

46 Ivan Sergeevich Turgenev (1818-1883). Writer. ANS, n.p., n.d., to an unidentified recipient, regretting his inability to attend a supper, 1 p., in French; ANS [Paris], n.d., to an unidentified person, an invitation to a dinner with Mérimée and Augier, 1 p.; ALS, Moscow, 15 June 1874, to Henry Holt, concerning translations, enclosing Memoirs of a Sportsman (Hunter's Sketches), 1 p.; ANS, Paris, 12 January 1879, to an unidentified recipient, enclosing a requested quotation; ALS, Paris, 17 February 1875, to Frau Seegen, asking if she and Frau M. Hartman received a copy of Hunter's Sketches, complaining about his health, hoping to see her in Karlsbad, 2+ pp.,

in German; and a letter, Paris, 29 September 1855, to Maria W. Chapman (copy, in French).

47 Richard Davis Webb. ALS, 24 December 1861, to [Anne Warren Weston?], wanting to know N.(?) Turgenev's address.

48 Winthrop Family. Copy of a letter from William Winthrop (1753-1825), Boston, 11 December 1798, to Captain Nathaniel Goodwin, mentioning a voyage to Russia.

49 Sir James Wylie. ANS, Aix la Chapelle, 7 October 1818, to Thomas Clarkson, referring to Tsar Alexander I, 2 pp.

MA 6
MUSIC DEPARTMENT
BOSTON PUBLIC LIBRARY
P.O. Box 286
Boston, Massachusetts 02117
(617-536-5400 x 316)

1 Frédérick Bonnaud. "Marche russe" for orchestra. Partition. Ms. Paris [187-?], 11 pp.

2 Aleksandr Tikhonovich Grechaninov (1864-1956). 3 items: "Gimmn Svobodnoi Rossii" [Hymn of Free Russia] for mixed chorus with piano accompaniment. Ms. M.? 1917, 2 pp.; "Kolybel'naia" [Lullaby] for voice and piano. M. 1887. Ms. 2 pp.; "Step'iu idu ia" [Over the Steppe] op. 5 no. 1 [St. Petersburg 1893, i.e., N. Y. 1953] 3 pp.

3 Johann August Alexander Klengel (1783-1852). 4 items: "Air russe." Varied for pianoforte by [J]A. A. Klengel. Ms. [185-?] 10 pp.; Polonaise for pianoforte. Ms. [185-?]. 12 pp.; Ronde for pianoforte. Ms. [185-?] 14 pp.; Rondeau militaire. Ms. [185-?] 11 pp.

4 Henry Peter Kreiner. Typescript: "Russian ballet. Notes for a bibliography." Newark, New Jersey, 1915, 13 pp.

5 Lazare Saminski (1882-1959). 2 items: Littanies [sic] des femmes (for voice and chamber orchestra). Op. [34]; Partition d'orchestre. [N. Y. 1926], 19 pp. Text of songs in Russian.

6 Dmitrii Dmitrievich Shostakovitch (1906-1975). [Lady Macbeth of Mtsensk, or Katerina Izmailova. An opera. 4 parts of the original Ms. in vocal score.] Autograph Ms. [Moscow?] 1935. 55-58 pp. Text in Russian.

7 Nicolas Slonimsky (b. 1894). Ca. 12 items. Impressions. La fuite de la lune, words by Oscar Wilde (Boston, 1926), 7 pp.; ms. copy, for voice with piano acc.; I owe a debt to a monkey, words by Kathleen Lamb (Boston, 1928), 4 ll., ms. in blue, red, and green pencil; Modinha russo-brasileira (Boston? 1942?), holograph, for piano, with a TLS from the dedicatee, 3 p., Marina Fernandez, to Slonimsky laid in; Moto perpetuo, for violin and piano, published volume (1939) autographed by the composer; "Music for junior" (from the Christian Science Monitor, February 1939-February 1941), compiled by the library's Music Department (Boston, 1941), 1, 28 pp. in a scrapbook; 3 anti-modernist songs, words from the book Music Since 1900 (1938) by Nicolas Slonimsky, music by Henry Cowell (New York? [1938]), 17 pp., reproduced from ms. copy, cover-title in ms.; My little pool, a song with pianoforte accompaniment, words by Paul S. Nickerson, holograph (Boston 1928), 3 pp.; My toy balloon, variations on a Brazilian tune (Boston? 1942), score, for orchestra, holograph, 20 pp.; the same, reproduced ms., with clippings; My toy balloon, variations on a kindergarten tune, for piano ([Boston] 1942), 4 pp., ms. copy; Four picturesque pieces for ambitious young pianists (Boston, 1930), 4 vols. in 1, ms. copy; Prelude (St. Petersburg? 1914), for the piano, holograph, 4 pp.; and Russian nocturne (Boston, 1943), for the piano, holograph in pencil, 7 pp.

8 Henri Wieniawski (1835-1880). 2 items: Danses Bohémienne, for violin with orchestral accompaniment, partition, ms., 30 ff.; Polonaise for violin with orchestral accompaniment, ms., 30 ff.

Finding Aid: Dictionary Catalog of the Music Collection, 20 vols. (Boston: G. K. Hall, 1972).

MA 7
SPECIAL COLLECTIONS
MUGAR MEMORIAL LIBRARY
BOSTON UNIVERSITY
771 Commonwealth Avenue
Boston, Massachusetts 02215
(617-353-3696)

1 Elie Abel (b. 1921). Papers, 1946-69, 3 ft. (additions expected). News commentator and writer. Correspondence with public figures and typescripts of writings, including The Missile Crisis (1966). Collaborated with W. Averell Harriman on Special Envoy to Churchill and Stalin 1941-1946 (New York, 1975), materials about which will probably be added to the collection. Unpublished inventory (NUCMC 70-11).

2 Gar Alperovitz (b. 1936). Papers, ca. 1956-present, 51 boxes (additions expected). Writer. Includes typescript (and carbon) drafts of his Atomic Diplomacy: Hiroshima and Potsdam (1965); holograph and typed notes plus bibliography for this book; subject files of printed pieces, clippings, and correspondence

kept while he was legislative assistant to Congressman Robert Kastenmeier of Wisconsin, including some of Kastenmeier's correspondence, 1961-62. Access is restricted. Unpublished inventory.

3 Stewart Johonnot Oliver Alsop (1914-1974). Papers, 1957-73, 84 boxes. Journalist. Notes on Kremlinologists, the Sino-Soviet struggle, Khrushchev's remarks during his Hungarian tour, and Alsop's interview with Chernyakov, a Soviet diplomat. Also, correspondence between Alsop and his brother Joseph during the latter's tour of the Soviet Union in 1957-58, and letters to or from George F. Kennan, Isaac Don Levine, and Charles E. Bohlen. In part, photocopies. Unpublished inventory (NUCMC 70-13).

4 Bortman Manuscript File. Collection, ca. 1650-1890, 440 items. Includes Secretary of State Thomas Pickering's instructions (manuscript copy with Pickering's signature) to Rufus King to negotiate a treaty of amity and commerce with Russia (4 May 1799). (NUCMC 61-1086)

5 Boston Symphony Orchestra. Archives, 1890s-present, 48 ft. Contains a holograph score of Sergei Prokofiev, Symphony no. 4, op. 47, in C major, full score, 64 pp., at end: June 23, 1930. 1:15 PM. Paris. S.P.; and the holograph of Igor Stravinskii's Symphonie de Psaumes, dedicated to the Boston Symphony Orchestra on its 50th anniversary, 1930, 1 l., 60 pp. (Additions expected)

6 Guy Daniels. Papers, 1952-68, 1 ft. (additions expected). American writer, critic, and translator of Russian works. Includes holograph notes; typescripts of his works, with manuscript corrections, published and unpublished; galleys; and correspondence. He has translated works of A. S. Pushkin and Russian children's literature. Unpublished inventory (NUCMC 70-27).

7 Mischa Elman (1891-1967). Papers, 1906-67, 4 ft. Russian-American violinist. Extensive correspondence, personal and business, with major artists, public and literary figures; scrapbooks of memorabilia, 1928-55; photographs of the artist and his family; autographed concert programs; posters; and memorabilia. Unpublished inventory (NUCMC 70-31).

8 Emma Goldman (1869-1940). Papers, 1911-14, 314 items. Anarchist and author. Mainly correspondence with Dr. Ben L. Reitman and Almedia Sperry. Includes an English translation, possibly by Goldman, of Leonid Andreyev's "In the Dreary Distance." Unpublished inventory (NUCMC 67-318).

9 Ralph Isaacs Ingersoll (1789-1872). In papers of Ralph McAllister Ingersoll, 1900-62, 30 ft., 152 boxes. R. I. Ingersoll was U.S. minister to Russia in 1846-48. His part of the collection includes substantial holdings relating to his service in St. Petersburg, including correspondence from President James K. Polk, a scrapbook of calling cards, pamphlets, and typescript copies of diaries he kept in Russia. Also, original journals of his son, Colin Macrae, who accompanied his father to Russia at the age of 27; and a box of painted wooden toys, brought back by Ingersoll and his son, representing a roughly scaled model of the Kremlin. Unpublished inventory (NUCMC 66-385, for R. M. Ingersoll only).

10 Flora Lewis (b. 1922). Papers, 1937-present, 101 boxes (additions expected). Journalist and foreign correspondent. Includes photographs taken in Moscow during a visit in 1957 and a list of her contacts there. Also 2 folders of notes, correspondence, newspaper clippings, reports, and other material on communism and the USSR. Unpublished inventory (NUCMC 67-325).

11 Joseph North (1904-1976). Papers, 1934-76, 19 boxes. Founder and editor of the New Masses and American Dialog. Includes correspondence and manuscript articles on the Soviet Union and on V. I. Lenin. Unpublished inventory (NUCMC 70-57).

12 Paul C. Richards. Collection, 1490-present, 55 boxes (additions expected). Contains letters and/or documents signed by Catherine II, 1793, Dmitrii Borisevich Kovalevskii, 1961, Peter I, 1711, Sergei Prokofiev, 1930, N. Rimskii-Korsakov, 1905, P. I. Chaikovskii, 1893, Ivan Turgenev, 1882, and Leo Tolstoi. Unpublished index.

13 George Bernard Shaw (1856-1950). Papers, 1918-50, 2 boxes (additions on occasion). Playwright. Includes an article by Jaya Deva, "Talks with Bernard Shaw on Moscow Trials," typescript, 5 pp., with an ANS from Shaw on the first page, 8 March 1938, repudiating the article. Unpublished inventory.

14 Tad Szulc (b. 1926). Papers, 1947-68, 24 boxes (additions expected). Foreign correspondent and writer. Correspondence, notes, outlines, and typescripts of writings, including "Impressions of the Soviet impact on the Iberian World," an address given at the Conference of the Institute for the Study of the USSR in Munich, 21 May 1968. Unpublished inventory (NUCMC 70-72).

Finding Aid: Some of the preceding collections are listed in Boston University. The Twentieth Century Archives (1973).

MA 8
KRESS LIBRARY OF BUSINESS AND ECONOMICS
BAKER LIBRARY
BUSINESS SCHOOL
HARVARD UNIVERSITY
Soldiers Field Road
Boston, Massachusetts 02163
(617-495-6360)

1 F. J. Brunner Print Collection. Includes the following items: Bourse de Saint-Petersbourg, n.p., after 1805, wood engraving, plate cut from unidentified French periodical (AE r3); Moscou. Bourse et Corps des Boutiques, lithographed by Arnout (probably Louis Jules Arnout, b. 1814) after a drawing by Dietz, published after 1805, hand colored, title also in Russian (AE r5 xx); Petersburg. (Die Börse), engraved by Joseph Jung, n.p., after 1805, hand colored, trimmed to plate mark, a view of the St. Petersburg exchange which was begun in 1805 and completed in 1810 (AE r2); Vue de la Bourse, St. Petersburg, signed: AM, n.p., after 1805, lithograph (AE r4 x); and Vue de la Bourse et du Magazin des Marchandizes, en remontant la petite Neva (St. Petersburg), engraved by Pierre Laurent Auvray (b. 1736), after a drawing by Louis Nicolas de Lespinasse (1734-1808), probably a plate from Leclerc's Histoire physique, morale, et politique de la Russie moderne (Versailles and Paris, 1783-85), which Auvray illustrated (Paris? 178-?) (AE r1 x).

2 (Jean François Magenthies). Prospectus of a company for trade with Russia, Avignon, 1780, 15 pp. Bound at front is a printed circular letter, 2 pp., signed by Magenthies, soliciting subscriptions.

3 Russia. Laws, statutes, etc., 1801-25 (Alexander I). An extract of the principal articles which are allowed to be imported by the tariff of 20 November 1819 [St. Petersburg, printed by Charles Kray, 1820], 28 pp., interleaved and annotated copy of Edward Spalding, a merchant of Bristol, Rhode Island. Also contains rules and regulations concerning the customs.

4 St. Petersburg government iron foundry. Specimens of iron work from this foundry, n.p., 1826, 13 ll., drawn by J. Reed. Consists of plates, including ink and watercolor drawings, of the products of the foundry.

5 Note: The Kress Library reportedly holds other manuscript tracts and/or rare publications concerning the trade of Riga and St. Petersburg, materials not located for this guide.

MA 9
MANUSCRIPTS AND ARCHIVES DEPARTMENT
BAKER LIBRARY
BUSINESS SCHOOL
HARVARD UNIVERSITY
Soldiers Field Road
Boston, Massachusetts 02163
(617-495-6411)

1 Winthrop W. Aldrich (1885-1974). Papers, 1918-59, 126 ft. Chairman of the Chase National Bank and frequent government advisor. Aldrich was active in U.S. foreign relations. Materials on the Bretton Woods monetary conference, Business Advisory Council, Citizens Committee for Reciprocal World Trade, International Chamber of Commerce, and the Marshall Plan Committee, most of which concerns Soviet-American relations in the post-World War II (Cold War) era. Correspondence from this period might also be pertinent. (NUCMC 70-1211)

2 John Jacob Astor (1763-1848). Business records, 1784-1892, 7 ft. Fur trader and capitalist. Includes material pertaining to fur trade with the Russian-American Company, Pacific Fur Company, and American Fur Company. (NUCMC 60-1738)

3 Thomas William Lamont (1870-1948). Papers, 1894-1948, 144 ft. Investment banker and chairman of J. P. Morgan and Company. He took part in the Versailles Peace Conference ending World War I and served on later monetary and reparations commissions. One of his interests was the Committee for Protection of Holders of Imperial Russian Government 6.5% Credit Notes; another was the question of U.S. recognition of the USSR. He studied Russian war relief in World War II. Among his correspondents were Woodrow Wilson, Edward M. House, and, during World War II, the Russian ambassador and consul general in the U.S. Guide to the Papers of Thomas William Lamont (1966), compiled by J. V. Miller, Jr. (NUCMC 74-341)

4 Ocean Shipping. Log Books. Listed under this heading in the card catalog: (1) 1793. Apollo, brig. Albert Smith. On this voyage from Boston to England and Russia, the Apollo received warning of the outbreak of war and the threat of French privateers; and (2) 1839, 2 vols., No. 2: 1839. Argo, ship. Joseph K. Farley. Trip from Boston to Russia and return.

5 Prices, Baltic region, 1708-88. 6 vols. in 1 box. Continuous record of prices kept for the use of a Dutch firm.

6 Jeffrey Richardson (b. 1789). Papers, 1812-32, 2 ft. Includes his correspondence and bills concerning, inter alia, the purchase of sail cloth in St. Petersburg. (NUCMC 60-1573)

7 Ropes Family. Papers, 1789-1875, 2 ft. William Ropes moved to St. Petersburg in 1832, establishing his own firm there to engage in commerce with the Russians. Includes correspondence from ca. 1810-41. Unpublished inventory (NUCMC 76-2048).

8 Samuel Sanford (fl. 1820s). Merchant. Sanford dealt in Russian goods (e.g., cloth). Letterbook for 1818-25 shows correspondents in St. Petersburg.

9 Elias Smith (fl. ca. 1800). Montreal merchant. Letterbook from 1799-1800. He did business with Russians.

10 Israel Thorndike (1755-1832). Business records, 1778-1899, 5 ft. Shipping merchant in Beverly and Boston. Includes several documents on trade with St. Petersburg ca. 1800 and lists of prices current in St. Petersburg, 1800-35. (NUCMC 60-1739)

11 Nathan Trotter and Co. Records, 1798-1929, 205 ft., 140 boxes, 1,348 vols., and 19 cases. Marketing firm that bought and sold at wholesale. From ca. 1830 they began to specialize in metals (chiefly iron, steel, copper, brass, and tin). They imported from England and Wales, later the Malacca Straits, Rotterdam, and Russia. (NUCMC 60-164)

12 John Walsh, Jr. (fl. 1780s). Boston merchant. Engaged in commerce with Russia. Letterbook, 1781-86.

13 Wendell Family. Business records, 1722-1865, 39 ft. Materials pertaining to commerce with Russia included. The ship Wonolancet traveled to Russia in 1800 and again in 1809-10; the ship Prince Madoc also engaged in Russian trade. Unpublished inventory (NUCMC 60-1724).

Note: There is good reason to believe that many other collections may hold varying amounts of Russian-related material.

Finding Aid: R. W. Lovett and E. C. Bishop, compilers, A Guide to Sources for Business, Economic and Social History (1978).

MA 10
RARE BOOK DEPARTMENT
THE FRANCIS A. COUNTWAY LIBRARY OF MEDICINE
HARVARD UNIVERSITY
10 Shattuck Street
Boston, Massachusetts 02115
(617-732-2170)

1 Anonymous Manuscript. Undated piece on the Russian Imperial College of Medicine.

2 Henry Pickering Bowditch (1840-1911). Papers, 1863-1911, several thousand items. Physiologist. A typed letter, 1906, to Bowditch from H. W. van Loon, in St. Petersburg, describes the European and Russian political situation.

3 Walter B. Cannon (1871-1945). Papers, 1891-1945. 50,000 pieces. A few folders of correspondence between Cannon and I. P. Pavlov. Unpublished finding aid.

4 Florence Nightingale (1820-1910). Papers, 1856-97, 150 items. Nurse. Includes letter by Nightingale from Crimea, 1856, with information on conditions there during the Crimean War.

5 Radiographs of Nicholas II and Alexandra. 8 X-rays of the emperor and empress, 1898, made by a Russian physician who studied in Germany.

6 Hugh Stalker (b. 1893). Papers, 1920-70, ca. 550 items. Doctor. Includes a 1923 ALS from Ivan Petrovich Pavlov to Stalker that discusses the state of Russian medicine, and a 1938 letter from Vasilii Nikolaevich Boldyreff to Stalker concerning Pavlov. There are also photographs of Boldyreff.

7 Note: The library has a large amount of manuscript materials, many of which are uncatalogued; the possibility exists that there are other materials pertaining to Russian science and medicine.

MA 11
ISABELLA STEWART GARDNER MUSEUM
2 Palace Road
Boston, Massachusetts 02115
(617-566-1401)

1 The Archive of the Museum is in part on display in cases in the galleries and rooms of the building. Comprises material collected by and papers of Isabella Stewart Gardner (1840-1924), American collector of art.

Personal correspondence of Gardner includes letters from Boris Anisfeld, 1; Ossip Solomonovitch Gabrilowitsch, 2: 4 April 1918 and n.d.; Charles Martin Loeffler, 114; Ignace Jan Paderewski, 2, n.d.; Ivan Panin, 2; Anna Pavlova, 1; Baron Roman Romanovich Rosen, 10; Baroness Elizabeth Rosen, 2; and Amélie Rives [Princess Troubetzkoy], 1. (NUCMC 65-1944)

Among correspondence collected by her is 1 letter of F. M. Dostoevskii.

2 Musical holdings include: Theodor Leschetizky--autograph score of Suite de morceaux pour piano, op. 46, no. 9, "Hommage à Chopin" (from Contes de jeunesse), dedicated to I. J. Paderewski, 12 ff.; and a photograph of him autographed with the incipit of his Serenata, op. 43, no. 1 (?) for piano; Anton Rubinstein--Miniatures: 12 morceaux pour piano, dedicated

to Mme. Aglae Massart, 13 ff., bound in leather, holograph score (also, a photograph of him); and P. I. Chaikovskii--Sextet for two violins, two violas, and two cellos, op. 70 (from Souvenir de Florence), autograph folio from the first version, composed 1887-90, including material not in the revised version, 1891-92, beginning in the middle of the third movement and continuing to the end of the movement, holograph in black ink with corrections in purple ink and pencil, 1 f.

3 Pictorial holdings include: Leon Bakst--Costume for Ida Rubinstein, pencil and watercolor on white paper, inscribed, 1911, and Costume for Anna Pavlova, pencil and watercolor on white paper, inscribed, 1913; and John Singer Sargent --pencil sketch of Jascha Heifetz at his premiere in Boston, ca. 1917?. There is also a photograph of Elizabeth Feodorovna, grand duchess of Russia, n.d.

Note: All of the personal correspondence is available on microfilm through the Archives of American Art in Washington, D.C.

Restriction: Serious scholars and researchers only.

Finding Aids: Personal correspondence and a few other items are listed in Correspondence of Isabella Stewart Gardner at the Gardner Museum (Boston, n.d.), a small brochure printed by the Museum. A published catalogue of musical holdings is in preparation by Ralphe Locke of the University of Rochester's Eastman School of Music. There is also an unpublished partial case list.

MA 12
THE JOHN F. KENNEDY LIBRARY
Columbia Point on Dorchester Bay
Boston, Massachusetts 02125
(617-899-2234)

The John F. Kennedy Library was created to preserve materials pertaining to John F. Kennedy and his administration. Its holdings can be divided into 4 parts: the papers of President Kennedy; collections of personal and organizational papers; oral history interviews; and audiovisual records. All these materials have, to a varying extent, references to Russia/USSR.

The Papers of President Kennedy

1 The Presidential Papers (1961-63, 3,351 ft.) contain the following groups of documents pertaining to Russia/USSR:

President's office files, countries series. 16 ft. 1.5 ft. of Soviet-related materials include unclassified and declassified letters, memoranda, cables, and reports divided into "general" and "security" material; background documents, briefing material, and memoranda of conversations from the 1961 Kennedy-Khrushchev Vienna meeting; material relating to Adzubei meetings and interviews; reports on Khrushchev; Kennedy-Khrushchev correspondence; and a small amount of published material. Although a small amount of this file remains security classified, most of it is available for research use without restriction.

National security files, countries series. 84 ft. 7 ft. of Russian-related materials include unclassified and declassified cables; Khrushchev correspondence; materials relating to Khrushchev, Dobrynin, Gromyko, Kuznetsov, and Mikoyan talks; and papers on other topics, including satellites and grain sales. Only 1.5 ft. of these materials are presently open for research.

White House central files. Consist of a subject file, 440 ft., a name file, 1,247 ft., a chronological file, 8 ft., closed, and a security classified file, 30 ft., closed. The subject file contains material on foreign affairs, 11 ft., human rights, 10 ft., national security defense, 20 ft., outer space, 2 ft., peace, 6 ft., and trips, 9 ft. The name file serves essentially as an index to the subject file.

White House staff files. 456 ft. Consist of correspondence, memoranda, and reports relating to the issues and problems on which White House staff members were working. Included are the files of McGeorge Bundy, special assistant to the president for national security affairs, 1 ft., closed pending review; Chester Clifton, military aide to the president, 1 ft.; Christian Herter, special representative for trade negotiations, 16 ft.; Godfrey McHugh, air force aide to the president, 17 ft., closed pending review; Howard Petersen, special assistant to the president for international trade policy, 22 ft.; and Walt Rostow, deputy special assistant to the president for national security affairs, 1 ft., closed pending review.

Collections of Personal and Organizational Papers

2 The following papers, some of which pertain to foreign affairs, the State Department, and the Department of Defense, have references to Russia/USSR: Robert H. Estabrook, editor and correspondent, papers, 1959-69, 1 ft., closed; John Kenneth Galbraith, economist and diplomat, papers, 1930-63, 45 ft.; Roswell Gilpatric, deputy secretary of defense, member, President's Task Force on Nuclear Proliferation, adviser to President Johnson, papers, 1956-67, 4 ft.; Roger Hilsman, assistant secretary of state for Far Eastern affairs, director of Intelligence and Research, State Department,

papers, 1961-65, 6 ft.; Arthur M. Schlesinger, author, historian, special assistant to the president, White House subject and speech files, 1961-64, 13 ft., papers, 1948-65, 53 ft., permission required; James P. Warburg, author, banker, adviser to Franklin D. Roosevelt, papers, 1920-69, 33 ft.; Edward Weintal, co-author of Facing the Brink, USIA official, papers, 1927-72, 3 ft., closed; Jerome Wiesner, special assistant to the president, director, Office of Science and Technology, papers, 1961-63, 8 ft., closed. There are inventories to all these papers.

3 The following records of U.S. government agencies have references to Russia/USSR: Arms Control and Disarmament Agency, records, 6 rolls of microfilm and 3 ft., closed; Central Intelligence Agency, records, 6 rolls of microfilm and 19 ft.; Department of Defense, records, 70 rolls of microfilm and 8 ft., microfilm closed; National Aeronautics and Space Administration, records, 11 rolls of microfilm and 17 ft., portions of microfilm closed; Office of Science and Technology, records, 73 rolls of microfilm, closed; Department of State, records, 129 rolls of microfilm and ca. 1 ft., closed; United States Mission to the United Nations, records, 8 rolls of microfilm and ca. 1 ft., closed; United States Information Agency, records, 237 rolls of microfilm and 1 ft., portions of microfilm closed, hard copy closed; and National Aeronautics and Space Council, records, 11 rolls of microfilm, portions closed, may have references to Russia/USSR. There are inventories to all these records.

Oral History Interviews

4 The following oral history interviews have references to Russia/USSR: Dean Acheson, presidential adviser on foreign affairs, 34 pp.; George Aiken, senator from Vermont, 42 pp.; Robert Amory, deputy director, CIA, chief, International Division, Bureau of the Budget, 153 pp.; John Badeau, ambassador to the United Arab Republic, 27 pp.; David Bell, director, Bureau of the Budget, administrator, AID, 169 pp., permission required to cite, quote, or paraphrase; Kenneth Birkhead, finance director, Democratic National Committee, assistant to the secretary of agriculture for congressional liaison, 91 pp.; Hale Boggs, representative from Louisiana, vice-chairman, Democratic National Committee, member, President's Commission on the Assassination of President Kennedy, 39 pp.; Henry Brandon, journalist and editor, The Sunday Times of London, 22 pp.; James MacGregor Burns, chairman, Department of Political Science, Williams College, Massachusetts political figure, Kennedy biographer, 54 pp.; John Moors Cabot, ambassador to Brazil, 1959-61, ambassador to Poland, 1962-65, 27 pp.; Lucius Clay, general, U.S. Army, president's representative, Berlin, 1961, 24 pp.; Maurice Couve de Murville, minister of foreign affairs of France, 15 pp.; Cardinal Richard Cushing, archbishop of Boston, 22 pp.; George Decker, general and chief of staff, U.S. Army, 45 pp., permission required to quote; William Douglas, associate justice of the Supreme Court, 39 pp.; Sir Alec Douglas-Home, minister of state for foreign affairs prime minister of Great Britain, 7 pp. and 11 pp., closed; Hugh Dryden, deputy administrator, NASA, 31 pp., references to the Soviet space program; Allen Ellender, senator from Louisiana, 50 pp.; Adrian Fisher, deputy director, U.S. Arms Control and Disarmament Agency, 28 pp.; John Glenn, Project Mercury astronaut, 32 pp., references to the Soviet space program; Lincoln Gordon, ambassador to Brazil, 144 pp., portion closed; Roger Hilsman, 36 pp.; Nicholas Hobbs, member, President's Panel on Mental Retardation, director of selection and research, Peace Corps, 32 pp.; Luther Hodges, secretary of commerce, 117 pp., portion closed; Solis Horwitz, member, JFK presidential campaign staff, director, Office of Organizational and Management Planning, Department of Defense, 31 pp., portion closed; Robert Hurwitch, special assistant for Cuban affairs, Department of State, 221 pp.; Constantinos Karamanlis, prime minister of Greece, 4 pp.; George Kennan, ambassador to Yugoslavia, 141 pp., portion closed; Nikita Khrushchev, chairman, Council of Ministers of the USSR, 5 pp.; Joseph Kraft, columnist, 31 pp.; Walter Lippman, journalist, 18 pp., portions closed; Robert Lovett, member, General Advisory Committee, U.S. Arms Control and Disarmament Agency, presidential adviser, 59 pp.; George Low, deputy director (Programs), Office of Manned Space Flight, NASA, 32 pp.; Henry Luce, editor in chief, Time Inc., 42 pp.; George S. McGovern, director, Food for Peace, senator from South Dakota, 51 pp.; Norman Manley, premier of Jamaica, leader of the Opposition Party, 11 pp.; Mike Mansfield, senator from Montana, senate majority leader, 46 pp.; Thomas Mboya, minister of labor, minister of justice and constitutional affairs of Kenya, 8 pp.; George Meany, president, AFL-CIO, 53 pp.; Edward Morgan, news commentator, American Broadcasting Company, Washington, 37 pp.; Charles Murphy, undersecretary of agriculture, 31 pp.; William Proxmire, senator from Wisconsin, 17 pp.; Hyman Rickover, chief, Bureau of Nuclear Propulsion, Bureau of Ships, chief, Naval Reactors Branch, AEC, 12 pp.; Leverett Saltonstall, senator from Massachusetts, 72 pp.; Robert Seamans, associate administrator, NASA, 46 pp., references to the Soviet space program, closed to newspaper reporters and writers in current periodicals; Theodore Sorensen, special counselor to the president, author, 69 pp., portions closed; Elmer Staats, deputy director, Bureau of the Budget, 36 pp.; Dirk Stikker, secretary general of NATO, 76 pp., permission required; Llewellyn Thompson, ambassador to the USSR, ambassador at large, 62 pp.; Sir Humphrey Trevelyan, deputy undersecretary,

Foreign Office, ambassador to Iraq and the USSR from Great Britain, 13 pp.; William Tyler, assistant secretary of state for european affairs, 40 pp.; Edward Welsh, executive secretary, National Aeronautics and Space Council, 51 pp. There are indexes to all these oral history interviews.

5 In addition, there may be references to Russia/USSR in the following oral history interviews: Charles Bohlen, special assistant to the secretary of state for soviet affairs, ambassador to France, 38 pp.; Chester Bowles, undersecretary of state, 107 pp.; McGeorge Bundy, special assistant to the president for National Security Affairs, 1961-66, 7 pp.; Averell Harriman, undersecretary of state for political affairs, 261 pp., permission required; Edward McDermott, director, Office of Emergency Planning, member, National Security Council, 67 pp.; George McGhee, undersecretary of state for political affairs, ambassador to Germany, 24 pp.; and Robert S. McNamara, secretary of defense, 1961-68, 5 pp., permission required. There are indexes to all these oral history interviews.

Audiovisual Records

6 These records include still photographs, sound recordings, motion picture films, and cartoons, some of which refer to Russia/USSR.

Finding Aid: Historical Materials in the John F. Kennedy Library (1978).

MA 13
MASSACHUSETTS DIOCESAN LIBRARY
1 Joy Street
Boston, Massachusetts 02108
(617-742-4720)

Charles Lewis Slattery (1867-1930). Papers, 1860-1930, ca. 2,500 items. Protestant bishop of Massachusetts, 1927-30. Letter from the Right Rev. Edward Parsons, bishop of California, refers to Sofia Zenova, who was seeking aid for the Russian Theological School in Paris. Access to collections by appointment only.

Finding Aid: Protestant Episcopal Church in the USA. Massachusetts (Diocese) Library. A description of the Manuscript Collections in the Massachusetts Diocesan Library (W.P.A., Boston, 1939).

MA 14
MASSACHUSETTS HISTORICAL SOCIETY
1154 Boylston Street
Boston, Massachusetts 02215
(617-536-1608)

1 Adams Family. Papers, 1639-1889, 171 ft. Available on microfilm (NUCMC 62-1621). Includes papers of the following individuals:

2 John Adams (1735-1826). Third president of the United States. Throughout his career he dealt with problems of European and Russian diplomacy. His "Letters Received and Other Loose Papers," letterbooks, and diary for 1779-84 contain correspondence with the Continental Congress, Francis Dana, at the Russian court, 1781-83, Golitsyn, and others. Materials concern armed neutrality, Russian recognition of the United States, trade, and the proposed, but abortive, mediation of Russia and Austria in the American war for independence. When members of his family were in Russia in 1809-15, Adams and his wife Abigail both corresponded with them, unofficially.

3 John Quincy Adams (1767-1848). Sixth president of the United States. In 1781 he accompanied the U.S. envoy, Francis Dana, to Russia; he was 14 years old. In St. Petersburg he acted as secretary and translator. He was minister to Russia in 1809-14 and secretary of state in 1817-25. Diaries and letterbooks from these periods, and as president, include data on Russian politics, banking, coinage, weights, measures, and vital statistics. He kept notes on his travel to Russia, books bought and read, the weather, agriculture, and the Russian language. Some materials (in part, copies) are about Russia and the Balkans, the Russian-America Company, U.S.-Russian commerce, Russian hemp manufacturing, U.S. trade in the Baltic area, the American consul Levett Harris, and the court of Alexander I. Among his correspondents and acquaintances were Aminov, Bakunin, Balaschev (Balashov), Brzozowsky, Campenhausen, Daschkov, Guriev, Koslodovlov, de Krudener, Princess Kutuzov, Naryshkin, Rumiantsev (an exchange of over 200 notes and letters), and the Emperors Alexander I and Nicholas I.

4 Louisa Catherine Adams (Mrs. John Quincy Adams) (1775-1852). She accompanied her husband to St. Petersburg, 1809-15. Her diary in Russia, October 1812-February 1814, a "Narrative of a Journey from Russia to France, 1815," and a long autobiographical sketch ("The Adventures of a Nobody") are included, as are her letters from Russia ("Letters Received and Other Loose Papers" file) and some notes and drawings by either her sister (Catherine Johnson, later Mrs. William Steuben Smith) or herself.

5 William Steuben Smith (1787-1850). Nephew and later brother-in-law of J. Q. Adams, legation

secretary during Adams's mission to Russia. Includes his diary for January-September 1814 and his letterbook for 1811-14. A privately owned Smith diary, July-October 1809, on deposit at the Society, is kept with this letterbook.

Note: All the Adams Family papers are available on microfilm from the Massachusetts Historical Society. The "Brief Survey of Materials of Russian Interest in the Adams Papers and Related Collections" in John Quincy Adams and Russia (Quincy, Mass., 1965) is pertinent.

6 John Albion Andrew (1818-1867). Papers, 1772-1886, 15 ft. Massachusetts governor, 1861-66, and statesman. Letter from Cassius M. Clay, 18 February 1867, and letter from Nathaniel Thayer, 25 March 1867, discuss Russian railroads, particularly their financing.

7 Appleton Family. Papers, 1696-1941, 17 ft. Includes some material on early Russian-American relations. Also, papers of Nathan Appleton, Jr., who wrote Russian Life and Society (Boston, 1904).

8 Thomas Astin Coffin. Papers, 1769-1818, 1 ft. Merchant. Includes 3 letters written in London, 1800-1801, which concern conditions in Russia and the tsars.

9 Dabney Family. Papers, 1716-1904, ca. 75 items. Merchants. Letterbook from 1831-34 contains copies of letters from Osgood Carney which include accounts of cargoes shipped between Cuba, St. Petersburg, and Boston. The goods are mainly sugar, coffee, fish, and candles. Unpublished guide (NUCMC 65-180).

10 Dana Family. Papers, 1658-1933. Francis Dana (1743-1811) was America's first, though unrecognized, envoy to Russia, 1781-83. His papers, 1780-1824, ca. 1 ft. plus scattered items, include private and official letterbooks from 1780-84; foreign state papers, 1780-82; correspondence from his stay in Russia; an account book; and journals from 1781 and 1783. Includes his original instructions as minister to Russia, trade proposals, reports on Russian-American diplomacy and relations, and prices of imports and exports at the ports of Riga and St. Petersburg, 1781-82. Note: Related materials are in the Dwight and Gerry (II) collections. Much of the Dana material has been published.

11 Caleb Davis (1738-1797). Papers, 1684-1830, 15 ft. Merchant. Includes a letter from William Cramp and J. M. Bulkeley in St. Petersburg to William Cheevers, 7 January 1788, that notes the annual increase in trade between the U.S. and Russia. Also, a letter of Samuel A. Otis, 27 May 1788, New York, speaks of conditions in Russia.

12 Alexander Hill Everett (1790-1847). Papers, 1804-74, ca. 100 items. Editor and diplomat. Served as secretary to J. Q. Adams, when the latter was minister to Russia, in 1809-11. Journals, correspondence, notebook, and an expense account book. Also, records of negotiations Everett had as minister to Spain, 1825-29, with the Russian minister there. Consult the "Brief Survey" noted in the Adams Family papers for a finding aid. (NUCMC 72-1556)

13 Thomas Jefferson (1743-1826). Papers, 1705-1826, 15 ft. U.S. president, 1801-1809. Includes some material pertaining to early Russian-American relations. Available on microfilm.

14 Thomas H. Perkins (1764-1854). Papers, 1786-1853, 20 ft. Boston merchant. Includes letter of 1816 which speaks of Alexander Barnaov at length.

15 Timothy Pickering (1745-1829). Papers, 1731-1927, 29 ft. Army officer and statesman. Family and general correspondence, official documents, journals, etc., part of which pertains to early Russian-American relations. Available on microfilm. Published finding aid (NUCMC 68-761).

16 Wetmore Collection on Rhode Island Commerce. 1706-1835, 5 ft. Includes some data on commerce with Russia.

17 Note: The Society also holds the logbooks of many ships, some of which engaged in trade with Russia and called at Russian ports. Records of these voyages must be traced through the name of the vessel.

Finding Aid: Catalog of Manuscripts of the Massachusetts Historical Society, 7 vols. (Boston: G. K. Hall, 1969).

MA 15
DEPARTMENT OF ASIATIC ART
MUSEUM OF FINE ARTS
Huntington Avenue
Boston, Massachusetts 02115
(617-267-9300 x 221)

Armenian Manuscripts. (a) Grigor Tat'ewac'i's Book of Questions (fragments), 16th-17th c. (accession no. 26.113); (b) four Gospels and Revelation of St. John, A.D. 1237 (acc. no. 30.2); and (c) 1 leaf from a lectionary, A.D. 1671 (acc. no. 46.51). Access by appointment only.

MA 16
HARRIET M. SPAULDING LIBRARY
NEW ENGLAND CONSERVATORY OF MUSIC
33 Gainsborough Street
Boston, Massachusetts 02115
(617-262-1120)

Preston Collection. Contains a letter from the pianist and composer Anton Rubinstein, Peterhof, 29 (?) April-13 May 1874, and a letter of Adolf von Henselt, the German-born court pianist at St. Petersburg, 10/22 November 1870. Both letters are in German.

MA 17
ARCHIVES OF AMERICAN ART
SMITHSONIAN INSTITUTION
87 Mount Vernon Avenue
Boston, Massachusetts 02108
(617-223-0951)

This repository, like each of the regional centers of the Archives of American Art, has microfilms of much of the original materials kept at the Archives' Washington Center. It also holds items on microfilm from originals in other hands. Some of these materials pertain to the Russian Empire/Soviet Union. For details, see the entry under the District of Columbia.

MA 18
ARCHIVES OF THE ARCHDIOCESE
ARCHDIOCESE OF BOSTON
2121 Commonwealth Avenue
Brighton, Massachusetts 02135
(617-254-0100)

Chancellor's Office, Central Subject Files, 1900-76. Scattered items relating mostly to Russian immigrants in this country and to relations with the Russian Orthodox and other Eastern rite churches. Also, material dealing with anti-communism in the U.S. in the 1950s.

MA 19
GRAY HERBARIUM
ARNOLD ARBORETUM
HARVARD UNIVERSITY
22 Divinity Avenue
Cambridge, Massachusetts 02138
(617-495-2366)

Letters of the Gray Herbarium file. Ca. 1800-1930, ca. 14,280 items. Includes 10 letters, 1846-50, between Asa Gray and the Russian scientist F. E. Fischer. The subject of the letters is entirely botanical, dealing with specimens that Fischer was sending to the United States. (NUCMC 75-1978) The file may contain other correspondence between Russian and American botanists. The Herbarium prefers to be contacted by mail.

MA 20
FARLOW REFERENCE LIBRARY AND HERBARIUM OF CRYPTOGAMIC BOTANY
HARVARD UNIVERSITY
Cambridge, Massachusetts 02138
(617-495-2368)

Cryptogams of the United States North Pacific Exploring Expedition. Collection, 1853-56, ca. 200 pp. Includes diagrams and descriptions of specimens gathered by the expedition of Charles Wright and James Small from various North Pacific sites, including Ayan, Petropavlovsk, and the Bering Strait. Published by Donald H. Pfister (ed.) as Cryptogams of the United States North Pacific Expedition, 1853-1856 (1978).

MA 21
RARE BOOK COLLECTION
HARVARD-YENCHING LIBRARY
HARVARD UNIVERSITY
2 Divinity Avenue
Cambridge, Massachusetts 02138
(617-495-2756)

1 Hsia yü so t'an ("Ramblings over Distant Frontiers"). Manuscript, 4 vols., with a preface by the author, Ch'ung-yüan Shih (pseudonym), written in the 42nd year (1777) under the reign of Emperor Chien-lung (1736-95). Contains a considerable number of comments about Russia. In graceful handwriting.

2 Meng ku lü ("Code on Mongolia"). Manuscript, 4 vols., with the endorsement of the governor of Shansi and Kansu provinces in the 29th year (1764) under the reign of Emperor Chien-lung. Bears slightly on the Russian Empire. In graceful handwriting.

MA 22
THE HOUGHTON LIBRARY
HARVARD UNIVERSITY
Cambridge, Massachusetts 02138
(617-495-2440)

1 Ivan Afanasev. "Grammatika ruskago i nemetskago iazykov." London, 1725. 1 vol., 37 ff. (71 pp.). (MS Russ 5)

2 Akademiia khudozhestv, Leningrad. "Privilegium, Reglament, und Etat de kaiserlichen

Akademie der Künste von 1764 bis 1840." Ms. (copy), St. Petersburg, 1843. 70 ff. (138 pp.). Contains rulings by Catherine II, Alexander I, Nicholas I, and others, in German. (Kilgour MS Russ 32)

3 Alexander I. Orders transmitted to Major Derby (MS Russ 2). Also, a decree bestowing a decoration, St. Petersburg, 23 May 1808. D. s. 1 s., 1 p.

4 American Board of Commissions for Foreign Missions. Records, 1810-1960. Ca. 50,000 items. 21 vols. of documents, 1838-59, deal with a mission to Armenia. Checklist. Restricted. (NUCMC 61-1964)

5 Apostol. 16th c. octavo manuscript, paper, 595 pp.

6 Armenian Church. 1 vol. [Synaxarion], [16th c.]. (MS Armenian 12)

7 Autograph File. Ca. 200 boxes. Included are autographs of several Russian authors, among them Turgenev, Tolstoi, and Gorkii.

8 Konstantin Dmitrievich Bal'mont (1867-1943). 1 vol. of correspondence, 1928-32, from Bal'mont to Ruth P. Bailey and from Leonid Vasilievich Tulpa to Bailey. (MS Russ 45)

9 Michael Andreas Barclay de Tolly (1761-1818). Barclay de Tolly's military journal for the year 1812, "Izobrazhenie voennykh deistvii 1-oi Armii." 30 ff. (59 pp.). (Kilgour MS Russ 33)

10 Ivan Barkov (1732-1768), attributed author. "Zhenskoe uchilishche." 1 vol. (Kilgour MS Russ 43)

11 Aleksandr Mikhailovich Beloselskii-Belozerskii (1752-1809). 1 album. Contains 127 poems, letters, dedications, and other items signed and/or written by various persons, including: Prince Aleksandr Mikhailovich Beloselskii-Belozerskii, Duke Pavel Petrovich, Catherine II, Prince Aleksandr Vrourakiskii, Maria Dmitrievna Tatischevvi, Frédéric César Laharpe (1754-1830), Count Grigori Aleksandrovich Stroganov (1770-1838), Princess Anna Grigorevna Beloselskaia-Belozerskaia (Kasitskaia), Princess Zinaida Aleksandrovna Volkonskaia (Beloselskaia-Belozerskaia) (1792-1862), Maria Aleksandrovna Vlasova (Beloselskaia-Belozerskaia) (b. 1787), Lole Kristovoskii, Platon, metropolitan of Moscow (1737-1812), Aleksandrine Chvostov, and many others, including non-Russians. (MS Russ 47)

12 Bible. Manuscripts, Armenian. Four Gospels. 1 vol., 1899. (MS Armenian 3)

13 Bible. Manuscripts, Armenian. Four Gospels. 1 vol. 1643. [Lectionary of the Gospels]. (MS Armenian 11)

14 Bible. Manuscripts, Georgian. Four Gospels. On vellum [n.p., ca. 1100], 158 ff. (315 pp.), Khutsuri script, with illuminations. (MS Georgian 1)

15 Bible. Manuscripts, Russian. New Testament, Revelations. 1 vol., ca. 1600. [Apocalypse, with illustrations]. (Kilgour MS Russ 15)

16 Bible. Manuscripts, Slavonic. New Testament, Mark. 1 vol., 18th c. [The gospel according to St. Mark]. (MS Slavic 1)

17 Bible. Manuscripts, Slavonic. Old Testament, Psalms. 1 vol., 17th c. [Psalter]. (Kilgour MS Russ 36)

18 Bible. New Testament, Gospels. 1 vol. (MS Armenian 8)

19 Alexander Calamato. [A new forest of thoughts]. 1 vol., 1741. (MS Armenian 9)

20 Carrapeat. [Authentic statement of the affair of M. Bore]. (MS Armenian 2)

21 O. E. Cesare. 51 drawings, mostly of persons and scenes in the USSR, made in 1922. Represented are Chicherin, Kalinin, Krupskaia (?), Lenin, Litvinov, Lebedev, Trotskii, Vorovskii, Zinoviev. (Kilgour MS Russ 28)

22 [Clippings concerning massacres]. 3 vols., [1895]. (MS Armenian 10)

23 Edward Estlin Cummings (1894-1962). 272 boxes. Writer. Includes a manuscript and typescript of Cummings's work, "Eimi," which deals with the Soviet Union, where Cummings travelled.

24 Vladimir Ivanovich Dal' (1801-1872). [Collection of Russian Proverbs]. MS (unidentified hand); [n.p.], 1852, 8 ll. (29 pp.). Belonged to Pavel Konstantinovich Simoni, who prefixed an explanatory statement (fMS Ital 75).

25 Jirc David (1647-1713). [Russian grammar]. 1 vol. (Kilgour MS Russ 53)

26 Natal'ia Borisovna Dolgorukova (Sheremet'eva) (1714-1771). The princess' "Commonplace book," 1 vol. (MS Russ 10)

27 Fedor Mikhailovich Dostoevskii (1821-1881). "The House of the Dead." Holograph manuscript, large quarto, 4 pp., of the beginning of the second chapter of Part II. This is the only known surviving portion of the manuscript. (MS Russ 1)

28 Aleksei Petrovich Ermolov (1776-1881). "Mes Observations." 1 vol., [n.d.]. (MS Russ 17)

29 G. Galitskii. "Posle sluzhby . . ." 1 vol. St. Petersburg, 1897. MS, unidentified hand, 8 ff. (16 pp.). (MS Russ 9)

30 Garrison Family. 1 box. Includes the copy of a letter, 1905, to Leo Tolstoi, thanking him for writing the introduction to Chertkov's life of Garrison. (bMS Am 1169 - 85)

31 Gatchina, Russia. 1 box. [Collection of Russian folklore]. MS (various hands), n.p., n.d. A collection of Russian folklore put together by a professor at Gatchina Academy between 1893 and 1897. There are reports on folklore from Novgorod, Pskov, St. Petersburg, and Kazan'.

32 Archive of the Republic of Georgia. 1880-1921, 90 cartons, 450 ft. Contains the official state papers of the independent Georgian republic. The materials concern all aspects of governmental policy, including relations with neighboring states. The archive has been on a 30-year loan to Harvard from the exiled government of the Republic of Georgia since 1974. Inventory. Access is by permission of the librarian of the Houghton Library and by permission of Mr. N. K. Tsintsadze and his representative.

33 Aleksandr Glazunov (1865-1936). [Symphony no. 7 in F major]. 10 May 1902, 18 ff. (53 pp.), 1 vol. A working draft; lacks part of the first three movements. Because of the fragility of the paper, the manuscript cannot be consulted without permission of the librarian.

34 Maksim Gorkii (1868-1936). "Aus meinem Tagebuch." Though headed in German, these "Pages from my diary" are written in Russian. 1 vol., [n.d.]. (Kilgour fMS Russ 16)

35 Greek Church. Liturgy, 1 vol., 1588 (MS Slavic 4); Liturgy [Octooechus, or Parakletike], 1 vol. [1353] (MS Slavic 2); and [Menologium; the Codex Suprasliensis], 1 vol. (MS Slavic 6).

36 Joseph Grew. 1909-48, 153 vols. American diplomat and twice undersecretary of state, 1924-27, 1944-45. Materials that shed light on wartime atomic policy and diplomatic policies regarding the Soviet Union. (MS Am 1687)

37 Aleksandr Sergeevich Griboedov (1795-1829). 2 manuscripts of his play, "Gore ot' uma": one dated [182?], the other 1839. (Kilgour MSS Russ 23 and 23.1)

38 Imperial Family. Correspondence, 1850-1905, 1 box. 24 ALS, in Russian, from Alexander II to his son the Grand Duke Vladimir, 1855-79; 22 ALS from Maria Aleksandrovna, empress consort of Alexander II, to her son, 1852-79, 5 letters in Russian, 17 in French; 5 ALS from Grand Duke Vladimir to his father, 1874-80, with pencil notes by Alexander II; and 33 ALS from various persons to Grand Duke Vladimir, 1873-1907. Accession list. (Kilgour MS Russ 26)

39 Innokentii, metropolitan of Moscow (1797-1879). "Zamechaniia o koloshenskom i kadiaksom iazykakh." Ms, unidentified hand, 1849, 69 ff. (136 pp.). Evidently transcribed from a printed edition. (MS Russ 8)

40 International (Second) Congress. 1893-1914, 1 box. Printed and mimeographed documents concerning the Second International. Inventory. (bMS French 224)

41 Joseph Ishill. Letters of Sophie Kropotkin, Nikolai Aleksandrovich Rubakin (1862-1946), and Peter Aleksandrovich Kropotkin (1842-1921). There is also Emma Goldman's "A Woman Without a Country," Maksim Gorkii's "Protest against the Assassination of Francisco Ferrer" (August 1910), 1 p., and English translations of works on P. A. Kropotkin. Accession list.

42 Ivan the Terrible (1530-1584). [Response to Jan Rokyta, of the Confraternity of the Bohemian and Moravian Brethren]. Ms. (unidentified hand); [n.p., ca. 1600], 82 ff. (164 pp.). Accession list. (Kilgour MS Russ 19)

43 James Family. Correspondence. Includes 15 ALS of Ivan Sergeevich Turgenev to Henry James, 1874-84. Unpublished index.

44 [Georgii Kolesov]. "Sbornik trudov myslitel'nykh . . ." Ms., unsigned, Vladivostok, 1897, 11 ff. (41 pp.). (MS Russ 101)

45 A. Krotkov. [The Russian fleet under the reign of Peter the Great]. 1 vol. (fMS Russ 38)

46 Mikhail Iur'evich Lermontov (1814-1841). "The demon. An Oriental tale." Quarto manuscript copy, 100 pp., ca. 1850. (Kilgour MS Russ 24)

47 Log books. Includes log books of ships that travelled to Russia in the beginning of the 19th c.

48 Sherry Mangan (b. 1904). Material pertaining to the Fourth International. Also, a typescript by Terence Phelan, "Wilson and the Soviet Union."

49 Manuscript Maps of Siberia, Collected by Leo Bagrow. Includes (1) the Godunov map, 1667, the earliest Russian general map of Siberia; (2) the Spatharios map, 1682, the only known map by the first Russian ambassador to Peking; (3) Semen Ul'ianovich Remezov's map of Siberia, ca. 1699; (4) the Shestakov map, 1726, showing Kamchatka, the Kuriles, and the Bering Straits before Bering's expedition; (5) Ivan Kirilov's map of northeast Siberia, 1726; (6) Semen Ul'ianovich Remezov's "Khorograficheskaia kniga," containing 165 sketch maps in pen and ink and watercolor, a world map, and several drawings, 1696-97. Accession list. (*55M-174: 1-6)

50 Thomas Garrigue Masaryk (1850-1937). 4 boxes. Manuscript of chapter III of The Spirit of Russia. (MS Slavic 5)

51 Ivan Stepanovich Mazepa-Koledinsky (1644?-1709). Confirmatory charter to the possession and usufruct of a water-mill situated on the river Oster Ms., D. S., Baturin, Ukraine, 14 October 1691, 1 1.); a letter patent granting a monopoly on the sale of wine and on keeping taverns where wine and tobacco could be sold in the village of Svetilnoye Ms, D. S. Baturin, Ukraine, 8 October 1695, 1 1 ., to pan Fedor Gregorievich); confirmatory charter given to Gregory Karpovich for a landed estate that he purchased from Kornei Lapieka, including a homestead, meadows, and bee-trees. (MS Russ 106, 106.1, 106.2).

52 Dmitrii Sergeevich Merezhkovskii (1865-1941). "Gete." 1 vol., [n.d.]. (Kilgour MS Russ 25)

53 Miscellaneous Manuscripts. 1 box, 2 envelopes. Contains Russian-related materials. (MS Russ 100)

54 Alan Moorehead (b. 1910). 1 box. Galley-proofs and printer's copy for the New York (Harper) edition, 1958, of Moorehead's The Russian Revolution. (MS Russ 27)

55 [Ossianic poems]. 1 vol. (Kilgour MS Russ 52)

56 Palladius (d. ca. 430). Successively bishop of Helenopolis and of Aspona. [Homilies], of which Palladius is the supposed author, in Church Slavonic and with 62 pictures in ink and watercolor, 58 ff. (81 pp.), ca. 1700.

57 Walter H. Page (1855-1918). U.S. ambassador to England, 1913-18. 1 diary discusses the "collapse of Russia," March 1917-8 March 1918. Accession list.

58 Boris Leonidovich Pasternak (1890-1960). [The Passing storm], 1 vol., 1958; crayon drawing of Pasternak, 24 December 1924; 9 ALS by Pasternak to George Reavy, 1931-60; 3 letters, in French, to Henri Mathot, 1959. (Kilgour MS Russ 18, 29, 34, 34.1)

59 Paterikon of Solovki Monastery. Life and miracles of various saints. Quarto manuscripts, waxed paper, 348 ll., 17th c. Has not been published.

60 Peter I (1672-1725). Proclamation to the Baltic peoples urging their support in the war against the Turks. Ms, D. S., Jaworow, 8 May 1711, 1 l. (1 p.). (Kilgour MS Russ 39)

61 [Prayer of healing]. 1 roll, [1708]. (MS Armenian 7)

62 Psalter with nocturn prayers divided in 8 parts. Incomplete and in poor condition. Illuminated. (MS Armenian 5)

63 Pseudo-Callisthenes. "History of . . . Alexander the great." 1 vol., [ca. 1903]. (MS Armenian 13)

64 Aleksandr Sergeevich Pushkin (1799-1837). "Moriu." Holograph manuscript of the poem, written on the sides of a folio leaf. (MS Russ 4)

65 "Raznyia zagadki." Ms. (unidentified hand), n.p., 1805. 22 ff. (41 pp.). (MS Russ 6)

66 John Reed (1887-1920). Papers. American journalist and eyewitness to the Russian Revolution. Included are pp. 1-165 of Reed's Ten Days that Shook the World; 2 scrapbooks of passports, passes, tickets, programs, decrees, collected in Russia, 1917-18; maps of Russia; unpublished manuscripts, "Scratch a Russian," 4 September 1917, and "Red Russia"; proofs of articles on Kerensky, the army, the Bolsheviks; pamphlets by Nikolai Bukharin, Emma Goldman, George V. Lomonosoff, Karl Marx, Leon Trotskii; Russian notebooks, 1917, 1919-20, with comments on Moscow conditions and a trip to the Volga; notes for Ten Days that Shook the World and on the Russian Revolution; letters to Louise Bryant; and a note from Reed to Lenin and a reply by Lenin. There are also typed Russian government releases on various matters, including the Kornilov attack, social insurance, banks, the "Vologda" meeting, German soldiers, People's Commissars, the principles of the Bolshevik government; privately made translations of documents on the Kerensky cabinet, Russian soldiers in France, Trotskii, V. A. Ovseenko-Antonov, Petrograd taxes; "later documents on the Russian Revolution" which pertain to the White and Red Terrors, Kharkov under the rule of A. I. Denikin, Japanese socialists and the Russian Revolution, Russian unemployment insurance, the economic consequences of Brest-Litovsk, A. I. Spiridovich, and other matters; "American documents, 1913-19," with material relating to Amos Pinchot, Hiram Johnson, George Creel, and "liberal editors"; manuscripts on Russia by Louise Bryant; and manuscripts concerning John Reed by Angelica Balabanova, Harry Kemp, and Edwin J. Mayer. Unpublished finding aid.

67 Aleksei Mikhailovich Remizov (1877-1958). "Something Unknown. The Tale of Tsar Dodon," a typescript, 14 ll., 1912, corrected by the author; 14 ALS from Remizov to Ariadna (Tyrkova) Williams, 1925-53; and 23 ALS of Vasilii Vasil'evich Rozanov (1856-1919) to various persons, 1905-17. (Kilgour MS Russ 21, 31, and 42)

68 Nikolai Andreevich Rimskii-Korsakov (1844-1908). 14 ALS of Rimskii-Korsakov to Aleksandr Tikhonovich Grechaninov, St. Petersburg 6/18 November 1898-3 December 1905; page-proofs, signed, with corrections and additions of "Pan Voevoda," [n.p.], 1903, 147 ff. (150 pp).

69 Russian autographs. 1 box. Various materials --letters, poems, drawings--signed and/or written by: Ivan Konstantinovich Aivazovskii (1817-1900); Pavel Vasil'evich Annenkov (1812-1887); Aleksei Nikolaevich Apukhin (1841-1893); Konstantin Dmitrievich Bal'mont (1867-1943); Aleksandr Aleksandrovich Bestuzhev (1797-1837); Aleksandr Aleksandrovich Blok (1880-1921); Vladimir L'vovich Burtsev (1862-1942); Anton Pavlovich Chekhov (1860-1904); Gavril Romanovich Derzhavin (1743-1816); Marina Ivanovna Efron (1892-1941) (several letters); Nikolai Vasil'evich Gogol' (1809-1852); Ivan Logginovich Goremykin (1839-1917); Maksim Gorkii (1868-1936) (several letters); Vladimir Vasilevich Lebedev (b. 1841); Ivan Stepanovich Mazepa-Koledinsky (1644?-1709); Vasilii Ivanovich Nemirovich-Danchenko (1848-1936); Boris Leonidovich Pasternak (1890-1960); Aleksandr Ivanovich Polezhaev (1805-1838); Alexandr Sergeevich Pushkin (1799-1837); Aleksei Mikhailovich Remizov (1877-1958); Dimitri Dimitrievich Shostakovich; Konstantin Mikhailovich Simonov; Petr Il'ich Chaikovskii (1840-1893); Leo Tolstoi; Leon Trotskii (1879-1940); Ivan Sergeevich Turgenev (1818-1883)--several letters to Maria Ageevna Miliutina; Vasilii Vasil'evich Vereshchagin (1824-1904); Prince Petr Andreevich Viazemskii (1792-1878); and Vasilii Andreevich Zhukovskii (1783-1852). Accession list. (Kilgour bMS Russ 11) Some of the items in this collection are described in detail in The Kilgour Collection (1959).

70 Russian charters. 1 box. A private file of business documents, 1543-1775, containing 104 scrolls and 6 conventional documents, all in vernacular Russian. (MS Russ 30)

71 Russian composers' autographs. 1 box. Includes letters and musical scores by Aleksandr Profi'evich Borodin (1834-1887), Aleksandr Sergeevich Dargomyzhskii (1813-1861), Aleksandr Glazunov (1865-1936), Anatol Konstantinovich Liadov (1855-1914), Modeste Petrovich Moussorgskii (1839-1881); Sergei Rachmaninoff (1875-1943); Nikolai Andreevich Rimskii-Korsakov (1844-1908); Igor Stravinsky (1882-1971); Sergei Ivanovich Taneyev (1856-1915); and Petr Il'ich Chaikovskii (1840-1893). Accession list. (Kilgour MS Russ 20)

72 "Russkiia pesni." 1 vol., 18th c., n.p., unidentified hand. (MS Russ 7)

73 Kondratii Fedorovich Ryleev (1795-1826). "Dumy" (St. Petersburg, 1832). Manuscript copy, 100 ll., which follows very closely the published texts. In this manuscript several of the lines suppressed by the censor are reproduced. (Kilgour MS Russ 12)

74 Aleksei Saltykov (1806-1859). "Les aventures de Lors Elphinstone." Manuscript, 1 vol.

75 [Service book of liturgical rules with . . . chants of the Armenian Apostolic Church]. (MS Armenian 6)

76 St. Sagis Shnorhali. [Commentaries on the 7 Catholic Epistles]. (MS Armenian 4)

77 Hryhoryi Savych Skovoroda (1722-1794). "Razgovor, nazyvaemyi alfavit ili bukvar' mira . . ." 1 vol., [1781]. Manuscript, quarto, 119 pp., unbound. (Kilgour MS Russ 22)

78 "Sudebno sledovatel' po osobo vashnym . . ." (Documents of the Sokolov investigation on the death of Nicholas II). 7 vols. of documents that came out of the White Army's investigation of the death of Nicholas II and his family in Ekaterinburg in 1918. (Kilgour MS Russ 35) Inventory.

79 Time Archive. 1942-55, 58 cartons. U.S. weekly news-magazine. Contains materials pertaining to Russia/USSR.

80 Ahmet Zeki Velidi Togan (b. 1890). "Turkestan today." 1 vol. (Kilgour MS Russ 49)

81 Lev Nikolaevich Tolstoi (1828-1910). MS. LS to Ernst Schramm, 7 April 1899, in German, 7 pp., on the subject of military conscription. (MS Russ 40)

82 Lev Trotskii (1879-1940). 157 boxes and 19 vols. Revolutionary and Soviet government leader. The Trotskii material can be divided into the following categories:

a) Trotskii papers. 94 boxes. (bMS Russ 13):

Works (manuscripts, typed excerpts, occasional clippings of Trotskii's writings, and unpublished documents of a general nature).

Ephemera (printed, mimeographed, and typed miscellany, largely for Trotskii's exile period; periodicals, leaflets, clippings, etc.).

Soviet correspondence, 1917-29. Trotskii's exchanges with individuals, or on specific matters. Authors and recipients of letters include: Aleksandr Gavrilovich Shliapnikov (1884-1943), Georgii Vasil'evich Chicherin (1872-1936), Adolph Abramovich Ioffe (1883-1927), Iakov Mikhailovich Sverdlov (1885-1919), Efraim Markovich Sklianskii (1892-1925), Grigorii Zinoviev (1883-1936), Khristian Georgievich Rakovskii (1873-1941), Mikhail Vasilevich Frunze (1885-1925), Lev Borisovich Kamenev, Trotskii's son Lev Sedov, Ivan Denisovich Smilga (1892-1938?), Ivan Nikitich Smirnov (1881-1936), Grigorii Konstantinovich Ordzhonikidze (1886-1937), Karl Radek (1885-1939), I. V. Stalin, V. Molotov, and many others.

Papers of Trotskii's exile period. 45 boxes. Inventory.

b) Van Heijenoort Papers. 6 boxes. Van Heijenoort was Trotskii's last secretary,

1932-39. These papers were separated from the main body of Trotskii papers during World War II. They were recovered and added to the collection in 1958. They consist mainly of works of Trotskii's exile period. The boxes have been opened. (MS Russ 13.2)

c) Harper manuscripts. 5 boxes. Materials dealing mainly with Trotskii's Stalin and its translation by Charles Malamuth. Includes 1 box of correspondence with Harper & Brothers regarding this work. (MS Russ 13.3 and 13.8)

d) Dewey Commission Exhibits. 7 boxes. The unpublished exhibits of the Mexico, New York, and Paris hearings of the Commission of Inquiry into charges made against Leon Trotskii in the Moscow trials, with some related material from Trotskii's papers. (MS Russ 13.4)

e) Letters from Trotskii to Sara Weber. 1 vol. (Kilgour MS 48)

f) Concordance of Guides. 1 vol. (MS Russ 13.5)

g) Trotskii's diary, printer's copy. 1 box. (MS Russ 13.7)

h) Work-sheets by Trotskii. 16 vols. (MS Russ 13.6)

Finding Aids: There is an unpublished guide, 2 vols., to the papers by George Fischer that is also available on microfilm and was used extensively in writing this entry.

83 Hohannes Vartabed. Letter concerning his abduction from Constantinople. (MS Armenian 1)

84 Oswald Garrison Villard (1872-1949). Papers, ca. 1886-ca. 1949. 150 boxes and 1 vol. Editor of the Nation. Some Russian-related materials.

85 [Sergei Iulievich Vitte (Witte) - Autograph album]. 358 ff. (441 pp.). This album, which contains documents signed and/or written by prominent Russian historical figures, has been partially published in Aleksandr Barsukov, "Avtografy izvestnykh i zamechatel'nykh liudei," Starina i novizna, VIII-IX (1904-1905), 271-398. Accession list. (Kilgour MS Russ 50)

86 Zinaida Aleksandrovna Volkonskaia (Beloselskaia-Belozerskaia (1792-1862). 1 box. Correspondents include notable Russian political, artistic, and religious figures. There is also correspondence and albums of drawings and poetry of Maria Aleksandrovna Vlasova (Beloselskaia-Belozerskaia). Unpublished index. (Kilgour MS Russ 46-46.14)

87 Feliks Vadimovich Volkhovskii (1846-1914). 5 boxes. Volkhovskii's correspondents include Vladimir L'vovich Burtsev (1862-1942), Nikolai Vasil'evich Chaikovskii (1850-1926), Vera Dolina, Egor Egorovich Lazarev (1855-1937), Vasilii Maslov-Stekoz, M. Mendel, B. Olenin, Semen Raichin, Count Lev Nikolaevich Tolstoi F. Trostin, Ivan Sergeevich Turgenev, and foreign-born correspondents, including Robert Spence Watson (1837-1911) and Herbert Metford Thompson. There are also letters to Ego Egorovich Lazarev from various people. Accession list. (Kilgour MS Russ 51)

88 Vasilii Andreevich Zhukovskii (1783-1852). Travel notebook with pencil sketches and miscellaneous notations made by Zhukovskii during his travels through Europe in 1839. (Kilgour MS Russ 104)

89 Note: Additional Russian-related materials at the Houghton Library could probably be found in a number of papers and collections of American public figures, diplomats, and travellers.

Finding Aids: The Kilgour Collection of Russian Literature (Cambridge, Mass., 1959), used in writing this entry. Many of the materials cited in this book have been published, including in D. Cizevsky and M. Karpovich, eds., Russian Literary Archives (New York, 1956).

MA 23
LAW SCHOOL LIBRARY - ILS
INTERNATIONAL LEGAL STUDIES BUILDING
HARVARD UNIVERSITY
Cambridge, Massachusetts 02138
(617-495-3177)

The materials described below, arranged in call number order, are collections of documents printed but not published, i.e., they circulated among a handful of high tsarist officials. The legal projects and proposals are accompanied by ministerial reports, materials of conferences or commissions created to consider the question, and related items. The items which follow are in call-number order, listed by subject (approximate at times), and not in chronological sequence.

1 Copyright (Rus 340 F11). Materialy k 1911 zakonu ob avtorskikh pravakh.

2 Press and censorship (Rus 355). Proekt ustava o pechati i tsensure. Ob"iasnitel'naia zapiska k proektu novogo ustava o pechati 1905. Proekt ustava knigopechatanii 1863.

3 Zemstvo (Rus 369 F01). Zemskoe polozhenie. Proekt novogo izdaniia 1901.

4 Municipalities (Rus 369). Gorodskoe polozhenie 1892. Gos. Sovet v soedinnennykh Departamentakh zakonov gos. ekonomii i grazhdanskikh i dukhovnykh del. Mai 1891; Ianv., Fevral', Aprel' 1892, 140 pp. MVD.

Departament khoziaistvennyi. Otdelenie VI. 1 Marta 1891, 45 pp. Svod mnenii Gubernskikh Nachal'stv ob izmeneniiakh v deistvuiushchem Gorodskom polozhenii 16 iiunia 1870, 246 pp. Ob"iasneniia po proektu novogo gorodskogo polozheniia, 47 pp. Spravka, 327 pp.

5 Civil order (Rus 370). Komissiia grafa Ignat'eva 1906. Zakony ob okhrane gos. poriadka. Zhurnaly 1905-1906, 184 pp. Materialy, 131 pp., 63 pp., 36 pp., 51 pp., 108 pp., etc.

6 Industrial tax (Rus 373 E99). Proekt polozheniia o gosud. promyslovom naloge. 1909 g.

7 Local courts (Rus 397 F112). Materialy po zakonu o vvedenii v deistvii zakona 15 iiunia 1912 g. o preobrazovanii mestnogo suda.

8 Council of Ministers (Rus 600). Vysochaishe utverzhdennye osobye zhurnaly Soveta Ministrov, 21 vols. I: 1907 Ianvar-Iiun'; II: 1907 Iiul'-Dekabr'; III: 1907 (sobst. vlast'iu); I: 1908 Ianvar-Iiun'; II: 1908 Iiul'-Dekabr'; III: 1908 (sobst. vlast'iu); I: 1909 Ianvar'-Iiun'; II: 1909 Iiul'-Dekabr'; III: 1909 (sobstvennoi vlast'iu); I: 1910 Ianvar'-Iiul'; II: 1910 Iiul'-Dekabr'; III: 1910 (sobst. vlast'iu); I: 1911 Ianvar'-Iiun'; II: 1911 Iiul'-Dekabr'; III: 1911 (sobst. vlast'iu); I: 1912; II: 1912 (sobst. vlast'iu); I: 1913; II: 1913 (sobst. vlast'iu); I: 1914; 1915 1-363, 364-783, 784-1107.

9 Municipalities (Rus 601). Zhurnal Gos. Soveta po predstavleniiam MVD k proektu gorodskogo polozheniia 1891-92. Svod mnenii gubernskikh nachal'stv ob izmeneniiakh v deistvuiushchem gorodskom polozhenii 16 iiunia 1870 g., 246 pp., 79 pp., 26 pp., 19 pp., and 13 pp.

10 Monetary reform (Rus 672). Volume I: Raboty komissii, Vysochaishe uchrezhdennoi 6 oktiabria 1895 g. (Zhurnal komissii; Soobrazheniia chlenov komissii; Zapiski sveduiushchikh lits, podannye v komissiiu; Materialy, sostavlennye dlia ko issii ee deloproizvodstvom). Volume II: Ocherk khoda dela ob ustroistve denezhnoi sistemy v Gos. Sovete 1837-39. Letter of S. Iu. Witte to V. K. Pleve (18 March 1896, 8 April 1896). Izvlecheniia iz vsepoddanneishikh dokladov byvshego ministra finansov Vyshnegradskogo komiteta finansov. Sessii 19, 27, 28 marta; 1 i 2 aprelia 1896. Protokoly zasedanii Soedinennykh Departamentov zakonov Gos. Ekonomii i Grazhdanskikh i Dukhonvnykh Del po delu ispravleniia denezhnogo obrashcheniia. Zasedanie 20 aprelia 1896. Ocherk denezhnoi reformy v Avstro-Vengrii. 1896. K voprosu ob ustoichivosti aktivnogo balansa russkoi vneshnei torgovli. Mezhdunarodnyi raschetnyi balans Rossii. Ministerstvo finansov. Osobaia kantseliariia po kreditnoi chasti. 19 oktiabria 1896 g.

11 Student disorders (Rus 677). Zapiski i zhurnaly, predstavlennye v soveshchanii ministrov i predsedatelei Departamentov Gos. Soveta po voprosu o preduprezhdenii i prekrashchenii massovykh besporiadkov v vysshikh uchebnykh zavedeniiakh. 1905 g.

12 Court reform (Rus 697 E64). Bound in 33 vols. (1863) are: Zamechaniia o razvitii osnovnykh polozhenii preobrazovaniia sudebnoi chasti v Rossii. Zamechaniia o primenenii v Sibiri osnovnykh polozhenii preobrazovaniia sudebnoi chasti. Raboty o vvedenii reformy: materialy --soobrazheniia Gos. Kantseliarii, soobrazheniia Komissii Vysoch. uchrezhdennoi pri Gos. Kantseliarii dlia nachertaniia proektov polozhenii o preobrazovanii sudebnoi chasti. Raboty iuristov-praktikov po preobrazovaniiu sudebnoi chasti. Zamechaniia ministra Iustitsii na proekt uchrezhdeniia sudebnykh mest. Zhurnal soedinnenykh departamentov zakonov i grazhdanskikh del Gos. Soveta s preobrazovaniem sudebnoi chasti. Sudebno-statisticheskie svedeniia po Khar'kovskoi gubernii. Ob"iasnitel'naia zapiska k proektu uchrezhdeniia sudebnykh mest. Proekt uchrezhdeniia sudebnykh ustanovlenii. Ustav ugolovnogo sudoproizvodstva. Ustav grazhdanskogo sudoproizvodstva. Zamechaniia. Ob"iasnitel'nye zapiski.

13 Court reform (Rus 697 E81). Zhurnaly vysochaishe uchrezhdennoi 17 iiunia 1881 g. komissii dlia izgotovleniia novogo izdaniia sudebnykh ustavov Imp. Aleksandra Nikolaevicha osoboi knigoi.

14 Court reform (Rus 697 E94). 2 sets of bound vols. are under this call number. The first, in 45 vols., 1894-1900, comprises: Vysochaishe uchrezhdennaia komissiia dlia peresmotra zakonopolozhenii po sudebnoi chasti (Podgotovitel'nye materialy; Ustav grazhdanskogo sudoproizvodstva; Ob"iasnitel'naia zapiska uchrezhdeniia). The second set (9 vols., 1905) consists of: Proekt novoi redaktsii uchrezhdeniia sudebnykh ustanovlenii; Vyrabotannyi Vysoch. uchrezhdennoiu komissiei dlia peresmotra zakonopolozhenii po sudebnoi chasti i izmenennyi Min. iustitsii; Proekt novoi redaktsii ustava grazhdanskogo sudoproizvodstva; Proekt novoi redaktsii ugolovnogo sudoproizvodstva.

15 Chernigov peasant office (Russ 748 E62). Zhurnaly Chernigovskogo gubernskogo po krest'ianskim delam prisutstviia, 3 vols., 1862-64.

16 Censorship (Rus 755 E70). Materialy dlia peresmotra tsenzury 1870 g., 5 vols.

17 Court calendar (Rus 766 E83). Pridvornyi kalendar' 1888-1917.

18 St. Petersburg Duma (Rus 769). Izvestiia 1876-1917.

19 Kakhanov Commission (Rus 769 E81). Materialy Kakhanovskoi Komissii. These materials, 1880s, come from an important commission investigating peasant self-government and village affairs; conservative officials succeeded in quashing its reform proposals while still in committee.

20 Municipalities (Rus 769 F03). Reformy SPB gorodskogo upravleniia. 1903 g. MVD. Departament Khoziaistvennyi. 1903 g., 139 pp. Proekt--polozhenie ob obshchestvennom upravlenii goroda SPB, 44 pp. Prilozheniia, 128 pp., 99 pp., 65 pp., 127 pp., 97 pp., etc. Pervonachal'nyi proekt, 56 pp. Zhurnal Soveshchaniia, 78 pp.

21 Note: The Hoover Institution at Stanford, California, also has the Osobye zhurnaly of the Council of Ministers; a microfilm copy is available for purchase. Nearly all remaining items cited above appear to be unique in the United States.

Finding Aids: The library has an unpublished descriptive list of holdings entitled "Harvard Collection 1800-1915" (from which the preceding information was drawn).

MA 24
MUSEUM OF COMPARATIVE ZOOLOGY LIBRARY
(THE AGASSIZ MUSEUM)
HARVARD UNIVERSITY
26 Oxford Street
Cambridge, Massachusetts 02138
(617-495-3946)

1 Archives. 1810-present, ca. 280 cu. ft. (additions expected). Contain correspondence between Russian and American scientists. Russian-born correspondents include Alexander Omfrievich Kovalevskii (1840-1901), Konstantin Dmitrievich Khrushchev (b. 1852), Sergei Ivanovich Ognev (b. 1886), Boris Stepanovich Vinogradov (b. 1891), and Sergei Sergeevich Turov (b. 1891). Correspondents on the American side include Alexander Agassiz (1835-1910) and Glover Morrill Allen (1878-1942).

2 Fish Department Records. In process. Include correspondence of Nikolai Borodin, curator (1928-35), with scientific institutions and individuals in the Soviet Union, ca. 1 ft.

3 Johan Koren. Papers, 1910-15, 18 items. Ornithological collector. Diaries of his expeditions in Alaska and the Bering Strait region. Notes on birds and mammals, and descriptions of village life; also photographs.

MA 25
HARVARD THEATRE COLLECTION
PUSEY LIBRARY
HARVARD UNIVERSITY
Cambridge, Massachusetts 02138
(617-495-2445)

1 Henry Wadsworth Longfellow Dana (1881-1950). Papers, ca. 1890-1945, 100+ boxes. Lecturer, New School of Social Research, 1921-32, and leading American expert on Soviet theatre. The bulk of the material relates to Russian/ Soviet theatre, drama, opera, and film (1895-1945). Includes hundreds of still photographs of major productions by V. Meyerhold, A. Tairov, and others; rare theatre posters; programs, pamphlets, and reviews--mostly collected on his trips to the Soviet Union, 1927-35; manuscript lecture notes and drafts of articles; correspondence with M. Gorkii, N. Evreinov, Alexandra Tolstoi, Upton Sinclair (concerning Que Viva Mexico!), and others; plays in script form, unpublished; clippings from a great variety of sources; and Dana's notebooks. Information on the Moscow Art Theatre, Kamerny Theatre, V. Mayakovsky, N. Pogodin, V. Katayev, V. Meyerhold, A. Afinogenov, Jewish theatre, ballet, the Moscow Children's Theatre, Moscow theatre festivals, opera, the Bolshoi Theatre, the films of Sergei Eisenstein, and productions of works by A. Chekhov, M. Gorkii, I. S. Turgenev, and N. Gogol. Much of the material was used in the compilation of Dana's Handbook on Soviet Drama, 1938. He also wrote Drama in Wartime Russia, 1943, and edited Seven Soviet Plays, 1945. Dana knew K. Stanislavsky, A. Lunacharsky, Eisenstein, Mayakovsky, and Meyerhold. He was a member of the American Russian Institute and of the American League for Peace and Democracy. Restricted while cataloguing is in process. Unpublished finding aids.

2 Nikolai Grigorevich Sergeev (1876-1951). Collection, 1892-1913, ca. 270 items. Ballet master at the Mariinsky Theatre and ballet producer. Materials on Russian ballet and ballet music, programs of the Mariinsky Theatre, production drawings by Konstantin Alekseevich Korovin, synopses by Sergeev, and dance notations by Vladimir Stepanov (1826-76). Roland John Wiley, "Dances from Russia: An Introduction to the Sergejev Collection," Harvard Library Bulletin (January 1976); and an unpublished finding aid.

MA 26
HARVARD UNIVERSITY ARCHIVES
PUSEY LIBRARY
HARVARD UNIVERSITY
Cambridge, Massachusetts 02138
(617-495-2461)

MASSACHUSETTS - HARVARD UNIVERSITY ARCHIVES MA 26

1 Sergius Ivanovich Chermayeff (fl. ca. 1895-1949). Papers, 1945-49, 1 folder. Architect. Material pertaining to the American Society of Planners and Architects. (NUCMC 76-1967)

2 Samuel Hazard Cross (1891-1946). Papers, 9 ft. and 30 vols. Harvard specialist in Slavic languages and literatures. Correspondence, teaching materials, writings, etc.

3 Merle Fainsod (1907-1972). Papers, ca. 1930-72, 33 ft. Harvard University librarian and teacher of government. In part, typed transcripts, photocopies, and notes from the Smolensk Archives (see also Widener Library) for his book Smolensk Under Soviet Rule (1958). Correspondence, notes, manuscripts of writings and speeches, and teaching material. Access restricted. (NUCMC 76-1952)

4 George Vasilievich Florovsky (b. 1893). Papers, ca. 1960s, 2 folders. Orthodox priest. Father Florovsky has written extensively on the history of the Eastern Church, Russian orthodoxy, and other religious themes. Biographical data, correspondence, and bibliographies. (NUCMC 76-1966)

5 Michael Karpovich (1888-1959). Correspondence, 1943, 2 items. Linguist and historian of Russia. (NUCMC 76-1967)

6 Wassily Leontieff (b. 1906). Papers, ca. 1920-68, 11 ft. Economics professor, winner of the Nobel Prize. Correspondence, notes, writings, and teaching material, a small part of which relates to Russia. Access restricted. (NUCMC 76-1982)

7 Russian Research Center. Administrative records, 1947-present, ca. 50 ft. (additions expected). Correspondence, financial records, etc. Includes material on the establishment and results of the Soviet refugee interview program run by Harvard scholars after World War II. More information about this project is under the entry for the Harvard Russian Research Center Library.

8 Harlow Shapley (1885-1972). Papers, ca. 1902-65, 126 boxes. Astronomer and director of the Harvard College Observatory. Includes materials he gathered on the American Committee for Emigré Writers and Arists and on the Program for Russian-American Amity. (NUCMC 71-106)

9 Leo Wiener (1862-1939). Papers, n.d., 2 ft. Teacher of Slavic languages and literature. Manuscripts of his scholarly writings, and notes.

Restrictions: Although some limitations have been noted above, details on the nature of the restrictions have not. Information on these matters is available from the archives staff. Write in advance for all collections.

Finding Aids: Descriptive Guide to the Harvard University Archives, compiled by Clark Elliott (1974). Shelflists and some inventories, unpublished, for the listed collections.

MA 27
RUSSIAN RESEARCH CENTER LIBRARY
HARVARD UNIVERSITY
1737 Cambridge Street
Cambridge, Massachusetts 02138
(617-495-4030)

The RRC has 11 file cabinets of questionnaires of interview transcripts and about 60 unpublished reports, all generated by the so-called "Refugee Program." After World War II Harvard scholars, supported by U.S. air force funds, gathered information from Russian displaced persons and "non-returnees" ("nevozvrashchentsy") then living in Germany. About 2,000 persons completed a general questionnaire in writing (schedule A). Of these individuals, professional people (doctors, lawyers, writers), priests, actors, and others were then asked to complete a second written questionnaire and to have an oral interview (schedule B). This involved 350 persons. Another group, representing a social and economic cross-section of the total number, went through a separate oral interview (schedule C).

The information gathered, from ca. 1945-54, covers such subjects as the Soviet family; health, medicine, and doctors in the USSR; religion; and work conditions. The material became the basis for 2 books, both published by the Harvard University Press: Raymond Bauer and Alex Inkeles, The Soviet Citizen (1959) and R. Bauer, A. Inkeles, and Clyde Kluchohn, How the Soviet System Works (1956); and the data have also been used in many other works of the Harvard Project on the Soviet Social System. Some of the material is duplicated in the Russian Research Center holdings of the University Archives. At present there is no access possible to these files; the collection is closed until final disposition and organization of the holdings can be arranged and a manual for using the archive can be reproduced.

Note: In addition, the library has 2 drawers of materials relating to the work of Professors Carl Friedrich and Merle Fainsod.

MA 28
TOZZER LIBRARY
PEABODY MUSEUM OF ARCHAEOLOGY AND ETHNOLOGY
HARVARD UNIVERSITY
21 Divinity Avenue
Cambridge, Massachusetts 02138
(617-495-2253)

Jaroslav Pasternak (1892-1969). Papers, in process, 37 file boxes and 3 notebooks. Ukrainian-born archaeologist. Field notes, diaries, and other papers, some relating to his work in the Ukraine and in Czechoslovakia, where he excavated at 72 sites. Unpublished finding aid. Currently closed because the archive has not been organized.

MA 29
UKRAINIAN RESEARCH INSTITUTE
HARVARD UNIVERSITY
1581-1583 Massachusetts Avenue
Cambridge, Massachusetts 02138
(617-495-5224)

1 Michal Bazansky (b. 1910). Papers, 1949-74, ca. 700 folders in 8 boxes. Literary scholar and political-social activist in Detroit, Michigan. Letters and clippings.

2 James D. Bratush (b. 1893). Correspondence, ca. 160 items in 2 boxes. Rochester political leader. With Ukrainian political leaders in Galicia and in emigration.

3 Stepan Duszenko. Papers, 1 folder. Ukrainian community and political leader, Buffalo, New York.

4 George M. Kossatch (b. 1909). Photoarchives, in 1 box, ca. 30 items. Writer. Photographs document his trips to the Ukraine.

5 Bohdan Krawciw (1904-1975). Collection, 1950-74, 27 boxes. Poet, literary scholar, and bibliographer. Contains ca. 2,200 folders of clippings dealing with Ukrainian humanistic studies, and relating to his work Ukraine: A Concise Encyclopedia.

6 Zenon Kuzela (1882-1952). Correspondence, 1914-20, 2 folders. Philologist in Berlin. Relates to his activities in Ukrainian publishing. Items are photocopies.

7 Mykhailo Lomac'kyj (b. 1886). Papers, 1 box. Writer. Closed until 1 January 1982.

8 Mykola Ponedilok. Papers, 1960s, 5 boxes. Satirist, living in New York. Correspondence with publishers and drafts of his novels.

9 Avhustyn Stefan (b. 1893). Papers, 1950s-present, 4 boxes. Carpatho-Ukrainian political leader. Correspondence, clippings, and notes for his scholarly works.

10 Ukrainian Student Movement (CESUS). Records, 1920s-1974, ca. 27 cartons. Information about life in emigration from the 1920s. Published and unpublished material.

MA 30
M.I.T. HISTORICAL COLLECTIONS
Room N52-260
265 Massachusetts Avenue
Cambridge, Massachusetts 02139
(617-253-4444)

Harvard-M.I.T. Eclipse Expedition to Ak Bulak, Soviet Central Asia, in 1936. An expedition undertaken in 1936 under the leadership of Donald H. Menzel of the Harvard Observatory. Included are photos of Ak Bulak (80 photos); Armenia (3); Bakhchisarai (23), with scenes of the khan's palace; Batum (3); Crimea (56), with scenes of Vorontsov's palace, Alupka, and of the tsar's palace; Livadia (19); Kiev (14); Kuibyishev (5); Leningrad (30); Moscow (43); and Rostov-on-Don (9). There are also films of the eclipse expedition and of accompanying travel in Europe.

MA 31
UNIVERSITY FILM CENTER
MASSACHUSETTS INSTITUTE OF TECHNOLOGY
18 Vassar Street 20B-120
Cambridge, Massachusetts 02139
(617-253-7612)

The University Center houses an archive of 600 films, a very small portion of which consists of Russian films. These include:

Alexander Nevsky (S. Eisenstein), 1938, 107 min., b/w, English subtitles; Battleship Potemkin (S. Eisenstein), 1925, 67 min., b/w, English subtitles; Bed and Sofa (Abram Room), 1935, 72 min. b/w, English subtitles; Bezhin Meadow (S. Eisenstein), 1935, 30 min., b/w, English subtitles; Cranes are Flying (M. Kalatozov), 1957, 94 min., b/w, English subtitles; Earth (A. Dovzhenko), 1930, 54 min., b/w, English subtitles; End of St. Petersburg (V. I. Pudovkin), 1927, 80 min., b/w, English subtitles; Man with a Movie Camera (Dziga Vertov), 1929, 66 min., b/w, English subtitles; Mother (V. I. Pudovkin), 1926, 116 min., b/w, English subtitles; Strike (S. Eisenstein), 1925, 90 min., b/w, English subtitles; Ten Days (October) (S. Eisenstein), 1928, 125 min., b/w, English subtitles; Storm over Asia (V. I. Pudovkin), 1928, 90 min., b/w, English subtitles.

Note: These films are circulated among schools (e.g., Boston University, Wellesley) that are members of the Center.

MA 32
ARTHUR AND ELIZABETH SCHLESINGER LIBRARY ON THE HISTORY OF WOMEN IN AMERICA
(formerly, THE WOMEN'S ARCHIVES)
RADCLIFFE COLLEGE
3 James Street
Cambridge, Massachusetts 02138
(617-495-8647/8648)

1 Alice Stone Blackwell (1857-1950). Papers, 1888-1911, 2 folders. Editor of the Woman's Journal, a suffrage organ, 1881-1917. Primarily material about her work with The Friends of Russian Freedom, including letters to Isaac A. Hourwich, 1904-1908, and to George Kennan, 1906-11. Also, an ALS from Frances Willard to Kennan. All letters to Kennan are photocopies. (NUCMC 77-1727)

2 Vera (Micheles) Dean (1903-1972). Papers, 1929-[61], 6 boxes plus 3 cartons (unprocessed addenda). Writer. She traveled extensively in Europe and published widely on foreign affairs. Manuscript of her book on Russia, some travel notes, speeches, and articles. Material on the USSR during World War II. (NUCMC 61-3507).

3 Ruth Holden (1890-1917). Papers, 1907-61, .5 box. Red Cross nurse. In January 1916 she went to Russia with the first Millicent Fawcett Medical Unit to establish maternity hospitals for Polish refugees. She learned Russian and Polish, and served as interpreter and courier for the unit. From Petrograd she later went on to Kazan, working at a hospital for Polish refugee children and also studying paleobotany at the university there. She traveled extensively in Russia to distribute supplies. Stricken with typhoid fever in January 1917, she caught meningitis when nearly recovered and died at Kazan in April. Mainly letters written by her, 1907-17, to her parents or to Louise Hodge Lahee, a Radcliffe classmate. They speak of the hardships involved in her work. Unpublished inventory.

4 Lena Kontorovitch. Violinist. Autograph, 21 February 1911, and autograph with musical notes, February 1911. (Part of the E. H. Smith Collection)

5 Anne Kalen Krich (b. 1895). Papers, [ca. 1960], 1 folder. Autobiographical sketches entitled "Stories from the Shtetl," dealing with a Jewish family's life in a Ukrainian village, family and village relationships, and the pogrom of 1905.

6 Mary Melinda (Kingsbury) Simkhovitch (1867-1951). Papers, 1850-51, 4 ft. and unprocessed addition, ca. 3.5 ft. Social economist. Married to the Russian-born economic historian Vladimir Simkhovitch (d. 1959). Includes folder with photos and letters of Vladimir Simkhovitch. (NUCMC 61-3458)

7 Louise Stoughton (1851-1886). Papers, 1877-79, 66 items. Niece of Edward Wallace Stoughton, U.S. plenipotentiary to Russia in the 1870s. She accompanied him. 63 letters and 3 stories describe her travels in Europe, social life, customs, and her experiences in Russia. (NUCMC 61-1784) Available on microfilm.

8 Eliza Ingersoll (Bowditch) van Loon. Papers, 1906-1907, 69 items. Wife of the journalist and author Hendrik Willem van Loon, who was an Associated Press correspondent in Moscow and Warsaw. Her personal letters describe political and social events in Russia and Poland. Unpublished inventory (NUCMC 74-941). Available on microfilm.

9 Mary Winsor. Papers, 1917-40, 13 folders. Suffragist. Personal papers and articles concerning women in Russia, etc. Unpublished inventory (NUCMC 61-3502).

Finding Aid: Arthur and Elizabeth Schlesinger Library on the History of Women in America. The Manuscript Inventories and the Catalogs of the Manuscripts, Books and Pictures, 3 vols. (Boston: G. K. Hall, 1973).

MA 33
MR. OSVALDS AKMENTINS--PRIVATE COLLECTION
P.O. Box 48
Dorchester, Massachusetts 02122
(617-266-1762, LPS)
(617-825-6346, home)

Mr. Akmentins, vice-president of the Latvian Press Society in America, has a collection, 1 box at present, of correspondence, newspaper clippings, and other material pertaining primarily to the relations between Latvia and Soviet/Russian authorities. Included are lists of Latvian intellectuals who were deported to Siberia by the Soviet Union during the years 1940-41 or were "imprisoned, deported, killed or persecuted after the end of . . . World War II in Latvia under Soviet occupation"; information on the deportation of farmers; and material on the dissident movement in Latvia, 1940 to the present. Access is restricted and letters of recommendation are required.

MA 34
LATVIAN HERITAGE FOUNDATION (LATVISKĀ MANTOJUMA FONDS)
c/o Olgerts Kutcers, Treasurer
14 Orchard Street
Jamaica Plain, Massachusetts 02130
(617-522-0315)

The Foundation's archives include the original tapes of its radio program, "Spotlight on Latvia," which features Latvian music and artists with English commentary. The program began in 1969 and continues to the present. (Copies of the first 7 years of broadcast tapes are in the Boston Public Library under restricted access conditions.) Access requires letter stating purpose of research; appointment made at least 1 month in advance; and letters of recommendation.

MA 35
INTERNATIONAL MARINE ARCHIVES, INC.
Old Town Building
Nantucket, Massachusetts 02554
(617-228-1821)

Russia Company, London, England. Records, 1667-1955, 15 microfilm reels. Complete set of the court minute books of the British company which traded with Russia (also known as the Muscovy Company and the Company of Merchants Trading with Russia). Materials cover the period 2 March 1667-10 November 1955. Originals are in the Guildhall Library, London. Only 2 or 3 complete sets exist at present in the world. To cite or reproduce, permission must be obtained from the Guildhall Library. (NUCMC 75-703)

MA 36
PROFESSOR NIKITA D. ROODKOWSKY--PRIVATE COLLECTION
10 University Drive
Natick, Massachusetts 01760

Professor Roodkowsky is in possession of the following materials: (a) A collection of correspondence, newspaper clippings, and other materials pertaining to the activities of anti-communist organizations in the United States during the late 1920s and early 1930s. Among the groups documented are the Circle of Russian Culture, of which Roodkowsky was a member, and the National Russian Student Christian Association (composed of the alumni of the Russian Students' Fund). (b) 25 letters from Mikhail Fedorov, minister of commerce before the Revolution, pertaining to his anti-communist activities. (c) An album of photographs taken on a large Russian estate in the Kaluga government, 1898-1902. All the photographs are well-preserved and show scenes of daily life such as outdoor games, teas in the afternoon, outings. (d) The diary of Roodkowsky's father for the year 1911. Most of the diary deals with everyday activities of the family, but it also documents Roodkowsky's work as a member and a secretary of the council of the military governor of St. Petersburg, General Drachevsky.

MA 37
FREE PUBLIC LIBRARY
613 Pleasant Street
New Bedford, Massachusetts 02741
(617-999-6291)

1 Memoranda and Other Documents Connected with the Local History of New Bedford (Library safe, shelf 3, envelope 26). Contains an unpublished document with information on the Hoffming, a Russian cartel ship which delivered American prisoners from Dartmoor Prison in England to New Bedford (1813).

2 William Rotch, Jr. (1759-1850). Papers, 1772-1810, 5 vols. Merchant. Includes ca. 6 manifests on ships he sent to St. Petersburg and Archangel (account book, letterbook, ledger, invoice book, and journal). Index to letterbook.

MA 38
OLD DARTMOUTH HISTORICAL SOCIETY
18 Johnny Cake Hill
New Bedford, Massachusetts 02740
(617-997-0046)

1 George Howland (1781-1852). Business records, 1803-50, ca. 2 ft. Merchant. He sent vessels to Archangel from 1810 to trade with the Russians.

2 Thaddeus Pickens (1774-1810). Papers, 1800-1809, 2 boxes. Sea captain. Commanded vessels trading with St. Petersburg in 1802, 1804, and 1805. 1 letter from Cronstadt ca. 1808 includes a manifest and list of prices.

3 William Rotch, Jr. (1759-1850). Letterbooks, 1796-1808, ca. 3 ft. New Bedford merchant. Letters contain substantial amounts of data on trade with Russia and on the involvement of Quakers in this commerce. Rotch sent as many as 3 vessels a year to Russia, sometimes chartering others for the same purpose. Trade was chiefly in hemp.

MA 39
COLLEGE ARCHIVES
SMITH COLLEGE
Northampton, Massachusetts 01063
(413-584-2700 x 502)

Sophie Satin (1879-1975). Papers, ca. 1900-76, 1 box. Botanist and feminist. Taught at Moscow University and Smith College. Includes typed memoirs with her handwritten emendations; photographs of her (in Russia and the U.S.) and her mother, Mrs. Alexander Satin; biographical material; Russian and English versions of her unpublished book on women's education in Russia; clippings; and a scrapbook honoring her, presented to the Archives by Satin's relatives, Oxana and Kyriena Siloti. The memoirs concern Satin's career, the Rachmaninoff family (relatives), and the zemstvo reforms in Russia.

MA 40
SOPHIA SMITH COLLECTION
WOMEN'S HISTORY ARCHIVE
SMITH COLLEGE
Northampton, Massachusetts 01063
(413-584-2700 x 622)

1 Madeleine Zabriskie Doty (1879-1963). Papers, 1907-62, 1 ft. Author, World War I newspaper correspondent, and social reformer. She was in Russia in 1917-18. Letters to her family describe her trip there, experiences in the revolution, and impressions of events. Also includes her press credentials in Russian from the U.S. ambassador (she represented Century Magazine and The Atlantic Monthly); a document giving her permission from the Committee of Inquiry of the Military-Revolutionary Committee to enter the Peter and Paul Fortress; and the same, to enter sessions of the Revolutionary Tribunal court and of the Constituent Assembly. There are photographs of 1917 events, such as the May 1st celebration on the Nevsky Prospect, a demonstration of soldiers' wives, mass meetings, and a soldier's funeral; and her incomplete, unpublished autobiography. A few photos are of Doty in Russia and one is of A. Kerensky. (NUCMC 67-556)

2 William Lloyd Garrison (1838-1909). Family papers, 1830-1967, 70 ft. (additions expected). Businessman and reformer. Correspondence, diaries, speeches, photos, printed matter. Includes an ALS of Henry George, Jr., New York, 18 September 1909, to Garrison, which speaks of having a meal with Leo Tolstoi on his Tula estate and of Tolstoi's saying he expected soon to see George's father, 3 pp.; an appeal on behalf of the Society of American Friends of Russian Freedom, signed by Garrison as treasurer, for contributions to aid Russians suffering from the famine, 1892?; and a TL to Tolstoi, 1905, signed with the initials W. L. G[arrison]., sending him a collection of William Lloyd Garrison's works and praising Henry George. (NUCMC 69-487)

3 Emma Goldman (1869-1940). Papers, 1911-36, 1 box. Anarchist and feminist. Chiefly printed matter; also, correspondence and biographical material. (NUCMC 77-1785)

4 Florence Haskell (Corliss) Lamont (1873-1952). Papers, ca. 1880-1968, 9 ft. Philanthropist, author, world traveler, and wife of Thomas William Lamont. Family ALS and typed letters, 1920s-1952, concern the USSR and the possible overthrow of the Bolsheviks in 1921. Also, miscellaneous speeches and pamphlets from 1946 relating to conditions in Russia and Soviet-American relations. Access restricted. (NUCMC 69-490)

5 National Council of American-Soviet Friendship. 2 mimeographed works: Women in the Soviet Union (New York, 1952), 9 pp.; and Family Life in the U.S.S.R., a study guide for leaders (New York, n.d.), 5 ll.

6 Sophie Satina (1879-1975). Botanist, geneticist, and pioneer in female higher education. Born and educated in Russia, Moscow University teacher, emigrated in 1921 and became Smith College professor. "Education of women in pre-revolutionary Russia" (translated from the Russian by Alexandra F. Poustchine), offset, 153 pp.

7 Ukrainian National Women's League of America, Inc. Reports, 1960-67, 1 box. Typed copies of reports given at annual meetings of the National Council of Women (not every year).

8 Mary van Kleeck (1883-1972). Papers, 1904-72, 71 ft. Social reformer. Correspondence, printed matter, speeches, and miscellaneous documents. Letters from the 1930s of P. A. Bogdanov, S. V. Shakhnovskaya, R. G. Tugwell, T. Paul-Sachs, Paul Douglas, E. C. Lindeman, and van Kleeck speak of the USSR; 1 TL of van Kleeck to M. L. Cooke (5 April 1933) mentions recognition of the Soviet Union. Includes 4 addresses given by van Kleeck: "Observations on Scientific Management in the USSR," 1 December 1932; at a meeting of the Why Club, 7 April 1933, on the USSR; "NIRA vs. PIATILETKA," August 1933; and "World Democracy Needs the Soviet Union," July 1941. Other pertinent materials include radio broadcasts, printed matter, clippings, a collection of signatures for a petition to the president about the USSR, 1934, and a signed statement urging the USSR be invited to a World Economic Conference, n.d. Other references: National Council of American-Soviet Friendship, Russian War Relief, and V. I. Meshlauk. (NUCMC 77-1832)

9 Ruth Woodsmall (1883-1963). Papers, 1906-63, ca. 72 ft. YWCA executive. Includes a letter to or about Countess Vera Tolstoi, 28 March 1922, an ALS of Merlen Neumann, 17 September 1959, to Woodsmall, about N. Kruschev [Khrushchev], and some photos of Russian scenes, including a nun and the entrance to the Moscow YWCA. Unpublished index (NUCMC 69-507).

10 Note: Under the names of individual Russian/Soviet women (e.g., Alexandra Kollontai, Lesya Ukrainka [Larissa Kossach], Sofia Kovalevskaya, and N. Krupskaya) and specific subjects (communism, Ukrainian women) and countries (USSR), the card catalogues list a variety of materials, mostly printed,

including articles and reprints, clippings, and pamphlets.

Finding Aid: Catalogs of the Sophia Smith Collection: Women's History Archive, 7 vols. (Boston: G. K. Hall, 1975); vols. 6-7 for manuscripts.

MA 41
JAMES DUNCAN PHILLIPS LIBRARY
ESSEX INSTITUTE
Salem, Massachusetts 01970
(617-744-3390)

1 John H. Andrews (b. 1775). Papers, ca. 1719-1874, 5 boxes. Salem merchant. Primarily correspondence, business and personal, regarding his shipping operations. Letters from Jeremiah Page on the brig Patriot concern the shipment of oil from Naples and Tripoli to St. Petersburg. Letters from commission merchants (1822) refer to bankruptcies in Russia, conflicts between Russia and Turkey and the interruption of trade with Russia, particularly in oil. (NUCMC 62-3372)

2 John Bagley (fl. ca. 1810). Papers, 1807-12, 1 envelope. Sea captain. Personal letters written from Russia, Havana, and Bordeaux. (NUCMC 62-3672)

3 Crowninshield Family. Papers, 1767-1903, 18 ft. Contains material on early Russian-American relations.

4 Derby Family. Papers, 1715-1858, 12 ft., 34 vols. Merchants. Had commercial relations with Russia.

5 Nathan Endicott (b. 1790?). Letterbook, 1838-41, 1 vol. Salem merchant. Includes shipping information about Russian trade, and letters to St. Petersburg.

6 Samuel A. Fabens (1812-1899). Letterbook, 1842-53, 1 vol. Sea captain. Letterbook and some sailing orders relate to his trading voyages in the ship Ariosto. St. Petersburg, Havana, Rio de Janeiro, and New Orleans were among his ports of call. Unpublished finding aid. (NUCMC 62-3559)

7 William Rufus Gray (1783-1831). Letterbook, 1818-30, 1 vol. Salem merchant. Includes business correspondence discussing trade with St. Petersburg.

8 Hale Family. Papers, 1773-1907, 16 boxes. Merchants of Newburyport, Massachusetts. Had commercial dealings with Russia in the first half of the 19th c.

9 Marine Logbooks. Ca. 1,500 items, 18th-19th c. Under this heading in the card catalogue the researcher will find many logbooks containing information relating to voyages to Russian ports and references to trade with Russia.

10 Josiah Orne (1768-1825). Papers, 1747-1878, 4 ft. Includes some correspondence relating to early Russian-American relations.

11 John Osgood (1758-1826). Papers, 1802-1808, 1 box. Salem ship's captain and merchant. Includes shipping papers, accounts, legal documents, etc. relating to the ship Commerce, which traded in Russia (Cronstadt). Also, correspondence and financial papers on Osgood's acting as agent for Countess Apraxin and her son Basil, who visited the U.S.

12 Benjamin Pickman (1740-1819). Papers, 1762-1842, 4.5 ft., 12 vols. Salem merchant. Includes some shipping papers on Russian trade; and ca. 50 letters between Richard Rogers at Archangel and his brother John at St. Petersburg, 1811.

13 Pingree Family. Papers, 1700-1933, 360 ft. Merchants and businessmen. Had some commercial contacts with Russia ca. 1820-60. Inquire at the Essex Institute.

14 John Prince. Papers, 1732-1838, 3 ft. Salem merchant. Includes shipping material related to Russian trade.

15 Salem Customs House. Records, 1789-ca. 1900, thousands of documents, uncatalogued and unprocessed. Customs papers from the Massachusetts ports of Essex, Gloucester, Marblehead, Newburyport, Ipswich, and Salem-Beverly. A substantial, but undetermined, portion of local trade was with St. Petersburg. On deposit from the Salem customs house. Restriction: Inquire at the Essex Institute.

16 [Richard Wheatland]. "The Wheatlands of Salem and Their Voyages," typescript, pertaining in part to the first American voyage to Archangel.

17 Richard G. Wheatland. Logbook, 1831-32, 1 vol. Includes voyage to St. Petersburg on the brig Eliza.

MA 42
PHILLIPS LIBRARY
PEABODY MUSEUM
East India Square
Salem, Massachusetts 01970
(617-745-1876)

1 John L. Bates and Company. Records, 1807-96, 12 ft. Correspondence, invoices, contracts, crew accounts and lists, cargo and account books for ca. 300 vessels of a world-wide shipping company of Boston. Includes data on Russian-American commerce in the second quarter of the 19th c. (NUCMC 72-1172)

2 Charles Endicott. Account books and letters, 1858-61. Salem merchant of the firm Phippen and Endicott. Some information on commerce with Russia.

3 John and Robert Hooper. Letterbook, 24 April 1824-January 1831 and 5 May 1831-4 January 1839. Marblehead (Mass.) merchants. Includes references to trade with Russia.

4 Joseph Moseley. Accounts, ship Grand Turk, 1792. Some voyages to St. Petersburg.

5 Thomas B. Osgood. Letterbook, voyage to Russia of the bark Mary, which was captured by Danes and condemned, 1809-11. Sea captain.

6 Thomas Pritchard, Jr. Letterbook, barks Hesper and Massachusetts, 10 July 1850-58 and October 1853, 1 vol. Sea captain of Newburyport, Mass.

7 Note: There is additional information on Russian-American commerce in the second quarter of the 19th c. in 2 other collections which could not be examined: Philemon Putnam Papers and Benjamin Schreve Papers.

MA 43
FOGG LIBRARY
WEYMOUTH HISTORICAL SOCIETY
Columbian Square
South Weymouth, Massachusetts 02190
(617-335-4804)

Ships Commerce & Hector. Correspondence, ca. 1825-40, 41 items. Letters and a few printed items concerning claims against the Russian government arising from the seizure of 2 ships by Russian vessels. The Commerce, owned by Eliphalet Loud and Samuel Bailey, was seized in 1807; the Hector, owned by Israel Thorndike, later. Includes correspondence with the U.S. State Department, Henry Clay, and Daniel Webster. One suit was eventually successful and the Russian government made restitution of 50,000 rubles (MS 30a-d). Researchers are requested to contact Chester B. Kevitt, 41 Columbian Street, South Weymouth, Massachusetts 02190 for information about access.

MA 44
CONNECTICUT VALLEY HISTORICAL MUSEUM
194 State Street
Springfield, Massachusetts 01103
(413-732-3080)

Daniel Harris (1818-1879). Papers, in process, ca. 4 vols. Engineer. Diary and several letters document his trip to Russia in 1859, where he studied the construction of railroad bridges. The letters contain many comments about life, religion, and tourist attractions in Russia. Available by appointment only to qualified scholars. Transcript available on microfilm.

MA 45
ROY G. JINKS
SMITH & WESSON
P.O. Box 2208
Springfield, Massachusetts 01101
(413-781-8300 x 222)

Smith and Wesson was a major arms supplier to Imperial Russia. The firm sold hand weapons to the tsarist regime in 1871-78. It is possible that Smith and Wesson guns, supplied by the U.S. government, not S & W, were used by Russia during World War II. Of nearly 1 million items in the corporate archive and Mr. Roy Jinks's collection, perhaps 1% relates to Russia/USSR. There are relevant letters and sales contracts. Some correspondence with General Alexander Gorloff, a military attaché, concerns sales of revolvers to tsarist security forces.

The materials are owned by Mr. Roy Jinks, Product-Manager-Handguns and Historian, whose permission (and the company's) is necessary to use the holdings. Some indication of the contents of the papers may be obtained from John E. Parson's Smith & Wesson (New York: William Morrow & Co., 1957), Roy G. Jinks's History of Smith & Wesson (Los Angeles: Beinfeld Publishing, 1977), and Jinks's three-part article "Smith & Wesson's Model Three" in the Arms Gazette (August 1974 and succeeding issues).

MA 46
AMERICAN JEWISH HISTORICAL SOCIETY
2 Thornton Road
Waltham, Massachusetts 02154
(617-891-8110)

1 Cyrus Adler (1863-1940). Papers, 1887-1934, 3 ft. Founder of the American Jewish Historical Society, 1892, first president of Dropsie College, Jewish Theological Seminary president, and leader of conservative Judaism in the U.S. Correspondence and other material on Jews in Russia. Correspondents include Theodor Herzl, Max J. Kohler, and Stephen S. Wise. (NUCMC 68-117)

2 American Jewish Congress. Records, 1916-present, 125 ft. and growing. Correspondence, minutes, publications, tape recordings, photos, phonograph records, clippings, and other matter relating to the organization and its work. One of its national commissions is on International Affairs and Israel. There

are references to the Warsaw ghetto and to Soviet Jewry. The Society expects to receive continuing additions to the collection; current holdings go up to 1971. (NUCMC 72-1363)

3 American Jewish Relief Committee for Sufferers from the War. Records, 1914-17, ca. 400 items. Some correspondence concerns requests for help from Americans' relatives in Russia and German-occupied Europe, obtained through the Jewish Colonization Association office in Petrograd and the Hilfsverein der Deutschen Juden. Includes appeal leaflets, circulars, addresses (speeches), and other papers. (NUCMC 72-1364)

4 Baron de Hirsch Fund. Records, 1885-1935, 30 ft. Fund to aid Jewish immigrants. Letters, minutes, reports, financial records, etc. cover both the Fund and a large number of related Jewish organizations. Some items relate to charitable work in Russia. (NUCMC 72-1365)

5 Board of Delegates of American Israelites. Records, 1859-80, 2 ft., 1,500 items. Includes information on pogroms, anti-Semitism, famine, and poverty afflicting the Jews in Russia (and elsewhere). Several letters from a Rabbi Isaac Elhanan Spektor appeal for help for a Jewish community near Kovno. (NUCMC 68-121)

6 Central Committee of America in Aid of Starving Jews in Russia. Receipt book, 1900.

7 Philip Cowen (1853-1943). Papers, 1876-1934, 3 cartons, ca. 1,500 items. Journalist and U.S. immigration official. Correspondence and published material, in English, German, and Russian. Some items concern Count Arthur Cherep-Spiridovich, Russian anti-Semitism, the Russian passport question, ca. 1911, the National Citizens Committee, loans from Jewish bankers to the Russian regime, and immigration to the U.S. from Russia and Eastern Europe. (NUCMC 68-124)

8 Solomon Eudovich (d. 1959). Papers, 1902-40, 50 items. Ritual slaughterer, Torah reader, and adult education teacher. Correspondence and miscellaneous papers, in Hebrew and Yiddish, primarily concerning his emigration from Vilna to England and to South America and his career.

9 Bernhard Felsenthal (1822-1908). Papers, 1856-1920, 2 cartons, 800 items. Rabbi. Material, primarily correspondence, about Jewish religion, social life, and history in Russia and Poland. Letters are in English, German, Hebrew, and French. Cyrus Adler was a correspondent. Index of correspondents. (NUCMC 68-129)

10 Jacob Fishman (1888-1962). Theater collection, 1915-60, 1 ft. Dramatist and director. Includes manuscript translations, in Yiddish, of plays by F. M. Dostoevskii and M. Gorkii. (NUCMC 68-130)

11 Sol Grossbard (b. 1889). Engineer. Typescript, 123 pp., written while with the U.S. Army Signal Corps in Siberia in 1918-19. Attached to the staff of General W. S. Graves, he was in charge of transportation and communication. The manuscript analyzes Allied attitudes and policies toward Russia and its political factions, the intervention, and alternatives to the unsuccessful U.S. policy.

12 Myer Samuel Isaacs (1841-1904). Papers, 1878-98, 73 items. Lawyer and communal leader. Correspondence and clippings concern, in part, Russian anti-Semitism. (NUCMC 68-138)

13 Kishinev Protest Meeting Committee. Records, 1903, 22 items. Correspondence and other papers relating to the committee and its meeting, held 27 May 1903, at Carnegie Hall in New York City. Includes addresses of Robert Stuart MacArthur and former president Grover Cleveland, meeting resolutions, a copy of the appeal sent to Nicholas II, and letters of Lyman Abbott, Newell D. Hillis, and Carl Schurz. (NUCMC 68-142)

14 Max James Kohler (1871-1934). Papers, 1888-1934, 11 ft. Historian, lawyer, and communal leader. Correspondence, reports, notes, and scrapbooks. 2 major interests for him were the liberalization of U.S. immigration and naturalization laws, and the condition of Jews in Russia. (NUCMC 68-143)

15 Jefferson Monroe Levy (1852-1924). Papers, 1901-39, 560 items. Lawyer and U.S. congressman from New York City. Letters, certificates, photos, and clippings. Material covers the suffering of Russian Jews and efforts to help them. (NUCMC 69-606)

16 Lucien Moss (1831-1895). Collection, 1840-95, 12 scrapbooks of newspaper clippings. Contains information on persecution of Jews in Russia, and other subjects.

17 National Citizens Committee. Records, 1911, 777 items. Committee organized to protest Russian abuse of travel and trade provisions of the Treaty of 1832 (e.g., Russian refusal to recognize passports of American Jews). Correspondence from U.S. federal, state, and local government officials, educators, lawyers, businessmen, and non-Jewish religious leaders; also published material, including a report on a mass meeting at Carnegie Hall, 6 December 1911. (NUCMC 68-157)

18 National Committee for the Relief of Sufferers by Russian Massacres. Records, 1905-1909, ca. 1 ft., 1,200 items. Correspondence and reports concern the committee's fundraising efforts in the U.S. on behalf of Russian pogrom survivors, particularly orphans, in both Russia and the United States (émigrés). Some correspondence is with the Russo-Jewish Committee in London. Letters are in English,

Russian, French, German, Hebrew, and Yiddish with various foreign groups. Information on conditions of Jews in Russia during and after the pogroms, the self-defense movement and defense fund, relief action, and emigration. Baron Horace G. Gunzburg in St. Petersburg was among those active in this work. (NUCMC 68-159)

19 People's Relief Committee (Jewish). Records, 1915-24, ca. 24 ft., 55,000 items. Correspondence (international, national, and intra-committee), in Yiddish and English, concerning relief work for Eastern European Jewry (arranged geographically). Among the correspondents: the All-Russian Jewish Public Committee, Central Jewish People's Relief Committee of Courland (Latvia), the Yiddishe Arbeite Helfskomite for Bukovina (Rumania), the Kulture League (Warsaw), and the Kultur League of Lithuania. Also includes newspaper clippings (U.S. and Canadian) and printed matter. (NUCMC 68-165)

20 Union of Orthodox Jewish Congregations of America. Records, 1933-68, 3 ft. Correspondence, minutes, and printed matter. Some relates to Soviet Jewry. (NUCMC 72-11)

21 Selman Abraham Waksman (1888-1973). Papers, 1886-1969, 1 ft. Marine bacteriologist. Some documents in Russian concern his life before emigrating to the U.S. ca. 1910. Travel diaries for 1924-69 cover trips to Europe, Asia, and the Near East. On his travels he met and had discussions with prominent individuals Like Marc Chagall and Vera Weizmann. (NUCMC 72-1389)

22 Stephen S. Wise (1874-1949). Papers, 1841-1968, 191 boxes. New York City rabbi. Correspondence, speeches, articles, etc. pertaining to Zionism, world affairs, and American Jewish issues. Some relate to Russia. Unpublished finding aid (NUCMC 77-50).

23 Simon Wolf (1836-1923). Papers, 1861-1923, 2 cartons, 342 items. Lawyer, judge, communal leader, and U.S. consul general in Egypt. Includes letters exchanged with U.S. congressmen and government officials concerning anti-Semitism in the U.S. and abroad, and the 1832 treaty with Russia (abrogated in 1911). (NUCMC 68-183)

Finding Aids: Preliminary Survey of the Manuscript Collections Found in the American Jewish Historical Society (1967) and Manuscript Collections in the American Jewish Historical Society cataloged Jan. 1968-Jan. 1969 (1969).

MA 47
SPECIAL COLLECTIONS
BRANDEIS UNIVERSITY LIBRARY
415 South Street
Waltham, Massachusetts 02154
(617-647-2513)

William Prokocimer (b. 1883). Papers, ca. 1914-1950s, ca. 40% of 2 boxes. Medical doctor. Austrian imprisoned in a Siberian POW camp during World War I. Includes correspondence, photographs of the POW camp, located at Sretensk, and other items.

MA 48
ARCHIVES BRANCH
FEDERAL ARCHIVES & RECORDS CENTER, GSA
380 Trapelo Road
Waltham, Massachusetts 02154
(617-223-2657)

This repository has some of the microfilms of materials in the National Archives (Washington, D.C.) that pertain to Russia/USSR. For more details, see Charles South, List of National Archives Microfilm Publications in the Regional Archives Branches (Washington: National Archives and Records Service, 1975). Original Russian-related materials in this repository that are not found in the National Archives in Washington are located in RG 36, Customs Records - New England, 18th-20th c., 350 cu. ft. These records include a small percentage of materials relating to Russian-American trade, including impost books, records of goods imported and exported, inward and outward vessel manifests, and records of entrances and clearances of vessels. There may also be Russian-related materials, particularly of a commercial nature, in RG 21, Records of the United States District Courts and United States Circuit Courts, 1789-1945, ca. 7,000 cu. ft., which cover the 6 New England states.

MA 49
PAUL GRABBE--PRIVATE COLLECTION
Box 882
Wellfleet, Massachusetts 02667
(617-349-6823)

The memoirs of General Count Alexander Nikolaevich Grabbe (1867-1947), aide-de-camp to Tsar Nicholas II, are in the possession of his son, Paul Grabbe. They deal with General Grabbe's schooling, his years as aide to Grand Duke Mikhail Nikolaevich, son of Tsar Nicholas I, and his activities as commanding officer of the Konvoy Cossack Regiment, 1914-17. The memoirs, ca. 150 pp., are handwritten in Russian. In addition to the memoirs, Mr.

Grabbe has 250 photographs of the Imperial family taken by his father 1911-17. The photos have never been published, except for the 24 included in Paul Grabbe's memoirs of his early life in Russia, 1902-19, entitled Windows on the River Neva. Access restricted to accredited researchers with a legitimate reason for research. Prior appointment necessary.

MA 50
CHAPIN LIBRARY
WILLIAMS COLLEGE
Williamstown, Massachusetts 01267
(413-597-2462)

1 Bayard H. Christy. 3 letters, December 1918, by and to him, concerning translations and availability in America of Leo Tolstoi's works (2 from Maxwell E. Perkins to him, his to Olga Tolstoi). Also, Russian-English bibliography of Tolstoi's minor works published up to 1918.

2 Julia Ward Howe (1819-1910) and Samuel Gridley Howe (1801-1876). Papers, ca. 1830-1910, ca. 750 items. Author and reformer (J.W.H.); doctor, reformer, and philanthropist (S.G.H.). Includes ca. 100 letters and petitions from Poles in exile following Russian suppression of the revolt of 1830-31, received by Doctor Howe as director of voluntary relief services in Paris and London, 1831-32, and of the Polish Relief Committee in Boston, 1832-35. Unpublished finding aid.

3 Leo Tolstoi (1828-1910). Writer and moralist. "The Prayer for Granddaughter Sonitchka," a fair copy, in Russian and English, written out and translated by Olga Tolstoi for Bayard H. Christy in 1922.

MA 51
AMERICAN ANTIQUARIAN SOCIETY
185 Salisbury Street
Worcester, Massachusetts 01609
(617-755-5221)

1 Adams Family. Letters, 1673-1954, 211 items. Contains 2 letters from John Quincy Adams (1767-1848) when he was minister to Russia, 1809-14. (NUCMC 74-3)

2 Robert Fotherby (fl. ca. 1613). 1 vol., folio. English author and navigator. Kept a journal (attributed) recording 7 whaling ships' voyage from London to the Spitzbergen archipelago (Arctic Ocean) in 1613. The Muscovy Company financed the expedition. The journal, 21 ll., contains details of the geography, wildlife, weather, and whaling. Whaling activities and wildlife are illustrated by 12 watercolors. A map, in poor condition, of part of the Spitzbergen coast is kept loose in the notebook. The complete journal has been published by Samuel F. Haven in Transactions of the AAS ("Voyage to Spitzbergen"), vol. 4. The watercolors are reproduced in Edward Pellham's God's power a providence (1631).

3 Justus Forward. Diaries, 1762-1799. 1 folder, 4 items. Minister. The diaries contain references to political upheavals in Russia.

4 Taylor Family. Papers, 1880-1937. 3 boxes and 1 vol. Correspondence of Charles Henry Taylor (1846-1921) and Charles Henry Taylor, Jr. (1867-1941), who ran the Boston Globe from publishers and journalists, including some letters from Arthur Elliott Sproul, a news correspondent in Russia in 1917.

MA 52
UNIVERSITY ARCHIVES
ROBERT HUTCHINGS GODDARD LIBRARY
CLARK UNIVERSITY
Worcester, Massachusetts 01610
(617-793-7206)

1 Alfred Lewis Pinneo Dennis (1874-1930). Papers, 1887-1930, ca. 40% of 3 ft. Historian. Correspondence, typed transcripts of U.S. State Department archives material, and notes. Includes transcripts of sessions on Soviet foreign policy he chaired at the Williamstown (Mass.) Institute of Politics, July-August 1922. Also, 6 boxes of notes from various sources relating to his The Foreign Policies of Soviet Russia (1924). Unpublished list of folder titles (NUCMC 73-319).

2 Dwight Lee (b. 1898). Papers, 1908-69, 7 ft. Diplomat, professor, and dean of the graduate school, Clark University. Correspondence, research, and teaching materials. Includes materials on the San Francisco Conference of 1945. Lee was a member of the Secretariat. Minutes, reports, and notes on the work of Committee III and about the genesis of the veto, 2 boxes. Unpublished finding aid (NUCMC 73-321).

MICHIGAN

MI 1
ARDIS/RUSSIAN LITERATURE TRIQUARTERLY--
PRIVATE COLLECTION
2901 Heatherway
Ann Arbor, Michigan 48104

Carl R. and Ellendea Proffer have gathered a substantial amount of materials in this collection. Approximately 20,000 pp. of literary manuscripts (books, stories, poems, etc.) from the 19th and (primarily) 20th c. Correspondence with several dozen Russian writers (living) in the USSR and abroad, and with American writers concerning Russian literature and writers. Biographical information on Russian writers, diaries, and related papers. Ca. 1,000 photographs of Russian writers and other subjects. An archive of samizdat materials. Tapes of interviews with literary figures and tapes of poetry readings. Some original art work, illustrating Russian literary works, plus copies of same. In addition, the business correspondence and office records of Russian Literature Triquarterly and Ardis (ca. 1972-present). Written permission of one of the Proffers is required. Specific information on individual holdings is available by written request.

MI 2
GERALD R. FORD PRESIDENTIAL LIBRARY
1000 Beal Avenue
Ann Arbor, Michigan 48109
(313-668-2218)

The new Gerald R. Ford Library building was completed in 1981 and parts of the Ford collection will be opened for research late in 1981. Many of the Russian-related documents in the Ford materials are of a highly classified nature and will be restricted for several years.

Finding Aids: Unpublished finding aids to segments of the Ford papers are being prepared as the collection is processed.

MI 3
INTER-UNIVERSITY CONSORTIUM FOR
POLITICAL AND SOCIAL RESEARCH
P.O. Box 1248
Ann Arbor, Michigan 48106
(313-763-5010)

The archive of the Inter-University Consortium for Political and Social Research (ICPSR) receives, processes, and distributes machine-readable data on social phenomena for over 130 countries. Among its records pertaining to Russia/USSR are the following:

1 Edward E. Azar and Thomas J. Sloan. "Dimensions of Interaction, 1948-1973" (ICPSR 7426). 4 data files. These data files are event summaries derived from the Conflict and Peace Data Bank (COPDAB) Project. Russia is one of the countries included in the study.

2 Richard Cady, Franz Mogdis, and Karen Tidwell. "Major Power Interactions with Less-Developed Countries, 1959-1965" (ICPSR 5005). Data for 89 less-developed countries on 56 variables recorded for 1959, 1961, 1963, and 1965. Variables include such measures as imports and exports, diplomatic representation, visits, communication rates, and proportions of imports from and exports to the major powers. These data were supplied by the Social Science Department, Bendix Corporation. The data set contains selected interactions of the United States, the Soviet Union, the People's Republic of China, and Eastern European countries with the less-developed nations.

3 Nazli Choucri and Robert C. North. "Nations in Conflict: Data on National Growth and International Violence for Six European Major Powers, 1870-1914" (ICPSR 7425). The data were compiled as part of the investigators' study dealing with the dynamics of conflict and warfare and the role of national growth and expansion in that process. The annual aggregate data compiled for the period 1870-1914 on Britain, France, Germany, Italy, Russia, and Austria-Hungary are in 8 categories: national size, colonial size, economic and productivity profile, commercial activity, government budget, alliances, violence, and conflicts of interest.

4 Walter C. Clemens, Jr. "Prospects for Peace, 1973-1977" (ICPSR 5803). A survey of expert opinion on the prospects for peace, 1972-77, using 151 respondents drawn mainly from leading American university centers of international studies, although some U.S. government officials and non-U.S. scholars are also represented. The survey was conducted in early 1973, largely by mail, with a response rate of approximately 1 in 3. A series of 121 questions were asked concerning the likelihood of war and peace in different parts of the world; viability of 1972 SALT accords and prospects for other arms control measures;

alternate scenarios for U.S.-Soviet relations; ranking of the forces most dangerous and conducive to international peace and economic development; likely linkages between trade and political relations among the great powers; expected role of the UN and other international institutions.

5 Barry Hughes and P. Terrence Hopmann. "Dyadic and Multilateral Events, 1948-1970" (ICPSR 5403). Data on 10,000 dyadic and multilateral events involving NATO and Warsaw Treaty nations as well as People's Republic of China, Sweden, North Vietnam, Yugoslavia, North Korea, Mongolia, and Austria. Only actions are included, not purely verbal events such as speeches and resolutions. Events are coded with the Moses/Brody conflict-cooperation scale. The source of the data is Keesing's Contemporary Archive.

6 Milton Lodge. "Soviet Elites in the Post-Stalin Period, 1966" (ICPSR 7521). The data were collected in 1966 to facilitate the exploration of relationships between the demographic and career pattern attributes of the Soviet leadership and attitudinal variance within the leadership. 2 types of data were included in the study: attitudinal and demographic/career pattern data. The attitudinal data were generated by a content analysis of a sample of articles in "representative" Soviet periodicals for the year 1965. A total of 411 cases was obtained. Demographic and career pattern data were collected to supplement the information on the Soviet officials in the attitudinal sample. There were 268 completed cases for these data. The data were received from the Laboratory for Political Research, University of Iowa.

7 Franz Mogdis and Karen Tidwell. "Asia and Major Powers Dyadic Interactions, 1956-1968" (ICPSR 5406). 442 card-images. This study contains data for 221 nation-dyads; 17 Asian nations, 5 major powers (United States, Soviet Union, China, United Kingdom, France) at 13 time points. There are 20 variables of positive and negative interaction measures. Each dyad is coded for each year.

8 Franz Mogdis and Karen Tidwell. "Sino-Soviet Interaction: Project Triad, 1950-1967" (ICPSR 5016). This study consists of an aggregate data set and a perception-interaction data set. The first part of the aggregate data contains 7 measures of economic, demographic, military, and diplomatic national attributes of the Soviet Union and People's Republic of China by year 1950-57. The second part contains data on the trade of and visits by leaders of the USSR and China with 17 less developed countries by year 1959-67. The perception data set consists of information obtained by computer content analysis utilizing Inquirer II. Selected official statements and newspaper content were analyzed for the period 1950-67. Soviet and Chinese perceptions of each other and of the United States are coded as follows: strong, weak, active, passive, negative, and threatening. Each of these perceptions is presented in the original and weighted forms. The interaction part contains measures of Sino-Soviet diplomat communications and trade interactions by year 1950-67. The latter was supplied by the Social Sciences Department, Bendix Corporation.

9 United States Information Agency. "World Survey II: Attitudes Toward Domestic and Foreign Affairs, 1964" (ICPSR 7048). Information for the study was obtained from 466 respondents, 2 cards of data per respondent, in the form of approximately 80 variables. Data for the study were collected in February and March 1964 in Rio de Janeiro, Brazil. The sample consists of persons aged 18+ and explores the respondents' attitudes to such areas as Brazil's stand in the conflict between communist and anti-communist ideologies, and the economic influence of the United States and the Soviet Union on Brazil. Variables concerned with issues and affairs at the international level examine the respondents' comparisons of the achievements and foreign policy of the United States and the Soviet Union, as well as their opinions about the nuclear test ban and disarmament, attitudes toward Fidel Castro and his impact on life in Cuba, the position of the United Nations, and the treatment of blacks in France, U.S., Russia, and South Africa. The data were received from the International Data Library and Reference Service, Survey Research Center, University of California at Berkeley.

10 Raymond E. Wolfinger et al. "America's Radical Right, 1962" (ICPSR 7273). These data report the attitudes, political behavior, and demographic characteristics of 307 people, out of approximately 2,000 who attended and supported the "San Francisco Bay Region School of Anti-Communism" held by the Christian Anti-Communist Crusade in Oakland, California, from 29 January-2 February 1962. Information was collected by personal interviews (94) and mail questionnaires (214).

Note: Additional Russian-related data might be found in the following archival holdings: Census Enumerations; Conflicts, Aggression, Violence, Wars; Elites and Leadership; International Systems: Linkages, Relationships and Events; Legislative and Deliberative Bodies (includes data on the United Nations); Mass Political Behavior and Attitudes; Social Indicators.

Finding Aids: The ICPSR's valuable Guide to Resources and Services, 1978-1979, cited verbatim in this entry.

MI 4
MICHIGAN HISTORICAL COLLECTIONS
BENTLEY HISTORICAL LIBRARY
UNIVERSITY OF MICHIGAN
1150 Beal Avenue
Ann Arbor, Michigan 48105
(313-764-3482)

1 Several collections relate to the North Russian (Polar Bear) Expedition--the American Expeditionary Forces (AEF) in the Murmansk and Archangel regions in 1918-19. Unless otherwise indicated, individuals noted below as being with the AEF served in the 339th Infantry Regiment. Though not treated by the library as a single holding, these collections were collectively described for a NUCMC entry (NUCMC 65-609).

2 George Albers (b. 1891). 11 items. AEF. Anonymous diary (possibly of Fred Kooyers of Company E) and miscellaneous papers, 1918-19, plus papers of Howard H. Pellegram Post (no. 3734) of the Veterans of Foreign Wars (1940-45).

3 James Burrill Angell (1829-1916). Papers, 1845-1916, 13 ft. and 6 vols. Educator, editor, and diplomat. President of the University of Michigan, 1871-1909; minister to China, 1880-81, and to Turkey, 1897-98. 6 letters to Charles Kendall Adams (1835-1902), then a Michigan history professor and later president of Cornell University and the University of Wisconsin, and 6 letters to his son Alexis Angell, all 12 written 1880-81, nearly all mentioning Russia and/or the possibility of a Russo-Chinese conflict. Index to correspondents. (NUCMC 64-1413)

4 Edwin L. Arkins. AEF. Shorthand diary in North Russia, plus some clippings, 1 vol.

5 John W. Bigelow (1896-1918). 8 items. AEF. Letters, certificates of recognition, and obituary.

6 Jay H. Bonnell. AEF. Typescript copy of his reminiscences with account of his Russian experiences, and a photograph album of the expedition, 90 pp.

7 John Boren. 23 items. AEF. Materials from 1919 relate to the expedition; papers from 1958-62 concern attempts to obtain the bodies of men killed and buried in Russia. Also, some postcard views of Archangel.

8 B. F. Broaddus. 14 items. AEF. Photographs, field orders, newspaper clippings, and a Thanksgiving Day menu.

9 E. D. Bruce. 5 items, 1962-64. AEF. Letter and songs relating to the expedition.

10 Rodger Sherman Clark. Ca. 60 items. AEF, 310th Army Engineers. Miscellaneous documents, maps, and charts of the North Russian forces, 1918-19.

11 John Sherman Crissman. 28 items. AEF. Diary describing living conditions, and letters from his family.

12 Frank W. Douma (1893-1976). AEF, corporal. Typescript copy, 21 pp., of his diary for 1918-19.

13 Walter F. Dundon. AEF, president of the Polar Bear Association. Diary and reminiscences concerning his efforts to recover bodies of expedition members slain and buried in Russia, 1929 and 1931.

14 Edward Flaherty. 35 items. AEF. Field diary of Company H, 1919; plus photos of Archangel and the AEF, taken by the American Red Cross.

15 Harry Franck (1881-1962). Papers, 1910-39, 7 items and 10 vols. Author of travel books. Includes typescript of his "A Vagabond in Sovietland," published under the same title by Stokes, McClelland in 1935. It is the account of his trip to the USSR in the early 1930s.

16 Albert E. Geltz. 6 items. AEF. Miscellaneous historical documents.

17 Robert Gessner (b. 1907). Papers, 1931-32, 16 items. Professor and author. After a visit to the Soviet Union he wrote to Louis A. Strauss, 29 September 1932, about his trip and his views on the country.

18 Alex Heath. 4 items. AEF. 1 map and 3 photos.

19 Burke Aaron Hinsdale (1837-1900). Papers, ca. 2 ft. Professor of education. His 3 daughters traveled to the USSR in 1928. Papers include their observations on Russia. (NUCMC 65-318)

20 Henry Katz. 4 items. AEF. Military orders and resume of medical work in north Russia, describing treatment of sick and wounded (American military and Russian civilians) by U.S. medical personnel.

21 Michael J. Macalla. Letters and papers, 1918-56, ca. 200 items. AEF, officer in the Polar Bear Association. Includes material on the American committee sent to the USSR in 1929 to attempt to recover bodies of AEF members slain, and on the dedication of the Polar Bear Monument (Troy, Michigan).

22 Hugh D. McPhail. 36 items and 4 vols. AEF. Scrapbooks with clippings, etc.; orders, citations, casualty lists, field message book (in part photocopies).

23 Margaret Wilder Menzi (b. 1898). Papers, 1911-40, ca. 250 items. Includes an account

of her trip on the Trans-Siberian Railroad on the eve of World War I, 1914, and a travel journal describing her trip across the rest of the country that same year.

24 Howard E. Merrill (fl. ca. 1917). Papers, 1917-24, ca. 250 items. YMCA volunteer in Russia during the Bolshevik Revolution. Correspondence, diary, 1920, and miscellanea. Letters are to relatives in the U.S. Also, playbills and newsletters published by Russian soldiers in German POW camps, and some writings of Donald A. Lowrie, who was in Russia with Merrill.

25 Joel Roscoe Moore (b. 1879). Papers, 1917-52, 17 items. AEF, U.S. Army captain. Correspondence, citations, and orders.

26 Otto Arthur Odjard. 8 items. AEF. 2 letters from General Edmund Ironside, British commander of Allied forces; list of British citations awarded to American and other Allied soldiers; other citations and decorations.

27 Silver Parrish. AEF. Photocopy of a diary, 57 pp., kept while in service with Company B on the Dvina River front, 14 July 1918-27 April 1919, with battlefield notes and details on Russian peasant life.

28 James Kerr Pollock (1898-1968). Military government files, ca. 1947-49, ca. .25 of 6 ft. Adviser to General Lucius Clay during the post-World War II Allied occupation of Germany. There are frequent references to dealings with the Russians in the administration of the occupation.

29 Caleb Dwinell Randall (1831-1903). Papers, 1855-1902, over 325 items. Banker, state legislator, and educator. Chiefly correspondence. Attended prison congresses and traveled in Europe, including Russia, about which he comments. (NUCMC 65-501)

30 Jesse Siddall Reeves (1872-1942). Papers, 1853-1942, 17 ft., 5 vols. Professor of political science and international law. Correspondence, reports, lecture notes, manuscript writings, etc. Some items concern the Russo-Japanese War of 1904-1905. Reference to Baron S. H. Korff. (NUCMC 65-507)

31 Charles Brady Ryan (b. 1886). 70 items and 3 vols. AEF. Diary for 1916, 1918-19; and correspondence, 1917-19, including letters home.

32 Hugo K. Salchow. 15 items. AEF. Partial transcript of an interview, 1971, in which he recounts his experiences with the Polar Bear expedition; miscellaneous documents he collected in 1919.

33 Clarence G. Scheu. 2 vols. AEF. Diaries, July 1918-July 1919, covering his service in Company B on the Dvina front.

34 James B. Sibley. 10 items. AEF. Diary for 7 November 1918-14 January 1919, plus various documents about the end of his service in the 339th.

35 Kenneth A. Skellenger. 7 items. AEF. Diary of his activities with Company A, a lengthy letter to his family, and a petition addressed to Bolshevik soldiers.

36 Gordon W. Smith. 1 vol. AEF, sergeant. Diary, 1919, with day-by-day accounts of Company D's activities, maps, company roster, and clippings.

37 William H. Stoneman (b. 1904). Papers, 1928-74, 6 ft. Foreign correspondent for the Chicago Daily News. In Moscow in 1931-35. Letters and scrapbooks contain pertinent information, and there is a folder of notes on Russia, 1932-35. Other subjects covered: the end of World War II as seen from London and Paris, and the development of the 1956 Hungarian revolt. A photograph album relates to the Hungarian events as well. One of his correspondents was Charles Bohlen. Unpublished list of folder contents and partial name index.

38 Laurence Todd (1882-1957). Papers, 1932-52, 1 ft. Correspondent for TASS, the Soviet news agency, stationed in Washington, D.C. Correspondence for 1933-52 and diaries for 1934-36 reflect his journalistic career with TASS, 1932-52, and political or international affairs relating to the Soviet Union. Unpublished finding aid.

39 Edward Trombley. 4 items, 1919-20. AEF. Letters and diary from the North Russian expedition.

40 Arthur Hendrick Vandenberg (1884-1951). Papers, 1927-51, 8 ft. Republican U.S. senator from Michigan, joined Democratic administration in bipartisan foreign policy. Chairman of the Senate Foreign Relations Committee, and delegate to the U.N. Conference in San Francisco in 1945 and to the Paris Peace Conference of 1946. Correspondence, diaries, scrapbooks, and speeches related to Soviet-American relations in the 1930s and the formation of U.S. policy toward the USSR at the end of World War II. The Private Papers of Senator Vandenberg, edited by Arthur H. Vandenberg, Jr. (Boston: Houghton Mifflin Co., 1952) gives a good idea of the contents. Unpublished folder list, name index, speech index, and scrapbook index.

41 Andrew D. White (1832-1918). Papers, 1857-1918, 8 microfilm reels plus 82 letters. President of Cornell University. Several letters from him to Edward Payson Evans, a teacher and journalist, while White was minister to Russia, December 1892-September 1894. Originals are in the Regional History Collection at Cornell University, under which

entry there is a more complete description. Note: The James B. Angell papers in the Bentley Library include letters from White which may be relevant.

Finding Aids: Guide to Manuscripts in the Bentley Historical Library by Thomas E. Powers and William H. McNitt (Ann Arbor, 1976), no. 33; Guide to Manuscripts in the Michigan Historical Collections of the University of Michigan by Robert M. Warner and Ida C. Brown (Ann Arbor, 1963); and Guide to Manuscript Collections in Michigan, prepared by the Michigan Historical Records survey project for the Works Projects Administration (Detroit, 1941-42), 2 vols. For the North Russian AEF expedition collections, there is a "Bibliographic Note" in Richard M. Doolen's Michigan's Polar Bears (Ann Arbor, 1965), which is Bulletin no. 14 of the Michigan Historical Collections.

MI 5
DIRECTORY OF RECENT SOVIET ÉMIGRÉS
CENTER FOR RUSSIAN AND EAST EUROPEAN STUDIES
LANE HALL
UNIVERSITY OF MICHIGAN
Ann Arbor, Michigan 48109
(313-764-0351;8571)

The directory, located at the Center for Russian and East European Studies, is under the supervision of Professors Zvi Gitelman and William Zimmerman. It contains the names, addresses, and relevant biographical information of recent Soviet émigrés in North America, Israel, and Western Europe who have specialized knowledge of aspects of Soviet society and the Soviet system. Directory categories include occupation, area of residence in the Soviet Union, and nationality.

The purpose of the directory is to facilitate contact between Western scholars doing academic research on the Soviet Union and émigrés whose knowledge and experience are of interest and value to those scholars.

To protect the privacy of émigrés, only those who have agreed to be listed are included in the directory, and their inclusion does not imply assent to being interviewed by a particular researcher. Names and addresses from the directory shall be made available only to scholars who can demonstrate a legitimate research need. The researcher would then contact each émigré personally to request permission for an interview. Statements made by émigrés will not be for attribution unless permission for quotation is granted explicitly.

The directory also lists ongoing and completed research projects involving émigrés so that interested scholars can be informed of the research of colleagues.

MI 6
ENGINEERING-TRANSPORTATION LIBRARY
UNIVERSITY OF MICHIGAN
Ann Arbor, Michigan 48104
(313-764-7494)

Charles Ellet, Jr. (1810-1862). Papers, 1827-1926, 18,000 items. American civil engineer. He corresponded with representatives of foreign governments about military affairs, mainly his plans for the use of naval steam battering rams. One draft of a letter dated 16 January 1855 is to the Grand Duke Constantine, vice-admiral of the Russian navy; in it Ellet offers a plan to destroy the Allied fleet in the harbor of Sevastopol with his battering rams. A letter of 4 February 1855 to Count Karl Robert Nesselrode, the Russian foreign minister, concerns "the national defenses of Sevastopol and Odessa." The same month Ellet sent copies of a paper entitled "How to Destroy Sevastopol" to Lord Palmerston, Sir James Graham, and Lord Panmure in Great Britain. All items are in folders 184-185. Contact the library prior to a visit. (NUCMC 62-2071)

Finding Aid: Guide to Manuscript Collections in Michigan, prepared by the Michigan Historical Records survey project of the Works Projects Administration (Detroit, 1941-42), Vol. 2.

MI 7
DEPARTMENT OF RARE BOOKS AND SPECIAL COLLECTIONS LIBRARY
UNIVERSITY OF MICHIGAN
Ann Arbor, Michigan 48109
(313-764-9377)

1 Armenian Manuscripts. 5 items, 12th-17th c. Calendrical tables, A.D. 1661, vellum, with ornamentation (Mich. MS 91), 1 l.; Gospels, A.D. 1161, vellum, 276 ff., colophon: Copied at Edessa by the scribe (priest) Vasil for the patron Christopher and his wife Aygots, with portraits of Mark and John (Mich. MS 141); Gospels, 17th-18th c., 286 ff. including 4 blank flyleaves, paper, vellum leaves from Armenian Gospel used as endsheets, with full-page portrait of Matthew, small portraits of Mark and John (Mich. MS 142); Gospels (fragments), 13th c., 5 ll., vellum, from Luke 19-21, with ornamentation (Mich. MS 143); and Hymnal, A.D. 1679, 341 ff., vellum, musical notations and ornamentation (Mich. MS 156). Unpublished brief listing. (Medieval and Renaissance Manuscripts)

2 Dimitrii, Saint, Metropolitan of Rostov (1651-1709). Lietopis' keleinyi . . . ot nachala mirobytie do r[o]zh [des]tva Khr[is]tova (Velikii Ustiug, 1708), in Church Slavonic. The author was Ukrainian. Provenance note on pastedown dated 1754. Published in 1784.

(Mich. MS 205). Unpublished brief listing. (Medieval and Renaissance Manuscripts)

3 Zakhariia Kopystens'kyi (d. 1627). Palinodiia [n.p., 19th c.?], dated 1621 on title page, provenance note on flyleaf dated 1855, in Church Slavonic (Ukrainian), Ukrainian author; published in 1878 in Russkaia istoricheskaia biblioteka. (Mich. MS 206). Unpublished finding aid. (Medieval and Renaissance Manuscipts)

4 Joseph A. Labadie (1848?-1933). Collection, 19th-20th c., social protest materials. This huge and varied collection includes printed materials (books, pamphlets, and vertical file material) and a manuscript and archival collection in which Russian-related materials exist. Among the books and pamphlets are serials and pamphlets of the Social Democratic Labor Party (Rossiiskaia sotsial-demokraticheskaia rabochaia partiia), Socialist-Revolutionary Party (Partiia sotsialistov-revoliutsionerov), as well as books and pamphlets of the British Columbia community of Doukhobors, 9 titles, and the Russian anarchist movement; various call numbers, some uncatalogued, retrievable by author. The manuscripts and archives include papers of Russian immigrants, among them Alexander Berkman (1870-1936)--correspondence, 1907-36, ca. 25 items; Mark Clevans (also known as Klavansky and Mratchny)--correspondence, 1922-38, ca. 150 items, of which a quarter are in Russian; Emma Goldman (1869-1940)--correspondence, 1909-40, ca. 180 items; and Isadore Wisotsky (ca. 1895-1970)--Such a Life [1968?], manuscript autobiography by Russian immigrant labor union leader (early life in Russia, association later with Russian radical exiles in the U.S. and abroad); American Committee for Protection of Foreign Born archives, 1933-61, ca. 70 ft., with the Committee's additions as active files are retired, comprising business correspondence, reports, office files, and court and administrative records of individual deportation cases; uncatalogued, retrieval by name of person for court cases which make up about half of the total amount (inquire about restrictions). In various stages of cataloguing.

5 Alberto Vimina (17th c.). "Relatione della Moscouia di Alberto Vimina secretario" [n.p., 1657?], manuscript, 76 pp., included in the author's Historia delle guerre civili di Polonia (Venice, 1671). (Phillipps MS 5554)

6 Wladimir S. Woytinsky (1885-1960). Collection, 1905-67, 2 ft., 350 items. Russian-American economist. Collection of Woytinsky and his wife, Emma (Shadkhan) Woytinsky (1893-1968). Woytinsky was imprisoned for radical activities and exiled to Siberia, 1908-17; he was a member of the Socialist-Revolutionary Party. Imprisoned in 1917 for anti-Bolshevik activity, he escaped to Georgia in 1918, went to western Europe, and emigrated to the U.S. in 1935. Prolific writer, chiefly on economics, in several languages, from 1905; Mrs. Woytinsky was co-author, editor, and translator. Includes a photocopy of his "Pravda ob Orlovskom Tsentrale," 1912, original in the George Kennan papers at the New York Public Library, published only in Dutch; a typescript entitled "The Soviet of the Unemployed in Petersburg, 1906-1907," 342 pp., a translation by Mrs. Woytinsky of his "Peterburgskiy Soviet Bezrabotnykh, 1906-1907" (never published in any language); and "Lost in the Siberian Wilderness," 123 pp., her translation of his V Taige (Petrograd, 1916), never published in English. Most of the writings have been published, but some of the Michigan materials are rare or unique; some of these works are on 36 reels of microfilm. Also includes reports and correspondence. Several folders of correspondence related to consulting work for an automobile company and correspondence related to his work for government agencies are currently marked "Confidential" and access will be restricted until their status can be clarified. Emma S. Woytinsky's Bibliography of the Writings of W. S. Woytinsky (Washington, D.C., 1961) lists 425 items, 27 pp., but excludes manuscript material and posthumous publications.

7 Sergei Ivanovich Zimin (1876-1942). Collection, 1911-20, 3 vols. Theater owner. Bound original, printed, programs from operas performed at the Zimin Opera in Moscow, 16 September 1911-17 January 1917, and from selected performances at the Teatr Soveta rabochikh deputatov, the subsequent name of the Zimin Opera, 3 September 1917-1920. All performances with the orchestra conducted by Eugene Plotnikoff (1877-1951). Plotnikoff's bookstamp on flyleaf of vol. 3.

MI 8
MANUSCRIPTS DIVISION
WILLIAM L. CLEMENTS LIBRARY
UNIVERSITY OF MICHIGAN
Ann Arbor, Michigan 48109
(313-764-2347)

1 Sir Henry Clinton (1738?-1795). Papers, 1750-1812, 86 ft. British general, commander in chief in North America. Correspondence, documents, etc., 260 vols. Includes 1 letter of Catherine II. (NUCMC 60-1447)

2 George III (1738-1820). Papers, 1784-1810, 5 ft. British monarch. Typed transcripts of originals in the Royal Archives of Windsor Castle. Includes a copy of a letter from Paul I. (NUCMC 60-1427)

3 Levett Harris. Letters, 1814, 82 items. U.S. diplomat in St. Petersburg. Correspondence concerns Russia and his private financial and commercial affairs. Among his correspondents

were John Quincy Adams, James A. Bayard, Albert Gallatin, Christopher Hughes, and James Monroe. (NUCMC 61-1915)

4 William Petty, 1st marquis of Lansdowne, 2nd earl of Shelburne (1737-1805). Papers, 1663-1791, 34 ft., ca. 11,000 items. English statesman. Official correspondence concerning British, European, and American affairs, plus photocopies of correspondence with George III. Includes a letter of Catherine II. (NUCMC 60-314)

Finding Aid: Guide to the Manuscript Collections in the William L. Clements Library, compiled by Arlene P. Shy (Ann Arbor, 1978).

MI 9
FORD ARCHIVES
HENRY FORD MUSEUM
Dearborn, Michigan 48121
(313-271-1620)

The Ford Archives have substantial amounts of Russian-related materials. Most concern Soviet-American business dealings, technological exchange, and economic assistance. No complete inventory of pertinent holdings is available but the following descriptions, by the repository's accession numbers, indicate where basic holdings are.

1 Accession 49. Box 1 contains a folder of Amtorg Trading Corporation correspondence with Ford, 1919-43. It also has a contract, 14 March 1919, between Ford Motor Company and Ivan Stacheeff & Company. Box 1A holds the important Report of the Ford Delegation to Russia and the USSR, April-August 1926, typescript, 266 pp., with contemporary snapshots and "informed commentary." A preliminary draft inventory of contents is available.

2 Accession 199. 37 boxes contain correspondence, orders, billings, requisitions, and invoices for the Amtorg Trading Corporation. Most of the items appear to be for the late 1920s and early 1930s. An inventory of contents is at the Ford Archive.

3 Accession 531. Similar to the preceding, this one box contains summary data, weekly reports, correspondence, and agreements, 1929-35, relating to the Amtorg Trading Corporation. There is a Ford Archives inventory (preliminary draft).

4 Accession 550. Photographs of the Russian/Ford trip of 1926.

5 Accession 632. Amtorg Trading Corporation, 2 boxes--finance, 1931-32 (billings, charges, ledger). Preliminary draft inventory.

6 Accession 662. A general report on a December 1955 trip to the USSR by 3 American industrial engineers (Ford, Westinghouse, and Bendix). Part of a limited exchange of engineering personnel.

7 Accession 771. Russia/Ford Tire Plant Equipment. G. Spicer's inventory of equipment sent to Russia by Ford in response to a U.S. government request to donate to the USSR the Ford Tire Plant and all equipment. The arrangements were part of lend-lease.

8 Accession 818. Letters, memoranda, and other papers, 1 box, pertaining to a Russian delegation to the U.S. to study Ford production records, 1929-30.

9 Accession 848. Perhaps the most unusual item: an original typescript in Russian (including snapshots and photostats of supporting documents) of the N. S. Sokolov investigation into the murder of Tsar Nicholas II and his family at Ekaterinburg in 1918. It is, however, possible that this may be a partial copy only.

10 Oral History Program. The Ford Archives has an extensive collection of oral history interviews, perhaps amounting to several hundred at present. They are available in typed transcripts. Among the interviews, with Ford relatives, employees, and associates, are at least 2 of relevance to Russia. The first is with Bredo Berghoff, one of the Ford Motor Company delegates to the USSR in 1926. The other is with Frank Bennett, a Ford engineer/adviser to Russian industry in the early 1930s.

Though not a true finding aid, Allan Nevins's Ford: Expansion and Challenge, 1915-1933 (Scribners, 1956) has an appendix ("The Russian Adventures") that gives an idea of the nature of some materials in this repository.

MI 10
DETROIT PUBLIC LIBRARY
5201 Woodward Avenue
Detroit, Michigan 48202
(313-833-1480)

Automotive History Collection

1 Charles B. King (1868-1957). Papers, ca. 1895-1939, ca. 27 ft. Engineer, inventor, and builder of the first automobile in Detroit. Includes some photographs of American troops, taken in Russia about the time of World War I (box 8). Partial contents list (NUCMC 67-351).

2 William G. Wagenhals (fl. early 20th c.). Papers, 1903-39, ca. 1 ft., ca. 400 items. Automotive manufacturer. Includes some

patents issued by the Russian and other European patent offices (for a variety of manufactured items). Partial contents list (NUCMC 67-354).

Burton Historical Collection

3 Ossip Gabrilowitsch (1878-1936). Correspondence, 1920-37, 36 boxes. Musician, conductor of the Detroit Symphony Orchestra. Correspondence between him, his colleagues, friends, family, etc. Correspondents include his wife, Clara Clemens Gabrilowitsch (Mark Twain's daughter), and European personalities. Unpublished contents list (NUCMC 69-705).

4 George Van Ness Lothrop (1817-1897). Papers, 1847-99, 5 boxes. Lawyer, attorney general of Michigan, and U.S. ambassador to Russia, 1885-88. A few papers relate to his diplomatic service but most concern his legal career. Lothrop family papers, at present unsorted and unexamined by the staff, and the papers of the law firm of Lothrop and Duffield might also contain some pertinent items. (NUCMC 69-716; and 67-1197 for the law firm records)

5 Polar Bear Association. Records, 1921-68, 22 boxes. The Polar Bears was the nickname given to American troops (American Expeditionary Forces) sent to the north of Russia during the Russian Civil War and Allied intervention. This unit was the U.S. Army 310th Infantry Regiment. Materials primarily concern the effort to return the bodies of members slain and buried in Russia and to re-inter them in Michigan.

6 Lois Rankin (fl. ca. 1939). Papers, 5 boxes. Ethnologist. Correspondence, notes, and writings on her ethnic studies of Detroit groups, used in preparing articles for Michigan history magazine, spring 1939. Includes material on Armenians, Bulgarians, Croatians, Finns, Greeks, Hungarians, Latvians, Lithuanians, Poles, Rumanians, Russians, Syrians, Ukrainians, and Yugoslavs. (NUCMC 67-411)

Rare Book Room

7 Armenian Manuscript. Four Gospels, A.D. 1223 (Armenian MS. Uncat. 1955).

MI 11
ARCHIVES OF AMERICAN ART
SMITHSONIAN INSTITUTION
5200 Woodward Avenue
Detroit, Michigan 48202
(313-226-7544)

This repository, like each of the regional centers of the Archives of American Art, has microfilms of much of the original materials kept at the Archives' Washington Center. It also holds items on microfilm from originals in other hands. Some of these materials pertain to the Russian Empire/Soviet Union. For details, see the entry under the District of Columbia.

MI 12
ARCHIVES OF LABOR HISTORY AND URBAN AFFAIRS
WALTER P. REUTHER LIBRARY
WAYNE STATE UNIVERSITY
Detroit, Michigan 48202
(313-577-4024)

1 The Archives of Labor History and Urban Affairs at Wayne State University was established in 1959, and has become one of the world's largest labor collections. Among the collections at the repository are the records of the United Automobile, Aerospace, and Agricultural Implement Workers of America (UAW), including the papers of Walter P. Reuther and other union presidents. Reuther visited Russia 1933-35, working many months at the Gorkii plant. (NUCMC 66-1520 and 77-1339, in part).

A number of other labor unions and organizations have preserved their records at this depository as well. At present there is identifiable Russian- or Soviet-related material in several of these collections, including those of the Congress of Industrial Organizations (CIO) (NUCMC 77-1313) and of the Jewish Labor Committee (NUCMC 72-833). Other Russian-related materials can be found in:

2 Workers Defense League Collection. Ca. 3.5 ft. of materials on the Committee of Inquiry into Forced Labor. Information is on Soviet gulags and similar forced labor camps. Many of the studies are by escapees; some are statistical.

3 John Nicholas Beffel (b. ca. 1895). Papers, 1943-54, ca. 14 ft. Freelance editor and officer of the League for Mutual Aid (New York). Includes manuscripts about Russia written by various individuals. Nearly all of these manuscripts appear to have been published in some form. They include: Voline [Vsevolod Mikhailovitch Eichenbaum], "1917: Russian Revolution Betrayed"; Joseph Cohen, "From My Left-Hand Pocket" (incomplete); "Mariam Freed" (unattributed and incomplete); and fragments of Rose Pesotta's autobiographical writings. All of these last 3 items include accounts of childhood and youth in Russia by American immigrants. (NUCMC 77-1302)

4 Raya Dunayevskaya. Papers, undated, 3 ft. Marxist author. Correspondence and literary manuscripts. Dunayevskaya, quondam secretary

of Leon Trotskii, has written several books (Philosophy and Revolution, Marxism and Freedom, etc.). She was a founder of the Johnson-Forest tendency; J. R. Johnson was C. L. R. James, and Dunayevskaya was Freddie Forest. She has also been chairman of the News and Letters Committee (Detroit), which puts out various newspapers. Approximately two-thirds of the collection consists of analyses of the Russian (Soviet) economy. There are also photostatic copies of letters to Dunayevskaya from Trotskii, 1937-39. Other materials include articles by her and James, her translations of Russian works, printed items, and manuscript writings. The entire collection is available on 2 microfilm reels from the archives. For the collection and the microfilm there is a guide written by Dunayevskaya herself, 17 pp. (NUCMC 73-274).

5 Edward J. Falkowski. Papers, 1916-38, temporarily in New York City. Miner who spent the years 1929-38 in Germany and the Soviet Union. As he is currently writing a book about his experiences, the diaries for these years may temporarily be removed from the collection.

6 Nemmy Sparks (Nehemiah Kishor) (1899-1973). Papers, 1942-73, ca. 5 ft. Labor organizer and official in the Communist Party of the U.S.A. He went to Siberia in 1922 on the Kuzbas project. Boxes 8-10 contain manuscripts, letters, clippings, and other items on Kuzbas from the early 1970s; articles and excerpts from his 2 books Common Sense About Communism and The Nation and Revolution; and his autobiography, in 2 parts, entitled Prelude and Epilog. Some of the Kuzbas correspondence is with American communist "survivors" still there at the time of writing. Note: 4 reels of tape recordings (partly blank or inaudible) of Sparks's Critical History of the CPUSA are on file with the archives' collection of magnetic tapes. A detailed finding aid is available for the collection (Accession No. 617).

Finding Aid: A Guide to the Archives of the Labor History and Urban Affairs, Wayne State University, compiled and edited by Warner W. Pflug (Detroit, 1974), 14 pp.

MI 13
SPECIAL COLLECTIONS DIVISION
MICHIGAN STATE UNIVERSITY
East Lansing, Michigan 48824
(517-355-3770)

1 Ernest Howard Crosby (1856-1907). Papers, in process. Writer, poet, novelist, and social reformer. Includes photostat copies of 17 letters, ca. 1896-1908, to him from Leo Tolstoi, whom Crosby had visited ca. 1893. Originals are in the Vassar College Library in Poughkeepsie, New York.

2 Ivan A. Il'in (b. 1883). Papers, ca. 72 boxes. Philosopher and literary critic. Taught at the University of Moscow until 1922; emigrated to Switzerland. Includes 1 folder of photos, mainly of Professor Il'in, and a large package, which is closed until 1982. The collection also includes a library of ca. 400 books.

MI 14
UNIVERSITY ARCHIVES AND HISTORICAL COLLECTIONS
MICHIGAN STATE UNIVERSITY
East Lansing, Michigan 48824
(517-355-2330)

1 Lester Paige Breckenridge (1858-1940). Correspondence, 1892-1925, 45 folders. Professor of mechanical engineering. Some letters discuss the development of Russian and Chinese railways; one correspondent was Keme Tien Yow, chief engineer for the Imperial Peking-Kalgan Railway. (NUCMC 70-1624)

2 Simon Cameron (1799-1889). Papers, 1738-1889, 22 microfilm reels. Financier, cabinet member, diplomat, and U.S. senator (Pennsylvania). Minister to Russia 1862-63. One correspondent was Charles A. Dana, the envoy to Russia. Originals are in the Library of Congress, under which entry there is more detailed information about these papers.

3 Eugen Ficket (fl. 1860s). U.S. Army officer. Letter dated 13 October 1869 from Ficket when he was stationed at Fort Kodiak, Alaska, 11 pp. He describes a trip to the north, his experiences, the natives, and the arctic environment. Passing references to American and Russian influences.

4 Francis H. Gambell (fl. ca. 1900). Papers, 1898-1959, 10 folders. Physician. In 1899 the U.S. sent him to give medical help to the Laplanders in Alaska, then tending reindeer newly introduced from Siberia. In 1919 he accompanied American forces to Siberia as a Red Cross physician. Diary, 1899, and reminiscences concern these experiences. (NUCMC 70-614)

5 Mortimer A. Waldo (1891-1963). Papers, 1904-59, 1.5 cu. ft. U.S. vice-consul in Helsinki in 1918. In 1916-18 he was with the YMCA Prisoners' Aid Society in Russia. 3 journals, 1916-17, discuss the fall of the Kerensky government and the rise of the Bolsheviks. Letters to family and friends concern life in Siberia. Some correspondence (e.g., with the historian Samuel E. Morison) and an official report, 1918, detail the economic, social, political, and military situation in Finland, and Finnish, Russian, and German relations. Also, notes for talks on Russia which Waldo presented to Rotary Club meetings in 1951 and after. (NUCMC 70-682)

Finding Aids: A Guide to the Historical Collections of Michigan State University, William H. Combs, director, and Anthony Zito, compiler (East Lansing, 1969), and A Guide to the Michigan State University Archives and Historical Collections, edited by Frederick L. Honhart, Suzann M. Pyzik, and Saralee R. Howard (East Lansing, 1976). There are also unpublished finding aids for each of the collections listed.

MI 15
DIOCESAN ARCHIVES
600 Burton Street, S.E.
Grand Rapids, Michigan 49507
(616-245-5347)

The archives of the Roman Catholic Diocese of Grand Rapids holds ca. .5 ft. of correspondence concerning Lithuanians, Latvians, and Ukrainians in various parishes of this 11-county diocese in western Michigan. Letters date from 1883, when the diocese was founded. They are not categorized according to nationality but form parts of different parish and personal files. There is also information about Bishop Jazeps Rancans, exiled auxiliary bishop of Riga, Latvia, who lived in Grand Rapids for nearly 20 years before his death in 1969. Assistance of the archivist would be necessary to locate relevant items. Access by appointment only.

MI 16
WAYNE ANDREWS--PRIVATE COLLECTION
521 Neff Road
Grosse Pointe, Michigan 48230

Mr. Andrews has photographic negatives of some 30 pictures he took, summer 1968, of Russian architectural monuments. These include 15 shots of Leningrad buildings (the Winter Palace of Rastrelli, the Smolny Cathedral--Rastrelli again, the New Admiralty--Zakharov, Imperial Stables--V. P. Stasov, General Staff Arch--Rossi, the Stock Exchange--Thomas de Thomond, and St. Isaac's Cathedral--Montferrand); 1 of the Novodevichy convent belfry; 3 of Charles Cameron's work (Palace, Temple of Friendship) at Pavlovsk; 2 of the Peterhof Palace by Rastrelli; 6 of the Tsaritsyno palace and pavilion by Bazhenov and Kazahof; and 4 of the Tsarskoe Selo Palace of Rastrelli, with the Cameron Gallery. The pictures are available for purchase either as 2x2 slides or as 8x10 prints.

MI 17
FINNISH AMERICAN HISTORICAL ARCHIVES
SUOMI COLLEGE
Hancock, Michigan 49930
(906-482-5300 x 58)

Finnish Relief. Records. 14 boxes. The Finnish Relief provided financial and material aid to Finland during the Winter War and World War II. The records, which are mostly in Finnish, include minutes of meetings, account books, correspondence, and other materials of American organizations.

MI 18
HOPE COLLEGE ARCHIVES
VAN ZOEREN LIBRARY
Holland, Michigan 49423
(616-392-5111 x 2130)

Oral History Collection. Currently in process, and held in the History Department by Professor G. L. Penrose, are 14 interviews with survivors of the 339th U.S. Infantry and 310th Engineers who saw action in north Russia during the intervention. Only 7 are complete, averaging 25 pp. of typescript. In final form they include pictures, biographical sketches, and indexes. Also, some personal diaries, copies of The American Sentinel published at Archangel'sk, and a rare copy of Capt. Joel Moore's The History of the American Expedition Fighting the Bolsheviki: Campaigning in North Russia 1918-1919 (Detroit, 1920). When the project is completed, all materials will be transferred to and available in the Hope College Archives.

MI 19
AMERICAN INSTITUTE FOR EXPLORATION
MAIN ADMINISTRATIVE OFFICE AND LIBRARY
1809 Nichols Road
Kalamazoo, Michigan 49007
(616-381-8237)

The Institute has ca. 20 original pages of diaries written by Aleuts in the 1700s and early 1800s. The diaries, which focus primarily on village life, refer to Russian customs and activities in Alaska. Also, 10 pp. of Russian manuscript, ca. 1810-20, detailing sailing plans of a Russian fur hunting group at Unalaska-Umnak in the eastern Aleutians; and ca. 450 Aleut archaeological artifacts dating from A.D. 1741 and showing Russian influence. Materials are available for inspection by qualified scholars upon application to the Institute.

MI 20
UPJOHN LIBRARY
KALAMAZOO COLLEGE
Kalamazoo, Michigan 49007
(616-383-8482)

Maynard Owen Williams (1888-1963). Papers, ca. 1890-1963, 2 filing cabinet drawers and several shelves. Journalist, world traveler, and chief of Foreign Staff of National Geographic magazine. As a foreign correspondent for the Christian Herald, he journeyed from Sakhalin Island to the Tibetan border, ca. 1916-17. He was a witness to the Russian Revolution in Petrograd, Moscow, and the Caucasus. Williams directed relief work in Van, the capital of Armenia, in 1917-18, and was the only American correspondent to cross Siberia with the Czechoslovak legionnaires. Includes ca. 200 of his articles in manuscript, about 40 of which pertain to Russia/USSR before 1940, many of them published in the Christian Herald. They concern Armenia, Georgia, Erzerum, Van, Merv, Tiflis, Etchmiadzin, Samarkand, the Siberian intervention, Central Asia, Russian peasants, "Russia's New Czar," and "The Spirit of Russia and the Soul of France." There are also 2 photograph albums, with pictures chosen and captioned by Williams of Armenia, Latvia, Russia, and other countries. Also, a signed portrait of Williams by Vasilii Nikolaevich Iacovleff, an artist who accompanied the Citroen-Haardt Expedition across Asia, 1931, which followed the Marco Polo route from Beirut to Peiping, plus letters, field notes, reports, a scrapbook, and printed matter about this expedition. Published finding aid: Maynard Owen Williams: Class of 1910 Kalamazoo College, by Lawrence H. Conrad, Sr. (1968).

MI 21
ARCHIVES AND REGIONAL HISTORY COLLECTIONS
WESTERN MICHIGAN UNIVERSITY LIBRARY
Kalamazoo, Michigan 49008
(616-383-1826)

1 Charles Garrett and Reint Schuur (Oral History Collection). Typed transcript, 43 pp., of a 1965 interview, 2 tape reels, with 2 soldiers who served in the 339th Infantry Regiment in Archangel, 1918-19. See also the Schuur collection below.

2 Louis C. Loetz. Letter, 12 February 1919, from Supply Sergeant Emil L. Storck, in Archangel with the 339th Regiment.

3 Ruth Paulsen. Letter, 22 November 1918, from her husband, George Paulsen, with the 339th Infantry in Archangel.

4 Reint Schuur. Memoirs of his experiences with the 339th Infantry Regiment in Archangel in 1919, typed, 31 pp. Note also the first listing above.

5 Robert S. Simonds. Papers, 1918-19, 51 items. U.S. Army Band leader stationed with the American Expeditionary Forces at Archangel. Correspondence and other items. (NUCMC 68-1007)

MI 22
CLARKE HISTORICAL LIBRARY
CENTRAL MICHIGAN UNIVERSITY
Mount Pleasant, Michigan 48859
(517-774-3352)

1 Thomas I. Beddow. Lectures, n.d., late 1960s, 7 items. Teacher. Collection of lectures on the USSR, emphasizing primarily the differences between the educational systems in the U.S. and Russia. Delivered to the World War I Veterans Barracks No. 40.

2 John W. Ellison. Papers, 1921-35, 9 items. Socialist Party leader. 8 letters, 1931-35, from him to his friend Jack Rand in Moscow describe poor living conditions in the U.S. and party work. 1 letter from Rand, 1935, concerns the cultural life of workers in Soviet Russia, 6 pp. Also, pamphlet with the Socialist Party platform in Ashtabula, Ohio, in 1921, 4 pp.

3 Russian posters. 15 large, colorful posters from the 1930s, brought back to the U.S. by Chester G. Finster, a registered architect and civil engineer who worked in the Soviet Union.

4 John M. Sill (b. 1831). U.S. ambassador in Korea. Letter, 25 January 1897, Seoul, from Sill to Don M. Dickinson discussing Russian and Japanese intrigue and internal strife in Korea, and defending his own conduct as ambassador, 30 pp.

MINNESOTA

MN 1
HILL MONASTIC MANUSCRIPT LIBRARY
BUSH CENTER
ST. JOHN'S UNIVERSITY
Collegeville, Minnesota 56321
(612-363-3514)

1 [Armenian Manuscripts on microfilm]. Several items from repositories in Oregon, Austria, and the Vatican.

2 Austrian National Library, Vienna. Microfilms of 186 Slavic manuscripts, 34 Armenian manuscripts, and 5 Georgian manuscripts. These are copies of manuscripts that apparently came into Austrian hands at some time during the Renaissance (before A.D. 1600). 115 of the 186 Slavic manuscripts are indicated as being written in Serbian Old Slavonic, 10 in Bulgarian Old Slavonic, 10 in Glagolithic (Croatian Old Slavonic), 15 in Russian Old Slavonic, 8 in Russian, 7 in Serbian, 2 in Rumanian, and 19 in a language not indicated (but probably Serbian Old Slavonic). 91 are of liturgical content (including psalters and menaea), 27 are biblical, 5 are biblical commentary, 10 are patristic, 10 ascetical, 13 hagiographic, 4 theology, 9 canon law, 6 profane, and 1 unidentified. Of the Armenian holdings, 15 are liturgical, 7 biblical, 4 theological, 1 hagiographical, 1 historical, 1 a dictionary, and 4 are unidentified. Finally, the Georgian manuscripts include a Gospel and a lectionary of the Gospels, 2 menaea, and 1 collection of translations of patristic homilies. (The German name of this repository is the Osterreichische Nationalbibliothek.) Copies of the materials may be purchased by scholars if the Viennese grant permission.

3 Mekhitarist Monastery Library, Vienna. Microfilms of 1,193 Armenian manuscripts (of a collection of 1,304 items). These items cover a variety of subjects and are not as heavily concentrated in liturgy and scripture as those in the Austrian National Library.

Finding Aid: Checklist of Manuscripts Microfilmed for the Monastic Manuscript Microfilm Library, St. John's University, Collegeville, Minnesota, vol. 1: Austrian Monasteries, compiled by Julian G. Plante, part 2 (Collegeville, 1974).

MN 2
MANUSCRIPTS DIVISION
LIBRARIES
UNIVERSITY OF MINNESOTA
Minneapolis, Minnesota 55455
(612-376-7271)

Charles Stuart, Baron Stuart de Rothesay (1779-1845). Papers, 1785-1845, 471 items. British diplomat, ambassador to the Netherlands, 1815, France, 1815-30, and Russia, 1841-45. Nearly all correspondence, with a few clippings, dealing with such subjects as Gibralter, Portugal, Mexico, the West Indies, and France. Among his correspondents were Castlereagh, George Canning, and William Pitt. Unpublished inventory (NUCMC 75-2025).

MN 3
SOCIAL WELFARE HISTORY ARCHIVES CENTER
LIBRARIES
UNIVERSITY OF MINNESOTA
Minneapolis, Minnesota 55455
(612-373-4420)

1 Paul Underwood Kellogg (1879-1958). Papers, ca. 1884-1958, ca. 15 ft. Journalist, editor, and social reformer. Correspondence, biographical information, and financial records. Material on his work with Survey Associates, foreign policy, and international relations. 1 folder, 1915, contains a report on the Russian Extraordinary Commission of Inquiry on German war atrocities. Items pertaining to the Foreign Policy Association, 1917-49, include scattered references to Russia. Also, correspondence ca. 1921 concerning a special issue on the USSR of Survey magazine, which he edited. In 1936 he traveled to the Soviet Union; there may be materials pertaining to this trip in the collection. (NUCMC 70-1652)

2 Harry Lawrence Lurie (1892-1973). Papers, 1927-58, 2 ft. Social worker, teacher, and editor. Correspondence, writings, reports, and speeches. His professional correspondence (especially in the 1930s) reflects his interest in foreign affairs, Russia, communism, and fascism. In 1936 he led a study tour of the Soviet Union for social workers. (NUCMC 67-1848)

3 Survey Associates. Records, 1891-1952, 44 ft. Organization for the advancement of social welfare through research and publication, especially its Survey magazines. Correspondence, corporate and membership records, administrative and financial records, and editorial files. Contact with the Foreign Policy Association, of which Paul Kellogg, the Survey editor, was a founding member. Includes correspondence, 1924-37, with Anna Louise Strong about travel in and writing on the USSR, 1 folder. Ca. 1 ft. of material, 1918-51, concerns the Foreign Policy Association. Ca. 1 ft. concerns a February 1944 issue of Survey devoted to the USSR (correspondence of the editors, Richard B. Scandrett and Albert Rhys Williams). (NUCMC 67-1849)

4 Savel Zimand (1891-1967). Papers, 1917-67, ca. 1 ft. Journalist and educator. Visited the Soviet Union in 1922 and subsequently wrote State Capitalism in Russia, a booklet published by the Foreign Policy Association in 1926. Correspondence regards preparation of this booklet. (NUCMC 70-1655)

Finding Aid: University of Minnesota Libraries, Descriptive Inventories of Collections in the Social Welfare History Archives Center (Westport, Conn.: Greenwood, 1970).

MN 4
COLLEGE ARCHIVES
RÖLVAAG MEMORIAL LIBRARY
ST. OLAF COLLEGE
Northfield, Minnesota 55057
(507-663-3229)

Lars W. Boe (1875-1942). Papers, 1909-42, 65 ft., ca. 60,000 items. President of St. Olaf, 1918-42. Dr. Boe was a member of the executive committee of the Lutheran World Convention (established in 1923), in which capacity he was active in the cause of international Lutheran cooperation. (The organization is presently known as the Lutheran World Federation.) In Box 103 of his papers are 2 pertinent file folders. The first concerns the plight of the "Harbin refugees," some 200 German-Russian Lutherans who fled the Russian Civil War and were stranded for a time in Harbin, Manchuria. Correspondence, 1932-34, some in German, details efforts to resettle this group in Brazil in 1934. The second folder contains letters and reports on the "Russian Situation," i.e., freedom of worship in the USSR. There are letters, copies, in German, from Bishop Th. Meyer of Moscow to Dr. John A. Morehead of the LWC office in New York. Other letters are between different LWC officials concerned about the "Russian Situation" and the Lutheran Church in the Soviet Union. Materials are from 1931-35.

Some items are translations and/or copies. It is possible that other documents interspersed in the Boe papers relate to the USSR. Box list/inventory (NUCMC 73-862).

MN 5
ARCHIVES OF THE BAPTIST GENERAL CONFERENCE
BETHEL THEOLOGICAL SEMINARY
3949 Bethel Drive
St. Paul, Minnesota 55112
(612-641-6282)

Beginning in 1923, the Baptist General Conference, then known as the Swedish Baptist General Conference, supported a missionary effort to Russians. Begun in Vladivostok, it soon moved to Harbin. In 1934 the work was transferred to Tientsin, and in 1939 to Shanghai. The archive files contain several folders relating to this effort: photos, correspondence, manuscripts, and clippings. In the files of the denominational newspaper are periodic accounts of the "Russian Mission." Some of the material is in Swedish. Open to qualified researchers.

MN 6
DIVISION OF ARCHIVES AND MANUSCRIPTS
MINNESOTA HISTORICAL SOCIETY
1500 Mississippi Street
St. Paul, Minnesota 55101
(612-296-6980)

1 Charles W. Brandborg (1847-1916) and Family. Papers, 1887-1970, 1 box. Swedish-born member of the Minnesota Socialist Labor Party. 2 sons were also active in the party. Correspondence, reports, transcripts of speeches, and printed material, including newspaper articles commemorating the 50th anniversary of the 1917 Revolution. Unpublished inventory (NUCMC 60-1033).

2 Hascal Russell Brill (1846-1922). Papers, 1805, 1849-1964, ca. 9 ft. Lawyer and judge. His nephew, William Hascal Brill, as a journalist covered the Russo-Japanese War of 1904-1905. Manuscripts, dispatches, diaries, scrapbooks, and photographs about the war. Unpublished inventory (NUCMC 70-1633).

3 Charles S. Bulkley. Correspondence, 1865-67, 2 vols. and 1 item. Leader of the U.S.-Russian Telegraph Expedition. Copies of letters exchanged between members of the group, one of whom was George Kennan.

4 Joseph Alfred Arner Burnquist (1879-1961). Papers, ca. 1884-1960, ca. 12 ft., 14,000 items. Lawyer, attorney general, and governor of Minnesota, 1915-21. Includes a letter from Stanley Washburn, in the consular service in Russia, on Russian military service, 5 March 1916. Correspondence from November 1918 concerns the suppression of a demonstration marking the successful Russian October Revolution. Some letters of 1918-19 relate to Alexai Eustophiaoich (sic) of Minneapolis, an alleged Russian communist. Unpublished inventory. (NUCMC 69-1687)

5 Central Labor Union of Minneapolis and Hennepin Co. Records, 1912-62, 61 boxes. Some of the materials concern Russia. Access is restricted; permission must be obtained in advance of visit. Unpublished inventory.

6 Otto Augustus Christensen (1851-1918) and Family. Papers, 1854-1964, ca. 3 boxes. Teacher and farmer. Includes a copy of a speech by Maurice Jacobsen describing his visit to the USSR, October 1933; a 1952 printed booklet entitled The Diary of General Grow, purportedly the diary of a military attaché at the U.S. embassy in Moscow telling of his espionage work in the Soviet Union; and a reprint, 1937, of Leon Trotskii's "I Stake My Life" speech, concerning the great show trials of the 1930s. (NUCMC 60-1242)

7 Citizens Alliance of Minneapolis; Minneapolis, Minnesota. Records, ca. 1903-present, 27 boxes. Information about the 1917 Russian

Revolution included. Unpublished inventory (NUCMC 70-1634).

8 Peter W. Copeland (1868-1930). Papers, 1905-39, 4 folders and 2 vols. Member of the Russian Railway Service Corps, a paramilitary group sent to restore order along the Trans-Siberian Railway after the Revolution. His diary, 1917-18, and letters to his sister discuss the trip from St. Paul to Vladivostok, Japan, and back to Vladivostok. Photos, reports, and clippings also relate to his trip. Unpublished inventory.

9 William Fuson Davidson (1825-1897) and Family. Papers, 1817-1919, 134 ft. Grain elevator manufacturer and real estate operator. Various Russian companies corresponded with Davidson 1911-18 about settling on his land and about obtaining relief from the First World War. Letters are indexed in an unpublished inventory (NUCMC 61-2787).

10 William Blake Dean (1838-1922). Papers, 1806-1937, ca. 3 boxes. Merchant and Minnesota state senator. Some letters to him from his grandson, William Winter Dean, with the American Red Cross's Inter-Allied Commission, 1919, concern the repatriation of Russian prisoners of war in Germany. Unpublished inventory (NUCMC 70-254; also 60-1043).

11 William C. Edgar (1856-1932). Papers, 1832-1949, 6 boxes, 7 vols., and 1 microfilm reel. Business manager and editor of the Minneapolis Northwestern Miller, 1882-1924. Letters, reports, and scrapbooks, 1891-94, concern his project to collect flour from U.S. millers and distribute it in Russia during the great famine of 1891-92 (Edgar himself visited Russia to help the work); 6 telegrams from Prince Cantacusene; 5 letters from Andre Bobrinskoy; and a menu autographed by the Grand Duke Alexander, 13 May 1839. Also autographed pictures of Bobrinskoy and Cantacusene. Letters of 12 February and 23 March 1894 describe construction of the Trans-Siberian Railroad, and 1 from 16 April 1892, Moscow, details a Russian Easter celebration. Letters are on microfilm; originals are in the Minneapolis Public Library. Unpublished inventory (NUCMC 62-4915).

12 Hamilton Fish (1808-1893). Typed copies of 4 items, 1873. American statesman. Material on Russians in the U.S. Originals in the Columbia University Butler Library.

13 Great Northern Railway Company. Records, 1854-1970, ca. 5,000 ft. Office files of the president, vice-president-operating, treasurer, comptroller, law department, some branch lines, and related companies hold materials about Russian railroads, visits of Russians to the U.S. and of Americans to Russia, and the Russian Railway Service Corps. Includes some applications for employment with the Great Northern from Soviet citizens, 1930-31. Unpublished finding aids for catalogued portions of the records; microfilm index of the president's subject files. Access is restricted in part.

14 Lynn Haines (1876-1929). Papers, 1909-31, 61 boxes. Editor of Searchlight on Congress. He collected a few pamphlets on U.S.-Russian relations. Unpublished inventory (NUCMC 60-1374).

15 Clarence A. Hathaway (1894-1963). Papers, 1928-40, 1 box. Tool and die maker, member of the American Communist Party from 1921, and editor of the Daily Worker, 1934-39. He was in Moscow in 1928. Includes 15 transcripts of speeches he delivered in 1928-40 on socialism, communism, and world peace. Also a copy of his manuscript, "The American Negro and the Churches," written in Moscow, 1928, and subsequently published in Russian. Unpublished inventory.

16 Oscar Ferdinand Hawkins (1872-1964). Papers, 1888-1963, 5 ft. Minneapolis teacher and politician. Includes material on the National Council of American-Soviet Friendship and on Russian war relief. Unpublished inventory (NUCMC 69-1705).

17 Frank T. Heffelfinger (1869-1959). Papers, 1900, 1 vol. Grain trader. He and Charles F. Haglin traveled to Europe, January-April 1900, to determine the feasibility of building concrete grain elevators in Russia. He met with Russian leaders and discussed the plan, which broke down when the Russians insisted that they operate the storage facilities.

18 Walter Henry Judd (b. 1898). Papers, 1939-62, 88.5 ft. U.S. representative from Minnesota, 1942-62. Some correspondence, reports, and office files concern his work on the House Committee on Foreign Affairs: State Department letters critical of Russian expansionism and occupation of Poland; letters about Alger Hiss; data on Nikita Khrushchev's 1959 visit to the U.S.; and letters revealing mistrust of Russia and fear of a Soviet attack on the U.S. Access is restricted; permission must be obtained in advance of visit. Unpublished inventory.

19 Frank B. Kellogg (1856-1937). Papers, 1890-1942, 35 ft. on 54 microfilm rolls. Lawyer, ambassador, secretary of state, 1925-29, and judge on the Permanent Court of International Justice, 1930-35. Correspondence with Robert E. Olds discusses the Russian Revolution, 1917-23. Letters from 1925-29 refer to recognition of the USSR and the admission of communist aliens into the U.S. A 1927 report outlines the Soviet offer to sign a pact renouncing war, and an undated report is entitled "The Essential Factors Involved in Establishing Normal Relations with the Soviet Regime." Published guide (NUCMC 60-2030).

20 Charles Augustus Lindbergh (1858-1924) and Family. Papers, 1808-1971, 7.5 ft. Minnesota congressman. Some items relate to the 1917 Revolution. Access is restricted; permission must be obtained in advance of visit. Unpublished inventory (NUCMC 65-672).

21 William Lochren (1832-1912) and Family. Papers, 1852-1925, 5.5 ft., 4,000 items and 23 vols. Judge. Letters to the family from the David Mercer family, which visited Russia on a European tour (June-October 1899). Also information on the Russo-Japanese War. Unpublished inventory (NUCMC 60-1039).

22 George Edward MacKinnon (b. 1906). Papers, 1933-60, ca. 34 ft. Lawyer, state legislator, and U.S. representative. Correspondence, speeches, reports, office files, and clippings concern communism, foreign aid, immigration, and the military. Access is restricted; permission must be obtained in advance of visit. Unpublished finding aid (NUCMC 76-2063).

23 Northern Pacific Railway Company. Records, 1861-1970, 9,000 ft. Files of the Land Department, which among other functions was concerned with immigration and colonization, include correspondence about a Mennonite sect in Russia which wanted to emigrate, 1872-73. The president's subject files have records regarding locomotives and cars built for Russian use, the Elihu Root Russian Commission, steamship business between North America and Russia, and World War I. Access is restricted in part. Unpublished finding aids for catalogued portions of the collection.

24 Quetico-Superior Council, Minneapolis, Minnesota. Records, 1906-64, 108 boxes. Some circular letters and other miscellanea, 1 folder, relate to Russian war relief in 1941-42. Access is restricted; permission must be obtained in advance of visit. Unpublished inventory (NUCMC 67-844).

25 Wilhelm Rosenberg. Passport issued to him in Finland, 1890.

26 Birdella M. Ross. Collection, 1961-63, 2 folders. Family histories, including some Russians living in Minnesota.

27 Russian Manuscripts. 10 items, 1886-1911. Includes the statute for an ecclesiastical teachers' school; stationery of the Pochayevo monastery; extract from a parish register relating to a Jewish girl converted to Orthodoxy, who married a peasant; statutes of the ecclesiastical school at Zhitomir, 1908; and a letter from the Uman Agricultural School to a prospective student, 1911. Unpublished inventory.

28 Russian Orthodox Cemetery Association. Certificate of organization of the body, dated 26 June 1900, Minneapolis, typed, 3 pp.

29 Francis Monroe Smith (1904-1951). Collection, 1936-51, 1 ft. Lawyer and political activist. Printed matter about communism, U.S.-Soviet relations since 1949, the American Committee for the Protection of the Foreign Born, the Subversive Activities Control Act, the Committee for Free Political Advocacy, the Communist Party, and the Bill of Rights Conference in New York City. Unpublished inventory.

30 Socialist Workers Party. Records, 1914-64, ca. 4 ft. plus 2 microfilm reels. Printed booklets and pamphlets, including "Down with the Stalin-Hitler Pact! Down with the War!" (protesting the 1939 Nazi-Soviet Non-Aggression Pact). Also newspaper clippings (on the Moscow purge trials of 1934-35, Albert Boldman's "Why We Defend the Soviet Union" from 29 March 1940, etc.) and some Leon Trotskii pamphlets. Materials indicate the relations between the SWP, the USSR, and world communism. Unpublished inventory (NUCMC 69-1723).

31 Stanley Washburn (1878-1950). Papers, 1890-1977, 6.5 ft. Journalist and diplomat. Scrapbooks and photos include information on the Russo-Japanese War and Russia in World War I. Typescript on Russia's role in World War I.

32 Howard Yolen Williams (1889-1973). Papers, ca. 1924-70, 48 boxes. Congregational minister and social and political activist. Letter of 26 December 1928 advocates recognition of the USSR by the U.S., urging the League for Independent Political Action to adopt this position. Copies of letters by Sherwood Eddy and Jerome Davis recount their impressions of the USSR in 1929-33 and the effects of the Soviet regime on all aspects of Russian life. Letter from E. S. Davies to John Dewey, June 1931, encloses a manuscript, 33 pp., with Davies' views on world affairs, U.S.-Soviet relations, and similar subjects. Letter from A. F. Burdoin to Dewey, April 1932, includes a copy of an anti-Bolshevik, anti-Semitic pamphlet entitled Secret Nature of Peace Agitation, an exposé of the financing of the 1917 Revolution. Letters of Williams while on a tour of Europe in 1947 stress the importance of American aid to Europe to prevent Russian dominance on the continent. In 1967 he took a trip to the Soviet Union, about which he wrote "A Visit Behind the Iron Curtain" (draft and reprint included). Unpublished inventory (NUCMC 61-2750).

33 William Windom (1827-1891). Papers, 1861-1943, 2 boxes and 2 vols. Minnesota congressman, senator, and U.S. secretary of the treasury, 1881, 1889-91. In 1888-90 he represented the U.S. in an arbitration case involving Russia, America, and the Alaska seal fisheries. Unpublished inventory (NUCMC 60-212).

34 Works Project Administration, Minnesota. Records, 1849-1942, 345 boxes. Body gathered some information about Minnesota residents, including some Russians. Unpublished inventory.

35 Raphael Zon (1874-1956). Papers, 1887-1957, 6 ft. Born in Simbirsk, studied at Kazan University, specialist in comparative embryology, and forester. He emigrated with his wife, Anna Abramovna Puzyriskaya, in 1898. Includes information on his education in Vilna and Kazan, comparisons and observations about Russian forestry, and material on Russian-American relations. Zon also had an interest in Russian science and affairs. During World War II he worked on relief efforts for Jews and Russians. A letter sent to Louis Adamic concerns life as a Russian Jew. Unpublished inventory. (NUCMC 66-876)

Finding Aids: Guide to the Personal Papers in the Manuscripts Collections of the Minnesota Historical Society (Guide no. 1), compiled by Grace Lee Nute and Gertrude W. Achermann (1935); Manuscript Collections of the Minnesota Historical Society (Guide no. 2), compiled by Lucile M. Kane and Kathryn A. Johnson (1955); Manuscripts Collections of the Minnesota Historical Society (Guide no. 3), compiled by Lydia A. Lucas (1977); and Guide to the Public Affairs Collection of the Minnesota Historical Society, compiled by Lucile M. Kane (St. Paul, 1968).

MN 7
IMMIGRATION HISTORY RESEARCH CENTER
UNIVERSITY OF MINNESOTA
826 Berry Street
St. Paul, Minnesota 55114
(612-373-5581)

1 The Immigration History Research Center, founded in 1964 as the Center for Immigration Studies/Immigrant Archives, has a vast and unique collection of materials on American ethnic groups originating in Eastern Europe. At present its library holds over 35,000 volumes, 4,000 reels of microfilm, and 2,500 ft. (3,000,000 items) of unpublished manuscripts. Among the groups for which the IHRC has holdings are Russians, Ukrainians, Estonians, Latvians, Lithuanians, Armenians, Byelorussians, Carpatho-Ruthenians, and Jews (also other Eastern and Southern Slavs, Poles, and Finns). Because the focus of collections is ethnic groups in America, most of the materials shed only indirect light on the respective homelands of these peoples. Even so, these collections represent major archival resources for the study of the Russian Empire and the Soviet Union.

Holdings are divided into "General Collections," which are records of agencies and individuals active in refugee resettlement, intercultural education, immigration policy, and similar work, and "Ethnic Collections," which currently cover 24 different nationalities. Collections may contain both published (usually books, newspapers, and serials) and unpublished items. Most are in the native languages but sizeable amounts are also in English.

A detailed listing of all relevant holdings would only duplicate existing published guides, which are excellent and readily available (see under Finding Aids at the end of this entry). This description will be brief, listing the names, sizes, and some further information for various collections under the individual ethnic groups and in the "General Collections."

General Collections

2 American Council for Émigrés in the Professions. Records, ca. 1938-65, 165 ft. Case records from the ACEP and 2 preceding organizations: National Committee for Resettlement of Foreign Physicians, and American Committee for Refugee Scholars, Writers, and Artists. The ACEP helped immigrant professionals find jobs in the U.S. Collection closed.

3 American Council for Nationalities Service, New York City. Records, 1918-present, 180 ft. and growing. Includes material from the period before it bore this name: Foreign Language Information Service, 1918-39, and Common Council for American Unity, 1940-59. The largest single collection now at the IHRC. Records of an organization devoted to all aspects of American immigration. Also includes the archives of the American Federation of International Institutes, which merged with the CCAU in 1958.

4 Assembly of Captive European Nations. Records, 1954-present, 60 ft. plus 13 scrapbooks and growing. Group seeking the liberation of Central and Eastern European nations from communist dictatorship and Soviet domination.

5 Bureau for Intercultural Education, New York. Records, ca. 1940-60, ca. 1.5 ft. Correspondence, reports, minutes, interviews, articles, and BIE publications.

6 Stewart G. Cole (b. 1892). Papers, ca. 1937-70, 1 ft. Concerned with intercultural education.

7 Rachel Davis DuBois (b. 1892). Personal papers and agency records, ca. 1932-57, 6.5 ft. Concerned with intercultural education.

8 Kenneth J. Enkel. Papers, ca. 1947-1958, 1 ft. Attorney on immigration cases. Legal briefs, documents, and correspondence. Detailed inventory.

9 George Graff. Papers, ca. 1931-47, .5 ft. plus 1 tape cassette. Involved in intercultural education.

10 International Institute of Boston. Records, ca. 1920-40, 21 ft. Materials concerning immigrants assisted in the Boston area.

11 International Institute of Minnesota, St. Paul. Records, ca. 1920-60, 60 ft. Organizational papers.

12 International Institute of St. Louis. Records, ca. 1919-61, 24 ft. Organizational material and record of activities.

13 U.S. Committee on Public Information. Records, 1916-19, 1 microfilm reel. Also known as the Creel Committee. Papers, letters, and publications of the committee's Division of Work With the Foreign Born.

Carpatho-Ruthenian

14 Holy Ghost Greek Catholic Church, Cleveland, Ohio. Marriage records, 1909-67, 1 microfilm reel.

Estonian

15 Minnesota Eesti Selts, Minneapolis, Minnesota. Records, ca. 1964-74, ca. .33 ft. Records and commemorative material of the Minnesota Estonian Society and its Estonian House.

Jewish

16 Marmarosher Jewish Center, Cleveland Heights, Ohio. Records, 1911-66, 1 microfilm reel. Financial records, minutes, etc.

17 Sherit Jacob Israel Synagogue, Cleveland, Ohio. Records, 1919-38, 1 microfilm reel. Financial records, minute books, miscellaneous items.

18 Temple of the Heights, Cleveland, Ohio. Minute book, 1891-1920, 1 microfilm reel.

Latvian

19 American Latvian Association in the U.S., Washington, D.C. Records, ca. 1951-present, ca. 20 ft. and growing. Cultural and charitable organization. Correspondence, records, and publications.

20 Amerikas Latviesu Palidzibas Fonds (Latvian Relief Fund of America), Philadelphia, Pennsylvania. Records, 1955-69, 1 notebook.

21 Daugavas Vanagi A.S.V. (Latvian Welfare Association), Chicago, Illinois. Records, 1956-68, 2.5 ft. Works for displaced persons of Latvian descent. Includes minutes of board meetings.

22 Magdalena Rozentals. Papers, ca. 1945-present, ca. 1 ft. Latvian immigrant librarian/bibliographer. Materials deal mainly with Latvian refugees worldwide.

23 Leonids Slaucitajs (b. 1899). Papers, 1947-69, 1 ft. Latvian-born geophysicist. His published works and data on Latvian culture in Australia.

Lithuanian

24 Jonas Cesna (1897-1975). Papers, 1950-74, ca. 5 ft. Former officer in Lithuanian and Ukrainian armies. Immigrated to the U.S. after World War II. Includes his writings and information on Polish-Lithuanian disputes.

25 Antanas J. Jokubaitis (Anthony J. Jacobsen) (b. 1887). Papers, ca. 1921-73, ca. .5 ft. Lithuanian-American poet.

26 Vitalis Zukauskas. Papers, ca. 1949-present, ca. 5 ft. and growing. Lithuanian-American playwright and author. Correspondence and clippings.

Russian

27 Mikhail Eisenstadt-Jeleznov (1922-1970). Papers, ca. 1922-70, 8 in. Russian-American writer (pseudonym: M. K. Argus). Correspondence, manuscript copies, and published editions of his writings.

28 Federated Russian Orthodox Clubs. Records, 1943-65, 2.5 ft. Records of the Executive Board, Board of Trustees, and conventions.

29 St. Nicholas Russian Orthodox Cathedral.

30 Alex Simirenko (b. 1931). Collection, 1961-64, ca. 1 ft. Sociologist. Materials, including photos, used for his book Pilgrims, Colonists and Frontiersmen (Free Press of Glencoe, 1964) about the "Russians" of Minneapolis.

Ukrainian American Collection

31 Peter Anderson. Papers, 1923-58, 2 in. Leader of the Minneapolis Ukrainian community. Correspondence and other material of the Ukrainian American Citizen's Club, the United Ukrainian Organization of the Twin Cities, and the Inter-Racial Service Council.

32 K. Bryzhun. Papers, ca. 1946-present, 2.5 ft. and growing. Concerns Canadian Ukrainians and the Ukrainian War Veterans League, Inc.

33 Alexander Bunka. Papers, 1925-69, 1.5 ft. Former officer of the Tucson (Arizona) Ukrainian Society.

34 Central Representation of Ukrainian Emigrants in Germany. Records, 1945-60, 6 ft. Some items touch on U.S. immigration also.

35 J. Chegensky. Papers, ca. 1950-65, 1 in. About Canadian Ukrainians.

36 Peter Feshchenko-Czopiwsky. Papers, ca. 1925-65, ca. 1.3 ft. Letters, music scores by M. Arkas and others, etc.

37 Dmytro Fodchuk. Papers, ca. 1958-present, ca. 2.5 ft. and growing. Materials on Ukrainian social activities (U.S. and Canada).

38 Alexander A. Granovsky (1887-1976). Papers, ca. 1900-76, 145 ft. Ukrainian activist, poet, and entomologist. Correspondence and other material on his activities in the Ukrainian American communities of the U.S. and on Ukrainians in the diaspora. He was the major sponsor of Ukrainian displaced persons to Minnesota.

39 Wasyl Halich (b. 1896). Papers, 1921-71, 2.5 ft. and supplemental papers, ca. 1973-present, ca. .5 ft. and growing. Wisconsin State University history professor and author of Ukrainians in the United States. Correspondence and published materials. Detailed inventory.

40 Mykola H. Haydak (1898-1971). Papers, ca. 1945-70, 10 ft. Entomologist. Concerns such topics as Ukrainian research and education centers, the Ukrainian Folk Ballet in Minnesota, Ukrainian-Jewish relations, and Ukrainian immigrants. Some letters are to/from his mother and relatives in the Ukraine.

41 Jacques Hnizdovsky. Papers, ca. 1966-present, .5 in. and growing. Ukrainian-American graphic artist. Samples of his woodcuts and exhibit programs.

42 Orest Horodysky. Papers, ca. 1960-present, 15.6 ft. and growing. Material, including photos, on the Chicago Ukrainian community, their Ridna Shkola, and the Ukrainian National Association.

43 Dokia Humenna. Papers, ca. 1928-73, 5 in. Ukrainian-American writer. Scrapbooks, 2 vols., with book reviews, publication announcements, epigrams, and correspondence.

44 Peter Kapschutschenko (Peter Enko). Papers, 1947-present, 1 in. and growing. Sculptor, in Argentina and then the U.S.

45 Konstantyn Klepachivsky (b. 1887). Collection, ca. 1919-56, 6 ft. Born in Poltava. Correspondence and material on Poland and Ukraine.

46 Reverend Vladimir Klodnycky (1891-1973). Papers, ca. 1917-73, 11.5 ft. Ukrainian-American priest and former officer of the Ukrainian Galician Army. Diaries, letters, and clippings. Came to the U.S. in 1925, ordained an Orthodox priest in 1930.

47 Michael Komichak. Papers, 1938, 1 in. Manuscript of his "Polkovnyk Konovalets, 14 June 1891-23 May 1938, Arnold, Pa. 26 June 1938."

48 Roman Kuchar. Papers, ca. 1950-present, 3 in. and growing. Language teacher.

49 Pawlo Kukuruza. Papers, 1946-47, .5 ft. Correspondence with various Ukrainian émigrés and their organizations.

50 Marian Kurochka (b. 1899). Papers, ca. 1900-66, 1 in. Manuscript of his work "Tsyhans'-kymy dorohamy" and other items.

51 Stephen Kuropas (b. 1900). Papers, ca. 1940-present, 1 ft. and growing. Correspondence, cultural events programs, etc.

52 Denys Kwitkowsky. Papers, 1971-present, 1 in. and growing. Michigan lawyer. Includes typescript of his Human Rights: Theory and Practice.

53 Myron Leskiw. Papers, ca. 1948-58, 2 in. Correspondence, clippings, and printed works.

54 Myron Malaniuk. Papers, ca. 1939-present, 11 ft. and growing. Materials on Ukrainian community life and activities in Chicago and elsewhere.

55 Manor Junior College, Jenkintown, Pennsylvania. Typescript history of the college, written in 1972, 1 in.

56 Evhen Onatzky (b. 1894). Papers, ca. 1918-1960s, 37.5 ft. Diplomat of the Ukrainian National Republic, professor, and editor. Ukrainian-born Onatzky attended the Paris Peace Conference and was a cultural attaché of the Ukrainian National Republic in Rome. Lived in Italy until 1943, when he emigrated to Argentina, becoming editor of Nash Klych. Correspondence with many Ukrainians in the Western Hemisphere.

57 John Panchuk (b. 1904). Papers, 1933-55, 3 ft. Chairman of the Michigan Commission on Displaced Persons and president of both the United Ukrainian American Relief Committee and Ukrainian Relief Commission of Michigan. Materials on these and other U.S. and Canadian groups, including Ukrainian War Relief. Detailed inventory. Supplemental papers, ca. 1932-present, 5.2 ft. and growing. Concern the Bandurist Chorus, Ukrainian cultural and political activities in Detroit, the Ukrainian Congress Committee of America, displaced persons, the Ukrainian Youth League of North America, and other organizations. Correspondence with prominent Ukrainians.

58 Lena Pechak. Papers, ca. 1917-67, 1.3 ft. Material on U.S. and European organizations,

clippings, Ukrainian currency of the Ukrainian National Republic, 1917-20, and ephemera.

59 W. J. Perepeluk. Papers, ca. 1960-73, 1.3 ft. About Ukrainians in Dauphin, Manitoba, Canada.

60 Petro Plewako. Papers, ca. 1920-68, 7.5 ft. Mainly related to Europe, but some correspondence is with U.S. and Canadian Ukrainians about building projects in Paris.

61 Youry Pundyk (1918?-1973). Papers, ca. 1940-73, ca. 6.5 ft. Economics professor. Correspondence, writings, clippings, and publications.

62 George Royick. Papers, 1957-66, 1.3 ft. Memoirs, correspondence with Ukrainian groups, and miscellanea.

63 Julian Sochocky. Papers, ca. 1950-70, 2.5 ft. Primarily newspaper clippings and other printed matter on Ukraine and Ukrainians.

64 Vera Stetkevicz Stangl. Papers, ca. 1910-72, 1.5 ft. Daughter of Joseph Stetkevicz, editor of Svoboda in the early 1900s. Includes musical scores.

65 P. Sydorenko. Papers, ca. 1903-67, 1 in. Includes copy of a history of early Ukrainian settlement in Saskatchewan, Canada.

66 Omelan Mychajlo Tyshovnytskyj. Papers, 1970-present, 2 in. Materials on Ukrainian cultural life in Los Angeles, California.

67 Ukrainian Congress Committee of America, Minnesota Branch. Records, ca. 1950-present, 7.5 ft. and growing. Correspondence, minutes, and other information on its activities.

68 Ukrainian Students' Club, University of Minnesota. Papers, ca. 1939-present, 7.5 ft. and growing. Correspondence, minutes, activities of the club.

69 United Ukrainian American Relief Committee. Records, ca. 1945-60, 260 ft. U.S.-based group with European representatives founded in 1944 to aid displaced Ukrainians, political refugees, and other war victims. Correspondence, financial records, photographs, and other agency records.

70 Philip and Anna Wasylowsky. Papers, ca. 1940-?, ca. 10 ft. Letters and minutes of the American Ukrainian Republican Association, other material on the Ukrainian National Association.

71 George Wynnyk. Collection, 1960s, 1 in. Items gathered by a Ukrainian in Massachusetts.

72 Alexander Wallace Yaremko. Papers, 1924-69, 1.3 ft. President of the Ukrainian Culture Center in Philadelphia. Correspondence and clippings about this group and on the Ukrainian Youth League of North America.

Ukrainian Foreign Collection

73 Association of Ukrainian Political Prisoners. Records, 1948-49, 1.2 ft. Group based in Munich.

74 Federation of Ukrainians in Great Britain. Records, 1949-54, ca. .5 ft. Includes correspondence, the constitution, and other material of the Federation.

75 Hetmanite Association of Germany and Austria. Records, 1947-67, 1 ft. Operating in Munich.

76 Miscellaneous Ukrainian Collections. Currently contains papers of 6 individuals or agencies.

77 Ukrainian Veterans Association. Records, 1945-46, 1 ft. Another Munich group.

Finding Aids: Immigration History Research Center: Guide to Manuscript Holdings (University of Minnesota, January 1976) for all the general and ethnic collections; and the IHRC Ethnic Collections Series (1976): no. 1 is The Baltic American Collection, compiled by Joseph D. Dwyer, and no. 9 is The Ukrainian American Collection, compiled by Halyna Myroniuk and Maria Samilo. (For those interested in materials on Finns and Poles, which might indirectly relate to the Russian Empire and Soviet Union, nos. 3 and 6 in this series respectively are germane.)

MN 8
GUSTAVUS ADOLPHUS COLLEGE ARCHIVES
St. Peter, Minnesota 56082
(507-931-4300 x 598)

Gustav Otto Richard Reusch (1891-1975). Papers, ca. 1914-75, ca. 2 boxes and 26 manila envelopes. Russian-born Lutheran missionary, pastor, and teacher. Hundreds of letters, manuscripts of writings, lectures, sermons, diaries, memorabilia, clippings, etc. Bulk of the material relates to his missionary work in Tanganyika, Africa, and to his teaching at Gustavus Adolphus College. Born in Samara of German Lutheran parents, raised in Georgia, educated at a military school and at the University of Dorpat, Estonia, where he taught and where he was also a pastor (St. John's Lutheran congregation). As a member of the Cossack Guard in Georgia, he had served in a battalion once sent in pursuit of the young radical Joseph Djugashvili (Stalin). In 1918 he fought the Bolsheviks under Field Marshall Mannerheim of Finland. In 1922 he went to Sweden, then to Denmark.

He was in Africa in 1923-47 and 1948-54, and in St. Peter, Minnesota, in 1947-48, 1954-75, retiring from teaching in 1964.

MISSISSIPPI

MS 1
MITCHELL MEMORIAL LIBRARY
MISSISSIPPI STATE UNIVERSITY
P.O. Drawer 5408
Mississippi State, Mississippi 39762
(601-325-4225)

Calhoun-Kincannon-Orr Family. Papers, 1837-1959, 179 items. Includes a typed copy of a letter, 19 March 1873, from U.S. Minister James L. Orr (1822-1873) in St. Petersburg to his brother Jehu. The letter describes his journey to Russia from the U.S. and his first meeting with the tsar. Orr died in St. Petersburg on 5 May. Unpublished guide.

MISSOURI

MO 1
JOINT COLLECTION: WESTERN HISTORICAL MANUSCRIPT COLLECTION, COLUMBIA-STATE HISTORICAL SOCIETY OF MISSOURI MANUSCRIPTS
23 ELMER ELLIS LIBRARY
UNIVERSITY OF MISSOURI
Columbia, Missouri 65201
(314-882-3660)

1 Green Clay. Papers, 1861-62, 4 folders. Secretary to the American legation in St. Petersburg, summer of 1861. His uncle, Cassius M. Clay, minister to Russia, headed the legation. His journal for 1861-62, photostat, 68 pp., covers most of his stay in Russia. He gives impressions of the capital and its surroundings, the Peterhof summer palace, and an industrial exhibit; assesses Russian craftsmanship and manufacture; and comments on the manners, customs, and conditions of life of the Russian people. The journal includes observations on Prince A. M. Gorchakov, the Russian foreign minister, and of the Duc de Montebello, the French ambassador. The description of Alexander II is long and favorable. Also, a letter, 24 July 1861, from William Seward informing Green Clay of his appointment to the St. Petersburg post. Unpublished description.

2 Fred Morris Dearing (1879-1963). Papers, 1897-1961, 1,624 folders, 28 vols. Diplomat. He served with the U.S. foreign service in Russia, 1916-17. Unpublished memoirs detail his work on the embassy staff. He records his impressions of Petrograd and Moscow, travels through Russia, the embassy's administration, war relief efforts, the situation of the Jews, a projected Russian-American trade treaty, and the decline of the Russian government. Personalities mentioned in the memoirs include Nicholas II, the Empress Alexandra, G. Rasputin, Sergei D. Sazonov (Sagonoff), A. D. Protopopoff, and the American Ambassador David R. Francis. The papers are completely closed during the lifetime of Dearing's son, Donn. Unpublished finding aid (NUCMC 61-2834).

3 Arthur Mastick Hyde (1877-1947). Gubernatorial papers, 1919-24, 32 ft.; and papers, 1886-1949, 477 folders. Governor of Missouri and U.S. secretary of agriculture. Correspondence, reports, and printed materials in the gubernatorial papers contain some items relating to Herbert Hoover's charges that the American Committee for Russian Famine Relief was communistic. The second collection, containing his papers as secretary of agriculture under Hoover, includes data on wheat production in the USSR and on Soviet efforts to manipulate grain prices in the 1920s-1930s. (NUCMC 60-2334)

4 Olive Gilbreath McLorn (b. 1883). Letters, 1915-34, 47 folders. Letters she received from William L. Cazalet, a British businessman living in Russia. Primarily love letters but also including impressions of World War I, the Russian Revolution, and British refugees and creditors of Russia. Restricted.

5 Duke Needham Parry (1893-1932). Papers, 1923-24, ca. 1 ft. Foreign correspondent for the International News Service. Correspondence, unpublished articles, and clippings from his tour in Japan, including some items about Russo-Japanese relations. (NUCMC 68-1347)

6 George N. Peek (1873-1943). Papers, 1911-47, 10 boxes, 3,088 folders. Public servant, special adviser to President Franklin D. Roosevelt on foreign trade, 1934-35, and president of the Export-Import Bank of Washington, 1934-35. His correspondence, particularly with Boris Said in 1934-35, concerns, in part, Russian-American trade, the Russian economy (especially oil and steel industry), and Roosevelt's reaction to the breakdown of trade negotiations with Russia. (NUCMC 60-2466)

7 William Benjamin Smith (1850-1934). Papers, 1876?-1933, 22 folders. Educator and philosopher. He spoke out for recognition of the new Soviet government in 1918. Autobiography, addresses, etc. (NUCMC 60-2641)

8 Fred H. Walden. In Stockholm in 1791, he witnessed a naval battle between Russian and Swedish ships. 1 letter, photostat, describes the engagement.

Finding Aid: Guide to the Western Historical Manuscripts Collection, Bulletin nos. 6 and 7 (1952, 1957).

MO 2
THE HARRY S. TRUMAN LIBRARY
Independence, Missouri 64050
(816-833-1400)

The Truman Library was established to preserve materials pertaining to Harry S. Truman and his administration. Russian-related materials can be found in 3 of its holdings: manuscripts; oral history interviews; and microfilms.

Manuscripts

1 Dean Acheson. Papers, 1933-71. 61 ft. Assistant secretary of state, 1941-45; undersecretary of state, 1945-47; secretary of state, 1949-53. 1 ft. of correspondence, memoranda, and speeches pertaining to the Soviet Union. (NUCMC 76-97)

2 George V. Allen. Papers, 1944-69. Ca. 1 ft. U.S. ambassador to Iran, 1946-48. Some letters pertaining to U.S.-Soviet relations towards Iran.

3 Allied Commission for Austria. Selected records (duplicates), 1946 and 1949-50. 1 ft. Included are the minutes of the Allied Commission for Austria and the minutes of the Executive Committee of the ACA. The originals are in the National Archives, Washington, D.C.

4 Thomas C. Blaisdell, Jr. Papers, 1933-51: 5 ft., 1933-51. Assistant secretary of commerce, 1949-51. Ca. 1 ft. of materials pertaining to commerce with communist countries. (NUCMC 66-1149)

5 Will L. Clayton. Papers, 1926-1966. 74 ft. Under secretary of State for Economic Affairs, 1946-47. Ca. 1 ft. of correspondence, memoranda, and reports shed light on the USSR. (NUCMC 66-1151)

6 Clark M. Clifford. Papers, 1946-52. 16 ft. Special counsel to the president, 1946-50. Includes 2 ft. of correspondence, memoranda, reports, and drafts of speeches pertaining to Russia. (NUCMC 68-1619)

7 George M. Elsey. Files, 1941-53. 42 ft. Administrative assistant to the president, 1949-51; director for Mutual Security, 1951-53. 4 ft. of correspondence, memoranda, notes, reports, and minutes of meetings relating to the Soviet Union. (NUCMC 77-901)

8 Bryn J. Hovde. Papers, 1940-50. 2 ft. Chief, Division of Cultural Cooperation, Department of State, 1944-45. 1 ft. of reports on the World Conference of Intellectuals, 1948. (NUCMC 75-594)

9 Charles M. Hulten. Papers, 1942-63. 12 ft. Deputy director, Office of War Information, 1944-45; deputy assistant secretary of state, 1946-51. Ca. 1 ft. of reports, memoranda, and information programs of the State Department (through the Voice of America) pertain to Russia. (NUCMC 76-102)

10 Joseph M. Jones. Papers, 1947-48. 1 ft. Special assistant to the assistant secretary of state for public affairs, 1946-48. 1 ft. of Russian-related materials, including correspondence, memoranda, reports, and copies of official documents used by Jones for writing his book, The Fifteen Weeks. There is also documentation on the Marshall Plan. (NUCMC 65-117)

11 Milton Katz. Papers, 1932-52. 9 ft. Special U.S. representative to Europe, 1950-51. Ca. 1 ft. pertaining to the Soviet Union, including correspondence, articles and notes, directories, and other materials relating to ECA operations. (NUCMC 74-325)

12 Edwin A. Locke, Jr. Files, 1941-53. 2 ft. Personal representative of the president to China, 1945; special assistant to the president, 1946-47; ambassador in charge of the U.S. Mission to the Near East, 1951-52. Some materials pertaining to Russia/USSR. (NUCMC 65-122)

13 Frank McNaughton. Papers, 1938-52. 10 ft. Correspondent for Time magazine, 1941-49. Includes a small amount of material on U.S. policy toward the USSR. (NUCMC 66-1158)

14 Frederick Osborn. Papers, 1947-54. 1 ft. U.S. deputy representative to the United Nations Atomic Energy Commission, 1947-50. 1 ft. of correspondence, briefs, and speeches have references to Russia. (NUCMC 76-103)

15 J. Anthony Panuch. Papers, 1931-73. 9 ft. Held various posts in the government. 1 folder containing a memorandum on Russia dated 1932. (NUCMC 77-902)

16 Walter A. Radius. Papers, 1948. Ca. 1 ft. Chairman of the U.S. Delegation, Danube Conference, 1948. Russian-related materials include documents pertaining to the International Conference on the Navigation of the Danube River, held at Belgrade, Yugoslavia, 1948.

17 Samuel I. Rosenman. Papers, 1945-66. 4 ft. Special counsel to the president, 1945-46. Some materials pertaining to Soviet-American relations toward Eastern Europe. (NUCMC 65-135)

18 John W. Snyder. Papers, 1918-71. 87 ft. Secretary of the treasury, 1946-53. Contains some materials on Treasury-related foreign policy matters. (NUCMC 65-142)

19 Sidney W. Soeurs. Papers, 1925-72. 2 ft. Executive secretary, National Security Council, 1947-50. Russian-related items include ca. 1 ft. of correspondence regarding the National Security Council.

20 State, U.S. Department of. Office files of the assistant secretary for Economic Affairs and the under secretary for Economic Affairs, 1944-48. Ca. 1 ft. of correspondence relating to Russia. (NUCMC 77-912)

21 Harry S. Truman. Papers as president of the United States from the central files of the White House (partly on microfilm), 1945-53. 2,713 ft. 15 ft. (estimated) of correspondence, memoranda, notes, reports (press releases), and speeches pertaining to Russia. (NUCMC 65-145 and 77-910)

22 Harry S. Truman. Post-presidential papers, 1953-72. 404 ft. 2 ft. of transcripts of interviews with Truman administration officials that pertain to the Soviet Union. (NUCMC 77-910)

23 In addition, there may be scattered references to Russia/USSR in the following manuscript collections: American Institute of Public Opinion (Gallup Poll), selected public opinion news service releases, 1945-52, ca. 1 ft.; Everett H. Bellows, U.S. representative in Europe, Mutual Security Administration, 1951-53, papers, 1951-60, ca. 1 ft.; G. Lyle Belsley, executive secretary, War Production Board, 1942-45, papers, 1938-45, 3 ft.; Edward L. Bowles, consultant to the secretary of war and special consultant to the commanding general, Army Air Force, 1942-47, papers, 1945-50, ca. 1 ft.; Committee for the Marshall Plan, records, 1947-51, 1 ft. (NUCMC 65-101); Nathaniel P. Davis, minister to Hungary, 1949-51, papers, 1916-57, ca. 1 ft. (NUCMC 65-104); Thomas K. Finletter, secretary of the air force, 1950-53, papers, 1943-69, 4 ft.; John W. Gibson, chairman, Displaced Persons Commission, 1950-52, papers, 1935-54, 19 ft. (NUCMC 65-111); A. Robert Ginsburg, member of the staff of the secretary of defense, 1949-53, papers, 1944-53, 6 ft.; Stanton Griffis, ambassador to Poland, scrapbook files, 1936-67, 5 ft.; Dan A. Kimball, assistant secretary of the navy for air, 1949, under secretary of the navy, 1949-51, secretary of the navy, 1951-53, papers, 1949-53, 3 ft. (NUCMC 72-897); Korean War, copies of selected documents from the files of the Department of Defense and the Department of State pertaining to the records, 7 ft., 1947-52 (NUCMC 72-911); John L. McKee, U.S. Army officer, headquarters, European command, 1949-53, papers, 1917-54, ca. 1 ft.; Cornelius J. Mara, assistant military aide to President Harry S. Truman, papers, 1944-50, ca. 1 ft.; Francis P. Matthews, secretary of the navy, 1949-51, papers, 1932-52, 29 ft. (NUCMC 68-1626); National Security Committee, records, 1947-50, ca. 1 ft. (NUCMC 65-129); Navy, Secretary of the, and Secretary of Defense, public statements, 1945-52, 3 ft.; John E. O'Gara, official, Central Intelligence Agency, 1949-61, papers, 1919-61, ca. 1 ft.; Frank Pace, Jr., secretary of the army, 1950-53, papers, 1946-53, 7 ft. (NUCMC 65-131); Richard C. Patterson, Jr., ambassador to Yugoslavia, 1944-48, papers, 1918-66, 9 ft. (NUCMC 75-599); Sumner T. Pike, member, Atomic Energy Commission, 1946-51, papers, 1920-61, 6 ft. (NUCMC 65-132); Henry Reiff, legal specialist in international organization, Department of State, 1944-46, papers, 1943-46, 5 ft. (NUCMC 75-601); Theodore Tannenwald, Jr., assistant director and chief of staff to the director for mutual security, 1951-53, papers, 1947-57, 3 ft. (NUCMC 65-143); Myron C. Taylor, personal representative of the president to the Vatican, 1939-50, papers, 1938-52, 1 ft. (NUCMC 75-603); United Nations Command (Korea), G-3 operations reports, 1951-52, 7 ft., closed; U.S. Senate Committee on Foreign Relations, 80th and 81st Congresses, selected documents, 1947-50, 2 ft.; George L. Warren, adviser on refugees and displaced persons, Department of State, 1930-72, papers, 1944-68, ca. 1 ft.; James E. Webb, undersecretary of state, 1949-52, adminsitrator, National Aeronautics and Space Administration, 1961-68, papers, 1928-75, 229 ft. (NUCMC 65-149); John C. Young, presiding judge, Tribunal V, U.S. Military Tribunal, Nuremburg, Germany, 1948, papers, 1947-48, 32 ft. (NUCMC 77-914).

Oral History Interviews

24 The Truman Library has oral history interviews that have or may have references to Russia. Among these are the following: John Abbott, Navy Department liaison officer to the Special U.S. Senate Committee investigating the National Defense Program, 1942-46, 173 pp.; Nathan M. Becker, economic adviser, Board of Economic Warfare and Department of State, 1941-47, economic adviser, general staff, U.S.-U.N. forces, Korea, 1952-53, 99 pp.; David K. E. Bruce, undersecretary of state, 1952-53, 49 pp.; O. Edmund Clubb, consul general, Vladivostok, 1944-46, 95 pp.; William H. Draper, military government adviser to the secretary of state, Moscow Conference of Foreign Ministers, 1947, 87 pp.; Josiah E. DuBois, Jr., member, Allied Reparations Commission, Moscow, 1945, member, U.S. delegation to the Berlin Conference (Potsdam), 1945, 39 pp.; George M. Elsey, special assistant to the president, 1947-49, administrative assistant

to the president, 1949-51, 477 pp.; Thomas K. Finletter, secretary of the air force, 1950-53, 84 pp.; Roswell L. Gilpatric, assistant secretary of the air force, 1951, under secretary of the air force, 1951-53, 48 pp.; Gordon Gray, assistant secretary of the army, 1947-49, secretary of the army, 1949-50, special assistant to the president, 1950, 57 pp.; Walter H. Judd, member of Congress from Minnesota, 1943-62, U.S. delegate to the 12th General Assembly of the United Nations, 1947, 123 pp.; Carroll H. Kenworthy, editor of the foreign department of United Press International, Washington, D.C., 1941-67, 65 pp.; Halvard M. Lange, minister of foreign affairs, Norway, 1946-65, 14 pp.; M. Leva, assistant secretary of defense, 1949-51, 97 pp.; Edwin A. Locke, Jr., personal representative of the president to China, 1945, special assistant to the president, 1946-47, 67 pp.; Isador Lubin, U.S. associate representative with the rank of minister, Allied Reparations Commission, Moscow, 1945, U.S. representative to the Economic and Employment Commission, U.N. Economic and Social Council, 1946-49, special assistant to the assistant secretary of state, 1949-50, U.S. representative with the rank of minister, U.N. Economic and Social Council, 1950-53, 12 pp.; Roger Makins, assistant under secretary of state, Foreign Service, Great Britain, 12 pp.; Cornelius J. Mara, assistant military aide to President Harry S. Truman, 1949-52, 125 pp.; Edward S. Mason, economic consultant to the Department of State, 1946-47, chief economic adviser, U.S. delegation, Conference of Foreign Ministers (Moscow), 1947, 46 pp.; Clifford C. Matlock, political officer, Department of State, 1946-62, 195 pp.; Philleo Nash, special assistant to the director, Office of War Information, 1942-46, 795 pp.; Louis H. Renfrow, assistant military aide to the president, 1947-49, assistant to the secretary of defense, 1949-50, 158 pp.; James W. Riddleberger, chief, Division of Central European Affairs, Department of State, 1944-47, counsellor of embassy and chief, Political Section, American Military Government, Berlin, Germany, 1947-50, political adviser to the Economic Cooperation Administration, Paris, 1950-52, director, Bureau of German Affairs, Department of State, 1952-53, 120 pp.; Arthur R. Ringwalt, chief, Division of Chinese Affairs, Department of State, 1946-48, 41 pp.; Charles E. Saltzman, assistant secretary of state for occupied areas, 1947-49, 25 pp.; Durward V. Sandifer, deputy director, Office of United Nations Affairs, Department of State, 1947-49, deputy assistant secretary of state for United Nations affairs, 1949-54, 139 pp.; R. Burr Smith, economist, Department of State, 1946-49, member, U.S. delegation, Austrian Treaty Conference, 1949, 77 pp.; Harold E. Stassen, member, U.S. delegation to the United Nations Conference on International Organization, San Francisco, 1945, 40 pp.; Lewis L. Strauss, member, Atomic Energy Commission, 1946-50, chairman, Atomic Energy Commission, 1953-58, 58 pp.; John L. Sullivan, assistant secretary of the navy for Air, 1945-46, undersecretary of the navy, 1946-47, secretary of the navy, 1947-49, 90 pp.; Theodore Tannenwald, Jr., assistant director and chief of staff to the director for mutual security, 1951-53, 31 pp.; J. William Theis, chief of the U.S. Senate staff of the International News Service, 1945-58, and of the U.S. Senate staff of the United Press International, 1945-58, 48 pp.; Constantine Tsaldaris, prime minister, Greece, 1946-47, 10 pp.; Eugene Zuckert, assistant secretary of the air force, 1947-52, 83 pp.

Microfilms

25 The Truman Library also has microfilm collections with Russian-related materials. These include microfilms of presidential papers, as well as microfilms of the Adams Family papers, 608 reels (NUCMC 62-1261), originals at the Massachusetts Historical Society; of transcripts of press conferences of U.S. Secretaries of State, 1933-53, 7 reels, originals at the Department of State; of the papers of Edward R. Stettinius, Jr., 2 reels, originals at the Univeristy of Virginia; and of the papers of Henry L. Stimson, 1 reel, originals at Yale University.

Finding Aids: Unpublished shelf lists for each manuscript collection are available at the Harry S. Truman Library. See also Historical Materials in the Harry S. Truman Library (January, 1979).

MO 3
ARCHIVES
JACKSON COUNTY HISTORICAL SOCIETY
Independence Square Courthouse, Room 103
Independence, Missouri 64050
(816-252-7454)

Simon Few (1810-1882). Papers, 1810-86, ca. 1 ft. Steamboat captain. 4 letters from Russia, 1875, written by Few, who was in charge of steamboats on the Volga River. Also, his visa, license, and photographs of Few and his family.

MO 4
ARCHIVES BRANCH
FEDERAL ARCHIVES & RECORDS CENTER, GSA
2306 East Bannister Road
Kansas City, Missouri 64131
(816-926-7271)

This repository has some of the microfilms of materials in the National Archives (Washington, D.C.) that pertain to Russia/USSR. For more details, see Charles South, List of National Archives Microfilm Publications in the Regional Archives Branches (Washington: National Archives & Records Service, 1975).

MO 5
DEPARTMENT OF ARCHIVES AND HISTORY
CONCORDIA HISTORICAL INSTITUTE
LUTHERAN CHURCH--MISSOURI SYNOD
801 De Mun Avenue
St. Louis, Missouri 63105
(314-721-5934 x 320/321)

1 Lutheran Church--Missouri Synod. Board for European Affairs. Records, 1847-1966, 21 ft. Ca. 1 ft. of the correspondence concerns pre-World War II Estonia and missions among displaced persons from Estonia, Latvia, and Lithuania. Unpublished inventory (NUCMC 62-1563, 66-98, and 69-654).

2 John (Jaan) Sillak (1864-1953). Papers, 1901-53, 7 ft. Lutheran missionary. Diaries, manuscripts, and printed matter, including the Estonian periodical Laulu ja Maengu Leht. Materials relate to his mission work in western Canada among Estonian and Latvian immigrants. Unpublished inventory (NUCMC 61-2516).

Restriction: Access to accredited researchers only.

MO 6
MISSOURI HISTORICAL SOCIETY LIBRARY
Jefferson Memorial Building
St. Louis, Missouri 63112
(314-361-1424)

1 William Keeney Bixby (1857-1931). Autograph collection includes 1 of Nicholas I of Russia.

2 David Rowland Francis (1850-1927). Papers, 1868-1919, 20 ft., ca. 50,000 items. Governor of Missouri, and U.S. ambassador to Russia, April 1916-April 1919. Ca. 50% of the correspondence, reports, and other papers concern embassy business and U.S.-Russian diplomatic relations. Many Russian subjects and personalities are noted. Includes a signed letter of V. I. Lenin (Lenine) to Francis, 14 January 1918. (NUCMC 68-1284)

3 Earl Maynard Johnston (1890-1955). Papers, 1916-19, 32 items. Secretary to David R. Francis, ambassador to Russia, from mid-1916 to 1919. Materials concern Russian-American relations and other subjects related to the diplomatic service.

Restriction: Access to accredited researchers only.

MO 7
VATICAN FILM LIBRARY
PIUS XII MEMORIAL LIBRARY
ST. LOUIS UNIVERSITY
3655 West Pine Boulevard
St. Louis, Missouri 63108
(314-658-3090)

The Vatican Film Library comprises microfilm duplications of ca. 75% of all manuscripts (5th-19th c.) in Greek, Latin, and Western European languages held in the Vatican Library in Vatican City (Rome), Italy. (Holdings of the Vatican Archives, a separate repository for the Vatican's "state papers," are not included.) Arabic, Ethiopic, and Hebrew manuscripts have also been microfilmed. The Film Library continues to microfilm on a small scale, so new acquisitions are expected for some time. In addition, the collection of manuscripts on microfilm is supplemented by color slides of the Vatican Library's illuminated manuscripts and slides from many other British and European manuscript libraries, currently numbering ca. 49,500 items.

Materials relating to Russia from the 17th and 18th c. are scattered throughout the various collections making up the Vatican Library's manuscript collection. They are not separately catalogued, and considerable searching through published and unpublished catalogues and indexes would be required to locate them.

MO 8
RARE BOOKS AND SPECIAL COLLECTIONS
WASHINGTON UNIVERSITY LIBRARIES
Skinker and Lindell Boulevards
St. Louis, Missouri 63130
(314-889-5495)

1 Vladimir Nabokov (b. 1899). Papers, 1958-64, ca. 10 items. Russian-American writer. Includes letters, March 1958-June 1959, from Vera (Mrs. Vladimir) Nabokov to Peter Russell concerning Nabokov's books and translations; transcript of an interview with the writer by Jane Howard which appeared as part of a 1964 Life magazine article, 7 pp., and a few other items. Among topics discussed by Mrs. Nabokov are her husband's views of translation, both of his own work and of others' (e.g., of Ezra Pound). Unpublished finding aid (NUCMC 70-2066, cited as part of a larger collection).

2 William Jay Smith (b. 1918). Papers, ca. 1924-68, ca. 40 boxes (additions expected). Author, poet, translator, editor, and lecturer. Correspondence, translations, journals, drafts, etc. He has traveled to the USSR and been involved in publishing works of the poet Evgenii Yevtushenko in English translation in the U.S. Some materials pertain to these Russian connections.

Correspondents include Guy Daniels, Babette Deutsch, and Philip Rahv. Unpublished finding aids (NUCMC 70-2067).

MO 9
ARCHIVES AND LIBRARY
EDEN THEOLOGICAL SEMINARY
475 East Lockwood Avenue
Webster Groves, Missouri 63119
(314-961-3627 x 65)

1 Fort Collins Seminary for Russians. Financial records, 1913-18, 20 pp., plus several promissory notes. Kassenbuch des Seminars für die Deutsch-Russen, in German. The notes, signed by J. Erbes and William Werner, are for construction on the seminary.

2 Reverend F. Freund. Correspondence with J. Baltzer, president of the Evangelical Church, November 1919-November 1920, 8 pieces. Pertains, inter alia, to Russian churches and to Reverend H. Rosenbusch. All are typewritten in German.

3 National Mission Brief Leaflet. Undated leaflet gives a history and explains the problems of the Volga-Germans and of mission work among them.

Note: It may be possible to arrange for interlibrary loan of the materials described above.

MONTANA

MT 1
ARCHIVES
MONTANA STATE UNIVERSITY LIBRARY
Bozeman, Montana 59717
(406-994-2841)

Milburn Lincoln Wilson (b. 1885). Papers, 1914-33, ca. 46 cu. ft. Professor of agricultural economics at MSU. He served as an adviser for the Grain Trust of the USSR on the organization and management of large-scale mechanized grain farms, spending the summer of 1929 in visits to proposed sites for such farms in southwest Russia, near Rostov. Materials include correspondence, reports, and lantern slides. They shed light on Russian-American relations generally in 1928-33. Some items contain his recommendations for machinery purchases, data on Soviet plans for model farms and training schools, and orders for U.S. machinery. Papers note the Amtorg Trading Corporation as well as the Grain Trust. Arrangements to use the papers should be made in advance. Unpublished inventory and index (NUCMC 67-493).

MT 2
ARCHIVES
MONTANA HISTORICAL SOCIETY
225 North Roberts Street
Helena, Montana 59601
(406-449-2694)

1 Fred Barton (fl. early 20th c.). Horse wrangler. Oral history interview, 1955, 1 hr., 2 cassettes, with 3 interviewers. Reminiscences of work on horse ranches in the Miles City, Montana, area and accounts of his horse raising in Siberian Russia, 1911-12, and, primarily, in China, 1917-37. R. Miracle, "Asian Adventures of a Cowboy from Montana," Montana Magazine of Western History, vol. 27, no. 2 (Spring, 1977).

2 Jesse B. Roote (b. 1870). Papers, 1919, 56 items. Lawyer and U.S. Army officer. In 1919 he was stationed with the infantry at Camp Bautzen, Germany, as representative officer for the Interallied Commission for Repatriating Russian Prisoners of War. In this position he was responsible for the welfare of as many as 2,000 Russian prisoners per month. General correspondence, primarily between Roote and Commission headquarters in Berlin; official incoming memoranda, orders, and instructions; messages from the Russian prisoners; reports to the Commission; outgoing supply requisitions and miscellany. These materials concern administration policies, camp conditions, and the numbers and attitudes of prisoners. Unpublished finding aid.

MT 3
ARCHIVES
MANSFIELD LIBRARY
UNIVERSITY OF MONTANA
Missoula, Montana 59812
(406-243-2053)

1 Michael Mansfield (b. 1903). Papers, 1943-77, ca. 4,200 boxes, 283 scrapbooks, and 107 photo albums, plus transcripts of all his radio and television interviews/appearances, and printed matter. U.S. senator, majority leader of the Senate, 1961-76. Contains information on the formation of American foreign policy, particularly in the foreign relations and speeches series. At this writing papers are not fully processed and accessible. Unpublished finding aid.

2 Note: The archives hold papers of other congressional figures, such as James Murray, which may well contain Russian/Soviet-related material.

NEBRASKA

NE 1
HAMILTON COUNTY HISTORICAL SOCIETY
PLAINSMAN MUSEUM
210 16th Street
Aurora, Nebraska 68818
(402-694-6531)

Hamilton County Russian Mennonite Settlement. A short account of the group's emigration from southern Russia in 1874. The preliminary edition of the Guide to Depositories of Manuscript Collections in the United States--Nebraska, compiled by the Historical Records Survey of the Works Projects Administration (Lincoln, 1940), notes this collection.

NE 2
NEBRASKA STATE HISTORICAL SOCIETY
1500 R Street
Lincoln, Nebraska 68508
(402-471-3270)

1 Henry J. Amen (1876-1975). Collection, 1904-48, 8 items on 1 microfilm reel. Merchant, grocer, steamship ticket agent, insurance salesman, and informal banker for the German-American community in Lincoln. Includes account books with the names and travel itineraries of Russian-German immigrants to the U.S. and other relevant information. Unpublished descriptive inventory and list of folders (NUCMC 76-242).

2 Lincoln, Nebraska. First German Congregational Church. Records, 1889-1919, 2 vols. on 1 microfilm reel. Organized in 1876, the church was composed of Russian-Germans who had migrated to Lincoln from the Volga region of Russia. The volumes are church registers. Several unpublished finding aids (NUCMC 76-3430).

3 Nebraska Breuder Konferenz. Records, 1887-1974, 7 vols. on 1 microfilm reel. The Konferenz, founded in 1887, is a prayer-discussion group of Russian-Germans in Nebraska. Designed to provide fellowship, protection, and social stability, it is modeled after organizations the Volga Germans developed while still in Russia. Programs, executive committee minutes, and printed histories of the group. Unpublished finding aids (NUCMC 76-434).

4 Arthur L. and Harry O. Palmer. Papers, 1873-1961, ca. 5.5 ft. Harry O. Palmer (1886-1951) was a lawyer, army major, and judge advocate of the American Expeditionary Forces to Siberia and China, 1918-21. Includes correspondence and his diary for the phase of his career in Siberia. Unpublished finding aid. (NUCMC 76-465 superceded by 78-450)

5 Raymon O. Parker. Scrapbook of clippings from 1904-1907 (Lincoln newspapers) relating to the Russo-Japanese War, and national and international politics.

6 Sutton, Nebraska. Emmanuel Reformed Church. Church registers, 1874-1946, 2 vols. on 1 microfilm reel. Congregation of Germans who emigrated from Russia in the late 1860s. They began to hold church services and established the German Reformed Church under the Reverend William Bonekeeper, son of a Reformed minister in Russia. Organized on 20 February 1877, the church later changed its name as above. Descriptive inventory, general description, and volume listing, all unpublished. (NUCMC 76-319)

7 John Milton Thayer (1820-1906). Papers, 1886-92, ca. 5.5 ft. Governor of Nebraska. Among the papers are letters outlining a plan to send supplies to aid suffering Russians in the famine of 1891. Unpublished finding aid.

8 Karlis August Ulmanis (1877-1940?). Latvian president and an exile in the U.S. In this country he worked in agriculture at the University of Nebraska. Includes correspondence and memorials, 1934-65. Unpublished finding aid (NUCMC 76-424). (Part of the Miscellaneous Papers, 1825-1967)

9 William F. Urbach (1888-1972). Collection, 1876-1900, 20 items. Materials about Russian-German immigrants to the United States: histories of the Urbach and Gabel families, 2 passports, some parish documents, and copies of passenger lists of the steamships Frisia and Nurnberg. Unpublished descriptive inventory and other finding aids. (NUCMC 76-424)

10 Hattie (Plum) Williams (1878-1963). Papers, 1884-1959, ca. 31 ft. Sociologist. Research notes on Russian-German immigration to the U.S., Williams' 1909 M.A. thesis on the German-Russian colony in Lincoln, and her Ph.D. thesis, "The Czar's Germans," 1915. Several unpublished finding aids (NUCMC 65-1509).

11 Thomas Frederick Arthur Williams (1871-1969). Papers, 1861-1964, 8 ft., ca. 3,000 items. Lawyer, husband of the preceding. Includes information on the migration of Germans in

Russia and the U.S. (presumably gathered by his wife Hattie), 1913-14; research notes; and a census of the Russian-German population of Lincoln, 1914-15. Unpublished descriptive inventory, biographical notes, and folder list (NUCMC 69-411).

Finding Aids: The society has published a series of bulletins under the title A Guide to the Manuscript Division of the State Archives, Nebraska State Historical Society (1974-).

NEVADA

NV 1
NEVADA HISTORICAL SOCIETY
1650 North Virginia Street
Reno, Nevada 89503
(702-784-6397)

1 John V. Ciceu (1924-1972). Papers, 1962-65, 2 boxes. Chapter leader of the John Birch Society at Reno, member of the Nevada Anti-Communist Freedom Forum. Materials, concerning anti-communism in the U.S., include fairly complete records of the Birch Society's chapter's and members' activities (correspondence, reports, office files, and account books). Ciceu corresponded with a number of prominent international and national political leaders. (NC 142)

2 John Hensley DeTar (b. 1925). Papers, 1956-73, 8 boxes. Organizer and director of the John Birch Society in Nevada. Letters, reports, literary manuscripts, miscellaneous documents, and considerable printed matter (many Birch Society publications), relating to anti-communist, right-wing political groups and activities, mostly in Nevada. Includes correspondence with many Nevada political leaders. Until 1983, access is by written permission from the donor only. (NC 113)

3 Alma Goble. Undergraduate thesis, University of Nevada (1906), entitled "The Fur Trade as a Factor in the Development of the Pacific Slope," 42 pp., with references to Russia. (0739)

4 George Thomas Marye (1849-1933). U.S. ambassador to Russia, 1914-16. Official photograph album given to him (?) by Nicholas II: Iz moego al'boma. Shest'desiat fotograficheskikh snimkov eia imperatorskago velichestva gosudaryni imperatritsy Aleksandry Feodorovny (Petrograd and Moscow, M. O. Vol'f, n.d.). Facing the title page, in hand of the empress presumably, is the short title and her signature. Photos are from 1912-15, all 60 captioned in Russian. They show scenes of the war, nurses, and the wounded.

Finding Aid: A Guide to the Manuscript Collections at the Nevada Historical Society (1975).

NEW HAMPSHIRE

NH 1
NEW HAMPSHIRE HISTORICAL SOCIETY
30 Park Street
Concord, New Hampshire 03301
(603-225-3381)

1 William E. Chandler (1835-1917). Papers, 1829-1917, 22 ft., ca. 25,000 items. Lawyer, politician, and U.S. senator. Includes a few letters referring to the Peace Conference at Portsmouth, New Hampshire, in 1905, where President Theodore Roosevelt helped negotiate a peace treaty between Russia and Japan. Unpublished guide (NUCMC 69-418).

2 Jacob Harold Gallinger (1837-1918). Papers, 1862-1919, 3 ft., ca. 1,000 items. Physician, U.S. representative and senator. Contains some correspondence concerning the Portsmouth Treaty Conference to end the Russo-Japanese War, 1905. Unpublished guide (NUCMC 69-420).

NH 2
SPECIAL COLLECTIONS
BAKER MEMORIAL LIBRARY
DARTMOUTH COLLEGE
Hanover, New Hampshire 03755
(603-646-2571)

1 Edwin Tappan Adney (1868-1950). Papers, 1887-1907, 1 ft. Artist, journalist, and researcher on North American history. Some correspondence is with John J. Healy (1840-1909), chief advocate of a railroad through Alaska, across the Bering Strait (by tunnel) and across Siberia. Also materials on the Alaska Northern Railroad Company and the Alaska and Siberian Development Company. Collection is described in the Dartmouth College Library Bulletin, NS, vol. 6 (January 1966). (NUCMC 74-297) (In the Stefansson Collection)

2 Ralph S. Bartlett. Family papers, undated, 1 box. Boston lawyer, art importer, and antique dealer. He ran the Old Russia antique shop in Boston, visited Russia in 1912 and again in

the 1920s. (In the Anthropology Department of Dartmouth College are letters and other papers about the Russian art objects Bartlett donated to Dartmouth, as well as the objects themselves --statues, porcelain, silverware, textiles, medals, icons, cassocks, and silver, 4 boxes.)

3 Grenville Clark (1882-1967). Papers, 1882-1967, ca. 244 ft. International lawyer and public servant. Correspondence, records, biographical materials, etc. Clark worked for world government after World War II, was an unofficial leader of the United World Federalists, tried to stem the Cold War, and produced, with Louis B. Sohn, the treatise World Peace through World Law (1958). He was friends with such American political leaders as John J. McCloy, John Foster Dulles, Averell Harriman, and Dean Acheson. He became involved briefly in the Cuban Missile Crisis of 1962 and afterward helped to establish the World Law Fund to encourage disarmament. Details of restrictions at the library. Published and unpublished finding aids (NUCMC 76-1830).

4 Robert Steed Dunn (1877-1955). Papers, 1896-1955, 5 ft., ca. 1,600 items. Journalist, author, and traveler. Served in the U.S. Navy in both world wars. Among the papers are over 500 diplomatic dispatches to and from U.S. naval forces and the U.S. embassy in Istanbul, 1920-21, concerning revolutions in the Near East, the Armenian Question, and other matters. (NUCMC 74-299) (In the Stefansson Collection)

5 John Ledyard (1751-1789). Papers, ca. 1772-88, ca. 30 items. Explorer. Sailed with Captain James Cook on his third voyage, as a corporal of marines. He was apparently the first American to make contact with the Russians in Alaska; Cook sent him to the Russians' trading settlement in October 1778. Furs obtained from Alaskan Indians were traded to Canton for large profits, leading Ledyard to try to set up his own fur trading company. In 1786 he traveled through Scandinavia to St. Petersburg, where he was unable to obtain a visa to continue to the Pacific. Undaunted, he pushed on anyway, to Moscow, Kazan, Tobolsk, Barnaul, Irkutsk, Lake Baikal, the Lena River, and Iakutsk. While awaiting spring to complete his journey to Alaska, Ledyard was seized by order of Catherine II and banished from the empire. The library has his journal and some of his letters. (Available evidence suggests that some of his writings remain in the USSR.)

6 Ernest Poole (1880-1950). Papers, 1905-37, 1 box. Journalist and novelist. He was a foreign correspondent in Russia before World War I. He wrote 2 novels about Russia, The Dark People (1918) and The Village (1918). Includes some literary manuscripts and articles.

7 Sergei Prokofiev (1891-1953). Correspondence, 1937-40, ca. 12 items. Composer. Letters to and by Prokofiev relating to Hanover's Prokofieff Society.

8 Kenneth Roberts (1885-1957). Papers, ca. 1919-1920s, 2 vols. Novelist. Served with the American Expeditionary Forces in Siberia, 1918-19. "Notebooks of a Foreign Correspondent." Restricted. Typed inventory.

9 Stefansson Collection on the Polar Regions. Ca. 528 ft. and growing, 1900-present. Vilhjalmur Stefansson (1879-1962) was an Arctic explorer, scholar, and writer. Collection holds correspondence, draft articles for his Encyclopedia Arctica, translations, U.S. government reports, journals, and printed material relating to Russia/USSR. While he maintained a polar library in New York City, Stefansson was in continous contact with Russian diplomats in New York and Washington, D.C. His letter files have annual folders labeled "Russia" or USSR" from 1927-50 and intermittent files through 1962. Among embassy personnel with whom he exchanged information on polar regions were Andrei Gromyko and Constantine Oumansky. Other correspondence relates to Stefansson's participation in the National Council of American-Soviet Friendship, Inc., the American Russian Institute, American-Soviet Science Society, and American Society for Russian Relief, Inc. There are Encyclopedia articles on the botany of Siberia, many individual Russian scientists or explorers, and the Soviet North in general. (The Encyclopedia Arctica and Stefansson's expedition journals are available on microfilm from Xerox University Microfilms in Ann Arbor, Michigan.) Much Russian material on the Arctic appears in translations by the Stefansson Library and in preliminary reports prepared for U.S. agencies, from the 1930s and 1940s mainly. One example is a typescript, 6 vols., Guide Book for Arctic Siberia done for the War Department. Some journals and other papers concern the wreck of the Karluk and its survivors' stay on Wrangel Island (1914), and the Wrangel Island Expedition of 1921-23 sponsored by Stefansson. The collection also includes the papers of Ernest deKoven Leffingwell, 1900-66, letters, journals, and notes, a geologist and explorer who took part in the Baldwin-Ziegler Expedition to Franz Josef Land in 1901-1902. The USSR claimed this territory in 1926. The Dictionary Catalog of the Stefansson Collection on the Polar Regions, 8 vols. (Boston: G. K. Hall, 1967) does not cover material added since Dr. Stefansson's death in 1962. (NUCMC 76-1839, for Leffingwell only)

10 Charles W. Tobey (1880-1953). Papers, 1933-53, 175 ft. Governor of New Hampshire, 1929-30, U.S. congressman, 1933-39, and senator, 1939-53. Tobey was closely connected to commercial and financial affairs in his political career. In 1944 he was a member of the U.S. delegation to the International Monetary Conference at Bretton Woods, New Hampshire. He

was also a member of the Senate Foreign Relations Committee in 1951-53. Letters, reports, speeches, photographs, printed matter, and memorabilia concern, among other subjects, the Cold War (the Dies and McCarthy committees), lend-lease (correspondence with Edwin Wendell Pauley, petroleum coordinator for the USSR and England in 1941), and American foreign policy. Inquire at the library. Typed inventory and list of major correspondents (both unpublished but available on inter-library loan). (NUCMC 70-151)

NH 3
DANFORTH LIBRARY
NEW ENGLAND COLLEGE
Henniker, New Hampshire 03242
(603-428-2344)

Styles Bridges (1898-1961). Papers, 1923-60, 124 file drawers. U.S. senator from New Hampshire, 1937-61, chairman of the Joint Committee on Foreign Economic Cooperation and a member of the Senate Foreign Relations Committee and Senate Armed Services Committee. The collection includes a considerable amount of material (used mostly for speeches) on lend-lease, Russian education, U.S. wheat to Russia, U.S. and Soviet ICBM output, Russian scientific equipment, and Soviet satellites. Khrushchev and Mikoyan are also mentioned in the papers. The material is open for the use of qualified researchers with a stated purpose, but prior arrangements should be made with the editor of the Bridges Papers, Mr. James J. Kiepper, at 9-3 Woodlake Road, Albany, New York 12203 (phone: 518-456-5915 or 518-457-5860). Unpublished register.

NH 4
THE MANCHESTER HISTORIC ASSOCIATION
Manchester, New Hampshire 03104
(603-622-7531)

A few pictures of the Japanese delegation to Portsmouth for the negotiations to end the Russo-Japanese War.

NH 5
DR. R. KRYSTYNA DIETRICH--PRIVATE COLLECTION
R.F.D. No. 1, West Farms Road
West Canaan, New Hampshire 03741
(603-632-7156)

Dietrich Collection. 12,000 items. 700 Russian-related items, 1760-1979, include paintings, drawings, graphics, slides, photographs, books, periodicals, published and unpublished bibliographies pertaining to the painter Alexander Orlowski (1777-1832).

Finding Aids: The Dietrich Collection has been described in a number of publications, including the following exhibition catalogue: Candace Ingals [and] Michael Hanitchak, Alexander Orlowski, 1777-1832. A Selection of his Work from the Collection of Dr. R. Krystyna Tolczynska Dietrich and the late Albert George Dietrich. Hanover, New Hampshire, The Hopkins Center Art Galleries, Dartmouth College, 1973. Dr. Dietrich is presently preparing a monograph on her collection. Material can be used only by permission of the owner.

NEW JERSEY

NJ 1
ARCHIVES BRANCH
FEDERAL ARCHIVES & RECORDS CENTER, GSA
Building 22-MOT Bayonne
Bayonne, New Jersey 07002
(201-858-7251)

This repository has some of the microfilms of materials in the National Archives (Washington, D.C.) that pertain to Russia/USSR. For more details, see Charles South, List of National Archives Microfilm Publications in the Regional Archives Branches (Washington: National Archives and Records Service, 1975).

NJ 2
NEW KUBAN, INC.
COSSACK MUSEUM AND ARCHIVE
Don Road
Buena, New Jersey 08310

Construction is currently underway on this repository. When completed the archives should hold important materials relating to Cossack history and personalities obtained from Cossacks in this country and abroad. Examples of the kinds of items one may expect to find in the archives in the future: correspondence, diaries, photographs, maps, literary manuscripts, and historical documents. Further information concerning holdings and conditions of access will be available only after the construction is finished.

NJ 3
CHARLES J. HOFFMAN--PRIVATE COLLECTION
540 Fulton Street
Elizabeth, New Jersey 07206

Mr. Hoffman is in possession of over 150 magic lantern slides, mostly taken by L. D. Woodridge ca. 1895-1914, that pertain to the Russian Empire. These include 88 slides of Moscow, 62 slides of St. Petersburg, 7 slides of Warsaw, and 1 slide of a police permit to photograph Moscow, 15 August 1913. Mr. Hoffman also has a TLS, 19 December 1917, from W. S. Crosley, U.S. naval attaché in Petrograd, to Mrs. Marion McAllister-Smith, 3 pp. (Note: Mr. Hoffman has a 14x18 in. oil painting, scribed on reverse "W. Borisoff, Moskau, 18-7-1919," of half-clad women.) Letter in advance requested.

NJ 4
ARMY MUSEUM AND ARCHIVE OF THE RUSSIAN IMPERIAL ARMY
R.D. 2, Alexander Avenue
Howell, New Jersey 07731

Like the Russian Naval Museum with which it is housed (see following entry), the Army Museum and Archive holds materials in each of its component parts. In display cases within the museum are documents and memorabilia of the Imperial Russian Army, from the 18th-20th c. Included are photograph albums of Cossacks, the Nikolaevsk Cavalry Academy, the Kadet Corps, and the Romanov family. On exhibit also are medallions, models of uniforms, and textual material. Among the latter are decrees signed by Catherine II, 1785 and 1790, and Anna, 1735.

The archive has 37 books, typed and handwritten, of military service records of all officers of the Russian Imperial Army in all military districts 1904-14. It also holds the papers of General Schultz, consisting of 10 notebooks from his service in the army in the Russo-Turkish War of 1877-78 and later years.

Miscellaneous collections in the archive include military orders--printed, typed, or hectographed--from 1908, 1911, 1917-18, particularly for the Caucasian front, and promotions; the rodoslovnaia kniga of General Nilov; personal papers of officers on education and military service, 2 ft.; a list of officers killed in 1914, 3 books; the career records of Junker Academy graduates, 6 books; military orders and promotions for 1915-16, 2 books; miscellanea on the Kadet Corps, 3 ft.; various cavalry charters; a typed history of the Semenovsky regiment; maps; and a collection of newspaper clippings of Boris A. Nikolaev, a captain of artillery. Arrangements to use materials must be made in advance with the museum's curator.

NJ 5
RUSSIAN NAVAL MUSEUM
R.D. 2, Alexander Avenue
Howell, New Jersey 07731

This museum, created in 1966, is run by the Association of Russian Imperial Naval Officers in America and the American-Russian Welfare Society "Rodina." The museum forms an annex to the "Rodina" main building and itself shares building space with the separate Army Museum and Archive (q.v.). Organized into 3 divisions--museum, library, and archives--this repository holds a large number of rare and valuable items, mainly connected with the military history of Russia.

In the museum proper are numerous objets d'art, military paraphernalia, ship models, uniforms, weapons models, and medallions, as well as textual materials. Among the paintings are portraits of all Russian monarchs from Peter the Great to Nicholas II and also of most important figures in Russian naval history (e.g., Count F. M. Apraksin, co-founder of the Russian navy with Peter I). 18th c. engravings and lithographs portray people and incidents related to Russian history. The large photograph collection covers such topics as the Russo-Japanese War of 1904-1905, World War I, the Revolution and Civil War, and émigré Russians.

The museum has an impressive documents and autographs collection as well. A manuscript letter to Prince Romodanovsky, 30 December 1715, and an ukaz addressed to Brigadier Francis Lefort, 1 December 1718, are both from Peter I. There are 2 holograph letters of Catherine the Great, one an imperial rescript to Prince Alexei G. Orlov, 23 February 1773, and the other, fragmentary only, to Rear Admiral Prince Nassau-Siegen. A signed letter of Paul I to Eugene of Württemberg is dated 17 October 1796, in French. From Alexander I there are an ukaz to the Lithuanian military-governor General Rimsky-Korsakov, 21 April 1812, and citations issued to Prince Vorontsov and Peter Nadgoft for service against Napoleon I. The signatures of Nicholas I and Alexander II also appear on documents in the museum collections.

Other items include an incomplete letter dated 14 November 1709 of Count F. M. Apraksin; an ukaz of 30 September 1788 to Governor Piel of Pskov; a letter to Baron Grimm, 30 September 1785; and a letter to the elector of Trier announcing the birth of the Grand Duchess Ekaterina Pavlovna, 23 May 1788.

The archives hold materials divided into 20 sections. The first 7 are office/business files of the association, and the last comprises correspondence and papers relating to the library and archives. Sections 8 and 9 hold letters, manuscripts, and illustrations from Morskiia zapiski, the association's own journal, and from S beregov Ameriki (New York, 1939), a commemorative publication. Section 10, with personal and family papers, is arranged alphabetically by donors' names. It fills several file drawers currently. Among these letters and documents are data on the education of Russian naval officers and sailors, the Russo-Japanese War, the First World War, the Revolution and Civil War, and émigré life. Further items in section 11 (originals and copies) concern the Romanovs, naval voyages, Russian naval history (arranged chronologically), the history of military-educational institutions, ships' histories, naval and other military biographies, history of the army and air force, classified official publications, and other topics. Sections 12-15 contain items about the Russian naval emigration. Newspaper and journal clippings are in section 16. The Naval Bibliography section (17) has indexes, catalogues, and other bibliographic aids for naval research. Finally, there are graphic materials (portraits, paintings, photographs, albums) in sections 18 and 19.

Arrangements for use of the collections must be made in advance with the curator. John W. Long has published a description of the museum ("The Russian Naval Museum, Lakewood, New Jersey") in the Slavic Review (June 1971), from which the above details come directly.

NJ 6
ESTONIAN ARCHIVES IN THE U.S., INC.
607 East 7 Street
Lakewood, New Jersey 08701

This repository contains both published and unpublished materials. Archival material includes documents published by the government of independent Estonia, 1918-44; records of displaced persons camps in the American, British, and French zones of occupied Germany, 1945-50; and papers of Estonain immigrants in North America (e.g., of Peter A. Speek, a socialist newspaper editor who fled tsarist Russia). Inquire concerning access.

NJ 7
JOHN L. BATES--PRIVATE COLLECTION
86 Durand Road
Maplewood, New Jersey 07040
(201-763-4189)

Mr. Bates has an extensive collection of materials (letters, photographs, and printed works) about the Russian Boy and Girl Scout movement in Russia and in emigration. Included are photos and publications of the Scout Assn. in Russia, 1909-22, and correspondence, photos, and memorabilia of the Assn. in exile, 1920-74. The main correspondent, with contacts in some 30 countries, was the founder, 1909, and chief scout, 1919-32, Col. Oleg I. Pantuhoff. Mr. Bates also has family letters, photographs, and manuscripts relating to the O. Pantuhoff book O dniakh bylykh (1969), as well as a small collection of Col. Pantuhoff's rare, old books on Russian architecture, crafts, and history. There are also 10 large M. Mikheyev engravings, 1753; 10 old maps, all of St. Petersburg; and finally, a collection of paintings, drawings, and photos of portraits by the late Russian-born artist Igor Pantuhoff (1911-1972), who painted Princess Grace of Monaco, Mrs. J. V. Forrestal, and many other prominent personalities. The Russian Scout collection is in small boxes. Letters are arranged by country of origin, some by name, ca. 35 ft. Prospective researchers would do best to contact John L. Bates by letter, but not in July, August, January, or February. There are no copying facilities.

NJ 8
MORRISTOWN NATIONAL HISTORICAL PARK
P.O. Box 1136R
Morristown, New Jersey 07960
(201-539-2016)

1 The Lloyd W. Smith Collection at Morristown is a large and unusual group of papers, with some rare Russian-related items:

2 John Quincy Adams. ALS, St. Petersburg, 18 December 1810, 4 pp., to Hon. Samuel L. Mitchell with a detailed account of the English and French blockades to shipping, plus an ALS of his wife Louisa; and an ADS, St. Petersburg, 31 March 1812, 2 pp., containing an itemized account for his diplomatic services to the U.S., 1811 and first quarter of 1812. (Nos. 3342 and 3343)

3 Madame de Campan. Author of Memoires, reader to Marie Antoinette, and sister of "Citizen" Genet. Autograph manuscript, Paris, 27 October 1801, 16 pp., describing her brother's experiences at the court of Catherine II of Russia and early events of the French Revolution; plus an unsigned note in her hand. (No. 695)

4 Charles Carroll. Carroll, of Carrollton, signed the Constitution for Maryland. An ALS of 9 May 1829, 3 pp., discusses tobacco and flour shipments and a Russo-Turkish War. (No. 99)

5 Ulysses S. Grant. ALS of this U.S. president from Rome to "Dear Fred," 22 March 1878, 4 pp., concerning Greece, Turkey, Turkish and Russian affairs, and his family. (No. 42)

6 Andrew Johnson. Signed letter to General U. S. Grant, secretary of war ad interim, asking him to be present that day when questions about

the newly acquired Russian territory will be considered, 12 August 1867, 1 p. (No. 44)

7 James Madison. Broadside: "National Intelligencer . . . Extra," 25 May 1813, Madison's message to Congress about the St. Petersburg Conference, Tsar Alexander in his role of mediator, and other affairs of state (No. 842; shelved with Rare Books); also, in papers from members of his cabinet ("The 6th Administration"), an item of Albert Gallatin on his acceptance of a mission to Russia, 1813. (No. 2987)

8 Maria Feodorovna. Signed letter of the tsarina of Russia, St. Petersburg, 27 October 1789, 1 p., to the playwright August von Kotzebue, in French; with a fine portrait. (No. 750)

9 Maria Paulovna. The tsarina's signed letter, dated Belvedere, 17/29 July 1831, in Russian, 1 p. (No. 749)

10 Russian (No. 2851). 23 pieces, 1719-1835, including documents, letters, portraits, clippings, a biographical sketch of Nicholas I in English, and an unsigned letter concerning autograph collecting. This extraordinary folder contains: a signed letter, 1 October 1719, and an ALS to Count Golovkin (?), 12 [?] October 1719, of Peter I; a DS by Catherine II, 20 February 1770, promoting one Grigorii Geikin, her LS to the governor of Pskov General-Colonel Pil', 19 April 17--, 2 pp., and a fragment of an ALS of Catherine in French; a DS of Paul I, 21 July 1797, promoting Aleksandr Ivanchikov, translator in the ministry of foreign affairs, with his LS to Prince Maintsskii, 21 October 1799; a DS by Alexander I, 17 August 1805, concerning Prince Avgust de Broglio-Revel; an ALS of Marie, wife of Alexander I, to her daughter Anette, 21 May 1810, with addressed envelope, 1 p.; a DS by Nicholas I, 17 June 1835, in Russian and Polish, conferring the order of St. Stanislav second class on Humbert, adviser to the Prussian embassy (also signed by Prince Aleksandr), 2 pp.; a DS by Alexander II conferring the order of the White Eagle on Lieutenant General Baron Edwin von Manteuffel; an ALS of Princess Eudosee Galitzin to the historical painter Henry Fuseli, 1 p., in French, with addressed envelope; and an account by Mr. Balmann (?) of how he came into possession of the Galitzin letter and others.

All of these documents are originals. However, the entire Smith Collection has been microfilmed and there is a published finding aid for the microfilm: Bruce W. Stewart and Hans Mayer, A Guide to the Manuscript Collection. Morristown National Historical Park (Morristown, New Jersey, n.d.).

NJ 9
KARL VON LOEWE--PRIVATE COLLECTION
23 Courtlandt Street
New Brunswick, New Jersey 08901
(201-846-3098)

Professor von Loewe is in possession of a substantial collection of microfilmed materials on 15th-17th c. Lithuanian history from archives in Warsaw, Krakow, Vilnius, Leningrad, and Kiev. Some of these films are duplications (negative and positive) of microfilms in the Oswald Backus Collection in the University Archives, Spencer Library, of the University of Kansas. The originals are in the following repositories: Mokslu Akademija Centrine Biblioteka (Vilnius), Leningradskoe Otdelenie Institut Istorii Akademii Nauk SSSR, Archiwum Główne Akt Dawnych (Warsaw), TsDIAK (Kiev), and Archiwum Państwowe Miasta Krakowa i Województwa Krakowskiego. There is an unpublished list of the fondy materials duplicated. (The Vilnius microfilm is not a copy of Backus Collection holdings.) Access is by written request.

NJ 10
SPECIAL COLLECTIONS DEPARTMENT
ALEXANDER LIBRARY
RUTGERS UNIVERSITY
New Brunswick, New Jersey 08903
(201-932-7510/7527)

1 Finnish Relief Fund, Inc. New Jersey State Committee. Records, 1939-40, 4+ boxes. Fund set up to aid victims of the Russian invasion of Finland in winter of 1939-40. Correspondence, 3 January-12 April 1940; correspondence, acknowledgements, memoranda, reports, programs, bulletins, mailing lists, lists of newspapers, financial records, etc., December 1939-August 1940. Several letters are from Herbert Hoover, national chairman for the Relief Fund.

2 John Frederick Charles Fuller (1878-1966). Papers, 1893-1965, 18 boxes and 9 vols. Officer and military authority. Includes his journal of a military tour, 22 October-2 December 1926, of India and present Pakistan, 48 pp., detailing his conversations with General Sir Andrew Skeen and other officers about military matters, Afghanistan, Russia, and Indian affairs. He was attached to the British War Office at the time.

3 Herbert Hoover (1874-1964). U.S. president. Holograph of an extemporaneous address delivered by him at the San Francisco "Yama" Conference of the National Industrial Conference Board, November 1945, typed transcript, 6 pp. A few references to "the great slave state of Russia" and the threat of collectivism in the form of communism.

4 William David Lewis (1792-1881). Papers, 1802-66, 57 items and 17 vols. Merchant, banker, and politician from Philadelphia. His brother John D. Lewis was a merchant in St. Petersburg. Includes John's letter book and accounts, 1 vol., 22 ll., for 1806-11 in St. Petersburg, and letters from Sir Robert K. Porter, 1822-31. (NUCMC 65-1670)

NJ 11
THE NEW JERSEY HISTORICAL SOCIETY
230 Broadway
Newark, New Jersey 07104
(201-483-3939)

1 Chew Family. Papers, 1735-96, 26 items. Includes the autobiography of Beverly Chew (1794-1844), vice-consul in Russia under President James Madison. The original title of this item, transcribed and edited by Morris R. Chew in 1890, is "Notes and Memorandums for Reference 1794-1844," 71 pp. (MG 596)

2 Reeve Schley, Sr. (1881-1960). Papers, 1904-44, 25 ft. Banker, lawyer, and president of the American-Russian Chamber of Commerce (1923-40). Ca. 5 ft. of the collection pertains to the organization he headed. Unpublished inventory. (MG 870)

3 Stevens Family. Papers, 1663-1959, 60 ft. (microfilmed in 46 reels). In the business correspondence of Colonel John Stevens (roll 19) for 1817 there are documents from his contacts with Tsar Alexander I concerning the possible use of steam frigates and elongated shells in naval warfare with the Turks in the Black Sea. Count Andrew Dashkoff, Russian minister to the Court of St. James (London), served as intermediary in these discussions. On roll 20 is a reference to "railroads (including the experimental Montagnes Russes)"--which may refer to roller coasters, an amusement item introduced into Russia during Alexander's reign. Guide to the Microfilm Edition of the Stevens Family Papers, edited by M. Studley, C. Cummings, and T. Krom (1968); W.P.A. Calendar of the Stevens Family Papers, 3 vols. (Newark, 1940); and unpublished W.P.A. calendars. (MG 409)

4 William Turk. Papers, 1824-33, 61 items. Naval surgeon. His journal pertains in part to a voyage aboard the U.S.S. Concord (under Matthew Perry's command), taking John Randolph (1773-1833) to St. Petersburg to take up his duties as minister extraordinary to the Imperial Russian Court. The ship departed Portsmouth, New Hampshire, in 1830. (MG 182)

5 Edward H. Wright. Correspondence, 1850-51, 30 pp. U.S. secretary of legation at St. Petersburg. Several letters in typescript copies, written to his family in Newark when he was serving in Russia. Published in Proceedings of the New Jersey Historical Society, vol. 82 (1964), pp. 75-100, 153-79, and 241-71. (MG 637)

Finding Aid: Guide to Manuscript Collections of the New Jersey Historical Society (1957); new edition in preparation.

NJ 12
PROFESSOR NINA BERBEROVA--PRIVATE COLLECTION
44 Stanworth Lane
Princeton, New Jersey 08540

Nina Berberova maintains 3 file cabinets in her private collection. These contain lecture notes, literary manuscripts, and her personal correspondence with Russian literary figures. The material dates from after 1960 and will eventually be given to the Beinecke Library at Yale (additions to the bulk of her papers already there, donated in 1960). Her other papers and materials are at the Hoover Institution (given in 1950) and the Library of Congress (including letters of M. Gorkii to V. Khodasevich and Berberova; given in 1951). Researchers should request access by letter in advance.

NJ 13
ETS ARCHIVES
Educational Testing Service B-008
Princeton, New Jersey 08541
(609-921-9000 x 2744)

Educational Testing Service has been involved in educational exchanges with the Soviet Union since the late 1950s. In 1958, for example, Henry Chauncey, president of ETS from 1948 to 1970, was a member of the first official U.S. educational delegation to the USSR. Mr. Chauncey made subsequent trips to the Soviet Union in similar capacities in 1965 and 1976. His papers in the archives include dictated (typed) notes on both the 1958, 312 pp., and 1965, 236 pp., trips. The latter notes are entitled "Interviews with Soviet Educators on Recent Developments and the Current Status of Education in the U.S.S.R." Archival files for reports, photographs, tape recordings, and other materials include taped seminars by participants in the 1976 trip (recorded after their return), as well as papers prepared for a Soviet delegation that came to the U.S. in 1958, notes by Americans who have visited the Soviet Union (Alex Inkeles in 1956 and Edwin Fleishman in 1960), and translations of Soviet educational publications. Many educational officials and institutions in the USSR are mentioned in the holdings. Prominent among them is A. I. Markushevich, former deputy minister of education and vice-president of the Academy of Pedagogical Science.

Relevant material continues to accumulate; present Soviet-related holdings total about 2 ft. Items more than 30 years old do not require permission to examine unless special restrictions apply; those less than 30 years old may be examined by permission of the archivist. There are several unpublished finding aids, including a shelf list of folder titles, a descriptive bibliography of speeches and writings by Mr. Chauncey, and an inventory.

NJ 14
SPEER LIBRARY
PRINCETON THEOLOGICAL SEMINARY
P.O. Box 111
Princeton, New Jersey 08540
(609-921-8300)

1 Sheldon Jackson (1834-1909). Papers, 1856-1908, 48 vols. (bound) and 6 folders. Missionary and first U.S. superintendent of public instruction for Alaska. In 1891-92 he was involved in the purchase of reindeer from Siberia. Collection includes 22 vols. of correspondence relating to "The Pioneer Presbyterian Missions West of the Mississippi and Missouri Rivers and in Alaska."

2 Robert Elliott Speer (1867-1947). Papers, 1878-1947, ca. 85 ft. Secretary of the Board of Foreign Missions of the Presbyterian Church, U.S.A.; president of the Board of Trustees of Princeton Theological Seminary, 1937-47; author; and educator. Includes correspondence, etc. on the Russo-Japanese War, 1904, 1 folder (Doc. .S745 R96); and correspondence on Armenia, 1903-10, 1 folder (Doc. .S745 A51). Partial unpublished finding aid.

Restrictions: Inquire concerning access.

NJ 15
MANUSCRIPT DIVISION
FIRESTONE LIBRARY
PRINCETON UNIVERSITY
Princeton, New Jersey 08540
(609-452-3184)

1 Louis Adamic (1898-1951). Papers, in process, 37 cartons and 8 boxes. Slovenian-born author in America. Correspondence, notes, and writings concern immigration, acculturation, labor, unions, ethnic identity and diversity in the U.S., domestic and foreign policy, Yugoslavia, and, especially in the 1930s, the USSR. Requires permission of the librarian. Finding aid in preparation.

2 Armenian Manuscripts. The William Scheide Library, privately-owned but housed in the Firestone Library, includes 2 items: four Gospels, preceded by the letter of Eusebius to Carpianus and Canon Tables, on paper, 251 + 2 ff., written in the church of Holy Sion and the Life-giving Cross in Cilicia by Kostandin (Constantine), A.D. 1219 (Armenian era 668), illuminations (including 6 full-page miniatures of the four Evangelists) (M74); and four Gospels, on vellum, Canon Tables misbound at the end, 332 ff., written from 1627 to 1633 at the monastery of Tathev (old form Statheus) in northeastern Armenia by the monk Luke, who signed it, dated 1076 (Armenian era), copied from a manuscript by Gregory of Tathev (14th or 15th c.), with 3 full-page miniatures and 25 pen and ink drawings by the artist Khatchatur of Julfa (M80). Other Armenian manuscripts include: 2 ll. from a Menologium, A.D. 1683 (AM 13658) and four Gospels, A.D. 1730 (AM 14399). Also, see infra, the Robert Garrett Collection.

3 Ray Stannard Baker (1870-1946). Papers, ca. 1905-39, 18 boxes. Journalist, author, and biographer of Woodrow Wilson. Correspondence, reports, writings, and notes. Includes material pertaining to Wilson, Russia, and the Tyrol region (box 18). Unpublished guide (NUCMC 72-594).

4 Archibald F. Becke (b. 1871). Typescript with autograph corrections and additions, 281 pp., entitled [Notes on Development of Tactics, 1740-1907]. Includes sections on the Crimean War, 1854-55; Turkish War, 1877; and some tactical lessons and deductions from the Russo-Japanese War, 1904-1905; with maps and illustrations. (AM 19023)

5 Claude Bragdon (1866-1946). Architect and writer. Miscellaneous material in the general manuscripts collections. Includes letter, 24 June 1904, to him from Willard Straight, war correspondent, describing the situation in Korea during the Russo-Japanese War.

6 John Foster Dulles (1888-1959). Papers, 1888-1959, 215 ft. U.S. secretary of state, 1953-59. Earlier diplomatic career included involvement in the Versailles Peace Conference, League of Nations, United Nations, and NATO. In many phases of his career he had close contact with the Soviet Union, particularly during the Cold War. Correspondence, conversation memoranda, notes, drafts of writings and speeches, and clippings. Inquire concerning restrictions. Unpublished guide (NUCMC 71-385)

7 Dulles Oral History Collection. 279 items, 1964-67. Interviews with such figures as Allen Dulles, Herbert Brownell, Elliott V. Bell, John C. Bennett, Charles Bohlen, Loy Henderson, Foy Kohler, and James Reston. Covers subjects similar to those noted in the

preceding collection. Restrictions. The Dulles Oral History Collection: A Descriptive Catalogue (1967). (NUCMC 71-384)

8 Robert Garrett. Collection of Medieval and Renaissance Manuscripts. Includes the following Armenian manuscripts: four Gospels, late 17th c. (No. 17); four Gospels, A.D. 1449 (No. 18); psalter and breviary, 16th c. (No. 19); breviary, 17th c. (No. 20); hymnal, 17th c. (No. 21); psalter, 16th c. (No. 22); and 6 ll. from the Alexander Romance, A.D. 1526, with miniatures (No. 23). The Garrett Collection Armenian Supplementary Series includes: Discourses by St. Gregory the Illuminator, 10th-11th c. (No. 1); four Gospels, early 11th c. (No. 2--Dep. 1466); Astronomy, A.D. 1774-75 (No. 3); 11 miniatures from a phylactery, 18th c. (No. 4); and 1 l., with miniature, from a Gospel, A.D. 1311 (No. 5). Also, a Georgian manuscript: hymns, on vellum, 99 ff., 11th c., mostly palimpsest, the underwriting mainly a Greek theological text (no. 24); and a Slavonic manuscript: missal, on vellum, 1 f., ca. 1480 (No. 25). Cited in De Ricci.

9 Old Church Slavonic Manuscripts. Holdings have not been fully investigated by the library staff.

10 Aleksei Mikhailovich Remizov (1877-1957). Papers, ca. 1930-34, ca. 25 items. Novelist and essayist. 19 letters, 3 postcards, and other material, including Turgeniev Snovidetz: K Pyatidesyatiletiyu So Dnya Smerti (1930), a booklet of Russian printed text published in Volya Rossii, 46 pp., with a manuscript of a "New Introduction" by Remizov entitled O Pozabytom i Nechitayemom, no Zhivom Sovremennon, 3 pp. (AM 18646)

11 Russia. Foreign Office. Passport issued at St. Petersburg, 2 July 1846, to Edward E. Rankin, an American citizen (AM 14512); and Russo-Chinese preliminary agreement of 10 May 1909, in regard to the administration of the lands of the Chinese Eastern Railway Co., copy of text given informally by Mr. Kozakoff of the Russian foreign office, 7 pp. (AM 14243)

12 Russia, 1793. Permit to an officer to stay in Warsaw from 3 April 1792 to 1 January 1794; signed by General Dolgorukij, commander in chief of the Russian army, 10 April 1793. (AM 13973)

13 Russian Manuscripts. Information on holdings unavailable at time of this writing.

14 Frederick G. Sikes, Jr. (1893-1957). Princeton Class of 1915. TLS, 12 April 1918, to L. Fredericks, written while Sikes was stationed at Vologda, Russia, in the U.S. army. (AM 17932)

15 Irina Skariatina (Mrs. Victor F. Blakeslee). Papers, ca. 1890s-1940s, 2 boxes. Russian noblewoman, writer, and journalist. Corrected typescripts, drafts, and correspondence relating to her writings: First to Go Back (1933), Skyroad to Russia (1942), "Doctors, Stalin and Important People and Views," "The Red Navy," and "First to go Home." Also, other articles and papers relating to her childhood in Russia and work as a war correspondent for Collier's during World War II. (AM 20966)

16 Evgenii Ivanovich Zamiatin (1884-1937). Author. Papers, 1922-34, ca. 17 items. Manuscripts, correspondence, and other papers. (AM 18810)

NJ 16
SEELEY G. MUDD MANUSCRIPT LIBRARY
PRINCETON UNIVERSITY
Olden Street
Princeton, New Jersey 08540
(609-452-3242)

1 American Civil Liberties Union. Archives, 1912-present, 1,861 albums, ca. 950 cartons (additions expected). Records include only a few relevant items, such as: an immigration case in 1950 involving a "Russian war bride"; correspondence in 1951 about American correspondents with Russian wives; 1959 cases involving the prohibition of demonstrations during the visit of Soviet Premier Nikita Khrushchev in Ames, Iowa, and Washington, D.C. Annual guides averaging ca. 50 pp. (NUCMC 60-1525, in part)

2 Bernard M. Baruch (1870-1965). Papers, 1905-65, 169 boxes, 121 cartons, and 521 vols. U.S. government adviser on economics and U.S. representative to the U.N. Atomic Energy Commission in 1946. The section of his papers pertaining to his U.N. post includes a few items concerning the attitude and position of the Soviet Union toward international control of atomic energy. (NUCMC 71-378)

3 Arthur Bullard (1879-1929). Papers, 1905-29, ca. 8 ft. Journalist and public servant. As a member of the Committee on Public Information (Creel Committee), he worked in Russia in 1917-18. From 1919-21 he was in the State Department's Russian Division, then joined the Secretariat of the League of Nations, 1926-27. Among his travel diaries, writings, reports, correspondence, and clippings are many items pertaining to Russian affairs, the League of Nations in the 1920s, foreign affairs, disarmament, and related topics. (NUCMC 71-379, superceding 62-321)

4 Fight for Freedom. Archives, April-December 1941, 6 boxes and 126 cartons. Includes a few appeals by the organization to support President Franklin D. Roosevelt's policy of extending war aid to the Soviet Union after June 1941; also, a limited number of items

encouraging Finland to make peace with the USSR during November 1941. (NUCMC 60-1521)

5 Louis Fischer (1896-1970). Papers, 1896-1970, 94 boxes. Journalist, author, and lecturer. Spent some 14 years in the USSR during the 1920s and 1930s, specializing in Soviet affairs. Articles, drafts of books, and a limited amount of correspondence. 6 boxes of family papers restricted until 2000.

6 James V. Forrestal (1892-1949). Papers, 1940-49, 139 boxes and 9 cartons. Secretary of the navy (1944-47) and the first secretary of defense, 1947-49. His diaries are rich with information on U.S. diplomatic and foreign policies in this period. Telephone conversation memoranda, letters, and other papers also pertinent. Some items concern his reactions to the ideas of George F. Kennan. A large part of the diaries has been published: Walter Millis, The Forrestal Diaries (1951). (NUCMC 60-2502)

7 George Frost Kennan (b. 1904). Papers, 1912-49, ca. 3 ft. Diplomat and scholar. Official and semi-official materials relating to the U.S. Foreign Service, 1934-49 (but not, at present, to Kennan's abortive ambassadorship to the USSR in 1952). Correspondence, reports, diaries, notes, lectures, writings, and clippings. Restriction: Inquire at the library. (NUCMC 71-392)

8 Robert Lansing (1864-1928). Selected papers, 1915-21, ca. 2 ft. Lawyer, public servant, and U.S. secretary of state, 1915-20. An authority on international law, he was U.S. counsel in the Bering Sea arbitration, 1892, in the Alaska Boundary Tribunal, 1903, and in negotiations on North Atlantic Fisheries, 1909-10. Correspondence, manuscript memoirs, and reports refer to the Soviet Union, World War I, Woodrow Wilson and his foreign policies, and the Paris Peace Conference. Inquire at the library. (NUCMC 71-394)

9 Ivy Ledbetter Lee (1877-1934). Collection of clippings, 1924-33, 16 boxes. All clippings pertain to the USSR. 1 box also contains handwritten memos to or from Lee. Some of the material is arranged chronologically, some by subject.

10 John Van Antwerp MacMurray (1881-1960). Papers, 1715-1960, ca. 51 ft. U.S. minister to China, 1925-29, to Estonia, Latvia, and Lithuania, 1933-36, and to Turkey, 1936-42. Extensive correspondence, writings, photos, and printed matter cover his public and private life (and that of his father, Junius, an American Civil War participant). (NUCMC 71-396)

11 Hugh Lenox Scott (1853-1934). Papers on Russia, 1910-23, 1 box. U.S. Army chief of staff. Member of the Elihu Root Special Diplomatic Commission to Russia in 1917, which encouraged the Russian people to continue fighting World War I. Correspondence, reports, speeches, and news releases relate primarily to this mission. (NUCMC 71-399)

12 Howard Alexander Smith (1880-1966). Papers, 1902-66, 275 cartons. U.S. senator from New Jersey. Traveled to Europe in 1947. Memoranda and daily reports concern his visits to Eastern European nations. (NUCMC 71-400)

13 Harry Dexter White (1892-1948). Papers, 1930-48, 13 boxes. Government official under President Harry S. Truman. Includes memoranda on the Russian loan question and the fate of post-war Germany. Relevant for the origins of the Cold War. Some items written by Secretary of the Treasury Henry Morgenthau, Jr. (NUCMC 61-2058)

Finding Aids: A Descriptive Catalogue of the Papers in the Area of Twentieth Century American Statecraft and Public Policy, rev. ed. (1974). All collections listed above have unpublished guides and/or descriptions.

NJ 17
ARCHIVES-LIBRARY
THE UKRAINIAN ORTHODOX CHURCH, U.S.A.
P.O. Box 240
South Bound Brook, New Jersey
(201-469-7555)

Organized in 1966 by the Most Reverend Archbishop Mstyslav Skrypnyk, the Archives-Library contains both published and manuscript materials dealing primarily with Ukrainian history, culture, religion, language, and politics. Approximately 75% of the material is in Ukrainian, 15% in Russian, and 10% in English. Items include correspondence, office files, literary manuscripts, miscellaneous documents, photographs, Orthodox ritual books, and maps. There are some rare religious and political manuscripts concerning the Ukraine during the Middle Ages and dating from the 15th to the 18th c. Much of the material relates to the UAPTsA (Ukrainian Autocephalic Orthodox Church in America). There is also documentation on the Ukrainian Liberation Movement of 1918-22 and the dissident movement in the Ukraine, 1960s-1970s. A card catalogue is in preparation. It is advisable, for lengthy research projects, to make advance arrangements with the Archives-Library.

NJ 18
ARCHIVES AND LIBRARY
BYELORUSSIAN ORTHODOX CHURCH OF STE. EUPHROSYNIA
South Whitehead Avenue (Mail: P.O. Box 26)
South River, New Jersey 08882

The archives holds some papers and documents, primarily material of Byelorussian immigrants who fled Soviet Russian persecution in their homeland. Among these holdings are papers of Iurii Stukalich that pertain to Byelorussian churches in the interwar period, 1919-39. Write in advance concerning access conditions.

NJ 19
EDISON NATIONAL HISTORIC SITE ARCHIVES
NATIONAL PARK SERVICE
Main Street and Lakeside Avenue
West Orange, New Jersey 07052
(201-736-0550)

Thomas Alva Edison (1847-1931). Papers, 1868-1931, ca. 505,000 items. Inventor. Incoming correspondence files include ca. 16 letters relating to Edison's inventions and Russia. For example, there are letters from Russian officials or engineers to the Edison Electric Light Co. (New York), inquiring about establishing lighting systems and the costs of certain manufactured items, 1 letter each in 1883, 1885, 1888, and 1890. 10 letters in 1890 and 1 in 1894 are from Julius H. Block, a Moscow importer of machinery and hardware, telling of phonograph demonstrations he had given and recommending ways to market phonographs. Edison replied in 1 note to Block, 1894. Researchers should contact the site archivist at least 1 week in advance, detailing research topics and files they wish to see (in this case, "Electric Light - Foreign - Russia, 1883-1890" and "Phonograph - Foreign - Russia, 1890-1894"). (NUCMC 66-797)

NEW MEXICO

NM 1
ARCHIVES
NEW MEXICO STATE UNIVERSITY LIBRARY
Box 3475
Las Cruces, New Mexico 88003
(505-646-3839)

Herbert James Hagerman (1871-1935). Papers, 1808-1935, 18 in. Second secretary at the U.S. embassy in St. Petersburg, 1898-1901. Contains his typescript "Memoirs of the Old Regime in Russia"; a photoalbum with 60 postcards and photoprints of the Imperial family, dignitaries, and other subjects; a notebook, August 1898, on the "Czar's proposal for arms reduction"; a second notebook, October 1898, labeled "People in St. Petersburg"; and a scrapbook with letters received, invitations, programs, broadsides, menus, calling cards, lists of diplomatic corps members, and pamphlets.

NEW YORK

NY 1
ALBANY INSTITUTE OF HISTORY AND ART
125 Washington Avenue
Albany, New York 12210
(518-463-4478)

Genet Family. Papers, 1778-1909, 40 items. Includes an original signed letter, Paris, 20 September 1791, from Louis XVI of France to Catherine II of Russia, in Latin but addressed in French (plus a copy, handwritten), 1 f. The letter, nearly half of which consists of the honorific salutation and titles of the empress, concerns the French National Convention's representation of the will of the people, Louis's assent to the Convention, his assurance to Catherine that French developments will not affect the friendly relations between them, etc. Unpublished finding aid (NUCMC 61-514).

NY 2
STATE RECORDS SECTION
NEW YORK STATE ARCHIVES
Cultural Education Center, 11th Floor
Albany, New York 12230
(518-474-8955: Ref.; 474-1195: Admin.)

1 Joint Legislative Committee to Investigate Seditious Activities (Lusk Committee). Records, ca. 1917-21, ca. 20-25 cu. ft. Official state body created to investigate seditious activity within New York State after World War I and during the Red Scare. The Committee interpreted its mandate broadly and investigated a large number of "leftist" organizations, many of which pertained to Russia, Bolshevism, communism, etc. Perhaps 50% of the materials--office files, reports, pamphlets, and publications--relate to the USSR. Many are photostats in poor condition. Subjects covered include: the Communist Party of America, Russian Soviet Bureau, Bolshevists, Union of Russian Workers, All-Russian Zemsky Union, Russian Information Bureau, the Russian

Revolution, the Russian revolutionary movement in the U.S., the Communist Labor Party, Soviet-American relations, Finnish Information Bureau, Leon Trotskii, and radical publications. Unpublished inventory of boxes by subject listing, broken down to folder heading level. Contact the Section for detailed information on specific subjects. (Accession #281)

2 Russian Insurance Companies. Records of ca. 9 Russian insurance firms that established branches in the New York area in order to carry on business in North and South America, ca. 1899?-1926, undetermined amount. The following companies established branches in New York City (unless otherwise noted), on the dates indicated, and terminated business in the manner and on the dates stated: First Russian Insurance Company, founded in 1827, of Petrograd, admitted 13 February 1907, U.S. branch placed in liquidation by Insurance Department of N.Y. State in 1925; Insurance Company of Salamandra of Petrograd, admitted 30 December 1899, reinsured all outstanding liabilities with Reinsurance Company of Salamandra (U.S. branch) of Copenhagen, Denmark, on 30 September 1919; Jakor Insurance Company of Moscow, admitted 20 June 1908, reinsured by Anchor Insurance Company of New York and withdrew 10 February 1922; Moscow Fire Insurance Company of Moscow, admitted 29 December 1899, U.S. branch in liquidation by Insurance Department in 1925; Northern Insurance Company of Moscow, admitted 24 November 1911, U.S. branch liquidated in 1926; Russia Insurance Company (U.S. branch--Hartford, Connecticut), admitted 5 February 1904, business transferred to Russia Insurance Company of America 1 April 1919; Russian Reinsurance Company of Petrograd, admitted 6 March 1907, U.S. branch in liquidation by Insurance Department in 1925; St. Petersburg Insurance Company of Petersburg, admitted 2 February 1900, withdrew 23 April 1901; and Second Russian Insurance Company of Petrograd, admitted 10 December 1913, U.S. branch in liquidation by Insurance Department in 1925. The records of State Insurance Department are in the custody of the state archives but maintained in a storage facility physically distant from the Archives. Though specific holdings could not be ascertained, the archives staff has indicated that Russian-related items should appear in the following series: Reinsurance Schedules. New York and other states and foreign fire insurance companies, 1885-98, 1906, 15 vols.; Annual Statements. Life, casualty, credit and title guarantee companies, companies doing new business, receivers. New York and other states and countries. 1859-1915 [without 1861], 57 vols.; Annual statements of life insurance companies of other states and countries. 1906-15. 20 vols.; Annual Statements. Casualty, credit, title and mortgage guarantee companies, mutual compensation companies, New York and other states and countries. 1905-15. 25 vols.; Annual Statements. Mutual fire insurance companies of the State of New York and of fire and life insurance companies of foreign countries. 1870. 1 vol.; Annual Home Statements. U.S. branches. Foreign fire, life, marine, casualty, credit insurance companies. 1871-1915. 49 vols.; Annual Home Office Statements. Foreign insurance companies. 1900-15. 10 vols.; Annual Statements. Foreign fire, N.Y. marine, marine insurance companies of other states and countries. 1868. 1 vol.; and Capital Statements. Foreign fire insurance companies. 1887. 1 vol. The records are bound (mostly), handwritten, legible, and have finding aids for the various series. Individual volumes but not series are indexed. Prior notice from researchers concerning their needs requested. (Accession #15)

NY 3
FRANK WUTTGE, JR.--PRIVATE COLLECTION
3021 Radcliffe Avenue
Bronx, New York 10469
(212-547-8811)

Mr. Wuttge has a collection of family photographs that pertain to his grand-uncle August Leuchterhandt, who was official photographer at the Russian Navy Yard in Sebastopol, ca. 1880-1906. He also has the personal notebook with formulas for developing collodion plates and prints used by his father, who worked for his uncle (Leuchterhandt) in his youth. (Materials for a biography of Frank Wuttge, Sr. are in the unprocessed Wuttge papers in the Manuscripts Division of the New York Public Library.) Researchers are requested to write in advance for permission to examine the papers and photos.

NY 4
HENRY R. HUTTENBACH--PRIVATE COLLECTION
321 Sackett Street
Brooklyn, New York 11231
(212-624-2301)

Collection of microfilms of documents pertaining to 16th c. Muscovy. Includes numerous reels from such archives/libraries as the Swedish State Archive, the Vatican Library, the Lenin Public Library in Moscow, British Museum, and Public Records Office in London. Also, microfilms from Vienna, Brussels, Copenhagen, Paris, and Venice. Among the subjects covered are border negotiations between Sweden and Muscovy, the Heresy of the Judaizers, Anglo-Muscovite relations, and the Schlitte expedition. Inquire concerning access.

NY 5
JAMES A. KELLY INSTITUTE FOR LOCAL HISTORICAL STUDIES
ST. FRANCIS COLLEGE
180 Remsen Street
Brooklyn, New York 11201
(212-522-2300 ext. 202)

John J. Rooney (1903-1975). Papers, 1943-75, 750,000 documents and 200 photographs. Congressman; member of the subcommittee on appropriations for the Justice and State Departments; involved in local Eastern European ethnic groups in the U.S. Some materials pertaining to the USSR and to ethnic groups in the Soviet Union, including Lithuanians. Finding aid.

NY 6
PAUL F. STIGA--PRIVATE COLLECTION
62 Montague Street, Apt. 8-C
Brooklyn, New York 11201

Chauve-Souris Collection. Ca. 325 items plus clippings, some in scrapbooks, ca. 1921-43. The Chauve-Souris, or Bat Theatre of Moscow, was a cabaret/revue begun as an offshoot of K. Stanislavskii's Moscow Art Theatre. It later emigrated to Paris and then to New York under the direction of Nikita Balieff. Most of the material comes from the estate of Oliver Sayler, who wrote books about the new movements in the theatre in Russia and Europe in the early decades of this century and who served as publicist for the Chauve-Souris.

Includes manuscript in English by Elene Komisarjevska, n.d., 7 pp., about the first C-S season in New York; typescript, carbon, 3 pp., description by Sayler of a C-S parody called No-Siree, performed in New York on 30 April 1922; souvenir programs and playbills, 1921-43, London, New York, and Paris, one with covers designed by S. Chermayeff; typescript, notes, and source materials on C-S, ca. 70 ll., including drafts of parts of Sayler's projected book on Morris Gest; ca. 190 photographs of different sizes showing C-S productions, performers, and staff; other photos of murals by Nicolas Remisoff, 4, n.d., of Balieff (signed), and of Sergei Soudeikine, 2, n.d.; a large poster by Soudeikine; 2 ll. of penciled biographical notes on Remisoff by Sayler, photo of a caricature portrait of Gest by Remisoff, and a receipt signed by Remisoff for his $100 fee; original drawings by Serge Tchekhonine, Remisoff, and Soudeikine; catalogs for exhibitions by Tchekhonine (Paris, 1928) and Remisoff (New York, 1922), plus Sayler's penciled comments on Tchekhonine's work; rehearsal script, typed, carbon, 46 ll., for A. Pushkin's "The Queen of Spades," adapted by G. Saint Ours, stage directions underlined in red pencil; ADS of Georges Annenkoff, n.d., 2 ll., a program note (?) explaining his design of scenery and costumes for "The Queen of Spades," plus Sayler's typed transcript; program for a benefit performance by C-S for destitute Russian artists, New York, 1922, autographed by stars who appeared (including Al Jolson, Leon Errol, Lenore Ulric, Marilyn Miller, and Dorothy and Lillian Gish); pencil caricature head of Balieff; ca. 105 ll. (office carbons) of Sayler's press releases concerning C-S; 14 handbills relating to C-S; transcript of an interview with Helene Pons about her career as a theatrical costumer, including remarks by her husband George, 19 ll.; TLS of Balieff, Paris, 31 August 1931, to Sayler concerning a projected American production of "The Queen of Spades," 1 p.; text of a curtain speech for a C-S revival, n.d., 2 pp., in an unknown hand; 2 article offprints; and hundreds of newspaper and magazine clippings, most in scrapbooks and concerning the first New York appearances of C-S (1922).

Unpublished list. Researchers should write in advance to arrange a visit.

NY 7
RARE BOOK ROOM
BUFFALO AND ERIE COUNTY PUBLIC LIBRARY
Lafayette Square
Buffalo, New York 14203
(716-856-7525)

1 William Ewart Gladstone (1809-1898). British statesman, leader of the Liberal Party, 1868-1894. Signed manuscript of "Russia and England," a review of Mme. Olga Novikoff's book Russia and England. Published in the Nineteenth Century, vol. 7 (March, 1880).

2 Henry James (1843-1916). American novelist and critic. Signed essay on Ivan Turgenev, first published in the Atlantic Monthly, vol. 53 (January 1884) and later reprinted in James's Partial Portraits.

NY 8
RARE BOOK ROOM
OWEN D. YOUNG LIBRARY
ST. LAWRENCE UNIVERSITY
Canton, New York 13617
(315-379-5451)

Frederic Remington (1861-1909). Papers, ca. 1889-1903, 155 items. American artist and author. Traveled through Italy, Germany, North Africa, Germany, and Russia in 1892, in company with Poultney Bigelow, a journalist, author, and historian. Their trip resulted in a series of articles for Harper's magazines, 1893-97, written by Bigelow and illustrated by Remington. Includes copies of letters from Remington to Bigelow concerning arrangements for the trip. Restriction information available at the library. (NUCMC 62-767)

NY 9
BASILE DENISSOFF--PRIVATE COLLECTION
764 Brookside Circle, RD #1
Elmira, New York 14903
(607-562-8206)

Basile Denissoff is the son of the scholar and priest E. V. Denissoff. His grandfather was V. I. Denisov, a member of the State Council in the early 20th c. and author of books on Russian commerce and industry. The family, of Don Cossack origin, includes many military men in its history.

The collection comprises ca. 1,900 manuscript and printed documents, bound, 5 vols., arranged chronologically (by family member) and topically. Tables of contents for each volume and a personal name index in one are useful finding aids. The oldest materials date from the mid-18th c., but the bulk is from ca. 1850 to World War I. There are also archival transcripts for the earlier period.

The majority of items are genealogical, including official documents (promotions, awards, orders, etc.) relating to the careers of family members. One such document is signed by Catherine II, others by A. V. Suvorov and G. A. Potemkin. Other large holdings concern the family's landownership in the Don region (ca. 6000 desiatiny and 400 serfs) in the mid-19th c. and the reforms (land settlement) of the 1860s. Some material relates to legal matters at the end of the last century. All material is in Russian except part of 1 volume which is translated into French.

Researchers must contact Mr. Denissoff in advance, stating the purpose of their work. Unpublished brief descriptions.

Note: After this entry was written, Mr. Denissoff placed his collection with Cornell University.

NY 10
BORIS SCHWARZ--PRIVATE COLLECTION
50-16 Robinson Street
Flushing, New York 11355
(212-445-7430)

Mr. Schwarz, a musicologist who has written the book Music and Musical Life in Soviet Russia, 1917-1970 (New York, 1972), has a small collection of photographs of Leopold Auer, Mischa Elman, Efrem Zimbalist, Gregor Piatigorsky, and the young Jascha Heifetz. He also holds supporting documentation for the 20 articles on Russian and Soviet composers and musicians he contributed to the New Grove (6th ed.). In addition, he has personal knowledge of musical resources in the United States.

NY 11
PROFESSOR VERA VON WIREN--PRIVATE COLLECTION
3 Northfield Road
Glen Cove, New York 11542
(516-759-1059)

Dr. Vera Von Wiren-Garczynski, a professor at the City University of New York and the granddaughter of Admiral Robert Wiren, maintains a collection of materials relating particularly to Russian naval history. Among the holdings is 1 box of family and official correspondence, ca. 1916-19, containing letters from Admiral Robert Wiren, naval commander in chief of the eastern defenses of the Baltic Sea and military governor of Kronstadt, the Russian consulate in New York, and Russian naval agents in Washington, D.C., Paris, and London. There is also a typescript copy of a memoir, in English, by the admiral's son, Alexis Wiren, entitled "Recollections of a Russian Naval Officer," several hundred pages. The memoirs concern Alexis's life in Russia and the U.S., 1901-76; he graduated from MIT in 1921 and also taught there. (The original of this item is in a vault in Malta.) The collection also holds the memoirs, in Russian, of Admiral Robert Von Wiren's wife, covering his visit to the U.S. as a young naval officer, involvement in the Russo-Japanese War, and other phases of his life; a document (from the admiral's visit?) entitled "Resolution providing for inviting Admiral Farragut and the officers of the Russian frigates now in, or to arrive at New York harbor to visit the City of Baltimore" ("Approved October 5, 1863"), printed, 1 p.; materials on the Mikhailovsk Artillery School, including the memoirs of its commanding officer, Vladimir Aleksandrovich Avrinskii, and some photographs; a family photo album with pictures of Kronstadt, Russian ships, and members of the Naval Aviation Commission of 1915; photos of the Von Wiren and of the Imperial families, from the late 19th c. on; and 2 folders of typed ship's logs from the vessel Baian' (27 September 1917-October 1917). In addition, Professor Von Wiren has some Russian art work, a Russian coin collection, medals, promissory war notes (1905), and émigré publications.

Note: Portions of Professor Von Wiren's original collection have been given to the Russian Naval Museum, which her father helped found, and to the Hoover Institution. Scholars should contact Dr. Von Wiren well in advance concerning conditions of access, detailing research interests and providing credentials.

NY 12
SPECIAL COLLECTIONS
CASE LIBRARY
COLGATE UNIVERSITY
Hamilton, New York 13346
(315-824-1000)

Maurice Hindus (1891-1969). Collection, ca. late 1930s-mid-1960s, ca. 6 to 8 boxes. Russian-born student of Soviet history and affairs. This collection apparently comprises only clippings, with no personal papers.

NY 13
THE FRANKLIN D. ROOSEVELT LIBRARY
Hyde Park, New York 12538
(914-229-8114)

The Roosevelt Library was created to preserve materials pertaining to Franklin D. Roosevelt and his administration. Russian-related materials can be found in at least 2 of its holdings: manuscripts and oral history transcripts. All estimates of the size and inclusive dates of Russian-related materials within these manuscript collections and microfilms should be considered approximate.

Manuscripts

1 Adolf A. Berle (1895-1971). Papers, 1912-74. 92 ft. Assistant secretary of State, 1938-44. 750 pp. of materials, 1946-71, pertain to Russian and United States foreign policy. Unpublished finding aid. (NUCMC 77-252)

2 Francis Biddle. The papers of this lawyer have been willed to the Library, but it has not yet received them.

3 James M. Carmody (1881-1963). Papers, 1900-58. 146 ft. Chief engineer, Civil Works Administration, 1933-35; administrator, Rural Electrification Administration, 1936-39. 3 ft. of documents on U.S. recognition of the Soviet Union and on economic conditions and industrial management in the USSR. Unpublished finding aid. (NUCMC 65-27)

4 Oscar Cox (1905-1966). Papers, 1938-66. 84 ft. General counsel, Foreign Economic Administration, 1943-46. 1,450 pp. of materials, 1944-45, pertain to U.S. aid to the USSR, the San Francisco Conference, and other Soviet-related matters. Unpublished finding aid. (NUCMC 74-310)

5 Wayne Coy (1903-1957). Papers, 1934-57. 10 ft. Special assistant to the president, 1941-43; assistant director, Bureau of the Budget, 1942-44. Lend-lease to Russia is documented in 150 pp. from July-August 1941 to 1946. Unpublished finding aid. (NUCMC 65-31)

6 Mordecai Ezekiel (1899-1974). Papers, 1918-75. 19 ft. Economic advisor to the secretary of agriculture, 1933-44. 300 pp., 1930-32, pertain to agricultural and economic planning in the USSR. Unpublished finding aid.

7 Henry Field (b. 1902). Papers, 1920-76. 100 ft. Anthropologist; director, "M" Project, 1944-45. 5 ft. of materials, 1920-77, contain miscellaneous studies of anthropology in Russia and documentation on Field's trips to the USSR. Unpublished finding aid. (NUCMC 65-36)

8 Louis Fischer (1896-1970). Papers, 1938-49. Ca. 1 ft. 270 pp. 60 pp., 1938-49, relate to the emigration of Fischer's wife and of members of her family from the USSR. Unpublished finding aid. (NUCMC 75-526)

9 Anna Roosevelt Halsted (1906-1975). Papers, 1886-1974. 20 ft. Daughter of Franklin D. Roosevelt. 300 pp., 1945-51, pertain to U.S.-Soviet relations, including the Yalta Conference. Unpublished finding aid.

10 Harry L. Hopkins (1890-1946). Papers, 1928-46. 140 ft. Administrator, Works Progress Administration, 1935-38; secretary of commerce, 1938-40; adviser to the president, 1940-45. 5 ft., 1936-46, pertain to U.S. trade with the USSR, lend-lease aid, U.S.-Soviet military arrangements, post-war conferences (at Teheran, Yalta, and Potsdam), and to Hopkins's special missions to the USSR. Unpublished finding aid. (NUCMC 65-43)

11 Isador Lubin (1896-1978). Papers, 1924-61. 146 ft. Special statistical assistant to the president, 1941-45. 400 pp., 1945, pertain to German war reparations to Russia. Unpublished finding aid. (NUCMC 65-48)

12 Robert Walton Moore (1859-1941). Papers, 1933-40. 12 ft. Assistant secretary of state, 1933-37, and counselor of the Department of State, 1937-41. 600 pp., 1933-40, pertain to the U.S. recognition of the Soviet Union and to Soviet debts to the U.S. Unpublished finding aid. (NUCMC 65-53)

13 Henry Morgenthau, Jr. (1891-1964). Papers, 1866-1948. 91 ft. Undersecretary, 1933-34, and secretary of the treasury, 1934-45. 6 ft., 1934-45, on U.S. lend-lease to Russia, U.S.-Soviet trade, Soviet gold production and reserves, Soviet debts to the U.S., and post-war planning in the Soviet Union. Unpublished finding aid. (NUCMC 65-54)

14 Herbert Clairborne Pell (1884-1961). Papers, 1912-61. 25 ft. Minister to Portugal, 1937-

41, and Hungary, 1941; American member on U.N. Commission to Investigate War Crimes. 300 pp., 1933-46, pertain to the recognition of the Soviet Union by the U.S. and to the U.S. Commission to Investigate War Crimes. Unpublished finding aid. (NUCMC 65-57)

15 President's Soviet Protocol Committee. Records, 1941-45. 12 ft. Records, 1941-45, relating to war supplies for the Soviet Union. Unpublished finding aid. (NUCMC 75-582)

16 Anna Eleanor Roosevelt (1884-1962). Papers, ca. 1877-1964. 1,330 ft. Wife of Franklin D. Roosevelt. Materials, 1945-62, pertaining to U.S.-Soviet relations and to Mrs. Roosevelt's trip to the Soviet Union. Unpublished finding aid. (NUCMC 74-317)

17 Franklin D. Roosevelt. Papers as assistant secretary of the Navy, 1913-20. 53 ft. 1 item, n.d., pertaining to the Provincial Siberian Assembly and to German and Austrian prisoners in Russia. Unpublished finding aid. (NUCMC 75-550)

18 Franklin D. Roosevelt. Papers as president, official file, 1933-45. 1,174 ft. Materials on the USSR and the United States, 1933-45. Unpublished finding aid. (NUCMC 75-579)

19 Franklin D. Roosevelt. Papers as president, president's personal file, 1933-45. 608 ft. Materials on Russia and the United States, 1933-45. Unpublished finding aid. (NUCMC 75-562)

20 Franklin D. Roosevelt. Papers as president, president's secretary's file, 1933-45. 130 ft. 3,000 pp., 1933-45, pertain to the USSR and the United States. Unpublished finding aid. (NUCMC 75-581)

21 Franklin D. Roosevelt. Papers as president, press conferences, 1933-45. 15 ft. Contains materials pertaining to the USSR. (NUCMC 75-580) The press conferences have been published by DaCapo Press, New York, 1972.

22 Franklin D. Roosevelt. Papers as president, Map Room file, 1941-45. 81 ft. 3 ft. of materials, 1942-45, pertain to Roosevelt and Stalin, the Teheran and Yalta Conferences, the Churchill-Stalin Conferences, Russia and Poland, convoys to the Soviet Union, World War II, and occupied zones in Germany. Unpublished finding aid. (NUCMC 75-578)

23 Samuel Irving Rosenman (1896-1973). Papers, 1928-48. 36 ft. Special counsel to the president, 1943-46. Russia, the Yalta Conference, and the future of Poland after World War II are dealt with in 25 pp. of these papers. Unpublishing finding aid. (NUCMC 65-64)

24 Whitney Hart Shepardson (1890-1966). Papers, 1910-66. 4 ft. Special assistant to the ambassador to Great Britain, 1942. 30 pp., 1955-57, deal with Russia and the Free Europe Committee. Unpublished finding aid. (NUCMC 75-570)

25 State, Department of. Records pertaining to foreign gift items, 1937-45. 40 ft. Includes materials on gifts given to and received from the Soviet Union. The records are not yet fully processed. (NUCMC 75-576)

26 Charles W. Taussig (1896-1948). Papers, 1928-48. 65 ft. Chairman, National Advisory Committee, National Youth Administration, 1935-43. 230 pp., 1922, 1932-34, 1945, pertain to mineral deposits in the Soviet Union and the San Francisco Conference. Unpublished finding aid. (NUCMC 65-66)

27 Elbert D. Thomas (1883-1953). Papers, 1907-50. 135 ft. U.S. senator from Utah, 1933-51. 200 pp., 1943-50, pertaining to the Cold War and to American public opinion toward the Soviet Union. Unpublished finding aid. (NUCMC 65-67)

28 United Nations. Papers relating to Mrs. Roosevelt, 1946-63. 10 ft. Printed materials (agendas, minutes of meetings, press releases, reports) concerning the work of the United Nations. The papers are not yet fully processed. (NUCMC 75-574)

29 War Refugee Board. Records, 1944-45. 46 ft. 150 pp., 1944-45, pertain to the condition of Jewish refugees in areas controlled by the Soviet Union. Unpublished finding aid. (NUCMC 75-584)

30 John Cooper Wiley (1893-1967). Papers, 1898-1967. 5 ft. Foreign Service officer and minister to Estonia and Latvia, 1938-40. 1,100 pp., 1928-41, 1950-51, deal with Soviet debts to the U.S., lend-lease negotiations with the Soviet Union, 1950-51, and Russian relations with Eastern Europe. Unpublished finding aid. (NUCMC 75-587) There are security classified materials on the subject of lend-lease negotiations with Russia, 1950-51.

Oral History Transcripts

31 Russian-related oral history transcripts include interviews with John Franklin Carter, with the "M Project," 29 pp., and Samuel I. Rosenman, special counsel to the president, 1943-46, 233 pp.

Finding Aids: In addition to the unpublished finding aids mentioned above, the library has published its Historical Materials in the Franklin D. Roosevelt Library (October, 1977).

NY 14
PROFESSOR WILLIAM W. AUSTIN -- PRIVATE COLLECTION
DEPARTMENT OF MUSIC
LINCOLN HALL
COLLEGE OF ARTS AND SCIENCES
CORNELL UNIVERSITY
Ithaca, New York 14853
(607-256-4097)

Professor Austin is in possession of a small file of letters, musical scores, and recordings sent by musicologists and composers in the USSR since 1971. A few of the scores are photocopies of things not yet published. The most extensive correspondence is with the writer Grigori Shneerson. Other correspondents (whose scores are in the collection) include Galina Ustvol'skaya and Andrei Eshpai. Interested researchers may write to Professor Austin.

NY 15
DEPARTMENT OF MANUSCRIPTS AND UNIVERSITY ARCHIVES
JOHN M. OLIN LIBRARY
CORNELL UNIVERSITY
Ithaca, New York 14853
(607-256-3530)

The Collection of Regional History and the University Archives together hold the following pertinent items. (Some are small parts of very large collections.)

1 Carl L. Becker (1873-1945). Papers, 1894-56, 8.4 cu. ft. American historian, professor at Cornell. Some letters from Mr. or Mrs. Leo Gershoy to Mr. or Mrs. Becker, 1932?-45, discuss Russia and the Russians. A letter from Louis R. Gottschalk to Becker, 24 August 1933, speaks of conditions in Russia and about the French people. (NUCMC 62-2359 and 70-1052)

2 George Lincoln Burr (1857-1938). Papers, 1861-1942, 16.8 cu. ft. Cornell professor. Letters, ca. 21 items, of Alexis Babine to Burr (1894-1930) concern his studies at various American universities and at the Sorbonne. Several from 1921-22 describe Russian conditions. An additional series of letters to Burr from Ralph Charles Henry Catterall contains at least 1, 7 September 1907, about the latter's trip to Russia. (NUCMC 62-2342 and 66-1029)

3 Karl Douglas Butler (b. 1910). Papers, 1935-64, 14 ft. Agricultural consultant, businessman. One of his files concerns alleged communist influence in American education during the 1950s. Substantial printed and mimeographed information is on Russian agriculture and other aspects of Soviet economic and cultural life.

4 Ralph Charles Henry Catterall (1866-1914). Papers, ca. 1906-14, 236 items. Cornell history professor. Traveled in Germany, Poland, and Russia in 1907. His diary for 27 June-28 November 1907 discusses in detail conditions in Russia. He also records his interviews with, among others, Russian revolutionary leaders. Among his lectures and writings are: undated "Report on Russian Emigration" covering June-August 1907, 1 rough draft in script, 162 pp., 1 typescript, 52 pp.; "Why Russia in Revolution . . .," typed, 10 pp.; "Differences between French and Russian Revolutions," rough draft, typed, 2 pp.; and "Russia," typed, 5 pp.; 3 lectures from 1908; and "Women in Russia," typed, 23 pp., 21 December 1908. Unpublished finding aid (NUCMC 64-846).

5 Henry Stern Churchill (1893-1962). Papers, 1929-62, ca. 6 ft. Architect and city planner. Correspondence speaks of the 1958 Moscow Congress of the Union Internationale des Architectes, which he attended. (NUCMC 71-1616)

6 Carolynne Helen Cline (b. 1915). Papers, 32 in. Includes mimeographed diary, 76 pp., of her trip to the Soviet Union in July 1956. Restriction.

7 Ezra Cornell (1807-1874). Papers, 1778-1952 and 1969, 28 cu. ft., plus 5 microfilm reels. Mechanic, businessman, and philanthropist. In his account books, 18 vols., 1831-74, he details his work with various telegraph companies, including 1 involved in the Siberian Extension. 49 letters, 1864-67, relate to the Russian Extension Company. Also printed reports on the Russian-American Telegraph. Unpublished finding aid. (NUCMC 62-2374)

8 Gustavus Watts Cunningham (1881-1968). Correspondence, 1911-27, 66 items. Philosophy professor. Includes correspondence with famous philosophers. Some letters discuss the situation in Russia in 1917. Calendar of contents. (NUCMC 73-329)

9 Edmund Ezra Day (1883-1951). Papers, 1923-50, 72.7 cu. ft. Cornell president, 1937-49. Correspondence concerns Russian language courses and the Russian program at Cornell, 1940-47, the controversy surrounding these courses, 1943-50, and acquisitions of Russian publications. Supporting material on some subjects includes clippings, articles, reports, speeches, pamphlets, and minutes of meetings. Also data on Russian studies in Iowa, 1938-45. Restriction. Unpublished (computerized) finding aid. (NUCMC 62-3868 and 66-421)

10 Livingston Farrand (1867-1939). Papers, 1917-39, 46 ft. Cornell president, 1921-37. Scattered correspondence concerns the education of both Russian émigré students and students from the USSR. Occasional references to visiting lecturers and research work. Restriction. (NUCMC 66-426)

11 David Rowland Francis (1850-1927). Ambassador extraordinary and minister plenipotentiary to Russia, 1916-18. Report concerning his experiences extracted from letters written by Francis's "major domo" Philip Jordan, typescript, carbon copy, 4 pp.

12 Francois-Jules Harmand (1845-1921). Papers, [1845]-1956, 4.5 cu. ft. Physician in the French navy, natural scientist, diplomat. While minister plenipotentiary to Japan, 1894-1906, he tried to aid Russians imprisoned there, 1904-1905. 32 letters are from wives and other relatives of Russian prisoners of war. All but one, in Russian, are in French.

13 History Department. Records, 1956-65, over 1,200 items. Correspondence relates in part to the selection of a professor of Russian history for Cornell. One correspondent is Sir Isaiah Berlin. Restricted in part.

14 Elias Huzar (1915-1950). Correspondence, 1942-49, 45 items. Cornell professor of government. David M. Ellis (Cornell Ph.D., 1942) letters include discussions on the study of Russian language and literature, international affairs, World War II, and other matters.

15 Hyde Family. Papers, 1863-1957, 3.6 cu. ft. 3 letters are from Alfred Sao-ke Sze to Florence E. Hyde, written in St. Petersburg. On 29 August 1899 he writes of the cold weather there; on 13 March 1900 he speaks of his duties at the legation, his liking for the city, and functions he has attended; the last letter is dated 22 June 1900. Unpublished finding aid (NUCMC 64-882).

16 Deane Waldo Malott (b. 1898). Papers, 1923-66, 69 ft., 42 microfilm reels, and 13 reels of tape recordings. Cornell president, 1951-63. Includes copies of his journals and notes from a State Department-sponsored trip to the Soviet Union in 1958. The trip, made with 6 other college presidents, was for the purpose of studying higher education in the USSR. Other items discuss increased academic exchanges between Cornell and institutions of higher learning in the Soviet Union. Partial restriction. Unpublished finding aid (NUCMC 73-352).

17 McCormick Family. Papers, 1900-41, 8.4 cu. ft. A few letters from Frederick McCormick, who reported the Russo-Japanese War for Reuter's from the Russian side, to his brother Howard, an artist and engraver, speak of the fight at Port Arthur on 9 February 1904 which opened the war, Newchang, China, 2 March 1904, of being in Mukden after escaping from the Japanese lines, 1 October 1904, and of his relief at getting away from "all the restrictions and suspicions of these people" on board a ship outside Vladivostok, 26 October 1905. A letter of 24 May 1907 from Frederick to Howard discusses visits to the Tretiakoff Gallery, the Hermitage, the Museum of Alexander III in St. Petersburg, and a large private collection in Moscow; Russians' talent in painting and music; their personal "savagery"; and Russian architecture. (NUCMC 62-3452)

18 McGraw Family. Papers, 1854-1956, 114 items and 3 vols. 1 letter from Jennie McGraw, 1840-81, later Mrs. Daniel Willard Fiske, to an aunt recounts her visit to Moscow in September 1878. She talks about churches (interior and exterior) and the Kremlin. (NUCMC 73-351)

19 Isidore Gibby Needleman (1902-1975). Papers, 1927-75, 2 boxes, 32 in. Attorney, Amtorg Trading Corporation official. Business files concern his association with Amtorg.

20 Charles Nathaniel Pinco (1879-1975). Miscellany, 1932-34, 1 box, 3 in. Engineer. Maps, tourist guides, Russian newspapers, photographs, sheets from a scrapbook of correspondence, receipts, memoranda, and ticket stubs--all from 3 trips Pinco made to the USSR in the early 1930s.

21 Augustus Loring Richards (1879-1950). Papers, 1872-1951, 9 ft. New York lawyer and dairy farmer. Includes information about Soviet-American relations. (NUCMC 62-4422)

22 Richard Brown Scandrett (1891-1969). Papers, 1907-66, 10 ft., 8 microfilm reels, and 4 tapes. Attorney and political activist. Scandrett was the first chief of the United Nations Relief and Rehabilitation Administration (UNRRA) Mission to Byelorussia in 1946. Previously he was a member of the Allied Reparations Commission, which met in Moscow in 1945. His legal firm (Scandrett, Tuttle, and Chalaire of New York City) lobbied for the American-Russian Chamber of Commerce and the Amtorg Trading Corporation. Papers include correspondence, speeches, articles, and 2 taped interviews. Various items reveal his views of pertinent subjects (e.g., critical of Edwin W. Pauley, the oilman who headed the Reparations Commission delegation, impressed by German devastation of Russia in World War II). In the recorded interviews from 1966, typed transcripts, 307 pp., Scandrett discusses his work in foreign affairs. In 1962-63 the writer and critic Kornei Ivanovich Chukovskii sent Scandrett 2 postcards from Moscow that speak of his (Chukovskii's) great admiration for the poet Robert Frost. Unpublished finding aid (NUCMC 73-368).

23 Jacob Gould Schurman (1854-1942). Papers, 1878-1942, 22.4 cu. ft. Cornell president, 1892-1920, and diplomat. 2 letters to him from Alexei Vasilyevich Babine in St. Petersburg, 9 October and 13 November 1905, request and then thank him for sending a copy of the Cornell University Charter for the Russian Ministry of Education (Professor A. A. Tihomiroff). Babine was Cornell class of 1892. Also, Schurman's address at the first

Citizen's Mass Meeting concerning the passport issue in Russia, 6 December 1911. (NUCMC 66-1042)

24 Goldwin Smith (1823-1910). Papers, 1844-1915, ca. 50 boxes. Cornell professor. Primarily correspondence; also writings, scrapbooks, clippings, and bibliographic works about him. Extensive correspondence (typed copies) with George William Curtis from 9 July 1864 to 20 December 1887, 56 items, includes some references to Anglo-Russian relations and British foreign policy, especially in the Near East. There are many letters from James Laister who, with Smith, engaged in a journalistic controversy about the Jewish problem in Russia and elsewhere, 1880-87. There are references to the Bering Sea question (settled in favor of Britain) in letters from 1894-95. Correspondence from late 1905 and 1906 notes the turmoil in Russia and settlement of the Russo-Japanese War. A letter to Charles Francis Adams, 2 January 1906, points out the role Russia played in preventing French intervention in the American Civil War; and a letter to Andrew Carnegie, 6 January 1906, is critical of Anglo-Japanese relations toward Russia. The bulk of this collection, plus supporting materials from other repositories, is now available in microfilm, 28 reels. Published guide to the microfilm. (NUCMC 62-4432)

25 Raphael Soyer (b. 1899). Papers, 1949-54, 288 items. Russian-born artist. Correspondence, minutes, articles, reprints, and clippings collected by him as an organizer and member of the editorial board of the art magazine Reality. (NUCMC 70-1128)

26 Henry Morse Stephens (1857-1919). Papers, 1894-1922, .4 cu. ft. Professor of Modern European History. Copy of a letter, 20 December 1899, to him from Alfred Sao-ke Sze concerning Russia, its climate, Russian hatred of England, and the large German minority. Original in the University of California Library, Berkeley.

27 Willard Dickerman Straight (1880-1918). Papers, 1857-1925, ca. 50 cu. ft. Diplomat, financier, philanthropist. Correspondence, reports, diaries, scrapbooks. Straight served in the Chinese imperial customs service, with Reuters in the Russo-Japanese War, and in Korea and Manchuria for the U.S. State Department. Papers cover all aspects of his career, particularly his reporting in the Russo-Japanese War. Also, a 3-month trip in 1908 through Northern Manchuria studying transportation, agriculture, trade, and Russian and Japanese penetration (diaries, 4 books). Other references: navigation of rivers of the Russian Far East, 1909 memorandum; observations on a 1906 trip through Siberia and northern Manchuria (lengthy report to President Theodore Roosevelt); objections of Russia and Japan to the Chinese Currency Loan Agreement, memorandum of 20 January 1912; E. H. Harriman's interest in the Far East, note to George Kennan, 17 March 1916; settlement of lands along the Chinese Eastern Railway, copy of the agreement between China and Russia, 11 May 1909; and the Tokyo riots following publication of the terms of the Portsmouth Treaty, letter of Frederick Palmer, late September 1905. There are also summaries of interviews Straight conducted in St. Petersburg with the Russian ministers of war, finance, and foreign affairs, and with P. A. Stolypin, minister of interior and premier, late June 1910. Part of the collection is available on microfilm, 12 reels. Unpublished finding aids and published guide to the microfilm. (NUCMC 62-1103)

28 Robert Henry Thurston (1839-1903). Papers, 1859-1902, .4 cu. ft. Cornell professor of mechanical engineering. ALS to him from Ambassador Andrew D. White, St. Petersburg, 13 March 1894, describes the Russian court balls and dining, 6 pp.

29 John Bennett Tuck (1868-1955). Papers, 1890-1948, 13 ft. Lawyer. 3 letters describe the Russian Revolution of 1917. (NUCMC 70-1136)

30 George Frederick Warren (1874-1938). Papers, 1900-38, 12.2 cu. ft. Cornell professor of agricultural economics and farm management. Material on the Fourth International Agricultural Economics Conference, 1936, includes reports of A. B. Lewis on a Russian collective farm, visit to Theleman Collective Farm on 18 July 1936, written 13 August 1936, 7 pp.; on his interview with O. M. Targulian of the Soviet Commissariat of Agriculture, 6 pp.; and on Moscow in general. (NUCMC 62-3411 and 66-459)

31 Andrew Dickson White (1832-1918). Papers, 1825-1920, ca. 94 cu. ft., 100,000 items. First Cornell president, scholar, diplomat, statesman. Correspondence, diaries, scrapbooks, and photographs. White was an attaché in St. Petersburg under Thomas Hart Seymour in the mid-1850s and was himself ambassador to Russia in 1893-94. He also served as secretary of the U.S. delegation to the Russian-sponsored First Hague Conference on peace and disarmament, 1899. There is correspondence on the following topics: the American legation in St. Petersburg, Russian court life, and Russian politics (letters of Herbert H. D. Pierce from 17 January and 9 February 1895 and 11 August and 18 December 1896; and of Henry T. Allen, 1 and 23 March 1895); the Dukhobor sect, letters from John Bellows, a Quaker, compares his faith to theirs, notes the influence of L. Tolstoi, 15 November 1895 and 4 March 1897; Russian Jewish policy and the passport dispute of 1911, letters from Lewis Abraham, Oscar Straus, Henry Dodge, Philip Cowen, Rabbi J. L. Magnes, Representative Henry M. Goldfogle, Samuel Stern, Reverend T. Joseph, James Whiton, Curtis Guild, and William McAdoo, 1895-1912; plus White's replies to

Henry Green, Edward Lauterbach, and some of the preceding, typed copies; a Rothschild loan to Russia, Russian loans, and Jewish bankers, letter of 9 August 1905; the Russian Revolution of 1905, letter to R. W. Gilder, 18 April 1906; letters from Hendrik Willem van Loon, 5 February 1907, Friends of Russian Freedom and Arthur Bullard, 19 March 1907, and Lyman Abbott, 18 April 1907; prospects of an Anglo-Russian war, letter from Adolph Sutro, 19 April 1897; war in the Far East, U.S. relations with Germany, France, and Russia, especially in the Spanish-American War, and the U.S. embassy at St. Petersburg, letters from Minister Ethan Allen Hitchcock, 1897-98; and U.S. help for the new Russian government in 1917, letters from Oscar Straus, 5 and 12 April 1917. About the Russo-Japanese War there are letters from Theodore Roosevelt, 1 June 1905, and J. B. Jackson, 7 May 1911, as well as White's article "Situation and Prospect in Russia," 11 February 1905. Other references and/or correspondents: George Kennan, Baron de Hirsch, F. J. Garrison, Maksim Gorkii, and George von Bunsen. Available on 149 rolls of microfilm. Several unpublished finding aids, published guide to the microfilm (NUCMC 66-795).

Finding Aids: The library has published a series of Report[s] of the Curator and Archivist of these two collections (1945-74), many quinquennial, with detailed information on accessions and additions to holdings in 1942-66. A semiannual Documentation Newsletter has replaced this title (1975-), for accessions since 1966.

NY 16
DEPARTMENT OF RARE BOOKS
JOHN M. OLIN LIBRARY
CORNELL UNIVERSITY
Ithaca, New York 14853
(607-256-5281)

1 Theodore Dreiser (1871-1945). Papers, 1892-1975, 24.5 ft. American writer. The author of acclaimed fictional works, Dreiser became interested in socialism, visited the Soviet Union in the 1920s, and wrote commentaries about the USSR and America. Among the items located by the library's staff, who excluded manuscripts known to have been published (copies unless otherwise noted): 25 TL from Dreiser to Sergei Dinamov, 1927-37; 2 TL to Peter A. Bogdanov, 13 January and 26 April 1933; 3 TL from Dinamov to Dreiser, 1935-37; "To Russia [1927-28]" (1 microfilm reel of his diary kept during his trip to the USSR); TL to Pravda, 14 January 1933; cable to Pravda, 2 June 1934; telegram to Joseph Stalin, 16 May 1945; mimeographed typescript, ["Concerning Russia and the United States"], 2 ll. [March 1939?]; typed answers to questions from Pravda, 2 November 1932; typescript about M. Gorkii, written in response to a request from Pravda, 2 ll., after 12 June 1937; typescript of unpublished (?) article on Hitler in Russia, 1 l., 23 November 1942; 2 typescripts on the subject of individual liberty in Russia, sent to Pravda, 2 ll. each, ca. 29 April 1936; unpublished (?) article on/to Russian youth, 1 l. typed, 23 August 1944; typescript of unpublished (?) article on A. S. Pushkin, 3 ll., 17 January 1931; a typescript, 1 l., on Russia as saviour "Sent to Walt Carmon--for Russian newspapers, September 9, 1936"; unpublished (?) article on Soviet youth, 1 l., 15 October 1938; TL to Dreiser from Pravda, 25 November 1932; and TL from Smena (Leningrad) to Dreiser, 21? August 1932. (NUCMC 64-953)

2 Jean Frédéric Phelypeaux, Comte de Maurepas (1701-1781). French minister of marine and secretary of state. Papers, 1731-51, ca. 3 ft., 626 items. Maurepas was interested in French commerce with other countries, including Russia; letters and reports pertain to naval affairs, shipbuilding, cartography, finances, and officers' service. There are 4 relevant documents: Boet de Saint Leger's "Mémoire sur le commerce de Russie," ca. 1733, 4 ll.; document with same title and date, 11 ll.; French Marine Ministry's "Mémoire sur le commerce de Moscovie," ca. 1733-36, 4 ll.; and the ministry's "Mémoire concernant le commerce de la France avec la Russie," 1733-36, 5 ll. Unpublished finding aid (NUCMC 64-956).

3 George Bernard Shaw (1856-1950). Papers, 1878-1978, 17.5 ft. British (Irish) dramatist. Includes autograph notes for a lecture on "The Rationalization of Russia," 1 February 1932, 5 ll.; and a TL, copy, from Leo Nikolaevich Tolstoi to Shaw, August 1908, 2 ll.

NY 17
PAUL BARATOFF--PRIVATE COLLECTION
88-11 34th Avenue, Apt. 3F
Jackson Heights, New York 11372

Mr. Baratoff is in possession of the papers, 1882-1932, of his father, General N. N. Baratoff (Baratov), in 2 large metal containers. These include: handwritten diaries, mainly private in nature; documents pertaining to all phases of the general's career, beginning with his peacetime service in the Russian army, activities in the Russo-Japanese War and World War I (in Turkey and Persia), participation in the Civil War (representing the "Government of the Armed Forces of South Russia" at the independent Transcaucasian republics of Georgia, Armenia, and Azerbaidjan, with headquarters in Tiflis, Georgia), and years in exile--he was the founder, 1920, and first president of the Association of Russian Invalids in Exile (Abroad); photographs; correspondence; clippings; and published matter. The collection is not yet fully arranged; materials are mostly in Russian. Access can be arranged by contacting Mr. Baratoff directly.

NY 18
THE HOLY TRINITY ORTHODOX SEMINARY
Jordanville, New York 13361
(315-858-1332)

The Seminary, which is now planning to build a museum and archive facility, has a growing collection of archival materials. Numerous church and émigré organizations are interested in depositing materials at the Seminary.

NY 19
CONGRESS OF RUSSIAN AMERICANS, INC.
P.O. Box 5025
Long Island City, New York 11105

This organization, formed in the early 1970s, represents ethnic Russians in the United States. It conducts studies of the cultural and spiritual life of Russian-Americans and gathers biographical information for publication. It defends the human rights of Russian-Americans and freedom of Russians throughout the world. Materials held by the group at present include: biographies of Russians who have contributed to science, art, technology, literature, "the spiritual life," and social work in the U.S.; correspondence with federal and state government agencies concerning the interests of the Russian ethnic group in this country; and correspondence with Russian clergy, scholars, and cultural associations throughout the United States, U.S. senators, congressmen, and other officials. Besides the correspondence, there are reports, office files, diaries, literary manuscripts, oral histories (interviews), documents, photographs, and maps, dating from 1741 to the present. Among the groups and bodies in contact with the Congress are the Association of Russian-American Scholars in the USA, Inc., Association of Russian-American Engineers in the USA, Inc., Holy Synod of the Orthodox Church in America, and Holy Synod of Bishops of the Russian Orthodox Church Outside Russia. The Congress of Russian Americans has over 20 chapters scattered around the U.S. Its materials will be made available to researchers in general only after publication. Its quarterly, The Russian American, publishes holdings as funds allow.

NY 20
R. POLCHANINOFF--PRIVATE COLLECTION
6 Baxter Avenue
New Hyde Park, New York 11040
(Work: 212-867-5200 x 317)
(Home: 516-488-3824)

Mr. Polchaninoff's collection consists of diverse materials dating from before World War II and, mainly, the period after 1951: books and periodicals, documents, correspondence, diaries, memoirs, postcards, calendars, private postage stamps, seals, labels, cacheted covers, matchcovers, badges, medals, lottery tickets, bookplates, and other artifacts. Subjects covered: World War II, D.P. camps in Germany, 1945-51, Russians in the U.S. and abroad, Russian Boy Scouts and other youth organizations, the N.T.S. (National Workers Alliance), Pravoslavnoye Delo (Orthodox Action), and names of Russian origin for places and streets outside the Soviet Union (toponymics). Some of these materials have been described in Novoye Russkoye Slovo, "The Collector's Corner," since 1968. Scholars may write to Mr. Polchaninoff (preferably in Russian; English and German acceptable), stating in detail the aims of their research; recommendations desirable. For reply, please enclose return postage.

NY 21
HUGUENOT-PAINE HISTORICAL ASSOCIATION
983 North Avenue
New Rochelle, New York 10804
(914-632-5376)

A diary of Peter Allexander Allaire documenting his journey to Russia in 1774. The diary will be published in Russian History/Histoire russe in the near future.

NY 22
ARCHIVES
AMERICAN ACADEMY AND INSTITUTE OF ARTS AND LETTERS
633 West 155 Street
New York, New York 10032
(212-368-5900)

The Academy-Institute archives hold correspondence, citations, press clippings, a few manuscripts, and assorted other items for such members or honorary members as Bella Akhmadulina, George Kennan, George F. Kennan, Boris Pasternak, Harrison Salisbury, Dmitri Shostakovich, Alexander Solzhenitsyn, Igor Stravinskii, and Andrei Voznesensky. Also, notes on the Soviet American Writers' Conference sponsored by the Kettering Foundation, held in the Academy building, 25-27 April 1978. Recommendations requested; access by appointment only.

NY 23
AMERICAN BIBLE SOCIETY
1865 Broadway
New York, New York 10023
(212-581-7400)

1 In the Society's files is a folder of correspondence relating to the distribution of bibles in Russia, 1816-70. One of the letters is from Alexander Tourguéneff (Turgenev) to Elias Boudinot, first president of the ABS, 21 August 1816, in French. Also, a small collection of printed annual reports, most in German, of Bible Societies in Russia. These comprise: "The Russian Bible Society, 1814-21"; "Evangelical Bible Society in Russia, 1848-1902" (incomplete); "EBS in Russia, Estonian Section, 1858-84" (incomplete); "EBS in Russia, Riga Section, 1860 and 1879"; "EBS, St. Petersburg Section, 1878"; and "The Society for the Distribution of the Holy Scriptures in Russia, 1878-1901" (incomplete). (The Historical Bible Collection includes a number of Russian Bibles, i.e., published works.)

2 In addition, the ABS holds the following manuscripts:

Armenian: Gospels, 14-15 c. Paper, 274 ff., 2 cols., 23 lines. Illumination: life of Christ, 15 pp., Evangelists' portraits, incipits. (No. 1816)

Church Slavonic: Matthew (1:1-22:21). 14-15 c. Parchment, 24 ff., 1 col., 25-27 lines. Illumination: rubrics. (No. 35077)

Kohlossian: Matthew plus the Decalogue. Ca. 1860. Copybook, paper, 92 ff. + 2 pp. Translation by Ivan Nadezhdin, in Alaska, with space left for Church Slavonic parallel text but only the first verse in each chapter entered. Note: This is the language of the Tlingit tribes, whom Russians call Koloshi or Kaliuzhi. (No. 18020)

NY 24
AMERICAN GEOGRAPHICAL SOCIETY
Broadway at 156th Street
New York, New York 10032
(212-234-8100)

The archives of the AGS include materials from Russian scientists as well as items by American scholars specializing in Russian geographical matters. There are also materials on Frank A. Golder's Bering's Voyages, 2 vols., published by the AGS in 1922, and items about the Russian Arctic in various polar files.

NY 25
THE NIELS BOHR LIBRARY
CENTER FOR HISTORY OF PHYSICS
AMERICAN INSTITUTE OF PHYSICS
335 East 45th Street
New York, New York 10017
(212-661-9404)

1 The library maintains a collection of transcripts of tape-recorded recollections of individuals significant in the history of 20th c. physics and astronomy. Among these are some that pertain to Russia/USSR:

2 George Gamow (1904-1968). Includes ca. 20 pp. on his early life in Odessa, his work at the University of Leningrad, and his leaving Russia in 1933.

3 Lew Kowarski (b. 1907). Several pages concern his childhood in St. Petersburg, 1907-17.

4 A. G. Massevitch (b. 1918). 1 hr., with considerable information on his career and education at the University of Moscow through the 1940s, as well as on scientific careers in the Soviet Union.

5 E. R. Mustel (b. 1911). References to his childhood and astronomical education in Russia.

6 Léon Rosenfeld (1904-1974). Contains passing references to Soviet nuclear physics in the 1930s.

7 Stanislav Vasilevskis (b. 1907). Some pages on his childhood and education in Latvia; the Russian impact on Riga, 1907-44; and his departure from Latvia during World War II.

The original tape recordings are preserved in the repository. Additions to the collection are expected. Unpublished finding aids (NUCMC 70-1438).

8 Note: The library also holds scattered correspondence from Russian/Soviet scientists, ca. 1900-1950, in its microfilm and manuscript collections; and a card index, the National Catalog of Sources, on physicists and astronomers, which might be useful in locating the papers of scientists who have had contacts with Russia/USSR.

Restrictions: Individual oral history transcripts may have special restrictions; inquire at the library. Access to all manuscript materials and oral history interviews is restricted to persons who have completed an application for access which has been approved by Center staff.

NY 26
WILLIAM E. WIENER ORAL HISTORY LIBRARY
THE AMERICAN JEWISH COMMITTEE
165 East 56 Street
New York, New York 10022
(212-751-4000)

1 Established in 1969, the Library has a rapidly expanding collection of oral history materials, currently numbering about 600 memoirs,

representing hundreds of taped hours and over 61,000 transcribed pages. Holdings concern American Jews, many of whose pasts are traceable to Eastern Europe. Individual items are often parts of larger projects, which are designated in abbreviated form in parentheses after the individuals' names. The cited Russian/Soviet-related parts of memoirs may frequently be minimal.

2 Celia Adler (b. 1899). 125 pp., 1974. Actress. Daughter of Yiddish theatre actors Jacob P. Adler and Dinah Fineman. On tour in Vilna, Warsaw, etc. Impressions of Boris Thomashefsky, others. Permission required to see.

3 Brigitte Altman (Holocaust Survivors). 51 pp., 1975. Housewife. Born Lithuania, Kovno ghetto, sheltered by Lithuanian peasants.

4 Hanan J. Ayalti (East European Jewish Communities; hereinafter, East Europe) (b. 1910). 91 pp., 1977. Writer. Born Sapetkin, Russia; description of town, family home, Russian and Polish peasants, Zionism, move to Bialystock, political involvement, anti-Semitism, Yiddish theatre, and the Jewish community. Permission required to see.

5 Jacob Ben-Ami (1890-1977). 195 pp., 1973 and 1974. Actor. Born on grandfather's farm in Russia; youth in Minsk; street circuses; bit player in Russian theatre at 15; member of Peretz Hirshbein's Yiddish theatre in Odessa; emigration to U.S. in 1912. Recollections of Yiddish actors, including Celia Adler. Permission required to see.

6 Harry Bock (Holocaust Survivors). 209 pp., 1975. Diamond merchant. Kovno ghetto. Permission required to see.

7 Louis Bogart (b. 1918). 69 pp., 1975. Textile designer and manufacturer. Recollections of life as student and textile designer in Lodz; Soviet-occupied Poland; Siberia. Permission required to see.

8 Joseph Brodsky (b. 1940). 105 pp., 1973. Soviet poet, translator. Family; early jobs; beginnings of writing career; life of a poet in the USSR; relationships between the regime and individuals; Russian legal system and anti-Semitism; work of other Soviet poets; Israel; and coming to America. Permission required to see.

9 Dora Trilling Chary (East Europe) (b. 1897). 90 pp., 1978. Actress. Born Dnepropetrovsk, Russia. Childhood memories; lack of anti-Semitism in Dnepropetrovsk; anti-Jewish regulations in Kiev; religious observances; gentile friends; education; move to Warsaw; performances in the Caucasus; star of Russian Yiddish theatre; return to Russia in 1914, as war starts; refugee flight from Warsaw; pogroms; family flees Cossacks; feelings about the tsar; 1917 Revolution; emigration to the U.S. in 1929. Permission required to see.

10 Benjamin V. Cohen (b. 1894). 143 pp., 1970. Lawyer and government official. In part concerns the Potsdam Conference of 1945; Paris Peace Conference, 1946; work as American delegate to the 1948 San Francisco U.N. Conference and as an aide to Secretary of State James F. Byrnes; appraisal of U.S. foreign policy and U.N. activities. Restriction.

11 Richard Cohen (Politics) (b. 1923). 49 pp., 1973. Organization executive. Comments on Soviet Jewry as U.S. political issue. Closed until 30 November 1999.

12 Harry Cokin (East Europe) (b. 1895). 64 pp., n.d. Born Senno, Byelorussia. Describes life as son of large, poor family in poor, small Jewish town. Emigrated to U.S. in 1922. Closed until publication or for 5 years, whichever is shorter.

13 Misha Dichter (b. 1945). 60 pp., 1972. Concert pianist. Musical training and teachers; Tchaikovsky Competition in Moscow, 1966; cultural attitudes toward music; discussion of Soviet musicians; anti-Semitism in the Soviet Union.

14 Akiva Egozi and Wife (Holocaust Survivors). 168 pp., 1975. Rabbi. Born Lithuania. Permission required to see.

15 Vladimir M. Eitingon (East Europe) (b. 1899). 33 pp., 1977. Banker. Born in Moscow; hereditary citizenship of family; education; awareness of numerus clausus; Jewish assimilationist home life; Jewish refugees in World War I; radical politics; Jewish community of Moscow; Orthodox grandparents; emigration in 1918. Permission required to see.

16 Benjamin R. Epstein (Politics) (b. 1912). 31 pp., 1973. National director, Anti-Defamation League of B'nai B'rith. Media treatment of Jewish vote issue, Soviet Jewry, Israel.

17 Lasar Epstein (East Europe) (b. 1886). 156 pp., 1976. Bund leader. Born Vilna, Lithuania. Educated by tutors; joined bund in 1902; activity in Jewish socialist politics, organizing workers, education; experiences in Minsk, Lodz, and Warsaw in early Jewish labor movement; Warsaw Jewish community; emigration to Japan, Manchuria, and China after the 1917 Revolution; to U.S. in 1938. Permission required to see.

18 S. Andhil Fineberg (b. 1896). 286 pp., 1974. Rabbi. In part covers Soviet anti-Semitism, a "Message to Khrushchev," and the American Jewish League Against Communism.

19 Richard N. Gardner (Jacob Blaustein) (b. 1927). 42 pp., 1972. Columbia University professor of law and international organization. Comments on Jacob Blaustein's development, in the Kennedy Administration, of the concept of a high commissioner of human rights or inter-

national ombudsman. Studied by the U.S. State Department in 1963, the idea, now known as the Blaustein Plan, was introduced by the U.S. in the UN Human Rights Commission, 1967. The General Assembly failed to adopt it because of objections by the Soviet bloc, India, and Arab countries.

20 Manya Gersen (b. 1888). 150 pp., 1977. Dentist and artist. Childhood memories of Riga.

21 Leopold Godowsky, Jr. (b. 1900). 149 pp., 1971. Musician and chemist. Reminiscences of childhood in Europe and of the career of his father, the composer. Permission required to see.

22 Boris Goldovsky (b. 1908). 350 pp., 1975. Musician, conductor, director. Born Moscow; mother a violinist; career in the U.S. under S. Koussevitzky at Tanglewood; critical analyses and reminiscences of conductors Koussevitzky, A. Rodzinski, and others. Closed until 1 January 1987.

23 Israel Goldstein (b. 1896). 186 pp., 1973. Rabbi. Reminiscences of boyhood in Philadelphia; shtetl life in Russia; founding of Israel.

24 Betty Goodfriend (Holocaust Survivors). 36 pp., 1975. Community leader. Born in Lithuania. Permission required to see.

25 Mordecai Gorelick (b. 1899). 99 pp., n.d. Theatrical set designer. Life in shtetl on the Russian-Polish border; emigration to U.S. in 1905 with family.

26 Victor H. Gotbaum (b. 1922). 78 pp., 1977. Union leader. Russian-Jewish background, childhood in East Flatbush, N.Y. Permission required to see.

27 Esther Green (East Europe) (b. 1894). 46 pp., 1977. Born Potkamian, Poland. Small-town life in Poland under Russian invasion. Permission required to see.

28 Leonard Green (East Europe) (b. 1899). 31 pp., 1977. Typewriter salesman. Born in Riga, Russia; childhood in Riga; home religious life; contacts with gentiles; education; anti-Semitism; entrance to and withdrawal from university; move to Germany and return to Riga because of anti-Semitism. Permission required to see.

29 Chaim Gross (b. 1904). 164 pp., 1973. Artist and teacher. Childhood in Austria and Poland; Cossacks; refugee experiences.

30 J. B. S. Hardman (1882-1968). 39 pp., 1966. Labor leader and writer. Traces development of People's Council, offspring of Russia's Workmen's Council; Judah Magnes involvement; U.S. Socialist Party; political life in Russia; 1908 exile by the tsarist government as a Marxist organizer.

31 Dora C. Hemley (East Europe) (b. 1898). 16 pp., n.d. Born in Orlovietz, Ukraine. Daughter of a poor family with 9 children, whose living conditions were similar to those of the surrounding peasantry but whose life was qualitatively different. Emigration to the U.S. in 1908. Closed until publication or for 5 years, whichever is shorter.

32 Masha Henley (Holocaust Survivors). 188 pp., 1975. Medical assistant. Born in Lithuania. Permission required to see.

33 Elmer Hering (East Europe) (b. 1904). 73 pp., 1977. Dental technician. Born in Hungary; Hungarian Catholics vs. Russian Catholics; family flees Russian invasion in World War I. Permission required to see.

34 Arthur Herz (Holocaust Survivors). 119 pp., 1974. Butcher. Born in Latvia; in concentration camp in Latvia.

35 Ruth Rosenblatt Hockert (Holocaust Survivors). 159 pp., 1975. Radiologist. Born in Poland, fled to Russia with her parents following Nazi invasion of Poland; interned in Siberia. Permission required to see.

36 B. K. (name withheld) (East Europe) (b. 1900). 70 pp., n.d. Born Priluki, Ukraine. Daughter of a well-to-do family; student social life in the shtetl and in Odessa before the 1917 Revolution; emigration to U.S. in 1923. Closed until publication or for 5 years, whichever is shorter.

37 Max M. Kampelman (Politics) (b. 1920). 56 pp., 1974. Lawyer. Adviser in Senator Hubert H. Humphrey's 1972 campaign. Comments on Senator George McGovern's campaign and relationship to the Soviet Jewry issue.

38 Sholom Katz and Wife (Holocaust Survivors). 52 pp., 1975. Cantor. He was born in Rumania, was interned in a series of Ukrainian concentration camps. Permission required to see.

39 Bel Kaufman. 288 pp., 1976 and 1977. Teacher, author, and lecturer. Born in Berlin; childhood in Odessa; recollections of Russian Revolution; early life with grandfather Shalom Aleichem; excerpts from mother's diary. Permission required to see.

40 Matthew Kaufman (East Europe) (b. 1895). 28 pp., n.d. Born Priluki, Ukraine. Son of parents in general merchandising; life in pre-World War I Russia; emigration in 1912 to join a brother in the U.S. Closed until publication or for 5 years, whichever is shorter.

NEW YORK - AMERICAN JEWISH COMMITTEE NY 26

41 Alfred Kazin (b. 1915). 208 pp., 1960. Literary historian and critic. Includes reminiscences of Leon Trotskii and Chaim Weizmann.

42 Alexander Kipnis (b. 1891). 27 pp., 1971. Russian basso. Born in Russia, emigrated to the U.S. in 1923.

43 Benjamin Koenigsberg (b. 1884). 42 pp., 1964. Lawyer and communal worker. Reference to the Kishinev pogrom.

44 Theodore Fred Kuper (b. 1886). 161 pp., 1974. Lawyer, foundation director, and author. Memories of childhood in Moscow; steerage trip to the U.S. in 1891.

45 Lautenberg Oral History Collection of East European Jewish Communities. Formal name of ongoing project, some of whose individual collections are listed herein with designation "East Europe" in parentheses.

46 Gita Lemo (East Europe) (b. 1893). 85 pp., 1977. Wholesaler. Born Vilna, Russia. Childhood memories of middle-class household; family lineage; high school; anti-Semitism of some classmates; rejection by the university because of numerus clausus; life in Vilna, theatres, culture; World War I relief work for Jewish refugees; news of pogroms; political activity and movements in Vilna; memories of early Zionist leader Leibitchke Yaffe. Discussion of occasional intermarriage in Vilna. Permission required to see.

47 Thomas F. Lewinsohn (Holocaust Survivors). 69 pp., 1975. City official. Born in Germany, escaped in 1941 through Poland, Russia, and Korea.

48 Jacques Lipchitz (1891-1973). 137 pp., 1970. Sculptor. Born in Lithuania to an Orthodox Jewish family.

49 Baruch Lumet (b. 1898). 271 pp., 1976. Actor, director, composer, and playwright. Memories of youth in Poland, anti-Semitism, participation in Warsaw dramatic groups, Yiddish theatre, Vilna Troupe. Came to U.S. in 1921.

50 Richard Maass (Politics) (b. 1919). 59 pp., 1974. Business executive. Chairman of the National Conference on Soviet Jewry. Discusses Senator Henry Jackson amendment; Pepsi-Cola and the Soviet Union; impressions of Richard Nixon and George McGovern; Nixon's approach to Israel and the question of Soviet Jewry; relation of domestic policy to international agreements.

51 Joseph A. Margolies (East Europe) (b. 1889). 67 pp., 1977. Librarian and publishing executive. Born in Brest-Litovsk, Russia. Home life with religious parents and 9 children; father an ironworker; neighbors; Jewish education; the Dreyfus case; anti-Semitism and pogroms; departure from the shtetl; varieties of Jewish life; schooling; Jewish organizational structure. Permission required to see.

52 James Marshall (b. 1896). 258 pp., 1974. Lawyer, educator, and honorary vice-president of the American Jewish Committee. Recollections of fighting discriminatory Russian treaty; the World War I peace conference; Henry Ford and the Protocols of the Elders of Zion; experiences in Palestine, 1927; Agro-Joint farm colonies in Russia, 1929. Closed during lifetime, plus 10 years.

53 Max Miller (1878-1975). 63 pp., 1971. Pioneer Texas businessman. Arrival in U.S. from Russia in 1903.

54 Jennie Muraven (East Europe) (b. 1900). 34 pp., n.d. Born Uman, Ukraine. Excitement of World War I, politics, literature, leaving for U.S. in 1914 at age 14. Closed until publication or for 5 years, whichever is shorter.

55 Elizabeth Newman (East Europe) (b. 1895). 62 pp., 1977. Teacher. Born Brestowitz, Russia. Memories of grandmother; cheder; further education; Orthodox home; rabbi's lifestyle; arranged marriages, dowries, change in customs; Jews and gentiles in the shtetl; rich and poor Jews; education and the poor; use of Yiddish and Russian; Jewish-gentile relations; pogroms; Jewish migration to America; 1905 Revolution and Jewish revolutionaries; life after the Revolution; Jewish quotas in schools; no intermarriage in Brestowitz; misery of Jewish life; Zionist sentiment; assimilation and conversion; the Wolkovisk high school; career as a teacher; World War I in Brestowitz; the Germans; impact of 1917 Revolution on the town; Polish anti-Semitism after the war; Bolsheviks loot the town; life under the Poles vs. life under the Russians; Passover and Yom Kippur in Brestowitz; emigration to the U.S. with her husband; feelings of nostalgia.

56 Morris S. Novik (b. 1903). 74 pp., 1975. Radio consultant. Arrival in U.S. from Russia in 1914. Permission required to see.

57 H. P. (name withheld) (Holocaust Survivors). 122 pp., 1975. Tobacconist. Born in Poland, Lodz ghetto; Siberian camp.

58 Simon Palevsky (East Europe) (b. 1903). 107 pp., 1977 and 1978. Jeweler. Born in Warsaw, family moves to Vilna; middle-class Hasidic background; cheder, yeshiva; religious views; relations with gentiles; family life; father's role in education; political awakening; joining of Tsukunft, the youth arm of the Jewish Workers' Bund; political and union activities; work as organizer; social and cultural life of Vilna. Permission required to see.

59 Jan Peerce (b. 1907). 185 pp., 1973. Opera and concert tenor. Born in New York City,

Russian-Polish extraction. Permission required to see.

60 Roberta Peters (b. 1930). 295 pp., 1972. Opera and concert soprano. Recollections of Metropolitan Opera experiences, performances in Israel and the Soviet Union. Closed until 1 January 2000.

61 Jacob S. Potofsky (b. 1894). 140 pp., 1970 and 1971. Labor leader. Son of a factory manager in a small Russian town; family immigrates to Chicago in 1907. Closed during lifetime.

62 Bessie Pupko (East Europe). 88 pp., 1977. Teacher and organization official. Born in Vilna, Lithuania. Studied engineering in Kherson, Ukraine, 1918-21; vital communal and cultural life of 80,000 Jews in Vilna between the world wars; schools, libraries, theatres, sports clubs, synagogues, hospitals, and other social services; Polish anti-Semitism; Kherson during the early days of communism. Permission required to see.

63 Rose Radin (b. 1885). 213 pp., 1975. Realtor. Parents' life in Minsk; family name-change to Minsky; parents' arrival in U.S.; New York Jewish theatre and start of Minsky Burlesque. Closed until 15 April 1992.

64 Tony Randall (b. 1924). 187 pp., 1976. Actor. Includes impressions of Konstantin Stanislavsky.

65 Ed Robbins (Holocaust Survivors). 83 pp., 1974. Camp director. Born in Rumania; concentration camp in the Ukraine.

66 Eli G. Rochelson (Holocaust Survivors). 81 pp., 1974. Born in Lithuania; Kovno ghetto. Permission required to see.

67 Bella Nemanoff Rochline (East Europe) (b. 1900). 29 pp., 1977. Professor of languages. Born in St. Petersburg; wealthy family background, father a lawyer; education, high school, private tutors; father's influence with the government; assimilationist background; political activity; October Revolution; travels during the war; absence of Zionist influence; return to Russia in 1965; Beilis affair in 1913. Permission required to see.

68 Ruth Rosenberg (Jacob Blaustein). 28 pp., 1972. Younger sister of Jacob Blaustein. Mother came from Riga, Latvia; father from Russia. Jacob was the second child in a family of 5. Permission required to see.

69 Joseph and Raisa Rothenberg (East Europe). 212 pp., 1977. Joseph (b. 1894) born in Zhitomir, Russia; life prior to and immediately following the Russian Revolution; childhood, Jewish, general education; short career as a lawyer in Russia; flight from Russia in 1918. Raisa born in Vilna, Lithuania; family; childhood; education; career as lawyer and judge in Poland between the wars. Covers lifestyle of Jewish upper class; relationships with non-Jews; and anti-Semitism. Permission required to see.

70 Ruth Rubin (b. 1908). 217 pp., 1976. Folklorist; archivist of Yiddish songs; singer and lecturer. Born in Montreal, Canada, of Russian immigrants. Impressions of Kalman Marmor, Chaim Zhitlowsky, etc. Her folklore collections are in the Library of Congress. Permission required to see.

71 Joseph Saul (East Europe) (b. 1902). 94 pp., 1977. Menswear retailer. Born in Suwalki, Lithuania/Poland, a town of 11,000 on the German border, with a Jewish population of 9,000, supporting 15,000 Russian soldiers. Father an attorney; opportunities for secular education better for girls than for boys; Jewish community, theatre, library, singing society; Yiddish-speaking culture activities; Bund; Socialists and labor Zionist movement; uncle who was the national arbitrator of the brewery industry of Poland, Lithuania, and Russia; Jewish Polish-Russian attitudes; polylingualism (Yiddish, Hebrew, German, Russian, Polish); Jewish ownership of 500 stores in town; Jewish courts of law; medical care; holiday observances. Permission required to see.

72 Herschel Schacter (Politics) (b. 1917). 73 pp., 1974. Rabbi. Chairmanship of Conference on Soviet Jewry; importance of Soviet Jewry issue in 1972 presidential campaign; meeting with Richard M. Nixon; impressions of George McGovern.

73 Gertrude Schneider (Holocaust Survivors). 193 pp., 1974. Writer and lecturer. Born in Austria; Riga ghetto. Closed during lifetime.

74 Harry Schneidermann (1885-1975). 276 pp., 1969. American Jewish Committee's first secretary, editor. AJC involvement in passport question; abrogation of commerce, navigation treaty between Russia and the U.S.; immigration problem; AJC fundraising; formation of the Joint Distribution Committee; establishment of American Jewish Congress; World War I Peace Conference.

75 Israel Schochet (East Europe) (b. 1898). 77 pp., n.d. Born Strijavka, Ukraine. Highly educated as first-born son and oldest child; disruptive effects of the Revolution; flight; unique description of shtetl life; emigration to the U.S. in 1924. Closed until publication or for 5 years, whichever is shorter.

76 George Schwab (Holocaust Survivors). 89 pp., 1974. College professor. Born in Latvia; Lvov ghetto. Permission required to see.

77 Irving S. Shapiro (b. 1916). 254 pp., 1975. Corporation executive (chairman of E. I. du

NEW YORK - AMERICAN JEWISH COMMITTEE NY 26

Pont de Nemours & Company). Discusses parents' life in Lithuania; arrival in U.S. Closed until 1 January 1985.

78 Gregor Shelkan (Holocaust Survivors). 87 pp., 1975. Cantor. Born in Latvia; Riga ghetto. Permission required to see.

79 Joseph Sisco (Jacob Blaustein) (b. 1919). 21 pp., 1972. Assistant secretary of state for Middle East and South Asia, 1969-74; undersecretary of state for political affairs, 1974-76; president of American University, 1976-80. Blaustein named member of U.S. delegation to the U.N. General Assembly, helped negotiate settlement of Korean War; Blaustein's attitude toward the Soviet Union .

80 Joel Sissman (East Europe) (b. 1886). 92 pp., 1977. Dentist. Born Mogilev, Russia. Mother ran a grocery store in a central courtyard of the city; lifestyles of poor Jews; public baths; Sabbath and Passover observances; Jewish education; pogroms; political atmosphere; vocational training; apprenticeship as a land surveyor and as a pharmacist; medicine; concerts, Yiddish and regular theatre; founding of haskole; Jewish and gentile death rituals. Permission required to see.

81 John Slawson (b. 1896). 159 pp., 1969. Social welfare executive; officer of the American Jewish Committee. Brief biographical data: born in Russia, came to U.S. in 1905.

82 Boris Smolar (b. 1896). 362 pp., 1977. Journalist and editor. Born Rovno, Ukraine; early interest in journalism; correspondent for a Jewish publication in World War I; active in the Bund and communal organizations in Rovno and Petrograd; post-war work of the Joint Distribution Committee and U.S. Morgenthau Committee in Poland; came to U.S. in 1919. Describes economic, religious persecution of Russian Jews. Permission required to see.

83 Raphael Soyer (b. 1899). Artist. In progress.

84 Isaac Stern (b. 1920). 57 pp., 1971. Concert violinist. Soviet policy on Jewish emigration and Jewish Defense League reactions; U.S. foreign policy. Closed at present.

85 Henry and Florence Strick (Holocaust Survivors). 95 pp., 1974. Trailer salesman and housewife, respectively. Florence born in the Ukraine. Permission required to see.

86 George M. Szabad (East Europe) (b. 1917). 40 pp., 1977. Business executive and lawyer. Born in Gorki, Russia; grew up and attended school in Warsaw.

87 Majsze Szwejlich (East Europe) (b. 1910). In progress. Actor. Born Vilna, Lithuania; resides in Warsaw. In Yiddish.

88 Milton Taichert (b. 1893). 102 pp., 1975. Dealer in hides, fur broker. Arrival in U.S. from Lithuania at 13. Permission required to see.

89 Sol J. Taishoff (b. 1904). 30 pp., 1977. Magazine publisher. Born in Minsk suburb, Russia; family immigrated to Washington, D.C. Permission required to see.

90 Laina Temchin (Holocaust Survivors). 249 pp., 1975. Housing development manager. Born Lithuania. Permission required to see.

91 Michael Tilson Thomas (b. 1944). 80 pp., 1970 and 1972. Musician and conductor. Recollections of grandmother, actress Bessie Thomashefsky, widow of Yiddish actor Boris Thomashefsky; influence of teachers Gregor Piatigorsky, Sviatoslav Richter, etc. Closed during lifetime.

92 Sholom Traub (East Europe) (b. 1904). 68 pp., n.d. Born Ryzhesh, Ukraine. Life as a Jew during birth, death of Ukrainian Independent Republic; emigration to U.S. in 1921. Closed until publication or for 5 years, whichever is shorter.

93 Hilda Sissman Twig (East Europe) (b. 1889). 69 pp., 1977. Saleswoman. Born Mogdolev, Russia. Education as a major goal; cheder; private school; female education; study and work in a pharmacy; mother's grocery store; herring as food staple; Sabbath observance; "extended family" of cousins, aunts, etc.; Jewish holidays deeply religious; daily hygiene; dating and social life; gulf between Jews and Christians; cultural activities, concerts, lectures; fear of pogroms on Easter Eve; Jewish reaction to 1905 Revolution. Permission required to see.

94 Sender Wajsman (Holocaust Survivors). 91 pp., 1975. School director. Born Lithuania; Vilna ghetto.

95 Morris Wax (East Europe) (b. 1905). 40 pp., n.d. Born in Chashwatowa, Ukraine. Account by son of upper-middle class shtetl family caught between marauding pogromchik bands and the Red Army. Left Russia in 1923. Closed until publication or for 5 years, whichever is shorter.

96 Florence Weinberg (East Europe) (b. 1901). 58 pp., 1977. Housewife and volunteer worker. Born Odessa, Russia; Jewish self-defense activities; family traditions; servants; education; feelings for Russia; exposure to Jewish culture; grandparents; Zionism and political influences; the October Revolution. Permission required to see.

97 Gertrude Weissbluth (Holocaust Survivors). 215 pp., 1974. Housewife. Born Silesia; forced labor in the Ukraine.

98 Pauline Wenger (East Europe) (b. 1906). 58 pp., 1977. Artist. Born in Nicolaieff, Russia; childhood memories; family business; household maids; education; father and brother leave for America; World War I prevents emigration of remaining family members; pogroms; the Revolution; brother forced into army and never heard from again; Kosher home; anti-Semitism before and after the Revolution; a gentile saves her from Cossacks; results of the Revolution; life under the tsar; Sabbath memories; Nowy Odessa synagogues; religious, rich, and poor Jews in Nowy Odessa; Jews arrested after the Revolution; false accusations made by anti-Semites; husband flees Russia during the Revolution; rabbi assists her in emigrating, joins husband in New York. Permission required to see.

99 Elijah Wisebram (b. 1892). 55 pp., 1972. Merchant and civic worker. Childhood impressions of Bialystok; immigration to the U.S.

100 Harry L. Woll (East Europe) (b. 1898). 50 pp., n.d. Born Gomel, Byelorussia. Account of a well-organized, intelligent, closely-knit Mitnagged family; emigration to the U.S. in 1920. Closed until publication or for 5 years, whichever is shorter.

101 Rivka Woll (East Europe) (b. 1900). 38 pp., n.d. Born Lyelchitz, Byelorussia. Daughter of the rabbi of a shtetl; Passover matzoh made in the home. To the U.S. in 1920. Closed until publication or for 5 years, whichever is shorter.

102 Angela Yaron (Holocaust Survivors). 145 pp., 1975. Sociologist, researcher. Born Rumania; survived German and Russian regimes.

103 Manya Yassen (East Europe) (b. 1905). 45 pp., 1977. Secretary. Born in Vilna, Poland. Childhood memories; grandparents; life under Poles, Russians, and Germans; education; Jewish homelife; memories of Vilna; father's business dealings with Jews and gentiles; anti-Semitism in Warsaw; Polish pogroms in Vilna; Passover and Chanukah in Vilna; intermarriage; increasing use of Yiddish in Poland; Jewish culture in Vilna; Yiddish theatre. Permission required to see.

104 Note: The William E. Wiener Oral History Library of the American Jewish Committee is currently embarking on a 2-year oral history project (funded by the National Endowment for the Humanities) to interview recent Soviet Jewish émigrés to the United States. Results of this project will be available on completion.

Finding Aid: The preceding information has been quoted from: Catalogue of Memoirs of the William E. Wiener Oral History Library (1978).

NY 27
AMERICAN JEWISH JOINT DISTRIBUTION COMMITTEE ARCHIVES
60 East 42nd Street
New York, New York 10017
(212-687-6200)

1 The Joint Distribution Committee was formed during World War I to help displaced persons and other civilians suffering from the conflict. Russia was a limited focus of its attention. It continued to operate in the USSR until ca. 1938. Office files, correspondence, reports, and account books are arranged chronologically and described in 3 catalogues. The holdings on Russia outlined in the 3 catalogues cover the following subjects:

2 For the years 1914-18, relief (money, food, clothing, and medical supplies) to Jews in German-occupied lands. Materials relate to JDC fund-raising efforts, the political and military difficulties involved in sending aid, and the JDC organization in Europe (the Central Jewish Committee for the Relief of War Sufferers in Petrograd was known as EKOPO). General files on Poland (129-42a) also cover cities listed as Polish but currently in the USSR (e.g., Vilno). The "Russia-General" files (143c-47) have information on clothing for Siberia, EKOPO, persecution of Jews, and pogroms. Among the correspondents in these papers are H. Bernstein, a New York Herald journalist and JDC delegate to Russia; Professor E. T. Devine, head of the U.S. embassy's relief division in Petrograd; David R. Francis, the U.S. ambassador to Russia; Baron Alexander de Guinzburg, chairman of EKOPO; Baron Theodore de Guinzburg, of the Russian embassy in Washington; and the State Department.

3 For 1919-21 (catalogue 2) there are materials on European Russia (files 247-61) and Siberia (files 262-80). In April 1919 Dr. Frank Rosenblatt was sent as JDC representative to Vladivostok. He remained there until November of that year, working with the Harbin Relief Committee (an auxiliary which he organized) and the Jewish National Council in Irkutsk. In 1920 the JDC appointed a representative to arrange for repatriation of POWs in Siberia. The JDC joined with other U.S. groups in the Siberian War Prisoners Repatriation Fund, which worked with the League of Nations' Nansen Commission. Documents cover administration of relief efforts, finances, relations with the U.S. and foreign governments, aid appeals, persecution and pogroms, POWs, and POW camps in the Far East (at Biysk, Nikolsk-Ussuriisk, Pervaya Rechka, Petropavlovsk, Tomsk, Turinsk, Achinsk, Barnaul, Irkutsk, Kansk, and Krasnaya Rechka). Some items relate to Admiral A. V. Kolchak.

In 1920 Dr. Rosenblatt became regional director for Russia. He and the JDC overseas unit no. 1, along with the JDC's Ukraine Commission, went to Russia in the spring. Unit no. 1 reached Kiev in April, organizing relief distribution at once. The Ukraine Commission then entered the country, reaching an agreement with the Soviet government's Moscow Relief Committee about relief distribution. In July 1920 the JDC established an office in Reval, Estonia, to transmit supplies (in cooperation with the British Society of Friends). The materials again cover pogroms (in Ukraine and Byelorussia), the relief work, finances, political conditions throughout Russia, reconstruction efforts, cooperatives, emigration, and relations with the Soviet regime. There are appeals of Russian Jewish organizations for all kinds of assistance--child care, medical, cultural, religious. Correspondents in these files include Allen Wardwell of the American Red Cross, and M. M. Vinaver. 1 memorandum is from General A. I. Denikin.

4 Catalogue 3, for 1921-38, includes official correspondence, account books, memoranda, reports on relief administration and cooperation with Soviet authorities, information on Jewish agencies receiving assistance, files of Agro-Joint (numbers 508-67), and data on the American Relief Administration (ARA). Between 1921 and 1938, JDC appropriations and individual subscriptions earmarked for the USSR totaled over $20 million. In 1921-22 alone, the JDC contributed $3.6 million for nonsectarian relief in the Soviet Union, this in cooperation with the ARA to counteract the 1921 famine (files 488-91). When the ARA began withdrawal from the USSR, the JDC arranged with the Soviet regime to continue independent activities (relief and reconstruction), for which it appropriated $4.22 million. Its aid went to agricultural settlements, loan associations, trade schools, hospitals, homes for the aged, orphanages, and other institutions. In July 1924 the JDC organized the American Jewish Joint Agriculture Corporation (Agro-Joint) to act as its operating arm in the Soviet Union. This operation spent roughly $5.88 million to the end of 1928 (files 508-09). In 1928 the American Society for Jewish Farm Settlements in Russia (ASJFS) was formed; it raised some $8 million privately in support of the Agro-Joint program (files 539-44 and 554-64). ASJFS ended its work on 31 December 1935, while Agro-Joint terminated operations in the USSR in 1938. Much additional JDC material relating to Russian activities, not detailed in this description, are in files 447-51 and 468-87.

Restrictions: Access by prior clearance and appointments only.

Finding Aids: Catalogue of the Archives of the American Jewish Joint Distribution Committee by Rose Klepfisz (and Eleanor Mlotek, vol. 2, and Emil Lang, vol. 3), 3 vols. (1964-74), covering 1914-32; vol. 4, for 1933-45, in preparation.

NY 28
AMERICAN NUMISMATIC SOCIETY
Broadway and 156th Street
New York, New York 10032
(212-286-3130)

1 Peter I. License badge, 1705. Copper disk, 24.1 mm in diameter, 1.7 mm thick. Issued by the regime, it had to be worn (carried) to show that the bearer had paid the necessary tax to wear a beard or mustache. The object is stored in a vault. Also, a document describing the token.

2 Russian Veterans' Society of the World War, Inc. Ca. 7 items. Typescript entitled "Information of the Russian (Disabled) Veterans Society of the World War," 5 pp.; 2 letters from the Veterans' Society president Alexander Elshin to Sawyer Mosser, the ANS librarian; a "Declaration" establishing the Order and Cross of the Compassionate Heart, with accompanying illustration; an "Application" for the award of the decorations of the Russian Orders; and a copy of the award certificate of the Order of the Compassionate Heart granted to Elshin, ca. 1933.

Finding Aid: The American Numismatic Society, Dictionary Catalogue of the Library (Boston: G. K. Hall, 1962), plus supplements.

NY 29
BUND ARCHIVES OF THE JEWISH LABOR MOVEMENT
ATRAN CENTER FOR JEWISH CULTURE
25 East 78th Street
New York, New York 10021
(212-535-0850)

1 The Bund Archives, established in Geneva in 1899, soon after the founding of the Bund in Vilna, collects primarily materials relating to the history of the Jewish labor movement in Eastern Europe and the Western Hemisphere. Among its holdings are printed and unpublished matter in Yiddish, Russian, Polish, English, French, German, and a few other languages.

2 Jewish Labor Bund. Archives, ca. 1840-present, ca. 2,000 ft. (additions expected). Includes manuscripts, reports, documents, photographs, and correspondence from before the start of the Bund (ca. 1850) to its elimination in the USSR in 1921; convention minutes, 1906-14; a nearly complete collection of the Bund's underground press in Russia; complete run of the Bund's legal publications, 1906-21, including periodicals and dailies; leaflets, proclamations, and booklets, many illegal. Materals relate to the Bund's Central Committee, its hundreds of local organizations, the Foreign Committee, the Russian Social Democratic Labor Party, and individual members.

3 Miscellaneous. Publications and documents of Jewish bourgeois parties (e.g., Der Fraynd of St. Petersburg and Warsaw, 1903-13; Der Vayter Mizrekh of Kharbin, 1921-22); documents, reports, and publications of the Poale-Zion, the S.S. (Socialist-Territorialists) in Russia and Poland; the Sejmistn; Di Fareynikte (United Party); Russian, Lettish, Georgian, Armenian, and Ukrainian Social Democratic movements; Osvobozhdenie Truda; Soyouz Russkikh S.D.; Socialist Revolutionary Party; Bolsheviks; Mensheviks; and anarchists. A main subject covered is the attitude of such groups to the "Jewish Question" and problems of nationalities. Additional collections concern revolutionary activities in tsarist universities and high schools; Jewish communists in Russia and elsewhere; the colonization of Biro-Bidzhan and the Crimea, 1920s; reaction of socialists. (Jewish and non-Jewish) to the 1939 Stalin-Hitler pact; anti-Semitism in Russia, Poland, and other countries (from 1890); pogroms, 1903-39; the secular Yiddish school system in Lithuania and Latvia; the Jews in Eastern Europe; and the Zubatov movement (police unionism). Among the items in these holdings are photographs, posters, a survey on Jewish self-defense compiled in Russia 1904-1905, letters and statements of prominent political leaders, and literary manuscripts (for example, writings of Marc Chagall). The archive also has individual biographical files on numerous socialists and revolutionaries, both Jews and non-Jews. There are files with newspaper clippings, letters, photographs, and manuscripts, on such figures as Raphael Abramovitch, Mendel Beilis, Alexander Berkman, G. Gershuny, Emma Goldman, Vladimir Kosovsky, A. Kremer, Peter Kropotkin, N. Lenin, Julius Martov, Vladimir Medem, M. Olgin, G. Plekhanov, H. Rogoff, Anna and Pavel Rosenthal, David Shub, V. Zhabotinsky, Chaim Zhitlovski, and Aaron Zundelevitch.

Restriction information available at the Bund Archives.

Finding Aid: A Great Collection; The Archives of the Jewish Labor Movement (New York, 1965).

NY 30
THE BETTMANN ARCHIVE, INC.
136 East 57th Street
New York, New York 10022
(212-758-0362)

The Bettmann Archive is a commercial institution, basically oriented toward the marketplace, working with publishers, editors, advertisers, and people in the television industry. The pictorial collections, including photographic and other still pictures, cover most nations of the world and most significant historical personalities, as well as a broad range of subjects. While Russia is not a specialty, pertinent material in the collections is extensive. Access for research purposes may be granted on an individual basis; contact the archive in advance, stating the nature of the research and material sought. Reproductions are available at the established rates.

NY 31
MRS. ALEXANDER CHEREPNIN (TCHEREPNIN)--
PRIVATE COLLECTION
170 West 73rd Street, Apt. 8-B
New York, New York 10023

Mrs. Cherepnin holds the papers of both her late husband, Alexander Cherepnin (1899-1977), and her father-in-law, Nicolas Cherepnin (1873-1945). Some papers are in Europe but a large amount is in the United States. The composers' papers include holograph musical scores, letters, diaries, and other writings. There is also information about the third generation of Cherepnin family composers, Serge (b. 1941) and Ivan (b. 1943). Ultimate disposition of this collection has not yet been determined. Because materials are presently stored, full access to holdings is not possible. However, specific inquiries from scholars concerning the collection will be answered.

NY 32
AVERY ARCHITECTURAL AND FINE ARTS LIBRARY
AVERY HALL
COLUMBIA UNIVERSITY
New York, New York 10027
(212-280-3501)

1 Nikolai Dimitrievich Fediushkin. Drawings, 1856-65 and n.d., ca. 350 sheets in 7 bound vols. Architect. These mounted plates are original architectural drawings of Russian churches, their decorations, and equipment. Some drawings are dated; many have Russian inscriptions. They include plans, elevations, sections, and details. The plates are in pencil on paper, some with watercolor. (Rare Book; call number AA/2635/F31/folio)

2 Nicholas N. Gvosdeff. Miscellaneous work, including original drawings, photographs, and manuscript material. 20th c. architect. The collection is uncatalogued. (Archive; drawers 157, 159, and 167; hereafter, DR)

3 Leningrad. A plan of the city of St. Petersburg, 110 x 110 cm., mounted on cloth, from 1868. (Archive; DR 136.I)

4 Moscow. Khram Khrista Spasitelia. 69 pp., plates, a plan, and tables in 1 vol., bound:

Istoricheskoe opisanie postroeniia v Moskvie khrama vo imia Khrista Spasitelia (1869). (Rare Book; AA/5681/M85/folio)

5 Vera Nikiforova. 57 watercolors on paper, drawings of Russian churches, most labeled with name of church and its date of construction (ca. 8 x 10 in., though size varies). Mrs. Nikiforov, wife of a well-known assistant professor of church archaeology at the Theological Faculty of the St. Vladimir Institute (Harbin), drew these pictures to illustrate her husband's lectures (ca. 1910). They are of ancient churches of different periods and various styles from the 12th c. forward. (Archive; DR 122)

6 Observations on the designs submitted for proposed opera house at Odessa, Russia, by "Solo Deo Salus". 14 mounted plates, bound, 1 vol., with English and French text accompanying the plates (187-?). (Rare Book; AH7/Od2)

7 Photographs of Russia. Ca. 70 items in 1 album, 19th and 20th c., of various subjects; donated by Frank Erb. (Archive; AH47/A112)

Restrictions: Inquire concerning access to the Rare Books and Archival material.

Finding Aids: Catalog of the Avery Memorial Architectural Library of Columbia University, 2nd ed., enlarged, 19 vols. (Boston: G. K. Hall, 1968); first supplement, 4 vols. (1972); second supplement, 4 vols. (1976); and third supplement, 3 vols. (1977). Also, unpublished card file for archival material.

NY 33
THE BAKHMETEFF ARCHIVE
COLUMBIA UNIVERSITY
801 Butler Library
New York, New York 10027
(212-280-3986)

The Bakhmeteff Archive has developed by means of gifts and purchases from a great many private individuals, including both persons who left Russia and also a number of Americans. The archive is open to qualified scholars in accordance with the policies of the Rare Book and Manuscript Library of Columbia University. A certain number of collections also have additional restrictions placed on them by their donors; these are indicated by the word "Restrictions" at the end of the collection. Interested scholars should contact the curator of the archive in advance concerning access. In addition to the listings that follow, the archive holds a great deal of Russian-related materials of an archival nature, primarily printed matter and issuances of organizations. Moreover, there are many files of rare and unusual periodicals or serials that have been omitted. It should also be emphasized that the listings that follow are based on preliminary inventories completed by the staff shortly before research for the guide in hand began. The reader is forewarned that some of the entries are incomplete.

1 V. K. Abdank-Kossovskii (d. 1962). Papers, 7 boxes, ca. 2,000 items. Émigré in France. Materials on émigré cultural life in Paris, émigré ballet, and the politics of the emigration (photos, correspondence, clippings). Some items also relate to the Volunteer Army, the Civil War in the South, and the White movement, the Russian Orthodox Church in emigration, ca. 1920-50, and the adult courses taught in Paris in 1931 by General N. N. Golovin. The collection further includes correspondence of the All-Russian Union of Cities (Vserossiiskii Soiuz Gorodov) in 1918-21, documents concerning the White northern forces in the Civil War, and letters concerning the unity of the early post-revolutionary emigration.

2 Raphael A. Abramovitch (1880-1963). Papers, 4 boxes, 1,300 items. Includes notes for a book on the Revolution, Civil War, and Soviet Union in the 1920s (his The Soviet Revolution); and a typed work by B. Dvinov, "Oppozitsiia v VKP, 1917-1924." The materials, covering 1914-39, concern Bolshevik intraparty politics, the 1917 Pre-Parliament, the working class, TsIK meetings, and foreign policy.

3 Mark Aleksandrovich Aldanov (pseud. of M. A. Landau) (1886-1957). Papers, 37 boxes, ca. 6,700 items. Author. Mainly writings and correspondence. Among his correspondents, ca. 1926-57: Don Aminado, B. A. Bakhmetev, Ivan Bunin, Marc Chagall, S. P. Mel'gunov, A. I. Konovalov, A. F. Kerensky, A. L. Tolstoi, Somerset Maugham, W. Lednicki, V. V. Nabokov, N. A. Teffi, B. K. Zaitsev, M. V. Vishniak, M. M. Karpovich, S. A. Kusevitskii, V. M. Zenzinov, S. V. Rachmaninoff, V. A. Maklakov, P. I. Miliukov, G. Struve, the editors of Novoe Russkoe Slovo. There are manuscripts (and reviews), in English and Russian, for most of Aldanov's major works, including Nachalo kontsa, Istoki, The Fifth Seal, Before the Deluge, Zhivi kak khochesh; many short stories ("Rubin," "T'ma," "Fel'd-marshal," "Greta i tank," etc.); and some plays (The Lie Detector--in Russian--and Rytsar' svobody). Restrictions.

4 Grigorii Alekseevich Aleksinskii (1879-1967). Papers, 15 boxes, ca. 2,400 items. Bolshevik spokesman in the second duma. Aleksinskii later left Lenin and joined Bogdanov and Lunacharskii in the Vpered group, emigrating to France after the Revolution. The collection includes photocopies of his memoirs for 1905-10, and substantial material (correspondence, documents, petitions, pamphlets, etc.) on the Russian Social Democratic Party, ca. 1907-14. Subjects covered: the socialist movement and anarchists in World War I, German

influence and propaganda in Russia, the assassination of Nicholas II, Russian soldiers and prisoners in Germany and France during World War I, the London Congress, the Vpered group, the SD Capri school, and the Okhrana penetration of the SD party. There are letters from Maksim Gorkii, G. Plekhanov, V. I. Lenin, Iu. Martov, D. Z. Manuilskii, A. Lunacharskii.

5 Alexander II (1818-1881). Handwritten copies of Alexander's letters to A. I. Bariatinskii, vice-regent of the Caucasus, bound, in French, with typed transcriptions. The correspondence has been published by Alfred J. Rieber in The Politics of Autocracy. Letters of Alexander II to Prince A. I. Bariatinskii. 1857-1864 (Paris, 1966).

6 Ekaterina Grigovevna Andersen. A tape recording, ca. 1972, of her reminiscences of childhood and adult life and Soviet conditions under Stalin, ca. 1905-38.

7 Leonid Mikhailovich Andreev. Short personal reminiscences of the Russo-Japanese War of 1904-1905 and of the 1917 Revolution.

8 Vladimir Mikhailovich Andreevskii. Papers, 2 boxes, ca. 300 items. Member of the State Council. Contains diaries, correspondence, memoirs, and handwritten reminiscences. Also includes a typescript entitled "Iz vospominaniia B. N. Chicherina" by N. I. Krivtsov.

9 Leonid L. Andrenko. Papers, 24 items. Photos, Soviet newspaper clippings, correspondence mostly concerning K. E. Tsiolkovskii.

10 Leonid Vladimirovich Andrusov. Papers, 20 items. Emigré scientist. A short typed autobiography plus printed copies of his scientific papers in French and German, 1950s.

11 M. D. Andrusova. Typed memoirs ("Moi vospominaniia") cover World War I, the Revolution, and foreign intervention in the Civil War, 1914-19. Restrictions.

12 Sofia Ivanovna Anichkova-Taube (188?-1957). Papers, 4 boxes, ca. 400 items. Poet. Include material on Petrograd in 1917-24 (literary and cultural life), her manuscripts, and also correspondence with P. Gnedich, Professor V. Speranskii, and V. Bulgakov (L. N. Tolstoi's secretary). There is also information on the emigration in Czechoslovakia. Also ca. 3 boxes of E. N. Taube, editor of Ves' mir in St. Petersburg before 1917. Poems, drawings, leaflets, correspondence (including one signed by Eleanor Roosevelt), her obituary, and an autograph of A. Kuprin; typed material on Baron E. N. Taube's family in the Czech emigration, 1940-46; photos; issues of Russian journals, 1903-17; and printed matter (books and pamphlets).

13 Oleg Anisimov. Typed memorandum: "Plight of the Russian Refugees in Germany" by O. V. Anisimov, and a mimeographed "Otchet gamburgskogo komiteta po delam bezhentsev" (1949) about Russian displaced persons in Germany.

14 B. P. and Iu. P. Aprelev. A typed copy of B. P. Aprelev's diary for 1915-19; the typed text of Iu. P. Aprelev's memoirs ("Zametki o sobytiiakh vo Rossii, 1917-19"); handwritten essays on World War I, the Revolution, and the Civil War.

15 O. Aptekman. Typescript (and carbon) of an unfinished biography of the social-democratic leader P. B. Akselrod, 1870-1905, 200 pp., attributed to Aptekman.

16 Asta Aristova. Newspaper articles and a typed account of a visit to the USSR, 1960s.

17 A. P. Arkhangel'skii. Papers, 5 boxes, ca. 2,500 items. General, former head of the Russkii Obshchevoinskii Soiuz (ROVS). Primarily relates to ROVS and particularly to its fifth section (Belgium). Correspondence, memoranda, orders, reports, notes, photos, membership lists, mimeographed circulars, and publications, 1920s-1950s.

18 Evgenii Porfirovich Arkhipenko (1884-1959). Papers, 63 boxes. Brother of the sculptor Alexander Arkhipenko, and minister in the Ukrainian People's Republic. He continued his political activity in the emigration in West Germany after 1945. The collection includes papers, minutes, and publications of such émigré organizations as the Ukrainian Red Cross, the Democratic Union of Former Politically Repressed Ukrainians under the Soviets (DOBRUS), Ukrainian Peasants Party (USP), Ukrainian National State Union (UNDA), Ukrainian Revolutionary-Democratic Party (URDP), Union of Christian Youth (IMKA), Ukrainian Orthodox Church (UPT), and the Ukrainian Technical Economic Academy (UTHI). A founder of the Ukrainian Heraldry Society, Arkhipenko also gathered many drawings of family crests, biographical materials on prominent Ukrainians, coats of arms, and bookplates of Ukrainian families. The papers further include correspondence, clippings, and a genealogy of the medieval prince Daniil of Galich. Restrictions.

19 Mikhail Nikolaevich Arkhipov. "Vospominaniia o pervoi mirovoi voine."

20 Iulii Iosifovich Aronsberg. Russian lawyer. Handwritten memoirs 1900-14. They describe his meetings with the poets V. Briusov and Anna Akhmatova as well as his legal career.

21 Grigorii Iakovlevich Aronson. Collection, ca. 75 items. Includes a description of the archive of S. P. Melgunov, manuscripts and notes of V. I. Lebedev, letters, and a typescript by P. Garvi, "Rabochaia kooperatsiia, 1917-21."

22 Nikolai Sergeevich Arsen'ev. Papers, 2 boxes, ca. 50 items. Some pamphlets plus handwritten and typed manuscripts on Russian Orthodoxy. Restrictions.

23 Ol'ga M. Artamonova. Contains typed notes and memoirs on her family, youth, education, and the Civil War in Siberia; and life in the emigration in China, Manchuria and the U.S.

24 Viacheslav P. Artem'ev (Artemjev). Manuscript of Ispravitel'no-trudovye lageria MVD.

25 Viacheslav Vasilevich Babushkin. Handwritten memoirs (1885-1919) covering his early life, service in the Russo-Japanese War, garrison life in Chita, army reforms, the battle of Mukden, events of 1905-1907 in Chita and Simbirsk province, and Russian diplomacy (Japan, Manchuria, and Mongolia), the Revolution and Civil War.

26 Viktor M. Baidalakov. Head of the Narodno-Trudovoi Soiuz (NTS), 1931-55. Papers contain his history of the founding and organization of NTS. Restrictions.

27 Anatolii Vasilevich Baikalov. Papers, 25 boxes, ca. 6,200 items. Member of the Russian Social Democratic Labor Party before 1917 and active in the Siberian cooperative movement. Sent to England in 1919 to study cooperatives there, he decided to remain in the West. The collection includes Baikalov's manuscripts, correspondence with A. I. Guchkov, the duchess of Atholl, Bernard Pares, the Labor Party of the United Kingdom, M. Muggeridge, the American Slavic Colonization Trust, W. M. Citrine and the TUC General Council, Russian émigrés, British authors and politicians, including Sidney Webb, and Boris Nicolaevsky. Restrictions.

28 N. D. Bakhareva. Papers, 40 items. Includes a typescript concerning N. S. Leskov.

29 Boris Aleksandrovich Bakhmeteff (Bakhmetev) (1880-1951). Papers, over 84 boxes, ca. 32,000 items. Last ambassador to the United States of pre-Soviet Russia (the Provisional Government). His papers contain official documents and materials of the Russian embassy in Washington, correspondence, items relating to the Natsional'nyi Fond and to the Humanities Fund, Inc.; and various books and pamphlets. Restrictions.

30 Sofia Markovna Bakunina. Papers, 17 boxes, ca. 5,000 items. Contains materials on Russian military and political history, émigré military organizations, the emigration, and the Staritskii, Rodichev, Herzen, and Bakunin families. Restrictions.

31 Angelika Balabanova. 13 tape reels. Tape recordings of 1958 interviews with Balabanova, in which she discusses V. I. Lenin, the Communist International, B. Mussolini, G. Zinoviev, I. Stalin, Giacinto Serrati, John Reed.

32 Boris K. Balakan. Papers, 29 items. Contains typed manuscripts of his novels, stories, and memoirs.

33 Silvan F. Baldin. Memoirs about the Russian Military Engineering Commission in the U.S., which Baldin headed 1914-17; and the Revolution and Civil War.

34 A. P. Balk. Last mayor of Petrograd. Typed diary for February 1917, with handwritten additions.

35 Zinovii Ivanovich Baltushevskii (Baltusauskas). Manuscripts on World War I; memoirs, in 4 parts, of military education (Vil'no military academy) and service, 1913-16.

36 Pavel Ilich Baranovskii. Typed memoirs about his military training and career, ca. 1900-20, and emigration on the island of Cyprus, in Bulgaria, and in Egypt. Restrictions.

37 Petr L. Bark. Finance minister under Nicholas II. Typed memoirs for 1890-1914, particularly describing his service as minister of finance.

38 Iraida V. Barry. Papers, 13 boxes, ca. 2,700 items. Includes correspondence and diaries from 1880 to 1920s. Among the items are Barry's typed reminiscences of 1914-18; a diary for 1858-59; the diary of Lieutenant P. N. Kondratovich, 1915; notebooks and essays by her father, Viacheslav Nikandrovich Kedrin, on music, ballet, esthetics, and theater, plus some of his poetry; photos of the Kedrin family and of A. Kerensky with Russian troops.

39 Aleksandr A. and Maria N. Bashmakov (Baschmakoff). Papers, 25 boxes, ca. 8,000 items. Bashmakov was an ethnographer in Russia and France. The collection holds information on his life and works, and many of his manuscripts. In addition, the archive contains materials of A. K. Bentkovskii, with documents on the Russo-Japanese War, and papers of the Grand Duke Kiril Vladimirovich and his Imperial Chancery. Also, the manuscript (and French published text) of Maria Bashmakova's Mémoires, 1958. The collection also includes correspondence, materials on her husband's life and works.

40 Vladimir Aleksandrovich Bazilevskii. Imperial army lieutenant general. 2 letters to him from General P. N. Krasnov, 1923, plus handwritten memoirs about the White movement near Orenburg and Semirech'e by Bazilevskii, 1918-20.

41 Nadezhda I. and Vladimir M. Bek. Papers, ca. 75 items. Her handwritten memoirs, 1880s-1920. Also papers of her husband, V. M. Bek, including materials on the Kuban Cossacks in the Civil War, and A. I. Denikin's armies.

42 A. Bekhteev. Manuscripts on rural life in Russia before the Revolution.

43 Natalia Borisovna Bekker. Handwritten memoirs by the widow of an NKVD engineer. Bekker herself became a political prisoner. The memoirs cover the years ca. 1919-40.

44 Anatolii Petrovich Beklemishev. Papers, 3 boxes, ca. 700 items. Includes typed "Vospominaniia," ca. 500 pp., about pre-1917 life, the Revolution, Civil War, and emigration by this engineer and journalist. His pseudonym was Kas'ian Proshin. Restrictions.

45 Sergei Ivanovich Bel'deninov. Papers, 7 boxes, 3,300 items. His memoirs for 1890-1919 student days, Irkutsk life in World War I, the Revolution, and the Civil War. There are typed and handwritten essays. Other items include correspondence and printed materials.

46 Boris N. Beliaev. Doctor. Typed manuscript on his work with the Empress Alexandra during World War I, and a pamphlet by Beliaev regarding help to war victims.

47 Nikolai S. and Sergei S. Beliaev. Nikolai's typed memoirs on the Beliaev family, who operated an important lumber business and were patrons of Russian music, and on the emigration in Finland, ca. 1890-1964. Also handwritten and typed memoirs of Sergei concerning St. Petersburg musical life, 1890-1914, the Revolution, and life in the emigration in Finland.

48 Nikolai T. Beliaev. Papers, 1 box. Clippings, notes, and offprints on archeology.

49 Aleksandra Nikolaevna Belli. Handwritten reminiscences on rural landowning families in the late 19th and early 20th c. Restrictions.

50 Sergei S. Belosel'skii-Belozerskii. Papers, ca. 45 boxes, 14,400 items. Émigré scholar. Papers of General M. D. Skobelev concerning the conquest of Central Asia in the 19th c.; memoirs of Princess Marie Galitzine; materials concerning many of the great aristocratic families of Russia, including the Cherkasovs, Lievens, Chernyshevs, Laptevs, and Stroganovs; memoirs about World War I, the USSR after World War II, and military history; Belosel'skii-Belozerskii's papers from his work with émigré organizations, particularly the Russian Immigrants' Representative Association in America, Inc.; plus clippings, newspapers, periodicals, and books.

51 V. D. Belov. Imperial Army officer. His memoirs cover tsarist military education, World War I, and post-World War II repatriation.

52 Emmanuil Pavlovich Bennigsen. Papers, 2 boxes. Extensive memoirs of government and Red Cross service and the emigration (France and Brazil); correspondence on the emigration in France, 1920s-1930s.

53 Georgii Pavlovich Bennigsen. Papers, 2 boxes. Typed essays and clippings on Russian history and politics in the 19th and 20th c.; letters and essays of V. L. Burtsev.

54 Gleb Alekseevich Benzeman. Papers, 130 items. Officer in Grenadiers Regiment of the Life Guards, 1917. A biography, family history, and typescript on the Corps of Cadets and the visit to Russia of Prince Hirohito of Japan. Typed reminiscences of Benzeman's military training and career. There is correspondence (and printed matter) concerning Russian émigré monarchist circles.

55 Nikolai Berdiaev (1874-1948). Papers, ca. 50 items. Philosopher. Correspondence, 1923-47, with A. Remizov, M. Osorgin, L. Shestov, and others.

56 Evgeniia I. Berestovskaia. Short typed, carbon, memoirs.

57 Boris Georgevich Berg. Count. Memoirs; family photos; and the handwritten original, and a typed copy, of a biography of Field Marshall F. F. Berg by Boris Berg, 462 pp.

58 Andrei Fedorovich Berladnik-Pukovskii. Papers, ca. 1 box. Colonel and engineer in the Imperial army, emigrated to Constantinople and then France after 1917. Material on the Caucasus, the emigration in Constantinople, and military history.

59 Pavel Abramovich Berlin. 2 boxes. Reports collected by Pavel Berlin as head of the economic department of the Soviet Trade Mission in Germany, France, and England, 1925-30.

60 Kezar K. Bernard. Construction engineer in Vinnitsa. Handwritten memoirs, in 7 parts, ca. 1914-43. They concern the sugar industry, World War II, and the Ukraine.

61 Mikhail Vladimirovich Bernatskii. 2 boxes, ca. 400 items. The papers are largely from his service in the Provisional Government; his tenure as chairman of the Financial Board in 1919-20 for the White government in southern Russia; and the emigration in Europe in the 1920s.

62 Alexander Lvovich Bertier-Delagarde. Papers, ca. 10 items. Includes typed history of the family, which emigrated to Russia after the French Revolution.

63 Aleksandr Vasil'evich Bessel'. Papers, ca. 8 boxes, 500 items. Includes the papers of Sergei Efimovich Kryzhanovskii, last state secretary of Imperial Russia and editor of the émigré journal Russkaia letopis'. Kryzhanovskii's memoirs are entitled "Zapiski chinovnika Imperatorskoi Rossii" (1862-1920). There are also copies of memoirs by A. V. Gerasimov and V. I. Gurko. The rest of the collection includes memoirs, manuscripts, documents, and correspondence. Restrictions.

64 Ayaz Ishaki Bey. Handwritten autobiography, 29 pp., covers his childhood, education, Tatar customs, tsarist policy toward Moslems, the political and cultural awakening of the Tatars, the 1905 Revolution, and formation of the First Moslem Union (ITTIFAKA).

65 Ignat Arkhipovich Bilyj. Papers, ca. 8,000 items. Supreme Ataman of the Cossack National Liberation Movement. Includes correspondence, documents, subject files, clippings, manuscripts, and printed matter. Most correspondence concerns his activities as ataman, the journal Kazak, the anti-communists groups. There are reminiscences, drafts of appeals and proclamations, and texts of speeches.

66 Artur Georgevich Bittenbinder. Handwritten memoirs concerning his childhood and youth, military career, World War I, and the Civil War in the South, plus an essay on A. Guchkov as minister of war in the Provisional Government.

67 Chester Bliss. Papers, ca. 25 items. American entomologist, worked in the Soviet Union during the 1930s. Contains copies of his letters to his family describing working conditions in Soviet scientific institutions, his contacts with Soviet scholars and his reactions to communism and the Soviet political situation, 1935-37.

68 Andrei Grigorevich Blok. 3 letters from Ivan Bunin to Blok, 1935-43, 2 letters to him from A. Grechaninov, 1931-33, and a poem by Bunin in French.

69 Aleksei Alekseevich Bobrinskoi. Papers, ca. 50 items. Includes reminiscences, manuscripts, documents, and photographs on a range of topics.

70 Mariia Aleksandrovna Bocharnikova. Typed memoirs and documents relating to her reminiscences of the Women's Battalion and the Civil War.

71 A. P. Bogaevskii. Papers, 17 folders. Don Cossack ataman. Correspondence, documents, and writings, 1920-34. Correspondents include the Generals P. N. Krasnov, P. Wrangel, F. F. Abramov, P. N. Shatilov, E. Miller, and A. P. Kutepov. Other information is on the Cossack Congress in Paris, 1933-34, Ataman A. M. Kaledin, and the Russian Historical Union (Russkii Istoricheskii Soiuz).

72 Boris A. Bogaevskii. Collection, ca. 130 items. Contains several handwritten manuscripts: "Iz proshlogo," Lt. Milnikov, Bogaevskii's "Pervyi kubanskii pokhod," and N. D. Khomutov's "Iz dalekogo proshlogo," 89 pp., on the Civil War in the South. There are also a printed letter of Colonel Bogaevskii and a pamphlet history of the Kalmuks.

73 Mitrofan Petrovich Bogaevskii. Papers, ca. 35 items. Material on his life as a student in St. Petersburg and on St. Petersburg University, ca. 1900-1906, and on the Civil War.

74 Mitrofan Ivanovich Boiarintsev. Papers, 3 boxes, ca. 600 items. Imperial Army officer. Memoirs of Boiarintsev's experiences as a young officer in World War I and the post-Revolutionary disintegration of the army; his service records; documents, articles, and ephemera on the war, the Civil War, General L. Kornilov and his troops, and émigré military organizations (Ob"edinenie kornilovtsov, Russkii obshchevoinskii soiuz).

75 Boris J. Bok (Bock). Papers, ca. 20 items. Reminiscences of the Russo-Japanese War and the fall of Port Arthur; diary of General V. N. Nikitin; memoirs of other participants in the siege of Port Arthur; minutes of the commission investigating the fall of the port. Full text of Dmitrii Ivanovich Abrikosov's memoirs concerns his childhood, diplomatic service (mainly in Japan), and life as an émigré in the Far East after 1917. All but the last part appeared in Revelations of a Russian Diplomat, edited and published by G. A. Lensen (University of Washington, 1964).

76 Maria Bok. Manuscript of Bok's personal recollections, 1890-1911, of her father, Petr A. Stolypin, as family man and statesman; and a 1909 photograph of Stolypin. Her memoir appeared as Vospominaniia o moem ottse P. A. Stolypine (Chekhov Publishing House, New York) in 1953.

77 Simon A. Bolan. Collection, ca. 320 items. Contains a broad range of items on many topics in Russian and Soviet history, such as description of Alexander I's death, plus printed documents on his succession; photos and documents about Jews in Kherson in 1917; and proclamations from the Civil War. Restrictions.

78 Aleksandr A. Bol'to (Boltho-Hohenbach). Papers, ca. 10 items. Passports and family documents; typed reminiscences--"Puti i pereput'ia, polveka emigratsii"--concerning his childhood, the Revolution, and Africa, ca. 1890-1940.

79 Vera Mikhailovich and Mikhail K. Borel'. Papers, ca. 150 items. Includes photocopies of letters to General M. V. Alekseev, from A. I. Denikin and others, ca. 1918; reminiscences by Mikhail Borel', and his brother Georgii Borel', on the Civil War; and minutes of a September 1918 military conference in Georgia of the Volunteer Army. Restrictions.

80 Vladimir Aleksandrovich Borisov. Handwritten diaries, apparently written in Constantinople, covering the emigration to Turkey, 1920.

81 Arkadii A. Borman. Printed materials concerning the Denikin government in southern Russia, 1918-19; typed memoirs, "Vospominaniia o strashnykh godakh, 1917-18," 274 pp.

82 Lidia Mikhailovna Borshch (Borchtch). Papers, 2.5 boxes, ca. 150 items. 2 biographies of Viktor B. Oks, a lawyer, writer and journalist (typed and handwritten); a typed bibliography of Oks's works; manuscripts of his novels and plays; and Oks's reminiscences of Lenin, Stalin, G. Zinov'ev, L. Krasin, and A. Enukhidze.

83 A. P. Brailovskii. Papers, ca. 50 items. Papers, photos, correspondence, and printed matter relating to the Civil War and the emigration in New York, 1919-1920s. Includes an appeal from the American Communist Party after the murder of S. Kirov.

84 Aleksandr P. Bragin. Papers, ca. 1 box, ca. 90 items. Typed memoirs about military service in Siberia before the Revolution, the Boxer Rebellion, and the Russo-Japanese War; personal documents of Bragin; correspondence concerning his mission to northern Persia in 1920.

85 Evgenii L'vovich Brazol. Handwritten and typed essays on Russian legal education, international politics, and the Brazol family genealogy.

86 Ekaterina Breshkovskaia. Originals and copies of 8 letters to Arthur Bullard and his family, 1912-29.

87 Evgeniia Mikhailovna Briunelli. Papers, ca. 250 items. Some 120 letters from her sister from Leningrad, 1922-40; notebooks of memoirs of Briunelli, an educator and wife of a retired guards officer, Pavel A. Briunelli. Restrictions.

88 Aleksandr M. Brofel'dt. His typed "Moi vospominaniia o sluzhbe v stavke verkhovnogo glavnokomanduiushchego 1916-1917."

89 E. M. Brofel'dt. Papers, 20 items. Handwritten essays about his service in the tsarist prison administration, as vice-governor of Volhynia, and in the Civil War.

90 Aleksei A. Brusilov. Papers, ca. 25 items. Handwritten and carbon copies of Brusilov's memoirs (vol. 3), about the Bolshevik Revolution and the early Soviet regime; letters to his wife, 1914-18; memoirs and letters of his wife, Nadezhda Vladimirovna Brusilova (nee Zhelikhovskaia). Restrictions.

91 Emilia V. Bruzinskaia. Reminiscences of her Siberian childhood.

92 Konstantin Bruzinskii. Typewritten essay "O moem dedushke" concerning the adventures of his grandfather Jakob Geishtor in Lithuania and in Siberian exile after the 1863 Polish uprising.

93 Boris Ivanovich Buchinskii. Handwritten essays/reminiscences concerning the Corps of Pages, tsarist hunts, and military events.

94 Ia. V. Budanov. The typescript of his Slovar' novykh slov i vyrazhenii voshedshikh v russkii iazyk v SSSR (n.d.), on the Russian language 1920-50.

95 G. Bukhantsov. His personal reminiscences, typed, 51 pp., of the German invasion and the course of the war, 1941-44.

96 Bureau of Applied Social Research. Papers, 36 boxes, ca. 7,000 items. Among the studies prepared by this bureau for the U.S. government was the War Documentation Project on the partisan movement in the USSR behind German lines in World War II. There are reports on specific geographic areas, the origins, organization, and morale of the partisans, and the military potential of East European and other nations. Additional military studies are in the collection. Restrictions.

97 Stepan Burian. Papers, 1 box, ca. 40 items. Mostly essays of an autobiographical, philosophical, and religious nature.

98 P. A. Buryshkin (Bouryschkine). Typed copy of Buryshkin's Ph.D. thesis, "Les sociétés russes nationalisées" (1944) and a typescript of his biographical sketch of S. N. Tretiakov.

99 Vasilii Fedorovich Butenko. Papers, 1 box, ca. 200 items. Typescript on the history of General S. L. Markov and the Markovtsy in the Civil War, 830 pp.; correspondence of S. S. Maslov, A. A. Argunov, F. I. Kolesov, and N. N. Somburov, 1900s-1940s, much of it concerning the Trudovaia Krest'ianskaia Partiia (Working Peasants Party), its central committee, and the émigré publication Krest'ianskaia Rossiia; and other printed materials.

100 Inna Konstantinovna Buttler. Memoirs of collectivization, the purges of the 1930s, and World War II.

101 Jane Perry Clark Carey. The diary of this legal scholar during a trip to the USSR as a student in 1929 has information on the Soviet legal system and on conditions in the Volga region.

102 P. P. Chechulina. This typed manuscript is entitled "Vospominaniia o sem'e Velikogo Kniazia Konstantina Konstantinovicha."

103 Aleksandr O. Chekan. Papers, ca. 4 boxes. Includes the archives of the Union of Russian Graduates of VUZy (Paris), also known as OROVUZ, its correspondence, and a 1929 questionnaire survey of its members; and the typed and handwritten memoirs of Grigorii Lomaka, also a father in the Russian Orthodox Church in France, for 1920-22, 206 pp.

104 Chekhov Publishing House. Papers, 1 box, ca. 500 items. Correspondence, arranged in alphabetical order, with such figures as M. Aldanov,

I. Bunin, V. Maklakov, V. Nabokov, A. Remizov, N. Teffi, and G. Struve.

105 Rakhil Samoilovna Chekver. Papers, ca. 2 boxes, ca. 750 items. Among the correspondents of this poetess, whose pseudonym was Irina Iassen, were: V. N. Bunina, A. M. Remizov, M. L. Slonim, I. Odoevtseva, and G. Adamovich. Restrictions.

106 V. N. Chelishchev. Includes brief typed essays on the Civil War.

107 St. Chemer (pseud. of Fedor Nikolaevich Tkachenko). Typed copy of his memoirs, "Dva goda pod znakom svastiki," 76 pp., actually covering 1941-45; a bound volume of typed memoirs--"Dvadtsat' piat' let pod serpom i molotom"--about life in the Soviet Ukraine, 1917-41.

108 Iurii Appolonovich Cheremshanskii. Papers, 2 boxes, ca. 630 items. Typed and handwritten essays on émigré politics, Russian military history, and the Cossacks in the Civil War, 1918-50; reminiscences of 1917; materials on the emigration in Japan and China in the 1930s and 1940s.

109 Igor Mikhailovich Cherkasskii. Papers, ca. 65 items. The archive holds manuscript and typed reminiscences mostly on World War I, the Civil War, and other materials.

110 Mariia Nikolaevna Chernysheva-Bezobrazova. Papers, ca. 2 boxes, 500 items. Handwritten memoirs and a family history of the princess, whose father was Prince N. S. Shcherbatov, director of the Moscow Historical Museum. There is also correspondence in the collection.

111 Erast Chevdar. Typed reminiscences: 1 of Berlin under Soviet occupation, 1945-46, the other of the Civil War in southern Russia, 1918-20. Restrictions.

112 Aleksei E. Chichibabin. His "Avtobiografiia," 62 typed pp., concerns his education and youth. Chichibabin became a chemist in Russia.

113 Dmitrii Dmitrevich Chikhachev. An album of photographs taken by G. H. Rogers of Russian troops in Manchuria 1904-1905 and of the Russo-Japanese War.

114 Pavel Nikolaevich Chizhov. Papers, ca. 20 items. Contents include the colonel's handwritten memoirs and essays on military history, World War I, the Civil War, and emigration.

115 Tikhon Kuz'mich Chugunov. Papers, ca. 50 items. Chugunov was a peasant's son, raised in a Soviet village, who became a trained agronomist. The collection includes typed and handwritten manuscripts on cattle-breeding in the USSR, 1917-62, and agrarian history in general for this period (part of a longer work: "Stoletnii plan russkoi derevni"); on the peasantry, 1900-40; and on Soviet labor and education. Restrictions.

116 Anton Ciliga (b. 1898). Carbon copy of the typescript "Le communisme yougoslave de son début jusqu'à la révolte de Tito (1919-1951)." Ciliga was the former chief editor of the Yugoslav Communist Party newspaper Borba. Restrictions.

117 Columbia University Russian Institute. Papers, 87 boxes. Transcriptions of interviews with Hungarian refugees concerning their personal backgrounds, political views, participation in the 1956 revolt, and evaluations of the Hungarian system.

118 Committee for the Education of Russian Youth in Exile. Papers, 51 boxes. The files of this organization, directed by Thomas Wittemore, contain biographical information on students, correspondence, financial records, photographs, etc. for 1920-39.

119 Communist Party, France, Jewish Section. Papers, 3 boxes, ca. 1,900 items. Leaflets, correspondence, membership cards, pamphlets, notes, and ephemera 1928-39.

120 Charles R. Crane. Papers, ca. 365 items. Memoirs of this prominent American businessman for 1907-37, carbon copy, 348 pp.; carbon copy of a diary of a trip to Siberia and European Russia in 1921; correspondence, carbon copies, 1877-1939.

121 Nikolai Trofimovich Dakhov. Papers, ca. 34 items. Autobiographical manuscripts on his life, from Gallipoli to Brazil, with photos. Dakhov was a White Army officer, author of a book on the Vlasov movement, and editor of the Sao Paulo Russkaia gazeta.

122 Evgeniia Moiseevna Dalina. Papers, 3 boxes, ca. 1,000 items. Correspondence, statutes, financial records, documents, and name indexes for the Nadejda Mutual Aid Society, a U.S. voluntary charity for émigrés, plus clippings on the same, 1940-60.

123 David Iul'evich Dalin. Papers, 1 box, ca. 20 items. Essays written by Soviet displaced persons in 1947 explaining why they chose not to return to the USSR. Most are typed and with English translations. They describe the authors' personal experiences as students, doctors, army commanders, peasants, workers, and scientists. Some attempt to generalize about the Soviet system. They provide valuable

124 Alexander Dallin. Papers, 1 box, ca. 110 items. A typed manuscript on Soviet judicial institutions in the 1930s--"Femida bez poviaski"; materials on both the USSR and Germany in World War II; and 5 lectures, typed, 1924-27, given at the Baptist seminary in Leningrad. Restrictions.

information on wages, living conditions (in towns and rural areas), political terror and controls in the 1930s, and the life of Soviet POWs and displaced persons in Germany. Restrictions.

125 Avgusta Filippovna Damanskaia. Papers, 2 boxes, ca. 150 items. Memoirs in 17 typed essays, 1956-57, of this émigré writer, journalist, and translator cover 1905-17 Russian literary, stage, journalistic, and political life, as well as the same topics for post-revolutionary Russia and the emigration, Berlin, 1920-23, and Paris, 1923-1950s; published and unpublished works of Damanskaia; her personal documents; notebooks for 1938-54 with jottings; and photos (including the editorial board of Russkoe bogatstvo).

126 Petr Danilchenko. Typed memoirs about his service in the Izmailovskii Guards regiment, the organization of regimental cultural evenings in St. Petersburg, the Grand Duke Konstantin Konstantinovich, literary activity, and the composer A. Glazunov (1897-1915).

127 Dmitrii Iosifovich Daragan. Papers, 4 boxes, ca. 1,500 items. Field diaries of General F. F. Palitsyn, 1916-21 (he was military representative in Paris); a handwritten interview with a participant of the Kronstadt revolt (done in 1960); personal documents, etc., from 1890-1960; correspondence for 1970-73 and for 1918-19; memoirs of Daragan's childhood in Warsaw, life on a family estate in Byelorussia, service as a naval officer, the Civil War in the North, and the emigration, ca. 1900-73. Restrictions.

128 Malcolm W. Davis. Papers, ca. 25 items. Davis served with the Carnegie Endowment in the 1930s. The collection contains typed essays by N. Grigorev on the history of Ukrainian nationalism and materials of I. Efremov on the Russian Orthodox Church and the ecumenical movement.

129 Marianna A. Davydova. Handwritten essays: "Moi ded," 5 pp., reminiscences of her grandfather, Ivan Orlov, and life on a large estate, ca. the 1870s; on popular discontent in southwest Russia in 1905, 10 pp.; and about the February Revolution in Kiev and St. Petersburg, 12 pp.

130 Anton I. Denikin (1872-1947). Papers of Anton and Ksenia Denikin combined, ca. 45 boxes. Denikin was one of the organizers and commanders of the White Army in the Civil War of 1918-20. His papers include correspondence, speeches, clippings, and other materials on World War I, the 1917 Revolution, Civil War, Provisional Government, Kadet Party, General L. Kornilov, the Ukraine, and the emigration, 1920-40. Restrictions.

131 D. L. De Vitt. A staff cavalry captain who served in the Imperial Guards Dragoons Regiment and in the Chechnia Cavalry Division in the North Caucasus during the Civil War. The collection includes manuscripts on military service during World War I and the Civil War.

132 D. F. Diadiun. Notebooks containing his "Vospominaniia" of Russia before 1914, the Civil War, and emigration.

133 Mikhail Diderikhs. A typed copy of an order issued by Diderikhs (ruler of the Zemskii Priamurskii Krai), 11 October 1922.

134 Helena Didisheim. Letters, including 1, undated, from M. Gorkii to George Foster Peabody.

135 Vitali Fedorovich Ditianin. 2 notebooks with the handwritten text of a speech for a celebration of Den' Russkoi Kul'tury; and 2 manuscript fragments. These are products of the emigration.

136 Erast Dlotovskii. Papers, ca. 25 items. Original documents of General Dlotovskii's promotions and decorations, 1825-79; his short history of the Kirasirskii Regiment, 1710-1826, 65 pp.; and his memorandum proposing the establishment of irregular troops in the 1860s, 11 pp.

137 Georgii Vasil'evich Dmitrenko. Papers, 1.5 boxes, ca. 90 items. Manuscripts and notes of a lawyer active in the Soiuz russkikh advokatov zagranitsei, ca. 70 notebooks and 2 folders. There are notes, articles, and reviews, 1900-64, about World War I, the Revolution and Civil War, the Volunteer Army, I. Stalin, the peasants, World War II, émigré political organizations, and world history/international relations in general.

138 Petr Petrovich Dmitrenko. A Russian railroad engineer. The archive includes his handwritten "memoirs" on railroads in Russia, 1899-1912, hydro-electric power, electrification, water transportation, and Russian economic history, 326 pp. He wanted to run a railroad through the central Caucasus. His writings also shed light on the professional organizations and activities of Russian engineers, the Ministry of Transport, elections to the first duma, the mood of railroad workers and the political activities of engineers in both the 1905 Revolution and the events of 1917, international conferences/meetings he attended, and the early history of the Kadet Party.

139 Nikolai Vsevolodovich Dmitriev. Head of the Russkii Narodnyi Universitet in Prague. Handwritten memoirs and notes, concerning the Union of Towns in the Civil War.

140 A. Dneprovets. A typescript on the purges in Dnepropetrovsk in 1936-37, based on personal experiences, and a second typed manuscript entitled "Kak sozdaiutsia 'Sputniki'"--on the NKVD supervision of classified scientific

research, 1938-40, again drawing on his own experience.

141 Mstislav V. Dobuzhinskii. Papers, 19 boxes. Leading Russian painter and stage designer. Contents include his essays on the World of Art group and its individual members; his sketches and illustrations of Russian literary and architectural styles and of historical costumes; catalogues of his exhibits; personal and business correspondence (mostly closed); official documents; memoirs on major modern Russian artists, musicians, and writers, written in the 1930s and 1940s. Among his correspondents were M. Karpovich, Mark Aldanov, Ivan Bunin, A. Grechaninov, V. Nabokov. Restrictions.

142 B. I. Dodov. A typescript, "The monetary reform and tax on capital in Bulgaria" (1946).

143 Mikhail Petrovich Dolgorukov. Papers, ca. 10 items. Photos and information about his father, Petr Dmitrevich Dolgorukov, who was vice-president of the duma, and about his family; clippings with excerpts of the diary of Fr. Nikolai Ryzhkov's daughter concerning her father's life and career in the Orthodox Church, ca. 1890-1945.

144 Margarita Oskarovna Domashkevich (Domaschkewitsch). Typed and bound copies of her literary works.

145 Nina S. Don. Memoirs, typed and carbon copy, of the wife of a tsarist naval officer, covering their life 1910-14, experiences during the Revolution (in Finland) and the Civil War (Ukraine), and in the emigration in France; also her trip to the USSR in 1968.

146 Don Aminado (pseud. of Aminad Petrovich Shpolianskii) (1888-1957). Papers, 1 box. Émigré satirist and poet. Contains materials 1920-57 on the Russian emigration, its literature and theater, newspapers and journalism, plus the manuscript of his autobiography Poezd na tret'em puti (Chekhov House, New York, 1954). The bulk of the collection is correspondence: over 100 letters from his readers worldwide, and such other correspondents as Ivan Bunin, 69 items, 1920-53, Mark Aldanov, 17 letters, 1920-56, Zinaida Gippius, 3 items, 1933-35, K. Bal'mont, 1 item, 1920, N. A. Teffi, 22 items, 1920-38, A. Tolstoi, 11 items, 1920-21, A. Remizov, 10 items, 1929-35, I. Repin, 1 item, 1920, P. Struve, 1 item, 1921.

147 Evgeniia Dostoevskaia. "Tiur'my, ssylki i kontslageria SSSR"--a carbon copy typescript, 152 pp., about the 1930s.

148 Mihail Dragomirov. Handwritten notes about Russian military history, 1856-81.

149 Vladimir Nikolaevich von Dreier. The typed memoirs ("Zapiski") of the general, whose father served in the tsarist administration of Turkestan, 350 pp. They cover his father's service, his own military education, his career in the Balkan Wars, World War I, and the Revolution, 1880-1920.

150 Mikhail Aleksandrovich Drizo. Papers, ca. 6 boxes, ca. 2,800 items. Drizo, whose pseudonum was MAD, was a Russian caricaturist. Among his correspondents were Ivan Bunin, P. Miliukov, M. Aldanov, N. Teffi, A. Benois, and N. Evreinov. There are also a number of his caricatures and illustrations. Restrictions.

151 Nadezhda Iakovlevna Dubakina. Papers, ca. 20 items. 2 manuscript reminiscences of Nicholas II's visit to Suwalki and of her experiences in the Crimea during the Civil War; documents issued to her and her husband in the Civil War in southern Russia. Also in this collection: papers of Evgeniia Tuliakova-Danilovskaia, including the typescript "Pervyi god v Germanii," about a flight to Germany from Pskov in World War II and a German labor camp.

152 E. Dune. "Zapiski krasnogvardeitsa"--about his experiences in the Red Guard, 1917-19, typed.

153 Duving. A typescript on internal opposition in the USSR and the Vlasov movement, 1936-46--fictionalized personal experience ("Velikaia skorb'"), 600 pp.

154 Sergei Grigor'evich Dvigubskii. Papers, 18 items. A miscellany largely consisting of family documents, memoirs, and some photographs.

155 L. P. Dzhunkovskii. "Vospominaniia generala Aleks. Aleks. Smagina," memoirs written by Dzhunkovskii, the general's friend, based on conversations with and notes of Smagin. They concern the Don Cossacks, the Revolution, and the Civil War, 1917-20.

156 Evgenii Ambros'evich Efimovskii. Typed memoirs about his studies at Moscow University (history faculty), V. O. Kliuchevskii and A. A. Kizewetter, the 1905 student movement, his work for the Kadets, and being a lawyer in 1917 and during the Civil War. Also typed essays on political thought and émigré affairs; photocopies of his writings.

157 A. Efremov. A typed and mimeographed manuscript on the agrarian problem ca. 1906-14, 19 pp.

158 N. N. Egerov. Handwritten "Vospominaniia o russkikh uchebnykh zavedeniiakh v Pol'she" (1920-45).

159 I. Eikhenbaum. His handwritten memorandum concerning the origins of the White movement in Russia in 1919, submitted to the International Congress of Jurists in 1950, along with a typed explanatory note. Both relate

to the disposition of Soviet displaced persons after World War II.

160 Irina Elenevskaia. "Vospominaniia" about pre-1917 life in St. Petersburg plus the emigration in Finland and Sweden, 1900-60, typed and bound.

161 Evgeniia Markovna Enno. Handwritten memoirs by the widow of the French consul in Odessa ca. 1918, covering the period of roughly 1900-18, ca. 60 pp.

162 Nikolai A. Epanchin. Memoirs, "Na sluzhbe trekh imperatorov," about the army, military campaigns, politics, the Imperial family, and foreign policy in the reigns of Alexander II, Alexander III, and Nicholas II, ca. 1860-1917, and about the emigration in France, to 1940.

163 Natalia Lazarevna Erenburg (b. 1884). Autobiographical essays.

164 B. P. Eriksen. Short, impressionistic, typed memoirs concerning his Cossack ancestors back to the 18th c., including I. V. Turchaninov, who was a brigadier general in the U.S. Civil War, and his emigration from Russia ca. 1920.

165 Konstantin Aleksandrovich Ermans and Varvara Ivanovna Ermans-Strakhova. Papers, 1 box. Contains her memoirs describing her work with the Mamontov opera; family documents; photographs and information about F. Shaliapin; memorabilia; material on the Russian conservatory in Paris; and correspondence with, for example, F. Shaliapin, A. Grechaninov, 1939, S. Rachmaninoff, 1928, Olga Knipper Chekhova, 2 items, 1946 and undated.

166 Boris Nikolaevich Ermolov. Papers, 55 items. Documents, reports, proclamations, correspondence, and other items on the Orthodox Church, the Revolution, and the Civil War, 1917-21.

167 Nikolai Frantsevich Ern. Papers, ca. 20 items. 6-part memoirs, handwritten, ca. 138 pp., of this Russian general who served in the Caucasus before and during World War I and under the Provisional Government. He was also chief of staff of the Russian Expeditionary Force in northern Persia.

168 Ivan Petrovich Eryzhenskii. His manuscript, "Moia odisseia," is on the Civil War in 1918-20.

169 Abbess Evgeniia. A carbon copy of the typed diary of Oleg Pavlovich Mitrofanov, the abbess's son, for January-4 July 1917, when he was a lieutenant in the Russian army. He discusses the Revolution.

170 Nikolai N. and Anna A. Evreinov(a). Papers, ca. 12 boxes, 4,600 items. Primarily a theater collection, this archive contains galleys of the book Histoire du théâtre russe and its Russian typescript; manuscripts on theater, art, aesthetics; and correspondence with artists and writers. Restrictions.

171 Nikolai N. Evseev. Clippings about publications and public readings by this poet in the emigration, 1962-63.

172 Nikolai V. Falkovskii. Autobiographical accounts, handwritten, of his participation in A. Denikin's army in the Ukraine and Crimea, 1918-20.

173 Mariia Vasil'evna Fedchenko. Handwritten memoirs about her aunt, E. N. Geringer, favorite lady-in-waiting of the Empress Alexandra. There is also reference to Archbishop Feofan of Poltava. The work covers the years 1872-1939.

174 Mikhail Mikhailovich Fedorov. Papers, 15 boxes, 6,700 items. Includes correspondence with Russian émigré students and about student aid; reports of the Tsentral'nyi Komitet po Vysshemu Obrazovaniiu, 1922-23 and 1928-29; materials about the commission on Russian schools and students in Poland, the Union of Russian Students in France, 1920-1930s, and the Russkii Natsional'nyi Komitet, 1933-34; and other manuscripts and correspondence.

175 Vasilii Mikhailovich Fedorovskii. Papers, ca. 1 box, 440 items. 2 handwritten essays about the Civil War in the South, 1917-20; material on Russian military activity in the Balkans in the 1870s (the Russo-Turkish War) and in the Caucasus in the early 20th c., including maps and orders of General Berkhman in the Sarkamysh operation in the Caucasus in 1914-15, during World War I.

176 Georgii Petrovich and E. N. Fedotov(a). Papers, ca. 6 boxes, 1,300 items. There are offprints and articles by Fedotov about Russian history, church history, religion, literature, and political questions, 1850-1940s, written for émigré publications, plus a photocopy of Svobodnye golosa No. 1 (April 1918), which he published and edited. Additional holdings include Fedotov's monograph and article manuscripts, lecture notes, and translations. Correspondents include S. Bulgakov, G. T. Struve. There are also letters relating to Fedotov's conflict with the Bogoslovskii Institut in Paris, 1935-39. Finally, there is reference to F. D. Maurice and Christian Socialism. Restrictions.

177 Dmitrii Nikolaevich Fedotov-White (1889-1950). Papers, 90 boxes, ca. 31,000 items. Fedotov-White was a teacher of the "naval art" before 1917; he worked for the Cunard Lines after the Revolution and wrote about Russian and Soviet military history. Contents include his memoirs, entitled "Survival," covering his experience as a naval officer, in the Civil War with Admiral A. V. Kolchak, as a Soviet prisoner, and as a Soviet academic and

administrator in 1920-21. His correspondence contains much information about Cunard business, also about affairs of the emigration and aid to the USSR in World War II. 2 of his correspondents were G. T. Robinson and G. V. Vernadskii.

178 P. N. Finisof. Papers, 40 items. Bound collection, 12 vols., of 29 lectures delivered in Paris in May 1921: Trudy Obshchago S"ezda predstavitelei Russkoi Promyshlennosti i Torgovli v Parizhe. Also, collection of 11 unbound lectures given by members of the Central Organizational Committee at a session of the Russian Exile Congress (Rossiiskii Zarubezhnyi S"ezd) in Paris, March 1926.

179 Finliandskii Polk. Papers, ca. 30 boxes, 10,800 items. Materials largely on the regiment's history in the 19th and 20th c.

180 Irina Viktorovna Fleginskaia. Typed reminiscences of Fleginskaia, the daughter of V. I. Karpov, a gentry member of the Council of State, concerning the early days of the February Revolution and some incidents prior to it, 1916-17.

181 N. N. Flige. Papers, ca. 80 items. Typed essays and documents about 1905, 1917, and the Paris emigration; Flige's memoirs about Russian high financial circles (Flige was related to both V. Kokovtsev and N. Bunge); typed materials on the Imperial family, including eyewitness accounts, in 1917-18; essays on other topics from the early 20th c. in Russia.

182 Michael T. Florinskii. Papers, 1 box, ca. 500 items. Correspondence with S. N. Prokopovich, 1938-46; the typed text of Prokopovich's work on the fourth Five-Year Plan; Florinskii's correspondence with Bernard Pares, V. Maklakov, J. Chamberlain, A. Gurkov, S. Sazanov, V. Kokovtsev, M. Karpovich, D. Mirskii, A. Meiendorff, D. Nabokov (6 in 1948 about Alexander II and Alexander III), and Professor Otto Hoetzsch, 1939.

183 Elizabeth Williams Foxcroft. Papers, ca. 20 items. Materials mostly dealing with the Russian emigration in South Africa.

184 Semen Liudvigovich Frank. Papers, 17 boxes, ca. 6,500 items. Papers of this Russian philosopher and religious thinker, a liberal who contributed to Osvobozhdenie 1903-1905, privat-dotsent at St. Petersburg University 1907-17, participant in the famous Vekhi symposium, 1909, professor in philosophy at Saratov University 1917-21, collaborator with N. Berdiaev's Free Academy of Spiritual Culture in Moscow, 1921-22, exile from the Soviet Union, and founder of the Russian Academy of Philosophy and Religion in Berlin. Includes a short autobiography; personal documents; correspondence with P. B. Struve, N. Berdiaev, G. P. Fedotov, S. Bulgakov, V. N. Losskii, F. Stepun, M. Aldanov, A. M. Remizov, Albert Einstein, and others; biographical materials; manuscripts and published works on philosophy, religion, history, etc.; other notes; and printed matter. Restrictions.

185 Mikhail E. Fridieff. Notebooks of handwritten memoirs for 1919-24, about the Civil War in the South and the early emigration, written in 1921 and 1970.

186 Evgenii Nikolaevich Gagarin. Papers, ca. 160 items. His sketches about the Neva and Volga Rivers; a typed copy of a letter by a peasant soldier from Bessarabia to a medical sister in Petrograd who had tended him; short typed memoir by Gagarin about Simferopol' in 1917-18.

187 Aleksandra Gagarina. Papers, ca. 53 items. Family papers (including dinner invitations from the Romanovs); material dating from 1827-36, when Prince A. A. Gagarin was Russian ambassador to Rome; plus other letters and documents.

188 Ekaterina Grigorevna Garina. Papers, ca. 1 box. Typed memoirs of the Decembrist Nikolai Ivanovich Lorner (1794-1873), in Russian, 82 pp.; typed memoirs of his granddaughter, Nadezhda von Grotthus-Foelkersam, 309 pp., in German. Restrictions.

189 Nikolai I. Gasfel'd (Gasfield). His experiences working for the French military in Persia, organizing Armenian troops to fight the Turks, are chronicled in the typed manuscript "Un An en Persie." Part of it was published as Polveka (Paris, 1950).

190 Aleksandr Nikolaevich Gasler. Papers, ca. 23 items. Handwritten reminiscences/memoirs concerning family life on a Finnish estate and local affairs from 1877 to the turn of the century; military education and service, 1904 through the Civil War; and the emigration and Orthodox Church in France ca. 1930-60. The colonel also discusses his trip to Japan in 1912, plus his trips to France and the Russian Expeditionary Force and Technical Supply Division in France.

191 Grand Duke Gavril Konstantinovich. Papers, ca. 4 boxes, 100 items. Original typed and photocopies of the grand duke's memoirs concerning the lives and careers of his father Konstantin Konstantinovich and his grandfather Konstantin Nikolaevich (ca. 1825-1918). Also, typed copies of official documents and correspondence of his father and grandfather, 1890-1910.

192 Konstantin N. Gavrilov. Papers, ca. 2 boxes, ca. 400 items. An engineer who emigrated during World War II. His diaries describe life in Stalingrad and other cities of that region. The collection also contains personal documents of Admiral Nicholas Horthy, regent of Hungary in World War II, when he was a political refugee after the war.

193 Vasili Grigorevich Gavrilov. Papers, ca. 19 items. Includes manuscripts about a broad range of topics in Russian history.

194 Marina Geiden. Comprises 2 sections of her typed memoirs, in French, about Russian high society 1907-12.

195 Gedvig fon Geiking. Her memoirs, typed, discuss her experiences in Germany under American and Soviet occupation, 1945, arrest and deportation to the USSR as a spy, and life as a political prisoner there until 1954.

196 K. M. Geishtor. Papers, ca. 20 items. Memoirs about military history, K. Pobedonostsev, the Imperial family, St. Petersburg life, the Russo-Japanese War, railroads in the Far East, the Civil War. Restrictions.

197 Aleksei Alekseevich Gering. Papers, ca. 2 boxes, 380 items. Mimeograph copy of his report as chairman of the Obshche-Kadetskoi Ob"edinenie vo Frantsii at the organization's ninth annual assembly in April 1960; Gering's correspondence; and manuscripts about Russian military history.

198 Iulia A. Gersdorf. Original handwritten and typed "Vospominaniia" about her husband, a deputy governor of Podolia.

199 Aleksandr Sergeevich Gershel'man. Papers, ca. 43 items. Typed memoirs concerning the Civil War and the emigration; memoirs, notes and essays by various persons on the Imperial court, World War I, and emigration, late 19th and early 20th c.

200 Boris L'vovich Gershun. Papers, ca. 6 boxes, ca. 1,500 items. Correspondence and other materials about the Ob"edinenie russkikh advokatov vo Frantsii, 1929-1950s; minutes of meetings of the Congress of Russian Jurists Abroad from 1922; Gershun's memoirs, 1903-17, about his work as a lawyer and membership in the Kadet Party; correspondence and biographical sketch of O. O. Gruzenberg.

201 G. Iu. Gerts. Memoirs: "10 let advokatury v Kitaiskom Sude," covering the early 20th c. in the Far East, typed copy.

202 Boris Vladimirovich Gerua. Papers, 6 boxes. Correspondence, ca. 1904-1972, discussing military history, the Revolution and Civil War, and the emigration. There are also copies of letters written by Gerua while serving in the Far East in the Russo-Japanese War of 1904-1905; caricatures (prints and originals) of émigré political and cultural figures, done at the 1926 Zarubezhnyi Kongress in Paris.

203 Vikentii Ivanovich Gets. 30 items. Memoirs of V. I. Gets, who served as an officer in the Imperial and White armies during World War I and the Civil War. His memoirs deal with World War I, the Civil War, the emigration in Bulgaria, and his experiences as a Russian translator for the Germans during World War II.

204 Oscar Oskarovich Gil'de. Notebooks with "Stikhi" and a "Kratkaia russkaia istoriia" by Gil'de, plus poetry by M. Domashkevich-Gil'de.

205 Aleksei Fedorovich and Liubov Aleksandrovna Girs. Papers, ca. .5 box. The archive contains his memoirs, reminiscences, and family history materials; official documents, including a general report and a typed annual report on the nationalities problem in Minsk province, 1913. The diaries of L. A. Girs discuss Odessa 1905-1906; the assassination of P. A. Stolypin in 1911 (which she witnessed); her husband's administration of Minsk, 1914-15, and of Nizhnii Novgorod, early 1917; the Revolution and her husband's arrest; also, her handwritten memoirs, ca. 1900-1911.

206 Ol'ga Pavlovna Glazenapp. Handwritten reminiscences of her family, commercial life in Nizhnii Novgorod, and her youth, ca. 1890-1917.

207 Ekaterina Osipovna Glinka. Papers, ca. 50 items. Family papers of pre-1917 Ukrainian landowners--family finances, bills of sale, and bank books. They were refugees in Turkey and France.

208 E. Glinskii. Manuscript, typed, carbon, entitled "Za piat'desiat' let'"--concerning the 50th anniversary of the Bolshevik Revolution and Svetlana Allilueva, 1967.

209 N. K. Globachev. Typed copy of General K. I. Globachev's memoirs 1914-20.

210 Grigorii Petrovich Godin. Papers, ca. 50 boxes, 11,700 items. Correspondence, reports, accounts, and published material about the Russian Expeditionary Force in France and Salonika during World War I, the Civil War, Russian émigrés and refugees in France, and émigré organizations (military and charitable).

211 Aleksei Aleksandrovich Gol'denweiser. Papers, ca. 83 boxes, over 11,000 items. A prominent lawyer. His legal correspondence, Russian refugees after World War II, compensation claims from the Revolution and for war damages, the Union of Russian Jews, citizenship questions, and the Kruzhok Russkikh Advokatov v Niu-Iorke. Other holdings: 2 letters of Dmitrii Bogrov, Stolypin's assassin, to his parents, 1 and 10 September 1911; portions of the memoirs of V. M. Bogrova ("Moe rannee detstvo") about Kiev ca. 1900, her work in the revolutionary movement, and relations with her brother-in-law, Dmitrii Bogrov; documents and a will of the Bogrov family. Restrictions.

212 Vladimir Avgustinovich Gol'dgaar. A secret report published by the quartermaster general

of the White Armies command in the South: "Ocherk vzaimootnoshenii vooruzhennykh sil Iuga Rossii i predstavitelei frantsuzskago komandovaniia," May 1919; concerns the Civil War and Allied intervention.

213 Aleksandr Dmitrevich Golitsin. "Vospominaniia kniazia A. D. Golitsina," 450 pp., covering the zemstvos, the Revolution, and other aspects of Russian history, 1880-1917; and handwritten memoirs in 2 notebooks: "2-oi god Russkoi Revoliutsii (1918). Bolshevizm na Ukraine. Khetmanskii perevorot. Petliurovshchina."

214 Mstislav Petrovich Golovachev. Papers, ca. 10 boxes, ca. 2,350 items. Documents, correspondence, reports, etc. of and about the Siberian Civil War, emigration to the Far East, émigré efforts to reestablish an independent Siberian government, 1918-38, the Bratstvo russkoi pravdy, Soviet administration and the Red Army in Siberia, the Soviet consulate in Manchuria, 1929-34, Russian/Soviet refugees in China, 1926-45.

215 Mikhail A. Golubov. Papers, 11 items. Memoirs and essays on Civil War, displaced persons after World War II, and the forced repatriation of Cossacks in 1945.

216 Boris Viktorovich Gontarev (b. 1879). The general's memoirs cover his childhood on a large estate and service on the Caucasus front in World War I, handwritten.

217 Emiliia Khristianovna Goppe. Typed memoirs of her late brother, Evgenii Kh. Tal'--his experience working on the Tatianinskoi Komitet dlia okazaniia vremennoi pomoshchi postradavshim ot voennykh bedstvii," 1915-17.

218 F. I. Gorb. Reminiscences, typed, about his and his family's life in the USSR in the 1930s and World War II.

219 N. A. Gorchakov. Papers, ca. 351 items. His "Istoriia sovetskogo teatra," typed, of which a short English version was published in Columbia Slavic Studies. Much in this manuscript, covering 1917-50, did not appear in print. Also 2 typescripts: "Tipy zakliuchennykh NKVD" by A. T. and "Pod znakom perspektivnoi illiuzii" by A. V. Lipskii, about L. Tolstoi's novels, 296 pp.

220 Georgii Adamovich Goshtovt. Papers, ca. 9 boxes, ca. 2,500 items. Goshtovt was a military historian. Correspondence for 1925-52; memoirs about World War I, 1914-15, and the Civil War (Whites and partisans in the South, 1919); information on émigré military and veterans organizations.

221 A. A. Govorov. 2 notebooks, handwritten, and a typescript on the Russian military in Turkestan ca. 1890-1919.

222 Nikolai Stepanovich Grabar. Typed memoirs of this civil servant, chairman of the Kiev circuit court, 1904-12, and member of the Senate, 1915-17; a list of former members of the Senate in emigration, 1922; and typed reminiscences about Grabar by A. P. Vel'min. Subjects discussed include Poland and Ukraine under tsarist administration, the Revolution, and the Civil War.

223 G. K. Graf. Manuscripts on Russian naval history, ca. 1906-17, on the Revolution, and the emigration.

224 Vladimir Ivanovich Granberg. Papers, ca. 2 boxes, ca. 840 items. A member of the State Council. Typed memoirs about World War I, the Revolution, and Civil War.

225 Georgii Dmitrevich Grebenshchikov. Papers, 30 boxes. Many of this author's literary works are in this collection ("The Turbulent Giant," "The Churaev Brothers," Russian and English, "Gonets," "Tsarevich," and some short stories); his diaries and notebooks; typed copies of 6 letters of I. Bunin to him, 1937-40; materials on Prague archives, 1930s-1950s.

226 Iakov Aleksandrovich Grebenshchikov. Illustrated memoirs about the Pavlovsk Voennoe Uchilishche ca. 1790-1911, typed, with an historical introduction, 571 pp.

227 G. A. Grekov. Photocopy of his memoir entitled "Moe postuplenie i 7-mo-letnee prebyvanie v Voronezhskome Velikago Kniazia Mikhaila Pavlovicha kadetskom korpuse" and further sections of the same manuscript, ca. 1907-14.

228 Vladimir Konstantinovich Grigor'ev-Trudin. Papers, ca. 200 items. Manuscripts on broad range of topics.

229 Erik Grimm. "Iz vospominanii Leib-gvardii Dragunskogo polka," ca. 1910, about military history, handwritten, 4 pp.

230 Evstafii Vladimirovich Grishkevich-Trokhimovskii. Short typed biography, curriculum vitae, and bibliography of works by this émigré scientist.

231 Leonid Vladimirovich Griunval'd (Gruenvald). Short, typed biography of General N. N. Iudenich.

232 Ksenia Grundt. Papers, 1 box, 150 items. 7 notebooks of handwritten memoirs, 1958-60, describing her ballet career in tsarist Russia (ballet training in general and hers at Kharkov in particular), the Revolution and Civil War, her work as a dancer and teacher in Yugoslavia and France.

233 Aleksandr Aleksandrovich Gubarev. Papers, 11 items. Short typed reminiscences/essays of

childhood before 1917, diary excerpts about social history and the Civil War in the South, poems, and a typescript on the Civil War.

234 Iurii G. Gudim-Levkovich. Typescript concerning Soviet peasants and anti-Bolshevik propaganda in the 1950s; photostat of his essay on Soviet kolkhoz production, typed, in Russian, undated.

235 E. O. Gunst. Papers, ca. 25 items. Russian musician, founder of the Russian Conservatory in Paris. There is correspondence and an essay about him. Restrictions.

236 Valerian I. Gureev. "Ekaterinoslavskii pokhod" in the Civil War, 1918-19, a typed study, by Lieutenant Gureev (about the Ukraine and P. P. Skoropadskii); his typed and handwritten memoirs about the White Army in the Crimea, 1919-20.

237 Boris Gurevich. His fictionalized memoirs (or a novel)--"Krasnyi sfinks. Povest' o sud'be russkoi revoliutsii i russkikh evreev"--an interpretation of the Revolution, its causes and effects, from a liberal viewpoint.

238 P. P. Haensel. Typed article, "The Truth about Tsarist Russia."

239 Fannina Halle. Papers, ca. 20 items. Materials on her contacts with the Russian Archeological Society and the Academy of Arts; correspondence with art historians and institutions.

240 Vera Harteveld. Mimeographed copy of her memoirs about life in musical, artistic, and literary circles of Russia; includes reminiscences of I. Repin, A. Glazunov, A. Akhmatova, F. Sologub, I. Severianin, S. Esenin, K. Balmont, V. Meierkhold, and V. Maiakovskii (1886-ca. 1920).

241 Harvard University Russian Research Center. Papers, ca. 21 boxes, 335 items. Data from the "Refugee Interview Project," 1950-51, including correspondence, mimeographed summaries of each interview, and a bound qualitative file (interviews coded according to selected categories). These interviews with Soviet émigrés cover social history, family life, nationalities, political history, and education 1900-50.

242 Sinclair Hatch. Typed copy of his diary, which recounts a trip to Leningrad and Odessa in the summer of 1931. Restrictions.

243 John N. Hazard. Papers, 11 boxes. In World War II this legal scholar was an important officer in the lend-lease program. The collection has a complete record of the office diaries, July 1941-46, during Hazard's tenure. There are also some office correspondence, January 1943-46, and reports on shipments. One report by the Foreign Economic Administration concerns German administration in the Baltic Area, November 1943, 23 pp. Most or all of these items are duplicates of documents in the National Archives in Washington, D.C. Also included are Hazard's class notes from the Moscow Juridical Institute in 1934-37.

244 Vladimir Heppener. Documents and certificates issued to him (in Czech and German) plus 2 photos, 1935-48.

245 Alexander Herzen (Gerzen). Papers, ca. 1 box, 325 items. About 300 letters from Herzen and his wife Natalie to the family of T. A. and N. I. Astrakov, from the Herzen children to the Astrakovs, and from the Astrakovs; letters of M. Bakunin, 1837-77.

246 Kira Vasil'evna Hickox. Largely papers of George Kumming, including manuscripts on Biblical topics.

247 Jacob B. Hoptner. Papers, 13 boxes, ca. 3,850 items. Manuscripts, statistics, and books on the economy, history, and geography of Yugoslavia and Central Europe; and mimeographed papers for a 1939 conference on Central Europe, the Little Entente, and diplomatic history 1920s-1930s. Sponsored by the Institut Internationale de la Coopération Intellectuelle and the League of Nations. Restrictions.

248 Arkadii Nikolaevich Iakhontov. Papers, 2 boxes. Handwritten and typed transcriptions, plus typed copies, of his minutes of State Council meetings in 1914-16, 346 pp. Other holdings: originals and copies of correspondence from former members of the Council of Ministers about the publication of Iakhontov's memoirs relating to Council work in 1914-16 (P. L. Bark, V. I. Gurko, V. N. Kokovtsev, and S. E. Kryzhanovskii), 1922-35; typed copies of 2 letters from Paris minister A. P. Izvol'skii to Minister of Foreign Affairs S. D. Sazonov, 1/14 December 1914.

249 I. S. Iakovlev. Typed history of the Russian emigration in Australia, 6 pp.

250 Sofia Iakovleva. Handwritten manuscript about the life of Russian émigrés in a French convent in the 1950s.

251 Konstantin V. Ialyshev. Papers, ca. 210 items. Issues of the mimeographed Informatsiia of the 18th Army Corps in Emigration (Armeiskii korpus v Emigratsii), 1930-37, with biographical information on the corps, ca. 1900-1918; minutes and other data on the Russian Brotherhood of St. Nicholas in Constantinople, 1921-23, and about a Russian refugee camp in Marseilles, 1923-25; 3 notebooks of handwritten memoirs about the revolutionary movement among students and the 1905 Revolution, 1900-1905; lectures on Ukrainian and Russian political questions, 1930s; and materials concerning General Bulak-Balakhovich's army, which fought

on the Polish side in the Russo-Polish War of 1920.

252 Vera Sergeevna Ianitskaia. Papers, 2 boxes. Materials by Alexandra M. Petrunkevich, typed essays on S. T. Platonov, her translation of the Slovo o polku Igoreve, a typescript on Russian verbs, and correspondence about her books and lectures (she taught in the Bestuzhev women's courses at St. Petersburg University). In addition there are correspondence of A. Petrunkevich and Miss A. F. Rodicheva. Restrictions.

253 Avraam Savelievich Iarmolinskii. Papers, ca. 128 items. Correspondence of E. Zamiatin, N. Roerikh, M. Aldanov, P. Miliukov (1929), V. Nabokov, Vladimir Markov (about V. V. Khlebnikov), G. Struve (on a translation of Anna Akhmatova's work), M. Karpovich, S. Esenin (1922), and George Rapall Noyes; photographs: Isaac Babel and his daughter Natalie (with negative), I. S. Turgenev, Madame P. Viardot, L. N. Tolstoi, handwritten notes on Turgenev; letters about Iarmolinskii's book A Russian's American Dream; Narkompros documents about education in 1924. Restrictions.

254 Maria Alexandrovna Iazykova. Genealogy of the Iazykov family; and 4 notebooks of handwritten diaries about childhood, the Revolution, and the Harbin emigration, 1918-38.

255 Sergei Ivanovich Iliushkin. This former Imperial Army officer's memoirs cover his military career, the 1905 Revolution, and the tsarist army, 1900-14, typed, 19 pp.

256 Aleksandr Pavlovich Iordanov. Papers, ca. 1 box, 28 items. Typed minutes of a Paris meeting of the Russkoe Obshchestvo Literaturnykh Rabotnikov, December 1914, with a speech by A. Lunacharskii; photocopies of an ukaz of 1707 and another of 1756 (by Elizaveta Petrovna), documents on military history, 1799-1813, gramoty of Alexander I, documents of Paul I, 39 letters of General A. Suvorov, 1788, 2 proclamations of Count F. V. Rostopchin (governor general of Moscow in 1812), an 1808 letter of Alexander I, and a 1744 map of St. Petersburg.

257 M. Iordanskii. Mimeographed copy of his eyewitness account of the Bolshevik takeover in Moscow, 1917.

258 Elizaveta Vladimirovna Isaakova. Typed memoirs of this daughter of a liberal landowner in northwest Russia regarding her life in Russia and the emigration (Poland and Western Europe), the 1905 Revolution, World War I, 1917 in Petrograd, and the Civil War in the Ukraine, 1900-50.

259 P. P. Isheev. The prince's memoirs, typed, in 2 sections, concern his military training and career, his family and social acquaintances, political events, the director V. Meierkhold, and the emigration in Bulgaria, France, and the United States, 1882-1938.

260 Natalia Konstantinovna Iskander. Papers, ca. 19 items. 4 chapters of her husband's memoirs, "Videniia proshlogo" (he was Prince Aleksandr Iskander, illegitimate son of the Grand Duke Nikolai Konstantinovich); correspondence concerning publication of these memoirs; a typed and handwritten account of the grand duke's life in Tashkent, ca. 1900-14; letters and military memoirs about World War I and the Civil War; and a "Voenno-okhotnichii dnevnik" with photos by the prince. Items cover the period ca. 1900-1953.

261 Nikolai N. and Aleksandra N. Iudenich. Papers, 5 boxes, ca. 2,000 items. White Russian general. Correspondence, mimeographed material, and other items on the Northwest Army as well as on émigré politics and cultural affairs; personal correspondence; photos of the tsarist army and Caucasian front in World War I. Also his widow's memoirs ca. 1862-1933.

262 Fedor Konstantinovich Iur'ev. Papers, ca. 40 items. The colonel's biography (clipping); photos; manuscripts of his music and poetry; about 10 official documents relating to his career in Russia and the emigration (Germany); and a handwritten supplement to the biography, penned by his widow.

263 Vladimir Ivanovich and Ol'ga Vsevolodovna Iurkevich. Papers, 2 boxes, ca. 800 items. Iurkevich (1885-1964) was a Russian marine engineer. His wife, nee Krestovskaia, was active in the Russian Red Cross in Europe during and after World War I and was also a writer (pseudonym: Ol'ga Iork). The archive includes his biography, plus documents and biographical materials on him; Ol'ga's memoirs of life in Paris and her correspondence (several letters from V. A. Maklakov); manuscripts and clippings of her short stories.

264 Ivan Fedorovich Iurtaev. Papers, 2 boxes, ca. 50 items. Unpublished studies by this metallurgist, a student of N. T. Beliaev, on his specialty, in French, ca. 1925-45.

265 Aleksei Mikhailovich Iuzefovich. Papers, ca. 1,600 items. 3 albums containing personal documents, letters, clippings, and photographs relating to this general's military career in Russia and émigré life in the U.S.; his service record, 1922, and related items; material on the Iuzefovich family; material on the siege of Port Arthur.

266 K. Ivanenko. A story/memoir entitled "Shlema," about a Soviet prison camp in the late 1930s; and a poem, "Beglets," 1930s.

267 Nikolai N. Ivanoff. Papers, ca. 34 items. Handwritten account of the formation of the

Russkaia narodnaia armiia by the Germans in the USSR during World War II; handwritten memoirs on events leading to the February 1917 Revolution and the Civil War; handwritten reminiscences in 2 sections: "Mezhdu maloi i bol'shoi revoliutsiei" and "Sobytiya v litsakh" for 1905-17; and data on Russian émigrés interned in France during World War II. Restrictions.

268 A. M. Ivanov. A typescript describing his experiences in the Civil War in the region of Astrakhan, 1918-20, based on diaries, written as day-by-day accounts, 170 pp.

269 L. E. Ivanov. Travel notes, handwritten, and sketches of a military topographer on a surveying expedition to Central Asia (Bukhara, Tashkent, Chimkent), 1900-1901.

270 Alexandra A. Ivanova-Soboleva. Typescript about a 1927 excursion of Russian émigré high-school students from Finland to Estonia.

271 Izmailovskii Polk. Papers, ca. 15 boxes, 4,200 items. Memoirs of members of the regiment; data on the history, organization, and membership of the regiment, 1711-1920s; lists of officers; 2,428 cards with information about officers, officials, doctors, and priests; biographies of 203 officers; correspondence; and over 250 photos. Subjects noted: the campaign of 1812, the Russo-Turkish war of 1877-78, World War I, and the Civil War.

272 I. Kachalinskii. "Prolozhenie k 'Kazachei zhizni'; protiv zlostnoi klevety v zashchitu pravdy i chesti V. G. Glazkova" (1958)--about the Cossack emigration in the U.S.

273 Olga Vladimirovna Kachalova. Her handwritten "Zapiski emigrantki" discuss family life in pre-1917 St. Petersburg and the Civil War in the South, 1905-20, 172 pp.

274 Pavel G. Kalinin. Papers, ca. 13 items. Personal documents, memoirs, and manuscripts about his service in the Imperial navy, 1905-15; typed copies of articles on the Russian navy.

275 A. N. Kalishevskii. "Prisiazhnaya advokature dorevoliutsionnoi Rossii advokatura SSSR," ca. 1860-1941, 1955, typed 43 pp.

276 O. Kallynyk. Typescript on the Bolshevik administration of Ukraine in 1948 ("Communism, enemy of mankind").

277 Vasilii Mikhailovich Kamenskii. Papers, ca. 4 boxes, ca. 1,475 items. Sections of his memoirs concern student days, military service in World War I (Siberia in 1916 and then the Southwest Front), the revolution in Iaroslavl, the Civil War in the Northwest, and the emigration (Estonia and the United States), ca. 1908-1970s. He was active in the Russian Orthodox Church in Russia and the U.S. Restrictions.

278 Vladimir Aleksandrovich Kamenskii. Papers, ca. 33 items. Handwritten memoirs: military education, including school schedule for the Corps of Pages; social-cultural life of St. Petersburg ca. 1890-1914; 7 short sketches/reminiscences of the Leib-gvardii egerskii polk, its organization, duties, and activities in World War I, ca. 1910-17.

279 Dmitrii Konstantinovich Kapatsinskii. Papers, ca. 3 boxes, 1,070 items. Personal documents, his master's thesis on social insurance in Czechoslovakia, minutes and correspondence on Russian war relief, 1941-46; also records of the Russkoe Ob"edinennoe Obshchestvo Vzaimopomoshchi Ameriki, 1920s-1950s; and materials on ROOVA, the ROOVA farm, the Russkoe Obshchestvo "Nauka," and the Obshchestvo Russkikh Bratstv v S.Sh.A. Restrictions.

280 Mikhail Dmitrevich Karateev (Karachevskii-Karateev). Papers, ca. 6 boxes, 1,410 items. This historical novelist's papers contain typed reminiscences of the emigration in Yugoslavia and Bulgaria in the 1920s, Paraguay in the 1930s; books and manuscripts in Spanish on mineralogy by his father, Dmitri Vasil'evich Karateev, who taught at the University of Lima, ca. 1920-40. Restrictions.

281 Mikhail Kantor. Materials of this writer include a manuscript (and typed copy) of 15 sonnets ("Venok somnenii").

282 Mikhail Vasil'evich Karkhanin. Papers, ca. 600 items. The colonel was chief of staff for representatives of the Russian supreme command in France, 1916-17. The collection includes mimeographed orders and documents of the REF, France and the Salonika front, 1915-19; handwritten "Materialy po istorii prebyvaniia russkikh voisk vo Frantsii, 1915-1919"; documents, correspondence, orders, etc. on the army of General A. Dutov in Siberia, 1919-20; a short biography of Karkhanin by his widow.

283 G. G. Karpoff. "Le Drame d'un Grand Peuple. La Russie et le Système Soviétique," typed, carbon, 1920-40.

284 Vladimir Ivanovich Karpov. Information about Karpov, his life, and his work.

285 Anton Vladimirovich Kartashev. Papers, ca. 40 boxes, ca. 16,300 items. Kartashev chaired the Russkii Natsional'nyi Komitet. There are financial records, accounts, correspondence, contributors' lists, and more for the RNK, ca. 1921-35, and for their international conferences and other activities. The holdings also include materials on the 1921 S"ezd Russkogo Natsional'nogo ob"edineniia in Paris; reports, correspondence, etc. of the Vserossiiskii soiuz gorodov and the Vserossiiskii zemskii soiuz; much information on refugee aid; letters from Ivan Bunin, B. Zaitsev, and other writers; Kartashev's personal papers and

correspondence from the 1930s; the diary of V. D. Kuzmin-Karavaev. Restrictions.

286 V. N. Kasatkin. Parts of the general's autobiography, covering his military education, World War I, the year 1917, and refugees in Harbin, 1900-1930s, handwritten.

287 Nikolai Timofeevich Kashtanov. O sukonnom fabrikante N. T. Kashtanove (Paris, 1942), a mimeographed volume, on the period ca. 1890-1941.

288 K. A. Katin. Handwritten memoirs of a Russian officer.

289 G. Katkov. "The political opinions of Soviet citizens" (Oxford, ca. 1950), a mimeographed essay.

290 Petr Terent'evich Kazamarov. 2 memoir pieces about the Revolution and Civil War: "Ekaterinodar--Nachalo 1918 goda i nachalo Beloi Bor'by na Kubani" and "Sud'ba."

291 Iakov I. Kefeli. In a bound volume and in loose sections, typed Vospominaniia s generalom A. V. Shvartsem v Karse, Trapezunde i Odesse, osen' 1915-vesna 1919 g.g. (Odessa, 1918-19); 2 notebooks with typed memoirs on medical student days and World War I in Trapezund, 1900-17; and 2 bound manuscripts: Oktiabrskii perevorot (on the Bolshevik coup in 1917) and Port Arturtsi o byloi stradie (on the Russo-Japanese War).

292 Antoni Antonovich Kersnovskii. Papers, ca. 21 items. Parts of a manuscript on Russian history 863-1942; plus typed and mimeographed essays on Soviet military history and the emigration in France.

293 Konstantin Nikolaevich Khagondokov. Papers, 69 items. 67 notebooks contain the handwritten memoirs of this general, a Kabardian, 1891-1920; the 944 pp. (and a typed carbon copy of the same) concern World War I, the Caucasus, and Turkestan.

294 Adrion Ksenofontovich Kharkevich. 2 typed poems, a book review, and a typed diary about the Orthodox Church in Florence, 1930-45.

295 Ivan Mikhailovich Kheraskov. Papers, ca. 20 items. Notebooks, in Russian and French, with clippings and handwritten accounts of World War II by this émigré in France.

296 Evgeniia Sergeevna Khmel'nitskaia. Papers, ca. 90 items. Letters from the USSR, 1920s; printed text of her story of the Bolshevik underground; her autobiography, in English and Russian; her articles and essays on Russian history and linguistics (teaching Russian); "From the letters of William Frey, 1839-1888," a typescript; offprints and handwritten drafts of her articles; letters to E. Mogilat, 1954-56, from Khmel'nitskaia.

297 Vladimir Sergeevich Khitrovo. His bound memoirs, "Vospominaniia i materialy dlia istorii: Leib-gvardii konnaia artilleriia. Chast' II-aia. Voina 1914-17. Pokhod k Vostochnuiu Prussiiu," typed, with photos; plus a microfilm of maps for the same.

298 Vladimir Veniaminovich Khoromanskii. Papers, ca. 44 items. Handwritten reminiscences of the start of World War I; typed reminiscences of service in Ekaterinoslav in 1919; leaflets appealing to Ekaterinoslav citizens; letters, documents, notes on the Russkoe khristianskoe dvizhenie in France, 1930s; the memoirs of his father, 1918-22, handwritten, with a photo of P. A. Stolypin; his essay, with documentation, on Russian refugees on Malta and Cyprus and on journalism, handwritten; a typed essay, "Poslednii otpusk, 1911 g."; plus other handwritten or typed reminiscences.

299 Edigei Kirimal. Typed copy of the 1918 Law Code adopted by the Crimean Parliament; essay by Dr. Kirimal concerning the Soviet treatment of the Moslem Crimean Tatars, typed and handwritten copies.

300 Fedor F. Kirkhgof. Notebooks with the typewritten reminiscences of Kirkhgof: "Vospominaniia adiutanta . . . verkhovnogo glavnokomanduiushchego," "Pokhod leib-gvardii izmailovskogo polka, 1914-1918," "Poslednii period leib-gvardii izmailovskogo polka," "Moe vozrashchenie s voiny," all on World War I, plus "Moia zhizn' v Petrograde v 1918-19 gg i kommandirovka v Berlin" and "Moia zhizn' na Ukraine v 1919."

301 V. V. Kirkhgof. Her memoirs on V. K. fon Vitte (von Witte) family genealogy, her childhood in St. Petersburg, education at the women's gymnasium of Emiliia Pavlovna Shaffe in the capital, and contacts with M. L. Goffman, one of her teachers who became a Pushkin scholar after emigrating to Western Europe.

302 Georgii M. Kiselevskii. Papers, ca. 48 items. Typed reminiscences of his education, work in the Russian railroad administration, and the life of émigré engineers, 1890-1920; diary and documents, copies, about his service at the Northwest Front (Reval) in the Civil War; historical documents, 1652-1872, of Peter I, Anna Ivanovna, etc.

303 N. N. Kissel-Zagorianskii. Bound volume of the general's memoirs: military and civil career, ca. 1910-30, governor of Riazan province in 1917, and the emigration ("Les mémoires du general Kissel-Zagorianskavo"), typed, 300 pp. Restrictions.

304 Vasilii Fedorovich Klement'ev. Papers, ca. 25 items. His handwritten and typed essays, mimeographed poems, and clippings about World War I, B. Savinkov's Soiuz Zashchity Rodiny i Svobody, the Civil War, and the emigration in

Poland; handwritten memoirs 1917-18, in 4 sections, and for the 1920s (Polish emigration); and an essay on the Civil War in 1918, "V 33 pekh. Divizii, II," handwritten, 6 pp.

305 Vasilii Mikhailovich Kliuzhin. Papers, ca. 10 items. Short, handwritten essays concerning early childhood and life at the Krasnoufimsk district factory, factory serfs, cottage industry, and the Dukhobors, 1800-1917.

306 Irina Vladimirovna Kol' (Coll). Papers, ca. 5 boxes, 1,000 items. A bibliography (on index cards) on the murder of the Austrian Archduke Franz Ferdinand in Sarajevo in 1914; a list of readers and their books at the Bibliothèque russe in Lausanne, Switzerland for 1912, bound volume; 3 microfilm rolls of materials about Gavril Princip and the Sarajevo assassination, much of it clippings; papers of her father, Vladimir Ivanovich Lebedev, minister of the navy in the Provisional Government and a journalist after the Revolution, including photos, clippings, fiction, and political articles. Restrictions.

307 Aleksandr A. and Anastaziia P. Kolchinskii. Papers, ca. 40 items. Include the lieutenant's typed poems, personal documents, a copy of a 1913 military manual, diaries for 1952 and 1954, text of L. Kornilov speech in August 1917, a typed essay about the Pavlovsk military academy, plus notes and a book on the same.

308 Iurii Aleksandrovich Kolemin. Papers, ca. 200 items. Russian diplomat in Paris and Madrid, and a scholar; the stepson of V. P. Bakhrat, last tsarist emissary to Switzerland. The diplomatic papers of his stepfather (and his own) concern Russo-German and Russo-Swiss relations before 1917. Kolemin's correspondence and manuscripts also relate to his scholarly interest--Russian Orthodoxy, 1892-1950s.

309 S. I. Kolokol'nikov. Papers, ca. 1 box, ca. 75 items. The private and business papers of this former member of the first state duma contain data on his business interests in Siberia (in the grain trade) and with U.S. firms, before and after the Revolution; the Civil War in the Far East; and the duma. Restrictions.

310 Petr L. Koniskii. Fragments of memoirs, typed, about Soviet labor camps and political prisoners in the 1930s.

311 Joseph Korbel. Memoranda of conversations with V. Clementis and A. Bebler; a Czech-Yugoslav trade treaty and typed essay about their trade relations.

312 Alexei Koriakov. Typed copies of his novel "Za Rossiiu i svobodu."

313 Alexandra Konstantinovna Korostovets. Papers, ca. 6 boxes, 1,100 items. Correspondence of George Lukomskii, Sir Philip Gibbs, Maksim Gorkii, Alexander II, Rudyard Kipling, Marie Curie, and Nicholas II; writings of Vladimir Korostovets (including Russia Past and Present with Reginald Hoare, Seed and Harvest), articles 1940s-1950s, essays on Soviet domestic and foreign policy, 1930s-1950s.

314 Veniamin Valerianovich Korsak-Zavadskii. Papers, ca. 2 boxes, 560 items. This writer's correspondence and handwritten works.

315 Sofia Vikent'evna Korsunets. Copies of her fiction, mimeographed, short stories, and plays.

316 Boris Sergeevich Korvin. Papers, ca. 25 items. Archive of this former artillery colonel includes manuscript of memoirs, typed in English, recounting his military education, service in World War I, Civil War in the Ukraine, arrest by the Cheka, and emigration.

317 E. N. Kosatkina-Rostovskaia. Papers, ca. 25 items. Papers of the late F. N. Kosatkin-Rostovskii, a poet and dramatist: a published book of his verse; handwritten diaries for 1940; memoirs of the literary, theatrical, and aristocratic life of St. Petersburg ca. 1910-40; correspondence from 1920 and after; and "Moi put' sluzheniia teatru," about the Russian theater in 1910-18, typescript, 400 pp.

318 Ivan F. and Olga Ivanovna Koshko. Papers, ca. 52 items. A governor and high civil servant of Imperial Russia and his daughter. 4 memoir notebooks concern his governorship of Perm province, 1911-14, 2 contain "Vospominaniia gubernatora, 1905-1914" starting with his Novgorod service in 1905. Her memoirs cover student life and revolutionary circles in St. Petersburg ca. 1910, life in Novgorod, social conditions in Penza and Perm, life in Perm during World War I, the Revolution, Civil War, and the emigration in Constantinople and Paris in the 1920s; memoirs of her brother, B. I. Koshko, relating to his service in the chancellery of the Council of Ministers; and the typed memoirs of Metropolitan Evlogii, his childhood, seminary education, career as bishop of Kholm and archibishop of Volhynia, service as a delegate in the third and fourth state dumas, World War I, the Revolution, the Civil War, and his tenure as metropolitan of the Russian Church in Exile, 1920-21. There are many papers of Dr. I. I. Manukhin (b. 1882), including a Russian typescript of his book "Samozashchita organizma." Restrictions.

319 Nikolai Nikolaevich Kostylev. Papers, ca. 440 items. Handwritten memoirs for 1876-1917; letters.

320 Aleksandr Efimovich Kotomkin. Papers, ca. 4 boxes, ca. 1,600 items. Songs, verse, correspondence, personal documents, notes, and books, 1885-1964.

321 Sofia Iu. Kovalevskaia. Papers, ca. 60 items. Basically the archive of General Iu. N. Pliushchevskii-Ploshchik, with his handwritten memoirs about the army, the Provisional Government, and the Kornilov Affair, 1918-23; and documents on World War I, the February Revolution, and the Civil War.

322 Maksim Maksimovich Kovalevskii. Papers, 2 boxes. Includes extensive correspondence, some in typed transcripts, with, among others, Petr Lavrov, ca. 75 letters, ca. 1890, Petr Struve, M. Tugan-Baranovskii, and P. Miliukov. Also, 35 handwritten notebooks of memoirs, with typed transcripts of same, entitled "Moia zhizn'" and "Vospominaniia." In addition, there is a typescript by S. Iu. Witte on Russian financial problems in 1880, submitted to the future Alexander III.

323 Petr Evgrafovich Kovalevskii. Papers, ca. 11 boxes, 3,050 items. This professor was in the emigration in Paris. His papers contain autobiographical material; materials of the Comité central d'aide aux étudiants russes, 1930s; family information and genealogy; family correspondence, 1845-60.

324 P. Kovan'ko. "Voiny i finansy," a typescript.

325 Il'ia Nikolaevich Kovarskii. Papers, ca. 200 items. Kovarskii was a member of the central committee of the Socialist Revolutionary Party. This collection of materials belonged to him and to M. V. Vishniak: A. Argunov's "Iz perezhitogo"--a memoir about ideological disputes between internationalists and defensists in the Russian socialist emigration in Europe during World War I and about the situation in Petrograd ca. 1917-18; correspondence, 1940s, with M. A. Aldanov, G. Grebenshchikov, M. Vishniak, and others.

326 Vladimir Fedorovich Kozlianinov. Papers, over 2 boxes, ca. 785 items. Correspondence with the Grand Prince Gavriil Konstantinovich, the Grand Princes Dmitrii Pavlovich and Dmitrii Konstantinovich, members of the monarchist movement, and various émigré veterans organizations; memoirs of his military career, 1900-17; historical documents, including one signed by A. Lunacharskii in 1918 about the confiscation of property; 29 notebooks describing political and personal events 1918-1940s. Restrictions.

327 K. N. Kramarenko. Memoirs in 5 parts, handwritten, about Kramarenko's experiences in Soviet industry as an industrial safety inspector and about trade unions, 1930s. Restrictions.

328 A. A. Krants. Handwritten memoirs describing life in Petrograd under War Communism, 1918-20.

329 Pavel Sergeevich Krasnikov. Papers, ca. 100 items. Writer (pseudonym: Karelin) and editor of the San Francisco Russian Life. Materials on World War I.

330 N. L. Krasnokutskii. Memoirs about his meetings with Leo Tolstoi, ca. 1907, 12 pp.

331 P. N. Krasnov. Papers, ca. 90 items. The general's letters to P. V. Kartashev, 89, 1921-37, concerning the Civil War and the Don Cossacks, plus a photocopy of a letter of July 1918 from the general and Don ataman to Kaiser Wilhelm, also about the Civil War.

332 Liudmila Aleksandrovna Kravtseva. Papers, ca. 40 items. Letters from Andrei V. Kravtsov in the USSR to relatives in Paris, 1925-28, describing domestic conditions; and issues of Soviet provincial newspapers. Andrei Kravtsov was a member of the Narodnaia Svoboda Party before 1917.

333 V. A. Kravtsev. Papers, ca. 180 items. Mimeographed and printed matter on the Soviet economy and foreign relations of the USSR, 1920s-1940; and materials on such émigré groups as the Russkii zarubezhnyi s"ezd, 1926, Obshchii s"ezd predstavitelei russkoi promyshlennosti i torgovli (Paris, 1921), and the Federatsiia soiuzov russkikh inzhenerov zagranitsei.

334 Aleksandr Vasil'evich Krivoshein. Minister of agriculture under the tsars and in the White governments of A. I. Denikin and P. Wrangel. Photocopies of 7 letters, ca. 1920, concerning the fall of the White government in the South and Russian refugees in Europe. Among the correspondents were Denikin, Wrangel, V. A. Maklakov, and Maurice Paleologue. Handwritten and mimeographed essay on his life and career, the Stolypin reform, Revolution, and the Civil War by his son, Kirill Aleksandrovich Krivoshein, published in Paris, 1973.

335 Konstantin Romanovich Krovopuskov. Papers, ca. 5 boxes, ca. 2,150 items. Minutes, proclamations, and reports of the Vserossiiskii natsional'nyi tsentr, financial records, law projects, and decrees, 1918-20, relating to White governments in the Civil War, materials from ca. 1949-55 on the "Russkii Ofis" of K. and V. A. Maklakov, which attempted to aid Russian refugees in France.

336 Vladimir Pavlovich Kruzenshtern. His typed memoirs about Russians in Manchuria; excerpts of his diaries when he was an officer in a regiment guarding the Russian railroad lines in Northern Manchuria, 1900-14, and while serving in the trans-Amur River cavalry, 1910, all typed.

337 Vera Georgievna Kugusheva. Typed memoirs of life in a liberal intelligentsia family ca. 1865-1923; reminiscences of V. P. Al'tovskaia and Tat'iana Isakovich; Kugusheva's short reminiscence about the Bolshevik capture of Vladivostok in 1919.

338 Aleksandr Kuksin. Papers, 2 boxes, ca. 800 items. Kuksin served in the P. P. Skoropadsky government in the Ukraine, was later active in émigré anti-Bolshevik politics. The archive includes correspondence (e.g., family letters from the USSR ca. 1935); diaries for roughly 1941-59; memoirs and memoir material; a signed copy of a 1921 treaty among anti-Bolshevik groups in Turkey and the Ukrainian rada.

339 Nikolai Kupfer. Memoirs of the ROA brigade in Italy; handwritten manuscripts--"Tole" and "Marzabotto"--on the Vlasov movement, Russian soldiers, and prisoners in World War II; and other material. Restrictions.

340 A. P. Kutepov. Papers, ca. 6 boxes, ca. 3,000 items. The general's archive, ca. 1918-28, contains his personal and professional correspondence with such figures as A. I. Denikin, P. Wrangel, P. N. Shatilov; orders of the Black Sea military governor, 1918, and of the Volunteer Army, 1920; materials on the Far East, Ataman G. M. Semenov, the Japanese intervention in 1921, the monarchist movement in the emigration, ROVS, and the Eurasian movement. Restrictions.

341 Iu. A. Kutyrina. Papers, ca. 50 items. Typescripts on Ivan S. Shmelev, a writer; typed essays about Shmelev by Kutyrina, his niece; photocopies of correspondence with P. B. Struve.

342 D. D. and Olga A. Kuzmin(a)-Karavaev. Typed essays and reminiscences by this lieutenant in the Imperial Army include: family history; childhood in army garrison towns and St. Petersburg; "Voennoe obrazovanie v Imperatorskoi Rossii v 20 stoletii," 1900-14, in 2 parts; "Invalidnyi dom v Sovetskom soiuze" (his arrest in 1945 in Finland); and "10 let v zakliuchenii," 1945-55, Butyrsk prison and the Mariinskii razpredelitel'nyi punkt. Also typed diaries of his wife who was arrested after the Russo-Finnish war and deported to the USSR. They concern the emigration in Finland and Soviet-Finnish relations.

343 Boris Mikhailovich Kuznetsov. Papers, ca. 170 items. Memoirs and essays, typed, of General K. K. Akintievskii; Kuznetsov's published memoirs on the Civil War in Daghestan in 1918; correspondence and documents relating to émigré military and monarchist organizations, especially ROVS (Russkii obshchevoinskii soiuz); correspondence and other materials on the Civil War. Restrictions.

344 Elena Ivanovna Lakier. Memoirs of Lakier ("Otryvki iz dnevnika--1917-1920") and of Sofiia Aleksandrovna Sushchinskaia ("1920-i god. Begstvo iz Odessy v Sevastopol' i evakuatsiia iz Rossii v Egipet").

345 A. A. Lampe. Papers, ca. 56 boxes, 21,000 items. The general's papers contain correspondence with ROVS, earlier émigré military groups, and members of the Romanov family after 1917; materials on the Vlasov movement and displaced persons in post-World War II Germany; his diary for 1945-61. A small amount of material in this collection concerns the Volunteer Army and the Civil War. Restrictions.

346 Olga Lang. A curriculum vitae and an essay, based on personal memoirs, on the Makhno army in Ekaterinoslav in 1919, both typed.

347 Illarion Sergeevich Lanskoi. Papers, ca. 10 items. A typescript about the émigré architect R. N. Verkhovskoi and a pamphlet on the same.

348 Aleksis V. Laptev (Lapteff). Papers, ca. 10 items. Typed memoirs, photos, and documents about the American Relief Administration in Ufa and the Urals, 1922-23.

349 Georgii Pavlovich Larin. Papers, ca. 1 box, ca. 560 items. Correspondence (the Shanghai branch with other branches) and information on the Bratstvo Russkoi Pravdy, an anti-Bolshevik organization established in the early 1920s by Metropolitan Anigonius Khrapovitskii and General P. N. Krasnov, 1920s-1930s; data on a mutual credit society in Shanghai, 1938-39; issues of émigré publications, photographs, correspondence, pamphlets, and mimeographed material on the emigration in China and Australia, 1920s-1960s.

350 Petr L. Lavrov. Papers, 1 box, 49 items. 48 of his letters to the revolutionary Aleksandra Vasil'evna Bauler about political theory and the potential for revolution in Russia, 1876-82, typed copies, and a catalogue of his library in Prague, 1938.

351 Adol'f Lazarev. His Zhizn' i Poznanie, a collection of reviews and articles on philosophical and theological subjects, written between 1905 and 1938, most published in journals, with an introduction by N. A. Berdiaev, and copies of correspondence between Lazarev and L. Shestov; issued in 1964 in 4 copies, including a bibliography of his works and a biographical note.

352 Konstantin S. Leiman. A handwritten essay on the Vilno Military Academy; others on military subjects.

353 Valentin Iosif Lekhno. Papers, ca. 43 items. His typed memoirs concern his experiences as a lawyer, 1915-1920s, the emigration in Poland and Yugoslavia, and World War II, to 1950.

354 A. N. Lenkov. "Rol' chekhoslovakov"--a typescript about the Civil War in 1919, and a pamphlet.

355 Evgeniia K. Leontovich. Papers of her brother-in-law, Boris L'vovich Baikov: typed essays in

English on claims to the Imperial throne, and a typed English translation of his manuscript about experiences in Persia in 1920.

356 Viktor K. Leontovich. Papers, ca. 90 items. Documents, books, and memoirs about the Russian administration in the Novorossisk region in 1910 and the Revolution in Transcaucasia; ca. 50 stereopticon pictures of Russo-Japanese War scenes; and a handwritten manuscript entitled "Skitaniia po delu russkogo intelligenta v Severnoi Persii."

357 B. V. Levenets. Papers, ca. 25 items. Diaries, documents (copies) and memoirs concerning World War I, Civil War and Soviet regime.

358 A. A. Levitskii. Handwritten reminiscences by this lieutenant about the Russo-Japanese War and his life to 1913.

359 V. L. Levitskii. Notebooks with memoirs: "Vospominaniia polkovnika 155-go pekh. Kubanskogo polka," typed and handwritten, 1914-17.

360 Mikhail Lidin (Fomichev). A typescript and 2 photocopies of an essay by "M. Fomichev" entitled "Iz vospominanii antonovtsa," about the peasant anti-Bolshevik revolt in Tambov, 1921-22, 34 pp.

361 Aleksandra Vil'gelmovna Linden. Memoirs about the family's flight from Petrograd in 1918, life in a dacha in the Crimea under the Whites and Allies, and the establishment of the Bolshevik administration there, 1917-25.

362 V. Linden. A biographical sketch of her husband, Mikhail Vil'gelmovich Linden, brother of Aleksandra, a bureaucrat in the tsarist ministry of trade and industry; other reminiscences about her family, south Russia 1917-19, and other topics.

363 Filip Linnik. Papers, ca. 26 boxes. Correspondence and ephemera of primarily religious organizations, 1950s-1960s. Restrictions.

364 Mikhail Aleksandrovich Lipskii. Papers, ca. 2 boxes. Personal correspondence. Restrictions.

365 L. Lishin (Lischin). His handwritten essay, "Bolshevizm i religiia"; issues of a newspaper put out by the concentration camp administration.

366 Aleksei Alekseevich Litvinov. Papers, 30 items. A typed family history to the 15th c.; handwritten essays by family members about military history; and official documents to the 1920s.

367 G. A. Liubarskii. The colonel's handwritten memoirs on military history 1914-20, ca. 450 pp.

368 Dmitrii Nikolaevich Liubimov. Papers, ca. 4 boxes, 200 items. "Russkaia smuta nachala deviatisotykh godov. 1902-1906," memoirs dictated by this former senator and head of the Ministry of Interior chancery, based on recollections, notes, and documents, primarily about the 1905 Revolution; also memoirs about his governorship of Vil'no, 1906-14, tenure as assistant to the governor general of Warsaw, 1914-15 and as senator 1914-17, plus the emigration in France; materials and documents concerning aid to refugees and émigrés, 1921-58, typed, 479 pp. Restrictions.

369 Aleksandr N. Lodygin. Papers, ca. 6 boxes, ca. 2,025 items. Papers of this Russian inventor of the incandescent light bulb, ca. 1872, engineer, and chemist, include: family documents; his personal documents; biographical material and a biographical sketch of Lodygin by Alma Lodygina, his wife; papers of two of his daughters--Vera (photos, notes, reminiscences of childhood, correspondence) and Rita (Faust); printed matter, including items apparently gathered for a law suit against Edison's patents, and material relating to his invention of the incandescent light.

370 Iurii Il'ich Lodyzhenskii. Papers, ca. 6 boxes, ca. 1,200 items. Typed reminiscences ("Zapiski vracha") of medical education and career in Russia and the Civil War in the Ukraine and Crimea, 1908-23, 2 notebooks in French; "Iz razskazov A. N. Tulub'eva," typescript, 17 pp., concerning life and mores on an estate ca. 1900; his articles, 1929-50, on Soviet espionage, the Comintern, and the anti-communist emigration; his mimeographed work on the church in Russian medieval history; and 2 essays by V. M. Pronin about the Crimean War and the Civil War. Restrictions.

371 Nataliia Apollonarievna Logunova. Papers, ca. 16 boxes, 1,850 items. A bibliography of her published and unpublished works; her poems, short stories, and novels of the 1950s and 1960s; the diary of a former displaced person for 1945-52 ("Proidennyi etap"), parts of which have been published; correspondence with readers and publishers; and published works, including memoirs of Odessa in World War II. Restrictions.

372 I. V. Lopukhin. A bound volume, composed 1809, with the manuscript "Zapiski nekotorykh obstoiatel'stv zhizni i sluzhby deistvitel'nogo tainogo Sovetnika, Senatora I. V. Lopukhina" about government service 1775-1807.

373 N. I. Lorer. A notebook containing the second part of Lorer's memoirs; he was a Decembrist, exiled to the Caucasus, who returned to Central Asia.

374 Iosif Grigorevich Loris-Melikov. Papers, ca. 4 boxes. Printed matter, documents, and

handwritten material about World War I, the Civil War in Siberia, the northwest front, German plans for Russia after World War I, the emigration in Western Europe, 1918-1920s.

375 Aleksandr Petrovich Lukin. Papers, 4 boxes, ca. 2,000 items. The archive of Lukin, a former tsarist naval officer, contains clippings and unpublished manuscripts of memoirs and reminiscences about the Black Sea fleet ca. 1900, World War I, the Revolution, and Civil War; also, materials on Russo-Turkish relations.

376 M. A. Lunin. A notebook with copies of letters from this former Decembrist to his sister in the 1830s and an essay on Polish conditions written in 1840. Restrictions.

377 Lollii Ivanovich L'vov. Papers, ca. 200 items. Manuscripts on Ivan Turgenev and miscellanea, including typed copies of 3 letters of the Tsaritsa Evdokiia, wife of Mikhail Romanov, ca. 1627.

378 M. N. Lyons. Papers, ca. 60 items. Map collection dating from ca. 1890-1920--Russian Central Asia, Mongolia, Afghanistan, China, and Japan as well as Galicia, Bukovina, and the Sea of Marmora.

379 Marshall MacDuffie. Papers, ca. 9 boxes. A mimeographed and typed transcript of his tape-recorded recollections of a USSR trip in 1946 to Central Asia and Minsk; mimeographed report on his 1953 trip. Note: See also the UNRRA papers in Columbia's Lehman Library.

380 MAD. See under Mikhail Aleksandrovich Drizo.

381 Vladimir I. Maiborodov. Papers, ca. 60 items. His memoirs cover his career as a zemskii nachalnik, 1904-16 ("Moia sluzhba pri starom rezhime i vo vremia smuty"), childhood in Orel and Chernigov provinces and his education, 1890-1910, and the years in the emigration in Yugoslavia, 1930-44 ("V otstavke").

382 Ekaterina Ippolitovna Maidel' (Maydell). Papers, ca. 1 box, ca. 985 items. Typed and handwritten memoirs/reminiscences, ca. 1890-1920, about women's education and her family (she was married to a naval officer and her father was also in the navy); a manuscript by S. E. Vittenberg on a mission to exchange Russian POWs for arrested Finns, July 1918, 6 pp.; typed memoirs of B. V. Berkelund, a Finn in the Imperial navy, about his family life in St. Petersburg pre-1917, the Revolution, the economy in War Communism, 1895-1918, his arrest by Soviet agents in Helsinki in 1945, and his term in Soviet prisons and camps until 1953; documents from the Provisional Government's 1917 investigation of the Kornilov affair. Restrictions.

383 Aleksandr Ivanovich Makhonin. Memoirs of childhood, youth (the family was Cossack), education at the naval engineering academy in St. Petersburg, service as a naval officer in World War I, time with the Volunteer Army in the south during the Civil War.

384 Petr Semenovich Makhrov. Papers, ca. 1.5 boxes, 600 items. Materials on military schools in tsarist Russia; a typescript of his SSSR, 1917-1945. Krushenie starogo mira, much of it on World War II; Makhrov's memoirs about Generals A. Brusilov and A. M. Kaledin, 1915-16; a handwritten biography of General M. V. Alekseev; memoirs, photos, maps, and other items about Germans in the Ukraine in 1917, A. I. Denikin, P. N. Wrangel, the Nikolaevskii Military Academy of the General Staff, the emigration, and World War II; and notebooks, mostly handwritten, about other military topics.

385 Charles Malamuth. Papers, ca. 17 boxes. His translations of Russian literature; data on Radio Free Europe, Radio Liberty, and the Voice of America (Malamuth was a director of VOA broadcasts); interviews concerning Soviet prison camps; information on L. Trotskii, including correspondence with him regarding translation; Malamuth's articles and writings about the USSR and the Jews in Eastern Europe; typescripts; a Boris Pilnyak short story and a scenario of Viktor Shklovskii; personal correspondence; photographs, 1900-1960s, including some Bolshevik leaders.

386 Irina Ivanovna Malina. Papers, ca. 30 items. Papers on her father, General I. P. Romanovskii, A. I. Denikin's chief of staff, 1918-20.

387 Vladimir Fedorovich Malinin. Papers, 24 items. Letters from M. V. Chelnokov, 18; 1930-34; typescripts entitled "Zabastovka vodoprovoda v Moskve 1905," "Pamiati printsa A. P. Oldenburgskogo," and "Velikaia kniaginia Elisaveta Feodorovna." Restrictions.

388 A. Malinovskii. Russian manuscript edition of a history of the administration of the Empire under the Secret State Council, 1726-30.

389 Sergei Aleksandrovich Malloi. Papers, ca. 420 items. Photo, typed biographical information, correspondence, and other items (some biographical) relating to Vladika Sergei (Korolev) of Prague (later archbishop of Vienna and of Kazan and Chistopol') in the 1920s; mimeographed and printed matter, plus photos, about the Orthodox Church in France, Prague, and Austria, 1940-65. Restrictions.

390 Sergei Ivanovich Mamontov. Typed memoirs, in French and English, about childhood on a country estate, service as an officer in Moscow during the Revolution, flight from Moscow, service in the White Army in the South, and the early emigration in Western Europe, ca. 1900-20; plus short sketches on peasant customs and agriculture.

391 Konstantin Mandrajy (Mandrachi). "Begin at the Beginning"--typed memoirs about his military career, World War I, and the Revolution, ca. 1880-1920.

392 I. I. Manukhin. Handwritten memoirs of this medical doctor, covering his training, medical students in the 1905 Revolution, family connections with such cultural figures as M. Saltykov-Shchedrin and F. Dostoevskii, the Moscow Art Theater, and S. Botkin, 1889-1914; a continuation of the memoirs, revised by his wife, for the years in emigration, 1921-42. Also memoirs ca. 1913-21 concerning his treatment of the upper class and "ruling circles"; he knew M. Gorkii, A. Kerensky, N. N. Sukhanov, L. Trotskii, G. Zinov'ev, and the Grand Duke Gavriil Konstantinovich. They also cover his work abroad before World War I. Restrictions.

393 Vasilii Pavlovich Marchenko. Papers, 21 boxes, ca. 8,000 items. This collection of an émigré Ukrainian scholar and journalist includes a short autobiography; personal documents; correspondence; notes and materials for articles; drafts and typescripts about the Soviet Union, Ukraine, international politics, émigré political groups such as SBONR (Soiuz bor'by za osvobozhdeniia narodov Rossii); and a diary for 1935-43 and 1945-49 (about the USSR under German occupation and the author's emigration to Germany).

394 Anatolii L. Markov. A bound, typed manuscript: "Zapiski o proshlom," vol. 1 being the "Istoriia roda dvorian Markovykh," 1473-1930; and a typescript entitled "Krepostnoi teatr v Rossii," on serfdom and the theater, ca. 1750-1861.

395 Nikolai Evgen'evich Markov. Papers, ca. 120 items. Letters in the French emigration, 1930-54; biographical sketches and writings on the state duma (he was a member, 1907-12, on the extreme right), anti-Semitism, and émigré politics; a handwritten biographical sketch of him by his nephew; anti-Masonic and anti-Semitic ephemera.

396 Nikolai Andreevich Martynov. Papers, ca. 55 items. His typed reminiscences of the Civil War in Siberia and the Far East; typescript in 2 parts, ca. 900 pp., "O zhizni i politicheskikh sobytiiakh v Kharbine, v Manchurii i voobshche na Dal'nem Vostoke s uporom na Beliiu Armiiu, 1923-1948," about the emigration; his diaries for 1951-52. Restrictions.

397 Nikolai Vitalevich Maryshev. Papers, ca. 80 items. Handwritten memoirs about childhood, youth, and education (Odessa, Vil'no, Warsaw) and "22 goda pod sovetskim itogom," carbon; handwritten memoirs about the emigration in Germany, 1941-57; poems and religious works; and information about displaced persons in Western Europe, 1942-60. Restrictions.

398 Nikolai Nikolaevich Mashukov. Papers, 9 boxes, ca. 3,000 items. A rear admiral in the tsarist Black Sea fleet. His personal documents; biographical material; memoirs of various naval officers; correspondence, ca. 1919-1960s.

399 Evgenii Vasil'evich Maslovskii. Papers, ca. 6 boxes, ca. 2,065 items. Typed memoirs of this general, bound, 3 vols., about an intelligentsia family, military education, diplomatic and military activity in northern Persia 1909-14, service on the staff of the Caucasus front in early World War I, and the Civil War in the South, ca. 1890-1920; 2 vols. of a typed diary--the Russian emigration in southern France and Nice, émigré political life, ROVS, the abductions of Generals A. P. Kutepov and E. K. Miller; copies of articles (and correspondence) relating to General N. Iudenich; drafts of typed reviews and reactions to Maslovskii's Mirovaia voina na kavkazkom fronte, 29 pp. Restrictions.

400 Mikhail Georgevich Mavrodi. A notebook contains handwritten memoirs about his naval training and career, 1914-17; and memoirs of his service on a Black Sea transport ship during the Revolution and Civil War and of the French intervention in the South, 1917-20.

401 Galina Nikolaevna von Meck (fon Mekk). 5 typed essays by the granddaughter of P. I. Chaikovskii's patroness (the widow of a wealthy railroad engineer). Galina's father married a niece of Chaikovskii, thus making her also a grandniece of the composer. The essays concern Russian railroad development in late 19th c. Russia. There are also her memoirs about Chaikovskii, life in Russia and the USSR, and exile in forced labor camps of Siberia, 1882-1930s; and an explanatory letter from before 1911.

402 Alexander Feliksovich Meiendorf. Papers, 1 box. A zemstvo and duma member (an Octobrist). The collection contains: a manuscript entitled "A brief appreciation of P. Stolypin's tenure of office," typed, 150 pp., plus notes and correspondence relating to this work, including a letter of 7 December 1938 from Olga Borisovna Stolypin, the premier's widow, comments of Count V. N. Kokovtsov, and a letter of Ariadna Tyrkova-Williams dated 5 June 1947.

403 Iurii K. Meier. Memoirs by General A. M. Mikhailov on Russia in Central Asia; writings on the Russian emigration in Yugoslavia, the founding of ROA and KONR, the start of World War II, and A. A. Vlasov.

404 Zinaida Andreevna Melik-Ogandzhanova. Papers, ca. 78 items. Handwritten memoirs about her husband, L. D. Melik-Ogandzhanov, his judicial career in Siberia, the Civil War, A. V. Kolchak, Ataman G. M. Semenov, and the emigration in the Far East.

405 Nikolai A. Mel'nikov. Papers, 2 boxes. Memoirs about his service in the Kazan zemstvo

--"19 let na zemskoi sluzhbe. Avtobiograficheskie nabroski i vospominaniya," written 1936-39, 371 pp., covering the years ca. 1898-1917 and such subjects as S. Witte, G. Lvov, A. V. Krivoshein, P. Stolypin, A. Guchkov, D. Shipov, the third duma, and the zemstvo delegation to Nicholas II in 1913; and a typescript, "Notes of a Dreamer" (1949), about Russian political, religious, and historical development problems, with proposals for a future government, 390 pp.

406 Nikolai Mikhailovich Mel'nikov. Papers, ca. 13 boxes. Headed the southern Russian government under A. I. Denikin during the Civil War, and close friend of the Don Cossack Ataman A. P. Bogaevskii. Correspondence of Mel'nikov, Bogaevskii, and Ataman V. Naumenko; Mel'nikov's "Grazhdanskaia voina na iuge Rossii"; his typed memoirs, carbon, entitled "Pochemu Belye na Iuge ne pobedili Krasnykh"; 8 vols. of financial accounts of the Don government; and a typed biography, plus 2 photos, of General Aleksei Maksimovich Kaledin, 330 pp.

407 P. P. Mendeleev. Papers, ca. 13 boxes. Zemstvo figure, member of the chancellery of the Committee of Ministers and, later, of the Council of Ministers, under S. Witte and P. Stolypin, ca. 1890-1917. Correspondence, photos, personal documents, diaries, typed essays, and clippings; 7 notebooks with handwritten memoirs, and a typed version, on the zemstvo movement before and during World War I. Minutes of meetings of the Union of Russian Gentry, 1926-41. Restrictions.

408 Vladimir Danilovich Merzheevskii. Papers, ca. 5 boxes, 960 items. Typed reminiscences of Generals A. P. Kutepov and E. K. Miller, and of ROVS and its espionage/sabotage activity in the USSR in the 1920s; manuscripts on military topics and émigré military groups. Restrictions.

409 Viktor Ivanovich Meshchaninov. Papers, ca. 24 boxes. Materials on the Semenovskii Regiment and its veterans' organization. Restrictions.

410 V. P. Meshcherskii. Papers, ca. 150 items. Original (and copies) of correspondence with members of the Imperial family, including Alexander II, Alexander III, and Nicholas II, ca. 1860-1905.

411 Ella Genrikhovna Messe. Papers, ca. 225 items. Papers of the Russian singer Evgeniia Foresta: memoirs ca. 1900-60 about F. I. Chaliapin, Raoul Czinsbourg, Hendrik W. Van Loon, and émigré culture.

412 Evgenii E. Messner (Moessner). Papers, 7 boxes. Typed memoirs about family history, youth, high school education, his early military career, World War I, the Volunteer Army, the Civil War in Odessa, World War II and Russians in Yugoslavia and Serbia; biographical data on General N. Golovin, plus the general's typed "Gallitsiiskaia bitva, 1914"; typed essays from, and the archive of the South American branch of, the Institut po issledovaniyu problem voiny i mira im. Gen. N. N. Golovina. Messner's diaries, written in Argentine emigration, with his views on contemporary questions.

413 Roman Grigorevich Miagkov. Papers, ca. 150 items. Memorabilia, objects, and photos relating to military regiments and military history.

414 Aleksandr Vasil'evich Miakin. Handwritten and typed memoirs of a Russian journalist associated with A. S. Suvorin and his Novoe vremia; 3 typed essays on the Union of Russian Journalists in Yugoslavia, and 2 journalists connected with Novoe vremia and Russkoe slovo, A. Ksiunin and E. Zhukov, ca. 1910-30.

415 Petr P. Migulin. Papers, 2 boxes. Manuscripts about the Russo-Japanese War, Russian and Soviet financial and agrarian policies, Nicholas II's reign, and correspondence and pamphlets relating to émigré monarchical circles and education in France (Migulin was a professor). Correspondents include N. Astrov and V. N. Kokovtsev.

416 D. M. Mikhailov. His typed reminiscences concern 1905 in Grodno and its boarding school for officers' children, 1918 and the start of the Civil War, the Pekinskaia dukhovskaia missiia over 250 years and the Russian Orthodox Church in China in 1945, and Archbishop Viktor.

417 Vasilii Aleksandrovich Mikhailov. Papers, ca. 60 items. Handwritten essays about the reign of Nicholas II, education, and the Mendel Beilis case; and reminiscences of Admiral A. V. Kolchak and the defeat at Omsk, 1919-20.

418 Vladimir Gavrilovich Mikhailov. Mimeographed volumes of his poetry, plus a long curriculum vitae, 1950, on his life and activity in the South American emigration.

419 Paul N. Miliukov. Papers, ca. 8 boxes. Scholar and political leader. Documents and correspondence, 1918-37, involving E. P. Dzhunkovskii, A. I. Denikin, E. Sablin, V. A. Maklakov, P. Struve, B. A. Bakhmetev, N. Astrov, S. Panina, A. I. Konovalov, V. D. Nabokov, I. Gessen, C. Crane. Documents and correspondence, 1900-1930s, of the Kadet Party, including draft programs, constitutions, reports, publications; Miliukov's speeches in exile on literature and his "Vospominaniia F. I. Rodicheva o 1917"; Miliukov's diaries for May 1918-April 1920; his memoirs, mostly published in the Chekhov edition of the memoirs, edited by M. Karpovich and B. Elkin (New York, 1955) and in the abridgement edited by A. Mendel (Political Memoirs: 1905-1917, Ann Arbor, Michigan, 1967); and a notebook relating to the Congress of Constituent Assembly Members in Paris. Restrictions.

420 Elena Aleksandrovna Miller. Papers, ca. 550 items. Miller was the widow of a former marshall of the nobility in Grodno and president of Warsaw. Family correspondence, papers of General M. D. Nechvolodov, including correspondence, reports on Civil War conditions, minutes of meetings of the Soiuz Russkikh Patriotov, ephemera of émigré political groups, monarchists, 1919-40; reports and correspondence on the Civil War, Russians fighting for Germany in World War II, the White movement, and the emigration in France; proclamations of the Kolchak government; and information about anti-Bolshevik terrorism in the USSR, 1920s-1930s, and the Orthodox Church in Russia and in exile. Restrictions.

421 Elizaveta Leonidovna Miller. Papers, ca. 3 boxes. Typed memoirs and reminiscences of St. Petersburg life, social history, women in Russia, women's education, women writers, dress, the legal system, life in France, World War II, and the emigration in South Africa, ca. 1900-60; personal correspondence, family documents, photos, and biographies of Miller's grandfather (a military engineer) and husband (a lawyer), 1860s-1920s; the Almanach de St. Petersbourg for 1911; essays on G. L. Lozinskii, his family, and works, 1900-55, including correspondence and a bibliography, typed; 4 notebooks with the handwritten diaries of Baron A. L. Frederiksen for 1938-40, in English, concerning world events; correspondence of Baron Frederiksen, Marshall Gustaf Mannerheim, late 1930s, and A. V. Romanova; notes from French police archives about terrorism and the ROVS and General E. K. Miller's abduction. Restrictions.

422 Karl Karlovich Miller. Papers, ca. 200 items. A commercial attaché in the Imperial Russian embassy in Japan. The archive contains accounts, correspondence, and reports about the liquidation of the embassy and consulates in China, Russian government financial transactions in Japan ca. 1916, and other affairs in Japan, 1920-21.

423 Nil Valentinovich Milovskii. Memoirs, signed "Aleksandr Sushkevich," about the city of Drissa on the Western Dvina during World War I, experiences in the Civil War (northwest front), the emigration in Vilno, and the Soviet and Lithuanian occupations of Vilno in 1939.

424 Catherine Chapatte Milton. 2 sections of memoirs about a childhood in Livny, family life in Perm (the father was a general), and women's education, 1900-14.

425 E. A. Milton. Part of typed memoirs of the life of her family in Moscow, 1914-17, where her father headed the Moscow Evacuation Point for wounded returning from the front in World War I.

426 Ivan N. Minishki. Memoirs, "Illiuzii ili deistvitel'nost'," 1910-40, typed, 387 pp.

427 Iurii Petrovich Miroliubov. Papers, ca. 20 items. Handwritten essays about early Russian history, religion, the Russo-Japanese War, folklore.

428 Petr Vasilevich Mironov. Papers, 2 boxes, ca. 800 items. Printed and typed documents of the Russkii Pravitel'stvennyi Komitet in London, which purchased arms for Russia in World War I, and Mironov's typed account "Boevoe snabzhenie russkoi armii v voinu 1914-1918."

429 Grigorii Grigor'evich Mitkevich. Papers, ca. 350 items. Collection of German press photos, of German armies on the eastern front in World War II, the occupation of the USSR, Russian collaboration with the Germans, and other subjects.

430 Leon Mitkiewicz. His typescript entitled "Powstanie Warszawskie w Sierpriu 1944 roku w swietle dokumentow Polskiej Misji Wojskowej w Stanach Zjednoczonych," with 40 transcribed government documents, in Polish and English. Mitkiewicz was the chief of the Polish Military Mission in the U.S. in 1944.

431 Elena Tikhonovna Mogilat. Papers, ca. 3.5 boxes, 1,260 items. Papers of this Russian language teacher at Columbia University include correspondence with students and with the Museum of Russian Cavalry and Other Services (New York), teaching materials, personal photographs, articles by and about Mogilat, and translations of Poe into Russian, 1960s-1970s.

432 Il'ia Nikitich Mokin. Papers, 1 box, ca. 350 items. Correspondence, accounts, membership lists, etc. for the émigré group Stavropol'skoe zemliachestvo (former residents of the Stavropol' region) in France, 1934-41.

433 Philip E. Mosely. Papers, ca. 24 boxes. Photos, field notes, correspondence, copies of articles, and genealogical items relating to the USSR, Eastern Europe (Soviet bloc), and China; correspondence with V. M. Chernov, ca. 1934-35; copies of letters of the British diplomatic representative in St. Petersburg, 1781; 2 boxes on the Soviet-American student exchange (profiles and projects of students, reports on the exchange from both countries, travel information), 1959-61; reports on the Germans in Eastern Europe and the USSR and on local resistance, ca. 1941; correspondence of Mosely, Svetlana Allilueva, her lawyer, and George F. Kennan; letters and reports on the 6th Dartmouth Conference in Moscow, January 1971. Restrictions.

434 A. K. Moskalenko. Materials on his acquaintance with the Chekhov-Knipper family.

435 Nataliia Murav'eva. Photocopy of "Koleso zhizni"--handwritten account of the emigration in Japan (autobiographical fiction), 1909-1950s, published in Japan in Japanese in 1969 as "Love, Revolution, and War."

436 Vitalii Il'ich Mushketov. Papers, 16 items. Typed, carbon copy of his biography, 1 p., a handwritten biography by his wife, typed notes and an album of drawings on Smolensk history (Istorii drevnego Smolenska v kartinakh, 1938).

437 V. S. Myl'nikov. Typed and handwritten manuscripts about the White Army in the southern Civil War, 1919-20.

438 Sergei Sergeevich Nabokov. Photocopies of letters from Sergei Witte to V. D. Nabokov, 1906, and from Lord Miller to Nabokov, 1918.

439 Elizaveta Alekseevna Naryshkina. Papers, 1 folder. Lady-in-waiting to the Empress Alexandra Fedorovna. Her diary, written in 1917, describes the moods of the tsar and tsarina, political personalities, reactions of court circles to domestic affairs, and the impact of World War I. Part only of the diary was published in the last chapter of her book Under Three Tsars (New York, 1931). The diary is typed in French.

440 Nikolai Dmitrevich Nelidov. Papers, ca. 87 items. Material about émigré political activities in France and youth organizations, 1920s; and documents on anti-communist and anti-Makhno movements in the northern Crimea, 1919-20.

441 Vladimir Ivanovich Nemirovich-Danchenko. Papers, ca. 30 items. His letters to Dr. Vladimir Veinberg, 1933-37, and to Nikolai Alexeev about the Soviet theater.

442 Lia I. Neustroeva. Her typed memoirs, in English, of life in Russian banking circles, ca. 1900-17.

443 Andrei Gennadevich Nevzorov. Papers, ca. 1 box, ca. 410 items. Handwritten essays on the 1905 Revolution and World War I; typed "Vospominaniya, 1918 g." by D. M. Mikhailov on the Siberian Civil War; materials relating to World War I and the Leib gvardii 3-ii strelkovyi polk; items concerning Russian émigré veterans' organizations; and Nevzorov's manuscript "O staroi russkoi armii," about his own military education and the tsarist army in World War I.

444 Vasilii Petrovich Nikitin. Papers, 19 boxes. Nikitin (1885-1960) was a diplomat, economist, and scholar of oriental languages and history. His diary and memoirs concern diplomatic service in northern Persia, 1911-19. Correspondents include the Soviet committee for return to the homeland, 1956-59, M. Aldanov, V. A. Maklakov, B. E. Nolde, P. N. Miliukov, P. E. Kovalevskii, N. Evreinov, Baron M. A. Taube. Other holdings: drafts for books on Cossack history and the writer A. M. Remizov; family history and correspondence; all of his published work; reminiscences and autobiographical writings; and documents of Petr Aleksandrovich Nikitin (d. 1912), a high tsarist official in Poland before 1914, including diaries.

445 A. M. Nikolaev. Papers, ca. 15 boxes. A military agent at the tsarist embassy in the U.S. Telegrams, 1916-19; arms supply data, reports, historical data in 1917; correspondence of tsarist agents in the U.S., 1917-20, and with émigré military organizations, 1920s; 2 notebooks with handwritten reminiscences of N. K. Borshchevskii, Nikolaev's father-in-law, an estate manager, and on the Revolution, 1917-18; petitions of American citizens to join the Russian army in World War I; a diary for the year 1915 (at the London embassy); memoirs for 1921-23 in the U.S. emigration; typed transcripts of V. O. Kliuchevskii's 1899 history lectures on the 11th-18th c.; manuscripts on Napoleon in 1812, A. Suvorov, World War I, and the Civil War; correspondence 1944-45. Restrictions.

446 Konstantin Nikolaevich Nikolaev. Papers, ca. 115 items. Part of his typed memoirs on the Revolution and Civil War, late 1917-20; memoirs of others on General Kornilov; Nikolaev's autobiographical writings for the years 1919-45 in the emigration, typed; typed memoirs/reminiscences of the Civil War, General L. Kornilov, White armies, military units in Serbia, ROVS and its history in the 1920s and 1930s, the emigration in Yugoslavia, and World War II; and correspondence and reports relating to an émigré jurists organization that Nikolaev headed in the U.S., 1950s-1960s. Restrictions.

447 N. N. Nikolaev. Papers, 1 box. Kadet, deputy to the fourth state duma. Papers include items gathered for his biography about work in the fourth duma, the Kadet Party, and his service with the Russian Mutual Aid Society in the U.S. Other materials: his poems; essays on Russian liberalism, G. Rasputin, and the Civil War in the Kuban area; correspondence; typed notes on the Provisional Government, Civil War, émigré politics, and the emigration in the United States.

448 Boris Nikolaevskii. An anonymous typed manuscript about the USSR 1939-45, army service, and the Vlasov movement, "V doliakh za rodinu i za Stalina."

449 Boris Aleksandrovich Nikol'skii. Papers, ca. 12 boxes. A commercial counselor in the Stockholm Russian embassy before 1914; after the war he was active in right-wing émigré activities and founded the Russian Christian Labor Movement. Included are correspondence and reports relating to the Russian Christian Labor Movement, 1930-41.

450 Iu. A. Nikol'skii. Papers, ca. 50 items. Papers of this literary critic include articles on A. A. Fet and I. S. Turgenev, copies of Fet-Turgenev correspondence, articles on enlightened absolutism, and a copy of a letter of Nicholas II.

451 B. I. Nil'skii. Typed sketches on daily life in the Soviet Union and political persecution, 1930-40.

452 M. Nilskii. "Pobeg," about Soviet labor camps, 1920-41, typescript, 266 pp.

453 Boris Nol'de. An essay, in French, on Russian foreign policy and diplomatic history, 1700-1940: "Questions russes," typed.

454 Aleksandr Leonidovich Nosovich. Papers, ca. 13 items. 3 essays with reminiscences of military life and photos of Nosovich in uniform, ca. 1900-20.

455 Taras Novak. Papers, 6 boxes, ca. 110 items. Typed, handwritten, and mimeographed writings largely on physics.

456 Mikhail M. Novikov. Papers, ca. 8 boxes. Novikov, a biologist, was rector of Moscow University in 1919-20. His typed curriculum vitae and memoirs cover his youth, education, early academic career in biology at Moscow, and the emigration. There are also lectures, handwritten and typed, correspondence, a handwritten summary of his work, 1876-1911, photos of Russian scientists, and his works.

457 Mariia Georg'evna Novitskaia. Papers, ca. 3 boxes. Correspondence, reports, photographs, biographical information and reminiscences of her father, Georgii Shavel'skii, a priest for the Imperial family, and on such topics as the Orthodox Church in emigration.

458 Evgenii Fedorovich Novitskii. Papers, ca. 20 items. Letters of General A. Lampe, S. Sollogub, G. Siunnerberg, and a handwritten account of the 1914 Battle of Lublin.

459 Evgenii Isakevich Novitskii. Papers, ca. 40 items. Letters of A. and P. Kartashev, and Novitskii, copies; émigré press articles on political and church affairs (Holy Trinity Monastery, New Jersey).

460 Vera Vasilevna Onoprienko. Papers, ca. 60 items. Her family's archives for 1827-1914 contain correspondence, photos, and documents about army careers and the Russo-Turkish War of 1877-78.

461 Georgii Aleksandrovich Orlov. Papers, 1 box. Diaries for 1918-21, typescript, 400 pp.; poems; correspondence, 1948-64; a typed essay on General P. N. Wrangel; and other items about the Civil War, military history, and the emigration. Orlov was a representative in Prague of the survivors of the Gallipoli campaign and an associate of Generals Wrangel and A. P. Kutepov.

462 Mikhail Petrovich Osipov (Ossipoff). Papers, ca. 3 boxes, ca. 2,220 items. Materials on the Russian Civil War and ROVS activities in the West, 1918-1940s; papers of the Soiuz kavalerov imperatorskago voennago ordena Sv. V. i P. Georgiia i georgievskago oruzhiia; soldiers' memoirs from World War I and Civil War; manuscript of a novel about Soviet refugees following World War II; publications of émigré military groups; and some documents relating to the White armies 1918-23.

463 Osobyi komitet po delam russkim v Finliandii. Papers, ca. 3 boxes, ca. 2,000 items. Correspondence, reports, minutes, accounts, etc. of this committee and of the Soiuz predstavitelei promyshlennosti i torgovli and the northwestern White Army and government of General N. Iudenich (including correspondence of Iudenich, A. V. Kartashev, A. N. Fenu, V. A. Maklakov, and M. Girs; printed transcript of the 1881 trial of A. Zheliabov; a Russian consular code book; autobiography of General M. G. Cherniaev; memoirs of E. F. von Mendt, a Finnish baron serving the Imperial family before 1917. Restrictions.

464 Dmitrii Kondratevich Ovdenko. Papers, 17 items. Notebooks with handwritten, semi-fictional reminiscences about Russian courts, the legal profession, Odessa, student life, the Jewish question, city administration, and the Paris emigration, 1900-early 1920s, by this émigré jurist.

465 Nikolai Aleksandrovich Palchevskii. Papers, ca. 95 items. Handwritten diary about Russian POWs in France, 1918-20; personal documents and correspondence, from before and during the years of emigration in France, 1910-50.

466 Sofiia Vladimirovna Panina. Papers, ca. 12 boxes. Contains much material on the Kadet Party in the Civil War, 1917-21, including protocols of the central committee; reports of local party conferences; manuscripts, papers, and correspondence of F. F. Kokoshkin, F. I. Rodichev, V. D. Nabokov, M. M. Vinaver, P. N. Miliukov, and other Kadet leaders; correspondence of Count Nikita Panin and other Panins, 1714-1801; family photos and letters from the 19th c.; the countess' speeches about émigré culture and her trial by the Bolsheviks in 1917; correspondence of N. I. Astrov, General A. I. Denikin, and Mrs. Ksenia Denikina (1919-46); N. I. Astrov's manuscripts, his memoirs, letters, and biographical notes; data on Russian education and women's education, pre-1917; and information about Moscow administration.

467 Oleg Pantiukhov. Founder, in 1914, of the Russkie Skouty-Razvedchiki. Letter dated ca. 1909.

468 S. D. Pavlov. 3 photographs from 1903-04 (1 of a military unit in the Russo-Japanese War, the other 2 of people on ships); and 2 broadsides--"Portmutskii traktat" (n.d. but ca. 1905) and another on the death of Nicholas II's uncle Vladimir Aleksandrovich in 1909.

469 Sergei Ivanovich Pavlov. Papers, ca. 200 items. Includes Sergei Gubinskii's typescript Moia Rossiia (Harbin, 1929), which discusses Russian literature; information on the emigration in Greece.

470 Vasili E. Pavlov. Papers, ca. 18 items. Notebooks with handwritten memoirs about Pavlov's youth and the Civil War, 1900-72.

471 Vera Nikolaevna Pavlovskaia. Handwritten manuscripts about the St. Catherine Academy for the education of young women in Moscow, where she studied, with photographs.

472 Petr Vasilevich Petrashin. Short, handwritten essays on the USSR, secret police, prisons, World War II, and foreign trade, 1939-45. Restrictions.

473 Rafail R. Petrov. "Dagestanskii konnyi polk, 1916-17" and "6 let voiny," about World War I and the Civil War, both handwritten, and "Aleksandrovskii khuzarskii polk."

474 Sofia Borisovna Pilenko. Papers, ca. 77 items. Part of typed family memoirs, "Moi vospominaniia," about politics and culture in the reigns of Alexander I, Nicholas I, and Alexander II, 1820-80; 11 manuscripts by Mother Mariia (Elizaveta Skobtsova), Pilenko's daughter, on the Revolution and the emigration; a biography of Mother Mariia, recounting her arrest and execution by the Nazis in France, 1943, typed, 4 pp.; poetry, religious essays, drawings, and notes on Russian authors (P. Chaadaev, N. Danilevskii) by Mother Mariia.

475 V. K. Pilkin. Papers, ca. 1 box, ca. 600 items. The admiral's papers include financial records of émigré naval organizations, 1920-25 (in Finland) and of the ship "Kitoboi" (1920), plus material on the Civil War in the Northwest. Restrictions.

476 Elena Sergeevna Pil'skaia. Papers, ca. 15 items. Typed essay in literary criticism (on Russian authors) and memoirs/reminiscences, handwritten and typed, about her husband and the Russian theater ca. 1860s-1920s. Pil'skaia was an actress at one time.

477 Richard Pipes. Typed copy of a report by Philip Makhardze to the central committee of Soviet Georgia, 6 December 1921; correspondence and notes on this report.

478 Aleksandr Alekseevich Pleshcheev. Papers, ca. 30 items. Essays and correspondence on the theater and ballet and clippings of Pleshcheev's articles, 1908-1940s.

479 P. A. Pletnev. Sections of his memoirs, written in quasi-novel form: "Den' v Peterburge," "U moria," and "Den' v Gaage," ca. 1900-40, about life in St. Petersburg and in the emigration (Netherlands).

480 N. V. Plevitskaia. Handwritten memoirs, in notebooks, of childhood and the start of her career as a singer, ca. 1890-1916.

481 Aleksei Ivanovich Pliushkov. Papers, ca. 1 box. His stories, verse, and novels; essay and photo of his father, a doctor who treated Maksim Gorkii; memoirs of A. A. Blok, E. P. Ivanov, and their circle; typed essays on S. Esenin, Soviet lawyers, L. Andreev, St. Petersburg, music, and the Revolution.

482 S. E. Plotnikov. "Nikolaevskoe Voennoe Inzhenerskoe Uchilishche," covering the years 1900-17, handwritten, 187 pp.

483 Aleksandr Abramovich Poliakov. Papers, ca. 100 items. Correspondence, 1930s-1950s, with P. Miliukov, Don Aminado, M. Aldanov, I. Bunin, A. Kuprin, and M. Tsvetaeva. Poliakov worked for Miliukov's Poslednie novosti and then Novoe Russkoye Slovo.

484 Vladimir Ivanovich Poliakov. Papers, ca. 107 items. Correspondence on military topics; handwritten reminiscences of the years 1903-45 and handwritten essays about various Russian topics.

485 I. F. Polianin. Papers, ca. 10 items. Short typed and handwritten essays on the Bulgarian emigration, World War I, and the Civil War, 1914-1920s, based on personal reminiscences.

486 Aleksandr Nikolaevich Polianskii. Papers, 12 items. Handwritten memoirs of his service in the Russian Corps in Yugoslavia (founded by the Germans) and of World War II; a photo and 8 typed letters from General A. P. Kutepov, 1920s, about the Bolshevik threat and the emigration; and a manuscript in Russian concerning life in Nizhnii Novgorod and the Volga steamers ca. 1900.

487 Mikhail Pavlovich Polivanov. Handwritten essays on Soviet higher education and universities 1919-42.

488 Boris N. Polozov. Essays on military life 1906-13 and the army in the Transcaucasus.

489 Andrei Fedorovich Ponomarev. Papers, ca. 2 boxes. Materials on the history and émigré activities of the Don Cossacks; correspondence and serial publications relating to the Tersk Cossack army and the Tiflis Kadets Corps, 1920s-1930s, plus more information about the Tiflis Corps 1890-1960.

490 Elena Antonovna Popandopulo. Papers, ca. 25 items. Handwritten memoirs of General A. N.

Shuberskii, in 6 notebooks; an essay on Nicholas II; and copies of 6 reports on Russian transportation in the 1830s.

491 Aleksandr Popov. Papers, 1 box. Paris antique dealer. Accounts, bills, and correspondence plus photos of Russian icons and old furniture, 1924-39.

492 Claudio Iosifovich Popov. Typed essays about his family (descended from a factory serf), the Vlasov movement, and the language of the Russian émigrés, ca. 1850-1950.

493 Grigorii Efimovich Popov. His memoirs of childhood in Tomsk and life in Mongolia, where he worked for a Russian company (much detail is on the life style of Mongolians), ca. 1901-21.

494 Vladimir Vladimirovich Popov (Popoff). Papers, ca. 5 boxes. Includes the archives of the Soiuz Byvshikh Sudebnykh Deiatelei Rossii (minutes of meetings, membership lists, reports, correspondence, accounts), 1925-68; his typed "Vospominaniia 1889-1957." Apparently a lawyer in Odessa before 1917, he was an associate of the Grand Duke Nikolai Nikolaevich, P. N. Wrangel, and E. K. Miller in the emigration. Also reminiscences of S. Matsylev, A. Dzhuliani, A. Lebedev, A. Derevitskii, and others; typed report for General E. K. Miller, P. N. Wrangel's chief of staff, 1922, on the Bulgarian political situation and difficulties the White armies might have in being received there; and handwritten "Vospominaniia matrosa sluzhby 1914 goda" by Trofim Isidorovich Gonoratskii (1932), in 11 notebooks, concerning naval education, the navy, and the Revolution, 1914-21.

495 Vera Aleksandrovna Popova. Handwritten family and personal memoirs: "Popovskaia khronika," ca. 1900-1920s, about a Moscow textile merchant family, Popova (a sculptress), and the Paris emigration, her life, contacts in the art world, the theater, etc., and a biography of her cousin, P. S. Popov, a Soviet philosopher.

496 Natalia Ivanovna Potresova. Papers, 4 boxes, ca. 1,400 items. The archives of the Soviet and émigré journalist Sergei Viktorovich Iablonskii (Potresov) include 3 albums of clippings of his newspaper articles about cultural and political questions, 1920-50, drafts, typed and handwritten, of his articles about literature, the theater, and other topics; album entries written by K. Bal'mont, I. Bunin, I. Bilibin, and others, 1908-1920s, and correspondence of A. Remizov, A. Kuprin, I. Shmelev, N. Teffi, V. Nemirovich-Danchenko, and I. Bunin. Restrictions.

497 Stoyan Pribichevich. 6 rolls of microfilm contain documents from the Czech Ministry of Foreign Affairs concerning the history of the Communist Party of Czechoslovakia, Balkan history and diplomacy, Yugoslav history, and Czech history, ca. 1939-45. Restrictions.

498 Nikolai Prokof'ev-Pylaev. "Zheltye zvezdy"--a typescript on World War II and experiences in the Vlasov movement, 1941-43.

499 Ekaterina Dmitreevna and Sergei Nikolaevich Prokopovich. Papers, ca. 6 boxes. 2 photo albums of such émigré figures as P. N. Miliukov, E. D. Kuskova-Prokopovich, M. A. Osorgin, A. I. Guchkov, and M. A. Aldanov, ca. 1900-55; some 95 manuscripts by S. N. Prokopovich on economic topics, published and unpublished. Restrictions.

500 Vasilii Mikhailovich Pronin. Papers, 15 items. Typed, 64 pp., and handwritten, 10 pp., manuscript on General M. V. Alekseev, World War I, and the Revolution, 1916-17; typed essays ("General Lavr G. Kornilov" and "Miting Gen. Brusilova"); handwritten autobiography, 5 pp.; handwritten manuscripts on the administration of émigré affairs in Serbia, 1941-44, Trotskii assassination plans, 1929, and Russian émigrés in Yugoslavia, 1920-40.

501 Lidia Aleksandrovna Protich. Her memoirs of marriage to a pre-1914 Serbian diplomat, typed, in French.

502 T. Protoponov. Military nurse. Memoirs describe her training, service in World War I, the Revolution and Civil War in the South, and the evacuation of the Crimea by White forces, ca. 1912-22, bound in 2 folders.

503 D. V. Pruzhan. A short, handwritten biography of the ethnographer A. Efimenko (1848-1918), and 2 portraits, one of the daughter of the poet V. Zhukovskii.

504 Boris I. Puzanov. Typed memoirs in several parts (1960): "Iz vospominanii sledovatelia po delu massovykh ubiistv v Evpatorii v Ianv. 1918 g." concerning Bolshevik summary trials for naval officers and well-to-do citizens, 23 pp.; "Moya zhizn'," 57 pp., about childhood in Eupatoria, law study at Kharkov, Odessa career (1909), evacuation from Eupatoria to Constantinople in 1920; the emigration in Yugoslavia, World War II, and finally, life in France and Belgium.

505 Ol'ga Rachinskaia. Her personal memoirs of childhood in Samara, education, pre-1917 Simbirsk, Moscow life under the Soviet regime in the 1930s, and the emigration, ca. 1900-77.

506 A. N. Radishchev. 1 vol., bound, handwritten copy of the Puteshestvie, retitled Kniga prichinivshaia neschastii, n.d.

507 Marc Raeff. Typed copy of an unpublished manuscript by A. E. Nolde--a biography of M. M.

Speransky, 239 pp.; and a photocopy of a 1783 document of Catherine II, rewarding a subject for his service.

508 S. Raev. Manuscript entitled ". . . I v Khrista i v Boga . . ." concerns his experience in Soviet concentration camps.

509 A. Rakhalov. "Zhemchuzhina zapoliariia"--a typescript about Soviet camps in the Polar region, 1930s.

510 Irina Sergeevna Rakhmaninova-Volkonskaia. Papers, ca. 100 items. Correspondence, 1950-68, from Ivan Bunin, 3 letters, 1948-49, Eugene Ormandy, Vladimir Horowitz, Leopold Stokowski, Sviatoslav Richter, Friz Kreisler, Emil Gilels, Vladimir Ashkenazy, and others.

511 Grigorii Efimovich Rasputin. Part of a letter written by him, original and photocopy, n.d.

512 Sergei Il'ich Razhev. Pages from his memoirs, particularly on experiences in post-World War II Soviet "kontslagery."

513 Nikolai Rebrov. Handwritten "Kratkaia biografiia moego zhiznennogo puti s 1914 goda" (1956).

514 E. M. Reeve. Memoirs, in English, of the Revolution and Civil War.

515 Nikolai Aleksandrovich Reimers. Professor. A short, handwritten biography with his photo; a philosophical pamphlet by him; and bibliographies of his scholarly work.

516 Iurii Aleksandrovich Reingardt. Typed essays/reminiscences of the Civil War and biographies of various generals, ca. 1890-1920s.

517 Aleksei Mikhailovich Remizov. Papers, 2 boxes. Writer. Literary manuscripts in various stages of preparation (Podstrizhennymi glazami [reminiscences], Pliashushchii demon, Kochevnik, Iveren', Shurum-burum, and others), dating from the 1930s to the 1950s; notebooks with ideas, lists of foreign authors, bibliographic references, etc.; 3 letters of Gorkii to Remizov, 1922-23; and miscellanea, including a letter draft to B. K. Zaitsev about his literary activity. Helene Sinany has published an excellent guide to this (and 5 related collections): "Archives de l'Université de Columbia (New York) relatives à Aleksej Remizov," Cahiers du Monde russe et soviétique, XVII (I), Jan.-Mar. 1976, pp. 113-23.

518 Andrei Mitronovich Rennikov. Papers, ca. 25 items. Correspondence, 1914-1950s. Journalist. Restrictions.

519 A. Repin. Photocopies of chapters of a work on the organization of the NKVD ca. 1930-40, typed.

520 F. P. Rerberg. Papers, ca. 14 items. Copies of a mimeographed speech delivered on the anniversary of the death of the Grand Duchess Ol'ga Aleksandrovna; information on emigration in Turkey and Egypt.

521 N. F. Rerberg. Typescript on the Russo-Japanese War by a participant and member of an investigating commission on the war, ca. 350 pp.

522 Research Program on the History of the CPSU. Papers, ca. 8.5 boxes. Materials on the history of the Communist Party of the Soviet Union, Soviet politics, and social history; typed accounts from former Soviet citizens; a list of all the essays, authors, and titles in this collection; and L. L. Sabaneev manuscripts on the Revolution and social freedom in the USSR.

523 Research Program on the USSR. Papers, over 54 boxes. Mimeographed and typed reports by Soviet émigrés on Soviet domestic life, the nationalities, Stalinism, the economy, and World War II, 1920s-1950s, with a list of holdings by subject. These items were published in 1952. Also, ca. 25 organizational charts of the Soviet secret police and security Organs (NKVD, KGB, etc.) 1945-60.

524 Sergei Nikolaevich Riasnianskii. Papers, ca. 20 boxes. Head of ROVS in the U.S. Includes personal and ROVS correspondence of the 1950s-1960s; correspondence, photos, and other materials on émigré military organizations (including ROVS) and the Russkii Politicheskii Komitet, 1950s-1960s; and information on military history. Restrictions.

525 Fedor Izmailovich Rodichev. Papers, 28 boxes. Zemstvo leader and Kadet liberal. Personal and political correspondence; political documents; copies of letters relating to the family of A. I. Herzen; account books; essays, for example, on refugees in the Crimea in 1920; correspondence, 1920s-1930s, with George Vernadskii, I. I. and A. Petrunkevich, Countess S. Panina, V. Maklakov, N. I. Astrov, A. V. Kartashev, Natalie Herzen; autobiographical and biographical information, plus memoirs, of Rodichev, 1900-1920s (duma career, youth); his speeches in the duma; handwritten copies, in French, of correspondence between Alexander and Natalie Herzen before their marriage. Restrictions.

526 Liubov Vasilevna Roehr (Rer). Carbon copy of Count V. N. Kokovtsev's memoirs of childhood and lycée education, ca. 1860-90.

527 Andrei Iakovlevich Romankevich. Short reminiscences of a childhood in rural Russia, student life in Moscow in the Revolution, the Ukraine during the Civil War, the Polish emigration, arrest and imprisonment by the Soviet regime in World War II, and exit from the USSR as part of General Anders's Polish army.

528 Elena Petrovna Romanov. Papers, ca. 10 items. Text, in French, typed carbon, of memoirs by Duchess Helene of Serbia, daughter of King Paul, who married the Russian Duke Ioan Konstantinovich, son of the Grand Duke Konstantin Konstantinovich.

529 Vera Meletovna Romanovich. Typed and handwritten memoirs about life and military affairs in the Don region, particularly the Civil War, 1914-20; and information about Viktor Sevskii and journalism.

530 Maria Ronseval. Typescript by Mariia Belozoskaia--"Na strashnyi sud istorii: Delo Anny Akhmatovoi," smuggled out of the USSR ca. 1951 and concerning events in 1946.

531 Ernest C. Ropes. Papers, ca. 35 items. Correspondence relating to his efforts to start courses on the USSR and an Institute of Slavic Studies in the U.S. in the 1940s; a diary for 1919-20 on the administration of Russian refugee relief in Estonia and Arkhangel'sk; a photo album; and a typescript by Ropes, "The Russia I Have Known," about the Soviet Union, based on his visits there in 1938 and 1946.

532 Ekaterina Nikolaevna Roshchina-Insarova. Papers, ca. 1 box, ca. 300 items. The prominent Russian actress's memoirs (and autobiographical essays) of childhood, her professional career before and after the Revolution; A. Pleshcheev's biography of her; correspondence with prominent cultural figures, including N. A. Teffi, 1922-51, ca. 50 letters, Boris Bakhmetev, K. Balmont, V. Bunina, M. N. Benois, V. Burtsev, O. Dymov, N. N. Evreinov, G. Grebenshchikov, A. Grechaninov, A. Kuprin, N. Kedrov, and S. Iablonovskii; theater programs; a memoir on V. Meierhold's staging of Lermontov's Maskarad in February 1917.

533 Ksenia Nikolaevna Rossolimo. Papers, 4 boxes, ca. 1,200 items. Typed excerpts from a diary for 1891-1923, part or all of which has been published; drawings and photographs; personal documents; business and other correspondence, mostly from 1948-53, with such figures as Professor M. Karpovich, R. Gul, V. Bunina, and B. Unbegaun.

534 Vasilii V. Rozanov (1856-1919). Literary critic, publicist, and philosopher. 5 letters written by him, with typed transcripts, 1918, and 2 envelopes.

535 A. N. Rozenshil'd-Paulin. Memoirs of this general, who commanded the 29th Infantry Division, concern military operations of the Russian army in Eastern Prussia, 1914-15.

536 Aleksandr Nikolaevich Rozhdestvenskii. Papers, ca. 130 items. Information on A. N. Silin; Rozhdestvenskii's memoirs about his service in the Ministry of Justice in the Caucasus before and during the Revolution, World War I (especially in the Caucasus) and the emigration; an account of his research in Venezuela on General Francisco de Miranda, a Latin American revolutionary who went to Russia for aid in the reign of Catherine II; photos; correspondence; a typescript about Rozhdestvenskii's 10 years in the Caucasus procurator's office.

537 Lev Stepanovich Rubanov. Papers, ca. 15 items. Typed essays/reminiscences about the Revolution and the Civil War in the South, 1917-20; later writings on Russian/Soviet political questions; and materials on the Soviet committee "Za vozvrashchenie na rodinu," 1957.

538 Iakov L'vovich Rubinshtein. His speech honoring V. A. Maklakov and the latter's refugee work, 1917-1920s, typed copy.

539 Vasilii Nikolaevich Rudskii. Copy of "Kratkii otchet o rabote otdela Dezhurnogo Generala Shtaba Osoboi Armii so vremeni eia sformirovaniia do 1 fevralia 1918," 1916-18.

540 N. S. Rusanov. "K istorii mirnoi kampanii sovetskoi demokratii sredi evropeiskikh sotsialnykh partii"--a typescript on World War I, the socialist movement, and the Stockholm Conference, 1918.

541 Russian Civil War Memoir. Photocopies of a fragment of a typed memoir about the Civil War in Tambov province, the forces of Antonov, and the peasants' role in the fighting.

542 Russkaia Mysl'. Papers, ca. 40 items. Paris-based émigré publication. A leaflet--"K russkomu narodu"--from 1918 with an appeal by Western ambassadors, information about the Allied intervention, texts of exchanges with Soviet foreign minister G. Chicherin; and letters to the editors, 1950-56.

543 Russkii Obshche-Voinskii Soiuz (Paris) (ROVS). Records, 1919-72, mostly from the 1930s, ca. 156 boxes. Correspondence with other organizations; information on members and other branches (in Poland, England, Sweden, Yugoslavia, Norway, Denmark, Holland, Finland, Belgium, Czechoslovakia, France, and the Far East); financial reports; reports on the USSR; and publications. Restrictions.

544 V. Ryndin. Handwritten manuscript entitled "Rabota NKVD," ca. 115 pp., including an organizational scheme and a description of the work of the Soviet secret police in the 1930s.

545 S. E. Rynkevich. Handwritten memoirs about the Russo-Turkish War: "Voina 1877-1878."

546 Zinaida Aleksandrovna Rzhevskaia. Sections of handwritten memoirs about life and thought in St. Petersburg high society, World War I, and G. Rasputin, 1914-18.

547 V. N. Rzhevskii. Manuscripts about his life, Nicholas II's death, and the Revolution, ca. 1907-60.

548 Leonid L. Sabaneev. Papers, ca. 2 boxes. Historian of Russian and Soviet music. Typed essays on revolutionary events, personalities, 1917-20; articles and pamphlets by Sabaneev; 4 letters from A. Glazunov, A. Grechaninov, and K. Medtner; books by various authors, including Sabaneev, on Russian music, ca. 1920-50.

549 Evgenii Vasil'evich Sablin. Papers, ca. 49 boxes. Last Russian diplomatic representative in London before the Bolsheviks took power. Contains some of the archive of the former Imperial embassy in London for 1886-90 and 1919-ca. 1930.

550 Georgii Mitrofanovich Sadovskii. Papers, ca. 52 items. Typed essays/reminiscences concerning his work on one of the Stolypin land reform commissions, the Civil War, Vitebsk in the early years of Soviet administration, his imprisonment by the Cheka, emigration ("Latvia, 1921-39"), and life in Germany and Brazil.

551 Elena Vladimirovna Safonov. Personal documents of Safonova (nee Bystrova) and her husband, M. S. Safonov, 1912-20.

552 Konstantin V. Sakharov. General. Books, in German, about the Kolchak campaign and the Czech legion; 2 biographies by his wife and a bibliography of the general's works; and his typed essay "Die Herrgottsbienen."

553 Vladimir Vladimirovich Sakharov. Papers, 12 boxes, 1926-43. Art historian. Materials for a comprehensive dictionary of Russian art and artists from the 10th c. to the 1930s, in 50 notebooks with handwritten notes; manuscripts on individual painters; catalogues of exhibits in London, Paris, and elsewhere; Sakharov's diaries for 1932-42; a 1924 list of émigré artists, arranged by geographical location, with many addresses. Restrictions.

554 Iurii K. Sakhno-Ustimovich. Papers, 3 boxes, ca. 10 items. General. Typed memoirs of the Russian army in World War I, political decay of tsarism, the Revolution and Civil War, particularly the Polish and Rumanian fronts, the Volunteer Army in the South, General A. Denikin, and the Ukraine, ca. 1914-20.

555 Vladimir N. Salatko. Parts of typed memoirs for the period 1920-40 ("Zapiski sovetskogo advokata"), concerning the Soviet legal profession and system.

556 Valerii F. Salatko-Petrishche. Papers, ca. 220 items. A short reminiscence of I. S. Turgenev (author unidentified), ca. 1900; typed reminiscences by Salatko-Petrishche of prerevolutionary Russian society, the Chinese emigration, and the Orthodox Church in Russia and the emigration, ca. 1910-1950s. Restrictions.

557 Boris Markovich Sarach. Papers, ca. 412 items. Correspondence, 1930s-1950s, partly copies, with and about N. P. Vakar, the early days of the German occupation of Paris in 1940, and the Ob"edinenie russkikh adokatov vo Frantsii (with biographical data on members in questionnaires for the French police); documents; and 2 pamphlets/reports of the Moscow "Kollegiia zashchitnikov" about Soviet jurisprudence, 1922-23.

558 Il'ia Grigorevich Savchenko. Papers, ca. 17 boxes. Memoirs of the V. V. Andreev balalaika orchestra by Prince P. A. Obolenskii; Savchenko's memoirs; the archive of the Russian Juridical Faculty in Prague, 400 pp.; the archive of the Soiuz ob"edinenii russkikh okonchivshikh vysshie uchebnykh zavedeniia (OROVUZ), which Savchenko headed, 1,200 pp., 1925-32; 2 handwritten essays by a Kuban Cossack officer in the White movement on the Civil War in the South, 1917-18; and correspondence with such prominent émigré cultural figures as Ivan Bilibin, I. A. Bunin, A. T. Grechaninov, A. I. Denikin, V. I. Nemirovich-Danchenko, F. I. Shaliapin, Lev Shestov, S. and G. D. Grebenshchikov, ca. 200 letters from the 1940s, and I. S. Shmelev.

559 Dormidont Matveevich Savin. Papers, ca. 26 notebooks. Writings on history, moral values, science, and religion.

560 Petr Panteleimonovich Savin. Papers, ca. 110 items. Materials on General E. K. Miller's death in 1937; and correspondence concerning research on politics and Soviet infiltration of émigré monarchist-military organizations, 1920s-1960s.

561 B. V. Savinkov. Papers, ca. 5.5 boxes. Documents, correspondence, financial accounts, minutes of meetings, proclamations, reminiscences, and newspapers relating to the history and activity of the Socialist Revolutionary Party in Russia and in exile, ca. 1890s-1920s. Holdings include a letter of E. Azef, seals of the SR Party abroad, a large photo of and letters to S. P. Postnikov, and 10 photos of such revolutionary figures as A. Herzen, N. Ogarev, and E. Breshkovskaia. Restrictions.

562 Vera V. Savitskaia. Typescript about women's gimnaziia, founded in St. Petersburg by Princess A. A. Obolenskaia, and "Moi vospominaniia," about Savitskaia's family and the Russian gentry, ca. 1830-1931.

563 Andrei Kazimirovich Savitskii. Papers, ca. 180 items. Engineer. Mimeographed and handwritten materials of the Obshchestvo liubitelei russkoi voennoi stariny (Paris), 1944-1960s, about Russian military history; his writings, typed, on military history and

Alexander I; his memoirs: "Isskustvo v moei zhizni"; documents and other items of K. A. Savitskii, his father, who was chairman of the Northern Donets Railroad, ca. 1907-20, concerning the Revolution and Civil War.

564 Semen Konstantinovich Sazhin. Medical doctor. Curriculum vitae and his collected essays, on such topics as the University of Kazan, Russian medicine, general medical questions, philosophical problems, and his arrest and imprisonment in China in 1954.

565 Leonid Seifulin (Seifullin). Typed memoirs of his military career and World War I, 1900-17.

566 Vladimir Ivanovich Sekara. Papers, over 1 box. Memoirs: "Smotr kavaleriiskoi divizii generala Barbovicha v Krymu" and another memoir on Sekara's capture by the Red Army during the Civil War in the South and his escape; anecdotes about meetings with British military men in World War I.

567 K. V. Semchevskii. Papers, ca. 30 items. Memoirs describing childhood in the Caucasus, education and service in the Imperial Corps of Pages (with some history of the latter), service in the Imperial Horse Guards before and during World War I, the February Revolution at the front, and emigration in the Far East, the U.S., Germany, and Austria; and documents.

568 Viktor Ivanovich Semenov. Notebooks with diaries for September-December 1939, when Semenov was in Warsaw, describing the German invasion and occupation.

569 Nikolai Dmitrevich Semenov-Tian-Shanskii. Typed memoirs about service with the Imperial family, 1903-14.

570 V. P. Semenov-Tian-Shanskii. Papers, ca. 500 items. Handwritten and typed memoirs--"Stranitsy semeinoi khroniki" (1800-1917), about the ancestors of his father, P. P. Semenov-Tian-Shanskii; manuscripts on V. Semenov-Tian-Shanskii's activities in the Finnish emigration, 1920s; an essay by Z. Gippius, 1930; Semenov-Tian-Shanskii's lectures in emigration; diary for 1941-44, handwritten and typed, by Semenov-Tian-Shanskii's son on the Russo-Finnish War and the son's letters, 1941; typed excerpts of a diary, 1917-19; and correspondence. Restrictions.

571 Viacheslav G. Seniutovich. Papers, ca. 133 items. Handwritten and typed essays on Ukrainian history and political situation, and other historical topics; and mimeographed memoirs of Seniutovich's father, 1921-22.

572 Aleksandr Vasil'evich Serapinin. Papers, ca. 40 items. Writings about religion and the Orthodox Church in Australia; a memoir-history ("Vozdushnaia gvardiia") about early Russian aviation history and his service as a military aviator in World War I and the Civil War.

573 Metropolitan Seraphim (Lukianov). Handwritten memoirs, 1879-1950, entitled "Moi vospominaniia. Istoriia moei zhizni."

574 A. N. Serebrennikova. Worked in the Siberian Provisional Government, emigrated to China. Biography and autobiography, 1882-1953.

575 B. V. Sergeevskii. Papers, 1.5 boxes, ca. 500 items. Officer in the Russian air force in World War I. Includes his autobiography (World War I, the Revolution and Civil War); reminiscences of others about him; ca. 70 of his military documents, 1916-21, in Russian, English, French, and Ukrainian; and correspondence with various émigré organizations (ROVS, Cossacks, etc.).

576 Father Innokentii Seryshev. Papers, ca. 7 boxes. Memoirs and autobiographical writings concerning Japan and Siberia before 1917, Japan and China in the early 1920s, and émigré life in Australia, 1922-66; correspondence with figures in the Esperanto movement.

577 Ivan Mikhailovich Shadrin. Notebook with handwritten description of the Imperial Court Choir; other writings concerning the Romanovs, 1900-17; and handwritten memoirs about service in the reserves in World War I, the 1917 Revolution at the front, the Civil War in the South, evacuation from the Crimea, and the emigration in northern Africa, 1914-28.

578 Vladimir Ivanovich Shaiditskii. Papers, ca. 120 items. The official historian of the Vsezarubezhnoe ob"edinenie vilentsev, an organization of alumni of the Vil'no military academy. Holdings include manuscripts on this academy and its alumni.

579 Varvara Alekseevna Shakhovskaia. Papers, ca. 22 boxes. Papers of the lawyer M. M. Filonenko, best known for defending N. Plevitskaia in the General E. Miller kidnapping trial: diary, 1918-19 (begun in Arkhangel'sk), about the Civil War; and professional papers (arranged in folders by client, mostly from the 1930s). Papers of Georgii Alekseevich Polianskii, former lieutenant-colonel of cuirassiers; diaries of Polianskii for 1919-20 (on the Civil War in the South) and for 1938-45; documents, etc. on the cuirassiers regiment (Kirasiry eia velichestva) and its veterans' organization in the emigration. The archive of Nikolai N. Chebyshev--pre-revolutionary procurator in Kiev and Moscow, senator in the Provisional Government, and writer for Vozrozhdenie in the emigration--holds his diaries for 1921 and 1926-34; correspondence (some with the Mladorosskaia party organization); and a diary and letters of N. Plevitskaia, with some other materials about her.

580 Ivan I. and Valentina Pavlovna Shali. His handwritten account, "Spets- i Trudposeleniia v severnom Kazakhstane v 1931-36 gg."--his

experiences as an agronomist and political prisoner and the forced resettlement of peasants and political prisoners in the 1930s; his "Pol'skie evreibezhentsy v Tomsk-Asinskikh lageriakh, 1940 god" (handwritten also), concerning life as a veterinarian and Siberian camp conditions for Jewish refugees from Poland in World War II; and her memoirs about Czechoslovakia, Hungary, Romania, Bulgaria, and Albania in 1945-58.

581 Vladimir Vasil'evich Shapkin. Typescript on the Cossack Obshchefrontovyi kazachii s"ezd in October 1917 and the Ukrainian Rada, plus a manuscript about the last days of the tsarist high command.

582 Pavel N. Shatilov. Papers, ca. 3 boxes. General. Typed memoirs, carbon copy, 1,110 pp., of childhood, education, military career under Nicholas II, Revolution, Civil War, the Crimea, ROVS, and the Plevitskaia trial in the 1930s; documents and correspondence from 1921-22 concerning the evacuation of the White Army from Russia and Constantinople and settlement in Hungary and the Balkans; "Vospominaniia armeitsa"--a typescript about the Irkutsk military school ca. 1905-10; correspondence, typed, carbon copies, from 1923-38; and documents, letters, and clippings on the Civil War, General A. P. Kutepov, and the Crimea, 1919-1930s. Restrictions.

583 Georgii I. Shavel'skii. Papers, ca. 40 items. Orthodox priest. The original typescript of his "Russkaia Tserkov pred revoliutsiei" (Sofia, 1937) and a copy, 540 pp.; his typed reminiscences about life in the Orthodox Church, its organization, his experiences in World War I and the Revolution, 581 pp., 1911-18; a typescript on the Volunteer Army, ca. 1920, 62 pp.; "Pokhod protiv Rasputina," 435 pp., another typed essay; more personal memoirs of life before World War I and the emigration in Bulgaria, 387 pp.; and typed biographies of Father Shavel'skii by F. Bokach.

584 Vadim Vsevolodovich Shchavinskii. 2 mimeographed volumes, 1931, plus some chapters of Istoriia Markovskoi Artilleriiskoi Brigady--about the Civil War in the South.

585 Nadezhda Aleksandrovna Shcherbacheva. Typed memoirs of the widow of a general who commanded the Rumanian front in World War I, written in 1919.

586 Irina Petrovna and A. A. Shebeko. Papers, ca. 5 boxes. Typed reminiscences of N. N. Shebeko, former ambassador to Vienna, about the origins of World War I, published in French as Souvenirs, in 1936, plus his correspondence; personal correspondence from 1914-37; Shebeko's official reports on the Balkan situation in 1913-14; and his notes on events 1918-19 and the activities of former Russian officials in the West. Restrictions.

587 Valentina Shelepina. Handwritten memoirs by a nurse in World War I, 1917-22.

588 E. N. Shendrikov (Shendrikoff). Typescript about the Revolution in Turkestan, 1917-18, 32 pp.

589 Ivan Aleksandrovich Shepetkovskii. Memoirs on military history, 1906-14, with many poems--"Russkaia imperatorskaia gvardiia," typed.

590 Shevchenko Scientific Society, Inc. Microfilm of materials on collectivization of agriculture in the Ukraine, 1929-33.

591 Marie Shevich. Typed memoirs in French: Sans retour (social history of 1880-1920).

592 Olga N. Shilo-Nudzhevskaia. Handwritten personal reminiscence of the Civil War, a meeting with General A. G. Shkuro, and World War II, 1918-20, 1941-44.

593 Vera Ivanova Shiraeva. Papers, ca. 18 items. Papers of Grigorii Ivanovich Shiraev, Russian botanist who worked in Prague, including short biographies, 1882-1954, a bibliography, and offprints of about 10 short scholarly works.

594 Sergei R. Shishmarev. Papers, ca. 12 items. His wife's memoirs, "Zhizn' i tvorchestvo Sergeia Shishmareva," typed; some typed manuscripts, including the novel "Korvet Eruslan"; and typed personal memoirs.

595 Mstislav Stepanovich Shitov. Papers, ca. 25 items. Military engineer. Typed, handwritten and illustrated memoirs, 2 vols., about his experiences in World War I, plus his ideas on military education and technology, 1914-70; and correspondence and documents of ROVS in Argentina.

596 F. V. and E. P. Shlippe. Typed memoirs, 1900-17, ca. 250 pp., by F. V. Shlippe, who was in the Moscow provincial zemstvo and the Ministry of Agriculture, about local government and the Stolypin reform; and the reminiscences of his wife, E. P. Shlippe, of social life and aristocratic political views in the 1890s, 6 pp.

597 Mikhail M. Shneerov. "V pogone za sinei ptitsei," "My last arrest and state prison in Kursk," and "When I Was Young"--all typed--about the SR Party and the revolution in 1902-1908, and 1917-18. Restrictions.

598 Philip Shorr. Handwritten essay by Professor J. Saposnekov, 1920s, about N. Novikov; a bibliography on Novikov; and a letter from P. Sorokin about Novikov.

599 I. Z. Shteinberg. Papers, 11 folders. Documents, memoirs, and essays by Left SRs and a history of the party, 1917-21.

600 Pavel P. Shteingel'. Handwritten manuscript entitled "Andron" contains observations on the national question in the Caucasus, Russian administration there, and Armenians in Russia, ca. 1909-19, 154 pp.

601 Konstantin Fedosevich Shteppa. Papers, ca. 3 boxes. History professor. The first part of his typed memoirs, 161 pp., concerns domestic conditions in the USSR in the 1930s and the historical profession. Other items: typed bibliography of historiographic books and works on history in the USSR, 1948-60, and of works by émigré historians; his reviews and articles, some published, on religion, the Ukraine, anthropology, nationalism, Marxism, Soviet ideology, and politics; and 2 typed essays--"Volna massovykh arrestov, 1937-38" about the purges and "Velikaia revoliutsiia nashei epokhi" on Burnham's The Managerial Revolution.

602 Vladimir Shubut. Papers, ca. 22 items. Documents, including autographs, of A. Glazunov, E. Roshchina-Insarova, A. Pavlova, F. Shaliapin, H. Sienkiewicz; documents about estates and landownership in Poland; and a letter from G. Danilevskii.

603 Ivan Nikolaevich Shumilin. Papers, ca. 1 box, ca. 825 items. Typed sections of his memoirs and reminiscences about childhood in Warsaw ca. 1900, the Kiev Cave Monastery (he was its jurisconsultant), Petrograd in the October Revolution, the Civil War, Soviet academic life, ca. 1917-45, and the emigration. Shumilin's pseudonym was Ivan Nikodimov. Restrictions.

604 Antonina Vasil'evna Shvarts. Papers, ca. 200 items. Wife of General A. V. Shvarts. Contains memoirs of her husband's military career in World War I (the Baltic, Byelorussia, Caucasus, and Petrograd), 1914-16; telegrams, letters, and orders of the general, 1915-16; memoir excerpts and documents about the childhood and youth of Alexander III (some Ministry of the Court archival documents), ca. 1845-78.

605 Evgeniia Alekseevna Sidorova. Papers, ca. 25 items. Handwritten memoirs of acquaintance with the painter K. S. Petrov-Vodkin; a photo of E. Sidorova, whose pseudonym was Evgeniia Mor; 2 poems, 1917-50; handwritten essays from the 1920s-1930s by the playwright Evgenii Shvarts; and handwritten essays/reminiscences of the Imperial family, Evgenii Shvarts, Ivanov-Razumnik (Razumnik Vasilevich Ivanov), A. Pliushkov, and World War II.

606 Vladimir A. Silin. Manuscript about the death of Alexander III and coronation of Nicholas II.

607 Igor' Vsevolodovich Simonovich. Diary for 1920-24 in Constantinople and Prague, handwritten, 5 vols.; notebook of poetry, ca. 1916-55; handwritten memoirs of the Revolution, Civil War, and evacuation of White armies in the South, 1917-20; and a notebook with literary fragments and essays, handwritten, 1920-23.

608 Sergei Vsevolodovich Simonovich. Papers, 2 boxes, ca. 300 items. Letters to him from Yugoslavia in the 1950s; documents about refugees in the 1920s; orders and information relating to ROVS, Obshchestvo Gallipoliitsev, and other émigré military organizations; Simonovich's notes on his experiences in the Civil War and prominent Russian women he knew.

609 Skorodumov. Typed essays/memoirs on the start of World War II in the USSR, the author's flight from the Soviet Union to Germany, and Soviet opposition to Stalin, 1941-45.

610 Oleksandr Skoropis'-Ioltukhovskii. Papers, 2 boxes, ca. 25 items. Photo albums about World War I and the Civil War; books and pamphlets on Ukrainian history; and typescripts about the Ukrainian problems in the 1930s and Poland, in German, by various authors.

611 Aleksei Ivanovich Skrylov (Skrilov). Information on his and his sons' careers in the U.S., ca. 1950; a note on the Kuban campaign of General L. Kornilov; other Kornilov items, including a copy of a photo of the general in Austrian captivity and data on his escape from Austria in 1916.

612 Rudolf Slansky. Typed, 2 vols., in Polish, of the proceedings of his trial, 1952, plus an English version, printed, both based on radio transmissions.

613 Iurii A. Slezkin. Short handwritten essays on military history; and his novels.

614 Mariia Andreevna Slivinskaya. Memoirs for ca. 1917-46 (Moi vospominaniya), typed, in a bound volume.

615 Nikolai P. Smirnov. His short, handwritten "Ocherk istorii fenologii v Rossii"; "Istoriia Iosifa, zapisannaia na iazyke derevev," on the science of phenology, late 19th c. to 1950.

616 Vladimir Nikolaevich Smirnov. Handwritten memoirs of the Russian Expeditionary Force on the Salonika front in 1916-18; 5 photos of the REF and of a Russian military cemetery on the Marne; a typescript, "Vernye dolgu," on the Russian legion in France, 1918.

617 Tat'iana A. Smirnova-Maksheeva. Papers, ca. 25 items. Her published literary works, including Taina Kazbeka (Paris, 1947), Dushoi i sertsem, and Rasskazy i povesti; biography of her husband, Vladimir Smirnov; her poetry, 1900-55; and typescripts about Russian women's education and Russian industry, 1812-1900.

618 I. S. Smolin. Army officer. "Vospominaniia starogo ofitsera," typed essays/reminiscences

of childhood in Iakutia, Siberia, the Russo-Japanese War, and military history and training, ca. 1900-17, plus other essays on military history. Restrictions.

619 Alexandra Smugge. Notebooks with handwritten memoirs of her grandfather and other ancestors in Irkutsk and Eastern Siberia and of her husband in Turkestan, ca. 1890-1917. Restrictions.

620 Jaromir Smutny. Papers, 22 Boxes. Chancellor to President Eduard Benes of Czechoslovakia, ca. 1938-48. After the February 1948 revolution, he emigrated to London, founding the Eduard Benes Institute (Ustav). The archive contains many of the Institute's published volumes; also, notes and lectures by Smutny; typed manuscripts on Czech politics and diplomacy, 1915-65, the February 1948 revolution, death of Jan Masaryk, the London government in exile in World War II, the Munich crisis of 1938, Benes's visits to Moscow in 1943 and 1945, and the Sudeten Germans in 1945; "Zpravy o situace v Rusku, 1942-43" and more zpravy (reports) of the London government in exile, 1941-43; and other materials concerning Thomas G. Masaryk, H. Pika, S. Osusky, V. Krajina, M. Hodza, B. Lausman, and H. Ripka. Restrictions.

621 Petr Grigorevich Sobolev. Papers, 12 items. "Zapiski zhurnalista," about a rural childhood, St. Petersburg journalism, the February Revolution, and the Civil War in the Murmansk area, ca. 1905-20. Restrictions.

622 Sergei Ivanovich Sobrievskii. Typed biography about the army, a musician's life, musical circles, and the emigration in Egypt, 1872-1951.

623 Soiuz pazhei. Papers, over 11 boxes. Archives of the Corps of Pages Union; mimeographed volumes with excerpts from memoirs of members of the Corps; copies of letters of V. Balabin concerning diplomatic service ca. 1840; L. V. Islavin's handwritten account of his mission to King Nikolas of Montenegro in 1915-21; photos of the Corps; and material on military and administrative history.

624 Soiuz russkikh pisatelei i zhurnalistov v Parizhe. Papers, 4 boxes. Correspondence, much of it to B. Zaitsev and V. Zeeler, reports, and accounts, 1928-51.

625 Soiuz russkikh shoferov v Parizhe. Papers, 16 boxes. Card file of members of the Union of Russian Chauffeurs in Paris ca. 1929-60; accounts, correspondence, and protocols of commissions, 1920s-1940s; a mimeographed history of the group.

626 B. A. Sokolov (B. Snezhin). "Pobedit' li Galileianin?"--a typescript; philosophical notebooks and pamphlets, 1910-50, with thoughts on cosmopolitanism.

627 B. N. Sokolov. This engineer's mimeographed reports on "Industry in the U.S.S.R. in 1931" and "Soviet Dumping" (Paris, 1931).

628 Pavel Alekseevich Sokolov. Printed and typed memoirs of military service, World War I, and southern White armies in the Civil War, ca. 1914-20; plus a typed novel, "Valeriia i Vera." Restrictions.

629 Pavla Andreevna Sokolova-Popova. Manuscript of a novel entitled Kazaki Ermakovy, in 3 notebooks, about Cossack families in the Don region; part of it has been published in the émigré press.

630 A. A. Sollogub-Dovoino. Manuscript about the Russian emigration in Poland, 1920-26, 175 pp.

631 Igor Konstantinovich Solomonovskii. Papers, ca. 30 items. Handwritten essays based on memoirs concerning the Vlasov movement and anti-communism in the Soviet Union in 1941-45; more of the same on Soviet espionage in France in World War II, Russian military history, and the defense of Kiepaja, Latvia in 1945; and a biography of Solomonovskii, 1901-45.

632 Dmitri D. Sonzov. Papers, ca. 30 items. Notebooks with handwritten "Zapiski psovago okhotnika," ca. 1890s-1920s; a book, photos, and drawings of dogs, their care and breeding, and hunting; and correspondence.

633 Ivan Petrovich Sozonovich. Taught comparative literature in Warsaw before World War I and in Prague after 1917. The collection contains his personal documents, a short biography of him and his wife, and handwritten lecture notes.

634 Maria Sozonovich-Kozhin. Papers, ca. 25 items. Personal and family archive, with photos (e.g., of Professor Konstantin Vasilevich Bestuzhev-Riumin, founder of the St. Petersburg women's higher education courses), and memoirs.

635 Aleksei Aleksandrovich Spasskii-Odynets. Employee of the southwestern railways and protégé of S. Iu. Witte, who helped create the semi-official newspaper Russkoe gosudarstvo, 1905-1906, and later joined the staff of Strana. Typed memoirs. Restrictions.

636 V. E. Sproge. Mimeographed copy of the autobiographical "Zapiski inzhenera" (Zurich, 1963), about World War I, the Civil War, and World War II in the USSR, 1913-41.

637 Iuliia Sergeevna Squibb. A brief memoir entitled "Anna Fedorovna"; a handwritten piece about the years 1900-50 ("Makarych"); a typescript on military settlements in Novgorod province (apparently in the 20th c.); "Nasha kukharka Tatiana"; and other items on the Russian-Asiatic Bank and South Africa.

638 Egor Egorovich de Staal. Papers, ca. 2 boxes. Baron. Correspondence, ca. 1883-93; materials on events of 1870-71 (concerning Constantinople, Persia, Armenia, and the Baltic provinces); personal documents, 1860-90; and a handwritten essay on the new military law of 1874, in Russian. Restrictions.

639 M. S. Stakhevich. Papers, ca. 75 items. A book on Russian naval history, with personnel lists, Petrograd, 1916; the émigré Morskoi zhurnal (Naval Journal), Prague, 1927-42; documents, clippings, memoirs, and printed matter about naval history, 1890-1940.

640 Aleksandra Aleksandrovna Stakhovich. Papers, ca. 2 boxes. Typed reminiscences of the Civil War, 1918-20; printed proclamations and clippings on the Siberian Civil War, 1919-20; and the archives of the Russian Lawn Tennis Association, founded in Paris in 1929 (correspondence, programs, documents from the 1930s).

641 Simeon Starikov. Manuscript, in Russian, on Russian public opinion about the Boer War, ca. 1900, 10 pp.

642 Pavel A. Staritskii. Papers, 2 boxes. Personal correspondence, 1970s, of the former head of the Union of Russian Chauffeurs in Paris (see also Soiuz russkikh shoferov v Parizhe).

643 V. N. Stefanov. Memoirs about his service in the Volunteer Army, part 1 of which is entitled "Neuviadaiushchie list'ia," part 2 is "Odesskaia evakuatsiia."

644 Andrea-Aleksandra Stegman. Carbon copy of memoirs of childhood, education, her Baltic German family (the father, Baron Armin Foelkersam, was curator of the Hermitage Museum before 1917), her service as a nurse in Petrograd in World War I, the family's life in Finland after the February Revolution, and a Red Cross mission for POWs in Moscow and Kiev during the Civil War; additional memoirs about arrest and imprisonment by the Cheka in 1919-20 and about her brother's experiences in Lubianka prison as a German POW after World War II; reprints of articles, 1966-67, by her husband Helmuth, including his memoirs on the Baltic states and the German population there, ca. 1919-39; a translation of a statement by P. A. Valuev about the Baltic Question in Alexander II's reign: and a publication of the Union of Baltic Nobility, 1968. Restrictions.

645 Sergei Mikhailovich Stepniak-Kravchinskii. Papers, ca. 110 items. Revolutionary and writer. 58 undated letters of Stepniak to his wife Fanni Markovna, about personal affairs, and the revolutionary movement in Russia and Western Europe; an additional 25 letters to his wife, 1860s-1930s; 10 letters to Stepniak, 1890-91, correspondence with E. Bernstein, Eleanor Duse, E. E. Lazarev, G. Plekhanov, Semen Vengerov, and A. Kornilova-Moroz; notes from Petr Kropotkin; a Stepniak 1905 speech; clippings; and 13 photographs. Restrictions.

646 Vasilii Pavlovich Stetsenko. Papers, ca. 30 items. Typed memoirs about General Kantserov, commander of the Markov Officers' Division, and the Civil War, 1918-20, with photos; typed memoirs of Admiral I. K. Grigorovich, in French, written in 1929; 2 notebooks with handwritten diaries of Stetsenko, 1918-20; short typed essays on military events of World War I and the Civil War; "Mrachnye vospominaniia o gen. Biskupskom . . ." by Stetsenko; and about the Bulgarian communist uprising of 1923.

647 Leonid Ivanovich Strakhovskii. Papers, ca. 50 items. Baron S. F. Korf's essays and speeches about Russian law and constitutional matters; papers of E. Francis Riggs, on the U.S. military mission to Russia in 1916-18; and a typescript by Count Paul Nikolaevich Ignatieff, former minister of education.

648 G. P. Struve. Photocopies of 4 letters of Archbishop Sergei of Prague to Nina Aleksandrovna Struve, 1926-31, and a letter of the archbishop to Arkadii Petrovich Struve, 1946.

649 Lev Petrovich Sukachev. Military officer. Memoirs (partly published in Vestnik Pervopokhodnika) about the Revolution and Civil War and the emigration, where he was a major in the Albanian army of King Zog and then a general in the Italian army, 1939-47; photos; and a memoir about the role of a Russian unit in Akhmet Zog's conquest of Albania.

650 Anna Matveevna Sukhanina. Papers, ca. 210 items. "Teni proshlogo"--handwritten memoirs of Bessarabia ca. 1887-1917 and later life, to 1945; plus newspapers and clippings on world affairs, 1939-53.

651 Ilia Dmitrevich Surguchev. Papers, 11 boxes. Playwright and novelist. Includes his literary manuscripts in French and Russian, notebooks, photos of play scenes and personal photos, and his correspondence with such figures as I. Bunin, A. Kuprin, N. Evreinov, and V. I. Nemirovich-Danchenko.

652 Iustin'ia Sushcheva. Papers, 18 notebooks. Handwritten notes for lectures on Russian and European history, physics, and Russian and French literature, 1968-72, in Russian and French.

653 P. B. Sushil'nikov (Souchilnikoff). "Astrakhanskie grenadery v boiu i bytu, 1900-1920," 1942, handwritten, and 10 short stories, typed, by Lieutenant Sushil'nikov about Russian military life, the Revolution, and Civil War.

654 S. G. Svatikov. Papers, ca. 61 boxes. Contents include his published books and article manuscripts; correspondence and other papers of V. Burtsev; reports on the Allied intervention and the economy of the Far East, 1912-19; a handwritten and typed manuscript, 143 pp., about "General Kornilov" and the Civil War in the Don and Novocherkassk areas; photos of Nicholas II, V. L. Burtsev, A. Gertsen, and E. Azef; photocopies of Svatikov's manuscript on Okhrana activities in Paris and Europe in 1881-1917; and bibliographic materials. Restrictions.

655 Mikhail Andreevich Svechin. Papers, 14 items. Typed memoirs--"Vospominaniya starogo kirasira eia velichestva" (Nice, 1958) and photos, 1890-1917, plus more memoirs for 1876-1919 covering education, the Imperial family, military training, the Civil War, Kiev, Ukraine, and the Don River region; and materials on the Soviet army in the 1920s and 1930s.

656 Ekaterina Ivanovna Sverbeeva. 3 documents of Sergei Sverbeev, last tsarist ambassador to Berlin (note signed by A. Sazonov and a report on German-Turkish relations in 1913).

657 M. K. Sverbeeva. Papers, 11 items. Letters from Tatiana L'vovna Tolstaia-Sukhotina (Count Leo's daughter) to Svergeeva's husband; and Tolstaia-Sukhotina's typed essay on A. S. Pushkin, with reminiscences of her father, 1940s.

658 Nikolai Vladimirovich Sviatopolk-Mirskii. Papers, ca. 6 boxes, over 700 items. Miscellanea relating to many different aspects of Russian history: photographs and graphic materials of Nicholas II and his family, the French invasion of Moscow in 1812, Russian clergy in the 1920s, a Russian church in Belgrade, Orthodox icons, Nicholas I; papers of the Finnish Notbek (Nottbek) family relating to agriculture, trade, and industry (ca. 1844); correspondence of General A. M. Dragomirov, 1950s; letters, grants, and decrees of emperors from Nicholas I to Nicholas II; a handwritten genealogy of the Sviatopolk family; Basil N. de Strandman's reminiscences of diplomatic service in the Balkans, 1908-15, 2 vols., 525 pp., in Russian; a photo and correspondence of the oceanographer Iu. M. Shokaevskii; and a variety of pamphlets, journals, and other printed matter.

659 Aleksandr K. Svitich. Papers, ca. 380 items. Materials, including typed memoirs, about the Russian Orthodox Church in Poland, France, and Russia ca. 1920-50, and the Ukrainian Autocephalous Church in exile; Svitich's memoirs of World War II; a German World War II circular to Orthodox Lithuanians ordering their help; and a telegram of Metropolitan Sergei to a Lithuanian diocese ordering compliance with the German circular, 1943.

660 Z. Szajkowski. Papers, ca. 1 box. Ephemera, leaflets, posters, and newspapers, in Russian, French, and mostly Yiddish, about Jews in Russia and the USSR, 1900-1920s; handwritten essay by A. Lozovskii on the trade union movement in the West, in Russian with French documents, 1911; revolutionary, conservative, and soviet proclamations and leaflets from the period 1904-1905; and documents of the Comité Général de la Colonie Russe, 1917.

661 G. A. Tal' (Thal). Papers, ca. 68 items. Notebooks with handwritten memoirs of childhood in St. Petersburg in the 1880s, court life, education, military career (lieutenant in a Hussar regiment); material based on diaries of Tal''s father concerning the assassination of Alexander II; data on serfdom taken from notes of Tal''s grandfather (1822); and information about the Jewish question in Russia, the emigration in Yugoslavia, and Russian military history, 18th-19th c.

662 Georgii Ferdinandovich Tanutrov. Memoirs, in 4 notebooks, typed, of the Caucasus and Daghestan (where his father served in the administration and he was born), of military training, Tbilisi, the cavalry in World War I, and the Civil War, 1895-1920.

663 Iadviga Iosipovna Tanutrova. Handwritten memoirs--"Na pol'skoi zemle"--about the turn of this century.

664 Tat'iana N. Tarydina. Papers, ca. 3 boxes, ca. 500 items. Actress, began her career in Moscow's Malyi Teatr and continued her career in the emigration after 1917. Includes correspondence (A. Tolstaia, A. Sedykh, E. Mogilat, and R. Berezov); photographs; published and unpublished short stories of Tarydina in manuscript; materials on her father, General N. A. Marks, other ancestors, and the poet Maksimilian Voloshin.

665 Mikhail Aleksandrovich Taube. Papers, ca. 20 boxes. Materials for a Taube family genealogy; manuscript biography of Johann Georg von Taube, founder of the family; binder with correspondence, printed matter, and ephemera on the Nicholas Roerich (Nikolai Rerikh) Museum and on his peace activities; handwritten and typed copies of von Taube's reminiscences--"Vospominaniia o tragicheskoi sud'be predrevoliutsionnoi Rossii"--for 1890-1917 and also for the years in emigration, 1918-56; and notes on Russian history.

666 Graham Taylor. Papers, 2 boxes, ca. 800 items. Mostly printed matter related to the U.S. intervention in the Far East during the Civil War (including the newspaper Druzheskoe Slovo, published by American authorities in Vladivostok; and reports on local attitudes, U.S. activities, and the local press.)

667 Nadezhda Alexandrovna Teffi (1892-1952). Papers, ca. 10 boxes. Pseudonym of N. A.

Buchinskaia, émigré writer and journalist. Contains many literary manuscripts (some published in whole or in part), largely from the period in emigration; typescripts of movie scenarios, in French (including "Gnock le bienfaiteur" and "Les Héritiers de la Jument Grise"); and correspondence with such figures as the Chekhov Publishing House, Metro-Goldwyn-Mayer movie studio, M. Aldanov, G. Adamovich, I. Tsvibak, A. Remizov, I. Shmelev, I. Bunin, Iu. Trubetskoi, F. Rodichev, E. Kuskova, B. Zaitsev, 1920s-1950s.

668 Nikolai I. Tereshchenko. Handwritten memoirs about World War I, the Civil War, N. Makhno, the Foreign Legion, World War II, and the Vlasov movement, 1914-45.

669 Aleksandr Il'ich Terskii. "Bat'ke Makhno"--a typescript based on his personal recollections of his experiences in a region where Makhnovtsy were active in the Civil War; included is a copy of a message to the Makhnovtsy from General P. N. Shatilov, 18 July 1920.

670 Georgii Aleksandrovich Teslavskii. Papers, ca. 58 items. Writer. Memoirs concern his education, World War I, and the northwest front in the Civil War, 1907-19; more memoirs under his pseudonym Iurii Pskovitianin; his literary works, including sections of the autobiographical novel "Burelom," on the Revolution, Civil War, and emigration, and the novel Smuta (written under his pseudonym).

671 Thomas Day Thacher. Papers, 5.5 boxes, ca. 1,000 items. Red Cross worker in Russia. Official materials, correspondence, and reports concerning the personnel, travel, and work of the American Red Cross Mission in Russia, 1917-18. There are photograph albums with pictures of the Russian army, Red Cross Mission, street scenes, the Women's Battalion, and architecture in major cities (Kiev, Moscow, Nizhnii Novgorod, Odessa, and Yaroslavl). Restrictions.

672 Georgii S. Tikhanovich. Secret documents of the general headquarters of General P. N. Wrangel, including 2 letters from General E. K. Miller concerning German policy, 1920-21. Restrictions.

673 Dmitrii Nikolaevich Tikhobrazov. Papers, ca. 1 box, ca. 165 items. Lieutenant general. Handwritten memoirs entitled "Iz vospominanii," about his family, military career, the Revolution and Civil War. Also diaries of Admiral M. A. Lavrov, who was on the F. P. Vrangel' expedition around the world, 1825-27, and Tikhobrazov's biography of Lavrov; handwritten diaries of Adrian M. Lavrov covering his naval career, 1864-66, and exploration of the Barents and Kara seas, 1870; handwritten essays on naval history, 1880-1905, by A. M. Lavrov; letters and diaries of Lieutenant Lavrov in the Russo-Turkish War of 1877; and correspondence with A. N. Alekseeva, V. M. Borel' (daughter of General M. D. Alekseev), 1963-74, and with General B. N. Sergeevskii, 1960s. Restrictions.

674 Tatiana Aleksandrovna Timchenko-Ruban. Papers, ca. 21 items. Memoirs of her aunt, E. S. Shaikevich-Ostrovskaia, about the life of a family with connections in cultural, political, business, and Jewish circles ca. 1890-1920, handwritten in pencil, in 1929, in 15 notebooks; personal documents of S. V. Danilova, widow of an adjutant general, and of S. K. and O. I. Lazarev.

675 Vladimir Nikolaevich Timchenko-Ruban. Memoirs of service in the Preobrazhenskii Regiment, Civil War, and French emigration, ca. 600 pp., 1889-1945, and an essay on the Preobrazhenskii Regiment on its 275th anniversary, 1683-1958, both typed.

676 Aleksandr A. Titov. Papers, ca. 3 boxes. Member of the Moscow city duma and of the central committee of the All-Russian Zemstvo and City Union (in charge of hospital supplies). After emigrating, he was a professor of chemistry in Russian courses organized by the Institut d'Études Slaves at the University of Paris. Correspondence, 1921-58, some official, with such people as Metropolitan Evlogii, V. I. Kokovtsov, A. I. Denikin, V. A. Maklakov, E. Kuskova, A. Kerenskii, V. Chernov, S. I. Bulgakov, I. Bunin, B. K. Zaitsev, I. S. Shmelev, A. M. Remizov, M. M. Karpovich, Lidia Dan, and P. N. Miliukov; diary of S. Tolstoi; correspondence and other papers of the publishing house "Russkaia zemlia," 1922-24; financial records of the Soveshchanie byvshikh russkikh poslov; and the archives of Tikhon Ivanovich Polner, an intimate of G. E. L'vov. Restrictions.

677 Mstislav Titov. Correspondence, notes, and writings concerning the emigration in Argentina, ca. 1959-73.

678 Zeledi V. Togan. Typescript about Azerbaijan, signed by Togan, 88 pp., and a typed essay on the same subject, 1800-1920, 3 pp.

679 Il'ia L'vovich Tolstoi. Papers, ca. 100 items. Letters to Count I. Tolstoi; notebook with handwritten notes; typed piece entitled "Democratic Peace," 3 pp., and a telegram text, ca. 1920-45.

680 Olga Tomashek. Her genealogy of the Struve family, published in German in 1960 (she was the grand-niece of Georg von Struve, the astronomer).

681 Konstantin A. Tomilin. Papers, ca. 26 items. Professor. Handwritten autobiography; typed essays on Soviet art and Russian fables; letters from G. Grebenshchikov; poems; handwritten manuscripts on Russian and Soviet education, ca. 1900-1920s, and on the education of Russian refugee children in World War II.

682 P. A. and Natalia Arkadievna Tomilov. Papers, ca. 20 boxes. He was a general. Chapters, typed, with duplicates, of his manuscript about the last days of the northwest front in the Civil War; documents, leaflets, and typed material about the end of the Civil War; her handwritten reminiscences of the taking of Erzerum in 1915; some 30 maps and charts from World War I; and the archive of General N. Iudenich. This collection holds the entire operational and political part of the so-called Archive of the Northwest Front.

683 Sergei Aleksandrovich Toporkov. Papers, ca. 8 boxes. Typed memoirs, 1881-1921, of youth in the northern Caucasus, military service, 1905-17, and participation in the Civil War, ca. 440 pp.; A. Vel'min's short biography of Toporkov; papers of a union of members of the Fifth Gusarskii Aleksandrovskii Polk and correspondence with other émigré military groups, 1928-34 and 1940-51; typed biographies, 2 boxes, of members of the Hussars regiment, 1775-1917; typed essays by Toporkov, a colonel and military historian, on the history of the Nikolaevsk cavalry school and other topics of military history; handwritten reminiscences of Fedor V. Severin on the Russian navy in the Russo-Japanese War; Toporkov's typescript about the abduction of General E. K. Miller, written in 1938, 115 pp.; typed reminiscences of World War I by V. A. Karamzin; and typed diary for 1914-17 by V. A. Petrushevskii. Restrictions.

684 Edvard Ivanovich Totleben. Papers, 43 items. General. Family documents from the 19th c.; bound notebook with his letters to his wife during the Crimean War, 1854; and 9 notebooks with Fieldmarshal Count E. I. Totleben's diary, with notations, kept in the Russo-Turkish War of 1877-78.

685 Vakhan Totomianz. Typed memoirs/essay on the cooperative movement and his private life, 1890-1954.

686 Boris Nikolaevich Tret'iakov. "Proizvodstvo v ofitsery," typed memoirs of the Russian Corps of Pages ca. 1900.

687 Nataliia Nikolaevna Troitskaia. Typed "Vospominaniia" dealing with the history of women's education, especially institutions run by the Imperial family for the nobility, 1764-1914; plus letters, typed essays, and photos concerning the education of Russian émigré children in Indianapolis, ca. 1950s-1960s.

688 Konstantin K. Troitskii. Handwritten memoirs/essays on the agrarian question, the administration of the Stolypin reform, V. I. Gurko, N. N. Kutler, and secondary education and university life in St. Petersburg in the late 1890s.

689 S. E. Trubetskaia. Letters about Russian political and cultural history from A. K. Tolstoi, A. Benois, Professor B. Nolde, and Professor P. Struve, 1830-1945.

690 Sergei Grigor'evich Trubetskoi. Largely materials on the genealogy of the Trubetskoi family.

691 Iraklii Georgievich Tseretelli. Papers, ca. 65 items. Menshevik leader. Typed chapters of memoirs on the February Revolution, Ukrainian crisis, and the nationalities question, 187 pp., also on the foreign and domestic policies of the Provisional Government; parts of these memoirs are in published form--Recollections of the February Revolution (1952: reissued, Paris, 1963?). Restrictions.

692 Isidor L'vovich Tsitron. Letters from M. A. Aldanov and V. A. Maklakov, 1945-56; and 2 manuscripts--"Biografiia Isidora L'vovicha Tsitrona, prisiazhnogo poverennogo Peterburgskogo sudebnogo okruga, i dolgoletnogo sotrudnika O. O. Gruzenberga" and "V. G. Korolenko v Kishineve" (reminiscences), both by Tsitron

693 S. Tukholka. Typescript entitled "Ancient Turkey; memoirs of a Russian Consul General" and 6 short essays, typed, in Russian, about the Russian diplomatic service in the Balkans in the late 19th-early 20th c.

694 Vasili V. Tulintsev. Papers, ca. 44 items. Handwritten autobiography/reminiscences of childhood in the Ukraine, folk customs and religious holidays, his military career, World War I, the Caucasus, Siberia, the Volga region, and Russian culture to 1919; essays on similar topics of Russian history, 1600-1919; and his grandmother's reminiscences of St. Petersburg and its Ekaterinskii Institut for the education of young women, 1870s-1880s.

695 Pavel Pavlovich Tutkovskii. Papers, ca. 3 boxes, ca. 100 items. Personal documents; correspondence; photos; music notes for Tutkovskii's compositions; reminiscences of her husband by Mrs. Tutkovskii; handwritten texts of Tutkovskii's writings; texts of 2 novels in French and 6 other books by Tutkovskii. Restrictions.

696 Ariadna Vladimirovna Tyrkova-Williams. Papers, ca. 23 boxes. Political leader and writer. Memoirs, largely unpublished, about the liberation movement, work in the Kadet Party, the dumas, the Revolution, and the Russian Liberation Committee in emigration; correspondence with V. A. Maklakov, E. V. Sablin, A. V. Kartashev, P. Struve, F. Rodichev, N. A. Teffi, S. Mel'gunov, S. Panina, B. Pares, Boris Zaitsev, M. Rostovtsev, G. Vernadskii, M. Karpovich, V. Shklovskii, G. L'vov, P. Miliukov; manuscript of the novel Vasilissa premudraia, A zhizn' tekla . . ., and other literary works; dispatches and materials of Tyrkova-Williams's husband, Harold Williams, a British journalist and correspondent of the London Times in Russia, 1904-26; and orders,

documents, and papers relating to the Kadet Party and to the Volunteer Army in the South during the Civil War; correspondence, reports, and pamphlets of the London Komitet osvobozhdeniia Rossii. Restrictions.

697 Uchreditel'noe sobranie. Papers, 1 box, ca. 150 items. Material from a 1921 meeting of former members of the 1918 Constituent Assembly, printed bulletin, appeals, typed minutes of the meetings of various commissions, mimeographed documents, and documents issued by the SR Party in 1921.

698 N. P. Ukraintsev. Colonel, a military jurist on the commission investigating General L. Kornilov's attempted coup in 1917. Handwritten memoirs about St. Petersburg society, military history, jurisprudence, the Revolution and the Provisional Government; handwritten reminiscences, entitled "1941" and "Raskol," concerning service as an interpreter with German occupation troops in the USSR; and several handwritten manuscripts, including "1905-yi god," based on personal memoirs of the revolution, 49 pp.; "Desiat' let v ispravitel'nykh trudovykh lageriakh," ca. 200 pp., on life in Soviet camps after being arrested in Poland, 1945-55.

699 Vladimir Nikolaevich Unkovskii. Papers, ca. 9 boxes. Émigré writer. Diary for 1925-27; handwritten reminiscences of social and cultural life in Kharkov and Kharkov University ca. 1907, World War I, and work in French West Africa after the evacuation from the Crimea; correspondence; literary manuscripts, including short stories; the manuscript and galleys of his novel Ikary, 1942; notebooks with autobiographical writings; handwritten reminiscences of A. M. Remizov, V. L. Burtsev, and Gallipoli, 1900-1930s; correspondence of A. Remizov and M. Aldanov.

700 Aleksandr L'vovich Urusov. Papers, ca. 1 box, ca. 550 items. Papers of the prince's father, Prince Lev Pavlovich Urusov, Russian ambassador or diplomat in Paris, Rome, Vienna, and Romania; correspondence; zapiski of the Budapest Consul-General A. L'vov about Hungary and events of 1905. Restrictions.

701 I. N. Urusova. Princess. Memoirs; and P. V. Vogak's memoirs about Red Cross work in 1914-21. Vogak's memoirs also cover his father's life under Alexander III and Nicholas II.

702 Natalia V. Usachova. Papers, ca. 15 items. Papers of Natalie Usachova-Gurliand, nee Sekerina, with whom A. N. Skriabin was once in love, letter from Skriabin, musical notes, books on Skriabin, and a handwritten biography of her former husband, I. Ia. Gurliand (a writer of history and fiction) by Usachova, 10 pp.

703 Varvara Uspenskaia. Papers, ca. 53 items. Typescript by the protoierei Ioann Chepelev about Uspenskaia's father, Metropolitan Platon, and work among the Russian Orthodox in America, 1918-30; clippings and printed matter about the Orthodox Church in the U.S.; and material on church history, religious thought, and the church in the USSR.

704 Nina Vladimirovna Vadbol'skaia. Typed and handwritten memoirs of the widow of General N. P. Vadbol'skii, commander of Russian troops in northern Persia in 1907, concerning Russian-Persian relations, Georgia, N. N. Iudenich.

705 Evgeniia Ignatevna Vagner. Papers, over 60 items. Correspondence with friends and scholars (on the life and work of her husband, Iu. N. Vagner, a noted entomologist); documents (including an official service record) and photos of her husband relating to Russian science, and the emigration in Yugoslavia and Germany before World War II, ca. 1800-1970s.

706 Nicholas P. Vakar. Papers, ca. 45 items. Scholar. Typed copies and newspaper clippings with his articles on Soviet politics, diplomacy, and international politics, 1930s.

707 Sergei Vasil'evich Vakar. Papers, ca. 38 items. Memoiristic writings about the city of Tambov, World War I, Revolution and Civil War, the White evacuation, émigré life in Yugoslavia, the Nazi Russian Corps; additional memoirs entitled "Nasha generatsiia," about World War I; handwritten essays on World War I, Russian military life and traditions, and the emigration in Argentina, 1920s-1960s, 10 pp.

708 V. Valentinov. Typed memoirs--"Wie ich 'Kollaborateur' wurde"--concern World War II, 1941-44, 70 pp.

709 Konstantin Efimovich Val'kov. Papers, ca. 30 items. Some of the personal effects of protoierei Vsevolod Perovskii, Perovskii's own publications, and 4 notebooks with handwritten essays on calendar reform.

710 A. A. Venovskii. Memoirs, entitled "Vospominaniia uchastnika revoliutsii 1905 goda," typed, 23 pp.; and essays on Shakespeare, mythology, and ancient history, handwritten and typed.

711 Aleksei A. Varzukevich. Typed memoirs about his early military career, the 16th Strelkovyi Polk, the Russo-Japanese War, and revolutionary agitation among students in 1905 (1904-10); 30 pp.

712 Maria Alexandrovna Vasil'chikov. Lady-in-waiting to the last Russian empress. Photos of her, and her handwritten essay in French on "The Empress Alexandra Fedorovna."

713 Illarion Sergeevich Vasil'chikov. Papers, 30 items. Autobiographical sketches on family

history, the Revolution, Civil War, and political life in the emigration; his "Moe naznachenie Gubernskim Predvoditelem Dvorianstva Kovenskoi Gubernii"; "Sebastopol. Souvenirs du Chef d'État Major de la garnison de Sebastopol Prince Victor Wassiltchikoff, écrites à Moscou en 1875-77," typed copy; and historical and biographical essays/reminiscences, typed, about the senatorial reviziia of Turkestan, 1908, the Red Cross and the Orthodox Church, both 1917, the Revolution, and the Civil War.

714 Mikhail Fedorovich Vasil'ev. Memorabilia concerning the Vlasov army (medal, identification book, 3 photos); and 2 notebooks with reminiscences of World War II.

715 S. V. Vasil'ev. Handwritten memoirs of the revolutions of 1905 and 1917 in the Ukraine and southern Russia, the pogroms, Civil War, and Soviet agrarian policy; plus a short story, "Russkaia zhizn'."

716 Evgenii Aleksandrovich Vechorin. Papers, ca. 8 boxes. Russian engineer. Taught at the Polytechnical Institute in St. Petersburg before the Revolution and in Paris after emigrating. His mimeographed memoirs of the Polytechnical Institute; materials of a group of its graduates in Paris; related materials.

717 Vladimir Nikolaevich Velikotnyi. Typed memoirs concerning education in a classical gymnasium, the Nikolaevskoe kavaleriiskoe uchilishche, February and October Revolutions in Petrograd, and the Civil War in the South with the Volunteer Army, 1907-20.

718 Anatoli Petrovich Vel'min. Papers, ca. 2 boxes. Correspondence, 1925-60, mostly with the émigré community worldwide, including B. Nicolaevskii and M. Karpovich; a biography of V. Maklakov by G. Adamovich (Paris, 1959); a German manuscript on the Smolny Institute, 4 pp., 1943; typescript on American famine aid and the emigration in Poland and Germany, 1920s-1940s; and a report and diary on the emigration in Latin America. Restrictions.

719 Vladimir Alexandrovich Vereshchagin. Papers, ca. 15 items. Correspondence with Prince F. Iusupov and the Grand Duke Gavril Konstantinovich, 1950s-1960s; and reminiscences ("Iz proshlogo," 123 pp.) of St. Petersburg cultural life in 1890-1923, typed carbon.

720 George V. and Nina V. Vernadskii. Papers, ca. 205 boxes. Émigré historian and his wife. Correspondence of both Vernadskiis, his father Vladimir (a noted geologist), their relatives (including the Bakunin, Staritskii, and Rodichev families); materials on the scientific work of George's father Vladimir, and émigré cultural life in Czechoslovakia and the U.S.; literary manuscripts of friends and relatives, including verses of V. I. Staritskii and stories of N. D. Shakhovskaia; papers of G. V. Vernadskii's graduate students in Russian history at Yale University; incomplete typescript with notes and drafts of G. V. Vernadskii's "Ocherki russkoi istoriografii" plus materials (including correspondence) on such historians as A. A. Vasil'ev, A. A. Kizevetter, M. P. Dragomanov, M. Rostovtsev, and S. G. Pushkarev and on the Seminarium Kondakovianum in Prague; family and personal documents of the Vernadskiis; articles and lectures in manuscript on many topics from Russian and Byzantine history; and notebooks, memoirs, and diaries of F. I. Rodichev. Restrictions.

721 Aleksandr Aleksandrovich Vetlits. Papers, ca. 30 items. Horse breeder and racer of horses, with large estates in Novgorod and Tver provinces. Reminiscences concern horsebreeding and racing, social relations in the countryside before 1917, the Revolution, and life in the emigration in Yugoslavia (including the role of White émigrés in King Zog's conquest of Albania); and reminiscences of service in the Russian Corps in Yugoslavia in World War II--"Kak partizany veli menia na razstrel." Restrictions.

722 Mykhailo O. Vetukhiv (d. 1960). Papers, 38 boxes. Geneticist active in Ukrainian émigré organizations, and president of the Ukrainian Academy of Arts and Sciences in New York (UVAN). Correspondence, published works, manuscripts, lectures, and scientific experiments of Vetukhiv; material on the history of genetics in the USSR; papers of the Ukrainian Free Academy of Sciences in the U.S.; personal materials; and documents of Ukrainian émigré organizations. Restrictions.

723 Galina L. Vigand. Papers, ca. 200 items. Handwritten Vospominaniia, 2 vols., bound, concerning life in the Northern Caucasus and Ternopol' regions, 1921-24; and letters to her from friends and relatives in the USSR, describing domestic conditions, 1925-36. Restrictions.

724 Maksim Moiseevich Vinaver. Kadet Party leader. Contains typed transcripts of his correspondence with another prominent Kadet, I. Petrunkevich. The letters, dated 1919-26, discuss the Civil War, intra-party politics, and foreign policy. There are also: typed stenographic report of Vinaver's speech to the First State Duma, 20 pp., typed copy of reminiscences about the October Manifesto and the first KD party congress, 4 pp., and a handwritten article dealing with politics, Paris, n.d., 7 pp.

725 Viktor Viktorovich Vinter. Papers, ca. 2 boxes, ca. 700 items. Engineer. Includes personal documents (from the period of Revolution and Civil War but mostly from the years in emigration), scientific articles and patents relating to his work in the

food-processing industry, family photos, and correspondence; diaries, 1930s-1940s; materials on World War I in Russia, the Volunteer Army in the Civil War, and the emigration in Czechoslovakia, ca. 1914-1950s. Restrictions.

726 S. E. Vittenberg. 4 notebooks with Vittenberg's diaries while in Finland, April 1918-May 1919, in a military post during the Civil War; typed essay by Ekaterina Maidel with background information on Soviet-Finnish relations and Finnish developments after October 1917; and documents. See also under E. I. Maidel for reminiscences of Vittenberg's visit to the Soviet Union in 1918.

727 V. V. Vladimirov. Papers, ca. 30 items. Typed memoirs of military espionage in the Russian navy, 1914-15, military service, the Revolution, and life under the Soviet regime, 1890-1921. More of the same on the Russo-Japanese War.

728 Nikolai Kirillovich Vlodarskii. Papers, ca. 25 items. Mathematician. Offprints and photocopies of scholarly papers and articles; and essays about Soviet scientific life, the NKVD, and a meeting with N. S. Khrushchev in Kiev during World War II, handwritten. Restrictions.

729 Petr V. Vogak. Papers, ca. 18 items. Handwritten memoirs covering his career in the Russian administration, World War I, the Red Cross, and the Civil War, 1900-18; additional memoirs going back to his father's life under tsars Alexander II and Nicholas II.

730 Mariia Vladimirovna Volkonskaia. Papers, ca. 6 boxes. Family archive of the princess and her father, Professor Vladimir Fedorovich Luginin. Includes his memoirs, correspondence, and family papers. Born in 1834, Luginin went to the Mikhailovsk Artillery School in 1849-53, fought in the Russo-Turkish war of 1853-56, knew L. Tolstoi at the siege of Sevastopol, left the military, was educated abroad in chemistry and physics, became a friend of A. M. Herzen, returned to Russia, and became a professor at Moscow University, dying in 1911. Also village church documents from Kostroma province; Volkonskaia's memoirs for 1875-1911 and an Italian translation of her diary for 1914; financial records of credit societies in Kostroma and Vetluga; and correspondence from the 1920s-1959 relating to the emigration in France. Restrictions.

731 Petr Mikhailovich Volkonskii. Papers, ca. 1 box. Documents, proclamations, etc. on the Civil War, 1918-20; and religious writings.

732 Marianna Volkov. Papers, 22 items. Photos of such personalities as Lili Brik, A. Khachaturian, E. Evtushenko, Iuri Liubimov, and V. Shklovskii.

733 A. A. Volzhanin. Papers, ca. 2 boxes, 325 items. Lengthy typed memoirs--"Grozy i buri moria zhiteiskogo," 500 pp., covering his military service as an officer in World War I, participation in the White movement in Siberia, arrest and imprisonment by the Soviet regime (to 1937), life in Soviet society before World War II, desertion to the Germans, and anti-Soviet military activities during the war. Restrictions.

734 A. M. Volzhenskii. Papers, ca. 35 items. Typed copies of telegrams and documents relating to Red Cross work in the Soviet Union, 1920; photocopy of a Karl Bohm letter to Volzhenskii in 1913; and a photo of Konstantin S. Ermolaev, 1912.

735 N. I. Vorobev. Papers, ca. 6.5 boxes. Materials on agriculture, southern Russian flora, and the Orthodox Church in Nice; émigré ephemera in French; typed and handwritten notes on the Kuban and Cossack affairs; lectures; curriculum vitae and related documents; diaries for 1931 and 1943-45; maps (including some of Central Asia); handwritten essay on Caucasian beekeeping; items relating to the Jewish question and to anti-Soviet activity. of Russians in World War II; and notes for a dictionary of prominent people from the Caucasus and Black Sea region. Restrictions.

736 Nikolai Voronkov. Military engineer in World War I. Short, handwritten autobiography (service for the Provisional Government, then A. I. Denikin; the Civil War in Siberia); and typed poems in Russian, ca. 1960.

737 Boris Vorontsov-Viliaminov. Colonel. Handwritten memoirs, 39 pp., for 1917-20, when he was an administrator of arms factories.

738 Vladimir Vostokov. Papers, ca. 16 items. Handwritten autobiographical essay; 2 typed reminiscences of tsarist days and the Orthodox Church under the Soviet regime, ca. 1900-20, plus a manuscript on the church in 1890-1917; miscellanea about Vostokov, an émigré clergyman.

739 Stepan Vasil'evich Vostrotin. Papers, ca. 4 boxes. Short biography of him; typed pages concerning the food supply question in World War I, the Revolution, and Civil War; 15 maps of Siberia and other places (showing resources and railroads); materials on the Chinese Eastern Railway, including official documents and treaties; stories of Vostrotin's grandfather about goldmining in Siberia; items relating to the Far East emigration; and typed and handwritten memoirs of youth and education in Siberia, ca. 1870-90, World War I, Revolution, and Civil War, General Khorvat's government (in which Vostrotin was active), work in Japan for the White government, and Russians and Japanese in Manchuria; papers of the Far East government and General Khorvat;

materials on the Obshchestvo Sibiriakov i Dal'novostochnikov in Paris; and manuscripts about arctic exploration and the Polar explorers F. Nansen and the Englishman Joseph Wiggins.

740 Vserossiiskii Zemskii Soiuz. Papers, 7 boxes, 1916-46. Minutes of meetings; reports on the union's activities; its bulletin; correspondence; photos of survivors of the Gallipoli campaign; and information about American aid, the credit union of the organization, and émigré welfare in Constantinople and elsewhere.

741 V. Vynnychenko. Papers, 138 boxes, 1900-50. Materials relating to Ukrainian studies. Restrictions.

742 Boris Petrovich Vysheslavtsev. Papers, ca. 1 box. Emigre philosopher. Texts of his articles and lectures on philosophy, typed and handwritten; issues of émigré publications containing his pieces; handwritten notes on his readings and lectures; correspondence from the 1940s-1950s with such people as the painter Konstantin Korovin, D. Merezhkovskii, and B. Zaitsev; and his manuscripts on Marxism, Stalinism, mass psychology, the Russian national character, Russian religion, Christianity and Judaism, Hindu mysticism, and esthetics, 1920s-1960s. Restrictions.

743 Allen Wardwell. Papers, ca. 8 boxes. Red Cross worker in Russia. 2 notebooks with typed diary excerpts--"American Red Cross Mission to Russia, 1917-1918"; diary of a trip to the USSR in 1922 in connection with a famine; 2 photo albums with almost 500 photos taken during 1917 Red Cross mission; typed account of the ARC in Russia, 1918; official correspondence and documents; materials on ARC relief distribution and on the Russian Famine Fund, 1921-23; correspondence and other items concerning Soviet-American trade in 1920; typed reports on the Russian internal situation and news summaries, 1918; and Wardwell's typed diary, with carbon, of his trip to the USSR in October 1941 with the Beaverbrook-Harriman Mission. Restrictions.

744 George E. Warren. Framed photocopy, with translation, of a document signed by A. G. Belosordov, chairman of the Ural District Soviet, 30 April 1918, acknowledging his receiving in custody Nicholas II, Empress Alexandra, and the Grand Duchess Mariia Nikolaevna (in Ekaterinburg).

745 G. Wierzbicki. His typescript, edited by M. Bernard, entitled "Deux ans dans les camps nazis d'extermination," n.d., 90 pp., on World War II, 1943-45.

746 Sergei Iul'evich Witte. Papers, 13 boxes, ca. 500 items. Finance minister under Alexander III and Nicholas II, negotiator of the Portsmouth Peace of 1905, and premier from October 1905 to April 1906. Primarily the original typed manuscript and photocopies of Witte's memoirs, which have been published. Witte's extensive correspondence with many statesmen of Imperial Russia are also in the collection, as are documents he gathered to support and illustrate the memoirs. Other holdings include essays (one is a 2-volume work on the origins of the Russo-Japanese War, from 1907); letters of Prince Nicholas of Herzegovina; his direct reports to the tsar as premier; telegrams and diplomatic correspondence, 1905; and a copy of the 17 October 1905 Manifesto. Additional reports and documents are by or about N. Bunge, the Finnish Question, the peasant question, 1898-1906, the Fundamental State Laws of April 1906, the gold standard, relations with Kaiser Wilhelm II and negotiations for a commercial treaty with Germany, the taking of Port Arthur, General A. N. Kuropatkin.

747 YMCA in Siberia. Photos taken by Charles Riley of YMCA activity in Siberia and the American Expeditionary Forces, showing Vladivostok, Tomsk, and Czech troops.

748 Elena Konstantinovna Zagorskii. Papers, ca. 2 boxes. Typed memoirs--"Koe-chto iz proshlago"--for 1910-20; short, typed autobiography of her husband, A. P. Vorobchuk-Zagorskii, 1954; and materials concerning the emigration in China.

749 Boris Konstantinovich Zaitsev. Papers, ca. 5 boxes. Émigré writer. Correspondence with I. Bunin, R. Gul', G. D. Grebenshchikov, V. A. Maklakov, Ivan Shmelev, N. A. Teffi, D. Merezhkovskii, A. Remizov, V. Khodasevich, V. Bulgakov, K. Bal'mont, Metropolitan Vladimir, Archbishop Kiprian, M. Aldanov, Z. Gippius, A. Grechaninov, M. Dobuzhinskii, M. M. Karpovich, B. Pasternak, photocopies, E. N. Roshchina-Insarova, and A. V. Tyrkova-Williams, 1920s-1940s; literary manuscripts and typed diaries for 1939-45, carbons. Restrictions.

750 Aleksandr Naumovich Zak. Papers, ca. 6 boxes. Documents and clippings concerning the Soviet-Estonian peace conference at Iurev in 1920; printed legal materials about the case of the Equitable Life Insurance Company (U.S.) vs. Russia, and the case of Lehigh Valley Railroad Company vs. Russia, 1927-1930s; and Soviet financial policies.

751 V. A. Zambrzhitskii. "Voennaia podgotovka SSSR v mirovoi voine i revoliutsii," about the period 1917-41, typescript (carbon), 309 pp.; and 3 handwritten essays about the 2 world wars and before.

752 Evgenii Ivanovich Zamiatin. Papers, ca. 900 items. Writer. Literary manuscripts--stories, articles, and other writings; correspondence, 1920s-1930s, including some with Charles Malamuth regarding a film of Zamiatin's story "The Captured Tsar" (1935); materials for the novel Attila; and his typescript about

meetings with Russian and foreign literary figures (Litsa, published in 1955). Restrictions.

753 Nikolai Vasil'evich Zaretskii. Papers, ca. 6 boxes. Autographs and letters of prominent Russian literary and cultural figures, including V. A. Zhukovskii, M. P. Pogodin, N. I. Grech, A. I. Turgenev, N. Gnedich, B. Pilniak, A. M. Remizov, and V. V. Rozanov; autobiographies of V. Khodasevich and B. Pilniak; writings of other 20th c. authors; correspondence, 1920s-1950s, with V. Bulgakov, S. Melgunov, N. Evreinov, A. Remizov, E. Zamiatin, N. A. Teffi; materials on the Museum of Russian History and Culture in Prague; short typed autobiography of Zaretskii; items relating to A. S. Pushkin and his times, ca. 2,300 prints, photos, cards, etc.; materials on military history, especially as it relates to Russian culture. Restrictions.

754 Evgeniia Sergeevna Zarina. Book of her poems; clipping relating to her novella; and typed excerpts of her diary (San Francisco emigration in the 1950s).

755 Vladimir Feofilovich Zeeler. Papers, ca. 7 boxes. Zemstvo and Zemgor leader, and a lawyer in the Paris emigration. Includes manuscripts and letters by leading Russian émigré writers and artists; the correspondence and materials of the Ob"edinenie russkikh advokatov vo Frantsii, 1928-33; correspondence with such émigré cultural figures as L. Pasternak, V. Nabokov, A. Glazunov, V. A. Maklakov, V. Nemirovich-Danchenko, A. M. Remizov, Marc Chagall, N. Roerich, Fedor Rodichev, A. F. Rodichev, N. A. Teffi, Mark Aldanov, N. I. Astrov, Konstantin Balmont, Aleksandr Benois, Ivan Bunin, M. Dobuzhinsky, V. F. Khodasevich, A. A. Kizewetter, Serge Koussevitsky, A. Kuprin, P. Miliukov.

756 N. P. Zemtseva. Papers, ca. 15 items. 3 notebooks containing handwritten memoirs of her father, General P. I. Bastieno, who participated in the Russian conquest of the Caucasus, 1863-65; mimeographed press releases, Tiflis, 1919, about the Civil War in Georgia; and a handwritten memo on Sukhumi and Georgia.

757 Aleksandr V. Zenkovskii. Papers, ca. 26 items. Zemstvo member. Handwritten "Vospominaniia o moei rabote v 1918 g. v soveshchanii zemskikh deiatelei"; similar writings about "visitations" ("poseshchaniia") of provincial and district zemstvos, 1903-15, 90 pp.; materials relating to P. A. Stolypin and the zemstvos; handwritten manuscript on service in the Kiev zemstvo, 1911-17; and memoirs dealing with a broad range of Russian political figures in the early 20th c.

758 V. V. Zenkovskii. Scholar. Sections of typed reminiscences, in Russian, concerning cultural figures he met in Prague, Belgrade, Paris, and the U.S., 1920-40; "Piat' mesiatsev u vlasti. Moe uchastie v ukrainskoi zhizni" (1918); materials on his participation in the Russian Christian Students' Movement, ca. 1900-1930s, and on the Russian church in Western Europe, 1950s; and manuscripts relating to pedagogical work in the emigration. Restrictions.

759 Vladimir Mikhailovich Zenzinov. Papers, ca. 52 boxes. Correspondence, 13 boxes, from the 1940s; reminiscences of Amalia Fondaminskaia, plus materials about her of V. Nabokov and Z. Gippius; letters of G. A. Gershuni, typed transcripts, 1903-1904, to his brother Viktor Andreevich, from the Petropavlovsk Fortress; letters, diaries, and photos of the Socialist Revolutionary Party, Zenzinov, and Russian students, 1903-1905; typed protocols of SR central committee sessions, September 1917-January 1918; a report on finances and statistics on elections to SR Party congresses, 1917-18, plus information on the Petrograd collective; typescript about the February Revolution and the SR Party, 93 pp.; correspondence, accounts, and mimeographed and handwritten materials from the 1950s concerning the Liga Bor'by za Narodnuiu Svobodu; plans for a united émigré center, 1951; Zenzinov's diaries, 1940s-1950s; manuscripts of his writings; photos, correspondence, texts of articles, and autobiography, 1923, of E. Breshkovskaia, with a bibliography of her works; typed "Vospominaniia" of B. Savinkov; letter from A. M. Remizov; documents on the founding of the Literaturnyi fond, 1946-47.

760 Nikolai Mikhailovich Zernov. Papers, ca. 3 boxes. Correspondence with autobiographical material on émigré leaders (writers, scholars, clerics), 1950s-1960s; typescript on V. Lenin's death according to the testimony of I. P. Pavlov and another neurologist; memoirs of Sofiia Aleksandrovna Zernov (1865-1942); report on Russian and Armenian refugees in France in 1935; materials on G. G. Kullman and the World Student Christian Federation, 1920s; and manuscripts of Zernov's articles, mostly published, on the Russian Orthodox Church in the USSR and in emigration, relations between the Anglican and Russian Orthodox churches, and other topics. Restrictions.

761 Sofia Mikhailovna Zernova. Papers, ca. 120 items. Typescript on visits to the USSR in 1961 and 1966 and on conditions there; typed memoirs for 1910-40 concerning the Civil War in the South, Georgia under the Mensheviks, the emigration in Constantinople, Europe, and the U.S., work for the Russian Student Christian Movement; letters of A. M. Remizov to his wife and his autobiographical sketch in English; and letters of N. A. Berdiaev and his wife to M. M. Zernova. Restrictions.

762 Aleksandr Borisovich Zharkovskii. Photograph of a delegation of Russian scientists

(including Ivan Pavlov) to the International Physiological Congress in Boston, August 1929; typed letters of D. I. Abrikosov while in the Pekin embassy, 1910; typescript biography, 266 pp., of I. Pavlov by Boris Petrovich Babkin.

763 Nikolai Vasil'evich Zheleznov. Papers, 2 boxes. Captain on the Russian general staff. Handwritten memoirs concerning the organization of the 13th army in World War I, the northern front in 1915, the Brusilov offensive, the Rumanian front, Revolution in Petrograd, disintegration of the army, and the Civil War in the South, ca. 1914-18.

764 Vera Vladimirovna Zherebtsova. Papers, ca. 36 items. Book with reminiscences of a Russian dentist, A. V. Frolov; and typed biography of Vladimir Vasil'evich Margoit.

765 A. Zherbi (Louis-Alexis Gerby). Typescripts in German about his activities for the SD Party in the 1905 Revolution as well as meetings with P. Miliukov in 1906 and after.

766 Pavel Zhestovskii. Architect for the king of Afghanistan. Typed account ("12 let v Afganistane") of his personal experiences, 1937-50, with illustrations and an historical introduction.

767 Nikolai Vasil'evich Zhigulev. Papers, ca. 3 boxes. Pseudonym of N. V. Matviichuk, an émigré journalist. Includes correspondence from the 1950s-1970s (some with Aleksandra Tolstoi); "Ushedshee"--recollections of childhood on the Don, ca. 1905, typed; and papers of the diplomat G. N. Gul'kevich regarding the Russkoe trudovoe khristianskoe dvizhenie, plus his correspondence with Zhigulev.

768 A. Zhukovskii. Typed and handwritten essays on such subjects as the Russo-Turkish War of 1877, the Caucasian front in World War I, military discipline, and gymnastics in the army, ca. World War I.

769 Aleksei A. Ziablov. Papers, ca. 150 items. Graduate of the Imperial Technical School, made a career in the Russian railway system and in the heavy machinery industry. His autobiography, handwritten and transcribed, 39 pp., discusses his technical education and later career (he taught in a provincial technical school after 1888). The autobiography also speaks of working conditions and labor unrest at the Kolomna heavy machinery plant ca. 1905, Russian personnel and investment in railroading, and the same in heavy industry. Other holdings include photos; official documents relating to his career; lecture notes about railroad mechanics; and a handwritten diary from an 1886 summer trip to the Caucasus. Restrictions.

770 O. A. Zinger. Photocopy of a typed manuscript by V. N. Pavlova about her youth and work in the Moscow Art Theater, ca. 1900-1930s, written in 1940 in Berlin, 200 pp.

771 Valentina Evgen'evna Zlinchenko. Poetry manuscripts, copies. Her pseudonym was Zlin.

772 M. M. Zolotarev. Papers, ca. 4 boxes. Government official. Correspondence concerning the unification of émigré organizations; materials concerning I. L. Solonevich, a former Soviet journalist who was sent to a prison camp and then fled the Soviet Union; membership lists, correspondence, statutes, etc. of Berloga--an émigré New York group seeking the overthrow of communism in Russia, 1939-40; documents on the 1914 Congress of Representatives of Russian Industry; papers from Zolotarev's tenure as a controller of the port of Vladivostok during World War I--about service in the State Control in the Far East, the Volunteer Fleet, etc., 1914-20; notes, reports, and minutes of meetings of the Russian Financial and Commercial Association in America, 1922-26; materials of the Rossiiskii Finansovo-Promyshlenno-Torgovyi Soiuz, 1922-23; and list of members of the Priamur National Assembly and other items on the Far East in the early 1920s.

773 Valentin P. Zubov. Typed "Souvenirs de la révolution russe (1917-1927)," 191 pp.; offprint of a Novyi zhurnal piece--"Institut istorii iskusstv. Stranitsy vospominanii"; and memoirs of the dwarf of Prince P. A. Zubov ("Karlik Favorita. Istoriia zhizni Ivana Andreevicha Iakubovskogo, Karlika Svetleishego Kniazia Platona Aleksandrovicha Zubova, pisannaia im samim," with preface and notes by V. P. Zubov. Restrictions.

774 S. de zur Muhlen. Baron Vladimir Knorring's essay entitled "Imperatorskaia Rossiia i ee otnoshenie k Lifliandskomu dvorianstvu i nemetsko-baltiiskomu natsionalizmu," 18th-20th c.

775 Larissa Dmitrievna Zvereva. Typed memoirs of life in Russia on her father's estate in Nizhegorod province, conditions there, the 1905 Revolution, and life in St. Petersburg with her husband, a deputy to the state duma (ca. 1885-1918; her father was a zemskii nachal'nik); and additional memoirs about events in Yugoslavia and the assassination of King Alexander in 1934.

NY 34
HERBERT H. LEHMAN PAPERS
COLUMBIA UNIVERSITY
406 International Affairs Building
New York, New York 10027
(212-280-2263/3060)

1 Hugh Jackson (1912-1966). Papers, 1942-45, 28 folders. Lehman's chief assistant at the

time of organization of OFRRO and its successor UNRRA. Became deputy director-general of UNRRA. Memoranda, conference reports, and (primarily) correspondence, all concerning relief efforts for war-torn nations after World War II. Information on the USSR, Balkan affairs, Poland, and other political matters. (NUCMC 74-291)

2 Commander Sir Robert G. A. Jackson. UNRRA Papers, 1945-48, 55 folders. Senior deputy director general of UNRRA. Reports, memoranda, etc., concerning the work of UNRRA, including missions in Byelorussia and the Ukraine. Some material involves Russian nationals who worked for UNRRA. In an oral history interview, ca. 300 pp., Sir Robert discusses his work as head of the Middle East Supply Centre and overseer of the Persian Gulf Supply Route to Russia during World War II.

3 Herbert H. Lehman (1878-1963). UNRRA Papers, 1943-44, 2 drawers and 25 folders. One of the initiators of the United Nations Relief and Rehabilitation Administration, and its first director general. Personal correspondence and general file of the director general of UNRRA. Reports, statements, speeches, and photographs. Lehman dealt with authorities in the Ukraine and Byelorussia concerning relief efforts in those areas; also with the Soviet government as UNRRA member and aid recipient. (NUCMC 74-292)

4 Marshall MacDuffie (1909-1967). Papers, 1944-48, 4 folders. Lawyer and UN official. First chief of the UNRRA mission to the Ukraine. Reports, correspondence, memoranda, and a history/review of the mission's work, covering February-August 1946 (including the months he was actually in the USSR, 20 March-late June). (NUCMC 74-294)

5 Charles Poletti (b. 1903). Oral history interview, 1978, ca. 600 pp. Allied military governor in Italy. Discusses the considerable contact with Russian officers he had in that post. They were observing American methods of military occupation to help plan their own methods after liberating Eastern Europe. There is a considerable amount of anecdotal material about Andrei Januarovich Vishinsky, one of the observers. Note: apparently the Poletti papers (NUCMC 74-295) contain no references pertinent to the USSR.

6 Richard B. Scandrett, Jr. (1891-1969). Papers, 1945-46, bound, 4 vols. Lawyer, first chief of the UNRRA mission to Byelorussia. Member of the Allied Reparations Commission, which met in Moscow in 1945. Includes reports and correspondence. (NUCMC 74-296)

Finding Aids: All collections have checklists, which may be obtained by writing the office.

NY 35
ORAL HISTORY RESEARCH OFFICE
COLUMBIA UNIVERSITY
Room 221M, Butler Library
(Mail: Box 20)
New York, New York 10027
(212-280-2273)

1 Columbia's oral history project, begun by Professor Allan Nevins, was the first such endeavor in this country. It remains the largest collection. Some of the listings below, though given separately, are also part of larger group projects (e.g., the "Eisenhower Administration" interview project). The larger project is indicated in parentheses after the individual name. In many cases, Russian/Soviet-related information forms a very small part of a total interview. The designation "Micro" at the end of a listing means that the transcript is also available in microform from the New York Times Oral History Program (Microfilming Corporation of America in Sanford, North Carolina). Many research libraries around the country will have some or all of these microforms. PRCQ means permission required to cite or quote.

2 Air Force Academy. 5,754 pp. at present, 1968-present. Concerns strategy and tactics in the air during World War I, World War II, and the Korean War. Individual restrictions apply.

3 Ralph Albertson (1866-1951). 46 pp., 1950, plus papers on microfilm. Clergyman. Traveled in Russia in 1918-19. Permission required to cite or quote (hereinafter, PRCQ). Micro.

4 John Richardson Alison (b. 1912) (Aviation Project). 132 pp., 1960. Air Force officer. In the USSR during World War II in connection with lend-lease. After 6 months in the Soviet Union, he was in Persia for 6 months, assisting the Russians (on assignment from the U.S. embassy in Moscow). He taught the Russians how to assemble and disassemble American aircraft. PRCQ. See also under Air Force Academy Project.

5 George Venable Allen (1903-1970). 77 pp., 1962, and 213 pp., 1967. Diplomat. 2 separate interviews. In the first he discusses the Potsdam conference of 1945 and his foreign service career. In the second, for the Eisenhower Administration project, he covers his tenure as director of USIA, the U.S. exhibition in Moscow and famous "Kitchen Debate" between N. S. Khrushchev and Richard M. Nixon, and his impressions of various secretaries of state (including John Foster Dulles). PRCQ. Micro.

6 Dillon Anderson (1906-1974) (Eisenhower Administration). 130 pp., 1969. Lawyer.

Speaks of the Geneva Summit Conference, President D. D. Eisenhower, and John Foster Dulles. PRCQ. Micro.

7 Orvil A. Anderson (1895-1965) (Henry H. Arnold Project). 113 pp., 1959. Air Force officer. Mostly on military subjects, World War II, and, in part, lend-lease. Permission required to see. See also under the Aviation Project. Micro.

8 Paul Henson Appleby (1891-1963). 360 pp., 1952. Political scientist. Lend-lease and the State Department. PRCQ. Micro.

9 Joseph Charles Aub (1890-1973). 566 pp., 1957, plus papers. Physician. Aub knew and gives his impressions of Ivan Pavlov. PRCQ. Micro.

10 Evan Peter Aurand (b. 1917) (Eisenhower Administration). 138 pp., 1967. Naval officer. N. Khrushchev's visit (1959) and the "Spirit of Camp David." PRCQ. Micro.

11 Aviation. 5,200 pp., 1961. More than 110 American and foreign figures important in the history of aviation recorded their memories of early flight, aerial combat (World War I, World War II, Korea), commercial aviation, and much more. No Soviet participants appear in the list of contributors. PRCQ in most cases. Many in Micro.

12 Boris Alexander Bakhmeteff (1880-1951). 568 pp., 1950. Engineer and diplomat. Early life in Russia, engineering studies in Switzerland and the U.S., Russian political affairs in 1903-14, and Russia in World War I. He came to the U.S. as part of the War Supply Mission, 1915-16, and, after the February Revolution, became ambassador to this country, in which post he remained until 1922. He discusses the Kerensky government, his ambassadorial service, the Woodrow Wilson administration, Edward Stettinius, Sr., and John Spargo. Permission required to see.

13 Angelica Balabanova (1878-1965). 100 pp., 1958. Russian socialist. Taken separately but now grouped with the Radio Liberty project. Balabanova was one of Lenin's closest colleagues and the first chief secretary of the executive committee of the Comintern. She discusses the 1917 Revolution, V. I. Lenin the man, the Comintern, the Zimmerwald Conference during World War I, John Reed, I. V. Stalin, and L. D. Trotskii. She also compares Bolshevism and fascism. Permission required to see.

14 Roger Nash Baldwin (b. 1884). 666 pp., 1954. Political reformer and sociologist. Traveled to Russia in 1927. Though he met some political prisoners, his book Liberty Under the Soviets (1928) is generally favorable toward the regime. PRCQ. Micro.

15 James William Barco (b. 1916) (Eisenhower Administration). 1,061 pp.; 1963. Lawyer and ambassador. Impressions of Nikita Khrushchev; discussion of various international questions and crises (World War II, Hungarian revolt of 1956) of the mid-20th c. Closed until 1 January 1984.

16 Joseph Barnes (1907-1970). 300 pp., 1953. Newspaperman. Entered the London School of Slavonic Studies in 1927; traveled to the Soviet Union the next year to study the peasant commune, staying for 8 months. He returned to the USSR in 1931, representing the New York Herald Tribune for nearly a year. He was again in the Soviet Union in 1934-39 and 1946-48. He discusses reporting from Russia and coverage of the N. Bukharin show trial (and others) in the purges. PRCQ.

17 Chester Bowles (b. 1901). 866 pp., 1963. Diplomat and government official. Discusses his long career, including work on the Defense Council, with the UNRRA, 1946-47, and in the John F. Kennedy administration. PRCQ. Micro.

18 John Brophy (1883-1963). 1,036 pp., 1955. Labor union official. He visited Russia in 1927. He comments on labor's view of socialism, communists, the labor movement, and William Z. Foster. PRCQ. Micro.

19 Earl Browder (1891-1973). 525 pp., 1964, plus papers. U.S. communist leader. Discusses the Russian Revolution of 1917, the Communist Party in 1919, the 1921 International Trade Union Congress in Russia, the third congress of the Communist International, the United Front and seventh congress of the Comintern, 1935, the Stalin-Hitler pact of 1939, World War II, postwar changes in the Communist Party, ideology, American radicalism, and various communist leaders. PRCQ. Micro.

20 Cass Canfield (b. 1897). 417 pp., 1966. Book publisher. Canfield interviewed Leon Trotskii in 1940. PRCQ. Micro.

21 Bennett Alfred Cerf (1898-1971). 1,029 pp., 1968. Book publisher. Traveled to Russia after World War I and the Revolution. Permission required to see.

22 Andrew Wellington Cordier (1901-1975). 532 pp., 1964. Educator and assistant to the UN secretary general in 1946. He also served in the UN in later years. He assesses such Russian leaders as Nikita Khrushchev, Andrei Gromyko, and other UN deputies. Comprehensive discussion of the early UN, its creation, the Hungarian (1956) and other crises. PRCQ. Micro. See also under Dag Hammarskjold and International Negotiations Projects.

23 Ted Cott (1917-1973). 297 pp., 1961. Radio and television executive. Speaks of the David Susskind interview of Nikita Khrushchev on the program Open End. PRCQ. Micro.

24 Frederic Rene Coudert (1871-1955). 170 pp., 1950, plus papers. Lawyer. Impressions of Boris Bakhmeteff. PRCQ. Micro.

25 James Freeman Curtis (1878-1952). 334 pp., 1951. Lawyer. Impressions of Efrem Zimbalist. PRCQ. Micro.

26 Malcolm Waters Davis (b. 1889). 435 pp., 1950, plus papers. Government official and statesman. In 1916 he went to Russia with a War Prisoners Aid Group (YMCA- and Red Cross-sponsored). After 6 months (in charge of Austrian and German prisoners for Russia), Davis went to work for the Russian Division of the United States Information Service (USIS), with which he served from 1917-19. Thereafter he worked for different international bodies. At the UN conference in San Francisco in 1945, Davis met the Soviet negotiators. He speaks of European and Siberian Russia in 1917-22, and of A. Kerensky, V. I. Lenin, M. Litvinov, Dmitrii (Dimitry) Zakharovich Manuilsky, P. Miliukov, V. Molotov, I. V. Stalin, L. D. Trotskii, A. Gromyko, the Grand Duke Michael, and George Vernadsky. PRCQ. Micro.

27 Theodosius Dobzhansky (1900-1975). 637 pp., 1962. Russian-American geneticist. In part 1 of the interview, he talks about his childhood and education in Russia, his early interest in genetics, experiences during the revolutionary and postrevolutionary years, and his genetics training in the USSR. He came to the U.S. in 1928 on a Rockefeller fellowship. In part 2 he gives his impressions of certain scientists, especially geneticists. PRCQ. Micro.

28 Kenneth Wayne Dryden (b. 1947). 58 pp., 1976. Athlete. Family background, public interest activities, the Montreal Summer Olympics of 1976, Official Secrets Act, Canadian national hockey team and Canadian hockey structure, impressions of Moscow and Leningrad in 1969, an incident during the Soviet Army-Philadelphia Flyers hockey game, and the Soviet Sport Institute. PRCQ, some pages closed.

29 Eleanor Lansing Dulles (b. 1895) (Eisenhower Administration). 973 pp., 1967. Economist. She served in the State Department in 1942-62. Covers such topics as the UNRRA, the Morgenthau Plan, post-World War II displaced persons, and internal security investigations. Permission required to see.

30 Donald Duncan (1896-1975). 981 pp., 1964. Naval officer. He was at the Yalta Conference. Much information about military affairs (e.g., missiles and aeronautics, the Korean War, the atom bomb).

31 Leslie Clarence Dunn (1893-1974). 1,086 pp., 1960. Columbia genetics professor. In 1927 he traveled to the Soviet Union. Discussion of Soviet science and scientists, the history of genetics in Russia, plant breeding in Russia, the end of the Gorki Institute of Medico-Genetics and the crisis of 1938, the Lysenko school versus the Mendel-Morgan-Weissman school of genetics, scientific debates in Russia in 1936, 1938-39, and 1948, and the American-Soviet Science Society. He speaks of Alexander Serebrovskii, Nikolai Vavilov, Theodosius Dobzhansky, H. J. Muller, and Trofim Lysenko. PRCQ. Micro.

32 Eisenhower Administration. 35,597 pp. at present, 1962-present, plus papers. Testimony gathered from General Dwight D. Eisenhower, his family, and those who played important roles in his 2 terms as president, 1953-61. More than 270 persons have participated. Among them:

33 Dwight David Eisenhower (1890-1969). 114 pp., 1967. Army officer and U.S. president. Discusses many international crises and problems of his administration. Certain pages closed.

34 John Sheldon David Eisenhower (b. 1922). 144 pp., 1967. Army officer and the president's son. Recalls anecdotes and personal aspects of his father's career and presidency, Korea, weapons development, and the Geneva Conference. Permission required to see. Various diplomats discuss their service in the USSR and negotiations with Soviet leaders. Some materials are closed; some require permission to see, others--PRCQ.

35 Henriette Epstein. 120 pp., 1976. Discusses her husband Abraham Epstein, his emigration from Russia to the United States, involvement with the workers' education movement in 1920, impressions of Russia (1921), job as research director for the Pennsylvania Old Age Commission, 1920-27, founding of the American Association for Old Age Security, 1927, fight for old age pension laws; and the Social Security Act of 1935. Permission required to see.

36 Bela Fabian (1889-1967). 447 pp., 1951, and papers. Hungarian political figure. In 1918 he escaped from a Russian POW concentration camp to Petrograd. Discusses these experiences, Russia and Hungary in 1918, the Tashkent and Krasnaia Rechka camps where he was interned, A. Kerensky, V. I. Lenin, A. V. Kolchak, A. M. Kaledin, Aleksei A. Lebedev, Miasoedov, G. Rasputin, I. V. Stalin, and L. D. Trotskii. PRCQ. Micro.

37 Paul F. Foster (1889-1972). 373 pp., 1966. Naval officer. Impressions of Vyacheslav Molotov. Permission required to see.

38 Osmond K. Fraenkel (b. 1888). 144 pp., 1974. Lawyer. Discusses education at Harvard,

1904-1908, and Columbia Law School; early law practice; Soviet cases; Norris, Patterson, Trop, and Leyra cases; communism in America; impressions of Alger Hiss and U.S. Supreme Court justices. PRCQ.

39 Charlotte Garrison (1881-1972). 58 pp., 1967. Educator. Traveled as a tourist to Russia in 1929, visiting schools, hospitals, and prisons. PRCQ. Micro.

40 Andrew Jackson Goodpaster (b. 1915) (Eisenhower Administration). 137 pp., 1967. Army officer and White House aide. Speaks of U.S. relations with the Soviet Union during the Eisenhower administration. PRCQ. Micro.

41 Michel Gordey (b. 1913). 106 pp., 1962. Journalist and author. Experiences in the Office of War Information during World War II and in Budapest during the Hungarian revolt of 1956. Impressions of Nikita Khrushchev. Permission required to see.

42 James C. Hagerty (b. 1909) (Eisenhower Administration). 569 pp., 1968. Journalist and presidential press secretary. Talks of travels with President Eisenhower as press secretary and of Nikita Khrushchev. Permission required to see.

43 Dag Hammarskjold Project. 230 pp., 1962. Colleagues reminisce about Hammarskjold (1905-1961), Swedish statesman and secretary general of the UN, 1953-61, his approach to administration and the executive challenges of his post, especially staffing the secretariat, the Congo crisis, and the Russian troika proposal. PRCQ.

44 J. B. S. Hardman (1882-1968). 83 pp., 1962. American labor leader born in the Russian Empire. Discusses his early life in Vilna; his father was in the lumber business. His years in Russia, 1900-10, were punctuated by arrest, 1906, as a union leader and by a trip to London, 1907, for a Social Democratic Party conference, where he saw V. I. Lenin and L. D. Trotskii. Open.

45 W. Averell Harriman (b. 1891) (International Negotiations). 353 pp., 1969. Statesman and official. He was present at many World War II conferences with I. V. Stalin and other Allied leaders. He assesses the use of the presidency in international affairs from 1933-69, talks at length about the nuclear test ban agreement, and discusses the Vietnam peace talks. Permission required to see.

46 Luther Hartwell Hodges (1898-1974) (Eisenhower Administration). 39 pp., 1968. Secretary of commerce under Eisenhower. Visited the Soviet Union as secretary of commerce. PRCQ.

47 International Negotiations. 1,677 pp., 1970-present. Edward W. Barrett, director of the Communications Institute of the Academy for Educational Development, conducted these interviews with individuals well versed in international negotiations and mediation of disputes. The single largest transcript is that of W. Averell Harriman (q.v.). Others interviewed include: Manlio Brosio, 24 pp., Arthur J. Goldberg, 51 pp., Sir Geoffrey Harrison, 34 pp., Joseph E. Johnson, 120 pp., Theodore W. Kheel, 43 pp., John J. McCloy, 24 pp., Llewellyn Thompson, 29 pp., and Vladimir Velebit, 80 pp. Permission required to see.

48 Hans V. Kaltenborn (1878-1965) (Radio Pioneers). 248 pp., 1950. Radio commentator and editor. He speaks of his visits to the USSR in 1926 and 1929. The second trip was under the auspices of the Russian-American Chamber of Commerce. He comments on American engineers in Russia, the friendliness of Russians to foreigners, and the strength of the Bolshevik regime. Detailed table of contents and index. PRCQ. Micro.

49 Nikita S. Khrushchev (1894-1971). 2,516 pp. Plus the original tape recordings. Soviet Communist Party leader and premier. Khrushchev tape recorded his reminiscences in the Soviet Union, then sent them abroad to be published. He discusses his career in the Communist Party of the Soviet Union from its beginnings to his tenure as first secretary, 1953-64. Among the topics covered are the purges and terror of the 1930s, World War II, famine in the Ukraine, Stalin's last years and the struggle for succession, and Soviet foreign relations. Much of this material has appeared in the 2 volumes entitled Khrushchev Remembers (Little, Brown and Co, 1970 and 1974). However, many details and stylistic flourishes were deleted when the cumbersome and disordered manuscript was prepared for publication. Name index and topical outlines. Permission required to see.

50 Alexandra Kollontai Project. 259 pp., 1978. Series of interviews on the life and career of Alexandra Kollontai (1872-1952), undertaken by Sonya Baevsky as part of a larger project on the Russian revolutionary and diplomat, involving also a documentary film. Some of the taped interviews are with persons who knew Kollontai; others discuss the significance of her career to Russian history, revolutionary movements, and women's history. Participants and pages: Erik Boheman (3), Barbara Clements (110), Runa Haukaa (5), Meridal Lessueur (61), Just Lippe (4), Alva Myrdal (7), Eva Palmaer (15), Margit Palmaer-Walden (11), Margit Palmaer-Walden and Alva Myrdal (2), Kenneth Rexroth (9), Gloria Steinem (26), and Aksel Zachariassen (6). Permission required to see.

51 Arthur Krock (1887-1974). 102 pp., 1950. Newspaperman. Was present at the Yalta Conference in 1945. PRCQ. Micro.

52 Corliss Lamont (b. 1902). 165 pp., 1960. Author and teacher. Discusses his visits to the Soviet Union. Permission required to see.

53 William Leonard Laurence (1888-1977). 148 pp., 1954 and 395 pp., 1964. Science editor for the New York Times, born in Russia. He talks about his early years in Russia and about his coverage of the development of atomic energy, the Manhattan Project, and the dropping of the atomic bomb. PRCQ. Micro. Note: The oral history collection also contains interviews with men who worked on the development of the atomic bomb (the Manhattan Project): Kenneth Bainbridge, Harvey Bundy, Charles Coryell, and Norman Ramsey. None of these interviews is listed separately in this entry.

54 Herbert Henry Lehman (1878-1963) (Herbert H. Lehman Project). 785 pp., 1961. Governor of New York and U.S. senator. Lehman was one of the initiators of the United Nations Relief and Rehabilitation Administration (UNRRA) after World War II. He became that agency's director general, in which capacity he had dealings with the Soviet Union (as member and aid recipient) --through the governments of the Ukraine and Byelorussia. Full topical index. PRCQ. Micro.

55 Lewis L. Lorwin (1883-1970). 479 pp., 1961. Economist. In 1921-23 he conducted a survey of the Soviet Union. He was later chief economist for the International Labor Organization, 1935, and served the ILO and the League of Nations in 1935-39. Permission required to see.

56 Branko Lukac (fl. 1930s) (League of Nations). 124 pp., 1966. Official of the League of Nations. Discusses the organization's role and work, including details of the Russo-Finnish War of 1939-40. PRCQ.

57 Marshall Plan. 103 pp., 1947-61. Collection includes material on the origins and implementation of the Marshall Plan. Emphasis is on the role of the State Department and particularly of Will Clayton. Participants and pages: Dean Acheson (5), Will Clayton (32), Emilio G. Collado (14), Lewis W. Douglas (2), Livingston Merchant (3), Norman Ness (5), Paul Nitze (8), Arthur Stevens (4), James Stillwell (5), Leroy Stinebower (6), and Ivan White, 19. PRCQ.

58 Livingston Tallmadge Merchant (1903-1976) (Eisenhower Administration). 86 pp., 1967. State Department official. Impressions of President Dwight D. Eisenhower, John Foster Dulles, and Vyacheslav Molotov, among others. PRCQ. See also under Marshall Plan and International Negotiations.

59 Edward P. Morgan (b. 1910) (Eisenhower Administration). 53 pp., 1967. Writer and broadcaster. Covered such events as the "Kitchen Debate" between Vice-President Richard Nixon and Nikita Khrushchev in 1959. Permission required to see.

60 Naval History. 17,921 pp., 1960-69. Concerns modern naval history, intelligence, scientific development, strategy and tactics in both world wars and the Korean conflict, major battles, the Russian navy, and American and foreign political and military figures. Among the 36 participants (with pages) were Alan G. Kirk, 386, and Chester W. Nimitz, 89. Individual restrictions apply.

61 David Rowan Nimmer (1894-1975). 199 pp., 1970. Marine Corps officer. Nimmer was naval attaché at the American embassy in Moscow in 1934-35. He also went on missions to Warsaw, Leningrad, and Sevastopol. Permission required to see.

62 John Bertram Oakes (b. 1913). 64 pp., 1962. Newspaper editor. Visited the USSR in 1936. Permission required to see.

63 DeWitt Clinton Poole (1885-1952). 490 pp., 1952. Diplomat. Served in Russia during the Revolution, 1917-18. Detailed account of these events and the Allied intervention at Archangel, 1919. Later he served in the Russian Affairs division of the State Department. PRCQ. Micro.

64 Popular Arts Project. 7,819 pp., 1958-60. Includes references to the Stanislavsky method of acting and Soviet silent films. One interviewee is the actor Akim Tamiroff (55 pp.). Most memoirs open.

65 Jacob Samuel Potofsky (b. 1894). 883 pp., 1965. Union official. Covers his family background and education in Russia, subsequent emigration to the U.S. PRCQ. Micro.

66 Max Rabinoff (1876-1966). 48 pp., 1963. Impresario. Toured with the Ballet Russe until 1917, helped introduce the Russian ballet to the United States in 1909-11. Open.

67 Radio Liberty. 1,495 pp., 1964-65. Transcripts, in Russian, of interviews conducted in Europe by Radio Liberty and the Munich-based Institute for the Study of the USSR. The occasion for the project was the coming 50th anniversary of the Revolution. The 75 participants (with page totals) included: Pavel Ivanovich Anov, pseudonym (32), Nikolai Yakovlevich Galay (23), Alexandr Karlovich Plakhe (25), Semyon Stepanovich Kabysch (18), Roman Vladimirovich Sagovsky (26), Oleg Alexandrovich Kerensky (14), Georgi Yakovlevich Kiverov (48), Maria Samoilovna Davidova (23), Vassili Tsouladze (19), Yuri Petrovich Denicke (54), Mikhail Matveyevich Ter-Pogosian (51), Alexander Osipovich Marchak (50), Arkady Petrovich Stolypin (20), Alexandra Petrovna Kaiserling (nee Stolypina) (15), Lev Nikolaevich Duwing (26), Vadim Alekseevich Kungurvew (25), Nikolai Sergeevich Kozorez (15), Andrei Vasilevich Svetlanin (7), Vasiliy Vasilyevich Orekhoff (21), Alexei Nikolaevich Tchebycheff (18), Sergei Alexandrovich Kasyanov (14), Wladimir Vasilyevich Weidle (16), Wilhelm Karlovich Mutsenek (20), Genrikh Gansovich Laratei (20), Bruno Pavlovich Kalnins (21), Georgii

Dmitrievich Adamovich (33), Mark L'vovich Slonim (54), Nikolai Sergeevich Arsen'ev (38), David Natanovich Shub (52), Prof. N. D. Polonskoi-Vasilenko (31), Mamed Mikheich Sadykov (10), Ekaterina Nikolaevna Roshchina-Insarova (45), Iurii Romanovich Disterlo (25), Evgenii Vasil'evich Maslovskii (16), Petr Grigor'evich Sobolev (48), Aleksei Aleksandrovich Golovin (24), Iurii Evren'evich Dzhunkovskii (26), Vladimir Vladimirovich Popov (21), Aleksei L'vovich Mishchenko (43), Aleksandr Aleksandrovich Lodyzhenskii (49), Mikhail Germanovich Kornfel'd (10), Mark Veniaminovich Vishniak (66), Solomon Meerovich Shvarts (40), Grigorii Iakovlevich Aronson (42), Aleksandra L'vovna Tolstaia (15), Sergei Germanovich Pushkarev (28), Aleksei Aleksandrovich Gol'denveizer (57), Roman Borisovich Gul' (28), Boris Vasil'evich Sergievskii (16), Sergei Georgievich Romanovskii (19), Sergei Viktorovich Grotov (26), Mikhail Iur'evich Rodionov (12), and others. Materials also include an excerpt from a letter written from the front, 9-15 March 1917, Old Style, by Aleksandr Aleksandrovich Drenteln, commander of the Preobrazhenskii Regiment, 15 pp. The original, 32 pp., is held by Count Kochubei in Rome. Interviewees discuss not only events of 1917 but also biographical details (childhood, education, emigration). Participants held a variety of positions in Russian society and came from all over the empire. Subjects covered in the interviews include the student draft, World War I, Petrograd's mood in 1916, the February Revolution, the Kornilov affair, the October Revolution, Civil War, Estonian independence movement, establishment of the hetmanate in the Ukraine, the Bolshevik occupation of Kiev, the Caucasus, and the New Economic Policy. Persons mentioned: A. Kerensky, A. R. Gots, V. Chernov, A. Zenzinov, A. Protopopov, Grand Duke Nikolai Nikolaevich, M. Gorkii, V. Mayakovskii, M. A. Vatsetis, P. I. Stuchka, K. Kh. Danishevsky, P. A. Stolypin, A. Lunacharsky, A. Blok, F. Dzerzhinsky, A. Belyi, A. V. Krivoshein, P. Miliukov, A. Guchkov, V. I. Lenin, and I. V. Stalin. Permission required to see. See also under Angelica Balabanova.

68 Nelson Aldrich Rockefeller (1908-1979). 730 pp., 1952. New York governor and U.S. official. Discussion of the Soviet Union and the San Francisco Conference establishing the UN, 1945, his State Department service, and questions of foreign relations. Closed until 1997. In 2 other memoirs, 40 pp., 1967--Eisenhower Administration, and 52 pp., 1978, he discusses international affairs during the 1950s.

69 Richard Rodgers (b. 1902). 392 pp., 1968. Composer. Impressions of George Balanchine. PRCQ; some pages closed during his lifetime.

70 Harrison Salisbury (b. 1908) (Journalism Lectures). 65 pp., n.d. Editor of the New York Times. Describes Nikita Khrushchev's 1959 visit to the U.S., particularly his trip to the Garst farm to inspect corn ("The Battle of Coon Rapids"). Salisbury talks about the problems of covering this event, the distorting effect of the journalists' presence, and his impressions of Soviet journalists. PRCQ.

71 Roger Huntington Sessions (b. 1896). 309 pp., 1962. Composer. Comments on Igor Stravinsky. PRCQ. Micro.

72 Max Shachtman (1903-1972). 522 pp., 1963. Trotskyite socialist. Discusses the development of socialist and radical groups in the 1920s and 1930s (Communist Workers Party, Workers' Council, Trotskyites); factional struggles; his trips to Moscow in 1925 and 1927; the International Labor Defense group; his expulsion from the Communist Party; the party split over the Nazi-Soviet pact of 1939; his visits to Leon Trotskii in Turkey, Norway, Paris, and Mexico; Trotskii's assassination; and the Independent Socialist League, 1948-58. Impressions of Joseph Stalin also. PRCQ. Micro. See also under Socialist Movement, Micro.

73 Ben Shahn (1898-1969). 154 pp., 1960. Artist. Discusses his early life in Lithuania. PRCQ.

74 Boris Basil Shishkin (b. 1906). 872 pp., 1957. Economist. Covers his early years in Russia, education, World War I, the Revolution, and his flight to Istanbul. PRCQ. Micro.

75 Socialist Movement. 1,141 pp., 1965. Project concerns the start and development of the Socialist Party, the party's relationship to unions, the Trotskyite movement, the Communist Party, and other groups. Those interviewed and pages: Irving Barshop (27), Daniel Bell (49), John Bennett (30), Travers Clement (39), Morris L. Ernst (33), Paul Feldman (23), Harry Fleischman (38), Samuel Friedman (54), Gerry Gelles (50), Maurice Goldbloom (37), Eric Hass (33), Adolph Held (28), Harry Laidler (50), Aaron J. Levenstein (43), David McReynolds (34), Nathaniel Minkoff (28), A. J. Muste (26), Robin Myers (53), Pauline Newman (33), D. Ernst Papanek (62), Joseph Schlossberg (51), Max Shachtman (76), Herman Singer (23), Mark Starr (42), Seymour Steinsapir (24), Irwin Suall (43), Paul Sweezy (14), Norman Thomas (25), Gus Tyler (28), and James Weinstein (45). PRCQ.

76 George Ephraim Sokolsky (1893-1962). 126 pp., 1962. Newspaper columnist and author. Reference to Russia. PRCQ. Micro.

77 Elvin C. Stakman (1885-1979). 1,687 pp., 1970. Plant pathologist. Discusses his interest in world food and hunger problems, agricultural science in Russia and other communist nations. Permission required to see.

78 George Stroganoff-Scherbatoff (1898-1976). 252 pp., 1974. Naval officer. Concerns radio

communications of the Russian naval general staff in 1916-17; the October 1917 Revolution; pre-revolutionary Russian society; family history and attempts to recover his inheritance; childhood and education; career as a U.S. naval officer in World War II; service as a translator at Yalta, Potsdam, Paris Peace, and Big Four Conferences; and "Arms of Friendship," a Soviet-U.S. veterans exchange program, 1958-67. PRCQ.

79 Thomas Day Thacher (1881-1950). 108 pp., 1949, plus papers. Judge. Comments on Russia in 1917. Closed until 1 January 2000.

80 Norman Thomas (1884-1968). 217 pp., 1950, and 152 pp., 1965. American socialist leader. Biographical memoir in 2 parts. PRCQ. Micro. See also under Socialist Movement, Micro.

81 Mary Heaton Vorse (Mrs. Albert White) (1881-1966). 73 pp., 1957. Author. Speaks of anarcho-syndicalism and of the Soviet Union. PRCQ. Micro.

82 James J. Wadsworth (b. 1905) (Eisenhower Administration). 248 pp., 1967. Government official. Discusses disarmament conferences, nuclear test ban treaty negotiations, Soviet relations, and his work with the United Nations. PRCQ. Micro.

83 Henry Agard Wallace (1888-1965). 5,197 pp., 1951, and microfilm papers, 36 items. Public official and U.S. vice-president. Scattered references to Britain and the USSR during World War II, his own trip to Siberia in June 1944, post-war Russia, his meetings with (and impressions of) Soviet and European diplomats, and major issues in Soviet-American relations. He comments on the problem of American recognition of the USSR, the Russo-Finnish War of 1939-40, Sikorski and the Polish Question, the disbanding of the Comintern, the Teheran conference, and trips to Russia by Wendell Willkie and Don Nelson. Impressions of M. Litvinov, J. Stalin, A. Gromyko, V. Molotov, and the Soviet Ambassador Constantine Oumansky. PRCQ. Micro.

84 Stanley Washburn (1878-1950). 201 pp., 1950. Journalist and businessman. Discusses Republican politics, 1890-1932; the Russo-Japanese War; service as a correspondent in Russia for the London Times, 1914-17; Stevens's railroad mission and the Elihu Root diplomatic mission to Russia in 1917. PRCQ. Micro.

85 John Campbell White (1884-1967). 139 pp., 1953. Diplomat and official. White was in the diplomatic service in Russia, 1915-16. He also talks about his experiences in Poland in 1919-21 (food distribution problems, Poles in the Ukraine, meeting with S. V. Petliura, the Bolshevik advance on Warsaw). He was first secretary at the Riga embassy, 1924-25, when that post was a main conduit for information about the Soviet Union. Back in Washington, he was with the East European division of the State Department in 1926. He comments on the question of American recognition of the USSR. PRCQ. Micro.

86 Eugene Edward Wilson (1887-1974). 974 pp., 1962. Naval aviator and aircraft industrialist. Impressions of Igor Sikorsky. PRCQ. Micro.

87 Milburn Lincoln Wilson (1885-1969), 2,165 pp., 1956. Agriculturist. Wilson went on an advisory trip to Russia in 1929, helping to set up an experimental tractor station near Rostov-on-Don. He participated in the Roerich expedition in the 1930s. The 1929 trip was backed in part by Alexander Legge, head of International Harvester, apparently hoping that Wilson would urge the Soviet Union to reimburse his company for its confiscated tractor plant near Moscow. Wilson also records his impressions of Birobijan, visited on the way home when he passed through Siberia to Vladivostok. PRCQ. Mirco.

Finding Aids: The Oral History Collection of Columbia University, edited by Elizabeth B. Mason and Louis M. Starr, 4th ed. (New York, 1979). Every memoir has a name index. In addition, a computerized name, subject, and topical index (combined) is in preparation but only for the memoirs available in microform (those labeled "Micro") at present.

NY 36
RARE BOOK AND MANUSCRIPT LIBRARY
COLUMBIA UNIVERSITY
801 Butler Library
New York, New York 10027
(212-280-2231/2)

Although the bulk of the Russian-related archival materials of the Columbia University Libraries is in the Bakhmeteff Archive, the Manuscript Department (and other divisions) also have significant holdings.

1 American Institute of Pacific Relations (1927-62). Office files, ca. 235,000 items. Primary concerns of the American branch and its international counterpart were the political, economic, and social problems of eastern and southern Asia and the South Pacific, and problems of American foreign policy. The institutes held international conferences, conducted research programs, and published works on these topics. Contains travel letters and reports on conditions in Russia and other countries, 1933-54. (NUCMC 64-1331)

2 Armenian Manuscripts (Smith Collection, Plimpton Collection, and separate holdings). The Smith Collection holds 2 leaves from a Gospel of John, ca. 12th c. (MS. Armen. [frag.] 1) and a miscellany from 1584 and later (MS. Armen. 5). The Plimpton Collection contains a

hymnal of 1659 (MS. Armen. 2), four Gospels, 17th c. (MS. Armen. 3), and a phylactery from 1636 (MS. Armen. 4). Separate holdings include a manuscript copy of the ritual of the Armenian church, 1628 (X892.9 Ar 5Q), theological lectures, n.d. (X892.9 L49), and an undated hymnal (X892.9 N35).

3 Nicolai T. Berezowsky (1893-1954). Papers, 1900-53, 9 boxes, ca. 1,250 letters and 15 vols. Violinist and conductor. Correspondence with Serge Koussevitsky (22 letters), Nicolai Lopatnikoff (72), Vladimir Golschmann, Alexander Gretchaninoff, Artur Rodzinski, Leopold and Olga Samaroff Stokowski, Paul Nordoff, and others. One TLS to him is from the Moscow First Symphony Ensemble (18 December 1930), 1 p. (NUCMC 71-927)

4 Louis Cowan Collection (1941-45). 45 items. Collection of Soviet World War II posters. Colorful propaganda works produced by such artists as Mikhail Cheremnykh for TASS, the Soviet Telegraph Agency. An artist collective would receive war news from TASS, quickly give it a graphic interpretation (usually within 24 hours), and hang the results in display windows of stores. The TASS Windows Collective in Moscow produced a total of 1,250 posters. There is a published brochure describing these posters, exhibited at Columbia's Russian Institute in December 1976, with commentary by Elizabeth Kridl Valkenier.

5 Malcolm Waters Davis (1889-1970). Papers, ca. 1883-1949, ca. 400 items. Author and international affairs specialist. Correspondence and literary manuscripts. Davis lived in Russia, 1916-19. His letters from these years contain observations about the country and particularly the Revolution. He later became associated with the Carnegie Endowment for International Peace. (NUCMC 74-267) Note: The Manuscript Department also holds the office files of the New York and Paris branches of the Carnegie Endowment for International Peace, ca. 1911-54; ca. 500 vols., 124 cartons, and 900 correspondence files, among which there may well be relevant materials. Time did not permit an examination.

6 Theodore S. Farrelly (1883-1955). Papers, ca. 1930-55, ca. 1,000 items. Writer. Collection of letters, prints, photos, and other materials relating to Alaska. Farrelly's research, resulting in books and articles, covered much of early Russian colonization in Alaska. (NUCMC 61-2939)

7 William Averell Harriman Papers on Special Envoy. Working files for the book Special Envoy to Churchill and Stalin, 1941-1946 (New York: Random House, 1975) by William Averell Harriman (b. 1891) and Elie Abel (b. 1920), Columbia University's dean of journalism. Typescript drafts with handwritten corrections of Harriman's recollections; typed notes; photocopies of American, British, and Soviet (in translation) diplomatic correspondence, memoranda, and reports; speeches and other writings by Harriman; and related background materials. Arranged in numbered folders (rough chronological order), some with subject headings. Some folders are lacking. Files cover 1941-46 and 1951-54. Includes photocopies of letters from Franklin D. Roosevelt, Harry S. Truman, Edward L. Stettinius, Harry Hopkins, Dean Acheson, Charles Bohlen, Joseph Stalin, Vyacheslav Molotov, Andrei Vyshinski, Winston Churchill, and Anthony Eden. An additional 5 letters from Harriman to Abel (1973-74) concern details of writing this book.

8 Lydia Holubnychny (1929-1975). Papers, ca. 1923-75, ca. 4,000 items. Sino-Soviet scholar. Include research materials for her dissertation; 5 boxes of Russian and miscellaneous files; a name file index, A-Z, 7 boxes; notes on China, 2 boxes; 2 boxes of bibliography cards; and a box of annotated books.

9 Herbert Renfro Knickerbocker (1898-1972). Papers, 1914-50, 8,000 items. Foreign correspondent. Notebooks, photos, clippings, 1927-45. Letters from Walter Duranty, Leon Trotskii, and Winston Churchill. (NUCMC 78-693)

10 Max Matthasia Laserson (1887-1951). Papers, 1932-46, ca. 1,000 items. Lecturer in legal and political philosophy at Columbia. Correspondence, notes, and drafts relate to his published works on international law and politics, especially of Russia. (NUCMC 66-1592)

11 Mikhail Lermontov (1814-1841). Collection of 3 albums containing poetry and drawings, many by the poet Lermontov. Such albums were kept at home so that friends could record their sentiments. Known as the "Vereshchagina Albums," only 2 actually belonged to the Vereshchagin family, which was distantly related to the Lermontovs. The third belonged to Varvara Lopukhina, a cousin of the Vereshchagins and an early sweetheart of Lermontov. Album I, 1808-22, belonged to Elizaveta Arkadievna Annenkova-Vereshchagina. It contains poems by Russian and French poets. Some of the verses by Russian poets are copies; others are autographs. Many poems have pencilled annotations identifying their writers (added later and not to be trusted). Besides verses this album contains many drawings (none of Lermontov). Other poets whose works are identified: N. Vakhrameev, Ivan Dmitriev, Davidov, A. Guselnikov, V. A. Zhukovskii, Popov, Vasilii Kapnist, Princess Nadezhda Pokhuznina, and S. Martinoff. Album II, 1831-33, belonged to Elizaveta's daughter, Alexandra [Alexandrina] Vereshchagina von Hügel (Baroness Karl), 1810-1873, who moved in the same literary circles as her cousin Lermontov. Contains Russian and French poems, also some English poetry, reflecting Russian interest in Lord Bryon and Thomas Moore. 1

poem has been identified as Lermontov's and there are 9 drawings by him. Other poets: Prince Alexei, Khovansky, A. S. Pushkin, E. Baratynsky, Offrosimoff, I. Kozlov, A. Bystren, Karlhof, and Glebov. Album III, 1825-40, was cherished by Lermontov's former sweetheart, Varvara Lopukhina, long after her marriage to Nikolai Bakhmetev, who never lost his jealousy of Lermontov. Her cousin Alexandrina eventually gained possession of this album. It contains no verses, only watercolors, ink and pencil drawings, all by Lermontov. A microfilm copy has been made; only with permission of the librarian for rare books and manuscripts can the microfilm (not the originals!) be used. The albums are described in Helen Michailoff's article "The Vereshchagina Albums," Russian Literature Tri-quarterly, no. 10 (Fall 1974).

12 John Milton (1608-1674). Letterbook, 1649-59, 1 vol. English poet and secretary to Oliver Cromwell. Copies (in a secretary's hand) of 156 letters written by Milton when he was Cromwell's secretary. All but 10 are in Latin, arranged by the name of the recipient. [Letter] 98 is "Instructions for ye Agent to ye Great Duke of Muscovy" (1657) and no. 99 is "Imp[er]atori Duciq[ue] magno Russiae" (To the emperor and grand duke of Russia, i.e., the tsar), ca. 1657. The tsar and grand duke would be Aleksei Mikhailovich. (NUCMC 61-3350)

13 Robert Minor (1884-1952). Papers, 1907-52, 15,000 items. Journalist, cartoonist, and founder of the American communist movement. Collection of notes, speeches, articles, and clippings. Covers his career as communist writer (including for the New York Daily Worker), party policies in the 1930s-1950s, and red trials of 1949-53. Extensive clippings on the Russian Revolution and the Spanish Civil War. (NUCMC 67-800)

14 Max Rabinoff (1877-1966). Papers, 1908-61, 975 items. Economist and musical impresario. Rabinoff was economic adviser to Estonia, Georgia, and Azerbaijan. He helped develop the Export-Import Bank and promoted trade with Russia. He was connected with the Ballet Russe in 1909-11. The correspondence, printed matter, photos, and oral history interview (transcript, 48 pp.) concern all phases of his life, but especially his introduction of Russian ballet to the U.S. in 1909-11 and the famous ballerina Anna Pavlova. (NUCMC 70-138)

15 Carl Remington (1879-1919). Papers, 1899-1905, ca. 100 items. Secretary to the American governor-general of the Philippines. Diaries, scrapbooks, letters, speeches, and reports (the last 2 in copies). Remington was involved in preparations for the arrival of Russian warships in Manila harbor after the battle of Tsushima Straits in 1905. Materials pertain to this event and to the Russo-Japanese War in general. (NUCMC 71-996)

16 Geroid Tanqueray Robinson (1892-1971). Papers, 1915-65, 25,575 items. Professor of history and founder of the Russian Institute at Columbia. Letters, lecture notes, and other writings for the major phases of his career. Drafts and proofs of his Rural Russia Under the Old Regime (1932). He participated in the Council on Foreign Relations, the Arden Conference, and the Research Program on the Communist Party in the Soviet Union. A letter from Popov in the Ministry of Agriculture, census division, concerns peasant resistance to a census of agricultural supplies, 14 August 1917. (NUCMC 73-99)

17 Manuel Rosenberg (1897-1967). Drawings and sketches, ca. 1920-50, 60 of 300 drawings. Chief artist (illustrator and cartoonist) and writer for the Scripps-Howard newspapers. Visited the Soviet Union in 1929 together with other journalists, producing 60 sheets of drawings on the trip. In his file of sketches and caricatures is one of Feodor Chaliapin.

18 James Shotwell (1874-1965). Papers, 1914-30, ca. 60,000 items. American historian. Individual Russian-related items not ascertained. Correspondence and documents concern the Paris Peace Conference, League of Nations, Locarno Pact, International Labor Organization, and other topics. Shotwell edited the Economic and Social History of the World War, 150 vols, 1919-29, which included several important books on Russia.

19 David Eugene Smith (1860-1945). Papers, ca. 1100-1939, ca. 40,000 items. Mathematics professor. Collected materials about mathematics and science. Many letters from Russian/Soviet scientists concern the history of science and other subjects. (NUCMC 62-4927)

20 Society for the Prevention of World War III (1945-72). Records, 12 boxes, ca. 5,000 items. Data on trade between Moscow and Bonn and about the Berlin crisis of 1961.

21 Boris Michael Stanfield (b. 1889). Papers, 1937-57, ca. 4 of 14 boxes, ca. 3,500 items. Columbia economics professor. Mimeographed material, clippings, and periodicals concerning economics, the labor movement, and the USSR (arranged by subject). (NUCMC 69-641)

22 Lincoln Steffens (1866-1936). Papers, over 50 boxes. Author and editor. Scrapbook of his 1916-17 lecture tour speaking on Russia contains letters and clippings. Correspondence files, manuscripts, and scrapbooks are available on microfilm for interlibrary loan. (NUCMC 61-3444)

23 TASS Windows. See under Louis G. Cowan Collection.

24 Leo Nikolaevich Tolstoi (1828-1910). Correspondence, 1897-1937, 124 letters. Russian

writer and religious philosopher. Letters from Tolstoi and members of his family to Aylmer Maude, the English translator of his works. They concern Tolstoi's health, art, censorship, John Ruskin, the "Resurrection" fund, the Dukhobors' banishment to Siberia, Jewish pogroms, Dmitrii Merezhkovsky, peasant misery, famine, the assassination of Alexander II, the doctrine of non-resistance to evil, and Tolstoi's attitudes toward slander and stimulants. Among the correspondents, besides Tolstoi himself (69 letters), are Maria Tolstaia Obolenskaia (6), Alexandra Tolstaia (3), Olga Tolstaia (5), Sergius Tolstoi (11), Tatiana Tolstaia (11), and Mrs. V. G. Tchertkoff (1). (NUCMC 61-3506)

25 Frank A. Vanderlip, Jr. (1864-1937). Papers, ca. 1890-1937, ca. 80,000 items. American financier. Information on American-Soviet economic relations in the early post-revolutionary years.

26 World War I--Posters. Ca. 500 items. Most of the posters are from Britain and the U.S. but some are French and Russian. Restrictions.

27 World War II--Posters. Ca. 700 items. Posters from the U.S., Great Britain, the USSR, Germany, and elsewhere, 1939-49. Restrictions.

28 World War II--Propaganda. Ca. 175 items. Materials from 1939-45, among them some pieces from the Soviet Union.

29 World War II--Russian War Posters. Ca. 75 items. Posters issued by TASS from 1939-45 (not TASS Windows as in the Louis G. Cowan Collection). A binder gives translations, authors, and other information for the posters. Restrictions.

30 Wladimir S. Woytinsky (1885-1960). Papers, 1906-1907, ca. 25 items. Russian-born economist and, in his youth, a radical. Russian and English manuscripts, with corrections, of his The Soviet of the Unemployed in Petersburg (1906-1907). (NUCMC 74-289)

31 Chan-han Wu (fl. 1920s). Correspondence, 1923-29, 28 items. Chinese student in Germany and USSR in the 1920s, member of the Chinese Communist Party, and Trotskyite. Letters written to his brother Chao Fa Wu. He apparently joined the Chinese Communist Party while in Germany and went to Moscow to study at the Sun Yat-sen University. Letters describe Chinese student life in Moscow during the revolutionary fervor of 1926-29. Also, letters from Wu's companion, Irene Petrashevskaya, in Moscow to Chao Fa Wu, 6 ALS, 1 TLS, 1927-28.

32 Note: Many collections in the Manuscript Department hold a small amount of Russian-related material (e.g., a calling card with brief signed note of P. Chaikovskii). Time did not permit identification of all such scattered holdings.

Finding Aid: Manuscript Collections in the Columbia University Libraries: A Descriptive List (New York, 1959) is brief and selective.

NY 37
COUNCIL ON FOREIGN RELATIONS, INC.
The Harold Pratt House
58 East 68th Street
New York, New York 10021
(212-734-0400)

1 The Council's archives contain correspondence, reports, memoranda, digests of meetings, and other materials pertaining to Russia from the 1920s on, and especially after World War II. Most of the material concerns foreign policy and international affairs. The archives are divided into 3 sections:

2 Records of Meetings. 18 vols., 1920-53. Each volume, loose-leaf binder, contains ca. 500-600 pieces of paper. Includes material relating specifically to Russia each year from 1926 to 1933 and from 1943 on, by at least one speaker every year. References to Russia also appear in speeches on other countries and on various issue areas.

3 Records of Groups. 45 vols., 1922-53. Includes material relating to study groups on Russia each year since 1944. Materials can also be found in groups primarily devoted to other subjects.

4 Records of Conferences. 4 vols., 1933-53. Contains no materials pertaining to Russia.

Restrictions: By resolution of the Council's Board of Directors, adopted 17 December 1974, all substantive records of the Council more than 25 years old are open for reference use during library hours at the Harold Pratt House, subject to the proviso that: "As a condition of use, the officers of the Council shall require each user of Council records to execute a prior written commitment that he or she will not directly or indirectly attribute to any living person any assertion of fact or opinion based upon any Council record without first obtaining from such person his written consent thereto." Each summer an additional year of records is opened for research under the guidelines stated above.

Finding Aid: A Table of Contents, available at the Council's library desk, lists groups by titles, arranged chronologically by program year (September-June) in which each group began; meetings alphabetically by speaker within each program year, including the title of the speech; and conferences chronologically.

NY 38
ESTONIAN HOUSE
243 East 34th Street
New York, New York 10016
(212-686-3356)

The Estonian House maintains the records of several Estonian organizations in the U.S.; some of these records, which include minutes of annual meetings, pertain to the political situation in Estonia.

NY 39
EDWARD FALKOWSKI--PRIVATE COLLECTION
70 LaSalle Street, 2A
New York, New York 10027
(212-864-3851)

Personal papers of Mr. Falkowski, Donbas coal miner and journalist, ca. 1929-37, ca. 45 large folders plus numerous early issues of the Moscow News. An anthracite coal miner in the U.S. (and also in Germany), Mr. Falkowski went to the Soviet Union in the late 1920s and spent several months in the Donbas mines. As he prepared to return to the U.S., Anna Louise Strong contacted him and asked him to work for the proposed English-language Moscow News, a post he accepted. He covered industry, the Industrial Party trials of 1930, and the later Promparty trials for the Moscow News. Among the writers he interviewed were F. Gladkov, Ilf and Petrov, Ilya Ehrenburg, and many others. There are ca. 20 folders of clippings and 20-30 folders of diaries and notes. Available to serious scholars. Note: These materials will eventually go to the Labor History Archives at Wayne State University (Detroit, Michigan).

NY 40
JAMES J. FULD--PRIVATE COLLECTION
300 Park Avenue, Room 2100
New York, New York 10022
(212-593-9216)

Mr. Fuld has a rich collection of music and dance materials. Among his holdings: Leon Bakst, signed card. Mikhail Baryshnikov, signed photograph. Fedor Chaliapin, signed photograph and numerous programs of his singing (operas), including one at the Marinsky Theatre, St. Petersburg, 5 March 1918. Sergei Diaghilev, letter, 31 October 1900, on stationery with a woodcut by L. Bakst. Mikhail Fokine, signed design. Aleksandr Glazunov, inscribed copy of Raymonda, published by Belaieff and a program for a performance of this work, 27 February 1918, at the Marinsky Theatre, with Tamara Karsavina. Reinhold Glière, letter, 14 May 1947. Mikhail Glinka, album leaf, Ruslan and Ludmilla. Tamara Karsavina, album leaf. Aram Khachaturian, Gayaneh Waltz, inscribed; album leaf; letter, 16 January 1961; and a program from 5 December 1954, London, when he conducted. Aleksei L'vov, letter, 31 March 1847; and the only known copy in the world of the first printing of "God Save the Tsar," the Imperial Russian National Anthem (K. Petz, St. Petersburg, ca. 1833). Modeste Moussorgskii, album leaf, Khovanshchina. Vaslav Nijinsky, album leaf. Rudolf Nureyev, signed program. Anna Pavlova, signed photograph. Programs, performances of Chaikovskii's Sleeping Beauty and Swan Lake at the Bolshoi Theatre, 30 December 1917 and 15 March 1918; performance of Rimskii-Korsakov's Snow Maiden, 12 February 1918, at the Marinsky Theatre; and Ballet Russe programs, 1910-11. Sergei Prokofiev, gavotta, signed. Sergei Rachmaninoff, Rapsodie sur un Thème de Paganini, signed, and numerous programs from his performances of his own concerti. Nikolai Rimskii-Korsakov, signed copy of The Tale of Tsar Saltan, published by Bessel. Anton Rubinstein, album leaf and program for his performance, 16 November 1872. Dmitry Shostakovich, dances, op. 1, signed. Igor Stravinsky, signed copy of L'Oiseau de Feu, published by Jurgenson; signed postcard; and numerous programs for concerts when he conducted his works. Petr Chaikovskii, letter to Katherine Laroche (n.d.) and program, 1888, from a concert when he conducted his own works. Open to serious researchers.

NY 41
ST. MARK'S LIBRARY
GENERAL THEOLOGICAL SEMINARY
175 Ninth Avenue
New York, New York 10011
(212-243-5150)

Paul M. Fekula Collection on Eastern Orthodoxy and Russian History and Culture. A large collection of primarily published works but including perhaps 20-25 manuscripts of a religious nature, some illustrated, including ritual books and musical materials; lithographs of costumes of the Russian Empire; and a number of photographs of Russian scenes. Also, published works, such as regimental histories, which were the emperor or empress's personal copies (from the Imperial library collection), and printed, bound ukazy and statutes from the 19th c. Access is to qualified scholars by application to Mr. Paul M. Fekula, 42-16 80th Street, Elmhurst, New York 11373.

NY 42
DR. WILLIAM GLASKOW--PRIVATE COLLECTION
206 East 9th Street
New York, New York 10003
(212-475-4789)

Dr. Glaskow, ataman and president of the Cossacks in the Free World, has in his possession over 150 ft. of published and unpublished materials pertaining to the history, culture, folklore, and art of the Cossacks. Unpublished materials include memoirs, diaries, correspondence, reports, office files, literary manuscripts, manuscript books, films, photographs, maps, tape recordings, miscellaneous historical documents, and copies of rare original manuscripts from libraries in London, Paris, and other countries. The material documents Cossack-Russian relations, as well as the activities of many Cossack state and political leader from 1926 to 1977. Ataman-President General Peter N. Krasnow, Prime Minister Nikolai M. Melnikow, and Wasil A. Charlamow, president of the Don-Cossack Parliament, plus the anti-Soviet Vlasov movement in World War II, are noted.

Note: Dr. Glaskow also has paintings and sculptures of various Cossack leaders and atamans, including Stepan Razin, Emelian Pugachev, Kondrat Bulavin, Ataman Krasnow, Alexis Ryabovol, the historian Sergey Boldyrew, and the conductor of the Don-Cossack choir, Serge Jaroff; very rare Cossack magazines and newspapers published during World War II, in territories occupied by the Germans; antique Cossack arms; objects symbolic of the Ataman's power (pernach and bulava); buntchuks (symbols of the Cossack supreme commander in chief); Cossack flags, standards, banners, emblems, etc.; and other Cossack objects. Advance written permission required, and recommendations requested.

NY 43
INTERNATIONAL LADIES' GARMENT WORKERS' UNION ARCHIVES
22 West 38th Street, Twelfth Floor
New York, New York 10018
(212-730-7310)

The archives hold ca. 500 ft. of materials relating to the Union and its activities, including correspondence, minutes of meetings, reports, and financial records. Perhaps 5 ft. of material relate to the Russian Empire and Soviet Union. Many members of this Union, established in 1900, were émigrés from Eastern Europe and the Russian Empire. Their interest in radical movements, socialism, and communism is reflected in these archival holdings. Some letters, post-1919, are from individuals in the Soviet Union to Union officers. Materials concern ideological questions, particularly communist influence in trade unions like the ILGWU, much more than conditions in Russia/USSR. Letters of recommendation or similar credentials requested.

NY 44
IREX (INTERNATIONAL RESEARCH AND EXCHANGES BOARD)
655 Third Avenue
New York, New York 10017
(212-867-0790)

Since 1968 American scholars in the Russian/Soviet field have been studying in the Soviet Union under the auspices of this organization (while their Soviet counterparts come here). In the course of their work, the researchers have examined large amounts of material on virtually all subjects, in a variety of archives and repositories. Many of them have brought back from their stays reproductions of these Soviet archival materials. Taken altogether, these photocopies and microfilm holdings may well represent one of the greatest resources in this country. But until now there has been no central record of which materials are in the U.S. Access to these items is enormously difficult, since they are in the hands of working scholars. Some years ago IREX attempted to compile a directory of these holdings, but responses to the circular inquiry were minimal. IREX is again planning to identify the materials that American scholars have used and duplicated. More information about this undertaking is available from the IREX staff, particularly the section how headed by Dorothy Knapp.

Other files and reports maintained by IREX that could be of interest to a researcher studying U.S.-Soviet exchange programs are generally kept confidential. However, some in-house reports are available for outside distribution. One current example is a bibliographic project that lists participants' published works based on research in the USSR. In addition, there are ways in which IREX can bring together researchers in fields of mutual interest. Thus, it might be possible to locate especially relevant duplicated materials in the U.S. on an individual basis, independent of the planned directory of such holdings. Such requests for specific information should again be directed to Dorothy Knapp.

NY 45
ARCHIVES
JEWISH THEOLOGICAL SEMINARY OF AMERICA LIBRARY
3080 Broadway
New York, New York 10027
(212-749-8000)

1 Altstok Family. Papers, ca. 1874-1902, 4 items. Green booklet with regulations, rights, and privileges for Russian military reservists according to the law of 1874; travel permit of Moshe Yutkovsky, son of Itzak, to go to various towns and places in Russia, October 1902-October 1903, indicates nationality, issued in Grodno region (1 brown sheet); identity paper of Liebe Hayimoff, a soldier of the lowest rank (enlisted 1 January 1894, released in 1897), 1 green sheet. All 3 items in Russian. Also, brown booklet with Austrian passport permitting travel to Germany from Buczacz in East Galicia, 1900, in German and Polish. In poor physical condition.

2 Anti-Semitica. Collection, 1920-34, ca. 30 items. Includes papers of Arthur Cherep-Spiridovich, 1 file, a conservative Russian monarchist active in the U.S. after the Revolution, who played a major role in dissemination of the spurious Protocols of the Elders of Zion.

3 Menahem Mendel Beilis (1874-1934). Trial account, 1913, 4 items. Victim of a blood libel charge in Russia in 1911. Tried and acquitted in Kiev in 1913.

4 Israel Friedlaender (1876-1920). Papers, 1888-1955, 8 ft. Semiticist and American Jewish communal leader. Professor of Bible at J.T.S.A., 1903-20. Contains a diary from 1920 kept while on a mission for the American Jewish Joint Distribution Committee visiting war-ravaged Jewish communities in Eastern Europe. His party spent some time in Russia. In July 1920 the group was waylaid by bandits in the Ukraine and Friedlaender and Bernard Cantor, an American rabbi, were murdered.

5 Jewish Theological Seminary of America Library. Records, 1898-72, 5 boxes. Includes 1 box of correspondence pertaining to an attempt to purchase the Judaica library of Baron David de Guenzburg from his widow, Baroness Mathilde de Guenzberg of St. Petersburg, 1911-17. The effort failed and the collection is now in the Lenin State Library, Moscow.

6 Eugène Manuel (1823-1901). Papers, 1860-1900, 1 box. French poet. A founder of the Alliance Israélite Universelle, 1860, a group which assisted Russian Jews in emigrating.

7 Print and Photograph Collection. Ca. 5,000 items, 17th-20th c. Includes portraits of individuals, Jewish communities, maps, posters, and original prints, some by Marc Chagall.

8 Note: Other archival collections pertain to East European Jewry and possibly to Russian/Soviet Jews as well.

Finding Aid: Preliminary Listing of Holdings, compiled by Judith E. Endelman (February 1978).

NY 46
JACQUES KAYALOFF--PRIVATE COLLECTION
40 East 78th Street
New York, New York 10021
(212-628-1223)

Collection of books and manuscript material pertaining to Armenia 1917-21, in Russian, French, and English. Includes memoirs of General Georgii Kvinitadze, commander of the Georgian Army; Colonel Alexander Chneour, "The story of Armeno-Turkish War in 1918"; an article written by Yakov V. Arakelian after his escape from Erevan in 1921; a large part of the archives of General Grigori Korganov; and photographs of military men active in Armenia 1918-21. Inquire concerning access.

NY 47
KHRONIKA PRESS
505 8th Avenue
New York, New York 10018
(212-722-9120)

Khronika Press (Valery Chalidze, editor-in-chief) publishes materials about and from the human rights movement in the Soviet Union. Its archives contain primarily samizdat material--articles, complaints, and legal records. Some are originals, typed and handwritten, but a large number are carbon copies (the usual form of samizdat) and some are photocopies. Most of the holdings date from 1973-78, a few from earlier years. Most of these items are also held by the Arkhiv samizdata of Radio Liberty in Munich, the most comprehensive collection of samizdat materials in the world. Access to the archive is controlled by Mr. Chalidze. Write in advance, c/o Mr. Edward Kline at the above address. The journal Khronika zashchity prav v SSSR lists most new acquisitions of the archive.

NY 48
MARIE T. LAMPARD--PRIVATE COLLECTION
161 West 75th Street
New York, New York 10023
(212-362-3866)

Collection on the Russian sculptor Sergei Timofeevitch Konenkov (1874-1971), including:

some pieces of his work, both sculpture and watercolors; photographs of his works, in Moscow and the United States, many professional, some personal; scrapbooks, posters, and letters (originals and photocopies); telegrams; interviews with friends, relatives, other artists, and acquaintances of the Konenkovs in Moscow and the U.S. (some tape recorded only, others transcribed); catalogue-file on his works in the U.S., with documentary photographs of all pieces located, ca. 65 at present; and most books written by and about him published in the USSR, some articles, and clippings. The collection, assembled for a monograph on Konenkov's American years, is currently closed to outside researchers but inquiries will be answered. Ultimate disposition of the materials is undetermined.

NY 49
JANET LEHR, INC.--PRIVATE COLLECTION
P.O. Box 617
New York, New York 10028
(212-288-6234)

Ms. Lehr is in possession of ca. 200 photographs pertaining to Russia. These include ca. 100 photos of a Russian military road in the Caucasus by D. Ermakov, Tiflis, ca. 1870; ca. 100 photos of people, towns, and landscapes in Russia, including St. Petersburg and Moscow 1870-80; and other photographs, some of which relate to the Crimean War. Telephone for an appointment, indicating the nature of the research project.

NY 50
LEO BAECK INSTITUTE ARCHIVES
129 East 73rd Street
New York, New York 10021
(212-744-6400)

1 Julie Braun-Vogelstein (1883-1971). Collection, ca. 1850-1971, ca. 35 ft. Includes 1 letter, 2 June 1912, from Leon Trotskii to Victor Adler, Vienna, handwritten. Concerns personal matters. Unpublished finding aid.

2 Sam Echt (d. 1975). Collection, ca. 1929-ca. 1950, ca. 2 in. Jewish community leader in Danzig. Includes materials about a trip to the Soviet Union by a trade delegation from Danzig, 6-15 July 1929: the delegation's summary report, 20 pp., with verbatim notes of discussions with M. Kalinin and others; reports about the delegation's meeting with the German ambassador in Moscow, von Dirksen, and the Polish ambassador, Patek; notes on discussions with A. Mikojan, people's commissar for foreign trade, typed, 8 pp.; notes of a visit with Mr. Tolokonzeff, Presidium member and head of "Maschinenbauwessens," 3 pp.; notes on discussion with Mr. Tschubar (Chubar), chairman of the Council of People's Commissars, 2 pp.; other notes; and several Soviet newspaper clippings, most with German translations.

3 Emigration 1864-1952. Artificial collection, over 170 items, ca. 900 pp., about half in German. Includes materials on the persecution and situation of Jews in Eastern Europe (e.g., Russia, Lithuania, Poland, and Roumania), much of it generated by organizations founded for their relief. Among the holdings are resolutions, circulars, and reports of several German groups helping Russian Jews. Russian-related items, mostly typed, printed, and mimeographed ephemera, 1882-1929. Unpublished inventory.

4 Emigration 1881-1914. Artificial collection, 62 items. Similar to immediately preceding collection. Unpublished inventory.

5 Efraim Frisch (1873-1942). Archives, 1894-1967, ca. 4 ft. Includes the papers of his wife, Fega Frisch, nee Lifschitz (1878-1964), born in Grodno. She translated many Russian authors into German. Among her typed translations: "Charakter und Eigentümlichkeiten der judischen Folklore," by S. A. Anskii, with handwritten corrections, 63 pp., the original of which appeared in St. Petersburg, 3 vols., 1908-11; "Der Weg," "Zwischen Zweien," and "Mikita" by Baruch Hager, each 6 pp.; and letters from Anton Chekhov to his wife, with handwritten corrections, 14 pp. Other translations are of Pushkin, Lermontov, and Tolstoi. There are also critiques of her translations, a diploma from a Grodno girls' high school, and some printed matter with her published translations. Note: Other parts of the collection, Efraim Frisch's papers and the editorial archives of the Neue Merkur, 1922-29, which he edited, would hold some related material. Unpublished finding aid (NUCMC 70-1589).

6 Hirsch of Gereuth Family. Papers, 1835-1966, ca. 1 ft. Includes the papers of Baron Moritz Hirsch (1831-1896), German Jewish railroad builder and philanthropist. Photostatic copies, positive, of originals in Vienna archives. After 1869 he was building railroads in Turkey, Russia, and Austria. Among the mainly Jewish causes he supported was the Jewish Colonization Association (ICA), which he established to aid Jewish farmers emigrate from Russia and set up agricultural settlements in South America and Palestine. (NUCMC 70-1600)

7 Jacob Jacobson (1888-1968). Collection, 18th c.-1960s, 18 ft. Historian and archival curator. Section III, 37-40 and 97, includes items on Koenigsberg (present Kaliningrad): typed copies of records concerning the citizenship rights of Jews in Koenigsberg, 1798 and

1814; election list, contributors' list, accounts, including for the burial society, ca. 1800/1801, handwritten in German and Hebrew; copies of regulations on Jewish given names; requests for birth, marriage, and death certificates, 1847, originals; and typed excerpts from the Findbuch concerning the Jewish question. Section IV contains some material on the Prussian administration of territories gained in the partitions of Poland, including Bialystok and Plock, and on South Prussian Jews.

8 Jewish Colonization Association (ICA). Records, 1802-92, 7 items. Comprises 7 pertinent reports: handwritten historical summary, ca. 1891-92, 37 pp., of the expulsion of Jews from Russian villages after 1802, with texts of various laws and edicts about Jewish affairs and Jews, 1804, 1807, 1812, 1845, 1848, 1853, and 1882; undated handwritten report, 41 pp., on the magnitude of the Jewish problem and the emigration of over 100,000 Russian Jews to the U.S.; report about prospects of emigration from Russia and negotiations with Baron von Hirsch, written in Koenigsberg, 29 January 1892, signed M. Grodsenski, 16 pp.; report, carbon copy, 23 pp., Koenigsberg, June 1892, with emigration statistics from Russia via Berlin and Hamburg to the U.S. from 1820-90, data on emigration to and from Argentina, 1871-90, and estimates of Jewish population and potential emigration figures, signed M. Grodsenski; undated fragment in German, 3 pp., and 2 Russian reports, 11 pp. and 12 pp. Note: The main body of ICA archival material is in London but currently inaccessible to scholarly use because of severe water damage.

9 Eric Muehsam (1878-1934). Papers, ca. 1896-1968, 2.5 in. Anarchist and writer, murdered in Oranienburg concentration camp. Includes some correspondence and papers of his wife Kreszentia (Zenzl Muehsam, nee Elfinger; 1884-1962). After his death she fled to Prague and then, 1935, to Moscow, at the invitation of Hélene Stassowa of the International Red Help (MOPR). Imprisoned in 1936 and again in 1938, she survived 17 years of prison and hard labor, emigrated to East Berlin in 1955, and died there. Includes 9 letters from her to Erich's family during her Moscow years; correspondence from this family (Charlotte and Leo Landau), Stassowa, Sophie Zinkiowicz, and Hans Muehsam (10 letters, 1 of which was returned by Soviet authorities); and newspaper clippings about Zenzl's experiences under Hitler and Stalin. Unpublished finding aid.

10 Joseph Roth-Bornstein. Collection, 1917-39, 5 in. Includes materials of Joseph Roth (1894-1939), Austrian journalist and author, and Joseph Bornstein, who was Roth's literary agent during the 1930s. There are loose diaries and notebooks, handwritten, 129 pp., from 1927 concerning Roth's Russian trip of the previous year, plus his certification of registration as a correspondent for the Frankfurter Zeitung, 1926, in Russian. Unpublished finding aid.

11 Leopold Schwarzschild (1891-1950). Papers, 1933-62, ca. 7 ft. Political publicist, economist, and journalist. Correspondence, 1941-49; personal documents and photos; and manuscripts, in German and English, of writings on World War II and of his books The Red Prussian (a biography of Karl Marx) and Gog and Magog: The Nazi-Bolshevik Twins, the printing of the latter by Oxford University Press in 1941 being stopped after Hitler invaded the USSR. (NUCMC 72-237)

12 Zosa Szajkowski. Collection, in process. Manuscript, 1,500 pp., and research notes concerning diplomatic efforts of German Jews on behalf of Russian and Polish Jews seeking to emigrate to North and South America, mid-19th c. to ca. 1928.

Finding Aid: Inventory List of Archival Collections, no. 1 (1971) and no. 2 (1976); a published catalogue of manuscript, memoir, and archival collections of the LBI is in preparation.

NY 51
ADELE LOZOWICK--PRIVATE COLLECTION
30 East 9th Street, Apt. 6MM
New York, New York 10003

The collection includes a short manuscript about Lasar (El) Lissitsky written by the artist Louis Lozowick. 75-80 photographs relate to the Russian theater and cinema: other photos are of paintings by Russian artists, of M. Kissling, N. Altman, and Chana Orloff. In addition, 50-60 photographs are of Moscow, Russian people, parades, and other scenes, including 1, 1928, of Louis Lozowick and David Shterenberg. Advance written permission required.

NY 52
MISCHA ELMAN MEMORIAL STUDIO
MANHATTAN SCHOOL OF MUSIC
120 Claremont Avenue
New York, New York 10027
(212-749-2802)

The widow of the Russian-American violinist Mischa Elman (1891-1967) donated some of his effects to the school. The studio holds photographs of Elman and his associates, a scrapbook of clippings, and musical scores once owned by Elman. Most of the music is printed but a few items are in manuscript (not Elman's hand). It is possible that some of the printed music has Elman's notations and fingering marks.

hand). It is possible that some of the printed music has Elman's notations and fingering marks.

NY 53
METROPOLITAN MUSEUM OF ART
Fifth Avenue at 82nd Street
New York, New York 10028
(212-535-7710)

Scattered holdings in various departments of the Museum pertain to the Russian Empire/Soviet Union. Among holdings pertaining to this guide (excluding much of the art works) are: Armenian manuscripts (No. 16.99 and No. 38.171.2); 53 watercolors of American scenes by Pavel Svinin; a wax mask of Anna Pavlova (35.105); another wax sculpture--Pavlova Gavotte (26.105); a poster by Leon Bakst; and a number of costumes for Ballets Russes productions.

NY 54
DEPARTMENT OF FILM
THE MUSEUM OF MODERN ART
11 West 53rd Street
New York, New York 10019
(212-956-4212, for study on premises)
(-4204, 4205, for film rentals)
(-4209, for film stills)

The Department of Film has extensive holdings on the subject of Russian and Soviet films and filmmaking. The facilities of the Film Study Center are available to graduate students or equivalent scholars. Films may be viewed on flatbed viewing tables or in projection rooms and a service fee is charged. The film-related documents may be consulted without fee. In both cases an appointment is necessary. Photocopying services available. A selected group of Russian and Soviet films are available in 16mm copies for rental to educational institutions for study purposes. A catalogue of circulating films is available on request.

Films:

The collection of films of Soviet or Russian origin, or relating to the subject, number more than 100 titles. They include fiction, documentary, newsreel and animation films and cover the period 1906 to the 1970s. A catalogue of holdings is in preparation.

Film-Related Materials:

Books and periodicals; clippings of U.S. newspaper reviews for most major Soviet productions; copies of New York State censorship records for Soviet films imported to U.S.; scripts, title lists, dialogue lists; advertising materials for films imported to U.S.; records of the Artkino Corporation (importer of all Soviet films to U.S.); motion picture stills from most major Soviet film productions, copies available for purchase for serious study or publications; a very small selection of film posters.

NY 55
LIBRARY
THE MUSEUM OF MODERN ART
21 West 53rd Street
New York, New York 10019

1 The library holds exhibition catalogues and miscellaneous uncatalogued material for such Russian Empire-born artists as Alexander Archipenko, Saul Baizerman, Ilya Bolotowsky, David Burliuk, Marc Chagall, Nathalie Goncharova, Arshile Gorky, John D. Graham, Wassily Kandinsky, Mikhail Larionov, Alexander Rodchenko (exhibition catalogues only), Nicholas Roerich, Mark Rothko, Moses and Raphael Soyer, and Adja Yunkers. The catalogue also states that the repository has much uncatalogued material in Slavic languages.

According to the published catalogue, there is also miscellaneous uncatalogued material for the following subject headings: Art, Lithuanian; Art, Russian (and exhibition catalogues); Art, Ukrainian; Painting, Russian (and exhibition catalogues); Russian War Relief, Inc.; and Sculpture, Russian, 20th c., as well as exhibition catalogues for Constructivism, Russian.

In addition, there are these collections/items:

2 Alfred H. Barr, Jr. (b. 1902). Archive, uncatalogued at present. Art historian. Includes 20th c. Russian art books, art exhibition catalogues from the Soviet Union, announcements, photographs, letters, notes, and ephemera that pertain to the USSR. Inquire concerning access.

3 Ballet russe de Monte-Carlo. Programs, 1938-45, 1 vol.

4 Ballets russes Diaghilew. Programs, 1911-29, 2 vols.

5 David Burliuk. Miscellaneous pamphlets published by the artist, in Russian and English, about his own work and that of other contemporaries.

6 Sergei Mikhailovich Eisenstein (1898-1948). Albums, uncatalogued at present. Film director. Original materials comprising family snapshots, memorabilia, original film scripts in the filmmaker's hand, related notes,

production sketches, correspondence, etc. Inquire concerning access.

7 [Arshile Gorky]. Scrapbook of statements by and about Gorky, with photographs and 45 illustrations, compiled by William Agee, 122 pp., n.p., n.d. (Special Collections)

8 J. P. Hodin. "The Soviet attitude to art"--typescript, 34 ll., 1951, consisting of a transcript of a statement by Vladimir Kemenov on art and Soviet society (made in London, 1951) and Hodin's analysis of Kemenov's remarks.

9 A. Kruchenykh. A book, Slova kak takovije ([n.p., n.d.]), 15 pp. plus plates, by A. Kruchenykh and V. Chlebnikov, with an illustration by K. Malevich ("Zhnitsa") attached to the cover and an illustration by O. R[osanova] inserted on page 3.

10 John Palmer Leeper. Leeper wrote the introduction to a work entitled Adja Yunkers (New York, 1952), 4 ll., unbound. (Print Room) Note: The Print Room also holds original prints of Adja Yunkers for a volume entitled Prints in the Desert.

11 Fernand Mourlot. The ongoing publication The lithographs of Chagall (1960-present) contains original lithographs by Chagall: 12 in vol. 1, 11 in vol. 2, etc.

12 Oslinii khvost i Mishen. Book, 153 pp. (The Donkey's Tail and the Target) published in Moscow in 1913 has a manuscript note in French on the title-page with a translation--a manifesto signed by N. Goncharova and M. Larionov. (Special Collections)

13 Paris. Federation internationale des archives du film. 1 item. A typescript entitled "Filmographie russe, 1907-1932," 37 ll., Paris, 1950. (Special Collections)

The preceding is not an exhaustive listing, only a sample culled from the published catalogue of the library: Catalog of the Library of the Museum of Modern Art--New York City, 14 vols. (Boston: G. K. Hall, 1976).

NY 56
NATIONAL BOARD OF YOUNG MEN'S CHRISTIAN ASSOCIATION (YMCA) HISTORICAL LIBRARY
291 Broadway
New York, New York 10007
(212-374-2042)

1 Chekhov Press (New York). Collection, 1945-55, ca. 8 ft. Business correspondence with its authors and manuscripts of books, mostly Russian émigré memoirs. In process.

2 Russian Work. Collection, 1900-1920s, 2 ft. Includes correspondence and reports from YMCA secretaries working in Russia and Western Europe, primarily from before the Revolution but also from later years when the YMCA was involved in the Russian émigré communities. Pre-revolutionary holdings deal mainly with the "Mayak" Society in St. Petersburg, founded by James Stokes in 1900, and closely tied to the American YMCA (it was also known as the Society for Cooperating with St. Petersburg Young Men in the Attainment of Moral and Physical Development) and with the "Student Work" of the YMCA in Russia. Some of the subjects covered are physical education and sports, general education (arithmetic, languages, music), and social service. From the start of World War I the YMCA was increasingly involved in humanitarian and relief work. Though headquartered in Petrograd, the YMCA and its War Prisoners' Aid division operated in such other cities as Moscow, Odessa, Kiev, Minsk, Kazan, Orenburg, Tashkent, Perm, Omsk, Tobolsk, Tomsk, Krasnoiarsk, Irkutsk, Chita, and Khabarovsk. It also helped Russian POWs in enemy hands. After the spring of 1917 (and the visit of the Root Mission in the summer), the YMCA worked more and more with the Russian army and engaged in war-related non-combat support. Among the administrators and secretaries of the YMCA Russian operations were Ethan T. Colton, Russell M. Story, Crawford Wheeler, Paul Anderson, Arthur Eugene Jenny, Reverend William L. Tucker, G. Sidney Phelps, Arthur P. Kempa, Raymond J. Reitzel, Franklin Gaylord, Sherwood Eddy, A. M. Craig, A. C. Harte, E. T. Heald, John R. Mott, Jerome Davis, Donald Lowrie, Louis Penningroth, and Herbert Sidney Gott. Correspondents with various YMCA offices and personnel: Maddin Summers, American consul in Moscow; Ernest L. Harris, consul in Omsk; and Boris Bakhmeteff, Russian ambassador in Washington. Toward the end of its work in Russia, the YMCA was particularly active in Siberia. There is much material on the Revolution and Civil War, relations with the Bolsheviks, contacts with Admiral A. V. Kolchak, the Czech troops in Siberia, the Cheka, and Russian émigrés. Preliminary inventory.

3 YMCA Press in Paris. Archives, 1921-present, ca. 1 ft. of documents plus a complete set of its published Russian-language books. Additions expected.

4 YMCA Work in Paris for émigré Russians. Collection, 1925-55, ca. 5 ft. Includes correspondence and other materials on the Russian Student Christian Movement (RSCM), Russian Superior Technical Institute, and the Russian Theological Academy.

Restrictions: Most of the above materials are restricted; information is available at the repository.

Finding Aid: The description of the Russian Work Collection was taken largely from Donald E. Davis and Eugene P. Trani, "The American YMCA and the Russian Revolution," Slavic Review (September 1974).

NY 57
NATIONAL CONFERENCE ON SOVIET JEWRY
Suite 907
10 East 40th Street
New York, New York 10016
(212-679-6122)

The organization's work focuses on helping Jews who wish to emigrate from the Soviet Union and helping those who wish to remain in the USSR to retain their cultural and religious identity as Jews. Its office files contain materials reflecting this activity: correspondence with Soviet Jews, including written testimony on the condition of Jewry and Jews in the USSR; translations of pertinent information and sources; and analyses of Soviet policies and conditions. Most of the material has been gathered since 1971 but reveals the situation of Russian/Soviet Jews extending back into the 19th c. Vertical file material is organized primarily into individual case files for hundreds of individuals, including refuseniks and prisoners of conscience. Advance appointment requested.

NY 58
NEW REVIEW (NOVYI ZHURNAL)
2700 Broadway
New York, New York 10025
(212-666-1692)

The archives of this quarterly review, founded in 1942, are at present closed to outside researchers. Inquiries concerning the material should be directed to the editor, Roman Goul.

NY 59
MANUSCRIPT DEPARTMENT
NEW YORK HISTORICAL SOCIETY
170 Central Park West
New York, New York 10024
(212-873-3400)

1 William Bainbridge (1774-1833). Papers, 1800-33, ca. 100 items. Naval officer. Includes material relating to his stay in Russia in 1811.

2 George Bliss (1830-1897). Lawyer. His autobiography, typed, describes his 1846 trip to Russia and Western Europe, 3 vols.

3 Neill S. Brown. U.S. minister to Russia. ALS, 25 October 1850, from him to A. O. P. Nicholson, describing St. Petersburg and Moscow, the weather and the people.

4 George Washington Campbell (1769-1848). Correspondence, 1808-20, 14 items. U.S. secretary of the treasury, minister to Russia in the reign of Alexander I. Letters to Albert Gallatin discuss Russian affairs.

5 Luigi Palmer di Cesnola (1832-1904). Correspondence, 1870-73, 50 items. Archeologist. Typewritten copies of letters exchanged between Cesnola, the Imperial Hermitage Museum, and the Museum's agents, all concerning archeological matters, primarily Cesnola's excavations on Cyprus. A proposed sale of a Cypriot collection and some other Mediterranean art objects to the Hermitage did not materialize.

6 George Coggleshall (1784-1861). Life and voyages, 1799-1846, 2 vols. Includes account of his stay in Riga during the winter of 1810-11.

7 Francis Dana (1743-1811). Correspondence, 1778-87, 21 items. Diplomat and jurist, U.S. minister to Russia. Drafts of 11 letters he wrote to Robert R. Livingston while in Russia, 1781-83, some quite lengthy. Livingston was secretary for foreign affairs. 10 other letters, 1778-87.

8 William Darlington (1782-1863). Papers, ca. 1800-63, ca. 3,300 items. Physician and botanist. Among his correspondents was Professor Fischer of St. Petersburg, with whom he exchanged 5 letters, 1800-63.

9 Gustavus Vasa Fox (1821-1883). Papers, 1841-83, 8 ft. Assistant secretary of the navy. Traveled to Europe and Russia in 1866. Includes his diary for the time he was in the Russian Empire, plus related documents. (NUCMC 60-2751)

10 Albert Gallatin (1761-1849). Papers, 28 ft. and 17 vols. Statesman and diplomat. In 1813 he served as U.S. envoy to St. Petersburg to negotiate peace with England under Russian mediation. Includes letters from George W. Campbell, minister to Russia, 6 November 1818 and 26 October 1819. Other correspondents, primarily 1780-1849, were: John Quincy Adams, John Jacob Astor, André de Dashkoff, Comte N. P. de Romanzoff, and Madame de Staël (at one time an exile in Russia). The materials discuss European affairs, Polish relief in 1834, and an American-Russian commercial treaty, 1813-14.

11 Maltby Gelston. Collection, 1806-10, 1 vol. New York notary public. Book of protests (37 in all) made by ships' masters arriving in New York. Protests record details of voyages and damage to ship and cargo. Some relate to Cronstadt. (Marine Protests)

12 Levett Harris. Correspondence, 1804-19, 12 items. U.S. consular official in St. Petersburg. Primarily letters to or from Albert Gallatin, secretary of the treasury in 1802-14. Most date from 1813-14.

13 Charles Heartmann. Collection, 1770s-1870s, ca. 4,000 items. Includes 3 letters exchanged between Karl Robert Nesselrode, Russian foreign minister, and William Pinkney, U.S. minister to Russia, ca. January 1817, concerning a crime of theft.

14 Hendricks Family. Papers, ca. 1790-1938, ca. 12 ft. and 30 vols. Includes papers of Harmon Hendricks (1771-1838), a New York merchant and copper entrepreneur. His business correspondence, office files, and account books, late 1790s-early 1800s, reveal aspects of his trade in Russian linen and sheeting.

15 Isaac Hicks (1767-1820). Papers, 1791-1808, ca. 30 ft. and ca. 40 vols. Quaker merchant. Correspondence and other items relate to his trade dealings with Russia in 1799 and 1803-1806.

16 Wickham Hoffman (1821-1900). Papers, 1863-66, ca. 40 items. Army officer and diplomat. Contains a translation of the memoirs of the Countess Choiseul-Gouffier, which have been published in English, 1900, about Alexander I and the Russian court.

17 Christopher Hughes (1786-1849). Correspondence, 1815-27, 21 items. Diplomat. Letters from Stockholm and Brussels, mostly to Albert Gallatin. References to Russia.

18 Rufus King (1755-1827). Papers, 1785-1826, 12 ft. and ca. 66 vols. American statesman and diplomat, minister to Great Britain in 1796-1803 and 1825-26. Includes correspondence concerning the 1799 commercial treaty negotiations (abortive) and letters to him from Joseph A. Smith in Russia.

19 Randall J. LeBoeuf, Jr. (1897-1975). Robert Fulton Collection, 1764-1857, ca. 215 items. Includes letter, 24 February 1810, from Fulton to André de Dashkoff; letter, 26 July 1812, from Fulton to Chevalier Svinin about the development of Fulton's steamboats in Russia; and letter, 28 July 1815, from John Q. Adams to Levett Harris in St. Petersburg enclosing a letter from William Cutting, Fulton's executor, asking that Fulton's grant for constructing steamboats in Russia be confirmed for the benefit of his family.

20 John Ledyard (1751-1789). Papers, 1772-91, 22 items. Explorer, traveler in Siberia. Includes 6 letters to Thomas Jefferson concerning his explorations.

21 Robert R. Livingston Family. Papers, ca. 1685-1885, ca. 65 ft. and 100+ vols. Primarily papers of Robert R. Livingston (1746-1818), member of the Continental Congress and secretary of the Department of Foreign Affairs. Includes instructions to Francis Dana as minister to Russia, 1781-83, and related items.

22 Henry C. McLean (1887-1955). Diaries, 1940-45, 4 vols. U.S. army intelligence officer. First volume, February-June 1940, includes comments on the attitude of Asians toward the U.S., Britain, Russia, etc.

23 Hoyt and Meacham Families. Correspondence, 1830-70, ca. 700 items. Includes some correspondence, 1860s, from Timothy Smith in Odessa, Russia.

24 Naval History Society. Generic, not integral, collection. Includes an ALS, 12 October 1839, to James Barnes from George Washington Whistler, introducing a Colonel Melnikov of the Russian engineers.

25 George Newbold (d. 1858). Papers, 1801-58, ca. 2,900 items and 19 vols. Merchant and banker. Includes some letters from Charles S. Todd in St. Petersburg.

26 Jonathan Ogden. Business records, 1800-24, ca. 9 vols. Merchant. Letterbook for September 1811-April 1817 includes frequent correspondence with Vincent Lassalette in St. Petersburg. Available on microfilm.

27 David Parish (d. 1826). Letterbooks, 1802-16, 7 vols. Merchant. Among his correspondents were the Brothers Cramer in St. Petersburg.

28 Joel Root (b. 1770). Seaman. An account, 1 vol., of his sealing voyage to St. Petersburg, etc. and return, 1802-1806.

29 Russian Fleet in New York. Collection, 1863, 50 items. Letters from public officials, military officers, and leading citizens, responding to invitations issued by a reception committee to accompany an admiral and officers of the Russian fleet on a trip from New York City to Niagara Falls. Addressed to Watts Sherman, Daniel Drew, and J. C. Bancroft Davis, members of the committee.

30 Gulian Crommelin Verplanck (1786-1870). Correspondence received, ca. 1805-57, ca. 2,000 items and other papers, early 18th-mid 19th c., ca. 900 items. Author, politician, lawyer, and reformer. Includes 9 letters, 1829-31, from secretary of state Martin Van Buren to the U.S. minister to Russia.

31 Edward Wyer. Letterbook, 1813-16, 1 vol., 179 pp., and correspondence, 1825-38, 15 items. American consul in the port of Riga, September 1813-March 1816. Contains copies of letters he wrote during this period. They touch on such questions as debt settlements, difficulties in obtaining passage to the U.S., his

low opinion of Russians (and of Levett Harris, U.S. chargé d'affaires in St. Petersburg), his brief partnership with a St. Petersburg merchant named John Venning, and other personal matters, especially his complaints and animosities. Correspondents include Harris, James Monroe, John Graham, John D. Lewis, Henry Clay, various naval officers, friends at home, and people in Europe.

Finding Aid: Arthur J. Breton, A Guide to the Manuscript Collections of the New York Historical Society, 2 vols. (Westport, Conn.: Greenwood Press, 1972).

NY 60
ARCHIVES
NEW YORK LIFE INSURANCE COMPANY
51 Madison Avenue
New York, New York 10010
(212-576-5036)

Company Archives total ca. 500 ft. of material, of which about 34 ft. are Russian-related. Records of the company's business in Russia, 1883-ca. 1935, include correspondence, policy forms, premium history cards, accounts for Russian branch office, Russian account books, claims and policy settlements, claim against the USSR and other litigation. Also, records relating to the Russian government's regulation and taxation of insurance. Open by appointment only to qualified researchers with advance permission. Address inquiries to Pamela Dunn Lehrer, archivist.

NY 61
BERG COLLECTION OF ENGLISH AND AMERICAN LITERATURE
NEW YORK PUBLIC LIBRARY
Room 320
42nd Street and Fifth Avenue
New York, New York 10018
(212-790-6281)

1 Russia. Foreign Office. Diplomatic passport issued at St. Petersburg 24 October 1896, to Norman Douglas, secretary of the British embassy, 2 pp.

2 Ivan Sergeevich Turgenev (1818-1883). Russian author. ALS to George Eliot, Paris, 25 February 1874, 1 l.; and ALS, Spasskoie (Orel province, Uzensk village), 20/8 May 1880, also to George Eliot, 1 p. Both have been published.

Finding Aid: Dictionary Catalog of The Henry W. and Albert A. Berg Collection of English and American Literature, 5 vols. (Boston: G. K. Hall, 1969).

NY 62
DONNELL LIBRARY CENTER-FILM CENTER
NEW YORK PUBLIC LIBRARY
20 West 53rd Street
New York, New York 10019
(212-790-6418)

Among the audio-visual materials held by the Donnell Library Center are the following films:

1 Alexander Nevsky (107 min.), 1938. Dir. Sergei Eisenstein.

2 Battle of Russia, 1944. Sixth in Frank Capra's series "Why We Fight," with coverage of the Nazi attack on the USSR, Russian music, footage from feature films, ending with the Siege of Leningrad.

3 Battleship Potemkin (60 min., silent), 1925. Dir. Sergei Eisenstein, plus the "Odessa Steps" sequence from this film (8 min.).

4 Bed and Sofa (112 min., silent), 192?. Dir. Abram Room. Fantasy of life in early Soviet Russia, showing the nearly Bohemian freedoms extolled but not actually existing.

5 The Birth of Soviet Cinema (49 min.), 1972. Compilation of excerpts from classics of the 1920s (including films of Eisenstein, V. Pudovkin, and A. Dovzhenko), by Richard Schickel.

6 Committee on Un-American Activities (45 min.), n.d. A history of the House Un-American Activities Committee (HUAC), produced by Robert Cohen, from newsreels and interviews, covering 25 years.

7 Counterpoint--The U2 Story. No details available.

8 Jaraslawa (10 min., color), 1975. Portrait of Jaraslawa Tkach, an old Ukrainian woman in New York state, by DeeDee Halleck.

9 Kremlin (54 min., color), 1963. Photographed by J. Baxter Peters for NBC-TV; a documentary showing the construction, design, and art work of the Kremlin in Moscow.

10 Last Year of the Tsars (19 min.), 1971. Newsreel footage plus scenes from Eisenstein's October and Strike; directed by Norman Swallow (from the Granada TV series Ten Days That Shook the World).

11 Lenin and Trotsky (27 min.), 1964. CBS News production describing their work for the Revolution, consolidation of communist power, and their "eventual split."

12 Man With a Movie Camera (55 min., silent), 1928. Dir. Dziga Vertov. One day on the streets of Moscow, using the "kino-eye" technique.

13 Marc Chagall (25 min., color), 1964. The artist and his art from inspiration to final works (canvas, sculpture, and stained glass windows).

14 March-April: The Coming of Spring (9 min., color), 1963. Spring scenes in rural, forested areas of the USSR, stressing the beauty of the land, animal activities, forest life, and elements of nature (Central Film Studies, Moscow).

15 Matrioska (5 min., color), 1971. Animated short--a nest of wooden dolls splits apart and they perform a stately peasant dance (made for the National Film Board of Canada).

16 Meet Comrade Student (54 min.), 1963. The Soviet educational system, curriculum, stress on competition, discipline, physical fitness; shows classes in session, education at a technical school, and extracurricular cultural and recreational activities of young Pioneers (produced and directed by Nicholas Webster for ABC-TV).

17 Moiseyev Dancers in "The Strollers" (6 min., color), 1954. The troupe performs lively folk dances.

18 Mother (80 min., silent), 1926. Dir. Vsevolod Pudovkin. Based on M. Gorkii's novel of the 1905 Revolution.

19 The Nose (11 min.), 1963. By the French-Russian animator Alexander Alexeieff, based on the N. Gogol short story.

20 Pysanka--A Story of the Ukrainian Easter Egg (10 min., color), 1975. The history, symbolism, and techniques of dyeing Ukrainian Easter eggs (Marco Pyrema).

21 Religion in Russia (20 min., color), 1968. Brief history of Russia's 5 major religions, using rare footage and recently filmed scenes of restrictions on worship today.

22 Revolt in Hungary (26 min.), 1958. Filmed during the October 1956 revolt, shows events leading up to the uprising and the severity of repression (CBS-TV, The Twentieth Century).

23 Russia (24 min., color), 1958. Pre-revolutionary Russia from 1904-1905 newsreels, present-day agriculture, industry, medicine, housing, education, and religion (produced by J. Bryan).

24 The Russian Peasant (20 min., color), 1968. The peasant in history (photos and paintings), his modern role, and a background of peasant music (J. Bryan, producer).

25 Siberia: A Day in Irkutsk (51 min., color), 1967. Vivid documentary of Irkutsk, with representative individuals spotlighted, showing their "resourcefulness and skills," and depicting the development of the city (NBC-TV).

26 Stanislavsky: Maker of the Modern Theatre (28 min., color), 1972. History of the actor/director's role in the modern theater, especially the founding of the Moscow Art Theater, with original photos and footage of MAT productions (Mosfilm production; English version by Harold Mantell).

27 Steppe in Winter (13 min.), 1965. Poetic evocation of winter life on a collective farm in the steppes--farmers at work with farm animals, at home, and at the community recreational center.

28 Stravinsky (49 min.), 1965. Informal portrait of his life and work--a recording session at which he conducts and reminiscences of his musical career. Dir. Roman Kroitor; produced by the National Film Board of Canada.

29 Tchaikovsky Nutcracker. Utilizes Ben Shahn illustrations.

30 Ten Days That Shook the World (October) (60 min.), 1927. Dir. Sergei Eisenstein. The October/November Revolution of 1917.

31 Women of Russia (12 min., color), 1968. Without narration the camera scans a cross section of Russian women at work, relaxing, with their families, and at their studies (occupations include crane operators, brick layers, field workers, ballerinas, and university students). (Produced by J. Bryan, conceived and edited by Yehuda Yaniv)

All of the preceding titles are available for in-house viewing; most can be checked out. Researchers should inquire at the library for all details of access and use.

NY 63
GENERAL RESEARCH DESK, ROOM 315
NEW YORK PUBLIC LIBRARY
42nd Street and Fifth Avenue
New York, New York 10018
(212-790-6161)

Vinkhuizen Collection. Ca. 15th-20th c., 32,236 plates, 762 vols. Illustrations of military costume, cut from books and other printed matter plus original watercolor drawings. Arranged in scrapbooks, chronologically by country, including Russia.

NY 64
MANUSCRIPTS AND ARCHIVES DIVISION
NEW YORK PUBLIC LIBRARY
Fifth Avenue at 42nd Street
New York, New York 10018

Annex Building
521 West 43rd Street
New York, New York 10036
(212-790-6338)

One of the earliest and largest collections of Russian holdings in the United States, the New York Public Library has an impressive number and range of pertinent archival materials, scattered in several different divisions. It began the serious collection of Russian-language materials long before any other major U.S. repository and has continued to add to its riches over the years.

Manuscript materials not in the Manuscripts and Archives Division collections are described in other NYPL entries. Some of the Manuscripts Division's holdings are not physically located in the 42nd Street building but are in the Annex. As materials continue to be shifted to the Annex, some items described hereinafter as in the division may eventually go to the Annex. Collections known to be in the Annex already are so designated.

1 Aleksandr Viktorovich Adiassewich (Russian historical archives) 14 items. Unpublished essays on Russian/Soviet economic affairs, all but 1 in Russian: "A sketch of the Russian petroleum industry from the earliest times to the present day," 1922, 17 pp.; "Story of the Cossacks in Russia," 1917, 114 pp.; "General notes on trade," [19--], 122 pp.; "Cotton growing and cotton industry in Russia," 1922, but revised to 1929, 7 pp.; "Economic sketch of Georgia in the Caucasus," 1922?, 125 pp.; "Economic sketch of Turkestan," 1922, 36 pp.; "Two articles upon economic aspects of the Ukraine," n.d., 29 pp.; "Economic sketch of the Crimean peninsula," n.d., 33 pp.; "A description of Daghestan in the Caucasus," n.d., 11 pp.; 3 articles on Armenia (its mineral wealth, 15 pp.; general description, 10 pp.; and description of the Caucasian Turkish part, 15 pp.); and an unfinished manuscript on Turkey collected from official sources, 1922?, 268 pp.

2 Aleksandriia. A late Russian half-uncial manuscript, 17th c., 150 ll., n.p., with initials, chapter headings, and running titles in red. Some leaves are missing. This is a translation of the Serbian version of the Romance of Alexander the Great into the Russian variant of Church Slavonic. An inscription from 1746 carries the names Ivan Nikolaevich Buturlin (praporshchik) and Petr Shkragutov (?). Bound with an item described below under Pieter Goos.

3 Robert J. Alexander. Ca. 2 boxes total. Interviews with labor leaders, almost all from South America but also from Latvia and other European countries, ca. 1952-54. Restricted.

4 Horace Newton Allen (1850-1932). Papers, 1855-1915, ca. 12 boxes. Medical missionary in Korea, secretary of the Korean legation in Washington, D.C., and minister to Korea. Diaries, letter books, account books, correspondence, photos, and native periodicals. There is information on T. Roosevelt and the Russo-Japanese War.

5 Armenian Manuscripts. (a) David, called the Philosopher, Philosophic hints. Aristotle, About virtue, to King Alexander. Commentary on the New Testament; ms. on paper, 17th c., 121 ll. (b) Song book of the Church of Armenia, 14th c., ms. on parchment, 366 ll.

6 Austrian Papers, 1781-83. 189 items. Transcripts made in 1868 of correspondence between the Austrian emperor, his ambassadors in London and Paris, and other individuals. The originals, in German, are in Vienna repositories. They concern the mediation of Austria and of Russia in continental disputes. (NUCMC 70-1702)

7 Alexander Bakshy (b. 1885). Translations of Russian plays (Falcons and Ravens; and a drama by Alexander I. Sumbatov and Vladimir Ivanovich Nemirovich-Danchenko).

8 Angelica Balabanoff (1878-1965). Socialist. Typescript with manuscript corrections and interlineations of her My Life as a Rebel, ca. 380 ll. (Annex)

9 Bancroft Collection. One part, 3 vols., of this large collection contains 135 transcripts of manuscripts (diplomatic correspondence) of the British ambassador to Russia. The letters, exchanged between Sir Robert Gunning, Sir James Harris, Lord Suffolk, Lord Stormont, and others (1774-83), concern the American war for independence (Britain's attempt to obtain Russian troops to serve in America) and European affairs in general. Originals are in the British Public Records Office in London. Another holding is listed as "Great Britain: Embassy to Russia" and has 21 pp. of extracts, transcripts, of dispatches between the Russian College of Foreign Affairs and its embassy at the Hague, 1782, again relating to American affairs. Eugene Schuyler made these copies from Moscow archives in 1868. A volume headed "Prussia: Embassy to Russia" has transcripts of dispatches of the Prussian ambassador to Russia about America, 1779-81; while the volume labeled "Prussia. Foreign Relations, 1776-1782" has transcripts of correspondence of Frederick II and ministers and courts of Prussia, Russia, and Sweden, 1781-82, on the armed neutrality agreements, 302 pp., copied from Prussian archives. "France, Ministry to Russia" has correspondence, in French, of Juigné, Corberon, and Vérac with Count Vergennes (Charles Gravier) and others, 1775-82, transcribed from French archives ca. 1850, 73 items. Unpublished finding aids.

10 James Asheton Bayard. See under U.S. Mission to Russia.

11 John Bigelow (1817-1911). Papers, 1839-1912, over 38 boxes and 63 vols. Includes his letters to Secretary of State W. H. Seward, confidential, 1862-66, and official, 1866; Seward's letters to Bigelow, 1856-68, all bound; and Bigelow's diary for 1843-53 and 1859-1911, 39 vols. There is information on the purchase of Alaska from the Russians. (NUCMC 73-671)

12 Poultney Bigelow. Signed holograph entitled "The German Emperor and the Russian Menace," 18 pp., and an ALS, bound, 1 p.

13 Robert Blakey (1795-1878). Historical sketches on various European countries, including Russia, ca. 1830(?). (Part of the DeCoursey Fales collection)

14 Dorothy Blumenstock. See under Harold D. Lasswell.

15 Ekaterina Konstantinovna Breshko-Breshkovskaia (1844-1934). Correspondence, 1923-34, 1 box. Russian revolutionary (pseudonym: Verigo). 174 letters and postcards to Mrs. Irene Dietrich, plus photographs, news clippings, and a letter from George (Egor) Lazarev to Dietrich, 1928, which discusses Breshkovskaia's life and work (and his own). The "little grandmother of the revolution" emigrated to Czechoslovakia after the Bolshevik coup and established a school for Russian children in the Carpathians. The correspondence concerns mostly Russian refugees, especially children, and Breshkovskaia's efforts to aid them with clothing and schooling. In some letters she also discusses her past life, philosophy, revolutionary figures (e.g., A. Kerensky), Russian and world affairs in general, the Russian national character, and other matters. Arranged in folders by date. (NUCMC 68-1076)

16 Herma (Hoyt) Briffault (b. 1898). Papers, ca. 1951-73, 1 package. Author and translator. Includes a typescript entitled "To the Yukon and Beyond," about the Russian-American telegraph expedition to the Arctic regions of Alaska and Siberia; copies of source materials relating to this expedition; correspondence about publication of the manuscript; and related items. There are some letters of Vilhjalmur Stefansson. (NUCMC 76-1500)

17 Izrail Bril'on. Typed and handwritten manuscript--"Forced Labor; the memoirs of a revolutionist," ca. 370 pp. Published in modified form in Moscow in 1927, the book lacks Chapter 1 and its last chapter differs from the corresponding one in this manuscript. (Annex)

18 Sergei Nikolaevich Bulgakov (1871-1944). A Marxist in his youth, Bulgakov became a priest and religious philosopher and teacher. His typescript, in Russian, entitled Ob imeni i Imeni (The Philosophy of the Sacred Name), has handwritten corrections, ca. 1937?, 400 pp. It was published as Filosofiya Imeni (Paris, 1953). (Annex)

19 Century Magazine. Records, 1870s-1914, 207 boxes. Includes correspondence and contributions of various writers, among them George Kennan (1886-1912). List of correspondents. (NUCMC 69-810)

20 Nikolai Gavrilovich Chernyshevski (1828-1889). Radical writer. Die Nihilisten oder was thun?, a translation by Alexander Schlesinger, 1878.

21 Chess. St. Petersburg Quadrangular Tournament. 1 item. A manuscript about the tournament (1895-96) between E. Lasker, W. Steinitz, H. N. Pillsbury, and M. Tschigornin, 41 pp.

22 Yevgenii Nikolayevich Chirikov (1864-1932). Novelist. 18 letters and a short story ("Oduvanchik") by Chirikov; a letter to V. Chirikova; and 2 letters by Vasilii Nemirovich-Danchenko. Materials are handwritten and typed; many letters are to Nikolai Sergeevich Karinskii.

23 James Chrystal (1832-1908). Papers, 1871-1908, 3 boxes and 4 vols. Episcopal minister. Includes clippings about "God's judgment on Russian idolators." (NUCMC 68-1093) (Annex)

24 Giovanni Francesco Commendone (1524-1584). Diplomatic correspondence, 1563-65, 1 vol. Catholic cardinal, envoy to Poland in the mid-16th c. Correspondence, in Italian, from Warsaw and other Eastern European sites to Cardinal Borromeo, discusses ecclesiastical and political affairs in Poland and Eastern Europe, including Russo-Polish relations. These are handwritten transcripts. (NUCMC 74-526)

25 James Copland. Logs, 1818-21, 1 vol. Sea captain. Log of a voyage from New York to Hamburg and to St. Petersburg, kept by Copland, the commander of the brig Boxer, employed by J. J. Astor. Includes his observations and information on social entertainment in the ports, 1 March-9 May 1818 for Russia.

26 Elmer Lawrence Corthell (1840-1916). Papers, 1872-1916, 4 boxes and 16 vols. Civil engineer and consultant. He became involved in the projected Trans-Alaska-Siberian Railway of Baron Loicq de Lobel. Many high tsarist officials and diplomats took part in negotiations for right-of-way concessions. Among the figures noted are Prince Obolenskii (director of his majesty's chancellery); Baron Fredericks; V. N. Kokovtsev (minister of finance and later premier); V. Lamsdorf (foreign minister); Khilkov (transport minister); and Cassini (Russian ambassador in Washington, D.C.). Papers, 1901-12, include correspondence, reports, photographs, maps of the planned route, a printed brochure on the railway, a copy of

Nicholas II's decree, 12 December 1905, approving Sergei Witte's report on the project, and reports on the economic and resettlement potentials of the railroad. (NUCMC 68-1101)

27 Stella Marek Cushing. Papers, 1928-37, 1 box. Journals, or letters, of her travels in Europe; collection of folk-songs, dances, costumes, etc. for lecture-concert programs in the United States; letters to her; and program notes. She visited most Eastern European countries, including Russia, 1928-34. (NUCMC 68-1107)

28 "D" Papers. 135 items. Documentation for footnotes to David Dallin's Soviet Espionage (New Haven, 1955).

29 Tello Jaen D'Apéry (1876-1949). Correspondence, 1889-97 and 1902, ca. 200 items. Editor and publisher of The Sunny Hour, a monthly for children. From contributors, subscribers, and others, mostly in Europe, 1889-97, 1902; some are from Russia. (NUCMC 76-1505)

30 Gherardi Davis (1858-1941). Papers, 1828-1940, 6 boxes and 6 vols. Lawyer, state legislator, and deputy police commissioner of New York City. Correspondence, notes, and illustrative material about flags of Russia (and other nations), plus a typed copy of The Story of My Life, ca. 106 pp., which includes recollections of conversations with German army officers about the Russo-Japanese War, ca. 1904. (NUCMC 68-1680)

31 Mstislav Valerianovich Dobujinsky (1875-1957). Papers, ca. 1914-52, 2 boxes. Painter, costume and stage designer. Includes notes for his apparently unpublished memoirs; notes; costume sketches; drawings; information about Russian stage designers and artists of the 19th and 20th c.; reminiscences of Constantin Stanislavsky and the Moscow Art Theater; and a chronology of the Russian art movement Mir Iskusstva. In Russian, English, and French.

32 Archimandrite Dosifei (d. 1845?). "Otkrytie bogomerzskoi i bogoprotivnoi skopecheskoi eresi"--composed in the Solovetsk monastery in 1834 by the archimandrite and kavaler Dosifei Nemchinov (Solovki, 1834). The manuscript, in 2 parts, folio, 101 and 44 pp., appeared in Chteniia v Imp. obshchestve istorii i drevnostei rossiiskikh pri Moskovskom universitete, vol. I, in 1872 (P. I. Mel'nikov's "Materialy dlia istorii khlystovskoi i skopecheskoi eresei"). All of part 2 but not all of part 1 were published. (In the Methodist Episcopal Church Manuscript Records)

33 B. (?) P. Dudorov. See under V. R. Kachinskii.

34 Eastern Orthodox Church, Russian. 1 item. Manuscript liturgy and ritual: "Lectionary of the Acts and Epistles" [Apostol] for the whole year, including weekday readings, beginning with lessons for Easter Week, 14th c. On vellum, 296 ll., unnumbered, double columns of 19 lines, in Russian uncial (Slavonic, in 2 hands?), with an illuminated headpiece at the start and illuminated initials (in the original wooden boards). Provenance: Novgorod or northern Russia (?).

35 Ilya Ehrenberg (b. 1891). Typescript of "The tempering of Russia," 426 pp., plus a corrected copy of the same, 424 pp. (Annex)

36 DeWitt Clinton Falls (1864-1937). Writings and scrapbooks on European armies and their uniforms, including Russian.

37 A. Fiodorov-Puntzev. 2 fairy tales: "Iablon'ka; skazka," 8 manuscript ll. with illustrated covers, and "Skazka-byl'," 10 ll., with illustrated front cover; both [Iarosl. pol. izol., 1925].

38 Harold Manchester Fleming (d. 1971). Papers, 1922-71, 12 cartons. Financial writer. Includes family correspondence, 1922-24, during his service in the American Relief Administration in Russia and as a journalist in China, plus a memoir of this period. (NUCMC 74-528) (Annex)

39 Basil Fomeen. Life's Worth Living--unpublished reminiscences of life in Russia and the United States, written in 1936, typescript, 1 vol.

40 William Frey (1839-1888). Papers, ca. 1860-88, 4 vols. Russian-American social reformer and Positivist. Born Vladimir Konstantinovich Heins, Frey came to America at the age of 29, forsaking a promising academic career, with the idea of founding or joining a communal agrarian settlement. He became a U.S. citizen; worked in both New York City and St. Louis, Missouri; founded 1 farm commune in Oregon and another in Cedar Vale, Kansas; and converted from a romantic socialism to Positivism (influenced by H. Spencer and A. Comte). He returned to Russia in 1885 to preach a new "religion of humanity," became close to Leo Tolstoi, and died in 1888. The library has ca. 375 items of correspondence, 1860-88, with Russian liberals and revolutionaries, American communists, and British and American Positivists, mainly discussing the Cedar Vale community, 1870-72, and his philosophical-religious ideas, many in Russian; plus his biography of Auguste Comte, over 196 pp. in Russian, and a few manuscript tracts on Positivism. Note: The library has an important mimeographed tract, in Russian, n.p., n.d., 100 pp., entitled "The Correspondence and Personal Interviews of William Frey with L. N. Tolstoy, 1886," donated by George Kennan. (NUCMC 69-861) (Annex)

41 Gershoy Family. Papers, 5 boxes. Letters, 1912-35, to Miriam (Lioubarski) and Morris

Gershoy, immigrants from Russia in New York City, including some from relatives in Russia--Sophia Lvovna Baranova, Berta and Valentin Rakita, in Russian. Restricted until 1981.

42 Giers (Girs) Family. Papers, 1859-95, 7 reels of microfilm. Reproduction of manuscripts, mostly letters, of Nikolai Karlovich Giers and his family (in French and Russian).

43 Richard Watson Gilder. 4 letters of George Kennan (1888-93); 1 letter, n.d., concerning Russian players; 1 letter about Russia and a question of extradition, 1893; and a letter from Russia about the Tolstoi Fund, 1892. (NUCMC 69-875)

44 Benjamin Gitlow. I Confess: the Truth About American Communism, typescript with manuscript corrections, 789 pp., for his book published by E. P. Dutton (New York, 1940).

45 Fedor (?) Gladkov (1883-1958). Typescript entitled "Marusya Makes Mischief." (Annex)

46 Edward F. Glenn. Papers, 1918, 20 items. U.S. army officer. Includes correspondence with I. Paderewski. References to Russia and Central and Eastern Europe.

47 Emma Goldman (1869-1940). Papers, 1906-40, 2 boxes and 1 microfilm reel, negative. Anarchist and author. Correspondence, address books, and other papers, collected by her niece Stella Ballantine, arranged in chronological order. The Russian-born Goldman emigrated to the United States in 1886, went back to the Soviet Union in 1920, became disillusioned and left, returning to the United States in 1922. Letters and postcards to Bayard Boyesen reveal Goldman's views of postwar conditions in Russia and Germany, 1917-28. Some letters concern the work of her friends who took up permament residence in the USSR. There are also letters to Mabel C. Crouch, Stella Ballantine, and Frances Perkins from prominent people; correspondence from Goldman concerning Spain and the Soviet Union; and microfilm (positive and negative) of manuscript letters of Goldman in the International Institute of Historical Sciences in Amsterdam. 1 letter, original, in this collection is to Roger Baldwin of the American Civil Liberties Union about American naivete over Russia, 1924; there are similar letters from 1937. Other items include 2 address books, condolences on her death, a typescript of Alexander Berkman's The Russian Myth, and the index to her own book Living My Life. (NUCMC 70-328)

48 Edward Goold and Company. Letterbook, 1797-98, 1 vol. Commission merchants of New York City. Holds communications to other merchants, especially in New England; concerns trade with Europe, China, India, and Russia (iron, ginger, brandy, etc.). Items date from 29 May 1797 to 3 September 1798.

49 Pieter Goos. [Pere]vo s"knigi imen ema vo//ny mir. Sirech'krakoe opi//sanie o obreteni pervago mo//rskago karabelnago kho inovy neznatny zemel', [sic] (n.p., 1667). Cursive manuscript, 59 ll. (In the Alexander the Great Collection, bound with the Church Slavonic manuscript described above under Aleksandriia.)

50 Francis Vinton Greene (1850-1921). Papers, 1776 and 1837-1921, 6 boxes and 13 vols. Army officer, historian, and engineer. Some correspondence concerns the Russo-Turkish War of 1877-78. Unpublished inventory (NUCMC 76-1512).

51 Anthony Jerome Griffin (1866-1935). Papers, 1883-1935, ca. 6 vols. and 49 boxes. Lawyer and U.S. congressman (from New York City). He toured the Soviet Union in 1931 with his wife Katharine (nee Byrne). During July and August they visited Leningrad, Moscow, Nizhnii Novgorod, Stalingrad, Rostov, Verblud Farm (a camel farm?), Tiflis, Batumi, Sochi, Yalta, Sevastopol', Balaklava, Odessa, Kiev, and Warsaw. Box 29 contains materials for a book about Russia, letters, and notes, all written by his wife. Box 7 contains his correspondence, 1930-32, in which there is discussion of the question of recognition of the USSR, Soviet slave labor, grain dumping, and American groups' opposition to trade with the USSR. Unpublished inventory (NUCMC 71-1204).

52 Bolton Hall (1854-1938). Papers, 1895-1938, 32 boxes and 3 vols. Lawyer, author, lecturer, and social reformer. His correspondence concerns Henry George and the single tax, the teachings of L. Tolstoi, and agricultural cooperation. He corresponded with scholars, writers, publishers, anarchists, and government officials. (NUCMC 70-1727) (Annex)

53 Stedman S. Hanks (b. 1889). Papers, 1956-67, 53 vols. Correspondence, photos, documents, clippings, etc. about the history of Borzoi dogs and introduction of the Borzoi into the U.S. Unpublished listing (NUCMC 70-333). (Annex)

54 Isabel Florence Hapgood (1850-1928). Papers, 1886-1922, 5 boxes. Author and translator. Contains correspondence with prominent Russians, including artists, writers, musicians, and churchmen, mostly in Russian, about their own cultural fields and world and Russian political affairs. Some letters are of Petrovo Solovovo Perovsky (Count Mikhail Mikhailovitch), written between 1906-22, concerning politics and particularly the start of the Revolution of 1918 [sic] and its later effect on the Russian nobility. There are photographs and papers on the women's education movement in Russia and about the "Kate Marsden Case" as well. Among Hapgood's correspondents and persons noted in the papers were Count Leo N. Tolstoi, countesses Sophia,

Alexandra, and Tatiana Tolstoi, Baroness A. Budberg, G. Bakhmeteff, Sophie Davydoff, Countess Speransky, Maksim Gorkii, M. M. Ipollitoff-Ivanoff, Alexandra Lvoff, Grand Duchess Maria Pavlovna, Prince Alexander K. Meshcherskii, E. Naryshkin, Alla Nazimova, K. P. Pobedonostsev, Nicholas II, Empress Alexandra Feodorovna, I. E. Repin, Baron R. R. Rosen, Count A. D. Scheremetieff, S. Stepniak (Kravchinskii), Sergius Witte, and General A. V. Verestchagin. Materials date from 1886-1926. Unpublished finding aid (NUCMC 71-1214).

55 J. Harris. Logbooks, 1807-10, 6 vols. British midshipman. Logs kept while on board HMS Temeraire on a long voyage around Europe. The ship went from England to Ireland, Sweden, Denmark, Norway, and Russia. From Reval it set out again for Spain and was in Russian waters ca. late 1809 or early 1810.

56 Levi Hayden. Diaries, 1864-84, 4 vols. Marine engineer from New York City. In 1878 he traveled widely in the Russian Empire for business purposes (viz., river and harbor dredging). Some 25 pp. of handwritten diary entries describe his impressions of Moscow, Taganrog, the Azov Sea, Mariupol', Kerch', Yalta, Sevastopol', Odessa, Nikolaev, and St. Petersburg. (NUCMC 73-676)

57 Alexander Herzen (1812-1870). Socialist and author. Typed copy of his letter to the editor of the London Daily News, 28 October 1854, concerning conversations with Russian prisoners at Plymouth. The piece appeared anonymously, bearing the signature "A Cosmopolitan Traveler."

58 Granville Hicks. Typed draft with his revisions of his book John Reed: the making of a revolutionary (21 chapters and appendix, ca. 450 ll.). John Stuart assisted him in the writing; Macmillan published it (New York, 1936). (Annex)

59 John Rogers Hudson (b. 1784). Papers, 1778-1829, Massachusetts merchant. Letters, 1803-29, and accounts, 1778-1813, relating to Atlantic coast towns, the West Indies, Russia, Holland, Sweden, and Great Britain (box 2).

60 International Committee for Political Prisoners. Records, 1923-42, 7 boxes. Materials detail its investigations into conditions and treatment of political prisoners in the Soviet Union and other countries (e.g., Canada, China, France, and India). 4 of the more interesting cases reported on were those of A. DeWit, 1937-38, Styopa Diebetz, 1938, Julius Simon, 1938, and Zensl Muhsam (Muehsam), 1936-40. Press releases, minutes of executive committee meetings, and correspondence deal with this same theme of political repression. The collection also holds a typescript by R. Abramovich, undated, entitled "Persecution of Russian Socialists by the Soviet Government." Among the group's correspondents were Henry G. Alsberg, Alexander Berkman, Harold Denny, Felix Frankfurter, L. S. Gannet, Emma Goldman, Z. Muhsam, Bertrand Russell, Upton Sinclair, Harry F. Ward, and the Soviet diplomat Alexander Troyanovsky. In 1925 the committee published its book Letters from Russian Prisoners. Unpublished inventory (NUCMC 76-1517).

61 Theodore P. Ion (d. 1940). Historian. Typescript of some chapters, with parts of a preliminary draft (revised) and references to sources in his hand, of The Political and Diplomatic History of the Eastern Question. (Annex)

62 Waldemar Jochelson (1855-1937). Collection, 1909-11, 6 boxes and 12 card files. Russian ethnographer. Aleutian linguistic and ethnographic materials collected on the Riabushinskii expedition of 1909-11. There are 81 coherent texts of folklore, tales, and traditions, plus Aleut-Russian and Russian-Aleut dictionaries in 9 card files. Roman Jakobson has supplied these Aleut holdings with a descriptive catalogue summary and they have been published by Avrahm Yarmolinsky as the Aleutian Manuscript Collection (New York, 1944). In addition, the collection has 3 card files of notes and writings, in English and Russian, on the language, customs, history, geography, and exploration of the Kamchadal people of the Kamchatka Peninsula in Siberia from 1910-11. Materials include many folk tales in the Kamchadal language with English translations. Part of these have appeared as Kamchadal Texts Collection by Waldemar Jochelson, published by Dean Stoddard Worth (Mouton, 1961). Unpublished index cards (NUCMC 68-1658).

63 Viktorin Romanovich Kachinskii (b. 1891). Typescript of a book edited by Nikolai Sergeyevich Karinsky--Istoriia letnago dela v Rossii do padeniia Imperii (New York, 1944-45). 3 illustrated volumes contain essays by Karinsky (history of flight in Russia to World War I), B. (?) P. Dudorov (aviation in the Baltic Sea area, 1912-17), Kachinskii (aviation in the Black Sea region, 1912-17), Boris Vasil'evich Sergievskii ("Zapiski voennago letchika /voiny 1914-1917 g.g./"), and Piotr Evgrafovich Stogov (radio and sea flying).

64 Nikolai S. Karinsky. See under V. R. Kachinskii.

65 George Kennan (1845-1924). Papers, 1866-1919, 5 boxes. Explorer, author, journalist, and authority on Russia. First traveling to the empire (Siberia) in the late 1870s as part of a surveying party for a telegraph line, Kennan returned to do research, especially on political prisoners in Siberia, in 1885-89. The collection has his correspondence, reports,

photographs, and other papers--most in Russian but many with translations. Of the substantial holdings on Russian prisoners and political exiles and trials, Kennan estimated that only about a quarter found its way into his famous 2-volume study Siberia and the Exile System. This collection contains lists of names of political exiles (1886), sketches on the history of socialist thought in Russia and on the treatment of political criminals (including administrative exiles), and eyewitness accounts of tsarist atrocities at Kara, Nerchinsk, and Iakutsk. Also, copies of ca. 40 letters of Ekaterina Breshkovskaia. A. Yarmolinsky published a description of the Kennan papers (and published materials) in the library ("The Kennan Collection") in the Bulletin of the New York Public Library, vol. 25 (February 1921). There is also an unpublished finding aid. (Annex)

66 Nikolai M. Khrabrov (1869-1940). Papers, 1916-37, 1 box. Russian army officer (major general) stationed in the U.S. during 1916-17, first as president of the artillery section of the Russian Supply Commission in the U.S. and then as head of the entire supply organization. Remaining in America until 1919, he returned to Russia, whence he again came to the U.S. after a 1-year stay in Siberia. Personal correspondence, 1916-17, discusses his work on supplies and a suspicious explosion that destroyed a storehouse of Russian munitions in 1917. His memoirs, handwritten, 163 pp., concern his Siberian sojourn; part of these was published in Prague ca. 1930. (NUCMC 71-1243)

67 Aleksandr Lachinov. "Zhalovannaia gramota na dvorianskoe dostoinstvo i dvorianskii gerb, dannaia polkovniku Aleksandru Lachinovu za revnostnuiu voennuiu sluzhbu ot imeni Imperatora Aleksandra I." Signed by Nicholas I in St. Petersburg, 14 October 1827, written in ink with gold lettering, these letters patent are on folio-sized parchment, with decorated borders, illuminated by the Imperial arms and by Alexander I's Imperial monogram. The arms assigned to Lachinov also appear on the pages.

68 Harold D. Lasswell and Dorothy Blumenstock. Typescript with manuscript corrections: "World Revolutionary Propaganda," 413 pp.; published by A. Knopf (New York, 1939). (Annex)

69 Log Books. Log of the brig Czarina, a merchant ship, commanded by Captain Wolston Dixey, master, for 13 January 1834-6 July 1837, 167 pp. 3 voyages from Boston to Cronstadt, Russia, the first and last via Cuba. Cargoes included hemp from Russia and sugar from Cuba.

70 Eugene Lyons. Typescript, with corrections in pencil, of his Assignment in Utopia, 951 pp., published by Harcourt, Brace and Co. (New York, 1937). (Annex)

71 Jan Waclaw Machajski. Unfinished essay--a critique of socialism--translated by his wife from Polish into Russian [Paris, 1911], 51 pp., mostly in her hand; plus a photostatic copy of the essay.

72 Gustav Manteuffel. Outline history of Livonia, 12th-19th c., in Polish, 2 vols., entitled Zarysy z dziejow krain dawnych inflanckich.

73 Alexander Hume (Campbell), Second Earl of Marchmont (1675-1740). Papers, 1722-24, ca. 400 items. Correspondence and diplomatic papers which discuss European affairs, especially the Congress of Cambray (with Baron Charles Whitworth); in English and French. (NUCMC 72-1056) (In the Hardwicke Collection)

74 Nicholas N. Martinovitch (1883-1954). Papers, 1935-51, 1 box. Orientalist. Biographical sketch, correspondence, and manuscripts of monographs on Turkish subjects. Includes copies of Oriental and Persian manuscripts.

75 Patrick McCartan. Doctor, envoy of the Republic of Ireland to Russia in 1921. Report on his contacts with Russia, typed copy, 34 pp. (In the Garrison-McKim-Maloney Collection/Irish Historical Collection--Miscellaneous Papers)

76 Vladimir Ivanovich Nemirovich-Danchenko (1858-1943). Translation of his My Life in the Russian Theatre by John Cournos, typed with manuscript corrections, ca. 185 pp., plus the typescript in Russian as published in Moscow in 1936. (Annex)

77 Florence Nightingale (1820-1910). British nurse and hospital administrator. Letter, 1867, asking for the address of the widow of a Surgeon Major French, who served at Scutari in 1854 and died in 1860. (In the Miscellaneous Collection)

78 Owen Family. Papers, 1829-72, 2 vols., 70 ll. Family living in New Harmony, Indiana, a communistic colony founded by George Rapp, 1814, and sold to the British reformer and socialist Robert Owen in 1825. Probably this family was that of his son, Robert Dale Owen. Includes a diary, September-November 1869, possibly written by Richard Owen, on a trip through southern Russia (Yalta, Kiev, and Odessa) and thence to the Near East.

79 Michael Pankiw (1894-1956). His Ukrainian poetry, plus Dr. A. Sokolyszyn's "Ukrainian poetry of Michael Pankiw," original manuscript, typescript, and galley-proofs.

80 Bernard Pares. Typescript of chapters 24-26, ca. 90 pp., of Sir Bernard's A History of Russia, with galley-proof and author's proof of index. (Annex)

81 M. R. Parkman. Diary, 5 March-23 April 1871, of a young woman traveling through Egypt and the Holy Land. She describes the Armenian and Russian quarters of Jerusalem, 3 vols.

82 Rose Pesotta (1896-1965). Papers, 1922-65, 45 boxes and 3 packages. Labor union official. Some family letters are in Russian. Correspondents include Emma Goldman, Alexander Berkman, and David Dubinsky. Unpublished inventory (NUCMC 76-1536).

83 Bernard Peyton. Typed, carbon copy, letters from Peyton to his wife in Charlottesville, Virginia, while on a journey through Russia and Siberia to establish trade relations, June 1856-April 1857, apparently transcribed in New York in 1934.

84 Vasilii Aleksandrovich Potto. Istoriia Novorossiiskago dragunskago polka, 1803-1865 [St. Petersburg, 1866], 2 vols., with tables--a manuscript presented to the Grand Duke Vladimir Aleksandrovich. Engrossed copy of a printed work which is in the NYPL Slavonic Division.

85 Andrew Pranspill. 1 box, ca. 185 items. Letters, most in Estonian, to Pranspill from leading 20th c. Estonian writers Eduard Wilde, S. Snglous (?), Kitzberg, Raudupp, Tammsaare, Kangro, Hindrey, Kiojad, Kampmann, Adson, Aavik, Wallak, Weiler, Rehang, Pass, Jurgenstern, Anderhopp, and Kallas.

86 Arthur James Putnam (b. 1893). Papers, 1942-63, 2 folders, ca. 300 items. Lend-lease administrator in Africa in World War II and editor of the Macmillan Co. Miscellaneous correspondence, including some letters of Immanuel Velikovsky relating to his book Worlds in Collision.

87 Rand School of Social Sciences. Ca. 6 items. a Bolshevik calendar, 6 pp., undated; "The Economic Work of the Soviets" (ca. 1918); Harry Wellington Laidler (?), "Russia" (1919?), typed, 55 pp.; Y. Stekloff's editorial on the attitude of Soviet leaders to the U.S. as compared with Germany (English translation from a Canadian Russian paper; original appeared in Izvestiia and was reprinted in Rabochii narod); Thomas D. Thacher, "Russia and the war" (New York City, 4 June 1918), a typescript, 11 pp.; and a "Letter from Alexander Trachtenberg to the Editor of The Evening Post, New York, on the Russian Revolution, 1917," carbon, 9 pp.

88 Aleksei Remizov (1877-1958). Correspondence, 1924-34, 21 items. Writer. Letters and postcards written from Boulogne to Nicolas Slonimsky, the composer.

89 John Ridley. 1 vol. British mariner. Log of the brig Tirzal for 23 May-23 July 1849, with expense accounts on sundry voyages, 1849-50, primarily between Liverpool and ports on the Black Sea. Written in "Old Moore's improved New Almanac for 1844."

90 John Jacob Robbins. Papers, 1893-1953, 13 boxes and 1 package. Author and translator of Russian literature. At least 3 boxes contain letters, photos, and manuscripts of interest. Box 1 holds typescript articles on Mikhail Lermontov, Konstantin Stanislavsky, and Russian war poetry, plus a short sketch on "My Friend Soudeikine," holograph, presumably the painter Sergei Iu. Sudeikin. In box 3 are translations of Russian verse, including works of Lermontov, A. Blok, V. Ivanov, I. (?) Krylov, Kuzmin, Voloshin, and A. S. Pushkin (Boris Godunov). The original typescript in Russian (incomplete) of Stanislavsky's My Life in Art--with corrections in Stanislavsky's own hand--is in box 8. There are also manuscripts and typescripts in English translation of B. Lavrenev's "The Road Begins," Vladimir Solovyov's "Field Marshal Kutuzov," 5 acts, N. Pogodin, "Chimes of the Kremlin," 3 acts, and Pushkin's "Feast of Death," "The Miser Knight," and "Mozart and Salieri." Unpublished inventory (NUCMC 73-703).

91 Rossiiskoye Bibleiskoye Obshchestvo. General Committee. 2 ff. contain a manuscript translation of the original Russian source concerning revision of the Esthonian Quarto Bible; and there are reports on the work of the General Committee, 21 ff., n.p., n.d. Materials are from 1870-74.

92 Russia--Libraries. Cablegrams, 1944, 7 items. From librarians in Moscow addressed to the Library Journal, New York, 9 July-22 August 1944, reporting successful efforts to preserve public and private libraries in the USSR. They note the destruction wreaked by the German army, and discuss student use of libraries in war conditions and the impact of the weather.

93 Russian Artillery Commission of North America. Records, 1917, of an investigation made by Lt. Boris Brazol of the Russian Supply Committee of the Russian Artillery Commission into allegations that an official of the Commission had engaged in espionage and treason against the Russian government with agents of the Central Powers in New York. Included are copies of reports of verbal examinations made by Brazol and other documents relating to the investigation, typescript copies in Russian and English.

94 Russian Lawyers' Association in U.S.A. Records, 1922-47, 1 box. Correspondence, etc., largely in Russian, of an organization of émigré Russian attorneys. They worked to establish contact and cooperation with American lawyers' groups.

95 Russian Literature. Under this heading the catalogue lists an 18th c. manuscript entitled "Raznost' i priiatnost'" which contains selections from Trudoliubivaia pchela and other Russian periodicals of the late 18th c.

96 Russians in U.S. Ca. 1 box. This rubric covers 2 separate holdings: issues of "Gazeta

'Ostrova Slez'," a daily newspaper in manuscript, edited by a group of deportees, mainly Russians, at Ellis Island, New York (numbers 2-4; 7-9 January 1920)--text in Russian, Ukrainian, Yiddish, German, Lithuanian, and English; and a box of "Materialy dlia istorii Federatsii russkikh organizatsii v Amerike, ee Filadel'fiiskogo otdela i Obshchestva izucheniia russkoi immigratsii" (New York, 1918-24). These latter papers include correspondence, protocols of sessions, and communications of members. The Society for the Study of Russian Immigration was New York-based. (The catalogue also lists this holding under the heading "Federation of the Russian Organizations in America.")

97 Boris Vasil'evich Sergievskii. See under V. R. Kachinskii.

98 Innokentii Nikolayevich Seryshev (b. 1883). Orthodox priest. Typescript of his "Strana samuraev; peshkom po iaponskim shkolam" (Sydney, Australia, 1948), with the title in Japanese also--it concerns 20th c. Japanese education; and "Problema mezhdunarodnogo iazyka" in 2 parts (Sydney, [1949]).

99 Albert Shaw (1857-1947). Papers, 1874-1947, 200 ft. Editor of the Review of Reviews (New York) 1891-1937. He corresponded with the Council on Foreign Relations, 1918-46, and with Near East Relief, 1919-44. There is information on Armenian history in these papers. (NUCMC 76-1544)

100 Vladimir Nikolayevich Smol'yaninov. "Vospominaniia" in manuscript.

101 Aleksandr Sokolyvych (pseudonym of A. Sokolyszyn). "A.F.A.B.N. Strength. On the Occasion of the Congress of American Friends of Anti-Bolshevik Bloc of Nations, Inc." (New York, A.F.A.B.N., 1958), 38 pp. with illustrations, and 37 autographs of prominent Ukrainians and others.

102 Yaroslav S. Stetzko. Outline of his life with his signature and that of the donor, Dr. A. Sokolyszyn ("Freedom for every nation and social justice for every human being").

103 Piotr Evgrafovich Stogov. See under V. R. Kachinskii.

104 Mary Stoughton (Mrs. Edwin Wallace Stoughton). Diary, 1878-79, 2 vols. Wife of a U.S. minister to Russia. Diary for 23 May 1878-16 February 1879 describing travel in western Europe and official life at the Russian court in St. Petersburg.

105 Ivan Strigutski. Manuscript entitled "Ocherk Ropshi, imeniia Gosudaria Imperatora." Compiled by I.S. (Ropsha?, 1881; 200 pp.), with the bookplate of the Grand Duke Vladimir Aleksandrovich.

106 Anna Louise Strong. Typescript--My Native Land. (Annex)

107 Vasilii Nikolayevich Stroyev (?). Manuscript presumably written by Stroyev; bears the heading "Veselovskie: Avraam, Issak i Feodor--russkie gosudarstvennye liudi XVIII stoletiia,' n.p., n.d., 8 ll.

108 Otto Wilhelm von Struve (1819-1905). Papers, 1852-98, 2 folders, ca. 60 items. Director of the Pulkovo Astronomical Observatory in Russia. Includes miscellaneous documents relating to the scientific and civil service career of Struve (certificates of appointment to diplomatic posts and to honorary orders, signed by Alexander II and Alexander III); papers relating to his membership in the Imperial Russian Geographic Society; diplomas; birth certificates; curriculum vitae; and drafts of his letters requesting favors and appointments for his sons. In Russian, French, and German.

109 Joseph Gardner Swift (1783-1865). Papers, 1815-58, 1 box. Soldier and civil engineer. Had some business contacts with Russia. One correspondent was George Washington Whistler.

110 Norman Thomas (b. 1884). Papers, ca. 193 boxes. Author, lecturer, and leader of the Socialist Party in the U.S. Includes information on L. Trotskii's right of asylum and Russian history, plus criticism of communism and the Soviet government. 1 box in the Thomas family papers has biographical data on Norman Thomas. List of correspondents. (Annex)

111 Anne Thomson (Mrs. James Thomson). Papers, n.d., 1 box. Letters sent to Anne Thomson, an American living in Paris, from Americans, Englishmen, Russians, and Spaniards distinguished in art, letters, and the professions.

112 Alexei Nikolayevich Tolstoi (1883-1945). Writer. Typescript of "Hyperboloid of the Engineer Garin," apparently published by A. A. Knopf. Text identical to "The Death Box," translation by Bernard G. Guerney (London, 1957). (Annex)

113 Ariadna Tyrkova-Williams. Part 2 of her biography of A. S. Pushkin, typed, 466 pp., with handwritten corrections, in Russian. (Annex)

114 U.S. Mission to Russia, 1813. Official papers of John Quincy Adams, Albert Gallatin, and James A. Bayard, envoys extraordinary to the tsar. Includes letters of credence; notes between the Americans and Count Nikolai Romanzoff (Rumiantsev), chancellor of the empire, about Russia's offered mediation to the U.S. and Great Britain during the War of 1812; and dispatches to the secretary of state. Bound with these 24 transcripts, 57

pp., are copies, 46 pp., of Bayard's letters to Caesar A. Rodney, 1802-14. (NUCMC 68-1050, under James Asheton Bayard)

115 U.S. Treaties. 5 items. Photostat copies (made in 1932) of papers in Russian governmental archives concerning proposed negotiations for a treaty with the United States that became the Treaty of 1832. There are correspondence between U.S. minister to Russia James Buchanan and Count Karl Robert Nesselrode, Russian foreign minister; Nesselrode's confidential report to the tsar; the draft of a dispatch from Nesselrode to Baron Sacken, Russian chargé d'affaires in Washington; and a summary of views concerning the principles of neutrality. The originals date from 14 June-18 December 1832. 4 of them are in French.

116 Piotr Demyanovich Uspensky (1878-1947). Typescript entitled "Wheel of Life" (apparently published by A. A. Knopf). (Annex)

117 Marcia van Dresser-Gertrude Norman. Collection, 1 box. Correspondents include Clara (Clemens Gabrilowitsch) Samossoud.

118 Lillian D. Wald (1867-1940). Papers, 1893-1940, 47 boxes. American social worker and pioneer in public health care. Wald founded a visiting nurse service in 1893 in New York City and also a settlement house. Includes correspondence with Jane Addams about the Russian Revolution and with Mrs. Vladimir Simkovitch (wife of a Russian agrarian historian). Unpublished finding aid. Note: The entire collection is available on master negative microfilm.

119 Alexander Werth. Typescript of his "Moscow Diary." (Annex)

120 Anna Matilda McNeill Whistler. Diaries, 1843-48, 2 vols. Wife of the succeeding and mother of James McNeill Whistler, the painter. Her journal while in St. Petersburg, 28 November 1843-27 September 1844 and 12 March 1845-September 1848.

121 George Washington Whistler (1800-1849). Photostat copy of the "Report by Major George Washington Whistler to his Excellency the Count [R.] Kleinmichel on the gauge of Russian railways, St. Petersburg, September 9, 1842," 9 pp. The original is in the files of the Transport Archives in Leningrad. Also a mimeograph of a typed copy of the report and correspondence regarding its acquisition. The report concerns railroads in the Caucasus.

122 Sergei Iulevich Witte (1849-1915). Typescript portions, ca. 100 pp., of the count's memoirs, translated and edited by Abraham (Avrahm) Yarmolinsky (whose edition appeared in 1921) plus some notes used in the translating work.

123 Bertram Wolfe (b. 1896). Papers, 1925-37, 2 boxes. Author, teacher, lecturer, and specialist on Soviet Russia. Correspondence, typescripts, clippings, and mimeographed material concerning such subjects as the Workers (Communist) Party of America and the All-American Anti-Imperialist League.

124 James F. C. Wright (b. 1904). Typescript entitled "Slava Bohu, the story of the Dukhobors" (published by Farrar and Rinehart, 1940).

125 Frank Wuttge. Papers, in process. Includes biographical information about Frank Wuttge, Sr., a photographer's helper in Imperial Russia.

126 Aleksyei Grigoryevich Yevstafiev (1783-1857). 67 items. Russian consul in Boston and New York. Personal and official correspondence; documents (photostats); incomplete biographical sketch of Yevstafiev by Leo Wiener; family tree, 1680-1880, of the Wilson family (Emily Wilson married Yevstafiev); a photo of the Yevstafiev home in Buffalo, New York; and miscellanea. There is also a holograph, 120 pp., of his "The Great Republic Tested by the Touch of Truth" (an examination of ideas of government of Russia, England, and the U.S., 1848-52). In the Slavonic Division, bound at the end of the book Memorable Predictions of the Late Events in Europe (Boston, 1814), 108 pp. (call number *KF 1814). Manuscript, 37 ll., entitled "Appendix. More predictions concerning the second downfal [sic] of Buonaparte," extracted from Yevstafiev's private correspondence with General Humphreys (his name is given as Alexis Eustaphieve in the book, whose contents were also extracted from his writings). The appendix consists of a publisher's preface, 21 August 1815, and 7 letters dated Portland, Boston, and Sandwich, 7 May-10 August 1815.

127 Miriam (Shomer) Zunser (d. 1951). Papers, ca. 1900-1907, 1 box and 1 package. Author. Includes reminiscences of her mother's family and their life in Russia in the 19th c.; a journal of her European travels; and some genealogical notes. (NUCMC 71-362)

Finding Aids: The New York Public Library Research Libraries have published the Dictionary Catalog of the Manuscripts Division, 2 vols. (Boston: G. K. Hall, 1967).

NEW YORK - NEW YORK PUBLIC LIBRARY NY 65

NY 65
DANCE COLLECTION
PERFORMING ARTS RESEARCH CENTER
NEW YORK PUBLIC LIBRARY
111 Amsterdam Avenue
New York, New York 10023
(212-799-2200)

The Dance Collection in the New York Public Library at Lincoln Center is the most comprehensive, for all forms of dance, in the United States, perhaps in the world. The amount of Russian/Soviet-related material in the repository is extensive; the description that follows cannot do the collection justice. The Dance Collection comprises textual material, photographs, motion pictures, prints, original designs, sculpture, and sound recordings. Items are listed in the card catalogue under 4 rubrics: names (persons--dancers, choreographers, authors, composers, artists, designers; companies; organizations; etc.), titles (ballets, concert works, folk and ethnic dances, films, books, etc.), topical subjects (folk dancing, history and criticism, etc.), and geographical place names. In general, one can say that for every major Russian/Soviet dancer, choreographer, impresario, and ballet there are archival holdings in the New York Public Library. (Not all pertinent materials, however, are physically located in this division.) A selected listing of holdings, which follows, can give only the barest idea of the size and scope of relevant materials. Note: Many items are part of much larger collections. When known, these collections are indicated in parentheses at the appropriate point in descriptions. But the catalogue and published guides used in compiling this list were not always clear about this matter.

1 Gabriel Astruc (1864-1938). Papers, 1904-25, 123 folders, ca. 1,300 items. French impresario, journalist, publisher, and director of the Théâtre des Champs-Elysées (Paris) in 1913. Includes correspondence, financial papers, inventories, notes and plans, programs, contract drafts, reports, and clippings. Much relates to the early activities of Sergei Diaghilev, who brought Russian ballet and opera to Western Europe. Most items are from 1907-14, none from 1915-24. Astruc and Diaghilev became close collaborators. The collection has detailed information about the first Saison Russe of Diaghilev at the Théâtre du Châtelet in Paris, 1909, including inventories of costumes and scenery and even Astruc's report to Baron Frederiks, minister of the Russian court. Among correspondents and others mentioned in the papers are Ida Rubinstein, Natasha Trouhanova, Baron Dmitri Günzburg, Vaslav Nijinsky, Anna Pavlova, Fedor Shaliapin, and Boris Shidlovskii. Requires special handling. Published register: Bulletin of the NYPL, 75 (Oct. 1971). (NUCMC 72-255)

2 Leon Bakst (Lev Samoilovich Rosenberg) (1866-1924). Manuscripts include several autograph letters, signed, 1917-21, some to George Wague in Paris, which discuss costumes, S. Diaghilev, his designs for the ballet Sleeping Beauty, and his designs for the ballet Firebird. There are also his pencil and watercolor sketch, signed in pencil, of a "Man in Spanish Costume," St. Petersburg, 1902-1903, and his Cretan Sketch Book, Greece, ca. 1907. The latter, in pencil and watercolor, is annotated. Bakst sketched the palace of Knossos on Crete, the site of major archeological discoveries just at this time. Hellenic inspiration showed in 3 of his ballet collaborations in 1912: M. Fokine's "Narcisse" and "Daphnis et Chloë" and V. Nijinsky's "Faune."

3 George Balanchine (Georgii Melitonovich Balanchivadze) (b. 1896). A rare ALS to S. Diaghilev, Paris, 1925, discusses recruitment of dancers in Latvia and Germany among Russian exiles, in Russian, but signed in French; a telegram from Igor Stravinsky to Balanchine, 1957, concerns the first performance of "Agon" by the New York City Ballet; photo by Gjon Mili of the Stravinsky-Balanchine "Movements for Ballet and Orchestra" (New York, 1963); and the complete working correspondence between the painter Eugene Berman in Rome and Balanchine in New York during their collaboration on "Pulcinella," 1971-72. (Collections such as that of José Limón hold letters and other items to, from, and about Balanchine.)

4 [Ballets performed at the Maryinsky Theatre, Leningrad, 1800-1903. New York? 194-?], 14 ll.

5 [Ballets produced Jan. 1, 1945-April 18, 1954 by Ballet Russe de Monte Carlo, Ballet Theatre and New York City Ballet (Ballet Society). New York, 1955?], 20 ll.

6 André Bauchant (1873-1958). Miscellaneous manuscripts, in French, including letters to Aleksandr Shervashidze.

7 Alexandre Nicolaivich Benois (1870-1960). Painter and writer. Watercolor, signed twice in ink, of a set design for scene II of "Le Pavilion d'Armide" (St. Petersburg, 1908); the ballet's libretto was also by Benois.

8 René Blum (1878-1942?). Miscellaneous manuscripts, including an ALS, 26 August 1936, which mentions the de Basil Ballet Russe de Monte Carlo, Karinska, and Yurek Shabel'evsky.

9 Jean Börlin (1893-1930). Holograph letter, signed, to Michel Fokine, 17 June 1918; Copenhagen, 1 p., in French, asking to study with Fokine.

10 Cesare, Enrico and Giuseppe Cecchetti. Several ALS and signed postcards are from

Enrico Cecchetti (1850-1928) to his pupil and godchild, Gisella Caccialanza, Milan, 1926-28; his manuscript book "Manuel des exercices de danse théâtrale a pratiquer chaque jour de la semaine à l'usage de mes élèves" (St. Petersburg, 1894), 102 pp., with a chapter on dance notation; there is also his volume, unpaged, entitled "Elenco delle allieve della Accademia di Ballo del Teatro alla Scala di Milano, 1925-1928" [Milan, 1928]. A TLS in Italian from Cesare Cecchetti to Cia Fornaroli (Milan, 13 December 1928) concerns Anna Pavlova. (In the Walter Toscanini Collection/ Cia Fornaroli Collection)

11 Tatiana Chamié. Papers, 1926-50, ca. 100 items. Photos, letters, notebooks, diaries, contract, and cards. Dancer, teacher, and choreographer. Items on the Ballet Russe de Monte Carlo and her own ballets, in Russian, English, and French. Unpublished register and folder list.

12 Jean Cocteau (1889-1963). 2 posters (colored lithograph by Verneau and Cochoin) of V. Nijinsky and T. Karsavina, designed by the poet and draftsman to advertise the third Diaghilev season in Paris (Paris, 1911); and a signed holograph article by Cocteau on the third season of the Ballets Russes (Paris, 1911)--in the Lincoln Kirstein Collection.

13 Edward Gordon Craig (1872-1966). Craig-Duncan Collection, 1901-57, 360 folders. Theater artist and author. Material relating to the dancer Isadora Duncan includes correspondence, 1904-1905, from Duncan when she appeared in St. Petersburg and Moscow. Special handling. Published register: Bulletin of the NYPL, 76 (1972), pp. 180-98. (NUCMC 72-256)

14 Victor Dandré (d. 1944). Correspondence of Dandré, the husband of Anna Pavlova, includes 4 holograph letters signed, 1913-28, 3 in French and 1 in Italian to Cia Fornaroli (in the Walter Toscanini Collection/Cia Fornaroli Collection); and an ALS dated 7 February 1931, in reply to a letter of condolence on Pavlova's death.

15 Aleksandra Dionisievna Danilova (b. 1904). Russian-born ballerina. Miscellaneous manuscripts; scrapbooks, 15 vols., of clippings, programs, and photos from 1937-56; scrapbook of clippings from U.S. tours, 1954-56; and photo scrapbook from a 1957 tour of Japan. Plus microfilm copies of the scrapbooks.

16 Agnes De Mille (b. 1918). 5 notebooks and 3 folders of material. American dancer, choreographer, and writer. Correspondence, scenarios, choreographic notes, and other writings. "Russian journals" kept by De Mille in 1966 and 1969, the latter diary from her trip to Moscow by invitation to judge an international ballet competition, handwritten and typed. The finished 1969 diary appeared as "Judgment in Moscow" in Dance Perspectives (New York, 1970, no. 44, Winter). Permission required.

17 Irving Deakin (1894-1958). Correspondence, 1934-55, 83 folders, ca. 1,245 items. In holograph, manuscript, and typescript, primarily relating to Deakin's work in association with Hurok Attractions and as general manager of the San Francisco Civic Ballet, 1947-48. Arranged chronologically, the letters concern Deakin's relations with the Original Ballet Russe, the Ballet Russe de Monte Carlo, Tamara Toumanova, and Adol'f Bolm. Unpublished register.

18 Gleb Derujinsky (b. 1888). Artist. Sculpture --a bronze portrait figurine--of the American dancer Ruth Page, Chicago, ca. 1930.

19 Sergei Pavlovich Diaghilev (Dyagilev) (1872-1929). Papers, ca. 1909-29, 600 items. Impresario. Correspondence, 1918?-29, 195 items, with such people as Lady Juliet Duff, Lady Rothermere, Ernest Outhwaite, and William Luck Warden (on the financing of his company, especially in 1928-29), Dorothy Archer, Cyril William Beaumont, Gerald Hugh Tyrwhitt-Wilson (Baron Berners), Irene Frances Adza Denison Mountbatten (Marchioness of Carisbrooke), John Alden Carpenter, Mario Castelnuovo-Tedesco, Sybil Halsey (Lady Colefax), Diana (Manners) Cooper (Viscountess Norwich), Elizabeth Theresa Frances Courtauld, Dorothee Coxon, Edward Gordon Craig, Anton Dolin, Rupert Doone, Elinor Dunsmuir, Powys Evans, Diana Isobel Erskine (Lady Fitzherbert), Sir Eugene Goossens, Felicity Gray, Ruth Holland, Sir Randle Fynes Wilson Holme, Gordon Jacob, Evelyn James, Sir Geoffrey Langdon Keynes, Constant Lambert, Berkeley John Talbot Levett, Ena Wertheimer Mathias, Violet Florence Mabel (Goetze) Melchett, Rose Schiff Morley, Celia Brunel James (Lady Noble), Sir Saxton Noble, Margot Asquith (Countess of Oxford and Asquith), Ruth Page, Aimée Phipps, Cole Porter, Walter Archibald Propert, Henry Prunières, Philip John Sampey Richardson, Harold Sidney Harmsworth (Viscount Rothermere), Florence Emily Henderson Grenfell (Baroness St. Just), Elinor Shan, Sacheverell Sitwell, Odette Tchernine, Sir Basil Home Thomson, George Herbert Thring, Countess Sophia de Torby, Sir William Turner Walton, Herbert Francis Wauthier, Mary Hoyt Wiborg, and Laura Wilson. The letters are in French, English, and Russian, holographs and typescripts, business and personal. They concern his ballets, dancers (e.g., V. Nijinsky), and social life. The Black exercise book, in Diaghilev's holograph, was written in St. Petersburg, Paris, and elsewhere, 1909-11. In great detail it reveals his business and artistic negotiations, casts and programs for planned ballets and operas, financial records, budgets and plans for the 1910-11 season, lists of members of the Ballets Russes de

Diaghilev, projected schedules through 1913, salaries, matters of decor and costume, etc.--with his doodles on many pages, 177 pp. Mostly in Russian, it is written in pencil and ink. (The contents are described by Brian Blackwood in the NYPL Bulletin, vol. 75, no. 8 [October 1971].) A microfilm of this book is also available. Diaghilev's small brown notebook, London-Paris, 1921-23/24, also in his autograph, contains notes on programs, schedules, finances, and many names. Some 400 letters and documents accompany these 2 notebooks, bearing the signatures of Leon Bakst, George Balanchine, Vaslav Nijinsky, Igor Stravinsky, and others. In addition, there are photos of Diaghilev's ballet companies, various productions, the 1916/17 American tour, and individual dancers. Finally, the collection has 2 autograph schedules for ballets and rehearsals, for London in 1921 ("La Belle au Bois Dormant") and for Paris, 1924. Special handling. Unpublished register. (Lincoln Kirstein Collection)

20 Mstislav Valerianovich Dobuzhinskii (Dobujinsky) (1875-1957). Stage designer. Miscellaneous manuscripts, including letters to Sol Hurok and David Lichine concerning Graduation ball, a list of Russian stage artists, a list of stage designers before 1900 and in later years, before and after the Revolution in Russia and abroad, and stage decoration sketches.

21 Vladimir Dukelsky (1903-1969). Composer. Various items, including an autograph letter, signed, giving a brief biography and his ideas on music.

22 Irma Duncan Collection of Isadora Duncan Materials. 183 folders, ca. 300 items. Manuscripts, photographs, programs, correspondence, memorabilia, and clippings relating to the lives and careers of Isadora and Irma Duncan. 1 group of manuscripts relates primarily to the years Isadora Duncan spent in Russia, 1921-24. Among the correspondents are Gordon Craig, Sergei Esenin (Isadora Duncan's husband), Eleanora Duse, Ellen Terry, Ivy Low Litvinova (Moscow, 1921), and Anatolii Lunacharskii. Permission required. Unpublished register.

23 Isadora Duncan (1877-1927). Miscellaneous manuscripts, including a letter to Augustin Duncan in which she discusses the Duncan School in Moscow. Note: There is much Isadora Duncan material in other collections such as the Edward Gordon Craig papers.

24 Sergei Dyagilev. See under Sergei Diaghilev.

25 Anna Evreinoff. Papers include a TLS, 7 July 1964, which speaks of Pedro Pruna's designs for L. Massine's ballet Matelots.

26 Sophie Fedorovitch (1893-1953). Costume-sketch in watercolor and pencil, unsigned, for Sir Frederick Ashton's ballet "A Child of Light" ("Dante Sonata" music of Lizst), London, 1940.

27 Mikhail Mikhailovich Fokin (Fokine) (1880-1942). Papers, 1914-41, 52 items in 14 folders. Choreographer, dancer, and teacher. Includes letters from Arnold L. Haskell, Cyril W. Beaumont, Sara Yancey Belknap, Alexander Levitoff, and others; essays and articles by Fokin and others; bookplates; calling cards; hotel bills; an invitation from Ruth St. Denis; and miscellaneous items, holograph and typescript, in English, French, and Russian. Subjects covered in the papers: Mary Wigman, Isadora Duncan, the evolution of modern dance, Fokin's ideals when creating, Sergei Diaghilev, Les Ballets Russes, and Les Ballets Russes at Teatro Colon (Buenos Aires). Special handling. Unpublished register and folder list.

28 Serge Grigoriev (Grigorieff). Régisseur of the Diaghilev (Ballets Russes), De Basil, and other ballet companies, 1909-52. 8 exercise books, ca. 1,100 pp., in Russian, contain journals of all performances of the companies. Included are statistics on all performers, production notes, and information about more than 50 Diaghilev shows (49 ballets) from 1916-29. Grigoriev used these basic sources for his book on the Diaghilev Ballet, 1909-29 (London, 1953).

29 Sergei Ismailoff (b. 1912). Papers, 1929-47, ca. 50 items. Dancer and teacher. Includes letters from Bronislava Nijinska, N. Singaevsky, S. J. Denham, and the Marquis de Cuevas; contracts; biographical notes; identity cards; and memorabilia, in English and Russian. Unpublished register and folder list.

30 Tamara Platonovna Karsavina (b. 1885). Dancer. Among the papers is a receipt for final payment from Sergei Diaghilev of all claims of back salary due Karsavina up to 1921.

31 Lincoln Kirstein (b. 1907). Besides important Diaghilev materials, this collection also contains such additional items as the autograph manuscript, 42 pp., bound, of Kirstein's biography Fokine (New York, 1932), requested by the British critic Arnold Haskell. Although Fokin dictated much of the material in a series of interviews, he did not care much for the end product, which was published in London in 1934. (Kirstein had studied under Fokin briefly in 1931-32 in order to write the book.) There is also a bronze portrait head of Fokin rendered by Emanuelle Ordono Rosales (New York, 1929?).

32 Mathilde Kshessinska (1872-1971). Ballerina. Photographs, at least 1 autographed.

33 Leonid Mikhailovich Lavrovski (1905-1967). Manuscripts in Russian (in process). Includes letter to G. Oswald.

34 David Lichine (1910-1972). Papers, in French and Russian. Includes photocopy of his holograph notebook on Graduation ball, with his description of the choreography, illustrated by small drawings throughout. This was the first ballet choreography accepted for copyright in the U.S.

35 Irène Lidova. Miscellaneous manuscripts, in process.

36 Serge Lifar (b. 1905). Dancer. Miscellaneous manuscripts, in French.

37 Allan Ross Macdougall (1893-1957). 65 folders, ca. 250 items. Collection of holographs, typescripts, and photographs, especially notes and drafts for his biography of Isadora Duncan entitled Isadora: A Revolutionary in Art and Love (New York, 1960). Also correspondence about the work, including letters to him from Irma Duncan concerning the Isadora Duncan School in Moscow, 1928, from Sergei Essenine, typed copy, and copies of original Isadora Duncan letters in the Irma Duncan Collection (q.v.).

38 Alicia Markova (b. 1910). British dancer. Miscellaneous manuscripts, including a holograph letter, 22 July 1941, to Cyril Beaumont discussing her first summer at Jacob's Pillow, Anton Dolin, Mikhail Fokin, Antony Tudor, and a revival of B. Nijinska's "The Beloved." (Real name: Alice Marks)

39 Leonide Massine (1896-1979). Choreographer. Miscellaneous manuscripts; photographs; motion pictures; oral history interviews; and a typescript ballet scenario--the prompt-book (with manuscript notes) for La boutique fantastique [New York, 192-?], 16 ll., performed at the Alhambra Theatre, London, 5 June 1919. Permission required for some items.

40 Joan Miró (b. 1893). Painter. Miscellaneous manuscripts, including 2 ALS to Serge Grigorieff, régisseur of Le Ballet Russe de Monte Carlo, concerning the company's productions, Barcelona, 1933-34.

41 Lillian Moore (1911-1967). Papers, ca. 1936-67, 20 drawers. Dance historian and critic. Includes correspondence between Moore and 2 Soviet colleagues, Natalia Roslavleva (pseud.) and Vera Krasovskaia.

42 Bronislava Nijinska (1891-1970). Sister of Vaslav Nijinsky, dancer, and choreographer. An ALS to Richard Pleasant about working again with his Ballet Theatre (Hollywood, 1940). (Isadora Bennett Collection)

43 Vaslav Nijinsky (1890-1950). Dancer. Assorted manuscripts, in French, including a signed receipt, 22 September 1917, for payment from S. Diaghilev and sheets of jottings from 1948; Nijinsky's red and blue wax crayon design (ca. 1922, Switzerland) entitled "A Mask of God"; documents relating to his association with Les Ballets Russes; photographs, including 1 from 1908 supposedly taken on the day of his graduation from the Imperial Dancing Academy in St. Petersburg; and a bronze portrait head of him by Una, Lady Troubridge, London, 1913, in the Lincoln Kirstein Collection.

44 Rudolf Nureyev (b. 1938). Dancer. Charcoal and conté crayon drawing of him by Lisa Rhana (New York, 1966?).

45 Oral Interviews with Dancers. Tape recorded interviews with such figures as Alicia Markova ("The Art of Ballet," 80 min.), Natalia Dudinskaia (with Marian Horosko, 25 min., about the Kirov Ballet and the training of dancers), Olga Spessivtzeva and Tamara Karsavina (M. Horosko, 12 min.), I. Youskevitch and L. Danielian (M. Horosko, 25 min.), and Leonide Massine (M. Horosko, 23 min., about S. Diaghilev, E. Cecchetti's system of teaching, American modern dance, and Isadora Duncan). (Oral History Archives)

46 Pavley-Oukrainsky Ballet Russe. Records, 1915-50, 5 folders, 73 items. Holographs, typescripts, business records, itineraries, and correspondence of Serge Oukrainsky and Adolf Schmidt among others. Includes a small notebook with income and expense records for 3 tours of the company between December 1927 and January 1929.

47 Anna Pavlova (1882-1931). Dancer. 2 scrapbooks, 1917-24, of the ballerina with photos and clippings (in French, Russian, Italian, and German) articles, programs, and postcards; extensive collection of photographs; a dry-point etching, signed, of Pavlova by Troy Kinney (New York, ca. 1930), also bearing the dancer's autograph; charcoal drawing with gouache highlights, signed, by Francis A. Haviland (London, 1910)--in the Cia Fornaroli Collection; and Pavlova's bronze death-mask (The Hague, 1931), from the original plaster now in London.

48 Marius Ivanovich Petipa (1819-1910). Choreographer. Miscellaneous manuscripts, in French, including a photostat of a letter, signed, to an unknown correspondent, 31 March 1870, mentioning a Léon (probably Léon Espinosa).

49 Pablo Picasso (1881-1973). Painter. 2 ALS to Jean Cocteau, Paris, 1917, about the Ballets Russes, S. Diaghilev, and his own work on the ballet "Parade."

50 Maia Mikhailovna Plisetskaia (b. 1925). Dancer. Programs; photos; 2 interviews, 1966, 1 with M. Horosko (15 min.) and the other with W. Terry (20 min.), the second concerning the Bolshoi Ballet.

51 Natalia Roslavleva, pseud. Isadora Duncan Collection, mainly 1904-1905, 322 items in 22

folders. Soviet dance historian. Reviews and material relating primarily to Duncan's performances in St. Petersburg and Moscow. Typescript and holograph copies of Russian newspaper and periodical articles, most with English translation, obtained from Russian archives and sent to Francis Steegmuller for his book "Your Isadora": The Love Story of Isadora Duncan and Edward Gordon Craig (1974). Unpublished register.

52 Joseph Schillinger (1895-1943). Composer and author. Holograph and typescript of his "Graph method of dance notation" [ca. 1934 and 1942], ca. 17 ll. plus diagrams.

53 Francis Steegmuller (b. 1906). Author. Correspondence, 1974-present, including some from Irma Duncan and Natalia Roslavleva relating to Isadora Duncan, especially her times in Russia. Also, papers relating to his book "Your Isadora," 1972-75, 94 folders. Includes correspondence with Irma Duncan and the Soviet dance historians Vera Krasovskaia and Natalia Roslavleva (pseud.). Permission required for the second collection.

54 Helen Tamiris (1905-1966). Ca. 190 folders. In folders 40 and 41 there are get well wishes to Tamiris, 1966, from, among others, Valentina Litvinoff.

55 Pavel Tchelitchev (1898-1957). Artist. Signed costume designs, Paris, 1933, in gouache and pen and gouache for the Balanchine-Schubert-Koechlin ballet "L'Errante": Hero and child, and Hero companions.

56 Walter Toscanini Collection of Research Materials in Dance. Ca. 30 vols. Contains a holograph letter, signed, of Ayenara Alexeyeva and Holger Alexeyev to Arturo Toscanini, 2 pp., 31 October 1927; a holograph letter, signed, from Ileana Leonidoff, Rome, 30 December 1930, 1 p., in Italian; a typescript telegram of Anna Pavlova to Fano Teatrale in Milan, 2 October 1913, in French; and 4 letters of Olga Iosifovna Preobrazhenskaia, 1912-22, 3 holographs, all signed. (Cia Fornaroli Collection)

57 Tamara Toumanova (b. 1919). Dancer. Chalk and charcoal drawing of her by August von Munchhausen, New York, 1941. (Irving Deakin Collection)

58 Galina Ulanova (b. 1910). Dancer. Photos of her teaching, in "Romeo and Juliet" (ca. 1960), and as "Giselle" (Moscow, 1960-61), taken by Albert E. Kahn. Kahn took hundreds of photos of her professional and private life for his 1962 monograph. Permission required. (Robert W. Dowling Collection)

59 Agrippina Yakovlevna Vaganova (1879-1951). Miscellaneous manuscripts, in French.

60 Mary Wigman (1886-1973). Miscellaneous manuscripts, including a poetic essay, signed, in remembrance of Anna Pavlova.

61 Igor Youskevitch (b. 1912). Miscellaneous manuscripts.

62 Furthermore, under such headings as "Russian Ballet," "Ballet--Russia to 1917," "Ballet--U.S.S.R.," and "Ballet Russe," the catalogue often has scores of entries, including photographs, motion pictures, scrapbooks, clippings, programs, and oral interviews. For virtually every Russian/Soviet ballet (i.e., with music, choreography, or libretto by Russian/Soviet artists) there are again materials. Thus, not only does the library hold large quantities of items for such standards as "Swan Lake" and the "Nutcracker," but it also has photos and a motion picture for "The Little Humpbacked Horse."

Note: The photo, print, picture, and clippings holdings of the library exist for virtually all of the persons, ballets, and subjects mentioned in the preceding description.

Finding Aid: The Dictionary Catalog of the Dance Collection, 10 vols. (Boston: G. K. Hall, 1974). In 1973 the library published A Decade of Acquisitions: The Dance Collection 1964-1973. All of the information contained in this entry came from these 2 published finding aids.

NY 66
MUSIC DIVISION
PERFORMING ARTS RESEARCH CENTER
NEW YORK PUBLIC LIBRARY
111 Amsterdam Avenue
New York, New York 10023
(212-799-2200 x 223)

A selected listing, taken from published finding aids, follows. Other divisions of the library hold related materials.

1 Joseph Achron (1886-1943). A kapelle Konzertisten [n.p., 1928?], facsimile, 9 pp.

2 Fiodor Stepanovich Akimenko. Mélodie élégiaque for violoncello and piano, op. 47b, no. 1, in G minor [1912?], score, 7 pp., and part, 4 pp.; and Romance, score, 2 pp., and part, 1 p., 1911.

3 Ivan Belza. Arsenal [192-?], 52 pp.

4 Nina Borovka. Autograph on her compilation of Crimean Tatar folk songs and dances (Stockholm, 19--), 8 pp.

5 Pëtr Ilich Chaikovski. Aveux passionné, n.p., n.d., 2 ll. (facsimile of autograph manuscript); and a photostat reproduction of 3

measures of his Andante cantabile from the String Quartet, in his hand, signed P. Chaikovskii, 1 p.

6 Aleksandr Nikolaevich Cherepnin. [Duo for violin and violoncello ?], copyist's manuscript, 3 ll. [n.d.].

7 Charles Davidoff (i.e., Carl Iulevich Davidov?). ALS from London, 15 May 1862?, 2 pp.

8 Karl Dondo. "Marsh dlia fortepiano" dedicated to the Grand Duke Vladimir Aleksandrovich by the band-master of the 111th Don Infantry Regiment, Karl Dondo (Kovno, 1888), 2 ll., full score; and "Marsh dlia orkestra" with the same dedication (Kovno, 1888), 3 ll., full score.

9 Mischa Elman (b. 1891). Approximately 9 letters and postcards to Sam Franko from the Russian-born violinist, 1910-16 and n.d., including 1 ALS from London (?), 4 pp., 10 December, no year. (In the Sam Franko Collection of programmes of performances . . .)

10 John Field. [Fragment], 13 pp., autograph manuscript (?) for piano, a score partly in another hand; [Nocturne, piano, no. 5, B-flat major; arr.], for piano and orchestra (1815?), a score, 47 ll.; facsimile of the same, Serenade, 3 pp.; facsimile of Nocturne no. 6 in F major, ca. 1814, 12 pp. on 6 ll.

11 Michael Fokin. Autographed presentation copy (to P. L. Miller) of his biography of Feodor Chaliapin, 23 pp. (New York, 1952).

12 B. A. Frisek. "Marsh 'Vladimir,'" composed by the bandmaster of the 90th Onega Infantry Regiment, B. A. Frisek, n.p., late 19th c., 2 ll., for piano, dedicated to the Grand Duke Vladimir Aleksandrovich.

13 Ossip Gabrilowitsch. ALS of 13 November 1900 and 11 December 1902 (in Mason Collection) and ALS to Mr. W. Weyman, Berlin, of 1 and 29 October 1908.

14 Aleksandr Konstantinovich Glazunov. [Cortège solonnel] (Torzhestvennoe shestvie), an 1894 score, 47 pp.

15 Mikhail Ivanovich Glinka. Russische National-Gesänge (n.d.), 1 l.; and a facsimile of the same or a similar piece (Russian national airs) in his own hand, n.d., 2 pp.

16 Ludwig Goede. "Vladimir Aleksandrovich, marsh," composed by L. Goede, n.p., 1882, 5 ll., full score, dedicated to the grand duke.

17 Aleksandr Tikhonovich Grechaninov. "Arise," for soprano and piano, text by Elizabeth Nathanson, holograph in ink, 3 pp.; "Crépuscule," for low voice and piano (poetry of Luc Durtain), holograph, 4 pp.; "Dobrinia Nikititch, suite symphonique" [1944?], 97 pp., orchestral score reproduced from his autograph manuscript; "Grande fête," overture, op. 178, score, holograph in ink on transparent paper (New York, 1945), 26 ll.; same, score, 26 pp. [1945?], reproduced from holograph with title-page in his own hand; "Lamentations de Jaroslavna" (text of Denis Roche), from the Slovo o polku Igoreve, holograph in ink with pencil corrections, 4 pp., for voice and piano; "Zhenit'ba" (Marriage), full score, 486 pp., and vocal score, 155 pp., in English and Russian, reproduced from holograph, a comic opera in 3 acts based on N. Gogol's "A bachelor's room" (op. 180, [1946?]); "Missa oecumenica" for 4 voices solo, choir, organ, and orchestra (op. 142, [1944?]), score, 148 pp., reproduced from holograph; "Les oeillets roses," for low voice and piano (poetry of Diana Tichengoltz), holograph in ink, 3 pp.; "Poème élégiaque" for orchestra, op. 175 [1945?], score in ink, holograph, 27 pp.; "Poème lyrique" for orchestra [op. 185], score, 64 ll., holograph in ink on transparent paper, and reproduction of same, New York, 27 March 1948; Polka-vocalise for soprano and piano [1933?], holograph in ink, 4 pp.; Septet, op. 172a [1948?], score, 34 ll., holograph in ink on transparent paper; "Slavlenie S. A. Kusevitskago. K 20-ti letiiu dirizhirovaniia Bostonskim orkestrom. Slova i muzyka A. Grechaninova" (English translation added in pencil: Glorification of S. A. Koussevitzky for his 20th anniversary as conductor of Boston symph.), for voice and piano, holograph in ink with corrections and additions in pencil, 16 May 1944, 3 pp.; Sonata for balalaika and piano, op. 188, no. 1 [1948?], 1 vol., reproduced from autograph manuscript; Sonata no. 1 for clarinet and piano, op. 161 [1940?], holograph in ink, 18 and 25 pp.; Sonata no. 2 for clarinet and piano, op. 172 [1940?], 19 pp., reproduced from holograph; Symphony no. 5, op. 153, score, holograph in ink (February 1938), 190 pp.; Symphony no. 6 [194-?], holograph in ink plus additional leaves in pencil, 28 pp.; "Towards victory," full score, "heroic poem" for orchestra and male chorus, in English and Russian, text by A. Pushkin, holograph in ink, New York, 1943, plus photostatic reproduction of same, 56 pp.; and 5 reels of microfilm with his collected manuscripts and published works, n.d., 134 items, and the same, ca. 150 items, 3 ft.

18 Louis Gruenberg. Signor Formica [1910], piano-vocal score in German, 165 pp.; and Volpone, score, various pagings (1948-59).

19 Aloysius Hauptmann. "1814, 19go Marta 1889. Iubilei marsh; po sluchaiu semidesiatipiatiletiia polka vsepokorneishe posviashchaet Ego Imperatorskomu Vysochestvu velikomu kniaziu Vladimiru Aleksandrovichu, Avgusteishemu Shefu leib gvardii Dragunskago polka, kapel'meister Aloizii Gauptman," n.p., 1889, for piano, 5 pp.

NEW YORK - NEW YORK PUBLIC LIBRARY NY 66

20 Vladimir Heifetz. Babi Yar, score [196-?], 17 pp.

21 Herbert Reynolds Inch. A bibliography of Glinka [New York, 1935], typed, 16 ff., with annotations, plus a supplement bound with this item.

22 J. Karnavicius. "The impostor," a ballet in 1 act (Samozvanets), 127 pp., copyist's manuscript in ink, signed on last page: J. Karnavicius, Kaunas, 1940, with superlinear descriptive text in English and Russian and a typed scenario in Russian inserted, 4 pp.

23 Kogda. "Kogda moia radost' nachnet govorit' vorkuia nezhnee golubki . . .," n.p., late 19th c., 3 ll.; these are the first lines of a song with Russian words, music for 1 voice with piano accompaniment.

24 Serge Koussevitzky. TLS, Boston, 15 March 1927 (Sam Franko Collection).

25 W. Labunski (b. 1895). Impromptu [1925?], 2 pp. (facsimile).

26 Theodore Leschetizky. Visiting card with several words in script; [Arabesque, piano, op. 45 no. 1 in A-flat major] (Deux arabesques), [1899], [2], 4 pp.; and [Souvenirs d'Italie], 10 pp. [ca. 1888].

27 Anatolii Konstantinovich Liadov. [Morceaux, piano, op. 31] (Deux morceaux pour le piano), [ca. 1893], 16 pp. (5 blank).

28 Sergei Mikhailovich Liapunov. Reproduction of Concerto for violin (ca. 1915), score, 31 pp.

29 Alexander Lipsky. Sonata for violin and piano (192-?), score, holograph in ink, 19 ll.

30 Arthur Lourié (b. 1884?). Song of Mitya Karamazov, ca. 1950, 9 ll., music (sheet); and Toska Vospominaniya [1941], 10 ll.

31 Samuil Moiseyevich Maikapar. "Prélude in Des dur fur Clavier," Vienna, 13 May 1895, in manuscript (probably Maikapar's hand), with presentation note to Ossip Gabrilowitsch, 2 ll.

32 Nicolas Nabokov. [Sonata no. 2 for piano], (1940?), 24 pp., reproduced from his manuscript, autographed presentation copy to Andor Foldes.

33 Karl Nawratil. Autograph musical quotation (Andante from "C moll Konzert"), undated, received in 1929, 1 p. (Miscellaneous Collection)

34 Vaslav Nijinsky. Autograph (W. Nizhinski) in Roberto Montenegro's biography Vaslav Nijinsky (London, 1913?).

35 Nikolai Platonovich Ogariov. Facsimile of his autograph "Romance," setting of M. Lermontov's poem "Tuchki" (Clouds) for 1 voice with piano accompaniment (original apparently in the Moscow Gosudarstvennyi literaturnyi muzei).

36 Henryk Pachulski. Meditation, score, 9 pp., for string orchestra, op. 25, n.d., and 2 parts.

37 Sergei Puchkov. "Marsh 'Razsvet'," dedicated to the Grand Duke Vladimir Aleksandrovich (n.p., 1880), autograph manuscript, for piano; title-page design in water-colors, 3 ll.

38 Max Rabinoff. Signed postcard to Mr. Robinson Locke and TLS to Locke, New York, 14 February 1919.

39 Sergei Rakhmaninov. Christmas card, visiting card, and his wife's visiting card with a few autograph words (Lambert Collection).

40 Nikolai Andreevich Rimskii-Korsakov. Act 3 from the opera-ballet Mlada, n.p., 1914, score, 98 pp.

41 Anton Rubenstein. ALS of 7 June 1892 (Lambert Collection); photostatic reproduction of an AL, 12 December 1888, 3 pp.; and a reproduction of 3 morceaux de salons [n.d.], 1 part, 2 pp.

42 Vassily Ilyich Safonoff. ALS, 11 April 1907; APS, 10 October 1906; ALS of 4 August 1908 (Mason Collection); and ALS to Mr. W. Weyman, 15 May 1910.

43 Lazare Saminsky. Autograph on "Little Sorele's Lamb," op. 2, no. 3 (New York, [ca. 1922]); autograph presentation copies of 3 works: Sabbath evening service (New York, 1930)--to Virgil Thomson, Three Shadows [1935] (London, [ca. 1938])--to Richard Singer, and The vision of Ariel (New York, [1951, 1950])--to Thomson and photostat reproduction of his IV Symphonie, op. 33, autograph manuscript score, 93 pp. (Vienna, 1927).

44 Joseph Schillinger (1895-1943). Papers, divided into 3 broad categories: Joseph Schillinger Collection of Posters and Charts (in the Iconography Collection of the Music Division), including items on his work and posters relating to Russian/Soviet music (e.g., jazz in the late 1920s); in the Musical Manuscript Collection--his holograph musical scores, 36 folders, 24 notebooks for the Schillinger system of composition, 33 notebooks with other writings, some in Russian, and some notebooks of his students; and in the Letter Collection: correspondence, ca. 170 items, documents, ca. 60 items, 7 typescripts of general writings, some on Russian music, and miscellaneous notes and other papers, ca. 700 items.

45 Kurt Schindler. Autograph presentation copy of The Russians in America, paraphrased by Kurt Schindler [n.p., n.d.], 7 pp., song text

in his hand, set to printed score of S. Rachmaninoff's Prelude in C# minor (first line: "Chaliapine! Sergei Rachmaninoff, he heads the roster").

46 Abel' Abramovich Silberg. "Marsh," composed by the band-master of the 96th Omsk Infantry Regiment, n.p., late 19th c., 5 ll., full score, dedicated to the Grand Duke Vladimir Aleksandrovich; title-page design in watercolors.

47 Igor Stravinsky. [Capriccio for piano and orchestra, arranged for 2 pianos], 1929, holograph, 53 pp. Symphony in 3 movements, completed in 1945, 107 pp., signed holograph dedicated to Arthur Sachs, full score; and Symphonie des psaumes [1930], song and piano arrangement by his son Sviatoslav, holograph, 40 pp.

48 Joseph Strimer. Musical manuscripts, ca. 50 items, in process.

49 Nikolai Topusov. Reproduction from typed copy of his Berlin dissertation Carl Reinecke [Sofia, 1943], cover printed, with author's autograph (one of 100 copies), ca. 461 pp.

50 Il'ya Tyumenev. "Sbornik khora uchenikov Imperatorskoi Akademii khudozhestv" [St. Petersburg, 1883], iv + 40 pp., reproduced from manuscript. Tyumenev was a pupil at the Academy.

51 Elias I. Tziorogh. "Ja rusyn byl; karpatorusskij hymn" for piano, mixed chorus, female voices, and male chorus--words of A. V. Duchnovich, arranged by I. I. Tziorogh [New York?, ca. 1927], 3 pp.; and "Podkarpatskiji rusyny, karpatorusskij hymn," a march for mixed chorus, arranged by Tziorogh, words by Duchnovich [New York?, ca. 1927], 5 pp.

52 Pauline Viardot-Garcia. "Der Gartner. Lied von Morike, Musik von Pauline Viardot," song with piano accompaniment, 3 pp.

53 Vladimir Rudolfovich Vogel. Losung (Devise), full score, for brass and percussion, Strasbourg, 1934, 23 pp.

54 Henri Wieniawski. Le carnaval russe, 1873, 2 ll., 11 pp.; and musical quotation with autograph signature (New York, 21 May 18--?).

55 In addition, the library has the Toscanini Memorial Archives, which contain microfilm reproductions of the following items:

56 Petr Il'ich Chaikovskii. Aveux passionés for piano; Concerto for piano no. 1 in B♭ minor; Concerto for violin, Op. 35; Manfred; The Nutcracker; Overture 1812; Quartet, strings in D major, op. 11; Quartet, strings in F major, op. 22; Quartet, strings in E♭ minor, op. 30; Romeo and Juliet Overture Fantasy; Sextet for strings "Souvenir de Florence" in D minor; Suite no. 1 for orchestra in D minor; Suite no. 2 for orchestra in C; Suite no. 3 for orchestra in G; Swan Lake; Symphony no. 3; Symphony no. 4; Symphony no. 5; Symphony no. 6 (first draft and final version); Trio for piano and strings in A minor, op. 50; and Variations on a rococo theme for cello and orchestra.

57 John Field. Nocturne no. 5 in B♭ (piano alone and arrangement for piano and orchestra).

58 Modeste Moussorgskii. Kinderscherzo for piano.

59 Igor Stravinsky. Capriccio for piano and orchestra arranged for 4 hands; Le chant du Rossignol (ballet); Danses concertantes; L'oiseau de feu (original version); Symphony of psalms, arrangement for piano and voices; and Symphony in 3 movements.

60 Note: The Julliard School in New York at present holds some manuscript material of the composer Arkadii Dubenskii which it intends to give to the New York Public Library in the near future.

Restrictions: Persons requesting copies of manuscripts in the collection will be asked to outline their purposes and agree not to duplicate further or publish without specific permission.

Finding Aids: The library has published Dictionary Catalog of the Music Collection, 33 vols. (Boston: G. K. Hall, 1964) and a supplement, 13 vols. (1973). "A selected list of microfilms currently available in The Toscanini Memorial Archives of The New York Public Library, November, 1969" appears in College Music Symposium, 17 no. 2 (1977). Finally, manuscript acquisitions for all divisions since 1971 are listed in the Dictionary Catalog of the Research Libraries, an automated book catalogue.

NY 67
THEATRE AND DRAMA COLLECTIONS
PERFORMING ARTS RESEARCH CENTER
NEW YORK PUBLIC LIBRARY
111 Amsterdam Avenue
New York, New York 10023
(212-799-2200 x 213/214)

The catalogue of these 2 collections lists an impressive amount of Russian/Soviet-related material under a variety of headings, 30 vols. The catalogue is divided into book and non-book listings, but even the first section has unpublished items. The descriptions which follow, taken directly from the catalogue, differentiate material according to the way the catalogue lists them; this listing is not exhaustive.

NEW YORK - NEW YORK PUBLIC LIBRARY NY 67

1 Drama Collection: Listing by Cultural Origin

Under "Drama, Russian" and "Drama, Russian--Translations into English" (or other language): Sergei Gerasimov--"The teacher." Vladimir Mikhailovich Kirshon and A. Ouspensky--"Red Rust." Boris Andreyevich Lavrenev--"The road begins."

2 Under "Drama, Ukrainian--Translations into Carpatho-Russian": Antonii A. Bobul'ski--"N'imaja nevista"; with Mykhaila Starytz'kyi--"Oj ne chodi Hricu, ta na vecernici."

3 Theatre Collection: Books on the Theatre

Under "Drama--Promptbooks and typescripts" (i.e., working scripts for play productions) and under "Drama, Russian--Translations into English" (or German): Leonid Nikolayevich Andreyev--"He who gets slapped." Mikhail Petrovich Artzybashev--"Enemies." Aleksandr Aleksandrovich Blok--"Love poetry and civil service." Mikhail Afanas'yevich Bulgakov--"Days of the Turbins" and an adaptation of Gogol's "Dead Souls." Anton P. Chekhov--"A marriage proposal"; "The cherry orchard"; "Ivanov"; "I forgot"; and "The seagull." Mikhail Chekhov--"The witch" by A. Chekhov with manuscript corrections and notes in Russian, plus "The adventures of Samuel Pickwick, esq." Jacques Deval--"Tovarich." Fedor Dostoevskii--adaptations: by Jacques Copeau ("The brothers Karamazov"), George Shdanoff ("The possessed"), and Boris Tumarin. Osip Dymov--"The Bronx express; a local comedy"; "The spirit of the city"; "Nju"; "Revolution in Coney Island"; "Ezra"; "In our time"; "The last woman"; and "Invitation to error." Aleksei Mikhailovich Faiko--"The man with a portfolio." Nikolai Vasil'yevich Gogol'--"The inspector-general"; "A madman's diary"; and "Dead souls"; plus other adaptations by Arthur Adamov ("Dead souls") and M. Bulgakov ("Dead souls"). Maksim Gorkii--"Night lodging" and "Queer people." Valentin Petrovich Katayev--"Die Defraudanten"; The last of the Equipagew"; and "The path of flowers." Konstantin Yakovlevich Khal'fin--"Secret weapon." Piotr Korvin-Krukovski (pseudonym: Pierre Newsky)--"The honour of the humble"; "The Danicheffs"; "Danischeffs"; and "Rurik" (an adaptation of "The Danischeffs" by Pierre Newsky and Alexandre Dumas fils). A. J. Kosorotow--"Café chantant." August Friedrich Ferdinand von Kotzebue--"Count Benyowsky; or The conspiracy of Kamtschatka. A tragi-comedy." Albert Lortzing--"Tsar and carpenter" (English libretto). Lev Natanovich Lunz--"The city of truth" and "The outlaw." Princess Alexandra Melikoff, duchess of Leuchtenberg--"A fire in the dark" (a picture of the Russian revolution). Her pseudonym was Zamtary. A. Nabatov--"The portrait of Izim-Yoo." Attila Orbok--"Der Volkskommissar." Mendel Osherowitch--"Czarevitch Feodor" (opera). Aleksandr Nikolayevich Ostrovski--"The forest." Yevgenii Petrovich Petrov--"The island of peace." A. S. Pushkin--"The feast of death." S. Semionov-Polonski--"On virgin soil." George Shdanoff--adaptation of Dostoevskii's "The possessed." Konstantin Mikhailovich Simonov--"The whole world over" and "The Russian people." Vladimir S. Solov'iov--"Field Marshal Kutuzov." Aleksandr Vasil'yevich Sukhovo-Kobylin--"The death of Tarelkin." Il'ya Dmitriyevich Surguchev--"Autumn." Aleksei K. Tolstoi--"The death of Ivan the Terrible." Sergei Mikhailovich Tret'yakov--"Roar China." Boris Tumarin--adaptations of F. Dostoevskii. L. Tur--"Showdown." Ivan S. Turgenev--"A month in the country." Lev Nikolayevich Urvantzov--"Vera" and other works in German. I.M. Voikov--"Love in the country." Nikolai Nikolayevich Yevreinov--"The chief thing" and "The radio kiss." Gerald Zoffer--"The end of all things natural; a drama of contemporary Russia" (1969).

Note: Under "Drama, Russian," nearly all citations are of published works. However, some of these books include the author's autograph (e.g., Ivan Yegorovich Bel'tzman).

4 Under "Drama, Lithuanian": Balys Sruoga--autographed copy of Aitvaras teisejas (Kaunas, 1935).

5 Under "Drama, Lettish": bound, uncatalogued pamphlet collection.

6 Non-Book Collection and Cage File

For the selected list of individuals, subjects, and works listed below, the collections include such material as photographs, clippings, programs, reviews, and articles. In some cases, specific holdings are noted.

Acting--Speech--[Dialects]--Stage dialects recorded by (?) Jerry Blunt (5" tapes). Tape 5, track 2, has Russian and German dialects (Rodgers and Hammerstein Div.). Actors and Acting--Russia. Chingiz Aitmatov. Aleksei Arbuzov. Brooks Atkinson--Correspondence from the 1950s about the Russian theater, A. Chekhov, etc. A. Chekhov. The Cherry Orchard--Correspondence, business papers, graphics, etc. concerning U.S. productions of this play, actors and actresses in it, etc. Cinema--Russia/Russian. Cinema--Stars--Russian. Circus--Russia. Sergei Mikhailovich Eisenstein--Original caricatures. Alexandra Exter--Original design (curtain) for Moscow's Kamerny Theatre (1914). Hallie Flanagan--Scrapbook with programs, clippings, manuscript notes, and letters relating to her trip to visit Russian theaters (1926). N. Gogol. Maksim Gorkii. Boris Goudounov--Color costume sketch by Leon Bakst; and wash drawings of costumes for Boris (Kate Friedheim Collection). Vassily Ivanovitch Katchaloff (also, Katschalow)--Autographed photographs, one of him as Vershinin in "The Three Sisters."

Vsevolod Meyerhold. Sonia Moore--Typescript of "Eugene B. Bakhtangov. Director, Actor, Teacher, Man" (n.d.); signed letter concerning a 1970 U.S. production of "The Cherry Orchard"; and signed letter, 1961, with reviews of her The Stanislavski Method. Moscow--(many subheadings). Moscow Art Theatre--Painting by George A. de Pogedas from June 1926 (Morris Gest originals); material relating to a 1900 MAT production of "Uncle Vanya"; original poster; filmstrips of MAT productions in 1965; and autographed photos of Olga Knipper-Chekhova and V. Kachalov. Alla Nazimova--Autographed photo; undated caricature (in Alfred Frueh originals); caricature of her in "The Cherry Orchard" (1928); ALS to Nila Mack ca. 1917; and a program. V. Nemirovich-Danchenko. Vera Mentchinova. Puppets for Proletarian Revolution. Radio--Russia. John Reed--Leaflets and periodicals with play casts from Moscow in 1917. Nikolai Vladimirovich Remizov --Photographs of original drawings by N. V. Remizov for a photoplay, "The gambler," after Dostoyevskii . . . [n.p., 193-?], 8 leaves and 16 plates, with a typewritten description of the drawings by the owner, Mr. Remizov (catalogue listing under "Cinema: Stills"). Soviet Circus. Stage--Russia. Konstantin Sergeyevich Stanislavski (real name Constantin Sergeivich Alexiev)--Photographs of him, his productions, and later Moscow Art Theatre productions; scrapbooks; clippings; articles from around the world; text of "Stanislavsky and America," a broadcast by N. Solntsev, 7 August 1958; pencil sketch for "The Mistress of the Inn"; tape recording (7") of a series of 12 talks given in Hollywood (1955) by Michael Chekhov (actor, director, and teacher at the MAT for 16 years and head of the Second Moscow Art Theatre); medals; and stamps. V. Stanitsin (Stanitzyn). Aleksandr Tairov (Tairoff). Theatrical Postage Stamps--Honoring the Soviet film industry, 1969, for the second international Tchaikovsky competition, 1962, and others. Yevgenii Bogratinovich Vakhtangov--See also under Sonia Moore.

Note: The collections include a number of phonodisc recordings of plays by Russian/Soviet authors (e.g., Anton Chekhov). (See listings under "Theatre--Recordings.") There are also related materials--for ballets and musical works--in the New York Public Library's other collections for Music and Dance and in the holdings of the Manuscripts and Archives Division and Prints Division.

Finding Aid: All of the preceding information came, as noted, from the Catalog of the Theatre and Drama Collections, 3 parts, 30 vols. (Boston: G. K. Hall, 1967), and from the 2 supplements issued in 1973.

NY 68
PRINTS DIVISION
NEW YORK PUBLIC LIBRARY
Fifth Avenue and 42nd Street
New York, New York 10018
(212-790-6207)

1 The Prints Division holds original prints and drawings by artists born in the Russian Empire and Soviet Union, and clipping files (by artist), separate descriptions for which follow. Original graphic material includes:

2 Alexander Archipenko (1887-1964). Lithographs: portfolio entitled Dreizehn Steinzeichnungen (Berlin, 1921), no. 59 of 60 printed, with artist's autograph (1 l., 13 plates); and "Figürliche Komposition."

3 Nick Bervinchak (20th c.; Ukrainian). 2 etchings: "Employed" (1940) and "Reflections" (1940).

4 Caricatures. Russian cartoons from the Napoleonic era; a few items. (Caricatures arranged chronologically by country)

5 Mykola Butovych (1895-1961; Ukrainian). 2 woodcuts (?): cover for the women's magazine Nova Khata (1932, no. 5) and bookplate for M. Khomyn, M.D.

6 Eugene I. Charushin (b. 1901). Lithograph: "Crow" (1938), in color.

7 Mstislav Dobuzhinski (1875-1957; Lithuanian extraction). Original drawings: 2 illustrations for "The Steel Flea . . ." of Nikolai Leskov, in pencil, unsigned (1943); and 2 illustrations to the Wonder Book by Nathaniel Hawthorne, in pencil, not signed (1949).

8 Nataliya Sergeyevna Goncharova (1881-1962). Portfolio of 14 lithographs--Misticheskiye Obrazy Voiny (V. N. Kasin, Moscow, 1914), with yellow board cover and title page. Subjects include Saints George the Victorious and Alexander Nevskii, The White Eagle, The English Lion, The French Rooster, Angels and Airplanes, The Condemned City, Archangel Michael, Christian Soldiers, The Pale Horse, and Mass Grave.

9 Yakiv (Jacques) Hnizdovsky (b. 1915). Ukrainian. 16 woodcuts, including 10 bookplates (for Jean Thiebault, W. E. Holiyan, I. W. Manastyrsky, Ihor Kostetzky, N. and I. Ivakhniuk, Bohdan Kravtsiv, and the Ukrainian Free Academy), a book cover with scribe, 3 items from 1944 (a study of trees, an old man, and "Youth and old age"), "The Cat" (1968), and "Great Horned Owl" (1973).

10 George Sviatoslav Hordynsky (b. 1906). Ukrainian. 2 woodcut covers for the women's magazine Nova Khata, 1935-37, and a bookplate for R. G. Berezovsky.

11 Vytautas Kazys Jonynas (b. 1907). Lithuanian. 1 lithograph, "Bacharach on the Rhine" (1951), in color; and 4 woodcuts: "L'Etoile de l'Amour" (1951), a Christmas scene; "The Shepherds in the Field" (1949); "Saint Antoine" (1950), artist's proof; and "Fifth Avenue, N.Y." (1957).

12 Vasilii Vasil'yevich Kandinski (1866-1944). 3 etchings from "Kleine Welten" in 1922 ("Compositions IX, X, and XI"), 4 woodcuts ("Composition VIII" from "Kleine Welten"--1922; "The Archer" from 1908/1909, in color; a 1913 abstraction, in color; and 2 horseback riders, 1913, in color, both from "Klange"), and a lithograph entitled "Composition with Chessboard-Orange" (1923), in color.

13 Anatoli Lvovich Kaplan (b. 1902). 2 lithographs: "The Village of Anatovka" (1961) and "Man of Air" (1957/61).

14 K. A. Klementeva (b. 1897). A lithograph entitled "Funeral Procession of S. M. Kirov, Dec. 3, 1934" (1934).

15 Moissey Kogan. 5 linoleum cuts: "Tanzende in langem Gewand" (1922); 2 kneeling figures, "Thais," Greek deity with deer, and 2 standing nudes, all 192-?

16 Myron Levytsky (b. 1913). Ukrainian. 5 bookplates (woodcuts)--for M. Denysiuk, Tetyana Mohylnytska, M. K. Levytska, Ilse Fumanelli, and O. Mokh.

17 Karin Luts-Arumaa. Lithographs: Portrait of Gustav Suits, Estonian poet and literary historian (1943), and 3 illustrations for the poems of Betti Alver "Art and Life," 1944.

18 Antin Maliutsa (1908-1970). Ukrainian. 2 etchings: of a steeple in the Carpathian Mountains and of a wooden church, same locale, both 1946.

19 Halyna Mazepa (20th c.). Ukrainian. Cover for the women's magazine Nova Khata, 1934 (woodcut?).

20 Nikolai Semionovich Mosolov (1846-1914). Etching.

21 N. N. Nagorsky. Wood engravings: "Ex Libris Eremina" (1923), and 2 theatrical designs (1924).

22 Alexander (Aleksandr Ossipowitsch) Orlowski (1777-1832). 12 lithographs: battle between Asiatic horsemen and fighters on foot (1829), "Un Voyageur en Quibitka, ou Traîneau à trois Chevaux" (1819), 2-horse sleigh with driver and officer passing a sentinel (1820), more Asiatic horsemen (1816), a bust-length self-portrait with oval frame (1820), and 6 pieces from Collection de Dessins Lithographies (1819) in original printed wrapper with Orlowski's signature in ink.

23 Ivan Padalka (1895-1961). Ukrainian. Woodcut (photostat?) of Cossacks.

24 Peter Simon Pallas (1741-1811). Flora Rossica, n.p., 18th c. 104 original drawings in pencil, ink, and wash, 74 colored, by Karl Friedrich Knappe, and 3 related items.

25 Eduard Rüga. 2 linoleum cuts: "Woman with the mirror" (1952) and "Tüdruk lindudega" (Girl with the birds; 1953), both in color.

26 Russkii narodnii lubok 1860-kh-1870-kh g.g.; al'bom. Collection of 200 lithographed picture sheets, 33 printed by A. A. Abramov, 21 by I. G. Gavrilov, 31 by I. A. Golyshev of Mstera, 32 by P. A. Glushkov, 26 by A. V. Morozov, and 52 by Ye. Ya. Yakovlev.

27 Russkii narodnii lubok 1870-ky--1880-kh gg.; al'bom (Binder's title: Les images nationales de Sitin et Co.). Collection of 62 lithographed picture sheets colored by hand: 41 printed by V. A. Vasil'yev, 12 by A. V. Morozov, and 9 by V. V. Ponomariov.

28 Gabriel Skorodumov (1748?-1792). Stipple.

29 Yurii Solovii (Jurij Solovij). 8 linocuts: "Pantocrator," "Princess Yaroslavna," and "Cymbal" from 1950; and "Crucifixion" (2), "Madonna and Child," "Horned Fish," and "Nude" from 1958.

30 Peter (Piotr) N. Staronosov (b. 1893). Wood engraving (linoleum block print) entitled "Airplane over the Taiga forest, Siberia" (1938), in color.

31 Vasilieff. Stipple engraving--"Susanna at the bath"--printed in sanguine.

32 Georgi Vereysky (Georgii Semionovich Vereiski). 2 lithographs, both 1922: "Portrait of the painter Constantin Somoff" and "Constantin Somoff at work before easel."

33 Arno Vihalemm (b. 1911). Estonian. 2 woodcuts: "Homage to Rilke" (1955) and "Keerub" (Cherub; 1954); 1 lithograph--"Lilith" (1955); and 4 serigraphs in black--illustrations to the short stories of Jaan Oks (1956).

34 Eduard Wiiralt (1898-1954). Estonian. "Arkeia"--a 1938 drypoint; "Berber Girl and Dromedary," etching from 1940; and 2 wood engravings: "Head of a Negro" and "The Absinthe Drinkers" from 1933.

35 Ossip Zadkine (1890-1967). Woodcut figures; and 3 lithographs: "Le Rêve (1955), "Trois Personnages" (195-?), and "Les Rois Mages" (1952 or 1953), all in color.

36 Sergei Zalshupin. 10 lineoleum cuts: portraits of Aleksandr Blok and Andrei Belyi (both 1922); street scene (192-?), signed

"Salschupin"; and illustrations for Belyi's St. Petersburg (192-?).

37 Many of the preceding items are signed by the artists. In addition, for individual artists, the division holds clipping files (in envelopes) with such materials as exhibition announcements, dealers' catalogues, reviews, reproductions, and some letters (from or about the artists). Among those for whom there are such files are: A. Archipenko, Ya. Hnizdovsky, V. Jonynas, A. Kaplan, M. Kogan, N. Mosolov, N. Nagorsky, A. Orlowski, Yu. Solovii, G. Vereysky, A. Vihalemm, E. Wiiralt, and O. Zadkine.

Restriction: Inquire about application for access.

Finding Aid: Dictionary Catalog of the Prints Division, 5 vols. (Boston: G. K. Hall, 1975).

NY 69
RARE BOOK DIVISION, ROOM 303
NEW YORK PUBLIC LIBRARY
42nd Street and Fifth Avenue
New York, New York 10018
(212-790-6296)

1 Ivan Belogonov. [Original water color paintings of Russia, n.p., 1848-56]. 30 mounted colored plates, 29 with manuscript Russian titles, signed by the artist, 23 dated in manuscript. (Call no. *KW)

2 Decorations of Honor. Includes the Russian orders of St. Stanislaus (3), St. Vladimir, Ste. Anne, and the White Eagle.

3 Fiodor Grigor'yevich Solntzev (1801-1892). 326 water-color illustrations for the book Odezhdy Russkago gosudarstva [St. Petersburg?], 1869, which bears the bookplate of Nicholas II. These original drawings show folk costumes, military and ecclesiastical costumes, apparel of the nobles and tsars, etc., ca. 1820-79. Signed, with manuscript captions. "List of drawings" and "Names of governments, cities and villages to which these drawings relate," 2 ll., in Russian manuscript, laid in. (Call no. *KW)

Finding Aid: Dictionary Catalog of the Rare Book Division of the New York Public Library, 21 vols. (Boston: G. K. Hall, 1971), plus supplementary vol. (1973).

NY 70
SCHOMBURG CENTER FOR RESEARCH IN BLACK CULTURE
NEW YORK PUBLIC LIBRARY
103 West 135th Street
New York, New York 10030
(212-862-4000)

1 Ira Frederick Aldridge (1807-1867). Black tragedian. Includes typescript, 37 pp., "List of theatres and plays in European cities where Aldridge, the African Roscius, acted during the years, 1824-1867," compiled by Arthur A. Schomburg (New York, 193-?), with Russian cities listed on pp. 31 and 34-37. Also, Marie Trommer, Ira Aldridge, American Negro tragedian and Taras Shevchenko, poet of the Ukraine. Story of a friendship (Brooklyn, 1939), a printed pamphlet, 14 pp.

2 Paul Robeson (1898-1977). Actor, singer, and political activist. Unprocessed papers include some correspondence and printed matter (e.g., press releases from the Soviet embassy) pertaining to Robeson's connections with and tours of the USSR and to the World Council of Peace.

3 Richard Wright (1908-1960). Papers, 1939-67, ca. 1,500 items. Author. Correspondence, writings, notes, etc., in part photocopies. Includes his typescript notes on Ross Poindexter entitled "Biography of a Bolshevik," 2 pp., and Wright's introduction to Pan Africanism or Communism by George Padmore. Requires permission of the chief or assistant chief of the Schomburg Center. Unpublished register (NUCMC 72-265). Note: The collection has been microfilmed on 2 reels, negative and positive.

NY 71
SLAVONIC DIVISION
NEW YORK PUBLIC LIBRARY
Fifth Avenue at 42nd Street
New York, New York 10018
(212-790-6336)

Like nearly all the major divisions of the Research Libraries of the New York Public Library, the Slavonic Division holds a large amount of unpublished or archival materials relating to the Russian Empire/Soviet Union. It is impossible to estimate how much and what kind of archival material is deposited in the Slavonic Division, since no distinction is made between archival or manuscript materials and published titles. Even the subject heading "Manuscripts" is of limited usefulness. All manuscripts, unpublished typescripts, albums of photographs in bound form and other archival materials in original form or in photoreproduction are treated the same way as published monographs, i.e., they are catalogued by author, title, subject, bound and classed according to the subject with published books.

There is also a large quantity of unpublished short articles, personal biographies, and memoirs, bound, in the Division's pamphlet volume collections. These pamphlet volumes are all physically located in 1 area (though again catalogued separately). Below are listed some examples of specific holdings of archival materials found in the collection of the Slavonic Division:

1 Anna Akhmatova (1888-1966). Poetess. "Amedeo Modil'iani," 15 ll., typescript with manuscript corrections, at end: Bolshevo 1958- Moskva 1964; accompanied by a typewritten copy of N. I. Khardzhiev's "O risunke A. Modil'iano."

2 Alexander II (1818-1881). Emperor of Russia. "Pis'ma Imperatora Aleksandra II, pisannyia Im v bytnost' Ego Naslednikom Tsesarevichem k S. A. Iur'evichu, v 1847 g." [St. Petersburg?] 1847, 3 ll.

3 Avtografy. Autographs of Andrei Belyi, Valerii Briusov, Riurik Ivnev, Pimen Karpov, A. Lunacharskii, Ivan Novikov, Matvei Roizman, Semen Rubanovich, Ivan Rukavishnikov, Fedor Sologub, Marina Tsvetaeva, and Ilya Erenburg (Moscow, 1921), 15 ll.; also, a microfiche (negative) of this item.

4 Cracow Union of Help for Political Prisoners in Russia. Tsirkuliarnoe pis'mo, no. 6 (Krakow? 1914), manuscript.

5 Saint Demetrius (1651-1709). Letopis' keleinyi preosviashchennago Dimitriia, mitropolita rostovskago i iaroslavskago, ot nachala Mirozdaniia do Rozhdestva Khristova, ego zhe arkhiereiskimi trudami sochinennaia [n.p., n.d.], 7 pp., 369 ff. + 21 ll., with 2 miniatures; film reproduction (negative) of an 18th (?) c. cursive manuscript, text written in red and black by various hands, compiled by Saint Demetrius.

6 [Yelizaveta Alekseyevna (Ashanina) Drashusova] (d. 1884). Al'bom Elizavety Alekseevny Karlgof. Peterburg, Moskva, Kiev, Parizh, Vena, Rim, Praga, Drezden, 1832-44, n.p., n.d., 83 ll. Photostatic reproduction on 97 ll. of an autograph album with 55 inscriptions, mainly in Russian and in verse, by Russian and non-Russian notables. An indication of the contents can be gleaned from her "Zhizn' prozhit' ne pole pereiti" in Russkii vestnik, 1881, vol. 5, pp. 133ff.

7 Grigorii, a monk of the Spaso-Yevfimiyev monastery (16th c.?). Zhitie i zhizn' blagovernykh velikiia kniazhny Evfrosinii Suzdal'skiia (St. Petersburg, 1888), 148 pp., with hand-colored plates.

8 Georg de Hennin (fl. 1730s). Manuscript dated 1735, 2 vols., on mines and metallurgical plants in Siberia. A. Yarmolinsky article describes the manuscript in detail, NYPL Bulletin, vol. 40 (1936).

9 Ivan IV Groznyi (1530-1584). [Otvet tsaria Ioanna Vasil'evicha Groznogo, dannyi protestantu Ianu Rokite v 1570 godu iiunia 18 dnia], 83 ll. Photostatic reproduction of the original now found in the Harvard University Houghton Library. Jan Rokyta (or John of Rokycan) was archbishop of Prague and a leader of the Moravian Brethren, ca. 1440.

10 George Kennan (1845-1924). Collection of clippings from different publications, mostly American and English, on contemporary Russian history, most for the period of World War I and the Russian revolutions, 1914-18; manuscript documents; and letters to Kennan. These materials are in envelopes, arranged alphabetically by subject, New York?, 1923. In addition there is a bound volume of portraits of Russian political exiles and convicts, with some photos depicting the life of both political and common criminals in Siberia, collected by Kennan and given to the library in 1920, 2 pp., 60ff., photos mounted.

11 Pomorskiye otvety. Copy of a work completed in 1723 by Andrei Denisov (with Semion Denisov and Trifon Petrov), leader(s) of the Vyg community of Old Believers (Priestless) near the White Sea. The full title of the manuscript is "Otvety pustynnozhitelei na voprosy ieromonakha Neofita," n.p., 176-?. The work is ca. 400 ff., with colored illustrations.

12 Pravda. Biulleten' "Pravdy," no. 1-4 (Vienna, 1912), typescript.

13 Yevgenii Mikhailovich Prilezhayev (b. 1851). "Kratkaia istoricheskaia zapiska ob Olontse" [Olonets, 1887], 16 ll., in honor of the visit to Olonets of their Imperial Highnesses Grand Prince Vladimir Aleksandrovich and Grand Princess Mariia Pavlovna, 29 June 1887.

14 [Rodoslovetz]. "Nachalo i koren' velikikh kniazei rossiiskikh" [n.p., n.d.], 14 ll. The text begins: "Iz variag priide Riurik . . ." Photostatic reproduction (negative) of a cursive Russian manuscript, probably executed in the first third of the 17th c.

15 Russia. Armiya. Gvardeiskaya strelkovaya brigada. Prikazy otdannye po Gvardeiskoi strelkovoi brigade . . . (Tsarskoe Selo, 1872-73). Orders issued by His Imperial Highness the Grand Duke Vladimir Aleksandrovich, 21 April 1872; some orders issued at Krasnoe Selo; in manuscript.

16 Russia. Armiya. Opisanie deistvii otriadov sostoiavshikh pod nachal'stvom Ego Imperatorskago Vysochestva Velikago kniazia Vladimira Aleksandrovicha na bol'shikh manevrakh 1871 goda v sostave sil iuzhnago korpusa, n.p.,

1871, 77 pp., chart, 9 colored mounted plans, a colored mounted plate, in manuscript, bound in black grained morocco.

17 Russia. Armiya. . . . Prikazanie po Uchebnomu pekhotnomu batalionu. S 1go iiulia po 8e avgusta 1864 goda, n.p., 1864, 39 ll., manuscript, at head of title: Kopiia; bound with: Russia. Armiya. Prikaz po Uchebnomu pekhotnomu batalionu (n.p., 1864); with bookplate of Grand Duke Vladimir Aleksandrovich.

18 Russia. Ministerstvo vnutrennykh del. Departament obshchikh del. Tret'ye otdeleniye. "Zapiska o sovremennom sostoianii raskola, sostavlennaia po delam III otdeleniia Departamenta obshchikh del," n.p., 1862, 417 pp., including tables. The manuscript is signed by Aleksandr Vishniakov.

19 Russia. Ministerstvo vnutrennikh del. Departament politzii. [Sbornik sekretnykh tsirkuliarov obrashchennykh k Nachal'nikam gubernskikh zhandarmskikh upravlenii, gubernatoram i pr. v techenie 1902-1907 g.g.], n.p., n.d. [New York, 1929], 266 ll., photostat copy by the New York Public Library, December 1929; most of the circulars are typewritten, some are printed; folder containing this collection reads: Delo 191 goda po opisi No. Nizhegorodskago gubernskago zhandarmskago upravleniia. . . . Concerns the Russian secret police, revolutionary movement, and criminology.

20 Mykyta Iukhymovych Shapoval (1882-1932). Sociologist and author. Contains his published and unpublished works; correspondence with family members, political and literary associates; and books, pamphlets, magazines, and newspapers edited by him. A large part consists of minutes and reports of institutions he founded, such as The Ukrainian Technical Institute (Ukrains'kyi tekhnichno-hospodar'kyi instytut) and the Ukrainian Sociological Institute in Czechoslovakia. Also, some material unrelated to Shapoval (published and unpublished) found in his library after his death by Sava Zerkal, who donated the collection to the library. Ca. 200 titles have been catalogued.

21 [Ivan Kornil'yevich Shusherin] (ca. 1630-1690). "Izvestie o rozhdenii i o vospitanii, i o zhitii, sv. Nikona patriarkha," n.p., 171-224 ll. The manuscript has caption-title and initials in red. Composed about 1687, the first printed edition of the work appeared in 1784. Biographical data on Nikon appears on leaf 224 in a different hand.

22 Ivan Dmitrievich Sytin (1851-1934). Autographed copy of his own book Polveka dlia knigi (Moscow, 1916).

23 Leo Nikolaevich Tolstoi (1828-1910). Autograph on the title-page of the translation of Henry George's works into Russian: Izbrannyia rechi i stat'i Genri Dzhordzhe (Moscow, 1906).

24 [Triod tsvetnaia]. Photostatic reproduction of a manuscript on vellum, written probably in the 14th c.; uncial, with headpiece and ornamental initials. This Triodion relates to the liturgy and ritual of the Russian Orthodox Church, 108 ll., n.p., n.d.

25 Leon Trotzky (Trotskii) (1879-1940). The first 6 items are all electrostatic reproductions of typescripts: "Pis'mo frantsuzskim rabochim; izmena Stalina i mezhdunarodnaia revoliutsiia," 10 June 1935, 6 ll.; "Pered vtorym etapom," 9 July 1936, 6 ll., concerning French politics; "Novaia moskovskaia amal'gama," 22 January 1937, 11 o'clock, 17 ll., written Mexico, about the show trials; "Terror biurokraticheskogo samosokhraneniia," 6 September 1935, 7 ll., on Russian internal politics; "Iaponiia dvizhetsia k katastrofe," Prinkipo, 12 July 1933, 9 ll., with manuscript corrections, concerning social conditions in Japan; and "Zaiavleniia i otkroveniia Stalina," 18 March 1936, 8 ll., on international relations; an anonymous bibliography of Trotskii's writings published in English in the press and in bulletins, n.p., 1959, 61 ll.; and a photostatic reproduction, on 19 ll., of a published pamphlet: Sowjetrussland und Polen (speeches of Kamenev, Lenin, Trotskii, Marchlevski, Sokolnikov, Radek, and Martov, 5 May 1920), n.p., 1920, 38 pp.

26 [Andrei G. Ukhtomskii]. "Sobranie fasadov," 2 vols. of plates, 100 aquatints, printed from copper (or steel?) plates.

27 Vidy. "Vidy Valaamskago monastyria," n.p., n.d., 40 photos on 21 ll., letterpress in manuscript, with bookplate of Emperor Nicholas II. Views of the Valaam, Finland, monastery.

28 Semion Alekseyevich Yur'yevich (1798-1865). Tutor to the children of Alexander II. "Pis'ma ob Avgusteishikh synov'iakh Imperatora Aleksandra II, pisannyia S. A. Iur'evichem v 1847 g. k Ego Velichestvu v bytnost' Ego Naslednikom Tsesarevichem" [St. Petersburg? 1847], 138 pp., reproduced from typewritten copy.

29 Vladimir Mikhailovich Zenzinov (b. 1880). 17 letters to Red Army soldiers gathered by Zenzinov in Finland during the Russo-Finnish War, n.p., 1939, 43 ll., illustrated, photostatic reproduction, includes envelopes; 9 letters are in the languages of the minorities of the USSR, 8 are in Russian. The letters became part of Zenzinov's book Vstrecha s Rossiei (New York, 1945).

Note: Many of the preceding items are on Reserve; for conditions of access, please inquire at the Slavonic Division.

Finding Aid: A revised and enlarged 2nd edition of the Catalog of the Slavonic Division, 47 vols. (Boston: G. K. Hall, 1974).

NY 72
SPENCER COLLECTION
NEW YORK PUBLIC LIBRARY
Fifth Avenue at 42nd Street
New York, New York 10018
(212-790-6110)

1 Armenian Manuscripts. Four Gospels, A.D. 1301; hymnal, 14th c.; four Gospels, A.D. 1623; four Gospels, A.D. 1661; "The Jewish Bride," 18th-19th c.; and four Gospels, 17th c.

2 Japanese Manuscripts. Includes: Roshia Zokkoku Jimbutsu Zu (Picture book of People in the Territories of Russia). Sketches of people in Siberia and Kamchatka, made during the later years of the Edo Period (Edo, ca. 1845), 1 vol. (Jap. MS 233)

3 Slavonic Manuscripts. In order, Slavonic MSS 1-10: Gospel according to Saint Luke, MS on paper in Church Slavonic, 98 ll., 1 miniature, n.p., n.d., but Russia, 15th c., contemporary binding; four Gospels, MS on paper in Church Slavonic, 320 ll., 4 full-page miniatures of the four Evangelists, other illustrations, n.p., n.d., Russia, 15th c., contemporary binding; The ladder by Saint John Climachus (ca. 525-600), MS on paper, 210 ll., 1 full-page miniature and other illustrations, n.p., n.d., Russia, 16th c., 18th c. (?) binding; Johannes Damascenus: Philosophia (Fountain of Knowledge), MS on paper, 308 ll., 1 full-page miniature, diagrams, n.p., n.d., Russia, 17th c., contemporary binding; The Life of St. Basil the Younger, written by Gregorius, the monk, 10th c., bound with selections from the Synod, MS on paper in Church Slavonic, 377 ff., 283 full-page colored drawings, headpieces, initial letters, n.p., n.d., Russia, 18th c., contemporary binding; Canticles of the Eastern Orthodox Church, Liturgy and Ritual "for the sweet singing and the solemn hymns for the good holidays of Our Lord," MS on paper in Church Slavonic, 287 ll., 1 full-page decoration and other illustrations, n.p., n.d., Russia, 18th c., contemporary binding; Canticles and Chants of the Eastern Orthodox Church, MS on paper, in Church Slavonic, 2 vols., illustrations, n.p., n.d., Russia, 18th c., contemporary binding; Kniga-Tzvetnik (Garden of Flowers; The Passion of Christ; the Last Judgement), MS on paper in Church Slavonic, 354 ll., 133 full-page watercolor drawings, initial letters, n.p., n.d., Russia, 18th c., contemporary binding; Apocalypse, MS on paper in Church Slavonic, 212 ll., preceded by 6 and followed by 5 ll. with notes in a contemporary hand, in Russia, 63 full-page water color drawings, n.p., n.d., Russia, 19th c., contemporary binding; and Paul I's gramota (grant), signed and dated: Gatchina, 24 October 1797, MS on vellum, in Russian, 3 ll., border decorations, many signatures at end, bound in silk.

Finding Aid: Dictionary Catalog and Shelflist of the Spencer Collection of Illustrated Books and Manuscripts and Fine Bindings, 2 vols. (Boston: G. K. Hall, 1971).

NY 73
FALES LIBRARY
ELMER HOLMES BOBST LIBRARY
NEW YORK UNIVERSITY
70 Washington Square South
New York, New York 10012
(212-598-3756)

Sean O'Casey (1884-1964). Papers, 1933-48, 149 items. Irish dramatist. Includes material, such as correspondence, reflecting his interest in World War II, particularly Russian participation, and his pro-communist sympathies. Reference(s) to socialism and nationalism as well. (NUCMC 68-795)

NY 74
TAMIMENT COLLECTION
ELMER HOLMES BOBST LIBRARY
NEW YORK UNIVERSITY
70 Washington Square South
New York, New York 10012
(212-598-3708)

1 The Tamiment Collection is devoted to materials on labor history and radical movements primarily, comprising published works, a large number of pamphlets and ephemeral printed matter, and manuscript holdings. Among the individual manuscript collections are the following:

2 American Friends of Russian Freedom. Papers, 1891-96, 56 items. Organized to protest the Russian Extradition Treaty of 1893. Correspondence, broadsides, pamphlets, flyers, and clippings. Correspondents include members of the group, Julia Ward Howe, Edwin D. Mead, Francis J. Garrison, Lloyd Garrison, Edmund Noble, and Stephen Stepniak.

3 American Trotskyism, 1928-1970. Title of the Bulletin of the Tamiment Library, issue 47 (April 1971). Basically a directory of groups associated with American Trotskyism and thus an excellent finding aid to materials on this subject scattered throughout the vertical files of the Tamiment Collection.

4 League for Industrial Democracy. Records, 1920-present, 33 boxes (additions expected). Office files, minutes of board meetings, correspondence, reports, membership lists, etc. Specific Soviet-related holdings not ascertained but believed to hold such material interspersed throughout. Unpublished finding aid.

5 Algernon Lee (1873-1954). Papers, 1896-1954, 8 boxes. Educational director of the Rand School of Social Sciences. Correspondence, speeches, notes, autobiographical fragments, transcriptions of his diary containing his philosophical and social views, and printed matter. Specific Russian-related items not ascertained. Correspondents include European socialists. Unpublished finding aid.

6 Rand School of Social Science. Records, 1905-62, 76 boxes. Office files, minutes, reports, correspondence, data on courses and faculty, etc. Believed to contain Russian/Soviet-related material interspersed throughout.

7 Russia and Religious Freedom. Collection, 1928, 1 folder. Includes a bibliography of selected publications containing information on freedom of religion in Russia, compiled by the U.S. State Department for Frederick W. Ninde; and selected translations and transcriptions by the State Department on this subject from Russian sources. (Part of Miscellaneous Manuscripts)

8 Russian Artillery Commission in North America. Records, 1915-17, 2 boxes. Imperial government arms purchasing group, based in New York, negotiated purchases of artillery supplies, primarily munitions. Collection, mostly in Russian, includes reports and notes of Ordnance Colonel V. Nekrasov. Correspondence with U.S. and Canadian firms discusses manufacturing specifications and procedures, equipment, production estimates, inspection and order arrangements. Unpublished inventory.

9 Max Shachtman (1904-1972). Papers, in process, 4 boxes, additions expected. Socialist leader and Leon Trotskii's literary executer. Personal files, manuscripts of his books, notes for his history of the Third International, a Trotskii bibliography, and ca. 1,000 carbon copies of Trotskii letters. Also, books and printed matter.

NY 75
NICHOLAS ROERICH MUSEUM
319 West 107th Street
New York, New York 10025
(212-864-7752)

The Nicholas Roerich Museum archives contain some material relating to Nicholas Roerich (1874-1947), painter, explorer, and archeologist. Manuscripts of his books, in Russian and English, are apparently no longer in this country. The correspondence of Mrs. Sina Fosdick, executive vice-president of the museum, with Professor Roerich is closed to researchers. The museum has a large collection of Roerich's paintings from various periods.

NY 76
NOVOYE RUSSKOYE SLOVO
243 West 56th Street
New York, New York 10019
(212-265-5500)

Inquiries concerning the contents and possible use of the archives of this newspaper should be directed to the editor, Andrei Sedykh.

NY 77
COUNSELOR--INTERNATIONAL AND REGULATORY SERVICES
PAN AMERICAN WORLD AIRWAYS, INC.
Pan Am Building
New York, New York 10017
(212-880-1294)

On 4 November 1966, the United States and the USSR signed an air transport agreement that provided for direct flights between the 2 countries. Pan Am was designated in the agreement as the sole American carrier, Aeroflot as the Soviet carrier. This agreement has been published in the Department of State Treaties and Other International Acts Series as TIAS 6135. Subsequent amendments published in this series are numbered 6489, 6560, 7287, 7609, 7658, 8058, 8217, 8996.

By the terms of the intergovernmental agreement, a considerable number of technical and commercial matters were left for resolution between the 2 airlines. An Agreement for Bilateral Provision of Services between the Transport Department of International Air Services of Civil Aviation of the USSR and Pan American World Airways, Inc. was concluded on 23 January 1967. Pan Am began service to the Soviet Union (Moscow) on 15 July 1968 and Aeroflot commenced service to New York about the same time. Pan Am's service was suspended in 1978. Aeroflot continues to serve New York and Washington.

Copies of the carrier agreement and amendments thereto are on file with the United States Civil Aeronautics Board, but have had no general distribution. Individual scholars may contact Pan Am's Counselor-International and Regulatory Services for advice in connection with specific research needs. However, the files of this office are not at present open to the public.

NY 78
PIERPONT MORGAN LIBRARY
29 East 36th Street
New York, New York 10016
(212-685-0008)

NEW YORK - PIERPONT MORGAN LIBRARY NY 78

1 This repository began as the private library of the famous financier and banker J. Pierpont Morgan. In 1924 Morgan's son made it a public institution in memoriam to his father. The library is particularly rich in early, illuminated manuscripts and in the holographs of well-known cultural figures.

2 Armenian Manuscripts. The library holds the following 13 items (with their respective identifying numbers): Sermons concerning the angels and the rational soul, 16th c. (M 437). Four Gospels (incomplete), 13th c. (M 620). Four Gospels, 17th c. (M 621). Menologium, A.D. 1348 (M 622). Four Gospels, A.D. 1658-59 (M 623). Four Gospels, A.D. 1588 (M 624). Scholium and epistles of St. Cyril of Alexandria, A.D. 1688 (M 625). Four Gospels, A.D. 1274 (M 740). Four Gospels, A.D. 1461 (M 749). 3 leaves from a Gospel, 10th c. (M 789). Fragment from a commentary on the epistle of St. James by Sargis Vardapet, 13th c. (M 802). Lectionary, A.D. 1334 (M 803). Lives of the saints and Christ, 17th c., vellum, 118 ll. (M 949).

3 Leopold Auer (1845-1930). Hungarian violinist and teacher. ALS, dated St. Petersburg, 17 April 1891, to an unidentified correspondent, 4 pp.

4 William Bainbridge (1774-1833). American naval officer. ALS, 19 September 1811, addressed to Messrs. Willing and Francis, 1 p., concerning his sales of indigo in Russia.

5 Enrico Modisto Bevignani (1841-1903). Conductor and composer. ALS, St. Petersburg 26 November 1884, to Josiah Pittman, accompanist at Covent Garden, about operatic matters, 3 pp. (Ford Collection)

6 Otto Eduard Leopold, prince von Bismarck (1815-1898). German chancellor. ALS to an unidentified friend, mainly concerning the Polish question, 4 pp., from St. Petersburg, 4 April 1861.

7 Nikolai Nikolayevich Blokhin (b. 1912). President of the Soviet Academy of Medical Sciences. TLS (Moscow, 22 December 1965) to Dr. Curt F. Bühler, thanking him for his interest in Blokhin's article on Vietnam in the New York Times, 1 p.

8 François Adrien Boieldieu (1775-1834). French composer. ALS from him in St. Petersburg to M. Delamarre in Moscow--about his success in Russia and his musical compositions, 8 May 1805, 3 pp.

9 Aleksandr Konstantinovich Glazunov (1865-1936). Composer. Ruses d'amour, ballet in 1 act, opus 61, piano score, 59 pp. Date stamped on front cover: 1898.

10 Maksim Gorkii (1868-1936). Writer. Incomplete, unsigned letter, 2 pp., to Walter Mett, 15 January 1922, concerning the organization of intellectual forces in Europe and world understanding.

11 Gabriel Theodore Joseph, comte d'Hedouville (fl. ca. 1803). French general and diplomat in St. Petersburg. ALS to an unknown woman ("Madame"), sending her a box of China tea, 24 February 1803, 1 p.

12 Petr Nikolaevich Krasnov (1869-1947). Tsarist general and anti-Bolshevik Cossack leader in the Civil War. 15 ALS, 1927-47, to Mr. and Mrs. Gregory P. Tschebotarioff.

13 Medieval Russian Manuscripts. Among the illuminated and other manuscripts in the library are: Gospels and prayers, 30 September 1471, 287 ff. In Russian but with covers (wooden boards and black stamped leather) apparently coming from 16th c. Austria (M 694).

Psalms and commentary, 15th (?) c., vellum, 219 ff. In South Russian, with original wooden boards and stamped leather (M 695).

Hymnal, in Greek, ca. 1600, manuscript on paper with musical notation, written and illuminated in a Greek monastery. 350 services for the principal feasts of the church year, as sung in Constantinople; tooled with stamp of Byzantine double-headed eagle, with folding flap and clasp, for Russian use (?) (M 350).

Bible. The four Gospels preceded by chapter headings and prefaces, followed by canon tables and a table of lections; manuscript on paper, written and illuminated in Russia, 1608, original red velvet over boards. (M 794)

6 sermons, ascribed to Saint Simon, the New Theologian (d. 1032). Manuscript on paper, in Church Slavonic, Bulgarian, written and rubricated in Russia, 19th c.; illuminated title-heads, initials, tail-pieces, 113 ll.; light brown morocco over boards, tooled in gold and silver, 2 clasps (M 704).

14 Boris Pasternak (1890-1960). Author. "Night," an autograph poem in Russian, plus portions of 2 other autograph poems.

15 Sergei Prokofiev (1891-1953). Composer. 2 music manuscripts, "Pas d'acier," op. 41, 1925, 22 pp., piano score; and "Chout," op. 21, 1915, 53 pp., short score--owned by Mr. Robert Owen Lehman and on deposit only.

16 Anton Grigorievitch Rubinstein (1829-1894). Composer. Album leaf with 4 bars of music, for voice and piano, signed and dated: Ant. Rubinstein. Naples 16 Janvier 1874, 1 p.

17 Russia. Army. A manuscript list entitled "The Empire of Russia's Army," dated 14 October 1764.

18 Russia. Sovereigns. Autographs and portraits of Russian emperors and empresses from Peter I to Nicholas II (stored in a vault).

19 Russia. Treaties. Manuscript copy in translation of a treaty dated Moscow, 11 December 1742, between George II of England and Elizabeth of Russia, 20 pp.

20 Igor Fedorovich Stravinsky (1882-1971). Composer. [Le baiser de la fée], added in pencil; original title, La Vierge des Glaciers, crossed out; ballet in 4 scenes, piano score for 2 hands, in pencil, title page and first page in ink, 76 pp., 1928. L'oiseau de feu, dance story in 2 scenes, manuscript reduction for piano, 2 hands, 49 pp., signed and dated at end 1910, second title page dated Morges 6 December 1918. L'oiseau de feu, printed piano arrangement with many autograph corrections and additions, Moscow/Leipzig, n.d. Persephone, manuscript dedicated to Victoria Ocampo, dated Buenos Aires/Rio de Janeiro Mai-Juin 1936; incomplete, note at end explaining he has no time to finish, dated Augosto 30/[19]60 San Isidro. Petrouchka, signed and dated at end: Igor Stravinsky Hollywood October 14/[19]46, 147 pp. Ragtime, signed and dated at end: Igor Strawinsky (Hiver) 1918 Morges, dedicated to Madame E. Errazuriz, 8 pp. (All items in Robert Owen Lehman Collection, on deposit in The Pierpont Morgan Library)

21 Jacques François Joseph Swebach (dit Fontaine) (1769-1823). Artist. ALS, St. Petersburg 26 July 1819, to Louis l'Archer de St. Vincent, concerning his personal and financial affairs, conditions in Russia, his plans to return to France, etc., 2 pp.

22 Leo Tolstoi (1828-1910). Author. ALS, n.p., 13 May 1904, 1 p., to Sydney Carlyle Cockerell, thanking him for sending books by John Ruskin and for forwarding a letter from the grand mufti of Egypt; plus a translation by Lady Anne Blunt of this philosophical letter to Tolstoi from the Grand Mufti Mohammed Abdul in Cairo, 8 April 1904, 3 pp.

23 Ivan S. Turgenev (1818-1883). Author. Letter of thanks, in French, to an unknown correspondent 15 April 1868, 2 pp.; the subject is Turgenev's contacts with Thomas Carlyle.

24 The Mary Flagler Cary Collection contains the following musical items:

25 Anton Stepanovitch Arensky (1861-1906). ALS, Nice 23 March 1905, to Alexander Siloti.

26 Aaron Avshalomoff (1894-1965). ALS to M. Cary, Shanghai 27 August 1934.

27 Mily Alexeyevich Balakirev (1837-1910). "Sibirskii kozachek" (The Siberian Cossack), 1 l., dance for piano; unidentified sketches on verso. Written ca. 1891 for a Christmas party at the St. Petersburg court chapel, of which Balakirev was director. Alexander Lopatin found the manuscript on the floor and sent it, 1912, to the composer Alexander S. Taneyev. Also, ALS from 1898 and ALS, St. Petersburg 17 December 1907.

28 Michael Balfe (1808-1870). ALS, St. Petersburg 6 March 1856, to a Mr. Smith.

29 Adolf Joseph Marie Blassmann (b. 1823). ALS to the Russian composer Youri von Arnold (1811-1898), Dresden 21 December 1866.

30 Alexander Porfirievitch Borodin (1833-1887). ALS, Tula 23 August 1881 and ALS, St. Petersburg 23 May 1886.

31 Sergei Eduardovitch Bortkiewicz (1877-1952). ALS, Vienna (n.d.), to the music publishers Breitkopf and Härtel.

32 Henri Casadesus (1879-1947). ALS, Moscow 30 January 1913.

33 P. I. Chaikovskii. See under Peter Ilyich Tchaikovsky.

34 César Antonovich Cui (1835-1918). ALS, n.p., 2 February 1886, to an editor; and ALS, n.p., n.d.

35 Alexander Sergeyevich Dargomyzhsky (1813-1869). ALS, St. Petersburg 15 August 1865 and ALS, n.p., n.d.

36 Karl Youlievitch Davidov (1838-1889). ALS, n.p., n.d.

37 Sergei Pavlovitch Diaghilev (1872-1929). Miscellaneous musical fragments, printed and manuscript, relating to productions of the Ballet Russe. See also under P. I. Tchaikovsky.

38 Issay Alexandrovitch Dobrowen (Dobroven) (1893/4-1953). ALS, Dresden 5 January 1928 and ALS from Mrs. Dobrowen in New York to Mr. Flagler, 5 January 1933.

39 Anna Nikolayevna Essipoff (Annette Essipova) (1851-1914). Essipoff married her teacher Theodor Leschetizky in 1880; they separated in 1892. Autograph postcard, signed, from Vienna, to Karl (Karel) Navrátil, 27 November 1889.

40 Clara (Clemens) Gabrilovitch (1874-1962). Mark Twain's daughter was married to the Russian-born pianist and conductor Osip Salomonovich Gabrilovitch in 1906. He headed the Detroit Symphony Orchestra from 1918-36. TLS, n.p., 27 November 1935, to Mr. Flagler.

41 Alexander Konstantinovitch Glazunov (1865-1936). ALS, St. Petersburg (?) 23 June and 6 July 1905 to Alexander Siloti; ALS, n.p., 19 October 1928; and TLS, n.p., 27 June 1935, to Alfred Cortot.

NEW YORK - PIERPONT MORGAN LIBRARY NY 78

42 Mikhail Ivanovitch Glinka (1804-1857). ALS, n.p., n.d., to Adolph von Henselt and ALS, n.p., n.d., to M. Olfers.

43 Leopold Godowsky (1870-1938). Musical autograph, signed: Milan 7 December 1913.

44 Alexander Fedorovitch Goedicke (1877-1957). DS, Moscow 14 January 1911.

45 Alexander Tikhonovitch Gretchaninov (1864-1956). Musical autograph, signed, Moscow 23 May 1911; and ALS from Mrs. Gretchaninov in New York, n.d., to Mrs. Flagler.

46 Moritz Karasowski (1823-1892). Born in Warsaw. ALS, Dresden 2 August 1877, to Karl Mikuli.

47 Aram Khatchaturian (1903-1978). Recitative and Fugue, for piano, signed twice, 4 pp.

48 Paul Kochanski (1887-1934). Pole, lived in St. Petersburg in 1913-19. ALS, New York 1 February 1931 and 26 January 1933, to Mr. Flagler.

49 Sergey Alexandrovitch Koussevitsky (1874-1951). Director of the Boston Symphony Orchestra, 1924-49. Autograph postcard, signed, Berlin 1 June 1911, to Herr Gutmann.

50 Wilhelm von Lenz (1809-1883). ALS, St. Petersburg 27 June 1873.

51 Theodor Leschetizky (1830-1915). Polish-born pianist and teacher (Osip Gabrilovitch was a pupil) was in St. Petersburg 1852-78. ALS, Vienna 18 November 1883.

52 Anatol Konstantinovitch Liadov (1855-1914). ALS, Borovichi 18 June 1906, to Alexander Siloti.

53 Sergei Mikhailovitch Liapunow (Liapunov) (1859-1924). ALS, Paris 8 May 1924.

54 Félia Litvinne (Litvinova) (1861-1936). ALS, n.p., n.d.

55 Alexey Feodorovitch Lvov (1798-1870). ALS, St. Petersburg 4 October 1833, to M. Peters; and ALS, Dresden 8 September 1842.

56 Nikolay Andreyevitch Malko (1888-1961). ALS, New York 4 January 1939 and 13 June 1940, to Mrs. Cary.

57 Nikolai Karlovitch Medtner (1880-1951). Autograph postcard, signed, n.p., n.d.

58 Sophie Menter (1846-1918). "Zigeunerweisen," composed by Menter, a German pianist and composer (protegee of F. Liszt), with instrumentation by Chaikovskii. Full score in Chaikovskii's autograph, 64 pp. At end: P. Chaikovskii. 2 October 1891. Schloss Itter (Menter's Tirol residence). First performed in Odessa 4 February 1893, under Chaikovskii's direction. Also, ALS, St. Petersburg, n.d.

59 Erik Meyer-Helmund (1861-1932). ALS, St. Petersburg 29 March 1898.

60 Eduard Nápravník (1839-1916). ALS, Bad Wildungen, 2 July 1907, to Alexander Siloti.

61 Vaslav Nijinsky (1890-1950). ALS to an otherwise unidentified Michail Dimitrievitch, concerning an Ollendorf language textbook, 3 pp., n.p., n.d.

62 Vladimir de Pachmann (1848-1933). Musical autograph, signed: n.p., 28 September 1899.

63 Ignace Jan Paderewski (1860-1941). 6 ALS and APS, Morges, New York, and Paris, 1897-1938, including 3 to Mr. and Mrs. Flagler, 1938; 1 to Alfred Cortot, 2 September 1928; and a musical autograph, signed: New York 18 March 1917.

64 Alexander Petschnikoff (1873-1949). ALS, n.p., 2 August 1912, to Herr Gutmann.

65 Sergei Sergeevitch Prokofiev (1891-1953). Autograph postcard, signed, Samoreau 8 April 1926, to F. Wever; and ALS, Kansas City (Missouri) 22 January 1926, to Mr. Flagler.

66 Sergei Vassilievitch Rachmaninoff (1873-1943). ALS, St. Petersburg 24 August 1907, to Alexander Siloti; ALS and 3 TLS, New York, 1924-25, to Mr. Flagler; and ALS, Hertenstein 10 May 1939, to Alfred Cortot.

67 Max Reger (1873-1916). Autograph postcard, signed, Munich 14 June 1904, to Ossip Schnirlin; ALS, Munich 9 November 1905, to Alexander Siloti; and ALS, Leipzig 31 May 1907, to Herr Salter.

68 Nikolai Andreevitch Rimskii-Korsakov (1844-1908). ALS, St. Petersburg January 1879; ALS, Munich 20 February 1906; ALS, Paris 22 May 1907, to Albert Carré; and ADS, St. Petersburg March 1905. [Krasavitsa, op. 51, no. 4, after Pushkin], song with piano, at end: [31 July 1897. Smychkovo. N R-K.], 4 pp.

69 Anton Grigorievitch Rubinstein (1829-1894). ALS, various places, 1856-93, including 1, 29 August 1856, to Princess Sayn-Wittgenstein, another to a Mr. Schirmer, 14 December 1872, and a third, 20 June 1893, to a Herr Bock. Quartets, for strings (2 violins, alto, and violoncello), op. 47, dedicated to Son Excellence Monsieur le Comte Mathieu Wielhorsky, 27, 28, 24 pp. Thème et Variations pour le Pianoforte, op. 88, dedication to Jules Behrens, 27 pp.

70 Anton Grigorievitch Rubinstein (1829-1894). ALS, various places, 1856-93, including 1,

29 August 1856, to Princess Sayn-Wittgenstein, another to a Mr. Schirmer, 14 December 1872, and a third, 20 June 1893, to a Herr Bock.

71 Nicolay Grigorievitch Rubinstein (1835-1881). ALS, n.p., n.d., to a Herr Wolff.

72 Vassily Ilyitch Safonov (1852-1918). ALS, Moscow 21 September 1897, to Eduard Hanslick.

73 Lazare Saminsky (1882-1959). 5 ALS, various places, 1927-43 and undated, to Mr. Flagler.

74 Alexander Saslavsky (1876-1924). ALS, San Francisco 26 November 1918, to Mr. Flagler.

75 Arnold Schoenberg (1874-1951). Autograph postcard, signed, to S. Koussevitsky et al.

76 Alexander Nikolayevitch Scriabin (1872-1915). Signed document, Moscow 11 May 1911.

77 Giovanni Sgambati (1841-1914). ALS, St. Petersburg 16 October 1903.

78 Jean Sibelius (1865-1957). ALS, Järvenpää 19 July 1907, to Alexander Siloti.

79 Alexander Siloti (1863-1945). ALS and 7 autograph postcards, signed, New York, 1922-31, to Mr. and Mrs. Flagler. Also, several letters to him, listed above.

80 Igor Stravinsky (1882-1971). Full orchestral score of "L'oiseau de feu," 164 pp., not autograph, with 76 manuscript and printed orchestral parts. This score and the orchestral parts were used for performances by the Ballet Russe until its demise in 1929. As of 1970, the work in ballet form had never been published in full score. Also, prelude and rondo of the princesses from "L'oiseau de feu" for violin and piano, transcribed by Stravinsky and dedicated to Paul Kochanski, 2 ll. + 20 pp., unpublished. (Kochanski, 1887-1934, was a Polish violinist at the St. Petersburg Imperial Conservatory; after 1921, he taught at the Juilliard School in New York.) Copy of the first printed edition (Moscow-Leipzig, 1910) of the piano score for L'oiseau de feu with choreographic directions on several pages, possibly in the hand of Michel Fokine; the score has many corrections and additions in Stravinsky's hand and markings of various conductors. [Études, piano, op. 7, nos. 1-3], 16 pp. Each étude has a dedication at the beginning and is signed and dated at the end. No. 1: Stepan Stepanovich Mitusov; Ustilug [i.e., Ustiug?], 1 May 1908. No. 2: Nicolay Ivanovich Richter; Ustilug, 29 August 1908. No. 3: Andrey Nicolayevich Rimsky-Korsakov; Ustilug, 8 September [1908].

81 Peter Ilyich Tchaikovsky (1840-93). First edition of the piano score of "Le lac des cygnes," Paris, n.d. (1895?), probably incomplete, with extensive alterations in the hand of Sergei Diaghilev, whose copy this was; and Diaghilev's copy of the orchestral score to the same ballet (Moscow and Paris, 1895), 2 vols., with Diaghilev's annotations. Both scores were used by conductors of the Ballet Russe. Also, Tchaikovsky's ALS, Klin 4 March 1893, and ALS, n.p., 18 January, no year, to Alexander Siloti.

82 Ignaz Tedesco (1817-1882). ALS, Odessa, 20 September 1869, to Karl Mikuli.

83 Pauline Viardot-Garcia (1821-1910). 3 ALS, various places, 1849 and undated; plus a musical autograph, signed: Leipzig 20 August 1843.

84 Henri Vieuxtemps (1820-1881). [Fantaisie-Caprice for violin and orchestra], 71 pp., full score; at end: Fini. St. Petersbourg ce 21 février 1840. H. Vieuxtemps. Completed in his 20th year, during his second concert tour in Russia; published ca. 1841 as op. 11.

85 Henri Wieniawski (1835-1880). Lublin-born musician, court violinist in St. Petersburg, 1860-71, died in Moscow. ALS, Brussels 2 January 1876, to M. Zilcken.

86 Wladislaw Zelenski (1837-1921). ALS, Warsaw 10 April 1879, to Karl Mikuli.

87 Alma (Gluck) Zimbalist (1884-1938). 3 ALS, New York and New Hartford, Connecticut, 1919 and undated, to Mr. and Mrs. Flagler and to Mrs. Cary.

Finding Aids: For some of these holdings, the 1969 A Review of Acquisitions, 1949-1968, published in New York by The Pierpont Morgan Library, will be useful. Most of the musical listings came directly from The Mary Flagler Cary Music Collection (The Pierpont Morgan Library, New York, 1970).

NY 79
PILSUDSKI INSTITUTE OF AMERICA
381 Park Avenue South
New York, New York 10016
(212-683-4342)

1 Belvedere Archives. Ca. 15 ft., 1918-22. Also known in Polish as Akta Adiutantury Generalnej Naczelnego Dowództwa. Records of the general headquarters of the Polish army's supreme command, including dispatches, reports, diplomatic and military materials, most submitted to Marshal Jozef Pilsudski as commander in chief of the army. Battle plans and orders, documents on the organization of military forces, and data on the Polish-Russian War of 1919-20 (Battle of Warsaw, Kiev campaign, etc.). Also includes some of Pilsudski's own manuscripts and foreign

policy reports submitted to him as chief of state from the Ministry of Foreign Affairs and from Polish legations and missions abroad. The records have been microfilmed (negative and positive) on 30 reels; Yale University's Sterling Library has the microfilm. Unpublished register (NUCMC 72-1203).

2 Zygmunt Guze. Papers, 1918-45 and n.d., 9 files. Polish engineer employed in Imperial Russia just before World War I. Materials relate to European and Asiatic Russia and the Soviet Union, and to his interests in history, geography, and ethnography. The handwriting is very difficult to decipher.

3 Katyn Forest. Records, 1940, 6 files. Material on the Polish prisoners of war captured by the USSR during the 1939 campaign and on the Katyn Forest Massacre of 1940.

4 Apolinary Kielczynski (1904-1968). Collection, 1941-56, 16 files and 6 vols. Diplomat and journalist. He was vice-consul of the Polish government in exile in Istanbul after World War II. The files concern his journalistic work; the volumes of "Balkan Materials" (1952-56) contain many items related to Russian and Balkan affairs.

5 Jozef Lipski (1894-1958). Papers, 1933-58, 19 ft. Polish diplomat, ambassador in Berlin, 1933-39, and representative of the Polish government in exile in Washington. Part of the 93 files relates to his service in Berlin and has been published, 1968. In the other part are many items related to Russian and Eastern European diplomacy or international affairs in which the Soviet Union played a role. (NUCMC 72-1197)

6 Valerian Platonov. Collection, 1837-65, 1 ft. Letters, documents, and clippings, originals and copies, relating to the Polish revolt of 1863 as well as economic, financial, and judicial conditions in (Russian) Poland. Includes proclamations of the Polish National Government, pronouncements of military leaders of the uprising, articles of the Polish press, and letters of Count F. Berg, A. and/or M. Gorchakov, Count M. N. Muraviev, I. F. Paskevich, E. Sievers, and Alexander Wielopolski. (NUCMC 72-1202)

7 Polish Consulate General in New York. Archives, 1939-45, 40 files. Materials related to routine office work, including some on activities of Russian ethnic groups from Eastern Europe.

8 Polish Embassy in London. Records, 1920-32, 10 folders. Political reports sent to the embassy by the Polish foreign office. Copies of the reports, originally received from Moscow or written by the foreign office itself, were distributed to all major embassies.

9 Polish Government in London. Records, 1940-present, 11 files (additions expected). Includes some items dealing with Russian and Eastern European diplomacy or international affairs.

10 Polish Wars. Archives, 1918-45, 9 files and 4 vols. 1 file concerns the Polish army in the USSR, 1943-44; the remainder relates to the Polish-Soviet War of 1919-21.

11 Jerzy Ponikiewski (1907-1965). Collection, 1945-54, 7 binders. Polish journalist. 1 volume concerns the USSR, chiefly the "Promethean Movement" for national self-determination among Soviet nationalities.

12 Press Collection. 19 vols., 1943-47. Press clippings, volumes I, XVII, XVIII, and XIX of which concern Polish-Soviet relations.

13 Aleksandr Prystor (State of Central Lithuania). Papers, 1920-22, 120 items. Reports of all departments of a government comprising Wilno (Vilna) and surrounding Lithuanianian territory, founded by General Lucjan Zeligowski (1865-1947), who became its chief of state. Originals and copies. Some documents concern Polish-Byelorussian and Polish-Ukrainian relations. There are posters connected with the elections to the Polish Diet in 1922. (NUCMC 72-1210)

14 Tadeusz Rozwadowski (1866-1928). Papers, 1920, 107 items. Polish army officer. Chief of the general staff of Polish forces in the Polish-Soviet War, 1920. Correspondence, reports, and other papers concern the Battle of Warsaw and the Riga peace conference. Marshal Jozef Pilsudski and General Maxime Weygand of the French military mission in Poland are 2 of the correspondents. (NUCMC 72-1206)

15 Russia-USSR. Records, 1939, 3 files. Documents concerning the deportation to the USSR of Polish citizens from Soviet-occupied Poland; also press clippings.

16 Edward Smigly-Rydz (1886-1941). Papers, 1920 and 1935-39, 2 ft. Marshal of the Polish army, commander in chief in 1939. Reports, orders, maps, and description of "Operation Winter" conducted in the winter of 1919-20 against Dünaberg, under his command, in the Polish-Soviet War; and correspondence, speeches, memoranda, and other papers from 1935-39 when he was general-inspector of the Polish army. In part, copies. (NUCMC 72-1207)

17 Michal Sokolnicki (1880-1967). Papers, 1908-45, 4 ft. Polish historian, diplomat, and author. Ambassador and mission chief to Turkey, 1923-45. In part, records of the Polish embassy in Ankara (office files, letters, military and diplomatic intelligence reports); also, personal correspondence and diaries. Many items concern Russian and

Eastern European diplomacy or international affairs in which the USSR played a role. (NUCMC 72-1208)

18 Julian Stachiewicz (1890-1934). Collection, ca. 1914-18, 16 files. General, historian, and director of the Historical Office at the Polish Ministry of War. Records concerning the participation of Poles in the Russian, Austrian, and German armies during World War I.

19 Ukraine. Collection, 1914-present, 3 files and growing. Records and press clippings related to living conditions in the Ukraine and to the Ukrainian ethnic group in the U.S.

20 Ukrainian Military Mission in Poland. Archive, 1920, 193 items. Ukrainian army sent into Poland by the nationalist government of S. V. Petliura. Originals and copies, mainly in Ukrainian, of the government's orders, notes, reports, maps, correspondence, and appeals to the Polish regime. Some letters are from Petliura himself. (NUCMC 72-1211)

21 Jan Weinstein (1903-1974). Papers, 1921-45, 60 files. Polish diplomat and historian. Includes some items related to Russian and Eastern European politics.

22 World War I. Collection, 1914-18, 5 files. Material about the military operations of Russian and Austrian armies on Polish territory.

NY 80
POLISH INSTITUTE OF ARTS AND SCIENCES OF AMERICA, INC.
59 East 66th Street
New York, New York 10021
(212-988-4338)

1 Waclaw Lednicki (1891-1967). Papers, in process, 6 boxes. Scholar specializing in Slavic literatures. Correspondence, writings, teaching materials, etc., some pertaining to Russia. Also, papers of his father Alexander, a member of the state duma, Kadet Party leader, and lawyer in tsarist Russia. Russian-related materials include correspondence, manuscript books, and miscellaneous other items from 1903-18. There is a photocopy of a memoir written by Alexander Lednicki in 1906 while in prison for his part in issuing the Vyborg manifesto. Among his correspondents were, in 1908, Nikolai Ivanovich Antsyferov, Pavel Pavlovich Korenev, and Petr Andreevich Petrovskii. These letters, and some telegrams from the same date, are originals. In addition, the senior Lednicki's papers include some copies, photostats, of material in Polish repositories, the British Foreign Office, and, handwritten, the French Foreign Ministry archives. Access requires advance written permission.

2 Note: The Polish Institute has 2 large collections of materials that include some pertinent holdings: over 300 microfilms relating mostly to East European history and society, in 9 languages; and the oral and sound history collection, ca. 240 cassettes and tapes. Among the microfilms are manuscripts of Kazimierz Baginski on the trial of the 16 Polish Underground leaders in Moscow in 1945 (he was one of the accused), and of I. Nekrasov on Russian labor camps in Dmitrovsk and Samara. In the oral and sound history collection are the taped memoirs of General Michal Tadeusz Karaszewicz-Tokarzewski, commanding officer of the Polish Resistance Movement during World War II. Additions are expected in both these collections. There is also a biographical file which might hold data relating to the Russian Empire and Soviet Union.

Finding Aids: The Institute's Annual Reports describe archival acquisitions and current holdings.

NY 81
MARK POPOVSKY--PRIVATE COLLECTION
2 Ellwood Street
New York, New York 10040
(212-569-5171)

Archive of peasant disciples of Leo Tolstoi, ca. 1918-77, over 3,000 pp. of typescript. Includes memoirs, diaries, autobiographical notes, letters, testimony and speeches at trials, poems, and songs composed by the peasant Tolstoians. Contemporary correspondence reflects their views on the relationship between society and government, collectivization, and the fate of Tolstoi's heritage in the USSR. Also, photographs, and lists of young Tolstoians drafted into the army and shot in the 1920s and in 1941-42 for refusing to bear arms. Materials concern: relations between the Tolstoians and the Soviet authorities over 60 years; the history of Tolstoian agricultural communes, 1918-39; history of Tolstoian schools for children, 1930-35; persecution and deliberate annihilation of Tolstoians throughout the USSR; the philosophical, social, religious views and everyday life of the peasant Tolstoians; and some of the most colorful figures in the movement. Also, some additional manuscripts concerning the Russian intelligentsia that could not be published in the Soviet Union. Inquire concerning access.

NY 82
PROLOG RESEARCH CORPORATION
254 West 31st Street
New York, New York 10001

Founded by the Ukrainian Liberation Council in 1957, Prolog holds a collection of materials dating from ca. 1941 to the early 1950s. The holdings, in approximately 2 4-drawer filing cabinets at present, include documents and publications of the anti-Nazi Ukrainian underground in World War II; typed reports of the underground Ukrainian Insurgent Army (an organization of Ukrainian nationalists); photographs of Ukrainian leaders, military formations, and related subjects; correspondence from the war years and to about 1950; leaflets--anti-Nazi and anti-Soviet of the underground, plus Nazi and Soviet matter; and some German official announcements (e.g., death sentences pronounced against members of the Ukrainian underground). All of these materials remain the property of the Ukrainian Liberation Council; they are open to qualified researchers.

NY 83
MRS. JOSEPH SCHILLINGER--PRIVATE COLLECTION
340 East 57th Street
New York, New York 10022

Schillinger Collection of Russian Memorabilia. Joseph Schillinger (1895-1943) was a theorist, composer, conductor, lecturer, teacher, and artist. His widow maintains a collection of the following items: 3 large Russian concert posters, 1926-28; 3 Russian concert program booklets and 1 program leaflet, 1926-28; a Horowitz-Milstein program, with a sketch of A. Glazunov on the cover, 1921; 2 lengthy, handwritten letters to her, 1967, from Leon Theremin in Moscow (perhaps the only letters written by him to anyone in the U.S. after his return to Russia); some notes for March of the Orient, op. 11, 1927; and 7 concert programs, leaflets, and pamphlets from demonstrations of the Theremin (musical instrument) in the United States, 1929-30. At present the collection is closed to outside researchers. Ultimate disposition of the material is undetermined. Other Schillinger collections at the New York Public Library, Museum of Modern Art, Archives of American Art, Fleisher Collection of the Free Library of Philadelphia, Columbia University, and University of Wyoming Library.

NY 84
SHEVCHENKO SCIENTIFIC SOCIETY--
AMERICAN BRANCH
312 West 13th Street
New York, New York 10003
(212-475-3699)

The Society maintains both an extensive library and a large collection of archival materials. The latter include minutes of meetings and other records of the organization itself as well as papers of members, photographs, and other documents. Holdings include papers of Professor Nicholas Chubaty, Prince Ivan Tokarzhevsky-Karasevych, and Professor Andriy Jakowliv; correspondence of Myhaylo Hrushevsky and S. Faryniak; documents of Bohdan Lepky; papers of Dr. Sophia Parfanovych; and some archives of the Voliansky family.

NY 85
KYRIENA SILOTI--PRIVATE COLLECTION
170 West 73rd Street
New York, New York 10023
(212-877-6994)

Collection of miscellaneous papers of her father, the pianist and conductor Alexander Siloti (Ziloti), plus her own papers. Materials of her father include a few musical manuscripts and some correspondence; also, a typed "program of new music performed in Russia, 1903-13," under the baton of Alexander Siloti. Materials are not arranged. Inquire concerning access.

NY 86
ARCHIVES OF AMERICAN ART
SMITHSONIAN INSTITUTION
41 East 65th Street
New York, New York 10021
(212-826-5722)

This repository, like each of the regional centers of the Archives of American Art, has microfilms of much of the original materials kept at the Archives' Washington Center. It also holds items on microfilm from originals in other hands. Some of these materials pertain to the Russian Empire/Soviet Union. For details, see the entry under the District of Columbia.

NY 87
SOLOMON R. GUGGENHEIM MUSEUM
1071 Fifth Avenue
New York, New York 10028
(212-860-1300)

1 Guggenheim Museum Collections. Hold works by the following artists: Alexander Archipenko. 4 sculptures and 1 gouache. Saul Baizermann. 2 sculptures. Ilya Bolotowsky. 4 paintings and 1 gouache. Marc Chagall. 8 paintings and 12 works on paper (including 3 prints). Ilja G. Chashnik. 2 drawings (watercolors). Naum Gabo. 8 sculptures. N. Goncharova. 1 painting. Wassily Kandinsky. 69 paintings, 52 drawings (watercolors), 12 prints, and 1 book.

Alexander Liberman. 1 sculpture, 1 painting, and 1 print. Jacques Lipchitz. 2 sculptures. El Lissitsky. 1 drawing (watercolor) and 2 portfolios of prints. Kasimir Malewitch. 1 painting. Antoine Pevsner. 2 sculptures. Alexander Rodchenko. 4 zinc plates. Mark Rothko. 1 painting. Vera Stravinsky. 1 painting. Adja Yunkers. 2 paintings.

2 Curatorial Research Files. Photographs of each of the works listed above (available for purchase); and correspondence (personal) with the following artists: Archipenko, Bolotowsky, Chagall, Gabo, Goncharova, Kandinsky, Lipchitz, Pevsner, and Stravinsky.

Restrictions: Access to serious researchers by appointment only.

Finding Aid: Joan M. Lukach's biography of Hilla Rebay, in preparation (1979), will list the artists included in the Archive.

NY 88
REBAY FOUNDATION ARCHIVE
THE SOLOMON R. GUGGENHEIM MUSEUM
1071 Fifth Avenue
New York, New York 10028
(212-860-1360)

Hilla Rebay (1890-1967) was Solomon R. Guggenheim's art adviser from 1929-49, curator of the S. R. Guggenheim Collection, and first director of the Museum of Non-objective Painting (i.e., the Guggenheim Museum), 1936-52. She was also a non-objective painter herself, ca. 1917-67, with a deep interest in W. Kandinsky. She knew personally and corresponded with many artists and others born in the Russian Empire or Soviet Union.

The archive holds materials about these artists, filed under the person's name or that of relevant organizations. Most of the holdings are letters but there are also photographs and miscellaneous documents, 1915-67.

Among those for whom the archive has material are the following (substantial holdings italicized): Ilya Bolotowsky, Marc Chagall, Sonia Terk Delaunay, Olga Egeressy, Naum Gabo, John D. Graham, Fannina Halle, Wassily and Nina Kandinsky, Olga Kotchoubey, Vladimir Korostevitz, Antoine Pevsner, Alexandra Povorina (Ahlers-Hestermann), S. Sigaloff, Esphyr Slobodkina, Daria Troubetzkoi, Alexandra Tolstoi (Tolstoi Foundation), Nicolai Vorobiov, and Abraham Walkowitz.

All of these items are autograph, first person documents (usually written to Hilla Rebay). Many other Russian artists and musicians are mentioned in the material, for example, Alexander Archipenko, Kazimir Malevich, and L. Massine. Interested scholars may write with specific requests about other possible holdings. Materials themselves are unrestricted but researchers must make an appointment in advance to use them.

NY 89
SOVFOTO/EASTFOTO
25 West 43rd Street, Room 1008
New York, New York 10036
(212-279-8846)

An extensive file of photographs, current and historic, from the USSR and Eastern Europe. They cover such topics as international trade, economic life, political affairs, agriculture, industry, science, geography, sports, culture, and the arts. Of recent vintage are photos on the Soyuz space program, SALT talks, cultural exchanges, summit meetings, leading personalities, workers, families, students, medicine and public health, weaponry, the armed forces, architecture, and atomic power. Over 800,000 photos are on file.

Sovfoto supplies these photographs for use by news agencies, newspapers and magazines, book publishers, television, U.S. government agencies, and a number of other organizations. Although access is unrestricted, a fee is normally charged for use of the collection. The originals may be rented for reproduction.

NY 90
IGOR AND VERA STRAVINSKY--PRIVATE COLLECTION
c/o Webster and Sheffield
One Rockefeller Plaza
New York, New York 10020
(212-582-3370)

Includes personal papers and musical materials. Scholars' written or telephoned requests for specific information concerning the collection will be answered if directed to the above address.

NY 91
STRAVINSKY-DIAGHILEV FOUNDATION and
PARMENIA MIGEL EKSTROM COLLECTION
525 East 85th Street
New York, New York 10028
(212-734-4167)

The combined collections of the Foundation and of Parmenia Migel Ekstrom are too large to detail fully in these pages. They contain the following materials concerning Russian dance and music: original stage designs by such artists as L. Bakst, A. Benois, B. Bilinsky, N. Goncharova, M. Larionov, N.

Roerich, B. Anisfeld, and others; correspondence of Igor Stravinsky and Serge Diaghilev (including approximately 800 telegrams to and from Diaghilev); some 15,000 business documents, bills, and records relating to Diaghilev and his Ballets Russes (among them, the contracts signed by his dancers, singers, and artists); a great quantity of original music scores; and a large number of photographs.

Useful finding aids might be the published catalogues for exhibitions of holdings of Roerich, Bakst, Bilinsky, and Stravinsky/ Diaghilev.

NY 92
STUDENT STRUGGLE FOR SOVIET JEWRY
200 West 72nd Street, Suites 30-31
New York, New York 10023
(212-799-8900)

This organization has materials on the situation of Soviet Jews from 1964 to the present. The material pertains primarily to the emigration of Jews from the USSR. There is also documentation on the situation of Soviet Jewish immigrants in Israel and the U.S. Most, but not all, of the material has been filed. Write or (preferably) telephone in advance, stating the purpose of research.

NY 93
TIME INCORPORATED ARCHIVES
Rockefeller Center
New York, New York 10020
(212-841-4122)

Office correspondence about the handling of news from Russia is in the archive. There are also drafts and background material prepared in the early 1940s by Time Inc.'s Postwar Department under the direction of Raymond Leslie Buell for an unpublished Fortune magazine supplement entitled "Relations with Russia." The archive, pre-1960, is sometimes open to qualified scholars upon written application.

NY 94
TOLSTOY FOUNDATION, INC.
250 West 57th Street
New York, New York 10019
(212-247-2922)

Researchers might be interested in both the records of the Foundation itself and the various manuscripts which scholars and literary figures have deposited with the Center over the years. Some years ago, Professor I. Shumilin prepared a preliminary list of holdings in the Foundation Archives. His headings were the following: Manuscripts "A" (concerning T.F.). Manuscripts "B" (other). Tolstoy Farm. Correspondence with welfare/ church organizations. Correspondence with various minor organizations. Confidential. Personal - Alexandra Tolstoi and Tatiana Schaufuss. Psychological warfare (psychological strategy in Cold War). Budget and financial reports. Statistical reports. Reports of T.F. Working plan of T.F. T.F. meetings - Tolstoy Foundation board of directors. Correspondence of T.F. with branches. Refugees relief. Laws and immigration documents - Legislation testimonies for hearings. Search - tracing department. Immigration: cases, sponsors, assurances, etc. (alphabetized and unalphabetized). Escapees and U S E P. I R O. American Council of Voluntary Agencies for Foreign Service (Foreign Operations Administration--F.O.A.). Material help, medical help, CARE, CRALOG, etc. Lists of DP--arrival and departure (Tolstoy Foundation and others) (alphabetized and individual items listed). Jobs, employments, recommendations. Resettlement of DPs (on farm, immigrat., etc.). Reports of new addresses. Miscellaneous materials about DP and immigration in general (outside U.S.A.). DP camps (outside U.S.A.). Exerptions (sic) from general DP-file: a) Nationality, b) Territory, c) Students. Personal and general correspondence of: a) A. L. Tolstoi, b) T. A. Schaufuss, c) E. I. Tomaschewskaja. Repatriation. Clippings of newspapers in 7 divisions (DP--varia; T.F.--activities; articles, notes, speeches of A. L. Tolstoi; laws, notes about a new immigration law; about Leo Tolstoi; "Berezoff's illness"; Varia). The news--Tolstoy Foundation (with general correspondence). Russian Language Program. Unclassified material. Information, books, newspapers, concerning refugees problems. Contributions.

The Foundation's archival material at present is located at the Center in Valley Cottage, New York. Access to these materials requires the written permission of the Foundation's management, which will reply to inquiries directed to the above address in New York City.

NY 95
LIBRARY AND ARCHIVES
UKRAINIAN ACADEMY OF ARTS AND SCIENCES
IN THE U.S., INC.
206 West 100th Street
New York, New York 10025
(212-222-1866)

1 Archival materials of the Academy, mostly from the 20th c. Ukraine, currently total over 500,000 items, making this repository the largest for Ukrainian materials in the U.S.

Holdings include personal papers, manuscripts, memoirs, family correspondence, photographs, graphic material, maps, philatelic items and other unpublished materials pertaining to Ukrainian history, literature, culture, and social-political thought. The archival materials are divided into: personal archives of individual persons; archives of organizations and institutions; and materials pertaining to the history of Ukrainian immigration in the U.S.

2 Among the personal archives are included: Archives of social-political figures - N. Hryhor'ev, Ya. Chuzh, B. Martos, K. Pan'kivs'kyi, E. Chykalenko, O. Skoropys-Ioltuchovs'kyi, H. Keller-Chykalenko, S. Drahomaniv, E. Prychod'ko, A. Zhyvotko, Shramchenko, B. Lepkyi, Rev. Danylenko-Danylevs'kyi, R. Genig-Berezovs'kyi, S. Demedchuk, A. Margolin, M. Rudnyts'ka (women's movement), K. Dats'ko, E. Onats'kyi, and others; archives of scholars - Dmytro and Natalia Doroshenko (among their archives is included an especially valuable monograph by D. Doroshenko, Hetman Petro Doroshenko), V. Doroshenko, D. Solovei, L. Chykalenko, N. Polons'ka-Vasylenko, P. Kurinnyi, V. Shuhaevs'kyi, L. Margolin, I. Sweet, L. Bykovs'kyi, V. Pavlovs'kyi, R. Genig-Berezovs'kyi, Rozhin, O. Arkhimovych, and others; archives of writers and poets - large archival collection of V. Vynnychenko, Yu. Klen, T. Os'machka, M. Orest, L. Kovalenko-Ivchenko, E. Malaniuk, O. Liaturyns'ka, D. Humenna, V. Barka, O. Stefanovych, K. Hrynevych, V. Chaplenko, and others. These archives also include the manuscript of the documental work, Khronolohiia zhyttia i tvorchosty Lesi Ukrainky by Olha Kosach-Kryvyniuk, the late sister of Lesia Ukrainka; archives of music-theatrical figures - composer P. Pechenihy-Uhlyts'kyi (holographs of his operas Viy and Vid'ma, compositions on Ukrainian and other themes, symphonic works, photos, programs, and clippings), composers M. Haivorons'kyi, V. Ovcharenko, Rev. H. Pavlovs'kyi, Nedzvids'kyi, and T. Koshyts' (materials about O. Koshyts'); among theatrical figures, the archives of O. Dobrovols'ka and Yo. Hirniak; archives of artists - large archival collections of V. Kyveliuk and V. Tsymbal, archives of the artist, poet-writer, founder of futurism D. Burliuk, and artist L. Gets.

3 Among the archives of Ukrainian organizations and institutions are included: archives of the Military Historical Institute, Union of Writers of Children's Literature (archives of Yu. Tyshchenko and Hoshovs'kyi); materials devoted to Sichovi Striltsi with valuable photographs relating to World War I (ca. 5,000) and other items; archives of the Ukrainian Artists Movement; archives of the editorial office of the weekly Nashe Zhyttia (Augsburg, Germany); archives of various camp, school and sports institutions. Of special note are numerous archival materials pertaining to life in DP camps after World War II, including documents and photographs which depict Ukrainian social and cultural life. Materials pertinent to the activities of Ukrainian-American organizations are systematically collected by the archives.

4 The numerous archival materials pertaining to the history of Ukrainian immigration in the U.S. are systematically supplemented with materials by the Academy's Commission for the Study of the History of the Ukrainian Immigration in the U.S.

5 Art work includes sketches for theatrical productions by Ia. Anchutin and graphic designs of Ia. Hnizdovs'kyi and O. Kul'chyts'ka, plus numerous paintings, drawings, pieces of sculpture, and sewn/embroidered items.

Restriction: Permission to use the archives may be requested by writing to the director of the archives at the Academy.

Finding Aid: V. Miiakovs'kyi, O. Voloshyn, T. Ivanivs'ka, Muzei-Archiv im. Dmytra Antonovycha (1945-1965). New York, UVAN, 1967, 12 pp.

NY 96
UNION THEOLOGICAL SEMINARY
3041 Broadway
New York, New York 10027
(212-662-7100 ext 276)

Armenian manuscripts. Four Gospels, A.D. 1293 (Cage Auburn CB58.5.1607), hymnal, A.D. 1646 (Arm. MS. No. 1), four Gospels, 15th-16th c. (Arm. MS. No. 2), liturgical service book, 15th-16th c. (Arm. MS. No. 3), Nerses Snorhali's works, sermons, and other texts, 15th-16th c. (Arm. MS. No. 4), and a phylactery, 17th-18th c. (Arm. MS. No. 5).

NY 97
UNITED NATIONS ARCHIVES
345 Park Avenue South
12th Floor
New York, New York 10010
(212-754-8685)

Though established in 1945, at a historic meeting in San Francisco, the United Nations has a "pre-history" dating to 1942. Some of the most important records of the organization come from these earliest years. The archives, like the United Nations as a whole, occupied its permanent headquarters in New York in 1952. The massive holdings of the repository currently total over 20,600 ft. of materials, mainly generated by the Secretariat.

NEW YORK - UNITED NATIONS ARCHIVES NY 97

1 Records of the United Nations Relief and Rehabilitation Administration (UNRRA), 1943-49. Established 9 November 1943, with 44 nations signing an agreement for the relief of war victims in areas under the control of any of the "united nations." Headquarters of the UNRRA became Washington, D.C.; a European Regional Office was established in London; and mission posts took up local work in the territories receiving aid. 4 of the most important UNRRA sets of records are:

2 Records of the UNRRA Headquarters. 1,089 ft. Reports, office files, account books, correspondence, and miscellaneous documents fall into 7 subdivisions (e.g., executive offices, bureau of administration, bureau of supply, bureau of areas). Interspersed throughout are materials on the Ukraine and Byelorussia; the total number of relevant items and/or their percentage cannot be stated.

3 Records of the European Regional Office. 320 ft. This office's records are of the same kind as headquarters' and are divided into 4 groups. Ukrainian and Byelorussian items are again interspersed.

4 Byelorussia Mission, 1946-47. 10 ft. Established in Minsk in April 1946, the mission was concerned exclusively with the receipt and distribution of relief supplies. Representatives of the Byelorussian government in Washington and London handled procurements and final disposition of supplies. A port office at Odessa also served the Ukraine mission. Largely completing its program by late 1946, and reorganized with fewer personnel, the Byelorussian mission closed 30 June 1947. The records are in 3 subdivisions: office of the chief, including subject files, monthly narrative reports, working papers, and correspondence; finance and administration; and supply.

5 Ukraine Mission, 1946-47. 5 ft. The mission, under Marshall MacDuffie, reached Kiev 20 March 1946. As with Byelorussia, the Ukrainian government negotiated through representatives in London and Washington and concerned itself with procuring and distributing supplies. The mission assisted in receiving and disposing of material. It also tried to publicize the program, making a newsreel film of activities and meeting with the newspapermen (see the separate entry for UN Headquarters--Film Footage Library). V. V. Khomyak was the mission's liaison with the Ukrainian Council of Ministers, headed at this time by N. S. Khrushchev. The mission helped to transfer $189 million worth of goods to the Ukraine. The records are in 3 groups, chief of mission, finance, and supply.

6 The following general archival groups contain, interspersed throughout, materials which bear on Soviet participation in UN activities:

UN Conference on International Organization, San Francisco, 1945. Working papers, correspondence, drafts, notes, verbatim minutes, delegations' comments on the Dumbarton Oaks Proposals.

UN Development Programme (UNDP). Includes some non-current registry files on operational assistance, plus files and working papers on evaluation of projects and reports, 1950-67. Closed to outside researchers for up to 25 years.

UN Preparatory Commission, 1945-46. Summaries of meetings (of the commission and of its committees), working papers, Secretariat correspondence and cables.

UN Secretariat. Registry files from all departments, since 1946 (especially the general ledgers); non-registry records, 1946-72, particularly for the secretary-general's office, the executive office, General Assembly affairs sections, the Office for Special Political Affairs, and the Protocol Section. These records are closed to outside investigators until a time limit (up to 20 years) expires.

Restrictions: Open to the public are those archives and records that were originally public at the time of their creation and those that are more than 20 years old and are not subject to restrictions imposed by the secretary-general. Inquire about specific holdings.

Finding Aids: For each holding there is a variety of unpublished finding aids such as inventories or guides.

NY 98
VISUAL MATERIALS LIBRARY
DEPARTMENT OF PUBLIC INFORMATION
UNITED NATIONS HEADQUARTERS
Room 814, Radio and Visual Service
New York, New York 10017
(212-754-6967)

UNRRA in USSR. Film, 1946-47, 6 reels. In the winter of 1946-47, the Ukrainian mission of the UN Relief and Rehabilitation Administration arranged for Julian Bryan and Peter Hopkinson to make a newsreel film to publicize the mission's activities. More than 16 reels of motion picture film resulted. Edited and condensed, selections appeared as The March of Time newsreel "The Russia Nobody Knows" (released in May 1947). Not all the original footage shot is in the Visual Materials Library. Covers the Ukraine, Dniepr River, a collective farm, Byelorussia, Minsk, Kiev, and Odessa. (Roll nos. 2-15 to 2-20)

Note: There is much more film material relating to the USSR in the UN scattered in various holdings of the library which could not be detailed in this entry.

Restrictions: Inquire at the library.

NY 99
UPI PHOTOLIBRARY
220 East 42nd Street
New York, New York 10017
(212-682-0400)

The Photolibrary maintains an extensive collection of photographs pertaining to pre- and post-revolutionary Russia. Use of the Photolibrary is limited to serious researchers who intend to publish its photographs.

NY 100
US-USSR TRADE AND ECONOMIC COUNCIL
1211 Avenue of the Americas
New York, New York 10030
(212-840-5500)

This non-profit organization was founded 1 September 1973 as a result of the protocol signed between the U.S. and the Soviet Union, June 1973, to promote trade. It publishes its own Council Journal and is composed, on the U.S. side, of private companies engaged in or wishing to encourage trade with the USSR. Correspondence, reports, photos, and office files in its archive are limited to use by members of the Council. The Council does offer, however, limited facilities to outside researchers.

NY 101
ARCHIVAL SECTION
HEADQUARTERS LIBRARY, 20th FLOOR
WESTERN ELECTRIC
222 Broadway
New York, New York 10038
(212-571-5115)

Western Electric's business dealings with Russia began in 1897 with the opening of a branch store in St. Petersburg. The same year it formed a partnership company with N. C. Heisler and Company in the same city. In 1925 Western Electric sold its foreign business to International Telephone and Telegraph. The records for Russian operations are very incomplete and currently not available to the public. The company's publication Western Electric News, however, is available to researchers; it contains articles on tsarist and Soviet Russia in the years 1912-25. Unpublished index cards in the library detail the holdings.

NY 102
ARCHIVES
YIVO INSTITUTE FOR JEWISH RESEARCH, INC.
1048 Fifth Avenue
New York, New York 10028
(212-535-6700)

1 YIVO, founded in 1925 as the Yiddish Scientific Institute in Vilno, has been in New York since 1940. Its extensive archival holdings today represent a major resource for study of the Russian Empire and Soviet Union. Materials are arranged in record groups, ca. 650 at present. The listing that follows is in numerical order to conform to this arrangement. These collections are only a selection, by no means exhaustive, of Russian-related holdings at YIVO.

2 RG 2. Lithuanian Jewish Communities. Records, 1844-1940, 40 ft. Primarily from the time of the Jewish National Autonomy in Lithuania, 1919-26, and from the Ministry for Jewish Affairs. Also, much material from local communities. A small amount relates to 1844-1918 and 1927-40. Includes records of the Jewish National Council, 1918-26; materials on political life and elections, the first conference of Jewish communities in Lithuania, 1920, and Jewish rights in Lithuania; records of the Historical-Ethnographic Society (Kovno) 1922-40; photographs; and other material on school systems, youth, theater, cultural activities, and professional-economic activities. Unpublished inventory.

3 RG 4. YIVO Collection of Autobiographies of Jewish Youth, 1932-39, 7.5 ft. YIVO-sponsored contests produced ca. 375 autobiographies of young Jewish men and women, aged 16-22, living mainly in Poland and Lithuania before 1939 (arranged geographically by author's place of origin). Some include correspondence, diaries, etc. sent in by the participants. Also, material relating to the contests and the YIVO youth research division. Unpublished inventory with name index and Moses Kligsberg's published guide, 1965.

4 RG 10. Jewish Community Board in Vilno. Records, 1820s-1940, ca. 11 ft. Minutes of meetings, correspondence, reports, financial records, printed matter, and miscellaneous documents relating to the activities of the Vilno Tsedakah Gedolah, 1844-1918, and to the Naye Kehilla, 1919-40--organizations that succeeded the Kahal (community administration) abolished by the government. Includes correspondence with the Lithuanian government, Jewish National Council in Lithuania, and Russian government. Unpublished inventory.

5 RG 12. Jewish Community Council in Minsk. Records, 1825-1921, ca. 3 ft. Includes registers of births, weddings, and deaths within the Jewish population of Minsk, Byelorussia; membership books from schools

and beth-midroshim; registers and correspondence pertaining to taxation of various economic strata of the Jewish population; and files relating to the Council's activities concerning the law on Jewish recruits to the army.

6 RG 22. Khevra Mefitzei Haskolo (Society for the Propagation of the Enlightenment). Records, 1909-38, ca. 2 ft. Founded in 1863 to unite "enlightened" groups among Russian Jewry to stem criticism of Jewish separatism in education and culture. Correspondence, reports, financial records, minutes of meetings, printed matter, posters, and other documents. Concerns cultural activities, schools, and World War I. Includes correspondence with the Russian government, 1909-11, and with towns around Vilno, 1909-18.

7 RG 24. Rabbinical School and Teachers' Seminary, Vilno. Records, 1847-1914, ca. 18 ft. Correspondence, reports, memoranda, financial records, and other documents. Curriculum of the Rabbinical School, established to train teachers for government schools for Jewish children, included secular subjects and Judaic subjects. In 1873 the seminary was converted into a teacher's institute only. Contains correspondence with the Ministry of Education's office for the province of White Russia; materials on courses, administration, and school activities; and much data on candidates for admittance.

8 RG 30. YIVO Vilno Collection on Russia and the Soviet Union, 1845-1930s, ca. 6 ft. Correspondence, reports, clippings, posters, documents, and printed matter relating to Jewish (and non-Jewish) affairs. Materials on Jewish political activities, 1845-1921; records relating to Birobidjan; government ukases and edicts relating to Jewish life; police reports about Jews and non-Jews under police custody, 1870-1911; materials about Jews in the Russian military, 1885-1915; police documents on Polish revolutionaries, 1863-70; and general records about different localities in Russia, 1902-17.

9 RG 46. Lithuanian Consistory of the Russian Orthodox Church. Records, 1807-1900, ca. 4.5 ft. Consists of 196 files for 290 persons, mostly women, residing in the former Pale of Settlement, applying to the Consistory for conversion to the Greek Orthodox faith. A few are cases of conversion of entire families, minors, former students of the Vilno Rabbinical School, Jewish soldiers, etc., and 2 are of converted soldiers (Cantonists?) who asked permission to return to Judaism (forbidden by the law). Unpublished inventory in Yiddish.

10 RG 80-89. Elias Tcherikower Archive. Described individually infra (not in its entirety).

11 RG 80. Central Archives of the Editorial Committee on Collection and Investigation of the Materials Relating to the Pogroms in the Ukraine. Records, 1802-1924, 61 microfilm rolls. Records relating to the daily operation of the Central Archive as well as documents, correspondence, minutes of meetings, manuscripts, memoranda, reports, etc. pertaining to the pogroms, 1903-21, and to Jewish life. Materials on the Kishinev pogrom, 1903; effects of the 1919-21 pogroms on various cities; lists of victims, 1919-21; statistics on relief work in the Ukraine; photos of destruction and victims; E. Tcherikower's notes on pogroms; records of official Jewish organizations (Jewish National Council, Jewish Ministry, Jewish National Assembly) and other Jewish organizations (United Zionist Labor Movement in Russia and various Soviet Jewish groups); historical documents; letters sent to the tsars; materials on the Beylis trial and Schwarzbard trial; memoirs of Shmuel Rabinovich, 1936-37; correspondence of the Eastern Jewish Historical Archive in Berlin, 1919-24, with individuals and organizations; and many other records of the editorial office. Inventory.

12 RG 81. Elias Tcherikower (1881-1943). Papers, 1903-63, 45 microfilm rolls. Historian, secretary and founder of the Eastern Jewish Historical Archive in Kiev and Berlin, founding member of YIVO, chairman of the Historical Section and Research Secretary of YIVO. Manuscripts, notes, correspondence, reports, clippings, and documents relating to his writings, 1910-40, plus personal correspondence of his family. Subjects covered: World War I and Jews in Russia; the Chmielnicki massacres, 1648-49; Jewish historiography; the Society for the Propagation of the Enlightenment; Aaron Liberman, history of the Jews in the Ukraine; various trials of Jews, including some involving the Protocols of the Elders of Zion; and the Jewish Colonization Association. Correspondents include Alfred de Ginzburg, Simon Dubnow, and Ilya Dijeur. Inventory.

13 RG 83. Marc Ratner. Papers, 1906-13, 3 microfilm rolls. Co-founder of SERP (Sotsialisticheskaya Yevreyskaya Rabochaya Partiya), the Jewish Socialist Workers' Party, in 1906. Correspondence, reports, minutes of meetings, circulars, manuscripts, and financial records relating to the activities of the Foreign Committee of SERP. The Party was based on a synthesis of nationalist and socialist ideas; after 1917 it joined with the Zionist Socialists, establishing the United Jewish Socialist Workers' Party. Correspondents include Ber Borochov, Z. Goldin, Pinkhas Dubinsky, Shimon Aronson, Virgilia Verdaro, Alexander Ziskind, Chaim Zhitlovsky, Michel Levitan, Yehuda Novakovsky, and Misha Fabricant. Inventory.

14 RG 84. Maxim Vinawer (1862-1926). Papers, 1918-23, 4 rolls. Lawyer, Kadet Party leader, historian, foreign minister in the Crimean regional government, 1918-19, and editor of the Yevreyskaya Tribuna, Paris, 1920s.

Correspondence, memoranda, reports, documents, and clippings. Includes records of the Partiya Narodnoy Svobody (Party of National Liberty), such as his correspondence with P. N. Miliukov and other members of the central committee of the Party about current political affairs; inter-office communications about his position as minister of foreign affairs in the Crimean regional government; and correspondence with, inter alia, the Institut d'Etudes Slaves, Chaim Zhitlovsky, the Conférence Politique Russe, N. Tchaikovsky, M. Rostovstev, and D. Merezhkowsky. Inventory.

15 RG 85. Sholom Schwarzbard (1886-1938). Papers, 1917-38, 4 microfilm rolls. Jewish political activist and writer who assassinated Simon Petlyura in May 1926. Poems about his assassination of Petlyura, poems by Anna Schwarzbard, personal documents, clippings, handwritten memoirs, typescripts entitled "At War with Myself," and correspondence with groups and individuals such as YIVO, the French ambassador to Moscow, Israel Ostroff, Noah Prilucki, Zalman Kalmanovitch, and Anna Schwarzbard. Inventory.

16 RG 86. A. Charash. Papers, 1912-18, 2 rolls. Doctor of sociology, author, and member of the Zionist Socialist Workers' Party and other groups. Includes records of the ZSWP, such as resolutions about émigrés returning to Russia through Switzerland and Germany, 1917-18, lists of members of the United Jewish Socialist Workers' Party and of its Emigration Committee, applications with photographs, minutes of meetings and circulars of the Western European League of the Party; and correspondence with Rafael Asch, Z. Gordin, Yitzchak Gorsky, Pinchas Dubinsky, Y. Zakalnik, H. Manilevitsch, Aron Syngalowski, and others. Some material on Russian-Jewish émigré students in the West. Inventory.

17 RG 87. Simon Dubnow (1860-1941). Papers, 1632-1938, 8 rolls. Historian, political writer, and educator. Community records from Mstislavl (his birthplace), 1760-1895, Pinczow, 1632-1740, Piotrowice, 1726-1809, and the Burial Society of Stary Bychow, 1686-1869--all original pinkeysim (record books); copies of record books of Tykocin, 1769-77, Zabludow, 1650-1783, Birze, 1755-96, and Dubno, 1670-71; partial records of the Lublin community from the 18th c., and other communities; documents from blood libel trials in Miedzyrzec, 1816, and Bobowno, 1829; documents from Nowa Uszyca, 1839-40; documents concerning restrictions, privileges, and other matters issued by East European rulers and governments for Jews in various localities; minutes of a commission to publish documents relating to blood libel trials in Russia, 1919-20; material on Gzerot Takh-Tat and Jewish massacres of 1648-49 during the Chmielnicki uprising; copies of archival documents of the Russian Ministry of Justice and Senate, 1799-1800; reports and documents pertaining to Russian pogroms of the 1880s, Kishinev pogrom, 1903, Homel pogrom, 1903, and pogroms of October 1905 and in Bialystok, 1906; Dubnow family papers, including material of Rabbi Benzion Dubnow, Simon's grandfather; and correspondence with, among others, Shmuel Alexandrovich, 1896, Yitschak Antonovsky, 1897, Chaim Zhitlovsky, Maxim Vinaver, 1922-23, Shmuel Silberstein, and Chaim Zuskind. Inventory (NUCMC 60-2386).

18 RG 88. Gregori Gurevitch (Gershon Badanes) (1852-1929). Papers, 1880-1929, 2 rolls. Early Russian-Jewish revolutionary, subsequently disillusioned and became a Jewish communal leader. Correspondence with Pavel Axelrod, 1925, Jacob Lestchinsky, 1929, N. Grinberg, 1924-28, N. Meisel, 1922, the Archives of the Russian Revolution, 1924-27, and others; materials about pogroms, including reports and memoirs, 1917-19; manuscripts and notes in Russian, ca. 100 pp., about individuals and political affairs; and printed matter, including his Yiddish translation of Mr. Aldanov's "St. Helena." Inventory.

19 RG 89. Baron Horace (Naftali Herz) Guenzburg (1833-1909). Papers, 1850-95, 2 rolls. Banker, philanthropist, head of the Jewish Committee in St. Petersburg, and chairman of the Jewish Colonization Association in Russia. Leader of the Khevra Mefitse Haskoleh (Society for the Propagation of Enlightenment), pertaining to which there is correspondence and minutes of meetings. Other correspondence between Guenzburg and various Russian authorities about unjust conscription of Jews into the Russian army, about the improvement of the political and legal situation of Russian Jews, with Jewish journalists about the Jewish press in Russia, with Jewish personalities in Russia about educational problems, and with others, especially rabbis of Russia and Poland concerning the creation of a rabbinical seminary in Russia; also, petitions to the government about Russian Jews' situation, notes on their legal situation and on educational activities among them, records, 5-22 October 1869, of the Vilno Committee for Improvement of the Situation of Russian Jews, and materials relating to anti-Jewish propaganda in Russia. Inventory.

20 RG 205. Kalman Marmor (1879-1956). Papers, ca. 1880-1952, ca. 37 ft. Yiddish writer, literary critic, editor, and lecturer. Member at various times of different political movements and parties, including The World Union of Poalei Zion, Communist Party of the U.S.A., and Mishagola (Russia). Diaries, correspondence, manuscripts, typescripts, clippings, posters, notes, identity and membership cards, photos, and bibliographical cards; about half the papers are arranged. Includes his diaries, journals, and portions of his autobiography (Lebens-geshikhte); family correspondence, from his wife, 1897-1909, and to his wife, 1899-1930; general correspondence, several

thousand letters, 1900-1950s; his manuscripts in Yiddish and Hebrew on various topics; materials on Joseph Bovshover (1873-1915), Yiddish poet; materials on Jacob Gordin (1853-1909), Yiddish playwright; papers of Morris Vinchevsky (1856-1932), Yiddish and Hebrew writer, socialist leader (traveled to Russia); materials on Aaron Liberman (1845-1880), early Jewish socialist; materials on Jacob Milch (1866-1945), Yiddish writer; materials on David Edelstadt (1866-1892), Yiddish poet, including his Russian poetry and letters to his sister Sonya; manuscripts of many writers, including M. Vinchevsky, D. Ignatov, Chaim Zhitlovsky, and Zalman Reisen. The unarranged portion of the papers contains material relating to the CPUSA, Friends of Soviet Russia, 1920s-1930s, Marmor's stay in Russia, 1931-35, and many other groups and subjects. Unpublished partial inventory in Yiddish (NUCMC 61-12).

21 RG 208. Chaim Zhitlovsky (1861-1943). Papers, 1886-1943, 30 ft. Russian-born philosopher, radical, and literary figure. He was a theoretician of socialism and Jewish nationalism in the Diaspora, one of the founders of the Jewish Socialist Workers' Party (SERP), and a member of the Socialist Revolutionary Party. Emigrated to the U.S. in 1908. Includes family and general correspondence, manuscripts of Zhitlovsky, his first wife, Vera Lonova, and other individuals, photographs, and clippings. Some materials and documents relate to the SR Party. Ca. 33% of the collection is in Russian. Unpublished finding aid.

22 RG 215. Berlin Collection, 1931-45, 24 ft. Records from the Reichsministerium für Volkaufklärung und Propaganda and the Reichskommisariat für das Ostland (i.e., for occupied territories in the East). Correspondence, memoranda, reports, minutes of meetings, clippings, documents, and printed matter, mainly relating to the Jewish question. Includes directives about German agricultural colonization in Eastern territories, 1940; instructions on policy for treatment of Jews in occupied territories, 1943; correspondence between the Propaganda Ministry and the Ministry for the Occupied Eastern Territories, plus an organizational scheme of the latter, 1941; German soldier's account of an attack on a Ukrainian village, 1941; memorandum of a high Soviet officer on the reasons for stubborn Russian resistance, 1944; reports on the morale of the Red Army; materials concerning the church in Latvia, Lithuania, and White Russia; reports and correspondence on the situation of the Jews in Estonia; letters from Ukrainians to Hitler, 1932 and 1941; list of 118 leading personalities of the Ukrainian emigration; and much more material on the Baltic countries, White Russia, Poland, Ukraine, and the USSR as occupied territories. Card catalogue in English and draft of detailed catalogue.

23 RG 220. Gershon Epstein. Collection, 16th-20th c., ca. 4.5 ft. YIVO's principal collector in France and Germany after World War II. Includes rare manuscript Judaica from Western and Eastern Europe, some relating to Jewish folklore. Unpublished inventory.

24 RG 223. Abraham Sutzkever-Shmerke Katcherginski Collection, 1806-1945, 7 ft. Jewish writers from Vilno active in Vilno ghetto life and in anti-Nazi resistance, 1941-45. Correspondence, manuscripts, reports, circulars, posters, and documents relating to Jewish life in Vilno from 1806 to the extermination of the ghetto. Includes 1942 map of the ghetto; diaries of Zelig Kalmanowitch, Herman Kruk, Yitzchok Rudashevsky, 1941-43; materials on the history, culture, schools, theater, health system, housing, etc. of the ghetto, ca. 1941-43; photographs; historical documents rescued from the destroyed Vilno YIVO; manuscript diary of Theodore Herzl; manuscripts of Simon Dubnow, Chaim Zhitlovsky, and others; pinkassim (community record books) of Jewish communities of Vilno and Shkud, 17th-19th c.; and much more. Unpublished inventory in Yiddish (NUCMC 61-3392).

25 RG 270. Union of Russian Jews. Records, 1945-60, 14 ft. Fraternal organization based in New York providing relief for relatives in the Soviet Union after World War II. General correspondence and minutes of meetings of the Executive Committee; correspondence with Soviet Jews; index of persons contacted in the USSR; manuscript on Russian Jewry, 1860-1917, and Soviet Jewry, 1918-61; and other correspondence and financial records.

26 RG 309. Leon Baratz (b. 1871). Papers, 1920s-1954, ca. .5 ft. Jewish-Russian lawyer, teacher, and publicist (pen name L. German) in Kiev and Western Europe. Writings, handwritten and typed, on such subjects as Jewish conditions in Soviet Russia, Zionism, the Diaspora, and the World Jewish Congress. Also, clippings, letters, autobiography, and materials on his father, Herman Baratz, historian and public figure in Kiev.

27 RG 335.2. American Joint Reconstruction Foundation (AJRF). Records, 1920-39, ca. 12 ft. Established as a joint effort of the Joint Distribution Committee and the Jewish Colonization Association in 1924 to aid economic reconstruction of Jewish communities in Eastern Europe after World War I by establishing cooperative credit institutions, commercial banks, and workers' cooperatives and rebuilding destroyed housing. Correspondence, financial reports, and reports on the situation in various communities from AJRF offices, divided into 19 series. Reports on Russia in the AJRF general records, 1921-28 (series 1); on Ukraine, 1920 (2); on Lithuania, 1920-25 (4); on Latvia and Estonia, 1922-26 (5); and on Agro-Joint, from the Moscow office, etc.,

1925-37 (12). Also, clippings, photos, and other material. Inventory.

28 RG 335.3. American Jewish Joint Distribution Committee. War Orphans Bureau. Records, 1919-23, 7.5 ft. on 14 microfilm rolls. Organized relief work for Jewish orphans mainly in Eastern Europe. Includes ca. 390 individual case files, correspondence, disposition reports, geographical files, internal records, and information on adoption in the U.S. Indexes by name of orphan and by foster parents' name.

29 RG 335.7. American Jewish Joint Distribution Committee, New York. Landsmanschaften Department. Records, 1937-40 and 1945-50, 15 ft. Memoranda, correspondence, reports, etc. Landsmanschaften are benevolent associations of emigrants from the same town. The Landsmanschaften Fraternal Division was originally created in 1919 to generate aid from the associations for their native towns. Discontinued in 1924, it was re-established in 1937 to aid the AJDC reconstruction program in Eastern Europe. Substantial portion relates to Russian Jewish localities. Unpublished inventory.

30 RG 348. Lucien Wolf and David Mowshowitch. Papers, 1890s-1950s, ca. 14 ft. Mowshowitch (1887-1957) was on the Jewish Board of Deputies in England, secretary to Lucien Wolf and later secretary of the Foreign Department of the Board of Deputies. Wolf (1857-1930) was a publicist, historian, and secretary of the Joint Foreign Committee formed by the Board of Deputies and the Anglo-Jewish Association. Correspondence, private papers, reports, minutes of meetings, manuscripts, etc. concerning the Joint Foreign Committee, the political situation of Jews in various countries, Wolf's work on the Paris Peace Conference, and the lives of both men. Includes Wolf's lectures on English-Russian relations, his correspondence with Prof. Simon Ashkenasy, 1921, and Maxim Vinaver (Vinawer), 1917; documents and correspondence pertaining to Soviet Jewry; materials relating to the Beilis Trial; Vladimir Jobotinsky's appeal about military service; and Mowshowitch's papers, including items on Russian anti-Semitism and translations of Russian poems into Yiddish. Published inventory in Yiddish; unpublished inventory in English.

31 RG 358. Joseph A. Rosen (1887-1949). Agro-Joint director files, 1921-38, 16 ft. Agronomist, leader of Jewish agricultural colony projects, and director of the Agro-Joint project for Jewish agricultural colonies in the USSR. Agro-Joint (American Jewish Joint Agricultural Corporation) was established by the American Joint Distribution Committee (JDC) as its operating agency in the USSR in 1924 to develop the land settlement of Russian Jews on a large scale. It also conducted general relief and professional training and worked for industrialization. Discontinued in the USSR in 1938, dissolved in 1954. Reports, surveys, financial records, minutes of meetings, correspondence, maps, and clippings. Includes various agreements with the Soviet government and with other relief organizations (YMCA, American Relief Administration); minutes of NKZ (Commissariat of Agriculture) meeting on results of JDC colonization work, 1923; essay by Louis Fischer, "The Forward to the Soil Movement of Jews in Russia" (1925); letter from Moscow to Felix M. Warburg on the worsening situation of Soviet Jews, 1927; Agro-Joint Main Office (AMO) annual and periodic reports, and files; records of the Agro-Joint Agricultural Department, including statistical summaries, 1924-38, of Jewish agricultural settlements in 10 western Soviet provinces; regional files for southern Russia (Crimea, Ukraine), White Russia, Moscow, etc.; and much more. Unpublished inventory (NUCMC 60-1116).

32 RG 366. Isaac N. Steinberg (1888-1957). Papers, 1910s-1963, 25 ft. Russian-Jewish political writer, leader of the Left Socialist Revolutionary Party during the 1917 Revolution, minister of Justice in the first Bolshevik government, leader of the Jewish Territorialist Movement and of the Freeland League for Jewish Territorial Colonization, and founding member of the YIVO Institute. Includes correspondence, manuscripts, and typescripts of books by him and others pertaining to Russia and the Russian Revolution (e.g., When I Was a People's Commissar), manuscripts on Maria Spiridonova, materials from the Left Socialist Revolutionary Party (correspondence, statements and resolutions by the party's Central Committee in Russia, 1918-20, and photos of some members); Steinberg's personal papers; family correspondence; manuscripts and typescripts of books and articles, essays, lectures, notes, etc. by Steinberg and others; diaries, calendars, photos; materials on the Freeland League; and material on Jewish colonization efforts. Unpublished inventory (NUCMC 60-2362).

33 RG 405. Dr. Mendel Sudarski (1885-1951) and Alta Sudarski. Papers, 1938-58, 5 ft. Physician, Jewish communal leader in Kaunas, Lithuania, chairman of the Federation of Lithuanian Jews in New York, and author; and his wife, active in Yiddish cultural organizations and in relief efforts for Jewish refugees in Shanghai and for Russian Jews. Correspondence, manuscripts, notes, and some photos pertaining to the book Lite (Lithuania, vol. 1, New York, 1951), which he co-edited; and correspondence and receipts for food and clothes packages for Jews in the USSR, 1950s.

34 RG 406. Julius Borenstein-Leah Eisenberg Collection on Early Jewish Migration, 1868-1930,

ca. 3.5 ft., 5 microfilm reels. Materials on the history of Jewish immigration, mainly 1860s-1914. Includes items on the reaction of European and American Jewish organizations to the persecution of Russian Jews and their efforts to assist emigration of these Jews to America. Relates to such organizations as the Comité de Secours pour les Israélites, Alliance Israélite Universelle, Deutsches Central Komitee für die russischen Juden, Baron de Hirsch Institute, Russo-Jewish Committee, and Jewish Colonization Association. Unpublished inventory.

35 RG 421. Daniel Charney (1888-1959). Papers, ca. 1920s-1959, ca. 6.5 ft. Yiddish writer and journalist. Includes his correspondence with such individuals as S. Dubnow, S. Nepomnyashtchy, Barukh Vladeck, and Shmuel Niger (the last 2 his brothers); family correspondence; his manuscripts; photos; correspondence of Vladeck (1886-1938) with Eduard Bernstein, Karl Kautsky, S. Asch, Marc Chagall, and others; and Charney's diaries, 1935-36, notebooks, and personal documents. List of correspondents.

36 RG 500. Alexander Pomerantz (1901-1965). Papers, 1920s-1960s, 2.5 ft. Yiddish writer and bibliographer, member of the faculty of the Institute for Jewish Proletarian Culture at the Ukrainian Academy of Science, Kiev. Comprises correspondence, including letters from Soviet-Yiddish writers (I. Fefer, M. Erik, and Abraham Kahan); correspondence with Yiddish cultural and political organizations in the U.S.; materials on the Institute for Jewish Proletarian Culture in Kiev (his notes for lectures, diplomas, clippings); notes for the biography of Max Erik, historian of Yiddish literature; manuscripts and notes on executed Jewish writers in the USSR; Pomerantz's published and unpublished articles in manuscript; correspondence and other materials concerning Grodno and the Grodno landsmanschaften in various countries; and other matter.

37 RG 557. Reichsicherheitshauptamt (RSHA) (Reich Central Security Office). Einsatzgruppen (task forces) in the USSR. Records, 1941-42, 2.25 ft. Task forces or mobile liquidation units of the RSHA that followed the army to carry out special tasks in various countries. Includes top secret reports of the chiefs of Security Police and the SD in the Soviet Union containing detailed information on task forces' activities, and reports from the occupied Eastern territories (Ostgebieten) by commanders of the task forces stationed in the USSR concerning anti-partisan operations and other problems of the Security Police. Card index.

38 RG 587. Isaac A. Hourwich (1860-1924). Papers, 1896-1924, ca. 4.5 ft. Yiddish, Russian, and English publicist, economist, lawyer, lecturer, and one of the organizers of the first American Jewish Congress in 1918. Manuscripts, documents, reports, minutes of meetings, memoranda, correspondence, etc. pertaining to Russia and the labor movement, the fifth Congress of the Jewish Labor Bund, 1903, the Russian Social-Revolutionary Party, and American Jewish affairs. Also, microfilm of his unfinished memoirs, published in the weekly Die Freie Arbeiter Stimme. Unpublished inventory.

39 RG 601. Leon Feinberg (1897-1969). Papers, 1920s-1968, ca. 14.5 ft. Yiddish journalist, poet, novelist, editor, and translator. Correspondence; writings; manuscripts of Feinberg, S. N. Feinberg (his father), Mani-Leib, and Moshe Nadir; speeches and lectures; and clippings, some of which relate to Russia, where Feinberg lived for part of his life. Unpublished inventory.

40 RG 713. Herman Bernstein (1876-1935). Papers, 1897-1935, 29 ft. Journalist, author, diplomat, and political leader. Includes correspondence, 1908-35, with many prominent cultural figures (e.g., the family of Leo Tolstoi, Leonid Andreyev and his wife) and other family/general correspondence; literary manuscripts; financial records; photographs, some of the Russian army in World War I; documents; translations of works by Tolstoi, Andreyev, M. Gorkii, and A. Chekhov; interviews (1 with Tolstoi); and clippings. Also, news dispatches from Russia and the Paris Peace Conference, filed when he was a correspondent for the New York Herald, 1917-20; materials concerning his libel suit against Henry Ford for publishing the Protocols of the Elders of Zion; and other items relating to the Russian Revolution, Russian Jews, pogroms, and Jewish journalism. Unpublished finding aid.

41 RG 725. Mendel Osherowitch (1887-1965). Papers, 1920s-1967, 10 ft. Yiddish journalist, poet, novelist, historian, organizer of the Federation of Ukrainian Jews in America (Association to Perpetuate the Memory of Ukrainian Jews), and editor of a book on Jews in the Ukraine. Correspondence, manuscripts, typescripts, photographs, printed matter, clippings, etc. Correspondents include Sholem Asch, Salo Baron, Albert Einstein, Aaron Glantz-Leyeles, Jacob Lestchinsky, Jacob Shatzky, Zalman Reisin, Abraham Sutzkever, Alexander Kerensky, and many organizations. Manuscripts and other material relating to the book Yidn in Ukraine; material on the Babi Yar Memorial, 1963, and of the Headquarters of the Russian Fascists, 1932; manuscripts by Abraham Cahan (Kahan), Dov Sadan, Moshe Starkman, and Hillel Rogoff; and other materials. Unpublished inventory.

42 RG 774. Maxim Kovensky Collection, 1906-13, ca. 1 ft. Former member of the Socialist Revolutionary Party in Russia. Contains original flyers and appeals of the Party,

clippings from Russian and Yiddish newspapers about the Socialist Revolutionaries, and typescript declarations of the Party.

Finding Aids: Guide to Major Collections in the YIVO Archives (New York, n.d.) and periodic newsletters entitled "Recent Additions to the YIVO Collections" (1974-present). Most important is the newly completed YIVO Archives Record Group Inventory (unpublished) that provides a full inventory of holdings on the record group level. The preceding descriptions quote verbatim from these registration sheets.

NY 103
ZIONIST ARCHIVES AND LIBRARY
515 Park Avenue
New York, New York 10022
(212-753-2167)

1 At present the archives, founded in 1939 by the Zionist Organization of America and Keren Hayesod, hold a small number of important collections relating to Russian Jews.

2 Zionist Organizations in Russia. 1 box, 12 in., of letters and reports from 1898-1906. This includes correspondence from the first All-Russian Zionist Conference, which was held in Minsk, 22-28 August 1902. In addition there are typed copies of Zionist reports and letters to party members in the Simferopol' and Ekaterinoslav regions 1900-1903. The collection also contains hectographed circular letters to Zionist groups in Moscow, St. Petersburg, Kiev, Lodz, and Vitebsk, Warsaw, Vilna, Kharkov, and Odessa, 1900-1904.

3 ZIMRO (Petrogradskii Kamernyi Ansambl', Obshchestvo Evreiskoi Narodnoi Muzyki). 12 in. In 1918 a chamber music ensemble, ZIMRO, was organized in Petrograd. This group toured Russia, the Urals area, Siberia, China, Japan, America, and Palestine. The collection comprises scrapbooks containing business correspondence, financial accounts, photos, programs, and reviews for the years 1918-19.

4 Photographs. The archives has a collection of photographs of the founders of the state of Israel, some of whom came from the Russian Empire.

NY 104
THE ROCKEFELLER UNIVERSITY ARCHIVES
ROCKEFELLER ARCHIVE CENTER
Pocantico Hills
North Tarrytown, New York 10591
(914-631-4505)

Duncan Arthur MacInnes (1885-1965). Papers, 1926-65, 8 ft. Chemist. A diary, photocopies of newspaper reports, and a mimeographed copy of "Trip to Moscow" by A. L. Nadai all concern his 1945 trip to Moscow to attend the 220th anniversary of the founding of the Russian Academy of Sciences (box 3). Scattered throughout the papers is correspondence that reflects MacInnes' continuing interest in the American Soviet Science Society. Unpublished description and container list (NUCMC 76-695). Note: The finding aids only can also be consulted at the Rockefeller University Archives Office, 1230 York Avenue, New York, New York 10021; telephone: 212-360-1554.

NY 105
MRS. SOPHIE KOULOMZIN--PRIVATE COLLECTION
38 Glen Byron Avenue
Nyack, New York 10960
(914-358-2439)

Mrs. Koulomzin is in possession of the following materials: (a) typewritten memoirs, 1857-88, by her grandfather, Andrei Alexandrovich Sabouroff, minister of education under Alexander II, 22 pp.; (b) private correspondence and memoirs, 564 pp., 1847-1907, by Sabouroff's wife, Mrs. Elizaveta Vladimirovna Sabouroff (Countess Sollohub), the daughter of the writer Vladimir Sollohub; (c) family photographs dating back to Mrs. Koulomzin's grandparents; (d) Mrs. Koulomzin's own 120,000-word memoirs, soon to be published, which deal in part with her contacts with Nicholas Berdyaev, Father Sergius Bulgakov, Father Alexander Eltchaninoff, and St. Vladimir's Seminary, where she worked as a lecturer. Note: A summary of the memoirs is available from Mrs. Koulomzin, 2 pp.

NY 106
REMINGTON ART MUSEUM
303 Washington Street
Ogdensburg, New York 13669

The Museum has a black and white watercolor or wash drawing by Frederic Remington (1861-1909) entitled "The Frontier Guard and the Custom House." The scene depicts the forced departure from Russia, 1892, of Remington and his traveling companion Poultney Bigelow, a writer. Bigelow apparently aroused suspicions by making too many sketches and taking too many notes about Russia for the series of articles he and Remington published in Harper's magazines, 1893-97. Any use or reproduction of the painting requires the written permission of the Museum's Board of Trustees.

NY 107
SHAKER MUSEUM
Old Chatham, New York 12136
(518-794-9100)

1 C. T. Chatfield and C. Lambert Heyniger, Headmaster of Darrow School. 3 letters, written 1949-59, in which Chatfield asserts that preliminary to the Russo-Japanese Peace Conference held in Portsmouth, New Hampshire, 1905, there was a peace conference involving the belligerents held at New Lebanon Shaker Village.

2 Anatoly Dobrynin, Soviet ambassador to the U.S., and R. Meader, Shaker Museum director. 3 letters, exchanged between them, January-June 1969. Meader suggests that C. T. Chatfield (see preceding) confused the Shakers' own peace convention of 1905 (held at New Lebanon Shaker Village) for a pre-conference to the Portsmouth Peace Conference of 1905.

3 Garden Diary (Mt. Lebanon, New York). Entry for December 1882 mentions a Shaker teaching English to young Russian believers.

Restriction: Researchers should make an appointment a few days in advance.

NY 108
ALEXANDER TARASSOV--PRIVATE COLLECTION
17 Old Mill Road
Poughkeepsie, New York
(914-462-3082)

Alexander Tarassov was a high school teacher of the Russian language in the Soviet Union before World War II. His book, Sotsial'naia religiia, was published in 2 parts, privately, in this country. The collection consists of the manuscript of this book. Researchers must obtain Mr. Tarassov's permission to use the materials.

NY 109
FRANCIS FITZ RANDOLPH RARE BOOK ROOM, BOX 20
VASSAR COLLEGE LIBRARY
Poughkeepsie, New York 12601
(914-452-7000 x 2135)

1 Armenian Manuscripts. Leaf from the epistle of Paul, 15th c., and 2 ll. from a lectionary, 1671.

2 Russian Manuscripts. Illustrated leaf from a Russian collection of Bible stories, ca. 1775, and illustrated leaf from a book of Russian holiday hymns, ca. 1790.

3 Leo Tolstoi (1828-1910). Correspondence, 1892-1908, 21 items. Russian writer and moralist. 15 ALS and 3 LS from Count Tolstoi to Ernest Howard Crosby, American social reformer, 9 January 1896 (?)-11 February 1908; and 3 ALS from Sophie Tolstoi to Crosby, 1892-94.

NY 110
THE AMERICAN BAPTIST HISTORICAL SOCIETY
1106 South Goodman Street
Rochester, New York 14620
(716-473-1740)

Correspondence and reports of missionaries to Russia, 1884-1929, sent to the American Baptist Foreign Mission Society. 2 folders, 1884-95; 3 folders, 1900-19; and 5 folders, 1920-29. Many letters are requests for financial assistance from missionaries in various parts of Russia; they contain vivid descriptions of the difficulties confronting the missionaries, including inflation, illness, family stress, and political persecution. The final item in the collection, 1929, describes the acute political repression of the day and includes a list of missionaries who had been imprisoned or had become "insane." The list of missionaries represented by correspondence: V. Pavloff, Sembal Bagdasarianz, Patvacan Tarainz, Herman Fast, A. R. Schiewe, F. Kiefer, Joh. Kepley, Julius Herrmann, M. Kerhe, J. Wolff, J. Blumberg, P. Marnowrky (?), Fried. Wirk, Robert Bahtz, J. Kessler, S. Lehmann (Lemann), Friedrich Brauer, W. Fetler (Wilhelm), and I. S. Prokhanoff. Most of the letters are handwritten in English. The material is available on microfilm through inter-library loan. Unpublished finding aid. Advance notice requested.

NY 111
ARCHIVES AND FILM DEPARTMENT
GEORGE EASTMAN HOUSE
900 East Avenue
Rochester, New York 14607
(716-271-3361)

1 The Archives hold both still picture and textual material. As none of it is arranged by subject or geographical area, it was difficult to ascertain the size of relevant holdings. Because collections are designated by individual photographers for the most part, the researcher would have to know in advance a specific photographer who visited Russia and took pictures there (one possibility is Margaret Bourke-White). Among the stereo views, however, which are in part filed under geographic areas, the staff was able to uncover, in a rapid check, some 30 views of

Russia (undated). There may be more pertinent holdings, either photographs or written matter (letters, diaries, manuscripts), in the Archives.

2 The Film Department holds the following Soviet films:

1916 Starewicz: PAN TWARDOWSKI, no English titles

1924 Protasanov: AELITA, no English titles

1925 Eisenstein: POTEMKIN, English titles

1928 Dovzhenko: ZVENIGORA, English titles

1929 Vertov: THE MAN WITH THE MOVIE CAMERA
Kozintsev-Trauberg: THE NEW BABYLON, flash Spanish titles
Eisenstein: OLD AND NEW, English titles, incomplete
Trauberg: THE BLUE EXPRESS, flash Danish titles

1930 Room: THE GHOST THAT NEVER RETURNS, no English titles

1938 Donskoi: THE CHILDHOOD OF MAXIM GORKY, English titles

1953 Rappaport: STARS OF THE RUSSIAN BALLET, 7 reels (excerpts from FOUNTAIN OF BAKHCHISARAI, THE FLAMES OF PARIS, and SWAN LAKE), Ulanova, Plisetskaya, and others

1955 Arnstam-Lavrovsky: ROMEO AND JULIET (ballet), excerpts, 1 reel, Ulanova and others
Stroyeva: BORIS GODUNOV, subtitled

1956 Yutkevich: OTHELLO, dubbed into English

1960 Heifits: THE LADY WITH THE DOG, subtitled

1961 (?) Daniela-Talankin: A SUMMER TO REMEMBER

NY 112
SIBLEY MUSIC LIBRARY
EASTMAN SCHOOL OF MUSIC
UNIVERSITY OF ROCHESTER
Rochester, New York 14604
(716-275-5789/3018)

The autograph letter file and photo collection contain items relating to Russian music and musicians. Among other relevant holdings are:

1 Nikolai Rimskii-Korsakov (1844-1908). Printed musical scores with the composer's own manuscript annotations (publishers' proof copies).

2 Anton Rubinstein (1829-1894). Holograph musical materials, mostly for piano.

3 Nicolas Slonimsky (b. 1894). Manuscript songs.

NY 113
DEPARTMENT OF RARE BOOKS, MANUSCRIPTS AND ARCHIVES
RUSH RHEES LIBRARY
UNIVERSITY OF ROCHESTER
Rochester, New York 14627
(716-275-4477)

1 Bragdon Family. Papers, 1819-1966, 24 ft. In the papers of Claude Fayette Bragdon (1866-1946), artist, architect, author, lecturer, stage designer, and philosopher, there is correspondence of Petr Demianovich Uspenskii, 42 letters, 1920-45, and of Nikolai Konstantinovich Roerich, 25 letters, 1922-41. Uspenskii's letters pertain to the translation and publication of his book Tertium Organum and to occult subjects; the Roerich letters pertain to painting and occult subjects, including Eastern religions. Unpublished finding aid (NUCMC 61-1634).

2 James Wood Colt (1858-1941). Papers, 1908-23, 1 box, 61 items. Railroad builder. Ca. 25 items (letters, reports, and contracts) relate to negotiations Colt carried on in 1915 for the sale of Spanish rifles to Russia. 4 items from 1917 concern his investigation of Russian resources. Unpublished finding aid (NUCMC 61-3010).

3 Edward Peck Curtis (b. 1897). Papers, 1919-75, 1 box. Rochester businessman; secretary to John A. Gade, U.S. commissioner to the Baltic states after World War I. Includes his diary for November 1919-June 1920, several hundred pp., with his record of events and observations of the Baltic region; and a typescript of reminiscences based on the diary, 10 pp., written in 1976. Unpublished finding aid.

4 Dexter Perkins (b. 1889). Papers, 1905-64, 1 box. History professor. Traveled as a graduate student in Europe before World War I. 3 (of ca. 60) letters are from St. Petersburg, 1 from Moscow, during his stay in Russia, October 1912. The Russian stay is recorded in his autobiography Yield of the Years (Boston, 1969). Unpublished finding aid.

5 William Henry Seward (1801-1872). Papers, ca. 1776-1910, 150 ft. and 11 microfilm reels. U.S. secretary of state, 1861-69. Negotiated the purchase of Alaska from Russia in 1867. A small but undetermined amount of correspondence concerns Russian-American relations and the transfer of Alaska. 1 folder (drawer E) holds prints made from a microfilm of material in the archives of the Russian Ministry of Foreign Affairs, including letters from Edouard de Stoeckl in the U.S. to Prince A. M. Gorchakov, the Russian foreign minister, in 1866-68. They concern the transfer of Alaska from Russia to the U.S. Unpublished finding aids (NUCMC 61-1621).

6 Hiram Sibley Family. Papers, in process. Papers of Hiram Sibley (1807-1888), American financier, organizer, and first president of the Western Union Telegraph Company, contain ca. 6 in. of material on the Russian-American telegraph line, on which his company expended ca. $3 million. Includes correspondence, mainly to Sibley, and other manuscript material, plus printed ephemera, documenting the negotiations between Western Union officials and the Russian government. Among the correspondents: Nicholas Abasa (at least 6 letters), Cassius M. Clay (at least 11 letters, 1865-67), and James Thal (at least 7 letters, 1865-66). There are also several family letters written by Sibley during an 1865 trip to Russia.

NY 114
ALCO HISTORIC PHOTOS
P.O. Box 655
Schenectady, New York 12301
(518-374-0153)

Photos of 12 locomotives built by the American Locomotive Company (Alco) and subsidiaries for Russia, mostly during World War I. A list of the locomotives is available (50¢ postpaid). Inspection of the collection is by appointment.

NY 115
MAIN LIBRARY AND CORPORATE PHOTO FILE
GENERAL ELECTRIC COMPANY
Schenectady, New York 12301
(518-385-8206)

The library has a small amount of miscellaneous documents relating to sales of electrical equipment, particularly generators, to the Soviet Union in the 1930s and 1940s. Most of the materials describe the equipment supplied. Also, photographs of the USSR, including the Dnieper Dam, 1930s. Holdings are restricted; access is granted on an individual basis. Approval is necessary for any public release.

NY 116
SCHAFFER LIBRARY
UNION COLLEGE
Schenectady, New York 12308
(518-370-6278)

The European Experience of American Jews in the late 19th through the mid-20th century. 60 oral history tapes. Approximately 50% of the tapes pertains to the experiences of Jews in Ukraine, Great Russia, White Russia, Lithuania, and other areas in the Russian Empire/USSR. The tapes were collected by Professor Lucille W. Brown with the guidance and collaboration of Professor Stephen M. Berk. The collection is closed to researchers. For more details, see Lucille W. Brown and Stephen M. Berk, "Fathers and Sons: Hasidism, Orthodoxy, and Haskalah. A View from Eastern Europe," Oral History Review (1977), pp. 17-32. (NUCMC 77-1954)

NY 117
ORTHODOX CHURCH IN AMERICA
P.O. Box 675, Route 25A
Syosset, New York 11791
(516-922-0550)

From 1794, when the first missionaries came to Alaska from Russia, until 1971, when it received autocephaly, this church was under the patriarchate of the Russian Orthodox Church. Although now separate, relations still continue between the Moscow Patriarchate and the Orthodox Church in America.

The archives of the Orthodox Church in America contain materials from the beginning to the present. They include such items as personal and business correspondence, office files, reports, diaries, literary and other manuscripts, financial records and account books, documents, autographs, and photographs. The total collection is in ca. 800 document cases, 15.25 x 10.5 x 5 in., with almost 20 additional filing cabinets full of material in need of sorting.

A breakdown of the correspondence shows the following holdings: with the Holy Synod and Imperial government in tsarist times; with local and diocesan church officials in this country; with other, ethnic Orthodox Churches (e.g., the Greek, Serbian, Bulgarian, and Syrian); with American government agencies, including the Interior Department, 1870-present; with or about Russians and other ethnic groups immigrating to the U.S.

Among Church records are resolutions dating from 1840; diaries and reports concerning early explorations, missionary activities, and the establishment of the church in America; financial records from around 1885; church calendars and yearbook directories from ca. 1905 on; and titles to church properties in Alaska.

Official church journals in the collection include Tserkovniya Vedomosti, 1870-1917, replies of diocesan hierarchs about proposed church reforms, 6 vols., 1905-1906, journals of the Russian Theological Academies, 1870-present, and the Russian-American Messenger, 1898-1974. In addition, there are proclamations--printed for original distribution and promulgation--of Alexander II (freeing the serfs in 1861) and Nicholas II (establishing the fundamental laws of 1905-1906), plus other Imperial manifestos and edicts.

The collection holds materials from or about the following persons: Metropolitan Innokenty; Archbishop Tikhon Bellavin (of North America and Canada, 1897-1907; patriarch of Moscow at his death in 1925); Metropolitan Platon Rozhdestvenskii (d. 1934); Professor Michael M. Karpovich of Harvard; the composer Sergei V. Rachmaninoff; Ambassador Boris Bakhmetev; Colonel S. Obolensky; and Metropolitan Leonty (formerly Fr. Leonid Turkevich).

Permission to use the archives must come from the archivist, Serge G. Troubetzkoy, at the above address. About 50% of the holdings has been catalogued at present, on ca. 11,000 general index cards.

NY 118
GEORGE ARENTS RESEARCH LIBRARY FOR
SPECIAL COLLECTIONS
E. S. BIRD LIBRARY, SIXTH FLOOR--
MANUSCRIPT DIVISION
SYRACUSE UNIVERSITY
Syracuse, New York 13210
(315-423-2697)

1 Margaret Bourke-White (1905-1971) and Erskine Caldwell (b. 1903). Papers of Bourke-White, ca. 1900-64, 88 boxes, ca. 44 ft., plus several thousand photographs and negatives, an American photographer, and of Caldwell, 1938-42 and undated, 13 boxes, author, are separate but linked collections. About .5 box of Bourke-White's papers (manuscripts, correspondence, financial, and biographical material) apparently relate to the Soviet Union. The photos are not yet fully processed and remain closed to researchers at present. Ca. 1 box of telegrams and manuscripts in the Caldwell collection relates to the Russian front in World War II. Unpublished finding aid.

2 Earl R. Browder (1891-1973). Papers, 1880-1967, 103 boxes. Author, lecturer, and leader of the American Communist Party until his ouster in 1946. Correspondence, office files, and literary manuscripts. Nearly the entire collection relates to communism. Some materials pertain to his work as representative of Soviet publishing firms in this country, 1946-50. These materials have been microfilmed and a restriction is in effect for the originals. Unpublished finding aid.

3 David Davidovich Burliuk (1882-1967). Papers, 1900-67, 10 boxes, 4.75 ft. Russian-American painter. Burliuk was a leader of avant-garde movements and chief exponent of modern art in Russia in the early 20th c., until his emigration in 1917. Settling in the U.S. in 1922, Burliuk (with his wife) continued to paint and later began publication of the art quarterly Color and Rhyme. Materials fall into 4 major groups: (a) correspondence, 1900-67: those in English or with transliterated Russian signatories are arranged alphabetically by sender's last name; remaining Russian items are in chronological order. Most of the letters are to Burliuk from art gallery directors, private collectors, fellow artists, family, and friends (including Henry Miller); (b) memorabilia, 1915-66: include scrapbooks of Russian newspaper clippings, genealogies of the Burliuk family, and exhibition catalogues; (c) writings, 1928-67: drafts of books, articles, and poems. Several diaries of the artist and issues of Color and Rhyme. Various authors of these manuscripts discuss Burliuk's art, the Blaue Reiter group (to which he belonged), and the development of modern Russian art; and (d) miscellanea, among which are the painter's financial records, with some data on sales of his work. Over 50% of the material is in Russian and remains untranslated. Detailed unpublished finding aid.

4 Ralph E. Flanders (1880-1970). Papers, 1923-67, 164 boxes. U.S. senator from Vermont. Relates to the beginnings of the Cold War in the post-World War II period. Includes typescripts of his radio broadcasts on foreign policy topics.

5 Robert C. Hendrickson (1898-1964). Papers, 1916-64, 281 boxes and 12 packages. U.S. senator from New Jersey. An anti-communist spokesman. Ca. .5 box has material relating to investigations of Senator Joseph McCarthy, whom Hendrickson opposed.

6 Granville Hicks (b. 1901). Papers, 1906-65, 4 of 36 boxes. Writer. Letters, subject files, and notes pertaining to Hicks's biography John Reed: The Making of a Revolutionary, with John Stuart (New York: Macmillan Co., 1936). Unpublished finding aid (NUCMC 67-112).

7 Eugene Holman. Papers, in process, 1 box. President of the Standard Oil Company of New Jersey. Speeches, in part concerned with U.S. foreign affairs and the USSR.

8 Eugene J. Keogh (b. 1907). Papers, 1937-67, over 400 boxes of different size. U.S. senator. Material concerning his work on the Herter Committee on Foreign Aid.

9 Irving R. Levine (b. 1922). Papers, 1946-64, ca. 6 of 21 ft. Television reporter and author. Broadcast scripts, notes, research materials, and clippings. In 1955 Levine became the first American television correspondent accredited to Moscow, where he served until 1959. The bulk of the papers comes from

these years. Some items carry the clearance stamp and occasional cut markings of Soviet censors (e.g., stories on the Hungarian uprising and on the launching of Sputnik). Among the literary manuscripts are several articles on Russian life and his 2 books Main Street, U.S.S.R. (1959) and Travel Guide to Russia (1960), both published by Doubleday (Garden City, New York). During Mr. Levine's lifetime, the researcher must obtain his written permission to examine the material. Unpublished finding aid.

10 Vermont Connecticut Royster (b. 1914). Papers, 1931-63, 17 boxes. Journalist and editor of the Wall Street Journal. Correspondence, journals, and notes. In 1962 Royster traveled to the Soviet Union and interviewed Nikita S. Khrushchev. His letters and journals discuss the trip. The interview appeared in the Wall Street Journal, 13 July 1962, the National Observer, and, slightly altered, in his book Journey Through the Soviet Union (New York: Dow Jones and Co., 1962). Unpublished finding aid (NUCMC 68-1751).

11 Dorothy Thompson (1894-1961). Papers, 1918-61, 139 boxes and some scrapbooks. Journalist. Correspondence, manuscripts, and photographs reflect a strong interest in the USSR and international affairs. In 1927 Thompson visited Russia to report on the 10th anniversary of the Bolshevik Revolution. Dorothy Thompson, an Inventory of Her Papers in Syracuse University Library, compiled by Stephanie Leon and Susan D'Angelo (Syracuse University Library Manuscript Collections, 1966) is issue 9 in the Manuscript Inventory series. (NUCMC 69-54)

NY 119
SYRACUSE UNIVERSITY ARCHIVES
E. S. BIRD LIBRARY
SYRACUSE UNIVERSITY
Syracuse, New York 13210
(315-423-3335)

1 George Babcock Cressy (1896-1963). Papers, 1919-67, 38 boxes. Geographer. Manuscript books, correspondence, and notes, including materials for his Soviet Potentials: A Geographic Appraisal (Syracuse University Press, 1962) and 2 earlier books on the USSR, 1945 and 1954. Also, slides and 2 folders of correspondence pertaining to the Soviet Union. Unpublished inventory.

2 Alexander C. Flick (1869-1942). Papers, 1895-1942, 39 boxes. New York state historian, professor of history at Syracuse University. Traveled to Russia during a world trip in 1912-13. Also, 1 folder of material relating to Russia in 1905. Reference(s) to Siberia. Published calendar (NUCMC 64-1169).

3 Warren Walsh (b. 1909). Papers, 1955-67, 7 boxes (additions expected). Professor of Russian history at Syracuse. Correspondence, writings, lectures, book reviews, notes, slides, etc. relating to his scholarly work on Russia.

NY 120
THE VAN HORNESVILLE COMMUNITY CORPORATION
Van Hornesville, New York 13475
(315-858-0030)

Owen D. Young (1874-1962). Papers, 1,076 cartons, 1880s-1962. Chairman of the General Electric Company. A friend of Col. Hugh Cooper, Young was interested in developing business relations with Russia and met with Amtorg representatives in New York. A few letters in the papers deal with U.S.-Russian industrial arrangement, 1917-1930s. For access, contact Mrs. Josephine Young Case at above address stating research plans.

NY 121
MAP AND MANUSCRIPT DIVISION
U.S. MILITARY ACADEMY LIBRARY
West Point, New York 10996
(914-938-2954)

1 Arthur Pendleton Bagby (1794-1858). Governor of Alabama and diplomat. Letter, 2 April 1849, to his son, Cadet Arthur P. Bagby, Jr., written while Bagby, Sr. was U.S. minister to Russia.

2 Benjamin Abbott Dickson (1897-1975). Papers, 1919-75, ca. 192 items. U.S. Army officer. Includes diary, 20 August-7 November 1919, 54 letters, and 138 photographs pertaining to the colonel's experience as an officer with the North Russian expedition.

3 William Sidney Graves (1865-1940). Papers, 1919-20, 10 items. Comander of American Expeditionary Forces in Siberia, 1918-20. Photograph of the 27th Infantry officers seated beneath the Siberian Expedition insignia, an insignia lapel pin, and some Russian currency.

4 Ernest Kuhn (1864-1935). Papers, 1885-1935, over 300 items. U.S. Army general. Includes 8 diaries and over 300 photographs covering the period he was military attaché to the U.S. legation in Tokyo for the purpose of observing the Japanese army during the war with Russia in 1904.

5 Amos Blanchard Shattuck (1896-1934). Son of an army officer stationed in the Philippines. Copy of the journal "From Manila to New York

via Trans-Siberian," 26 July-9 September 1913, 110 pp., accompanied by copies of a time table, map, and brochure from the International Sleeping Car Co. Young Shattuck was en route to Exeter via Manchuria, Siberia, Germany, and England.

6 George Evans Stewart (1872-1946). Papers, 1918-40, 1 box. U.S. Army officer. Participated in the North Russian expedition during the American intervention in the Russian Civil War. Ca. 205 items 1918-19, including official correspondence, documents, reports, and maps, pertain to his career and the North Russian expedition in particular. (NUCMC 70-1360)

Finding Aid: Preliminary Guide to the Manuscript Collection of the U.S. Military Academy Library, compiled by J. Thomas Russell (West Point, 1968).

NORTH CAROLINA

NC 1
SOUTHERN HISTORICAL COLLECTION
WILSON LIBRARY 024A
THE UNIVERSITY OF NORTH CAROLINA
Chapel Hill, North Carolina 27514
(919-933-1345)

1 Thomas Hart Benton (1782-1858). U.S. senator from Missouri. Letter, 1856, to Thomas Hart Seymour, U.S. minister to Russia, introduces Mr. and Mrs. Appleton of New York. (No. 61)

2 Lyman Atkinson Cotten (1874-1926). Papers, 1886-1947, 7,500 items. Naval officer. Correspondence contains a few references to Russian affairs, 1920. (NUCMC 64-988) (No. 182)

3 Duff Green (1791-1875). Papers, 1810-1902, 9 ft. (reproduced on 25 reels of microfilm). Journalist, politician, and industrial promoter. Undated business papers mention speculation on the St. Petersburg-Moscow railroad line and American investment possibilities in Russia. (NUCMC 68-808) (Nos. 993 and M-993)

4 Gwyn Family. Papers, 1779-1938, 720 items. Papers of James Gwyn include a letter, 1837, from his friend M. S. Stokes, in the U.S. Navy, visiting St. Petersburg. Stokes relates how the tsar boarded his ship incognito; he also speaks in detail of the court and the city. (NUCMC 64-512) (No. 298) Note: A typed copy of this letter is in the Gordon-Hackett Family Papers (No. 1040).

5 James Kimbrough Jones (1839-1908). Papers, 1900-21, 103 ft. U.S. senator from Arkansas. Attorney for Oklahoma oil developers at one time. He received letters, 1906, concerning Russian oil competition and the consulship at Batoum (Batum). (NUCMC 64-1036) (No. 387)

6 Alexander Robert Lawton (1818-1896). Lawton Family papers, 1774-1952, 2 ft. President of the American Bar Association. Although he had served as minister to Austria-Hungary, he was ruled ineligible for an appointment to the U.S. mission in Russia. Documentation is in correspondence of 1884-85. (NUCMC 64-544) (No. 415)

7 London Family. Papers, 1776-1933, 305 items. On microfilm only are typed copies of letters sent to the family from J. Carson Breckenridge, son of the U.S. minister to Russia, 1894-95. (NUCMC 64-552) (Nos. 2442 and M-2446)

8 Morris Randolph Mitchell (1895-1976). Educator and world traveler. Copies of 3 letters to his sister-in-law from her friend in Russia, 1922. The friend describes Moscow and also relief work in the Volga region. (NUCMC 77-595) (No. 3832)

9 Phillips Family. Papers, 1804-1928, 1,400 items. In 1886-94 the family received many letters from George Kennan, the Russian expert and Siberian explorer. In addition, W. H. Phillips (1853-1897) received 3 detailed letters from Supreme Court Associate Justice John M. Harlan about his work as arbitrator on the Bering Sea Commission in 1893. (NUCMC 64-613) (No. 596)

10 Pickens Family. Papers, 1800-89, ca. 160 items. Francis Wilkinson Pickens (1805-1869) was U.S. minister to Russia in 1858-60. His correspondence, 1859-60, contains information about his service and Russian-American diplomatic relations. (NUCMC 64-615) (No. 1492)

11 Robert Crooke Wood (1832-1900). Papers, 1807-1910, 2 ft. Includes a letter from H. B. Trist to a friend describing the visit of his uncle, Tom Cottman, to Russia in 1854 and his uncle's interview with Prince Doljarouki (Dolgorukii). (NUCMC 64-1546) (No. 800)

Finding Aids: Guide to the Manuscripts in the Southern Historical Collection of the University of North Carolina, prepared by the WPA (Chapel Hill, 1941); The Southern Historical Collection: A Guide to Manuscripts by Susan Sokol Blosser and Clyde Norman Wilson, Jr. (Chapel Hill, 1970); and The Southern Historical Collection: Supplementary Guide to Manuscripts, 1970-1975 by Everard H. Smith (Chapel Hill, 1975). There is an unpublished survey for each of the collections listed.

NC 2
MANUSCRIPT DEPARTMENT
WILLIAM R. PERKINS LIBRARY
DUKE UNIVERSITY
Durham, North Carolina 27706
(919-684-3372)

1 Allen-Angier Family. Papers, 1843-1971, 1,730 items and 7 vols. George Venable Allen (1903-1970) was a diplomat and director of the U.S. Information Agency. In the Allen section of the papers are a letter, 21 January 1948 attached to a letter of 29 September 1960, and a chapter of a book, Mission to Iran, that discuss Soviet-Iranian relations, and a speech of 15 October 1959 (USIA box) on U.S.-Soviet relations. In the Angier section are 3 letters, March 1950, January 1951, and February 1962, about Russian-American relations and 1, 21 March 1951, concerning Soviet relations with Yugoslavia. (NUCMC 72-862)

2 Anonymous diaries. 2 items. The first, from England, contains observations of a young man working on board hired British transport ships in the Crimean War. Entries dated 23 March 1854-22 September 1855. The writer, on different ships, was in Eupatoria, Sevastopol, and Balaklava. Much space is devoted to naval and military operations. At the end of the diary, 164 pp., are 2 ship lists, for the Black Sea fleet and for transports. Throughout the volume are colored drawings of ships and military personnel. The second diary is of an American woman traveling in Europe with a group of other women. They were in Russia (entering at St. Petersburg) for 9 days, starting 11 September 1878. The woman remarks on the Winter Palace, the Peter and Paul fortress, the Hermitage, the celebration of a saint's day in the capital, and the return of troops from the Russo-Turkish War. In Moscow she saw the Kremlin, St. Basil's Cathedral, and other churches.

3 Sir Edwin Arnold (1832-1904). Papers, 1870-1903, 136 items. British poet, journalist, and Orientalist. 3 letters discuss Russo-Japanese relations, 18 February 1895; ca. September 1895; and 30 September 1898. (NUCMC 71-50)

4 John Backhouse (1784-1845). Papers, 1740-1956, 4,473 items and 7 vols. British undersecretary of state for foreign affairs. In his correspondence are references to Circassia, 1835-36, British relations with Russia, 1833-36, and Russo-Turkish relations, 1834-36. In addition, letters from 1819-22 contain discussion of Jacques Augustin Galiffe's plans for travel in Russia and mention the Russian language. (NUCMC 69-1467)

5 Henry Dunster Baker (1873-1939). Papers, 1794-1953, 272 items and 8 vols. Consular officer, newspaper editor, and publisher. He traveled through Siberia in 1909. His Tasmanian Scrapbook contains clippings about Siberia. Assigned to the Petrograd embassy in 1914 as a commercial attaché, Baker filled his scrapbook for 1911-33 with printed matter, pamphlets, and pictures which include material about Russian commerce with the U.S. Some of the items are by or about Baker, 1916 especially. In 1930-31 he was opposed to trade with the Soviet Union. (NUCMC 71-52)

6 Sir Robert Barrie (1774-1841). Papers, 1765-1953, 729 items and 2 vols. British naval officer. Includes 1 letter, 2 January 1812, which refers to Russia's relations with Turkey. (NUCMC 68-1525)

7 George William Barrington, 7th Viscount Barrington (1824-1886). Papers, 1619 and 1822-1901, 463 items. Member of British Parliament. Includes a letter, 8 March 1886, discussing Russo-Turkish relations in 1844 and 1852 (enclosure). Other papers from 1876-86 pertain to Great Britain's links with Russia. (NUCMC 68-1526)

8 George S. Bernard (1837-1912). Papers, 1816-1912, 34 items and 3 vols. Undated scrapbook contains an item about Sevastopol harbor in the 19th c.

9 John William Ponsonby, 4th Earl of Bessborough (1781-1847). Papers, 1821-33, 22 items. MP and Home Secretary. Includes 1 letter, 29 August 1832, about Russo-British relations.

10 Sir George Biddlecombe (1807-1878). British naval officer. Memoirs, 368 pp., contain observations on the Crimean War and the fall of Cronstadt. In 1854 he was master of the Baltic fleet and conducted allied fleets to Cronstadt.

11 Turin Bradford Boone. Diaries, 1911-12, 2 vols. Member of the staff of Morgan Shuster, treasurer general of Persia. Diaries, typed, record his travel in Russia. Comments on art and architecture, politics, and religion. He discusses Russian efforts to penetrate Persia and Russian diplomats.

12 Sylvanus Bourne. Papers, 1799-1815, 12 items. U.S. consul in Amsterdam, 1799-1815. Includes a letter, 15 November 1815, with reference to the city of Archangel.

13 Sir John Nicholl Robert Campbell, 2nd Bart. (1799-1870). Papers, 1812-41, 257 items. British military officer and diplomat who served in Persia 1824-34. Correspondence in the early 1830s contains many observations on Russo-Persian and Russo-British relations, Russian efforts to expand west of the Caspian Sea, Russian officers replacing the British as military advisers to the Persian army, Central Asian affairs (Khorasan and Khiva), and the unlikelihood of a Russian invasion of India. From the earlier period there are letters discussing the Russo-Persian War. On 8 February 1828 Campbell, in St. Petersburg,

reported on his talks with Russian officials, and on British help in trying to end the war. Field Marshall Ivan F. Paskevitch had requested the British assistance. Also, a letter from Paskevitch, Count of Erivan, to Prince Nicolas Dolgorouki. (NUCMC 63-42)

14 G. Hope (Summerell) Chamberlain (1870-1960). Papers, 1821-1946, 3,397 items and 21 vols. Author, of Chapel Hill, North Carolina. Includes a letter, 20 February 1899, referring to Russian foreign relations; letter, 24 August 1905, on the Russo-Japanese War; and a 3rd about the 1905 Revolution, 21 December 1905. (NUCMC 71-58)

15 Francis Rawdon Chesney (1789-1872). British general. Manuscript volume, ca. 100 pp., entitled "Observations on Persia as an Ally, and the Cheapest as well as Most Important Frontier Line of Our Indian Empire" (ca. 1831-33). In it he discusses Russo-Turkish relations since 1717, Russo-British relations, and Russian domination of Persia.

16 Clara Mary Jane Clairmont (1798-1879). Papers, 1814-26, 7 vols. and 1 typescript. Governess in a Moscow family. Diaries for 1814-26 describe in detail her life, Russian social life, and customs in the early 19th c. Items are in part transcripts and photocopies (negative) of originals held mainly in the British Museum. (NUCMC 60-2192)

17 Stanley de Astel Calvert Clarke (1837-1911). Papers, 1846-1913, 91 items. British army officer. Includes an army contract with Russia, 3 January 1906.

18 John Clopton. Collection, 1629-1915, 11,734 items (Papers of the Clopton and Wallace families). Includes some material (amount and date unknown) on education in Russia. (NUCMC 61-87)

19 Richard Cobden (1804-1865). Papers, 1840-64, 42 items. English statesman. Includes a letter of 2 January 1853 about Great Britain's relations with Russia.

20 William Harris Crawford (1772-1834). Papers, 1790-1867, 126 items. U.S. senator from Georgia, secretary of war, 1815-16, secretary of the treasury, 1816-25, and unsuccessful presidential candidate, 1824. Letters from William Short to Alexander Hamilton, 1790, discuss Russian finances and foreign relations. Letter, 16 July 1815, from George William Erving, U.S. minister to Spain, to Crawford reports on Austrian and Russian intrigue in France. On 4 October 1821 Erving gave Crawford an analysis of the balance of power between Russia, Austria, Italy, Turkey, and England, and of Alexander I's intentions toward Constantinople. Letter, Paris, 1 November 1827, contains Erving's views on Nicholas I as a threat to Turkey. Letters of then secretary of state James Monroe in 1814 comment on his audiences with Alexander I. (NUCMC 60-2217)

21 John Wilson Croker (1780-1857). Papers, 1809-57, 2,251 items. British statesman and essayist. Received letters on the following subjects: Russian army, 24 October 1813, Russo-British relations, 29 April 1818, and the Crimean War, 1853-56. (NUCMC 68-1539)

22 John Bligh, 4th earl of Darnley (1767-1831). Papers, 1738-1858, 76 items. British House of Lords member. Includes an account of the "General State of the Russian Trade, 1771-1785," 3 pp. (NUCMC 63-46)

23 Francis Warrington Dawson (1840-1889). Papers, 1559-1963, 7,440 items and 65 vols. Includes papers of his son, F. W. Dawson II (1878-1962), journalist. 1 microfilm reel, negative, contains material on the Russo-Japanese War of 1904-1905. (NUCMC 69-1485)

24 Nathaniel Barksdale Dial (1862-1940). Papers, 1915-35. Includes information about Russian trade with the United States. (NUCMC 61-1360)

25 Frederick Commins Edwards (1863-1948). Papers, 1883-1945, 213 items and 79 vols. Episcopal clergyman. Vol. 45 of his journal contains observations on the Russian Revolution and Civil War, 1917-21. (NUCMC 72-869)

26 Robert Lawrence Eichelberger (1886-1961). Papers, in process. Army officer. Letters, reports, summaries, photographs, and maps concern the American intervention in Siberia, 1918-20, and military intelligence, 1918-24. Letters from Siberia to Mrs. Eichelberger, August 1919-February 1920, are on 2 reels of microfilm. Volumes 2 and 3 of an album entitled "Siberia" contain photos, 132 pp., from September 1918-January 1921. Access restricted.

27 Field-Musgrave Family. Papers, 1739-1966, 2,172 items and 15 vols. David Dudley Field (1805-1894), a lawyer and law reformer, traveled in Russia in the late 1830s and in 1851. His travel journals for those years describe his experiences. (NUCMC 62-1595)

28 Sir Thomas Douglas Forsyth (1827-1886). Papers, 1869-75, 2 items. British administrator in India. Includes a letter, 19 August 1869, concerning Russo-British relations.

29 Joseph Fuller (d. 1841). Papers, 1819-41, 32 items. British general. Includes material pertaining to a Russian grand duke.

30 Alfred Edward Garwood. British mechanical engineer. Draft of his memoirs, chapters 17-22, ca. 100 pp., dealing with Russia. He went to Russia at age 22, serving in turn as assistant master mechanic at Bologoe for the Nicolai Railway (St. Petersburg to Moscow);

assistant locomotive superintendent of the Dunaburg-Witepsk (Vitebsk) Railway, 1869; chief engineer in charge of locomotive construction at the Baltic Ironworks, St. Petersburg; manager of shops at Globuki; manager of locomotive service at Novi-Tcherkash (i.e., Tcherchassk); works manager of the Struve Brothers' Kolomna Engineering Works, near Moscow; district locomotive superintendent for the Orël-Graize Railway at Orël; and engineer in chief of the Locomotive, Carriage, and Wagon Departments of the Losova-Sevastopol Railway. In the last job, which opened the Crimea to rail transport, Garwood worked with Major Nicolai Yakolevitch Prochoroff, engineer in chief and general manager of the railroad. The memoirs have been published in revised form as Forty Years of an Engineer's Life At Home and Abroad, With Notes By the Way (Newport, Monmouthshire, 1903).

31 Francis Calley Gray (1790-1856). Diaries, 1811-15, 1 vol. Harvard graduate who accompanied John Quincy Adams to Russia in 1809 and became unpaid secretary for the U.S. legation in St. Petersburg. The diary describes his return home through Russia, Estonia, and Prussia, September 1811. Comments on living conditions and the decay of Russian travel vehicles.

32 Mark Green. Letters, 1855-56, 12 items. Sharpshooter in the British army during the siege of Sevastopol, 1855. Correspondence with a cousin in England. Ca. 8 letters describe his service in the front-line trenches, various battles, and the poor hospital conditions. The final letter, 25 February 1856, describes Sevastopol and the British camp there.

33 Sir Andrew Snape Hamond, 1st Bart. (1738-1828). Correspondence, 1783-1862, 229 items and 1 vol. British naval officer. Business correspondence for 1795-1803 (at least 12 letters) contains frequent references to the hemp trade with Russia and the importation of naval stores. A report to the Privy Council, 18 December 1800, quotes hemp prices in 1790-1800 for Riga and St. Petersburg. (NUCMC 71-1656)

34 Hinsdale Family. Papers, 1712-1973, 2,500 items and 52 vols. Includes a letter, 11 February 1904, referring to the Russo-Japanese War. (NUCMC 75-1960)

35 Henry Richard Vassall Fox, 3rd Baron Holland (1773-1840). Papers, 1809-39, 189 items. English politician. Includes a letter, 1837, concerning Russo-British relations. (NUCMC 68-1561)

36 John Mitchell Kemble (1807-1857). Collection, 49 items and 2 vols. Philologist and historian. Includes a manuscript entitled "Heads of a conversation with J. C. H. [John Cam Hobhouse] at the India Board. Feby. 10th 1839," 5 pp. It discusses Afghan affairs, establishment of an anti-Russian league beyond the Indus, Russia and Britain in Central Asia, and diplomatic relations in 1838 among Britain, Russia, Persia, and Afghanistan. Author of the piece was apparently Henry Reeve, though Kemble was probably the copier.

37 William Beatty Kingston (1837-1900). Correspondence, 1877-86, 26 items. British foreign correspondent for the Daily Telegraph. He received a number of letters from Sir Edwin Henry Egerton, second secretary in the British embassy at St. Petersburg, 1877, later secretary in the Istanbul embassy; from Demetrius Ghica, a Rumanian statesman; and from Lord Odo Russell, ambassador to Germany. Egerton writes in 1877 about Russian political affairs; the Russo-Turkish War, Russian navy, and the Daily Telegraph's coverage of the war; articles Kingston wrote on Russia and Germany; the opera; Russian reaction to Donald Mackenzie Wallace's book about the empire; the difficulty of obtaining accurate news; trials of radicals; taxation; the possibility of a revolution; and Britain's unpopularity. Ghica, in December 1877, also writes about the Russian war with Turkey and about a visit of Alexander II. In a letter of 20 December 1877 Lord Odo Russell explains European attitudes toward intervening in the Russo-Turkish War. In 1879 Egerton writes from Vienna about the departure of a man named Law from the Daily Telegraph and his knowledge of Russia. Letter, 27 June 1886, discusses British weakness in foreign affairs and India's frontier against Russia.

38 John Knight (1806-1864). Papers, 1788-1891, 1,323 items and 48 vols. Mississippi merchant. Traveled with his wife to Russia (Moscow and St. Petersburg) in 1858. Her diary describes the people, fashions, palaces, churches, and jewelry she saw. Her name: Mrs. Frances Zeruiah Susanna (Beall) Knight.

39 Levant Company. Records, 1768-1902, 134 items and 3 vols. Contains material on Turkey's relations with Russia.

40 Robert Banks Jenkinson, 2nd Earl of Liverpool (1770-1828). Papers, 1669-1900, 1 vol. British statesman. Pages of a scrapbook, 70 ff., concern Russian internal affairs and Russo-British relations, 1798-1814. (NUCMC 68-1575)

41 Lord Augustus William Frederich Spencer Loftus (1817-1904). Correspondence, 1871-84, 15 items. Secretary to the British legation in St. Petersburg, 1871-79. Letters, 26 June 1871; March-November 1877; and 7 May 1884, discuss Russo-British relations, particularly with respect to the Russo-Turkish War. Correspondence of 17 May 1872 discusses the coal and iron industries in the interior of Russia

and investments in them by Lord Alfred Paget. Reference to Konstantin Pobedonostsev.

42 Malet Family. Papers, 1832-1908, 1,287 items and 1 vol. Sir Alexander Malet, 2nd Bart. (1800-1886), was an unpaid attaché at the British embassy in St. Petersburg. His letters from 1824-26 refer to the Decembrist revolt (to which he was an eyewitness), the succession of Nicholas I, British diplomats in Russia, St. Petersburg life, bear hunts, horse racing, various festivals at the palace, a tournament, and the great flood of November 1824. Letter of an unidentified Russian from Taganrog, 19-27 November 1824, describes the illness and death of Alexander I. Sir Alexander's eldest son, Sir Henry Charles Eden Malet, 3rd Bart., was a Grenadier Guards officer at the siege of Sevastopol during the Crimean War. Ca. 80 of his letters, written from the Crimea, 1855-56, discuss his experiences. An album contains sketches, battle plans, and watercolor scenes of the war. Other letters of 1853-56 also discuss Russo-British relations in general and Russo-Austrian relations as well. 2 of Lady Malet's correspondents, Lord Stanley and Queen Sophia of the Netherlands, write about the Crimean War. In addition, ca. 27 letters in the "Queen Sophia Division" of the Malet papers contain references to Great Britain's relations with Russia, Russian foreign relations generally, and Russian government, 1844-77. See William Rector Erwin, "A Queen's Confidante: The Papers of Lady Malet and her family," Duke University Library Notes, no. 43 (November 1972). (NUCMC 72-877)

43 John Sanford Martin (1886-1957). Papers, 1917-58, 8,586 items and 6 vols. Newspaper editor. Includes a letter, 19 September 1936, about recent developments in the Soviet Union; and a "confidential transcription," 19 June 1945, of an interview with President Harry Truman concerning future relations with the Soviet Union and the United Nations. (NUCMC 68-1579)

44 Henry Dundas, 1st Viscount Melville (1742-1811). Papers, 1779-1813, 468 items and 1 vol. British statesman. Includes a paper, 7 September 1799, concerning the Russian army and navy. (NUCMC 63-109 and 72-878)

45 Henry Louis Mencken (1880-1956). Collection, 1901-21, 5,433 items. Editor, critic, and author. Clippings about the theater, including folders labeled "Andreev, Leonid"; "Chekhov, Anton Pavlovich"; "Gogol, Nikolai Vasilievich"; "Gorky, Maxim"; and "Theatre, Russian."

46 Edward Lacon Ommanney. Papers, 1810-30, 50 items. British general. Includes some references to Russian foreign relations.

47 William John Monson, 1st Viscount Oxenbridge (1829-1898). Papers, 1872-76, 204 items. British politician. Includes a letter, 20-21 April 1876, with enclosures, concerning Russo-Turkish relations. (NUCMC 72-883)

48 Henry John Temple, 3rd Viscount Palmerston (1784-1865). Papers, 1808-65, 44 items. British statesman. Materials in part concern relations between Russia and Great Britain.

49 Louisa Bouknight Poppenheim (1868-1957). L. B. Poppenheim and Mary Barnett Poppenheim Correspondence, 1871-1955, 955 items and 34 vols. Includes 1 letter, 6 August 1902, describing travel to Turkistan in Russia. (NUCMC 71-1666)

50 Posters. 43 originals and 9 facsimiles, ca. 1929-62. 29 items, donated by Dean Calvin B. Hoover, are propaganda posters issued during the transition from the New Economic Policy to the first Five-Year Plan. Subjects include the struggle against religion, public nurseries, the Russian Revolution and Civil War, women workers, Red Army training, Lenin, Stalin, alcoholism, industrialization, and the fight against imperialism. An additional 14 posters comprise electioneering placards on materials of the 22nd Congress of the Communist Party of the Soviet Union. They concern the transition from socialism to communism, the Seven-Year Plan, industry, agriculture, social welfare, electrification, and the collapse of capitalism and imperialism.

51 George Poulett (1786-1854). Letter book, 1807-10, 1 vol., 127 pp. British admiral. Contains copies of orders he received from autumn 1807 to winter 1810, while commanding the Quebec. Some items directly concern relations with Russia.

52 Purviance-Courtenay. Collection, 1757-1932, 2,361 items. Correspondence and other papers. Includes some reference(s) to Russia's relations with Brazil.

53 Recueils. Affaires Diverses du 18e Siècle, Particulièrement de Celles de Dauphine. 1 vol. Some pages concern Princess Charlotte of Brunswick-Wolfenbüttel, wife of Tsarevich Alexius Petrovich, son of Peter I.

54 Kurt Riess. Scrapbook, 1904-33, 1 vol. Includes material on the Russo-Japanese War of 1904-1905 and on the Russian navy.

55 Frederick Sleigh Roberts, 1st Earl Roberts (1832-1914). Letters, 1881-1910, 55 items. British army officer. Includes 2 letters, 6 and 18 September 1902, with comments on Russo-British relations. (NUCMC 72-886)

56 Raymond Robins (1873-1954). Papers, 1917-18, 1 microfilm reel. Head of the Red Cross mission to Russia. Correspondence and diary, 1 January 1917-31 May 1918, discuss the 1917 Revolutions and relief work. Originals in the Wisconsin State Historical Society.

57 William Govett Romaine (1815-1893). Papers, 1857-77, 12 items. British jurist. Includes

letter, 12 July 1877, that refers to the Russo-Turkish War.

58 Romanov Family. Correspondence, 1796-1852, 243 items. Transcripts of letters in French written by members of the Russian Imperial family. Made by Professor Sydney Wayne Jackson for his Romanov Relations, The Private Correspondence of Tsars Alexander I, Nicholas I and the Grand Dukes Constantine and Michael with Their Sister Queen Anna Pavlovna, 1817-1855 (London, 1969). The transcripts do not all appear in the book. Originals are in the royal house archives at the Hague, which restricts their use, and in the Thuringian state archives in the German Democratic Republic, which asks to be consulted before use. Copies or originals of the transcripts are also in the royal house archives. Letters comprise: Queen Anna to Alexander I, Nicholas I, Grand Duke Constantine, and possibly Grand Duke Michael, 1816-35, 110 letters; Nicholas I to Anna, 1820-46, 66 letters; Nicholas I to King Willem II of the Netherlands, 1815-45, 25 letters; Constantine to Willem II, 1816-30, 22 letters; Alexander I to Anna, 1817-25, 7 letters; Alexander I to Willem II, 1816-22, 5 letters; Nicholas I to Willem II and Anna, 1842-46, 2 letters; Nicholas I to Prince Hendrik of Orange, 1849-52, 2 letters; Anna to Princess Louise of Prussia, 1825, 1 letter, to King Friedrich I of Württemberg, 1816, 1 letter, and to Duke Friedrich Eugen of Württemberg, 1796, 1 letter; and Grand Duchess Maria Pavlovna of Saxe-Weimar to Anna, 1835, 1 letter. Queen Anna was both aunt and mother-in-law of Queen Sophia of the Netherlands (see the Malet Family papers). Besides the private and family life of the Romanovs, the letters reveal aspects of Russian politics, government, and foreign affairs.

59 Jay Rutherford (b. 1916). Papers, in process. Includes a video tape recording, 80 mins., of an interview with W. Averell Harriman (b. 1891), former ambassador to the USSR, 1943-46, in which he discusses his 50-year diplomatic association with the Soviet Union. This tape is part of a larger project of interviews with prominent figures who were involved in American foreign policy since 1914.

60 William Sandford (d. 1871). Papers, 1833-1914, 183 items. British author and expert on cotton growing in the Near East. Letters of 1952-63 discuss Soviet-British relations. (NUCMC 69-1540)

61 Albert Houtum-Schindler (1846-1916). Papers, ca. 1889-1912, 33 items. Telegraph inspector and army organizer in Persia, knighted by the British and made a general by the Shah. Primarily correspondence from George Nathaniel Curzon, 1st Marquis Curzon of Kedleston, to General Schindler. Letters from 1891-96 concern relations among Britain, Persia, and Russia. A draft memorandum Schindler wrote in January 1889, 15 pp., pertains to the opening of the Karun River to commerce, the Russian consular office at Meshed, the boundary problem with Russia in northeastern Persia, and internal Persian affairs.

62 Socialist Party of America. Records, 1897-1976, ca. 249,840 items and 177 vols. Includes national, state, and local party records (correspondence, minutes, resolutions, financial records, biographical sketches, speeches, printed matter, etc.); papers of the Youth and Young People's Socialist League; files of related organizations (e.g., the International Solidarity Committee); serials; audio-visual material (films, tapes, and recordings from the 1950s-1960s); and a "Picture File" with photographs of prominent socialists (individual and in groups). Topics covered in the "National Subject File" include communism, international socialism, war, peace, and totalitarianism. There is some information on the Russo-Finnish War of 1940. A selection of material from this foremost collection on American socialism is available on microfilm, over 140 reels, from the Microfilming Corporation of America. Unpublished finding aid and, for the microfilm collection, a printed index and guide. (NUCMC 62-1598, 75-1967, and 77-883)

63 Alexander Sprunt & Son, Inc. Records, 1779-1960, 5,851 items and 231 vols. Cotton exporters. Includes 1 item, 26 August 1909, on economic conditions in Russia. (NUCMC 71-85)

64 Strachey Family. Papers, 1776-1847, 2 microfilm reels. Richard Strachey (1781-1847) was a traveler and diplomat in India, Persia, and Russia.

65 John Banister Tabb (1845-1909). Papers, 1901-36, 16 items. Poet and schoolteacher. Contains references to the Russo-Japanese War of 1904-1905.

66 James Augustus Thomas (1862-1940). Papers, 1905-41, 29,231 items. Merchant and an authority on the Orient, where he spent much of his career. He was in China during the Russo-Japanese War, 1904-1905. Includes some letters, 1928, from John B. Powell about Russian influence with the Chinese Eastern Railroad in Manchuria. Letter, July 1930, from C. E. Harber in Shanghai concerns the completion of the Turkestan-Siberian (Turksib) Railroad and the probable increase of Russian influence that would follow. (NUCMC 62-919)

67 William E. Tolbert (ca. 1840-ca. 1900). Papers, 1820-1939, 1,413 items. Civil War soldier and businessman. Contains reference(s) to the Russian Revolution of 1917. (NUCMC 63-119)

68 U.S. Army. European Command. Historical Division. Foreign Military Studies, 1945-

1954. 329 items. Since the end of World War II, this program has gathered records of the European War by former high-ranking German officers. Among the materials at Duke (only a part of the entire collection) are items on Russian armed forces and the German occupation of the USSR in 1941-44. The Historical Division's Guide to Foreign Military Studies, 1945-1954, Catalog and Index (1954) contains indices of topics, authors, and military units, and also describes each manuscript.

69 John Fane, 11th Earl of Westmorland (1784-1859). Papers, 1837-76, 22 items. British diplomat. Includes a letter, 7 September 1853, which concerns Russo-British relations.

70 James Willis (fl. ca. 1800). Papers, 1799-1804, 63 items. British East India Company employee. Primarily correspondence between him and Harford Jones (Sir Harford Jones Brydges), also an East India Company employee and British diplomat. In 1801 Jones writes about war with France, possible complications with Russia, and British interests in India. Elsewhere he writes of Henry Dundas, who wants news of Russia and Afghanistan. Subjects of other letters from Jones include Russian designs on Turkish Armenia, January 1802; the Persian Shah's anger over Russian encroachment in Georgia, March 1802; Azerbaijan's rising against Persia and appeal for aid from Russia, 5 April 1802; and Russian expansion near the Caspian Sea, April 1804. Jones feared the outcome of a Persian-Russian war, or even a war by Persia and Turkey against Russia. He wanted a pact among Persia, Turkey, and Britain against the tsar. Letters of February 1802 concern the diplomatic work of the Russian ambassador at Constantinople, V. S. Tamara. Other letters, July 1802 and 7 May 1804, concern the Russians in the Near East. In 1801 Jones sent Willis a report, 2 pp., entitled "Substance of Information Obtained from an Armenian Merchant on the 16th May 1801." In 1795 the merchant traveled from Herat in Afghanistan to Astrakhan in Russia via Bukhara. Jones's summary discusses these regions, the people, relations with Russia, travel conditions, and especially potential for military operations (a Russian invasion of India through Astrabad and Gazna). (NUCMC 68-1616)

71 Sir Thomas Willshire, 1st Bart. (1789-1862). Papers, 1806-1935, 79 items. British army officer. Includes letters, 4 and 20 December 1839, that comment on Russo-British relations. (NUCMC 71-1669)

72 Sir Evelyn Wood (1838-1919). Correspondence, 1848-1919, 232 items. British field marshal. Publication of his history of Crimean War in 1895 brought him more than 15 letters from participants with details, corrections, and additions to his account. They concern the 18 June 1855 assault on the redan during the siege of Sevastopol; the rank and status of Sir William John Codrington, Crimean commander at one point (from his son); the service of Sir James Yorke Scarlett; the Battle of the Alma River on 20 September 1854; and criticism of the war history by Alexander William Kinglake. 1 letter, 2 January 1860, from Kinglake himself requests a copy of General Sir John Miller Ayde's book on the war. None of the correspondence is contemporary with the war. (NUCMC 63-148)

Finding Aids: All catalogued collections have unpublished descriptions. Published guide to the manuscript collections in preparation.

NC 3
RARE BOOK ROOM
WILLIAM R. PERKINS LIBRARY
DUKE UNIVERSITY
Durham, North Carolina 27706
(919-684-4134)

1 Armenian Manuscripts. Four Gospels, A.D. 1654 (Armenian MS. 1); and fragments, 4 pp., of an illustrated manuscript on paper, 15th c. (?), possibly a book of prayers (Armenian MS. 2).

2 Note: The rare book room also holds a Church Slavonic manuscript in Cyrillic on paper, hagiographic in nature, ca. 17th c., currently in process.

NC 4
ARCHIVES DIVISION
COMMISSION ON ARCHIVES AND HISTORY
UNITED METHODIST CHURCH
39 Lake Shore Drive (Mail: P.O. Box 488)
Lake Junaluska, North Carolina 28745
(704-452-5584)

1 Bishop William Burt (1852-1936). Papers, 1883-1935, 9,000 items. Minister of the Methodist Episcopal Church. Several folders relate to Russia. Published preliminary descriptive inventory. (NUCMC 71-1917)

2 Records of the World Division of the Board of Global Ministries of the United Methodist Church (and its antecedent bodies). Archives, 1819-1972, 1,100 cu. ft. Reports of the General Conference and Board of Missions, correspondence (particularly of missionaries), diaries, journals, and financial records all include some material pertaining to the Russian Empire/Soviet Union. (Cf. NUCMC 71-1916 and 71-1918). Application for release of information necessary in advance; write the Archives Division.

NC 5
DIVISION OF ARCHIVES AND HISTORY
NORTH CAROLINA DEPARTMENT OF CULTURAL RESOURCES
109 East Jones Street
Raleigh, North Carolina 27611
(919-733-2952)

1 Nell Battle Lewis (1893-1956). Papers, 1862 and 1920-56, ca. 10,000 items and 5 scrapbooks. Newspaper columnist. Includes some of her articles on the USSR. (NUCMC 66-1241)

2 Abraham Lincoln (1809-1865). Papers, 1852-65 and 1927, 2 items in 1 folder. U.S. president, 1861-65. Signed authorization by the president for use of the great seal of the United States for the recall of Cassius Clay as U.S. minister to Russia, 8 April 1862; and a printed pamphlet containing previously unpublished letters of Lincoln, 22 January 1852-February 1865, reprinted from the Congressional Record, 1927.

Finding Aid: Guide to Private Manuscript Collections in the North Carolina State Archives, prepared by Beth G. Crabtree (Raleigh, 1964); revised edition in preparation.

NC 6
SOUTHEASTERN BAPTIST THEOLOGICAL SEMINARY LIBRARY
Box 752
Wake Forest, North Carolina 27587
(919-556-3101 x 225/250)

Everett Gill, Sr. (1869-1958). Served with the American Relief Administration in Russia, 1921-22. Manuscript of his book "Protestants of the East: A Study of the Paulicians of Armenia and of the Bogomiles of the Balkans," 322 pp., typed. The book mentions Russia only in passing.

NORTH DAKOTA

ND 1
ARCHIVES DIVISION
STATE HISTORICAL SOCIETY OF NORTH DAKOTA
Liberty Memorial Building
Bismarck, North Dakota 58505
(moving within two years)
(701-224-2663)

Historical Data Project--Biography Series. Interviews with North Dakota "pioneers," ca. 1938-41, ca. 5-6,000 interviews. Perhaps 25-33% of the interviews are with Russian-Germans who came to the United States at the turn of this century. Questionnaire/answer sheets supply names of family members, birthdates, birthplaces, and other information, often supplemented by further biographical data on separate sheets. Partial finding aid (name and location index).

ND 2
DR. WILLIAM A. DANDO--PRIVATE COLLECTION
DEPARTMENT OF GEOGRAPHY
THE UNIVERSITY OF NORTH DAKOTA
Grand Forks, North Dakota 58202
(701-777-4246)

Dr. Dando, a specialist in Soviet climatology, agrometeorology, and agriculture, has a collection of more than 6,000 color 35 mm slides, taken every year from 1970 to 1979, of all geographic and ethnic regions of the USSR. The emphasis of the photographs is upon man's modification of and adjustment to harsh environments.

OHIO

OH 1
FIRESTONE TIRE AND RUBBER COMPANY
1200 Firestone Parkway
Akron, Ohio 44301
(216-867-8220)

The archives hold records (correspondence, reports, and photographs) of the firm's intermittent contacts with Russian and Soviet officials concerning the sale of tires and tire manufacturing equipment. Among the holdings are: reports of R. Q. Harris of the Motor Tire Department, January, March, and April 1915, about a contract with the tsarist government for tires--later cancelled as the Russians decided to buy direct from the manufacturers; a thick, uncatalogued folder of letters, agreements, work papers, etc., labeled "Amtorg Trading Corp." (1929) relating to Soviet plans to have Firestone build a tire factory in the USSR (the scheme fell through); reports, February-March 1932, to Firestone management concerning the production of Koksaghy Rubber in the Soviet Union and Soviet experiments with various rubber plants; and "Ford--Russia Equipment Purchase," 1940-43 and 1957, uncatalogued, relating to the October 1943 purchase of the Ford Motor Company's tire manufacturing plant for shipment to the Soviet Union as part of the lend-lease program. Materials are restricted to officers and top executives of the Firestone Company. The archives has unpublished inventories and finding lists for its collections.

OH 2
ARCHIVES OF THE HISTORY OF AMERICAN PSYCHOLOGY
THE UNIVERSITY OF AKRON
Akron, Ohio 44325
(216-375-7285)

1 The Manuscripts Collections (unpublished papers of individuals), Archives (unpublished papers of organizations), photographs, films, audio tapes, oral histories, and other materials in the repository include numerous references to Ivan Petrovich Pavlov (1849-1936), the Russian physiologist who pioneered the study of conditioned reflexes. Among relevant holdings are correspondence and other items of:

2 David P. Boder (1866-1961). Papers, 1927-56, 8 ft. Note of 10 March 1936 speaks of Pavlov, Ivan Sechenov, and Vladimir Bekhterev. The Boder Museum Collection holds a photo of Pavlov (1932). Unpublished finding aids.

3 Ernest A. Hilgard (b. 1904). Manuscript, 1934, on conditioned reflexes; letters from William H. Burnham and others listed here.

4 Karl S. Lashley (1890-1958). Letter, 14 May 1935, to Hilgard on Bekhterev and conditional reflexes.

5 Florence Mateer (1887-1961?). Letter of 19 May 1937 to Hilgard speaks of Pavlov, Bekhterev, and Krasnogorskii.

6 Everett F. Patten (1895-1966). Papers, 1932-39, 3 ft. Include a letter from Clark L. Hull, 20 February 1935, about Pavlov.

7 Irvin T. Schultz (b. 1892). His Reminiscences Concerning Psychology and Psychologists (February 1963) contain references to Pavlov, one from the 1932 Copenhagen Congress.

8 St. Clair A. Switzer (1902-1976). Papers, 1929-41, .25 in. Include a letter from Clark L. Hull, 25 February 1932, that mentions Pavlov.

9 W. Clark Trow (b. 1894). Amateur motion pictures taken at the Tenth International Congress of Psychology, Copenhagen, 1932, show Pavlov with P. S. Kupalov, his close associate, and G. V. Anrep, his former student, translator, and editor of Conditioned Reflexes (1927).

10 John B. Watson (1878-1958). Letter, 18 February 1937, to Hilgard about Pavlov's influence on him.

11 Robert M. Yerkes (1876-1956). Letter to Hilgard, 25 January 1937, about Pavlov.

12 In addition, the Gregory Razran (1901-1973) Papers, 1940-73, contain a few Soviet-related items. And the Archives maintains a Locator File listing historic materials held by other institutions or by individuals.

Restriction: Open only to scholars who have a bona fide interest in the history of psychology. Inquire about individual restrictions.

Finding Aid: Nearly all of the preceding information came directly from Joseph Brozek and Marion White McPherson, "Pavloviana in the USA: Archives of the History of American Psychology, University of Akron," Conditional Reflex, vol. 8, no. 4 (October-December 1973).

OH 3
SHELDON BENJAMIN--PRIVATE COLLECTION
3525 Middleton Avenue
Cincinnati, Ohio 45220

A large collection of printed and unpublished materials focusing on the Jews and other minorities of the Soviet Union, dissidents, and samizdat. Materials, for the years ca. 1893-1920 and 1965-present, include correspondence, clippings, translations, photos, reprints, and issuances (bibliographies, pamphlets, information bulletins) of human rights and Soviet Jewry groups, ca. 25 ft. (plus ca. 50 ft. of books and periodicals). Most archival material concerns the Cincinnati Council for Soviet Jews (complete archives), Union of Councils for Soviet Jews, Student Struggle for Soviet Jewry, and (to a lesser extent) the National Conference on Soviet Jewry and Amnesty International. Unpublished materials can further be divided into 5 general topics: (a) American reaction to Soviet restrictions on Jews (the largest collection of files); (b) Soviet abuse of psychiatry for political purposes; (c) events surrounding the Jackson-Vanik amendment to the Trade Act of 1973; (d) human rights provisions of the Helsinki accords; and (e) folksongs and customs of the shtetl Streshin in Byelorussia, including a large number of oral history taped recordings, maps, photos, folklore, and ca. 100 taped Yiddish and Russian folksongs native to the area ca. 1900. Unrestricted use on the premises; inventory in progress.

OH 4
CINCINNATI HISTORICAL SOCIETY
Eden Park
Cincinnati, Ohio 45202
(513-241-4622)

1 Joseph Pitcairn. Papers, 1796-1821, 201 items. Diplomat and merchant. Includes several pieces of diplomatic correspondence from John Quincy Adams before and during his ministry to Russia, 1809-14. A few other miscellaneous letters also concern Russia and diplomacy in the Napoleonic wars, 1798-1811. Unpublished calendar (NUCMC 62-4299).

2 Charles Stewart Todd (1791-1871). Todd family papers, 1809-1949, 343 items. Lawyer and minister to Russia. Correspondence, documents, and genealogical information. (NUCMC 63-194)

Finding Aid: Louis L. Tucker, "The Historical and Philosophical Society of Ohio; its Resources," Ohio History, vol. 71, no. 3 (October 1962).

OH 5
AMERICAN JEWISH ARCHIVES
HEBREW UNION COLLEGE
3101 Clifton Avenue
Cincinnati, Ohio 45220
(513-221-1875)

The Archives has material primarily concerning the history of the Jews in the Western Hemisphere. Among Russian/Soviet-related collections are the following:

1 Alliance israélite universelle. Records, 1887-1939, 17 microfilm reels. Correspondence. The group assisted Russian Jews in emigrating to Argentina. (NUCMC 68-8)

2 Harold Berman (1879-1949). Papers, ca. 1929-47, 7 boxes. Journalist and author. Includes essays about pogroms and Russian Jews. (NUCMC 66-1017)

3 Boris D. Bogen (1869-1929). Correspondence, 1921-24, 961 items. Educator and social worker; director general of the Joint Distribution Committee in World War I. Letters concern relief work for Jews in Russia and Poland and his travel with the Hoover Mission. (NUCMC 65-1721)

4 Stanley F. Chyet (b. 1931). Former associate director of the AJA. Materials on Soviet Jewry, 1967 (box 2355).

5 Gitelson Family. Papers, 1897-1963, 36,193 items. Letters and business (textiles) records, plus family papers, in part photocopies. Some papers are in Russian and Polish. (NUCMC 68-25)

6 Nelson Glueck (b. 1900). Papers, 1918-63, 220 items and 5 microfilm reels. Rabbi, archaeologist, and president of Hebrew Union College-Jewish Institute of Religion. Correspondence and other papers, in part microfilm of originals retained by Dr. Glueck. Includes his statement about the plight of Soviet Jews (box 2382). (NUCMC 68-26)

7 Samuel Kipnis (b. 1887). Papers, 1922-62, 1 microfilm reel. Partial autobiography and diaries contain Russian references. (No. 1685)

8 George L. Kline. Professor of philosophy, specialist in Russian and Soviet philosophy. Tape recording of 1964 lectures delivered at the Frank L. Weil Institute for Studies in Religion and the Humanities (Cincinnati). The topic: religion and anti-religion in the Soviet Union. Published in revised and expanded form (Chicago, 1968). (Tapes 171-82)

9 Louis Marshall (1856-1929). Papers, 1891-1930, 96 ft. Constitutional lawyer, philanthropist, and Jewish leader. Correspondence and other papers concern anti-Semitism worldwide, Zionism, and many political questions. On Russian affairs in general, 1891-1929, there are materials in 25 different boxes; 15 boxes hold correspondence to and from Marshall concerning Russian and Soviet Jewry, 1916-17 and 1920-29; references to efforts to abrogate the 1832 Russian-American Treaty in the period 1910-1920s are in items in 16 boxes; and 7 boxes contain, in part, letters on Russian relief efforts, the Russian Information Bureau, and a Russian hospital unit. Also, information about Jewish agricultural colonization in Russia is in box 85. Access restricted.

10 Jacob H. Schiff (1847-1920). Papers, 1914-20, 29 ft. Financier and philanthropist. Correspondence and other papers. Includes 22 items concerning a war loan to Russia in 1916 (box 453); 31 items, 1917, about a Russian Commission (Mayor's Committee) and the Russian Information Bureau (box 461); and 42 more items on the Russian Information Bureau in 1918 and 1920 (boxes 468 and 470). 6 items of J. J. Goldstein are Russian-related (box 465). (NUCMC 65-1739)

11 Samuel M. Schmidt (1883-1964). Papers, 1919-45, 987 items and 1 microfilm reel. Cincinnati businessman. Active in Joint Distribution Committee activities in Europe during and after World War I. In World War II he was again involved with relief work, aiding Polish and Lithuanian refugees. Correspondence and miscellaneous documents relate to all of this work. The picture collection at the AJA has related items. (NUCMC 68-1148)

12 Moishe Leib Schnitzer. Miscellaneous documents, 1890-99, 11 pp. Includes his military papers from the Russian army, 1890-93.

13 Felix M. Warburg (1871-1937). Papers, 1910-37, 103 ft. Philanthropist. Includes Russian-related material, ca. 24 items, from 1919 and 1926-27 in 3 boxes. References to A. I. Konovoloff (Konovalov), A. D. Margolin, A. J. Sack, Dr. Henry Sliosberg. Contains diary of James N. Rosenberg (copy) with reference(s) to Russia (box 236); and correspondence pertaining to Russia from Alexander de Guinzburg, ca. 16 items (box 182), Isaac Landman, 22 items (box 226), Walter E. Meyer, 4 items (box 227), and Milton J. Rosenau, 4 items (box 217).

14 Frank Leopold Weil (1894-1957). Papers, 1897-1955, ca. 19,310 items and 8 boxes. New York City lawyer. Correspondence, reports, minutes, notes, and printed matter pertaining to his life and work, and to agencies with which he was concerned, including the American Jewish Joint Distribution Committee, American Red Cross, and Committee on Public Information. (NUCMC 68-110)

15 In addition, the AJA has materials scattered in various collections by or about the American Jewish Committee, American Relief Administration, American Society for Jewish Farm Settlements in Russia, Inc., foreign affairs, Joint Distribution Committee, League of Jewish Youth of America, Russia, Russian Famine Fund, and Russo-Jewish Committee which, according to published catalogues, contain information on Russian/Soviet Jewry. Also, there are vertical file materials on Russian Jews in 1917, anti-Semitism in the USSR, etc. (mostly printed matter); tape recordings about Soviet capital punishment, 1964 (tape 183) and other Russian matters (tape 230); and microfilm holdings about Soviet Jewry (e.g., nos. 167-77).

Finding Aids: Manuscript Catalog of the American Jewish Archives (Cincinnati), 4 vols. (Boston: G. K. Hall, 1971), especially vol. 4, appendices; and First Supplement to the preceding catalogue (1978).

OH 6
COMPANY ARCHIVES
THE AUSTIN COMPANY
3650 Mayfield Road
Cleveland, Ohio 44121
(216-382-6600)

The company archives contain documentation on the production plant and workers' city built by the Austin Company for the assembly of Ford-type automobiles in Gorki (Nijni Novgorod) in the early 1930s. The material includes a small amount of correspondence, slides, movies, 2 Russian-captioned photo albums, a book of site and layout drawings, miscellaneous photographs, and some printed magazine articles. The contract awarded Austin by the Soviet state trust Avtostroi in August 1929 was for ca. $60 million, the largest entered into by the Soviet regime since 1917. At dedication ceremonies in January 1932 the plant was christened Molotov in honor of the premier. After 90 days of operation it closed, having produced just 2 of its planned 750 rear axles. Researchers should contact the company in advance so that stored material can be gathered. A brief introduction to the story of the Austin Company's Russian adventure is in the pages of Martin Greif's The New Industrial Landscape: The Story of the Austin Company (Clinton, New Jersey, 1978), pp. 97-102.

OH 7
BAKER, HOSTETLER & PATTERSON
Union Commerce Building
Cleveland, Ohio 44115
(216-621-0200)

Newton Diehl Baker (1871-1937). "Baker Collection," primarily books with his nameplate or signature, many volumes of newspaper clippings about him, and some original documents (mainly letters and telegrams on his death and tributes to him). Baker was U.S. secretary of war, 1916-21. Includes 3 vols. of original correspondence between Baker and General Tasker Bliss, U.S. representative on the Allied Supreme Command during World War I. Some letters apparently pertain to the Russian front. Write or phone in advance to arrange a research visit.

OH 8
ARCHIVES
CASE WESTERN RESERVE UNIVERSITY
2040 Adelbert Road
Cleveland, Ohio 44106
(216-368-4289)

Case Alumnus. This publication contains several Russian-related items, including 5 articles by Ray W. Stuck, an engineer and supervisor in charge of construction at a steel plant in Magnitogorsk for the Cleveland engineering firm of Arthur G. McKee. These pieces appeared, with pictures, in vol. 12, nos. 1-5 (October 1932-April 1933).

OH 9
SPECIAL COLLECTIONS
CASE WESTERN RESERVE UNIVERSITY LIBRARIES
11161 East Boulevard
Cleveland, Ohio 44106
(216-368-2993)

1 Donald J. Angus (1887-1966). Papers, 1904-63, 3 ft. Engineer and inventor. Correspondence,

report, laboratory notes, patents, and fiscal records pertaining to the Esterline-Angus Company of Indianapolis, Indiana, and to other matters. Some items relate to Angus's work on a steel plant in the Urals. Unpublished inventory (NUCMC 68-903).

2 Benedict Crowell (1869-1952). Papers, 1917-20, 20 boxes, 10 ft. Assistant secretary of war, 1917-20, and director of munitions, 1919. Correspondence, printed matter, and other items (mainly statistical) issued by the War Department. Unpublished contents list (NUCMC 60-2024).

OH 10
JOHN G. WHITE DEPARTMENT OF
FOLKLORE, ORIENTALIA AND CHESS
CLEVELAND PUBLIC LIBRARY
325 Superior Avenue
Cleveland, Ohio 44114
(216-623-2818)

The John G. White Department of Folklore, Orientalia, and Chess owns over 147,000 volumes and 1,500 manuscripts, with the largest chess library in the world, of approximately 21,000 vols. To speak of relevant materials by subject, one can start with the chess holdings, among which are:

1 Aleksandr Aleksandrovich Alekhin (1892-1946). Pencil manuscript in German with his articles cabled to the New York Times from the 1929 Karlsbad chess tournament (1929), 54 ll. (W789.24M S9s); a portfolio, n.p., 1932, 4 pp., of a chess play exhibition in New York City, 3 p.m., 8 November 1932, against 200 opponents at 50 boards (W789.21 AL25a); a German manuscript entitled Original-glossierungen, meisterpartien des Zürcher Turnierbuches, 1943 of 37 numbered ll. [1934] (Wq789.24M T4z2); and an autographed copy of Alekhine v. Euwe, 1937 (London, 1937, no. 15 of a limited edition) (Wq789.22 AL25e7).

2 Fedor Parfen'evich Bogatyrchuk (b. 1892). 8 Partiĭ velmistra Bohatyrcuka with annotations by M. L. Pachman (Prague, 1944), reproduced from typescript, 83 pp. (W789.21 B633o).

3 N. Bol'berg. Kolxoz stanbnada jal [Leisure in the camp of the kolkhoz], translated by Bajmoratof (Bashkir, 1935), 66 pp. (W789.77 B637k).

4 Mikhail Moiseevich Botvinnik (b. 1911). Match tournament for the absolute chess championship of the USSR Leningrad-Moscow, 1941; complete collection of games with detailed notes and foreword ([n.p., 194-?], edited by I. Maiselis and translated by A. Krivis (Wq789.24M U1b). Also, a copy of a limited edition of Botvinnik's Best Games, 1927-1934 (New York, 1937) (Wq789.21 B659).

5 David Ionovick Bronshtein (b. 1924). Reproduction from typed copies of Larry Evans' David Bronshtein's Best Games of Chess, 1944-1949 (New York, 1949) (Wq789.21 B789e); and of a description of his match with Boleslavski in 1950. Chess Student Quarterly, 1951, 30 pp. (W789.21 B789b).

6 Paul Keres (b. 1916). Reproductions from typescripts of 2 books: Dr. Emanuel Lasker on the Keres-Euwe Match in Holland (1939/40) (Wq789.22 K454e); and on Keres' Best Games, 1932/36 and 1937 (New York, 1937-38) (Wq789.21 K454r).

7 Aron Nimzowitsch (1886-1935). Autographed limited edition copy (no. 41) of Thirty-five Nimzowitsch Games, 1904-1927, edited by Fred Reinfield (New York, 1935), 57 pp. (W789.21 N619).

8 Russian War Relief, Inc. Publicity release for the U.S.A.-USSR radio match (New York, 1945), 27 ll., reproduced from typed copy. (Wq789.24 U5r)

9 Shakhmatnyi turnier v gor. Prianu posviashchennyi XV-letiiu Sovetskoi Estonii. Chess tournament in Pärnu dedicated to the 15th anniversary of Soviet Estonia, 13-31 July 1955. Carbon copy of manuscript, 34 ll.

10 Serge de Stchoulepnikoff. 2 manuscripts: Twenty Solutions of the Problem of the Knight's Tour, 10 pp., 9 numbered diagrams (Buffalo, New York, 1865) (W789.62M M5s); and Numerate Tables of All Symmetric Tours arranged with quarts, a record of an investigation in search of magic tours. Transcribed exactly as the original manuscript by John G. White in 1888 with a page of his own statement. 1885, 135 pp. (W789.63M 05s).

11 Savelii Grigorevich Tartakover (1887-1956). An autographed letter to Dr. Gerard C. A. Oskam with typed translation prefixed, 4 pp., 1924. (W789.691M T178)

One might note that the chess collection also includes literary works making significant references to chess, such as Gesta Romanorum (58 early editions); the Rubaiyat of Omar Khayyam (1,050 editions in 40 languages); an article from the Syn Otechestva for 1839, and other works relating to chess.

The Folklore and Orientalia collections of the White Department have extensive and important holdings on ethnology and explorations of Central Asia, Georgia, and the Caucasus published by the 19th c. Russian learned societies; literary works and language materials in Jagataic (51 titles), Armenian (122 titles), Uigur (18 titles), Georgian (67 titles), Turkish (Roman Script, 160 titles), Turkish (Old, 185 titles), Bashkir (7 titles).

The following manuscript items are in the collection:

12 Iamshchik ne goni loshadei. A manuscript of "Coachman, do not speed the horses," 19 pp., and 4 other gypsy songs, n.p., n.d. 5 songs with music in all. (Wq091.9917 Ia6)

13 Istoricheskiia i statisticheskiia svedeniia o Kirgizskoi Bukeevskoi orde. A collection of government reports (all but 2 in manuscript) about Russia's relations with the Kirghiz and Khan Bukei in the first half of the 19th c., n.p., 1806-48, 828 pp., and a map. (Wq091. 9917 Is7).

14 [Kamchatka and the Koryaks]. Russian manuscript copy of a journal of Siberian exploration, 1843-45, 109 pp. (Wq091.9917 K128).

15 Nikolai Savvich Tikhonravov (1832-1893). Istoriia drevnei russkoi literatury. N.p., 1878-79, comprising lectures on ancient Russian literature, 281 pp. (Wq091.9917 T449i).

16 Among the Chapbooks of popular works, tales, abridged editions of literary classics, 130 titles are in Russian--a unique collection in the United States.

Finding Aids: Catalog of the Chess Collection (including checkers), 2 vols., arranged by author and subject (Boston: G. K. Hall, 1964); and the Catalog of Folklore, Folklife and Folk Songs, 2nd edition, 3 vols. (Boston: G. K. Hall, 1978), a dictionary catalogue arranged by subject which supercedes the earlier 1965 edition.

OH 11
UKRAINIAN MUSEUM-ARCHIVES, INC.
1202 Kenilworth Avenue
Cleveland, Ohio 44113
(216-661-3038)

The Ukrainian Museum-Archives holds documents, chronicles, decrees, and papers of prominent Ukrainians, Ukrainian civic leaders, and local Ukrainian organizations.

1 Msgr. Eugene Bachynsky. Ukrainian Orthodox Archbishop in Switzerland. Diary, correspondence, photographs, clippings, etc. 1905-present, several thousand items.

2 Dr. Longin Horbachewsky. Ukrainian civic leader in Cleveland. Memoirs or biographical data.

3 Prof. Volodymyr Pawlusewycz. Local Ukrainian leader. Memoirs or biographical data.

4 Plast (Ukrainian scout organization). Records, 1950-present. Correspondence, minute books, etc. of the Plast Organization in Cleveland and in some other U.S. cities. Includes the archives of the late Professor Severyn Lewycky, former chief Ukrainian scout.

5 Jurij Roik. Ukrainian civic leader. Memoirs or biographical data.

6 Prof. Alexander Tysowsky. Local Ukrainian leader. Memoirs or biographical data.

Note: The Museum also holds a substantial collection of Ukrainian art works and objects, including folk art items.

OH 12
THE WESTERN RESERVE HISTORICAL SOCIETY
10825 East Boulevard
Cleveland, Ohio 44106
(216-721-5722)

1 Maria D. Coffinberry (1879-1952). Family papers, 1767-1930, 3 containers. Includes a copy of an ALS, 20 August 1786, from George Washington to Col. George Morgan concerning the Marquis de La Fayette, who was seeking information on American Indian languages for Catherine II of Russia. Unpublished register.

2 William Haven (1888-1973). Papers, 1916-72, 3 containers. Cleveland engineer and businessman. In 1930 he supervised the planning of the Magnitogorsk steel plant, largest in the USSR. In 1931 Haven traveled to the Soviet Union and remained there for a year. Autobiography, data about plant construction, clippings, and pamphlets. Unpublished register.

3 Myron Timothy Herrick (1854-1929). Papers, ca. 1827-1935, 17 boxes. Financier, industrialist, Ohio governor, and diplomat. Correspondence from the 1920s, when he was ambassador in France, refers to Russia, the Bolshevik government, and the American Food Relief Project. Unpublished register (NUCMC 62-4689).

4 Mrs. T. Ellis Minshall. Collection, 1724-1867 and n.d., 4 items. 3 Russian documents: 1 signed by Peter the Great, 28 December 1724; the second signed by Catherine II, 31 December 1793; the third signed by Alexander II, 4 November 1867, ennobling Peter Moritz, son of Alexis Moritz, who entered Russian service in 1840 and rose to become secretary and treasurer for Tsarina Maria Alexandrovna. Also, a writing album of Alexander II, undated.

5 Shaker Collection. Ca. 1723-1939, ca. 122 ft. Contains copies of 4 letters, 1889-91, from Leo Tolstoi to Alonzo G. Hollister of Mt. Lebanon, New York, in which Tolstoi discusses Shaker beliefs. Also, copies of 8 letters

written by Hollister to Tolstoi in 1889-92 (originals in the Tolstoi State Museum, Moscow). A Guide to Shaker Manuscripts, ed. by Kermit Pike (Cleveland, 1974). (NUCMC 75-1717)

6 Philander H. Standish (1835-1918). Papers, 1861-1948, 5 containers. Mechanical engineer and inventor. Includes letters of patent Russia issued to him for, among other things, his invention of a chain-making machine, a sewing machine treadle mechanism, and a steam cultivator. A patent grant of 19 August 1869 is for improvements in the chain-making machine. Unpublished register.

7 Leon Trotskii (1879-1940). Revolutionary. Photocopy of a TLS, 22 July 1921, possibly to the editor of the New York Times, concerning establishment of diplomatic relations between the United States and Soviet Union.

8 Selma Weiss (d. 1974). Papers, 1926-46, 1 box. Social worker in the Red Cross, World War II. Ca. 18 letters, notes, and many photos relate to her visit to the USSR in 1936. They concern Leningrad, the Central Park of Culture, the Prophylactorium for Prostitutes in the USSR, Soviet social insurance, trade unions, communes, collective farms, and marriage and abortion laws.

Finding Aid: Kermit J. Pike, A Guide to the Manuscripts and Archives of The Western Reserve Historical Society (Cleveland, 1972).

9 Note: The Society expects to receive in the near future the papers of Cyrus Eaton, ca. 700 ft., that contain Russian-related material.

OH 13
ARCHIVES-MANUSCRIPTS DIVISION
THE OHIO HISTORICAL SOCIETY
Interstate 71 and 17th Avenue
Columbus, Ohio 43211
(614-466-1500)

1 John W. Bricker (b. 1893). Papers, 1939-59, 185 ft. U.S. senator from Ohio, 1947-58. Includes some material on Russia/USSR and on communism. Restricted. Unpublished typescript inventory (NUCMC 68-1374). (Manuscript Collection 340; hereinafter, Ms Coll.)

2 Thomas Clarkson (1760-1846). Holograph manuscript account of an interview, 23 September 1815, Clarkson had with Alexander I, during which they discussed the slavery issue. Clarkson was a Quaker.

3 Warren G. Harding (1865-1923). Papers, 1888-1923, 250 ft., 263 microfilm rolls. U.S. president, 1921-23. Russian-related items are in Boxes 565-71 (microfilm rolls 181-82). These include files for 1921-23 with material on the Russian economic situation, Russian relief (with letters from Herbert Hoover), and Meyer Bloomfield's trip to the USSR. Materials consist, in part, of extensive State Department correspondence (much of it from Charles E. Hughes), and of reports of the Purchasing Commission for Russia. The Warren G. Harding Papers: An Inventory to the Microfilm Edition, ed. by Andrea D. Lentz, Madalon M. Korodi, and Sara S. Fuller (Columbus, 1970) gives cross references to box numbers and microfilm rolls (NUCMC 75-1019). (Ms Coll. 345)

4 Jewish History Project. Oral history materials, 1974-76, 75 interviews. Interviews with Jewish immigrants to the Columbus area, many of whom were born in Russia. 7 of the interviews are closed.

5 Peter Kaufmann (1800-1869). Papers, 1806-69, 4 ft. German immigrant to the U.S., 1820, and founder of the Teutonia community in eastern Columbiana County, Ohio. In 1823 he published a Latin ode to Peter the Great, Elogium Petri Magni, Russorum Imperatoris. Some of his papers may contain notes for this publication. Unpublished typescript inventory (NUCMC 68-1391). (Ms Coll. 136)

6 Frank J. Lausche (b. 1895). Papers, 1949-69, 226 ft. U.S. senator from Ohio, 1957-69. Some constituent correspondence on the Khrushchev visit to the United States; a tape of Dalles Townsend's report from Moscow on the Kennedy assassination. Restricted. Unpublished typescript inventory (NUCMC 75-1073). (Ms Coll. 341)

7 National Council of Jewish Women--Columbus, Ohio Chapter. Records, 1919-74, 11.5 ft. Contains some materials on Soviet Jewry. Unpublished typescript inventory (NUCMC 75-1114). (Ms Coll. 403)

8 Charles Emil Ruthenberg (1882-1927). Papers, 1906-66, 4 ft. American communist leader. Most of the collection consists of materials collected by Oakley C. Johnson for his biography of Ruthenberg, The Day Is Coming. Available on microfilm (8 rolls). Unpublished typescript inventory (NUCMC 75-1163). (Ms Coll. 163)

9 John Sherman (1823-1900). U.S. senator from Ohio. ALS, 10 October 1867, to an unnamed correspondent comments on the status and potentials of Russian-American relations, 3 pp. Unpublished typescript inventory to Ms Coll. 329, of which this item is part (NUCMC 75-1177).

10 Eli Todd Tappan Family. Papers, 1826-1904, ca. 2 ft. Box 3 contains more than 1 folder of correspondence from Russia by Charles Tappan (d. 1908), a mining engineer who went to Siberia in 1899 to inspect mining

properties. Unpublished typescript inventory (NUCMC 68-1411). (Ms Coll. 100)

11 Temperance and Prohibition Papers. 417 rolls of microfilm, 1830-1933. Collection of records and papers for a number of organizations and individuals. Roll 25 of the World League Against Alcoholism Series contains information on the liquor problem in Russia. Roll 28 of the same series contains miscellaneous material, some of which pertains to Russia. Guide to the Microfilm Edition of Temperance and Prohibition Papers, ed. by Randall C. Jimerson, Francis X. Blouin, and Charles A. Isetts (Ann Arbor, 1977). The microfilm and the published guide were produced in cooperation with: Michigan Historical Collections (University of Michigan Libraries), Westerville (Ohio) Public Library, Woman's Christian Temperance Union (Evanston, Illinois), and others. (Ms Coll. 411)

12 John M. Vorys (1896-1968). Papers, 1939-58, 105 ft. U.S. congressman from Ohio, 1939-59. Some materials relate to Russia/USSR. Unpublished typescript inventory (NUCMC 75-1218). (Ms Coll. 280)

13 Frank B. Willis (1871-1928). Papers, 1892-1928, 52.5 ft. U.S. senator from Ohio, 1921-28. Includes materials on Soviet-American relations in folder 38, box 18, and folder 46, box 28. Unpublished typescript inventory (NUCMC 75-1239). (Ms Coll. 325)

14 Note: Material concerning American reactions to Napoleon's invasion of Russia in 1812 and Russian diplomatic activities in the late 18th and early 19th c. can be found in the papers of early Ohio political leaders, including Ethan A. Brown, Return J. Meigs, Jr., Arthur St. Clair, Winthrop Sargent, and Thomas Worthington. For more details, see Linda Elise Kalette, comp., The Papers of Thirteen Early Ohio Political Leaders. An Inventory to the 1976-77 Microfilm Editions (Columbus, 1977).

Finding Aid: A Guide to Manuscripts at the Ohio Historical Society, ed. by Andrea D. Lentz (Columbus, 1972), lists the Society's manuscript collections through Ms Coll. 365; the Society currently possesses 641 manuscript collections.

OH 14
SPECIAL COLLECTIONS
MAIN LIBRARY
OHIO STATE UNIVERSITY
1858 Neil Avenue
Columbus, Ohio 43210
(614-422-5938)

Rosa Dembo. Papers, ca. 1914-76, ca. 1 box. Lithuanian immigrant to the U.S., 1939. Correspondence, and diary, in English, containing descriptions of the city of Kaunas, Lithuania, and recollections of the Russian Revolution and Civil War, 92 pp.

OH 15
HILANDAR ROOM
MAIN LIBRARY
OHIO STATE UNIVERSITY
1858 Neil Avenue
Columbus, Ohio 43210
(614-422-0634)

Hilandar Slavic Manuscripts, 12th-20th c., ca. 300,300 pp. on 150,150 frames of microfilm, covering ca. 800 complete manuscripts, 100 fragments, hundreds of lay and ecclesiastical edicts and charters, and a substantial number of icons, frescoes, and other religious art. Originals of the Hilandar manuscripts are located in the Hilandar Monastery Library on Mt. Athos in Greece; additional material added to this collection was filmed in such repositories as the Zograph Monastery, Iveron Monastery (Mt. Athos), National Library in Athens, Vatican Library (Rome), Rila Monastery in Bulgaria, Synodal Library, National Library, and Academy of Sciences Library (all in Sofia, Bulgaria). Primarily ecclesiastical and religious works. Of those in Church Slavonic, 322 are in Russian recension and 1 in Ukrainian. 13 other manuscripts are also in Russian. Among the edicts and charters are 9 from the 15th-16th c. issued by Ivan IV Vasilevich (Grozny), Fedor Ivanovich, Boris Godunov, Michael Fedorovich Romanov, and Alexei Mikhailovich Romanov. Professor Mateja Matejić and his associates photographed the materials in 1970-75. His detailed description, Hilandar Slavic Codices (OSU Slavic Papers No. 2; Columbus, 1976), includes a glossary, index of titles, and statistical data tables.

OH 16
UNIVERSITY ARCHIVES
305 HITCHCOCK HALL
OHIO STATE UNIVERSITY
1858 Neil Avenue
Columbus, Ohio 43210
(614-422-0634)

1 Mikhail V. Condoide (1898-1971). Papers, 1921-71, 2 boxes. Russian-born professor of economics at OSU. 1 box of correspondence, book reviews, and other materials on research and courses pertaining to the Russian Empire/USSR. 1 folder of material on his military service in Russia. Unpublished index.

2 History Department. Archives, 1934-73, 14 boxes. Includes material on Russian history

courses, 1942-44; the Soviet Union Summer Program, 1966; the Midwest Slavic Conference, 1966; and the Slavic Translation Program, 1967-68. Unpublished index.

Restriction: Material of a personal nature may be restricted in accordance with the U.S. Right to Privacy act.

OH 17
WRIGHT STATE UNIVERSITY ARCHIVES
UNIVERSITY LIBRARY
Dayton, Ohio 45435
(513-873-2092)

1 Carol Cline. Papers, 1956-57, 1 folder. Includes a diary of a visit to the USSR, 1956, entitled "The Adventures of Carol in Stalinland."

2 James Cox (1870-1957). Papers, 1920-57, 15 cu. ft., 42 boxes. Governor of Ohio and presidential candidate, 1920. Papers contain scattered references to Russia.

OH 18
MRS. ILIYA BULATKIN--PRIVATE COLLECTION
167 West Winter Street
Delaware, Ohio 43015
(614-362-4855)

Memoirs in the form of a letter, ca. 200 pp. closely written on both sides, by her husband's father, Foma Bulatkin, a Don Cossack who fought in the Imperial army during the Revolution and eventually emigrated to the United States. Includes family history, material on the folk customs of the Kalmucks and the Cossacks of the Don region, and personal observations on the events of the Civil War. As a young man Foma Bulatkin (1863-1944) was a census taker among the Kalmuck tribes east of the Don. He later became ataman of the town of Constantinovskaya, and emigrated to Prague ca. 1921. Note: Ultimate disposition of the original material will probably be at the Hoover Institution (Stanford, California), though Mrs. Bulatkin will retain a copy. Write in advance to inquire about access.

OH 19
MANUSCRIPTS DIVISION
THE RUTHERFORD B. HAYES LIBRARY
1337 Hayes Avenue
Fremont, Ohio 43420
(419-332-2081)

1 Rutherford B. Hayes (1822-1893). Papers, 1835-93, ca. 164 ft. U.S. president. Includes: letter, 21 August 1879, from Wickham Hoffman, member of the U.S. legation in St. Petersburg, to John Sherman asking him to intercede on Hoffman's behalf to gain reappointment to the Russian post; signed document, 25 August 1879, 1 p., concerning Hayes' letter to Alexander II congratulating him on the birth of a grandson; and reference in the Registers of Letters Received by the President to a letter, 26 January 1880, from William H. Edwards, consul-general at St. Petersburg, to the president, requesting appointment as consul-general in Paris because the Russian weather was too severe (the letter being sent to the State Department for further consideration). Unpublished finding aids (NUCMC 62-3472).

2 Webb C. Hayes (1856-1934). Papers, 1868-1934, 28 ft. and 15 boxes. President's son, army officer, industrialist, and traveler. Hayes went to Korea in March-April 1904 to observe the Russo-Japanese War. Several letters and postcards describe his travels there and his attempts to reach the front near Anju and the Yalu River. ALS, 23 April 1904, to Dr. Horace N. Allen, American minister to Korea, tells of his capture by Russian torpedo boats off the coast of China. In May Hayes was in China and Manchuria. In Newschwang, Manchuria, he visited a Russian garrison and had discussions with several officers. His diary entries for 23 March-19 May 1904 recount these Korean and Manchurian experiences. An annotated photograph album holds nearly 90 pictures taken in these 2 regions. Hayes's diary for 19 April 1877 describes in several pages a White House visit and state dinner in honor of a Russian entourage. Among the guests were the grand dukes Alexis Alexandrovitch and Constantine (son and nephew of Alexander II respectively), Rear Admiral Grigorii Ivanovich Boutaukauff (Butakov), Baron Captain Schilling (or Schilley), Flag Surgeon Koudrine, Fleet Captain E. I. Alexieff, Captain Gerloff, Commodore Blagodareff, minister Nicolas Shishkin, and members of the Russian legation in Washington. Unpublished finding aid. (NUCMC 61-3285)

OH 20
CHALMERS MEMORIAL LIBRARY
KENYON COLLEGE
Gambier, Ohio 43022
(614-427-2244)

Philander Chase, Jr. (1798-1824). U.S. navy chaplain and son of the founder of Kenyon College. Includes Chase's "Journal during a Cruise on the Frigate Guerrière, July 25, 1818, to June 30, 1819," which contains descriptions of St. Petersburg.

OH 21
ETHNIC HERITAGE PROGRAM
SCHOOL OF LIBRARY SCIENCE
KENT STATE UNIVERSITY
Kent, Ohio 44242
(216-672-2784)

The Program has gathered a substantial collection of Baltic materials. Lithuanian, Latvian, and Estonian collections are not separate and distinct but are all integrated into the University library's general collections. At present nearly 10,000 items are in the 3 Baltic collections. Holdings include a large number of printed books and serials but also literary manuscripts, letters, and ephemera.

Some examples of Lithuanian holdings: diaries of Ona Simaitis, a Lithuanian woman who saved many Jewish children from the Nazis in World War II, 29 vols., unpublished; papers, 1 box, of Albinas Treciokas, an American-Lithuanian who corresponded with displaced persons wishing to immigrate to the U.S.; transcripts of the radio program "Memories of Lithuania" (1947-69), hosted by Dr. Jack Stukas (b. 1906?); a collection on the University of Vilna, in process (an exchange program); and a modest amount of material on the Soviet occupation of the Baltic States in 1940.

OH 22
MASSILLON PUBLIC LIBRARY
Massillon, Ohio 44646
(216-832-9831)

Rotch-Wales Papers. Ca. 22 ft., ca. 1780-1882. Primarily papers of Thomas Rotch (1767-1823) and his family, plus papers of Arvine Wales (1785-1854). Includes 2 letters, 11 October and 31 December 1802, from William Rotch, Jr. to Thomas Rotch and a letter, 11 November 1812, from William Rotch, Sr. to Thomas Rotch, all of which refer to Russian trade. Unpublished preliminary inventory (NUCMC 72-964).

OH 23
OBERLIN COLLEGE ARCHIVES
Oberlin, Ohio 44074
(216-775-8285 x 247)

1 Edwin Michael Hoffman (1884-1977). Papers, 1917-74, 1 ft. Served with the YMCA in Yokohama, Japan, 1918-19, and in Harbin, Manchuria, 1919-20. He was in contact with the American Expeditionary Forces in Siberia and attempted to learn Russian. Includes 80 letters (mostly family correspondence), in which he comments on events and people he observed; a journal with photographs of Irkutsk; music for a few Russian songs; and recollections, 1972-74, of his overseas work. Collection available on microfilm, which must be used for the majority of papers because of the very fragile condition of the originals. Unpublished inventory card and box list (NUCMC 76-656).

2 George Frederick Wright (1838-1921). Papers, 1850-1921, ca. 17 cu. ft. Oberlin professor, Congregational minister, and geologist. Includes information about his trip across Russia in 1900. Unpublished finding aid.

OH 24
ANTIOCHIANA
OLIVE KETTERING LIBRARY
ANTIOCH COLLEGE
Yellow Springs, Ohio 45387
(513-767-7331 x 200)

Alumni Writings Collection. Includes a typed travel account, 77 pp., by Philena Weller Montgomery (Antioch class of 1930) and John Ferguson Montgomery (Antioch, 1927) entitled "Traveling through the USSR," a description of their trip to the Soviet Union in 1933.

OKLAHOMA

OK 1
WILL ROGERS MEMORIAL
P.O. Box 157
Claremore, Oklahoma 74017
(918-341-0719)

Will Rogers (1879-1935). Papers, 1900-35, 5,000 items. Humorist. Rogers traveled to the Soviet Union in 1926 and 1934, and wrote a book about his first visit--There's Not a Bathing Suit in Russia and Other Bare Facts (1927). Throughout the papers, most of which are on microfilm, there are scattered references to Russia. Restriction: Due to space problems, use of materials is limited to 1 researcher by appointment only. (NUCMC 75-2068)

OK 2
WESTERN HISTORY COLLECTIONS
UNIVERSITY OF OKLAHOMA
Monnet Hall, Room 452
630 Parrington Oval
Norman, Oklahoma 73069
(405-325-3641)

1 Patrick J. Hurley. Papers, ca. 600-700 boxes (in process at time of writing). U.S. army officer. Includes correspondence, memoranda, telegrams, certificates, reports, press releases, notes, and invitations relating to the general's trip to the Soviet Union in 1942.

2 Microform Collections. Contains reproductions from many repositories, including, on microfilm, from the National Archives in Washington, D.C.: records of the Russian-American Company, 1802-67 (NARS RG 261); and notes from the Russian legation in the U.S. to the Department of State, 1809-1906 (NARS RG 59). These holdings have the respective call numbers M-11 and M-39.

3 Stuart Ramsay Tompkins (b. 1886). Papers (1917-56), 7 ft. and 8 microfilm reels. History professor. Subject file on Russian history, manuscript and galley proofs of his The Russian Mind (Norman, 1953), manuscripts on Alaska, article reprints, a monograph Russia through the Ages (1940), and 3 scrapbooks, 1 in Russian, containing primarily newspaper articles on Russia. Also, maps, including 13 negative photocopies of maps of Russian cities and areas from the 9th c. to 1900. On microfilm are materials on the Russian occupation of Kamchatka, transcripts of Russian and Spanish correspondence, and documents, from 1761-73, and many excerpts from Russian periodicals. (NUCMC 62-3026)

4 The Collections also hold the papers of a number of Oklahoma senators and congressmen; most of these papers are currently being processed but preliminary surveys reveal documents on the USSR and the Cold War. Among these congressional papers are collections of Page Belcher, Helen Gahagan Douglas, Fred Harris, Robert S. Kerr, Mike Monroney, and Elmer Thomas. These papers are under various restrictions; inquire at the repository.

Finding Aid: A Guide to Microfilm Collections in the University of Oklahoma Library Western History Collections Manuscripts Division by G. C. Williams and Donald E. Ritz (1978).

OREGON

OR 1
SPECIAL COLLECTIONS
UNIVERSITY OF OREGON LIBRARY
Eugene, Oregon 97403
(503-686-3069)

1 Clarence Leroy Andrews (1862-1948). Papers, 1913-48, 3 ft. Employee of the U.S. Interior Department's Reindeer Service in Alaska and an expert and author of books on Alaska (especially the introduction of reindeer there). He wrote about Russian America (Alaska), penned a biography of A. A. Baranov, and gathered manuscripts and documents on Alaskan history (materials of Kiril T. Khliebnikov, Petr A. Tikhmenev, the Valaamskii Preobrazhenskii Monastery, and William T. Lopp). The collection includes letters, reports, and photographs as well, 1913-48. Ca. 2 ft. Russia-related. Unpublished inventory (NUCMC 70-1770).

2 Verne Bright (1893-1977). Papers, 1917-62, 3 ft. Author. Includes correspondence when Bright was an infantryman with the American Expeditionary Forces in Siberia, 1918-19. Ca. 64 letters discuss the Revolution and Civil War. Unpublished inventory (NUCMC 69-944).

3 Jerome Davis (b. 1891). Papers, 1915-63, 17 ft. Member of the YMCA-run International Committee for Work with Prisoners of War in Russia, 1916-19. He traveled to the Soviet Union again in 1943-44 to gather material for a book. From this time there are wireless dispatches, a diary, and some newspaper stories he sent to the Toronto Star Weekly. He wrote books about Russia and edited a Russian series for the Vanguard Press. The collection also includes some posters from Russia dating from World War I. Ca. 3 ft. of Russian-related items. Unpublished inventory (NUCMC 72-344).

4 John Frederick Finerty (1885-1967). Papers, 1910-61, 15 ft. Lawyer. Includes letters and documents (1937-38) connected with the Commission of Inquiry into the Charges Made Against Leon Trotskii in the Moscow Trials. In addition there are case files on matters involving Julius and Ethel Rosenberg, Thomas J. Mooney, the American Civil Liberties Union, and the Workers Defense League, 1952-53. Ca. 3 ft. of Russian-related material. Unpublished inventory (NUCMC 70-1786).

5 Emmett W. Gulley (b. 1894). Papers on the Dukhobors, 1950-55, ca. 2 ft. Representative

of the American Friends Service Committee, sent to Canada in 1950 to investigate relations between the Canadian government and the Dukhobor sect. Correspondence and printed matter (pamphlets and clippings) from 1950-55 concern this work. Unpublished inventory (NUCMC 69-973).

6 Leo Huberman (1903-1968). Papers, 1937-67, 18 ft. Professor of labor and economic history and the labor editor of the Monthly Review and the newspaper PM. There are letters and documents about the court case of California vs. Earl King, Ernest G. Ramsay, 1937-41, and the Harry Bridges deportation hearing, 1939; memoranda and documents concerning PM (1940-41); letters and papers relating to Huberman's appearance before the McCarthy committee; reports, 1942-45, on the National Maritime Union; and printed matter on the Communist Party, Cuba, India, and socialism. Ca. 14 ft. Russian-related. Unpublished inventory (NUCMC 74-839).

7 Grace Hutchins (1885-1969). Papers, 1898-1954, ca. 2 ft. Author and founder of the Labor Research Association. From 1926-27 there are letters written in Russia. Unpublished inventory (NUCMC 72-1125).

8 Eugene Lyons (b. 1898). Papers, 1937-64, 2 ft. Tass and United Press correspondent, author. Manuscripts of his books Assignment in Utopia (New York, 1937) and Our Secret Allies, the Peoples of Russia (New York, 1953). Also, the original typed and corrected copy of his interview with Joseph Stalin 22 November 1930, which Stalin signed, and 1 letter from Stalin. Unpublished inventory (NUCMC 69-1001).

9 Michael A. Meyendorff (1849-1908). Papers, 1861-1908, 1 box. Polish revolutionary exiled in Russia. Includes correspondence, a notebook, scrapbook, biographical manuscript, 10 pp., and some estate papers. In 1866 he was released and emigrated to the United States, where he became a college lecturer. (NUCMC 64-1135)

10 Henry B. Miller (1854-1921). Correspondence, 1904-1908, 65 items. U.S. consul-general at Newchang, China, 1901-1904, and Yokohama, Japan, 1905-1909. Includes 8 letters and reports about Russian-Japanese-Chinese relations and the Russo-Japanese War of 1904-1905. Unpublished register (NUCMC 74-846).

11 Harold Joyce Noble (1903-1953). Papers, 1918-47, 1 box. Historian. Contains materials (letters and reports) on the American Red Cross in Japan, 1918, Russian refugees in Korea, 1922-23, and the Far East, 1946-47. (NUCMC 62-4213)

12 Floyd Cleveland Ramp (b. 1882). Papers, 1903-49, ca. 2 ft. Oregon socialist and communist, visited Russia in 1920-22. A diary covers his Russian experiences. Letters and printed matter (broadsides, pamphlets) from 1918-65 concern his political activity. Unpublished inventory. (NUCMC 69-1028)

13 Kaye (Moulton) Teall. Papers, 1964-67, 1 box. Author and television educator. Includes the manuscript of her book From Tsars to Commissars (1966). Some correspondence with the Lenninger Literary Agency concerns its publication. (NUCMC 72-545)

14 Anne Terry White (b. 1896). Papers, 1963-68, ca. 2 ft. Author of children's books. Includes translations of Russian works for children. (NUCMC 70-1814)

OR 2
RARE BOOK ROOM
LIBRARY ASSOCIATION OF PORTLAND
801 S.W. Tenth Avenue
Portland, Oregon 97205
(503-223-7201)

Charles S. Bulkley. U.S. Russo-American Telegraph Expedition, 1865-67, 1 vol. Engineer in chief for the expedition. Letters from members of the Western Union Telegraph Company's expedition for the Russian extension; correspondents include Major (later Colonel) Abasa, in charge of the Russian party in Alaska, and George Kennan, crossing Siberia to meet the American-Russian party at the coast. Also, map of Russian Alaska (Alaska Territory) compiled from Russian charts and surveys by J. F. Lewis. Access to original restricted; photocopy and microfilm (negative) available (latter also at the Bancroft Library, University of California, Berkeley). (NUCMC 73-144)

OR 3
OREGON HISTORICAL SOCIETY LIBRARY
1230 S.W. Park Avenue
Portland, Oregon 97205
(503-222-1741)

The Society has an extensive microfilm collection, much of which relates to Russian America (Alaska) and the Pacific region, where Russians were active in the 18th and first half of the 19th c. The list following does not separate microfilm from original materials. In addition, the Society recently received some microfilms containing Russian-related material; these were not processed in time for inclusion.

1 Alaska History Documents, ca. 1795-1938. 8 reels of positive microfilm (originals in the Library of Congress and National Archives).

Correspondence, diaries, journals, records, reports, minutes, logbooks, statistics, indexes, and other papers. Most concern the Russian exploration and settlement of Alaska, expeditions (e.g., to the Bering Sea), Russian trade, the Orthodox Church in Alaska, and Russians in Alaska. Includes archives of the Holy Ruling Synod, St. Petersburg; Ministry of Foreign Affairs; Academy of Sciences; Ministry of the Navy; and (material from) Imperial Public Library; plus papers of Erastus Brainerd, Caleb Cushing, Ivan Petrov, and others. (NUCMC 72-1584)

2 Archivo General de Indias, Sevilla, Espana. 1 roll of microfilm, in process. Includes reports on Russian activity in the North Pacific, 1775-1817.

3 Archivo General de Simancas, Espana. Estado. 1 microfilm roll, in process. Contains reports on Russian activity in the North Pacific, 1814-17, and information on the Russian-American Company.

4 William Eden, 1st Baron Auckland (1744-1814). Papers, 1788-93, 1 microfilm reel. British statesman and diplomat, ambassador at Madrid, 1788-89, and at The Hague, 1789-93. Includes some items on the Nootka Sound controversy. (Micro 145)

5 Mikhail I. Belov. "Geograficheskoe otkrytie severnoi azii (Issledovaniia severnykh otriadov Vtoroi Kamchatskoi ekspeditsii Vitusa Beringa)," 17 pp.; and "Mangazeia--pervyi russkii zapoliarnyi gorod, po materialam arkheologicheskikh raskopok," 24 pp. The second also concerns the Siberian fur trade in the 16th-17th c.

6 Joseph Billings (1758?-1806). Photostat of a report, 8 pp., on the exploration of Russian America, 1787-95. Original in the National Library of Scotland. (Mss 1501)

7 Nikolai Nikolaevich Bolkhovitinov. Soviet historian. Tape recording, 30 min., of a lecture he delivered, 3 September 1975, at the Society on early Russian-American relations and research. (OHS Tape 906 066 sant)

8 Stratford Canning (1786-1880). Mission to the United States papers, 1820-25, 2 microfilm reels. British diplomat. Includes some information on Russia in 1825 and on boundaries, 1820-23. Originals in the British Foreign Office Records.

9 David B. Cole. "A brief historical background to the wood frame church building at 3605 NE Mallory Avenue and to other structures owned there by St. Nicholas Russian Orthodox Church, Portland, Oregon" (1975), 6 pp.; and, with Gabriel Krivoshein, "The beginnings of the Orthodox Church in Oregon," 4 pp., n.d. (Mss 2274)

10 E. A. P. Crownhart-Vaughan. Head of the Society's Russian Desk. Tape recording, 60 min., of her lecture, 1971, "Remote Kamchatka," concerning the Bering expedition, exploration of Kamchatka, Russian eastward expansion, and the explorer S. P. Krasheninnikov. (OHS Tape 957.7 C953r)

11 Henry Elliott. Photocopies of 8 unpublished drawings showing hunting and fishing in Alaska. They depict methods used by natives who supplied the Russian-American Company with furs.

12 James Judge (1866-1910). Papers, 1894-1910, 2 ft. Assistant U.S. Treasury agent for the seal fisheries of the Pribilof Islands. Includes correspondence, 1894-1903, pocket notebooks, 1897-1907, reports, 1895-1905, seal reports, 1896-1904, fox reports, journals, a census, receipts, and other documents.

13 Gavriil and Vera Petrovna Krivoshein. Russian émigrés, post-1917. Tape recording, 30 min., of their reminiscences of life in Imperial Russia, the Revolution, emigration, Harbin, Alaska, and the establishment of a Russian Orthodox parish in Portland, Oregon. Interviewed by Charles di Gregorio, 1976. (OHS Cassette 92 K925d)

14 Logbooks. Includes microfilm of original logs held in the Massachusetts Historical Society: the Atahualpa, 1811-15, commanded by John Sutter; and the Pearl, 1804-18, commanded by John Ebbets. Both vessels were involved in shipping for the Russian-American Company. The Atahualpa log includes information on the Russians in Hawaii, January-July 1815. (Micro 6 and 23, respectively)

15 Wilbur Morton (fl. 1870s). Papers, 1873-75, 1 box. American merchant, entrepreneur, and purveyor of goods, living in Siberia. Letters, diaries, and miscellaneous documents.

16 Jacob Pelleson. Russian immigrant. His 1880 citizenship oath.

17 Photograph Collection. Includes photos on the following subjects: Alaska (files 25-33); Fort Ross (file 407 in part); Russia, Russians, Siberia (file 925-A); and for the Belov and Derbyshire collections. Draft catalogue for the iconographic collection.

18 Alexandier Riel. German soldier. During World War I he sent a letter, 8 December 1914, from Berlin to Miss Benedict describing battles between Germans and Russians, German attitudes toward the war, and American support for German children. (Mss 2290)

19 Russian Advance into Alaska. Miscellaneous holdings, some on microfilm. Includes 2 letters, ca. 1785, from Peter Simon Pallas to Joseph Banks about the Russian exploration of America (microfilm; originals in the Botany

Library of the British Museum--Natural History division); material of Nikolai Petrovich Rezanov concerning Alaska (2 microfilm reels; originals are in the Library of Congress); items relating to Joseph Hatchett, Matthew Guthrie, Johann Friedrich Blumenbach, Russian exploration of America, the Billings Expedition, the Nootka Sound controversy, Russian advance into the Pacific, fishing rights treaties, boundary questions, and the northwest coast of America. Much of the material was formerly in the British Foreign Office. (Mss 1524 and Mss 1568)

20 Russian-American Company. Records, 1802-67, 77 rolls of microfilm purchased from the National Archives, under which entry they are more fully described. (Microfilm M-11)

21 Russian History Documents, 1600-1934. 24 reels of microfilm obtained through a Russian exchange program in 1968-79 (originals in Russian archives and libraries). Negative and positive film. Essays, articles, accounts, histories, bibliographies, and other material, mostly in Russian, concerning the Russian-American Company and its American colonies; Russian settlements in the Pacific; workers in Siberian gold mines; Siberian migration; Russian diplomatic relations with China and Japan; travel to and exploration of the Amur, Priamur, and Ussuri regions, the Kurile Archipelago, Sakhalin Island, Far Eastern Islands, and Siberia; the Bering Sea and other scientific expeditions, 18th-19th c.; and such cities as Irkutsk, Nerchinsk, and Petropavlovsk-Kamchatka. Unpublished guides to persons and geographic names (NUCMC 72-1674 and 73-804).

22 Smolensk Archives of the All-Union Communist Party. Ca. 1920-41, 68 reels of microfilm (originals in the National Archives). Seized by the Germans in World War II and then by the Americans. Described in the entry for the Widener Library, Harvard University (Cambridge, Ma.). Originals in the British Foreign Office Records.

23 United States Department of State. Dispatches of U.S. ministers to Russia, 1808-1906, 66 microfilm reels; originals in the National Archives (RG 59, in part). (Microfilm M-35). Related microfilm holdings obtained from the National Archives include: diplomatic dispatches. Russia, 1898-1906. U.S. Department of State, 1 roll, Microfilm M-486; consular dispatches, Vladivostok, 1898-1906, 1 roll, Microfilm M-486; dispatches from United States consuls in the Amoor River region, 1856-1871 and 1871-1874, 2 rolls, Microfilm T-111; and dispatches from United States consuls in Petropavlovsk (Kamchatka), 1875-1878, 1 roll, Microfilm T-104 (National Archives RG 84).

24 Thomas Vaughan and E. A. P. Crownhart-Vaughan. Correspondence, 1968-present, ca. 6 ft. (additions expected). Crownhart-Vaughan heads the Society's Russian Desk. Correspondence with scholars, institutions, and colleagues in the USSR. Currently not open for research.

25 Ivan Veniaminov (Innokenti, Bishop of Kamchatka and the Kurile Islands). Diary, 1821-37, 1 microfilm reel. Original at the Alaska Historical Library and Museum (Juneau).

Finding Aids: Oregon Historical Society Manuscripts Collections (1971); Supplement to the Guide to the Manuscript Collections (1975); Oregon Historical Society Microfilm Guide (1973); and an unpublished oral history catalogue.

OR 4
OUR LADY OF TIKHVIN CENTER
St. Benedict, Oregon 97373
(503-845-3300)

1 Avvakum Petrovich (1621-1682). Archpriest (protopop) and church reformer, leader of the Old Orthodox Believers. Fragment of an autograph manuscript (ca. 4 words). Believed to be the only item of its kind outside the Soviet Union.

2 Note: The Center also serves as a liaison for the Old Orthodox (Old Ritualist) communities of Marion County, Oregon, some of which hold unusual manuscript materials.

OR 5
ARCHIVES DIVISION
OFFICE OF THE SECRETARY OF STATE
1005 Broadway NE
Salem, Oregon 97310
(503-378-4240)

1 Centennial Commission. Administrative Assistant. Records, 1957-59, 6 boxes, 323 folders. Includes 1 folder relating to Russia, 1957-58. (Inventory 60-31; item 18)

2 Centennial Commission. International Trade Fair. Records, 1957-59, 2 boxes, 126 folders. Contains 1 folder pertaining to the Soviet Union, 1957-59. (Inventory 60-31; item 20)

3 Defense Council. Records, 1941-45, 21 boxes. Includes 1 folder on Russian War Relief, week of 5 February 1945. (Inventory 1; item A-1)

4 State Library. Out-of-state correspondence, 1930-46, 4 boxes. 1 folder on Russia, 1944. (Inventory 61-8; item 10)

5 U.S. Navy Department. Records relating to the exploring expedition under the command of Lt. Charles Wilkes, 1836-42, 27 microfilm reels,

945 ft. Positive microfilm from the National Archives. The expedition left in August 1838 for the Antarctic, islands of the Pacific, and the northwest coast of America, returning in July 1842. References to Russians in America. The expedition was sent by the U.S. Hydrographic Office. (Film 8)

Note: The Archives Division may have other microfilms obtained from the National Archives that contain references to Russia.

OR 6
WESTERN AMERICA INSTITUTE FOR EXPLORATION, INC.
ALEUTIAN-BERING SEA EXPEDITIONS RESEARCH LIBRARY
1821 East 9th Street
The Dalles, Oregon 97058
(503-296-9414)

Richard Henry Geoghegan (d. 1944). Correspondence, 1938-44, ca. 1,500-2,000 pp. Scholar and Sinologue. Typed copies of letters addressed to Jay Ellis Ransom, currently executive director of WAIE. They concern Russian, Siberian, Asiatic, and Aleut linguistics, and Geoghegan's translations of Bishop Ivan Veniaminoff's Aleutian writings. Originals are kept at the Department of Linguistics, University of Alaska, Fairbanks, Alaska.

PENNSYLVANIA

PA 1
DR. JOSEPH SATALOFF--PRIVATE COLLECTION
26 Overhill Road
Bala-Cynwyd, Pennsylvania 19044
(215-839-7668)

Collection of correspondence and miscellaneous documents, ca. 1790s-1815, perhaps 100-150 items. Includes letter of Paul I, fragments of notes of Catherine II, love letters of Alexander II's wife, and letters ca. 1810-15, many of which concern the French invasion of Russia by Napoleon. Also, some cablegrams and a copy of the 1812 peace treaty between Russia and Turkey. The preceding description is based on preliminary investigations of the collection and subject to modification. Access by appointment only; scholars should inquire concerning conditions of access.

PA 2
MORAVIAN ARCHIVES
41 West Locust Street
Bethlehem, Pennsylvania 18018
(215-866-3255)

1 O'77 Masland Collection. 1581-1887. 2 boxes. A letter of Andreas von Nartow (Andrei Nartov) of the Free Economic Society in St. Petersburg, to John Heckewelder, 21 March 1797; Heckewelder's certificate of membership in the Free Economic Society, 1 April 1797; and a draft of a letter by Heckewelder to St. Petersburg, 1797.

2 Andreas Schoute (1700-1763). Books on navigation and logbooks, 1708-55. Includes Schoute's logbook (when he was first mate) on the Russian Imperial ship Astrakhan, 14 April-22 October 1743. There is also a manuscript primer in Dutch for studying Russian, n.d.

PA 3
MANUSCRIPTS DIVISION
BRYN MAWR COLLEGE LIBRARY
Bryn Mawr, Pennsylvania 19010
(215-525-1000 x 304)

Trofim Denisovich Lysenko (b. 1898). Soviet agronomist and biologist. ALS, 1 May 1966, from Moscow to Conway Zirkle, 1 p., in Russian. On the occasion of Zirkle's 75th birthday, Lysenko writes: "The whole world knows that it is primarily through your efforts . . . that I have gained an international reputation."

PA 4
PROFESSOR DAN E. DAVIDSON--PRIVATE COLLECTION
DEPARTMENT OF RUSSIAN
BRYN MAWR COLLEGE
Bryn Mawr, Pennsylvania 19010
(215-525-1000)

Professor Davidson is in possession of photocopies of 34 letters, 1817-25, by Nikolai Karamzin. Originals are owned by a Russian-born private collector who now resides in Louisiana. Professor Davidson's material is available for inspection to qualified researchers only.

PA 5
SPECIAL COLLECTIONS
DICKINSON COLLEGE LIBRARY
High Street
Carlisle, Pennsylvania 17013
(717-245-1399)

1 James Buchanan (1791-1868). Papers, 1808-68, 359 items. U.S. president, minister to Russia in 1832-34. Letters and documents, some of which pertain to Russia. (NUCMC 66-465)

2 John Baldwin Hay. Album of clippings, 1878, 1 vol. Pertains to the Russo-Turkish War.

3 Soviet Russian Photos. 76 photos, early 1930s. Photographs of scenes and people in the Soviet Union, distributed in America by the Soviet Photo Agency.

PA 6
U.S. ARMY MILITARY HISTORY INSTITUTE
Carlisle Barracks, Pennsylvania 17013
(717-245-3601)

This facility holds over 300,000 books and more than 30,000 bound periodical volumes. Its manuscript holdings consist of 1,000 collections, aggregating over 9,000 boxes. Each year 500 more boxes of manuscripts are received.

1 Armor Magazine. Office files, 1861-1971, 9 boxes. Correspondence on, among other subjects, the Soviet invasion of Czechoslovakia in 1968.

2 Donald V. Bennett. Oral history, ca. 1940-74, 2 boxes. General. Memoirs mention 2 encounters with the Russians over Czechoslovakia. As lieutenant-colonel of the 62nd U.S. Armored Field Artillery Battalion, he helped occupy that country in 1945. As commanding general of the VII Corps, he confronted Russian forces that entered Czechoslovakia in August, 1968.

3 John C. Burwell. Papers, 1941-45, 1 box. Major in the Army Medical Corps. Memoirs discuss his medical service at the Russian repatriation camp in Cologne, Germany, in 1945.

4 Frederick Edward Bury (1874-1969). Papers, 1898-1941, 1 box. Army officer. Served with the American Expeditionary Forces at Murmansk and Archangel in 1919. Part of the collection is official correspondence (about promotions, transfers, duty assignments) and military orders. Also, a scrapbook of clippings. Not much is on actual military operations. (NUCMC 75-814)

5 Mark W. Clark. Oral history, ca. 1917-53, 2 boxes. General. Reminiscences cover his dealings with the Russians as U.S. high commissioner for Austria, 1945-47, and as a member of the U.S. delegation to the quadripartite Council of Foreign Ministers meeting in Moscow in 1947.

6 Bruce Cooper Clarke. Papers, 1941-78?, 6 boxes. Army officer. Commanded the U.S. Seventh Army and the U.S. Army in Europe. Bulk of the collection is speeches, essays, and articles on his philosophy of command and politics. Reminiscences cover the Cold War (German crisis of March-April 1962, resolved by his conference with Marshal Ivan Konev on 5 April). (NUCMC 75-827)

7 Lucius D. Clay. Oral history, ca. 1918-49, 2 boxes. Military governor of the U.S. Zone of Germany and the commander in chief/European Command, 1947-49. General Clay frequently mentions, in his recollections, his confrontations with the Russians in the early years of the Cold War.

8 Henry Cook (fl. ca. 1920). Papers, 1917-21, 1 box. Private in the 339th Infantry Regiment in World War I. Served in Russia, France, and England. Official papers and some printed matter relate to this service. (NUCMC 75-829)

9 Michael S. Davison. Oral history, 1939-75, 5 boxes. General. Memoirs record his impressions of the Russians with whom he dealt while he commanded the Seventh Army and the Central Army Group, 1971-75. Access restricted.

10 Harry Gilchrist. Papers, 1920, 1 box. Colonel in the medical corps. Commanded the American Polish Relief Expedition in 1920. Some of the material contains references to the Russo-Polish War of 1920.

11 Alvan Cullom Gillem. Papers, ca. 1888-1972, 16 boxes. Army officer. Served in Siberia in 1919-20. The transcript of a 1972 interview covers this subject in part. Other letters, reports, photos, maps, and clippings concern the Polish campaign of 1939, his tour with the XIII Corps in Europe in World War II, and his command of U.S. forces in China in 1946-47. (NUCMC 75-852)

12 Thomas T. Handy. Oral history, 1918-54, 2 boxes. General. Recollections of his service as commander in chief and deputy commander in chief/European Command, 1949-54, refer to various aspects of the Cold War, including the Berlin Blockade. Restricted.

13 Ernest Nason Harmon. Papers, 1894-1965, 3 boxes. Army officer. Commanded occupation forces in Czechoslovakia, June-December 1945. Correspondents from this period include Russian commanders. Some post-war letters contain reminiscences of military operations. Also, memoirs, which became the basis for his published book Combat Commander (Prentice-Hall, 1970). (NUCMC 75-861)

14 Sidney R. Hinds. Papers, 1920-74, 5 boxes. Army officer. A small part of the papers contains information about contacts in the 1950s-1960s between American and Soviet veterans who had first met on the Elbe in 1945.

15 Nick Hociota (Hochee) (1891-1969) (American Expeditionary Force--Siberia). Collection, ca. 1919, 18 items. Corporal of the 27th U.S. Infantry Regiment. Concerning the American intervention in Siberia during the Russian Civil War there are: 2 reminiscences by Hociota; reminiscences of Sergeant J. B. Longuevan (31st Infantry Regiment); memoirs by Sergeant Sam Richardson (medical corps); letter from Lieutenant Rodney S. Sprigg (replacement battalion) to his wife, 3 March 1919, Vladivostok; and 2 reminiscences of Captain Adlai C. Young (27th Infantry Regiment). See also under Joseph Burwell Longuevan.

16 John E. Hull (1895-1973). Oral histories, 3 boxes. General. Service in the military committee of the Yalta Conference in 1945 is 1 of the subjects discussed in his 2 autobiographies.

17 Harold Keith Johnson (b. 1912). Collection, 1800-1968, 140 boxes. General. Student of military history, particularly of operations on the Russian front in World War II. Notes, speeches, and articles relate in part to this topic. (NUCMC 75-871)

18 Edward Larkins. Papers, 1897-1971, 1 box. Engineer and army officer in various regiments. Includes his report on service with the American and Japanese forces in Siberia during the intervention, August-December 1918. Letter by Lieutenant-Colonel Ferdinand Reder, one of the Austro-Hungarian prisoners of war whom he guarded in Siberia, praises him. Letter from his wife discusses her experiences during World War I and the Russian Revolution, 5 pp.

19 Lawrence J. Lincoln. Papers, 1921-71, 1 box. Army officer, member of the Joint U.S.-Soviet Commission for Korea. Includes a commentary, ca. 1947-49, on a book concerning China in World War II and the Soviet-American occupation of Korea, 1945-47. He discusses the restoration of Korean home rule. (NUCMC 75-883)

20 Joseph Burwell Longuevan. Papers, 1917-78, 10 boxes. Sergeant in the 31st U.S. Infantry Regiment. Served in Russia during and immediately after World War I. Letters, reminiscences, and miscellaneous documents center on the American Expeditionary Force in Siberia (especially the 27th and 31st infantry regiments) but also units in Murmansk and Archangel. Some items are contemporaneous with the period of the Revolution and Civil War, 1918-20; most come from a later time, when veterans of the Siberian expedition (some famous by then) corresponded. Many references to World War II, Viet Nam War, Cold War, and particularly the Korean War. See also under Nick Hociota. (NUCMC 75-887)

21 Charles MacDonald (1873-1936). Papers, 1 box. Army officer. Contains material on his tour of duty on a transport carrying Czech and German soldiers from Vladivostok to Trieste in 1920.

22 John J. Maginnis. Papers, 3 boxes. Colonel. Wartime diary, supplemented by postwar reminiscences, recounts his service with civil affairs, military government detachments in Europe during and just after World War II. He dealt with Russian refugees behind American lines and with Russian forces in Berlin.

23 Peyton C. March. Papers, 1904-34, 1 box. Captain, military observer with the Japanese army in the Russo-Japanese War. Later, U.S. Army chief of staff. Includes a lecture, 6 April 1934, he gave at the Army War College in which he discusses his career, focusing on tsarist and Soviet Russia and the Russo-Japanese War, Allied and American relations with Russia in World War I, and the Russian Revolution (especially the Siberian intervention). He also spoke of the prospects of war between Russia and Japan in the 1930s.

24 McCann Collection on "Women in Uniform." 2 albums, 1938-44. Primarily newspaper clippings and brochures. In part pertaining to women in Soviet armed forces.

25 Floyd Lavinius Parks. Papers, 1944-45, 2 boxes. Chief of staff and commanding general, First Allied Airborne Army and military district of Berlin. General Parks's diaries, 3 June-29 August 1945, cover in great detail his experiences as commander of American forces in Berlin and as American representative on the Allied Kommandatura for that city before, during, and after the Potsdam Conference.

26 Sonntag Family. Papers, 1786-1841, 1 folder. Includes material concerning George Sonntag, who joined the Russian navy (after 1808), served on the Black Sea, and commanded a regiment of marines against Napoleon, 1812-14. He was later governor of the port of Odessa and admiral of the Black Sea fleet. Includes some comments about him by Russian officials. (Part of the Halstead-Maus Papers)

27 U.S. Army War College. Records, 1908-78, ca. 1,700 boxes. Archives of the Army's senior educational institution. Course material, student papers, plans, and lectures, some of which refer to or focus upon Russia and the Soviet Union. Also available are reports on the Soviet Union prepared by the Intelligence Division, U.S. War Department General Staff in the 1930s.

28 World War I Survey. 1917-21, 175 boxes. Within this collection, 1 box contains memoirs and letters by soldiers of the American Expeditionary Force, Siberia. Most material received so far concerns the 31st U.S. Infantry Regiment. One reminiscence deals with the 146th U.S. Ordnance Depot Company. The diary

of Lieutenant Douglas Osborn of the 31st recounts his experiences in Vladivostok and along the Trans-Siberian Railroad, 25 February-6 October 1919 and 13 January-7 February 1920, 5 vols.

29 Ivan D. Yeaton. Oral history, 1919-75, 1 box. Colonel. Recollections cover his tours as a lieutenant in the 27th U.S. Infantry Regiment in Siberia, 1919-20, and as military attaché in Moscow, 1939-41. He also mentions his dealings with the Russophile General Philip Faymonville.

30 Note: In addition to the papers cited above, the Military History Institute has the papers of many army generals serving in NATO and the Pentagon during the Cold War. Their material, too, may well touch upon U.S.-Soviet relations. Researchers are invited to inquire about these holdings.

Finding Aids: Manuscript Holdings of the Military History Research Collection by Richard J. Sommers, 2 vols. to date (1972 and 1975). Available only through the Superintendent of Documents, GPO, Washington, D.C. 20402 (Stock nos. 008-029-00101-2 and 008-029-0093-8 respectively).

PA 7
WIDENER COLLEGE ARCHIVES
Chester, Pennsylvania 19013
(215-876-5551 x 431)

Edward E. MacMorland (1892-1978). Papers, ca. 1918-42, 1 box. U.S. Army officer. As a major he took part in the American intervention in North Russia. Ca. 33 pp. of his World War I diary concern operations in Murmansk and Archangel, typed. References to Admiral N. McCully, British forces, and many individual officers. Published in part as "First War With the Russians," Collier's (13 October 1951). Also, correspondence, 1918-20, 23 pp., concerning World War I; correspondence with American forces in European Russia in World War II, ca. 56 pp.; and further correspondence from 1941-42 relating mostly to China in World War II, ca. 20 pp. The papers include a typescript by John E. Wilson, army chaplain in Russia with the AEF in 1918-19, entitled "When Murmansk Went Yank," n.d., 9 pp.

PA 8
HISTORICAL SOCIETY OF DAUPHIN COUNTY
219 South Front Street
Harrisburg, Pennsylvania 17104
(717-233-3462)

Simon Cameron (1799-1889). Papers, 1861-92, 4,100 items. U.S. senator, secretary of war, 1861-62, and minister to Russia, 1862. Correspondence and documents contain some information on Russian-American relations in the 1860s but this is only a small part of the total holdings. The entire collection has been microfilmed, for which microfilm edition there is a published finding aid. (NUCMC 64-1377)

PA 9
DIVISION OF ARCHIVES AND MANUSCRIPTS
(PENNSYLVANIA STATE ARCHIVES)
PENNSYLVANIA HISTORICAL AND MUSEUM COMMISSION
Third and Forster Streets (Mail: Box 1026)
Harrisburg, Pennsylvania 17120
(717-787-3023)

1 Simon Cameron (1799-1889). Papers, 1861-92, on microfilm. U.S. senator, secretary of war, 1861-62, and minister to Russia, 1862. Originals held by the Historical Society of Dauphin County in Harrisburg; see which for a description. (NUCMC 74-875)

2 Pennsylvania Collection (Miscellaneous). Ca. 7 cu. ft., 1626-1970. Includes an ALS, 20 September 1870, from Andrew G. Curtin, minister to Russia, in St. Petersburg, to General Adam Badan, consul-general in London, ca. 2 pp. Concerns Russian war preparations; attitudes of Sweden, Denmark, and Russia toward the French republic; and President U. S. Grant's proclamation of neutrality. (MG-8)

Finding Aid: Guide to the Manuscript Groups in the Pennsylvania State Archives, compiled and edited by Harry E. Whipkey (Harrisburg, 1976).

PA 10
QUAKER COLLECTION
MANUSCRIPTS DIVISION
HAVERFORD COLLEGE LIBRARY
Haverford, Pennsylvania 19041
(215-896-8125)

1 Stephen Grellet (1773-1855). Papers, 1796-1833, ca. 100 items. American Quaker minister. Includes letters, diary extracts, and travel accounts. ALS, 21 May 1821, to Daniel E. Smith refers to schools in Russia; manuscript account of a journey to Europe, 1832-33, made by Grellet and William Allen includes mention of Russia, 12 pp.; and other accounts of travel to Europe in letters or diary extracts also note Russia. (NUCMC 62-4691)

2 J. Rendel Harris (1852-1941). Collection, 1209-1836, 70 items. Includes 3 early Armenian manuscripts; a hymnal from the 17th

c., phylactery of 1687, and a second phylactery of the 17th-18th c.

3 Charles Roberts Autograph Letters Collection. Ca. 22,000 items, 1425-present. Includes a document signed by Catherine II, 1784. (Additions expected) (NUCMC 62-4331)

4 Daniel Wheeler (1771-1840). Copybook, ca. 1832, 1 vol. Letters pertaining to the death of his wife in Russia.

Finding Aid: Survey of Manuscript Collection at Haverford College compiled by Paul Bleyden et al. (1940-present), a loose-leaf typescript.

PA 11
JOHNSTOWN FLOOD MUSEUM ARCHIVES
304 Washington Street
Johnstown, Pennsylvania 15901
(814-536-1716)

Clara Barton (1821-1912). Humanitarian and founder of the American National Red Cross. Letter to a Johnstown resident commending the city for its donation to the Russian famine fund so soon after the city's own disastrous flood in 1889 (ca. 1892). (Barton's book The Red Cross has a chapter on the famine of 1891-92 in Russia.)

PA 12
FACKENTHAL LIBRARY
FRANKLIN AND MARSHALL COLLEGE
Lancaster, Pennsylvania 17604
(717-2-1-4217)

1 Reynolds Family. Papers, 1830-65, 3 ft. Included is a box of letters from James Buchanan to John Reynolds. Many of these letters are from Russia, where Buchanan was minister 1832-34. Unpublished calendar.

2 David McNeely Stauffer (1845-1913). Papers, 1862-1913, 24 items in 10 vols. and 2 portfolios. Artist, engineer, and editor. In 1890 he visited Nizhnii Novgorod and the oil-wells of Baku, where a former colleague was directing operations. This trip is described in Stauffer's memoirs. Material can be used only under the supervision of the librarian or reference librarian. (NUCMC 60-2841)

PA 13
LANCASTER MENNONITE CONFERENCE HISTORICAL SOCIETY
2215 Mill Stream Road
Lancaster, Pennsylvania 17602
(717-393-9745)

Archival materials of the society are not yet fully processed. However, staff members could assist researchers in locating pertinent items among the collections from various congregations in the Lancaster Mennonite Conference. There are scattered records within ca. 10 collections of, primarily, material and financial aid given to immigrant Russian Mennonites as they passed through southeastern Pennsylvania on the way to the American Midwest and Canada, 1874-1930. These include letters, diaries, account books, certificates, and other documents.

PA 14
THE ARCHIVES, BOX A-417
BUCKNELL UNIVERSITY
Lewisburg, Pennsylvania 17837
(717-524-1493)

David Jayne Hill (1850-1932). Papers, 1866-1930, 1 vol. Educator, diplomat, and historian. Includes an illustrated volume of autographs, letters, and photographs pertaining to the Second Peace Conference at the Hague, 15 June-18 October 1907. This large folio contains a signature of Nicholas II as well as a document bearing the coat of arms of Russia. The volume can be used only under the supervision of the Bucknell University archivist or his assistant. (NUCMC 61-2644)

PA 15
SUSQUEHANNA COUNTY HISTORICAL SOCIETY AND FREE LIBRARY ASSOCIATION
Monument Square
Montrose, Pennsylvania 18801
(717-278-1881)

Galusha A. Grow (1823-1907). Collection, 1856-1907, 17 items. Correspondence, speeches, etc. Letter, 6 August 1879, from William M. Everts, U.S. secretary of state, to Grow offers him the post of ambassador to St. Petersburg. Grow's response of 8 August declines the appointment.

PA 16
AMERICAN FRIENDS SERVICE COMMITTEE, INC. ARCHIVES
1501 Cherry Street
Philadelphia, Pennsylvania 19102
(215-241-7044)

The Archives of the AFSC are divided into a number of sections, many of which hold Russian-related material. Among the important divisions with pertinent holdings are:

1 Foreign Service: Conference for Diplomats, 1956-59, and Conferences and Seminars, 1959. Some materials relating to the USSR appear under these headings.

2 Foreign Service: Country--Russia. Records, 1917-37, ca. 6 ft. The American Friends Service Committee and British Friends undertook a major relief role in Russia about the time of the Revolution. The main part of the relief work, in the Samara and Buzuluk regions, lasted until 1926. After 1926 the British and American Friends maintained a center in Moscow until 1931. During the period 1931-37 the AFSC was involved in work for Russian refugees living outside the Soviet Union. Collection includes correspondence, reports, etc.

3 General Administration. Among these records are several collections with pertinent items: (a) Committees and Organizations: Doukhobors, 1921-31, ca. 2 in. Materials compiled by the Friends concerning the group of Doukhobors which emigrated to Canada from Soviet Russia and their problems in adjusting to their new lives. (b) Mission to the USSR. Items relating to the 1955 goodwill visit to the Soviet Union by a group of Quakers. (c) Quaker United Nations Office, 1947-present. Material representing contacts with Soviet diplomats and officials at the UN. (This heading is the most recent in a series for this set of items. Since 1960, the UN material falls under the International Division.) And there are other groups of holdings subsumed under the General Administration label, including a small file concerning N. S. Khrushchev's visit to the U.S. and his meeting with the Quakers in 1960.

4 International Division (until 1974, International Affairs Division). Besides United Nations business since 1960, this Division also holds Soviet-related materials under the headings Reciprocal and/or Tripartite Seminars and Conferences and Seminars for the years 1960-present (to 1976 for Reciprocal Seminars).

5 Youth Services Division. In 1961-69 this Division ran a School Affiliation Service which handled some teacher exchanges between the U.S. and USSR. In 1969-72 the International Affairs Division was in charge of the program.

Note: The AFSC archives also hold a large collection of glass slides dating from the 1920s that depict conditions prevailing in the Soviet Union.

PA 17
AMERICAN PHILOSOPHICAL SOCIETY LIBRARY
105 South Fifth Street
Philadelphia, Pennsylvania 19106
(215-627-0706)

1 Benjamin Smith Barton (1766-1815). Papers, ca. 1795-1815, 9 ft. Includes some material concerning early Russian-American relations.

2 Theodosius Dobzhansky (1900-1975). Papers, ca. 8,000 items and ca. 35 notebooks. Russian-born American geneticist. Expert on population genetics, evolution, and the origin of species. Includes his papers "Crisis of Soviet Biology" and "Concerning holes in academic gowns." There are many Russian/Soviet names in the unpublished list of papers and correspondents, 13 pp.

3 Leslie Clarence Dunn (1893-1974). Papers, 1930-74, ca. 10,000 items. Professor of genetics at Columbia University. Traveled to the USSR in 1927. He remained actively interested in Soviet genetic controversies, especially the Lysenko affair. Correspondence and other papers relate to American-Soviet scientific contacts, the T. D. Lysenko controversy, and national or international meetings of scientists. Table of contents, 58 pp., lists correspondents, etc. (NUCMC 69-1371)

4 Miers Fisher, Jr. (1787-1813). Papers, 1808-13, 2 vols. Includes 1 vol. of correspondence to Miers Fisher, Sr., from Spain and Russia, 200 letters, 1808-13; and the son's account of a trip to northern Europe, including Russia, 1809-10.

5 Benjamin Franklin (1706-1790). Papers, ca. 1700-1790, 78 ft. Statesman, inventor, scientist, writer, and printer. Contains some material pertaining to relations with Russia.

6 Stephen Girard (1750-1831). Papers, 1780-1831, 57,000 items, ca. 650 reels of microfilm. Early Philadelphia merchant and banker. Includes considerable material on commerce with Russia, including manifests of merchandise. Originals in the Girard College Library in Philadelphia.

7 Isadore Michael Lerner (1910-1977). Papers, 1945-77, over 1,500 items. Geneticist, closely involved with Soviet genetics. Some correspondence concerns a visit to the United States in 1967 by a group of Soviet geneticists. He later translated Zhores Medvedev's Rise and Fall of T. D. Lysenko. Several items relate to his translation and work with Medvedev. There is also correspondence with Anton R. Zhebrak, the Byelorussian delegate to the UN Conference in San Francisco in 1945, concerning improved relations between Soviet and American geneticists. A table of

contents, 4 pp., lists various correspondents, etc. (NUCMC 76-915)

8 John Lindsay, Earl of Crawford (1702-1749). Military journals and papers, 1691-1739, 3 vols. British soldier. Includes his journal of a voyage from the Thames to Russia and of campaigning with the Russian Army, 1738-39. The account includes 1 map and 25 plates, mostly plans of battlefields, 2 vols.

9 Jan Potocki (1761-1815). Journal, 1797-98, 1 vol. (plus addition). Polish historian, archaeologist, and traveler. The count journeyed to Russia 1797-98, in part to search for traces of the ancient Scythians. His journal, entitled "Voyage dans les steps d'Astrakhan et du Caucase . . . Histoire primitive des peuples qui ont habite anciennement ces contrees," 437 pp. The German orientalist and traveller, Heinrich Julius Klaproth, edited and published the account under the same title in 1829, 2 vols. Along with the journal is some corollary material photocopied from Polish archives. (NUCMC 62-3386, part of Papers on Travel and Exploration)

10 Richard Joel Russell (1895-1971). Papers, 3,000 items. Geographer and geologist. He attended an International Geological Congress in Moscow in 1937. Among his papers are notes he took while in attendance at the meeting.

11 Conway Zirkle (b. 1895). Papers, 1,600 items. Botanist. 2 of 3 boxes contain correspondence, printed matter, and other material that relate to Soviet genetics, the controversy surrounding Trofim Denisovich Lysenko, and Zirkle's own book on this subject: Death of a Science in Russia (1949). Many clippings and translations of newspaper items concern the Soviet rejection of Mendel-Morgan genetics, their support of Michurin's biological ideas, and the All-Union Academy of Agricultural Sciences. There is a copy of Sir Henry Dale's resignation from the USSR Academy of Sciences 22 November 1948 (over the Lysenko affair) and also excerpts from a letter of J. Coyne Mossige to L. C. Dunn about the visit of a "cultural delegation" from the USSR to Norway and a lecture by Professor V. N. Stoletov. Reprints of writings of L. C. Dunn, H. J. Muller, Theodosius Dobzhansky, and N. I. Vavilov concern the decline of Soviet science. Other persons and subjects noted in the papers include E. M. Chekmenev (Checkmenev), L. Davitashvili, S. F. Demidov, Albert Deutsch, Elena Dimitrova, I. E. Glushchenko, S. Kaftanov, M. B. Mitin, V. S. Nemchinov, I. I. Prezent, Brian Roberts, I. I. Schmalhause, I. F. Vasilenko, V. M. Yudin, V. Zhuravsky, Russian medicine, and Soviet science and technology. (NUCMC 76-960)

12 In addition, the library holds the following miscellaneous items:

a) 16 letters from or about the Imperial Academy of Sciences (1785-1911, but most are in the 19th c.), some copies, all 1-4 pp. These letters appear in the catalogue under "Saint Petersburg. Académie Imperiale des Sciences."

b) 45 letters, 1789-1910, copied from a microfilm, in a collection listed as "Letters of Scientists. Moscow . . ." Among the scientists are Benjamin Franklin, Cleveland Abbe, F. G. W. Struve (?), Aleksandr Nikolaevich Veselovsky, Thomas H. Huxley, Alexander Ross Clarke, Sir William Herschel, John Churchman, Joseph Henry, Mr. Radsoff, A. Belopolsky, John Couch Adams, Lewis Boss, John Murray Mitchell, Dr. Rost, J. O. Backlund, Abraham Valentine Williams Jackson, and Carl Salemann.

c) 7 letters to the American Philosophical Society from the Corps of Mining Engineers, 1841-55, all but 1 forwarding publications; the other forwards magnetic and meteorological observations made in the Russian Empire in 1846. These are listed in the catalogue under "Russia. Corps des Ingénieurs des Mines" and "Saint Petersburg. Corps des Ingénieurs des Mines - Etat-Major (du)."

d) 5 letters listed under "Russia (or Saint Petersburg). Observatoire physique central (Nicolas)" dated 1851-97, all to the American Philosophical Society, on exchanging publications.

e) 2 letters to John L. Le Conte from the Russian Entomological Society, 1861.

f) 1 letter to the American Philosophical Society from the Imperial Botanical Gardens, 1876, forwarding publications (under "Saint Petersburg. Jardin imperiale de botanique").

Note: A large number of the above letters are in French; many are printed but filled in in manuscript.

13 A microfilm from the collections of the Royal Society of London, listed under "Russia, Poulkova," apparently concerns the famous astronomical observatory at Pulkovo.

14 Correspondence with Princess E. R. Dashkova and Pavel Petrovich Svin'in.

15 A document from 1822, in the hand of John Vaughan, an early Librarian, relating to "Russian literature" and/or books from or about Russia.

16 An anonymous "Journal de la campagne de l'armée russe contre la Turquie, 1737-1739" contains also marching orders, plus (bound together) "Relation des opérations de la campagne . . . 1738 . . . par Chev. de Forrester" and "Initium diary . . . June 24, 1738-September 5, 1739," in German. (NUCMC 62-3386)

Restriction: Inquire about possible restrictions on recent acquisitions.

Finding Aids: The Society has published a Guide to the Archives and Manuscript Collections of the American Philosophical Society, compiled by Whitfield J. Bell, Jr., and Murphy D. Smith (Philadelphia: 1966); Catalog of Manuscripts in the American Philosophical Society Library, 10 vols. (Westport, Conn.: Greenwood Publication Corp., 1970); and Catalog of Books in the American Philosophical Society Library (Westport, Conn.: Greenwood Publication Corp., 1970).

PA 18
RESEARCH LIBRARY
THE BALCH INSTITUTE
18 South Seventh Street
Philadelphia, Pennsylvania 19106
(215-925-8090)

American Latvian Association. Records, ca. 1949-73, ca. 4 boxes. Correspondence, minutes, clippings, etc. Includes some materials on the Captive Nations.

Note: The Institute's library also holds archival materials that appear to be primarily printed and published (e.g., issues of periodicals) for many other ethnic groups of the Soviet Union (Armenian, Ukrainian, Latvian).

Finding Aid: There is an unpublished calendar of holdings prepared by Philip Mooney (n.d.).

PA 19
THE CHEW HOUSE
CLIVEDEN
6401 Germantown Avenue
Philadelphia, Pennsylvania 19144
(215-848-1777)

William White Chew (1803-1851). Papers, in process, 3 legal-size file cabinets, ca. 7,500 sheets. Secretary of legation (St. Petersburg) to George M. Dallas and chargé d'affaires ad interim. Correspondence, calling cards, pamphlets, and books, in part pertaining to his diplomatic service in Russia, 1837-40. (Part of the Chew family papers) These papers are privately owned and all inquiries should be directed to the administrator of Cliveden at the above address.

PA 20
CURTIS INSTITUTE OF MUSIC LIBRARY
1726 Locust Street
Philadelphia, Pennsylvania 19103
(215-893-5265)

1 Petr I. Chaikovskii (1840-1893). ALS, 5/17 February 1893, to an unidentified autograph seeker, with a 4-bar musical extract. By appointment only.

2 Note: Specific requests for information about the Efrem Zimbalist papers (not at the Curtis Institute) will be answered if scholars write to the above address.

PA 21
DROPSIE UNIVERSITY ARCHIVES (LIBRARY)
Broad and York Streets
Philadelphia, Pennsylvania 19132
(215-229-0110)

Ben-Zion Goldberg (1894-1972). Papers, in process, 40 ft. Journalist and member of the American Committee for Jewish Anti-Fascism. Includes ca. 20 ft. of correspondence, reports, diaries, newspaper clippings, and photos pertaining to J. Stalin, N. Khrushchev, and Jews in Russia. Unpublished inventory.

PA 22
ARCHIVES BRANCH
FEDERAL ARCHIVES & RECORDS CENTER, GSA
5000 Wissahickon Avenue
Philadelphia, Pennsylvania 19144
(215-951-5591)

This repository has some of the microfilms of materials in the National Archives (Washington, D.C.) that pertain to Russia/USSR. For more details, see Charles South, List of National Archives Microfilm Publications in the Regional Archives Branches (Washington: National Archives and Records Service, 1975).

PA 23
EDWIN A. FLEISHER MUSIC COLLECTION
FREE LIBRARY OF PHILADELPHIA
Logan Square
Philadelphia, Pennsylvania 19103
(215-686-5313)

This collection holds about 13,000 works of music, published and unpublished, at present. A selective list of items relating to the Russian Empire/USSR follows.

1 Joseph Achron (1886-1943). Hebrew Dance, op. 35, no. 1, score for orchestra (1913); Hebrew

Lullaby, op, 35, no. 2, score for orchestra (1913); Dance Improvisation, op. 37, score for orchestra (1916); Children's Suite, op. 57, arranged by D. Tamkin; Two Tableaux, from the Theatre Music to "Belshazzar" by Roche, score for orchestra (1931); Suite, from the Theatre Music to "Golem" by Leivick, for chamber orchestra, score (1931-32); Improvisation on "Jeanie with the Light Brown Hair," by Stephen C. Foster, for string orchestra (1939); Improvisation on "Tambourin," by Jean-Philippe Rameau, score for string orchestra (1938, but composed for violin and piano in 1910); Second Concerto, op, 68, for violin and orchestra (1932-34); and Third Concerto, op. 72, for violin and orchestra (1936-37).

2 Lan Adomian (b. 1905). Prelude, op. 2 ("Stage Music," no. 1), large folio score for orchestra (1929); and his arrangement (1936) of D. Shostakovitch's Five Preludes (for orchestra).

3 Feodor Stepanovich Akimenko (1876-1945). Suite de Ballet, in 3 parts, secured from the composer and copied from his original manuscript score (1916); Deuxième Nocturne, secured from the composer and copied from his original manuscript score (1920); and Nocturne, score for string orchestra (n.d.).

4 Modest Altschuler (b. 1873). See under S. Rachmaninoff, N. Rimskii-Korsakov, V. Sapelnikov, and A. Skriabin.

5 Nicholas Amani (1872-1904). Orientale, arranged for violin and orchestra by Mischa Elman (1917).

6 Anton Stepanovich Arensky (1861-1906). Suite, op. 15, transcribed for orchestra by Modest Altschuler, score, 74 pp., 1908.

7 George [i.e., Yuri Karlovich von] Arnold (1811-1898). Rêve de sorcière [Witches dream], op. 13, no. 1, score, 29 pp., ca. 1910.

8 Menahem Avidon (b. 1908). 3 holographs.

9 Aaron Avshalomoff (1894-1965). Peiping Hutungs, a Sketch in Sounds upon Chinese Themes and Rhythms for Symphonic Orchestra, 1931-32; Concerto in G, upon Chinese Themes and Rhythms, for piano and orchestra, 1935; First Symphony in C minor, score, 237 pp., 1938-39; The K'e Still Ripples to Its Banks, score for orchestra, negative photostat, 1936; A Maid Goes Hunting (Bow and Arrow Dance), orchestral score, 1937, negative photostat; The Soul of the ch'in (Symphonic Suite), drawn from music written for the ballet pantomime by Ken Nakazowa, score for orchestra, 1926, negative photostat; Concerto in D for violin and orchestra, score, 181 pp., 1937; Concerto for flute and orchestra, score, 139 ff., 1948; Symphony no. 2 in E minor, the Chinese, score, 218 ff., 1949; and Symphony no. 3, in B minor, score, 169 ff., 1953.

10 Pierre Marie François de Sales Baillot (1771-1842). [Russian air with variations, score for violin and string orchestra, op. 24], 32 pp., 1807.

11 Nicolai T. Berezowsky (1900-1953). Symphony No. 2, op. 18, score for orchestra, 1933; Symphony No. 3, op. 21, orchestral score, 1936; Symphony No. 4, op. 29, score for orchestra, 1942, black and white contact prints; Introduction and Waltz, op. 25, score for string orchestra, 1939; Fantasie, op. 9, for 2 pianos and orchestra, score, 1929-32; Concerto, op 14, for violin and orchestra, score, 1929-30; Concerto, op. 28, for viola or clarinet and orchestra, large folio score, 1941; black and white contact prints; Concerto Lirico, op. 19, for violoncello and orchestra, score, 1935; Toccata, Variations and Finale, op. 23, large folio score for string quartet with orchestra, 1938, photostat; Soldiers on the Town, op. 30, no. 1, score for orchestra, 1943, black and white contact prints; Christmas Festival Overture, op. 30, no. 2, score for orchestra, 1943, black and white contact prints; and [Concerto for harp and orchestra, op. 31], score, 59 ff., 1944.

12 Guillaume (Vassili) Vassilievich Bezekirsky (1835-1919). Concerto in A minor, op. 3, score for violin and orchestra, n.d.

13 Sergei Eduardovich Bortkievich (1877-1952). Five Russian Dances, op. 18, orchestral score, n.d.; Symphony no. 1, From my native land, op. 52, in D minor, score, 128 pp., n.d.; and Symphony no. 2, op. 55, in E flat major, score, 100 pp., n.d.

14 Israel Brandman (b. 1901). Der Pionier (Hechalutz), op. 10, score for orchestra, 1930; and [Variations on a theme of Joel Engel], score for piano and orchestra, 34 pp., ca. 1934.

15 Revol Samuilovich Bunin (b. 1924). [Concerto, piano and chamber orchestra].

16 Petr Ilich Chaikovskii. See under P. I. Tchaikovsky.

17 A. and N. Cherepnin. See under A. and N. Tcherepnin.

18 Cesare Ciardi (1818-1877). I carnevale di Venezia [Carnival of Venice], scherzo, op. 22, score, 18 pp., n.d.

19 Cesar Antonovich Cui (1835-1918). Berceuse from op. 20, Suite Miniature, arranged by William F. Happich, orchestral score, n.d.

20 Arcady Dubensky (1890-1966). Andante in F major, score for orchestra, n.d.; Armenian Dance, orchestral score, 1935; Dance Orientale, orchestral score, 1939; Old Russian Soldier's

Song, orchestral score, 1930 and later; Political Suite, orchestral score, 1936; Rajah (An Old Arabian Dance), orchestral score, 1930; Russian Bells (1st Movement), orchestral score, 1927; Russian Bells (2nd Movement), orchestral score, 1937; Andante Russe, score for string orchestra, 1925; Prelude (Nocturne), score for string orchestra, 1936; transcription of Zdenko Fibich's Poem, for string orchestra, n.d.; arrangement of Jean-Marie Leclair's Sarabande and Tambourin, score for string orchestra, 1934; arrangement for string orchestra of Jean-Baptist Lully's Gavotte, 1935; transcription of Ludwig Senfl's Canon, 1935; Suite for nine flutes (no orchestra), score, 1935; and Fanfare and Choral, for 4 trumpets, score, 1939.

21 Vladimir Dukelsky (Vernon Duke, pseud.) (1903-1969). Symphony No. 2 in D flat, score for orchestra, 1928; Ballade for piano and chamber orchestra, 1931-43, on microfilm; and Dédicaces [Dedications, for piano, orchestra, and obbligato female voice], 1934-36, negative photostat.

22 Mischa Elman (b. 1892). See under N. Amani.

23 Jacobo Ficher (b. 1896). 2nd Suite Symphonique, op. 6, orchestral score, 1926; Tres Bocetos Sinfónicos [Three Symphonic Sketches, Inspired by the Talmud], orchestral score, 1930; Segunda Sinfonia [Second Symphony], op. 24, score, 1933; Tercera Sinfonia [Third Symphony], op. 36, score, 1938-40; Dos Poemas [Two Poems, nos. 16 and 42, from "The Gardener" of Rabindranath Tagore], op. 10, score for chamber orchestra, 1928; Sinfonia de Cámara [Chamber Symphony], op. 20, score, 1932; Los Invitados [The Guests], op. 26, ballet score for chamber orchestra, 1933; Concerto, op. 46, score for violin and orchestra, 1942, negative photostat; Sulamita [Shulamite, Poem of Love], op. 8, orchestral score, 1927, negative photostat; [Symphony no. 4], op. 60, score, 111 ff., 1946; Symphony no. 5, Thus spake Isaiah, op. 63, score, 112 pp., 1947, inspired by World War II; and [Symphony no. 6], op. 86, score, 138 pp., 1956.

24 John Field (1782-1837). Concertos I, III, and IV in E♭ major, VI in C major, and VII in C minor, scores for piano and orchestra, n.d.

25 Isadore Freed (1900-1960). First Symphony, large folio score, 1941-42, black and white contact prints; Pastorales, Nine Short Pieces for Orchestra, score, 1933-36; Music for strings, score, 38 pp., 1937; transcriptions of Claude Goudimel's Huguenot Psalms LXII and CXXXIII, scores for chamber orchestra, 1936; arrangement for chamber orchestra of Ernest Schelling's Tarantella, score, 1936; Music for Strings, score, 1937-38; motet arrangements for strings of Tomás Luis de Vittoria's O Magnum Mysterium and O Vos Omnes, scores, 1935; and Concerto, large folio score for violin and orchestra, 1939, black and white contact prints.

26 Alexander Konstantinovich Glazounov (1865-1936). Orchestration of Robert Schumann's Carnival by Glazounov, A. Liadov, N. Rimskii-Korsakov, and N. Tcherepnin, orchestral score, ca. 1908-1909?; and transcriptions of 2 of his works: [Reverie, op. 24, transcribed for horn and orchestra by B. Jivoff], score, 13 pp., n.d., and Theme and variations [op. 72, in F sharp minor], transcribed for orchestra by Elizabeth Camerano, score, 69 pp., ca. 1962?.

27 Reinhold Moritzovich Glière (1875-1956). Krasni Mak (Pavot Rouge) [Red Poppy], op. 70, complete ballet score in 3 acts, 1926-27, plus scores for many individual numbers from the ballet; and Mélodie, free transcription for violin and piano by Arthur Hartmann, arranged for string orchestra by W. F. Happich, n.d.

28 Alexander Tikhonovich Grechaninov (1864-1956). Symphony III, op. 100, in E major, score, 1920-23; Fourth Symphony, op. 102, in C major [In Memory of Tchaikovsky], score, 1925-42; Triptique, op. 163 [or 161], score for string orchestra, 1940, black and white contact prints; and [Elegiac poem, op. 175], score, 24 pp., 1944.

29 Louis Gruenberg (1884-1964). Americana, suite for orchestra, op. 48, score, 114 ff., 1945; Concerto for piano and orchestra, no. 2, op. 41, score, 130 ff., 1938-63; Concerto for violin and orchestra, op. 47, score, 163 ff., 1944; Symphony no. 2, op. 43, score, 204 pp., 1941-63; and Symphony no. 3, op. 44, score, 184 pp., 1941-64.

30 Adolf von Henselt (1814-1889). Concerto in F minor for piano and orchestra, op. 16, score, completed at St. Petersburg before 1845.

31 Michael Michailovich Ippolitov-Ivanov (1859-1935). Yar-Chmel [Exhilarating Time], op. 1, spring overture, score copied from composer's original manuscript, 1881; Symphonic Scherzo, op. 2, score copied from composer's original manuscript, 1882; Episode from the life of Schubert, op. 61, symphonic picture for orchestra and tenor, the composer's own score and only known manuscript, 1929; [From Ossian, three musical pictures, op. 56], orchestral score, 91 pp., 1925; [Sur le Volga, musical tableau, op. 50], orchestral score, 1910; and [Quartet for strings, op. 13, in A minor, excerpt, intermezzo transcribed for string orchestra], score, 5 pp., 1894, transcriber unknown.

32 Dmitri Kabalevsky (b. 1904). Symphony no. 2, op. 19, score, 1934, photostat.

33 Jeronimas Kacinskas (b. 1907). Lento, for symphony orchestra, score, 31 pp., 1957; and [Song to light], score, 17 pp., 1947.

34 Aram Ilich Khatchatourian (1904-1978). Piano concerto, score for piano and orchestra, n.d., photostat.

35 Marcelo Koc (b. 1918). Preludio, intermezzo y fuga, for strings, score, 29 ff., 1951.

36 Gennari Ossipovich Korganov (1858-1890). In the Gondola, op. 20, no. 6 (Album lyrique), orchestrated by William P. Happich, violin and piano transcription by Arthur Hartmann, n.d.; and Mazurka in B minor, arranged for string orchestra and harp by William F. Happich, n.d.

37 Jacobo Kostakowsky (b. 1893). El Romancero Gitano [Gypsy Romances, suite in 4 parts], score (n.d.); Lascas [Fragments (Symphonic Poem)], score for orchestra, 1939; Clarin [The Trumpet (Choreographic Prelude)], score, 1935, microfilm; Concertino, score for violin and orchestra, 1938, negative photostat; Concierto, for violin and orchestra (also solo and piano reduction), negative photostat, 1942; La Creación del Hombre [The Creation of Man, Mexican Mayan Legend], ballet score, scenario by J. Gorostiza, 1939, negative photostat; Juventud [Youth, Symphonic Poem], orchestral score, 1937, negative photostat; (Marimba) Capricho, score for piano and orchestra, 1938, negative photostat; Musica de Camara No. 5 "Estampas Callejeras" [Chamber Music No. 5 "Street Sketches"], n.d., negative photostat; Sinfonieta Tropical, score for chamber orchestra, 1940, negative photostat; Taxco, Poem ("Al Caer la Tarde") [Poem ("At Sunset")], orchestral score, 1938, negative photostat; and [Concerto, no. 1, for violin, in C major], score, 56 pp., 1942.

38 Aristote G. Koundouroff (born in Greece, educated in Russia). Ikar [Icarus], Symphonic poem, score, n.d.; Conte No. 2 [Tale], score for orchestra, 1925-29; Suite Greque, orchestral score, 1930; and Symphoniette, orchestral score, 1934.

39 Fabien Koussevitzky. See under Fabien Sevitzky.

40 Serge Alexandrovich Koussevitzky (1874-1951). [Concerto, op. 3] for contrabass, score, 100 pp., 1902.

41 Boris Koutzen (b. 1901). Poeme-Nocturne, "Solitude," orchestral score, 1927; Symphony in C, large folio score, 1939, black and white contact prints; "Valley Forge," Symphonic Poem, orchestral score, 1931; Mouvement Symphonique, score for violin and orchestra, 1929; Concerto, large folio score, for 5 solo instruments and string orchestra, 1934, black and white contact prints; Concerto for violin and orchestra, score, 146 ff., 1946; Divertimento for orchestra, score, 114 pp., 1956; and From the American folklore, concert overture, score, 34 ff., based on American folksongs, 1943.

42 Tikhon Krennikov (b. 1913). Symphony, op. 4, score, 1933-35, photostat.

43 Wiktor Labunski (1895-1974). Symphony No. 1, op. 14, score, 1936; and Concerto in C major, op. 16, score, 1937.

44 Marc Lavry (b. 1903). Chasidischer Tanz, score for orchestra, 1928; and On the Banks of Babylon, op. 33, manuscript score for string orchestra with photostat inset, n.d.

45 Leonid Leonardi (b. 1901). All transcriptions: of 3 J. S. Bach works, 1935, of D. Buxtehude, 1935, of S. Scheidt, 1935, of J. N. Hanff, 1935, and of J. K. Vogler and J. G. Walther, 1935.

46 Theodore Leschetitzky (1830-1915). [Berceuse, op. 46, no. 1], transcribed for string orchestra by Poul Kroman, score, 6 pp., n.d.

47 Anatol Konstantinovich Liadov (1855-1914). Two preludes: 1. E major and 2. B-flat minor, transcribed for string orchestra by Bernard Morgan, score, 7 pp., transcription, 1939. See also under Alexander Glazounov.

48 Sergei Michailovich Liapunov (1859-1924). Lesghinka, arranged for orchestra by Josef Alexander, score, 1938.

49 Samuel A. Lieberson (b. 1881). In a winter garden, suite for large orchestra, score, 107 ff., 1932.

50 Charles Martin Tornov Loeffler (1861-1935). Les veillées de l'Ukraine, for violin and orchestra, score, 159 ff., ca. 1891?.

51 Nikolai Lopatnikoff (1903-1976). Opus Sinfonicum, op. 21, orchestral score, 1933-41; Symphony No. 2, op. 24, large folio score for orchestra, 1939-40, black and white contact prints; Deux Nocturnes, op. 25, large folio score for orchestra, 1939-40, black and white contact prints; Symphonietta, op. 27, large folio score for chamber orchestra, 1942, black and white contact prints; Concerto, op. 26, large folio score for violin and orchestra, 1941, black and white contact prints; Danton Suite (Suite from the opera "Danton"), op. 20, orchestral score, n.d., negative photostat; Concertino for orchestra, op. 30, score, 69 ff., 1944; Concerto for 2 pianos and orchestra, op. 33, score, 131 ff., 1950; Divertimento for orchestra, op. 34, score, 106 ff., 1951; and Symphony no. 3, op. 35, score, 153 ff., 1954. (Additions expected).

52 Nikolai Iakovlevich Miaskovsky (1881-1950). Concerto, op. 44, for violin and orchestra, score, 1938, negative photostat.

53 Michel Michelet (Mikhail Isaakovich Lewin) (b. 1894). [Elegy for string orchestra, op. 4], score, 8 pp., 1918.

54 Stanislas Moniuszko (1819-1872). Polonaise--Entr'acte, from the opera "La Comtesse," violoncello solo with accompaniment of 2 violoncellos, viola, and contrabass, score for string orchestra, ca. 1860?.

55 Iwan Müller (1786-1854). [Concerto, for clarinet, no. 4, in A minor], in 1 movement, score, 43 pp., n.d.; [Concerto no. 5 for clarinet in E-flat major], in 1 movement, score, 79 pp., n.d.; and [Concerto no. 6 for clarinet in G minor], score, 83 pp., n.d.

56 Modest Moussorgskii (1839-1881). [Songs and dances of death, no. 4], transcribed for voice and orchestra by J. Schwarzdorf, score, 16 pp., text in Russian by Count Arseny Golenishchev-Kutuzov, n.d.

57 Nikolai Nabokov (b. 1903). Les Danses de Polichinelle, suite of dances for symphonic orchestra, score, n.d.; Symboli Chrestiani [for baritone and orchestra], score, 51 pp., 1956; and his arrangement of J. S. Bach's Orchestersuite, 1938.

58 Leo Ornstein (b. 1895). Danse, orchestral score, 1936, photostat; and Nocturne, orchestral score, 1936, photostat.

59 Herman M. Parris (b. 1903). Concertino for piano and chamber orchestra, 1946; Concerto no. 6, piano and orchestra, 1949; Concerto for violin, 1946; Elegiac overture for strings, 1948; Elegiac rhapsody, 1960; Four etchings for orchestra, n.d.; Hospital suite, in 10 movements, 1946; In memoriam [Joshua Levitsky]; Invocation and lamentation, 1946; lament for string orchestra, 1955; Nocturne for bass clarinet and orchestra, 1946; Nocturne for clarinet and strings; Nocturne for string orchestra, 1958; Overture, America, 1946; [Rhapsody no. 1, Hebrew rhapsody], 1947; Rhapsody no. 2, Heart, for orchestra, 1947-48; Suite no. 1 for symphonic band in 9 movements, 1947; Suite for strings, in 4 movements, 1948; Suite for trumpet and strings, in 6 movements, 1960; [Symphony no. 1, Akiba, in 1 movement], 1946; Symphony no. 2, 1947; Symphony no. 3, 1948; Symphony no. 4, 1950; and Three orchestral abstracts, 1948.

60 Josef Piastro (1889-1964). Crimean rhapsody, Bachchissaray, score, 67 pp., 1920-38.

61 Gregor Piatigorsky (1903-1976). Variations on a Paganini theme for violoncello and piano accompaniment, transcribed for orchestra by Arthur Cohn, score, 65 ff., transcription, 1946.

62 Alfredo Carlo Piatti (1822-1901). Airs Baskyrs, Scherzo, op. 8, score for violoncello and orchestra.

63 W. Pogojeff. See under F. Sevitzky.

64 Sergei Sergeevich Prokofiev (1891-1953). Fanfare, for a Spectacle, 3 trumpets, score, ca. 1921?, negative photostat; and Suite, op. 12, orchestral transcription by Harold Byrns, originally composed for piano, 1908-13, 1941, black and white contact prints.

65 Jaan Raats (b. 1932). [Concerto for strings, op. 16].

66 Sergei Vassilievich Rachmaninoff (1873-1943). Polka de W[assili] R[achmaninoff], score, 15 pp., based on a theme of his father, transcription by an unknown composer, n.d.; [Prelude, for piano, op. 3, no. 2, in C sharp minor, transcribed for orchestra by Modest Altschuler, score, 12 pp., n.d.; and Prelude for piano, op. 23, no. 5, in G minor, transcribed for orchestra by Altschuler, score, 16 pp., n.d.

67 Eda Rapoport (1900-1968). The Mathmid, Symphonic Poem (after Chaim Nachman Bialik), orchestral score, 1935, black and white contact prints; Suite, large folio score for orchestra, 1942-43, black and white contact prints; Adagio, score for string orchestra, 1940; Lament (Revolt in the Warsaw Ghetto), score for string orchestra, 1943, black and white contact prints; Concerto for piano and orchestra, large folio score, 1939, black and white contact prints; Fantasie (originally, Concerto) for violin and orchestra, score, 1942, black and white contact prints; Lamentations, based on Hebrew themes, for violoncello and orchestra, score, 1933; Three pastels for string orchestra, 1947; and Israfel, Tone Picture after Edgar Allan Poe, for flute, strings, and harp, score, 1936.

68 Karol Rathaus (1895-1954). Suite from the ballet "Le Lion Amoureux," commissioned by Colonel de Basil's Ballet Russe, score, 1937; Polonaise symphonique, op. 52, score, 25 ff., 1943; Salisbury Cove, an overture, op. 65, score, 31 ff., 1949; and Vision dramatique, op. 55, score, 44 ff., 1945.

69 Nikolai Rimskii-Korsakov (1844-1908). [Sadko. Song of India], transcription by Modest Altschuler, 8 pp., n.d. See also under A. Glazounov.

70 Salomo Rosowsky (1878-1962). Chassiden (Chassidim), Phantastischer Tanz, large folio score for orchestra, 1914.

71 L. Julien Rousseau. Les petits Moukjiks.

72 Anton Gregorovich Rubinstein (1829-1894). Berceuse [Lullaby] in G major, score for string orchestra, n.d.

73 Lazare Saminsky (1882-1959). Pueblo, a Moon Epic, orchestral score, 1936; Hebrew Rhapsody, op. 3, no. 2, score for violin and orchestra,

1923; Overture in F# minor, op. 1, score, 1908, negative photostat; First Symphony, op. 10 (Symphony of Great Rivers), score, n.d., negative photostat; and Symphony IV, op. 33, score, n.d., negative photostat.

74 Vassily Lvovich Sapelnikov (1867-1941). Polka caprice, transcribed for orchestra by Modest Altschuler, score, 11 pp., transcription, 1916.

75 Joseph Schillinger (1895-1943). March of the Orient, op. 11, orchestral score, 1924; Symphonic Rhapsody "October," op. 19, score for large orchestra, 1917-27; North Russian Symphony, op. 22, orchestral score, 1930; and First Airphonic Suite, op. 21, for (RCA) theremin and orchestra, score, 1929.

76 Fabien Sevitzky (originally Koussevitzky) (b. 1893). Russian Folk Song, free transcription for string orchestra, score, n.d.; W. Pogojeff's Prelude in G sharp major, arranged by Sevitzky, score for string orchestra, 1929; and his arrangement for string orchestra of J. S. Bach's Prelude "Herzlich thut mich verlangen," score, n.d.

77 Rodion Konstantinovich Shchedrin (b. 1932). [Suite for accordion, harp, and strings], score, 23 pp., 1961.

78 Dmitri Dmitrievitch Shostakovich (1906-1975). Suite "The Nose," op. 15, score for orchestra, 1927-28, photostat; Suite from the ballet "The Bolt" (the ballet is op. 27), large folio score for orchestra, 1930-31, photostat; Five Preludes, arranged by Lan Adomian, score, 1936; Symphony no. 13, Babi Yar, op. 113, score, 223 ff., 1961; and [Symphony no. 14, op. 135], score, 153 pp., 1969.

79 Mark Silver (1892-1965). Funeral march (Marcia funebre), symphonic poem, 1915-16.

80 Anton Y. Simon (1851-1916?). Plainte Élégiaque, op. 38, no. 1, in memory of G. Fitzenhagen, score for string orchestra, ca. 1890?.

81 Alexander Nikolaievich Skriabin (1872-1915). [Nuances, for piano, op. 56, no. 3], transcribed by Modest Altschuler, 1 p., n.d.; and Two études, arranged by LaSalle Spier, 21 pp., transcription, 1940.

82 Nicolas Slonimsky (b. 1894). Little March for the Big Bowl (or: Marche Grotesque), edited by Arthur Cohn, orchestral score, composed for piano in 1928, 1933; Four Simple Pieces for small orchestra (original title: Four Compositions for Young People), score, 1931; Fragment of chorus from "Orestes" of Euripides, arranged by Slonimsky, score for chamber orchestra, 1933; Pequeña Suite [Suite for flute (and piccolo), oboe, clarinet, percussion, and a portable typewriter, score, ca. 1941?; Fanfarria Habanera para Despertar a los Trasnochadores [A Havana Fanfare to Wake Up Those Who Have Been Out All Night], edited by Arthur Cohn, score composed in 1933, 1944; Fanfare for the W.P.A. Music Copying Project of the Free Library of Philadelphia, edited by Arthur Cohn, score, 1942; and The Prince Goes Hunting (Ballet), written for the pantomime by Paul Horgan, score, 1925, microfilm.

83 Igor Fedorovich Stravinsky (1882-1971). Circus polka, composed for a young elephant, orchestral score, 1942, black and white contact prints; Four Norwegian Moods, orchestral score, 1942, black and white contact prints; Ode in Three Parts, score for orchestra, 1943, photostat; Fanfare for a Liturgy, score, n.d.; Fanfare, from the March Royale, score, n.d.; [Symphony in C], score, 209 pp., 1938-40; and [Fanfare for a new theatre], 1964.

84 Alexander Sergeievich Taneiev (1850-1918). Mazurka I, op. 15, no. 1, orchestral score, 38 pp., n.d.; and Mazurka II, op. 15, no. 2, orchestral score, 28 pp., n.d.

85 Peter Ilich Tchaikovsky [Chaikovskii] (1840-1893). Sleeping Beauty, op. 66, ballet in 3 acts, score, 1888-89; Mélancholie (Chanson triste), op. 40, no. 2, score for string orchestra, ca. 1878?; and In Autumn, Tone Picture, op. 37a, no. 10, arranged by Ludwig Sauer, score for string orchestra, 1876.

86 Alexander Nikolayevich Tcherepnin (1899-1977). Suite Géorgienne, score for string orchestra, n.d.; [Concerto for harmonica, op. 86], score, 88 ff., 1953; and [Symphony no. 2, op. 77, in E flat major], score, 130 ff., 1946-51.

87 Nicolai Nicolaievich Tcherepnin (1873-1945). See under A. Glazounov.

88 Eduard Tubin (b. 1905). Music for strings, score, 24 pp., 1962-63; [Symphony no. 9, Sinfonia semplice], score, 79 pp., 1969-70; and Symphony no. 10, in 1 movement, score, 88 pp., 1973.

89 Taavo Virkhaus (b. 1934). [Concerto for violin], score, 73 ff., 1966; and Overture to Kalevipoeg, score, 39 ff., 1957.

90 O. Warchavsky. Danse Russe, with flute, score for string orchestra, n.d.

91 Jacob Weinburg (1879-1956). Ora [subtitled: Palestinian folk dance]; and Palestine, rhapsody, op. 18.

92 Lazar Weiner (b. 1897). Prelude and Fugue, score for orchestra, 1938.

93 Henri Wienawski (1835-1880). Polonaise de Concert, in D major, op. 4, score for violin and orchestra, n.d.; and Polonaise brillante

No. 2, in A major, op. 21, score for violin and orchestra, n.d.

94 Richard Yardumian (b. 1917). Armenian Suite, score, 42 pp., 1936-37.

95 Arnold Zemachson (b. 1892). Chorale et Fugue en Re Mineur, op. 4 [Chorale and Fugue in D Minor], score, 1928; Concerto Grosso, op. 8 [in E minor, for large orchestra], score, 1932-33; and Suite in F major, op. 11, score for strings, 1936-38.

96 Efrem Zimbalist (b. 1889). Concerto for piano in E. flat major, score, 138 ff., 1953-59.

Note: For many of the preceding works, there are accompanying manuscript materials (solo, parts, strings, reductions, etc.) or reproductions of such additional material. Moreover, in numerous instances, for a published score of a composer (some not listed above), there are unpublished parts, etc.

Finding Aid: The Edwin A. Fleisher Collection of Orchestral Music in the Free Library of Philadelphia: A Cumulative Catalog, 1929-1977 (Boston: G. K. Hall, 1979), compiled by Sam Dennison et al.

PA 24
RARE BOOK DEPARTMENT
FREE LIBRARY OF PHILADELPHIA
Logan Square
Philadelphia, Pennsylvania 19103
(215-686-5416)

1 Hampton L. Carson Collection. Includes a New Testament in Russian, on paper, 16th c. There are 5 miniatures in the 249 ff. The manuscript bears the arms of an early Russian owner.

2 John Frederick Lewis Collection. Includes the following Armenian manuscripts: four Gospels, A.D. 1504; four Gospels (Armenian-Turkish), A.D. 1655?; four Gospels, A.D. 1563?; four Gospels, 16th c.; four Gospels (Armenian-Turkish), 17th-18th c.; psalter and prayer book, 16th c.; antiphonary, A.D. 1314; abbreviated liturgical book, A.D. 1257; poetical works of Nerses Snorhali, and texts by other authors, A.D. 1528; phylactery, A.D. 1816; phylactery, 18th c.; and 1 leaf from a ritual book, 16th-17th c. (The manuscripts are numbered 115-125A.)

PA 25
GIRARD COLLEGE LIBRARY
Girard and Corinthian Avenues
Philadelphia, Pennsylvania 19121
(215-236-6500)

Stephen Girard (1750-1831). Papers, 1780-1831, 57,000 items. Banker, merchant, mariner, and philanthropist. The papers contain a considerable amount of materials regarding Russian-American trade in the early 19th c. Originals are housed in a vault in Founder's Hall, Girard College. A microfilm of and index to the papers are kept in the Library building (and at the American Philosophical Society in Philadelphia). (NUCMC 61-530)

PA 26
MANUSCRIPT DEPARTMENT
HISTORICAL SOCIETY OF PENNSYLVANIA
1300 Locust Street
Philadelphia, Pennsylvania 19107
(215-732-6200)

1 Myer Asch. Papers, 1867-87, 50 items, 1 vol. Colonel, secretary of the U.S. Centennial Exposition. Letters and documents, including items from Russian (and other) envoys, expressing their government's high regard for Colonel Asch. (NUCMC 60-2034) (AM .0085)

2 Balch Collection. Ca. 2,000 items, 1699-1923. Thomas W. Balch was a lawyer, author, and collector. Includes a letter, 3 February 1899, from George Peirce concerning the Russian fleet's visit to New York in September 1863, and material on an Alaskan boundary dispute in 1854.

3 Rudolph Blankenburg (1843-1918). Papers, 1881-1918, 150 items. Philadelphia mayor. Includes several items relating to famine relief for Russia in 1892-93: letter, 2/14 March 1892, from E. W. Brooks about funds raised by the English Society of Friends for the famine-stricken population of Russia; letter, 3 March 1892, from C[ount?] Worongrow Daschkow [Vorontsov-Dashkov] regarding the sailing of the ship Indiana, carrying food for relief of Russian famine victims; letter, 17 March 1892, from Blankenburg to "Your Excellency" (Vorontsov-Dashkov?), presenting him with a photograph of the sailing of the Indiana from Philadelphia; letter, 27 May 1893, about honoring Blankenburg with a Russian loving cup in appreciation of his help in delivering flour to Russia via the Indiana; a pamphlet entitled Shall Russian Peasants Die of Starvation?; and an account of receipts and expenditures for J. P. Blessig's Famine Relief Fund, 1892. (NUCMC 61-1066)

4 Atherton Blight. Papers, 1849-56, 2 vols. Diary and account book. Includes notes on the Crimean War. (NUCMC 60-2015) (AM .02555)

5 [Boats and Cargoes]. Includes 2 inward manifests of goods from Russia, 1795. The first, 2 May, is for the brig Henrietta; St. Petersburg articles were consigned to F. H.

LeComte and Richard Gernor, and declared by Thomas Hunt. The second, 28 October, shows that the ship Sedgley from St. Petersburg carried cargo consigned to William Cramont of Philadelphia. (Part of Society Miscellaneous Collection)

6 James Buchanan (1791-1868). Papers, 1815-68, 114 boxes, ca. 25,000 items, on microfilm. Minister to Russia, 1832-33, and president of the U.S., 1857-61. 6 microfilm reels contain dispatches from U.S. ministers to Russia in the years 1830-34 and 1852-56. 1 box of Buchanan's own papers relates particularly to his service in Russia. His correspondence at the time was not voluminous. Letters, reports, notes, writings, speeches, scrapbooks, and other materials from various phases of his career are also in the collection. One of his correspondents was Secretary of State Edward Livingston. All the papers are microfilmed. For the microfilmed edition there is a published guide.

7 Cadwalader Collection. Ca. 100,000 items, 1630-1900. In 1 section of the collection, materials of J. Francis Fisher, there are 3 boxes (4, 5, and 8) that include letters of the sisters Mary Helen (Hering), Maria, and Eliza Middleton, daughters of Henry Middleton, ambassador to Russia. Mary Helen (d. 1850) wrote 14 lengthy letters from St. Petersburg, 1820-29, to another sister, Mrs. H. M. Rutledge. They discuss family and social concerns, the Russian court, and diplomatic affairs in Russia. All are ALS. There are over 200 items of Maria's correspondence, ca. 1821-33; she received letters from various people in England and Russia, in English and French. Eliza (1815-1890) corresponded and collected miscellaneous invitations, programs, and other papers during her St. Petersburg stay, 1820-30.

8 Citizens' Permanent Relief Committee, Philadelphia. Records, 1885-99, ca. 10,000 items. Philanthropic organization. Business correspondence and other records. One of its efforts was to aid suffering Russians in the great famine of 1892-93. (NUCMC 61-81)

9 Clifford Family. Papers, 1722-1832, 10,000 items. Philadelphia family engaged in trade worldwide, including with Russia, over several generations. Letters, invoices, bills, receipts, a diary, vessel charters, legal instruments, insurance policies, and printed matter. (NUCMC 60-1764)

10 Colonial-Revolutionary Manuscripts. Part of Society Miscellaneous Collection, 1738-1808, ca. 150 items. John Adams's letter, 10 April 1780, to Samuel Huntington encloses a mémoire/letter signed by Prince D. A. Gallitzin, Catherine II's envoy to the Estates General. The prince notes that the Russian position in the American Revolutionary War is one of neutrality but that Russia is determined to maintain her honor, commerce, and navigation. (NUCMC 60-1707)

11 Gilbert Cope. Historical and Genealogical Collection, 1682-1924, ca. 30,000 items. Includes consular papers, 1807-24, from U.S. consulates in London and Riga; ship registers; and materials relating to legal cases in Russia.

12 Tench Coxe (1755-1824). Papers, 122 microfilm reels. Assistant secretary of the treasury. Includes material on early Russian-American relations. Published guide.

13 Joseph Fels (1854-1914). Papers, 1865-1952, ca. 3,500 items. Soap manufacturer and philanthropist. In 1907 he lent money to the Russian Social Democratic Labor Party. Box 1 holds a receipt for the sum of £1,700 signed by all the delegates of the Last International Convention of the RSDLP in London, May 1907; and a September 1908 document, probably dictated by V. I. Lenin, explaining why payment of the loan had been delayed. Lenin, who presided at the 1907 meeting, did not sign the receipt, photocopy from Party archives in Moscow, 5 pp. The 1908 document is handwritten, 3 pp., accompanied by a typed translation, 2 pp. In box 5 are some notes of Arthur P. Dudden for his biography of Fels; they refer to the RSDLP (1907 loan folder). Papers also contain a letter of Mary Fels about Efrem Zimbalist. (NUCMC 70-1247)

14 Benjamin Franklin (1706-1790). Papers, in process, 1,000 items. Statesman, inventor, scientist, writer, and printer. Includes some material pertaining to early Russian-American relations.

15 Edward Carey Gardiner. Collection, 1632-1939, ca. 12,000 items. Includes, ALS, 10 October 1827, from Thomas Monroe to Thomas J. Baird describing Russian arms and telling of Baird's sending a musket to the Grand Duke Constantine; ALS, 10 March 1820, of Peter H. Schenck to Matthew Carey concerning the new Russian tariff; letter, 30 May 1858, from E. Penshine Smith to Henry C. Carey discussing the emancipation of the serfs in Russia; ALS, 18 January 1863, from Bayard Taylor to Henry C. Carey describing his experiences as chargé d'affaires in Russia and "the Emperor's wise rule"; and a letter, 29 July 1859, from Julia V. Wiltbank to Henry C. Carey which speaks of the Russians and their hospitality.

16 Gilpin Family. Papers, 1727-1872, ca. 20,000 items. Includes ca. 700 letters of Joel R. Poinsett (1779-1851), an American diplomat who traveled in Russia in the early 1800s. The Gilpins were distinguished in politics, scholarship, and commerce. Published guide. See also under Joel R. Poinsett.

17 Simon Gratz. Autograph collection, 1383-1921, ca. 175,000 items. Miscellany section includes documents on Russian and other celebrities and royalty. Also, 2 certificates of health, 1830, relating to Russia. Unpublished finding aid.

18 James M. Greene (Part of the Society Miscellaneous Collection). Includes an ALS, 11 March 1826, to him from George W. Backus discussing the death of Alexander I and efforts to place Nicholas on the throne in place of Constantine.

19 Joseph Harrison (1810-1874). Letterbook, 1844-65, 6 vols. Railroad engineer and locomotive designer. Includes information on commerce with Russia. (AM .07194)

20 George S. Hillard. Letter, 3 January 1872, to J. F. Fisher concerns Russia's treatment of the Poles. (Part of the Francis F. Hart Collection)

21 Charles Jared Ingersoll (1782-1862). Papers, 1803-62, ca. 675 items. Author and U.S. representative from Pennsylvania. Includes material on early Russian-American relations.

22 Charles Godfrey Leland (1824-1903). Papers, 1835-1906, ca. 5,000 items. American journalist. Contains an undated "memorial" to the Amon (i.e., the Russian Pacific Land) Company.

23 William David Lewis (1792-1881). Letterbook, 1821, 1 vol. Merchant, banker, politician and literary dilettante. Contains letters to his brother John D. Lewis, a merchant in Russia. (AM .09244)

24 Lewis-Neilson Collection. Papers, 1800-1918, 15,000 items. Includes papers of William D. Lewis (see preceding): Russian notebooks for 1815-18, with data on commerce, and 3 boxes of correspondence from his brother John in Russia.

25 Richard O'Bryen. U.S. consul-general in Algiers. Journal for 1789-91 discusses Russian and other European diplomatic interests, 1 vol. (AM .109)

26 Joel Roberts Poinsett (1779-1851). Papers, 1785-1851, ca. 4,250 items. Congressman from South Carolina, 1821-25, minister to Mexico, 1825-29, and secretary of war, 1837-41. He traveled to Russia, became a friend of Alexander I, and toured the Caucasus and Caspian Sea regions (including Baku), ca. 1807. Papers are arranged chronologically, in 16 vols. of correspondence and 7 vols. of miscellaneous papers. (The poinsettia is named for him.)

27 Jonathan Potts (1745-1781). Papers, 1766-80, 500 items. Army surgeon. Includes an intelligence report, 7 May 1777, from France that the courts of Spain, the Netherlands, Prussia, Austria, Sweden, and Russia have applied to Benjamin Franklin for ambassadors to be sent to their countries.

28 Powel Family. Papers, 1700-1925, ca. 50,000 items (4 sets of family papers under this heading). Includes the manuscript of the book Travels Through Part of the Russian Empire and Country of Poland (London, 1815) by Robert Johnston, who journeyed through northern Europe and Russia in 1814. (NUCMC 61-738)

29 Gustav Heinrich von Rosenthal (John Rose) (1753-1829). Russian baron of Baltic origin. He fled his homeland in the early 1770s and eventually came to America, where, as John Rose, he played an active role in the Revolutionary War. Some of his letters are in the Irvine Papers.

30 Richard S. Smith (b. 1789). Memoirs, 1 vol. Comprises his "Reminiscences of Seven Years of Early Life," ca. 1808-13, which contain information on wars of Russia and other countries. (AM .155)

31 Solomon Solis-Cohen (1857-1948). (Part of the Society Miscellaneous Collection) Includes a letter, 17 January 1942, to him from Helena Day concerning Russian war relief and a planned benefit for the USSR.

32 Charles Thompson (d. 1824). Papers, 1774-1811, 9 vols. Includes material relating to commerce with Russia.

33 Watermarks. 2 sheets of Russian paper, 1965, bearing watermarks.

34 Note: Professor Otto E. Albrecht of the University of Pennsylvania reports that in various collections of the Society, particularly the Dreer and Pennypacker collections, there are such Russian-related holdings as correspondence of Michel Asantchevsky, César Cui, Karl Iu. Davidov, Antoine de Kontski (3 letters), Alexis Lvov (2), Wassili Leps, and Sergei Rachmaninoff.

Finding Aid: Guide to the Manuscript Collections of the Historical Society of Pennsylvania, 2nd ed. (1949).

PA 27
MANUSCRIPT COLLECTIONS
LIBRARY COMPANY OF PHILADELPHIA
c/o MANUSCRIPT DEPARTMENT
HISTORICAL SOCIETY OF PENNSYLVANIA
1300 Locust Street
Philadelphia, Pennsylvania 19107
(215-732-6200)

1 Pierre Eugene Du Simitière (1736-1784). Collection, 1492-1783, 1 m., 681 items. Artist, antiquary, and collector. Includes: (a) "A

Summary Account of the Voyage of the Late Captain James Cook undertaken by order of the British Government. . .," which contains extract from a letter from Captain Clarke at Kamchatka to a friend in England; and (b) "Accounts of the Russian Discoveries between Asia and America. . .," which comprises copies of accounts published by the Westminster Magazine (August 1780), London Magazine (March 1780), London Public Advertiser (18 September 1781), and William Coxe's Account of the Russian Discoveries between Asia and America: to which are added, the Conquest of Siberia, and the History of the Transactions and Commerce between Russia and China (London, 1780). (YI 1411 Q/F8) Printed catalogue.

2 Stephen Grellet (1773-1855). Papers, 1790-1855, 1 ft., 1,300 items. Quaker minister. Includes some correspondence and a report, in French, on social conditions from his Russian mission in 1818.

PA 28
PHILADELPHIA JEWISH ARCHIVES CENTER
Curtis Building--625 Walnut Street
Philadelphia, Pennsylvania 19106
(215-923-2729)

1 Gerson Bergman (b. 1893). Interview, 1976, 1 cassette tape recording. In this interview, ca. 1.5 hrs., with his son Edward B. Bergman and Lindsay B. Nauen, PJAC archivist, he talks about his family and life in Russia, immigration to the U.S. in 1903, his father's occupations in Philadelphia, and his progeny.

2 Pearl Block. Papers, 1964-76, 1 folder plus photographs. Newspaper clippings, 1964, regarding the "New Jerusalem" section of Philadelphia, where Eastern European Jews first settled in the 1860s-1870s, and photographs of her family.

3 Pinchas Brodsky (1827-1924). Papers, 1897 and 1975, 1 folder. Copy of an 1897 photograph and a letter, 1975, containing biographical information about Brodsky, written by his great-grandson, Mitchell Snyderman. Brodsky was born in Russia, immigrating to Philadelphia in 1911.

4 Coats, Pants and Waist Makers' Union. Records, 1915-20 and n.d., 1 folder. Photocopies of meeting notices of the union, written in a combination of English, Yiddish, Italian, and Lithuanian. Originals at the Temple University Urban Archives.

5 Edith Deitsch. Papers, 1926-60, 1 folder. Newspaper clippings and playbills of Yiddish theater groups, including a Young Men's-Young Women's Hebrew Association program of Russian singer Nastia Poliakova.

6 Flitter Family. Papers, 1903-1906, 1 folder. Copies of immigration records of the family, including a 1903 Russian passport issued to Tova Davidovich Guralnik and a 1906 Russian travel permit issued to Itzko Abroovich Flitter.

7 Nathan Garber (1890-1947). Papers, 1918-46, 1 folder. Personal papers of a Russian immigrant: draft discharge certificate, 1918; marriage license, 1921; certificate of naturalization, 1926; and death certificate.

8 Glantz Family. Papers, 1905-1906 and 1916, 1 folder. Immigration and marriage records of various family members; a 1905 Russian passport; and a 1906 health inspection card for Reize Flerman.

9 Simon Glaser (ca. 1900-1977). Papers, 1931-77, 1 box. Includes autobiography written in 2 installments for the Jewish Exponent, describing his life in Russia before World War I and during the Russian Revolution.

10 The Jewish World. Records, 1914-44, 1 folder and 10 photographs. Photocopies of a newspaper clipping and correspondence, 1944, about the donation of the Jewish World press to Biro Bidjan, an autonomous Jewish state in the USSR. The Jewish World, Philadelphia's only Yiddish newspaper, ceased publication in 1942. Samuel Lipschutz, a former employee, purchased the equipment and, in 1944, donated the press and $300 to Biro Bidjan. Photos of the newspaper's (Philadelphia) headquarters and staff members are in the PJAC Photograph Collection; a few scattered copies of the newspaper are in the periodicals collection.

11 Jekabs Kucgalis (b. 1906). Papers, 1933-63, 1 folder. Photocopies of his personal papers. He emigrated from Latvia in 1939. Includes his school grades, birth certificate, and letters of recommendation from various jobs he held as a physical education teacher.

12 Elsie (Mrs. A. Harry) Levitan. Papers, 1892 and n.d., 1 folder. Immigration documents in Hebrew and Russian, 1892 and n.d., and an undated card written in Russian. 8 family photos are in the PJAC Photograph Collection.

13 Hershel Lichten (ca. 1872-1937). Papers, 1932, 1 folder. Photocopy of an autobiography, 1932, translated by his son, James Lichten. He tells about his family and life in Russia ca. 1872-1913 in great detail in the early part of the work.

14 Manuel Lisan (1882-1975). Papers, 1902-73, 1 box. Pioneer Philadelphia Zionist, born in Odessa. Emigrated to the U.S. in 1900. Includes original and drafts of his autobiography, covering the years 1897-1910, which recounts his journey from Russia through Finland, Denmark, and England to the U.S.

15 Melnick Family. Papers, 1901-20, 1 folder. Immigration application, health certificate, police release, and passage certificate of the Melnick family, including Sara Chmielnik, Zelig Chmielnik, Golali Chmielnik, Lora Chmielnik, Jospo Chmielnik, and Max Mulnick. Documents in both Russian and English.

16 Joseph Real (1891-1977). Papers, 1974-76, 1 folder. Autobiographical sketch written by a Philadelphian who left Russia in 1895. Includes anecdotes about his ancestors and insights about what it was like to be a Russian Jewish immigrant in Philadelphia.

17 Harry Richman. Citizenship document, 26 June 1896, of Richman, who was born in Russia.

18 Isadore Ross (b. 1899). Papers, 1976, 1 folder. Edited transcript of an interview with Ross, who was born in Russia, lived in Moscow during the 1917 Revolution, and later immigrated to the U.S. He describes his experiences in Russia, marriage, and journey to the United States, as well as his life in this country.

19 Harris Rubin (1847-1931). Papers, 1915-20, 1 folder. Translation, 1974, by his granddaughter's husband, Benson Schambelan, of his autobiography, originally written in Yiddish. Born in Lithuania, he immigrated to Philadelphia in 1882. First part of the autobiography describes in great detail life in Russia in the late 19th c.; the second part recounts the trip from Russia and life in Philadelphia and New Jersey.

20 Vitebsker Beneficial Association. Records, ca. 1897-1945 and n.d., 1 folder. Constitutions and by-laws, ca. 1897 and 1934; souvenir booklets, 1927 and 1937; letter, 1945; membership list, n.d.; and 12 undated letters. Composed of men who immigrated from the Vitebsk region of Russia.

21 In addition, the PJAC holds records of several beneficial associations and other groups founded by people who came from towns or regions of Russia and Eastern Europe. There is a subject file for Soviet Jewry, 1971-present; and the photograph collection holds some material pertinent to the Russian Empire/Soviet Union.

Finding Aid: A Guide to the Philadelphia Jewish Archives Center, edited by Lindsay B. Nauen (1977), from which all the preceding information was taken.

PA 29
PHILADELPHIA MUSEUM OF ART
26th and Benjamin Franklin Parkway
P.O. Box 7646
Philadelphia, Pennsylvania 19101
(215-763-8100)

1 Archives. Holds some material relating to the American-Russian Institute, Alexander Portnoff, and Christian Brinton. Most of it concerns Brinton's collection of Russian art which was given to the Museum in the 1940s.

2 Department of Prints, Drawings, and Photographs. Houses 2 early Armenian manuscripts: a psalter and perpetual calendar, 16th-17th c., and a second psalter, early 16th c. (Museum acquisitions, no. 45-65-20 and no. 53-128-7, respectively)

PA 30
PRESBYTERIAN HISTORICAL SOCIETY LIBRARY
425 Lombard Street
Philadelphia, Pennsylvania 19147
(215-627-1852)

Sheldon Jackson (1834-1909). Papers, 1856-1908, ca. 20 ft., ca. 8,000 items of correspondence and 65 scrapbooks. Missionary and U.S. superintendent of Education in Alaska, 1860-1908. Letters, reports, diaries, photographs, and other materials pertaining to missions, education, travel, and Siberian reindeer in Alaska, 1860-67. Ca. 8 ft., 2,450 items, concern Alaska before 1868. The complete collection is available on microfilm, as is an index. Unpublished thesis describes the collection (1951). (NUCMC 61-3120)

Finding Aid: Special Collections in the Presbyterian Historical Society (1955).

PA 31
HISTORICAL COLLECTIONS
AMERICAN CATHOLIC HISTORICAL SOCIETY
RYAN MEMORIAL LIBRARY
ST. CHARLES SEMINARY
Overbrook
Philadelphia, Pennsylvania 19151
(215-839-3760 x 283)

William Franklin Sands (1874-1946). Papers, 1875-1945, 6 ft. Diplomat, businessman, author, and teacher. Includes his notes on a trip to Russia for the American International Corporation, November 1917-January 1918, 4 items; letter, 26 July 1921, to J. P. Hutchins, Madrid, concerning the possibility of foreign-owned properties in Russia being restored, a possible anti-communist uprising, Herbert Hoover's conditions for undertaking to feed Russians, etc.; letter, 21 April 1922, to F. J. Whiting of Stone & Webster, Boston, discussing the Genoa Conference on reparations and suggesting a possible economic solution for Germany and Russia (exchange of materials and means of production); letter, 27 December 1921, to an unknown addressee,

Berlin, in French, briefing this person on life in Russia under the Bolsheviks (incomplete); Sands's "Country Life in Bolshevik Russia" (1921); and translations of Russian newspaper clippings, 35 items.

Finding Aid: Survey of the Manuscript Collections of the American Catholic Historical Society of Philadelphia, by Alice E. Whittelsey (n.d.).

PA 32
SPECIAL COLLECTIONS
PALEY LIBRARY
TEMPLE UNIVERSITY
Berks and 13th Streets
Philadelphia, Pennsylvania 19122
(215-787-8230)

1 Richard Aldington (1892-1962). Papers, 1912-62, 98 items. British author. Literary manuscripts and correspondence. Includes some postcards to his family, 1912-62, describing travels in France, Italy, and Russia. Access restricted, in part. Unpublished finding aids (NUCMC 76-2096).

2 Dallas Family. Papers, 1775-1926, ca. 2 ft., 200 items. Includes papers of George Mifflin Dallas (1792-1864), U.S. senator from Pennsylvania, vice president of the U.S., and minister to Russia, 1837-39. These contain: ALS, 2 March 1837, to him from Martin Van Buren asking for advice on replacing I. R. Clay as secretary of the Russian legation; and letter signed by James Buchanan, 7 March 1837, notifying Dallas of the Senate's confirmation of him as minister and of William White Chew (1803-1851) as secretary of legation. Typed register, photocopy available gratis. (NUCMC 71-1882)

3 Herbert Adolphus Miller (1875-1951). Papers, 1903-66, 5 in. Sociologist. He befriended many Eastern European immigrants in the years before World War I. In 1912 he visited Poland, Russia, and Finland. In 1925 he again traveled in Eastern Europe. Letter, 2 November 1925, written during his visit to the Soviet Union and the Baltic nations discusses his meetings with Karl Radek, Olga Kamenev (L. Trotskii's sister), and other minor officials; the funeral of General M. V. Frunze; and especially visits to educational institutions. The papers contain only a copy (in quadruplicate) of the original typed letter to his wife, 50 pp. Unpublished descriptive inventory.

4 Gerald D. Timmons (b. 1897). Papers, 1946-62, 4 ft. Dean of Temple University School of Dentistry. In June 1961 he led a U.S. dental mission to the USSR. Includes 2 mimeographed, undated copies of a "Report on a visit to the Soviet Union," 15 pp., and his "Diary of the Russian Trip, June 1, 1961 to June 29, 1961," 50 pp. Both deal primarily with his visits to dental services in the Soviet Union, his analyses of the characteristics of these services, and his general impressions of the country. Unpublished index.

5 William W. Tomlinson (b. 1893). Papers, 1943-77, 2 ft. Vice president of Temple University. Traveled widely, visiting the Soviet Union twice, in 1958 and in 1965. Includes "Shadows of the Kremlin," typescript, 26 pp., 1958?; and "Soviet Metamorphosis; a re-examination of life and the pursuit of liberty in the USSR," typescript, 12 pp., 1965? Unpublished index.

PA 33
MORRIS ARBORETUM OF THE
UNIVERSITY OF PENNSYLVANIA
9414 Meadowbrook Avenue
Philadelphia, Pennsylvania 19118
(215-247-5777)

The library of the Arboretum has 4 packages of materials sent to the United States in 1841 by Dr. F. E. L. Fischer, director of the St. Petersburg Imperial Botanical Gardens. The materials were intended for Dr. William Darlington of West Chester (Pennsylvania); Dr. John Torrey of New York; the Massachusetts Historical Society; and the Boston Society of Natural History. The packages, which include letters, seed samples, and pamphlets on botany and zoology, were carried to the U.S. by William Chew, secretary to the United States legation at St. Petersburg. For a fuller description of this material, see the article on which this entry is based, Hui-Lin Li and Ann F. Stanley, "Russo-United States Botanical Exchange of 1841," The Morris Arboretum Bulletin, Volume 26, no. 4 (December 1975), pp. 51-56.

PA 34
RARE BOOK COLLECTION
VAN PELT LIBRARY
UNIVERSITY OF PENNSYLVANIA
Philadelphia, Pennsylvania 19104
(215-243-7088)

1 Frater Thomas Campanells, O.P. Dominican friar. Manuscript book entitled La Monarchia Spagnola, containing chapters on relations with such countries as Poland, Russia, and Turkey (17th c.), in Italian. (Ital. 164)

2 Ludwig, Graf von Cobenzl (1753-1809). Papers of Ludwig von Cobenzl, Austrian ambassador to Russia, and Philipp von Cobenzl, vice

chancellor of Austria, 1786-1806, 105 items. Correspondence and documents concern diplomacy and political affairs, including relations between Austria and Russia, Prussia, and France. Among the correspondents are Count Nikita Ivanovich Panin, Andreas Razumovski, and Prince N. V. Repnin. (NUCMC 68-847) (French 55)

3 Theodore Dreiser (1871-1945). Papers, 1890-1945, 486 ft. Author. Includes letters, 1926-37, from Sergei Dinamov, ca. 50 items, and 8 letters from Sergei Eisenstein, 1931-41. Permission for copying, in any form, of the letters must be provided in writing by either the author of the document or his executor. Also, 2 folders of materials concerning Russian publishers of Dreiser's books, 1927-40. Dreiser's diary of his trip to Russia, November 1927-January 1928. Much of this material was used in Dreiser Looks at Russia (New York, 1928) and in Ruth Epperson Kennell's Theodore Dreiser and the Soviet Union (New York, 1969). (NUCMC 60-1134)

4 Horace Brisbin Liveright (1886-1933). Papers, 1927-33, 20 boxes. Publisher and theatrical producer. Letters received by Liveright from authors whose works were published by the firm of Boni & Liveright. Includes correspondence from Dr. Ivan Petrovich Pavlov, the physiologist. Unpublished finding aid (NUCMC 68-453).

5 Jurgis Saulys (1879-1948). Papers, in process, 34 boxes, ca. 16 ft. Lithuanian civic leader, statesman, and diplomat. Cosigner of the Lithuanian Declaration of Independence on 16 February 1918. Personal correspondence and historical documents, including much material on Lithuanian culture and political history, especially efforts to gain independence during World War I. Many items are from Lithuanian legations headed by Dr. Saulys--Berlin, Bern, Rome, and the Vatican. Representatives of Lithuanian culture noted include Jonas Biliūnas, Lazdynu Pelēda (pen-name of S. Psibiliauskienē), G. Petkevicaitē-Bitē, J. Tumas-Vaizgantas, Vydūnas (pen-name of V. Storasta), and Zemaitē (pen-name of J. Zymantienē). Among his correspondents were scholars, civic and political leaders: the linguists Jonas Jablonskis ("Father of the Lithuanian standard language") and Kazimieras Būga; archaeologist T. Daugirdas; literary historian Mykolas Birziska; jurist M. Roemeris; historian I. Jonynas; Jonas Basanavicius ("Patriarch of the Lithuanian national renaissance"); P. Grigaitis; P. Leonas; composer M. Petrauskas; V. Pozēla; Antanas Smetona (first president of the Lithuanian Republic); J. Vileisis; and Vincas Kapsukas-Mickevicius, foremost Lithuanian communist theoretician. For Kapsukas, there are materials not available even in Soviet Lithuania. Note: The library also holds a large number of rare, even unique, Lithuanian (and other Baltic) printed works, many from the Saulys collection.

6 Robert Williams (d. 1660/61). Manuscript book, 1632-54, 90 pp., bound. Merchant? Includes notes concerning trade, fiscal matters, weights and measures, and commodities in London in 1632, and in cities such as Moscow, Constantinople, Smyrna, Venice, Rome, Genoa, Madrid, and Tunis. (Eng. 21)

PA 35
HUNT INSTITUTE FOR BOTANICAL DOCUMENTATION
CARNEGIE-MELLON UNIVERSITY
Pittsburgh, Pennsylvania 15213
(412-578-2437)

1 Andrey Nikolaievich Avinoff (1884-1949). Papers, 1930-50 and n.d., 2 folders. Russian-born curator of the Carnegie Museum and author of botanical works. Includes biographical information (mostly from published sources).

2 Aleksandr Fedorovic Batalin (1847-96). Director of the St. Petersburg Botanical Garden. Letter, 16/28 March 1893, to an unknown colleague, 2 pp. (NUCMC 72-150)

3 Franz Gabriel von Bray (1765-1832). Correspondence, 1798-1831, 23 sets of letters (positive and negative photocopies). Letters from Russia included. Originals in Bavaria.

4 Nicholas Tiho Mirov (b. 1893). Botanist. Oral history interview, 1970, 17 pp., transcript. Interviewed by Lois Stone in Berkeley, California. In part covers his early years in Russia. (Part of Botanical Reminiscences) (NUCMC 72-154)

5 William Trelease (1857-1945). Correspondence, 1893-1944, 208 items. Director of the Missouri Botanical Garden, 1889-1912. Includes letters from Boris Lavrent'evic Isacenko, 1929, and Jurij Nikolaevic Voronov, 17 November 1929.

6 Frits Warmolt Went (b. 1903). Papers, 1950-67, 1 box. Botanist. Includes manuscript and typescript journal, carbon copy, pertaining, in part, to his travels in the Soviet Union. Also, correspondence.

7 Truman G. Yuncker (1891-1964). Correspondence, 1833 and 1895-1955, 340 items. Curator of De Pauw Herbarium, De Pauw University (Indiana), 1919-64. Includes correspondence from K. W. Kamensky, 2 letters, 1932, Botanical Institute and Garden of the Academy of Sciences, Leningrad; Ivan Sergeevic Kossenko, 1933; Boris Fedchenko, 1925-26; and Ivan Vladimirovic Palibin, 1926, Director of Botanical Museum in Leningrad.

PA 36
SPECIAL COLLECTIONS
ARCHIVES OF INDUSTRIAL SOCIETY
UNIVERSITY OF PITTSBURGH LIBRARIES
UNIVERSITY OF PITTSBURGH
Pittsburgh, Pennsylvania 15260
(412-624-4430)

1 Billy Adams (b. 1860). Papers, 1911-42, 1 ft. Socialist Party leader. Materials pertaining to the Socialist Party of Allegheny County, including a "Russian song"; pamphlets on Bolshevism and labor law in Russia, 1920s. Unpublished inventory.

2 American Service Institute of Allegheny County. Records, 1941-61, 50 ft. Materials on the Carpatho-Russian church in the U.S., the United Russia Orthodox Brotherhood of America, 1952-53, the Russian Orthodox Women's Mutual Aid Society, 1952-53, the Lithuanian Alliance of America, the Sons of Lithuania, 1952-53, the Lithuanian Society of Western Pennsylvania, 1952-53, the Lithuanian Citizens Association, 1952-53, and the United Lithuanian Relief Funds of America. There are also documents on customs and festivals of Lithuanians, Estonians, and Latvians in the U.S. Unpublished inventory.

3 Michael Cherniavsky (1922-1973). Papers, 1954-73, 6 ft. Professor of Russian history. Correspondence with Robert F. Byrnes, Leopold H. Haimson, Sidney Monas, Marc Raeff, Donald W. Treadgold, and other historians in the Russian field; unpublished writings; research materials; photographs. Restricted: Series VII of the Cherniavsky papers is closed to most researchers. Unpublished inventory. (NUCMC 77-2037)

4 Ethnic Fraternal Organizations Oral History Project. 1975-77. Tape recorded interviews conducted by the University of Pittsburgh's Department of History which explore the roles and influences of these organizations and ethnic communities in the Pittsburgh area. Some respondents are of Russian-Jewish and Polish background. Partly transcribed. Partial index.

5 National Council of Jewish Women. Pittsburgh Section. Oral History Project. 11 ft., 1893-1964. Materials by Jewish immigrants, many of them Russian-born, who settled in Pittsburgh between 1890 and 1920. The material was published in By Myself I'm a Book (1972). Restricted. Unpublished inventory.

6 Nechama Pearl Rothbart. "Reminiscences of my childhood (at the beginning of the century) . . ." Pittsburgh, 1971, 32 ll. Photocopy of typescript. Describes the life of old Jews in the Vilna district of Lithuania.

7 Slavonic Congregational Church of Pittsburgh. Records, 1901-70, partial microfilm reel. Includes legal papers, church registers, family members lists, correspondence, church committee minutes. Unpublished inventory.

8 Slavonic Immigration to Western Pennsylvania Research Project. .5 ft., 1953-54. Includes correspondence, reports of interviews, reports and extracts of books, card file of ethnic institutions, societies, and organizations in western Pennsylvania. Unpublished inventory.

9 Weaver Social History Collection. 11 ft., 1913-51. Includes minutes, March-June 1936, of the Campaign Committee to send a Mr. Hill as an observer to the Soviet Union, as well as miscellaneous materials on the National Council of American-Soviet Friendship. Unpublished inventory.

PA 37
FRIENDS HISTORICAL LIBRARY
SWARTHMORE COLLEGE
Swarthmore, Pennsylvania 19081
(215-328-2625)

1 William Allen. Quaker. Extracts from his memorandum book concerning a visit to Westminster Meeting in London by Emperor Alexander I and an interview with him, 19-21 June 1814. (Miscellaneous Manuscripts)

2 Thomas Clarkson. Material on his interviews with Alexander I at Paris, 23 September 1815, and at Aix-la-Chapelle, 9 October 1818. They discussed the slave trade and peace. (Miscellaneous Manuscripts)

3 Elkinton Family. Papers, 1736-1973, 47 boxes. Includes some items pertaining to the Doukhobors following their emigration from Russia.

4 Miers Fisher, Sr. Journals, 1803-18, several vols. Quaker. On 30 September 1813 he reports learning of the death in St. Petersburg of his son, Miers, Jr. (Manuscript Journals)

5 William Hubben (1895-1974). Quaker writer and editor, emigrated from Germany in 1933. Collection includes unpublished typescript, 304 pp., "The Making of the Russian Mind: Profiles from the Russian Past" and several articles about Russian history and literature, especially concerning the writings of Dostoevskii and Soloviev. (Record Group 5)

6 Janney-Timbres. Papers, ca. 1920-75, in process. Papers of Harry Garland Timbres, Quaker doctor, who died in Russia in 1937, and also of his wife, Rebecca Janney Timbres Clark. Included are several articles by Rebecca Janney Timbres Clark about life in the Soviet Union in the late 1930s. (Record Group 5)

7 Lucy Biddle Lewis (Biddle Papers). Lewis papers, ca. 1919, 24 items (of ca. 1,000 items in the Biddle Manuscripts). Member of the Swarthmore College Board of Managers. Includes

3 letters discussing Russian relief; a typescript (by John and Lydia Rickman?) entitled "Conditions in Eastern Siberia and Manchuria in the Autumn of 1918"; An Eyewitness from Russia, published by the People's Information Bureau (London, 1919); and a photostat of "Picture of Russian peasant life in the period August 1916-September 1918," apparently written by John and Lydia Rickman. 2 ALS, 26 and 30 April 1919, are to Lydia Rickman. The first speaks of an interview with Dr. Fridtjof Nansen and Herbert Hoover about Russian relief (Nansen headed the Neutral Commission to get supplies into Russia). The second recounts a meeting with Jane Addams, Lillian D. Wald, Emily Greene Balch, and others concerning relief efforts. Another letter of 30 April 1919 to Wilbur K. Thomas again concerns the interview with Nansen and Hoover. (NUCMC 60-2194, in part)

8 Rotch-Wales Collection. Papers, ca. 1780-1882, ca. 22 ft. on 4 microfilm reels. Includes correspondence of William Rotch, Sr. and Jr. to Thomas Rotch, 1802 and 1812, that relate to commerce with Russia. Originals in the Massillon (Ohio) Public Library. (NUCMC 72-964, for Massillon Public Library)

9 Wilbur Kelsey Thomas (1882-1953). Papers, ca. 1915-34, 1 ft. Executive secretary of the American Friends Service Committee, 1918-29. He was active in post-World War I relief efforts for Russia and Germany (the Friends Feeding Mission). A portion of his letters, addresses, and writings pertains to this humanitarian work and other public service. Unpublished checklist (NUCMC 67-2115).

10 Wheeler Manuscripts. Ca. 1 in., 1820-43. Quaker family. Includes description, dated 19 December 1832, of the death of Jane, wife of Daniel Wheeler (1771-1840) at Shoosharry (Shusharri), near St. Petersburg. Also a letter 13 January 1833 by daughters Jane and Sarah to an aunt, H. Brady, about the illness of their brother Charles and the need for postponing the burial of their mother. (Small Collections)

11 John Greenleaf Whittier (1807-1892). Papers, 1790-1957, ca. 700 items. Quaker poet and abolitionist. Includes letter of 22 April 1891 to Francis J. Garrison in which he admits misgivings about the Society of American Friends of Russian Freedom's campaign against Russian lack of freedom because "our treatment of seven million of colored Americans" was so similar; and a letter of 3 July 1891 to Garrison concerning Russian political exiles, Russian despotism, and George Kennan.

PA 38
SWARTHMORE COLLEGE PEACE COLLECTION
FRIENDS HISTORICAL LIBRARY
SWARTHMORE COLLEGE
Swarthmore, Pennsylvania 19081
(215-544-7900)

1 Jane Addams (1860-1935). Papers, 1838-1935, 90 ft. Social worker, co-founder of Hull House, a founder of the Women's International League for Peace and Freedom, and Nobel Peace Prize recipient. Includes materials on American reactions to the Russian revolutions of 1917 and other scattered items pertaining to Russia. (NUCMC 60-2187)

2 Emily Greene Balch (1867-1961). Papers, 1893-1961, 52 ft. Economist and sociologist, shared the Nobel Peace Prize with John R. Mott in 1946. Includes scattered items relating to Russia/USSR ca. 1917. (NUCMC 60-1200)

3 Anna Melissa Graves (1875-1964). Papers, 1919-47, 10 ft. Pacifist and worker for liberal causes. Includes correspondence from Angelica Balabanoff and Bertram Wolfe. (NUCMC 61-3533)

4 Abraham Johannes Muste (1885-1967). Papers, 1930-67, ca. 24 ft. Pacifist, minister, labor leader. Director of Brookwood Labor College, 1921-33. Materials concerning atomic energy questions relate in part to the Soviet Union. He had many other contacts with the USSR including the U.S.-USSR peace leadership exchange project.

5 Helene Stöcker (1869-1943). Papers, 1896-1943, 5 ft. Pacifist and feminist in pre-Hitler Germany and abroad. Correspondents include Emma Goldman and William Henry Chamberlin. (NUCMC 61-3543)

6 Sydney Dix Strong (1860-1940). Papers, 1914-40, 2 ft. Includes papers of his daughter, Anna Louise Strong (1885-1970), journalist, educator, and Russian publicist. (NUCMC 61-3544)

7 Time did not permit a thorough search, but it is probable that in various record groups in the Peace Collection, such as the American Friends Service Committee, 1917-47, 9 ft., the Women's International League for Peace and Freedom, 1919 to date, 100 ft., and A. Ruth Fry (1918-1962), 2 ft., there is additional Russian-related material. In addition, Collective Document Group B (secondary material) includes 5 document boxes of USSR material relating to Leo Tolstoi, Jan Gotlieb Bloch, Catharine Breshkovsky, Russian Reconstruction Farms (famine relief), international affairs, peaceful coexistence, and miscellaneous.

Finding Aid: Guide to the Swarthmore College Peace Collection (1947). Revised edition in preparation.

PA 39
THE HISTORICAL SOCIETY OF YORK COUNTY
250 East Market Street
York, Pennsylvania 17403
(717-848-1587)

Henry Lanius Smyser (1825-1900). Papers, 1849-58, 50 items. Physician and surgeon in York. Actively participated in Russian medicine during the Crimean War. Personal correspondence ca. 1854-55 includes references to St. Petersburg and the war. Unpublished inventory (NUCMC 61-2700).

RHODE ISLAND

RI 1
BRISTOL HISTORICAL PRESERVATION SOCIETY
48 Court Street
Bristol, Rhode Island 02809
(401-253-8825/5705)

De Wolfe Family. Papers, uncatalogued, ca. 4 file drawers. James and John De Wolfe, a sea captain. Includes scattered references to Russian commerce. Papers are arranged by name of ship. The Juno was engaged in Russian trade. Researchers should call or write in advance to arrange a visit.

RI 2
NAVAL HISTORICAL COLLECTION
NAVAL WAR COLLEGE
Newport, Rhode Island 02840
(401-841-4052/2435)

1 Record Group 4. Publications office curriculum files, ca. 1919-69, 112 cartons. Contains, inter alia, copies of lectures delivered at the college by leading scholars such as Zbigniew K. Brzezinski, Merle Fainsod, Henry A. Kissinger, Philip E. Mosely, Harry H. Schwartz, John Scott, Demitri B. Shimkin, Marshall D. Shulman, and Bertram D. Wolfe. Topics covered include Soviet history and politics, economy, foreign relations, navy, and role in Asia.

2 Record Group 8. Intelligence and Technological Archives, 1894-1945, 80 cartons. Included here are research source materials on naval warfare and related subjects collected and/or produced at the Naval War College. Among Russian-related items are: a report by N. C. Fuglede, a Danish Army officer who travelled through Russia 1918-19; compilation of articles on the Soviet Union from M.I.D. Summaries; and materials, some of them published, on the Dvina River and on German cooperation in the restoration of the military industry of Russia, 1926.

3 Record Group 14. Faculty and Staff Presentations, ca. 1892-1970, 31 cartons. In these lectures delivered by members of the College faculty there are some references to Russia/USSR.

4 Record Group 15. Guest Lectures, 1885-1971, 13 cartons. Some of these lectures, given by visiting authorities at the Naval War College, contain materials pertaining to the USSR. Post-1955 classified and restricted lectures are housed in the Classified Library, Hewitt Hall.

5 Record Group 24. Office of Naval Intelligence Records, 1914-18, 1943-45, 22 ms. boxes and 80 vols. Included here are State Department naval attaché reports dealing with the military situation of belligerent forces in World War I. There is some material, dated 1916, pertaining to P. N. Miliukov, Rasputin, the Duma, and political conditions in Russia. (RG 24 will soon be made a part of RG 8.)

6 Ms. Document 19. 1 vol. of clippings from the Yokohama newspaper The Japan Daily Mail (English) relating to the Russo-Japanese War, 1904-1905.

Restriction: Prospective researchers should send letters of introduction and intent to the president of the Naval War College.

Finding Aids: Card indices are available for the record groups cited above. A general guide (unpublished) to the collections is also at the repository.

RI 3
JOHN CARTER BROWN LIBRARY
BROWN UNIVERSITY
George and Brown Streets (Mail: Box 1894)
Providence, Rhode Island 02912
(401-863-2725)

1 Brown and Ives. Records, ca. 1750-1875, ca. 4-500,000 items. Providence merchants. Contains a large amount of material on Russian-American commercial ties, 1789-1815, including data for ca. 20 ships engaged in Russian trade, prices current, and correspondence with Edward James Smith and the Cramer Brothers in St. Petersburg. Partial unpublished finding aid (NUCMC 60-1421).

2 Arnold-Green Companies. Papers, ca. 1742-86, ca. 25,000 items. Welcome Arnold & Co./Samuel Green & Co., merchants. Includes

materials on several voyages of ships to St. Petersburg (letters received, bills, and invoices). Unpublished finding aid (NUCMC 66-95)

RI 4
JOHN HAY LIBRARY
BROWN UNIVERSITY
20 Prospect Street
Providence, Rhode Island 02912
(401-863-2146)

1 John Milton Hay (1838-1905). Papers, 1856-1905, ca. 10,500 items. Secretary of state, 1898-1905, and ambassador to England, 1897-98, also held diplomatic posts in Paris, Vienna, and Madrid, 1865-98. Some of his papers, which include personal letterpress copy books reflecting his diplomatic service, pertain to Russian affairs. (NUCMC 60-2193 and 78-82)

2 Harry Lyman Koopman (1860-1937). Papers, ca. 1890-1940 and in process, ca. 30,000 items. Literary scholar and librarian at Brown University. Includes correspondence from at least 1 individual who, as a St. Petersburg resident in 1902-13, was an eyewitness to the Revolution of 1905. Preliminary inventory.

3 Usher Parsons (1788-1868). Papers, 1611-1900 (1810-60), ca. 950 items. Professor of anatomy and surgery at Brown University. Includes descriptions of Russia and other European countries ca. 1818-19. Research guide.

4 Jonathan Russell (1771-1832). Papers, 1795-1832, 7,000 items. Merchant, Massachusetts congressman, chargé d'affaires at Paris, 1810, minister to Sweden and Norway, and member of the U.S. commission to draw up the Treaty of Ghent, 1814-18. Includes several hundred letters from Russell to Secretary of State James Monroe concerning commercial and diplomatic relations between the United States and Europe, the War of 1812, and the Treaty of Ghent. There are also letters from John Quincy Adams when he was minister to Russia, 1809-14, and correspondence from William David Lewis, 1792-1881, an American merchant in Russia in the 1810s, who sent Russell his translation into Russian of "Yankee Doodle." (NUCMC 60-2120)

5 Alexandra L. Tolstoi (b. 1884). Daughter of Leo Tolstoi and head of the Tolstoy Foundation in New York. Letter, 1939, to Mrs. Maud Howe Elliott concerning the Tolstoy Foundation.

6 Henry Wheaton (1785-1848). Papers, 1786-1899, ca. 275 items. U.S. chargé d'affaires in Denmark and minister to Prussia. Correspondence concerning diplomatic matters pertains in part to Russia.

7 John Brooks Wheelwright (1897-1940). Papers, ca. 1920-40, over 15,000 items. American poet and socialist. Contains several hundred manuscripts dealing with socialism and with his association with the Socialist Workers Party. Preliminary inventory (NUCMC 73-59).

8 Note: The library has miscellaneous papers of several U.S. presidents--Abraham Lincoln, James Monroe, John Quincy Adams, Rutherford B. Hayes, Grover Cleveland, William McKinley, Theodore Roosevelt, and John F. Kennedy. These may include materials pertaining to Russia/USSR.

Finding Aid: Stuart C. Sherman, "Guide to the Manuscript Collections in the Brown University Library," Books at Brown, vol. XXV (1977), used in writing this entry.

RI 5
COLLEGE ARCHIVES
PHILLIPS MEMORIAL LIBRARY
PROVIDENCE COLLEGE
River Avenue at Eaton Street
Providence, Rhode Island 02918
(401-865-2377)

1 Louis Budenz (1891-1972). Papers, 1953-72, 9,500 items. Editor of The Daily Worker in the 1930s and anti-communist crusader in the 1950s-1960s. As an authority on Russian (and Chinese) communism, he lectured and wrote extensively on the threat of world communism. Correspondence concerns primarily American communism; among his correspondents was Senator Joseph R. McCarthy. Unpublished register (NUCMC 71-404).

2 William Henry Chamberlin (1897-1969). Papers, 1912-69, 120 items and 40 diaries on 4 microfilm reels. Foreign correspondent for The Christian Science Monitor in Russia and author of the classic The Russian Revolution, 1917-1921, 2 vols. (1935), plus other studies of the Soviet Union and its economy. Diaries, 1913-19, 1940-69; notebooks on world events, 1949-65; and personal correspondence, 1940-69. These items contain many references to Russian communist affairs, policy, and leaders. Information on family finances in the diaries cannot be used. (NUCMC 71-405)

3 Nazi Bund. Records, 1930s, 300 items. White Russian Fascist Movement organization composed of Russian émigrés in the United States. Includes publications The Fascist, 1933-69, and Gentiles Review, 1923-24, personal correspondence of Anastase Andreivich Vonsiatsky, and memorabilia.

RI 6
RHODE ISLAND HISTORICAL SOCIETY
121 Hope Street
Providence, Rhode Island 02906
(401-331-0448)

1 Edward C. Carrington (1775-1843). Papers, 1813-ca. 1850, 221 ft. Merchant. Includes material on Russian-American commerce. Unpublished partial inventory, and published description in Rhode Island History, vol. 22, no. 1 (January 1963).

2 Champlin Family. Papers, 1712-1840, ca. 12 ft. (in process). Includes papers of Christopher Champlin (1731-1805) and Christopher Grant Champlin (1768-1840). Contains data on trade between the U.S. and Russia.

3 Custom House. Records, ca. 1785-1900, 441 ft. Information on commerce with Russia in the "Import Books" and records of "Entries and Clearances." Described by Earl C. Tanner in the New England Quarterly (March 1953).

4 James De Wolfe (1764-1837). Papers, 1751-1864, 3 ft. Merchant. Includes references to the ship Rambler, and 3 items from 1823 about Russian-American trade. Unpublished inventory.

SOUTH CAROLINA

SC 1
THE CITADEL ARCHIVES-MUSEUM
Charleston, South Carolina 29409
(803-792-6846)

Mark Wayne Clark (b. 1896). Papers, 1918-66, 40 ft. and 12 microfilm reels. General, UN supreme commander in Korea, 1952-53, and president of The Citadel (1953-present). Correspondents include Soviet Foreign Minister V. M. Molotov, General Zheltov, General L. V. Durasov, Marshall I. F. Konev, American presidents, congressmen, military leaders, and statesmen. Included are letters, diaries, and documents, plus 26 tape recordings (of speeches and lectures) and 21 motion picture films (on military operations and his career). Unpublished subject guide and cross index (NUCMC 71-1563).

SC 2
MIDDLETON PLACE FOUNDATION
Highway 61 and Route 4
Charleston, South Carolina 29407
(803-556-6025)

Middleton Family. Papers, 1789-1900, 31 boxes. Includes papers of Henry Middleton (1771-1846), minister plenipotentiary to Russia 1820-30, and of his son, Williams Middleton (1809-1883), attaché of the American legation in St. Petersburg during his father's service there. Russian-related items, probably in the hand of Williams, include: 6 pp., handwritten, n.d., about the Decembrist revolt, serfs and nobles, Nicholas I's respect for serfs, Nicholas's behavior to the insurgents, Mr. Nerischen's (Naryshkin?) horn band, Nicholas's temper and temperament, and the city of St. Petersburg, built on ice; "Memoirs of a Russian Court II" (skating on the Neva, no aid given to fallen or drowning people), n.d., 2 pp.; Easter customs and marriage rites, n.d., 2 pp.; incomplete, on Russian life, Laplanders, and the midnight sun, n.d., 1 p.; Russian marriages, 22 December 1877, 1 p.; another incomplete, on the same subject, n.d., 1 p.; and (incomplete) "Memoirs of a Russian Court," n.d., 6 pp., typed + 12 pp., handwritten. Inquire about access.

SC 3
CLEMSON UNIVERSITY LIBRARY
Clemson, South Carolina 29631
(803-656-3024)

James F. Byrnes (1879-1972). Papers, 1930-68, 115 ft. and 32 vols. Lawyer, U.S. senator, Supreme Court justice, director of the Office of Economic Stabilization and of the Office of War Mobilization (and Reconversion) in World War II, secretary of state, 1945-47, and United Nations delegate. The collection, comprising some 225 document boxes, plus scrapbooks of news clippings, phonodiscs, tapes, and photographs, includes correspondence, reports, book manuscripts, press conference transcriptions, and State Department memoranda. There are delivery texts of speeches, a log by Byrnes's assistant covering the Potsdam, Moscow, and London conferences; Byrnes's own shorthand (McKee's New Standard) notes on Yalta; copies of minutes of conferences at London, Berlin, Moscow, Paris, and New York, 1945-46; and State Department briefing books on individual countries for 1946, 4 vols. Among subjects covered are U.S. foreign policy, atomic bomb decisions, lend-lease, and the peace treaties. There is a Voice of America rebroadcast, 30 December 1945, of Byrnes's report on the Moscow meeting of the Allies' representatives; also a speech of 27 March 1946 (possibly before the UN) in which he discusses a Russian-Iranian dispute over Soviet troops. Gen. Lucius Clay was a correspondent. Joseph Stalin and V. M. Molotov are mentioned. Unpublished finding aids: name and chronological index for pre-1941 material; and a folder-by-folder analysis of contents for ca. 3,000 folders, 1940-54, of which only about 400 contain Russian-related items (interspersed). (NUCMC 77-849)

SC 4
MANUSCRIPTS DIVISION
SOUTH CAROLINIANA LIBRARY
UNIVERSITY OF SOUTH CAROLINA
Columbia, South Carolina 29208
(803-777-5183)

1 Milledge Luke Bonham (1815-1890). Papers, 1771-1940, 4,402 manuscripts. Lawyer, army officer, and statesman. Includes 10 letters to Bonham from Francis W. Pickens, minister to Russia, 1859-60. Pickens tells his close friend of his reaction to U.S. political developments and describes Russian court life. In part, copies. Unpublished calendar (NUCMC 67-945).

2 Josef Hofmann (1877-1957). Papers, 1893-1957, 60 items. Concert pianist, toured Russia in the early 20th c. (accompanied by his wife). In several letters to his wife Hofmann gives his views of World War I in Europe. His wife's diary for 1907-10, 4 vols., contains concert itineraries and accounts of Russian tours with observations about the people, the food, accommodations, cultural life, and travel conditions. (The entire collection is on microfilm.)

3 William Joseph Holt (d. 1881). Papers, 1799-1910, 118 items. Physician and military surgeon who served with the Russians during the Crimean War. In letters, diaries, and other papers, Holt discusses the war and the role of American doctors in the Russian army. The collection also includes pencil sketches of (presumably) the Crimea and a map of the same; some material is in French and Russian. (NUCMC 62-1132)

4 Francis Kinloch (1755-1826). Papers, 1787-1819, 8 items. U.S. congressman. AL, 15 November 1804, from Kinloch, traveling in Europe, to Dr. Levi Myers, in part about the possibility of war between France and Russia.

5 William Lowndes (1782-1822). Papers, 1818-42 and 1901, 7 items. Diplomat. AL, 9 April 1818, from President James Monroe offers him the post of ambassador to Russia or minister to Constantinople, whichever he chooses, because of the "confidence which I repose in your ability and merit."

6 Manigault Family. Papers, 1750-1900, 1,411 items. Includes correspondence and other papers of Mrs. Ralph Izard (Alice DeLancey), Margaret Izard Manigault, and Georgina Smith (Mrs. Joseph Allen), from ca. 1800-23, pertaining to Russians in the United States (especially Philadelphia, Pennsylvania, and Washington) and to events in Russia. References also to Joseph Allen Smith's interest in Russia based on several years spent there in the early 1800s. Unpublished calendar.

7 McCrady Family. Papers, 1821-1907, 262 items. Includes letter of William Henry Trescot, on a diplomatic mission to China, which relates rumors of a war between China and Russia, 12 August 1880. Unpublished calendar (NUCMC 62-1608).

8 Henry Middleton (1770-1846). Minister plenipotentiary to Russia, 1820-30. Miscellaneous items, including letter, 2 February 1820, from him to John Quincy Adams expressing his willingness to become minister to Russia although ignorant of the language, and his hope that his duties would not entail private expenditures for him; also indicates his acceptance of Charles Pinckney as secretary of legation, photostatic copy. Letter, 3 September 1829, to Martin Van Buren discusses the Russo-Turkish War.

9 Pickens Family. Papers, 1781-1929, 284 items. Largely correspondence and other papers of Francis Wilkinson Pickens (1806-1869), U.S. representative from South Carolina, minister to Russia, and Confederate governor. Ca. 20 letters, 1858-60, to his wife, Lucy Holcomb Pickens, discuss Russian court life, customs, and U.S. political events. Account books also contain some Russian-related material. Some letters are copies. (NUCMC 66-1375)

10 Pinckney Family. Papers, 1735-1922, 315 items and 7 vols. Includes some papers of Charles Pinckney (1757-1824), statesman and governor of South Carolina. ALS from him to James Monroe discusses "our having formed an alliance with Russia [and the] sensation here as it was not believed before," Spain, February 1805. (NUCMC 67-953)

11 Joel Roberts Poinsett (1779-1851). Papers, 1804-51, 60 items. Minister to Mexico, 1825-29, and secretary of war, 1837-41. Includes a letter to James Monroe, 8 August 1816, expressing his concern over "Russian settlements on the N.W. Coast, and . . . the utility of establishing a line of demarcation with that power."

12 Edwin Grenville Seibels (1866-1954). Cotton insurance agent. Seibels visited Russia in 1911. On 18 February 1933 he delivered a talk to the Kosmos Club in Columbia, South Carolina, called "The Great Experiment," in which he recalled his 1911 trip and his association with a Russian insurance company. The manuscript is in a bound volume.

13 Beaufort Taylor Watts (d. ca. 1869). Papers, 1822-79, 283 items. Secretary of legation to Russia when his fellow South Carolinian Henry Middleton was minister. He arrived in St. Petersburg in January 1829. His letters, ca. 10 items, 1828-30, document his disputes with Middleton and reply to the latter's criticisms. He served only briefly. These papers contain little information about Russia directly.

Finding Aid: John Hammond Moore, Research Materials in South Carolina (1967).

SC 5
WINTHROP COLLEGE ARCHIVES
DACUS LIBRARY
Rock Hill, South Carolina 29733
(803-323-2131 x 28)

Lucile Kathryn Delano (b. 1902). Papers, 1927-73, 50 items. Professor of modern languages. Visited the Soviet Union in 1966, 19 May-9 June. In her diaries she discusses Soviet customs, art, and sites she visited. Unpublished finding aid (NUCMC 77-1382).

SOUTH DAKOTA

SD 1
KARL E. MUNDT ARCHIVES
KARL E. MUNDT LIBRARY
DAKOTA STATE COLLEGE
Madison, South Dakota 57042
(605-256-3551 x 228)

Karl E. Mundt (1900-1974). Archives, 1927-72, 640 ft., 15,000 items. Congressman and senator, 1939-72, from South Dakota. Member of Subcommittee Number 2 of the House Foreign Affairs Committee, which in 1945 spent a month in the USSR and Soviet-dominated countries to report on the merits of Russia's claim for UNRRA relief. This visit, the first trip to Russia by a congressional committee since 1939, is well-documented in the papers. There is also material pertaining to the Yalta Conference, the compilation of the Yalta Papers by Bryton Barron and his dismissal by the State Department, the All American Conference to Combat Communism, the United States Information Agency, and Mundt's Voice of America legislation. Unpublished finding aid.

SD 2
GEOLOGICAL SURVEY
E R O S DATA CENTER
UNITED STATES DEPARTMENT OF THE INTERIOR
Sioux Falls, South Dakota 57198
(605-594-6511)

The E R O S (Earth Resources Observation Systems) Data Center stores image products acquired by the U.S. space and aircraft programs associated with earth resources. Among these are Landsat satellite images of the Soviet Union. The data base is constructed on a geographic retrieval system. To determine whether coverage is available over any area in the world, those seeking information should provide a latitude/longitude point.

SD 3
ORAL HISTORY CENTER
UNIVERSITY OF SOUTH DAKOTA
Room 16 - Dakota Hall
Vermillion, South Dakota 57069
(605-677-5208)

South Dakota Project. Oral history interviews, ongoing, ca. 1,970 interviews to date, with ca. 250 new interviews added each year. They cover such topics as homesteading, politics, history, agriculture, ethnic groups, the Rapid City flood and other natural disasters, and the role of women in the state. The following selected listing from published catalogues includes primarily those interviewed with a Russian-German or Russian-Jewish background. The cited Russian-related portions of the interviews may often be minimal. Tape recordings (and some transcripts) available for interviews.

1 Jeanette L. Agrant (MS 1108). 1976. Father came from Russia in 1880s.

2 Carl D. Anderson (MS 1057). 1974. Russian-Germans near Newell and Vale, South Dakota.

3 Anonymous (MS 1041). 1974. German-Russian family settlement in McPherson County; influx of German-Russians, exit of English-speaking people; feelings toward German-Russians by outsiders in World War I; ethnic feelings.

4 Solomon Bailin (MS 1189). 1974. Personal background, came to U.S. from Russia; pogroms in Russia; opportunities in the U.S.

5 Eva Berndt (MS 1004). 1974. Emigrated from Odessa, Russia, at age 14, in 1905; reasons for emigration; childhood recollections of Russia and Germany; ill feelings between Russians and Germans.

6 Arthur Bickel (MS 1019). 1974. Family background: parents emigrated from Russia; courtship customs; use of German language.

7 David Brosz (MS 1125). 1974. Reasons for family emigration from Russia.

8 Nellie May Christensen (MS 1112). 1974. Relations with German-Russian settlers in area of Leola; anti-German sentiment in World War I.

9 Judee Epstein (MS 1111). 1976. Family background, came to U.S. from Russia.

10 Christian J. Fischer (MS 1042). 1959. Tape in German dialect; see under David Fischer.

11 David Fischer (MS 1043). 1959. Translation of tape by Christian J. Fischer. German emigration to Russia; farming; education; conscription; Russian-German relations; religion; money; songs; service with coast artillery at Odessa, training; description of a state funeral; Lord's Prayer in Russian, song from church service; emigration to Eureka, South Dakota, in 1889; translator's comments.

12 Christian Flemmer (MS 1039). 1974. German-Russian family.

13 Ed Gall (MS 1010). 1974. Father emigrated from Russia.

14 Jacob M. Goehring (MS 1023). 1974. Family emigrated from Russia, 1890s; description of sod houses.

15 Karl Goehring, Sr. (MS 1024). 1974. Recollections of village life in Russia; Russian-German relations; brother in military service, taken out of Russia by mother; trip to U.S. in 1905; anti-German sentiment during World War I; depression; farm work and machinery in Russia; family members sent to Siberia.

16 Mr. and Mrs. Christian Grenz (MS 1017). 1974. Many German-Russians settled in area; anti-German sentiment in World War I.

17 Christian Gutjahr (MS 1116). 1974. Trip from Russia to U.S. in 1907; use of German language; explanation of clearing land of rocks.

18 Mr. and Mrs. Arthur Haas (MS 1300). 1975. Migration of family from Germany to Russia to the Dakotas.

19 Albert and Alma Hauffe (MS 1120). 1974. German-Russians are Republicans.

20 Henry G. Heib (MS 1033). 1974. German-Russian parents; sod house; education; discipline of children; feelings of other settlers toward German-Russians.

21 Edward and Rose Hoffman (MS 1113). 1974. Family emigrated from Russia; description of "Russian lignite"; arrangement of marriages.

22 Jacob Hohenecker (MS 1122). 1974. Born in Russia, served in Russian army during Russo-Japanese War, 1904-1905; reasons for emigrating; problems experienced by Germans in Russia, 1940-41.

23 Louise Huber (MS 1012). 1974. Family background, German-Russian immigrants; grew up in sod house, description and construction.

24 Fred and Rosa Jundt (MS 1129). 1974. German-Russian immigration to South Dakota; use of German language; taking rocks out of soil.

25 Nathan Kaplow (MS 1198). 1974. Came to U.S. from Russia; life in Russia.

26 Mrs. Elizabeth Kessler, Mrs. Magdalen Kline, and Miss Anna Stephan (MS 1126). 1974. Parents came to South Dakota from Russia in 1886; homesteading and farming in McPherson County.

27 Art Kluckman (MS 1014). 1974. German-Russian settlers in area (Mound City); German spoken in childhood home.

28 Paul O. Kretschmar (MS 1032). 1974. German-Russians: separate seating in church, schooling, class system, arranged marriages, changing social mores, male-female role.

29 Josef D. Lacher (MS 1095). 1974. Catholic German-Russians east of Ipswich.

30 Herbert J. Liedle (MS 1044). 1974. German-Russian emigration to South Dakota; reading, schooling, parents' attitudes toward education; music education, self-teaching, love of classical music.

31 Mildred Light (MS 1365). 1975. Childhood in Russia; Jewish life in Russia; trip to United States.

32 Leslie M. Lindley (MS 1128). 1974. German-Russian settlement in county.

33 Emil Loriks (MS 005). 1970. Relations with Karl Mundt; anti-communist crusade in 1950s.

34 Jacob Mayer (MS 915). 1973. Family came to U.S. from Russia; reasons for leaving Russia.

35 Jonathan Miller (MS 084). 1956. Trip from Russia to South Dakota, 1880s; Mennonite settlement in Hutchinson County, 1880-present; songs, etc.

36 Sara Moos (MS 774). 1973. Story of her family's move from Sicily to Odessa, Russia, thence to South Dakota via Quebec, early 1880s.

37 Fred Odenbach (MS 1035). 1974. German-Russian family background; homestead established and area described; building sod house; farming, flax and wheat.

SOUTH DAKOTA - UNIV. OF SOUTH DAKOTA SD 3

38 John Ottenbacher (MS 1036). 1974. German-Russian family background; homesteading; German-Russian neighbors, language problems; father came to U.S. to escape conscription.

39 Isadore Pitts (MS 1187). 1974. Family background, came to western South Dakota from Russia to homestead; other Jewish homesteaders.

40 Mr. and Mrs. Alvin Renz (MS 1005). 1974. Use of German language in childhood homes; German-Russians good farmers; grandparents' trip from Russia to U.S.; homesteading in the area.

41 Conrad Wenzel Renz (MS 1011). 1974. German first language, learned English; education; relations among ethnic groups in area; father's homestead; German-Russians excellent farmers; German-Russians predominantly Republican.

42 Calma Schamber Rettstatt (MS 1040). 1974. Explanation of why English settlers left Eureka and were replaced by German-Russians.

43 A. C. Rossow (MS 1013). 1974. Family background, father homesteaded in Campbell County; ethnic groups in area; German-Russians excellent farmers; present use of German language; German attitude toward draft and World War I; reading material in childhood home; description of sod house.

44 Charles Rossow (MS 1020). 1974. Father emigrated from Germany, homesteaded in area; lived in sod house, description; relations between Germans and German-Russians; anti-German sentiments in World War I.

45 Mr. and Mrs. Abe Rye (MS 300). 1971. Recollections of and description of building sod houses; "Russian" brick houses.

46 John A. Schick (MS 1037). 1974. German-Russian homesteading in McPherson and Campbell counties; German language at home; father drafted into Russian army; German-Russians liked Crimean weather better than that of South Dakota.

47 Jacob Schuetzle (MS 1009). 1974. Recollections of life in Russia; reasons for emigration to U.S.; comparison of military life in Russia and United States.

48 Christian Schumacher (MS 1119). 1974. Born in southern Russia, emigrated to U.S. at age 3; family homestead and sod house; arranged marriage; purchase of war bonds encouraged among German-Russians in World War I.

49 William Shapiro (MS 1368). 1975. Personal background, early life in Russia; trip to U.S.; Jewish community in Sioux Falls.

50 Andrew Stoebner (MS 1038). 1974. German-Russian emigration; homesteading and farming; anti-German feeling in World War I.

51 Theodore F. Straub (MS 1034). 1974. German-Russian funerals and marriage arrangements.

52 Mr. and Mrs. August Thorstenson (MS 279). 1971. Discussion of "Russian" bricks and house built thereof.

53 Abraham V. Tieszen (MS 050). 1970. Low German Mennonite settlement around Marion, South Dakota; description of farm life in German-Russian home, Russian oven.

54 Gottlieb Trautman (MS 923). 1973. Family's trip to Clay County from Russia, late 1880s; methods used in building sod houses; methods used to provide water, early 1900s; farm methods and machinery, early 1900s.

55 Irene Gerdes Treick (MS 1123). 1974. Father was a doctor; German-Russian immigration; English families in Eureka and why they left by 1910; anti- and pro-German sentiment in Eureka.

56 Dr. John Tschetter (MS 207). 1971. History of Hutterites in Austria and Russia; Hutterite settlement in South Dakota, 1870s; Mennonite revival meetings.

57 Art and Ramona Ruede Weishaar (MS 1127). 1974. Family emigrated from southern Russia; Hutterite colonies in McPherson County; anti-German sentiment, 1917-18; German-Russian families and land settlement among children.

58 August Wessel (MS 1015). 1974. Reasons for family's emigration from Russia; parents homesteaded near Mound City; German-Russians in area; reading materials in childhood home.

59 Karl Wolfer (MS 1007). 1974. Emigrated from Russia, age 15, father homesteaded in Dakota; lived in sod house, description; recollections of Russia.

Note: Recordings and some typed transcripts are available for research use under supervision in the offices of the Oral History Center, at the I. D. Weeks Library at the University of South Dakota (Vermillion), and at the Historical Resources Center library in Pierre, South Dakota. In addition, the Microfilming Corporation of America will, in future, make the transcripts available on microform. Copies of tapes may be made available to researchers with written permission from the interviewee(s) or members of the immediate family.

Finding Aids: The South Dakota Experience: An Oral History Collection of Its People (Pierre and Vermillion, 1972-), 5 vols. to date, was quoted for all the preceding information.

TENNESSEE

TN 1
ABRAHAM LINCOLN MUSEUM
LINCOLN MEMORIAL UNIVERSITY
Harrogate, Tennessee 37752
(615-869-3611 x 76)

Cassius Marcellus Clay (1810-1903). Papers, 1840-98, 650 items. Emancipator and U.S. minister plenipotentiary to Russia under Lincoln, Johnson, and Grant. Primarily diplomatic, political, and personal correspondence, much of it concerning Russian-American relations. Correspondents include William Seward, Abraham Lincoln, Henry Clay, and Count L. Tolstoi. Published list of correspondents (NUCMC 64-1383).

TN 2
TENNESSEE VALLEY AUTHORITY LIBRARY
400 Commerce Avenue, E2B7 C-K
Knoxville, Tennessee 37902
(615-632-3466)

TVA files include a typed report, 12 pp., on a delegation trip to the USSR in August 1962 led by secretary of the interior Stewart L. Udall which visited Soviet electric power stations in Irkutsk, Bratsk, Kuibyshev, Volgograd, and the Moscow area. Accompanying material includes correspondence of Mr. Fred Chambers, assistant to chief power engineer, TVA, and of Kenneth M. Klein of the Bonneville (Oregon) Power Administration; and 13 pp. of questions and answers concerning facilities visited on the trip, plus a map of the delegation's itinerary. Also, some slides taken on the trip by Mr. Charles F. Luce of the BPA.

TN 3
MEMPHIS/SHELBY COUNTY PUBLIC LIBRARY
AND INFORMATION CENTER
1850 Peabody Avenue
Memphis, Tennessee 38104
(901-528-2961)

Kenneth Douglas McKellar (1869-1957). Papers, 1911-53, 876 ft. U.S. senator, 1911-52. Correspondence and other materials pertaining in part to Russia. He favored U.S. recognition of the Soviet Union. Published register, 1974, and calendar of speeches, 1928-40 (1962). (NUCMC 64-257)

TN 4
DEPARTMENT OF SPECIAL COLLECTIONS
JOHN WILLARD BRISTER LIBRARY
MEMPHIS STATE UNIVERSITY
Memphis, Tennessee 38152
(901-454-2210)

George W. Grider (b. 1912). Papers, 1964-66, 33 cartons, 2 tape recordings, and 1 film. U.S. congressman from Tennessee. Includes 1 folder (carton 17) pertaining to the USSR.

TN 5
METHODIST PUBLISHING HOUSE LIBRARY
201 Eighth Avenue South
Nashville, Tennessee 37202
(615-749-6437)

Christian Advocate. Records and materials on Methodism, 1882-1937, ca. 3,250 items and 36 folders. Includes letters, reports, and printed matter of James Richard Joy (1863-1957), editor of the Christian Advocate, about the Methodist Church in Russia after the 1917 Revolution and Bishop Edgar Blake's trip to Russia, 1918-27, 460 items in 2 folders. Unpublished card index (NUCMC 64-966).

TN 6
DARGAN-CARVER LIBRARY
SOUTHERN BAPTIST CONVENTION
127 Ninth Avenue North
Nashville, Tennessee 37234
(615-251-2133)

1 Baptist and Evangelical Christians. Ca. 75 items, 1920-ca. 1955, pertaining to Russia/USSR, including: Historical Papers of Waldemar Gutsche (A.R. 240 and 244); Papers of I. V. Neprash (A.R. 341); Historical Papers of Mrs. I. V. Neprash (A.R. 342); typed documents of the All-Russian Union of Baptists (A.R. 242); copy of a typescript by Ilia Ivanov, "Baptists of the U.S.S.R. and Their Contacts with Christians in the U.S.S.R. and Other Countries"; and photos and news notes of the All-Union Council of Evangelical Christians-Baptists. These materials are all photo- and carbon copies; the originals and other materials related to the preceding are deposited at the Russian-Ukrainian Evangelical Baptist Union of U.S.A., Evangelical Baptist Camp, Mansfield Center, Connecticut 06250.

2 Brooks Hays (b. 1898). Papers, 1950-59, 4 ft., 4,900 items. Lawyer and U.S. representative from Arkansas. Chiefly correspondence relating to his term as president of the Southern Baptist Convention, 1957-59. Includes information about his trip to Moscow with Dr. Clarence Cranford, president of the American

Baptist Convention, in 1958. Unpublished register (NUCMC 64-1161).

TN 7
ARCHIVES AND MANUSCRIPTS SECTION
TENNESSEE STATE LIBRARY AND ARCHIVES
403 Seventh Avenue North
Nashville, Tennessee 37219
(615-741-2451)

1 Oswald Theodore Avery (1877-1955). Papers, 1867-1970, 600 items and 2 vols. Includes a letter (1948) pertaining to Harriett Ephrussi-Taylor and the USSR. Unpublished register (NUCMC 71-432).

2 Felix Grundy (1777-1840). Whitefoord P. Cole Collection, 1818-1951, ca. 800 items. Includes a letter, 1818, from George W. Campbell, U.S. minister to Russia, describing St. Petersburg. Unpublished register (NUCMC 66-946).

3 Speeches. Includes a speech by Lord Hailsham concerning the experiences of Neill S. Brown as U.S. minister to Russia, 1850-53. Also, clippings from Nashville Tennessean, 16 February 1958, relating to this speech.

TN 8
TELEVISION NEWS ARCHIVES
JOINT UNIVERSITY LIBRARIES
VANDERBILT UNIVERSITY
Nashville, Tennessee 37203
(615-322-2927)

The archive maintains a videotape collection of network newscasts over the past 10 years. Included are videotapes of U.S. television coverage of Russia from 5 August 1968 to the present. An index to the collection as a whole, Television News Index and Abstracts, is published monthly. Index entries are under the country name, persons, and places in the country.

TEXAS

TX 1
DIVISION OF SPECIAL COLLECTIONS
UNIVERSITY OF TEXAS AT ARLINGTON LIBRARY
P.O. Box 19497
Arlington, Texas 76019
(817-273-3391)

1 Carl Philip Brannin (b. 1888). Papers, 1915-69, 150 items. Humanitarian, reformer, journalist, and traveler. He was Socialist Party candidate for governor of Texas in 1936. The collection, in positive photocopies, consists of correspondence, articles, a scrapbook, biography, and typed transcript of a taped interview, 1967. Among the letters are 41 written on 2 trips to the Soviet Union, in 1925 and 1967. Brannin describes and analyzes living conditions, the political situation, and other matters. In the interview Brannin discusses, among other things, the Texas Socialist Party. Unpublished finding aids (NUCMC 73-875).

2 Dott E. Smith (1904-1971). Papers, 1944-46, 3 ft. Colonel in the United States Army. Commanded the largest prisoner of war compound in the United States from May 1944 through June 1946, during which time all German/Russian prisoners of war were repatriated through this camp. These prisoners were largely Russian soldiers captured by Germans and forced into German service. The records consist of transcripts of telephone conversations, and conferences, special orders, reports, statistics, and photographs relating to the prisoner of war camp and the repatriation of the Russian/German soldiers. Unpublished finding aids (NUCMC 77-2057).

TX 2
INSTITUTE OF MODERN RUSSIAN CULTURE
AT BLUE LAGOON
P.O. Box 7217
Austin, Texas 78712
(512-345-5123 Cables IMORCTEXAS)

The Institute of Modern Russian Culture (IMRC) was incorporated in May 1979. Its primary aim is to preserve and propagate the historical and esthetic values of Russian culture, especially of the 18th through 20th c. Archival storage and systematization play a key role in its activities.

The IMRC concerns itself with Russian culture as a whole, depending on 8 particular sections: 1) Visual Arts; 2) Cultural History; 3) Literary Science; 4) Literary Practice; 5) Architecture 6) Music; 7) Ballet; 8) Archives. The Library and the Archive of the IMRC concentrate (at this time) on art and literature of the 20th c.

Because of the recent establishment of the IMRC and because it is now moving into new premises, systematization of the archive is in a state of transition. What is outlined below, therefore, represents the general direction of the archival holdings, but is only a small part. Inasmuch as the IMRC receives constantly new materials, the focus and strength of the archive also changes. For example, within the next 12 months, the IMRC expects to receive the personal archives of 3 outstanding representatives of the artistic and literary avant-gardes from the first decades of this century, and these donations alone will shift the current focus of the archive.

1 Art

Unpublished articles on modern art by Mikhail Larionov (1881-1964), Pavel Filonov (1883-1941), Yuliia Arapova (1890-1977), David Burliuk (1882-1967), and other members of the Russian avant-garde, 2 boxes.

Manuscripts of published articles by Olga Rozanova (1886-1918), Kazimir Malevich (1878-1935), Nadezhda Udaltsova (1885-1961), Pavel Filonov, Aleksandr Rodchenko (1891-1956), and other members of the Russian avant-garde, 5 boxes.

Long unpublished article by the critic Nikolai Punin (1888-1953) on Russian Futurism; letters from Punin to Larionov; miscellanea concerning Punin the critic, 1 box, and Nikolai Akimov (1901-1968), stage designer.

Letters from contemporary Russian/Soviet artists living in the USSR and in the West; articles about them; questionnaires filled in by them for the IMRC; manuscripts of essays by them; descriptions of Soviet cultural life during the period 1950-79 by them (unpublished). Artists include Henry Ellinson (b. 1935), Francisco Infante (b. 1943), Mikhail Kulakov (b. 1933), Lev Nusberg (b. 1937), Alek Rapoport (b. 1933), Oleg Prokof'ev (b. 1928), Mikhail Shemiakin (b. 1943). The archive also includes many visual works by them in oil, gouache, watercolor, indian ink, lithograph, 10 boxes.

The archives has about 10 unpublished catalogues of informal or "semi-official" exhibitions of art in Leningrad and Moscow from the 1960s and 1970s, 1 box.

2 Literature

Large archive of contemporary Russian/Soviet poetry and prose (most unpublished at this time) by Leningrad, Moscow, and other writers covering the period 1950-79. Archive contains manuscripts of critical essays, descriptions of Soviet cultural life, reviews, commentaries on contemporary Soviet and non-Soviet artists and writers and musicians, letters both to and from such figures. Literati represented by unpublished manuscripts include Yuz Alechkovsky (b. 1928), Ilia Bokhshtein (b. 1938), Oleg Okhapkin (b. 1944), Petr Cheigin (b. 1948), Aleksandr Gladkov, Lev Khalif (b. 1930), Aleksei Khvostenko (b. 1940), Konstantin K. Kuzminsky (b. 1940), Eduard Limonov (b. 1943), Aleksandr Manusov, Aleksandr Okun', Henri Volokhonsky, and many others, 14 boxes.

The archive also has unpublished materials by and on literati of the 1920s and 1930s including Igor' Bakhterev (b. 1908), Daniil Kharms (b. 1905), and Aleksandr Vvedensky (1904-1941), 10 boxes. A correspondence to/from David Dar (b. 1910) contains information on Soviet writers, 1 box. 1 box of miscellanea on Lilia Brik and Vasilii Katanian.

3 Music

The archive is very rich in pre-revolutionary records on Amur and other labels (78s) of grand opera. Singers include Fedor Shaliapin (1878-1933), Leonid Sobinov (1872-1934), Dmitrii Smirnov (1881-1943), Vladimir Kastorsky (1871-1948), Antonina Nezhdanova (1873-1950), Ivan Ershov (1867-1943), Nadezhda Zabela-Vrubel' (1868-1913), and many others. Provincial recording labels (e.g., Kiev) are also included.

The archive also has 78 records from the 1920s and 1930s of opera and also of popular music, including jazz (e.g., Utesov) and transcriptions of American fox-trots, etc. There are some declamatory recordings by luminaries such as Leo Tolstoi and Iosif Stalin, i.e., first editions on 78s, ca. 200 records.

Among the musical holdings of the archive are items of sheet music, especially from the 1920s-1930s--jazz, dance music, popular songs --often carrying Constructivist and Art Deco covers, 1 box.

Original recordings (unpublished) include readings, vocal presentations and declamations by Aleksei Khvostenko (b. 1940), Oleg Okhapkin (b. 1944), Igor' Bakhterev (b. 1908), Viktor Krivulin (b. 1944), Viktor Shirali (b. 1945), Dmitrii Bobyshev (b. 1936), Vladislav Len (b. 1940), Vladimir Aleinikov (b. 1945). There are about 33 persons on 50 tapes.

4 Photographs

Photographs have not been catalogued yet. Concentration is on Soviet cultural life of the 1950s-1970s with photo-portraits of leading figures such as Yurii Zharkikh (b. 1938), Evgenii Mikhnov (b. 1932), Evgenii Rukhin (1943-1976), and many more. Ca. 200 photographs of exhibitions, poetry readings, apartments, happenings.

Also a large photographic record of churches, classical buildings, landscapes in various parts of Russia. Photographs date from 1950s onwards. Also ca. 100 photographs pertaining to art and design of the 1920s in Soviet Union (unpublished), especially in the field of stage and costume decoration (for productions by Tairov and Meierkhol'd). Artists represented include Aleksandra Ekster (1884-1949), Liubov' Popova (1889-1924), Isaak Rabinovich (1894-1961), Varvara Stepanova (1894-1958). Unpublished photographs of paintings and drawings and sculptures of the 1920s-1930s by Russian artists include works by Aleksandr Deineka (1899-1969), Iosif Chaikov (b. 1888), Natan Al'tman (1889-1970), Popova, Ekster, 3 boxes.

5 Video-Tapes

Basic materials and video-tapes for the movie Yuliia's Diary (Boston PTV). Interviews with poets and artists such as Konstantin K. Kuzminsky and Yakov Vinkovetsky (b. 1938). Interview with Aleksandr Ginzburg.

Restriction: No restriction of access except where stipulated by donor.

TX 3
KONSTANTIN K. KUZMINSKY--PRIVATE COLLECTION
403 East 30th Street
Austin, Texas 78705
(512-474-9839)

Collection of poetry, prose, and the visual arts of Russia, primarily Leningrad, ca. 1955-75. Includes 3 typescript anthologies of poetry and prose of Leningrad writers: R. Mandelstam, V. Ufliand, M. Yeriomin, G. Gorbovsky, V. Sosnora, E. Rein, J. Brodsky, A. Naiman, A. Kushner, E. Sneiderman, G. Alexeev, H. Volohonsky, L. Aronzon, K. Kuzminsky, O. Okhapkin, G. Trifonov, S. Stratanovsky, A. Ozhiganov, B. Kuprianov, V. Krivulin, M. Gendelev, V. Earl, V. Shirali, Y. Alexeev, B. Taigin, P. Cheigin, A. Nik, L. Bogdanov, V. Bukovsky, Y. Galperin, B. Dyshlenko, N. Koniaev, V. Lapenkov, A. Liubegin, N. Matrionin, A. Morev, V. Nemtinov, V. Nechaev, S. Nik, Y. Olshansky, B. Ostanin, O. Ofensky, N. Podolsky, F. Chirskov, and Y. Shigashov (these anthologies, ca. 1,290 pp., are entitled "The Living Mirror," parts 1 and 2, and "Leprozoriy"); additional typed and handwritten manuscripts, ca. 10,000 pp., of the preceding authors as well as some Moscow and provincial writers; microfilm of ca. 100 authors' works, mainly from Leningrad; ca. 10 original author's editions with autographs; ca. 30 tape cassettes of the poets in "The Living Mirror, II" and others; correspondence, 1975-79, with L. Nusberg, M. Chemiakine, E. Limonov, V. Gakhchanyan, H. Volohonsky, etc.; ca. 500 photos of Leningrad poets, readings, exhibitions, and other Russian scenes; ca. 500 slides of Leningrad, Moscow, and Ukrainian artists; photos and documentary material pertaining to the September 1974 exhibition "23" in Kuzminsky's Leningrad apartment; a December 1974 exhibition of 53 Leningrad artists, and the October 1974 exhibition of 13 photographers--"Under the Parachute"; and ca. 100 pieces of graphic art and oil paintings, including original works by Chemiakine, H. Elinson, A. Rapoport, V. Makarenko, E. Mikhnov-Voitenko, and others. Inquire concerning access.

TX 4
ILYA LEVIN--PRIVATE COLLECTION
DEPARTMENT OF SLAVIC LANGUAGES
THE UNIVERSITY OF TEXAS
Box 7217
Austin, Texas 78712
(512-471-3607)

Collection of literary manuscripts and other material, primarily from the 1960s-1970s, in 11 large boxes, plus 12 cassettes and 2 reel-to-reel tapes. Contents include poetry, mostly typed copies but some holograph, chiefly of Leningrad and some Moscow poets, ca. 5 boxes. Among the poets represented are Igor Burikhin, Leonid Aronson, Konstantin Kuzminsky, Juliia Voznesenskaya, and many others. There are also poetry and prose works of the oberiuty poets (e.g., Daniil Kharms and Aleksandr Vvedenskii) from the 1920s and 1930s (typed copies and some photocopies of originals). Other boxes contain prose and correspondence of Leningrad and Moscow writers of the past 2 decades, such as David Dar and Aleksandr Gladkov. Also, 1 box contains nonfiction, memoirs, diaries, essays, etc., and 2 boxes hold photographs pertaining to the Leningrad scene in the 1970s, particularly to the nonconformist cultural movement known as "the second culture." The cassettes and reel-to-reel tapes include poetry readings and memoirs of literary figures. Inquire concerning access.

TX 5
THE LYNDON BAINES JOHNSON LIBRARY
Austin, Texas 78705
(512-397-5137)

The Lyndon Baines Johnson Library was created to preserve materials pertaining to Lyndon Baines Johnson and his administration. Included in the library's holdings are the personal papers of more than 200 individuals and more than 400 oral histories. Among these holdings Russian-related materials have thus far been identified in the White House Files of the Johnson Administration, 9,500 ft., 1963-69. These files contain the following materials pertaining to Russia/USSR:

White House Central File, Countries 303 (USSR). Ca. 1 ft. of Russian-related materials. Partially closed.

White House Central File, Confidential File, CO 303. Ca. 1 in. of Russian-related materials. Partially closed.

National Security File, Country File, USSR. 5.5 ft. of Russian-related materials. Most of the material is closed and unprocessed.

National Security File, Head of State Correspondence File, USSR. .5 ft. of Russian-related materials. All unprocessed and closed.

President's Staff File, DPT, Head of State Correspondence File, USSR. 2 in. of Russian-related materials. All unprocessed and closed.

National Security File, Committee File, Special Committee on U.S. Trade Relations with East European Countries and the Soviet Union (Miller Committee). Ca. 2.5 ft. of Russian-related materials. Partially closed.

Additional Russian-related materials are scattered throughout the White House files, but the location and nature of this material can best be discussed with the researcher upon his arrival at the Library.

Finding Aids: There are finding aids to all the materials cited above.

TX 6
UNIVERSITY ARCHIVES
BARKER TEXAS HISTORY CENTER
SID RICHARDSON HALL 2.109
UNIVERSITY OF TEXAS
Austin, Texas 78712
(512-471-5961)

1 Mary Emma English. Bibliographies, 1905-1906, 1 vol. Typescript includes a bibliography on the Russo-Japanese War.

2 Joel Roberts Poinsett (1779-1851). Papers, 1807-51, 109 items. South Carolina political figure and diplomat. Includes personal letter, 20 February 1807, Poinsett wrote from St. Petersburg while traveling in Russia, typed copy. Original is in the Historical Society of Pennsylvania. (NUCMC 70-1928)

3 Note: There are a number of collections of transcripts and photocopies of documents from Spanish and Mexican archives which may contain information about Russians in California and in the Pacific Northwest.

Finding Aid: Chester Kielman, comp. and ed., A Guide to the Historical Manuscripts Collections in the University of Texas Library (1967).

TX 7
BENSON LATIN AMERICAN COLLECTION
SID RICHARDSON HALL 1.108
UNIVERSITY OF TEXAS GENERAL LIBRARIES
Austin, Texas 78712
(512-571-3818)

1 Lucas Alamán (1792-1853). Manuscript collection, 1615-1859, 364 items. Mexican historian. ALS from Carlos Beneski de Beaufort to Alamán, Paris 16 February 1832, 1 p., about Russia, Prussia, Austria, and other matters. Published finding aid.

2 Valentín Gómez Farías (1781-1858). Papers, 1770-1892, ca. 4,700 items. Mexican political leader. 4 letters, some drafts, from Valentín G. Farías to his sons Benito and Casimiro and to José Trinidad Muñoz, 1843-53, concerning European affairs and Russia, plus a draft of his letter to an unnamed friend, n.d. but ca. 1854?, on Russian designs on Constantinople and the Dardanelles; 8 ALS from Benito G. Farías to his father and 1 ALS from Benito to D. Julio, 1849-55, about the tsar's ambitions in the Danube region, the Russo-Turkish question, the Crimean War, Constantinople, the Dardanelles, the Black Sea, the bombardment of Odessa, and the Danubian principalities; an ALS from J. M. de Castillo y Lanzas to V. G. Farías, 2 January 1834, naming current foreign representatives in Washington, including Baron de Krudener of Russia; a translated excerpt (n.d.) from H. Chauchard's Géographie that concerns the Turkish empire, Russia, and the Black Sea; and a translation of a work on coffee, n.d., its origin, use, and adoption in Europe, with references to Dorpat and Russia. Published finding aid.

3 Juan E. Hernández y Dávalos (1827-1893). Manuscript collection, 1692-1865, ca. 3,000 items. Mexican government worker, amateur historian, and bibliophile. Correspondence, 17 items, 1823-31, of Tomás Murphy, José Mariano de Michelena, Manuel Eduardo de Gorostiza, Vicente Rocafuerte, Enrique P. Virmond, and Lucas Alamán on such subjects as the Holy Alliance, Russian influence on Mexican affairs, French and Prussian desires to restrain Russia, effects on Russia of British recognition of Mexican independence, Russian plans against Turkey and Greece, Russian agreement to aid Spain in exchange for the Californias, the decline of Russian influence in Spain, the danger of Russian advances in California, Russian attention turned to the East, the naval battle of Russia, France, and England against the Turks at Navarino, trade in grain with Russian ships, the port of Sitka, an otter-hunting agreement with the Russians, and Mexican-Russian relations; copy of ordinances for San Blas, Mexico 14 December 1789, with references to Russian settlements in northern California; 2 extracts from articles handcopied by Agustin de Iturbide, 1823, in part on Russian anti-constitutionalism and about Russo-Turkish relations; Spanish

translation of a speech of Lord Henry Brougham, lord chancellor of England, and other speeches, London 3 February 1824, with reference to a Russian agreement with Turkey, 6 ll.; 3 letters, March-April 1824, concerning the renting of a villa in Livorno by the Russian consul; the Junta de Guerra's plan for defending the coasts of Mexican lands, 21 August 1829, which mentions the Russian settlement at Puerto de la Bodega. Published finding aid.

4 Mariano Riva Palacio (1803-1880). Papers, 1716-1880, ca. 10,300 items. Mexican political leader. 2 telegrams from Manuel Rosas (Rozas) concerning European affairs and the end of a threat of war between England and Russia, November-December 1870; ALS of Ignacio Alvarez y Guerrero, 4 May 1871, 1 l., in part concerning illness and a prescription to take Russian baths; and court testimony in a case (Maumejean) involving a French national, Julián Larrede, married to a Russian woman, Mexico November-December 1857. Published finding aid.

5 W. B. Stephens (d. ca. 1937). Collection, 16th-19th c., ca. 20,000 pp. American geologist employed by a Mexican firm. A report, 1761, 13 pp., written by Ignacio Poyanos ("Carta escrita desde San Petersburgo por Don Ignacio Poyanos, Secretario de embajada del Duque de Almodovar") concerns Russian activities on the California coast.

Finding Aid: Carlos E. Castañeda and Jack Autrey Dabbs, Guide to the Latin American Manuscripts in the University of Texas Library (1939).

TX 8
HUMANITIES RESEARCH CENTER
THE UNIVERSITY OF TEXAS
Box 7219
Austin, Texas 78712
(512-471-1833)

1 Sir Maurice Baring (1874-1945). Papers, ca. 400 items. Diplomat, journalist, and author. He spent most of the years 1904-12 in Russia. Collection includes: diary for 1905-1906; 2 letters, typed, incomplete, from an unidentified author to Baring about conditions in Russia ca. 1918; correspondence from Aleksandr Ippolitovich Dmitriev-Mamonov, 31 items, 1909-23, M. Troubetzkoy, P. Ctentizon, Ludovic Naudeau, and Nicholas Popoff; and some translations into Russian.

2 W. S. Crosley (1871-1939). Correspondence, 1917-20, 1 folder. Military attaché at the Petrograd embassy. Letters of Walter S. Crosley and his wife Pauline to Mrs. McAlister Smith from Petrograd. Hers have been published as Intimate Letters from Petrograd (New York, 1920).

3 Edward Gordon Craig (1872-1966). Collection, ca. 1910-12, 2 vols. and correspondence. English scene designer and producer. Daybooks in part concern his production of Hamlet at the Moscow Art Theatre in 1912.

4 Stephen Graham (b. 1884). Papers, ca. 100 items. Traveler and writer. Includes typed manuscript, undated, entitled "Maxim Gorky," carbon copy, 2 pp.; notes, memoranda, and fragments, some about Russia, n.d., 38 pp.; and 68 letters to Terence Ian Fytton Armstrong (John Gawsworth), 1930-64.

5 Alexander Kerensky (1881-1970). Papers, 1917-68, 24 ft., 207 folders and 1 small box. Russian socialist and head of government in 1917. Collection includes:

Materials and documents on 1917: Minutes of the fourth duma session; manuscripts of works by Kerensky; materials on Rodzianko, Victor Chernov and the Socialist Revolutionary Party, Nicholas II, Lenin, the Russian economy before October 1917, the army - 1917, Kornilov, the German Foreign Office, etc.

Materials, mss. and documents on earliest years through 1912: Manuscripts and English translations of works by Kerensky; materials on the Russo-Japanese War, Osvobozhdenie, Witte, terror organizations, etc.

A. Kerensky's manuscripts, articles, and personal files: Kerensky's personal file "pro sebia"; file on "ideology"; manuscripts, letters to editors, clippings.

Photographs, tapes, newspaper clippings: Photographs of Kerensky family and relatives (including Kerensky's father); transcripts of tapes; 2 records of Kerensky speaking Russian; clippings, including of reviews of Russia and History's Turning Point.

Correspondence (mostly 1931-68): correspondents include M. Aldanov (Landau), Nina Berberova, Robert Browder, Doudoroffs, Fomichev, Frumkins, Helene Izwolsky, Juri Jelagin, Michael Karpovich, Dr. Kiffa and Brandt, Kirshner, Kurganoff, E. Lyons, V. Maklakov, S. Maximov, W. Nowikoff, Ter Pogossian, S. Soloveitchik, Frank and Victor Sosskices (?), B. Souvarine, Vladas Stanka (Stankevic), Sergei Vassiliev, M. Vishniak, Voronovich, Wyrouboff, V. Zenzinov.

Correspondence (miscellaneous): A miscellaneous folder with assorted correspondence of interest, e.g., Robert Bruce Lockhart, Suzanne La Follette, Herbert Hoover, George V. Ivanoff, Odoevskaya, Krukoff-Angorsky, Struve, Vol'skii, Vladimir Nabokov, Roudneff, Weinbaum, Zetlin, Benensen, Deriugina, Laurent, Strumsky, Keating, Fedotoff, Cheremetieff, Stepun, Sidney Hook, Max Eastman, David Shub; other materials.

Correspondence, university lectures; invitations to speak, write; course and outlines.

Family correspondence and mss.: Letters to and from Gleb, Oleg, and Mrs. Therese Kerensky; excerpts from memoirs by Mrs. Olga Lvovna Kerensky; poems and short stories by Mrs. Nelle (?) Kerensky; unpublished, 283 pp., ms. by Gleb Kerensky, "Only One Freedom."

Kerensky's personal business correspondence: Income taxes, bank statements, cancelled checks, appointment books, contract and correspondence with Duell, Sloane & Pearce and Meredith Press.

Political organizational work among émigrés: Correspondence and other materials regarding Narodnoe dvizhenie, Coordinating Centre of Anti-Communist Action, League for Free Russia, Union for the Liberation of the Peoples of Russia, American Committee, The Russian People's Movement. Correspondents include Kurganov, Voronovich, Abramowitch, Fedotoff, Roman Goul, Michael Karpovich, Konstantinovsky, Boris (?) Nicolaevsky, Vishniak, Zenzinov, and others.

On displaced persons and émigrés: Correspondence regarding DPs, 1947-1953, and Russian émigrés of Jewish origins.

Depositions, testimonials, and unusual documents not subject to classification: Persons mentioned in these documents include Stalin, Boris P. Doudoroff, V. Emoukhvari, Jacob F. Frumkin, Iliodor, Anna Vyroubova (?), M. Iordanskii, Dr. L. Kaschtanoff, Georg Kossatsch, E. D. Kuskova, A. R. Lednicki, Lokhvitskii, Maklakov, Martianoff, Merezhkovsky, Somerset Maugham, Anna L. Podozerov (?), M. Terestchenko, Illja Trotzky, Sergius A. Vassiliev, Bertram D. Wolfe, B. Wyrouboff, Ivan Bunin, Victor Chernov, and others.

Memorabilia: Alien registration card, Christmas cards, other items.

Émigré publications: Issues of Novaia Rossiia, Za Svobodu, Borba, Golos Naroda, Biulleten', Dni, Posledniia Novosti.

Kerensky's personal diary, handwritten, in Russian, 1941-42 and 1959-61, is also in the collection. Unpublished finding aid, compiled by Elena Ivanova, on which this description is based.

6 George Nathaniel Nash. Papers, 1917-19, 1 box. British army officer. Detailed diary ("From Palace to Prison"), 18 January 1917-10 December 1919, of his military activity in Russia during the Revolution, culminating in his being taken prisoner and then released in exchange for Raskolnikov, lord high admiral of the Russian fleet, original typescript, 128 pp. + 13 pp. of preface and table of contents, in a looseleaf notebook together with 85 pp. of newspaper clippings, translations, etc.; carbon typescript with corrections of the diary; scrapbook containing 85 items, including a rare V. I. Lenin pamphlet (Say! What Are You!), official permits, paper money, visiting cards of dignitaries, and clippings; and a photograph album containing 158 photographs illustrating events and scenes discussed in the diary. Nash traveled widely during this time; places noted in the diary include the Russian southwestern front, Petrograd, Siberia, Vladivostok, Tiflis, Georgia, Vladikavkaz, and Moscow. The diary is unpublished.

7 PEN. International writers' organization. Includes 3 typed letters from the group to Maksim Gorkii, dated 22 November 1926, 31 January 1933, carbon, and 14 March 1934, carbon.

8 Photography Collection. Includes ca. 200 slides and photographs taken by James H. Hare (1856-1946) of the Russo-Japanese War. Also, an additional 92 stereographs in a separate collection titled "Russo-Japanese War through the stereoscope" (New York: Underwood & Underwood, 1904-1905).

9 Edgar Allan Poe (1809-1849). Koester Collection, 1817-1900, ca. 350 items. Includes letter, 10 August 1904, of Maksim Gorkii concerning Poe, the American writer. Unpublished description (NUCMC 71-1908).

10 Poutiatine Family. Correspondence, 1890s-1910s, 2 cartons and 1 box. Letters of the Countesses Vera, Jackie, and E. Poutiatine, nearly all in English, apparently written after moving from Russia to Great Britain. Also, some letters of their aunts Olga and May.

11 Nikolai Punin (1888-1953). Papers, 1915-36, 1 box. Poet. Includes 10 notebook diaries, correspondence, numerous love letters from Anna Akhmatova, and newspaper clippings.

12 Elias Tobenkin (1882-1963). Papers, 1905-63, 63 boxes and 25 file envelopes, plus 1 shelf of miscellanea. Russian immigrant writer and journalist, expert in Russian/German matters. Collection is uncatalogued at present, but a rough finding list is available.

TX 9
THE SAM RAYBURN LIBRARY
P.O. Box 309
Bonham, Texas 75418
(214-584-2455)

Sam Taliaferro Rayburn (1882-1961). Papers, 1905-61, 240 ft. and 73 microfilm reels, 30 filing cabinets. U.S. congressman, 1913-61, and speaker of the House of Representatives. Files with Speaker Rayburn's correspondence with his constituents, copies of his speeches, and papers relating to legislation, politics, national and international affairs. Particularly for the years of the Eisenhower administration, 1953-61, there are materials that concern the Soviet Union. For example, there are letters from President Dwight D. Eisenhower, Secretary of State Christian A. Herter, and Soviet Prime Minister Nikita S. Khrushchev to Rayburn about the proposed summit conferences of spring 1960. A recently prepared biographical compilation of excerpts from Speaker Rayburn's letters, interviews, and speeches (Speak, Mister Speaker) may serve as a finding aid. (NUCMC 66-1344 and 74-965)

TX 10
DeGOLYER FOUNDATION LIBRARY
P.O. Box 396--S.M.U. Station
Dallas, Texas 75275
(214-692-2661)

In the interest of scholarship, the authors feel it is useful to indicate that formerly this library held an important collection of Russian-related materials that have, for the indefinite future, reverted to private hands and remain for now inaccessible. These materials included correspondence of Alexander II and his mistress Princess Catherine Yuryevskaya, ca. 140 items; the diary of Alexander III for 1894; and 15 ALS of Prince Peter Alexievich Kropotkin. The ultimate disposition of these items has not at present been determined (they may or may not remain in this country) and absolutely no queries concerning them can be answered by the library.

TX 11
ARCHIVES BRANCH
FEDERAL ARCHIVES & RECORDS CENTER, GSA
P.O. Box 6216
Fort Worth, Texas 76115
(817-334-5515)

This repository has some of the microfilms of materials in the National Archives (Washington, D.C.) that pertain to Russia/USSR. For more details, see Charles South, List of National Archives Microfilm Publications in the Regional Archives Branches (Washington: National Archives and Records Service, 1975).

TX 12
JOHN FISKE LOUD--PRIVATE COLLECTION
DEPARTMENT OF MODERN LANGUAGES & LITERATURES
TEXAS CHRISTIAN UNIVERSITY
Fort Worth, Texas 76129
(817-921-7355)

This collection of poetry by a contemporary Soviet writer, Yurij Nikolaevich Volodin, came into Professor Loud's hands in 1971. In one group of lyrics are 17 pp. of original verse, copied in Moscow under the author's supervision and typed in the U.S. A second group, which was received later, consists of 19 pp. of original verse in both longhand and typescript. Events and subjects memorialized in the poetry include the burial of Anna Akhmatova, at which the author was present; the exhumation and reconstruction of the bust of Ivan IV Groznyj by the anthropologist M. Gerasimov, whose official photographer the author was; and a catastrophic air disaster over the Caspian Sea 24 July 1970. Write or telephone to inquire about access.

TX 13
WOODSON RESEARCH CENTER
FONDREN LIBRARY
RICE UNIVERSITY
6100 South Main Street (Mail: P.O. Box 1892)
Houston, Texas 77001
(713-527-8101 x 2586)

William L. Clayton (1880-1966). Papers, 1898-1966, ca. 19 ft. Assistant secretary of state for economic affairs, 1944-46, and undersecretary of state for economic affairs, 1946-47. Played a significant role in the formulation of the Marshall Plan and participated in important post-World War II conferences. Primarily correspondence, formal statements, and reports, plus business correspondence, 1930-66, and family correspondence. Some copies of original material located elsewhere (e.g., the Truman Library in Missouri). Russian-related material is mainly in correspondence files for 1944-47. Access requires permission of the Rice University Provost. Unpublished finding aids (NUCMC 77-1746).

TX 14
SOUTHWEST COLLECTION
TEXAS TECH UNIVERSITY
Box 4090
Lubbock, Texas 79409
(806-742-3749)

Boyd Cornick Family. Papers, 1878-1964. 17,584 leaves. 773 leaves of correspondence, diaries, and photographs pertaining to the activities in Russia, 1921-22, of Boyd Cornick's son, George Cornick (1856-1933), who was a district physician of the Medical Division of the American Relief Administration in Tsaritsyn. Inventory.

UTAH

UT 1
SPECIAL COLLECTIONS AND ARCHIVES
MERRILL LIBRARY
UTAH STATE UNIVERSITY
UMC 30
Logan, Utah 84322
(801-752-4100 x 7559)

Jack London (1876-1916). Papers, 1894-1969, 10 ft. and 6 microfilm reels. Author. Original materials include notes he made as a newspaper correspondent in the Russo-Japanese War of 1904-1905. Published register (NUCMC 70-2037).

UT 2
ARCHIVES AND MANUSCRIPTS
HAROLD B. LEE LIBRARY
BRIGHAM YOUNG UNIVERSITY
Provo, Utah 84601
(801-374-1211 x 2984)

1 Georgi Phillipovitch Baidukoff (b. 1907). Typescript translation, from Pravda, by Nickoli Vishnevski, of a 1937 address Baidukoff delivered on his "Observations of USA and Capitalism" on returning from a polar flight to March Field, California, 3 pp. Also included are U.S. newspaper accounts of the flight. (MSS 773)

2 Charles George Gordon (1833-1885). Papers, 1 folder. British soldier. Includes an ALS, 11 January 1878, discussing Russia's alliance with Rumania, 3 pp., and a hand-drawn map of areas noted in the letter. (MSS 1335)

3 Franklin Stewart Harris (1884-1960). Papers, 1818-1960, 16 ft. Educator, author, and agricultural adviser. Contains diary, correspondence, notes, reports, photographs, press releases, and mementos, ca. 1 ft., covering a study mission to eastern Siberia in 1929 for the purpose of investigating the possibilities of establishing a Jewish colony in Biro-Bidjan. Dr. Harris, president of Brigham Young University, was asked to head the study commission by Benjamin Brown, a member of the National Executive Committee of the American Association for Jewish Colonization in the Soviet Union (ICQR). Collection can be used on approval of the archivist. Unpublished register (NUCMC 68-1514). (MSS 340)

UT 3
GENEALOGICAL SOCIETY OF UTAH
50 East North Temple
Salt Lake City, Utah 84150
(801-531-2896)

Founded in 1894 and funded by members of The Church of Jesus Christ of Latter-day Saints, this non-profit organization has the largest collection of original genealogical materials on microfilm in the world. Current holdings comprise 1,700 periodical subscriptions, 175,000 vols., bound, over 500 hrs. of oral family history tapes, and more than 1 million catalogued reels of microfilm. The USSR at present is one of the countries for which the society has only limited holdings, ca. 200 microfilm reels, mostly for the Ukraine with a few from Byelorussia. These are primarily microfilms of registers of Eastern Orthodox and Catholic churches filmed recently in Polish archives. There are also 1,000 reels of German parish registers for areas formerly in East Prussia, now part of Kaliningrad oblast. There is an ongoing research project for the Soviet Union.

The types of items found on microfilm for other areas of the world include census schedules; civil registrations; parish registers; land, probate, and tax records; notarial records; and family and local histories. More information about the society, its collections, and its services, is available in a brochure, in English and Russian, entitled "The Genealogical Society of Utah," issued in 1976.

VERMONT

VT 1
WILBUR COLLECTION
GUY W. BAILEY LIBRARY
UNIVERSITY OF VERMONT
Burlington, Vermont 05401
(802-656-2020 x 35/39)

1 Warren R. Austin (1877-1962). Papers, 1877-1962, 101 ft. Lawyer and senator, and the first U.S. ambassador to the United Nations, through 1952. He also helped to prepare the Lend-Lease Act, 1939-42, was in on the establishment of NATO, and became involved in other major U.S. foreign policy questions. Materials Austin collected while at the UN, 1949-52, include mostly printed matter (mimeo handouts, press releases, State Department memos and notes). Among the correspondence, speeches,

writings, notebooks, and other materials are items on his career, Bretton Woods, Dumbarton Oaks, the Korean War, and similar matters. There are memoranda of conversations with Secretary of State James F. Byrnes also. The collection is inventoried by folder but not in detail for folder contents. (NUCMC 71-1923)

2 Edward C. Carter (1878-1954). Papers, 1916-54, 14 ft. Head of the Institute of Pacific Relations, 1926-48 and president of the Russian War Relief 1941-50. Approximately 1 ft. of letters and other material relates to the Russian War Relief, 1941-45, and the American Russian Institute, 1946-51, in boxes 3 and 4. Some 6 in. each of newspaper clippings concern relief (box 14) and the USSR generally, in 1938-45 (boxes 20-21). Unpublished inventory of folders only. (NUCMC 71-517)

3 Hagar Family. Correspondence, 1840-80, 1 ft. Includes letters of Sarah G. Hagar (1827-1908), a governess, to her sister Kate. Sarah spent 12 years in Europe with the family of General Berdan, during which time she went to Russia. The relevant items were written from St. Petersburg in 1870-72. Unpublished inventory (NUCMC 74-1103).

4 John Spargo (1876-1966). Papers, 1890-1966, 21 boxes. Socialist before World War I. He wrote articles, essays, reviews, and letters about Russia, 1900-40. Among his 22 Russian correspondents were Gregor Alexinsky, Ekaterina Breshkovsky, A. Kalpaschnikoff, Marie Pechkoff, V. Tchertkoff (Chertkov), and V. Verestchagin (Vereshchagin), the artist. Concerning Russia Spargo corresponded with, among 14 persons, William H. Taft, Elihu Root, and Henry Cabot Lodge. Most of the correspondence is from 1900-20, but some Russia-related letters come from the 1930s. Unpublished list of correspondents and inventory of titles of his writings.

5 The Wilbur Collection also includes the papers of 2 long-time U.S. senators from Vermont, George D. Aiken (b. 1892) and Winston L. Prouty (1906-1971). These collections most probably contain some pertinent materials.

VT 2
ALEXANDER SOLZHENITSYN ARCHIVES
Cavendish, Vermont

The exiled Russian author has begun a major collection effort for memoir material, diaries, documents, and other items that concern primarily Russian history in the late Imperial period. No details of holdings were available at the time of this writing. The question of access to scholars has also not yet been decided. The address given above is not a mailing address.

VIRGINIA

VA 1
MANUSCRIPTS DEPARTMENT
ALDERMAN LIBRARY
UNIVERSITY OF VIRGINIA
Charlottesville, Virginia 22901
(804-924-3025)

1 Robert Loring Allen. Final draft of his book The Soviet Bloc Credit Program in Underdeveloped Countries, typescript reproduction, 104 pp., and a 1957 research report on the Soviet bloc foreign economic relations project of the University of Virginia's Woodrow Wilson Department of Foreign Affairs, typescript reproduction, 19 pp. (Accession no. 9337; hereinafter, Acc.)

2 Bagby Family. Papers, 1901-38, 5 items. Includes 1 typescript, 57 pp., carbon, of Philip Haxall Bagby (1888-1926), 1st lieutenant, 15th Infantry, on the Russo-Japanese War: I. The Combat Around the Fortifications of Liao-Yang From 1-3 September 1904, and II. The Retreat of the Russians. Apparently a summary of official German, British, and U.S. reports rather than a first hand account. (Acc. 6510-a)

3 Robert South Barrett (1851-1896). Papers, 1865-90, 12 items. Reverend. Volumes of sermons, religious essays, fiction, and a diary, ca. 1890, with his impressions of a trip to Germany, Sweden, and Russia. He visited St. Petersburg and Moscow. (NUCMC 71-571) (Acc. 6461-a)

4 Staige David Blackford (1898-1949). Papers, 1939-49, 800 items. Army officer, commander of U.S. Army Evacuation Hospital No. 8. Includes a letter to his wife, Lydia, about a Russian POW camp in Germany in World War II. Unpublished guide (NUCMC 77-1205). (Acc. 2170-a)

5 James Rives Childs (b. 1893). Papers, 1823-1977, 28 ft. Foreign service officer and author. After World War I, held diplomatic posts in several Near Eastern nations and served with the American Relief Administration in the Tartar (Tatar) Republic of the USSR. Includes a diary, n.d., containing notes on villages and towns near Kazan that Childs visited as part of his ARA work. It is filled with statistics on food supplies, illnesses, deaths, and people helped, and mentions a brief encounter with the Cheka. Also, some genealogical items about his wife's family. These materials are all in box 36. Among his correspondents were Edward Reilly Stettinius,

Jr., Henry Louis Stimson, Cordell Hull, and Yousuf Yassim. Unpublished finding aids (NUCMC 71-574). (Acc. 9256)

6 Hugh Smith Cumming (b. 1900). Papers, 1948-57, 200 items. Diplomat. Correspondence of Cumming and his wife, Winifred Burney (West) Cumming, for 1948-57, contains descriptions of diplomatic life in Moscow, Paris, Stockholm, and Indonesia. Her "round robin" letters, 1951-52, to family and friends in the U.S. describe events in their daily lives, impressions of Leningrad, diplomatic functions, etc., ca. 30 items. (Acc. 6922-s)

7 John Dos Passos (1896-1970). Papers, 1865-1970, 65 ft. Author. Correspondence, notebooks, and writings. Includes an essay on the failure of Marxism, typescript, 16 pp., post-1954; 2 pages of loose notes on Russian travel; and a 1921 travel diary, Persia, in which he jotted down a few thoughts on the breakdown of the Russian Revolution. Edmund Wilson was a correspondent. (NUCMC 71-1937) (Acc. 5950-ac)

8 Alfred Phillip Fernbach (b. 1915). 2 typescript drafts on the USSR and International Labor Organization: "Soviet Coexistence Strategy: A Case Study of International Labor Organization Experience" (1960), carbon, 81 pp.; and "Soviet Bloc Relations with the International Labor Organization," n.d., 72 pp. (Acc. 6011-a)

9 Carter Glass (1858-1946). Papers, 1821-1946, 125 ft. U.S. senator from Virginia, 1920-46, and secretary of the treasury, 1918-20. Includes some material concerning lend-lease to the Soviet Union in 1941. Unpublished finding aid, on microfilm (NUCMC 60-2401). (Acc. 2913)

10 Grinnan Family. Papers, 1740-1935, 5 ft. Includes a letter, 28 December 1897, of the Reverend Randolph Bryan Grinnan, a missionary in Japan, mentioning a fear among the missionaries that Russia would drive them out of Japan. (NUCMC 60-3332) (Acc. 2118)

11 Soto Guinard. Secretary of the European section of ARCA (Asociacion de Relaciones Culturales Americanas). Circular letter, mimeograph, 1 p., 10 July 1964, protesting the dismissal by the Uruguayan government of composer Alberto Soriano from Official Radio. Soriano was being punished for flying to Moscow for the premier performance of his Concertino by Mstislav Rostropovich. (Acc. 7672)

12 Colonel Valery Harvard. Papers, 1879-1905, 23 items on 1 microfilm reel. Assistant surgeon general of the U.S. Notebooks and correspondence, relating chiefly to service as American military agent and medical observer in Russia during the Russo-Japanese War and his subsequent imprisonment by the Japanese. Also, his 1905 report to the chief of the 2nd Division of the U.S. Army, general staff, and a lecture on his experiences in the war. (Acc. 5081-a and 5081-aa)

13 Lafcadio Hearn (1850-1904). Papers, 1849-1952, 8 ft. Author. Unpublished articles written for the Japan Chronicle, 1894-95, including ca. 12 on growing Japanese militarism, relate to events that led to the Russo-Japanese War a decade later. Unpublished listing (NUCMC 60-1713). (Acc. 6101) (Part of the C. Waller Barrett Library of American Literature)

14 Atcheson Laughlin Hench (1891-1974). Collection, ca. 1300-1974, 8,000 items. Includes a holograph, in French, from the 18th c., entitled "Prospect of a treaty of commerce between Peter I, Czar of Russia, and the King of England," 16 pp. (NUCMC 65-1028) (Acc. 6435-a)

15 George Cyril Herring (b. 1936). History professor. Typescript of his article, ca. 1967, "Lend-Lease to Russia and the Origins of the Cold War: 1944-1945" (based in part on materials in the E. R. Stettinius, Jr. papers in this library). (Acc. 8803)

16 Thomas Jefferson (1743-1826). Papers, 1732-1828, 3,300 items. U.S. president, 1801-11. Includes letter, 18 January 1784, to Edmund Pendleton discussing Russo-Turkish relations, photostat; and letter, 20 June 1813, from John Barnes, briefly noting Napoleon's defeat in Russia, holograph (Thurlow-Berkeley nos. 59 and 1234, respectively). Note: These papers also contain photocopies of the Jefferson-Thaddeus Kosciusko correspondence in the National Library, Cracow, Poland. Published guide, 2 parts (1973).

17 Louis Arthur Johnson (1891-1966). Papers, ca. 1917-64, 56 ft. Assistant secretary of war, 1937-40, and secretary of defense, 1949-50. Correspondence, memoranda, speeches, photographs, maps and charts, scrapbooks, phonograph records, and movies of speeches. Includes his annual reports for 1937-39, summaries of Defense staff meetings in 1950, and data on the decision to intervene in Korea. Among his correspondents were Presidents D. D. Eisenhower, Herbert Hoover, and Harry Truman, and such other figures as E. R. Stettinius, Jr., Cordell Hull, and Chester Nimitz. Unpublished guide (also on microfilm for interlibrary loan). (NUCMC 77-1227) (Acc. 8476)

18 Allen Kent and Robert C. Booth. "Trends in information services--U.S. vs. U.S.S.R. developments in scientific and engineering fields, 1957," typescript, 20 pp., a paper presented before the Symposium on Systems for Information Retrieval, 16 April 1957, in Cleveland, Ohio. (Acc. 6894)

VIRGINIA - UNIVERSITY OF VIRGINIA VA 1

19 Literary Autograph Collection. Ca. 50 items, 1852-1937. Includes 3 letters of Samuel Solomonovitch Koteliansky, July-August 1926. (NUCMC 61-2816) (Acc. 38-601)

20 Carl von Malachowski (1783-1844). Adjutant to Frederick William III of Prussia. Holograph memoirs, dictated to his son, entitled "Aus dem Leben des General-Lieutenants von Malachowski," 397 pp., giving an account of his life as adjutant, the Congress of Vienna, travel with the king, court life, the Russian royal family and court, and Russian politics. Published in German (Leipzig, 1897). (Acc. 8648)

21 Jane Walker (Stevenson) McIlvaine McClary (b. 1919). Papers, 1946-67, 6 ft. Author. Letters and clippings concern her 1953 trip to the Soviet Union, ca. 40 items. (NUCMC 71-1954) (Acc. 9559 and 9559-a)

22 James Clark McReynolds (1862-1946). Papers, 1819-1952, 2 ft. U.S. attorney general and Supreme Court justice. Includes a letter, 10 September 1931, from Edwin S. George concerning an article about Russia he would write, having spent 3 months there. (NUCMC 64-798) (Acc. 3577)

23 Mildred Nelson Page (1865-1959). Papers, 1879-1950, 210 items. Protestant missionary in Japan. She received ca. 18 letters from diplomat Charles R. Crane (1858-1939), a member of Wilson's special commission to Russia in 1917 (and present at the Paris peace talks). He describes both Russia and Paris events, and Russians in Egypt and Jerusalem, 1910. A 1914 letter from Count J. Rostovtsof describes the death of the father of Andrew Semenov. In 1917 Crane refers to the same count and speaks of a conference attended by Dr. John R. Mott, Samuel Harper, and Prof. Thomas (?) Masaryk, at which Mott addressed 2 Russian church conventions. (Jan Masaryk was Crane's son-in-law.) A later letter describes Russian refugees in Jerusalem, ca. 1923. Another correspondent was Amélie Rives Chanler Troubetzkoy. (NUCMC 71-1961) (Acc. 6287-b)

24 William Webb Pusey (b. 1910). College professor. Typescript of his article (1969) entitled "An innocent in Russia, 1929," 10 pp., describing a trip to Russia when he was 18 years old. (Acc. 9154)

25 John Randolph of Roanoke (1773-1833). Papers, 1788-1833, 719 items. U.S. representative, senator, and statesman. Includes a letter, 4 January 1831, from him to Elizabeth T. C. Bryan and others which briefly mentions that he hopes to return to Russia in the spring and that he tried to do a good job there but events beyond human control may cause his failure. (Acc. 3400)

26 Russian-American Company, New Archangel, Alaska. Records, 1802-35, 9 microfilm reels (positive). Correspondence between the company's board of directors in St. Petersburg and the governors general in Alaska. Originals are in the National Archives. (Acc. 8135-c)

27 Florence (Dickinson) Stearns (b. 1883). Papers, 1920-55, 3 ft. Poet and author. Typescript draft of her play Catherine of Russia, 60 pp. (NUCMC 67-2190) (Acc. 7494)

28 Edward Reilly Stettinius, Sr. (1865-1925). Papers, 1902-25, 40 ft. Financier and government official. Papers are divided into 4 series. In the fourth are materials from his service in World War I as Allied purchasing agent for J. P. Morgan, munitions purchaser, and then assistant secretary of war, and finally adviser to the committee overseeing liquidation of the financial affairs of the American Expeditionary Forces. Among his correspondents were Newton Diehl Baker, Winston Leonard Spencer Churchill, Herbert Hoover, and Prince Casimir Lubomirski. William D. Barnard has prepared "Guidecards" for the papers, a finding aid, available on microfilm for interlibrary loan. (NUCMC 71-589) (Acc. 2723-g)

29 Edward Reilly Stettinius, Jr. (1900-1949). Papers, 1918-49, 398 ft. Businessman and government official (like his father). In World War II he was U.S. secretary of state. The papers, divided into 6 series, contain information on the Lend-lease Administration (series III)--about which he wrote a book called Weapon for Victory; his work as undersecretary and then secretary of state, the London mission, and conferences at Dumbarton Oaks, the Crimea, Mexico City, and San Francisco (series IV--State Department files); the London Preparatory Commission, first General Assembly of the United Nations (series V); and other phases of his career. Correspondents included Andrei Andreevich Gromyko, Vyacheslav Mikhaylovich Molotov, Winston Churchill, John Foster Dulles, W. Averell Harriman, Franklin D. Roosevelt, and Harry S. Truman. Restricted; an access committee must approve research projects well in advance. Set of unpublished "Guidecards" to the papers available on microfilm for interlibrary loan. (NUCMC 71-590) (Acc. 2723)

30 Alfred Julius Swan (1890-1970). Papers, 1915-70, 1,500 items. Composer, scholar, teacher, and historian of Russian music. Born in St. Petersburg. Primarily materials for his Life of Nicholas Medtner (1967), but also letters of Alexander Cherepnin, M. I. Glinka, Sergei Rachmaninoff, and other modern composers. Unpublished guide. (Acc. 10093)

31 Amélie (Rives) Chanler Troubetzkoy (1863-1945). Papers, 1887-1945, 4 ft. Wife of the Russian

painter Prince Pierre Troubetzkoy (married 1896; her second husband), and American novelist. Some items relate to Prince Troubetzkoy, including a printed Troubetzkoy family genealogy: Les Princes Troubetzkoi (Paris, 1887), 327 pp. (NUCMC 62-3926). (Acc. 2495)

32 Edwin M. Watson (1883-1945). Papers, 1900-67, 21 ft. U.S. Army general and assistant to President Franklin D. Roosevelt. Includes material on American aid to the USSR, 1940-42, and typed report, 39 pp., on "The Influence of Brigadier General Philip R. Faymonville on Soviet-American Military Relations" (ca. 1943). Unpublished finding aid (NUCMC 74-1140). (Acc. 9786)

33 Hallie Erminie (Rives) Wheeler (1876-1956). Papers, 1908-52, 80 items. Includes 35 pre-World War I Russian postcards, about half of which show scenes of St. Petersburg, and half have views of villages and peasants. Mrs. Wheeler's comments are on the versos. (Acc. 8090)

34 Quincy Wright (1890-1970). Papers, 1910-65, ca. 5,000 items. Educator and statesman. Includes 12 items of correspondence with Percy Elwood Corbett and Frederick Sherwood Dunn, 1944-45, which mention Moscow, Teheran, and certain international organizations. Wright was deeply interested in U.S. foreign policy and international questions of human rights. There may be additional Russian-related items in his papers. Correspondents include E. R. Stettinius, Jr., and George W. Ball. (Acc. 6112 and additions; the 12 letters are 6112-d)

Finding Aids: Annual Report of the Archivist (1930-40); Annual Report on Historical Collections (1941-50); and "Monthly News Notes" (1951-present).

VA 2
ARCHIVES
GEORGE C. MARSHALL RESEARCH LIBRARY
Drawer 920
Lexington, Virginia 24450
(703-463-7103)

1 Frank B. Hayne (b. 1891). Papers, 1925-41, 38 items. U.S. Army colonel, 1942-47. Correspondence includes a letter, 3 June 1937, advising Hayne on the attitude he should maintain while serving at a new post in the USSR. Unpublished inventory.

2 George C. Marshall (1880-1959). Papers, 1932-59, ca. 200 ft. Army chief of staff, 1939-45, special ambassador to China, 1946, secretary of state, 1947-49, and secretary of defense 1950-51. Collection consists of personal papers for these years retained by General Marshall. Soviet-related papers have been identified in the following files: S. D. Embick; Secretary of War; William D. Leahy; Harry Hopkins; Dwight D. Eisenhower; Averell Harriman; Bernard Baruch; Charles G. Dawes; Frank B. Hayne; Leonard Gerow; Combined and Joint Chiefs of Staff; Robert Lovett; James Forrestal; John J. McCloy; Russia; Great Britain; Franklin D. Roosevelt; Harry S. Truman; and Directives. Card index for selected correspondence. Published guide in preparation.

In addition to the personal papers of General Marshall, selected copies (microfilm and paper) of Marshall-related records in the National Archives have been made and deposited in the Marshall Library. Approximately 1 million pieces, 1901-51, are accessible through numerous subject headings in a comprehensive card index. Soviet-related records for the World War II years include the following: U.S. Army chief of staff; secretary of war; secretary of war safe file-Russia; War Plans Division; Operations Division; Adjutant General's office; SHAEF; minutes of Allied conferences; minutes of Joint Chiefs of Staff and Combined Chiefs of Staff; and White House records of Fleet Admiral William D. Leahy, 1942-49. Records documenting General Marshall's mission to China in 1946 are also available. State Department records, 1947-49, related to Russia include: records of Charles E. Bohlen; fortnightly survey of American opinion on international affairs; Policy Planning staff; and the secretary's weekly summary. Marshall-related records from the Department of Defense, 1950-51, have also been identified and copied as well as other important records such as papers of the National Security Council, 1947-53.

3 Frank McCarthy (b. 1912). Papers, 1941-49, 14 ft. Secretary to the War Department general staff and military secretary to George C. Marshall, chief of staff. He accompanied Marshall to the Anglo-American-Russian conferences at Teheran, November 1943, Yalta, February 1945, and Potsdam, July 1945. Personal correspondence, reports, photographs, maps, and office files. Ca. 40 folders 1941-45 hold Russian-related material, including those labeled "Cairo-Teheran," "Yalta-Crimea," "Potsdam," and "Marshal Iosif Stalin." Also reference to Viacheslav Molotov. Unpublished finding aid.

VA 3
THE WAR MEMORIAL MUSEUM OF VIRGINIA
9285 Warwick Boulevard
Huntington Park
Newport News, Virginia 23607
(804-247-8523)

Ca. 80 photographs, 1913-17, of Russian Imperial Navy ships; photographs, 1917, of the Russian army; photographs, 1940, of Russian troops; current U.S. Army films on the Russian military; and a documentary film, "The AEF in Siberia," made from films produced in 1919 of U.S. troops in Vladivostok. The museum also has uniforms, weapons, insignia, newspapers, artifacts, and published materials pertaining to Russian military history.

VA 4
MacARTHUR MEMORIAL
MacArthur Square
Norfolk, Virginia 23510
(804-441-2256)

1 Douglas MacArthur (1880-1964). Archives, ca. 1930s-1963, 690 ft. American general. Soviet-related materials are in the following record groups: RG 5, records of general headquarters, Supreme Commander for the Allied Powers (SCAP), 1945-51, 124 boxes; RG 6, records of general headquarters, Far East Command (FECOM), 1947-51, 95 boxes; RG 9, collections of messages (radiograms), 1945-51, 169 boxes; RG 10, General of the Army Douglas MacArthur's private correspondence, 1932-64, 55 boxes of different size. Some of the material documents his dealings with the Soviet government and with Major General Kuzma Derevyanko when he (MacArthur) was occupation commander of Japan. The Soviet Union is also mentioned in the daily intelligence summaries submitted to the general by his intelligence staff during World War II and the Korean War. Some of the material may be security classified. Descriptive inventories for record groups. (NUCMC 77-382-396, *passim*)

2 Charles A. Willoughby (1892-1972). Papers, 1946-73, 15 ft. U.S. Army major general Record group 23 includes the drafts and final report entitled "Leftist Infiltration into SCAP," written by Willoughby.

VA 5
VIRGINIA HISTORICAL SOCIETY
P.O. Box 7311
Boulevard and Kensington Avenue
Richmond, Virginia 23221
(804-358-4901)

1 Charles Baird. Papers, 1914-38, 34 items. Includes correspondence of Charles Baird and Mrs. Lucy V. Baird (not husband and wife) concerning bonds of the Imperial Russian government, 1914-30.

2 Bouldin Family. Papers, 1737-1960, 3,757 items. Includes a letter, 21 March 1831, of John Randolph to Mark Alexander, signed holograph, in which Randolph notes his inability to return to Russia as minister.

3 David Kirkpatrick Este Bruce (b. 1898). Papers, 1918-71, 298 items. Diplomat. Includes typed copies of letters, 1921-22, he wrote while traveling in Russia, Finland, Hungary, and other European nations; addressed to Louise Este (Fisher) Bruce and William Cabell Bruce. Much of the collection is currently uncatalogued. Restricted at present because of the current nature of the materials. (NUCMC 77-621)

4 Vasyl Dubrowsky (1897-1966). Professor, émigré in U.S. Typed abstract, in English, of his article "The Centenary of a Russian Legend in America," *Shevchenko's Almanac* (Jersey City, Svoboda, 1964) about the 1863 visit of the Russian fleet to New York City and San Francisco.

5 Holladay Family. Papers, 1728-1931, 2,318 items. Includes some drawings, 1788, relating to the Battle of Oczakov, in which Lewis Littlepage served in the Russian navy against Turkey. Also, undated map of Warsaw, Poland, engraved by Pierre François Tardieu. (NUCMC 72-1794)

6 William Lee (1739-1795). Papers, 1683-1867, 684 items. Diplomat. Letterbook for December 1780-June 1783, 276 pp., contains reference(s) to Russia. Part of this bound volume is holograph. Partial index. (MSS 1L51f)

7 Laura Henrietta (Wirt) Randall (1803-1834). Papers, 1819-57, 74 items in bound vol. Daughter of the author and lawyer William Wirt. Includes a letter, 1823, to her from Maria H. Middleton, daughter of minister to Russia Henry Middleton, in St. Petersburg.

8 Archibald Stuart (1757-1832). Papers, 1786-1922, 51 items. Includes an ALS, 13 February 1799, to him from Thomas Jefferson on negotiations for commercial treaties with Russia, conducted by Rufus King, and with Turkey (by William Smith), 4 pp. (MSS 1St9102f)

9 Christopher Tompkins (1778-1838). Account book, 1801-1805, 1 vol. Ship captain. Record of his voyages, including sailings of the *Lucy Ann* to, among other ports, Kronstadt and St. Petersburg. (MSS 1T5996b) (Tompkins Family papers)

10 Frederick Williams (1800-1877). Papers, 1800-80, 27 items. Seaman. Includes an autobiography for 1800-34, written in 1855, concerning his voyages on various ships, one or

more of which went to Russia. Also, his diary for April 1818-June 1839.

VA 6
ARCHIVES AND RECORDS DIVISION
VIRGINIA STATE LIBRARY
Richmond, Virginia 23219
(804-786-2306)

1 Campbell-Brown Collection. Papers, 1793-1886, 148 items. (G. W. Campbell-Percy Brown, the donor) Includes negative photostatic copies of 115 letters to and from George Washington Campbell, some of which relate to his service as minister to Russia. Correspondents include J. J. Astor, 1819, and A. Gallatin. (Acc. 20799)

2 Virginia Colonial Records Project Microfilm. Project continues in progress. Includes scattered petitions, memorials, etc., ca. 1681-1782, generally relating to the Muscovy tobacco trade. Originals are in various British and French manuscript repositories. The entire collection is available on microfilm at the Virginia State Library, the University of Virginia (Alderman Library) in Charlottesville, the Virginia Historical Society in Richmond, and the Research Department of Colonial Williamsburg in Williamsburg. In addition, the Virginia State Library and the University of Virginia make the microfilm available through interlibrary loan. Unpublished finding aids.

WASHINGTON

WA 1
SKAGIT COUNTY HISTORICAL MUSEUM
Fourth Street
La Conner, Washington 98257
(206-466-3365)

Oral History Transcripts. Includes interviews with: Freda Lipke (No. PBH 18), in which she recalls a conversation with a Russian Orthodox priest in Alaska about conditions in Russia, 1918-30; and John Uitto (No. PBH 103), in which he mentions a Russian order for equipment in 1918.

WA 2
MANUSCRIPTS, ARCHIVES, AND SPECIAL COLLECTIONS
WASHINGTON STATE UNIVERSITY LIBRARIES
Pullman, Washington 99164
(509-335-6691)

1 Annie Heloise Abel-Henderson (1873-1947). Collection, 1860-1939, 8 ft. Historian. She collected notes, clippings, manuscript material, and printed matter pertaining to Russian history (ca. 550 items). One subject covered is the Revolution of 1917. Unpublished container list.

2 Catherine May Bedell (b. 1914). Congressional papers, 1959-70, ca. 280 ft. U.S. congresswoman. Contains several folders on wheat sales to Russia. Published register, 1972. (NUCMC 71-1976)

3 Walter Franklin Horan (1898-1967). Papers, 1943-65, 253 ft. U.S. representative. Includes materials on wheat sold to the USSR in 1962-64 (container 497), and on un-American activities in 1947-64 (containers 479-81). Published register, 1964 (NUCMC 66-1507).

4 Alfons Horten (fl. early 20th c.). Papers, 1905-26, ca. 2,500 items. Mining assessor for the German firm of August Thyssen. Business correspondence, including letter press file copies, typescript transcriptions, and originals. In letters between Horten and various members of the Thyssen family (August, Fritz, and Joseph), and others, there is discussion of technical aspects of mining and mining concessions in Russia, Turkey, and elsewhere. Also, information on the relationship between international politics and the Thyssen firm's mining activities. Unpublished container list (NUCMC 71-1983).

5 Edward Carl Johnson (1880-1962). Papers, 1896-1959, 4 ft. Dean of the College of Agriculture at Washington State University. During several months in 1937 he traveled in Western Europe and the Soviet Union. His diary for the year contains observations on agriculture as well as travel notes. Unpublished finding aid.

6 Paul P. Kies (1891-1971). Collection of autographs, 1621-1970, 1,500 items. Includes signed letter, 11 November 1850, of Nicholas I.

7 Napoleon I (1769-1821). French emperor. Signed letter, 18 July 1812, Ghloubokoe [Glubokoe], Russia to Eugene de Beauharnais concerning troop movements.

8 Carl Parcher Russell (1894-1967). Papers, 1920-67, 45 ft., 24,916 items. Historian, ecologist, and National Park Service administrator. Expert on the American fur trade, frontier, and mountain men. Includes works on Russians in North America (folder 56) and

notebooks with data on the Russian American Fur Company (folder 282), Russian fur trade (folder 281), and on Russian guns in Alaska (folder 249). Reference to Gregory Shelekof, Georg Heinrich von Langsdorff, and Russian axes and cannon (several for the last 2). Published register, 1970 (NUCMC 69-569).

9 Dame Edith Sitwell (1887-1964). Papers, 1917-67, ca. 2 ft., 335 items. English poet and literary critic. Includes correspondence of the artist Pavel Tchelitchew. Unpublished finding aid (NUCMC 76-840).

10 Spanish, English and Russian discoveries on the Pacific Northwest Coast. Microfilmed pages from the Survey of De Fuca Straits, 1790, 1 reel, negative. Original in the British Museum (Add. Mss. 13,974).

11 Anna Biedel Weitz (b. 1907). Papers, 1917-71, ca. 150 items. Local historian. Collection of materials about the settlement of Russian-Germans in the Pacific Northwest. Her hometown of Endicott, Washington, was a center of such emigrant settlements. Includes letters and miscellaneous historical documents.

Finding Aids: Selected Manuscript Resources in the Washington State University Library (Pullman, 1974). Microfilm material is listed in R. W. Hale, Guide to Photocopied Historical Materials in the United States and Canada (Ithaca, 1961).

WA 3
COAST GUARD MUSEUM/NORTHWEST
1519 Alaskan Way South
Seattle, Washington 98134
(206-442-5019)

The Museum has 10-15 folders of photographs of Russian Orthodox churches and the priests who served natives and Russian trade settlements in Alaska. The photos, which date back to over 100 years, were taken primarily in the 1930s and collected by U.S. Coast Guard crewmen on Alaska/Bering Sea Patrol. Patrons are not permitted to make copies or borrow originals from the collection.

WA 4
ARCHIVES BRANCH
FEDERAL ARCHIVES & RECORDS CENTER, GSA
6125 San Point Bay, NE
Seattle, Washington 98115
(206-442-4502)

This repository has some of the microfilms of materials in the National Archives (Washington, D.C.) that pertain to Russia/USSR. For more details, see Charles South, List of National Archives Microfilm Publications in the Regional Archives Branches (Washington: National Archives and Records Service, 1975). In addition, there are microfilms of Russian-related materials in the National Archives that are not mentioned in South's guide: RG 22, Fish and Wildlife Service, RG 36, United States Customs Service, District of Alaska, and RG 348, Alaskan Territorial Government. Finding aids are available to these 3 microfilms.

WA 5
SERGEI EUGENE HITOON--PRIVATE COLLECTION
2367 Hughes Avenue SW
Seattle, Washington 98116
(202-932-3900)

Mr. Hittoon holds the manuscript of his memoir (autobiographical in form) entitled Dvoryanskie Porosyata, which has been published in Russian (Sacramento, California, 1975), 315 pp. Also, an English translation of the work, at present unpublished. The book concerns historical events before and after the 1917 revolutions. The author, a student at Petrograd University, was later on guard duty in the Taurida Palace during the first 3 days of the February Revolution. Briefly imprisoned by the Bolsheviks, he was amnestied and moved to Siberia to join the forces of Admiral A. V. Kolchak. Subjects covered include the education of the Russian nobility, the end of the monarchy, Kolchak's southern army, Baron R. Ungern von Sternberg's Cossack forces, and the retreat of anti-Bolshevik forces into China. Also, the Lena Goldfields Massacre of 1912, in the legal battles surrounding which his father, a judge, played an important role. Hitoon had 2 interviews with Alexander Kerensky in 1966, described in this collection, and there are original photographs illustrating the book. Access is by advance written permission; recommendations requested.

WA 6
ARCHIVES AND MANUSCRIPTS DIVISION
UNIVERSITY OF WASHINGTON LIBRARY
Seattle, Washington 98195
(206-543-1879)

1 George Russell Adams (b. 1845). 1 microfilm reel. Copy of Adams's "The First American Exploring Expedition to Russian America 1865-1867," which concerns the Russian-American Telegraph Expedition. (In Charles S. Hubbell Collection)

2 Henry E. B. Ault (d. 1961). Papers, 1918-53, 6 ft. Journalist, politician, and labor leader. Material, primarily correspondence, concerns the Washington (state) Branch of

Russian Relief. Among his correspondents were William Z. Foster and Anna Louise Strong. 2 unpublished finding aids. (NUCMC 65-1031)

3 Thomas Burke (1849-1925). Papers, 1875-1925, 26 ft. Lawyer and judge. Letters, documents, speeches, writings, and financial miscellany. He corresponded with, among others, the Russian Club of Seattle, 1916-17, 1920, 5 letters; the Russian Student Fund, Inc., 1923-25, 38 letters with 20 non-letter enclosures; and the Polish Victims Relief Fund, 1916, 5 letters. The last 15 years of his life the judge was a trustee of the Carnegie Endowment for International Peace. The reference division has issued The Thomas Burke Papers, 1875-1925 (1960). (NUCMC 62-1028)

4 Stephen F. Chadwick (b. 1894). Papers, 1919-45, 15 ft. Seattle lawyer, politician, and civic leader. Information on Russian war relief, 1942-44. (NUCMC 64-1260)

5 Frank A. Golder (1877-1929). 4 microfilm reels. American historian of Russia. Collection of photostat copies of documents in Russian archives. Covers Russian international relations, travel, exploration, Alaska, Russian politics and government, commerce, and the Imperial Archives. Original photostats are in the Library of Congress.

6 Edwin William and Mary Hopkinson. Papers, 1923-64, 2 ft. and 1 microfilm reel. Mr. Hopkinson was a farmer, chicken rancher, and chairman of the Communist Party of Pierce County, Washington. Mrs. Hopkinson was an osteopathic physician, politically active in leftist movements. Notebooks, letters, documents, and articles concern the Autonomous Industrial Colony in Kuznetsk Basin, Kemerovo, Siberia, where Hopkinson was the colony's timber expert, in 1923 (microfilm). Among those associated with this Siberian colony were Tom Barker, Simon Hahn, William D. Haywood, Dr. William H. Mahler, Alfred Pearson, Jr., S. J. Rutgers, Samuel Shipman, and William A. Warren. There are also minutes and other materials on the Pierce County Communist Party in the 1940s. Unpublished inventory (NUCMC 66-976).

7 Charles S. Hubbell (d. 1954?). Collection, ca. 1866-1948, 1.5 ft. Alaskan materials, including Hubbell's private correspondence, 2 folders, 1935-50; diaries of Lieutenant George R. Adams, 1866-67, Captain F. M. Smith, 1865-67, and others in the Western Union Telegraph Company expedition to Alaska, in typescript by Hubbell with his introductory note; list of Alaska shipwrecks, 1786; 1 folder of photostats of Alaska cession documents; a Clarence L. Andrews translation of the life of Aleksandr Andreevich Baranov, typescript; and a copy, 115 pp., typed, of the diary of Stepan M. Ushin, a Sitka resident. Original of the Ushin diary is held by the Library of Congress. Unpublished inventory record and guide (NUCMC 66-1037).

8 Jacob Ilitowitz (b. 1878). 1 reel of tape. Lithuanian immigrant, tailor, laborer, and furniture refinisher. 45-minute interview, conducted by Karyl Winn in 1971, touches on the Russian population and an agricultural cooperative society in Washington (tape 51).

9 Nazary V. Kochergin (b. 1887). Papers, 1905-73, 3.5 ft. Former governor of Kamchatka. Correspondence, legal documents, notes, photographs, and clippings. Information on Russians in Seattle and American fisheries (salmon) in Alaska, 1924-52. Unpublished inventory.

10 Mark M. Litchman (1887-1960). Papers, 1914-60, 3 ft. Lawyer and politician. Letters, court papers, speeches, and writings, some concerning the Russian-American Industrial Corporation. Unpublished inventory record (NUCMC 65-1042).

11 Carl Mattson. Papers, 1919-52, 3 ft. Labor leader. Letters, clippings, and printed matter. Information about Russian industry, politics, and government. He was involved with the Industrial Workers of the World and the International Association of Machinists.

12 Bert G. Mitchell. Papers, 1927-32, ca. 2 in. YMCA leader in Russia in the 1920s. Correspondence, documents, in Russian, and miscellaneous materials.

13 John Rosene (1861-1918). Papers, 1901-10, 2 ft., ca. 1,760 items. Business and railroad executive. Involved in operations of the Northwestern Commercial Company (a successor to the Alaskan Commercial Company, formed in 1867 to replace the Russian-American Company). Materials relating to the North Eastern Siberian Company include general and interoffice correspondence, financial statements, and inventories, 1902-10; ca. 100 items. Correspondents include N. Matunin, Count Constantine Podhorski, and Count V. M. Wonlarlarsky. There is a scrapbook of articles, pamphlets, and promotional material for the Northern Exploration and Development Company, another Rosene venture, 1910. A book of survey maps and other items pertains to the Alaska Midland Railroad Company, a subsidiary of Northern Exploration. Rosene also had dealings with the Alaska Mercantile Company, the East Siberian Syndicate Ltd. (London), and the Transalaska-Siberian Railway Company. Unpublished inventory record and guide (NUCMC 66-982).

14 Anna Louise Strong (1885-1970). Papers, 1885-1967, ca. 20 ft. Journalist and political activist, author of books about China and the USSR. In 1921 she went to Moscow with an American Friends relief committee. There she began and edited the English-language daily Moscow News. She married the Russian journalist Joel Shubin and lived with him in Siberia

until ca. 1941. She was often back in the U.S., promoting leftist causes like the Loyalists in the Spanish Civil War. In 1949 L. V. Beria had her expelled from the USSR as a spy. For a time she lived in Los Angeles but eventually went to China, where she died. Correspondence, 1900-30 and 1942-58; notebooks on the Soviet Union, China, and the Spanish Civil War; diary for 1896-99; and typescripts of her published and unpublished writings. Among the subjects covered: the John Reed Colony for children in Russia, 1925, and the Moscow spy charges, 1949-50. Correspondents include her husband Shubin, Raymond Robins, and Eleanor Roosevelt. The collection is restricted; information available at the repository. 2 unpublished finding aids. (NUCMC 76-798)

15 Hulet M. Wells (b. 1878). 2 items. Labor leader and chairman of the Socialist Party of Washington. Traveled to the Soviet Union in 1921. Typed account of the trip, 70 pp., and his autobiography, typescript, 311 pp.

Finding Aid: A published guide to the collections is in preparation.

WA 7
PACIFIC NORTHWEST COLLECTION
SUZZALLO LIBRARY
UNIVERSITY OF WASHINGTON
Seattle, Washington 98195
(206-543-1929)

1 Papers relating to the Russians in Alaska. Petrograd, 1732-96, 21 vols. Photostat copies of documents selected from the Russian Archives by Frank Alfred Golder, in Russian. Contents: vols. 1-2. Vitus Jonassen Bering (1681-1741), Danish explorer in Russian employ, "Discovery of the Aleutian Islands"; vol. 3. Bering, Papers; vols. 4-6. Alexei Ilich Chirikov (d. 1748), Journal, 1733-42, Log of the St. Paul, and report to the Admiralty College on the voyage of the St. Paul, ca. 1741 and later; vol. 7. Miscellany; vol. 8. Nikolai Golovin, "Propositions of Count Nikolai Golovin to send ships to Kamchatka"; vol. 9. Imperial Archives materials; vol. 10. Sofron Khitrov, Log of the St. Peter, 1 September 1740-27 January 1743 (nautical journal of Tchitrev); vol. 11. G. F. Muller, report on the discovery of new islands near America by Captain Shmaleev; vol. 12. Papers on the missions in Alaska to 1799; vol. 13-15. Grigorii Shelikov (Shelikhov) (1747-1795), founder of first permanent Russian settlement in Alaska (1784, on Kodiak Island), Papers concerning Church affairs, the activities of Shelikov and A. A. Baranov in Alaska, and the early history of Russian Alaska, 1783-96; vol. 16. "Opinion of Vice Admiral Sanders" (1732-43); vol. 17-19. G. W. Steller (1709-1746), German naturalist on second Bering expedition, Journal, "Organization of first Kamchatka expedition, and Reise"; vol. 20. Sven Waxel (1701-1762), Danish captain in Russian navy and member of second Bering expedition, report, 15 November 1742, to the Admiralty College on the voyage of the St. Peter; and vol. 21. Kharlam Yushin, Log of the St. Peter, 1741, English translation in F. Golder's Bering's Voyages, 2 vols., 1922.

2 Serge N. Smirnoff. Chamberlain to the governor of Pavlovsk and secretary to Duke John of Russia. Diary concerning the Russian Revolution, murder of the Romanov family, and his escape from a Bolshevik prison to Stockholm in 1919. The journal proper ("Narrative"), 31 pp., is preceded by a biographical sketch, 23 pp., and followed by a "Letter to his wife, March 17, 1919," 196 pp., and "Freedom," 13 pp.

Finding Aid: The Dictionary Catalog of the Pacific Northwest Collection of the University of Washington Libraries, Seattle, 6 vols. (Boston: G. K. Hall, 1972).

WA 8
MOLDENHAUER ARCHIVES MUSICOLOGICAL INSTITUTE
1011 Comstock Court
Spokane, Washington 99203
(509-747-4555)

In process of organization. Inquiries concerning Russian-related holdings should be directed to Rosaleen Moldenhauer, executive director.

WA 9
TACOMA PUBLIC LIBRARY
1102 Tacoma Avenue South
Tacoma, Washington 98402
(206-572-2000)

1 Historic Poster Collection. Consists of 10 Intourist posters, 1935-36. They concern travel to the Soviet Union and cultural events in these years.

2 Note: There may also be relevant materials in a World War I collection of John B. Kaiser and some propaganda items from both world wars.

WEST VIRGINIA

WV 1
SPECIAL COLLECTIONS
JAMES E. MORROW LIBRARY
MARSHALL UNIVERSITY
Huntington, West Virginia 25701
(304-696-2320)

Allen C. Klinger (1885-1961). Papers, 1879-1957, 13 cu. ft. Marshall University history professor. Includes 2 postcards and a letter, 1946, from Thomas R. Senter, a diplomat in Russia. Descriptions of J. Stalin and Tito (whom Senter saw at M. Kalinin's funeral), and comments on life in Moscow and NKVD surveillance.

WV 2
WEST VIRGINIA COLLECTION
WEST VIRGINIA UNIVERSITY LIBRARY
Morgantown, West Virginia 26506
(304-293-2240)

1 Charles H. Ambler (1876-1957). Papers, 1834-1957, 50 boxes, 1 bundle, and 1 folder. Historian and writer. Includes transcripts of 12 letters, 1859-62, written from St. Petersburg by an agent of the Ross Winans Locomotive Works of Baltimore, Maryland. They concern Russian railroads. (NUCMC 60-40)

2 Israel G. White (1847-1927). Papers, 1867-1941, 30 ft. Geologist. Includes ca. 100 letters relating to his participation in geological congresses in St. Petersburg (1897) and in Paris (1900). (NUCMC 60-270)

Finding Aid: Guide to Manuscripts and Archives in the West Virginia Collection, by James W. Hess (Morgantown, 1974).

WISCONSIN

WI 1
CIRCUS WORLD MUSEUM
Baraboo, Wisconsin 53913
(608-356-8341)

114 Soviet circus posters, mostly from the last 20 years.

WI 2
ARCHIVES DIVISION
STATE HISTORICAL SOCIETY OF WISCONSIN
816 State Street
Madison, Wisconsin 53706
(608-262-9576)

The Archives Division includes collections of the Mass Communications History Center and of the Wisconsin Center for Film and Theatre Research, many of whose holdings appear in the listing that follows. It is important to note that, through a unique loan system, individual manuscript collections may be temporarily transferred to any one of Wisconsin's 13 Area Research Centers (or to this repository from the Centers) for use by researchers.

1 Stephen E. Ambrose (b. 1936). Historian. Photocopy of his review of The Last Battle (New York, 1966) by Cornelius Ryan and 5 letters relating to the review. One letter is from Dwight D. Eisenhower, 23 August 1966; another is a response to Ryan from the Soviet Union.

2 American Committee for Liberation. Radio scripts, 1960-61, 6 boxes. Russian-language scripts for Radio Liberty broadcasts from Munich, Germany, to the USSR, with English translations. Scripts are for every eighth day. (NUCMC 68-2305)

3 American Federation of Labor. Records, 1881-1952, 218 ft. Files of various offices or divisions of the AFL, including papers of presidents Samuel Gompers and William Green, economist Boris Shishkin, and research director Florence Thorne. Contains a general and book review file for the American Federationist, also materials on World War I, World War II, and post-war problems. Unpublished inventory (NUCMC 62-3458).

4 American League for Peace and Democracy. Madison Branch. Records, 1937-40, 3 boxes. Includes material dealing with the Russo-Finnish War of 1939-40 (the so-called Winter War). (NUCMC 62-1077)

5 George Lucius Anderson (1849-1934). Papers, 1897-98 and n.d., 1 folder. U.S. military attaché in St. Petersburg, 1897-98. Contains letters written home from Russia, photocopies.

6 Hilmar R. Baukhage (b. 1889). Papers, 1915-62, 4 boxes, 5 tape and 26 disc recordings. Journalist, radio news commentator, and lecturer. Letters, broadcast scripts, 1944-57, personal journals, 1915 and 1942-53, speeches, 1941-62, and other items. In box 3, folder 1 is material relating to Russia.

7 S. N. Behrman (b. 1893). Papers, 1924-56, 23 boxes. Dramatist. Includes the screenplay for the comedy Ninotchka, 1939, the film starring Greta Garbo. Detailed notes, drafts, and revisions of this and some 30 other plays or adaptations. Restricted. Unpublished inventory. (NUCMC 64-1597)

8 Alvah Bessie (b. 1904). Papers, 1947-63, 8 boxes. Reporter, screenwriter, and one of the Hollywood Ten. Among his letters, legal materials, scripts, speeches, and clippings are items relating to the confrontation between the House Committee on Un-American Activities (HUAC) and the Hollywood Ten.

9 Herbert Biberman and Gale Sondergaard. Papers, 182 boxes, several vols., 2 microfilm reels, and 1 film. Film director (1 of the Hollywood Ten) and his actress wife. Original deposit included correspondence, writings, and scripts relating to their careers in films and to their political activities. Includes a 10-minute film documentary entitled The Hollywood Ten. Additional papers, for 1946-65, are of Biberman's lawyers and concern, in part, the Council of Soviet-American Friendship (box 61, folders 4-5). Original papers are in part restricted in access. Unpublished inventory for the addition.

10 Creed C. Black (b. 1925). Papers, 1943-69, 16 boxes. Journalist and editor. Traveled to the Soviet Union in 1962. His private business files contain material on the trip. Unpublished inventory. (Papers are held on deposit only.)

11 Peter Bobrik (1880-1951). Imperial Russian Army general. Typed copy of his autobiography, "The Current of Life I Strolled By," 146 pp. Covers his early life, the tsarist educational system ca. 1900 (especially the cadet school at Simbirsk and Mikhailovsk Artillery College at St. Petersburg), his military training, churches (structures), and church holidays.

12 Bornett L. Bobroff (d. 1946). Papers, 1904-46, 1 box. Inventor and businessman. Emigrated from Russia to the U.S. in 1904. In 1917 the Bobroff voting machine was adopted by the Wisconsin Assembly, the first such device in the nation. He eventually became president of the Teleoptic Company of Racine, which manufactured his automobile turn signal invention. Most of the materials concern his patents and inventions.

13 David John Bradley (b. 1915). Papers, 1940-65, 1 box. Free-lance writer, interested in the Russo-Finnish War (Winter War) of 1939-40. He became a war correspondent for the Wisconsin State Journal, went to Finland (too late to cover the brief conflict), and ended up writing several articles about the Finns. In the 1960s he wrote a book about Finland and its people (Lion Among Roses); much of the collection concerns this book.

14 Hannah Brain Campbell (1880-1973). Papers, 1921-73, 1 folder. Siberian prospector. Letters, writings, and articles mainly concern Campbell and her family as goldminers in Siberia, 1917-18; the aftermath of the Bolshevik takeover there; and her freighter journey for the Red Cross, escorting European Russian children back to their families.

15 Marquis Childs (b. 1903). Papers, 1919-63, 29 boxes. Newspaperman and author. Correspondence, writings, speeches, scripts, interviews, and business files. Box 4 contains notes and memoranda on, inter alia, Moscow. Box 5 has news dispatches filed from Poland and Russia for the St. Louis Post-Dispatch. Box 6 holds a notebook of rough memoranda, apparently kept during a visit to the USSR in 1958. Much of the correspondence is with prominent political figures in the U.S. Some, in the period 1946-51, concerns charges that Childs had communist sympathies or belonged to communist organizations. For example, on 1 February 1951 he wrote HUAC to deny such accusations. Among his correspondents are Dean Acheson, Charles E. Bohlen, Hubert H. Humphrey, John F. Kennedy, Isaac Don Levine, Henry Cabot Lodge, Richard M. Nixon, Adlai Stevenson, and Harry S. Truman. In box 28 is correspondence, 10 April 1958, of Mikhail A. Menshikov. Boxes 21-27 contain St. Louis Post-Dispatch files, among which are items for 1941-46 on deteriorating Soviet-American relations, the European recovery, the Korean War, and Senator Joseph McCarthy. Requires permission of the director of the State Historical Society. Unpublished description. (NUCMC 68-2147)

16 John R. Commons (1862-1945). Papers, 1894-1937, 19 boxes. Labor economist. Includes some material relating to the Soviet Union. (NUCMC 62-5012)

17 Jeremiah Curtin (1835-1906). Papers, 1861-69 and ca. 1900, 3 microfilm reels. Secretary to the U.S. legation in Russia, 1861-69. Excerpts of his recollections. Published as Memoirs of Jeremiah Curtin, edited by Joseph Schafer (1940). (NUCMC 62-1972)

18 Domor (fl. ca. 1919). U.S. Army sergeant. Letter, 15 January 1919, from him to his commanding officer (Company F, 339th Infantry, American Expeditionary Force, Kholmogory, Russia) containing a list of men at Kholmogory and at Pinega.

19 Draper Manuscripts. Collection, ca. 1750-1927, ca. 500 vols. Subdivided into 50 series of materials. In the section of Frontier War MSS (Series U, 23 vols.) are letters of Charles S. Todd, American statesman and minister to Russia in 1841-46, in vol. 8. The Pittsburgh and Northwest Virginia MSS (Series MN, 10 vols.) have transcripts of correspondence of the Russian-born Baron Gustavus Henri de Rosenthal (known as John Rose in America).

Rosenthal, of Baltic origin, left Russia after a duel, came to Baltimore in 1776 and studied surgery, then joined Pennsylvania troops and fought in the American Revolutionary War. General William Irvine made him a staff officer at Fort Pitt in 1781. He returned to Russia in 1784, was pardoned by the tsar, and lived on his family estate until his death in 1830. Although he never revisited America, he corresponded with Irvine after his return home, discussing the war, the Crawford campaign of 1782, and other reminiscences. The volume in which the letters are kept has a detailed index. In Virginia MSS (Series ZZ, 14 vols.) are the manuscript "Letters of a Russian Spy," which were published in the Chillicothe Gazette in 1825-26. Published guide in preparation.

20 Robert H. Estabrook (b. 1918). Papers, 1949-66, 7 boxes. Journalist, foreign correspondent, and United Nations correspondent for the Washington Post. Letters, diaries, reports, interviews, speeches, articles, notes, clippings, and subject files. Reference(s) to the Soviet Union. Unpublished inventory.

21 Federated Trades Council of Milwaukee. Records, 1900-50, 18 vols. and 4 boxes. Includes a committee report on the Soviet form of government in Russia (1920). (NUCMC 62-4836 and 68-2184)

22 Stephen Feinstein (b. 1943). Correspondence, 1970, 5 items. Professor. Photocopies of letters written to him and graduate student Reno Rizzo by Soviet students and a Leningrad Intourist guide. Originals at the River Falls Area Research Center.

23 Ernest G. Fischer (b. 1902). Papers, 1941-66 19 boxes. Associated Press foreign correspondent in Europe. Correspondence, dispatches, diaries, and notes. Access restricted. Unpublished inventory.

24 John Fischer (b. 1910). Papers, 1945-63, ca. 3 ft., additions expected. Writer and editor of Harper's Magazine, 1953-67. At present about half the materials relate to his books and articles, particularly Why They Behave Like Russians (1947; published in Europe as The Scared Men in the Kremlin). Includes notes, original manuscript, typesetting copy, galley proofs, and articles about the book. Also, original manuscript and typesetting copy of his Master Plan: U.S.A. (1951). Much of the remaining material consists of correspondence concerned with his work for Harper's. (NUCMC 64-1604 and 62-3854)

25 James Archibald Frear (1861-1939). Papers, 3 boxes and 6 vols. Lawyer and U.S. congressman. He made an unofficial tour of Russia in 1923 with Senators Ladd (North Dakota) and King (Utah). Some correspondence, April-July 1923, concerns the trip. This "Unofficial Commission to Russia" was sponsored by the Hearst publishing firm. Also, the itinerary of the group, August 4-8. (NUCMC 62-2422) Note: The Society's museum holds a scrapbook of pictures taken by Frear on this tour of the USSR.

26 Gibbs Family. Papers, 1796-1903, 2 vols. and 4 boxes. 1 box, on deposit only, contains a diary of George Gibbs for 1918 which relates to the Russian Railroad Commission. (NUCMC 62-2787)

27 Boris S. Glagolin. Actor, chief director of the Moscow Theatre of the Revolution, and later a director in Milwaukee, Wisconsin. Includes an undated article, "The Liberty of the Russian Theatre," about his experiences ca. 1905-27; and an article by N. N. Evreinoff, "Boris S. Glagolin, the Actor."

28 Albert Goldman (1898-1961?). Papers, 1940-59, 1 ft. Labor attorney, socialist, and communist. Leon Trotskii's counsel in Mexico, 1936-40. As a Trotskyist he was convicted of sedition in Minneapolis in 1941 and expelled from the Communist Party as an anti-Stalinist. He was successively a member of the Socialist Workers Party, the Workers Party, and other groups sympathetic to socialism. A change of heart about Russia led him to try to become reinstated to the bar. Correspondence, 1940-59 but primarily 1948, ca. 300 letters, concerns these later phases of his career. The 1948 letters (and later ones) often refer to Trotskii, but no items to or from him are among these papers. Also, notes and trial briefs, annotated pamphlets by Goldman, and clippings. Unpublished inventory (NUCMC 64-1607).

29 Robert Goralski (b. 1928). Papers, 1953-60, 7 boxes and 1 tape recording (additions expected). Radio and television reporter. Correspondence, 1953-54, and scripts for the Voice of America, 1959-60, and other programs. The tape is an interview with Goralski about his life and career. Access restricted. Unpublished inventory.

30 Alexander Gumberg (1887-1939). Papers, 1904-39, 35 boxes. Russian-born U.S. immigrant, adviser to American financial and business concerns on political, economic, and cultural relations with the USSR. Probably the most important individual in the U.S. in promoting American business with Russia in the years preceding U.S. diplomatic recognition of the Soviet Union. In New York Gumberg had worked with Leon Trotskii on a newspaper. He returned to Russia in 1917-18, becoming involved with American businesses, the American Red Cross, and the (Creel) Committee on Public Information. At this time he became acquainted with Raymond Robins. His papers for 1917-18 contain some material on the Revolution and the emergence of the new economy. Correspondents include G. V. Chicherin, F.

Dzerzhinsky, V. I. Lenin, V. Molotov, and Trotskii. In papers for 1917-24 there are also data on Soviet-American relations, the Soviet Union Information Bureau, and the All-Russian Textile Institute. Gumberg was Senator William E. Borah's adviser and source of information on Russian conditions, once he returned to the U.S. Correspondents at this time include Borah, Robins, William Henry Chamberlin, Louis Fischer, John Reed, Boris Sivirsky, and Upton Sinclair. In the 1920s Gumberg promoted closer economic ties between the U.S. and USSR, and American recognition of the Soviet Union, particularly through his work with the American-Russian Chamber of Commerce. He was an assistant to both Reeve Schley and Colonel Hugh Cooper when they were president of that organization. (Schley was also with the Chase National Bank.) The collection is rich in materials on the American-Russian Chamber of Commerce and on Amtorg, the Soviet trading corporation in the U.S. Among other persons and subjects covered are: the Geneva Disarmament Conference of 1927-28 (Gumberg reported on it); the Moscow trials of 1936-38 and the political figures involved in them; his own brother, Veniamin Gombarg, vice-president of a Soviet chemical syndicate and purge victim; the appointment of Joseph E. Davies as ambassador to the Soviet Union; Dwight W. Morrow; Peter A. Bogdanov; Louis Adamic; James A. Frear; Maurice Hindus; L. A. Serebriakoff; Lincoln Steffens; Oswald G. Villard; and Albert Rhys Williams. Partial index. (NUCMC 62-2431)

31 John Gunther (1901-1970). Papers, 1938-44, 2 boxes. Journalist and author. Wrote radio scripts about all theaters of operation in World War II. Also, annotated typescripts of lectures, notes, and miscellany connected with a 1939 lecture tour; and disc recordings of 41 broadcasts of 1942-43. Unpublished inventory (NUCMC 68-2205).

32 Charles Henry Hawes (1867-1943). Papers, 1899-1906, 1 package. British traveler in Russia, 1901. Author of In the Uttermost East. Includes notes on his reading about Siberian tribes and Sakhalin Island, and on his conversations with Russian Empire inhabitants. (NUCMC 62-1788)

33 John M. Hightower (b. 1909). Papers, 1944-60, 4 ft. State Department and international affairs correspondent. Primarily notebooks he kept on press conferences, diplomatic gatherings, and news trips. There is much background information, such as confidential memoranda from, among others, John Foster Dulles, W. Averell Harriman, and George C. Marshall. In the correspondence is a series of letters to his wife, written while he was covering the Council of Foreign Ministers meetings in Moscow, 1947, and Berlin, 1954. Access restricted until 1982. Unpublished inventory (NUCMC 65-1061).

34 Morris Hillquit (1869-1933). Papers, 1899-1933, 10 microfilm reels. Leader of the American socialist movement in the 20th c. Born in Riga, he came with his family to the U.S. in 1886, later changing his name from the original Moses Hillkowitz. He joined the Socialist Labor Party in 1887, at the age of 18. He became a lawyer, representing labor leaders and organizations in legal cases throughout his career. Particularly after the Russian Revolution of 1917, Hillquit wrote about party tactics, Marxist philosophy, and related issues. Materials include photographs, biographical data, ca. 200 letters, writings, ephemera, press releases, and clippings. Several items pertain to Maksim Gorkii's fund-raising tour of America, his literary work, his acquaintance with Hillquit, and exiled Russian revolutionary writers. There are letters of Gorkii, Maria Andreevna Peshkova, Ivan Ladyshnikov (Ladyschnikov), and Raphael Rein Abramowitsch. Correspondence of Algernon Lee, Adolph F. Germer, Santeri Nuorteva, Gilbert E. Roe, Isaac A. Hourwich, and Ludwig C. A. K. Martens, 1918-19, sheds light on divisions among American socialists over Bolshevism, attitudes of Finnish-Americans toward V. I. Lenin and the Bolsheviks, "red-baiting" in the U.S., and charges against Martens as representative of the RSFSR Bureau in the United States. Papers are on microfilm, for which there is a published guide (1969). (NUCMC 62-2507)

35 International Workingmen's Association. Records, 1868-77, 2 microfilm reels. Divided into 4 sections: records of the General Council, 1871-74; records of the Central Committee, North American Federal Council, 1868-77; records of Section 26 (Philadelphia), 1871-76; and records of Section 1 (St. Louis), 1870-77. Correspondence, minutes, clippings, broadsides, convention resolutions and proceedings, financial records, and miscellany; some items in French and German. A few items relate to Friedrich Engels and Karl Marx. Entire collection is on microfilm, for which there is a published guide (1972). (NUCMC 62-1943)

36 Albert Aaron Johnson (1880-1963). Papers, 1884-1963, 5 boxes and 1 package. Agricultural economist, educator, and authority on the early Soviet Union. Family correspondence, diaries, writings, patents, and other materials. Some items concern his trips to the Soviet Union. Unpublished inventory.

37 George Hopkins Johnson (1901-1974). Papers, 1860s-1972, 4 boxes and 2 cassette tapes. Businessman (Gisholt Machine Company). Served on the War Production Board during World War II. In 1945 he went to Germany and Moscow as a member of the American delegation of the Allied Commission on Reparations. Papers include letters, a diary, reports, memoranda, speeches, and notes, covering his

family and his career. In the Gisholt Machine Company records (box 4) are correspondence and contracts for several balancing machines to be delivered to the Russians shortly after the end of World War II. Several folders (box 2) in his personal papers contain information about post-war production conditions in Eastern Europe. Unpublished finding aid.

38 Hans von Kaltenborn (1878-1965). Papers, 1883-1962, 100 ft. News broadcaster, became known as the "Dean of American Radio Commentators." Correspondence, 1902-64, radio scripts, 1927-60, television scripts, 1951-60, film scripts, 1939-61, notebooks, 1926-61, and scrapbooks. Ca. 500 disc and 23 tape recordings cover his broadcasts, mainly 1940-48, interviews, and panel discussions. International affairs and the Soviet Union are topics well represented in the collection. Descriptive brochure available on request. Unpublished inventory file (NUCMC 65-1062).

39 Robert Walker Kenny (b. 1901) and Robert S. Morris. Papers, 1940-57, 10 ft. California attorneys. Correspondence, legal briefs, memoranda, notes, depositions, and other items relating to the Hollywood Ten, the Hollywood Nineteen, and the appearances of these screenwriters, producers, and directors before the House Un-American Activities Committee (HUAC). Some of the material is on tape and disc recordings. Unpublished inventory (NUCMC 65-1063).

40 Elizabeth Poe Kerby. Papers, 1953-61, 1 folder. Unpublished summary of her findings in an investigation of the extent and impact of the Hollywood Blacklist resulting from HUAC hearings, 1952-53, plus copies of 4 published articles on this subject.

41 Austin H. Kiplinger (b. 1918). Papers, 1951-59, 2 boxes. Reporter and news commentator. He went to the Soviet Union in 1959. Includes notes on this trip, as well as radio and television news broadcast scripts, 1951-56, and correspondence, 1955-56. Scripts cover, in part, the Korean War, Senator Joseph R. McCarthy, and HUAC. (NUCMC 68-2247)

42 Howard Koch (b. 1902). Papers, 1937-76, 7 boxes. Author of radio scripts, plays, and film scripts. He wrote the screenplay for Mission to Moscow (1943), the movie adaptation of Ambassador Joseph Davies' book. The script, photographs, clippings, and notes on the film are among the papers. In addition, there are letters, statements, transcripts, and clippings relating to the Hollywood blacklist. Unpublished inventory.

43 Leo Lania (1896-1961). Papers, ca. 1930s-1950s, 13 boxes. Writer for films, the theater, and broadcast journalism. Among his plays is one entitled Comrade Ivan (January 1951), an outline and notes for which are in box 4 (folder 6). He wrote a number of radio scripts for Radio Free Europe and the Voice of America in 1950-52 (box 8). Box 9 (folder 7) contains a 1948 article about Sergei Eisenstein; and several other articles and clippings concern the Soviet Union 1932-36 and 1952 (box 11). One correspondent was Max Eastman.

44 Robert Lasch (b. 1907). Papers, 1940-71, 2 vols. and 13 boxes. Journalist and editorial writer for the St. Louis Post-Dispatch. Correspondence, subject files, office files, writings, notes, and clippings include analyses of the Korean War, McCarthyism, national defense, and the Vietnam War. In small part restricted. Unpublished finding aid.

45 Emmet Lavery (b. 1902). Papers, 1925-62, 5 boxes and 2 packages. Stage, screen, and television writer. Includes the complete transcript of his testimony before HUAC. Collection is on loan and is restricted. Unpublished inventory.

46 Albert W. Levin (b. 1887). Papers, 1962-63, 2 items. Russian Jew who immigrated to Racine, Wisconsin. Biographical sketches, written in 1962 and 1963. One has a description of the shtetl in Uzda and his life there until age 19.

47 Herman Levin (b. 1907). Papers, 1948-56, 183 boxes and 10 packages. Theatrical producer. Ca. 66% of the collection pertains to the Broadway musical My Fair Lady. Some files are on foreign and foreign-language productions, including the Russian tour. A film entitled "Tours of American Artists in Russia" is about The Liza Company (My Fair Lady). Unpublished inventory (NUCMC 64-1614).

48 Louis P. Lochner (b. 1887). Papers, 1905-61, 23 ft. Foreign correspondent, commentator, and author. Letters, diaries, book manuscripts, radio scripts, speeches, articles, and interview transcripts. Some materials pertain to his work as secretary on the Ford Peace Expedition. Also, reports on German-Russian relations, 1922-41, and on land reforms, economics, and POW treatment in the Russian-occupied zone of Germany in 1947, plus an eyewitness account of the fall of Berlin. Unpublished inventory (NUCMC 64-1615).

49 Roy L. Martin (fl. ca. 1918). Papers, 1901-54, 3 boxes and 1 vol. Includes a series of letters, 1918-19, written by Fayette Keller (to Martin?) while serving with the Russian Railway Service Corps in Siberia. They describe conditions in the Far East during the Civil War. (NUCMC 68-2272)

50 John K. M. McCaffrey. Oral history collection, 1956-57 and 1961-62, 9 tape and 15 disc recordings. 1 disc recording, ca. 1961, is

of an interview with George F. Kennan, in part concerning international affairs.

51 McCormick Collection. Records and family papers, 1600-1963, 3,692 boxes, 1,983 vols., and 4 packages. Business correspondence pertains, inter alia, to early development of the company's business in Russia, 1879-1902 (marketing only). For later years there are some duplicates of correspondence held in the International Harvester Archives of Chicago. International Harvester was the successor firm to the McCormick Company and established a large sales network plus a major factory at Lyubertsy in Russia, 1902-17. Personal papers of Harold F. McCormick and of Cyrus H. McCormick, Jr., should also contain Russian-related material.

52 Michael Myerberg (b. 1906). Papers, 1940-49, 10 boxes. Show business manager and producer. At one point he handled the Ensemble of the Red Army. Papers on deposit only. Unpublished inventory. 8 cartons unprocessed.

53 Edward P. Morgan (b. 1910). Papers, 1955-59, 109 boxes. News analyst, commentator, and correspondent. References to Soviet subjects occur in his news broadcasts. Unpublished inventory (NUCMC 61-2952).

54 N. Richard Nash (b. 1913). Papers, 1937-61, 10 ft., additions expected. Playwright and producer. Includes a letter, 28 November 1958, from Adlai E. Stevenson, representing 79 authors and dramatists, concerning Nash's efforts in Moscow to have Soviet users of American books and plays pay higher royalties. Unpublished inventory (NUCMC 64-1618).

55 National Aeronautics and Space Administration. Records of the Public Information Center, 1959-63, 6 boxes. Contains items relating to Soviet manned space flights. Access restricted. (NUCMC 68-2353)

56 National Association of Educational Broadcasters. Records, 1925-65, 83 boxes. During the 1950s many of this organization's activities were financed by grants from the Fund for Adult Education. In the Program file are correspondence, minutes of meetings, publicity clips, scripts, and printed materials, 1951-56, for the experimental radio lecture series, "People Under Communism," underwritten by the Fund for Adult Education. Scripts discuss Soviet drama, industry, literature, and other topics. Unpublished inventory.

57 National Educational Television (NET). Records, 1951-70, 618 boxes, 2 vols., 5 films, and 1 tape recording. A collection of records of an organization financed primarily by the Ford Foundation's Fund for Adult Education. The Public Information series contains a few newsclips on such topics as "Russia: The Unfinished Revolution" and "Conversation with Svetlana Alliluyeva." Program materials on Russian civilization, language, music, foreign relations, etc. are scattered through the programming series. Unpublished inventory.

58 John B. Oakes (b. 1913). Papers, 1932-65, 4 microfilm reels. Editor of the New York Times editorial page. Alphabetical subject file of correspondence, book reviews, reports, minutes of meetings, speeches, notes, article drafts, and other materials, some concerning the Soviet Union. Unpublished inventory.

59 Samuel B. Ornitz (1890-1957). Papers, 1919-57, 9 boxes and 1 vol. Author, playwright, and screenwriter. Contains material on the Hollywood Ten (legal papers, printed matter, Ornitz's undelivered statement to HUAC, and the transcript of the Committee's hearings). Unpublished inventory (NUCMC 68-2293).

60 DeWitt Clinton Poole (1885-1952). Papers, ca. 1920-52, 12 boxes. Diplomat and educator, served in the U.S. consular service in Russia, 1917-21. In World War II he was director of the Foreign Nationalities Branch of the Office of Strategic Services, 1941-45. Contains notes and drafts of Poole's lectures on, among other topics, the American mission to Russia, 1917-24; also, letters, articles, and notes of his career, the Russian Revolution, Soviet diplomacy and foreign relations, U.S. diplomatic recognition of the USSR in 1933, Kremlin-Vatican relations, and Stalin's plans for establishing a new Polish government. There are notes from 1951 of an interview with George F. Kennan on the need for foreign educational exchanges with the U.S. (NUCMC 62-2914)

61 Clarence J. Primm (fl. ca. 1918). Correspondence, 1918-19, 9 items. U.S. Army lieutenant stationed at Archangel as a member of the 339th Infantry in the North Russian Expeditionary Forces. Letters to his wife describe conditions he observed in northern Russia.

62 Radio Free Europe. Records, 1966-present, 35 boxes (additions expected). Includes background and situation reports, press surveys, and quarterly indexes on nations and areas of the world. Research departments of RFE prepare reports for use by editors and policy staff. Soviet-related material interspersed throughout. Unpublished inventory.

63 Radio Liberty Committee. See under American Committee for Liberation.

64 Paul Samuel Reinsch (1869-1923). Papers, 1835-1924, 20 boxes and 8 vols. Professor and diplomat. In 1903-1904 he received letters from O. A. Forstrom in Finland and other correspondents who wrote about Russian oppression in Finland starting in 1899. (NUCMC 62-2878 and 68-2309)

65 Raymond Robins (1873-1954). Papers, 1878-1951, 46 boxes. Social worker, social economist, politician, and lecturer; head of the American Red Cross mission to Russia in 1917. He became personally acquainted with V. I. Lenin and Leon Trotskii. In April-July 1933 he was back in the Soviet Union, where J. V. Stalin and other high-ranking officials received him. At this time (and earlier) Robins was promoting U.S. recognition of the USSR and closer economic ties between the 2 nations. Materials in the collection include: for 1917-18, diaries, letters to his wife, copies of diplomatic correspondence with U.S. Ambassador David R. Francis, and items by or about Lenin, Trotskii, and G. Chicherin, some of which are in Russian. Correspondents in the 1920s include Alexander Gumberg, D. Heywood Hardy, Thomas D. Thacher, William Boyce Thompson, and Allen Wardwell. His 1933 radio address about the USSR on NBC elicited letters from Soviet representatives Peter A. Bogdanov and Boris E. Sivirsky. (NUCMC 68-2313)

66 Edward Alsworth Ross (1866-1951). Papers, 1859-1951, 31 boxes and 9 vols. Sociologist. 4 notebooks for 1917-18 contain observations made in Russia. He refers to the Bolshevik Revolution, social conditions, and an interview with Leon Trotskii on 9 December 1917. Also, several letters about his trip (made under the auspices of the American Institute of Social Service) and about his articles on Russia. Unpublished inventory and shelf list (NUCMC 68-2317).

67 Dore Schary (b. 1905). Papers, 1950-61, 65 boxes, 28 vols., and 3 packages. Author, producer, stage and screen writer. Speeches, articles, and research materials concern, in part, the movie industry and communism. Unpublished inventory (NUCMC 64-1627).

68 John Scott (1912-1978?). Papers, in process, 62 cartons, 2 boxes, and 3 scrapbooks. Foreign correspondent and assistant to the publisher of *Time* magazine. Includes annotated drafts of a report on "The Soviet Economic Offensive," plus items pertaining to his books--e.g., *Handbook of Political Warfare* (1955) and *Democracy Is Not Enough* (1959). (Scott was the author of the classic *Behind the Urals* [1942].) Unpublished inventory (NUCMC 62-3120).

69 Alfred Senn. Papers, unprocessed, 6 cartons and 1 box. Linguist who specialized in Lithuanian language and culture. He lived and taught in Lithuania, 1921-30, and was active in both the political and cultural life of the newly independent state. Among his acquaintances were the philologists Max Niedermann (extensive correspondence in this collection), Jonas Jablonskis, and Kazimieras Buga; and the writers Juozas Tumas-Vaizgantas and Vincas Kreve-Mickevicius. Also, Professor Senn's diaries. He emigrated to the U.S. in 1930 but maintained ties with Lithuania and worked to aid Lithuanians before and after World War II. Note: Some papers of his son, Professor Alfred E. Senn of the University of Wisconsin, are eventually to come to the Society. These papers include some tape recorded oral history interviews (and transcriptions) with Mykolas Birziska and Vaclovas Sidzikauskas and correspondence with Steponas Kairys concerning Lithuanian politics, especially the Social Democratic movement.

70 Singer Manufacturing Company. Records, 1848-1943, 244 boxes, including 142 vols., and 178 additional vols. Contains correspondence, reports, and account books, ca. 1866-1918, pertaining to Singer's Russian operations, the development of its wholly owned Russian subsidiary (Manufakturnaia kompaniia zinger), and the latter's activities up to the Revolution. This Russian subsidiary was reputedly the largest firm, domestic or foreign, in Russia in 1914. Materials provide a detailed record of business operations, management of marketing structure and procedures, sales, and related matters. The Kompaniia zinger had a factory in Podolsk, for whose operations there are correspondence and some financial data, ca. 1905-12. The Singer collection is restricted; written permission to read or copy from the records must be obtained in advance from the president, vice-president, or secretary of the Singer Company, 30 Rockefeller Plaza, New York, NY 10020. Unpublished catalogue (NUCMC 68-2329).

71 Howard K. Smith (b. 1914). Papers, 1941-48 and 1957-61, 12 boxes (additions expected). News commentator and correspondent. Includes radio scripts 1941-45, some reporting the signing of the German surrender in Marshall Georgi Zhukov's headquarters in Berlin. Smith was the only American broadcaster present. Unpublished inventory. (NUCMC 68-2331)

72 Raymond Swing (1887-1968). Scripts, 1943-47, 2 boxes. Radio commentator. Includes analyses of foreign policy and international affairs questions, particularly disarmament, nuclear weapons, and the effect of Sino-Soviet relations on the U.S. after World War II. (NUCMC 68-2344)

73 Otto David Tolischus (1890-1967). Papers, 1926-42, 1 box. *New York Times* correspondent specializing in international affairs. Some of his letters contain observations while in the Soviet Union in 1930. Also, an account of the fall of Warsaw, 27 September 1939. Unpublished inventory (NUCMC 68-2351).

74 M. I. Veranick. Transcription of an oral history interview, 1967, 19 pp. In the Ukraine during the Revolution and Civil War. Original in the River Falls Area Research Center (see which entry for details).

75 Voice of America (radio program). Records, 1960-61, 22 boxes. Scripts used in broadcasts from 31 May-29 June 1960 and news copy from the International Broadcasting System, 11 January 1960-5 January 1961. Scripts describe primarily American life. (NUCMC 68-2363)

76 William E. Walling (1877-1936). Papers, 1871-1962, 3 boxes. Author, lecturer, and civic leader. In letters, post-1900, there are scattered references to the breakdown of tsarist rule and the development of revolutionary sentiments in Russia and Poland, 1905-1906. (NUCMC 68-2364)

77 William Appleman Williams (b. 1921). Writings, typed, 138 pp., 1 microfilm reel. Historian. Includes his typed essay "American Intervention in Russia," which has been published.

78 Matthew Woll. Acting president of the National Civic Federation in 1932. Letter, 5 November 1932, from Woll to a number of college professors, concerning U.S. recognition of the Soviet Union, 4 pp.

79 Helen Zotos (b. 1923). Papers, 1947-67, 6 boxes. Associated Press correspondent. She covered the Greek Civil War, 1946-49. Includes files from her work as news analyst and editor of Radio Free Europe's Daily Information Bulletin, 1955-57. Unpublished inventory (NUCMC 68-2392)

Finding Aids: Guide to the Manuscripts of the State Historical Society of Wisconsin (Madison, 1944); supplement no. 1 (1957) and supplement no. 2 (1966). Photocopies of inventories and registers (unpublished) are for sale by the Society.

WI 3
DATA AND COMPUTATION CENTER FOR
THE SOCIAL SCIENCES
DATA AND PROGRAM LIBRARY SERVICE
4452 SOCIAL SCIENCE BUILDING
UNIVERSITY OF WISCONSIN - MADISON
1180 Observatory Place
Madison, Wisconsin 53706
(608-262-7962)

Established in 1966, the University of Wisconsin - Madison's Data and Program Library Service (DPLS) is one of the oldest libraries and archives for social science machine-readable data in the U.S. Its Russian-related machine-readable data include the following:

1 Russian Imperial Bureaucracy. 1762-1881. 1 data file (1,417 logical records). The data, processed by John A. Armstrong from the Russkii biograficheskii slovar' (Moscow, 1896-98) and other published sources, provides information on 1,417 Russian administrators, including ca. 415 governors. The information includes dates of incumbency in various posts, dates of attaining each of the top 4 civil ranks (chin), education, birth/death dates, and year of entrance into civil service. Finding aid.

2 USSR Nationalities Data. Contains 4 data sets: (a) Aggregate Data on the Linguistic and Demographic Make-up of Basic National Areas and Groups, 1926 and 1959; (b) Native Language of Non-Russian Ethnic Groups by Urban-Rural, Sex, and Residential Differences, 1959; (c) Native Language of Non-Russian Ethnic Groups by Age, Urban-Rural, and Sex Differences, 1959; (d) Native Language of Basic National Groups in 5 Multiple-Oblast Republics (Ukraine, Byelorussia, Kazakhstan, Uzbekistan, Turkmenistan), by Sex and Urban-Rural Differences, 1959. The principal source of this data, gathered by Brian D. Silver of Florida State University, is the Soviet census for 1926 and 1959.

WI 4
ARCHIVES--443F MEMORIAL LIBRARY
UNIVERSITY OF WISCONSIN - MADISON
728 State Street
Madison, Wisconsin 53706
(608-262-3290)

Joseph E. Davies (1876-1958). Papers, ca. 1937-58, ca. .3 cu. ft. U.S. ambassador to the Soviet Union, 1937-38. Primarily correspondence between Davies and 3 presidents of the University (Davies was a graduate) concerning donation of his art collection. The Davies Collection of Russian art is now in the Elvehjem Art Center at the Madison campus. Unpublished folder-by-folder inventory list.

WI 5
SPECIAL COLLECTIONS AND UNIVERSITY ARCHIVES
MEMORIAL LIBRARY
MARQUETTE UNIVERSITY
1415 West Wisconsin Avenue
Milwaukee, Wisconsin 53233
(414-224-7256)

Charles J. Kersten. Papers, ca. 1940-65, 20 ft. "Anti-communist" Republican congressman from Wisconsin's 5th District. Kersten served in the 80th, 82nd, and 83rd Congresses, 1947-48, 1951-54. Author of the Kersten Amendment to "support resistance behind the Iron Curtain," he chaired a Congressional Committee to Investigate Communism in American Labor and Industry. In 1953 he became chairman of the House Select Committee on Communist Aggression. He was a White House consultant on foreign affairs in 1955-56. About 3 ft. of records (correspondence, reports, photographs, and other documents) relate to the USSR and its military and political domination of Eastern Europe. Much is secondary material or printed matter. Some of the items are restricted, though most of the Russian-related holdings are not. Collection in process.

WI 6
MILWAUKEE COUNTY HISTORICAL SOCIETY
910 North Third Street
Milwaukee, Wisconsin 53203
(414-273-8288)

1 Jeremiah Curtin (1835-1906). Papers, 1878-1952, 10 ft. Linguist with an interest in mythology. Secretary to the U.S. legation in St. Petersburg, 1864-69, timber merchant in Russia, 1872-77, employee of the Smithsonian Institution to collect materials on the Russian people, 1897 and 1900, and assistant to the Russian delegation in the negotiation of the Treaty of Portsmouth, 1905. Ca. 2 ft. of his papers pertain to his Russian activities 1864-1905. Materials include correspondence, diaries, literary manuscripts, photographs, maps, and miscellaneous historical documents. Individuals mentioned in the papers include Prince Gortchakov, Mikhail N. Katkoff, Leo Tolstoi, Count Serge Witte, Grand Duke Alexis, Prince Alexander Eristof, Konstantin P. Pobedonostsev, Count Nicholas P. Ignatiev, A. R. Fadeyev, Andrew White, Theodore Roosevelt, Charles A. Dana and John Fiske. There is a handwritten account copied by Curtin from Count Witte's personal papers regarding the construction of the Manchurian Railway and the Boxer Rebellion, 1898-1900. The account was copied at Witte's chancellery in France, 1902, 150 pp. Donor's permission needed for some items. Lists of files and letters in several series of Curtin documents.

2 Stella S. Matthews (1868-1948). Papers, 1918-49, 2 boxes. Nurse. Organized relief work in Eastern Europe after World War I and involved in the evacuation of Red Cross personnel from Warsaw at the time of the Bolshevik invasion of Poland in 1921. Correspondence, diaries, personal records, and clippings contain references to these subjects.

3 Social Democratic Party. Records, 1897-1940, 12 cu. ft. Includes correspondence of Victor Berger, a Wisconsin congressman.

4 Socialist Party. Records, 1879-1970, 7 microfilm reels and 8 vols. Minutes of state and local party organizations in Wisconsin, plus scrapbooks of newspaper clippings, containing references to communist and socialist activities in Russia.

Finding Aid: Guide to Historical Resources in Milwaukee Area Archives, edited by John A. Fleckner and Stanley Mallach (Milwaukee, 1976).

WI 7
AREA RESEARCH CENTER - SPECIAL COLLECTIONS
THE LIBRARY
UNIVERSITY OF WISCONSIN - MILWAUKEE
Milwaukee, Wisconsin 53201
(414-963-5402)

1 Lindsay Hoben. Papers, 1926-63, 2 cu. ft. Editor of the Milwaukee Journal. Includes correspondence, articles, photographs, and a manuscript entitled "10,000 Miles of Bolshevism." Currently unprocessed and held in Madison, Wisconsin.

2 Lizzie Black Kander (1858-1940). Papers, 1875-1960, 2 boxes. Social worker active among Russian Jewish immigrants. Letters, minutes of the Abraham Lincoln Settlement House, 1921-31, reports, and biographical materials. Unpublished inventory (NUCMC 68-2237). (Available on microfilm)

Note: Through a unique loan system, individual manuscript collections may be temporarily transferred to any one of Wisconsin's 13 Area Research Centers or to the State Historical Society (Madison) for use by researchers.

Finding Aid: Guide to Historical Resources in Milwaukee Area Archives, edited by John A. Fleckner and Stanley Mallach (Milwaukee, 1976).

WI 8
AREA RESEARCH CENTER
CHALMER DAVEE LIBRARY
UNIVERSITY OF WISCONSIN - RIVER FALLS
River Falls, Wisconsin 54022
(715-425-3567)

1 Stephan Feinstein (b. 1943). Professor. Copies of 5 letters, 1970, written to him and graduate student Rene Rizzo by Russian students and a Leningrad Intourist guide. The Americans met these correspondents on a university tour of the USSR in spring 1970. The letters concern personal interests.

2 M. I. Veranick. Oral history interview transcription, 1967, 19 pp. Student in the Ukraine during the Russian Revolution, and White Army volunteer in the Ukraine. Discusses the first Revolution, Duma, Bolshevik Revolution, Ukrainian independence movement, Volunteer Army, influenza epidemic in the army 1917-18, brief musical career in Europe, World War II, and career in the U.S. Most of his information on Leningrad and Moscow is rumor or second hand and of doubtful accuracy. Interviewed by Deryl V. Gease.

Note: Through a unique loan system, individual manuscript collections may be temporarily transferred to any one of Wisconsin's

13 Area Research Centers or to the State Historical Society (Madison) for use by researchers.

Finding Aids: W. Massa et al., Guide to Archives and Manuscripts in the University of Wisconsin-River Falls Area Research Center (June 1975); and Voices from the St. Croix Valley: A Guide to the Oral History Collection (1978).

WYOMING

WY 1
AMERICAN HERITAGE CENTER
THE UNIVERSITY OF WYOMING
BOX 3334
Laramie, Wyoming 82071
(307-766-4114)

Archives of Contemporary History

1 Harry E. Barnes (1889-1968). Papers, 1912-68, 201 boxes. Historian and educator. Correspondence, manuscripts of writings, memoranda. Includes "class notes" on the genesis of World War II and the Rosenberg case. Among Barnes's correspondents were N. S. Timasheff and P. A. Sorokin. Unpublished finding aid (NUCMC 66-2016).

2 A. Beeby-Thompson (b. 1873). Papers, 1894-1961, 22 boxes. Author (The Oil Fields of Russia, 1908) and known as the "father of the oil industry." He worked as an engineer for an Anglo-Russian firm operating in the Baku oilfields and had considerable business contacts with Russia during his career. His collection includes maps of the Caucasus; a legal document, 1913, on the Baku Wire Cable Company Ltd.; several folders of notes on "Russia and the Russians - early experience"; printed materials on Russian oil-field developments; a published article by Sallie McCabe, "With my Husband in Soviet Russia"; published yearbooks, 1903-1909, on engineering, irrigation, oils, etc. in Russia, and 2 boxes of correspondence. Unpublished finding aid.

3 Edward T. Devine (1867-1946). Papers, 1910-36, 3 ft. A founder of modern American social work. Helped establish American Red Cross program of national disaster relief. Manuscripts, correspondence, scrapbooks, journals, published works. In 1916 he was named special agent to the American embassy in Petrograd to arrange for relief of German war prisoners in Russia. Collection includes 13 personal journals, 8 of which record his experiences in Russia in 1916 and a return trip in 1923. Unpublished finding aid.

4 George D. Embree. Papers, 1959-73, 73 boxes. Scholar specializing in Soviet Union. Includes manuscripts on Soviet diplomats, Russian submarines, U.S. tour of the Soviet agricultural ministry, Soviet policy toward the oil crisis, Soviet views toward European security, and on Soviet pipelines, films, women, science, labor market, youth problems, railroads, social security, economic problems, and other matters. There are also 2,241 4x6 index cards of research notes for Embree's The Soviet Union Between the 19th and 20th Party Congress, 1952-1956 and 13 black and white negative photographs of a "Russian farm visit" and "Russian farm delegates." Unpublished finding aid.

5 Cedric W. Foster (b. 1900). Papers, 1940-72, 25 boxes. Radio news commentator. In part, transcripts. Contains oral history transcripts on Brezhnev, Central Asia, Khrushchev, Nixon's China visit and Russian reactions to it, Russian spies in Britain, Russians in Cuba, the Tchaikovsky Competition, Ambassador E. Durbrow, the Russian navy, and Russian art. There are also books and pamphlets pertaining to Russia. Unpublished finding aids (NUCMC 74-1179).

6 Gene Gurney (b. 1929). Papers, 1944-72, 37 boxes. U.S. Air Force officer and historian. Includes typed manuscript by Gurney and Clare Gurney, "The Launching of the Sputnik," 74 pp., and photos gathered for Gurney's The Pictorial History of the United States Army. These photos include pictures of Georgians from Russia captured by the American army in France and of Russian soldiers in Iran, 1944. Unpublished finding aid (NUCMC 75-2085).

7 Anthony Harrigan. Papers, 1 box. Railroad businessman. A few periodicals, newspaper clippings, and articles pertaining to Soviet naval power, U.S.-USSR agreements at Helsinki, Khrushchev's policies, Soviet Mediterranean strategy, and Soviet goals in the Middle East. Unpublished finding aid.

8 Valentine Hayes. Papers, 3 boxes. Mining engineer. Maps in this collection include the following: "Joined Map of Goldcontaining Districts in the Amour Region"; "Nemansky Region"; "Summary Map of Place Districts, Amoor Province"; and 47 unidentified maps, some of which are written and labeled in Russian. There are also reports: "Gold Dumps - Karisny Mines"; "Goldfields and Mines of the Nimansky Goldbearing System belonging to V. A. Khaeff"; "Lena Goldfields"; "Prospecting and Development of Silver and Lead Deposits in Eastern Zabaikal"; "Records of Gold Production from Amazar-Urium-Horogoch Group. Production from

1895 to 1919"; "Report on the Mines Belonging to First Gold Association 'Rudnik'"; "Report on Mines of the Transbaikal Province of Siberia"; "Report on the present condition of the silver lead mines which have been worked prior to the liquidation of silver lead mining in the Nerchinsk Mining District in 1906"; "Silver-Lead Mining in the Western Zabaikal"; "Undinsky Group"; "Urulginsky Group of Placers"; "Western Transbaikal - Lead and Silver." In the group called "Russian materials" there are various documents, including reports, notes, incompletes, and correspondence, all written in Russian, 1,073 items. Among the "miscellaneous materials," there is a ledger book, printed in Russian; a Russian checkbook, with the title "Banque de Commerce de Siberie"; and handwritten, unidentified notes, presumably on a particular mining area in Russia or eastern Siberia, 39 pp. Finally, there is a 5x8 in. photograph of Vasili A. Hayeff, and correspondence, 1921, from various persons to Alexei V. and Vasili A. Hayeff. Unpublished finding aid.

9 Ross Hoffman. Papers, 40 boxes. Mining engineer. Hoffman's correspondence, 1890-1939, contains 5 folders of letters and approximately 170 telegrams in Russian. Among Hoffman's correspondents were the Russo-Asiatic Bank and the Pioneer Company of Siberia Ltd. In the file boxes, where Hoffman kept his own records of various mines on file cards, there is 1 box of materials on Russia and Siberia. The drill and time logs contain 2 folders, mostly on Russian mines, for 1926. There are maps or data on Borovaya Claims, East Siberia, Kamchatka, Lena River, Nikolaievsk, Russia, Siberia, a tundra lake, Ural districts, Varinski, Vladivoski (Vladivostok?), Sybyriakoff and Lena Co., Valentinovsky, Okhotsk, and North Amur river. The materials on mines document the following: Amur-Orel Gold Mining Company, 1 folder with 2 reports on the company. Ayan Corporation Ltd., 6 folders containing miscellaneous notes written by Ross Hoffman, maps, 1 picture, a memorandum on the Articles of the Association, supply lists, and reports on the Okhotsk District, Andrich River, Kazyonny Mine, Pology Creek, Londonsky, and the Varvainsky Mine. Chibaschek Mine, 1 folder containing a cost sheet for that mine. Cu, Ag-Pb, and Lou Mines in Russia, 1 folder containing data on copper and zinc produced in the Akmolinskaya, Elizabetpolskaya, Erivanskaya, Ferganskaya, Ufimskaya, Kieletskaya, Kutaiskaya, Permskaya, Primorskaya, Semipalatinsk & Semireachinskaya, Sir-Darinskaya, Terskaya, Tomskaya, Turgaiskaya, Viatskaya, Viborgskaya, Yennesseiskaya, and Za-Baikalskaya Government regions. Eltsoff and Levashoff Mines, 1 folder containing an 1897 report. Empire Drill Holes, 1 folder containing prospecting reports on the Amka River, Dlinney Creek, Inya River, Marekan River, Ottav River, Rasvyet Creek, and Ulya River. Kalga Creek System, 1 folder containing a prospecting report, a map and a written report on the mine. Karadog Concession, 1 folder containing a Russian document and a letter to the Board of the Russo-Persian Mining Company. Lena Company Concession Agreement, 1 folder containing the document in Russian. Lena Company Mines, 1 folder containing 2 reports. Mariinsk, 2 folders containing an estimate for the mine and a 1912 report with a map. Marinsk District, 1 folder containing expense accounts, notes on the district, various German papers and maps. Maslofka Creek, 1 folder containing maps, prospecting and drill reports and a written report. Nikolaievsk, 1 folder containing a summary of claims, time and prospecting reports, and maps. Novo Udeel, 1 folder containing memos and maps, and Novo-Udyl, 4 folders containing expense accounts, various prospecting journals, maps, surveys of pits, contracts, original estimates. Nunoleeyski Coal Mines, 1 folder containing a paper on coal and a Russian report. Okhotsk, 2 folders containing pictures, several Russian reports, maps, and the prospecting itinerary for 1925-26. Ool River, 1 folder containing time logs, progress reports, prospecting reports, and 1912 reports. Pamir Gold Mining Company, 1 folder containing a 1916 report translated from Russian. Pantalamonskaya, 1 folder containing a 1917 report and shift reports. Patushinki Claims, 1 folder containing a 1912 report. Pioneer Company of Siberia Limited, 3 folders containing miscellaneous notes, accounts, summaries on holdings of the company, memoranda, first annual report of the company, maps, proposal contracts, and 1913 reports. Pokal Mine, 1 folder containing a 1929 report. Renkevitch Coal Deposit of Sachaline, 1 folder containing a map and a report. Russian Empire, 4 folders containing mining reports of ore 1884-90, bank statements and summary statements from Russia, Russian reports of copper and zinc production, and Russian tax laws of 14 May 1916. Russo-British Mining Companies, 1 folder containing notes copied from the 1915 yearbook, a map, and miscellaneous notes. Sachaline Coal, 4 folders containing a report on coal by P. Polevoi, miscellaneous notes by Hoffman, several maps, Russian papers, assay outfit and accompanying expense accounts, and reports. Semipalatinsk Company, 1 folder containing an inventory of goods, and various miscellaneous notes. Siberian Mining Company, 3 folders containing miscellaneous data, a report on possible methods of doing business, memorandum on dredging in Siberia, and a report on the mine. Somine River, 1 folder containing ore samples, time logs, prospecting reports, maps, a 1912 report. Somnine Gold Dredging Property (?), 1 folder containing a 1912 report and 3 maps. Sybyriakoff Properties, 1 folder containing various calculations, 10 exhibits sent by Hoffman on the mine. Summary of results of examination of the Niemtshyhoff, Bazanoff, and Sybyriakoff Company's mines.

Tchoussovskoi Swamps, 1 folder containing maps and a rough calculation for the Von Brevern Concession. Turkestan, 1 folder containing a 1917 report by John Hoffman. Uda River, 1 folder containing shaft and prospecting logs, ore samples, and a 1912 report. Urals, 1 folder containing a report on the Epitome of the Gold Mining Concessions in the Urals. Verkni-Amur Company, 1 folder containing a report on the properties, maps, and an extract from a letter from Mr. C. S. Purrington to the Board of the Company. Yuba River Exam, 3 folders containing a 1935 report, various notes and drill reports, and several maps. Znaminity Mine, 1 folder containing a cost sheet, inventory from 31 March 1916, assay lists, a pay roll and weekly reports.

Finally, the Hoffman collection contains many books and pamphlets pertaining to Russia and Russian mining. Unpublished finding aid.

10 Ira B. Joralemon. Papers, 19 boxes. Mining engineer. The collection includes correspondence with the Zyrianovsk Mine of the Russia Mineral Corp., 1917, and maps, notes, and diagrams on Russian and Siberian mines. There is also a manuscript, "Development in the Nonferrous Metallurgical Industry and Science in Old Russia and the USSR," by M. G. Corson. Unpublished finding aid. Restricted.

11 Robin Kinkead. Papers, 5 boxes. Includes newspaper clippings on the Soviet Union, a 3x5 in. photograph of Joseph Stalin, and a typewritten and annotated essay by Kinkead, "Road to Moscow, 1929," 17 pp. There are also 2 cablegrams pertaining to the Soviet Union: "Soviet Food Tantalus - Tighter Control of Supplies Today" and "Soviet Pleased with French Pact - Two Salient Clauses." Both cablegrams are dated 29 November 1932.

12 William Robert Moore. Papers, 30 boxes. Contains ca. 1 box of correspondence, 1957-63, research notes, galley proofs, and manuscripts pertaining to Russia.

13 Peter A. Morrison. Papers, 1 box. Includes a Rand report, May 1974, entitled "Soviet Military Management at the Troop Level."

14 C. Stribling Snodgrass. Papers, 210 boxes. 1 file folder with 14 items on Russia, 1945-68, and a letter from Dr. H. L. Malakoff to A. L. Regnier, 7 August 1957.

15 Harold A. Titcomb. Papers, 1904-16, 33 boxes. Mining engineer. This collection contains various materials (including notes, annual reports, accounts, and reprints of articles) on the Anglo-Siberian Company, Ltd., 1 item, Lena Goldfield, 1 item, the Nerchinsk Gold Company, Ltd., 1 item, Omsk Goldfields, 2 items, Russian mining, ca. 50 items, 1914-16, the Russian Mining Corporation, Ltd., 2 items, the Russo-Asiatic Corporation, Ltd., the Spassky Copper Mine, Ltd., 7 items, the Troitzk Goldfields, 1 item, and the great Russian mining boom, 1906-12. There are also 36 photographs, 1912, of Siberia, 8 postcards, 1909, of Russia, scientific articles on Siberian mines, and a map of mining and ore deposits in Siberia, 1903. Unpublished finding aid.

16 Donald N. Wackwitz. Papers, 10 boxes. Included are mimeographed and carbon copies of reports on Russian colonialism, Russian libraries, the Russian people, Soviet airpower, Soviet strategic intentions, and the "psychological effectiveness within the U.S.S.R. of the U.S.A.F. air offensive in 1953." Some of the reports were written by Wackwitz. Unpublished finding aid.

17 Charles A. Willoughby. Papers, 3 boxes. U.S. Army officer. Includes articles from the Foreign Intelligence Digest pertaining to Russia. Unpublished finding aid.

18 Charles Will Wright. Papers, 20 boxes. The collection contains reports on the industrial power of the Soviet Union, 1960, Soviet mineral potential, 1963, metal output of the USSR, 1968, and on "Russia in 1937." There are also maps, newspaper clippings, pamphlets, and magazines pertaining to Russia and its mineral resources. Unpublished finding aid.

Division of Rare Books and Special Collections

19 Joseph Schillinger (1895-1943). Collection, ca. 1918-77, 1 box. Russian-born composer and musical theorist. Includes negative photostats of holograph musical compositions: Northern Russian Symphony, op. 22, score and parts, 64 pp., 1930, with piano transcription, 26 pp.; Violin Sonata, op. 9, score and parts, 41 pp., 1921-22; and Poeme nocturne, op 7, 6 pp., 1921; also 11 photos, concert programs, 1 for 1918 and 1 for the first Russian jazz concert in 1927, photocopies and originals of Russian documents, passports, citizenship papers, patents, and other material.

20 Hugo Winterhalter (1910-1973). Papers, ca. 1935-72, 25 ft. Arranger, composer, and conductor. Includes material pertaining to N. Rimskii-Korsakov. (NUCMC 77-1274)

INDEX

Prepared by Nancy Nawor Blanpied
Edited by William Bruce Pitt

Repository Index